ISBN 978-1-332-22660-3
PIBN 10300999

Submerged Atlantis Restored

OR

RIN-GÄ' SE NUD Sİ İ KEL'ZĒ

(LINKS AND CYCLES)

A short treatise on the Over Spirit as the Cycle Supreme; the Over Soul as the Epicycle Supreme; Spirit, Soul and Matter as Links Supreme, and Time, Space and Life as Trinity Epicycles operating on the deferent of the Over Soul by Impulse from the Over Spirit in creative process, through the activity of Animation, Extension, Expression and Duration, as the source of all individualized form manifestation throughout the Universe.

Also an elaborate treatise on the Continent of Atlantis, including its Mountain Ranges, Valleys, Seas, Lakes, Bays, Rivers, Sections or States, Cities, Convulsions, Submergence, Geographic, Geologic, Ethnographic and Ethnologic conditions, Languages, Alphabets, Figures, Cardinal and Ordinal Numbers, Punctuation Marks, Calendar, Money, the six Flags of the Nation, Religion, Mummifying of Bodies, Enterprises, Air-Ships, Government, Temples, Monuments, Architects and Architecture; Botanic, Zoologic and Ornithologic conditions; Poets and Poetry, Authors and Prose; Tone Poets and Musicians, Painters and Paintings, Sculptors and Sculpture.

Various Illustrations accompanying the above-named subjects.

Other great features, such as the Pre-historic Convulsions and the periods of time when they occurred, that have established the present contour of the Continents and Islands of the Earth, and that have established the various bodies of water and deserts now in existence; the re-establishment and influence of the above-named subjects in Prehistoric ages, subsequent to the submergence of Atlantis, by remnant and migratory conditions; re-conceived and re-embodied ideas, through natural, material and spiritual influences, their continuation and development, or degeneration, as leading up to the Ancient, Modern-Ancient, and Modern periods of time, thus establishing the Pre-historic and Historic sections of the great Cycles of Life, from the period of Atlantian greatness, to that of the Twentieth Century A. D.

BY

J. BEN LESLIE

ROCHESTER, N. Y.
AUSTIN PUBLISHING COMPANY
1911

Press of the Bates Printing Company, 46 Stone Street, Rochester, N. Y.

CONTENTS

INDEX TO ILLUSTRATIONS

PREFACE.

Our object in this treatise is to consider spiritual and material facts, and their recognition by means of sensual forces, and to characterize the disquisition with personifications, cycles, epicycles, links and eclipses, in order to satisfy the general reader, who demands some of the idealistic in connection with the realistic, to insure his further contemplation of the theme. Furthermore, to give communications that we have received and are still receiving from spirits who in mortal dwelt as celebrities, in times far remote, pre-historic, historic, antequated and modern, who are turning the wheel, or cycle of records, to unfold and reveal the sequence of facts spiritual, material, physical and historical, to the mortal dwellers on earth.

In presuming to offer this work to the literary world at large for consideration, the author does so with some degree of apprehension regarding the total acceptance of the theme, particularly that portion characterized with spirit revelation.

Critics of merely a literary type, and those wedded to creedism, unacquainted with the laws governing spirit manifestations and unwilling to withdraw from long-accepted or established theories, will no doubt discredit these points, and only recognize them as incredible, or imaginary absurdities.

On the other hand, we feel that the theme will be accepted by those whose careful investigation and study into the philosophy and phenomena of spirit, have possessed them with a different understanding.

Those who do not recognize the fact that, at the so-called death, the active forces, the sensations and entire qualities of being that animated the material body before the disembodiment of the soul and spirit, remain an undissolved individuality, capable of manifestation by, and through, the laws governing the disembodied state of existence, we would invite with us, to feel, think and re-think, and penetrate deeper into Nature, thus seeking better understanding, reaching more perfect conclusions and enjoying much more satisfaction from the truth, knowledge, and wisdom therein obtained, that otherwise would be lost to our consciousness.

Let us all seek broader knowledge in the Sciences, and thereby the better realize how closely they blend in evidence of universal truth. By such means might the great brotherhood of man be united in religious understanding and acceptance, and creeds would then be conditions of the past.

The spirit of Philosophy would then blend into that of Science, and manifestations in the realm of Phenomena would the better reach the senses and ultimate conception of mortals.

Having confidence, therefore, in the spirit sources from which the inspirations, the impressions, the manifestations and revelations, through clairvoyant and clairaudient aid, have come to us, we send the work out in their behalf, and trust to their force of inspirational influence to use it as an instrument for good to all races of men.

If in this effort, we have led one mortal to unroll himself from the material blanket that hitherto had folded him, mentally, in the condition of non-development, and have caused him to expose his sensual faculties to the influence of the Infinite Over Spirit, as manifesting throughout the universe, thus aiding him to connect the cycles of life material and spiritual into that of the eternal, then shall our efforts be well rewarded.

In regard to the pre-historic and non-historic nomenclature having place in this work, of which there are 3,000 or more terms, we wish to state that about two-thirds of them were received by Mrs. C. C. Van-Duzee, thus given her by Alem Prolex, one of the four Atlantian spirits, in aid of this work, at our various private seances during the period of time that we have worked together in collecting data for this book. The remaining one-third of the terms were received directly by the Author as given to him by Kū-lī-ú'thüs, a Phœnician spirit who, when a mortal, dwelt in the then known section of Phinea, now known as along the shores and west of the Dead Sea, one of the helpers of Alem Prolex in search of nomenclature for this book.

As the length of the work will not admit of a grammatical treatise, or of a vacabulary giving the definition and proper pronunciation of the pre-historic and non-historic terms, we make the facts cognizant by their use in the book sections, with the peoples to whom they belong, the pronunciation being indicated by the accented syllables, and the sounds of the vowels by the usual marks, as they would be in a dictionary, which, if the reader is familiar with them, will be a great aid in reading the same.

As will be seen, plurals are often indicated by the accent mark being placed terminally.

The English conjunction "or" and the intransitive verb "is" have no corresponding terms in the Atlantian language, as will be observed in a few cases in this work.

It may seem at first sight that we have crowded the subject with Atlantian terms, but considering the fact that Atlantis and its people have been considered a myth, legendary, or fairy tale, the Atlantian Spirits in charge of the production of this work have thought best to use as much linguistic evidence as possible and not fatigue the reader, in order to prove their existence as remote dwellers on the earth plane, though the entire work could have been given in the Atlantian language, so far as the capability of the spirit revealers was concerned, or the ability of the Că-cĕl-lă´-zē (spirit sensitives) to receive the same. As it now is, the manuscripts have been cut down from what would have made a book of 1,300 pages to the present dimensions of the book, finance being the chief obstacle.

Despite all our care, a few errors will be found in the text, which in the next edition will be corrected.

Much might be said in relation to the various subjects herein set forth, especially the pre-historic, that would give evidence of the linkings of the past, present and future, but space forbids. Therefore, dear reader, we leave you to contemplate the subjects herein contained. Think! think with an unbiased or unprejudiced mind. Learn the forces that are hidden within the resources of thine own soul and thereby link thyself to the great Cycle of Thought; for knowledge is food to the spirit now, and ever shall be a life-giving Cycle without end.

J Ben Leslie.

A SHORT BIOGRAPHY OF MRS. CARRIE C. VAN DUZEE.

Mrs. Carrie C. Van-Duzee, born in Gouveneur, N. Y., Nov. 25, 1828, began her Spiritual work as a healer in Erie, Pa., in the spring of 1872.

In this phase of spirit work she operated as a Că-cĕl'lā or spirit sensitive for several years, during which time her spirit helpers, through her physical forces, co-operative with theirs, performed some most wonderful cures, among which the crippled were made to walk; the blind made to see, and various unfortunate sufferers, who had been given up by material physicians as hopeless cases, were freed from their diseases and thus made to rejoice, and give credit to the source of their relief.

In 1876 she began lecture service, both that of parlor gatherings and on the rostrum, through the influence of trance, clairvoyant and clairaudient qualifications, and also that of giving tests and private readings, a mission she faithfully and conscientiously carried out until in the year 1901 when, on account of physical inability to endure the strain necessary upon her nervous system to continue her public work, she retired from it, after having labored in twenty-four states of the Union in the great cause of Spiritualism, thus covering a period of twenty-five years unselfishly devoted to the cause. Wherever she had engagements she was sure of a full house of followers and earnest investigators, some of whom would come from ten to thirty miles to attend her lectures and readings, to receive tests and messages, from their disembodied loved ones—services she oftentimes rendered without monetary compensation, being in the pioneer days, not only of the country, but of spiritual work. One of her special features of service was that of establishing spiritual societies to carry on the good work, after she had served the people for a short period as a speaker or spirit Că-cĕl'-lā. When the exponent known as "*Light for Thinkers*" was established in Atlanta, Ga., she was chosen by Hon. A. C. Ladd, president of the company, and W. C. Bowman, editor, to fill the position of message receiver for said paper, a mission which she filled with satisfaction.

In 1906, in accord with the wishes of the Ancient Spirits (who some two years previously had inspired the author with the idea and title of this book, and had already designed and written parts of it), she consented to join issues with him, in order to aid where clairaudient and clairvoyant forces were necessary in giving the facts relative to a truthful revelation of pre-historic events; and he, under the guidance of spirit inspira-

Yours for all good.

Carrie C. VanDuzee

tion and other phases, as a spirit sensitive, to plan and carry out the literary and art details of the work. Therefore, the author feels himself under great obligation for the services so freely and unselfishly given him by her during a period of four years and more.

As to her characteristic qualities, the author would say that she might be termed a child true to nature; simple in her manner; not in sympathy with the rigid forms of fashionable etiquette or society; ever uninfluenced or governed by flattery; loving the society of young men and women whom she at all times sought to lead into purer living; free from ranting display; never sacrificing womanly delicacy, though dignified in manner; hostile to vice, crime and social impurity of every kind; pure in character to the extreme; kind, charitable and sacrificing unto all with whom she associated, or unto the worthy needy; manifesting womanly qualities both in the privacy of her home and when in public service, at all times seeking to influence all those with whom she came in touch with the idea of bettering the conditions that were to govern their lives.

All the foregoing biographic and eulogistic statements are facts that can be gathered from out a vast number of testimonials, eulogies, comments and reports, that appeared in both religious and secular exponents throughout her period of public work, which the author has at hand.

Having, as before stated, labored for small remunerations, the greatest reward she recognizes and which gives her the greatest pleasure, is in the fact that hundreds date their awakening unto the truth of Spiritualism to the various periods of her services unto them; therefore, she, with all the true pioneers in the cause, who in reality were martyrs on account thereof, should have, in memoriam, laurels placed on their brows and carpets of the choicest flowers upon which to walk, and brightest lights of of the spirit world to shine upon them throughout the ceaseless ages of Eternity, for no greater mission, be it imposed upon spirit or mortal, is there than to bring the light of truth to mortal seekers, especially that which concerns their spirit, soul and body interests.

IN RECOGNITION OF SPIRIT REVELATION.

Oh, Holy Angels! pure, sweet, beloved spirits divine,
Famed and revered in long ages agone as mortals;
From spirit land, to earth you come to aid mankind,
Teaching them through your opened spirit portals;
How to gather up the links that cycled the eternal past,
From your home-lands long submerged by oceans and seas,
Where now the great rolling billows still hold them fast,
There in the sands of time waiting for this, their release.
To our faithful guides A-lēm Prō-lĕx and Er-ō-thrō-dī-ä,
Co-operative with Zē-rē-chā, Yër-mäh and An-stä-ci-ä,
Who have led the band of pre-historic and ancient workers,
In revealing the truth of the past unto their modern brothers,
We give our earnest thanks and acknowledge profound adoration,
And hereby tender this work in behalf of every living nation,
Hoping to reach and impress some mortal with truth's influence,
And thereby free his imprisoned mental, or intelligence.

Links and Cycles

RE-ME'NA, OR BEGINNING.

TELTZIE I.

I, Rē-mē'nä, always was, am now and ever shall be,
For Creation and Evolution are perpetual as Eternity.
Numberless Ages have come and passed by,
Manifesting truths that creeds seek to deny;
But Science will prove them by logical ways,
And dispel such beliefs as in the Miracle of Seven Days.

Nĕn cie (time), *Lē măz* (space) and *Wōtz* (life, three infinitely related elements, co-operating, eternal, immaterial, with an unknown beginning or *E-ŭn-dū* (ending), unchangeable in their relative condition of co-operation or co-dependence, form the Infinite Cycle of Existence, while the links of beginning and ending blend to roll and unroll the sequences that have formed the Cycles and Epi-cycles of the past, developing them in the present, and shall extend them operatively for all time to come.

He who would enter into the analysis, or synthesis of those Cycles and Epi-cycles, must possess a mind tuned in harmony with the universal laws of Nature, and in addition to the influence brought to bear upon his faculties of sensation, impression and inspiration, must exercise his reasoning forces, thereby obtaining direct and indirect acquisition of knowledge arising from the result of the co-existence and co-operation of life and Sŭ-māze'lĕt (material) with time and space.

Many are the themes relative to the beginning and ending of universal existence, causes and effects, etc., both ancient and modern, of which the reader, no doubt, has knowledge; e. g., Anaxagoras of Clazomine, recognized one intelligence in opposition to the Pagan belief, in his day, in plural gods, their power and functions as controlling and governing material things, and all bodies in motion in the Universe, therefore separating matter and Quē-ĕl'ze (intelligence), making the latter the motive force of the former.

Zeno taught that there were two original principles of all things; viz., that which acts and that which is acted upon.

Antonenus, in conformity with this idea, recognized one common Bär'dër (substance) as being distributed among countless bodies, which resulted in the phenomena of all substantial, or material things visible to the material eye.

Plato, in speaking of material things, said, "Nothing ever is but is always becoming."

The Biblical narrative of Creation, together with the ideas set forth in isms, creeds and writings of the ancient Sages, or comments of the more modern Scientists, we leave non-quoted for research by the reader.

First, let us recognize the *Over Spirit,* or *Life,* as the animating or operating force governing creational existence.

Second, the *Over Soul* as the medium through which the *Over Spirit* operates.

Third, Substance or Matter as the foundation of form, or structural existence.

Fourth, Natural Law as governing the process of extension and growth.

Fifth, Constructed Form as the phenomenal result thereof, and the visible proof of the action of the *Over Spirit* force through the *Over Soul,* as having acted upon Matter through absolute Space, in the eternal duration of Time, as Triune Cycle.

Hence, the *Over Spirit,* or *Life,* the efficient force and quality of an existence in the womb of space unlimited, during time everlasting, has by its inherent quality of extension, shaped Substance or Matter into physical and organic structure, and ultimate individuality, an effort also from which we cognize cosmogonic and cosmographic proofs.

This animate principle, co-existing with the inanimate as eternities, neither could assume sire-ship, but the animate could utilize, control the inanimate in the creation of universal form existence, the act of which establishes the principle of universal Nature, the evidence of which, as before stated, is to be recognized by the phenomena of forms visible.

Therefore, in further pursuance of this great theme, let us consider it with reason, such as shall be free from skepticism, or prejudice, being governed by natural laws as the Cycles of Cause, on whose deferent move the Epi-cycle of Effect.

USH RED'ZE EL-NEPTHS'.

OR THE GREATER DEPTHS.

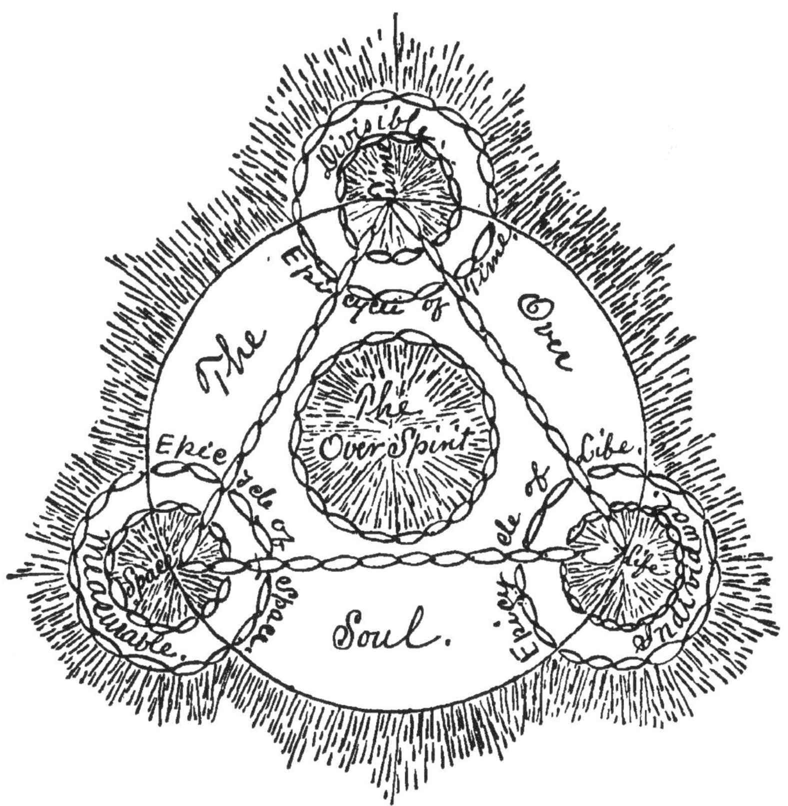

THE SUPREME CYCLES, EPI-CYCLES AND LINKS.

TELTZIE II.

The *Over Spirit, Life's* source of animation,
The original active Force, vital and immaterial,
The Electric Principle in universal Creation,
The Infinite Mind, manifest in Time, Space and Life Eternal.

Submerged Atlantis Restored

The *Over Soul, Life's* source of habitation,
The immaterial Form covering the spiritual,
The Magnetic Principle in universal Creation,
The Infinite Body, manifest in Time, Space and Life Eternal.

Spirit, Soul and Matter, Life's source of individualization,
The original Links in every Cycle and Epi-cycle,
The Developing Principle in universal Creation,
The Infinite Triangle, manifesting in Time, Space and Life
Eternal.

The individual portion of Electricity or the *Over Spirit* thus formed continues to move, operate and exist on the deferent of the great Electric and Magnetic Cycles or those of the *Over Spirit* and *Over Soul* embodied in the Epi-cycle of individulity, and further encircled by the ultimate Material form, a coarser quality of existence, which the force of the individualized Epi-cycle of Soul or magnetic form, and thence to the outer or Material form which it controls and operates from the period of the original nucleus formation, through the form development, dis-embodiment, and return of the Material to its original realm, and Spirit and Soul into the greater heights of life and development, during which periods of time it has moved, acted and existed individually separated from, but dependent upon the Great Whole, or Supreme *Over Spirit* and *Over Soul Cycles.*

Elemental Substances are material and spiritual portions of the Over Soul and Over Spirit respectively, collective by nature in the process of form construction, thus acted upon by the principles of Animation, Extension and Duration, finding their placement by the force of activity, throughout the realms of Time, Space and Life.

Polar action and reaction, under the influence of Animation and Extension, therefore, produces spirit and material forms, and also establishes functionary life of substances, forms of matter, etc., everywhere existent; therefore Animation is responsible for the vast differences in form and the phenomena of infinitude.

Nature operates in two laboratories, viz: what is usually termed the "unseen," and that which is "visible," usually recognized in a material or mortal sense.

There are attributes of nature visible only to the spirit sight, e. g., Electricity, the active principle as acting upon elemental substances or the electric vibrations, and the magnetic principle operating through its attractive and repulsive forces, by which act the two principles or forces meet and blend to form the life principle in all created existence throughout space; the first process of polar attraction, by which spirit and soul unites as the foundation principle of cosmic establishment, which induces molecular affinities; the fundamental active principles lying back of chemical spectrum, or the chemical rays of a solar spectrum; the constructive and destructive processes of metabolism relative to the established degrees of activity, and ultimatum of protoplasm, and still further, the activity which establishes complex organic substances intervening nutritive material and protoplasm, and ultimate material form which is inhabited by the spirit and soul individualities, that have through the process visible to spirit, developed in likeness and kind thereof, and in contradistinction to the former, the active process inducing decomposition, which scatters the complex substances into that of simple, and separates them from the protoplasm and excreta that composed the complex form, or activity that is the cause of disembodiment of the spirit and soul individualities from the material form thus breaking up, in which, therefore, they could no longer exist, hence pass from, or as an embodied individuality to that of a disembodied, leaving the former to return to its elementary laboratory and the latter to pass on into a higher development of the same individuality of spirit and soul.

By the co-united forces of that quality of the Over Spirit known as spectrum, induced by the light and heat, and the molecular change that takes place in the condition of darkness to material vision, but visible to spirit sight, Extension links spirit visibility of form existence to that visible to mortal sight, which is also the link between the individuality of the soul and body, the spirit and soul entities being visible to spirit, and the body or grosser material to that of the mortal; therefore, the Over Spirit forces and process of action which establishes chemical spectrum, is visible to spirit vision, whereby they cognize the Gä'lä principle that induces materialization, and therefore material or mortal visibility.

Chemical Spectrum being a quality of Electricity or the Over Spirit, is in the same ratio a quality of individual spirit existence and capable of development as such throughout an eternity, as it passes from one spirit zone to another, thus entering greater light at each advancement, which is a throwing off of all material influences such as it had to assist in its development in the material or mortal sphere, and which it does in the case of the soul body which accompanies it from zone to zone, the passing being made possible by the development away from the material conditions that passed with it from the material plane to the first zone of spirit, etc., until it is a pure entity belonging to spirit, or companion through which the spirit makes itself visible as an entity. Therefore, throughout the zones of Absolute Space, Limitless Time and Endless Life, exists the Over Spirit and Over Soul, extended, developed and perpetuated by spiritual energies and substances, that are embodied in the great Electric and Magnetic principles as infinite as Gä'lä, being quality principles thereof, operating as developing factors or formative princples in the spiritual elements as are necessary to the development and continuity of all spirit existence where the union, blending and development of Gä'lä principles, such as the Electric and Magnetic, and the natural laws by which it operates.

By the law of polar attraction the spirit mentally attracts thoughts from the electric currents or radiations passing through the magnetic system such as elevate or debase the intelligence by bringing to it truth, knowledge and wisdom, or degradation, ignorance, superstition and falsehood, as does the plant attract from the etheric atmosphere of space, the elements necessary for its physical growth, and, in the condition seen only by spirit, there is a finer system of polar attraction in the plant that brings to it the spiritual qualities of intelligence under conditional physical limitation according to its specific individuality.

So also is it with polar repulsion; the spirit has the mental force to repel thoughts not intended for all good, or based upon purity and truth, as the plant repels and refuses to assimilate elements and compounds not suited to its individual development, and as was the case in its attraction of spiritual qualifications, so likewise has it a spiritual force for repulsion, both qualifications or principles, as is the case with the animal and human races, exist after disembodiment, and belong to the sensibilities of spirit existence, and therefore govern the development of both spirit and soul.

The Over Soul or Magnetic entity, or material principle in nature, co-operative with the Over Spirit or electric entity, or electric principles such as activity and energy, that shapes all forms of spirit, soul and material, and which promotes growth or development of form, be it spirit, soul or material, has not only the original process visible to spirit, but a continuity of force which exists after disembodiment, relative to the spirit and soul development, still real Gä'lä principle within, which pulsates in rhythmic vibration throughout the molecular compound of the individualities, soul and body in material life and the soul which is the spiritual body after the grosser material disembodiment.

Therefore, the Electric or individualized portion of the Over Spirit which furnishes the energies that combine in the materially invisible spectrum, be it chemical or otherwise, governing every type of energy and form expression, be it simple or compound, commonly accepted as the energies and forces of nature, is the Gä'lă principle that controls the universe (for what the mortal mind grasps as the universe generally, is the earth, the sky-dome and planets that traverse it, and the stars and constellations that be-stud it; but which in reality is but one universal system among numberless similar organizations having place beyond this, throughout portions of absolute space), and therefore is the principle or spirit of Animation, whose mission it is to perpetuate activity, energies, or forces co-operative with the spirit of Extension, by action and reaction upon molecular existence, which ultimates as the formative principle or force in the realm of changing chemical spectrums, and is a part of electricity or the Over Spirit, recognized as regards visibility only by the ocular sense of spirit, and that only after certain degrees of development of the individual spirit after its material disembodiment, and recognized by them as the connecting link between spirit and material phenomena of form, belonging to nature.

Mē-ĕl-zō'rĭck (Electricity) in its supreme existence is motion without life.

Wĕl-zē-rĕt' (Magnetism) in its supreme existence is life without motion.

Electricity is the comprehensive force governing the soul of all existence or the Gä'lă within, controlling the Gä'lă without, for both Electricity and Magnetism co-united with matter are embraced in the compound principle of Gä-lă principles.

Electricity, the father principle, Magnetism, the mother, and Individuality the children thereof, which establishes the trinity of principles embodying all life energy.

Life itself is a triangle principle embracing all existence, be it in the material or spiritual condition, and Electricity, Magnetism and Individuality the embodiment of universal co-operative Energy.

Through the bounds of absolute Space, the calculations of unlimited Time, and the realms of Life Eternal, radiates the Electric force or motion of the Over Spirit, setting the Magnetic Over Soul into activity, scattering it into individualities which it illuminates or qualifies with the light of life, and further qualifies it with the qualities of Sŭl-cē-ăn'ä (Animation); Frē-dĕn'cē (Extension); Frē-nī'ĕt (Expression); and Gē-ī-rĭsh'ē (Duration), and possesses it with the ability to link itself with Matter, from which it develops its material mask or visible form; hence, by the Cycle of the *Over Spirit,* linked with that of the *Over Soul,* their individual dispersement into Epi-cycles, through the trinity principles of Time, Space and Life, which move on the deferent of the Cycles of the *Over Spirit* and the *Over Soul,* we recognize the great machine of Creation, which is automatic and perpetual to an endless degree; hence, the Gä-lä or Universal Cycle.

In further consideration of the Greater Depths of Existence, Alem Prolex informs us that the only beginning that can be claimed for either individual spirit or material life is that period when the nucleus of individual form is established, which is at the time that the electric force comes in contact with the magnetic principle, thereby inducing motion by attraction and repulsion, and ultimate asemblage of the two principles, Electricity and Magnetism, and their qualities.

Since the great Electric or *Over Spirit* force principle moves radiantly throughout the great Magnetic or *Over Soul* principle in absolute Space, it, therefore, operates originally in the invisible laboratory of the latter, so far as the material eye can recognize molecular processes, but visible to that of the spiritual; hence, the ability of our spirit advisers to acquaint us with these facts.

When a minute invisible electric current or radiation of the *Over Spirit* strikes a minute portion of the great invisible Magnetic *Over Soul* body it sets the invisible molecules into vibratory motion, according to the local conditions existing at the point of the co-union of principles, which under the further influence of Animation and Extension, establishes the nucleus that organizes individuality and develops the ultimate individual form of both material and spiritual existence in all the differentiations of life, for at the period of the co-union of the two forces, Electricity and Magnetism, individuality begins, the latter becomes charged with the super-quality of the former and are each separated from their parent cycle by the combustion that takes place at the time of the meeting of the two principles; hence the individuality.

Preparatory to further contemplation of the theme *Links and Cycles,* let us enumerate some of the fundamental principles upon which it is based.

The *Cycle Supreme,* or the *Over Spirit,* which is of boundless domain, embracing the Trinity Cycles of *Time, Space and Life.*

The *Epi-Cycle Supreme,* or the *Over Soul,* which operates in unison with the *Cycle Supreme.*

The *Epi-Cycles* of Individualized *Spirit, Soul* and *Matter,* which move on the deferent of the *Epi-Cycle Supreme.*

Links symbolize endless development and are the functionary principles belonging to *Cycles and Epi-Cycles,* and seal the eternal condition of *Cycles.*

Cycles and Epi-Cycles symbolize Eternity and are in ceaseless manifestation throughout the Universe, as conclusive evidence of the force of the *Over Spirit* to create.

Links form *Epi-Cycles,* and *Epi-Cycles* move on the deferent of the *Epi-Cycle* and *Cycle Supreme.*

Link within Link, and Cycle within Cycle, embodies the universal machine that creates, under the force of the *Over Spirit,* which propels it.

Nothing is created in all the worlds but that is based on the principle of *Links* and *Cycles.*

Nothing is created that does not in some way reproduce under the same law; hence the *Universal Cycle.*

Nothing is extended into Form without occupying Space; hence, the *Epi-Cycle* of *Space Measurable.*

Nothing is extended into Form without occupying time; hence the *Epi-Cycle* of *Time Divisible.*

Nothing is extended into Form without modes of Motion, Vibration or Animation; hence, the *Epi-Cycles* of *Life Individual.*

Nothing can be formed without Substance, Matter and Spirit; hence, the *Epi-Cycles Material* and *Spiritual.*

Nothing can be formed without an operator; hence, the *Epi-Cycles* of *Spirit Individual.*

Nothing has come into existence without the ruling of specific Natural Law; hence, the Principles of *Vibration,* or *Animation* and *Extension.*

Nothing exists without visible evidence of its specific individuality; hence, the Principle of *Expression.*

Nothing exists without an Infinite Counterpart; hence, the Principle of *Duration.*

ME-LEN'ZON SI USH VINZ LE-A'SA, ENT WOTZ SUL-MAZE'LET.

OR INFLUENCE OF THE OVER SPIRIT IN LIFE MATERIAL.

Gä-lä's Infinite plan for individual existence,
Co-relative with that of all bodies and souls;
Inhabiting space with forms and intelligence,
That develop in periods and ages as time unrolls.

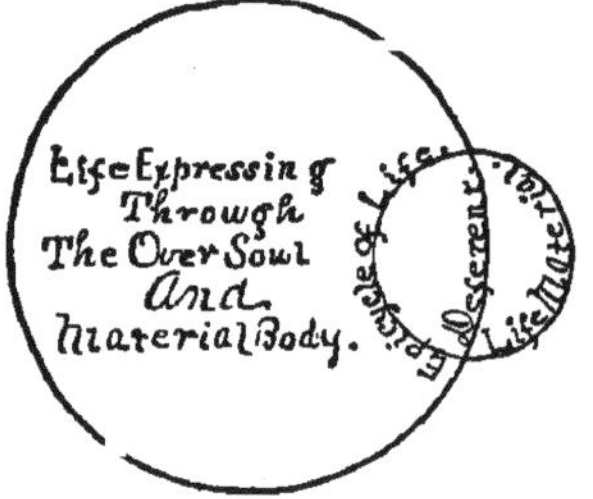

USH LE-A'SA SI SUL-CE-AN'NA, OR THE SPIRIT OF ANIMATION.

TELTZIE III.

An *Over Spirit Quality*, the motive force in Nature,
Expressing through the epi-cycles of Life Material;
By modes of motion, a life-giving feature,
The vital and mental spark, the Spiritual.

Mortal Intelligence! I, the Spirit of Animation speak unto thee from out the realms of Life Eternal. My language finds utterance through the silent and invisible modes of motion and ultimate materialization. I make declarations by manifestations, thus forcing truth upon the quality of sensation which is greater proof of the force of Life than are the materialized forms through which the manifestations are made.

I control the elements of nature and compound forms of matter by activity or polarity, a process by which I form entities of spirit, soul and body into individuality by the principles of electricity and magnetism.

I, therefore, establish individual life by the principles or influence of the Over Spirit through the electrodes of the Over Soul and Body, which under further control of my co-operative principle Extension, completes the individuality of the trio principles, which may be cognized in the existence of all kinds or forms of existence.

Life, when thus individualized, responds to the demand of Extension, in obedience to the same law of attraction and repulsion, according to the polarity of its invisible magnetic or Over Soul quality of being, whereby it collects elements reciprocal to its extension, from the atmosphere, soil, heat, light, moisture, etc. according to its individual or normal condition in the scale of visible form and variety.

In all the Epi-cycles of Life, I am the connecting link between Spirit and Matter, holding the two together as co-operative individualities. My mission with the Spirit Epi-cycle is to assist it in shaping and developing the material counterpart and qualifying it with the principles of activity and individuality. So long as I remain the connecting link, the spirit individual and its material partner remain co-operative and, therefore, will manifest together to the more perfect individuality of both, or *vice-versa,* according to the conditional environments.

By my acts you may trace Life or Spirit as it manifests itself through the vital functions co-operative with its material form. Therefore, contemplate me, the principle of Animation, as influencing the construction of animal, vegetable and mineral forms by the act of, or processes governed by natural laws, calling to your aid the sciences of Embryology, Botany, Zoology, Ornithology, Astronomy, Cosmography, etc., and the principles of Electricity, Magnetism, Motivity, etc., etc., leaving your intellectual forces to grasp the more profound consideration of the subject, especially modes of motion and the act of vibration, etc.

Your senses will suffice to bring you as an individual Spirit in touch with the universal whole; thus, according to your development, will you receive instruction, or experience pleasure, as you behold the various manifestations.

Is it enough to say, that is a shrub, a tree, or a cereal grain? a man, a woman, or a child? a cloud, a raindrop, or a snowflake, without knowing more about their whence and their whither, the why and the wherefore? No! The Infinite cause has endowed you as an individual spirit epi-cycle with the quality of sensation, that you may therefore place yourself in communication with the Great Over Spirit of all.

Therefore, I, the spirit of Animation, one of the chief representatives of the Over Spirit, declare unto you that through your functions of sensation, aided by spirit influence and inspiration, and other forms of manifestation, you may clearly recognize the truth and obtain perfect knowledge regarding the existence of the Infinite Active Principle, Electricity, which is the Over Spirit and the All Force in Nature and the Universe.

During all the cycles of past time, contemporaneous with mortal life, Ideas of the Infinite Principle have been cognized and contemplated, through natural impressions, inspirations, conceived and re-conceived, embodied and re-embodied ideas, cognized and further contemplated through natural impressions, sensual perceptions and mental consciousness, and further developed in accord with the conditions that influenced the mind of the recipient.

Strong nerve systems, strung and tuned in harmony with keen sensations, have been endowments of the past and present to man, and perceptive ideas have been infused into his mind by not only the means of phenomenal objective impressions, through the instrumentality of his physical senses, but by inspiration and other spirit aids acting direct upon his spiritual being and its higher sensations.

SAL-MA'SA LI USH LE-EN'CES
OR
COGNITION BY THE SENSES.

Both mortals and spirits by their ocular sense,
May cognize Ush Mē-Iĕn'sŏn Sī Ush Vĭnz Lē-ā'tä,
Whether in the form, or after departing hence,
They see it through Ush Frē'nī-tē Sū-cē-ăn'nä.
In the marvelous cycles and epi-cycles of time,
And in the immensity of space, profound, sublime.
They see it in all nature in the process of growth,
In future extension after the propagation and birth.
In the glorious Sun in its great diurnal flight,
And in the moon, stars and constellations by night.
They see it in the beautiful colors, shades and tints,
In the lights and shadows wherever nature re-prints.
In the valley, the plain and in the mountain range,

And in the erosions that have wrought them change,
They see it in the moving waters that cover the land,
In the waves that pebble the beach and pile the sand.
In the shrubs and trees that spring from the ground,
And in the grasses and the flowers that grow around.
They see it in material forms qualified with animation,
In every inanimate form existing throughout creation.
In the bright morning dawn and in the evening twilight,
And in the brightness of noon-day, or darkness of midnight.
They see it in the Spring verdure and golden glow of Summer,
In the tinted leaves of Autumn and the white robes of Winter.
In the dewdrops that freshen the leaves and wildwood flowers,
And in the mists that be-moisten the lawns and leafy bowers.
They see it in the tinted clouds of the gathering storm,
In the electric flash that illumines the mountain's form.
In the various kinds and colors of ancient fossils and shells,
And Indian arrow heads which to them antequated history tells.
They see it in the prismatic colors that form the rain-bow,
In the refracted and reflected rays from the Sun's bright glow.
In every effulgent manifestation influenced by natural art,
And in the beautiful, the sublime, expressing from its heart.
They see it in every object as they exercise their perspectivity,
In which act they recognize Ush Lē-ā'sä in its ceaseless activity.

USH RE-EL'CES LE-EN'CE,
OR
THE AURICULAR SENSE.

They hear it in the voice of animals and the song of the birds,
In their own vocal expressions, conveying their thoughts by words.
In the rustle of gentle zephyrs, and whistle of the cool breeze,
And from aeolian harps played by the wind god on rocks and trees.
They hear it in the wild current winds as they variably blow,

In their fiercer howl as they deeply pile the drifting snow.
In the gurgling brooklet, or murmuring stream on the mountain,
And the roar of the cascade, water-fall, or wave of the ocean.
They hear it in the distant thunder after the electric flash,
In its dreadful rolling and pealings with the near-by crash.
In the first descending raindrops as they so gently come down,
And the dashing showers, or rushing torrents that wash the ground.
They hear it in every sound or tone made audible by vibration.
In its emission they sense Ush Lē-ā'tä giving vocal expression.

USH CON'CEST LE-EN'CE,
OR
THE OLFACTORY SENSE.

They smell it in the perfume of the wild-wood flowers,
In the spicy odors from the leaves in the verdant bowers.
In the air that surrounds the garden, field, or wild-wood home,
And in the glens, the canyons, and valleys, from the watery foam.
They smell it in the earth as they bend low some trail to follow,
In the mosses on the rocks that serve them for bed and for pillow.
In the fields as they plow, harrow, and sow their various grains,
And as they cultivate their vegetables after refreshing rains,
They smell it in all the fragrant odoraments diffused by nature,
In which they recognize Ush Lē-ā'sä as the Infinite Creator.

USH CLETE LE-EN'CE, OR THE GUSTATORY SENSE.

They taste it in the luscious flavor of the ripened fruits,
In the starch of the cereals and delicious oils of the nuts.
In the pure crystal waters as they rush from the mountains,
And mineral impregnations that qualify Nature's fountains.
They taste it in the honey of the flowers, there formed and concealed.
In the sugar and the gums of forest trees where they are congealed.
In the juice from the fruits grown on vines and on trees,
And the flavor they sense from vegetable roots and leaves.
They taste it in all they partake of for sustenance and food,
In which they recognize Ush Lē-ā'tä providing for their good.

USH RENTZ LE-EN'CE, OR THE TACTILE SENSE.

They feel it as they handle forms of material, wood, or stone,
In the jar or force of the water-falls and radiance of the Sun,
In the force of the winds when blowing, or in gentle afflations,
And in the mists, the drizzling rain, or in its violent effusions.
They feel it in the soft, velvety blades of the grass and leaves,
In the waxy petals of the flowers they gently stoop to seize.
In the soft touch of the snowflake, or stroke of the cutting sleet,
And in the cold icy ground, or water that gives pain to their feet.
They feel it in all the changes that come to qualify each season,
In the knowledge thus gained through their faculty of reason.
In their affection and love, agitation of sensibility, or emotion,
And through natural susceptibility, and by mental impression,
They recognize Ush Lē-ā'sä by internal and external taction.

ME-LEN'ZON SI USH VINZ LE-A'SA ENT LE'MAZ LET-SAN'DE-US,

OR

INFLUENCE OF THE OVER SPIRIT IN SPACE MEASURABLE.

Gä'lä's Infinite Empire, resistless, immovable domain,
Boundless and endless as the cycles of life and time;
Thus absolute and limitless thou must forever remain
The relative kingdom of all cycles, marvelous, divine.

USH LE-A'SA SI FRE'DEN-CE,

OR

THE SPIRIT OF EXTENSION.

TELTZIE IV.

An *Over Spirit Quality,* a developing force in nature,
Expressing through the Epi-cycles of space measurable,
By modes of Materialization, the form giving feature,
The external form or body, the contour of the spiritual.

Out of the depths of absolute space speak I, the Spirit of Extension, unto thee.

I, as an Infinite Quality, co-adjutant with that of Animation, convey Bär'dër Sŭl-mä'cē-ä (substance or matter) into space where I qualify it with length, breadth, thickness, or ultimate form, in obedience to the will of the *Over Spirit,* by the process under the influence of that specific natural law.

Links and Cycles

Knowest thou that the grand old maple tree beneath which thou art reclining for rest, is closely allied to thee by the ties of nature—yea, even as a brother?

Hath thy senses awakened thy intellectual faculty, and thy mental forces in response thereto set into operation thy faculty of reason, thus causing thee to recognize the fact that the same generative forces hath brought both thee and the tree into material existence, each possessed with a spirit counterpart, through similar lines of development, thou from the uterus, the animal or material generator, and the tree from the earth, the vegetable or material generator, both representing a magnetic embodiment, or Clētz (soul) occupied by an electric spirit counterpart, which latter is the generative force of the former, and which as an individualized portion of the great Over Spirit has built the magnetic and ultimate material form which it inhabits into an individuality after its own individual electric form, vibratorially speaking, and therefore, each a counterpart of the other, under conditional influences giving the ultimatum of each, or a created individuality composed of spirit, soul and body, alike, according to the species to which it belongs, so far as regards form, differing only in the vibratory conditions natural to each as separate from the other, the law that governs the individuality of either spirit, soul or body as such, the former two continued after disembodiment from the latter, and it, in its material existence as a specific individuality, originally belonging to the two former.

Wouldst thou, dear mortal, know thyself better, thy whence and thy whither? Wouldst thou also know that of thy kindred tree? Then trace thy life line conditions, link by link, from the Over Spirit or Electricity, its action upon the Over Soul or Magnetism, and the further influence of Animation, Extension, and U-lĕn′zē (Vibration), which conditionally operates upon protoplasm, and thus establishes nuclei, to the perfect man or tree.

Profound and marvelous is Mē-ĕl-zō′rĭc (Electricity), or the Over Spirit, which is the divine, everlasting motivity or cause of all natural motion or vibration. The activity in the process of creation, the cognition of which fact can be deduced by such effects as produce the development of material form in Space Measurable, Time Divisible, and Life Individual, or by the rotation of worlds, as calculated from horizon to horizon by their changing altitude, by change of the Solar and Lunar orbs as they are revealed to mortal vision at morning or evening, links of Time Divisible, and by the Constellations and fixed Stars appearing to the earth dwellers during the various seasons. Or through the activity or motion of the Over Soul and Body in response to the

Over Spirit or the invisible motive force or impulse received during their existence as Epi-cycles of Life Individual.

When through sensation, mental conception and ultimate reason, thy consciousness hath concluded with truthful understanding, in regard to the laws and science of material and spiritual formation, physical construction, causation, effects and purposes relative to the nature of things, both material and spiritual, then canst thou embrace a tree, cherish its flowers and enjoy its fruits, and therefore call it thy kindred as an Epi-cycle of Life Individual, existing in Space Measurable, under the ruling of Time Divisible, according to the laws that govern the kindred principle of Duration, spiritually and materially. Then canst thou fondle the flowers in all their beauty and purity, press them to thy heart and call them thy soul mates; fondle and tenderly care for animals and call them thy soul companions; listen to the sweet songs of the birds and call them thy soul contemporaries in nature's choir, operating in unison with thy own melodious soul, whose vibrations reach into unlimited space—yea! until they blend and are lost in the embodiment of the Over Spirit, or Cycle Supreme.

Then canst thou contemplate the mountain range, the valleys, the plains, the oceans, the seas, the lakes and the rivers, and call them thy benefactors and teachers of facts relative to the past, present and future operations of the Over Spirit, in harmony with the wisdom displayed in their wondrous organisms. Likewise, the Solar and Lunar bodies, in company with the Constellations and countless (so termed) fixed Stars that inhabit all the innumerable regions throughout absolute space, and consider them thy influential counsellors, whose ceaseless operation should give thee knowledge through thy faculty of reason. Therefore, record the facts upon thy mental pages for further contemplation and reflection, that thy intellectual or spiritual being may be illumined with greater wisdom, as it develops and traverses the various regions of eternal life, as a human epi-cycle or intellective contemporary, co-adjutant with all creation as such, under the influence of the Over Spirit, moving on the deferent of the Over Soul as an individual Epi-cycle, co-operative with the great cycles of Time, Space and Life.

I, Extension, serve as a mediator between Spirit, Soul and Matter. I and the Spirit of Animation are the silent, invisible, evolutionary agents of the Divine Principle operating through the sub-principles of Activity and Process.

We are the chemists in the great laboratory of substances, the Grē-tie'zē (Architects) or builders of the Universe; the transmitters of Energy through universal form, and the preservers of individuality; the establishers of Histology, and the executors of its laws; the natural organizers of the science of Physiology, the dispensors of Life and Motion through the functional systems; the cause of all the Molecular processes, or phenomena of life, relative to the form and action of living beings, and are the establishers of the science of Mineralogy, the natural attractive force that induces cohesion and chemical affinity, which results in the establishment of inorganic bodies.

Our influence is cognizable, not only in evolution, but in dissolution and integration as well. We operate energy both for destructive and constructive purposes, to the establishment, reproduction and preservation of material individualities.

We are responsible for all the differentiations or modifications that establish histology, and the transmission of afferent impulses over the central nerve systems, causing molecular agitation or turmoil, to which the changes of consciousness respond, resulting in motion of the motor muscular systems in unison with that of the motor nerve system, thus establishing one of the principle laws in governing the science of physiology and the phenomena of physical movement; therefore, through the combination of invisible and visible motion we have brought Spirit, Soul and Matter into co-union, developed and extended them into individual animal and vegetable epi-cycles that move according to the force and quality belonging to the individual.

As chemists, architects and builders, we not only design and construct form, but by chemical process, qualify substances for the sustenance of the same. Our process to this end is by conversion through the principles of oxidation, the source of energy, resulting in reverse transmutation, viz.: breaking down to decay and raising again to living substance, which supplies the energy for both the unseen molecular thrills and visible muscular motion. "Each act of life is the offspring of an act of death."

Escaping energies bring the so-called "death and decay," which is a closely related phenomenon to that of life, and its principal eclipse, viz., disintegration, the servant for breaking down complex substances, necessary to the result of dissolution or decay, which in turn is the source of life and energy.

Simultaneous with the beginning of form construction, we establish functional forces and agents for development, growth, and sustenance.

Through the medium of Osmosis, our manifestations may also be cognized by the force of imbibition, whereby we diffuse food solutions into the cell systems.

Activity is the agent by which we unite the external and internal forces successively, establishing the specific absorbent capacity, and make the transmission of sustenance through the primordal utricle and tissues.

We deposit starch and other plastic products into vegetation, convert them into non-nitrogenous or nitrogenous reserves, which aids lfie in its process of maintaining the vegetable form through its natural duration.

By metabolic force we reverse products, and by the difference in constructive and destructive activity, we establish excretions and secretions.

Life hereby exercises energy for the present utility of the various forms it controls, and for the future use of those it generates, by the utility of non-nitrogenous and nitrogenous surplus or storage, such as seeds, spor and cells, as depositories of reserve materials to be utilized by the offspring during the early stage of generation.

Therefore, I, Extension, co-operative with Animation, by the force of activity and energy, move the machinery of metabolism and disperse, deposit and retain products necessary to the perpetuation of material life, for its natural time of duration, or as a specific material form.

Hence, observe that we have developed all human, animal, bird and vegetable forms, as well as those of mineral and other materials by molecular processes; hence the principle of Extension, which I personify, resulting in the co-operation of Wōtz Lūtesăn'dē-ŭs (Life individual), Nĕn'ciē Dē'bŭs (time divisible) and Lē'măz Lĕt-sān'dē-ŭs (space measurable), as a trinity epi-cycle dependent as an individuality upon the Over Soul and Over Spirit Cycles.

The first material link in this development is Fō-rĕn'thŭs (protoplasm) and Over Soul quality, or the sensitive, mobile, semisubstance or amoeba, an organism consisting of a network or framework of protoplasm, filled up with other matter, thus rendering it complex in character, and the life bearer to the primordial utricle and cell in the vegetable, and the nerve and muscular tissue in the animal, and is the throne or seat of the inner or invisible motion or activity which we utilize in the process of growth, and is the prime unit of organization in the animal and vegetable form structure.

This living matter is a soul link, centrally located within the body link, which by process of development ultimates in an individualized Over Soul Body, in co-union with that of an individualized Material Body, moving on the deferent of the Over Soul Cycle, thereby receiving the vital spark of Life, which electrifies and illuminates it in response to the impulse of the Over Spirit, transmitted through the Over Soul, which completes it as an individualized epi-cycle, a fac-simile of the Over Spirit, and Over Soul Cycles from which it was generated and developed in degrees of perfection made possible by the conditions attending the creation, and its endowments of quality, together with its force necessary to reproduce under the same law, which is governed by a natural unfoldment. First, in the animal or human epi-cycle, from the links of protoplasm and eveloping nuclei, to Sĕl-mē'zŭt (spermatoza), the fertilizing elements paternal, having active motion and characteristic form, which governs the species, and the quality to fecundify.

Second, from protoplasm and developing nuclei, to the primordial and mature U'lŭs (ovum), to the rudimentary polarizing elements material, having the quality of fecundity.

Third, from the union of these elements, to Gē-lĕn'tē-zē (segmentation) and I-lĭs'cē-ŭs (concrescence), through the marvelous development of the E-nŏ'ē-ĕs (embryo) to the perfect Rē-lū'măz (fœtus), and ultimate man.

Fourth, in the vegetable epi-cycle, from the link of protoplasm and developing nuclei, to the O'lŭm (pollen) grain, the male or fertilizing element, having the force to influence generation and the quality to fecundify.

Fifth, from protoplasm and the developing nuclei, to the U-lĭ'ŭs (ovule) or ripened seed, the female or rudimentary generative element, having the quality of fecundity.

Sixth, from gamogenesis, the marriage of these elements, to Tē-cē-ē'tē (cell), Yĕlz (duct), I-ĕn'cy (fiber), and Un'dŏd (wood) production, having place in the marvelous development of vegetable forms, from an embryo to the perfect plant or tree.

The second link in the construction of form is the nucleus, the seat or throne of individual process, or multiplication and reproduction, which we establish by the force of motion or activity, in response to the impulse of the Over Spirit upon the first link.

The third link is the living cell, the foundation of the material form through which, as before stated, the mediant Over Soul form, co-adjutantly develops with that of the material, and through which the Over Spirit makes manifest.

The fourth link is tissue, the throne or seat of life, and activity, from which all the phenomena of the body epi-cycle is performed, and the agent through which it is fed, controlled and supported as an individuality of Spirit, Soul and Body, as an extended and animated form or epi-cycle.

ME-LEN'ZON SI USH VINZ LE-A'SA, ENT NEN'CE DE'BUS,

OR

INFLUENCE OF THE OVER SPIRIT IN TIME DIVISIBLE.

Gä'lä's absolute measure and Wōtz's relative duration,
The Infinite Sī-ĭ'kĕl, linking the past, present and future;
Endless apparent, by the ceaseless records of motion,
And the positive causes operating in phenomenal nature.

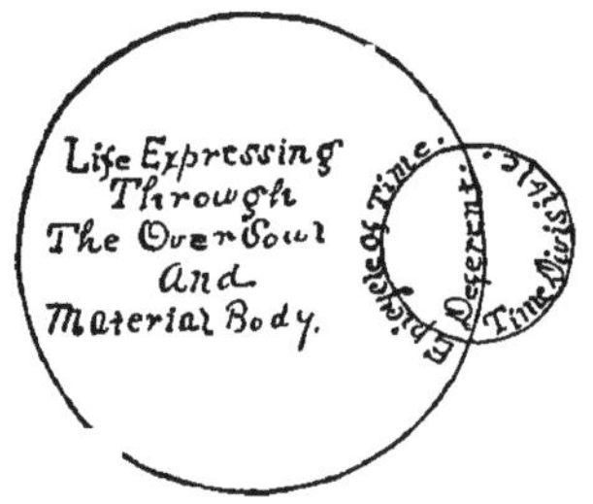

USH LE-A'SA SI GE-I-RISH'E,

OR

THE SPIRIT OF DURATION.

TELTZIE V.

An *Over Spirit Quality,* the force of continuity in nature,
Expressing through the Yĕt'ly Sī-ĭ'kĕl of time divisible,
By modes of cohesion and life's measuring feature,
The material form period, and absolute of the spiritual.

I, Ush Lē-ā'sä Sī Gē-ī-Rĭsh'ē (The Spirit of Duration), from out the depths of the hidden past, speak unto thee.

I am Nature's Scribe, who holds eternal record of facts, having existence through the operation of positive causes, specifically influenced by my contemporary Over Spirit qualities, viz: Animation and Extension, who measure the divisions of time by the principle of operative motion, which are to be occupied by all the individualized material forms having existence throughout my domain and through all the cycles of time.

As the Spirit of Duration, I am termed Rē-lĕn'tī-ē (Eternity) and am recognized by an aggregate of past, present and future time, the Kā-nĕr'ĕt (Infinite) Cycle within which all time cycles operate.

Positive causes, the innovate forces of the universe, co-existent and co-operate with myself, have established and individualized principle cycles the phenomena of which has further established compendious cycles which mortals in their degrees of recognition and further comprehension, have used to measure portions of my existence, and as the basis of their Nĕn'ciē Rē-lăn-sē'ŭs (Time Calendars), in periods past and present.

By these forces worlds without number, at various periods of time, have found existence and dispersement throughout space, as individual material cycles, there to rotate in cycles of time, relative to Infinite Duration, the cognition of which is deduced by mathematical calculation.

By the movement of these worlds in their orbits the cycles of Wīl'gĕt nŭd Yēte (night and day) were established, which further established compendious epi-cycles of time operating on the deferent of the great Cycle of Duration, the compendate result of which forms the operative time links, the extension of which unfolds Bĕl'zē (seconds) into Rē-nĕt'zē (minutes); Lŏnt'zē (hours); Yēte'zē (days); Sō-ĕt'zē(weeks); Ash-nŏr'zē (months); Yĕlt'zē (years); Vrĕx'zē (periods); O-jĕt'zē (ages); Rē-lĕn'tīe (eternity); or Absolute Duration, which embodies the foregoing Infinite system of time epi-cycles.

Every rising of the sun in the golden glow of the morning, or its setting in the glorious tints of the evening; every phase of the moon as manifested by its waxing and its waning, thus changing the perfect fullness of its silvery disc; every unveilment of the stars in the heavens to the eyes of the earth's dwellers, by the cessation of the light of the Sun at night, or their hidden view when it returns in the morning; every wave of the ocean that lashes the time-worn sands of the beach, or the tides that ceaselessly ebb and flow; every rock that is formed by the co-herence of material, and every metal that finds its bedding in the mountains and valleys; every animate or inaminate form of individualized creation, and the life that perpetuates its kind moves and operates in its own individual time cycles, each a unit link in the great Cycle of Duration.

Thus, by the motion of individual forms or natural phenomena, induced by positive causes under the influence of my contemporary principles, Animation and Extension, the intelligence of man has been induced to conceive ideas of time divisible, which latter he has, through mathematical calculation, aided by spirit inspiration and influence, utilized for calendar purposes, and a further knowledge of the Spirit of Duration.

But few peoples have ever inhabited the worlds of the universe, during all periods of the cycle of Duration, who have not in some way recognized and utilized different time compends, or sorts of compendium of the science. It is a part of the infinite spirit that embodies In-trō-săn'trä (creation), and its recognition has been inevitable according to the sensual faculties, or that quality belonging to life, or to human individuality, as well as an operative force of response to the influence, by all animate and inaminate individualities thus governed, according to their individual needs regarding development and continuity of existence and operation thereof.

Degrees of perfection have been reached in different worlds according to the development existing therein, and the natural influences brought to bear upon them. Therefore, knowledge gained and advanced, or retrograded and lost, has been limited by ideas in variance with records kept or lost by descended, or extinct peoples. As in the present, so it has been in the past. There have been records preserved and those that have been lost. Those pre-historic, and those historic, while some of the long-lost have been re-posessed by excavations, and others re-inspird by spirit intelligences, into the minds of mortals of subsequent generations, who have conceived the ideas and brought them forth again for future developments; *e. g.,* some that had been traced on stone and other materials in ages long agone, are being unearthed in the present period of time, while the individuals contemporaneous with the time of those records have passed into the zones of spirit life, and from thence are reaching out and inspiring sensitive intelllgences now in the mortal sphere, with facts concerning these lost links and cycle records, a condition which has existed in all ages of past time, though the mortal earth dwellers are not generally willing to give credence to the facts in the case, but rather recognize them as idealistic conceptions, used principally for legendary or traditional purposes.

Earthquakes and volcanic eruptions have archived many past records, some of which by recurring, or new conditions, will be re-possessed by future generations, as in the case of excavations at Pompeii, and many other places known to modern readers and travelers, while many more will be made known and reproduced, as this work is being given by spirit intelligences to mortal sensitives; for through this source has all the greatness ot the 20th century been originated, developed and perfected.

Links and Cycles

Cataclysms have submerged and obliterated records of greatness in times pre-historic and antequated, as well as in times modern, as was the case on the At'län-ti-än Continent long ages agone, and tablets containing some of their records have already been found along the borders or remnant portions of that illustrious country, and will in time be recognized as such. Conditions will yet come in future time which will enable moderns to possess themselves with records and further evidences of the so termed "lost arts" and scinces (not lost but archived by the works of nature), which now lie embedded beneath the sands of the Atlantic Ocean and other waters, which characterized the material and intellectual life cycles of that and other races of people.

No less changeable will be the conditions of the present and future centuries regarding the records of the past. Although the 20th century mortals boast of their greatness in records produced and preserved, yet printed as they are on flimsy paper, many will be destroyed and lost in the future by conflagrations; *e. g.*, as were those of the great libraries of Alexandria, Egypt, by which much was lost that otherwise would have linked past knowledge of the sciences, arts and philosophies with that of the present, and which former, future generations will earnestly endeavor to possess themselves with.

That which is lost can only be obtained in two ways, viz First, from disembodied intelligences who are in possession of the facts contemporaneous with their mortal lives, or have become acquainted with them after their disembodiment, who reveal the same unto embodied mortals yet on the earth plane. Secondly, by monumental evidences or remains being discovered in the above named natural archives by excavations and removed waters, or submarine explorations, the result of which must of necessity establish facts and not fiction, whether they be accepted as such or not.

Finally, every epicycle of life, through the Over Soul and Material Body or Form, represents an epi-cycle of time divisible, moving on the deferent of the Over Soul, according to its material and spiritual duration, both being infinite, never cease operation and development, the former changing at the end of its specific duration as an individual material epi-cycle, to form some new individuality in the material region, and the latter continuous in spirit zones, changing in quality or perfection of being as an eternal individuality or disembodied individual epi-cycle of life, the duration of which is Eternity.

The individual material epi-cycle, therefore, being of shorter duration than the spirtual as an individual, hence no longer a contour of the original spirit, which latter, like thoughts, has departed on the vibratory wings of life, (the mode of spirit transport or travel, the rapidity being governed by will) or absolute Duration.

Oo Ush Lĕ-ă'să Sĭ Gĕ-ĭ-Rĭsh'ĕ (I, the Spirit of Duration), therefore, am the quality, serving the Over Spirit in the establishment of all individualized existence, be it of Material or Spiritual Life, from all molecules cognized only by the sense of spirit vision to the smallest that can be recognized by mortal sight; from the most minute insect or bug, to the most majestic of the bird family; from the most tiny worm, to the greatest reptile; from the smallest animalcule, to the largest mammoth; from the most tiny vertebrate, to the largest whale; from the infant embryo, to the giant of mankind; from the smallest atom to the majestic rock and the stupendous mountain; from the humid particle, to the mighty ocean's breadth and depth; from the smallest seed, to the largest vegetable or mammoth tree; from the tiniest moss bloom to the largest flower; from soul original to that of individual being and from spirit Infinite, to that Eternal, all of which move and operate in epi-cycles of time, on the deferent of the great Cycle of Duration.

USH QUA'TE-OTS SI WOTZ,
OR
THE ECLIPSES OF LIFE.

When the grass and corn blades have grown yellow and gray,
And the forest trees don tints of red, golden and brown;
When the stubbled fields reaped of their cereals and hay,
And the weeds of the field are withered and breaking down;
When the wild purple aster and golden-rod solemnly appeals,
And the decaying herbs mingle with the quiet falling leaves;
When Nature thus pays a last tribute to verdureless fields,
And the caterpillar his last chrysalis cocoon covering weaves;
When the spider hides in the secret cell of his time-worn web,
And the crickets and grasshoppers have ceased their chirping;
When the bugs and insects to their secret hidings have fled,
And the nut-burrs have opened and their kernels are falling;
When thistles, flags, and milk-weeds on cotton pinion combines,
And other avolating seeds join in pursuit on the aerial plane;
When the yellow pumpkins cling to their frost-bitten vines,
And the corn-shocks are drooping with unhusked ripe grain;

Links and Cycles

When the moistened autumn leaves like tears of sadness fall,
In soft, rythmic accents to the low, sad sighing of the breeze;
When as they have thus fallen they cover the earth like a pall,
And all nature lamentingly responds to the sad funeral call;
When the distant dim hills in their marvelous, hazy outline,
And the veil-tinted valleys blend in their extent below;
When the sombre cloudlets join the mysterious, solemn combine,
And the be-shadowed waters mirror them as they gently flow;
When butterflies feebly hover over the fading clover fields,
And the bees lazily gather honey from the last wild flowers;
When the migratory birds fill their craws with cereal meals,
And rise from the stubble to take flight to fairer bowers;
When the human body totters and the venerable form is bent,
And the face is wrinkled, the hair turning to gray and white;
'Tis then the eclipse over spirit and soul, for disembodiment,
Creeps over their material forms like the sleep of the night;
A connecting link between the mortal and spirit visibility,
To conceal the passing of the latter from the former entity;
'Tis then Animation bids Life its material expression to cease,
And also Extension its developing force and control to release;
The spirit to pass on to zones of eternal light and Duration,
Gä'lä's ultimate placement for individualized spirit creation.

USH NAT'THUS NUD NELT'THER ZIN'ETH ITH'NA,

OR

THE PLANETS AND THEIR ZONE CONDITIONS.

TELTZIE VI.

In contemplation of the planets and their Space Zones, time and space will not permit of a general explanation thereof, as it would take volumes in which to record all the Spirit helpers would like to give us on the subject, but enough will be given however, to lead up to more scientific and general considerations in the future, which the author hopes to bring out, or perhaps may be by other Spirit Sensitives, who in subsequent time may be fitted by Spirit Inspirers and Helpers for the work.

The terms which we shall now use for the planets and the zodiac, are such as are known and only used by spirits who have passed beyond the Earth plane, for we are informed by A'lĕm Prō'lĕx that the terms used by mortal Astronomers, cease usage by those in spirit, who instead, adopt the nomenclature instituted by spirit Astronomers, which are one and the same to all nations of spirits having passed from any of the planets in the zodiac of the Sun, and that each succeeding zodiac system beyond this, is governed by changed nomenclature suited to the conditions and developments naturally, spiritually and scientifically in those regions of space.

Klŭm is therefore the term used for the Sun, meaning electric fire, and not only refers to that marvelous body of electric force which disperses light and heat throughout its zodiac, but also to the zone of space in which it is posed.

In regard to its influencive condition, spirit astronomers have further termed it Wĕnz, the term referring to it as the radiant centre of spiritual development.

Cŏn-cĕn′sū, likewise for the planet and zone of Mercury, meaning electric light.

Rē-lōw′, for that of Venus, meaning activity, or a dancing motion which is natural to that planet.

Crĕt-lōw′, for that of the Earth, meaning a circular motion, or orbit.

Cĕl-ē-mĕt′, for that of Mars, meaning density of the planet.

Lū-ē-ĕt′, for that of Jupiter, meaning transparency.

Lē-ō-lĕt′, for that of Saturn, meaning to encircle.

Kē-rĕn′ey, for that of Uranus, meaning ultimate, referring to the close of material education.

Mē-lū′nē-ä, for that of Nepture, meaning illumination, it being the last planet in the Sun's zodiac, as recognized by the earth dwellers, the term meaning effulgence.

The El-thē′ër (Atmosphere) surrounding each planet is characterized with chromatic conditions peculiar to the Kū-lĕt′ (orbit) in which it moves, being visible to spirit only, and that in its grandest sense or intensity; *e. g.*, that of Mercury which is ,a beautiful blue; of Venus, a very deep blue; of the Earth, a rosy hue, shading up to the crimson, such as oftentimes is reflected at morning or evening on the horizon and in the waters, visible to mortal vision; of Mars, a golden hue, which is caused principally from shades reflected into that orbit by Saturn; of Jupiter, a deep orange; of Saturn, a beautiful emerald or transparent green, which is caused by a great volume of water through which a golden light radiates, thus causing the atmosphere to have the transparent color; of Uranus, a white light, slightly tinged with yellow; of Neptune, that of a brilliant light commingled with the yellow-tinted white light of the atmosphere of Uranus, and that of the effulgent light reflected from Rē-plē′si-ä, the central planet in the next higher zodiac.

The colors above mentioned as qualifying the space zones of the various planest, are visible to spirits at all times, day or night, but were it possible for a mortal from the planet Earth to stand on the various planets, they could only see the colors at daytime. When thus viewed by material eyes, the changes in their intensity are best recognized at the morning and evening hours, as often seen on the horizon of the Earth, when at sunrise or sunset the rosy and crimson hues of the atmospheric condition are such as to afford it.

An Earth mortal, however, if on Mercury, could see the crystal light of the planet and the blue tint of the atmosphere surrounding it at daytime, but no change of tints at morning and evening, as on that planet there is scarcely any twilight as compared with that of the Earth, which brings quickly the sombre shades of night. There is no night on Mercury, as compared with that of the Earth, for the planet passes quickly into a condition similar to that of the latter-named planet on a very dark day when the Sun is obscured by the dense atmosphere, being a trifle darker, however, which to mortal vision would deaden the sparkle of the crystal molecules of which the planet is composed.

So it is to spirit or mortal vision on the planet Venus; however, being a generative planet, it has not the same brilliancy of Mercury. When the change from night to day is coming on, or vice-versa, the light retracts and returns, the radiations moving spasmodically as it were, thus coming on like shooting advances of light, and vice-versa, which is caused by the darker or denser condition of the planet and its surrounding atmosphere, which causes a change similar to that of the Earth as night comes on, which causes the blue to be more or less intense, or shadowed. There is therefore a little more twilight on Venus than on Mercury, being similarly caused to that of the Earth light and shadows according to the density or transparency of the atmosphere, and the distance they occupy from the Sun, and also lights reflected upon them from other planets, strongest at morning, evening, or night, when the angle, co-relative with the reflection from the water creates the difference to the vision.

The shades reflected from Saturn pass through the blue ether in connection with the rays of the Sun, giving the golden tint to the zone of the Earth.

Tints and colors on the planets are often reflected by worlds that are passing and re-passing (which latter will never be discovered by mortal Astronomers) that thus reflect their lights or shadows upon the other planets. It has been said that new worlds have been discovered at various times. They are not new, but are as old as the Earth itself, and some much older.

Submerged Atlantis Restored

Klũm, the mighty orb and king that governs the existence of all worlds and the individual life thereon, throughout its zodiac, is stationarily enthroned, has no revolutionary motion either on its axis or throughout an orbit, as is the case with its subjects, the planets, but has placement at a given point of equilibrium within the centre of an El-thē-ĕr-ĕc'ly (atmospheric) zone.

All existence has its being as such through some form of the conceptive principle, and Nature has made no exception to this operative law in the process of cosmic creation.

The space zone of the Sun is the original formative womb of the Electric principle materially, which produces orbs of the male order only. All planets and worlds of the Sun's zodiac have been, and will continue to be born into Absolute Space, within the space zone of the Sun, which is the cradle in its zodiac where they have been rocked into existence as such.

As they there gathered strength enough to establish them as infant worlds, they moved out, yet extremely slow, thus radiating from the point of their birth into the zodiac of the Sun, relatively aged, according to their distance from it, or the place of their birth. The movement outward is so extremely slow that earth astronomers have failed to cognize the fact. It has taken numberless millions of years for the planets to assume their present positions; therefore, even Mercury is an old planet according to the lapse of time; hence, in the same ratio, Neptune arrived in its present spaze zone during a period of time not easily comprehended by mortal minds.

There are now, though invisible on earth, spherical bodies being formed in the space zone of the Sun, some of which in ages to come, will occupy the zones now posessed by Mercury, Venus and the Earth, and so on, as each of these planets move on out to occupy the space zone of the next planet in order; a law of progression governing their movements, which is on and on into the succeeding zodiac of Qũin-tĕn'zē (worlds), etc., for in every argument relative to creation and the origin of all things, the law of progression must render the account and also balance the scale of facts.

Cŏn-cĕn'sū (Mercury) emits a very bright light (as has been observed by telescopic aid), though only occasionally visible on the earth plane because of its nearness to the Sun. The sides of the sphere present themselves to the Sun, which angle establishes its axis. The sphere is a little more eliptic than that of the other planets. Its body is composed of material atoms of the crystaline order, known to spirit geologists as Jē-lē'cŭs, or crystal atoms, and also by the term Fē-lē'di-ä, which refers to the male quality or influence, and which they affirm is the electric or male principle in cosmogonic creation, or spirit entities in an embryotic state, and of which Mercury is entirely composed, there being scarcely any magnetic conditions in the planet or its space zone, hence termed a male planet by spirit astronomers.

It being so much nearer the Sun than the other planets the male crystal atoms or molecules are impregnated or highly electrified therefrom, which condition endows them with the male principle or force, as it were.

There are no mountains on Mercury, as has been supposed by some earth astronomers. It being composed of the one elementary principle, viz., electric, there is no magnetic principle to attract and repel; hence no convulsive conditions to establish rocks and their upheavals; consequently no mountains.

What is supposed to be spots on this planet, such as discovered by Schröter, are simply shadows from passing material orbs or cosmic bodies, smaller than Mercury, not visible to earth astronomers.

The atmospheric zone through which Mercury passes is also highly electric, for no planet, not even the Sun, exists without an atmospheric condition surrounding it, and peculiarly adapted to its existence as such.

There are no streams or bodies of water on Mercury, and there being no magnetic or female principle in existence there, materially speaking, there is therefore no developed individual life creation, for in the absence of the latter-named principle, material individualities can never be formed on Mercury in its present location.

Rē-lōw′ (Venus) is known to spirit astronomers as Nē-ī-ĕn′tē, or the female planet in the Sun's zodiac, because it has taken on the Magnetic force which spirit intelligences recognize as the female principle in all cosmographic formations.

It is upon this planet that the original embryotic formative principle is established in relation to all forms of creation, and the principle of extension does its first work, but which only reaches the embryotic molecular degree of development.

Venus, like Mercury, is possessed of water, which conditions it as a body, and the atmosphere that surrounds it, necessary to the existence and development of the embryotic or life molecules developed on the planet, by the conjunction of the electric and magnetic molecules or entities.

The electric radiations from the Sun penetrate the atmospheric zones of Mercury and Venus, which furnishes them heat, and in the case of the latter in connection with the principle of moisture which further establishes the productive principle, and under the influence of animation, the electric principle from the sun-rays, establishes motion in the magnetic body, the ultimatum of which is warmth and health, according to the degrees of electric force.

That the reader may better comprehend the great creative principle in operation, we will say that it is the space zone in which a planet develops and further exists that gives it its degree of creative and developing force. When Venus had the position that Mercury now occupies, it was then all electric and a male orb; but when it passed to its present position it gathered the Magnetic Principle, which brought to it the female force for embryotic development. So it was with the Earth as it occupied the now positions of Mercury and Venus, and as it passed to its present position it took on further developing forces to the ultimatum of the present condition of material life in the form, subject to changes, etc. So it will be with Mercury as it passes on out into the positions now occupied by Venus and the Earth.

The electric condition of Venus, co-operative with those of the Sun, meet and penetrate the fluidic atoms of the magnetic principle belonging to Venus and the Space Zone in which it revolves, which established the conceptive principle of the planet in regard to individual life entities or formative prnciples generally.

The electric light from the Sun, co-operative with the electric and magnetic conception, establishes a circular or spiral motion which generates the magnetic heat and establishes further development, which is the life force of all existence. Therefore, Venus, so to speak, is the womb of the whole system of planets, and all life thereon, and throughout the atmospheric zones through which they operate.

When the electric or positive force comes in contact with the magnetic or negative condition, combustion takes place which throws off balls of light; hence the force which produces light, a condition that is controlled by quantity, intensity and conductivity, or natural process, whereby light is diffused into organic formative existence, or lost by opposing conductivity. Illustrative to this fact, note the balls of fire and light that at times fly in radiations from the trolley line at the point of its connection with the trolley pole, especially so when the wire is wet or icy, etc., when the negative and positive conditions come together. The same conditions may be observed with any electric machinery under the same influences; hence the force thus produces light.

Electric rays are set in motion by the rays of the Sun, no matter if the atmosphere is conditioned with clouds or density. These rays meet the magnetic element just the same. There is always the flash, whether the sun shines visibly or not. It is the excess electric element and force over that of the magnetic, whether in the atmosphere, or in the trolley, or electric machine, the excess becoming fire. When the current of electricity overpowers the magnetic element, the equilibrium is disturbed and the excess force terminates in balls of fire.

As the original electric molecules of Venus were attracted to the liquid magnetic element of the Space Zone, or the latter to the former, they retained their original form, for they are not dissolvable, but expand under the magnetic condition in the water, whereby the embryotic life entity is esatblished, the crystal entity being surrounded by an individualized portion of the magnetic element, much as the yolk of an egg is enclosed within the albumen, etc. Thus it remains for a long time varying according to the conditions surrounding the two united forces. Then animation proceeds with its work in the establishment of motion, as far as to the last stage of development natural to the planet of Venus, in which condition it fits the thus individualized con-junct forces or molecules of life for further transmission through the space zone of Venus, and further attraction into that of the Earth, and ultimately to the latter-named planet. This spiral motion established by the crystal or male spirit life germ, in the magnetic element surrounding it, is the process which ultimates in an individualized spirit entity within a magnetic globule or soul entity, and as such continues its motion and is caught up by the greater electric and magnetic forces or conveyed on the deferent of the Over Spirit and Over Soul to the region of the Earth, where as above stated they are further developed.

Neither the electric crystal or the magnetic element are in themselves productive. A co-union of these two forces becomes necessary with that of heat and moisture to establish the result. The influence is triple, for animation begins with the Sun, which has its effect upon Mercury, and the Sun and Mercury affect Venus, when the real birth of individuality follows these combined effects.

There would be no life entity established on Venus, originally speaking, were it not for the heat, a quality of the Sun or electric activity. Mercury exercises its force by dispersing its electric particles, co-adjutant with the heat of the Sun, by radiant electric force on to the planet of Venus.

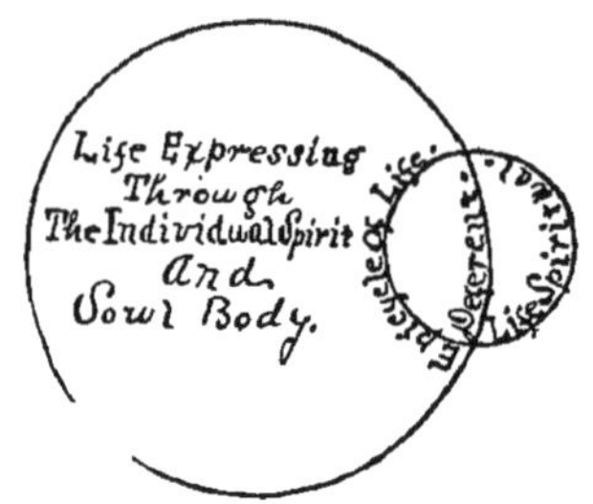

USH RED'ZE MI-ZETS'

OR

THE GREATER HEIGHTS.

Cĕl-ē-mĕt', (Mars) is known to Spirit Astronomers as Mĕz'-mŭs, the term referring to the trinity of developing forces, male, female, and child production, thus embodied under a higher and more spiritual order, or condition.

Mars is the only planet aside from the earth having on it material or physical birth, be it human or vegetable. All life on the following planets, there exists as spirit and soul individualized beings, under development as such. E. g., First, take a mortal on the plane of the Earth, let his or her soul pass out from the material Earth body, it is then ready for further development such as will fit it to pass on to the planet Mars, or into its space zone as a disembodied individuality ready for further development as such, where it may possess knowledge relative to that planet.

Second, take an individualized being, born materially or physically on the planet Mars, and after the term of years alotted the individual for remaining there in a material body natural to that planet, let the spirit and soul pass out from that Mars body, it also is ready for further development such as shall fit it to pass on from Mars to the planet Jupiter, or into its space zone, as a disembodied individual also, ready for further development as a soul and spirit, which may possess it with knowledge relative to that planet.

Therefore, as there is no material or physicial birth on any planet beyond Mars, the soul and spirit leaving it, having had a material on the planet Earth, and the soul and spirit having had a material or physicial birth on the planet Mars, may each pass individually to the plane of Jupiter as individualized spirits and souls, which latter planet they inhabit as such during the period of time necessary for that development as individualities, such as shall fit them to pass on to the other planets, as far as to that of Uranus, the conditions of each planet affording developing influences necessary to the animation, extension, and duration of the individuality of all life on the various planets, and that of the space zones that intervene them, a fact which must of itself denounce the dogmas of individual re-incarnation.

The inhabitants on Mars consist of but one race of white people; thus through the law of development, there are no colored souls after leaving the earth body they vacated, only temporarily, but when they wish to return to the earth plane to manifest as spirits to surviving mortals, for identification, they have the ability to take on or assume their original color condition, as they do garments and infirmities that belonged to them on the earth plane, that they may thereby be recognized by their friends, as the Că-cĕl'lä (spirit sensitive) thus describes them. They are kind, extremely spiritual and intelligent people, far superior to the earth races. The material conditions of Mars are finer than those on the Earth, consequently the people are less ponderous of body. They are some smaller than the people of Earth, and generally speaking, they live to greater ages as well. Their system of education is more like reformatory schools, when compared with that of the Earth peoples. It embraces science, arts, literature, spiritual and mental growth, etc. Their chief enterprise is simply that of agriculture, whereby they obtain sustenance for their material bodies, prefering rather to advance spiritually and mentally, than commercially, hence, when passing from their material bodies they are better prepared to advance rapidly as spirits and souls, than are those who pass from the material plane of the Earth. 'Tis thus they hold to one good principle as a great brotherhood, which is based upon forces in nature, as set forth in this book. No creeds or isms come in to divide them in opinion, for being highly spiritual, inspirational, and sensitive to various spirit influences, among whom are therefore many Că-cĕl-lä'zē (spirit sensitives), they are taught chiefly by spirit helpers, many truths they otherwise could not have become conscious of while in the body.

Mars, geographically, is not divided into district spherical zones as is the case on the Earth maps, for the reason that these materially differ in degrees of temperature. In the first place, the northern hemisphere is much milder than that of the Earth. The seasons are extremely changeable from year to year, which affects all parts of the globe differently as well as from time to time, hence the inequality which otherwise might cause the establishment of specified spherical zones. The seasons are greatly affected by reflective conditions that reach the planet from the other planets, as well as from the Sun. This fact has rendered it very changeable as the planets also sustain periodical changes, as is the case on the Earth, any one of the seasons is liable to changes, more or less intense in regard to cold and heat, according to the same influences, but more intense than on the Earth, especially in regard to heat. It is so intense in some parts of Mars at times that, the inhabitants wear very loose garments, and, in many instances, none at all, a fact never looked upon by the inhabitants as an immodest or improper act, they being so spiritually minded.

The ruddy appearance on the planet is caused by the light of the Sun and the manner in which it strikes the planet, similar to the rose and crimson that is seen on the earth at sunrise or sunset which is caused by reflected light. The greenish hue also seen at times on the planet, is caused by the pure light of the planet not under the condition of reflection from the rays of the sun.

The veil that the earth astronomers have observed as coming on at times over Mars in the winter, varying from hours to days, and even months at a time, was caused by intervening clouds.

Lū-ē-et′ (Jupiter) is known to spirit astronomers as Wē′zē-lŭs, or the elementary body for soul and spirit development.

Here the spirit and soul aspires to greater heights in regard to spiritual love for the grandeur and beauty in nature, such as has thus far unfolded to their vision, and yet to be seen and understood as having arisen from the operations of the Over Spirit and the Over Soul in relation to unfoldment or development in the realms of all life. Here they are wonderfully impressed with the principles of harmony; natural art; music of the spheres; beauty in nature; and especially that degree unto which the spirits and souls of all humanity may attain through the refining process natural to higher life; sexual and material advancement through which the individual recognizes the sublimity, the magnificence, the elegance displayed by natures unfoldments on that planet, and the blending of their own spirits and souls into the aura of that of the great Over Spirit and Over Soul, thus giving greater impulse or desire for research after general knowledge regarding the Gä′lä (God) principles.

The great size of Jupiter, when compared with the other planets, is due to its stronger electric and magnetic forces whereby it draws a greater quantity of material molecules, under spiritualized conditions, that have been thrown off from other planets, as it sweeps through the sun's zodiac during its revolutions about the latter.

This principle holds good in the case of all the planets, the size being due to the electric and magnetic forces of the planet body to attract to itself the refined molecules of its orbit, thrown off from other planets during their revolutions, and that have been attracted to the various space zones of the planets, some of them being strongest in the magnetic and some in the electric, hence the force necessary to the varied effects. However, these forces in Jupiter are nearly equal.

In these cases, an equilibrium of forces must be established, hence those planets having the greater magnetic, attract electric to that end, and *vice versa.*

Since Jupiter was naturally possessed with an equilibrium in this respect, it was, and is, therefore, able to draw a greater quantity of the material atoms from the space zone with which to build itself greater than those planets that were not naturally equally qualified with the two forces, and, therefore, had no exercise their stronger forces to replenish the weaker, hence, less able to gather excess material for their further engrossment of body. This principle or condition is the same in the nature of human bodies as well, and exists also in the vegetable and animal, hence difference in size and characteristices. In case of the human organism, the unusual possession of the two forces renders the individual incapable to act as a Spirit Sensitive, to any degree of certainty, for Spirit Operators who would otherwise use them as instruments through whose forces they would make manifestations, cannot do so without first supplying their beings with the neressary force lacking, which if done, or attempted, weakens the Spirit from whom the force must be given, which also disqualifies the operator and the instrument for further development, hence so many failures in case of desired development as Că-cĕl-lä'ze (Spirit Sensitives). Those who come most readily into the service, as a general thing, are those who possessed the equilibrium even at birth. Some, however, may be brought to greater degrees of manifesting ability through the equilibrium that arises from the blending of the two forces natural to the two Cacellaze, one being by nature the stronger electric, and the other magnetic, and when together, are used by spirit forces that likewise are blended to the same equilibrium established in the aura of the two Cacellaze (as is the case with instruments and operators who are bringing to light the contents of this work), the Spirit operators are therefore less hindered by opposing influences, and weakening of their own forces by otherwise necessary supplies.

There are material planetary bodies preparing for birth, as it were, into regions of the zodiac of the Sun, thus unequally balanced by the two forces, hence unable to draw to themselves the material necessary for further structure development, and therefore become extinct, as is the case with meteors, falling stars, etc., that seemingly fall to the Earth, which in reality the larger specimens do, but some of the weaker and less developed, find their repose on Mercury and Venus, and therefore do not become planets, for which they embryotically were intended, or organized. These embryotic bodies, therefore, are not parts of volcanic dislodgement from the Earth, or discarded matter thrown off from other planets, as generally supposed, but failures arising from the above named causes.

Some of these orbs, less weak, and, therefore, having passed beyond the planet Venus, have continued their existence as satellites. It is the electric and magnetic forces embodied in the various planets that have attracted to them the satellites which originally were among the infant cosmic bodies that were seeking a space zone for themselves, and which now hold them in co-operation with themselves as satellite accompaniments, otherwise they would have disintegrated, and have fallen in that condition of particles to the planet nearest to them, as do the meteors and falling stars on that of the Earth.

Therefore, what we term the Moon, and all the satellites now known to Earth Astronomers, come under this principle of establishment and continued existence, by borrowed forces, etc.

Those planets having no visible satellites, are not strong enough to attract and hold them as such.

All worlds become individual cycles only complete when they have drawn to themselves all the material that their specific forces are capable of.

As the axis of Jupiter is nearly perpendicular to its orbit, there is but little change in the seasons, hence its great force to continually attract material for development, and that more evenly, since the change from cold to heat and *vice versa* does not occur to such an extent as to consequently resist.

Some planets go out of existence as such, after having been long matured, in the event of which they become accellerated in motion, rotating faster and faster, by which means they throw off their material composition, which goes out into space, thus reduced to atoms again, which are attracted again unto new worlds in their process of formation, hence, like the human body, or that of all material forms, being changed to re-establish new ones, as throughout all time, disintegration and integration operates for that purpose.

Jupiter is composed of both land and water. The colored

strips as seen by Earth Astronomers, are caused by reflected light from the other planets, and the colorings are caused by different rays through which the light passes, as the planet changes its position. The Earth being between the Sun and Jupiter, produces a different coloring to the Earth vision, than it would be if the latter were between the Earth and the Sun. The copper color on Jupiter is caused by reflected light from the Sun, as it is passing through vapor.

Lĕ-ō-lĕt′(Saturn), is known to Spirit Astronomers as Tī-rēne, or place for greater unfoldment of spirit intelligence regarding the principle of love in its purest sense; elegance of spirit and soul, such as comes to the individual through research after the grandeur and higher conditions and influences of life, as belonging to the depths of the Over Spirit and Over Soul principles; natural laws; higher conditions in relation to harmony and order; beautifying the Spirit and Soul through higher refinements; intellectual advancement by higher development attained through the knowledge of, and adherence to, natural sciences there attained, all of which comes under the influence and inspiration rendered by spirit intelligence, for there are no material individualties on Saturn, excepting of the refined soul nature, the coarser having ceased when leaving the Earth, and next grade of refined on departure from Mars, and the body there inhabited.

While Saturn sustains and aids the revolutions of its satellites, it also throws off equally a magnetic force from all sides of its sphere, which meets the electric force in its space zone, and causes the rings to be established about the planet. The electric force being in excess to that of the magnetic, causes combustion which is continually taking place, and by the aid of the polarized light thus established, the rings become individualized and continuous.

A-lem Prō′lŏx here informs us that, a fourth and outer ring is being established at the present time, now visible to spirit vision, and that in time, it will also be visible to earth astronomers.

Part of the illumination however, is caused by reflected light from its satellites, which becomes brighter when they are nearest it.

The rings thus established are illuminated the strongest on the sides facing the satellites, as the penetrative force is not strong enough to pass through the whole body of the rings, therefore, the inner sides of the rings are apparently shadowed, thus darker, while the illuminated sides appear more opaque.

The rings are not directly back of each other, consequently

the space between them gives the appearance of dark stripes, each of which grows denser as it nears the planet, hence darker.

The inner ring is the largest, and brightest of the three, which is occasioned by being more opaque than the dense space or band back of it, which brings it out still brighter.

The inner shadows become brighter as they are located in nearness to the planet, the outer ones being less intense, because they are thinner, and, therefore, more penetratable by the light.

Ages agone, the planet was more eliptic in shape, but by force of rotation, attraction and repulsion during long ages, it is less intense in that respect, in a spheric sense, having thrown off more material at the region of the poles, than at the equatorial points, hence the present condition of the orb.

The apparent changes that have come on the surface of the planet, is from the fact that there were and still are great liquid upheavals.

There is a greater portion of water on the planet than of land, which gives place to great tidal waves, which move with great rapidity, thus causing the disturbance as observed by earth astronomers. The water is thus thrown outward by subterene convulsions in the form of waves, only it is a greater body of water which rises at once, and then reacts. The movement of the water is most wonderful to spirit vision, and known to them as being the result of subterene disturbances. Similar ones take place in the deep waters on the Earth plane, but are small indeed when compared with those of Saturn.

Kē-rĕn′ey (Uranus), is known to spirit astronomers as Cē-rĕl′zĕr, or planet where the material influences cease, and the spirit turns away therefrom, and the reverse motion of the planet to that of the preceding ones, is to them symbolic of the unfoldment of all spiritual matters through further mental effort which the individual spirit must exercise before passing on to Neptune.

When an individual spirit has reached Uranus he or she must have possessed themselves with a general knowledge of the laws and sciences relative to the operative principle in nature, so far as regards material formations, etc., such as the origin and extension of form, and the co-operative forces of the Over Spirit and Over Soul relative to their dispersment into individualized epi-cycles, and further unfoldment as they move on the deferent of the Supreme Cycles, in their development from Mercury to Mars inclusive, which takes ages for the most refined and progressive minds to accomplish.

After an individual spirit has attained to this degree of education or knowledge, he or she must return from Uranus, to the space zone of the Earth for the purpose of gaining further knowledge regarding the laws and sciences that govern all spirit existence, which they do as they pass to and fro through the various planets and their space zones, thus to attain to the greater heights of all spirit principles and forces, and therefore the better to understand the true relation that exists between the great Supreme Cycles, Over Spirit and Over Soul and their developments, the foundation upon which all creation stands, the principles that have established all individual epi-cycles, and that hold in keeping the charge of their eternal existence as unfolding entities of Spirit and Soul. When this education is obtained, they are then ready to pass on to Mē-lū'nē-ä (Neptune), also known to Spirit Astronomers as A-rē-ăn'thĕr, which refers to greater heights or attainment in knowledge relative to the eternal laws that govern the development and evolution of the spirit and soul of all things. Thus by these two schools, the spirits have acqainted themselves with the marvelous processes in nature such as involution and evolution, causes, effects and ultimatums.

Having passed through the schools, the spirits thus developed are ready to pass on into the second Lō-dū'cy (zodiac) or worlds, where they, generally speaking, inhabit the central planet, which is known to Spirit Astronomers as Rē-plē'si-ä, because of the effulgent condition that characterizes it, and the spirit life that inhabits it.

Replesia does not have the same provident mission in its zodiac that the Sun does in its, viz: as a central solar light or heat provider to the other worlds in its zodiac, for each planet or world and its individualized life are endowed with their own spirit light thus developed, which takes the place of light of a solar orb in the zodiac.

Thus positioned upon Replesia, the spirit does not of necessity have to pass on to the other planets in the zodiac of Replesia to obtain knowledge thereof. That is optional with the individual spirit, therefore, all are more or less inhabited.

The fact that, being spirits, they are capable of passing to and fro from planet to planet as such, and therefore able to teach facts relative to the planets they have visited, as they mingle with the spirits of Replesia, it being the centre of the zodiac, highly attractive by nature, powerful in electric and magnetic principles, affords communication through the law of thought transference.

Each planet is a sun of itself, being electrified by the great light of the Over Spirit, and therefore infinitely and eternally illumined as a whole. No words are adequate to its description, hence non-comprehensive to a mortal mind.

Therefore, the light being electric, dispersive and reflective from one planet to another, the whole system is thus wonderfully characterized. The condition in the zodiac, and within the planets and their space zones, as before stated is such as to afford communication from world to world practical and certain, hence a mode of obtaining knowledge of the various planets and their conditions. The force governing this mode of communication, is that of vibration, which latter is induced by the operative forces of higher electric and magnetic principles, than those known to the Sun's zodiac, as embodied in the great Over Spirit and Over Soul Supreme Cycles, the planets and inhabitants thereon, being reciprocal as epi-cyclcs belonging to the Supreme Cycles, may receive and impart knowledge through the modes of thought transmission and inspiration, whereby they further develop and unfold mentally as spirit epi-cycles on a higher plane or portion of the deferent of the Supreme Cycles.

So it is throughout eternity, spirits co-adjutant with finer and and finer souls, pass to the central planet in the Lō-dū-sy-ĕts' (zodiacs) lying still beyond in space, and as limitless in number as space itself, for the same order of spirit elevation in all these is to pass generally to the central planet of each successive zodiac throughout space, going at will to any of the planets in the zodiacs as they may desire (as they understand the law of governing electric currents, etc.), where as individual spirit and soul epi-cycles, they move on the deferent of the great Over Spirit and Over Soul or Supreme Cycles, which fact is positive proof against the theories relative to material or physical re-incarnation.

Alem Prolex informs us that, when leaving Neptune, en route to Replesia, the spirit passes through space zones of ether that grow finer and finer as they near the planet.

When approaching and entering the planet, the marvellous effulgence that pervades it and the space zone in which it revolves, is almost overpowering to spirit vision.

There effulgent light is the Spirit and the God. Color is the Soul and the Individual. Transparency a condition of the Color which admits the Light and makes them inseperable.

It is as though there was no solidity, but all light and illumination. There can be seen that which appears to be the movement of water, but it is light from the other planets moving across it. As this comes in contact with that of Replesia, it causes most beautiful and wonderful changes in the colors, in and through which myriads of spirit peoples are passing (who once inhabited the Earth plane) so softly, so gracefully they move, that a spirit even on the planet of Uranus would seem gross beside them. They have no solidity of soul or form, but composed of light and color under a perfect transparent condition. So with the elements, they are extremely pure and refined.

Each progressive step upward brings more light, more perfectly refined etehr, more beautiful colors and transparent conditions, grander, fuller and more perfect expressions of the Gä'lä principle, which is light in its greatest force of purity. The inhabitants, the trees, the shrubs, the grass, the animals, the birds, in fact all life known to the Earth dwellers, and many more exists on this planet, but as beautiful as the purest crystal, characterized with transparent colors, so pure that the spirit sight can penetrate through every form and look beyond it, as mortal can look through a pane of glass. The cities are masses of transparent colored architecture, through which the crystal light shines forth in dazzling rays, thus to further illumine the scene. Truly, these are "Mansions not made with hands, eternal in the heavens." No expression in words can make comprehensive the real beauty and grandeur of a spirit individual and the home on the planet Replesia.

Crĕt-lōw' (the earth) is known to spirit astronomers as Lēn'-zē-ly, which term refers to the planet as the real mother of individualized life and form. As the Earth became established in its new Space Zone, the Electric germs,, already clothed and developed into embryotic existence by aid of the magnetic fluidic principle natural to its former condition, again entered into new Space Zone conditions, which established the process of further development of all life embryos on the Earth, where they were brooded in the soils, rocks, waters, etc., where they further developed by electric, magnetic, atmospheric, terrestrial and aquatic conditions, which resulted in the origin of all created existence on the land, in the waters and atmosphere of the Earth. Those attracted to aquatic conditions, to inhabit the waters; those on terra-firma, to inhabit the land; those to atmospheric regions, to inhabit both land and air; and those beneath the surface of the land, to inhabit the soil and rocks; which was the origin of every form of individual life known to the Earth plane, and every one of which came forth in extremely minute form. As we are shown clairvoyantly, even the largest specimens of animal, vegetable and human life, originally on the Earth, did not exceed an inch in length or height, with corresponding breadth and thickness. Many were the ages that passed before the progressive development reached the normal size known to pre-historic, ancient and modern times.

At the stage of individual development, above mentioned, the Earth had assumed greater size, as nature at this stage had completed the original part of creation; it had therefore brought everything of the original existence in pairs, which fact established the functions necessary to the condition of procreation and its continuance as such, hence the continuity of all individual life originally established on the Earth plane, which has sustained many conditional changes since the time of the establishment of the law of procreation, as will be seen.

We wish to emphasize the statement that since the creative forces in nature, viz: electric and magnetic, were male and female principles, therefore the original life germs were possessed with one or the other characteristic as such, and that when under original process of individual formation on the Earth plane, the product thus established came in pairs. Just here is the point where the mortal mind is lost, or led astray, and theretore does not understand that sex principles were original points in the divine law of creation, belonging to the great Over Spirit and Over Soul principles from which all existence has originated.

The principles that govern origin, procreation and continuity of life, hold good in regard to planets or worlds, as well as in that of the individual form creation that inhabits them. Merccury and Venus, influenced by the forces of the Over Spirit and Over Soul, were the original influences answering to gender, which established the condition of procreation on the Earth, and as the latter developed by animation and extension, individual life advanced in strength and size, though the process to that effect was very intricate, marvelous and slow, as shown us clairvoyantly by spirit Epictetus, the Greek philosopher.

The picture is very difficult to explain; the materials thus employed come from many different sources operated by electric and magnetic forces, the minute particles slowly gather toward a given center, and in the process appear so minute that they are as imponderable as ether itself. As these particles took placement together, they assumed that of the human form, perfect in every detail but so extremely minute. The same process, generally speaking, occurs in all forms of creation in degrees of complexity and quality according to the orders, genera, species, etc., required at the original stage of existence. The movement of the material particles when taking their place in the process of origin, is that of a circular motion, one which is also conducive to all growth in its normal state, or all progression after its origin, which is in conformity with the motive forces, which latter also come from all directions like electric radiations, which they are; while the magnetic element passes through and commingles with the circular movements of the electric force. This circular formative motion is the cause of so many things in nature taking on the circular form, such as seeds or cereals, eggs, nuts, fruits and worlds. The same circular influence forms the bodies and limbs of trees, vegetables, animals and human beings, etc., and forms within all the ova that are to continue procreation.

Condition being the next step to that result, *i. e.*, placed in darkness under the influence of fecundity, the circular motion begins again, which induces progression, which is upward and outward. Within the earth is the electric and magnetic conditions, procreation will go on, and soon the result is made visible placed in frozen ground, destruction would have ensued and life unable to further the progression; but if placed in warm conditions, procreation will go on, and soon the rssult is made visible by extension. The conception was made in the earth by the electric and magnetic forces, which also brought it forth as individualized life—as these forces had originally done, or under similar conditions. When the light is reached by the form extension, it progresses onward, outward, and upward; thus the law of progression continues on the Earth plane.

When the Earth has moved out and up as far as to the space zone that Mars now occupies, the condition of the former planet and its inhabitants will be similar to that of the latter, having higher birth and more refinement in every way, and so on out, as it revolves in the space zones of the other planets, and they in turn have passed on to the second zodiac. It is thus the finite mind may better understand all indiviudal life questions.

Again, as Venus moves out to take the place of the Earth, and Mercury that of Venus, they will be similarly endowed with original forces such as belonged to the planet preceding them; and, likewise, Mercury will be replaced by one of the strongest of the planets now being formed, which ultimately will be endowed with the same quality that it now has, and so on will the cradle of worlds perpetuate the replacements, and, therefore, the progression *ad infinitum*.

U^{c}H RED'ZE MI-ZETS'.
OR
THE GREATER HEIGHTS.

Gä'lä's infinite plan for all life continuity,
Progression of individualized spirits and souls,
Throughout the countless ages of all eternity,
As each epi-cycle on the Over Spirit Cycle rolls.
Oh, Gä'lä! is it thus we reach the greater heights,
There to find that we have purer and wiser grown?
That our souls grew brighter on their upward flight,
As the light of the Over Spirit through them shone,
Doth Animation there operate as in the greater depths,
To energize all the life and individualized soul existence,
Freeing it from all the grosser magnetic elements,
Guiding it onward and upward by thy electric influence?
Doth Extension turn cycles and epi-cycles ever forward,
Never reversing thy infinite order of natural motivity,
Thus moving life individualities constantly onward,

On the deferent of the Over Spirit Cycle, by electricity?
Doth Duration forbid spirit and soul re-incarnation,
Lest it disorganize thy law of creating individuality?
Or limit thy natural froces of animation and extension,
And create disorder in thy automatic modes of eternity?
Yea! the mode of spirit an dsoul is eternal progression,
As epi-cycle entities they must seek the greater heights;
In obedience to the infinite law of eternal evolution,
Which conditions all life with the Over Soul lights.
Thy turn not back on the marvelous cycle of time,
For to them the material cycle hath ceased its polarity;
They dwell in etherial zones energized by Gä'lä divine,
Thus represented by the chemical spectrum of electricity,
Clothed with chromatic garments that beautify such souls,
And qualified with energy, motivity, sensation and mind,
Individually progressive as time into eternity rolls,
Epi-cycles of the Over Spirit and the Over Soul combined.

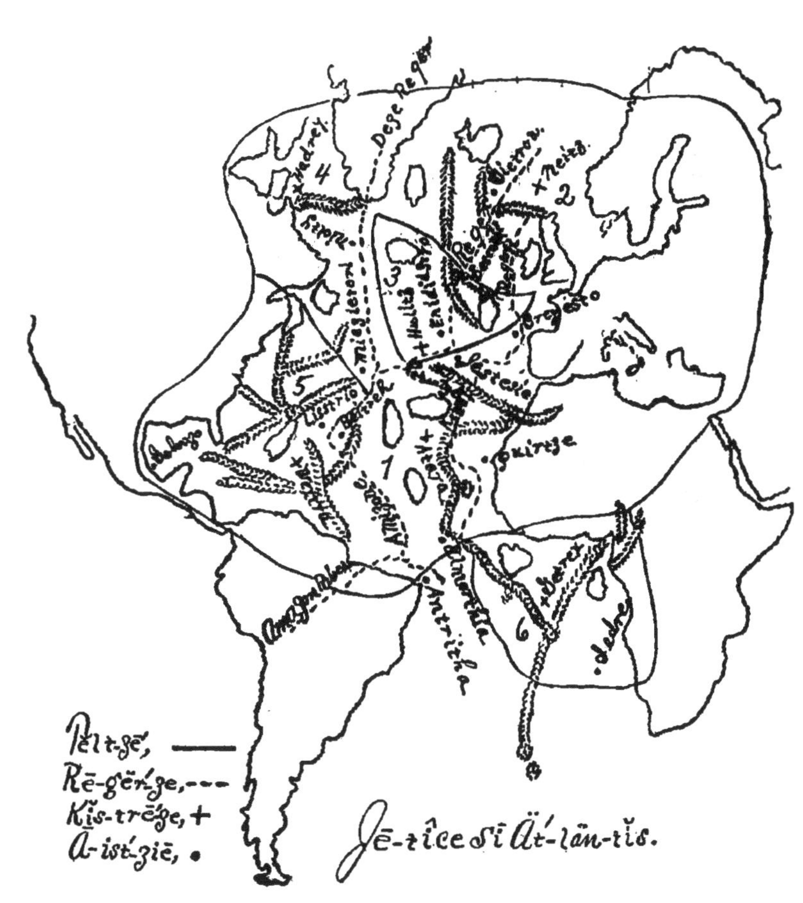

Jē-rīce sī Ät-lān-tīs.

USH NEL'DE LON-TI'DRI SI AT'LAN-TIS, OR THE GREAT CONTINENT OF ATLANTIS.

TELT'ZIE VIII.

The following information relative to the Geographic, Geologic, Botanic, Zoologic and Ornithologic links and cycles, have been given us by Er'ō-thrō-di-ă Prō'lĕx, At'lăn-tî-ăn Ev'li-am Lē-ā'sä Mŭl'tē-cĕn (Atlantian literary spirit inspirer) of the Author, who was the Kĕl-lăn'tră (daughter) of En-tî'thä Prō'lĕx, her Pē-ĭt'siē (father), and A-cē-lī'nä Prō'lĕx, her Mĕd'siē (mother) and the Sī-ĕs'tiē (sister of A'lĕm Prō'lĕx.

As shown on the foregoing Jē'tîce of Atlantis, the Lontidri was divided into 6 Tĕlt-ziē (Sections or States) which, relatively speaking, would correspond with the various state divisions of the United States of America, and were then known as Teltzie' Et, Wē, Sĕt, Kĕt, Zrĕt and Sŏt, or Sections 1, 2, 3, 4, 5 and 6.

Following is a short description of the Kĭs'trĕz A-ĭs'tiē (Capitol City) of the Lontidri, and those of the various Teltzie, and also the chief A-ĭs-tiē'zē (cities) of the Lontidri.

Beī'trĕh, a great resort for invalids, was located in the western central portion of Teltzie Et, east of the great Am'i-zōne Ri'gër (river). On the east side of the aistie was the beautiful Lū'krĕt (lake) of O-zĕn'ti-ō. The water was so clear and crystal like that it was a perfect mirror, and thus reflected the beautiful sunlight and image of every object near it. Its inlet was subterranean, and had never been discovered on account of its great depth. The water was strongly impregnated with sulphur and other mineral solutions, was always warm, hence its name, which meant light and heat. Its outlet was through the Pī-ĕs'cō Riger (the term meaning to come from unknown depths), which flowed southward, and emptied into the Amizone. By the foothills of the A-ĕl-kĕd'zē (mountains) west of the Lukret, were two thermal springs known as O-pĕn'ti-ō and Tĕl-mĕs'zē,, noted for their healing qualities. A vein from a large A-ĕl-kē'dē (mountain) near by, fed the larger Tĕl'mĕz (spring), the source of which was from subterranean waters. In the Aelkede depths were small basins, each containing a specific mineral substance in solution, deposited therein from a system of veins through which the minerals were collected and carried thence to the basins, which in turn emptied into one great lateral basin where all the mineral solutions became a compound, in which condition it flowed on into the exterior telmas proper. The water of the smaller telmas was from another Aelkede source. It flowed through crevices in the rocks in which were sulphur deposits, which highly impregnated the water, before it reached the outer basin of the telmas. The water from the large telmas was made famous by being of a general medicinal character of Aelkedze, was a resort for people who came there for a time to visit the Telmesze for treatment.

Quīrt'ze was an aistie located in the eastern central portion of Teltzie Et, was of medium size and its inhabitants were energetic in their pursuits, the chief manufacture being that of furniture.

Kē-rĕn'tē-zē, was a large aistie located on the north-central border of Teltzie Et, on the eastern side of the Amizone Riger. It was a great resort for the wealthy, many of whom had their permanent residences there. It was most noted for its schools and colleges, where students were educated in all the arts and sciences. It was an aistie consisting of fine architectural strue-tures, on account of the great wealth there assembled. Being on the Amizone, it was a great commercial exchange, and possessed one large, and several small artificial water courses through the aistie (like those of modern Venice, Italy,) the inlet of which was from the Amizone. They were used both for freight transportation and pleasure boating. The people were very intellectual and enterprising.

Jĕs-tē'siē, or Ush Aistie zē Fē'ste (The City of Light) was located on the Amizone River, northeast of the aistie of Kerenteze, in the northern portion of Teltzle Et. This aistie was noted for a natural phenomenal condition in the form of a great light, or illumined vaporous cloud that continually hovered over the aistie. The phenomenon was caused by an electric condition in that vicinity, from which the Atlantian scientists discovered the dynamic force of natural electricity and its motive power, which they utilized as such in various enterprises, and also for heating purposes.

Crey-ĕs'tō was an aistie located in the northern portion of Teltzie Et, on the Kentry Riger. It was also a great educational centre. Pupils came there from all parts of the Lontidri in pursuit of education in the arts and sciences. Its architectural and artistic display was grand and beautiful.

Neītz, was the Kistrez aistie of Teltzie We, located in the north eastern portion, east of the Quĭn'trō tĕr-răn'zi (range), and north of the Skeīt. It was a small aistie, having no special commercial enterprise, the principal interest being that of governmental affairs. The people who dwelt in the aistie however, were generally wealthy and intellectual.

Gī-ĕ'trō, was an aistie that was located in the northern portion of Teltzie We, between the Amizone Riger and the Quintro terranzi, though very near the Riger, from the aistie, to the north, could be seen the highest summits of the terranzi, now known as Iceland. The aistie was beautifully located, and built upon the site of a hamlet where dwelt a crude straggling people who had come there from the north east, and who knew nothing of their ancestry. They were called Săn'dē-ĕns by the Atlantians, the term meaning aboriginal. They were indolent and idolatrous, and as a people they became extinct by mixed race conditions with the Atlantians, who also settled in that section. After Yermah became Deltsanz of that Teltzie, he established schools and enterprises which wrought great changes with the people in general, especially those who were not mixed with Sandeen blood.

Dē-sĕn'trōw was a large aistie that was located in the southern-central border of Teltzie We, on the Amizone Riger. The chief enterprises were factories for converting metals into commercial utilities, the chief of which were Kurg (iron) for mechanical purposes; U'ziē (gold) for ornamental use, etc. Another enterprise was that of Ar-ī-dĕ'tē (boat) construction, such as were utilized on the Amizone Riger, and upon the various Yĕl'-măz (canals), the latter having place as inlets to parts of the aistie, thus affording connection with the Amizone for shipping utility, and also throughout portions of the Teltzie in the vicinity of the Amizone, where rapids and waterfalls made it impossible for the freighted Ar-ī-dē-tĕ'zē (boats) to float in continuation of the Amizone proper, hence the Yelmaz. They could leave the Riger above the rapids and enter it again below them. The aistie could not be said to be very beautiful in regard to fine architecture or artistic detail, though the structures generally, were substantansially built. The inhabitants were more disposed to amass wealth individually, than to lavish it on architecture and art. However, there were several fine temples, as the people were very religiously inclined, the finest of which was located on the side of the foot-hills of the Tū'tē-rōn terranzi, on the west side of the Amizone. The people were bright, busy, enterprising, etc., but did not pay so much attention to general education as they did to amassing wealth.

Hū'lĭtz, was the Kistrez aistie of Teltzie Set, and was located on the western side of the Amizone Riger, in the south-western portion of the Teltzie. It was a large aistie, beautifully laid out with streets at right angles, possessed very fine buildings, especially the Pĕl-zō'zē (temples) and the government buildings and dwellings of the wealthy inhabitants. There was no very great manufactury in the aistie, it being the Kistrez, was a place for wealthy residents. There were fine schools, and the people were very refined, intelligent and wealthy.

En-ĭd-ĭds'trō, was the principal aistie in Teltzie Set, and was located north-east of Hulitz on the west side of the Amizone Riger, in the southern portion of the Teltzie. The inhabitants were among the most intelligent and civilized in the Teltzie. They had fine Pelzoze, public buildings and residences. One of the Pelzoze was built in a hexagonal form and in the style of a great monument, which, in fact, it represented. Its roof was peculiarly shaped, being in the form of waves. Centrally, on its summit, stood an equestrian statue, with spear in hand, in representation of a warrior. The structure was utilized as a council chamber where preparations were made for war. The people throughout the Teltzie being war-like in nature.

Al-mör-thē'ä, was a commercial aistie that was located in the northern-central portion of Teltzie Set, on the west side of the Amizone Riger, and east of the slopes of the Tuteron terranzi, and near the aistie of Desento. It was very beautiful, the inhabitants were very bright and energetic, and always busy. It was a great musical aistie, and the location of the great instrumental factory of Atlantis. Various other aistieze were located along the Amizone Riger in this Teltzie, but the inhabitants were much more crude and uncivilized. One of these aistieze was very crude in construction, being that of clay structures. Its name was Al-mä'zä, and was located on the Amizone, in the northern central portion of the Teltzie, on the western side of the Riger, between it and the Tuteron Aelkedze.

Hā'drey was the Kistred aistie of Teltzie Ket, located in the north western portion of the Teltzie, east of the large Lukret of Gonzela. The aistie spread over a large area, as the inhabitants had homes on the order of gardens, containing from three to five acres, from which they obtained a livelihood, a fact that made the place very beautiful. It was an aistie for educational enterprises. There was one large school for general education, and one for the sciences. The streets were broad and beautifully kept. There were several fine parks, the best one being located opposite the Kistrez buildings, which latter were very large, but plain structures. All others throughout the aistie were plainly, though substantially built. There were two large Pelzoze. The people generally, were sun-worshippers, and so ornamented their Pĕl-zō-zē (temples) with that symbol, which they reverenced as representing the seat of all life. The people, though of the middle class were intelligent and industrious.

Miē-ziē-tō′ry, was a beautiful aistie on the south eastern boundary of Teltzie Ket, in size, comparatively speaking, with the aistie of Atara, the Kistrez of the Lontidri, and of Teltzie Et. Many people came to this aistie from Teltzie Zret, to transact business of all kinds, it being the seat of commerce in that part of the country, which caused a mixture of the populace; but the natives proper were highly civilized and very progressive. The streets and the buildings were of the purest white, being constructed with a material then known as Kintlin, a stone taken from the Aelkedze near the aistie, which was similar to lime-stone, excepting that in its native state was of the purest white. It was quarried in blocks for building purposes, and pulverized for cement in which the blocks were laid, and also for the surface construction of the streets, which ultimately were kept in perfect cleanliness. At the foot of the Aelkedze, bordering the aistie, was an immense market or exchange, from which the Kintlin was shipped, as well as great quantities of Cē-geī′lĕt (mineral water) to all parts of the Lontidri. The Cegeilet was taken from an immense pool formed in the rocks on the side of the Aelkedze. A beautiful plateau possessing all the charms of nature fronted the pool, which was a favorite resort for the people who visited it in great numbers to partake of the Cegeilet.

Nī′ōl-ty was a great manufacturing aistie, located in Teltzie Ket, on the western side of the Dē′zē Riger. Its most noted enterprise was the manufacture of all kinds of art in Zī′tē (mosaic) designs, such as statues, images, medallions and various ornamental designs in fine colorings; *e. g.*, a medallion subject famous in the Teltzie, was that of a beautiful lady represented as sitting in the foreground contemplating the rising sun and its beautiful light as it burst forth from the orient horizon, and thus shining upon a beautiful pelzo in the distance, between her and the horizon, which was to symbolize the light of truth shining out upon the souls of men. The pelzo was to represent the souls of men, and the lady that of Mother Wisdom as the teacher.

Teltzie Zret was a very beautiful portion of the Lontidri it being more tropical in nature than the foregoing Teltzie, and possessed exquisite flora. Even the wild shrubs of the Aelkedze were prolific in bloom and foliage. Grand Hĕl-trō-plŏx′zē (caves) characterized the Aelkedzie, over the entrance of which were creeping vines bearing flowers of violet and lavender hues. When entering them it was that the individual walked on carpets of moss, as it were, whose shadings were from a delicate green beneath, to a golden tint on top. Such was the case with the En'triē Kĕnd'trī-ō of Atlantian fame, located in an Aelkede of the same name, in the Hĕlt'zy terranzi east of the then known Bē-rūn'dí-ä peak (now the Bermuda Island) in Teltzie Kret.

Wĕx'trä, the Kistrez aistie of Teltzie Zret, was located on the eastern central portion of the Teltzie, southeast of the Tē-rä-ĕs'-tĭn Lukret, in the great fertile Tynger (valley) of Al-ē-lō'ōs, that had place between the Meztrie and the Gĕn-lē'cē-ī terranzi. It was a very large aistie, possessed very fine buildings of low, but beautiful structure, with flat roofs, the principal ornamentations being that of carved subjects from nature in relief, and many pillared porticoes and interior supportings. The Kistrez building was a very large structure, though not elaborately designed, excepting in the details of its pillared porticoes and diamond-shaped, four-sided cupola that rose over the front centre above the great main portals, which was sculptured with landscapes in relief, and painted in accord with the scene representation, a different representation having place on each plane of the diamond. Other carvings on the exterior and interior, with pillar, or column accompaniments, made the structure an imposing one. On the summit of the cupola floated the Gē'ĕl (flag) of the Teltzie. The aistie was a great winter resort for the people of the northern and eastern Teltzie, who sought the more tropical climate for that season. There were many beautiful parks in the aistie, one of which surrounded the Kistrez buildings, composed of tropical trees, shrubs and flowers. There were several beautiful artificial Lukretze. There were three principal Pelzoze, the principal worship being the same as the form used in Atara. The inhabitants were intelligent, energetic and highly civilized, though it was a tropical section. This difference was due to the mixed assembly of Atlantians of the north and east, with the natives, which latter caught the influence of the former and therefore were improved. They were all lovers of nature, hence did much to beautify their surroundings. They had good schools, but no very great advancement in manufacture.

Gō-lŏn'zō was a small aistie located in the southwestern portion of Teltzie Zret, on the site where now the city of Vera Cruz, Mexico, has place. In the Atlantian time, it was an ancient aistie, and has been destroyed and rebuilt several times since its existence as Golonzo, and the present city of Vera Cruz has sustained similar conditions by contentious peoples. We are here informed that conditions of a convulsive nature that now exist and are centered in the location of that city and its immediate surrounding country, point to a great convulsion that is likely to occur in time not far distant which will again destroy the city and tear up the country generally. The inhabitants of Golonzo had advanced only to a moderate degree in manufacture, education or general livelihood.

An-trī'thä was a large aistie situated on the western side of the Amizone near its outlet into the Southern Ocean, east of the now known Cape of St. Roque, then the southeastern portion of Teltzie Zret. The aistie was on the order of a large Mexican city of modern times. It was considered by the Atlantians of the third Efremetrum to be very antique. Having place by the Amizone, and by the Southern Atlantic, was therefore a great manufacturing and commercial point. It was in this aistie that the Tĕl'tä A'ētä (air ships) were built and from thence dispatched to all parts of the Lontidri, where they were to be owned and operated; when completed they were slowly elevated by their own electric machinery to the altitude necessary for departure, when they soared away rapidly to their destination.

Lĭs-tri'ō was a large aistie located on the Amizone near the eastern central border of Teltzie Zret. The location was a beautiful one, one that was highly cultivated, and a great fruit district as well. The Căn'tū-lŭs (a fruit similar to the modern grape) was one of the vintage growths, the juice of which was manufactured into El-dī'sō (a non-fermented drink), similar to grape juice of modern time, which was transported to other parts of the Lontidri. The inhabitants became well civilized and were, in regard to their customs, manners and general livelihood, much like the modern Germans. Many Ar-ī-dē'tē (water craft, the term meaning moving on the waters) were employed on the Amizone at this point, heavily laden with Eldiso and various fruits from the Teltzie.

Gē'trĕx, was the Kistrex aistie of Teltzie Sot, and was located east of the Yĕl'pĕt terranzi, and north of the O-tĕs'sĕn, in the triangular section of country formed by the junction of the two terranzi, the point of which is now marked by the St. Helena Island, which latter was the junction peak of the two terranzi. In regard to construction, the aistie was quite crude, for there were no aistieze of great importance in Teltzie Sot, and the people were of a crude and half civilized order, they being the most southerly races of the Lontidri. There were no Kistrez buildings of any account, and the government was simple in detail. There was very little enterprise or learning, except such as chanced to be established there by northern traders who bought and exported products from the more southern fisheries.

I-ē'dri was a crude settlement in the southeastern portion of Teltzie Sot, so named from the fisheries there located, the term meaning fishery. This was a great point for that enterprise, as very fine fish of various kinds were to be obtained in the waters of the South Atlantic at that period of time, which were caught, prepared and sent into the aistie of Detrex for distribution throughout the Teltzie. The fisherman and their families lived in very crude habitations, constructed something in the manner of the Adobes of modern times. The people in the northern portion were more intelligent than American Indians. They built their habitations out of limbs and sticks, woven or thrown together and filled in with mud to form the body of the structure. They were allowed to remain when vacated, or when the inhabitants went on their roving expeditions, and re-occupied again on their return.

LIM'PIRE NUD A-THU'RO RIN'GA NUD SI-I'KEL.

OR

GEOGRAPHIC AND GEOLOGIC LINKS AND CYCLES.

TELTZIE IX.

There always have been, and always will be geographical changes, such as are caused by the coming up and going down of portions of the earth's surface, submergences and recedings of its waters, conditions which have made it difficult for historians to substantiate or preserve facts relative to the present geographic aspect of the world.

Let the reader take his Atlas, scan the coast of the Eastern Continent, contemplate its present aspect in connection with that of Micronesia, Polynesia, Melanesia and Australasia, whose remnants of land protrude from the mighty waters of the Pacific Ocean, and there read from the present condition, the unwritten history of Nature's remote, secret compilation.

Likewise, turn to the map of the Western Continent, North and South America. Look across the great Atlantic to the coast of the Eastern Continent, adjacent Europe and Africa, and behold the remnants of land whose present condition, like all others of the world, are due to the mighty convulsions and submergences of Nature, whose mysterious protrudings, ragged, zigzag, wave-washed coasts bespeak the mighty forces of Nature to rend the lands, disperse the waters, and bring mighty changes upon the earth.

Further contemplate the Bays, Sounds, Gulfs, Straits, Channels, Inland Lakes and Seas, the unrecorded history of which is everlastingly being rehearsed by the roar of the mighty billows during the hours of Nature's tempestuous conditions.

One of the great questions of the 20th century is, what are the true links, past, present and future, that belong to the Great Cycle of human life, material and spiritual, to which Ethnographic and Ethnologic epi-cycles we must add those of the Geographic, the Geologic, the Zoologic, the Botanic, the Ornithologic, etc., etc.

These links are innumerable and in the absence of correct history, are very mystifying, indeed; and, therefore, can only be connected up by the aid of spirit intelligences who were contemporaneous with the times of their establishment and who are able to communicate with mortal sensitives, giving them facts such as shall render aid in the process of both material and spiritual research.

Many men and women have written upon these and other subjects in regard to the great universal laws and processes governing their establishment through causes and effects, thus recording their views upon the pages of history through their various works and forms of literature. Most of these, however, have thus conceived and written under spirit aid. and influence without the consciousness of the fact, and therefore have held their own mentality in supremacy to that of the guiding influence to such an extent as to weaken the power of the latter-named aid and influence, which, on the contrary, would establish truth, correct data, and prefix to the 20th century buried history of the so-called pre-historic past, renovate, correct, and glorify that of antiquity, bring out much that is non-historic, and ultimately establish the complete and perfect epi-cycles belonging to the Great Universal Cycle of Cause and Effect.

In connecting the Atlantian Lontidri with the now known Eastern and Western Continents, establishing its boundary line, and further to extend the Great Geographical Cycle of the globe to its present extent and condition, giving the causes and effects leading up to the latter, we do so by establishing Atlantis as the center of the cycle. (See the Jetice or Map.)

The Am'ĭ-zōne Rigĕr (meaning an immense river coming from the zone) was a great salt water course, having its rise from the

Arctic waters, that flowed through the Lontidri. It was the longest and broadest river ever known to the world. It flowed in meanderings from the North to the South, and was very rapid along some portions of its course. In its meanderings it passed west of the now known Azores, and east of the Bermudas, to the now known Amazon remnant of South America (the name having descended to the latter from that of the Atlantian Amizone, with only its orthographic change) when their confluent waters found an outlet into the South Atlantic ocean.

The great Amizone Riger was the dividing line between the Eastern and Western hemispheres of the Atlantian Lontidri. As it plunged through the Aelkedze terranzi near the peaks now known as the Azores Islands, it formed the then famous Dĕs-wī′-triē (meaning many falls in one). As the water gushed forth from this great gate-way(it plunged down a precipice of about eighty feet, then through a canon of palisaded rocks for two miles, through which it formed eddies, cascades, whirlpools and rapids, when came a second fall of about 160 feet into a great semi-circular basin where the water boiled and rolled by the force of its fall, casting a rainbow spray upon a great plateau on the west side of the foothills, back of which great rocks jetted out from their backward ascent, and over the trees, shrubs, flowers and mosses that characterized the undulating ground below.

The Dē′zē Riger was a large fresh water course that had its rise in the Aelkede regions of the now known country of Greenland, which flowed southward through Teltzie Ket, having its outlet in the great Amizone Riger, east of the aistie of Miezietori.

The Kentry Riger was a large fresh water course which had its rise in the Skeīt terranze region, in Teltzie We, or in the region now know as north of the British Islands and west of Norway, which in its meanderings southward, passed through the eastern extremity of Teltzie Et, and emptied into the Alt-lăck′ĕr (South Atlantic Ocean), east of the aistie of Almorthia.

Prior to the submergence of Atlantis, there was a great Prish (Bay) or inlet from the Trĕt-zĕl′zä (Arctic Ocean), then known as the Ex′ā-trŏn, about three leagues in width, located northwest on the now known sections of Norway and Sweden, from which the Amizone received its waters. The latter was about three leagues in width at its junction with the Exatron, and likewise varied in width on its course to the Altlacker.

The Rē-tĕx-ē-rī′ton was a Cō-lī-ē′tē Cē′lĕt (Inland Sea) that was located in the northeastern portion of the Lontidri, west of the sections now known as Portugal and Morocco, fed principally by subterranean sources, and the waters were of a thermal character, the temperature varying at times from medium to cooking heat.

This condition led to much scientific investigation, when it was discovered that, so far as soundings could be made, the sea appeared to be bottomless at a certain section. There was always a rumbling sound that came from beneath the waters in that section, and scientists claimed that the heat and sound was caused by the action of a subterranean sulphurous volcano, and that it was but a question of time when the fire of the volcano would cut its way through the bed of the sea, admit the waters through the aperture, when the great heat would so rapidly generate steam in such quantities and force that the sub-aqueous earth could not resist it, and that then it would explode the earth shell and follow the ramifications of the earth veins, until all that section of the earth in that region in a manner influenced, would be destroyed by the almost universal explosion. This claim, alas! proved true, which was the cause of the ultimate sinking and submergence of the great Lontidri of Atlantis, with which many cities, towns, hamlets and settlements, together with millions of people went down and were lost to the knowledge of subsequent peoples on the remnant lands.

Simultaneous with the fires reaching the waters of the Coliete Celet, the same condition and result occurred in the Exatron Prish, which caused a great convulsion that extended from the now known section of Norway and Sweden in Northern Europe, then a part of Atlantis, to the Straits of Gibralter, and still further south-westward.

Prior to the convulsion, a large stream of water in line with the now known Baltic and White Seas, had its course through a valley across the country of Europe, which practically rendered Norway and Sweden an Island belonging to the then known Tretzĕl'za (Arctic Ocean), and but for the existence of the then known Chē-rä'da Aelkedze, or now Orbay range, that section, or Island, would have gone down. At the time of the convulsion the great valley between the Baltic and White Seas rose, and that portion which before was an Island became permanently connected to the European Continent.

This convulsion (followed by those elsewhere mentioned by Alen Prolex), co-operative with the waters of the Retexeriton the Tretzelza, and the Altlackeer that flowed into the great crater of the sub-aqueous volcano, and other volcanoes, generated a marvelous steam and mighty force, such as the rock-bound soil of the Lontidri, where now the North Atlantic Ocean rolls, could not resist; hence the sinking and submergence of the Atlantian Lontidri.

Er'ō-thrō-dî-ä further informs us that the same condition now exists under the westerly waters of the now known Gulf of Mexico, and that it is only a question of time when the fires of that volcano, in like manner, will cut their way through the bed of the Gulf, when by an unspeakable explosion, the Continents of North and South America will disappear from the material world, and the waters of the Pacific will reach, together with the Atlantic, to the western confines of Africa. Then will the remaining portion of the At'län-ti-än Lŏn-tī'drî have disappeared with all the peoples and cities of the Twentieth Century Civilization. Thus may we understand what is the meaning of the term "being destroyed by fire."

USH A-EL-KE'DE TER-RAN-ZE' SI AT'LAN TIS,

OR

THE MOUNTAIN RANGE OF ATLANTIS.

TELTZIE X.

The Jăn'tī-zē was a terranzi that began with high peaks in Teltzie Et, which now form the Azores Islands and in their extension, embraced peaks now known as the Madeira and Canary Islands, and, further continuation, the remnant Atlas mountains in Morocco and Algeria of northwestern Africa; and but for the submergence that established the Mediterranean Sea, would have been a part of the great system in Europe and Asia, the link being broken at Sicily and lower Italy, by the waters of the Mediterranean.

Furthermore, tracing the ranges around the globe, through Asia, crossing the North Pacific via the Aleutian Islands into North America, through the great system of Rockies of the United States and Mexico, reaching the summits of the Aelkedze which formed the Bermudas, which link can only be connected through revelations of unwritten history, as gathered from the records of memory of spirits contemporaneous with the ages of the past, who give the facts through mortal sensitives, as at the present time.

The Gū-il'ī-tō extended from the western portion of Teltzie Et, in a zig-zag easterly course, to that of the Jăn'tī-zē terranzi.

The Yĕl'pĕt extended from the peaks now known as the Cape

Verde Islands, in a meandering course, embracing the peaks that now form the Ascension, St. Helena and Tristan d'Acunha Islands, the latter name being the result of a submergence that was of ancient date inAtlantis.

The O-tĕs'sĕn then extended from the now known Cameroon Mountains in Africa, into the Lontidri, then embracing the now known Islands in the Gulf of Guinea, and also the peaks that now form the St. Helena Islands, whose further continuation had also been submerged in the ancient days of Atlantis.

The Bĕn'tē-zē meandered from the peaks that now form the Bermuda Islands, extending to and embracing New-Foundland, which was the highest portion of the range at the northern extremity.

The Lŭ'tī-zē extended from the now known Bermudas to the State of Virginia, U. S. A., and further into the section now known as the Chesapeake Bay and its remnant Islands.

The Miē'ziē-tō-ry extended from the Bermuda peaks to the north-central border of Teltzie Ket.

The Hĕlt'zy extended from the Bermuda peaks south-west to the now known coast of Florida, and northeast to the southwest portion of Teltzie Ket.

The Gĕn-lē'cē-ī extended from the sections now known as Guiana, South America, to within a few miles of the then known Berundia Peak, the latter extension of the terranzi, to the Berundia Peak terminating with low spurs or foothills.

The U-zä'zăc extended from the Bermudas to North Carolina, to the point now known as Cape Hatteras.

The Mĕz'triē extended from the Sierra Madra branch to the great Rocky Cordillera, through Yucatan, embracing Hayti, Porto Rico, and that portion of the West Indies now known as the Caribee Islands.

The Mŭ'tī-zē extended from the section of Hayti to Honduras and Nicaragua in Central America, thus embracing Jamaica.

The Quīn'trō extended in a crescent from Ireland to Iceland, which latter was a high portion of the terranzi.

The Skeīt extended from Scotland, north to the group of Islands west of Norway, when a large valley had place between them and Iceland.

The Tŭ'tē-rŏn extended from the eastern-central portion of Teltzie Set, through the central portion of Teltzie We, to western Iceland.

The Tĭs-cŭn'dä from the north-central to the west-central portion of Teltzie Set, thus extending from the Tuteron terranzi.

The Rē-ē'tä from the southwestern portion of Greenland, in

a meandering course into the northwestern portion of Teltzie Ket.

The Trĭx'ŭh-lee extended southeast from the central point of the Rē-ē'tä terranzi in Teltzie Ket.

The Ep'zä was a branch that extended from the central portion of the Zentulu into the southewestern portion of Teltzie Et.

The Zĕn'tē-lū extended from northwest to southeast through Teltzie Zret. Between its northwestern portion and the Bermuda peaks, was a great valley then known as Cē-dē-lē'shē.

Before the submergence of Atlantis, the terranzi in the southwestern portion, from which the West Indies are remnants, were a part of the Rockies of North America. These and their adjacent land, connected Atlantis with these two Continents. The West Indies therefore, are simply mountain peaks of these ranges, located in the submerged portion of South Atlantis. The lower portion, or Caribee Islands, are remnants of the Gasibbee range known to the Atlantians. It had connection with South America and that portion of the West Indies known as the Caribee Islands.

The Zä-māy'cä Heights, now known as Jamaica, was the highest portion of the Mutize terranzi, and received its name from the system of springs located in that portion of the terranzi, of the same name. After the submergence, the Aborigines changed the name to that of Jamaica (Isle of springs), which in turn sustained several changes by modern possessors, and finally was re-possessed with its aboriginal name of Jamaica.

It will be observed that the name Xamayca is used in modern writings, and sometimes used in reference to the Island of Jamaica, which is but a re-inspired term. It was given to, and conceived by the mortal who re-established its use, by an Atlantian spirit who, in mortal life, dwelt in that portion of the Lontidri, and being desirous that the original name should be perpetuated, communicated it to the individual for that purpose, in the same manner that all the Atlantian terms, and those of prehistoric nomenclature have been given, such as appear in this work.

The two Gayman Islands were peaks of the Mutize terranzi, and their separation from each other and from Jamaica was cused by the water rushing through the lower portions between peaks, which tore away the earth, and left the peaks as Islands.

The Swan Islands belonged to the Andes range, which but for the Xamayca tynger, would have joined the Great Gayman, which latter terminated the Mutizse terranzi.

The great slope of the Mutize terranzi to the north, and that of the Meztrie to the south, divided the heights of Jamaica from those of Cuba, and formed the great Tynger of Yamayca, which extended in a hook shape around the two Gayman Islands and Cuba, between the Swan and the Great Gayman, the southwestern portion extending into a broad, rich area of the Tynger. At the time of the submergence, the Tynger went down, which accounts for the great depth of water now existing there.

The Dīn'gĭs, now known as Cuba, which latter name was given it by the aborigines, was the main portion of the Meztrie terranzi. Its shape, as is the case with most remnants of land forming Islands, is in conformity with the principal mountains, adjacent foothills and lowlands.

That portion of the West Indies now known as the Bahama Islands, was a part of the Meztrie terranz,i leading down to the large, rich and beautiful Tynger of Zā-ō'nē-ä, and various smaller ones, having place between the Meztrie and the Zentelu on the northeast, and the Heltzy on the northwest. The Zentelu bordered the great Tynger of Atara on the southwestern portion, and the Miezietory on the western.

The Berundia peak or Bermuda Island, was the highest point of the four terranzi west of the great Tynger of Atara. They radiated from it, where it stood, as it were, like a great Sentinel guarding the Tynger.

The Zentelu terranzi was noted for its Clē'tiē (silver) deposits, which was used for vases, urns dishes and ornamental mountings.

The Miezietory terranzi was noted for its beds of Kĭnt'lĭn (white stone) which was extensively used in constructing the city of Miezietory, some being shipped to other parts of the Lontidry for the same purposes. In the extension of the great Kintlin veins towards Berundia Peak, it changed in character to that of white Sig-nī'ti (white marble), then began a series of variegations, first white and ashen, or gray, the latter growing darker until a purple was lost in black, and the former to dark shades of yellow. These varieties were used extensively for Zī'tē (mosaic) work.

Many of the Aelkedze in Teltzie Et were natural depositories of mineral and chemical substances, crystalizations and other volcanic products of many varieties, which made wealth and enterprise for the people of the Lontidri.

The Quintro and the Skeit terranzi were noted for their extensive beds of Bezer (salt), the Reeta and the Miezietory for Zē'lēte (zinc).

From a compound of E'trēz (copper) and Zelete, the Atlantians produced a substance then known as Ate'ley, which in color was similar to gold, which was extensively used for various ornamentation. The Etrez was also mixed with U'zē (gold), which made it comparatively lighter in color, and less valuable.

The Jantize terranzi produced Uzie, Cletie and I-rē'ïz (sulphate of zinc) each extensively used for interior and exterior ornamentation.

The Lutize terranzi produced Yē-ē'trä (brass) and O-ē'trä (lead), which was used for mechanical purposes.

In the northern portion of the Jantize, great quantities of Neū'zūu (agate) was obtained. The colors were various, blue, green, orange and purple predominating. Nuzuu was much used for jewelry, and wealthy Atlantians used it largely for mantles, panels and other interior home decorations, as well as for vases, urns, etc. There was one Pelu (mine) owned by the Government, from which the black crystalline Nuzuu was taken, and was utilized for Getrex (money). There was but one Pelu of this product in the Lontidri, therefore limited in quantity and quality, hence its utility for Getrex purposes. Atlantian scientists claimed that its color was due to the degree of heat that characterized the lava as it flowed into the position where it became transformed into Nuzuu, a different condition or process from that which formed the other varieties of Nuzuu, in other Hĕl-trō-plŏx'zē (caves), viz: by chemical liquid droppings. The Atlantians did not use Cletie and Uzie for Getrex.

The terranzi in Teltzie Sot were never prospected, so far as is known by the spirit advisors.

Between the Heltzy and the Lutize, was the large Tynger of Shĕl'tē-ze. Between the Lutize and the Bentize, was the large rich Tynger of Dē-rū'frĕs.

North of the Reeta Terranzi was the very large Tynger of Reeta, which was characterized similar to valleys in the northlands of modern times, and south of the same range was the large Tynger of Zē-ē'tra. West of the Quintro terranzi was the large Tynger of Trē-zē'krē. Between the Quintro and the Skeit, was the large Tynger of E'ken; and extending from the southern portion of the Quintro, westward to the Deze Riger, was the large Tynger of Quĭn'tro.

There were many beautiful Lū-krĕts (lakes) dispersed over the Lontidri, a few of the principal ones were as follows.

The Op'síte was located north of Atara; the Skĕd'zē, west; and the Zī'dē, south of the same aistie in Teltzie Et.

The Wĭlt'zē was located in the north-western portion, and the Sēeth in the south-central portion of Teltzie We.

The Crĕt'zē was located in the northwestern; and the Mī-ī'tī in the eastern portion of Teltzie Set.

The Gōn-zē'lä, the largest Lukret in the Lontidri, was located in the north-western portion; and the Lā-măn'sä, another large Lukret, in the south-central portion of Teltzie Ket.

The Tē-rä-ĕs'tĭn was located in the central portion of Teltzie Zret.

The Gĭl'dä was located in the north-eastern portion; and the Or'zĕr in the north-western portion of Teltzie Sot.

About 22000 years ago, according to the traditions that were handed down to the Atlantian people of the third Efremetrum, a Teltzie of the pre-historic period of Atlantis, south of their historic Teltzie Sot, and of the southeastern extremity of Teltzie Zret, had been submerged by the waters of the then great Xä-mā'thrāy (original name of the South Atlantic Ocean, meaning great body of water), which was caused by convulsions in that section. The name of the submerged Teltzie was Gän-de'rō, or the Lost Lontidri, as it was said to have been a large portion of country.

The Atlantians believed that their Yelpet terranzi, which came to a sharp break off in the southern portion of Teltzie Sot, must have formerly extended into the great Xamathray beyond, and that it embraced the now known Tristan d'Acunha Islands, the larger one of which was known to the Atlantians as the Kendrew, and the smaller one as the Ill'tē-zē. At that time there were other Islands between these and the now known coast of Africa, which were said to have been submerged, two of which were inhabited at the time of their submergence, all being lost.

About 18875 years ago, or 3125 years subsequent to the traditional convulsion above referred to, there began a system of ten mighty periodical convulsions, accompanied by smaller ones at times, and locations, which therefore changed the contour of the country, the lakes; the inland sea; the channels between bordering islands and the main land near the Xamathray, or, later, Altlackeer; the Tretzelza, and a few straits; bays, sounds; gulfs and the zig-zag coast lines along them; but the main portion of the Lontidri remained non-submerged until the time of the tenth convulsion, when all went down.

The first of the ten convulsions above referred to occurred in Teltzie Zret, at the junction of the Heltzy, Uzazac, Benteze and Lutize terranzi; or southwest of the then famous Berundia Peak (then a great volcano; the name sustained several changes until it is now Bermuda). The force, however, was confined principally to the Uzazac and the Heltzy terranzi, and in its disastrous extension, brought geographic changes toward the section now known as North America, and also to the south, where it subsided in the region of the West Indies Islands.

The second convulsion occurred about 800 years subsequent to the first, and had place northeast of the Berundia Peak, in Teltzie Zret, which wrought changes in that region.

The third occurred about 500 years after the second, and had place at the junction of the southeast section of the Yelpet, and the southwestern section of the Otessen terranzi, in Teltzie Sot, or north of what is now known as the St. Helena Island. The force extended northeast along the Otessen terranzi, toward the section now known as the Gulf of Guinæ, and south of the junction, along the Yelpet terranzi, which caused a portion of Teltzie Sot to become submerged by the waters of the Xamathray.

The fourth occurred about 50 years after the third, and had place in the northwestern portion of Teltzie Sot, which seriously changed the geographical condition of the northwestern remnant, left by the latter convulsion.

The fifth occurred about 400 years subsequent to the fourth, and had place at the junction of the Tuteron and the Tiscuda terranzi, in the north-central portion of Teltzie Set, which brought changes to the north and northeastern regions of the Teltzie. The eastern, southern and southwestern regions did not sustain much change until the time of the convulsion that had place in the adjacent Teltzie.

The six occurred about 100 years after the fifth, and had place near the junction of the Quintro and the Skeit terranzi, near where the Amizone Riger burst through those Aelkede barricades in Teltzie We, which brought geographical changes in the western regions of the Teltzie.

The seventh occurred about twenty-five years after the sixth, and had place in the northwestern portion of the Skeit terranzi, west of the now known section of Norway, which brought changes in the northern and northeastern regions of the Teltzie.

The eighth occurred about 200 years after the seventh, and had place at the northwestern extremity of the Gelutic, and the southeastern extremity of the Trixuhlee terranzi, in Teltzie Ket, which affected the geographic aspect of the central and southern regions of the Teltzie.

The ninth occurred about 100 years after the eighth, and had place near the junction of the Trixuhlee and the Reeta terranzi, which brought geographic changes to the northern and western regions of Teltzie Ket.

The tenth occurred about 100 years after the ninth, and had

place in the Jantize terranzi near Atara (and was simultaneous with the great convulsions in the Coliete Celet and the Eratron Prish. This, in connection with the two above named, was the most mighty and overwhelming of the ten. It extended along the Jantize, north and south, and northwest along the Gurilito, to the aistie of Beitreh, at the point of the angle where the terranzi further extended southward, along which it also traversed that part of the terranzi, until it came to a very high and massive portion, when the force was spent, and the high section above mentioned was left standing as an Island, which also, after the lapse of another 100 years, sank into the ocean, not by cause of convulsions, but by the washing out of the sands, thus removing its foundation. When thus undermined, it slowly sank into the ocean with the other parts of the Lontidri subsequently submerged.

It will be observed that the time intervening the traditional submergence of Gandero, or the Lost Lontidri, said to have occurred 22000 years ago and, 18875 years ago, when the above-named system of convulsions began, that ultimately destroyed Atlantis, formed a period of 3125 years, and that the total number of convulsions covered a period of 2375 years, which would make a total of 5500 years, the period of time intervening the traditional Lost Lontidri and the last submergence of Atlantis; which if subtracted from the supposed time of the former, e. g., 22000—5500—16500 years, the remote period of time when the Lontidri of Atlantis as a whole became submerged.

Links and Cycles

I-E'TICE SI ATARA.

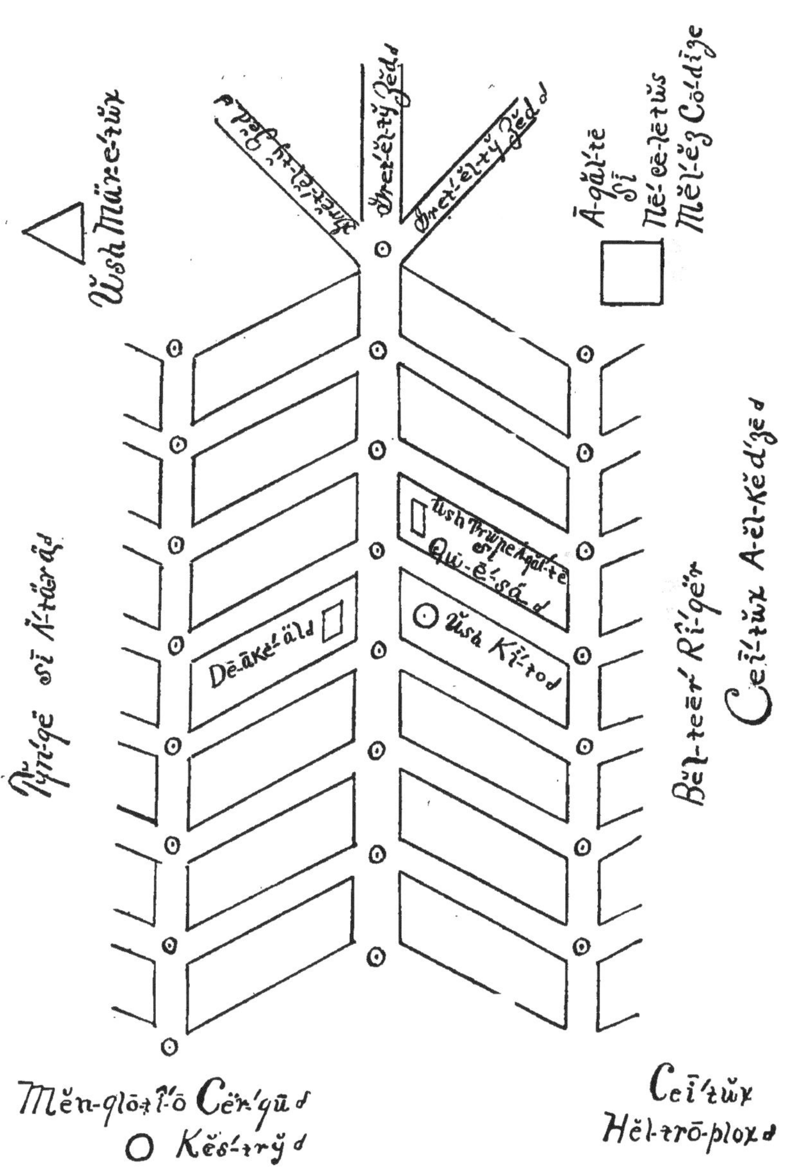

USH KIS'TREZ 'A-IS'TIE SI 'AT'L'AN-TIS, OR THE CAPITOL CITY OF 'ATLANTIS.

TELTZIE XI.

Many of the principal aistieze (cities) of commerce were situated along or near the great Amizone Riger, while the Kistrezie (capitol cities) were more interior, or centrally located.

A'tä-rā the Kistrez aistie of both the entire Lontidri and Teltzie Et, was located in Teltzie Et, west of the Jantize aelkedze, and between the Lukretze Atara, Ozentio and Seeth, and received its name at the beginning of the first Efremetrum.

During the first Efremetrum the population became much increased by immigrants from other parts of the Lontidri. This condition, the natural increase by nativity and race mixture—the latter being in the early history of the Efremetrum—made great changes in the inhabitants of Atara, regarding population and race conditions.

During the second Efremetrum, these conditions continued, which ultimately established a still more beautiful, intellectual and civilized race of people, whose activity was made manifest in the aistie and throughout the Tyngerze of the Teltzie.

During the third Efremetrum, conditions were such that every form of civilization changed for the better. At the close of this age, Atara was the abode of over one million of people; i. e., allowing the area of the aistie to extend from the Ceitux Heltroplox in the Jantize terranzi, to the Opsite Kelete, thus embracing the suburban portion. Furthermore, settlements were established all through the great Tynger of Atara. These people with those of the aistie, formed a large proportion in that portion of the Teltzie.

The main Xŏn'tĭs (street) of Atara was 150 coi'tĕx (feet) in width, and extended 15 Xē-trŭx'zē (miles) from north to south. Parallel with it, throughout the aistie, were others at equal distances apart, though varying in length according to their location in the aistie. Crossing these from east to west, were others laid out in similar form at proportionate distances apart (the longest of which extended a distance of 10 Xetruxze) so as to divide the aistie into parallelogramic I-x-rōl'tä (squares). The main Xontis was the location for the principal large business houses and other public buildings. On its west side, in the center of the aistie, stood the great Dē-āke'äl (capitol of the Lontidri). It and its subordinate buildings were all built of white Signiti or Altyna (Signiti means marble, and Altyna, white marble), the latter occupying the western portion of the Ixrolat, which was beautifully adorned with trees, shrubs and flowers. The Deakeal as a colossal structure, circular in form and 600 coitex in diameter, and from its base to the apex of its dome, represented a height architecturally proportioned with its diameter. Its majestic form symbolized a reaching up and out for strength and power. The roof and dome were very similar to a modern Mosque. The dome was adorned with a combination of Uzie symbols, viz., a central standard crowned with an As'tri-än, a fish noted for its swiftness. (It was known to the Ancients as the Dolphin.) It not only served as a weather vane, but as a symbol of the invisible force and motion of the atmosphere. Beneath this was a large globe, which symbolized the Sun, and all the spherical bodies of the heavens, from which geometrical and astronomical science originated, and applied mathematically in all spherical calculations. Still lower on the standard were three horizontal rods, on each end of which were triangles placed in a perpendicular position, which symbolized the super-realms as a source from whence knowledge was obtained and the science of geometry applicable in all angular calculations.

The exterior was very highly polished. The blocks of altyna were so perfectly joined and blended that the joints were not easily discerned. The doors and windows were arched and adorned with beautiful carvings. A portico covered the main entrance, leading up to which was a flight of altyna steps. On each side in the portico were two half pillars in high relief against the wall, and two in the round at the front corners to support the roof. On each side of the portico were altyna seats for public use by those awaiting entrance to the Deakeal on their business missions. On the facade, over the entrance, was the following inscription which, translated, read: "Here Justice is Given."

The walls beneath the roof, the door and window frames were sculptured or carved in designs of trees, shrubs, vines, flowers and fruits, exquisitely wrought in alternations so as to form a beautiful scene.

The interior was very plain, but rich in detail. Two-thirds of it, in conformity with the form of the structure, was devoted to public seats. The remaining third was occupied by an enormous stage, with the seats arranged as shown in the diagram on page 88. On each side of the auditorium, front of the stage, was a door for entrance and a system of altyna steps leading up to it. On the entire interior rose massive columns of altyna, as supports for the roof and dome, in addition to that of the massive walls. These were ornamented with massive capitals similar to those of the Grecian heads of fruit and flowers. The columns were similar to those of the Tuscan order, but massive and highly polished. The dome was decorated in sky blue, upon which the constellations were represented, which symbolized time, and the mathematical principles by which it was made divisible. On the wall at the rear of the Rē-ĕst'mē (stage) the recumbent form of a man was sculptured. He was represented as lying on his side knees drawn up, head resting on his right hand, and the left across his body. An altyna canopy covered the figure. This was wrought with fine carvings and decorated in harmony with the great dome. Beneath the figure was a platform corresponding in depth with that of the canopy. It was supported by altyna brackets and ornamented only by designs from nature. The recumbent figure symbolized a listening ear and a watchful care, such as should be exercised by those who are entrusted with public affairs. Entrance was made to the Reestme by two ways, viz., from the exterior by the side doors and also by the stairway, was a masive column, and one on each side of the canopy, similar to those in the auditorium. The arrangement of the seats on the Reestme was very commodious, as can be seen by the diagram. It was thus: At the rear center, in front of the recumbent statue, were three altyna seats, topaz in color, perfectly plain and highly polished, as was the case with all the other seats on the Reestme. On each side, one set of three. Center, one set of three. Center, three sets of three, thus forming parallel and angular aisles leading down to the Reestme front. The floor of the Reestme was a mosaic, beautifully designed and wrought from the choicest varieties of altyna that the Lontidri afforded. On the front center of the Reestme stood a massive Kĕt (table), also one on the right and one on the left. The Supreme Efremetrum sat at the center Ket, facing the audience, in company with the Sub-Efremetruzem (Teltzie Teachers or Governors). During the session, questions from the various Teltzie were taken up in order, beginning with the first Sub-Efremetrum on the left, who placed his questions, in writing, before the Supreme Efremetrum for disposal, and so on round the Ket, until all the Sub-Efremetruzem had done likewise. The questions of each Teltzie were entirely settled and disposed of before passing to the next one in order.

The side Kĕtzē′ (tables) were each occupied by three individuals, six in all, who had been chosen, one from each Teltzie, by the Sub-Efremetrum of the Teltzie. These six men acted as Cŏn-sē-mĕz′ (secretaries). Each Con-se-mez (secretary) acted for the Efremetrum of his Teltzie, as well as to note the general discussions and decisions before the assembly. The Consemez were also allowed to offer supplementary questions for consideration by the Supreme Efremetrum and general Council.

The numerous Sū′thē′ūs (seats) on the Reestme were for the utility of those who sat in council with the high officials who occupied the Sutheus at the Ketze.

Each Sub-Efremetrum chose from five to seven leading persons of his Teltzie to officiate on ordinary occasions but, in criminal cases more were chosen, according to the severity of the crime and the complicated conditions that attended it, so that perfect justice might be given the individual being tried for the offense against the laws of the Lontidri.

The arrangement of the Sutheus in sets of three each was instituted from the idea of the triangle, which symbolized the principles of Justice, Mercy and Love, which were three lawful Atlantian terms; hence, everything pertaining to official business was carried out according to them. There were always three principal representatives for each case, who acted as spokesmen. These occupied the central Sutheus, and the remainder of the Council those at the sides.

Furthermore, this arrangement of the Sutheus was to facilitate the entrance and exit during a session. The aisles extended in right angles, thus to symbolize a meeting of the principles of right and wrong at a point of law thus to establish a new condition.

As the councilor descended the perpendicular, so to speak, he opened the door of his soul for the influence of love to enter. As he turned the angle, for that of justice, and as he traversed the horizontal, for that of Mercy, knowing them to be attributes of then Gala Principle.

An arched Lē-ī′sē (vine) was carved on the back of each Suthe, beneath which the number of the Suthe was placed. The front of the Reestme was ornamented with the Lē-ī-sē′ūs (vines) in harmony with those on the Sutheus.

The front of the Mĕn′lä (Auditorium) was adorned with a

massive window in an arched frame, with ornamental carvings on top and down the sides. On each side of the Reestme and the Menla were windows ornamented in harmony with that of the front.

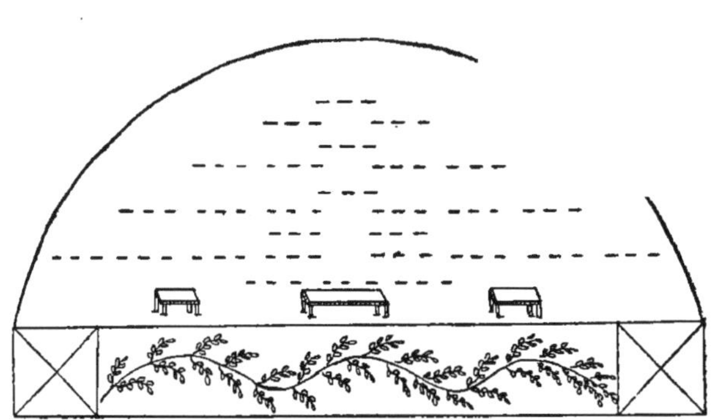

USH DE-AKE'AL RE-EST'ME.

N. B.—How the arrangement of seats carries out the idea of a triange and squares; also the facility for entrance and exit.

On the east side of the main Xontis, opposite the Ixrolta on which stood the great Deakeal was located a small Kergu (park) in which the Ki'tō (a shrine or place for prayer to which the people went before entering the Deakeal for business) stood.

Beginning the next Ixrolta north, on the east side of the Xontis, stood Ush Trŭne A-găl'tē Sī Qū-ē'sä (The New Temple of Peace).

On all the angular Xontisze were beautiful palaces and homes that varied in size, height and general architecture, in accord with the wealth of the possessors, which were built of different materials, such as blue, orange, and variegated, quarried from the Aelkedze near Atara. The blue and orange colors were so placed as to alternate in diamond figures diagonally across the buildings in meanderings and trellis-like work, with ornamental carving in designs of flowers, fruits, vine in scroll work wrought by a graceful arrangement of leaves and vines with headings of fruits, grains, and flowers. Care was taken to carry out the order of the alternation of colors, so as to maintain perfect symmetry.

The base, corners and summits of the walls were constructed from variegated material which much resembled the Scotch granite. The door and window caps were usually wrought in three pointed outlines. The ornamental work on these, aside from the scrolls of leaves and vines, were wrought in diamond and triangular-shaped figures, in the center of which balls were carved in representation of the Sun.

At the northeastern limit of the aistie, near the bank of the Belteer, a small river that had its rise in the Cutux terranzi, which flowed along the eastern boundary of Atara, was the Agalte Si Neceletus Melez Codize (Temple of Illustrate Dead Bodies).

In the Tynger of Atara, northwest of the aistie, stood the great Mär-ē'tŭx (Triangular Monument of the Government). North of this was the beautiful Opsite Kelete which was about three Xetruze in width and five in length. Many summer homes adorned the Kelete region. Beyond this, the Grĕt'ĕl-ty (country) was undulated and adorned with natural trees.

On the Ceitux Aelkedze, east of the aistie, and near the Ceitux Heltroplox, stood the Nez Agalte Si Qū-ē'sä (Old Temple of Peace).

The Aelkedze near Atara were very high. There were many crevasses, caverns and caves. Jutting rocks, some of which were rough and rugged, while others were symmetrically laid, as if by the hand of man. A profusion of shrubs and flowers blended with the verdure of the trees. The general view over the Tynger was extremely beautiful, revealing verdant grasss and foliage. Beautiful planes and undulating sections. Gardens of vegetables and flowers, especially Indraze (roses) of many varieties, fragrant and beautiful as they twined over the Weīt'zeē (trellises). Small aistieze; sections of fruits and grains; rigerze; keletze and adjacent aelkedze, such as characterized the homeland of Atara.

At the northern extremity of the aistie, two Zĕd'zē (roads) diverged from the continuation of the main Xontis, each forming a triangle with it, as the three were lost to view in their extent into the Tynger.

At the southern limit, the main Xontis was connected with the Grĕt'ĕl-ty Zĕd'zē (country roads) by bridges over the Riger.

At the southwestern limit of the aistie was the beautiful Mēn-glō-tī'ō Cĕr'gū (Menglotio Park). This large Cergu was adorned with choice flower trees and shrubs, drives and walks, monuments and statuary, vases and urns. Flowers of the choicest varieties that Atlantis could afford. Kĕs-trey'zē (fountains; the term "kestrey" signified purification) and artificial Keleteze, where aquatic birds and varieties of fishes played in the sparkling sunlit waters, or rested in the shadows along the verdant bordering banks.

In the center of the Cergu the famous Atlantian Kestrey was located. It was 100 coitex in diameter. The water was thrown up through metal pipes that varied from 10 to 50 coitex in height. These were arranged as follows: Centrally, the highest was one pipe. Next a shorter set of three. Next a shorter set of twelve, thus making three circular rows of pipes about the center one, which bore out the trinity idea and conical form. The water was entirely converted into spray, which was thrown upward from the top of the pipes, and downward from six arched pipes that were placed near the top of the perpendicular one. This resulted in a symmetrical combination of fountain sprays, that mingled to form one massive fountain of sprays. The great basin into which the sparkling spray fell was inhabited by a variety of fish, whose quiet and graceful movements symbolized contentment. It was constructed of White Signitie and adorned with a border of green mosses and small flowers simliar to the modern forget-me-not. The mosses symbolized humility of spirit in the presence of Gala, and the flowers, the graces that he would bestow upon it through this condition. Twelve walks radiated from the Kestrey, to the outer of three that encircled the Kestrey, thus symbolizing the radiant light of the Sun, whose image, power and source of radiation was symbolized in the momentum of the waters and their glistening surface in the circular basin. The triangular divisions of earth between the radiations of Signitie were massive floral beds. By their beauty and fragrance they symbolized the virtues that surround a life of purity, which latter virtue was symbolized by the great Kestrey.

AT-SI-AN'AS RIN'GA,

OR

BOTANIC LINKS.

TELTIZIE XII.

In establishing and connecting up the Botanic Links, such as were broken on the deferent of the great Cycle of Botanic Life in the regions of Atlantis, Erothrodia informs us that they had great varieties, some of which closely resembled the classes, orders, genera, species and varieties of modern times.

Passing by the mosses dispersed by Nature in aquatic depths, and forest regions, we begin with the Cletish (flowers) which were numerous and very beautiful on the Lontidri.

The Am'wä was a semi-aquatic family of plants that ranged over various district of the Lontidri, and compared closely with the now known genus Liliacea, or Lily families. Originally, the Amwa was distributed over the central, southwestern, southern and southeastern portions of the Lontidri, but some species were cultivated in the northern as well. In regard to species and varieties in each family, they varied in their forms and colorings, from the gross to the tiny, and from the richly robed to the more modest.

The Jĕlt was a species of the Amwa that was particularly attractive, and differed from any of the modern lily varieties. Its flower was trumpet-shaped, thus formed by five bright pink petals; a white pistle that terminated with a yellow, three-lobed stigma; five white stamens surmounted with bright golden anthers, etc. The leaves of the plant were of a linear lanceolate form, though larger, as was also the case with the bloom, than those of the modern lilies.

The Gĭst was another species of the Amwa family that was also very attractive. It bore a flower with five obovate petals with a bright, velvety, but medium purple color, the central base being white, which shaded up until it was lost in an exquisite blending with the purple. The pistil was white but the stigma as a delicate purple which, as it were, shaded down in dewy drippings over the upper portion of the pistle. The stamens were white, and were surmounted with light purple anthers, with similar shadings to those over the pistil and stigma. The plant leaves were peculiar. They were linear lanceolate, but the mid-rib extended through the leaf to the apex, much closer to the upper margin than the lower, which rendered the latter portion broader and gave it a thicker appearance than the upper.

The E-quē'trē was another species of the Amwa family, of many varieties, though the white and the orange were in the majority. The flower was solitary, thus nodding on a tall peduncle. The white variety consisted of six linear crenate and re-curved petals that formed the corolla in which stood a white style and pistil, thus terminated with a yellow, three-lobed stigma and five white stamens surmounted with yellow anthers. The plant leaves were eliptical lanceolate like such varieties of the modern lily.

The Equetre, especially the white variety was very popular with the Atlantian people, which was held sacred as a symbol of the motive influence of Gala; i. e., the intensity of the recurving of the petals were governed or influenced by the force of the sunlight, as the hours of the day advanced, which at midday was the most intense, and as the night approached the movement of the petals had reversed to nearly the form of a closed bud; hence, by that peculiar phenomenon symbolized the Gala principle operating upon that flower to the Atlantians who looked deeply into the nature of things for the Gala principle or motive quality in all beings.

Nearly every family of the genus now known as Liliaceae, or land lilies, were origanalyy semi-aquatic, having their origin in the shallow, still waters or marshes of the Atlantian Lontidri, and thus extended to pre-historic regions; but have acquired their changed characteristics in that respect from continuous transplanting and cultivating apart from the more natural or original aquatic conditions; yet, the Lily still turns back to the old habits of its ancestors, and thrives best when given plenty of fluidic nourisment. All the spotted-petals varieties of the lily tribe have been thus established through amalgamate conditions, attending the descending species, the origin having had place in the latter part of the Adamic Period.

Thus, from the original Amwa family, at the time of the submergence of Atlantis through the remnant plants left on the border lands of the different hemispheres, and those already indigenous and contemporaneous with those of the Atlantian Lontidri, have descended upon the Eastern and Western continents such varieties of the land-lilies as are represented by the various species known to modern botanists. See account in modern works, of the latter.

The Rôu'cē was an aquatic flower plant that inhabited the shallow waters of all the principal Keletze of the Lontidri. There were many varieties, some elegant and some more common, but we will only describe four of the most noted. Like most of the genera Nympha, or Water-lilies, the Rouce was a floating plant. The flowers, generally speaking, were of great beauty, were extremely fragrant, which latter condition was a charming aecompaniment to their marvelous beauty, as they graced the blue, clear waters of the Keletze, where they were much sought after by the people. The first of the four bore a flower that measured from four to five inches in diameter. The center bore a flat golden-colored stigma, that was surrounded by a numerous throw of white stamens, with golden anthers (though in some varieties the stamens were golden and the anthers were a light yellow) and further surrounded with numerous and very large, bright red, or rose-colored petals, all of which were gracefully supported by a throw of dark green sepals. Thus materialized, it was a flower of rich appearance, as the sunlight reflected from its perfectly color-blended form. The leaves of the plant were circular or shield-like, were much larger than those of the water lily, and were a bright red on the upper side, over which flashed a glistening reflection of a bright pink hue.

The second of the four species was formed similar to the first, only the leaves were some larger. Its pistil was white and was surmounted with a pale yellow stigma, over which was a reflection of pink. Its stamens were white and surmounted with pink anthers. Its petals were pure white and its sepals were a pale or sea green. Like the above variety, it was so perfect in its blending of colors as to be most charming in appearance, as the sunlight fell upon it on the blue waters of the Keleteze. The leaves of the plant were sagittata or arrow-shaped at the base, but slightly trilobate or three-lobed at the apex. They were of a glossy green color on the upper side, over which gleamed a yellow reflection, but the under side had a fuzzy coating.

The third of the four species was similar to the second. Its pistil was of a creamy white, and surmounted with a pale yellow stigma. Its stamens were also a creamy white and its anthers were a pale yellow. Its petals were of a pale, but very bright blue, and its sepals were of a lustrous pea-green, the bloom being very large. The plant leaves were about 2 feet long and 1 in breadth, and were formed like the now known leaf of the Lily of the Valley, differing only in their number on each plant, and greatness in size. The ribs were very marked which gave them a raised appearance. They were of a delicate green.

The fourth species was quite different from those already described. The leaves of the plant, two in number, of large eliptic form, surmounted a stalk from three to four feet in height, and was of a dark green, the surface being rough or velvety quality. From between the two leaves likewise rose from 6 to 10 flower stalks to a height of about 5 feet, each surmounted with a single bloom. There were however, several species. The flowers of all were formed similar to these of the now known Iris or Flower-de-luce. The outer surface of the petals folded upward, and were variegated in stripes that rose from the base of the petal to about its centre where they were lost in blendings with the color of the apex of the petal. The central strip was a velvety black, and on either side of it, and in conformity with it rose a velvety brown stripe. The inner side of the same petals were a light pea-green from the base to their centre, but shaded out to a very delicate sea-green around the margin and over the apex of the petal. The 3 outer reflex segments wore a golden sheen at the central base, that further shaded out over the petal thus terminating in a blended margin and apex of dark golden or orange hue.

Another variety had blended stripes on the upper petals of purple or dark lilac, from the centre stripe, and crimson or rose colored stripes on either side. The inner side of the same petals were of a rose color at the central base that shaded up into a bright lilac at the margin and apex of the petals. The 3 outer reflex segments were striped, but so perfectly blended that they appeared more like shadings, than distinct stripes. The central base was of a rose color that blended out to a bright lilac. The margins of all the petals of this variety were curled or reflex.

From this fourth species, have descended the now known Iris family of plants, of which there are many varieties. The original Rouce species was a bulbous plant, the bulb however being oblong instead of circular, and from this condition, the rhizomatous plants were established, by further elongation, or branching of the root-stocks through the ages of their evolution. The rhizomatous condition is a result established long after the Atlantian period of time, as well as the changes that have been established from the oblong bulbs to those of the more circular, a condition also arising from similar causes, but operating in diverse development; hence, the fourth species of the Rouce and their descendants, prehistorically known as the Grĕn'tă on the Eastern, and the Yĕl-tō'zē on the Western Continents, became the prehistoric ancestors of the now known Iris, or Fleur-de-lis, the image of which has long had place as an emblem of heraldic device among the celebrities of the Eastern Continent, as evidenced by its placement on sculptured head-dresses of the Egyption Sphinxes; as ornaments on the sceptres, seals and robes of not only the Merovingian, but Greek, Roman, German, Spanish and English Kings; a symbol employed by the nobility in various parts of Europe; the Coat of Arms of the city of Florence, Italy; and since the 12th century has been employed as a symbol of royalty in France.

Prior to the submergence of Atlantis, the Rouce was indigenous in certain districts of the now known Eastern and Western Hemispheres, and at the time of the submergence remnant plants were also left in the waters of the borderlands, from which two conditions, the Rouce takes its part as an ancestoral link of the descended Water-Lily species, pre-historically known as the Wē-ĕl'zĕr on the Eastern Continent, which name it bore until about the Adomic period, when it was changed to that of Lily by the peoples in the Nile region, the name having been carried from there into the south-western part of Asia, thence into Greece, and further handed down to the present time by migrating peoples. It was known on the Western Continent, pre-historically, as the Gĕs'lĭs, the name having been changed to that of Lily, by the early immigrants from the Eastern Continent, and its descendants, as well as those of the Weelzer, became the prehistoric ancestors of the now known Nymphaea, now inhabitants of all quarters of the globe. (See various works for the many descended modern links of the Lilium species.)

The Nē'mē was a plant belonging to the Amwa genus, and originally grew near the Kelteze of the Atlantian Lontidri. It closely resembled the now known species Convalearia Majalis, or more commonly known Lily of the Valley, only it was very much larger in the Atlantian time. Its present dimuinutive condition is a result from having been transplanted from semi-aquatic districts to those of drier soil. Originally, their large gamopetalous blooms of bell-shaped corolla, were divided, as now, at the top with 6 segments and were of pink, white, and purple varieties, and in their aggregation, distributed along the flower stem, which latter seldom rose above the plant leaves which also rose from the rizone, 2 in number, that were about 1 foot in length, 6 inches broad and veined as is now the case in the Lily of the Valley.

The extreme beauty, sweet perfume and great abundance of the Nimne, caused it to be much sought after, and utilized in decorative art, as in floral beds, about the homes, fountains and in public parks. The white variety was especially sacred to the people, and therefore used by them at all religious or spiritual gatherings, and particularly so on the occasion of weddings, it being symbolic of good and pure influences, as recognized in religious or spiritual services; but, in case of marriage ceremonies, it reminded the individuals that future rising generations should be brought forth as pure, if not more so, than the preceeding ancestors; hence, at the time of the marriage ceremony, one spray of the white Nimne was handed to both the bride and groom by the Deltsanz who performed the marriage ceremony, at the close of the same, which flower they wore until it had faded materially, when they were taught to hold to and cherish the fact that the spirit of the withered flower had not faded, but had entered the spirit realm there in its continuity to lend an influence upon their minds for good, thus prompting their acts in further material life, especially so, those that would in any way effect the lives and existence of their future generations, and ultimately to symbolize the link that should bind their souls together in the eternal bonds of spiritual love, as it had done in that of the conjugal during the material existence.

At the time of the submergence, the Nimne had extended into the border lands of the now Eastern and Western Continents, where it was left as remnants, the descendants of which were pre-historically known as the Snō'kē, on the Eastern, and as the Qū-zē'tē, on the Western Continents, whose ultimate descendants became the pre-historic ancestors of the species, Convalearia Majolis, or Lily of the Valley, as is now supposed to be an original plant of the mountains of Europe, and in its wild state, on the high Alleghanies of Virginia and Carolina, with further distribution through domestic influences. Many of the modern plants that bear similar flowers and leaves to the now known Lily of the Valley, enlarged or diminished in size, are descendants from the several species of the Atlantian Nimne.

The Pē-lē'sĕn was an aquatic plant that inhabited the stiller portions of the inlet waters along the Rigerze and Mū-zĕt'zē (marshes) of the southern and southeastern portions of the Lontidri, and closely resembled the species Nymphaea Alotus, or Water Lily of the Nile, Egypt, only that in every way it was much larger. There were several varieties, among which were three principal ones. The first of the three bore a flower with white stamens, yellow anthers and pink petals. Another of the three bore flowers with orange colored, flat stigma, or capsule, which was surrounded with white stamens, yellow anthers and golden-colored petals. The blooms, like those of the Rouce, were extremely fragrant. It was not only a native of Atlantis at the time of the submergence, but indigenous in parts of Egypt and southern Africa at that time, as well as in South America, from which, in connection with the remnants from Atlantis, established the species of their kind, pre-historically known as the Crē'shĕck, on the Eastern continent, and the Zĕl'lūs in South America, from which further descended the family Nymphæa Alotus of Egypt; the Nelumbium Speciosum, formerly a native of the Nile; the Lotus of India and China; the gigantic Victoria regina of South America, etc. So let the reader look up the great varieties of the Lily race, belonging to modern times, then meditate upon the source and antequated period from whence they have descended, viz., from the Atlantian Amwa, at that period of time.

The Crĕz'ĕs, was a flower plant that inhabited all parts of the Lontidri, both wild and cultivated. It resembled the now known genus Viola, only larger than the present violet family, and far more fragant. The smallest were even larger than the modern Pansy, which latter is a returning from the degenerate conditions of descendants toward the original. There was one species of the Crezes that in its original wild state was extremely tiny; so much so that a magnifying glass was necessary to aid in its analysis, and thus viewed, was wonderfully perfect and beautifully constructed. It grew among the mosses and, generally speaking, bore a white flower, tinted with pale yellow reflections, and in some cases there were pale yellow blooms, with a white reflection. From this tiny species, by cultivation and development, through the ages, all the white and yellow varieties of the Crezes of Atlantis were established, and finally developed to their grossest size.

Generally speaking, the Crezes was of all colors and varieties, belonging to the more modern times, yet they were much richer in color and markings, they being deeper and more reflective, sweeter in perfume, etc., than the latter. It had place with the Neme in decorative art about the homes, public grounds, vase ornamentation with cut flowers, and in its spontaneous distribution, beautified and made fragrant the wooded districts, charmed the aspect of dales and valleys, while its fragrance blended with the melodious songs of the birds, as beautiful qualities of the Gala in Nature.

At the time of the submergence of Atlantis, the Crezes had spread out into various districts of the temperate regions of the northern hemisphere, of both the Eastern and Western Continents, and some of the southern varieties of Atlantis had even found way into South America, all of which in continuation with the Atlantian links of extension, established through their descendants, the plant and flower, pre-historically known as the Cē-băl-ā-tē'ä on the Eastern and as the Căth-ā-măn'gĕs on the Western Continent, whose further descendants became the prehistoric ancestors of the now known extensive genus Viola, of which there are at least 1000 varieties. See various works for the modern links.

The Ar'i-ĕt was a flowering plant that ranged over the greater portion of the Lontidri, and was both wild and cultivated. It closely resembled the now known genus Tulipa, though much larger than the modern plants. There were many varieties of colors, among which was one that bore a bloom with a white style, crowned with a three-lobed stigma, numerous yellow stamens, surrounded with golden-colored anthers, broad obovate, crimson petals with crenate margins, slightly curved at the apex. The leaves of the plant were thick, linear-lanceolate, and rose in a cluster from the ground, amid which, from their center, rose an elevated peduncle that supported the beautiful flower. Like the Equetre, it was a symbolic plant. The circle or crimson petals symbolized the disc of the autumnal Sun. The yellow stamens, the tinted condition of the atmosphere that accompanied the rising and setting Sun. The golden-colored anthers, the illuminated cloudlets that floated in the Sun region, and the three-lobed stigma and white style, the source of natural light which produced these phenomena. Likewise of Gala and the sublime conditions that exist in that region. The spirits that draw from its inexhaustible supply of intellectual and spiritual light, through the source of life. The bulbs of the plant were used as an edible product, by some of the southern and eastern inhabitants of the Lontidri. It was also indigenous in North Africa and in certain parts of the British Islands prior to the submergence, and was further distributed in the now submerged regions of the Mediterranean Sea, Armenia, Caucasus, Persia, Central Asia and Afghanistan by the migrating peoples who used it for food, and thus established the wild species of those regions. Therefore, from the Ariet, has descended a large family of blooming plants, pre-historically known as the Nĭm′nē on the Eastern Continent, whose descendants became the pre-historic ancestors of the genus Tulipa, of almost endless variety. See various works for the modern links.

USH CLU ZE-LEN′TRES NUD A-E-EN′SES, OR THE FLOWER VINES AND SHRUBS.

TELTZIE XIII.

The Trĕck was an Atlantian vine, or leguminous plant that had place in the southern, southeastern, southwestern and central portions of the Lontidri. It closely resembled the now known species Wistaria, only its blossoms were pink and white, instead of purple and white. The blossom was a pendant cluster like the Wistaria, but the leaves were larger. At the time of the submergence, remnant seedlings and plants remained on the borderlands of Africa, South and Central America, and the southern United States, the descended species of which were pre-historically known as the Oŭ-ĭs'kä, on the Eastern, and the Cē-lŭ'-cē-ä on the Western Continent, which became the pre-historic ancestors of the species Wistaria, Sweet Pea and Wild Pea.

The Zū'ĭt was a twining shrub that had place in all portions of the Lontidri, excepting the extreme boreal districts. It closely resembled the genera Tecoma, or that species of it commonly known as the Trumpet Flower. There were several varieties, the principal one of which had at that period of time, linear serulate leaves, which condition was lost during the ages of its descendancy. The flowers were of distinct whirls, having a trumpet-shaped corolla; were of a deep purple, and the outer edges of the perianth leaves were striped with white. The flower was very attractive and sent forth a very sweet perfume. At the time of the submergence, remnant vines were left in the tropical and semi-tropical border regions of Atlantis, from which descended species pre-historically known as the Hō-lŭ'cē, on the Western Hemisphere, and as the Kĕn-zĕn'cē, on the Eastern, whose descended species became the pre-historic ancestors of those now known as Tecoma or Trumpet-Flower; the Lonicera sempervereus or Trumpet Honeysuckle and the Caprifolium Periclymenum or Woodbine.

The In'drä was a flowering shrub that had place throughout the Lontidri; it closely resembled the genera Rosa or Rose Shrub. There were many species of the Indra. One of the most beautiful varieties bore a bloom of pure white outer, and flesh-colored inner petals, it being very double and fragrant. The leaves of the various species were odd-pinnate, consisting of from three to seven (odd numbers) leaflets that were eliptic and serrate. Another variety much admired by the Atlantians was much larger than the modern American Beauty rose. It was a climber, and thus adorned the Kaleza (trellis) and walls of many Atlantian homes. It was a semi-double bloom with central yellow stamens, pure white inner petals, but the outer were white and variegated with a delicate pink. It was very beautiful and extremely fragrant, therefore much admired for all purposes. At the time of the submergence, remnants were left on both the Eastern and Western Hemispheres, from which descended the same genera, pre-historically known as the Kĭs'ly, on the Eastern, and the Crū'lĕt, on the Western, from which further descended the Wild Rose of the swamps and prairies, or Sweet briar of the fields, which in reality are degenerate diminutive descendants of the Atlantian

Indra. In pre-historic times, there began a cultivation of the wild varieties, continued through the Adomic and Historic periods, which has resulted in the re-production of varieties more like those of the Atlantian period, a return from degeneration toward the original.

The I-ĕn′drä was one of the choicest of the Atlantian flowering shrubs. It originally inhabited the central and southern portions of the Lontidri and was especially cultivated in the cerguze of the aistie of Atara. Originally it grew wild along the rigerze and keletze, its habits being much like those of the modern willow, relative to aquatic influences. It grew from ten to twelve coitex in height. Many stalks rose from its root region and the leaves of the shrub were of trifoliate, eliptic or magnolia-like form, and were closely arranged together on the stem. The flower was proliferous and composed of a calyx of bright scarlet reflect sepals and a corolla of short, alternating erect, bright golden-colored petals. In place of a style, rose a proles, or small flower, that took the place of a stigma, and that was composed of a cruciform calyx of white abcordate sepals. Its center was a capitulum of golden color. It was a deciduous bloom, thus giving place to a large red berry similar to the modern acorn in appearance and, notwithstanding its being slightly bitter, it was considered edible. At the time of the submergence it had become spontaneous in the region of South America, thus influenced by its growth in the southern portion of the Lontidri, and also became spontaneous in the tropical and sub-tropical regions of both the Eastern and Western Hemispheres, through borderland extensions from the Lontidri. The remnants in the South American region established a species pre-historically known as the Qū-ē′-rĭsh on that Continent, and those on the Eastern, then known as the Qū-ē′vĕr. Strange as it may seem, the descended species of the Quever and the Querish became the pre-historic ancestors of the Passion Flowers of South America and the tropical and sub-tropical regions of the Eastern Hemisphere. This, indeed, is one of the transformations among the many that have taken place in the botanic development of species, from remote pre-historic periods, to the ultimatum of the same conditions in the present time, and will therefore serve the purpose of informing the reader in regard to that branch of evolution, such as has, to a greater or lesser degree, changed the physical existence of the vegetable kingdom, during the succession of ages that were contemporaneous with their existence as periodical varieties. In this case we find the shrub greatly changed; e. g., the Tacsonias of the Andes, changed from a shrub to that of a climbing plant with wooded stalks, herbaceous or wooded branches and tendrils necessary to their habit of climbing. The leaves of the plant have drawn themselves closer together, thus evolving from their original trifoliate form, to that of a palmately-lobed and further possessed themselves with various stipules at the base of their stalks. Their inflorescence has changed from a reflex calyx, short erect corolla, proles bloom, etc., to that of a cymose character, the terminal branch being represented by the tendril, the side-branches by flower stalks or the inflorescence may be reduced to a single stalk. (See Encyclopædias for modern links.)

The O-gē'nē was an Atlantian deciduous flower shrub, and was one of the most beautiful, that inhabited the Lontidri generally. The flowers and leaves of the shrub resembled the genus Springa or Lilac species; however, the leaves in texture, were more like those of the Orange or Lemon. The form was eliptic-crenate, therefore the modern leaves are a degenerate result. In size, the shrub was about that of the Lilac. The flowers were of thyroid terminal pennicled form and were of dark purple, light purple, canary yellow and white; were much larger than the modern blooms, and fragrance much sweeter. The perfect harmony of the leaves and flowers made the Ogene a shrub of great beauty, and that harmony rendered it symbolic of the harmonious blending of soul and spirit with that of Gala, the Supreme or Infinite Principle of Life, whereby the individual might become more beautiful. Prior to the submergence, the Ogene had become spontaneous throughout the district now submerged by the Mediterranean Sea, from whence, to a certain extent, it had extended still further east. It was carried by migrators into the Mediterranean district originally, who settled along the then known Hammo Riger, that flowed through the Mediterranean district. Further descendancy of the shrub established the plant in Persia, Hungary and along the borders of Moldavia, and by European Colonists it was brought to North America.

Submerged Atlantis Restored

USH CLU E-EL-DES'SE
OR
THE FLOWER TREES.

TELTZIE XIV.

The Gū-ĭl'lō was an Atlantian leguminous flower and pod-producing tree, that inhabited the central, eastern, western and northern (excepting the extreme boreal districts) portions of the Lontidri, and closely resembled the *L. Ceratonia Siliqua* or Carab tree, especially the species now known as the Locust tree. It was larger however, its longevity far greater, and its epidermis or bark smoother. Its flowers were about the same in form, excepting that they were larger, the pendants larger and longer. One variety bore rose colored blooms; one pure white; one of white and pink variegation over which were strewn stops of brown. Their fragrance was so strong that it could be sensed at a great distance from the tree as it was carried away by the etherial currents. It was both spontaneous and cultivated. Its inflorescence made it ornamental, and its legumen were used as a choice edible by both man and beast, a utility that followed its descendants through all ages, the legume being the husks referred to in the story of the "Prodigal Son." It was the material with which Moses sweetened the bitter waters of Marah, Exod. XV. 25. It was the meat referred to in Matt. III, 4, that sustained John the Baptist. It is still used in its dried state, as a relish by the Hebrews and even other peoples, and in Sicily, a spirit and syrup are made from them. Prior to the submergence, the Guillo had become spontaneous in Europe and Africa. This condition, together with the remnants on the border-lands, established a species of trees, pre-historically known as the Skĕl-dē-lē'ŏn, whose further descendants became the pre-historic ancestors of the Carab or Locust-trees. It reached America by Colonists, who scattered the seeds when migrating. (See various works for modern links.)

The A-cū-lū'tĭve was a genera of trees and shrubs that inhabitated the central and southern portions of the Lontidri, with eastward and westward extensions, of which there were many varieties, that closely resembled the order Magnoliaceae. It was both spontaneous and cultivated. The principal variety grew to about 25 or 30 feet in height. The branches were more spreading than the modern varieties. Its leaves were Cē-lē-gā'cē-oŭs (fatty and glossy). Its flowers very large and white and were very fragrant. The principal one of the A-ē'ēn (shrub) order of the Aculutive, grew from ten to twelve coitex in height. The leaves and blossoms were about one-third smaller than the above-named E-ĕl'dē (tree). The flowers were a violet color, very fragrant, and hung in pendant form from the branches. At the time of the submergence, remnants of the Aculutive were left on the Eastern and Western Hemispheres, that with the indigenous growth on the southern portion adjacent to Atlantis, descended into a genera of trees and shrubs pre-historically known as the Mär'rŏth on the Eastern, and as the Frä-ē'frŭm on the Western, whose further descendants became the pre-historic ancestors of the now known fifteen or more species of the magnolia trees and shrubs. (See various works for the modern links.)

The Cē-lä-dĕn'cē was a genera including many species and varieties of coautchine bearing trees, shrubs and Zō-ĕng-ō'nĕs (plants,) that inhabited the tropic and semi-tropic districts of the Lontidri, and links into the various cycles of the natural order of caoutchine trees, shrubs, and plants, whose remnants now extend into South America, Africa and Asia, from which rubber is produced. Its value was well known by the Atlantians, for they extracted the Dĕl'zŏc (caoutchine) from their eeldesse, and when partly dried, they shipped it in balls for use as ball-bearings, or when conveying one piece of metal over the surface of another to roll between them. It was also made in sheets of various thicknesses for use in musical instruments, or anywhere that moderns use felting.

The Lŏ-ē'tiē was a small species of the Celadence genera, that resembled the species Manhot Glazeovii or Rubber-tree of South America. It was very beautiful. The leaves were odd-lobed, palmate in form, and of a silvery green color. The inflorescence was a one-sided raceme of nodding lilaceous blossoms of pink and white variegation. At the time of the submergence, remnants were left in the region of South America whose descendants established a genus of trees and shrubs, pre-historically known as the Măn-zē-ū'lĕs, whose further descendants became the pre-historic ancestors of the species Manhot Glazeovii or Ceara Rubber Tree of Rio Janeiro, etc. To the Atlantians the Loetie was a symbol of virtue, that quality of being which protects the spiritual and physical man when in conquest with vice, thus rendering him beautiful in character and a force among men, when influencing their acts in the interest of right against wrong, whereby they may deal justly in opposition to injustice.

The Et'lä was also a species of the Celadence, and was of several varieties, the principal one of which was a large Tăm-ī-dō-rĕs'ĕnt (Ornamental tree that resembled the species Hevea brasileansis, one of the caoutchine trees of South America, from which the Para rubber is obtained. Its leaves were trifoliate, its inflorescence panicle, being a compound raceme of five white sepals, or stella-shaped blossom. At the time of the submergence, remnants were left on the southern hemisphere, from which descended a species of trees pre-historically known in South America as the Gē-rĕn'zē-mŏs, whose further descendants became the pre-historic ancestors of the species Hevea brasileansia of several varieties in South America, from which Para rubber is obtained, etc. Its stately form, bedecked with white stellablooms, intermingling with large, glossy, verdant trifoliate leaves, and productive capacity, were qualities that made it symbolic of human character, such as distinguishes the life of the individual and makes him both useful and pure and an attractive influence mong men.

The Qū-ī'lĕt was a species of the genera Caladence that closely resembled the species Castilloa elastica of Central America. At the time of the submergence, remnants were left in regions of Central America, the West Indies Islands and South America, from which descended a species of trees pre-historically known as the A'shăn, whose further descendants became the prehistoric ancestors of the species Castilloa elastica; particularly those of the dense forests in the basin of the Rio San Juan, and also in Costa Rica, Guatemala, Honduras, Mexico, Cuba, Hayti, Panama, western coast of South America, etc., from which is obtained the Nicaragua rubber.

The Yĕn-dĭl'zē was a species of the Caladence that inhabited the southeastern portion of the Lontidri, and resembled the Voahere of Voa-canja and Voa-hine trees of Africa. At the time of the submergence, remnants were left on the Continent of Africa, whose descendants became the pre-historic ancestors of the African species of caoutchine trees and plants.

The Kär-dĕn'zē, another species of the Caladence genera, closely resembled the species Ficus elastica of India. At the time of the submergence, remnants were left on the Eastern Hemisphere, whose descendants were pre-historically known as the Wĭl-dē'zē, whose further descendants became the pre-historic ancestors of the species Ficus elastica of British India, and rocky valleys of the Himalayas, etc., from which Asam rubber is obtained. (For the many other distributions as modern links, see Encyclopædias on the subject.)

Links and Cycles

USH K-RUTE' E-EL-DES'SE,

OR

THE FRUIT TREES.

TELTZIE XV.

There was an abundance of fruits on the Atlantian Lontidri, nearly all of which were more oval in form than the modern. In color, they were similar. All were grown in orchards and gardens. The trees and vines were carefully and artistically planted so as to form various geometrical figures, for in all geoponies, as well as architectural pursuits, the science of Geometry was called into use in form establishment, that the extended forms might serve the purpose of symbols representing spiritual, principles. Thus recognized, they taught the people as they passed to and from their daily avocations.

The Gū-ĕltz' was an Atlantian perennial fruit-bearing plant that inhabited the greater portion of the Lontidri. The fruit and leaves resembled the genus Fragaria or Strawberry, though larger. At that time it was a low shrub instead of a creeping vine, the latter condition being a degenerate result through descendancy. Its fruit was extremely delicious and fragrant. There was but one variety, the color being a dark red. At the time of the submergence, remnant plant were left on both hemispheres, from which descended a genus of plants pre-historically known as the Kĕl'tĭsh on the Western, and as the Dĕnt'ry on the Eastern Continent, whose further descendants became the prehistoric ancestors of the genus Fragaria or Strawberry plants. (See various works for modern links.)

The On'thē was an Atlantian fruit-bearing plant that inhabited the southern or tropical portion of the Lontidri, that resemlbed the species Ananassa sativa or Pineapple. It was very plentiful, and was a great favorite with the Atlantians on account of its sweet juice, it being unlike the modern Pineapple in that respect, the latter being aciduous. At the time of the submergence, remnant plants and seeds were left in the South American, Central American and Mexican regions, from which descended a plant pre-historically known as the Gör'phy on the Western Continent, whose further descendants became the pre-historic ancestors of the Pineapple.

The Cŭ'rĭd was an Atlantian vine that inhabited the central and southern portions of the Lontidri, with some distribution eastward and westward. It resembled the Lycopersicum esculentum or Tomato-plant. Both the plant and its fruit was larger than the modern species. It was very plentiful ,and grew both spontaneously and under cultivation. The principal colors were red and yellow. At the time of the submergence, seedlings and remnant plants were left in South America, from which descended a plant pre-historically known as the Or-nō'thō, on the South American Continent, whose further descendants became the pre-historic ancestors of the Tomato or Love-apple plant.

The Căn'ti-lŭs was an Atlantian fruit-bearing vine that inhabited the southern, central and western central portions of the Lontidri, with some extension in the northern border. It resembled the genus Vitis, or Grapevines. It was larger in regard to both vine and fruit, which latter was finer and sweeter than the modern varieties of grapes. It was eliptic formed, and grew in massive clusters. The colors were similar to the modern, only one of the varieties was a milky-white and extremely delicious on account of its mild flavor. The vines were self-supporting and grew to a considerable height, being more on the shrub order, and drooped when laden with fruit. The leaves were similar, but larger than the modern grape. At the time of the submergence, remnants of the Cantilus were left on the Eastern and Western Continents, from which descended vines pre-historically known as the Gĭl'sey, on the Eastern, and the Gŏn'shy, on the Western Continent, whose further descendants became the prehistoric ancestors of the genus Vitis, or species of Vitis Vinifera. The remnants on the Western Continent developed into a wild species pre-historically, though in the latter part of that period it was cultivated some by the inhabitants of Central America and Mexico, and ultimately found its distribution into California by the Franciscan fathers. Later, French, German and Spanish varieties were introduced, which extended into the United States. The remnants on the Eastern Continent were dispersed by migrating peoples who pre-historically passed eastward (see our migrations); hence the great antiquity of viticulture over the Eastern Continent, which now figures in Portugal, Spain, France, Austria, Hungary, Germany, Italy, Southern Russia and Greece, Armenia, Eastern Pontus, and other parts of Asia, whose wine product was utilized in the lands of the Levant from the earliest memory of civilization, and was even more remotely used by the Egyptians in honor of their god Osiris; by the Greeks, in honor of their god Dionysus; by the Hebrews, to the Patriarch Noah, and was an accompaniment to the repast of corn and oil, as recorded in the Old Testament, all of which have their remote connection with pre-historic utility, through the Cantilus of Atlantis.

The Cē'trē was an Atlantian fruit tree, that inhabited the greater portion of the Lontidri, and resembled the species Pyrus Malus or Apple tree. There were several varieties, the difference being principally in flavor and color, the general form being that of an egg shape. By the time of the submergence, it had become spontaneous on both the Eastern and Western hemispheres, the descendants of which established a degenerate species pre-historically known as the El-zăn'ĭc, on the Eastern, and as the Cū-rē'zō, on the Western, whose further descendants became the pre-historic ancestors of the wild species commonly known as the Crab apples, degenerate and diminutive as it became, by cultivation of the less degenerative in the latter part of the pre-historic period, through the historic to the present time, it has reversed its condition of the species back toward the Atlantian Cetre, on both hemispheres, as now manifested in Europe, Canada, the United States of America, Northern India, China, Australia, New Zealand, etc., thus distributed by migrating peoples.

The Sū'tor (pronounced Tsutor) was an Atlantian fruit tree that inhabited the central and southern portions of the Lontidri, and resembled the Punica Granatum or Pomegranate, only a larger fruit. It was considered peculiar on account of its habits. It grew from ten to twelve coitex in height. Its branches in their extension of growth, turned toward the midday sun, which fact made it symbolic of all material life reaching out toward the solar light; a necessary influence to the development of material form; especially man, in his effort to reach out unto Gala for that spirit light whereby he might gain knowledge and understanding, and the development of his soul forces, unfoldment of his spiritual being, in the present and future time.

The Vrū'ēze was an Atlantian fruit-bearing tree that inhabited the productive valleys in the central, northeastern, northern and northwestern portions of the Lontidri, and resembeld the genus Cerasus or Cherry tree. It averaged in size with the modern trees. The fruit was more elongated in form, or similar to the modern Plum. There were three varieties, viz., pure white, red, and black, the former being the most delicate in flavor. At the time of the submergence it had become spontaneous on the borderlands of both hemispheres, thus influenced from the Atlantian growth. This, with the remnants, established trees pre-historically known as the Că-ū-rē'ă, on the Eastern, and as the Jăn-ā-ĕn'thēs, on the Western Continent, whose further descendants became the pre-historic ancestors of the Cerasus or Cherry trees. (See Encyclopædias for modern links.)

The Gū'lū was an Atlantian fruit tree that inhabited the central, eastern and western-central portion of the Lontidri, and resembled the species Prunus persica, or Peach tree. It was considerably larger than the modern Peach, more oblong in form, stronger in flavor, the skin was a purplish-red, and the meat more like the modern ',Blood-red Peach," which latter is the return influence of the original Gulu. At the time of the submergence, remnants were left on the Eastern Continent, whose descendants established a species of trees and fruit, pre-historically known as the Mĕr-sĕn'ză, the further descendants of which became the pre-historic ancestors of the Peach tree, pre-historically established by migrating peoples as they journeyed eastward into China, Persia, Asia-Minor, Afghanistan, India, etc. Hence, its distribution originally was eastward and not westward, as has been supposed.

The Nectarine or smooth-rind peach is an amalgamate condition caused by a mixture between the Atlantian Brest and Gulu, thus descended.

The Brĕst was an Atlantian fruit tree, then considered a species of the Gulu family, and inhabited the central and southern portions of the Lontidri. It resembled the species Prunus armenica, or Prunus Vulgaria, the Apricot tree. The fruit was much larger, however, and was of a deep orange color, very sweet and palatable. At the time of the submergence, remnants were left on the Eastern Continent, from which descended trees and fruit, pre-historically known as the Nō'dē, whose further descendants became the pre-historic ancestors of the Apricot tree, pre-historically distributed in Egypt, Armenia, Asia, etc., by migrating peoples.

The Clū'nĭs was an Atlantian fruit tree of several varieties, that inhabited the central, western and eastern portion of the Lontidri, and resembled the genus Prunus, or Plum tree. It was larger than the modern Plum, and was of purple, red, green, and white varieties. At the time of the submergence, remnants were left on the Eastern Continent, from which descended trees and fruit, pre-historically known as the Clē'mē, whose further descendants became the pre-historic ancestors of the Plum trees, as distributed into Antola, Caucasus, Southern Europe, Armenia and along the Casian regions, by pre-historic migrating peoples.

The Krĕt'ziē was an Atlantian fruit tree that inhabited the southern, central and tropical portions of the Lontidri, and resembled the genus Citrus Aurantium or Sweet Orange, and was about three times as large a fruit as the modern Orange. At the time of the submergence, remnants were left on the Eastern Continent and the Islands of the Atlantic, and the West Indies Archipelago, from which descended trees and fruits pre-historically known as the Cĕl'dĕ-nĭx, whose further descendants became the pre-historic ancestors of the Orange trees, as distributed into China, India, Western Asia, and eventually into Europe by pre-historic migrating peoples. The true Chinese variety, from the Azores, came through Spain and thence into China and Japan, and into the Indian Archipelago at the time of the submergence. It is the idea of nearly all writers upon the subject of distribution to reverse the order of migration from the east, westward, when it should be from west, eastward. This refers to pre-historic distributions.

The Quĭnt'sŭl was a fruit tree that inhabited the southern central and tropical portions of the Lontidri, and resembled the Bitter Orange, or so-called "Pummelo, or Grape Fruit." Originally it was about the size of the largest modern growth, and similarly characterized. At the time of the submergence, remnants were left upon the Eastern Continent, the Islands of the Atlantic and the West Indian Archipelago, from which descended trees and fruit, pre-historically known as the Trĕs'dy, whose further descendants became the pre-historic ancestors of the Bitter Orange, which was variously distributed by pre-historic migrating peoples.

Subsequently, by amalgamation between the Quintsul and Kretie fruits, the Citrus Lemonum or Lemon and Lime trees were established, the latter being a diminutive variety of the Lemon proper; hence, the Lemon and Lime fruits are not straight descendants from Atlantian species, but by amalgamation. These found their distribution also by migrating peoples, pre-historically who were passing eastward from the Azores, Portugal, Spain, Arabia, and subsequently throughout the Mediterranean regions, ultimately into California and Florida and sub-tropical countries by similar sources.

UŠH SU NUD KAL-LES'TE E-EL-DES'SE,
OR
THE NUT AND FOREST TREES.

TELTZIE XVI.

The Ex'tŏn was a nut-bearing genus of trees, represented by three principal species, viz: the Bŏn'zĕl, a native of the Eastern portion of the Lontidri; the Ex'ton and the Cū-rĭ'tä, that were contemporaneous natives of the western portions. The Bonzel closely resembled the genus Juglans or Walnut; the Exton that of the Juglans cinerea or White Walnut, commonly known as the Butternut; the Celuth that of the genus Carya, or Hickory nut. The Exton bore a nut much larger than the modern White Walnut and was more oval in shape, with a blunter end; the Bonzel was also larger and shaped more like the English Walnut; the Celuth was about the same as the modern Hickory nut, only larger, and the bark of the tree was smooth on all species. Prior to the submergence, the Exton had become indigenous on both the Eastern and Western Continents, as it was a native of both the eastern and western portions of the Lontidri. Its remnants and the indigenous growth, established similar species, pre-historically known as the Yĕlt'tē on the Eastern, and as the Yŏn-zō'ē on the Western Continent, that became the pre-historic ancestors of the Juglas nigra of North America, etc. The Bonzel became indigenous on the Western Continent, as it inhabited the western portion of the Lontidri, though some species were in the eastern, and thus reached the European districts. The remnants and indigenous species of the Bonzel, subsequent to the submergence, established a species of trees and nuts, then known as the I-ō'nē-zŏn, on the Western Continent, and as the Băl'săc, on the Eastern, whose further descendants on the Western became the pre-historic ancestors of Gray Walnut, or Butternut, commonly called the Oil nut and White Walnut of North America. The Celuth became indigenous on the Western Cnntinent principally, as it originally belonged to the western portion of the Lontidri, with some distribution on the eastern, which to a small degree left links on the Eastern Continent. The Atlantian remnants with the indigenous growth, established a species pre-historically known as the Wĕr-ē'sä on the Western Continent, and as the An-tō-sō'ĕn on the Eastern, that became the pre-historic ancestors of the Hickory nut trees of North America.

The Cū-rĕl'tä was a nut-bearing tree that, in the time of Atlantis, closely resembled the Exton species, and inhabited the northern, northeast and northwest portions of the Lontidri. Prior to the submergence it was indigenous on both the Eastern and Western Hemispheres. After the submergence the remnants and indigenous descendants established a species of trees, prehistorically known as the Gŏn-sō-lē'ĕm, on the Eastern, and as the Glō'tī-ē on the Western Continent, whose further descendants became the pre-historic ancestors of the genus Captanea, or Chestnut trees. The Atlantian Curelta, unlike the modern Chestnut, bore a nut that was covered with a non-echinsilate shuck, therefore entirely free from the prickles that characterize the modern Chestnut burrs.

The Kăl-lĭs-tē'nō or Wĕr-zē'lē (forests) and the E-lē-zăcs, or Rĕlt'zē (fields) of Atlantis, aggregated in a natural assembly of shade trees, that represented many genera, species and varieties, too numerous to give complete account of in this work; therefore, we will only give some of the principal ones, that the arborary links in the cycle of that branch of vegetation now existing may be linked back to its pre-historic severing, prior to the Atlantian submergence that rendered it broken.

The Atlantian Făn-ī-dō-rĕs'ĕnt (Ornamental) arboriculture was a scientific study with the people, who practised it in the culture of Jŭs-tē-zăc'zē (Orchards) and Căl-tē-lī'zē (Vineyards).

The Zĕl'zŭm was a beautiful forest tree, as well as an occupant of the principal parks, and along the streets in the principal cities of the Lontidri; but originally, in its wild state, it inhabited the central and northern portions. It resembled the now known genus Acer or Maple tree. There were several varieties. It was not then used for its saccharine product. The principal difference between the Atlantian Zelzum and the modern Maple tree was in their samara or seed formation, those of the Atlantian being but one-winged. Prior to the submergence, the Zelzum was also indigenous on both the Eastern and Western Hemispheres, which, in connection with the remnant links, established a genus of trees pre-historically known as the Dē-mĕl'trē on the Western Continent, which became the pre-historic ancestors of the now known Maple trees, ranging in Europe, North America, North Asia and Japan.

The Al'tē-zōne was a fine forest tree, very tall, graceful, large dimension, bore graceful leaves and was of several varieties. It inhabited the northern, northeastern and northwestern districts of the Lontidri, and so upon the northern portions of both the Eastern and Western Hemispheres, and this condition, with that of the Atlantian remnants, pre-historically established a species then known as the An-ăs-tē'trŭm, on the Eastern, and the Bŏn-ī-gĕl'ĕt, on the Western Continent, whose further descendants became the pre-historic ancestors of the genus Traxinus or Ash trees. The Altezone, unlike the Ash trees, had a smooth bark. The Altezone, through the Bonigelet, therefore, by the modern link of the Ash trees, has extended the Cycle into Europe, Asia, Greece, Turkey, Asia Minor, the West Indies, America, etc.

The Sīn'ā-bōre was a natural ornament of the forests. It was of the coniferous order of trees, and of several species, the term meaning evergreen. The principal species originally inhabited the lower portions of the Keletze and along the Rigerze, instead of the high altitudes as is the habit of its modern descendants. It closely resembled the genus Pinus or Pine trees. The principal species grew very tall, the trunks were limbless for many feet above the roots, and were crowned with a spreading cedal, glauceous foliage, which in contrast with its red brown bark made it very attractive. At the time of the submergence, remnants were left upon both the Eastern and Western Continents, that linked into the indigenous growth of the adjacent regions, from which descended a species of trees pre-historically known as the Yĕt-lä'cä, on the Eastern, and the Dĕn'zīc on the Western, whose further descendants became the pre-historic ancestors of the Pine trees. (For the vast number of modern species, see Encyclopædia Britannica.)

Remnants of one of the species of Sinabore, on the Eastern and Western Hemispheres, established a variety of trees pre-historically known as the Dŏm-tŏm'zēs, on the Western, and the Jĕn-zē-lū'cy, on the Eastern, whose further descendants became the pre-historic ancestors of the Fir or Spruce trees. (See Encyclopædia for the many varieties.)

The Kē'dē was a genus of the Sinabore order, represented by three principal species, and ornamented the forests, mountains, and valleys throughout the Lontidri. The first species closely resembled the Larix Americana, or Tamarac of the Western Hemisphere, and the Larix Europæa of the Eastern. This species had a straight, erect trunk, from 25 to 30 feet in height. The branches grew horizontally, spreading at irregular intervals from the stem, growing gradually shorter as they approched the summit. The points of all the branches drooped gracefully, so as to give them a pendant appearance in sections. The thick, studded whirl of narrow linear leaves, of bright light green, especially the young ones in the springtime, gave to the tree a fluffy, beautiful appearance. The cones were similarly arranged on the branches to those of modern trees, but were much larger. The second species closely resembled the genus Thuja and Biota or Arbor-Vitæ, only the trees were much larger, the leaves darker green and in more massive inibricated clusters, and did not grow as bushy in its wild state as the modern trees. It was very beautiful and therefore much cultivated in the parks and about the homes in Atlantis. At the time of the submergence, remnants of this species were left on the Eastern and Western Hemispheres, from which, in connection with the indigenous growth, descended a species of trees pre-historically known as the Cly'dŏx, on the Eastern, and as the Mĕn'drē o nthe Western, whose further descendants became the pre-historic ancestors of the genus Thuja or Thuya accidentalis, the Arbor-Vitæ of Western America. For the marvelous modern varieties and evergreen links arising from the foregoing pre-historic extensions, see the Encyclopædia Brittanica and other works. The third species closely resembled the genus Cypressus, or Cypress trees, and ranged in the central, northern, and southwestern portions of the Lontidri. About the same difference existed between the second and third species of the Sinabore, as now exists between the Cypress and the Arbor-Vitæ, etc. At the time of the submergence, remnants of the third species were left upon the Eastern and Western Continents, which with the already indigenous growth, established a species of trees pre-historically known as the Ab-boy'yä, on the Eastern, and as the Zĭt'yä, on the Western, whose further descendants became the pre-historic ancestors of the Cypress trees of Levant and Persia; North India; the East Indies; California; Mexico; North China, etc.

The Sinabore was a symbolic tree to the Atlantians, and thus represented natural artistic beauty and adornment, or the graces that fascinate the mind and charm the inner being or spirit of mankind. In its evergreen quality they recognized a symbol of the continuity of Spirit-life beyond the material existence. In the contrast between its glauceous foliage, red-brown bark and altitude, the symbol of Soul-beauty and adornment, such as comes to the aged individual by virtue of mental, moral, soul and spirit unfoldment, and therefore greater elevation of being.

The Cör-dū-lū'săc was a genera of amentaceous trees of several species that originally inhabited the north temperate zone of the Lontidri, and closely resembled genera Populus, or poplar trees. The O-lĭp'siē was one of its most attractive species on account of its restless, varied-colored leaves. It was very similar to the Aspen Poplar and, like it, its leaves danced and glistened in the sunlight to the rhythm of the breeze. There were three varieties of the Olipsie, the difference being in the leaves, catkins and bark. One variety possessed dark green, slightly trilobate, glossy leaves; dark green catkins, the scales of which were tinged with a light green; dark drab bark, generally smooth, but occasionally marked with seal brown knots or spots. Another variety had paltate or shield-shaped leaves, the upper side being of a mossy light green color and the under side white; the catkins were of a light green body, the scales tinged with a whitish glow; the bark was a very light tan-brown of bright lustre. Another variety had ovate leaves with a glossy olive green shade on the upper surface, and a very pale yellow below. The catkins were a medium green-colored body, the tips of the scales being lighted up with a darker shade of yellow than that on the under side of the leaves. The bark was white and marked with the dark spots, a variety now entirely extinct. These three varieties, with the Zelzy and the Zenzea, adorned the parks and city squares. They were symbolic of impulse, or external influences, operating momentarily upon the mind, causing the individual at times to be uncertain in character, and also brought into contrast the condition of restless impulse, with that of soul meditation and the calm, peaceful enjoyment occasioned by virtue of the recognition of all that is beautiful, and appreciation of the influence it had upon the soul and spirit, for its permanent unfoldment, and ultimate happiness. The Zĕl′zy was another very beautiful species of the Cordulusac. It was of medium height. Its body was alternated with circumferential stripes around them. The bark was of two colors, light black and dark drab or stone color. The black stripes were about four inches wide and the drab were twelve at the base of the trunk, each alternation growing narrower until they reached the apex; the limbs and branches similarly marked, and the whole form dotted promiscuously with black spots that made their appearance at the base of the trunk first, thus ascending, the trunk as a new set appeared in addition anually, until the age of the tree had endowed the entire trunk with the markings. The leaves were very small, of lanceolate, cerulate form, the upper surface being of a glossy green color, and the under side a light green. The catkins were a dark green, the tips of the scales being a light green. They also adorned the parks, city squares, home grounds and along the water-ways.

The Zĕn-zē′ä was a small tree that belonged to the Cordulusac genera, and was extremely beautiful. Its bark was smooth and a pea-green color. Its leaves were small, reniform or kidney-shaped, and of trifoliolate placement. They were a glossy, reddish bronze tinge on the upper side, and bright glossy red on the under. In place of the regularly organized catkins the inflorescence was solitary, took on the form of a flower that sprang out from the branches at the base of the leaf-stem, and were supported by a long stem. There were three varieties of the flowers. One bore white petals, white stamens and yellow anthers. One with pink ground petals striped with white, much as a modern "Morning Glory" is marked, white stamens and yellow anthers. One with purple ground petals, striped with white, white stamens and anthers, the latter slightly tinged with pale lilac. The stamens were short, capitate or inflorescence head-shaped, which gave the centre of the flower a fluffy appearance. It grew spontaneously by creeks, lakes, and was cultivated in parks and public places and about Där-ĕsh-ĕnzy'sŭm (reservoirs.) The adjacent grounds to the Dareshenzy (Reservoir) on the Aelkedze near Atara, were beautifully ornamented. A row of the dark green leafed Olipsie, interspersed with other ornamental trees marked the outskirts of the Dareshenzy district. About 100 coitex within was a second row of green and white-leafed Olipsie, with other interspersements. Still further, in about 100 coitex, bordering the outline of the Dareshenzy bank, was a third row of the light green and yellow leafed Olipsie that was interspersed with alternations of the Zenzea and the Zelzy trees. The area between the outlines or rows of ornamental trees were beautifully laid off with designs of flower shrubs, climbing flower-vines and plants, with accompanying stone and marble walks. The entire sloping bank of the Dareshenzy was devoted to the culture of trailing vines, so trained as to ascend the bank in their extension toward the water's edge, all bearing different colored flowers, harmoniously blended by arrangement. At the top of the bank, outlining the water's edge, was a broad walk for the people who visited the beautiful spot, and where they stood in contemplation of the scientific ornamentation. At the time of the submergence, remnants of the Zenzea were left on the Eastern and Western Continents, which with the spontaneous growth in the adjacent districts, established a genus of trees pre-historically known as the Bä-bō-kătch'ē-wä on the Western, and the Dĕl-kä-i'nō on the Eastern, whose further descendants became the pre-historic ancestors of the Poplar trees that range in the north temperate zone, such as the White Poplar of Abele; the Gray Poplar of central and southern Europe; the common Aspen of Europe, Northern Britain, Southerland, Lapland and from Siberia to the Arctic Circle, Norway; the large-leafed Aspen of America; and many others too numerous here to mention.

The Lū-ĕn-sē-ō'lĕs was a genera of both large and small deciduous trees and shrubs, that originally inhabited the central and northern portions of the Lontidri, extending east and west, with some distribution in the southern, and closely resembled the genus Salix or Willow trees. The leaves were deciduous, alternate, longer than broad, and varied in size and length according to the species. The flowers of the female were borne in catkins, and consisted of a bracket from whose axil rose a short stalk, surmounted by two carpels. That of the male was borne in amenta, and consisted of a small scale or bracket in the axil, of which rose two or more stamens according to the variety. In color they were brighter and deeper tinged than modern varieties. In nearly all species the branches were more inclined to be of a pendant or drooping character, than those of the modern trees, excepting the species Salix Babylonica, which has retained more of the character of the Atlantian trees in that respect.

The Crĕt'chiē was the most beautiful of the Luenseoles genera, that grew spontaneously and also under cultivation. It resembled the now known species Salix Babylonica, or Weeping Willow, though the leaves were longer and broader. Spontaneously, it grew along the rivers and lowlands of the central and northern portions of the Lontidri, but was cultivated in parks and public places. It was not only an ornamental tree, but used for medicinal purposes, in which case the juice was extracted from the bark, prepared and taken as a tonic, the quality being similar to that of sulphur. It was also a symbolic tree, being that of humility, such as beautifies and adorns the soul, enobles and dignifies the individual spirit, making it attractive among men, and as a spirit, loved and honored by the heavenly hosts. At the time of the submergence, remnants were left upon the Eastern and Western Continents. These with the spontaneous growth, established a species of trees pre-historcally known as the Bä-bō'rō, on the Eastern, and as the Gär-dĕn-cō'lēs, on the Western, whose further descendants became the pre-historic ancesors of the genus Salix of many varieties. (See Encyclopædias and other works for the modern links.)

USH LE-E'TRES, OR THE CEREALS.

TELTZIE XVII.

All Leetres were sown and cultivated in fields of various sizes, according to the needs of the Kĕl-lē'tä (tiller), and like the fields of Hē-lē-ŏn'zōs (vegetables), were formed into geometrical figures, symbolizing some life principle.

The E'trē was a cotyledonous, gramineous plant, or Lē-ŏn'trē (grain or cereal) that was grown in the central, northern, and northeastern portions of the Lontidri, and resembled the species Triticum sativum or Wheat, particularly the variety speltaas, cultivated by the aboriginal Egyptians, Romans, and Swiss Lake-dwellers, from which has evolved the dicoccum, tenax, and other varieties contemporaneous with pre-historic time, and on the cycle of cereal evolution, modernly. The principal difference between the Etre and the modern grain is that the grain rachis of the Etre were much longer and more pendulous than those of the modern growth, which latter condition was caused by the weight of the cereal, for it was a very productive plant. At the time of the submergence, remnants were left upon the Eastern Continent, from which descended a species of grain, pre-historically known as the I-ĭsh'ăm, in that region of country, from which decended the grain of the Egyptians.

The Quĭnt, cereal plant or species of graminæa, that was grown in the southern and southeastern portions of the Lontidri, resembled the species Zea Hays, or Indian Corn, and was of two varieties, viz: the yellow and the pnrple, the latter being the Atlantian Sweet Corn. The leaves were broader, thicker, and more prolific on the stalk than modern varieties, which latter bore from two to three ears each. At the time of the submergence, remnants and spontaneous plants were left on the Southern and Eastern Hemispheres, from which descended a grain, pre-historically known as the Brä-sē-ĕn'sēs, on the Eastern, and as the Sē-kĕl'săs, on the Southern.

The Krū'zē was a variety of the Quint species, and was contemporaneous with it in growth; differed from it and the modern Sweet Corn by having much narrower leaves, thicker ears of lobe-shape at the ends; each stalk bore from three to five ears of white kernels. The modern Sweet Corn is a descendant from an amalgamation between the purple Quint and the Kruze remnants; hence, both white and purple Sweet Corn of modern time. The yellow variety descended from the yellow Quint, through the pre-historic Braseences and Sekelsas, and the white variety, likewise from the Kruze, straight, which was of but one variety, viz., the white. The purple variety of modern corn descended from the purple variety of Atlantian Quint, and the modern striped variety by amalgamation from the yellow and purple varieties of the Quint species, having diverged from the parent varieties through the descendancy of the pre-historic Braseences and Sekelsas. Therefore, from the Atlantian Quint and Kruze, have descended four great classes or Flint varieties east of Lake Erie, and north of Maryland; the Dent varieties, west and south of these points; the Horsetooth varieties of the South; and the Sweet varieties of various distribution. The species known to the Eastern Hemisphere were introduced through Africa by the then migrating peoples who carried it into the Asiatic and European countries, and likewise to the East Indies. Its introduction onto the American Continent was also by migrating peoples from the West Indies, into Central America, South America and the Southern United States, and the present varieties have thus been established through mixed species, local cultivation, under modifications, having arisen from acclimatization, soil, and local in, fluences.

The Bō-rō'bē was a gramenaceous cereal that inhabited the borderlands, lakes, rivers and marshes in the central, southern, and southeastern portions of the Lontidri. It resembled the species Oryza sativa or Rice plant. It grew wild principally, and was very abundant, therefore obtained without cultivation. There were no high land varieties in Atlantis; that is a subsequent condition, caused by change of location, soil and culture, such as have changed from the original aquatic habit. Originally, it grew about three coitex in height; the leaves were longer and broader than on the modern varieties; the kernel or fruit was twice as large as the modern rice, more ovate in form, and also more prolific. At the time of the submergence, remnant seedlings and spontaneous plants were left in the now known region of Africa, form which descended plants pre-historically known as the Răs-sē'tĕs, whose further descendants became the pre-historic ancestors of the Rice plants. Their pre-historic introduction in to China and Japan was by the Lazerends and the Kentersends, when migrating across Africa, Arabi, Persia, etc.

and into India by the Timmenons and further into Java and Australia by their descendants (see migration of these peoples). Therefore all the Rice plants are descendants from the Atlantian Borobe, through their descendant plants, the Rassetes, etc.

The Kĕlt'zĭ-ē was a graminacious cereal plant that grew in the central and eastern portion of the Lontidri, and slightly resembled the genus Avenea or Oats. Through descendant conditions it has sustained greater changes than any of the cereal plants having their origin in Atlantis and existing modernly. Originally, it was a shorter plant and had broader leaves than the modern varieties. In place of the seed growth in panicle form on a single stalk like the modern Common Oats, there were from three to four stalks that rose from each plant, each of which terminated with a gram rachis; the spikelets were closely attached to the rachis, and contained more numerous glumes encasing the seeds or grams, which extended into a long stiff awn, twisted at the base. These changes are due to long descension under the influence of climate, soil, cultivation, etc., etc. At the time of the submergence, remnants were left in the region of North Africa, and the British Islands, whose descendants established a species of plants pre-historically known as the Cē'crū, on the Eastern Continent, whose further descendants became the pre-historic ancestors of the now known Oats plant. The distribution into northeastern America and South America was by modern migrators, from which has arisen many species. (See Encyclopædias, etc., for modern links.)

The cereals now known as Barley and Rye were not known in the Atlantian periods of time. Barley has its origin in Northern Egypt, it being an offspring from the pre-historic Itisham. Prior to the occurrence of the Biblical flood, in which Noah was the chief figure, it had become very plentiful in Egypt, and was then known as the Căs'tō-rĭx (see our account of the flood), and subsequent to that cataclysm, it was changed to Dū-frĕt, and so remained until the time of the mythical, or so-called Biblical writings, when it was changed to Barley-Corn. At the time of the above referred to cataclysm, which extended from the regions of the now known Black and Caspian Seas, southwestward through Turkey and Syria, into Egypt, seeds of the Dufret were transported and scattered by means of the fluviatic conditions, during the rising and subsidence of the waters, which established the plants termed Barley-Corn, which became the ancestor of the genus Hordium or Barley. (See Encyclopædias and other works for the modern links.)

The Rye plant, supposed by modern writers to have originated in the region between the Black and the Caspian Seas, had its origin in the regions of Denmark and Southern-Sweden, prior to the convulsions that shattered the region of Denmark and submerged portions of the then unbroken land of those districts, when an amalgamate condition took place between some of the pre-historic Itisham and Gecru of that region, which established a plant pre-historically known as the Cĕ′tŏx. Subsequently, it became distributed by migrating peoples, into various parts of Northern Europe, who began its cultivation, a condition that established a principal variety to which it has closely held in those regions, and is now the principal cereal of the peoples who occupy the regions of North Europe, especially Scandinavia, Russia and North Germany.

USH HE-LE-ON'ZUS,

OR

THE VEGETABLES.

TELTZIE XVIII.

The Atlantians subsisted principally upon vegetables, cereals and fruits, their spiritual development therefore being more rapid and perfect. They ate their fruit uncooked. Sometimes they cooked their cereals, and at others they were served in a natural state. In case of the former, they prepared them by taking them before they were ripe, so as to retain the milk, rolled and dried them. The process was a quick one, to prevent the loss of the milky substance, and was done by machinery. When dried, the substance was converted into a Kā'lĕt (flour) which was baked or cooked in various ways. The vegetables were usually cooked, though some were served as moderns do onions, celery, lettuce, radishes, etc.

The vegetables were cultivated in fields and gardens, geometrically arranged by the Kelleta, who sought thus to symbolize certain life principles.

The Păs'kĕt was a vegetable that resembled the species Solanum tuberosum, or Potato, and was grown in the central and northern portions of the Lontidri. It bore an esculent tuber. The plant grew from four to six coitex in height, and resembled those of the species Helianthus Tuberosus, or Jerusalem Artichoke, though the leaves and flowers were larger, more like those of the now known Sunflower. (All the species of the Helianthus have descended from the Atlantian varieties of the Pasket.) At the time of the submergence, tubers were swept by the submerging waters onto the coasts of South and Central America, from whence in its wild state it was subsequently carried into the regions of the Andes mountains by miners, from whence it was taken into Chili, Peru and Argentine Republic by migrating peoples, where it was pre-historically known as the Bō-nō-bē-zä'sō; and by similar means, from northwestern South America, into Costa Rica and the mountain regions of Mexico and southwestern United States of America, where it was pre-historically known as the Fī-zē-ăl'lŭs. Therefore, the Pasket, through the Bonobezaso and the Fizeallus, became the pre-historic ancestor of the Potato plants. It was a symbolic vegetable. The underground development of the tubers on radiating roots represented a propagating epi-cycle, independent of seeds, which had their development on the branches in the aerial element; was symbolic of both mortal and spiritual life, body and soul development, the former earthly and the latter heavenly, and the dark or negative condition represented the material or lower plane of life, and the light, or positive condition, that of the spiritual or the higher.

The Păs'kĕt Tē'sĕt (Sweet Potato) was a plant that had an esculent tuberous root, that grew in the southern porion of the Lontidri, and resembled the species Batatas edulis or Sweet Potato. The vine, however, grew from ten to twelve Cĕl'ăx(inches) in height. The leaves were odd-pinnate, eliptical, and serrate. It bore a small purple blossom. The roots grew long and branching and the tubers were attached singly in alternate form along them, instead of in clusters. At the time of the submergence, remnants were left on the West Indies, Central America and Mexico, where it had already began a spontaneous growth, especially so in the section of the West Indies, the descendants of which established plants pre-historically known as the Bä-bō-kä'yä, whose further descendants became the pre-historic ancestors of the species Convalyulus batatas or Sweet Potato plants. In its subsequent culture, it has gradually changed from a self-supporting stalk to that of a creeping vine, and the arrangement of its tubers more in clusters.

The El'tē-gĕn was an edible plant that grew in great abundance in the northern and central portions of the Lontidri, and resembled the species Brassica or Cabbage. At the time of the submergence, remnants plants were left along the coasts of England and central Europe, thus deposited by the Atlantic and Mediterranean waters, where in its wild state it degenerated into what is now known as the species Brassico oleracea or Wild Sea Cabbage, pre-historically known as the Gē-ĭl-dē'zē, from which by cultivation it has evolved into many varieties of culinary vegetables. It, therefore, is the pre-historic ancestor of the Wild Cabbage, of England and Central Europe; such species of Brassica as the Drum-head-Cabbage; the Red-Cabbage; the Portugal-Cabbage, etc., and diminutions such as Scotch Kail; German-Greens; Jersey or Branching-Cabbage; Brussel-Sprouts, which latter is an amalgamation between the Cauliflower and the Cabbage; the Kohl-rabi, an amalgamate form that was established through the grafting process, or thus uniting the white turnip and cabbage plants, a practice that began in the latter part of the pre-historic period, the seedlings from which union, established the now Kohl-rabi or Top-turnip. The spherical mass of the Eltegen symbolized the natural result of concentration, by virtue of central activity, its force to collect, condense and mature for the utility of man, and Gala, the concentricity of all nature, and also was symbolic of the spirits action within the soul, or spirit body, or material form, the mortal body, whereby all grades of development, spiritually and materially have their ultimatum.

The Ex'nŏt, was a plant that bore a sweet esculent root, that was grown principally in the middle and eastern portion of the Lontidri, and resembled the species Beta Maritima or Sea Beet. It was very nutritious and of three varieties, viz: red, yellow and white. At the time of the submergence, remnants were left on the Eastern Continent, where it degenerated into a wild state, the descendants of which established a race of plants, pre-historically known as the Sĕs'ē-lĭx, whose further descendants became the pre-historic ancestors of the Wild Beet, from which, through cultivation, climate, soil and local influence, has descended the species of Beta, such as the Mangel-wurzel, or mangold field and garden Beets, cultivated from very remote times, etc.

The Dĭ'ziē, was a vegetable that grew in the central portion of the Lontidri, and resembled the species Allum cepa or Common Onion only it grew in a flatter and larger form. It was used more in a medicinal way than as an edible. There were varieties that bore seeds, top bulbs, and lateral bulbs. There were white, reddish-purple and yellow varieties. At the time of the submergence, remnants were left in the British Island regions, whose further descendants established a bulbus genus of plants, pre-historically known as the Hĕl'tē-zō, whose further descendants became the pre-historic ancestors of the Onion-plants, etc.

The Cŭl-lū'rä was a leguminous plant that grew principally in the south-eastern portion of the Lontidri in its original state, but by cultivation, was distributed through parts of the central and eastern portions. It resembled the species Pisum sativum or Vegetable Pea, only the vines grew much taller, the flowers much larger and brighter in color. The legumes were broader and longer, and contained two rows of seeds or globular fruit. At the time of the submergence, remnant plants and seedlings were left on the now known coast of North Africa, from whence by means of migrating peoples, it was carried into Arabia, and Persia, where its descended plants were pre-historically known as the Gī-ū'lä. Thence by the same means, it was carried into Southern Europe, and south-western Asia, and thus handed down to the Aryans and the Semites. Therefore, the Culura, through the Giula, became the pre-historic ancestor of the Vegetable Peas.

The Gē-ĭltĕr was a vegetable that bore an edible root, that grew in the northern and central portions of the Lontidri, and resembled the species Raphanus sativus or Radish. It was of white, red, and light purple varieties, being round, spindle-shaped, and eliptic forms. At the time of the submergence, remnants were left on the Eastern Continent, from which descended a species of plants, pre-historically known as the Lē-ĕn'zē-ŏck, whose further descendants became the pre-historic ancestors of the Wild Radish of the Mediterranean coast, from which, by cultivation, has descended the Spindle and the Turnip-rooted varieties of the Radish. Further cultivation, climatic and soil influences, have established many varieties of these species on the Eastern and Western Continents.

The Căz-ē-kä'gē-wä was an herbacious vegetable that bore an esculent root, that grew in the northen and central portion of the Lontidri, and was of white and orange varieties, and resembled the species Dacus carota, or Carrot, and the genus Pastinaca, or Parsnip. At the time of the submergence, remnants were left on the Eastern Continent, whose descendants established a plant pre-historically known as the Jĕn'sĕy, whose further descendants became the pre-historic ancestors of the Wild Carrot, which by cultivation, climate, soil and local influences, has developed into the now known tribe of Carrots, that range in Southern Europe, Asiatic Russia and North America.

The species Brassica Rapa or Turnip, was not known to the Atlantian peoples. Subsequent to the submergence, an amalgamation took place between the white and purple varieties of the Geilter, which established what is now known as the white and purple mixed, or small bulbiformed Turnips, that were known to the aborigines only as a wild edible root, which after many generations was cultivated and brought back to its present state of existence. Another pre-historic amalgamation took place between some of the Geilter and the Kazekagewa plants, which established the Yellow Finland species, or Rootabegas.

The Glĕn'sŏn was a culinary vegetable, that was classed with the Eltegen, that grew in the northern portion of the Lontidri, and resembled the Cauliflower. At the time of the submergence, remnant plants and seedlings were left on the Eastern and Western Continents, which established a plant, pre-historically known as the Kĕl'tā-sŏc, on the Eastern, and as the Mĕl-tē-zū'ŭs on the Western, whose descendants became the pre-historic ancestors of the Cauliflower, and its ally, the Brocoli, and Brocoli-Sprouts, or offsprings of the Cabbage and Cauliflower amalgamation.

The Il'dĭx was an herbaceous plant bearing a milky, narcotic juice, that was grown in the northern and central portion of the Lontidri, and resembled the genus Lactuca or species Lactuca sativa, or Lettuce plant, and in the Atlantian time was classed with the Eltegen and Glenson. At the time of the submergence, remnant plants and seedlings were left upon the Eastern Continent, whose descendants established a plant pre-historically known as the O-ŏs'ĭc in that region, whose descendants became the pre-historic ancestors of the species Lactuca sativa or Lettuce plants.

The Cĕl-ē-rōux was a leguminous plant of several species that grew in the greater portion of the Lontidri, and resembled the genus Faba, or Bean tribe. At the time of the submergence, remnants and seedlings were left on the Eastern and Western Continents, that established a genera of plants pre-historically known as the Wrĕn'tē-sāy, on the Eastern, and as the U'nŭm on the Western (only in a wild state at that time), that became the pre-historic ancestors of the Bean plants. (See Encyclopædias for the modern links.)

The Băr-bē-dū'ä was a scandent plant that grew in the northern portion of the Lontidri, and resembled the genus Cucumis, or Cucumber, then classed with the Celeroux on account of its scandent habits. It grew from two to two and a half coitex in height. The stalks were thicker and heavier than those of the modern growth. The leaves were about the same, only very smooth. The shape of the fruit was similar, only smooth and glossy. At the time of the submergence, remnants were left on the Eastern and Western Continents, whose descendants established a species of plants pre-historically known as the Săn-mā-lū'ciē on the Eastern, and the Gē-ĭn'cē-lŏc on the Western, whose further descendants became the pre-historic ancestors of the common Cucumber, of exceedingly numerous varieties and were much esteemed by the Ancients, both as an edible and as a product of drink.

The Căl-tā-zook' was a scandent plant that grew in the central portion of the Lontidri, and somewhat resembled the species Cucumis citrullus, or Watermelon. Its vine grew about two and a half to three coitex in height, was of a climbing habit, and, like the Barbedua, had to be supported with a trestle. The stalks were heavier and thicker than those of the modern species. The leaves and vines differed by being smooth. The fruit was about the size of the modern Citron, was green on the exterior, and a bright salmon inside, had cinnamon-colored seeds, was of an oval shape and very palatable. At the time of the submergence, remnants were left on the Eastern Continent, whose descendants established a plant pre-historically known to the Egyptians as the För-lĕs'ā-cū, whose further descendants became the pre-historic ancestors of the Watermelon.

The species Cucumis Malo, or Muskmelons and Canaloupes, were not known in the Atlantian times. They are descendants from the Caltazook remannts, in the Egyptian and Arabian countries, where some of its fruit, grown near a fruit-bearing plant pre-historically known to the Egyptians and Arabians as the Trĕ'ē-lŏck (now extinct), mixed pollen from their blossoms, which established a plant pre-historically known as the U-rĕn'sĭc (an Egyptian and Arabian term), whose further descendants became the pre-historic ancestors of the Muskmelons and Cantaloupes of the scarlet, the white and the green varieties.

The Treelock above referred to was a plant about three coitex in height; bore leaves similar to the modern melon; the fruit was about the size of the Bitter Orange or Pumelo, and about the same shape. It was a brilliant yellow color on the exterior surface and of a light orange or salmon inside; was extremely fragrant or sweet-scented, and very palatable. The seeds were ovate, long and circumferential in form.

The En-rī-jō-nē'ŭs was a scandent plant that grew in the northern and central portions of the Lontidri, and resembled the species Cucurbita Melo or Pumpkin. There were two varieties, the green and the yellow. It being of a climbing habit, had to be supported on trestles. The stalks were thick and heavy and grew from four to five coitex in height. The fruit was about the same form as the modern, but smaller. The vine and leaves, however, were perfectly smooth. At the time of the submergence, remnants were left on the Eastern and Western Continents which established a plant pre-historically known as the Shĕl'-tē-ŏs on the Eastern, and as the Nē-tā-sä' on the Western, whose descendants became the pre-historic ancestors of the Pumpkin plants.

The Squash (known to the Indians of North America as the Askutasquash, prior to the settlement of the English on the Western Continent) was not known in Atlantis, it being an hybrid descendant from the Enrijoneus and the Caltazook, some of the descendants of which established a species from which descended the Squash.

Links and Cycles

USH IN-TOX-E-A'CI-A RINGA,

OR

THE ZOOLOGIC LINKS.

TELTZIE XIX.

In gathering up the links that are to establish the Zoologic Cycle, disclose its pre-historic conditions and account for its present variety of orders, sub-orders, families and species, so far as we are able to do within the limited space of this treatise, it will be necessary to note a few facts regarding the conditions that co-operate with facts established by and through the laws that govern descendant generations.

The general condition made manifest through the descended generations of the past, not only in the human races, but in those of the animal, bird, and even vegetable as well, has been that of a tendency to physical diminution or decrease in stature naturally; especially so when the descendants have passed through epi-cycles of the same genus, or order, free from any hybrid influences.

Hybrid conditions, in many cases, have retarded the rapidity of the diminution in size of all the foregoing-named epi-cycles of descending races, in co-operation with specific or local conditions such as climate and locality, having their influence upon the descendants of several generations, and in some instances, when the hybrid condition has taken place between the larger specimens of the two races, the development in the offspring generations turns back, or up toward the product of a grosser generation physically and in stature, for an indefinite time, when again the diminution physically will begin in the following generation.

Cold or hot climates have their effect upon the condition of diminution or extension. Cold produces flesh and fat, and heat the opposite, each being nature's provision to the physical being as protective agencies in accord with the respective natural conditions of climate.

A singular condition in the workings of the laws of nature is in the return of the physical characteristics such as belonged to generations of the past, after having apparently disappeared from the organisms of the intermediate generations of the descending epi-cycles, when again the ancestry blood seems to return in the epi-cycles of descendancies, when it manifests the characteristics, for three or four generations, thus making a complete change again in the species, the result of which may be either from the smaller to the greater, or vice versa, which is the case with physical diversities, even in the same family and the same generation of all races of existence.

The same principle holds good, not only in the physical organization generally, but in the mental and the spiritual development of the human race, in accord as those faculties become weaker or stronger through the conditions of descendancies.

At the present time the amalgamation between the European and American races is establishing a grade upward in regard to the physicl conditions of the descending generation, such as will, for a time, continue until the new race mixture becomes established as a unit, when ultimately a diminution will begin again.

There is another physical law that not only governs gender in all reproductive conditions, but that also, to a certain extent, throughout all time, governs the degrees of physical, mental, moral and spiritual development, viz., if at the time of conception, the male be stronger in any one or all of the above qualities of being, than is the female, the offspring will not only be of the male gender, but will take on similar nature and qualities. If on the other hand, the female be stronger than the male, her characteristics and gender will be developed in the offspring; hence, the proportionate division in the male and female existence, and the degree of distribution of their natural qualities such as belong to the races.

If the exercise or habit of reaching upward were practised from childhood, short statures could be elongated during the process of growth, hence making the individual taller at maturity than otherwise would be the case, and therefore further affect the stature of subsequent offspring, and so on through the generations.

This law was known and practised by the better classes of Atlantians, as one of their principal points in physical culture, and even after having reached maturity in regard to natural growth, the stature was further developed by the practise of reaching upward, etc.

In evidence of the fact that descending generations, through hybrid conditions, have a tendency to diminution in size and stature through subsequent descending species, we might state, that to take the male Tiger and the female Fox, or Lynx, let them enter into a hybrid condition, the diminution in size, for a time, will be retarded in the offspring species that follow; but reverse the order—take the male Fox, or Lynx, and the female Tiger, and the diminution will at once tend toward that of the smaller offspring, whose descendants will continue the condition of diminution. Hence, the greater variety of forms, from the mammoth down to the mouse; from the eagle down to the humming bird; from the giant down to the dwarf; from the mighty trees of the Yosemite valley to the mosses that exist on their barks, and that adorn the rocks that lie at their roots, have their respective physical dimensions through these and other co-operating influences, in connection with other natural laws, governing extension and diminution, that have wrought many changes in the living genus, orders, sub-orders, families and species, such as inhabit the earth to-day, too vast in variety to follow out and give in this short treatise, the hybrid and other links that have led down to the modern physical and other conditions of existing life on the terrestrial sphere.

Despite the conditions of degeneration and diminution, arising through specific causes, originalities are not always lost in what modern are wont to term "new race conditions;" e. g., take the black race, let them mix races with the white, and the offspring will have changed color through gradation to the unit of the mulatto, but as original beings they have not changed. On the other hand, it often occurs that the offspring is of a higher grade intellectually, capable of improvement when placed under proper conditions. So it is with the animal and the vegetable kingdoms. Much depends upon the influences brought to bear upon the spirit being, and its own forces, as operating in and through man, animal and vegetable beings in regard to the ultimatum, which is to manifest through man and animal physically, mentally and spiritually—yea, we will add the vegetable beings as well, for at the present time wonderful results in obtaining new races of fruits and vegetables, by and through the same law of mixing races, have been accomplished, but there remains a co-union to the original ancestors, though nectarized, yet divisible through the gustatory and olfactory senses. Thus man may grow finer in specimen physically, more beautiful, exercise greater intelligence; vegetation put forth more beauitful foliage, larger, sweeter edibles; and richer perfumes from the flowers, under the process of natural law and the co-operative force of intelligence. physical, mental and spiritual, each capable of further development through individual desire and effort, in accord with the conditions under which the developments are subject.

Another law of generative effect is in the influence brought to bear upon both the female and her offspring, through the manifested pride and dominant will, exercised at all times by the male of various races not even excluding that of the human, which not only affects the size of the offspring of the male gender, but has such an effect upon the female as to cause her to influence the offspring of the female gender to a certain extent, thus affecting the generations that follow, for a time, according to the conditions co-operative with that of the above named. In evidence of some of the foregoing statements, take for example the line of hybrid conditions of the races leading up to the establishment of the now known Giraffe. The paternal ancestor in each case, through the hybrid generations, was the stronger from the original predecessors that mated with the female of a different race of animals, and therefore carried certain characteristics into the next generation, such as had belonged to each of the co-united races formerly, or from the primitive Hittraina and Zeneletrix down to the now known Giraffe; e. g., the lofty elevation of the head of the Giraffe, as it now exists, has descended through three influences, first, the paternal ancestors of the Giraffe race, viz., the Dezne, Celplete, Cuisto and the Ketrox, all of which possessed the long neck characteristic, in various degrees, such as now characterizes the Giraffe, the Cuisto having been the one that possessed the greater force of elongating its neck at will, which fact had its effect in further developing that characteristic in each of the following hybrid generations, and ultimate Giraffe race, who thereby possessed its extremely long neck.

Secondly, the male Giraffe, as well as that of the preceding ancestors, was in each instance larger than the female, and was in every case dominant over her, exercising great pride in his supremacy, etc., which caused them to acquire the habit of head and shoulder elevation while guarding over his mate. This not only caused his further development physically, but influenced the same characteristic in the female to a certain extent through association with her proud companion, thus giving rise to a dual condition such as had further effect upon her offspring, and was the characteristic handed down in an intensified degree to the next generation, to the present time, there being no further hybrid conditions to break or change the developmnt.

Thirdly, the Giraffe, by constanlty reaching upward in his pursuit of food by browsing from elevated limbs, further elongated its neck and tongue (the latter characteristic being one that belonged to the Celplete, and that reappeared in the Giraffe), developed its shoulders, or intensified their stature (a natural development to both male and female through the same cause), and as each generation followed, the characteristic grew more marked in intensity, on account of the physical use to which the shoulders, neck and tongue were put in its daily pursuit for food, and made diminution impossible.

The elevation of the head and extension of the neck through the pride influence, such as is exercised by the male over the female, is observable in the Peacock, the Ostrich, the Goose, the common Cock, and in many other birds and animals, the human race not excepted.

In many instances the pride nature of the male and his disposition to dominate, not only over his opposite sex, but in the pursuits of life, will at times influence an increase in size physically which fact in turn has its influence on his descendants. This condition, however, is modified by co-operating influences of other characters, etc.

The Tĕx'rŏnz was an Atlantian ruminant mammal that inhabited the central and eastern portions of the Lontidri, on account of its utility for servitude, though it was a native of the southern climate. It closely resembled the species Camelus dromedarius, or Arabian Camel. At the time of the submergence of the eastern portion of Atlantis, remnants were left on the African continent, from whence they migrated into Asia, and their straight descendants have remained a distinct genus, unaltered to any extent. Originally, it was a more speedy animal than the present species of Camels. They had larger bodies, but no taller; were darker in color, especially those of the central and eastern portions, but their hair was not shaggy like modern species; their feet differed somewhat on account of general use, the sandy portions of the country being more solid than where the Camel now exists, and their transportation to non-sandy soil of the central and eastern sections of the Lontidri; hence, they developed more of a hoof or claw-like formation on the point of the foot which served the purpose of grappling with the earth or hard substances over which they traveled. The cushion-like foot that now characterizes the Camel, and the loss of the claw of the Atlantian species, were conditions co-operative with development to them after they became inhabitants of the desert regions. They, like the Elephants, were used as beasts of burden, and the more fleety ones were used to draw the Atlantian Rŏu'tĕx (carriage) in which the people traveled, when not by means of the air-ships. The Routex was a two-wheeled vehicle, with shafts, and covered body, and was beautifully decorated in golden designs, as was the harness worn by the Texronz; and it was the knowledge of this custom that caused the pre-historic and historic Oriental peoples to adopt the plan of similar ornamentations. The Texronz and its descendants became the pre-historic ancestors of the species Camelus dromedarius, or Arabian Camel.

The Zū'tē was a ruminant mammal that inhabited the southern and southeastern portions of the Lontidri, and closely resembled the now known Bactrian mammals, only its limbs were shorter; body larger and of a light brown color; had a very pretty shaped head; slender neck, and feet not so broad as the Camelus bactrianus species. Its straight descendants became the pre-historic ancestors of the Bactrian or South African Camel.

The Tĕz'ē-rĕt was a ruminant mammal that inhabited the middle and southern portions of the Lontidri, was similar to the Camel races, only it was about six feet in height; had a larger frame; broader back; larger limbs, but about the same in length; large head; bushy mane; long, bushy tail; of a cinnamon color, but some were spotted and some mixed with gray. They were of a semi-aquatic nature, hence stood in the water a great deal; were gregarious, very playful, happy and fleety when traveling. They were hornless; had a soft, melodious, joyous lowing, etc. They became extinct at the time of the submergence of Atlantis.

The A-lä'mä was a plantigrade, omnivorous mammal that inhabited the western and northwestern sections of the Lontidri, and was a degenerate, diminutive hybrid offspring from the An'zŏs (bear) and A-ĕx'tä (bison) species. Its limbs were similar to the now known dog and fox species; tail like the dog; head, feet and claws like the bear; large body and three feet in height; had a large, fleshy roll around its neck; colors dark brown and gray. Its remnant descendants inhabited the mountain districts of the western portion of North America, but became prehistorically extinct.

About the Adomic period, some of the Nyl'gäw or Texronz species, mixed breeds, the hybrid offspring of which were prehistorically known as the Qū'dĭx, whose further descendants became the pre-historic ancestors of the Guanaco Deer. Some of the male Guanaco Deer and the female Algazel mixed species, whose offspring were pre-historically known as the Zĕl'dĭx, on the Western Continent, and Kă'hĕl on the Eastern, and their descendants became the pre-historic ancestors of the Ibex or Capra genus. Some of the male Tezeret and the female Texronz mixed species, whose offspring were pre-historically known as the Cē-ī'dĭsh, on the Eastern Continent, and Gŏn'thāle on the Western, and their descendants became the pre-historic ancestors of the species Alpaca paco. Some of the male Zeldix and the female Ceidish mixed species, whose offspring were pre-historically known as the Quinset, and their descendants became the pre-historic ancestors of the genus Auchenia or Llama species. Some of the female Chamois and the male wild Deer mixed species, whose offspring were pre-historically known as the Wĕl'-dĭn-ĭx, on the Eastern Continent, and Gip on the Western, and their descendants became the pre-historic ancestors of the species Capra ægagrus or Wild Goat, from which the domestic Goat has descended. Some of the male Weldinix and the female Quinset mixed species whose offspring were pre-historically known as the I-zĕn'tĭs, on the Eastern Continent, and the E-ī'lū, on the Western, and their descendants became the pre-historic ancestors of the species Ovis or Wild Sheep, and ultimate domestic species.

The Zē-ŭn'stry was a large animal that in some respects would compare with the Walrus and the Elephant species. It had a larger body, heavy horns, that extended downward from the head like the tusks from the mouth of the Walrus; feet and legs about half the size of those of the Elephant, and body about two-thirds its size; was quite fleety; had short, black hair on body, but long bushy hair on the neck and down the back to the tail, that parted on top and hung down on both sides of the body, and was quite bushy two-thirds down the tail. Their remnants ultimately became extinct, but some of the species had mixed with that of the Lion, whose further offspring were pre-historically known as the A-ĕx'tä. This descendant had more of the long hair than the Zeunstry, but not under the belly. Its color changed to a dark, heavy brown, generally, some being very black. Its size was diminished. Its ultimate degenerate descendants became the pre-historic ancestors of the Bison, or Buffalo. The light brown color of the Lion, through the hybrid conditions of the ancestry, developed into the brown hue in the Bison. The fur-like condition became finer as they descended. The Aexta first inhabited the midland climate, in the mountain regions, and were quite harmless unless a rage was produced among them, when they, like the Bison, would engage in their stampedes. The Buffalo Bison, about 1000 years ago, was much larger and more ferocious than at the present time, they having greatly changed in modern time.

The northern, or American Bison, came over from the land south of the now known country of Greenland, now submerged by the North Atlantic or Greenland Sea, before the time of the convulsions that submerged that section or district of land. As they changed climate, the fur grew around the whole body and they shed it annually, as is the case with the Lion and the Bison of the present period. If you were to observe the female Bison and also the female Lion, when enraged, you could easily detect the clever resemblance in the two species, even at the present period of time. The resemblance is more marked in the females of the two species than in the males. Nature, in all its producitve or creative forces, is capable of hybridity; therefore, union of races should not create entire depletion or destruction.

The Nŏl-ō-kā-thē′rŭm was an amphibious reptile of large size that closely resembled the Crocodilia of the Eastern Continent and the Alligator of the Western. It inhabited the southern half of the Amezone Riger and other waters in the south, southeastern and southwestern portions of the Lontidri. At that time it was more of a saline water reptile. Prior to the submergence of the southern portion of the Lontidri, many of them had migrated into the regions now known as South America, by way of the now known Amazon and Orinoco rivers (which at that time extended into the Lontidri, and emptied into the Amezone), when they became fresh-water reptiles. At the time of the submergence of the southwestern portion of Atlantis, remnants were forced to migrate into the now known Central American region, whose descendants subsequently migrated through the waters of Central America, Mexico, and Southern United States. Prior to the establishment of the Great Sahara Desert of Africa, the Syrian and Sandy of Arabia, some migrated eastward out of Atlantis, across Africa, via the borders of the Karuntic Reende (Inland Sea), through the marshes which gave place to the Great Sahara Desert, into Egypt and Northeastern Africa. Subsequently, some of their descendants migrated still further eastward through Arabia, via the borders of the then known Kultezen and Amthaic inland seas that established the U-ĭsh-tē′cōs (deserts) now known as the Syrian and the Sandy, respectively, and thence into India, and ultimtely as far east as Australia, etc., whence they became fresh-water reptiles. Therefore, the Nolokatherum became the pre-historic ancestors of the families Gavials, Crocodiles and Alligators. (See Encyclopædias, etc., for the modern links.)

The Skē-ĕl′tē-zē was an hybrid, whose paternal ancestor was the Bison, and its maternal, the White Bear. The original hybrid condition took place in the polar regions, and the animal is now known to the inhabitants north of the 70th degree N. Lat., in the mountains of British America, by that name. It is about the size of a new-born calf, has curly, grayish brown hair that turns forward in its growth, and rather more closely resembles its maternal ancestor.

The Ex-că-tī′nä was a direct race of animals that resembled the modern Elephant, which former was its primitive ancestor, through the Extrefon. It inhabited both the northern and southern portions of Atlantis, those of the northern being the larger. It was used by the Atlantians for various forms of servitude, but more especially when conveying freightage, or produce from one city to another. They were, in their wild state, quite ferocious, but after being tamed became quite domestic. It never mixed races with any other animal, hence remained, comparatively speaking, a distinct race, having changed only through its own evolutions. Those of the southern portion had short, thin, light bronze-colored hair; the males only had tusks, which were short and grew downward; those of the north had quite dark, nearly black hair, thicker and longer than characterized those of the south; the males had extremely large tusks, that projected forward in their growth, and it was not uncommon for the aged females to develop small tusks. In time of danger, the male would give a call, understood by the female as a warning, when she would step behind him for protection, for the male was very loyal to the female.

The Ex-trĕ′fŏn was the continuation of the Excatrina after the submergence, and was the animal whose remains have been unearthed in modern times known as those of the Mastodon, now extinct.

The Wō′ĕx was a ruminant, ungulate mammal that in physical appearance resembled the family Bovidæ, or Cow, especially the genus Bos grunniens, or Yak, of Asia, in the Altai and Himalaya mountain regions. It, however, was not as large as the modern Cow, was between it and the Goat and, like the latter, had but two teats from which to extract milk. It had a beautifully shaped head, much like that of the Yak; short, stubby, drooping horns; expressive face, similar to the sheep; expressive eyes, almost human-like; long hair all over the body; long, bushy tail; limbs longer than the Yak; ungulate feet with hoofs broad and well separated in front; color gray and brown; carried its ears erect like the horse; was harmless and a great domestic animal.

The Tē-ī′tĕx was a land mammal, domestic by culture, for the utility of its milk. It resembled the modern Ram, especially the head, though the nose was more pointed; but in body it was more like the dog, though it had short, stocky legs. Its horns curled backwards like the Ram; had long, bushy tail; dark, brownish gray, curly hair; and slightly cloven-footed. It was centrally located in the Lontidri, with some distributions in the north and south sections.

The U-tŭs′kä was a semi-marine mammal that closely resembled the Sea Lion, and was originally in the northern waters of the Lontidri. It was continued in the Arctic Sea after the submergence of Atlantis. It had close, dark brown hair; flat head; blunt nose; small, roundish ears, more like the human; no tusks; no legs, but fin-like claws and tail, like the Sea Lion, which latter was its descendant.

The Swä'dĭsh was a marine mammal that closely resembled the modern Whale, and pre-historically inhabited the Arctic Sea regions, whose descendants became the pre-historic ancestors of the order Cetacea or whale family. A small species of the Swadish, pre-historically inhabited the Arctic Sea (now extinct, except in a few unexplored portions), and the Utuska, to a certain extent mixed species, and the hybrid offspring became the pre-historic ancestors of the Sea Elephant. The Utuska being both a land and water animal, frequented the shores in the sections inhabited by the Woex, where some of the females of the former, mated with the males of the latter, the offspring of which became the pre-historic ancestors of the Phocidæ, or Walrus family. The horn condition possessed by the paternal ancestor, and its influence upon the maternal, was developed in the tusk of the Walrus. The sub-branch of the Phocidæ, now known as the Seal, had its origin from the hybrid offspring, resulting from a mixed condition between the Sea Lion and the Sea Elephant.

The Gĕn'zē was a land mammal that closely resembled the modern Cow. It was a hybrid offspring from the male Tär-tē'-mŭs (Walrus) and the female Teitex. Being born to a maternal land parent, in her native abode, it remained a land mammal by assumed nature, and therefore adopted the habits of the Teitex. It was smaller than the modern Cow, and was a very pretty animal. The male had short horns that curved back like those of the modern Ram; short hair on their bodies, white, black, gray, red and spotted; long hair on top of their necks and under their bellies; long tails, bushy on the end. They ranged in the regions of the now known British Islands, where they became the pre-historic ancestors of the Bovine Genus of animals; hence the ancient Kine and the modern Cow. Under the hybrid conditions, the tusk influence of the Tortemus reverted backward in conjunction with that of the horn of the Teitex, which naturally was but a growth of scarce protrusion which caused the loss of the tusk and further developed the horn condition, such as now characterizes the Bovine genus.

A migration of the Genze mammals was established when they passed south-eastward from the British Island region into the lofty plateau of Asia, between the Altai mountains and the Himalayas, where never having further mixed races, as a whole, with any other mammals, they become straight descendants, during following generations, from the Genze family, with only such physical changes as would naturally occur during its long line of descendancy. Ultimately, their descendants became the prehistoric ancestors of the Yak, that originally dwelt in the above-named regions. Another migration of these mammals, from the northwestern regions, was instituted southward into the country of Arabia, where they mixed races with the pre-historic Arabian Camels, the former the maternal and the latter the paternal ancestors, whose offspring became the pre-historic ancestors of the Zebus, or "humped Indian Cattle," which further migrated into India, east into Japan, and west into Egypt as far as the African Niger.

The Hĭt'trä-ī-nä was a pachydermatous mammal that, in physical appearance, would resemble the genus Equus, or horse, in some respects, and in others that of the Tapir, and even the Rhinoceros. Its head was large, thick at the top, and it carried it in an extended manner, like the Rhinoceros, or Camel. Its neck was short and thick like that of the Tapir. It was not so handsome an animal as is the modern horse. The body was shaped more like that of an Elephant or Camel. Its legs were long, like the Camel; it was very speedy, and could endure much hardship; it was used for the same purposes as is the modern horse; it inhabited all parts of the Lontidri of Atlantis by nativity and further transportation. Some were black, some gray, and the hair was short, some curly and some straight.

The Jä'trĭx was a mammiferous quadruped that inhabited the southern portions of Atlantis. It was of medium size; long, round body; short, thick legs; tapering head, but bluntish nose; very small ears and eyes; short, thick neck; small claw-like feet; short tail; shiny drab and old-gold colored hair that grew short on the back and sides, but longer on the belly and down the legs; was a very fleety animal in its movements.

The Căs'tŭs was also a mammiferous quadruped that inhabited southern Atlantis. It was larger than the Jatrix; had a large, long, round body; peculiar legs, they being broad and massive from the knee up to the body, smaller at the knee, but long and very slender from the knee down; flat, broad and claw-like feet, but shorter than those of the Ja-trix; the two in front had short, sharp-curved claws, with which they caught and held their food; a dog-like head only a little more flat on top and rounding at the back; a longer tail than that of the Ja-trix; black and cinnamon-colored hair, that grew about three inches long on the back, but longer on the sides, belly and down the legs. At the time of the submergence of Atlantis, remnants of both the Jatrix and the Castus, that had migrated to those regions, were left on the Eastern and Western Continents, and some even reached southern Asia. Ultimately the two remnant races mixed breeds, the offspring of which were pre-historically known as the Vĕn-tē'lūs, and were very prolific. At one time they were very numerous in South and North America, in which latter-named region they increased to a great size. Their descendants became the pre-historic ancestors of a large variety of mammals through hybrid conditions, to the grosser species by development, and to the lesser by degeneration. The former were the ancestors of the extinct Magatheridæ family, such as the edentata mammals Megatherium; the Mylodon, etc., and the latter in the development of the Sloth; the Ant Lion; the Glyptodon and other Armadillo mammals.

The Ad'ū-ăc was a ruminant mammal that resembled the Antelope family and originally inhabited Teltzie Et of Atlantis. At the time of the submergence, remnants were left on the now known Continent of Africa. In size, it was larger than the Antelope Gnu species, or was about the size of an ox, only in that the body was slimmer. Its legs were more like the modern stag; feet more like the horse; dark brown hair; slightly aquiline nose, or more on the order of the horse; mane from the head down over the crest of the neck, that stood erect about five inches long; a Fretize extended down from the chin over the breast and upper part of the legs, the hair being about eight inches in length; two antlers in their extension circled to the right and left, up over, and, turning on the curve, met and sometimes lapped over the crown of the head; the tail was about one and a half feet in length, the hair being heavy on top, like that of the horse, but none on the other side.

The U'trĭx was a ruminant mammal similar to the Ox or Bos-taurus group of the Bos genus, that inhabited Teltzie Sot of Atlantis, originally, but later became dispersed to other parts of the Lontidri. At the time of the submergence, remnants were left on both the Eastern and Western Continents. Their descendants became the pre-historic ancestors of the genus Bos-taurus. Ultimately, some of the female Aduac and male Utrix mixed breeds, and their descendants were pre-historically known as the U-ī'gĕr. Their descendants ultimately migrated eastward into the regions of Southern India and the Bay of Bengal distriet, before its submergence. Ultimately, the small herds of Uiger were lost in mixed conditions with the group of Zĕn-ē-le'-trĕx (Rhinoceros) whose descendants became the pre-historic ancestors of the Javan Rhinoceros. Some of the Zeneletrex that remained in Africa, mixed breeds with the female Kĕl′-trō-zē (Mammoths), whose descendants became the pre-historic auces-tors of the common Rhinoceros of the wooded and watered districts of Africa. The two horns, prehensile upper lip, the non-plicate condition of the skin, etc., came through the influence of the maternal ancestor, Keltroze. Another mixed breed condition between the male of one of the smallest of the species of the Keltroze and the female Zeneletrex, whose descendants became the pre-historic ancestors of the Square-mouthed Rhinoceros, now inhabit the valleys and open districts in Africa south of the Zambesi.

The Zeneletrex was an ungulate mammal of Atlantis that resembled the species Rhinoceros unicornus of India, dwelt in the Shū-shăc′zē (jungles) and valleys along the mountains of Teltzie Sot, but in every way larger than the modern species. Prior to the submergence some had migrated into the African country, descendants of which continued to migrate eastward until they arrived in the country of Hindustan (the Arabian Sea and the Bay of Bengal not then having been established, through which districts of country they passed), where its descendants became the pre-historic ancestors of the Rhinoceros unicornus, that in its wild state now inhabits the terai region of Nepals, N. E. Hindustan and Bhutau, India; and in the valley of Brahmaputra, or the Province of Assam, British India; Southern India, Bay of Bengal district (not then submerged), Malay Peninsula, Sumatra, etc. Ultimately, some of the Zeneletrex migrated south from Hindustan, as far southeast as to Java, and remained unmixed as a race, where at the time of the submergence of that region of country, they were left as a remnant on the Island of Java, and became the pre-historic ancestors of the Javanese Rhinoceros. A small herd of the common Rhinoceros migrated across Africa, through the district now submerged by the Arabian Sea, and Bay of Bengal, where they mixed breeds with the Zeneletrex and Uiger in the Sumatran district, when at the time of the submergence of those sections they were left in Sumatra, and bcame the pre-historic ancestors of the Sumatran Rhinoceros.

The Keltroze was an Atlantian mammal of three species, such as the Proboscidæ order, and inhabited the northeastern, northern, and northwestern portions of the Lontidri. The first species was possessed of long black hair; small, medium-lengthed tail which was bushy at the end; tusks leaving the head, were directed downwards and outwards, then upwards and finally inwards at the tips, and a tendency to a spiral form, of great length.

The second species would compare, in size of body, with the

modern elephant of medium size. It was characterized with short, thick, dark mouse-colored hair, but had very little on the tail, which latter was shorter than the above-named species; feet similar to the elephant, only cut straight across on the rear, similar to that of the modern horse, presenting three toes, or rather hoof-like nails; long, slender neck; broad head at the top, but tapered downward to and continued into a prehensile proboscis, that generally was about three feet in length and used by the animal for the purpose of collecting its food, and on account of its long neck did not require so long a proboscis as the modern Elephant. Its mouth, like the modern Elephant, when closed, being close back under the proboscis, was not easily observable, excepting when feeding. Its eyes were small; ears large, round and flabby. Both the male and the female possessed two tusks, that of the former being much the longer, which were, on an average, about two feet in length. In leaving the head, they were directed at first downwards and outwards, then slightly upwards again. In addition to the two tusks, the animal was characterized by a peculiar horn that left the head at the upper portion, and was first directed perpendicularly, then curved back over the top of the head, and then slightly forward again, and was of a broad form, and smooth quality; its length was not over one and a half feet, some being considerably shorter.

The third species, in size of body, would about compare with a large Ox, or between that a medium-sized Elephant. Its body was bunchy, like hat of an Elephant; was of a fierce temper, restless and wandering by nature and habit; had short, dark hair on the body generally, but where the limbs joined the body and under the belly and from the breast up to the neck, it was longer; its tail was long, and tipped with hair; its eyes large, its feet round, flat, with four toes, or hoof nails; long, flattish head; nose that was of an aquiline form, projecting below the tusks, and which terminated in square, truncated lips; very peculiar tusks, not long, but when leaving the mouth they were first directed upward in a vertical growth so as to cross and form an X-shape above the head, but were not of great length.

At the time of the submergence of the northeastern, northern, and northwestern portions of Atlantis, remnants of the various species of the Keltroze were left upon the Eastern and Western Continents to which, prior to the submergence, they had begun to migrate. Their descendants became the pre-historic ancestors of the extinct species of the Mammoth, or Elephas primigenius; the Mastodon and other Proboscidea of pre-historic ages, and ultimate species of modern Elephants.

The Dĕz′nō was a ruminant mammal that inhabited portions

of Teltzie Sot, and was an hybrid from the male Hittraina and female Zeneletrex, which after a long and varied line of mixed descended species, became the remote ancestors of the now known Giraffe. It was slimmer and smaller than the horse, and developed larger during descending generations. It possessed a small, slim, well proportioned body like the horse; less neck, and more body than the Giraffe, the neck being longer and slimmer than that of the horse; head more like that of the camel; ears more like the deer or Giraffe; large full eyes; legs small below the knees, but heavier from the knees up to the body; tail about one foot in length, with long hair at the extremity; short uniformed hair over the body, some being black, some dark brown and some was a uniform mixture of black and white over the greater portion of the body; one spot up over each hip and over the spine just above the tail of white, and also nearly white under the belly; feet with slightly parted hoof, at the point of the two toes, the upper part being more in shape like that of the horse. The nasal condition of the maternal Zeneletrex was entirely lost in the hybrid Dezno offspring, hence not visible, and that influence upon the following hybrid, the Cĕl-plē'tē, in that regard, was directed upward to the establishment of the slight horn condition, in connection with that of the Sī'cŭsh, that characterized the Celplete.

The Celplete was the second hybrid descendant from the Hittraina and Zeneletrex through the Dezno, leading down to the Giraffe. It was an Atlantian ruminant mammal that inhabited the mountain regions of Teltzie Sot, and was a descended hybrid from the male Dezno and the female Sicush, the latter also being a ruminant mammal of the highlands of Teltzie Sot. The Celplete in size was about the same as that of the Dezno. It had a slim body, long slim neck, extremely long tongue which it used for the purpose of examination and pre-hension of its food, which latter it obtained by browsing the leaves and tendrils of trees; long, slim tail, with considerable hair at its extremity; head similar to that of a yearling heifer, only thicker through the upper portion, on which was a very slight protrusion of a hornish substance, that showed a degeneration from the horned condition of its maternal ancestor, the Sicush, though the latter was but slightly horned; feet of the ungulate order, yet the hoofs parted in the form of three toes, the center one being the longest; the skin was pachydermatous, but characterized with short, cinnamon-colored hair; legs somewhat heavy at the body, but slimmer below the knees.

The Gū-ĭs'tō was the third hybrid descendant from the original Hittraina and Zeneletrex, through the Dezno and the Celplete, leading down to the Giraffe. It was a ruminant mammal that inhabited the mountainous region of southern Teltzie Sot, and was a descended offspring from the male Celplete and the female Gō-gē-ăn'lēs, the latter being a ruminant mammal of the southern and eastern portions of Teltzie Sot. It was about the size of the Celplete, only it had a shorter, more chunky body; shoulders considerably elevated above the hips, and broader on top; neck longer, broader and thicker at the shoulders, and gradually tapered down to the head, than was the case with the Celplete. The skin on the neck being in folds of a coiled spiral form, enabled it to elongate its neck at will, when reaching for food, which was about two feet in length. Its legs were longer than those of the Celplete, a descended influence from its maternal ancestor the Gogeanles. It had two toes or short hoofs; gray hair, generally, characterized with black and old-gold spots on its sides, back and neck; but the limbs and belly were black, an influence descended from its maternal ancestor, the Gogeanles. It had a shambling walk, and moved the hind and fore feet on the same side at the same time, an influence from its maternal ancestor also.

The Kē'trŏx was the fourth hybrid descendant from the original Hittraina and Zeneletrex, through the Dezno, the Celplete, and the Cuisto. It was a ruminant mammal that inhabited the highlands of northern Teltzie Sot. It was an offspring from the male Cuisto and the female Ex-că-ē'rä, the latter also being a ruminant mammal in Teltzie Sot. It was about as large as a medium-sized modern Elk; light, brisk, or agile in its movements; slim body in front of the hips, but heavier through the shoulders; tall on its feet; small limbs; long neck, that was thick and broad at the shoulders, but tapered down considerably to the head; head, nose and ears very much like that of the modern deer, which former it carried extended forward in harmony with its out-stretched neck; long tail with a luxuriant hairy terminal; hair generally very short on the body, and of a glossy character, much like that of the modern seal, that differed in color, the male being brown and the female a grayish brown, some being mottled with white spots, while others were characterized with larger white spots on their necks, faces and other ports of the body, similar to the modern Arabian ponies, a characteristic that belonged to their maternal ancestors, the Ex-că-ē'rä, from whom it had descended to them. Their feet were of the ungulate order, parted hoofs with two short toes, some of their feet being possessed of tufts of fur, or fine hair about them, a characteristic that had descended to them from their maternal ancestors, the Excaera. Their skin was of a pachydermatous order, like that of the Dezno, the Celplete and the Cuisto, thus influenced by their remote maternal ancestor, the Zeneletrex. It was of a gregarious habit, being compelled to secure itself from the intrusion and danger of other animals that often sought its life, and like the modern Giraffe, would station its sentinels to give warning of approaching danger. It was of keen sight and scent.

Prior to the submergence of Atlantis, some of the straight descendants of the Dezno had migrated into Africa, and ultimately into northwestern India, thence south-wesward into the region of southwestern France, where they remained a distinct race, whose descendants became the pre-historic ancestors of the now extinct genus, Hallodotherium, whose remains have been found in the deposits of the Miocene period.

The Yŏn'ăx was a mixed species from three ancestor influences, viz., the Celplete, Cuisto and Ketrox. It was about the size of the modern Ox. At the time of the submergence of the southern portion of the Lontidri, remnants were left in both Africa and South America, whose straight descendants became the pre-historic ancestors of the Giraffe, and at that time ranged in Africa, Asia, South America, Central America and Mexico, all now extinct except those in Africa.

The Jä'trĭx was a pachydermatous ruminant mammal that pre-historically inhabited the Eastern and Western Continents, and was a hybrid from the male of one of the species of the Extrifon and the female Yonax, a singular coincidence that took place on both Continents about the same period of time. Its descendants became the pre-historic ancestors of the family of ungulata known as Palæotheridæ, or the Palaplotherium, whose remains have been found in the middle Eocene and the Anchitherium in the Miocene period deposits, in Europe and North America, and ultimately became the pre-historic ancestors of the various species of the Tapir families, of both the Eastern and Western Continents.

The Rī'ĕz'lĕth was a mammal that closely resembled the genus Hippopotamus amphibius, but much larger and stronger. It ranged along the Amezone, its tributaries and the Inland Sea, small herds had migrated eastward along the watercourses, into northwestern Africa and Spain, and at the time of the establishment of the Sea, some descended herds were left as remnants on both the African and European sections, and those left on the western side of the Sea, in Atlantis, became very numerous· Had it not been for the migrations into Africa and Europe, prior to the submergence of Atlantis, the race would have been entirely lost with the Lontidri. The descendants of the Riezleth, therefore, became the pre-historic ancestors of the Hippopotamus amphibius.

The Hē-zä-lō-tē'tō was a mammal of the Proboscidæ Ungulata order, that inhabited various portions of Teltzie' We and Set, and being near the frozen portions of the globe, had long black suits of hair; large, broad feet; long toes, four in number, with heavy, sharp claws to aid them in climbing the elevated portions of the country. Remnants were left in British America, and in time their descendants migrated into the Rocky Mountain regions, where they became very abundant. At the time of the convulsions which established the present conditions of the ranges in that region, they were principally lost, and the remains of many were buried in various depths of the earth by the depressions and upheavals of the earth's surface, where in modern time their fossilized forms have been unearthed, restored, and are now known as the remains of the genus Mastodon, the principal species of which are classified as the M. ohioticus, americanus, obscurus and productus. It was a great migrator, very prolific, the offspring usually being twins, and quite frequently triplets. They were semi-gregarious by nature, therefore went in immediate families and did not mix breeds; hence, descended through their own relationship, which was the cause of divergances in species. Prior to the submergence of Teltzie Set, some of the families had migrated southward into the region of the northern portion of South America, whose descended species are now termed Mastodon, andium and humboldtii.

At the time of the convulsions that caused the submergence of the eastern portions of Teltzie We and Set, remnants were left in the British Island regions whose descendants became the pre-historic ancestors of the species now termed Trilophodont series, viz.: M. angustidens, borsoni, pentelici, pyrenaicus, tapiroides, virgatidens; and the Tetralophodont series; viz., M. arvernensis M. dissimilis and longirostris, of Europe.

The migrations southward into India and further southeast, established families whose descendants became the pre-historic ancestors of the species now termed M. falconeri and pandionsis, etc.

The Zĕn'thä was a carnivorous mammal that closely resembled the genus Felis, especially the Lion. Originally, it inhabited the northern, northeastern and northwestern portions of the Lontidri. As the convulsions came in that region, they were driven centrally and eastward, and when the final submergence came, remnants were left in Europe and Africa, from whence they further migrated into Asia, where they entered the wilds of those regions; their descendants migrated further southward into the jungles of the hot climates. They were much larger than the modern Lion; more powerful and ferocious; limbs longer; head and body larger. (The colossal idea of the great Sphinx at Gizeh, Egypt, was conceived by Shemozan, through his knowledge of the physical grossness of the pre-historic Zentha.) It was of various colors. Some males were black and some old gold, and all males possessed the vī-ē'chä (mane). Some of the females were old gold, and some of both sexes were mixed with black and old gold ground, spotted with black. The all-black species were more ferocious than the other species. The straight descendants of the Zentha became the pre-historic ancestors of the various species of Felis leo genus and the variations of the species are due to climatic and local conditions and not hybridity. On account of its great strength, pre-historic nations used its image to symbolize strength, fierceness, energy and persistence, in opposition to other forces. Like the Hippopotamus, the Lion, on account of straight, non-hybrid conditions, is fast becoming extinct. Much of its ferociousness was induced by hunger, which former condition had a serious effect upon its offspring, and hence, generations that followed.

The Kăl-lū'tūs was an animal of the feline order, that originally inhabited the northern portion of Teltzie Sot. At that time it was very closely allied to the Zentha, only it was more ferocious; larger, longer, and slimmer in body; longer legs; more fleet, agile and graceful. In color, the ground was of a bright, yellowish orange; face, throat and under the belly were white; the whole body elegantly striped with a series of transverse black and gray bands, and bars; had no mane. At the time of the submergence of Teltzie Sot, a small remnant was left in the western-central portion of Africa, from whence they migrated eastward, through that continent into Asia, where some of the males mixed breeds with the females of the Zentha family that had migrated to that region from North Africa; their offsprings became the pre-historic ancestors of the genus Tigris regalis.

The An'zōs was a plantigrade of omnivorous and frugivorous habits that closely resembled the order Ursidæ. Originally it inhabited the northern and southern portions of the Lontidri, from whence it spread to the eastern and western portions. There were several species. Generally, they had stout, heavy, thick, bunchy bodies, larger than the modern species. There were black, brown or seal, and white-colored species. At the time of the submergence of the Lontidri, remnants were left on both the Eastern and Western continents. Some of each color were left in the British Island region; some of each color excepting white, in North America; some of the white in the Arctic regions of both Continents; and some of the black were left in the region of Morocco, Africa. In subsequent time, the white Anzos became the pre-historic ancestors of the Sea Bears, of which the Polar or White Bear is the sole representative; and never having entered into hybrid conditions, remains a fair specimen of the Atlantian White Anzos. The brown or seal-colored Anzos on the Eastern Continent migrated to the temperate and north-temperate regions of the Eastern Hemisphere, from Spain to Japan, and their descendants became the pre-historic ancestors of the species Ursus arctos or common Brown Bear. The brown and black Anzos remnants that were left on the North American Continent, migrated through the wooded parts of the Continent, and their descendants became the pre-historic ancestors of the species Ursus americanus, or the American Black and Brown Bears. The Gray Anzos of Atlantis (a mixed breed between the white and black Anzos) were left as remnants on the North American Continent, and mixed breeds with the brown remnants, whose descendants became the pre-historic ancestors of the now known species Ursus ferox, or Grizzly Bears. The fossil remains, such as have been found in the deposits of the Pliocene age, viz., those of the Great Cave Bear, Ursus spelæus of Central Europe and Asia, and its allied species, Ursus priscus of Britain, were among the pre-historic descendants of the Anzos remnants of those regions, which bear evidence of the superior size of the original Anzos, in comparison with the modern order of Ursidæ.

Subsequent to the establishment of the several varieties of the remnant Anzos in the British Island regions, there was a mixed condition of breeds between the species, the descendants of which established a variety pre-historically known as the Yăk'-ā-lĕt, which migrated into the regions of Norway and Sweden, the colors being black, white, cinnamon and black and white spotted. Ultimately, some of the males of the Wē-ī'zē-lĕx (tiger) family, mixed breeds with some of the females of the Yakalet family, whose descendants, subsequently known as the Gargus, became the pre-historic ancestors of the Pard, Panther, or Leopard, whose pre-historic range, during the early part of the Pleistocene period, was throughout the British Islands, the Norway, the Sweden, and the latter part of the same period, throughout the Spain, France, Germany, and England districts, which fact can be deduced from the fossil remains of those districts. Then began a migration of the animals that had grown numerous, when some went southwest, some south, and thence southeast, to the hotter climates, until they now range over the greater part of Africa, from Algeria to the Cape Colony; throughout southern Asia, from Palestine to China, including India, south of the Himalayas, and the Islands of Ceylon, Java, Sumatra, Borneo, etc. From the hybrid conditions that characterized their ancestors, they sustained changes of color, marking of the head, back, limbs and under parts with irregular black spots, and their sides with distinct numerous rosettes, or clusters of small spots, disposed in circular form, which have thus remained for generations, by no more hybrid conditions attending the descendance. Some diminutive, degenerate descended conditions, however, gave rise to the species now known as the Cheetah, the Panther, the Cat, etc., of the Eastern Continent. The pre-historic common Cat of the Eastern Continent, through the Cheetah species, tamed by the natives for the Antelope chase, established the pre-historic domestic Cat on the Eastern Continent; and later descendants, the domestic species.

The Jĕl-wā'gĕr was a carnivorous mammal that inhabited the southern and western portions of Teltzie Ket and Zret, and closely resembled a large breed of the modern Dog. Its colors were black, brown, and black ground spotted with gray. At the time of the submergence, remnants of the Jelwager and the Zentha were left on the eastern coast of British America, where some of the male Jelwager and the female Zentha remnants mixed, whose descendants were pre-historically known as the Gāz-ō-qū'quĕk. Its descendants became the pre-historic ancestors of the Jaguar or Felis onca of North and South America, through Mexico, Central America, and down into South America, whose descendants became the pre-historic ancestors of the Jaguar, Puma, or Felis concolar species, or Panther, Wild Cat, etc. The pre-historic common Cat of the Western Continent had its origin through domestic influences exercised upon the Wild Cats that were captured and retained by the Indian races. Straight descendants of the Jelwager, under degenerate diminutive conditions, were pre-historically known as the Skĕn'dĭsh on the Eastern Continent, and the Shū'shrăn on the Western, whose further descendants became the pre-historic ancestors of the digitigrade mammal, or genus Canis lupus, or Wolf of Europe, Asia and North America, from Greenland to Mexico and North America, of various species. The name Skendish was given to the true Wolf by the pre-historic peoples of Adamawa, Central Africa. The animal and its name were carried into the northern portion of the Continent, and thence it migrated into Europe and Asia, where later it was called the Wolf. As the true Jelwager, or Wolf, disappeared in the tropical regions, the Wolf-allied dogs became non-prevailing, through degeneration and diminution, which established small breeds such as the Jackals, the Foxes, and the Pariah Dogs of India and Egypt, between which no perceptible difference is manifest, except in their domestic habits. Jackals, like the Wolf, though to a greater degree, associated with dogs, and their offspring are not sterile. The wild species of dogs in tropical America, where the Wolves and Jackals have become extinct, are descendants from the Jelwager, Jĕz'mī-lĕt (pre-historic Dog) and Jĕf'ry (pre-historic Fox) ancestors, from which ultimate wild canine and the present domestic breeds have descended. At the present time, the Arawal Indians cross their dogs with the aboriginal wild species, in order to improve their domestic breeds, thus proving the close alliance and certain descendancy of the wild canine breeds from the Jelwager, or ultimate Canis lupus; Jezmilet, or Canis latrans, and the Jefry, or Canis aurens, and the present great variety of domestic breeds, having their origin through the influences brought to bear upon the captives from the wild breeds, by pre-historic means, and ultimatum reached by the modern, represented by 189 distinct varieties, according to Professor Fitzinger. (See Encyclopædias for modern links.)

In subsequent time, the true Shushran and Gazoququek mixed breeds and their descendants, pre-historically known as the Jĕz'-mī-lĕt, became the pre-historic ancestors of the species Canis latrans, the Coyote or Prairie Wolf of North America. Another species of the Jezmilet, pre-historically known as the Jefry on the Western Continent, and the Gŏn'thāle on the Eastern, by degenerative, diminutive conditions, became the pre-historic ancestors of the species Vulpes, or Fox families. Another species of the Jezmilet, pre-historically known as the Glăn'sō, on the Western Continent, and the Dăv'ē-näh on the Eastern, became the pre-historic ancestors of the species Canis aurens or Jackals.

The Lē'trū was an ungulate ruminant and deciduous mammal of the Carvidæ order, that originally inhabited the northern, northeastern and northwestern portions of the Lontidri, and closely resembled the genus Cerous, especially the two species, Alces malchis, Elk or Moose Deer, and Farandus rangifer, or Reindeer, though much larger. It had longer, stronger limbs than the Elk; a very flat, bushy tail that was feather-like in form, as it parted down the top, as the quill of a feather, the hair growing at right angles to it; both the male and female had horns that were extremely large, palmated and branching in form; hair generally of a fawn color, that grew heaviest around the neck, thus forming a muffler, called by the Atlantians a Frē'tī-ze, that generally was of a light brown color. Some of the animals were of a light brown ground, and had a dark brown Fretize. They had ungulated feet; short, thick necks; large heads; and had a proud, stately bearing of body when posed or silent, and when traveling as well. At the time of the submergence of those portions of the Lontidri, remnants were left in the region of Europe on the east, and British America on the west. They were contemporaneous on both Continents with the Keltroze and the Zeneletrix. The remnants left on the European side, migrated across the British Island region, to the southern portion of Norway and Sweden, and their descendants into all parts of Northern Europe and Asia, and into Prussia, the Caucasus, into the region of Germany and France, and later transported into China. The remnant left on the American side migrated over the regions of North America, from the New England States westward to British Columbia. The straight descendants of the Letru, became the pre-historic ancestors of the species Alces malchis, prehistorically known as the Dē-ä-lĕn'zä, and modernly as the Elk or Moose Deer. The fossil remains of the Deer species found in the lake deposits of Ireland; on the Isle of Man; in Scotland and England, such as the Cerous megacerous or gigantic "Irish Elk," are of the last descended species of the Letru remnant proper.

The Gē-lī'tē was an ungulate ruminant and deciduous mammal of the Carvidæ order, contemporaneous with the Letru, and very closely allied to it. It had very large, branching horns, but not palmated. In color, some were of a glossy dark, and some of a glossy light brown; very short, but bushy tails, and ungulate feet. At the time of the submergence, remnants were left in Europe and British America, and their straight line of descendants migrated into the same regions as did the Letru. Their descendants became the pre-historic ancestors of the general order of Carvidæ, the variance in species being due to hybrid, diminutive and degenerative conditions. Some of the male Letru and the female Gelite mixed breeds, both on the Eastern and Western Continents, whose descendants, pre-historically known as the Bē-ä-lĕn'zä, became the pre-historic ancestors of the Reindeer. Those on the Western Continent descended into two species, and are further represented by the Barren Ground Caribu and Woodland Caribu, or American Reindeer of the boreal regions of the western hemisphere, from Greenland and Spitsbergen in the north, to New Brunswick in the south. Those existing on the Eastern Continent, or Europe and Asia, descended into all the varieties known to the boreal regions of those sections.

The Zē-lyn'thä was an ungulate ruminant and deciduous mammal of the Carvidæ order, that originally inhabited the northwestern portion of the Lontidri. They were easily domesticated, when they never left the home unless taken away. They were often placed in the parks, and being harmless, were fondled by the children in safety. Their horns were flat, or palmated, branching, but short, and in their extension grew horizontally to the right and left from the head. Hybrid conditions in most cases cause the horns to change in form, some from round to flat, from straight to curved, spiral, and other divergent forms, as was the case with the Zelyntha. It was a hybrid offspring from the Letru and the Gelite, the condition having taken place in Atlantis before the time of the submergence, and in that country compared with the Reindeer of the Eastern and Western Continents. No remnants of the Zelyntha worth mention were left at the time of the submergence.

The An-zĭ'dä was another of the same order of mammals that inhabited the southern and eastern portions of Teltzie Sot. Its color was spotted, very much like the modern fawn. The ground was brown and spotted with gray, and the under part of the body was gray. A ruffle or tuft of long dark brown hair extended down from about six inches above on the legs, down to the hoofs, in beautiful contrast to the glossy gray on the remainder of the legs. The antlers were two in number, short, erect, and back curved, similar to the modern species Antelope corinna. Its tail was of medium length, with hair similar to Delthurz, only brown on the top, and gray underneath.

The Dĕl'thürz was another animal similar to the Anzida, that inhabited the eastern and southeastern portions of Teltzie Et. The males were much larger than the females. In color both were the same, the ground being of a dark seal brown, striped with gray. A heavy half Fretize, or breast mane, of dark brown hair extended from the throat and under jaw, down to the breast, and further hung down in pendant form over the upper portion of the legs, similar to the modern Antelope gnu. Its tail was medium large, with hair like that in front. The antlers were similar to those of the Antelope Koodoo, only a little shorter. At the time of the submergence, remnants were left on the now known western coasts of Africa. Ultimately, some of the female Anzida and the male Delthurz mixed breeds, which gave rise to a species pre-historically known as the Trō-ŏ'dĭge, which was almost an exact type of the Koodoo Antelope, and the female, that of the Harnessed Antelope. Their descendants became the pre-historic ancestors of the Koodoo Antelopes of south and west Africa, and later, that of the Harnessed Antelopes of Senegal.

The Cē'tē ū was a mammal closely allied to the Hittraina, and resembled the modern genus Equus that inhabited the southern and southeastern portions of the Lontidri, originally, but had spread out to the northeastern. It was about the size of the modern horse, only more clumsy and coarse in form. It had a shorter, but similar head; a thicker neck, of medium length; ears not so pointed; body more round, with hips less prominent; tail shorter, and the hair grew in a lapped form; limbs very similar; feet hoofed the same; color a reddish brown, and gray, glossy and sleek; mane similar, only shorter, and grew erect over the crest of the neck, about six inches in length. At the time of the submergence of that portion of the Lontidri, a remnant was left on the western coast of Africa. Ultimately, some of the male Ceteu and the female Delthurz mixed breeds, which established a new species that later, in the pre-historic periods, was known as the X-ä'lä, whose descendants became the pre-historic ancestors of the genus Equus Zebra, or Mountain Zebra of Africa. Some of the male Troodige and the female Xala mixed breeds, which established a new species whose descendants became the pre-historic ancestors of Burclell's Zebra of Africa. Subsequently, some of the male Kăn'trĭck and female Ceteu mixed breeds, the descendants of which became the pre-historic ancestors of the Quagga, or Cowagga of Africa. Subsequent to the establishment of the Delthurz and the Rē-ĕn'sŭc on the African Continent, some males of the former mixed breeds with the females of the latter, whose descendants were pre-historically known as the Kantrick. It and its descendants became the pre-historic ancestors of the Equus caballus, or Horse. A strange change took place in the Kantrick, through the hybrid influences of the Delthurz upon that of the Reensŭc, which was that of inverting the Fretize of the Delthurz from the under side of the neck, to the crest or upper part of that of the Kantrick, where it appeared as a standing viecha or mane, similar to that of the Zebra species of Equidæ. The straight line of descended Ceteu became the ancestors of a later pre-historic species, then known as the Reensuc, and its descendants became the pre-historic ancestors of the species Asinus Vulgarus, more particularly the species Asinus Tæniopus or Wild Ass of Assyria.

The barren condition of the female mule's organism is due to the re-amalgamation of the blood of the Ass race, with its hybridized half sister of the horse race, thus establishing a second hybrid condition, or dual generative force in the mule offspring that is chaotic to the reproductive unity of an offspring.

The same condition circumstantially, to certain extents, variable perhaps, would occur with the same lines of descension of any other two races thus conditionally related, and to a certain extent would occur likewise in that of the human race, if confined, or restricted to the same specific line of descension, and would also lead, in some cases, to degeneration, diminution and deformity of organism in the specific cases where barrenness had not been the result, an exception, of course.

The excessive degree in hybridized conditions that existed in the far remote ages of the past, in comparison with those of modern times, may be cognized through the existence of two facts, each contemporaneous with its own period of time, viz.: First, at the time of the great convulsions that established the submergence of the Atlantian Lontidri, most remnants of the various species of animals were comparatively few in number, which fact, under migratory conditions, brought them, as different races, more into immediate association; when their natural instinct, and under unrestrained generative influences, as wild, co-dispersed and co-mingling species, by natural forces, entered into the practise of hybridity, which caused the species subsequently to continue, either in a straight line of descension, or under further hybridity, to the establishment of new species, so long as they did not conflict in such a way as to bring barrenness. But in case of the latter, there being no continuance of the forced hybrid influences, that species, by virtue of its barrenness, became extinct.

Second, in the more modern periods of time, when the various genuses, orders, families and species, generally speaking, had become great in number, more widely spread, and collectively under a unit of generative conditions, wholly within their own species, non-hybridity was the natural result, when the specific lateral races continued in their line of descension, under their various conditions and influences, that either rendered degenerate, diminutive, retarded, fluctuating (such as for a time, elevated the development), as evidenced by the present great variation of existing animals, and the fossil remains, deposited during the past ages.

The Děz'ē-lět was an amphibious, rodent animal, of one principal and one sub-order, that originally inhabited Teltzie' Et and Set. The larger or principal genus closely resembled the genus Castor, though larger; nose and head more tapering, and ears more pointed. There were black and very dark reddish varieties, and in old age many turned a dingy gray. At the time of the submergence, remnants escaped from Teltzie Set, into North America. It and its straight descendants in the European region became the pre-historic ancestors of the genus Castor, or European Beaver of the British Islands and other parts of Europe. The remnants left on the American Continent, and their straight descendants, became the pre-historic ancestors of the species Castor canadensis, from whence they spread over the

Continent between the Arctic Circle and the tropic of Cancer. The fossil remains found in the Tertiary beds of the Continents, larger than the modern species, were descendants of the original Dezelet genera. The sub-order above referred to were not amphibious rodents, but dwelt in earth habitations apart from aqueous districts. In size they were about the same as the modern Beaver, similar in appearance to the genus Arctomys Monax of the Harmot genera, though larger. There were black, reddish brown, gray and pure white varieties. These became the prehistoric ancestors of the Arctomys Monax and their degenerate descendants, the Ground Hog, or Woodchuck; the Cynomys, or Prairie Dogs, etc., etc.

The Gū'ĭt was a rodent animal of arborial habits, that inhabited all parts of the Lontidri, and closely resembled the genera Sciurinæ, or Squirrel family. Its tail was longer, more bushy, and its head and nose were a little more tapering. There were several varieties, especially in color, each having its original abode—the black, orange and yellow, the eastern portions; the white the southern and southwestern, etc. At the time of the submergence, remnants were left in the regions of Europe, from whence they spread out over the whole Palæarctic region from Ireland to Japan, and from Lapland to northern Italy, where the specific colors, excepting white, have descended in straight lines, etc. The white species mixed families with the black, and thus, as a distinct colored species, were lost in the new species of gray, of the deep blackish order, such as are known to inhabit the mountain regions of southern Europe; and those of Siberia that are more of the clear, pale gray color, in accord with the degree of black blood in the mixture of the families; and the mixed families of yellow and orange varieties established the bright red species that inhabit the region of northern and western Europe. Through the condition of variety mixing, local influences, in regard to size and color, the brilliant markings and ornamentation with longitudinal stripes, were established in the species that inhabit the Malayan and Indian regions, etc. The same conditions, viz., mixture of colored species, occurred with the remnants and their descendants upon the western hemisphere, and are similarly represented in North and South America; hence, the black, the gray and the red species of those regions. There was no hybrid condition established with other orders of animals, the mixture being confined to that of the varieties of their own race; hence, the Gū'ĭt and its descendants became the pre-historic ancestors of the genera Sciurinæ, or the true Squirrel of the Eastern and Western Hemispheres.

In Atlantis, among the people where the white Gū'ĭt was a native, it was chosen sometimes as a symbol of purity and innocence, and thus retained as a domestic, living image of those principles.

The Cū'rēt was the principal one of several ungulate ruminant mammals that originally inhabitated the central portion of the Lontidri. It closely resembled the Antelope family, but was larger in every respect. Its hair was glossy, chestnut color, and laid close to the body like that of the modern seal. It had three horns, the two outer being triple-curved, with annulations like the Antelope carvicapa of the east. The central horn was small, and stood erect like that of the Antelope chickara of India. After the establishment of the Aduack and the Aexta in Africa, some males of the former and females of the latter mixed breeds. Their descendants became the pre-historic ancestors of the Catoblepas Gnu, and further degeneration and mingling of races established the Catoblepas Gorgon of Africa.

The Wăh was a plantegrade mammal of frugivorous herbatious and partially carnivorous habits, that originally inhabited Teltzie We, with later migrations to the western and southwestern portions of the Lontidri. It closely resembled the species Melus Taxus, or European Badger, only considerably larger in every way. In color some were black and some gray. It was nocturnal and solitary in its habits; slept by day and by night sought its food, which consisted of roots, berries, nuts, birds' eggs, frogs and insects. Its legs were short, body heavy but elongated; tail short, and bore short bristles, and the body was covered with very coarse bristles. At the time of the submergence, remnants were left in northern and northeastern Europe, North and South America, and Africa. Subsequently some of the male Yakalet mixed breeds with the Wah, the descendants of which were pre-historically known as the Krĕs'nä on the Western Continent, and the Lä-bä'tō on the Eastern, whose descendants became the pre-historic ancestors of the Suidæ, or true Pig family. (See Encyclopædias for the modern links.) Straight descendants of the Wah established the genus Melus, of Europe and North America. A mixed breed from the male Anzos and female Kelzutus genus, established a species pre-historically known as the Ic-thē'ŭs, which under further degenerate conditions, became the pre-historic ancestor of the family Procyinlotor of Storr, and Ursos lotor of Linnæus, commonly known as the Raccoon of North America, with migrations to Central and South America.

Links and Cycles

USH ZO'LI-ATH RIN'GA,

OR

THE ORNITHOLOGIC LINKS.

TELTZIE XX.

Many beautiful species of birds inhabited the Atlantian Lontidri. In fact, Erothrodia informs us that they had all the original ones from which ancient and modern-ancient orders have descended, such as still exist on the Eastern and Western Continents, though considerably changed in physical appearance from the original Atlantian ancestors, and also that there were many Atlantian species that never survived the submergence of the Lontidri. On the other hand, there are varieties of birds in modern time, not known to the remote ancient peoples, established by hybrid, degenerate and diminutive conditions, through descension, for the epi-cycles of evolution are continuous, and capable of establishing divergences to general lines; hence, the varieties and the changes that come to all physical life.

The Dĕl'ĭs was a diurnal bird of prey, represented by four principal genera, viz., the Delis proper, the Es'tē Bä'nō (Wild Bano); the Crē'tē Bano (Tame Bano); and the El-cē-ē'nä. It closely resembled the Falconidæ, or Eagle, as to size, manner and general habits, but its plumage was far more beautiful and it was considered one of the strongest and finest birds of the Lontidri. Originally it inhabited the central portion, but migrated into various parts of the Lontidri, which caused changes in some of the species. It was the national bird of Atlantis, and its image was used as a representative emblem of perfection, in Art, and the Nation's greatness, displayed in Governmental and Educational buildings, and was always a figure-head in decorative art on public occasions, and was also worn as a badge of brotherhood. The principal species of the family possessed golden-colored plumage on the upper portion of the body, and also on the upper part of the neck and head; the wing and tail coverts were also of a golden hue, shading out into a pure white that characterized the quill feathers; the under part of the body was of a pale, ashen gray; the under part of the throat and the sides of the neck, extending back under the wings, were of a pale lilac hue; the breast was a pure violet that shaded down into the ashen gray of the under part of the body; the leg feathers were also of a violet hue; the plumage, instead of being flat, was characterized with a curly or puffed appearance on the edges of the feathers. Its eyes were sharp and piercing, being of a golden color with black iris. Its beak and legs were of an ashen gray color and its feet were black.

The Jĕn'sĕt was the next most important species that originally inhabited the northwestern, northern and northeastern portions of the Lontidri. It was the largest and most common of the genera. It was a very dark brown or dingy black, except under the body and wings, which was a light brown. Its feet and beak were black. At the time of the submergence of Atlantis, remnants were left on the northern portion of both the Eastern and Western Continents, whose descendants were pre-historically known as the Queg, on the Eastern, and the Tē'zē-lē-ŏn on the Western, which became the pre-historic ancestors of the species Aguila chrysætus, the Golden or Mountain Eagles of the inland districts of Britain, the Palæarctic regions generally, and portions of the Nearctic, of both the Eastern and Western Continents. These have also sustained characteristic changes through descending influences.

The El-cē-ē'nä was the next in rank, and originally inhabited Teltzie' Et, Zret and Sot. Its body was a glossy dark blue, on the upper portion; breast mottled with red and violet, and the same condition on the under side of the body, only of a lighter hue. The wing and tail coverts, in their extent from the body, were blue; and the long quill feathers of the tail and wings were blue at the body, but shaded out into lighter hues, and were tipped with a rich blending of red into an ultimate violet, the blendings of which gave them the appearance of being in bands or stripes. A crest of blended red and violet feathers adorned the forehead and hung down over a portion of the beak, which latter was curved and notched. Its feet were black, but its legs were a dark yellow, shaded down into the black of the feet; its irides were crimson. Those that inhabited the higher altitudes were more swift of wing than those of the lower. At the time of the submergence, remnants were left on both the Eastern and Western Continents, whose descendants were pre-historically known as the A-dăm'wa, on the Western, and the Trē-mŏn'dāle on the Eastern, whose further descendants became the pre-historic ancestors of the Falcons proper, the Desert Falcons, Marlings, Hobies and Kestrels. The original beauty of the Elceena plumage has been lost to that of the above-named species, and otherwise changed in markings, by descending influences and local conditions. (See Encyclopædia for changes in modern species.)

The Este Bano originally inhabited the isolated places in the Aelkedze of Teltzie' Set and Ket, but some migrated to the eastern and western portions of the Lontidri, and were practically untamable. It was a light stone color. Its short wings and long tail were tipped with black and a ruff of fluffy feathers ornamented the base of the beak, which was black; the upper mandible sinuated, but not notched. Its feet were black and it was a very swift bird in flight. At the time of the submergence, remnants were left on the boreal portions of both Continents. Their descendants were pre-historically known as the Gä-frē'trä, on the Eastern (so named on account of the term meaning "Victory," the bird being in the habit of building its nest in holes and crevices in high and inaccessible rocks or mountain ledges, where man or beast could not destroy them, or rob them of their eggs), and Gär'dĕl, on the Western. Their descendants became the prehistoric ancestors of the sub-family, Buteoninæ, or Buzzards of the British Islands in northern Europe, and the degenerate subfamily known as the Harriers and the Kite species. Ultimately some of the Tremondale and the Gefretra descendants on the Eastern Continent, and the Adamwa and Gardel descendants on the Western, mixed families by inter-breeding, which established the now known species Astur palumbarius, or Gos-Hawks of Britain and its immediate allies; and the Astur articapellus of North America, and further degenerate, diminutive descendants, such as the species A. nisus, the common Sparrow Hawk that ranges from Iceland to Japan, northern India, Egypt, and Algeria; the A. brevipes adjacent to Asia-Minor and Persia; the Sharp Shining Hawk of Canada and the United States; the A. tinus of South America; the A. boduis of India, and others in Southeastern Asia; Indo-Malay Archipelago; Australia, etc.

The Cete Bano originally inhabited the northern portions of Teltzie We, and migrated to the eastern and western portions of the Lontidri. It inhabited districts well peopled, was very tame, and in many cases was kept by domestics as a pet. Its body was clothed with plumage of a dark green color, of the bright sheeny order on the upper portion, but shaded down to a light green on the under side and down the upper portions of the legs; the wings and tail were of a sheeny black, the feathers being long and very broad, especially those of the tail, as the barbs on the scapus, forming the shafts, or vexillium, were of equal length, while those of the wings, the barbs on the scapus forming the after shaft, or second vexillium, were much shorter than those forming the chief vexillium. Its beak was a dark green and its legs a light green, in harmony with the colorings of the under part of the body; but singular to say, its feet were black, shading up lighter until it met the green in a blend.

At the time of the submergence that established the West Indies, remnants of the Cete Bano were left in Central and South America, where to some extent they mixed breeds with the remnant Elceena of that region, and their descendants were pre-historically known as the Gŏn-sō-lăn'sō, which became the pre-historic ancestors of the sub-family, Cracine, the now known Curassow. (See Encyclopædias for the various species.) The now known species, however, are greatly changed physically, especially in colorings and markings, occasioned by descending influences, such as hybrid and mixed breed conditions, etc.

At the time of the submergence of Atlantis, remnants of the Delis family were left in the British Island regions, and also in the boreal regions of North America. Their descendants were pre-historically known as the Wä'nō, and became the pre-historic ancestors of the family of Sea or White-tailed Eagles, who likewise have sustained changes by descending influences. The species of Delis that escaped to the Western Continent and their descendants, were pre-historically known as the Wä-zĕs'sō, whose further descendants became the pre-historic ancestors of the Bald Eagles of the United States of America.

The Ax-'zē-lē was a bird similar to the genus Pavo or Peacock, only larger, that originally inhabited Teltzie Sot and the southern and eastern portions of Teltzie Et and Zret. No bird of A'tlantis was so proud and beautiful as the Axzele. Its body was more bunchy than that of the modern Peacock; its legs were longer; feet larger. It had three toes and a spur, the three toes being slightly webbed; the first two of the same length, the third shorter, and all containing sharp claws. The neck was long and broader at the shoulders, and tapered down to the head, which latter was longer and adorned with a long, heavy crest of feathers that fell gracefully forward from the crown and nearly covered the eyes, and down back from the head on the upper part of the neck, and in color were mixed blendings of purple and light green. Down the neck the feathers were very short and closely fitted, and were of a shiny blue; the base of the neck was adorned with a heavy ruff of feathers that in color were blended tints of cardinal and green. The body was adorned with a suit of feathers, the color of which was black and green tints beautifully blended; the tail was very long, and when spread measured from ten to twelve feet across, but instead of being round, as that of the modern bird, was more of a fan shape, or more elongated; the feathers were shaded out from a dark green at the base, to light green tips, and the tail coverts were shaded from base to tip in corresponding harmony of colors; the ocellated parts of the plumage were also more elongated than those of the modern Peacock; the little eyes, therefore, or elongated spots, were formed by colors within colors, viz: light green centrally, bordered with an orange band; next a white, then a pink, then a bright green, then a light purple; and the radiating parts of the feathers, in their extension, shaded out from the purple to a glossy black, and some were of a glossy green. The wing feathers at their extremity were marked similar to the tail coverts; i. e., with the ocellations, only the spots were smaller. The ends of the wings were carried up loosely from the body so as to show the markings of the tail coverts, and when the bird spread its tail the wings were also raised, so as to form a part of the erection of the tail. There were a few pied and mottled varieties that inhabited the northeastern portion of Teltzie Et. The body of the hen was black, and the upper coverts of the wings were a pale green, shaded down to the long quill feathers into a dark green, the rear part of the coverts was purple, and shaded out into a black at the ends of the quill feathers. The tail at the base was a light green, shaded out to a central purple, and terminated in black at the points of the quill feathers.

At the time of the submergence of the southern and southeastern portions of the Lontidri, remnants were left on the Continent of Africa, and being of a migrating nature, passed eastward before the establishment of the Arabian Sea, into the section of Hindustan, and ultimately into the Indian Peninsula and Island of Ceylon, and even farther into those regions. But eventually, limited in space by the submergence of that section, and the remnants few in number who were left in the African region, after the eastern migration of the main portion they became extinct as a species, through natural causes; hence the now supposed nativity of the Peacock is in India and Ceylon, where they are so abundant.

Therefore, the Axzele and their descendants, pre-historically known as the Pä-sĕn-ē'sä, on the Eastern Continent, became the pre-historic ancestors of the genus Pavo, or Peacocks, embracing several species. (See Encyclopædias for the same.)

The Nē'trē was a domestic bird that originally inhabited the central, northeastern and southern portions of the Lontidri. It closely resembled the Anitidæ family or Swan, only larger in every way. It had webbed feet, as it was a swimming bird, and beautiful plumage. The principal species was pure white, had a red bill that was surmounted with a black berry or knob; large, dark gray legs and black feet. Some had white bodies, light golden wings and tail, pink bill, light drab feet and legs. Some had dark orange bodies with white wings and tail; dark drab bill and legs, with black feet, and a white crest on the head. Some had the entire body clothed with dark gray plumage. Some with a light gray, both the latter having yellow legs, beaks and feet. Both the eggs and flesh of the Netre were utilized for food by certain classes of the Atlantian people. At the time of the submergence remnants were left in the region of the British Islands, Africa, South America and North America. Those on the Eastern Continent were pre-historically known as the Tē-ū-lē'ŏn; those in North America as the Kō-kē-ăn'ō, and those in South America as the I-ĭs'lĕm. From natural descending influences, their descendants became the pre-historic ancestors of the Cygnus order, the large Mute or Tame Swan; the C. musicus, the Whooper or Whistling Swan (the musical tones it utters have been celebrated from the time of Homer); the C. bewicki or Bewick's Swan; the C. buccinator or Trumpet Swan of North America; the C. melanocorypha or Black-necked Swan of South America, etc.

The Skŏl'wăsh was a swimming bird, so named on account of its hiding in the marshes, and diving out of sight, at the approach of the natives, who hunted it for food. The term means "water-bird." It inhabited the entire portion of Teltzie Sot. Its plumage was usually a glossy black on the upper portion of the body, and of a sooty black underneath. Its wings, legs, feet and beak were black. At the time of the submergence of Teltzie Sot, remnants were left on the now known Continent of South America. In subsequent times some of the Skolwash and the Netre species mixed breeds, whose descendants became the pre-historic ancestors of the species C. melanocoryha or Black-necked Swan of South America, pre-historically known as the Quĭn-zō'lă. It was much sought by the natives of that region, and therefore soon exterminated on that Continent. But a portion of the species migrated westward, throughout the Great Eastern Archipelago, until at last they reached the region of Australia, where they remained in a wild state.

The Un'dūke was a scansorial bird, consisting of five species, that originally inhabitated the extreme southern portions of the Lontidri, but migrated westward and eastward from that section, and was carried by the inhabitants into the central portions as a domestic pet. It closely resembled the Psittacidæ family or Parrot bird, particularly the genus Ara or Macaw species, only it was larger and more beautiful. When in captivity it learned to sing sentences of the Atlantian language, and much more distinctly than the modern Parrots talk. It sang the sentences more frequently than it talked them, and therefore learned many of the Atlantian melodies. For that reason their images were placed upon public buildings and in decorative Art, especially where music was the commercial enterprise; and on articles of commerce, such as musical instruments, etc.

The Am'wā was the principal one of the five species. The upper portion of its body was mottled with four colors, black, olive green, dark green and blue; the under portion the same, only lighter shades. The wing and tail coverts were based with a beautiful deep orange color that extended out into the bright green, then into a beautiful shade of pink, the terminal of the contour feathers being tipped with red. All the above-named colors extended in the form of blended bands across the coverts, from their base outward, respectively. The quill feathers of the wings and tail were black. A crest of feathers surmounted the head, the base of which was a light green, shaded up into a deep orange, and tipped with black. The tail feathers were considerably spread. At the time of the submergence, remnants were left on the South American Continent, where in time they mixed breeds with remnants of the second of the five species. This and continued inter-breedings established a family of birds whose descendants were pre-historically known as the Săn-gū'lä. These became the pre-historic ancestors of the Macaw Parrot of some fifteen or more species. (See Encyclopædias for description of modern links.) All of these had their ancestry in the Amwa and Unduke of Atlantis, and their present characteristics by the influence of long periods of mixed species and inter-breedings, in the regions of South America, Central America and Mexico.

The second of the five principal species were about as large as the Amwa. Nearly the entire portion of contour feathers, on the body, were of a bright red color; the feathers of the tail and wings were of medium length and were tipped with a beautiful shade of green; the upper part of the breast and under the throat were characterized with bright golden-colored feathers, so laid as to form a triangle; a black stripe, about two inches in length, extended downwards from the base of the head, terminating in a point on the back of the neck; a crest of purple feathers adorned the head; a massive beak of pale pink marked the contrast.

At the time of the submergence, remnants were left on the

African Continent and in northern South America. Those in the former region migrated eastward into the Indian Archipelago region, and those in the latter, into Central America and Mexico. This species and their straight descendants, became the pre-historic ancestors of the Lory, or Parrote, of the order Psittaci, that ranges over the Moluccas and New Guinea. A divergent, degenerative branch from this species established the now known sub-family Loriinæ, etc. (See Encyclopædias for modern links, etc.)

The third of the five principal species were garmented with a contour of white feathers. Their wings and tails were tipped with black. Under the head and throat was also black, and their beaks were massive and of a dnrk brown. Some of the third and fourth species mixed breeds, and their descendants became the pre-historic ancestors of the species Colyptorhynchus funereus—the "Funeral," or Black Cockatoos, of Australia.

The fourth of the five principal species possessed a contour of steel gray feathers over the entire body, but of a lighter shade underneath. The coverts of the wings and tail were shaded, in bars that extended crosswise, beginning at the forward end with a bright orange band which shaded back into a bright reddish pink, and lastly into white. Those across the tail were the same as those of the wings. The massive beak was a very light yellow. Their straight descendants, under degenerate, diminutive influences that arose from long inter-breedings, established the species Psittacus erithacus, or Gray Parrots.

Some of the second, third and fourth species mixed breeds, the descendants of which became the pre-historic ancestors of the species Cacatua Leadbbeatere, or Leadbbetier's Cockatoo, of South Australia.

The Kĭsh'hăm was a scansorial bird that originally inhabited Teltzie Et, and was closely allied to the Unduke. It was as large a bird as either of the five species of the latter. It was clothed with a contour of pure white feathers, had a high crest of golden-colored feathers, long tail of the same color, and a massive drab beak. It was a sacred bird with the Atlantians, on account of the color of its plumage. The yellow represented conjugal love, and also the light and knowledge that comes from spiritual sources. The white represented the purity of that love, and the truth that may be gained through the contemplation of spiritual teachings. At the home it thus governed as a domestic symbol. At the time of the submergence, remnants of the wild Kishham were left in sections of Central Africa, whence they subsequently migrated into the regions of the Indian Archipelago, New Guinea and Australia. Its descendants became the pre-historic ancestors of the species Cacatua Galerita, or the true Cockatts.

The On'tē was a scansorial bird, closely allied to the Unduke, but smaller. It was one of the most sacred birds of the Atlantians, on account of its vocal qualities. When taught it was far superior to any of the Unduke species in its more perfect utterance of words and sentences. Its language sounded more like the human voice speaking. The plumage on the upper portion of its body was a glossy, silvery white. That on the neck and shoulders shaded down into a light pink, under the body into a violet. The head feathers were white on top; but those on the sides of the neck and head were a light but bright purple. Its crest was composed of very fine feathers about one and a half inches in height, which fell back on the neck, and were of several colors, beautifully blended. The wing and tail bore a changeable lustre of green, the tips of the feathers being a pinkish red. The beak and legs were a light purple, but the feet were black. From the main stock of the Onte family, under degenerate, diminutive influences, has descended all the species of Parakeets.

The Skē-mē'drŭm was a bird of gigantic physique, the largest of all the Atlantian birds. It resembled the genus Struthio, or Ostrich, yet was considerably larger. It originally inhabited the greater portion of Teltzie Sot, and southeastern Teltzie Zret. Some were black and some white and a few were dark brown. Some had black bodies, white tails and wings, and others just the reverse. In the Atlantian period they were extremely wild, and never had been domesticated. At the time of the submergence of the southern and southeastern portions of Atlantis, remnants were left on the African continent. Their descendants were pre-historically known as the Kä-hō'gä (so named by the pre-historic natives on account of their song, or vocal utterance, which sounded like the term). Their descendants became the pre-historic ancestors of the Ostrich. Some of the white, brown, and a larger number of the black species, migrated westward from Teltzie Sot, and southward from southeastern Teltzie Zret, into the section of Brazil and South America. Their descendants established a genus of birds, pre-historically known as the A-dē-nōn'zō, whose further descendants became the pre-historic ancestors of the family Rheidæ, or American Ostrich of South America; the R. americana that ranges from Paraguay and southern Brazil into Patagonia; the R. darwini of Patagonia; the R. americana that associates with herds of deer, etc. Migrations of the Kahoga eastward, north-eastward and south-eastward, from their original home, established some extinct, and yet existing species, under changed conditions. Among them were the extinct Moas of the genus Dinornithidæ of New Zealand; the yet existing Cassowaries and Emeus of the genus Casuariidæ of the Island of Ceram, and more greatly removed from the original species, through diminutive and degenerative conditions, the Kiwis of the genus Apterygidæ, of New Zealand. The Ostriches of the genus Struthionidæ of Africa, the largest of modern birds, which seek the society of Zebras and Antelopes, are straight descendants from the Atlantian Skemedrum, as well as those of Arbia. The finest of these are natives of the neighborhood of Shomer and the uplands of Toeyka, or traversing acros the sands in files of from twenty to thirty.

The Hē'lĭ-tŏx was a very large, diurnal, accipitrine bird, that inhabited the entire Lontidri excepting Teltzie Zret. It closely resembled the family Vulturidæ, though larger; was of obscene habits, such as feeding on dead and decaying carcasses, dead fish, etc. It was about the size of the modern Condor. It was black and white mottled or pied, barred and striped. Some had all white wings and black bodies, others were mottled with black and white. Their beaks were longer than the modern Vulture's. Their heads generally were void of feathers, and the skin of some species was white, of others red, with nasal caruncles of the same color. Each species had a ruff of feathers around the neck, some being black with a white central stripe. In some it was white and black mottled or pied, and in others it was entirely a light gray. It was a bird of wonderful endurance in flight, which it made at various altitudes, from 25000 feet down to the level of the earth's surface. At the time of the submergence of the Lontidri, remnants were left on both Continents. Their descendants, pre-historically known as the Gŏn'sō-lēte on the Western, and as the Spū-gū'lŭm on the Eastern, became the pre-historic ancestors of the genus Vulture, including the Buzzards and the Condors. The descendants on the Western Continent became the pre-historic ancestors of the species Sarcorhamphus, or gigantic Condor; the Gypagus or King Vulture; the Catharisrista, embracing the so-called Turkey Buzzard and its allies or degenerate descendants; Pseudogry phus or great California Vulture, of the western slopes of North America, etc. Those of the Eastern, or Old World, represented the true Vulture of five genera, embracing the N. percnopterus or Egyptian Vulture, of India, Africa, the shores of the Mediterranean, England and Norway. (For the degenerate descended sub-families of Vulturine, etc., as modern links, see Encyclopædias.)

The X-y'ēs resembled the family Corvidæor Pigeon. It originally inhabited the northern, northeastern and northwestern portions of the Lontidri. Its contour feathers were black; wings, legs and beak white. Its head was adorned with a feather crest. It was a beautiful songster whose tones were soft and melodious. At the time of the submergence, remnants were left on both Continents. Those on the Eastern inhabited the British Island regions, and those on the Western, North America. Hybrid conditions between the Xyes, the Iista or the Due, already begun in Atlantis, more fully developed after the submergence in the remnants, which established the family Columbidæ or Pigeons and Doves. Those on the Western Continent were pre-historically known as the Kē-lē'tē, and those on the Eastern as the Sā'gä, which are mongrels of the three above-named Atlantian birds, the bright colorings being a descended influence from the Iista. All that is left of the beautiful song of the Xyes is heard in the cooing of the Dove; and the black and white contrasts of its plumage is now lost in the shadings and mixed blendings on the plumage of the Columbidæ family.

The Dūe was closely allied to the Xyes, and inhabited the central and southern portions of the Lontidri. It resembled the branch of the Columbidæ family, now known as the Dove. Its song was flute-like, plumage pure white; its crest was of white feathers, tipped with bright red, which extended across the head from right to left, just above the eyes. It has sustained but little change physically since the Atlantian time, excepting to its vocal qualities, due to inter-breedings, etc. At the time of the submergence, remnants were left on the Eastern Continent in the African regions, where it pre-historically was known as the Cē-rū'tē (the term meaning purity), from whence it migrated northeastward and eastward into Egypt, Europe and Asia. There it mixed breeds with the Xyes and the Iista remnants, whose descendants became the pre-historic ancestors of the Ring Dove, or Wood Pigeon of Britain and Europe; the small Stock Dove, the common Turtle Dove, the Barbary Dove, the Rock Dove, the Wild Races of Egypt and Asia, etc., all having had their distinctions through mixed breed influences. (See Encyclopædias for the many other modern links.)

A mixed breed condition between the Gafretra and the Tremondale families on the Eastern Continent, and the Gardel and the Adamwa on the Western, established a sub-family, having place as a dual or co-incident descendancy, on the two Continents, pre-historically known as the Pē-lē'zōn, on the Eastern, and the Kŭp'pēr on the Western, whose descendants became the pre-historic ancestors of all the Astur, or Hawk families, and further descended species on the two continents, to which must be added the Harriers and the Kites, as degenerate and diminutive.

The Lē'tē was a domestic fowl that inhabited all portions of the Lontidri, excepting Teltzie Sot. It resembled the order Gallinæ, especially the family Phasianidæ, or common Cock and Hen, or Jungle Fowl, though a larger and finer bird than the modern species. There were black, white, yellowish brown, reddish brown, mottled and striped varieties; some were black and white, some were gray and brown, and some were yellow and brown. The Cocks were considered songsters, in which they would raise the tones of the voice five steps, from a low to a high pitch, trilling the highest tone, which made the utterance more song-like than the crow of the common modern Cock. The image of the Lete was placed on medallions as a figure in the "coat of arms" of families, and on buildings, for the same purpose. At the time of the submergence, remnants were left on both the Eastern and Western Continents, whose descendants were pre-historically known as the Am-ā-lū'tŭs on the Eastern, and the Găs'trō on the Western. Their further descendants became the pre-historic ancestors of the Jungle Fowls and Pheasants. Through the influence of inter and cross-breedings of wild families and species, through their long descendancy, have arisen all the species and varieties of Pheasants known to moderns. (See Encyclopædias for the modern links.)

The Dē-ē'tē was a small domestic bird, a sub-family of the Leete, kept solely for its egg product. It inhabited the entire Lontidri excepting Teltzie Sot. Some had black wings and tails, but the contour feathers were a blending of black and dark green. Some had red and yellow blendings through the contour feathers, red tails and wings and single red combs and wattles; some had yellow and some drab legs, and black feet. At the time of the submergence remnants were left on the Eastern and Western Continents, where, by inter-breeding, they were lost in the Lete family. Degenerate, diminutive conditions born to the descendants of some of the inter and cross-bred species of the pre-historic Lete, or Amalutus and Gastro species, intermixed with those of the Deete, have established several species in the order Gallinæ, the Gray Partridge of Britain; the red-legged Partridge of Europe; the Barbary Partridge of Africa; the Black Partridge of Europe and India; the Snow Partridge of Asia, etc. Further degenerate, diminutive conditions produced the Grouse of the Eastern and Western Continents, of numerous species; still further degeneration and diminution established by inter and cross-breed influences, etc., the Quail species. (See Encyclopædias for the numerous modern links.)

The Lĕ-tĕ-mĕ'quä was a large wild bird that originally inhabited the central and southern portions of the Lontidri, but had migrated eastward and westward to the border-lands. In the Atlantian time it was a bird of flight, was very beautiful and had a peculiar song, similar in some respects to that of the modern Guinea-hen, but louder and much shriller. When frightened its cry was very much more like that of the modern Panther than of a bird. Its body was large, but chunky; legs and neck short; its contour feathers were mottled; some black and white, some red and black, and some golden and black. It had small head and eyes; short single comb, some being all red and some a pinkish red. At the time of the submergence remnants were left on both Continents, especially in Central Africa, and in the Cape Verde Islands when they were severed from Africa; in the West Indies, or section of the Greater Antilles, and the Ascension Islands, where in their wild state they further degenerated. They were pre-historically known as the Gŏn-sō-lĕ'ŭm, on the African Continent and as the Tĕ-ŭ'kä in the West Indies. Their further descendants became the pre-histric ancestors of the Ancient Avis or Gallina Numidica, and ultimately the Guinea-hen, a straight descendant from the Letemequa, with no connection with the Turkey, as has been supposed.

The Chĭl'lĕ was a tenuirostral bird that originally inhabited the central and southern portions of the Lontidri and closely resembled the Trochilidæ, or Humming-birds; only at that time they had not become so tiny as the modern Humming-bird. There were three principal species, the first and most beautiful of which was characterized with changeable colors, in accordance with its movements about, in the light; the upper portion of the contour feathers was of a greenish brown; those on the breast were changeable shades of blue and dark purple; the wings and tail were shadings of black and orange; the head was of a dark salmon; the beak was of a light drab and the legs were the same.

The second principal species possessed entire contour feathers of changeable red and blue shadings; the head was of a deep blue; the wings and tail were black and blue mixed; a cap-like crest of pinkish red feathers adorned the head; the beak was a pale green and drab, blended, and the legs were the same.

The third principal species had contour feathers on the upper part of the body, that were a mixed deep orange shaded with a light pink; and those on the under part of the body the same, but in lighter shades; the neck was blue and black, shaded up over the head; a straight, erect crest of dark orange tipped with black; the wings and tail were black, tipped with orange, with a blending of light pink that separated the black and orange.

At the time of the submergence remnants were left on the Western Continent, whose descendants, under various changes physicially, became the pre-historic ancestors of the now more than 400 species of the smallest, most wonderfully and brilliantly plumaged of all birds. (See Encyclopædias for these modern links.)

The Tē-lĕ'quĕm was a very large, wild, and also domestic bird, that originally inhabited the eastern, central and western portions of the Lontidri. It closely resembled the genus Meleagris, or Turkey, though much larger. Its plumage was varied, black, white and brown; mottled or pied, the latter being black and white, black and dark green, etc. Their caruncles were much larger than those of the Turkey, and those on the white varieties were a light red; those on the black, a purple, though changeable to red when excited; and those on the brown, a light drab, changeable to a bright pink under the same conditions. At the time of the submergence remnants were left on both Continents, whose descendants were pre-historically known as the Jĭb-ē-ō'tēs on the Western. Their descendants became the prehistoric ancestors of the genus M. Mexicana of Mexico; the M. gallo-pavo of North America; and the Melegrenæ of Northern Central America, etc. The remnants left on the Eastern Continent, pre-historically known as the Quäd'rū, being fond of flying over aquatic regions, migrated further eastward from time to time, until they reached Australia and the Great Eastern Archipelago. Their further descendants became the pre-historic ancestors of a great number of Eastern varieties.

The Qū-tē-zō'lĕm was a nocturnal bird of prey, that closely resembled the family Strigidæ, or Owls. It inhabited all parts of the Lontidri and was of several species. It was much larger than the modern bird; some were black, some white, some tawny, some mottled with black and white, etc. Its feet were larger and claws more hooked. Its eyes were very large and the male's were a dark green; the eyes were encircled with a large rosette of light-colored feathers. Its tail and wings were longer than the modern Owl's. At the time of the submergence remnants were left on both Continents, whose descendants were pre-historically known as the Lĕn-zē-ō'lē on the Eastern, and the Clī'gĕr on the Western. (See Encyclopædias for the great varieties of modern links.)

The I-ĭs'tă was a conirostral bird that inhabited the southern portions of the Lontidri, with some migrations north and east. It reesembled the family Oriolidæ, especially the Golden Oriole, though larger in every respect. There were several species. The principal one, the Shĕl'te, had bright golden feathers on its head and breast, which blended into the bright red on its neck; the tail and wings were a glossy black. The O'kōsh, another variety, had bright yellow and black plumage, the breast and under parts of the body being yellow and the wings, tail and top of the head black. The Rĕl'zē, another variety, had bright red plumage on the breast and under parts of the body; the wings and tail were black; the upper part of the body gray, with a semi-circular ruff of red feathers on the back of the neck at the base of the head. At the time of the submergence remannts from the northern and eastern portions of the Lontidri were left in the regions of Great Britain and Asia. Those in the southern portion arrived in the regions of South America, and those in the eastern, in Africa. Their descendants were pre-historically known as the Zrĕl'tŏx on the Eastern Continent, and as the Kē-sĕl-'să, on the Western. Their further descendants became the pre-historic ancestors of the Oriolidæ family. The Finches, Canary birds, Robins, Starlings, Buntings, Larks, Chaffinches, Yellow Hammers, Nightingales, Tanagers, Weaver-birds, etc., etc., are all descendants from the several spècies of the Atlantian Iista, established through inter and cross-breedings, diminutive, degenerative and climatic influences during the long lines of descendancy. (See Encyclopædias for these vast modern links.)

The Skăr'dĕnt was a bird that originally inhabited the central portion of the Lontidri, with migrations into the northern, northeastern and northwestern. It resembled the passerine birds of the Corvus genus, especially the Raven, but larger. Its plumage was a shiny black, over which was a purple reflection, changeable in the different rays of sunlight. In the Atlantian period it was a bird of fine song, as it piped its call tones in the evening and on moonlight nights. It was not a bold and sagacious bird, but rather loved to frequent the home grounds at eventide. Whenever it did not so appear, it was taken to be the omen of an approaching storm, hence was never molested by the people. The characteristics of the modern bird, however, have reversed, for it is now persecuted, on account of its change of morals, from that of domestic companionship to sagacious and bold plunder. At the time of the submergence remnants were left on both Continents, the descendants of which were pre-historically known as the Cŏn'zō on the Eastern, and the Skē'mŏt on the Western, whose further descendants became the pre-historic ancestors of the Raven species. Further degenerative, diminutive descendants were the sub-famliy Corvinæ or Crows; still further degenerative, diminutive conditions established the species Turdus Merula, or Blackbirds, etc.

The croaking call-tones of the Crow, so degenerative or changed, from the sweet song of the Atlantan Skardent, seem to revert back in the Blackbird, as in nature's attempt to reproduce some of the qualities of voice possessed by the Skardent in the vocal powers of the Blackbird. This is evidenced by the song of the Cock, who displays a peculiar liquid tone, though discontinuous, that makes it much admired. In many cases, in its wild state, it has been rightfully termed a "Mocking Bird," it having been known to imitate the song of the Nightingale, the crowing of a Cock, and even the cackling of a Hen. In confinement, it has been taught to whistle a variety of tunes, and even to imitate the human voice. Thus do we see that through descending generations, mixing of breeds and species, there is a disposition upon the part of Nature not only to degenerate, diminish and silence the vocal powers in some of the subsequent offspring, but to augment, unfold, expand; and to reach back, and connect up again, the severed links; to re-establish the supposed lost qualities of being, such as characterized remote ancestors; to reinstate all developments and unfoldments, productive of new forms of life, with new characteristics and life qualities, through which reflect those of the past. Hence, "natural unfoldment," in which the qualities of being are endowed with reflected re-incarnations by the light of spiritual influence, but not spirit being, or individuality, which is the true and only re-incarnation that can exist in any descended individual, or can possibly return from the spirit state of existence to that of the material from which it has passed. Therefore, "re-incarnation" is only past influence, reflected upon future being, both mentally and spiritually, and in the human race it is largely mental. As, for instance, in writing this book, the data and pre-historic facts contained therein are reflected from spirit intelligences contemporaneous with the period of their existence as such, and are therefore re-incarnations in the mind of the writer; who further re-incarnates them in the mind of the reader. So it may be, not only with facts of data, but qualities of being. A spirit, long since separated from the mortal body, may cause his qualities of being to be reflected upon a descended mortal, through the power of influence of one spirit upon another, though one be in the body and the other dis-embodied. Hence the true "re-incarnation" is conditional influence, operating through the qualities of being, and not spirit individuality, having taken on a new form of flesh.

The E-ū-tē'ä was a bird of sweet song and great beauty, that inhabited the mountains and valleys bordering the northern and eastern portions of the Lontidri. It closely resembled the family Pica caudata, or Magpie. There were two principal species. The first of these was larger than the modern Magpie. Its contour feathers were black, over which gleamed purple reflections. Its wing coverts and quills were scarlet, marked with a gold and white combination patch on the quill feathers. The scapulars and inner web of the flight feathers were golden and white, in place of the white alone that characterizes the modern Magpie. Its legs were a bright yellow. Its head bore a bright, narrow yellow stripe on top and a spot of yellow skin had place under its eyes; a bright conirostral and orange beak; yellow wattles formed a lappet back of its eyes, that resembled the Grackula, of the Sturnidæ family of India.

The second species bore soft, loose, bluish feathers underneath the body, and a ruffed crest of the same colored feathers crowned its head. Its upper contour feathers wing and tail coverts, were a dark bright blue, and the quill feathers of the tail and wings were the same color at the base, but were tipped with a light gray. Its legs and beak were also gray, but its feet were black.

At the time of the submergence remnants of both these species were left in the Great Britain regions. Their descendants were pre-historically known as the Gŭl'fē, some of which further migrated into Europe and Asia. Other remnants were left in northwestern Africa, whose descendants were pre-historically known as the Găl-sē-lĕt'. Another remnant was left in North America, whose descendants were pre-historically known as the Cŏn-nī-pŏn'ē-ŭs, whose descendants migrated into the western portions of the United States. Therefore, from these species of the Eutea, through the Gulfe, the Galselet and the Conniponeus, have descended all the species of the Magpie family in the above-named regions and their further migrations, including the Grackels of the Sturnidæ family, and their degenerate, diminutive species, the Rice Birds, or Bobolinks, the Greater Butcher Birds, Shrikes, the Jay Birds, etc.

The Pĕn-cĭp'ē-ŭs was a Wild Bird that inhabited the greater portion of the Lontidri, and resembled the family Anatidæ or sub-family Anserenæ, the Geese, though much larger. There were three species. One had all black plumage with black feet, legs and beak. Another had all white plumage; yellow feet, legs and beak. The third had all gray plumage and gray legs, but pink feet and beak; the latter being a mixed breed condition between the former two species. These birds were never domesticated in the Atlantian time, except as they frequented the waters of the Parks.

At the time of the submergence remnants of the various species were left on both the Eastern and the Western Continents, whose descendants were pre-historically known as the Al-să-sē-ă'tē on the Western, and the Squă-nē'drŭm on the Eastern, whose further descendants became the pre-historic ancestors of the sub-family Anserenæ, or Geese. (See Encyclopædias for the various species in the modern links.)

After the establishment of the Netre (Swan) and the Peneipeus, on the Eastern and Western Continents, some of the female Netre, or their descendants, the Teuleon, and the male Pencipeus, or their descendants, the Squanedrum, on the Eastern Continent, mixed species and cross-bred, which established a sub-family, or allied species, pre-historically known as the Sănd'clĕf. Likewise, upon the Western Continent, some of the female Netre, or their pre-historic descendants, the Kokeano, and some of the male Pencipeus, or their descendants, the Alsaseate, mixed species, and further inter and cross-bred, which estabilshed a sub-family or allied species, pre-historically known as the Rĕp'tă. The Sandclef and the Repta, therefore, became the pre-historic ancestors of the sub-families of the Anatidæ, such as the Anatinæ or Fresh-Water Ducks, Sea Ducks, Spiny-tailed Ducks, and common Wild Ducks, from which all domestic breeds have descended.

USH AT'LAN-TI-AN EX-AN'TA NUD SEL-DON'ZE REX'ZE, OR THE ATLANTIAN ALPHABET AND PUNCTUATION MARKS.

TELTZIE XXI.

The following pre-historic information has been given us by Zē-rē'chä Yĕr'mäh, our Cōl'tĕr-mūse Lē-ā'sā Gĭl'tör (co-operative spirit director), a Sū'ē (son) of Zō'lăx Yermah, his father; and A-lū'ghä Yermah, his mother; and the Es-săn'drä (husband) of Erothrodia Prolex, hence the Sū-ē-lēte' (brother-in-law) of Alem Prolex.

The following diagram represents the Atlantian Exanta, as it was employed by the people of Teltzie Et. Some differences, as was the case with the language existing in the other Teltzie, will be shown further on. The capital letters were distinguished from the others by simply being made larger. The "T," when being pronounced, was strongly aspirated. The terms for "G" and "J" were spelled the same, and also that of "A" and "T," the distinction being in the sound of the vowel, as marked in the diagram:

Ŭt, Bū, Sū, Dū, Se, Tū, Gū, Ĕlt.
A. B. C. D. E. F. G. H.

Tī, Jū, Dūt, Ĕt, Ŭm, Ŭn, Fō, Fā,
I. J. K. L. M. N. O. P.

Dā, Lĕt, Ēst, Ūt, Ūd, Fēt, Wī, Ăg,
Q. R. S T. U. V. W X

Wē, Sä,
Y. Z.

The differences that existed in the Ex-ăn-tă'zē (alphabets) of the various Teltzie, as above referred to, were as follows: That of Teltzie We corresponded to that of Teltzie Et, excepting the b, c, h, i, k, o, s, t, v, and y which were:

That of Teltzie Set corresponded with that of Teltzie Ket, excepting the a, b, g, i, m, p, t, v, w, x and z, which differed in form respectively as follows:

That of Teltzie Ket corresponded with that of Teltzie Et, excepting the d, g, m, n, o, r, u, w and y, which differed in form respectively, as follows:

That of Teltzie Zret corresponded with that of Teltzie Et, excepting the c, h, j, q, s, u, v and y, which differed in form respectively, as follows:

It must be remembered that these were the differences in the Exantaze in the latter part of the third Efremetrum. Other differences existed in the early part of the first Efremetrum, and even earlier, extending through the second, and into the first part of the third, as will be seen in the inscriptions on the Maretux of Atara.

The following diagram, as will be seen, represents the Atlantian Sĕl-dŏn'zē Rĕx'zē (punctuation marks), and terms, with the English translation:

Signs	Atlantian Terms	English Terms
	Vrĕx.	Period.
	Dŏx.	Comma.
	Zăn.	Colon.
	Gĕtz.	Semi-colon.
	Wrĕx.	Interrogation mark.
	Dĕx.	Exclamation point.
	Vĕn'ĕx.	Quotation mark.
	Nī'ĕt.	Apostrophe.
	Gwēt.	Parenthesis.
	Fēze.	Etc. or &c.
	Ax'tē.	Note.

The Atlantian alphabet has descended in fragments that have found re-establishment, in various others, pre-historic ancient and modern, in a similar way to other characteristics and utilities of that people. As, for instance, the Atlantian Ut, or A, which appears in a similar character in the Chalcidian inscriptions; Bu, or B, in the Greek alphabet, Phœnician, old Athenian, old Corinthian, old Chaldean, old Latin, etc., with slight changes nearing the form of modern X; Du, or D, in the old Hebrew rock-cut inscriptions, old Athenian, Greek, Chalcidian inscriptions, old Latin; Ie, or E, hieratic Egyptian; Tu, or F, in the old Athenian, and reversed in the Chalcidian and old Latin; Gu, or G, in the old Hebrew rock inscriptions; Elt, or H, in the old Greek, old Corinthian, slightly changed, and inverted in the Chalcidian and old Latin; Ti, or I, in the old Corinthian, Chalcidian inscriptions, old Latin and modern Alphabets; Gu, or Γ, in the Phœnician; Et, or L, in the hieratic Egyptian, Ancient Phœnician, and Moabitic; Fa, or P, in the old Corinthian, Latin, and modern, slightly changed; Let, or R, in the Greek with left oblique stroke added; Ut, or T, in the hieratic Egyptian, and Hieroglyphic numbers; Ud, or U, in the Ancient Phœnician, old Athenian, and old Corinthian, slightly changed, and also reversed; Az, or X, in the Phœnician; We, or Y, in the Syriac numbers; Sä, or Z, in the Greek letters, slightly changed.

The Atlantian notes, or musical characters, have reappeared in such cases as the ancient Phœnician, Moabitic and hieratic Egyptian alphabets; slightly changed in the Grecian inscriptions and old Hebrew rock-cut inscriptions, etc. And other cases of the above can be traced, if the reader cares to make the research.

These re-embodiments came principally through fragmentary inscriptions wrought by descendants of the remnant Atlantians, and subsequently discovered by pre-historic peoples, who utilized them, in part, in their subsequent inscriptions, such as preceded the remote ancient writings; whereby the few links have extended into the ancient inscriptions, and ultimately into modern usage. The time will come when some of the pre-historic, and even Atlantian inscriptions, shall be unearthed. Yea, some have already been discovered (though they have been attributed to Egyptian antiquities), that will give evidence of these facts!

USH AT'LAN-TI-AN LE-E'GRU U-RE'TA NUD RE-RE'TA RE-ELT'ZE,

OR

ATLANTIAN FIGURES FOR THE CARDINAL AND ORDINAL NUMBERS.

The following diagram and vocabulary will be sufficient to give the reader a very good idea of the Atlantian Cardinal and Ordinal Numbers, as used in the time of the third Efremetrum:

Ĕt Wē Sĕt Kĕt Zrĕt

1. 2. 3. 4. 5.

Sŏt Zŭm Ĕst Ŏnt Trŭm

6. 7. 8. 9. 10.

Ē-tēte Thrĭst Frwĭth Fē-tēte Dē-rēte

20. 30. 40. 50. 60.

Sĕn'-tē Ē'-the Nē'-thē Ŏn'-thre Tēlt'-tiē

70. 80. 90. 100. 1000.

Atl'n.	Eng.	Atl'n.	Eng.
Et	One	Etz	First
Wē	Two	Wĕz	Second
Sĕt	Three	Sĕtz	Third
Kĕt	Four	Kĕtz	Fourth
Zrĕt	Five	Zrĕtz	Fifth
Sŏt	Six	Sŏtz	Sixth
Zŭm	Seven	Zŭmz	Seventh
Est	Eight	Estz	Eighth
Ont	Nine	Ontz	Ninth
Trŭm	Ten	Trŭmz	Tenth

NOTE.—The ordinal numbers, from the first to the tenth, inclusive, are formed by adding "Ze" to the cardinal:

Et'zē	Eleven	Et-zē'	Eleventh
Wē'zē	Twelve	Wē-zē'	Twelfth
Sĕt'zē	Thirteen	Sĕt-zē'	Thirteenth
Kĕt'zē	Fourteen	Kĕt-zē'	Fourteenth
Zrĕt'zē	Fifteen	Zrĕt-zē'	Fifteenth
Sŏt'zē	Sixteen	Sŏt-zē'	Sixteenth
Zŭm'zē	Seventeen	Zŭm-zē'	Seventeenth
Est'zē	Eighteen	Est-zē'	Eighteenth
Ont'zē	Nineteen	Ont-zē'	Nineteenth

NOTE.—The only distinction between the cardinal and the ordinal numbers, from eleven to nineteen, inclusive, is in the accent of the syllables; the cardinal having the accent on the first, and the ordinal on the last.

E'tēte	Twenty
E-tēte-zē'	Twentieth
Et'nŭd ē-tēte	One and twenty
Etz'nŭd ē-tēte-zē'	First and twentieth
Thrĭst	Thirty
Thrĭst-zē'	Thirtieth
Et'nŭd thrĭst	One and thirty
Etz' nŭd thrĭst-zē'	First and thirtieth
Frū'ĭth	Forty
Frū-ĭth-zē'	Fortieth
Et'nŭd frū-ĭth	One and forty
Etz'nŭd frū-ĭth-zē'	First and fortieth
Fē'tēte	Fifty
Fē-tēte-zē'	Fiftieth
Et'nŭd fē-tēte	One and fifty

Etz'nŭd fē-tēte-zē'	First and fiftieth
Cē'rete	Sixty
Cē-rēte-zē'	Sixtieth
Et'nŭd cē-rēte	One and sixty
Etz'nŭd cē-rēte-zē'	First and Sixtieth
Sĕn'tē	Seventy
Sĕn-tē-zē'	Seventieth
Et'nŭd sĕn-tē	One and seventy
Etz'nŭd sĕn-tē-zē'	First and seventieth
E'thē	Eighty
E-thē-zē'	Eightieth
Et'nŭd ē-thē	One and eighty
Etz'nŭd ē-thē-zē'	First and eightieth
Nē'thē	Ninety
Nē-thē-zē'	Ninetieth
Et'nŭd nē-thē	One and ninety
Etz'nŭd nē-thē-zē'	First and ninetieth
On'thrĕ	One hundred
On-thrē-zē'	One hundredth
Et'nŭd ŏn-thrē-zē'	One hundred and one
Et'nŭd ŏn-thrē	First and one hundredth
Tĕl'tiē	One thousand
Tĕ-tiē-zē'	One thousandth
Et'nŭd tĕl-tiē	One and one thousand
Etz'nŭd tĕl-tiē-zē'	One and one thousandth

NOTE.—The above table can be made complete by prefixing a cardinal or ordinal number, from one to ten, and from first to tenth, to each denomination, e. g., We nud e-tete, two and twenty; Wez nud e-tete-ze, second and twentieth; Set nud, e-tete, three and twenty; Setz nud e-tete-ze, third and twentieth, etc.

The Atlantian figures, like the alphabet, have found re-embodiment in subsequent alphabets and numebrs; e. g., Et, or I, is found in the Phœnician and old Hebrew alphabets, and the modern eighth rest sign in music; We, or 2, in the old Hebrew alphabet, slightly changed obliquely; in the Phœnician and Moabitic, slightly changed, and in the modern sixteenth rest; Set,, or 3, in the Ancient Phœnician, Moabitic and old Hebrew alphabets, and modern thirty-second rest; Zret, or 5, in the ancient Phœnician and early Greek and Latin alphabets; Sot, or 6, in the hieratic Egyptian numbers and in Greek letters, slightly changed; Est, or 8, same as Sot, or 6, though with a little more change; Ont, or 9, in the hieratic figures; the Cipher, in the Egyptian, Phœnician, Moabitic, old Hebrew, Greek, Latin and English alphabets, etc.

USH AT'LAN-TI-AN RE-LAN'SE,

OR

THE ATLANTIAN CALENDAR.

The Atlantian Yĕlt (year) was established by civil, and not astronomical calculations. It was divided into 12 Ash-nör'zē (months) viz: (1) Qŭin (March); (2) Dĭn (April); (3) Lŭll (May); (4) Rĕ-sĕt', (June); (5) Lūte (July); (6) Gē-ĭst' (August); (7) Sĭn-lēte' (September); (8) Ar'bŭt (October); (9) Kā-mūte' (November); (10) Em-blēze' (December); (11) Yër (January); and (12) Alt (February).

Invariably there were 28 Yēte'zē (days) in each Ashnor. The Yētē (day) record began at 3 A. M., and the Wĭljĕt (night) at 9 P. M. The Yelt began with Quin, which therefore was the first Ashnor in the Atlantian Yelt, instead of Yer, as is the case with the modern Almanac, and it closed with Altz, instead of Embleze.

The Relanse divisions of time into 12 Ashnorze for the Yelt, and the Păn-tī-nū'sä, or ephemeris divisions, into 28 Yeteze for the Ashnor, established an Almanac of only 336 Yeteze to the Yelt. According to the modern Calendar there would yet remain 29 Yeteze, at the close of the 12 regular Ashnorze, and 30 at the expiration of every fourth year, before the solar period for the beginning of another Yelt.

This period of 29 Yeteze between the Ashnorze Alt and Din, was termed Ez-rē-mance' which meant intervening time, and in place of an intercalation record of one Yete in every four Yeltze, caused by the additional 5 Lŏut'zē (hours), 48 Rē-nĕt'zē (minutes), and 46 Bĕl'zē (seconds), of the solar time, which occurs annually, as accounted for in the Julius Cæsar period, or as in the present Calendar systems, and recorded at the end of every four years as that of the "leap-year" condition, the Atlantians made an intervening Ezremance of 30 Yeteze every fourth Yelt, which rendered a corresponding result. Therefore, at the close of the Ashnor of Alt, 29 Yeteze were passed over, or omitted from the Relanse for three successive Yeltzie, and 30 Yeteze for the fourth Yelt, when the civil Yelt began again on the first of Quin, March.

Just here Yermah informs us that "the now known Julian

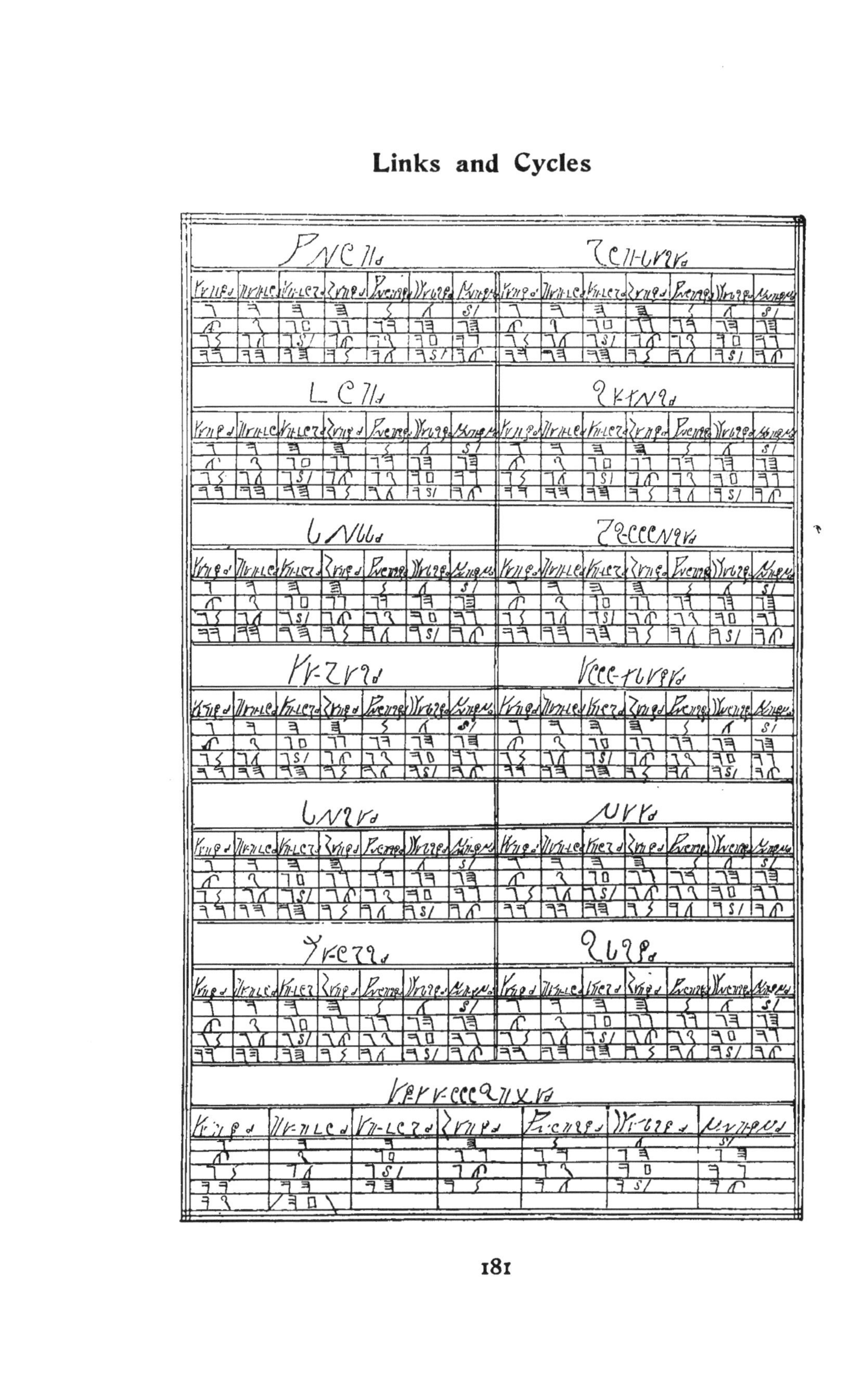

Calendar or division of time, is a re-embodied idea of the Atlantians, conceived and re-established through both spirit and historic influences;" viz., before the time of the Ptolemies, an Atlantian spirit, who as a mortal was known by the name of Ar-ē-tē′-pō′lŭs, revealed the idea of the Atlantian Relanse, or Calendar, unto an Egyptian by the name of A-man′zē-răs, who dwelt in the Nile region, between the Third and Fourth Cataracts, near the now known town of Merawi, who made a plan and record of it.

Through this revelation, as recorded by Amanzeras, as was the case with other remnant and inspired revelations that had been recorded from time to time, it found its way into the great Alexandrian Library, where it was archived as valuable evidence of Atlantian existence.

In subsequent time, Spirit Aretepolus influenced the minds of Sosigenes and Julius Cæsar, and revealed unto them, principally through the Cacellaship of Sosigenes, the idea of the Atlantian Relense, at the opportune time when the Roman Calendar, as established by Numa, was in such an indefinite condition. And he further informed them of the existence of the record of the Amanzeras, in the Alexandrian Library. Therefore Julius Cæsar sought evidence verifying the fact. He possessed himself of the knowledge that they there existed, by a copy of the same, after which he, Cæsar, by the advice and assistance of Sosigenes, abolished the intercalations, as per the Roman year Calendar, by Numa, and robbed the pontifices of their power to change the same to the convenience of themselves and their friends, and established the divisions of time now known as the "Julian Year."

He further informs us that the records as made by Amanzeras, which had been revealed to him by Aretepolus, and collected by the Ptolemies along with the other Atlantian records above referred to, were subsequently lost, during the time intervening between Cæsar, Caracella and Diaclatias, and the disgraceful pillage of the Library in 389, A. D., under the rule of the Christian Bishop, Theophilus.

USH AT'LAN-TI-AN MA-RE-TUX'ZE,
OR
THE ATLANTIAN MONUMENTS.

TELTZIE XXII.

Yĕr'mäh further informs us that, in the great Tyn'gĕr (valley) of Atara, suburban to the aistie of Atara, stood the great Mä-rē'tŭx (the term signifying "to learn"), or national Monument. This Maretux was triangular in form (see cut), so constructed as to symbolize the three principles, Wisdom, Love and Truth. It was composed of three parts, viz., pedestal, column and cap-stone, so placed as to further symbolize the trinity, Nencie, Lemaz and Wotz, or Time, Space and Life. The cap-stone was drawn to an apex, in harmony with the triangular form of the base and shaft of the Maretux. The height from the base to the apex was about 100 coitex or feet. The diameter of each of the three parts was of proportionate dimension. The material from which it was constructed was of a lava formation, having a sheen similar to that of the Obsidian formations, as now found in Ethiopia, and the Yellowstone Park of the United States of America. It was quarried from the Aelkedze near Atara, and afterwards transported to the place of its erection. This was done by animal force, as electricity had not come into use as a motive force at that period of time. This material was used principally for the construction of Maretuxze, or monuments.

The erection or construction of this great Maretux was begun by Găl-thä'zä, the first Efremetrum of the Lontidri, at the time he established the Atlantian Republic. He gave the structure the name of "Maretux," as being suitable for the Nencie of Dĕl-zē-mär-ĭc'sĕs, or "time of Governmental records."

At the time of its completion, Galthaza's effigy was sculptured on one side of it (the side not visible in our cut), together with three inscriptions, selected from his Delzemaricses principles, as follows:

First inscription:

The translation is, May my reign be in justice.

Second inscription:

The translation—Kā'lä give me wisdom.

Third inscription:

The translation—Kala help the people to be more like unto thyself.

According to the plan laid down by Galthaza, it became the custom at the beginning of the term of office, for each succeeding Efremetrum to place on the Maretux three inscriptions, giving expression to his chief thoughts, for the spiritual education of the people, who read them, and contemplated them together with his cffigy.

As was the case with all inscriptions placed in public places during the first Efremetrumze, and early part of the third, those on the Maretux were subjected to the condition of abbreviation, so far as the characters were concerned, some individual ones being understood by the peoples of those periods as "word signs," and some as "syllable signs," while in some cases the entire word was written out by characters belonging to the period of time and locality, when recorded. It must be remembered that the alphabet differed in the various Teltzie, even in the same periods of time; and furthermore it sustained changes under the management of the different Efremetrumze, developing into a better and more complete system of writing during each succeeding Efremetrum, until in the last half of the third, the language was written out in entirety, as is the custom in modern times. Therefore a parallel case with the developments from the pre-historic to the ancient; an ultimate result of the modern methods of inscription and chirography; which latter is but a re-embodied idea, or link from the Atlantian linguistic and chirographic epi-cycle, through which that connection must be made, the nearest representative being in the Egyptian method, of ancient periods, which latter is an offspring from the Atlantian.

Furthermore, differences in relation to the parts of speech are to be encountered, when translating from the Atlantian to the English, and other languages, which make the characters seem inadequate to syllabification, or word formations, in the early Atlantian writing or inscriptions, e. g., the words "or" and "is" of the English, which have no representative terms in the Atlantian, etc.

We have divided the words and characters in the inscriptions and translations of the ancient Atlantian, with commas, so that the reader may see how many characters are required for the translation of the words.

In the first Efremetrum and even prior to that time, the term Kā'lä was used in the sense of "God.". In the second, the term was changed to Gā-hä'lä, which continued into the early part of the third, when, under the teaching of Alem Prolex, it was changed to Gä'lä.

When Goĕt'lĕz, who was chosen from Teltzie Zret, came into office as the second Efremetrum, he brought the influence of the language, and character representation of the same, from his Teltzie, and according to the cutsom above referred to, his effigy and spiritual inscriptions were placed upon the second side of the Maretux, and were as follows:

First inscription,

The translation—Out, of, the, darkness, cometh, the, light.

Second inscription,

The translation—Have, you, found, the, truth, within, your, own, souls?

Third inscription,

The translation, Gabala, dwells, within, let, him, show, himself.

When Alem Prolex, who was chosen from Teltzie Et, came into office, as the third and last Efrmetrum of the Lontidri, his effigy and spiritual thoughts were sculptured similarly to those of his predecessors, upon the third side of the Maretux.

First inscription,

The tranlation, Gahala, within; Gahala, in all; Seek, in, thy, soul, the, greater, Gahala, you, will, find.

Second inscription,

The translation—The soul, in, nature, may, be, revealed, A, law, A, divine, truth.

Third inscription,

The translation—As, the, sun, gives, light, reaching, everywhere, so, let, the, truth, of Gahala, search, your, souls.

During the latter part of the second Efremetrum, an inscription was placed upon each side of the cap-stone of the Maretux, as follows:

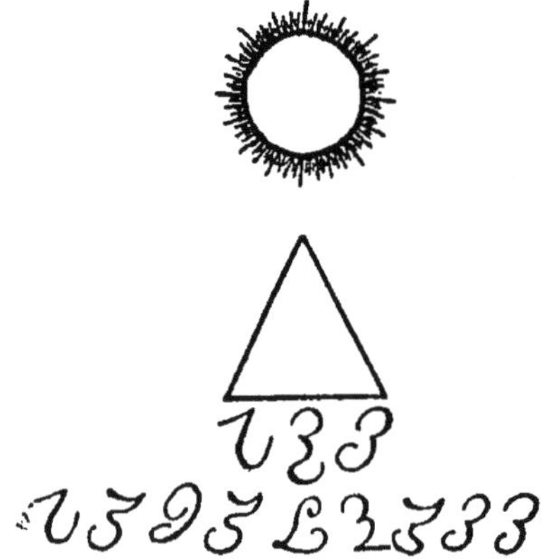

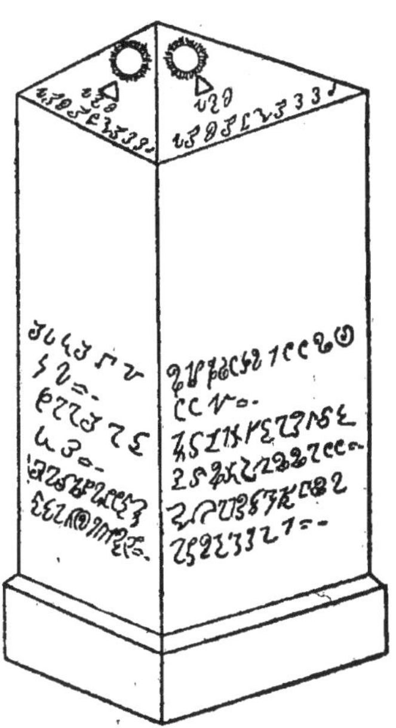

USH IN-THA-O'ZA MA-RE'TUX SI AT'LAN-TIS.

Following is a chirographic illustration of the foregoing inscriptions on the Maretux, as they appeared in the Atlantian language, written in Teltzie Et, in the third or last Efremetrum:

Following are the Atlantian and English translations of the nine inscriptions of the Efremetrumze, that had place on the Maretux, as written in the latter part of the third Efremetrum, which shows the development in the chirographic art, and the linguistic differences among the three Efremetrumze, in that respect:

1. Gēl cĕlt ĕn′ nĕt lē ĕnt kŭt′cē
   May my reign be in justice.
2. Kä′lä quĕt lĕt mĕn′dĕn.
   God give me wisdom.
3. Kä′lä lĕp ŭsh grē′āte ĕt lē frĕl lēse lĕs′ĕt trĭst.
   God help the people to be more like unto thyself.
4. Ors sī ush dĕz′ry zē-rē′ăth ŭsh sū-tly.
   Out of the darkness cometh the light.
5. Hăl ŭz grĕst ŭsh hĭst cör′ī-tĕn ŭz′ē tĕs′zē?
   Have you found the truth within your souls?
6. Gā-hä′lä lĕs′tĭs cör′ī-tĕn ŭt sī′tër ër′ŏn sī-tër-ŏn′tes lŭt′ĕnt.
   God dwells within, let him show himself without.
7. Gā-hä′lä cör′ī-tĕn Gā-hä′lä ĕnt nū krĕt ĕnt trī tēs ŭsh quĕl′tër Gä-hä′lä ŭz ĕlt clĕd.
   God within, God in all, seek in thy soul, the greater God you will find.
8. Ush tĕs ĕnt zä′tĕn gĕt lē lēd-mēde ĕnt ŏnts clăt tel′tä-ĕc hĭst·
   The soul in nature may be revealed in self, a law, a divine truth.
9. Tĕs ŭsh tĕt quē′trē sūtry mĭl-lĕnt′ vĕn′tī-lē ĕs kĕt ŭsh hĭst sī Gä-hä′lä păl′zy ŭz′ē tĕs′zē
   As the sun gives light reaching everywhere, so let the truth of God search your souls.

The reader will note that the term Kala in the second and third inscriptions of the first Efremetrum, is represented by three characters, a partial syllabication, a linguistic influence having arisen from the teachings of Galthaza, who had been chosen as Efremetrum from Teltzie Zret, and wrote and spoke the language of that Teltzie; also that the term Gabala, in the third inscription of the second Efremetrum, is represented with but two characters, entirely different from those of the first, a condition due to a change of language and characters by Goetlez, who had been chosen as Efremetrum from Teltzie Set; another example of partial syllabication, thus influenced by the language as spoken by Goetlez, who was more familiar with that used in Teltzie Set;

that the term Gahala, in the first and third inscriptions of the third Efremetrum, is represented by only one character, unlike any one of the above, due to abbreviated changes that had taken place during the latter part of the second Efremetrum, an example of single word signs; that the term Gahala, beneath the triangle in the cap-stone of the Maretux, is represented by three characters, unlike any of those above mentioned; so influenced by character changes that had arisen from linguistic developments natural to the period of time in which they were placed on the Maretux; an example of pure syllabication, viz., divided into three syllables, the first character representing "Ga,' the second "ha," and the third, "la."

Another idea entertained by Goetlez, when separating the inscription for Gabala into three characters, was to carry out the symbolic idea of the triangle, which latter was represented above the inscription. This was also the case on the Temple of the Illustrate Dead Bodies, the only difference being in the character writing that took place during the lapse of time intervening between the placements of the two, viz: those on the Maretux, during the latter part of the second Efremetrum, those on the Temple, during the early part of the third·

The disc above the triangle was intended as a representation of Ush Kĕn (the sun), and symbolized Gahala, of that period, and Gala, of the latter part of the third Efremetrum. The disc was formed by Zĭn'dē'lēte Zī-tē'zē (crystal mosaics), and the radiations of U'ziē (gold), placed to reflect the light of the sun so it could be seen for miles up the Tynger. The triangle, as represented beneath the image of Ken, symbolizd All Things; and the entire inscription, beneath the triangle, was descriptive of the entire thought as embodied in the two symbols above, viz: *Gahala, all things,* and later, *Gala, all things,* or *God in all existence.*

In the northern portion of the Tynger, between the Maretux and the Kelete, were numerous Maretuxze which had been erected from time to time for the purpose, as it were, of dramatizing religious, natural and scientific principles, in connection with various facts in Atlantian history.

One of these Maretuxze was known as the Kē'dĕst E-ŏn'try, the term meaning " a wayside shrine," and was a perfectly plain structure. It had only one main entrance, with an opening to admit the light. In the interior, against the rear wall, was a very large stone tank, which was constantly filled with water, and represented the Great Spring of Life. The continuous flow of water represented the everlasting Purity of Gahala, a principle which all mankind should seek to possess. Above the tank was an inscription read by the frequenters of the shrine, as follows: Zrī'ăld ĕt Gä-hä'lä (Sacred to God)· Beneath the inscription was the image of the Ken, represented with a disc and golden radiations.

This Kedest Eontry was for the utility of the people from the country, who, when passing to and from the aistie, would halt for the time, that they might rest, cleanse themselves, and worship Gahala. Before drinking of the water, each individual would, on bended knee, offer the following impressive prayer unto Gahala: "Tĕs vy vĕs'tē ĕnt ŭsh lū-tiē' vĕs'lĕy ĕx'ō Gä-hä'-lä lĕp ĕt lŭt-tē'ny tĕs nŭd bălt;" which, translated into English, is as follows: "As we bathe in the pure waters, so God help us to purify soul and body.

Another of the Maretuxze was known as the Ex'trē-phŏn, the term meaning an "up-reaching for greater purity." It was a lofty and impressive structure, about 100 coitex square, tapering at the top, and was built of enormous blocks of stone, the latter being so perfectly matched and highly polished as to give the structure the appearance of a giant monolith There were no inscriptions on it, but by its colossal form, it was understood to symbolize the greatness and wisdom of Gahala, and the force of that principle throughout creation; and thus played its part in the silent drama being enacted by the Maretuxze, for the benefit of the people who passed and re-passed, enroute through the great Tynger of Atara

Near the Kelete was another Maretux, known as the A-sē-nō'rĕt, the term meaning "a place of pleasure." It was a large and beautiful structure surmounted by the figure of an Ant'lī-ĕr (an Atlantian animal of the wilds), sculptured in recumbent position, with his feet projecting in front, and his head turned as if looking back toward the aistie. It was thus erected and held sacred as a memorial of "soul knowledge" and "educational attainments" that were possessed through its development; conditions that lead the individual from the crude, uncivilized state into which they have fallen to the condition of betterment, of both soul and body. Amid the adornments which Nature had placed about, and in the vicinity of the Maretux, seats were interspersed for the utility of those who sought the place for rest and quiet.

In the aistie of Listrio was another colossal Maretux, known as the An'tī-lē-ŏn, the term meaning "Place of Worship·" It was constructed under the direction of Yermah the Deltsanz of the Teltzie, and was a very beautiful structure, composed of gray Signitie (Marble), and ornamented with Kintlin (White Stone).

Its foundation was 100 coitex square. The foundation, or pedestal, was an elevation of three combined bases, each relatively smaller than the one on which it rested; i. e., each super-base was about 3 coitex less in dimension than its sub-base, and each of the three bases was about 6 coitex in height, thus making the combined base about 18 coitex in height. From the compound base rose a colossal shaft to the height of about 80 coitex. Each corner of the shaft was crowned with a block of Kintlin, and from these, of the same material, rose four smaller shafts, one from each block, that supported a large Kintlin basin, in which pure water from the rain-fall was gathered. On the front of the base of this great Maretux were three large steps of Kintlin which led up to a grotto-like opening in the first section of the base, through which one might enter. Within this section a flight of Kintlin steps ascended to the third, or upper section of the base, which was divided into four chambers. On one side of each chamber a large tank was located. Square Kintlin tubes or pipes connected these with the basin on the summit, through which the water passed from it into the tanks. These were also utilized as conductors of air from the lower chambers to the outer atmosphere at the summit. In connection with the basin there was an apparatus by which the flow of water was controlled. The walls and floors of the four chambers were of solid Kintlin. There was an exterior opening from each chamber, through which to admit light and air. These chambers were dedicated to the four seasons of the year, at which times, on stated days, or four times a year, the people from the aistie and surrounding country gathered there for religions services. Each individual brought a large vessel, in which to carry away some of the sacred water from the tanks for a bath at home. As each person entered to get his supply of sacred water, he first placed his vessel on the white tank, then knelt down on one knee, raised both hands, palms together, above his head, and uttered a prayer. This was in such words as the soul prompted. Then rising, he filled the vessel and departed in peace. Above each tank was the following inscription:

The following is a translation of the foregoing inscription, according to the language and characters, as utilized in Teltzie Zret, in the third Efremetrum:

Tēs mūse ĕnt ŭsh lĕr ĕl-zĕs′ĕs Gä′lä lĕp lĕt lĕr-rĕz′ clētz nŭd cō-dī′zē.

As I bathe in the pure waters, so God help me purify soul and body.

The tanks were at all times kept sacredly clean and pure. The only inscription on the exterior of the Maretux was as follows·

En′thŭs lĕs-ĕt′ Gä′lä.

Sacred unto God.

Small Maretuxze of this kind were erected all over the Lontidri, but were built in accord with the taste of the people in the Teltzie where they were located.

In a beautiful Cergu, in the center of the great white aistie of Miezietory, was a magnificent Maretux known as the E-lŏnkĕt′rē. It was constructed as a symbol of certain principles, and also as an artistic ornament, suitable to adorn the beautiful aistie. Its solitary base and approaches covered an area about 200 coitex square. The base was 10 coitex in width and the same in height. It was characterized with an opening in front, to which an approach was made by a flight of steps. The top was adorned with a square projection on the center of each side, the base conforming to their shape· In each projection, excepting the front one, was a large opening. Above the solitary base rose the main shaft, to the height of 50 coitex. Above this a shaft of lesser dimension rose to about 15 coitex. This was crowned with a beautiful dome, upon which were represented geometrical and astronomical characters; and finally, from the dome, rose a central standard of Cletie (silver), in the form of a cross, the three points of which outlined the triangle· From the three points were radiations of Uzie (gold), thus outlining three small triangles, which gave the effect of a triangle of triangles.

The exterior of the base and shafts was solid; but the dome was one great hall with arched openings on each side for observatory purposes, and furnished seats for public use. A rotunda extended from dome to base, around which was a spiral stairway, by which to reach the dome hall. The dome was supported by four walls, which thus divided the base and shaft into four rooms that extended in height from base to dome. Arched openings in each wall afforded entrance and exit from room to room, as well as to the rotunda. The exterior was adorned with equestrian statues, which were placed on either side the opening leading to the rotunda. The one on the right was that of a female figure, seated upon an Hittraina. She was in stately pose with garments gracefully floating backwards, as if in rapid flight. Her head was adorned simply with a wreath of leaves. She held out a partially unrolled manuscript, on which the following inscription was wrought in golden characters, for the people to read:

[illegible]

Following is the translation of the foregoing inscription, according to the language and character writing in Teltzie Ket, in the third Efremetrum:

Tŭn lū nĕh ŭsh cē'lūth sī nū mĕn'dĕn ŭn gĕlt ĕm sī thŭn nălt ŭn gēl tĭz nŭd kē-mē'lĕt nū nălt Gä'lä gĕlt lăv ŭn lē.

Thou who art the representative of all wisdom, we would ask of thee that we may know and understand all that God would have us be.

Note.—The term "un" was used for both pronouns, "we" and "us," the context governing the same.

On the left was a male figure, seated in a stately position upon a Zĕn'thrä (Atlantian animal), his only garment being a plain, loose robe, that extended down to his feet. Nothing adorned his head excepting a flowing suit of hair. He held a sceptre, crowned with a golden anchor, in his hand. This statue was intended to represent or symbolize Trust, or the anchorage of the soul in Gala; and that Gala had given to man the force to overcome all things, if he so willed it.

The general symbolic idea of the entire structure was in itself a drama to the people. In its height and beauty they saw that which portrayed the force of Gala to construct the "all beautiful," which through contemplation brought to them the light of truth; in its whiteness, the purity of the light of truth, such as came to them from above; in the sheen of the Uzie and the Cletie, the beautiful light that adorns the spirit after it has left the material form, as it gathers wisdom, and blends into conditions of knowledge and truth. In the Zenthra, they recognized strength and endurance. So should man, when going forth on his missions in life, do so with great determination, and by being forcible and strong in every effort, conquer all things. In the Hittraina, they recognized the quality of fleetness, which should attend their efforts in life. In the female who was represented as riding it, the affection and love that quietly and mildly conquer where all else fails; and a virtue that should at all times accompany the conquests in life, in whatever avenue they may be.

At'LAN-TI-AN MEL'LA-CES NUD EL-TA-ME'DES A-GAL-TE'ZE,

OR

ATLANTIAN PRIMITIVE AND ERECTED TEMPLES.

TELTZIE XXIII.

The primitive Mĕl-lā-cēs A-găl-tē'zē of Atlantis, Yermah informs us, were built without hands, and adorned without the aid of the wealth of mortals, for they were of Nature's formation.

All the Aelkedze of the Lontidri were characterized with Heltroploxze (caves), which the people held sacred because of their natural formation, and were therefore used as Mellaces Agalteze, in which the Deltsanza taught the people of the earlier periods, regardng the Gahala principle in Nature.

To an Atlantian, the Heltroploxze represented a coming nearer to the Gahala in all Nature, and were therefore used by them as Nature's Temples.

In the famous Ceitux Aelkede, of the Ceitux terranzi, adjacent to the aistie of Atara, was located a Heltroplox Kito (Cave Temple) for educational purposes. At certain times during the day, people could be seen going in and out, others standing at the entrance awaitng the hour for the beginning of special instruction. The Deltsanza entered the Heltroplox clad in their raiment of office, and ofttimes, just inside the entrance, could be seen some poor unfortunate mortals, posed in a crouched position, thus hoping to attract the attention of the Deltsanza as they passed to the interior of the Heltroplox. Being conscious of their unworthiness to approach the Deltsanza, or the sacred Kito where they taught the people, the unfortunate would halt just inside, hoping to speak to them as they passed by, that thus they might receive instruction such as would lead them into better conditions.

On a platform of Nature's own creation, far in the interior, in one of the chambers of the Heltroplox, the Deltsanza, in their procession, with the Efremetrum, or Supreme Deltsanz of the Lontidri, at the head, took their respective positions for the purpose of imparting knowledge to the people there assembled.

It was a beautiful sight to see the people in the act of assemblage, enroute to take their places before the Deltsanza, which latter were reverenced by the people as Deltsanza torze Gahala (Teachers from God).

The method of instructing adopted by the Deltsanz was to place large placards on various jutting rocks, as natural easels, before the people, on which were written certain principles and rules, which they proceeded to explain and comment upon, as the occasion afforded, and the needs of the people demanded. They taught that Gahala was the "enduring spirit of life," and that which was life should be light, in the sense of knowledge and understanding; that there must be a purity of principle, and that in order to rule, there must be child-like simplicity, especially in matters pertaining to the existence on the material side of life, or on the material plane.

This grade of instruction being completed, the people were taken into another chamber of the Heltroplox, which by its grandeur, symbolized the passing of the spirit and its soul-body from that of the mortal body.

The grandeur of this chamber was very impressive. It was brilliant with rare gems, crystals, stalactites and stalagmites, upon which a mysterious light was thrown, such as filled each soul with awe and reverence. In this chamber the people were taught that only those who were developed for it could enter the glorious condition of immaterial life; and that this condition did not exist on the earth plane; but development, like that of passing from one chamber to another, would ultimately bring them into grander conditions, as they would pass through the realms beyond the material.

By the great extent of this chamber, when contrasted with the preceding one, a comparison was made between the mortal and the spiritual existence; and it was also a symbol of the vastness of eternal Nencie (Time), Lemaz (Space), and Wotz (Life).

The people were taught that as the stalactites and the stalagmites met, in their process of formation, and varied in size and length, the principle was analogous to man and his conditions, and represented his development spiritually; that the downward probing of the stalactites, to reach the point of the stalagmites, symbolized forces as coming from the celestial realm to the terrestrial, where a union of forces from the two took place, for the ultimate uplifting of all souls to a higher condition; and that there was also symbolized the source of the guidance as coming from the higher realm, to influence growth and development spiritually and morally. It also represented knowledge of the past as coming from the same source.

The stalactites and the stalagmites having already met, symbolized the forces as having already begun their work. Those not having met, symbolized the natural aim of the forces to bring about that result. Those with no visible opposite formation, like positive forces without the negative, in co-operation, symbolized lives without reciprocal balance, and of no definite aim.

The people were also taught that the same forces, such as had blended in the ages past for the development of knowledge and wisdom, such as sustain the spiritual part of man, were in like manner operating in their time of life, and would so continue for all time to come; that by and through these forces, man could rise sufficiently high spiritually, to enter a condition wherein he might receive the light from the temple of wisdom and knowledge, which would enable him to see that he was a part of the Gahala, and Gahala a part of him; and that his purity of growth was the result of the blending of light and knowledge.

All the dark chambers symbolized conditions of mortal souls, before the spiritual development began.

The deep, unexplored chambers symbolized conditions into which a soul might be plunged during its material existence, by the influence of undeveloped spirits and mortal conditions, that might overthrow their material plans in life; a result neither easily gotten out of, nor away from. The submergence of parts of the Lontidri, and the depths to which the people had sunk, were often taken as a symbolic lesson, or as examples of the latter. This had a great influence over the people who dwelt in the remaining portions of the Lontidri, for the Atlantians, in their study of natural cause and effect, found an accompanying symbol of comparative principles. The former was demonstrated by restorations from obsession, made through treatment of the Atlantian healing Că-cĕl-lă'za (healing spirit sensitives), by spirit influence, in the Agalteze or Pelzoze (Temples) on occasions special for that purpose. In fact, all diseases were treated by "spirit influence," through the organisms of the Atlantian Cacellaza, who were developed for that purpose.

The Heltroploxze were used both as Primitive Temples and as repositories for the mummified bodies of the people generally, until the time of the erection of Pelzoze and Agalteze, for that purpose; after which they were used only for the bodies of the common people, and the Pelzoze and Agalteze, erected exclusively for that purpose, such as "The Temple of the Illustrate

Dead Bodies" at Atara, became repositories for the bodies of celebrities.

The Heltroploxze became sacred as Pelzoze and Agalteze of worship, from the fact that it was supposed by the Atlantian people that Gatlins, an Atlantian Geologist, when exploring them, conceived his idea of the Gahala Principle, which he established and taught to the people during his latter days as a mortal. From these the Gala, or God Principle, of the third Efremetrum was taken and re-established as such. The term "Gatlins" signified "revealer."

From the teachings of Gatlins there descended to the minds of the people the idea that Gahala had prepared the Heltroploxze for their utility, as places of worship, and repositories for mortal bodies; after the disembodiment of the spirit, which latter had departed unto the zone where Gahala dwelt; consequently they were used as such.

The erection of Pelzoze and Agalteze began in the second Efremetrum, and were crude in comparison with those of the third; but they were the links between the Heltroploxze, or primitive places of worship, and those of the grand edifices of the third Efremetrum.

The principal Pelzo (temple), of the second Efremetrum, was known as Ush Nĕz Pĕl'zō Sī Qū-ē'sä (The Old Temple of Peace), by the people outside of Teltzie Et; by those of Teltzie Et, as Ush Nĕz A-găl'tē Sī Qū-ē'sä, especially so in the time of the third Efremterum, when the term "Pelzo" was changed to "Agalte," in Teltzie Et only.

This old Pelzo was built upon the foothills of the Ceitux Aelkedze, overlooking the great aistie of Atara. From this location views could be had far up and down the great Tynger of Atara, in which the aistie lay, and up and down the Belteer Riger, which in its meandering course flowed southward between the Aelkedze and the east side of the aistie, and far away to the west, from south of the aistie, through the extent of the great Tynger, toward the great Amizone Riger, thus disclosing to view Nature in its marvelous beauty; giving to the individual who viewed it that divine inspiration that emanates from Gala, the God Principle in Nature, which lifts man higher, intellectually and spiritually. Over the Pelzo was an image of the Ken. The people, when entering the Pelzo, would uncover their heads, remain standing in silence for a moment before the image, believing it to be a representation of Gahala's light in the act of descending upon them, through which he saw and recognized them; and it therefore became the symbol of the act, a fact that made the symbol very sacred to them. For this reason the Ken, or Sun, was adopted as the principal symbol of Gala, during subsequent periods. As it was placed on this old Pelzo in the second Efremetrum, so it was placed on those of the third; as for example, on Ush Trūne A-găl'tē Sī Qū-ē'sä (The New Temple of Peace); Ush A-găl'tē Sī Ush Nē-cē'lē-tŭs Mĕl'zē (The Temple Of the Illustrate Dead); and also added to the great Maretux during the third Efremetrum.

The New Temple of Peace, in the aistie of Atara, was a structure of rare beauty, and was constructed out of Kintlin, or White Stone, from the Miezietory Aelkedze. In form, it might be said to have been hexagonal, though it had additional juttings on the walls of each side, similar to the bay-windows of modern strue-tures. On the exterior of each were arched windows, and the interior conformed to the same arched shape. Each exterior arch was adorned with a human statue, whose right hand was posed with the index finger pointing upward. On the arches of the windows, beneath the statues, were exquisite carvings in the stone, of various fruits and flowers, which gave to the exterior walls a charming appearance. The roof was somewhat on the order of the modern Mansard. Around the top were Kintlin balustrades, three coitex apart. These were most artistically carvd in designs of animal and human forms, with accompanying landscapes, which constituted an elaborate ornamentation. Each corner of the roof was adorned with additional spires of silver-colored metal, terminating with gold-colored points. Each balustrade was crowned with a quadrangular piece of Kintlin, adorned with carvings similar to those on the balusters, with the addition of miniature spires, of silver color, with golden-colored points, to harmonize with the corner spires. On the facade was a portico, with entrance, and a flight of Kintlin steps leading up to it. Massive pillars supported the top. Archways extended from pillar to pillar, on the front and sides, making three in number. The top of the portico extended up in form corresponding with the main roof, only that it terminated in the form of a spire of the silver-colored metal, pointed with the golden color. Upon the front of the portico roof, in the center, was a representation of the sun, about two-thirds arisen, with the rays extending upward and outward at the sides, over a clear horizon, thus to represent Morning. Just below this scene, on one side, was a male figure, and on the other, that of a female, each kneeling upon one knee, looking up to the sun, with hands clasped, palms togther, as if in the act of offering an invocation to Gala. This ornamentation was in bas-relief, and most beautifully wrought on the Kintlin.

All the carvings on this Agalte were wrought by some of the most talented Celporze (sculptors) of Atlantis, whose works are not surpassed by those of any historic sculptor.

The interior dimensions were about 100 by 150 coitex. The roof was supported by four massive Kĭs-ā-rē'zē (columns) with a small one on each side of it. The bases of the Kisareze were beautifully sculptured in representation of vines; and the flat stone Kĕn-dē-măz'ĕz (capitals) were in three sections, each smaller in succession and highly ornamented, in diamond-shaped lattice-like carvings, with a star inside each diamond. The Kendemazez were of Kistlin material. The four outer Kisareze were connected by a Gothic frame-work, which extended within 10 coitex of the top; thus forming four facades, as it were, facing the four points of the compass. Inside of these were angular stairs that led up to the openings in the Gothic frames, where the Deltsanza stood, as they taught the people. From the platform, the Deltsanza could pass through interior openings to any one of the other facades, and thus could speak from any side, during the service, as the occasion might demand. At times this was necessary, especially on occasions of large assemblies, when of necessity the people were seated in circular rows, and thus congregated on all sides. On occasions when the assemblies were small, the people were seated in semi-circular form. The Gothics were entirely constructed out of sculptured Kintlin. All the seats in the Agalte were of the same material, beautifully sculptured, in designs of various fruits and flowers. Beautiful Jēsts (urns) were placed at the entrance of the Agaite, which were always filled with flowers, or plants of perpetual bloom.

By the symbols on the Pelzoze, or Agalteze, and the Maretuxze, we can readily see that the Atlantians were a spiritual people, and that all their inner worship was of a spiritual character.

The most famous Agalte of the Lontidri was that of the Temple of the Illustrate Dead Bodies, as before stated, built in one of the suburban districts to the aistie of Atara (see map of Atara), as a repository for Somalez Codize (mummified bodies) of departed celebrities of Atlantis, to which it was dedicated. The basilica of this Agalte was 200 coitex wide and 600 long. The facade was surmounted with three magnificent towers of the Gothic order.

The massive towers were further adorned with towerets, or turrets, of the Gothic order, whose summits formed a triangle with the main tower. The entire summit of the basilica walls was adorned with statues, each an effigy of some departed celebrity, so posed as to carry out the idea of the Gothic triangles. at the top with Gothic caps, and additional turrets at the sides, Three portals gave entrance to the Agalte. These were adorned thus to bear out the idea of triangular form. Glass was placed in three divisions, to conform with the triangle on the cap. The upper division of glass was blue in color, and formed the upper triangular point of the triangle, and the two lower sections which divided the lower half of the triangle perpendicularly, were orange. The closings or screens to the portals were constructed of Ur'mē (a shrub much like the modern willow), woven in meandering lattice form and highly ornamented with floral paintings. High upon the central facade of the tower stood an immense statue, or effigy, of Aquelon, a follower of Gatlins, the establisher of the Gabala Principles, and the most celebrated of the "Illustrate Deltsanza of religious principles" that had place on the Agalte.

It might be well to state here that the "brotherhood of Deltsanza" was under the direction of a leader, similar to the modern diocese; having a bishop in authority, over the clergy of his jurisdiction; and therefore the same as a diocesan, or bishop, as he stands related to his clergy or flock. It was from this fact that, later in the religious periods of Atlantis, the Efremetrum carried out the same plan of leading the Deltsanza in the Pelzoze, or Agalteze, in continuation of the order established by Gatlins, and continued by Aquelon in the Heltroploxze Pelzoze, of the famous Ceitux Aelkede, near Atara.

Gatlins belonged to the second Efremetrum, and Aquelon was contemporaneous with him during the latter part of the same period, and extended into the first part of the third Efremetrum, whose influence was further carried out by Alem Prolex of the third Efremetrum, in the Eltamedes Agalteze of, and in, the vicinity of Atara.

On the facade, above the central portal, was a Gothic window. The upper portion of the triangle contained white glass, but the two portions of the triangle, divided perpendicularly, and the main body of the window, instead of being glass, were beautifully carved panels of wood, to carry out the form of the window. Very little sunlight was admitted into the Agalte, for the better preservation of the Codize, as well as to carry out the idea of light characteristic of the Heltroplox tombs.

Between this window and the top of the central portal was the following symbol, wrought in mosaics of gold and crystals:

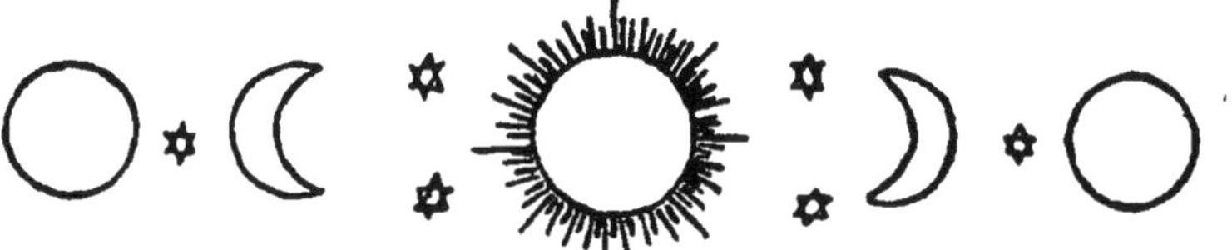

The image of the Ken symbolized Gahala, or Gala, and also Life. The crescent Oul or Moon (the Ou was pronounced like oo, or like o in move), in connection with the full discs, represented its waxing and waning, through the monthly periods, and therefore symbolized Time. The Sĕl'zē, or Stars, by their respective distances, symbolized Space. These symbols, collectively were arranged so as to represent triangles, which could be formed by imaginary lines, and symbolized Spirit, Soul and Body; and the mental exercise of tracing out the non-outlined triangles, symbolized the force of man to search into the processes of Nature, regarding the existence and co-operative principles of this Trinity of Life-epicycles.

Under the statue of Aquelon, above the central window, were the following characters, or abbreviated inscription, which the people readily understood as such, and recognized it not only in its literal translation, but as conveying the idea of the trinity, "Nencie, Lemaz and Wotz," or Time, Space and Life, as represented by the three characters. The inscription and its translation were:

Gahala Divine Spirit

On the cornice beneath the statue were carvings and sculptures in various designs, both spirit and mortal representations and scenes belonging to the same, as well as from the depository services, held on such occasions in the Agalte.

The entire exterior of the basilica was covered with tiers of statues representing the Sō-mā'lĕz Cō-dī'zē (mummified bodies) that had been deposited in the Agalte, which added a striking appearance to the edifice. The statues were in high-relief, thus sculptured on the blocks of stone that formed the walls.

The interior was in three divisions, thus formed by the aisles that extended from the portals to the rear of the auditorium. The three divisions were filled with Sō-mā'zē (mummies) of the Celebrities there deposited, which were placed in an erect position as thick as they could conveniently stand. Over the head of each Sō'mā (mummy) an inscription was placed in memory of the individual.

The services held in the Agalte, at the time the Somalez Codize were deposited, were as follows: The Cō'di (body) was brought into the Agalte and placed on a Kĕl-tī'zē (an altar about six feet long and three wide) that stood in the center of the Agalte, and covered with an exquisitely embroidered Clyst (altar cloth or pall). The embroidery was wrought with gold and silver threads, in raised designs of fruits and flowers, which had place on the four corners and around the edges of the Clyst. When the Codi was ready for consignment to the Agalte, it was brought in upon a Zī'ĕl (bier) which, with the Codi, was placed on the Keltize. The Codi was then covered with a long Clyst, excepting the face. This upper Clyst was also beautifully embroidered, the design being a large vase of flowers and ferns, wrought upon the center of the Clyst. It was narrow enough not to cover the embroidery on the lower Clyst. At the head of the Codi, on the Keltize, was placed a silver Jĕst, filled with natural flowers. This latter completed the preparation of the Somales Codi for the service.

All Codize deposited in this Agalte being those of Celebrities, were entitled to a service at which their brotherhood should officiate; therefore, the services began by the entrance of the officiating Deltsanz, who led the solemn procession, taking his station at the head of the Codi. Then followed the brotherhood, who took their station on the left of the Codi. Then came the relatives of the departed, who took their position on the right of the Codi. Then the musicians opened the service with a prelude on the Ethereleum, and the singers chanted a requiem (an idea re-embodied in the Catholic service, viz: that of singing a mass for the repose of the souls of the departed, as "Requiem æternam dona ist, Dimine," Give eternal rest to them, Lord), in memory of the departed spirit, during which the relatives and brotherhood stood with bowed heads, and the Deltsanz, with elevated hands and face upturned to the image of Ush Ken, offered a very impressive prayer, suitable to the occasion. Then followed a chant in the minor key, rendered by the chosen singers. This was made more spiritual and impressive by the singers' being positioned out of sight, which was effected by means of massive curtains, arranged for that purpose. Then the Deltsanz gave a short eulogy on the departed brother; the singers led the repository procession, singing as they proceeded; the Deltsanz and the brotherhood followed. Then the Ziel and Codi with the top Cloyt remaining over them, were lifted from the Kelteze and borne down the aisle by a portion of the brotherhood. The relatives, friends and people in attendance, followed in the procession. The singers, having separated into two lines, continued chanting until all the procession had passed between them, and gathered at the place of depository. Then the members of the brotherhood who had borne the Codi thence, on the Ziel, stepped aside, and other members placed the Codi in an erect position, where it was henceforth to remain. Then the Deltsanz spoke in the following words: "The soul has passed on to a higher and more beautiful realm. This, the house in which the soul lived, we have preserved, that at times we might behold the face. The soul is left in the care of Gala. The body, the friends have prepared for its last resting place." Then the singers chanted until all present had left the Agalte.

In regard to the process of mummifying bodies, as practised by the Egyptians and pre-historic Americans, Yermah informs us that it was not, as is supposed, original with them; for the origin dates back into the ages of Atlantian history. The Atlantian people preserved the Codi, as stated in the foregoing, in order that they might occasionally "look at the face," in memory of the past friendship and esteem held for the relative, friend or celebrity, and not in a superstitious way, as was the case with the ancient Egyptians and Americans, the erroneous idea of whose age was that the spirit often came back to the body which it had left; and that it could the more readily reach its surviving mortal friends, to communicate with them, by standing by the side of its own mummified body. It is the "surviving mortal friends," seeking communication, or having need of spirit protection or aid, and the obligation or pleasure of the spirit to perform some mission on the earth plane, that attracts the spirit thence, and not the mummified or otherwise disposed-of body, so long thrown off. True, the sooner the body becomes decomposed, the sooner the spirit is entirely free from all the environments that materially held it to the body; and no process, to this end, is better than cremation; fire being the quickest and best method for the dissolution, or separation, of the material body into its constituent elements, thus to set free the particles to find placement in new creative processes of material individuality.

The Atlantians preserved every Codi so perfectly that it retained its life-like appearance. They also preserved the garments worn at the time the Codi was thus preservd, with the Codi, by the same process. This art, as established by the Atlantians, and principally lost at the time of the submergence of the Lontidri, has never been re-established in its then perfect state, by any people who have practised it now known as having existed in Egypt, etc.; nor can it ever be, by future generations, on account of the non-existence now of some of the substances in any place accessible to mortals, for they lie embedded beneath the waters of the Atlantic Ocean, with the Atlantian Codize, once preserved by their marvelous qualities.

The Atlantian process of mummifying bodies was as follows: As soon as the spirit was known to have left the body, they filled the stomach, bowels and other intestines, with a liquid or solution of Cĕ'tē-liē, a volcanic substance which the Atlantians found in the Ceitux Aelkedze, a day's journey from the aistie of Atara. It was obtained by excavations made near an extinct volcano, known to them as the Cetelie, and the only one of its kind on the Lontidri. The substance therefore received its name from the volcano that had produced it. In a few hours, the above-named fluid would penetrate the entire Codi, and cause it to expand and round out to a natural form, hence disguising the condition of emaciation. When this condition of expansion had reached a satisfactory degree, the exterior of the Codi was washed with a powerful, poisonous preservative, which was distilled from a shrub then known as the Zī'tī-liē (which yet exists in small quantities in Egypt and Arabia). This arrested the dilatation of the Codi. The garments were then dipped in the latter solution and placed on the Codi, and the latter deposited in a dark room where it remained for a period of two months.

By penetration, inner and outer, the applied substances, or solutions, met and blended forces through the Codi, thus solidifying the flesh, which resulted in a sort of petrification, lasting as time itself.

The preservative force of the Cetelie was accidentally discovered, by finding bodies of animals that had fallen into pools or basins of water that were highly impregnated with the substance, which evidently had lain there a long time. Removing the bodies from the pools, it was discovered that, though they had been preserved for a long time, they eventually needed some additional compound to perfect the durability of the preservation, which finally resulted in the utility of the oil of Zitilie.

The preservative quality of the Zitilie was also accidentally discovered. An individual having a diseased arm, from which the skin and flesh were sloughing off, accidentally got some of the oil, or juice of the plant, on the afflicted limb, and it arrested the decay. This fact caused investigation of the plant, and especially of the preservative quality of its oil, which ultimated in its utility in connection with the solution of the Cetelie, to complete the process of Codi Somaelus.

The manufacture of Zitilie became a great enterprise in the aistie of Quirtz, whence it was transported to other districts of the Lontidri. The process of its manufacture was a very particular one, under the directorship or guidance of experts and by the utility of fine machinery, all of which made the product an expensive one.

As before stated, the supply of Cetelie was cut off at the time of the submergence of Atlantis, hence the art of Somaleus Codi was lost for a time, and for all time, in its more perfect state, on account of the lost substance of Cetelie.

The remnant Atlantians, though having some knowledge of the processes of Codi Somaleus, found themselves robbed of the one principal substance with which to carry on the art. They therefore resorted to other ingredients and processes, which though having long preservative forces, never equalled the original Atlantian art, and especially so in preserving the life-like appearance of the Codi. So it was with their eastern and western descendants, as evidenced by ancient remains examined in modern times; e. g., the mummies of Egypt, and those of the pre-historic and ancient American races, by their crumbling forms, and poorly-preserved features, certify to the use of an imperfect preservative.

As has been the case with the restoration of all the arts belonging to ancient periods of time, that of mummification was largely due to the influence of Atlantian Leasaza (Atlantian spirits), who in their mortal life had understood the original art as practised by the Atlantians. These spirits made it their first mission, from the spirit side of life, to aid and influence their surviving mortal brethren, after the submergence; then, later on, to influence the Egyptians and pre-historic and American races; but as before stated, the loss of the Cetelie substance brought a condition that weakened the influence, making it impossible to reach the perfection in the re-establishment that had existed in the Atlantian art.

NOTE.—Most volcanoes possess some specific substance natural to themselves, and so it was with the Cetelie.

USH AT'LAN-TI-AN TEL'TA A-E'TA, OR THE ATLANTIAN AIR-SHIPS.

TELTZIE XXIV.

In regard to the Atlantian means of travel, Yermah informs us that animals such as the Hittraina (Horse) and Telzic (Ox) were principally used as "beasts of burden," and to draw vehicles in which the people made local visits; that equestrianism was a favorite practice by both sexes; that the Atlantians generally preferred aerial navigation to that of water, and but few water craft were used for the accommodation of passengers on the local waters; that the Ar-ī-dē'tē (name of a water vessel, which means "moving on the waters") was used for freight transportation on the Rigerze (rivers) and Keletze (lakes); and that the Keīn (a large water craft, the term meaning "swiftness") was used for coast trips on the Alt-lăck'ē-ĕr (South Atlantic Ocean); Ex'ā-trŏn (Arctic Bay of Atlantis); the Rē-tĕx-ē-rī'trŏn (Inland Sea of Atlantis), and some of the largest Keletze of the Lontidri, all of which craft were propelled by electric force.

The Tĕl'tä A-ē'tä in the time of Atlantis (and from which re-embodied ideas have been extended through spirit influence and impression, from time to time, during the development of modern balloons and the ultimate aviators),* was employed to effect rapid transit to distant parts of the globe, not on the surface, but on air strata. Such a conveyance would accommodate from fifty to one hundred people, and the entire circumference of the earth's sphere could be traversed in a short space of time. It was not necessary to depend upon the direction of air currents in order to reach desired points. The force of electricity, by which the Telta Aeta was propelled, was sufficient to overcome the most violent gale, and propel the flying ship through storms, with as much facility as steam now propels vessels through placid waters.

The Telta Aeta was constructed from a model in representa-

*The principal part of this information, relative to the Tel-ta A-e-ta, was given us by Yer-mah in 1893, and the balance in 1904, when we revised the article. It will thus be seen that we have in no way been influenced by the later development of Aviators, etc.

tion of the Delis, or large Atlantian Eagle, and in exact mathematical proportions, though many times larger, in accord with the utility to which it was to be placed. The exact form and symmetry of the Delis were maintained. The legs and feet were used for rests when not in motion. The wings, when in motion, were operated by machinery, with a motive force of electricity, of which there was a constant supply ,as it was drawn direct from the atmosphere. This not only kept the Telta Aeta afloat on the air, but was also the means by which it was heated and lighted. The wings not only propelled the Telta Aeta through space, but were also the means by which it was guided. In its body, near the top, were compartments and saloons for passengers. Underneath and centrally, on the bottom, was a portion of the electric machinery, while the finer and more intricate parts had place in the wings, the former and the latter having respective electric connection. At the sides were storerooms for baggage or light freight.

The material of construction was a light metal, similar in appearance to modern aluminium, strong, impenetrable, and possessing great magnetic force, which virtues were exalted by low, and diminished by high temperature; hence, a material capable, in itself, of any temperature. This material was obtained by the action of sodium on the sesquichloride of chronium, as prepared by the Atlantians. It could not be oxidized by air ,and was of such specific gravity that it was not much heavier.

The Tĕlt′zä A-ĕt′zä (air-ships) in their flight, attained great speed, and at times great altitude, the average speed for ordinary commerce being from seventy-five to one hundred miles an hour, while a speed of from one hundred to one hundred and fifty miles an hour was frequently attained by the more venturesome.

Passengers were entirely protected, being excluded from the outside air, except what was admitted by air conduits, a system accompanied by ventilators through which the foul air escaped.

The machinery was worked by a cog system that was under perfect control at all times. That part utilized for the attraction and collection of the electricity, from the atmosphere, was the most complicated. It was materially aided, in its collecting process, by the magnetic forces of the material from which the Telta Aetza were constructed.

Externally, on the central top of each Telta Aeta, was a metal frame, from which, at each end, rose a standard ten or twelve coitex (feet) in height, composed of a coil of seven wires, the central one being the greatest in diameter. This trminated at the top with a powerful magnetic point, of a golden-colored material especially prepared as a magnet, in accord with the amount of force required; so was the force of the magnet established. The remaining six wires of the coil were qualified in like manner, and stood in a ramified position, out and up, grading downward in altitude from that of the central point.

Below the exterior plate, and on the interior of the Telta Aeta, the seven wires left each coil in radiations, those of one standard crossing through those of the other, thus forming a "V-shaped" network of fourteen wires. Each of these, in turn, connected with the outer wire in the "V," thus transmitting the entire force to the point of the "V," whence it was conducted by a continuous line to the machinery in the wings.

Beneath the "V" network of wires was a second metal frame, from which rose the metal standards, as supports to the conducting lines receiving the force from the "V." These lines connected the force to three large balls (of the same material as that of the frames), located in each wing, which received the electric force that set them into stationary rotation. Thus, by their connection with the intricate machinery in the wings, was maintained the mechanical force that propelled the Telta Aeta.

Ush Yē'dō (the controller) of the machinery had his position central, where, by mechanical appliances, he could change the position of the wings, as is used the rudder, on modern water craft, by the pilot. This guided the course of the Telta Aeta in any direction desired, or in its ascent and descent. One wing at a time could be operated, when so desired, or both, at will, according to the course desired.

Yermah informs us that he, when in the mortal, on several occasions, made a complete circuit of the earth in a Telta Aeta. He also informs us that the Atlantians, or some of them at least, had reached nearly all parts of the earth during their aerial travels, and that the fables mentioned in Grecian and other literatures of antiquity, were founded on knowledge then possessed, relative to the Atlantian Telta Aetza; and that in the Alexandrian Library there were models and descriptions of these Atlantian Telta Aetza, but they were included in the loss by conflagration when the Library burned.

Upon questioning Yermah in regard to the correctness of the supposition that the Atlantians could go farther west, in a day, in their Telta Aetza, than it would be possible to go in an easterly direction, taking advantage of the rotation of the earth, he informs us that we are partly correct in the surmise, and would be entirely so, were the earth a square or a cube, moving in a westerly direction. But as the earth is spheroid, and has a diurnal revolution toward the sun, which from modern local standpoints is an "easterly direction," at an angle of forty-five degrees from the polar star, it would seem more reasonable that an aerial vessel should travel, with greater facility, in the same direction the earth travels through space—that is, in an easterly direction. Yet as the Telta Aetza were constructed on the pricniple of a bird of flight, they could soar, if necessary, the perimetal air strata, and thus avoid the influence of the terrestrial revolution. Upon this hypothesis, the direction of flight would not be material.

In regard to the production and utility of electricity in contrast with that of modern times, he further informs us that the method employed, as before stated, to develop electricity, was to extract from the atmosphere, and naturally its dynamic force was as unlimited as the thunder bolts which shot across the summer skies. It was genuine, not artificial, electricity; hence, its energy was practically both unlimited and inexhaustible.

The reason that the dynamic force of modern electricity is so limited, in energy, is that moderns confine themselves to the products of the earth kingdom, in their development of electricity, viz., Cloride of Sodium, Clorides of Magnesium and Potassium Bromides of Magnesium, Sulphate of Magnesia, Sulphate and Carbonate of Lime, etc. Inequalities in lesser and greater degrees, through present or remote influences, enter into the composition of modern electricity. Of course the product is artificial, and depends for its dynamic force upon the durability and strength of the ingredients of which it is composed.

Meelzoric (electricity), among the Atlantians, was an obedient agent, made to conform to every use where light, heat, or dynamic force was required; hence it was a motive force for every mechanical apparatus.

GRE-TIC'ZE NUD GRE-TIC'TOR,
OR
ARCHITECTS AND ARCHITECTURE.

TELTZIE XXV.

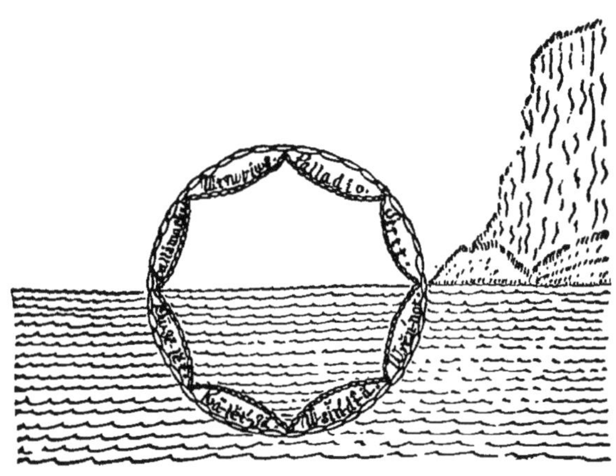

The Kid ze Greticior (Art of Sculpture) did not become manifest in a forcible manner until the latter part of the second Efremetrum, when it came forth rapidly, under both spirit and mortal influences. That such rapidity was possible to the Atlantians, can be realized by comparing that of modern nations with ancient times, especially the progress made in such things during the last sixty years of the nineteenth century and the beginning of the twentieth, which clearly demonstrates the fact.

So it is, and has been, in regard to the progression of civilization in all the ages past; i. e., the change from the original crudeness of long-standing periods, suddenly came into wonderfully rapid progress, when the minds of the people were in a proper and sufficiently prepared condition to receive the impressions, inspirations, and new ideas, thrown upon their receptive powers, from the intelligences that dwell upon the spirit side of the Art Cycle.

Wrĕn'nŏt was the most noted Grē'tĭc (Architect) at the close of the second Efremetrum, and his work, which was principally that of plain exterior ornamental designs, extended far into the third. His most noted Gretictor was that on the famous Pĕl'zo Ze Ush Jĕl-tē-rĕs' Mĕl'zē (Temple of the Greater Dead, or before-mentioned Temple of the Illustrate Dead Bodies), and the Jĕl'tē Dē-āk'ē-äl (Great Capitol Building) in the aistie of Atara, where much of his work in Gretictor was done, on account of that aistie being his home.

Some of his finest work was that on both the exterior and interior of the mansion home of Liū'srŏn, the Jelte Calluth (Great Painter), of Atara, and others as well, made manifest on porches, pillars, facades, etc., in which he wrought delicate designs in leaves, trailing vines, flowers, fruits, etc., such as were marvelously beautiful.

On the facade of the mansion home of Liusron he designed the word Cĕl'cē-mŭsh (Welcome), which he wrought with flowers. This was visible from quite a distance, to those who were approaching it. The flowers were re-tinted with gold by Liusron. Generally speaking, the Greticze (Architects) of Atlantis designed and also wrought the ornamentations on structures except in large contracts, where more workmen were necessary to complete the work within a given time. In such a case the principal Gretic did the finest portion of the work, and the balance was done under his immediate supervision.

U-sin'di-ä was the most noted Gretic of the northern portion of the Lontidri. He was located at Gletic (later known as Nietz), the Kistrez aistie of Teltzie We. He was famous for his beautiful ornamental designs, for both exteriors and interiors. His works and influence dated from the first quarter of the third Efremetrum. The most renowned of his designs were those he wrought on the Pelzo Ze Wē'sē (Temple of Light) in the aistie of Neitz. This Pelzo being a religious one, he made the ornamentation in harmony with the teachings therein given.

One of the principal of these designs portrayed the progress of the human soul. This had place on the facade of the Pĕl'zō, wrought within the space of an immense panel so as to give the symbol complete. In the center of the panel stood the figures of a male and female, in the attitude of contemplation. On each side of them were animals, represented as having been turned away, or in the act of leaving them—which was to symbolize the grosser material conditions as leaving the mortal individual, when his or her soul reached out for more light and knowledge. A bright light was represented as descending upon the two individuals, while the animals were departing into the shadows of a forest, thus symbolizing the two individuals as being endowed with the principle of purity, which would bring them into the ascendency of life, as spiritual beings, more perfectly governing the development of their souls and mortal bodies.

Lō'ū-ĕn-ō, a pupil of Usindia, was a noted Gretic, who continued to influence the Zē-ū-lē'ŭs (Art) thus established, to the close of the Efremetrum, which came to an untimely end by the great submergence.

Kạ̄-lĕt'zä was a Gretic, contemporary with Usindia, and a resident of Neitz. His work was not so much in ornamental designing as a finisher of designs laid out by Usindia; hence, his fame was always associated with that of Usindia.

Dū'zē-lĕt was the most noted Gretic of the southern portion of the Lontidri. He was a native of the aistie of Golonzo, in Teltzie Zret, now submerged by the Gulf of Mexico. His principal work was that of interior designing, both for ornament and utility conveniences, for both private and public structures.

No noted Gretic had place in Teltzie Sot. The early work there was very crude, indeed, especially the ornamental. It consisted simply in the placement of sticks in various forms to carry out some idea of ornamentation. Later, however, the people progresed some in the Zeuleus of structure, and in ornamentation, through the influence brought to bear upon the minds of those who wandered into Teltzie Zret, where they saw the more developed arts, and gathered ideas, and when they returned, tried to model after the styles that existed in Teltzie Zret.

Generally speaking, the Gretictor was grand as well as most beautiful, in many parts of the Lontidri. All Greticze were obliged to be well versed in the science of structure; one must in fact be a Kidstry, or Zeule (artist), by profession, as was the case with all the other Zeuleusze Nud Zeuleze (Arts and Artists), to ensure him employment in his profession. This was a fact that had great influence on the rise of all Zeuleusze, that led up to greatness, in that respect, that characterized the works of the Atlantian people, having place in the Lontidri at the time of the submergence.

A SPIRIT MESSAGE FROM AGATHA MENKARA.

Dear Mortals.—I am the daughter of Menkara, the great priest of the Nilus, who existed before the Pharaohs, and who gave to the world the wealth and knowledge of times that were before history was written; who gave to the world laws and sciences, and whose mortal remains yet lie in the sarcophagus, in

AGATHA MENKARA

the interior of the eastern pyramid of Egypt, near the ancient city of Cairo. The labyrinthian passages leading from the exterior to my father's tomb, cannot be fathomed by mortals of modern times; nor can the entrance on the exterior surface of the pyramid be discovered, so accurately are the joints blended. But there, hundreds of feet in the interior, and hundreds of feet beneath the surface, through polished granite passages, there are the remains of my father, Menkara, with hundreds of millions of wealth, in precious stones, surrounding his mummified form; wealth sufficient to redeem Egypt from the hands of the oppressor, could mortal Egyptians, of this day and age, but obtain possession of it.

I am Agatha, the daughter of that Menkara of whom I have written and of whose memory all Egypt is proud. I am Agatha, whose spirit-picture you have seen, and I have come to this genial race of mortal beings to testify to the greatness of the people of Egypt. I am Agatha who, when a mortal, was idolized by the brave and hardy sons of Egypt; who wore the royal purple of power, and sailed the Nilus, attended by many people. I am Agatha, the spirit now, who comes to earth-life scenes in the interest of humanity; to aid in establishing the truths of immortal life, and the facts of spirit presence, near every mortal; to establish the fact that guardian angels hover near the poor and weary to aid and comfort, and to lighten the pathway from one life to the other.

This is my mission,—I am to teach of the life so pure, so bright, so celestially sweet, in the balmy regions of ether, perfumed with the spirit of flowers, such as the earth can never know; of that life where the warm sunshine of love never grows cold; where hearts never break; where hopes are never disappointed; but where all is the fruition of every joy.

I am Agatha, who will visit you in those darkening hours of trial and care, and will brighten with silver lining, those clouds which press upon the soul.

In regard to your query, relative to the Great Sphinx at Gizeh, I will say that the Colossal Shemozan, or now known "Sphinx," at the base of the great Pyramid at Gizeh, Egypt, of which so little is known by mortals, was, in one sense, of Atlantian construction and sculpture, it having been designed and constructed by Atlantis Shemozan, the first Shacha (ruler), and his son, Atlantis Saban, the second, and subsequent Shachaza (rulers), descendants of the Cuzetens, which latter-named people were descendants from remnant Atlantians, who survived the great submergence of the Atlantian Continent, and had settled in the region now occupied by the Great Sphinx.

On account of the surnames, it may seem strange that Atlantis Saban should have been the son of Atlantis Shemozan. Yermah informs us that Saban was the surname of Atlantis Saban's mother, whose maiden name was Jĕn-cĕl'lä Saban, and who was the eldest daughter of Pĕl-zŏn'ä Saban, a wealthy Cuzeten. It was a custom with the Cuzetens, when there was no male offspring, to perpetuate the surname and inherit the wealth of the grandsire, which was made lawful by a son of the oldest daughter taking his mother's maiden surname, when he became heir of his grandsire's estate, and this was the case with Atlantis Saban, who retained the given name of "Atlantis," in order to become heir to both his father's and grandfather's estates.

With the Cuzetens, the term "Atlantis" was sacred to the memory of their departed Atlantian ancestors, and their original home of Atlantis. From the fact that the term Atlantis was thus rendered sacred, it was the custom of some of the early Cuzetens to name their first male offspring "Atlantis," and both Atlantis Shemozan and Atlantis Seban had thus received their names.

Subsequently, the term "Atlantis" descended, with but little change, to the body of water now covering the original Continent of Atlantis; viz., Atlantic.

The term "Atlantic" had its origin and adoption, in contradistinction to that of "Atlantis," from the fact that in the Atlantian language, the terminal syllable "tis," referred to land; and with the Cuzetens, the terminal syllable "tic," to water; and from the fact that Atlantis as a Continent was covered with "tis," or water, the term "Atlantic" was adopted to convey the meaning.

The term "Pacific," as applied to that body of water, though it has nearly the same terminal as Atlantic, was not derived from the Atlantian nomenclature, but had its origin proper through the Spanish term, "Pacifico," so given by the Spanish invaders who had entered Mexico, and in recognition of the peaceful and mild condition of the waters, in comparison with those of the Atlantic, as known to them in their Spain-land, etc., and the term was further extended into the eastern countries by translation into the Latin, Italian, French, English, etc.

Atlantis Shemozan and Atlantis Saban were the first two Shachaza of the Cuzetens, in that region, who were esteemed great, as mortal spirits, for having designed and established the constructing of the colossal Shemozan; and after their disembodiment as such, and after they had passed into the spirit existence, were recognized as "gods," under the title of "Atlantis." The surname of "Shemozan" was retained, to identify the now known Sphinx, on account of the illustrious disembodied man having been the first "Shacha," and the designer of the Sphinx, in the first period of its establishment.

Shemozanza, the plural of Shemozan, was the term used, in that sense, for many generations by the Cuzetens, after which both terms were changed to "Sphinx" and "Sphinxes."

The term "Sphinx" was adopted for that class of sculpture from the fact that it (like the Atlantian term Spŏnzä, from which it was derived through the Greek and Latin) represented sculptures, the forms of which were those of the human and the animal combined, such as Andro and Ciro-Sphinxes.

The terms Shemozan and Shemozanza, in reference to Sphinxes, was local, and used only by the Cuzetens, specific to their adoption and utility, and ceased, as such, in the pre-historic period, when they were superseded by other material changes. But, as above stated, the term Spŏn'zä, and its plural Spŏn-zä' (the distinction between the singular and plural being in the syllable accent only), was handed down, and retained, by other Atlantian remnant peoples than the Cuzetens of this section, after the submergence, and changed to that of Sphinx and Sphinxes, through Egyptian, Greek and Latin dialects and usages. And thus were established the now historical terms.

On an avenue leading from Luxor to Karnak, in my earth days, were "Andro-Sphinxes," much as trees now line a modern boulevard. They each and every one represented, in likeness, a leader of the Cuzetens, whether male or female; and sphinxes or statues, of my father, Menkara, and myself, were among the rest.

From the extremity of this avenue branched another avenue, leading to the temple of "Karnak," which term is a corruption of "Menkara," the name of my father, in whose honor this temple was built. In fact, what the moderns term "Karnak" was but the temple, with its dependent buildings for priests and retainers, and was occupied by my father and myself, and our retainers. The avenue last named was lined by Ciro-Sphinxes, of which fragments yet remain. These represented priests and priestesses of the remnant Atlantians, or Cuzetens, or what modernly would be termed *media*.

The five pylones, and four courts, of the temple, were my suggestions; and in those courts I entertained people who sought the consolation of the precincts of the temple.

In the southern chamber are the sculptures which compose the "Menkara tablets"—not of Thothmes, Dynasty IV, as moderns claim; those were destroyed by the vandals about five hundred years after the Christian era, and the tablets of Thothmes, in the "Hall of Ancestors," were found in recent years and removed to France.

Ancient history, written by modern authors, is so conflicting, that a spirit who, in mortal life, was contemporaneous with times of antiquity, is averse about speaking upon the subject, for fear of displacing pleasant delusions, and attracting from "accepted history" much that has given historians reputation for science and learning.

I would that it were different; but unfortunately for mankind, the modern mind is rather more pleased with fiction than a truth which contradicts long-accepted theories.

AGATHA MENKARA,
Nilus, Egyptus.

The picture shown is from a spirit-drawn crayon portrait of Atlantis Shemozan, whom we have described as the establisher of the great Shemozan, or now known Sphinx of Gizeh, the first great Ruler and Architect of the Atlantian remnant people who settled in the region of Găs'bí-ä, or now known district of Cairo and El-Gizeh. The reader will note that the head, the general pose of the head, the visage and the style of the hair* are all very similar to the same characteristics in the Sphinx of Gizeh. The crescent moon and single star, represented in the sky above the portrait, were to represent the celestial region, and home of departed ancestors. The object below, and to the right, represented an A-ō'so, or royal covering, for the head of the supreme ruler of the nation, and was in the style of the one worn by Atlantis Shemozan, the great architect and ruler, and ultimate god of the Cuzetens of Gasbia.

The two ensigns, at the right of the portrait, were indicative of the rank of office held by the individual who wore them. The upper one was always worn on the left breast, and represented the individual as being the high representative of spiritual matters and conditions, that would raise him to the rank of a god when he should pass to spirit life. The lower one was worn on the waist girt, in front, and represented the wearer as a

---

*The hair did not reprint well in the half-tone reproduction. It should flow back and down toward the shoulders; trace it by the dark outline in the cut.

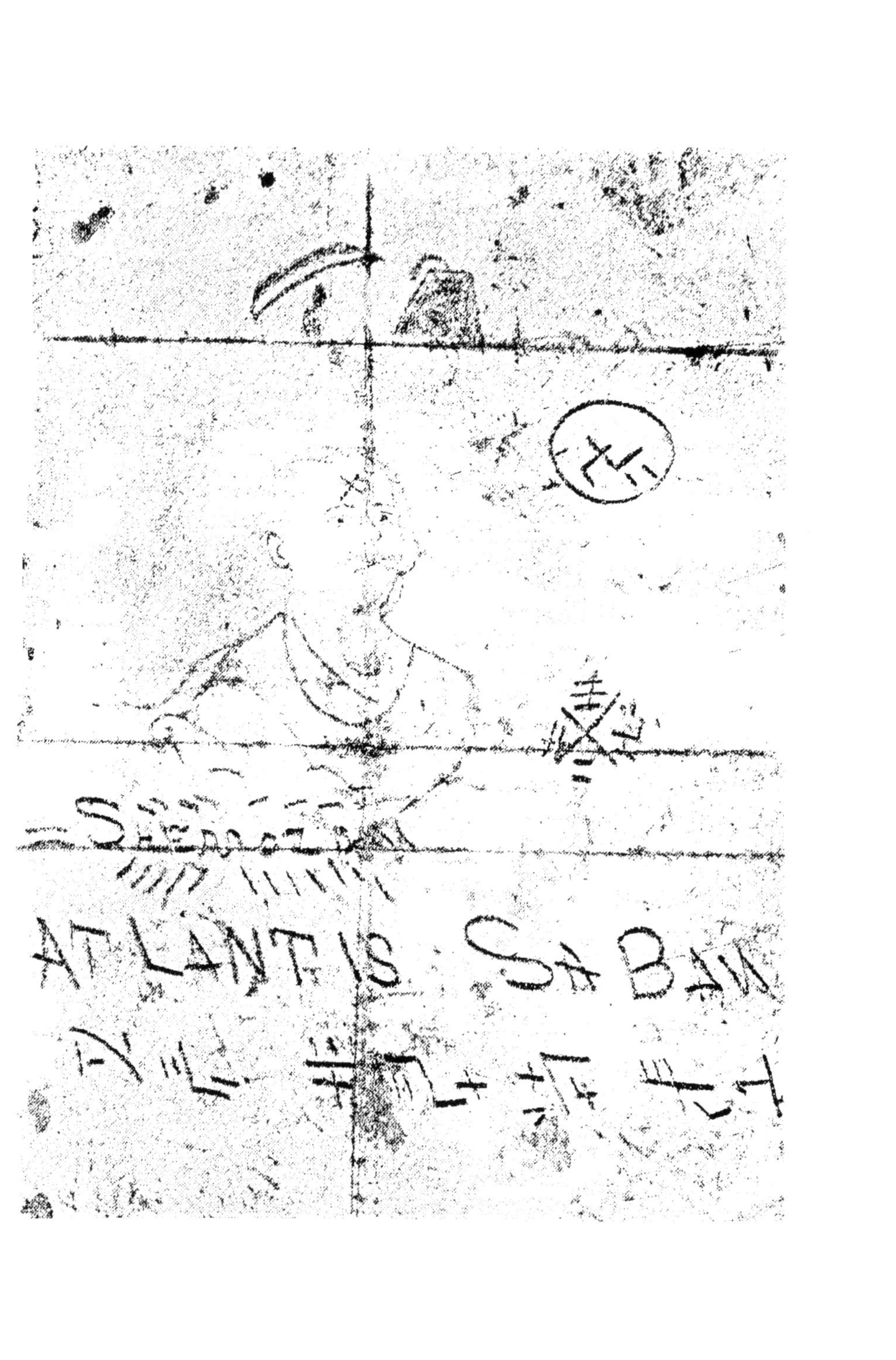
ATLANTIS

high ruler of material matters, or National conditions, and therefore raised the individual to the rank of "Supreme Ruler of State and Nation." The inscription at the bottom is written in the language, and alphabetical characters, used by the Cuzetens at the period of time when the Shemozan or Sphinx was constructed. The language and characters have thus changed and developed, from those of the Atlantian proper, from the knowledge the several generations had retained of the Atlantian characters and language, through their great migrations and changing conditions in life. The characters and language, when translated into English, make the name written above it, viz., At-län-tĭs Sā'băn.

The plus sign, on the forehead of the portrait, to have been correctly represented, should have been placed, by the spirit artist, on the upper left portion of the forehead near the hair, in place of centrally, as it appears in the portrait.

The sign was placed on the forehead of its wearer by means of an indelible stain, of royal purple; and was thus worn by Shemozan (and by subsequent rulers) in recognition of mental and physical greatness, so ordered by his people, in recognition of their estimation of him in that respect. However, he gave to it a greater significance, i. e., caused it to represent the power of the brain to act, and control matters both material and spiritual; and he so taught it; and further, established the four points of the sign as symbolic of the spiritual knowledge that must be given out to all the peoples who dwelt in the regions extent within the four points of the compass, and that the same was to be handed down, from generation to generation, by the subsequent rulers. Such was his method for acquainting the peoples with the greatness of mentality, and especially that of spirit intelligence, such as would return, to inspire and direct the rulers, and their associate priests and priestesses, in guiding the people generally. Therefore, the sign was worn by each of the succeeding rulers, from the time of Atlantis Shemozan and his son, Atlantis Saban, and on down, nearly to the time of the first Dynasty of Egypt.

Originally, the same sign had place on the Shemozan or Sphinx, but is now obliterated, erased by the force of the elements.

The Cuzetens who settled in Gasbia, or especially those who settled in the region of the Pyramids, were originally governed by a Shā'chā (god or supreme ruler), who rose to that rank by being the one of the nation who could originate or create the greatest architectural designs, by and through the aid of "spirit guidance," which capability entitled him to the degree of a "Shacha" during his mortal rule, and of a god in the spiritual, and so reverenced by the people subsequently. The honor, therefore, of being made ruler while in the mortal, at that period of time, was not obtained by conquest and bloodshed, but by individual mental greatness, both in creative and constructive development, and spirit sensitiveness.

The second greatest Shacha was Atlantis Shemozan, who was a descendant from the Cuzetens, who dwelt in the then known ancient city of Jĕlt'mĭs, east of the now known Sphinx, and where Jeltmis, the first great architect, had built the "Temple of Jeltmis," a thousand years before.

Atlantis Shemozan won his title of Shacha, or ruler, by drawing the plan of the great Shemozan, or Sphinx, now having place at Gizeh, Egypt; a plan which he executed by means of an indelible vegetable juice, and which when complete, was in the form of long tablets, then called Shăz; i. e., long strips of dried skins were used as the body or form, to which strips of prepared bark from a tree of the mountains, then known as the Qū-ī'lĭsh, were attached perpendicularly, in rows, and fastened to the body by strips of skin, until it was filled, and was then hung suspended to a frame. It was this Shaz method of preserving architectural drawings, that gave the idea of all the descended or subsequent tablet and monumental inscriptions and writing, stone being substituted for the bark, and strips for the Shaz.

Not only the diagrams of the various sections of the structure were delineated upon the Shaz, but full directions for the construction and sculptural development as well, so that in case of the disembodiment of Shemozan before the completion of the great image, his successors would be able to carry the plan to a finish.

When Shemozan was raised to the degree of supreme ruler, he immediately began work on the construction of the Colossal Image, which subsequently was named "Shemozan," after him, as having been the designer and ruler. This name the image bore, until about the time of the first Dynasty of Egypt, when it lost its great prestige as a sacred monument, or god image, that it had previously held, in memory of Shemozan, the "first ruler," and later, the "god," of the Cuzetens of that region.

The great Shemozan image was commenced about 13,000 years ago, and was 1,000 years under construction. At the disembodiment of Atlantis Shemozan, his son, Atlantis Saban, became ruler, and continued the work on the image, according to the plans delineated by his father, except that he made a change in the head and visage, from the original design of an animal, to the likeness of his father. This was to satisfy the wishes of the people. Atlantis Shemozan, when originating the image, chose the face of a Lion, since it then, as it had been with the Atlantian ancestors, was a symbol of great strength; a characteristic of the animal well known to the peoples of that region, and especially the ancestral portion, who had migrated through Sfury (Africa), to the region of Siloton (Egypt). Therefore, the idea was copulative with that of the choice of a ruler, or god, who was able to create and construct the greatest works thus planned.

All of the body-construction and sculpture of the Shemozan image, and that of the sub-structure, as yet unexplored, were wrought under the supervision of the various Shacha, subsequent to, and beginning with, Atlantis Shemozan, during the period of 1000 years.

The great shaft opening at the rear center of the Sphinx, which perforates the whole body, leads to a labyrinthian passage, and ultimately to a tomb-chamber of considerable depth, which will be discovered in the future, by excavations. The tomb-chamber is made accessible by a great flight of polished steps and several landings, according to the labyrinthian order. This labyrinthian chamber was the place of the entombment of the remains of all the mortal rulers, or gods, from the time of Atlantis Shemozan and Atlantis Saban, and other rulers who superintended the building of this image, to its completion (down even to the time of the erection of the early pyramids).

After Atlantis Shemozan passed to the spirit world, he, as the god of the people, or as a spirit, returned to the subsequent rulers, thus to inspire, direct and influence them, to carry out his original plan, to the finish, which completed his principal mission on the earth plane. For in that period of time, "spirit return" and "communion," as they were in Atlantis, were far in advance of modern times.

The image, therefore, of Atlantis Shemozan, was worshipped as one of the principal gods of that period of time. They had many, including the celebrated spirits of their original Atlantian ancestors, of whom, through spirit return and communication, they had learned; as also those of the 1000 years, who had passed to spirit life during the construction of the Shemozan image.

Many tombs of small dimensions, built for the priests and priestesses, in this section, as well as that of the Sphinx, are now buried beneath the drifting sands and changeable soil, of the desert, some of which will yet be discovered, in evidence of our present revelation.

Therefore, the Shemozan, or Sphinx of Gizeh, is the oldest

visible remnant left of the monumental products of the pre-historic Cuzetens of the Gasbian region, and having been established by them, the descendants of the remnant Atlantians, it serves as a proper link in the great "cycle of Architecture," with which to connect that of a remote, pre-historic antiquity, to our modern-ancient, where it stands, in evidence of veneration by peoples of the long ages past; similarly revered by the modern-ancient Egyptians and their descendants, as sacred to the memory of their ancestral greatness; admired and protected by the Greek and Roman invaders; contemplated by the Mohammedans as an establishment in representation of some principle held sacred by a pre-historic people. But alas! under the influence of the Mamelukes, who judged it to be an Afreet, or evil spirit, it was used as a target for their matchlock and cannon shot, a fact which established the beginning of its most serious decay.

We are also informed, by the spirit of Al'chē-lĕt, that the El-tē-zē' Cī-cĕn-tū'ĕs Mä Cī-cĕn-tū-ē'rē (Architects and Architecture of Arabia) differed from those of other countries, in that the Cicentues were not a class of Mĕl-sä-ĕst'ĕs (Artists) distinct from the Cĭs-tä-rē-ĕr'ĕs (Sculptors), from the fact that the exterior form of the buildings, at that period, varied but slightly; hence, each individual constructed according to one plan, in the majority of cases, and as the interior designs were so closely allied to those of the Cĭn'stry (Sculpture), being wrought out by plastic process, and therefore superintended by the Cistareeres proper. Therefore, the Cistareeres were also the Cicentues, hence the Melsa ses Cicentuere (Art of Architecture) pre-historically, was under one head, viz: that of Cinstry, and therefore superintended by the Cistareeres.

The Cicentuere differed somewhat, according to the region in which the structures had place. Those in the mountainous regions were built of stone, but those in desert places were built of blocks manufactured from the sand of the desert, under a cement process. The finest work of the plastic order was done on the interior of the structures.

The most noted Cicentues, during a period about 6000 years B. C., were pupils of Conetry, the famous Cistareer (Sculptor) of that period; but subsequently, the Melsa of Cicentuere was under the influence of the descended Melsaests of that order.

Passing into Siloton (Egypt), with the migratory influence direct from the Atlantian remnants, and not from Elteze or Zanzureta, as the other Art influences had come, co-operative with that of spirit-inspiration, we find the Lē-ĕl'vä mĕs Tē-lī-ū-sä'tĭc (Art of Architecture) in an original and crude state, but ready for development.

Links and Cycles

Hĭl-lō'thē-ăn was the most noted Tē-lī'ū (Architect) whose work and influence began about 6000 years B. C. He was a Silotonian by birth, and lived in a small Cĕl'zĭc (town or city) by the name of Fā-gä'rō, then located west of the Nile River, between the First Cataract and the town of Edfoo. He lived and worked through the century, and ultimately won renown as a Teliu, especially in wood structures. He established many styles of wooden ornamental work, particularly in archways and pillars on the facades of buildings. By nature he was very fanciful, which characteristic made him quite susceptible to that kind of spirit influence, or inspiration, which led him to conceive many ideas, and aided him in their development. He superintended a great many workmen, among whom a goodly number of Tē-lī-ū'-sä (Architects) developed the Leelva to a certain degree, and from Fagaro travelled into various parts of the country, where they aided in the further extension and growth of Teliusatic, in the districts of Siloton.

Căl-lū-ĕn'dĕn was a most noted Teliu, whose influence and works began about 5925 years B. C. He was an apprentice, under direction of Hillothean during his (Hillothean's) latter years, at which time he resided in Fagaro, but subsequently moved to the section northwest of the Fourth Cataract of the Nile, or between it and the northern course of the river, where he resided in a small Celzic by the name of Cĭs-mā'shăl-ly. He lived and worked into the fourth quarter of the next century. He further developed the ideas and styles of Hillothean, and also established styles, which he first wrought out of soft stone material, and later produced the same, in a developed form, from granite, marble and other hard stone material. He also employed many men as helpers, among whom some developed as Teliusa, and branched out into other districts of Siloton, thus aiding the influence of Hillothean, and his descended workmen, in further development of the Leelva of Teliusatic, by uniting the influence of Calluenden and his descended workmen to the ultimate establishment of the Leelva mes Teliusatic of that period.

Passing into Zăn-zū-rē'tä (Greece), we find the influence of Silotonian Teliusa (Egyptian Architecture), by migratory conditions, awakening ideas of the same kind in Zanzureta.

Cŏn-a-plū'ŭs was the first noted Mĕt'thä (Architect) there, whose works and influence began about 5750 years B. C. Being an apprentice to Calluenden, in Siloton, his early years were spent in the Celzic of Fagaro, Siloton, but subsequently he migrated to Zanzureta, where he located in a Sē-mā'sä (pre-historic Grecian term for "town") by the name of Tĕl-cī-cū'sĕs, then located in the district now submerged by the Ægean Sea, between what is now known as the Skyros Islands and the northeastern coast of Eubœa. He lived in the mortal form until the first quarter of the next century. He worked in both wood and stone, and originated the styles of that period. He was a well-developed spirit sensitive, a fact which he was conscious of, and depended more upon the inspiration he received thereby than upon his own individual genius, for the ideas which he conceived and developed. He superintended many workmen, among whom some fine Mĕt-thē'ŏn (Architects) developed, who, by dispersement throughout the country, lent their influence to the further development and completion of various forms of Mĕt-thē-ŏn'sĕs (Architecture), in the district of Zanzureta.

Nŏn-tā-sū'an was the most noted Mettha, whose works and influence began about 5590 years B. C. He was a Zanzuretan by birth, and being an apprentice under the direction of Conapluus, spent his first thirty years in the Semasa of Telcicuses. He moved to a Semasa by the name of Dē-lĕs-trē'ŏn, then located on the east side of the now known river of Aspru, about thirty-nine degrees North Latitude. He lived in the form about one hundred and fifty years, during which time he did a great work as a Master -Mettha, and therefore superintended many workmen, among whom some developed into good Mettheon, who migrated into various parts of Zanzureta, and adjacent countries, such as Italy, etc., and lent their influence in favor of the development of Mettheonses in those regions. His mission on the earth plane was that of general progression in the former styles of Conapluus; and being naturally a very talented individual, along the line of Mettheonses, he originated and developed ideas of his own. He was not as strong a spirit sensitive as Conapluus, but having worked so long under the direction of the latter, understood the laws of impression and inspiration, and therefore was able to gain considerable help from that source.

CE'MOZ SI USH KIS'A-RE NUD CE-MET'TE-ZA, OR ORIGIN OF THE COLUMN AND ARCH.

TELTZIE XXVI.

Returning to Atlantis, Yermah informs us that the Atlantian Gretictor had arrived at a point of perfection which embraced the grandest specimens of the orders, Tĭl'zē (similar to the Ionic), the I-thē'zē (similar to the Caryatic), both being prevalent in Teltzie Et, though the former was really the national style of that Teltzie; the Nŭ-zē'lĕth (similar to the Doric), the national style of Teltzie Set, though there was a dispersement of the Itheze style in parts of the Teltzie; and the Ad'mŭs (similar to the Corinthian), the national style of Teltzie Zret. A more composite, or mixed, order had become established in Teltzie We, thus influenced by Yermah, the principal Deltsanz (Teacher or Governor, of the Teltzie; i. e., he being a native of Teltzie Zret, and brother-in-law to Alem Prolex, the Supreme Efremetrum of the Lontidri, who dwelt in Atara, therefore became conversant with the national styles of both Teltzie Et and Zret. Furthermore, he encouraged emigration of Greticze from both Teltzie', to further develop the Gretictor of Teltzie We, hence the compound style that arose from mingled ideas of the three national styles, viz., Tilze, Itheze and Admus, which was termed the "I-ŏ'thē-ŭs." Some influence was carried, in a similar way, from Teltzie Et, into Teltzie' Set, Ket, and Zret, which made variations of styles, in those Teltzie', but not enough to change the national forms.

The Atlantian Kĭs'ä-rē (Column) was extensively used in its various styles, which were, by elaboration, made grand and beautiful in every detail, and of various uses. They had place as single shafts, or monuments, in the open areas, such as surrounded fountains or reservoirs, to mark the corners of the square, or rectangular plats of grass-covered ground or junctions of the walks. Those occupying such districts were usually of marble material, surmounted with golden capitals. Some were characterized by inscriptions, and such elaborate ornamentation as was characteristic of the order and style to which the column belonged. They were also extensively used on the interior and exterior of public buildings, and of some palatial homes.

The Atlantian Cē-mĕt′tē-zä (Arch) was also extensively used throughout the Lontidri, and varied, in detail, from simple forms to those of elaborate grandeur, and had place at the entrances, drives, or gateways, to private grounds and homes, as well as to those of public places. The ends were highly ornamented with sculptures of various forms, and also bore inscriptions, usually wrought in golden-colored letters, giving the name of the public grounds or home, the latter being more in use at that time, than the designation of dwellers by their individual names and numbers, as is common in modern times; and streets were always known by name instead of by number. Occasionally, the inscriptions were wrought with silver-colored letters, but as they tarnished much sooner than those of the golden color, the latter was more commonly used.

The Atlantian Cemetteza, instead of being circular at the top, as is the case with the modern forms, extended so as to form a triangular apex or gable covering, to the side Kĭs-ä-rē′zē (Columns). (See No. 5, Plate I.)

This is in representation of the one that had place at the entrance to the grounds of the great Deakeal, or Capitol, of the Lontidri of Atlantis, in the aistie of Atara. The Kisareze (Columns) and the horizontal Kisare, that extended from one perpendicular Kisare to the other, thus forming a cap-stone to them, and a sub-base of the pyramidal portion of the structure, were of equal dimensions, being five feet wide, six feet thick, and twelve in length, each composed of one solid block of white Signitie (marble). The top, or pyramidal portion of the structure, was formed by an assembly of Wilse Signitie (white marble). On the face of the horizontal Kisare, the following motto was engraved, in Atlantian characters, and embossed with Uzie (gold): "Dē′ĭt Nŭd Crĕst Lū Ush In-thä′ō;" the translation of which is: *Law and Order for the Nation.*

On the face of the left Kisare were sculptured images of two men, one representing the Supreme Efremetrum of the Lontidri, and the other, a Deltsanz of State, so posed as to represent the Efremetrum as coming from the Deakeal, and the Deltsanz as going to it. Having met on the way, the two individuals had paused to talk with each other, and thus standing, the Efremetrum was facing front, with a parchment, or roll document, in his left hand, the hand and arm posed at the point of repose at his side, and the Deltsanz was facing him, in a profile attitude to the observer. On the visage of the Efremetrum was the expression of one in deep thought, while the Deltsanz expressed earnestness in his conversational pose. The Efremetrum, thus represented,

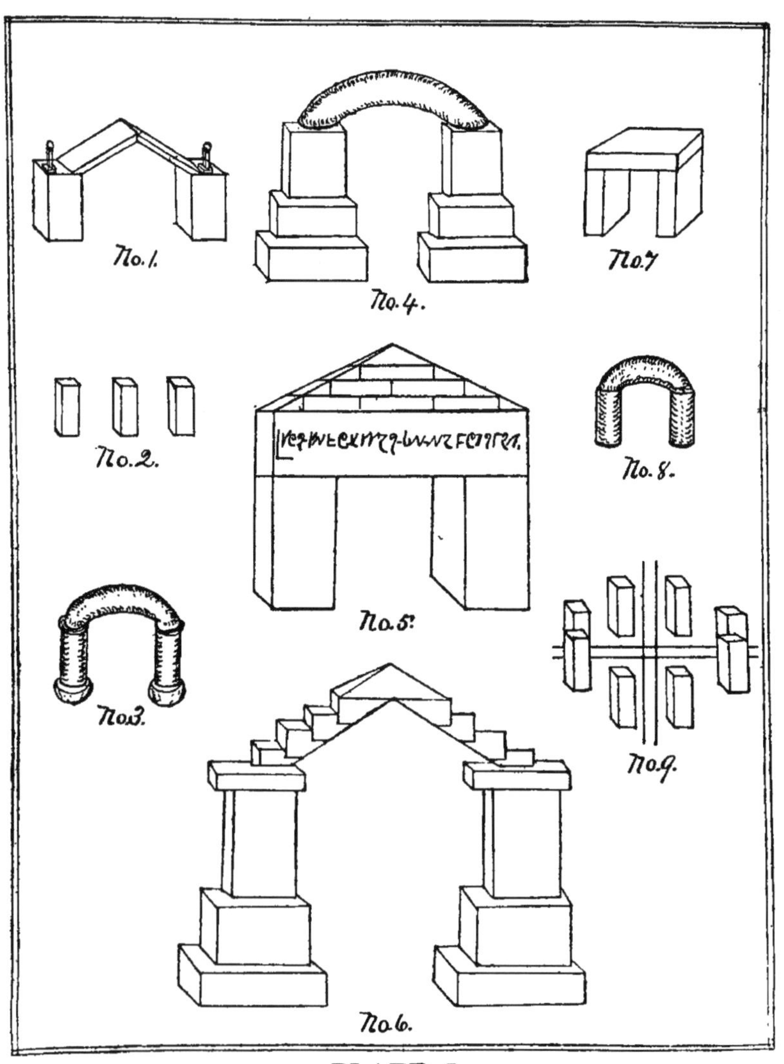

PLATE I.

was somewhat slender, being about six feet four inches in height, while the Deltsanz was of stouter build, and about six feet in height. Both individuals were represented clothed with outer garments similar to the now known Prince Albert coat, only the skirts extended down to their feet, like the modern Priest's Vesture. Each wore the Et'lä (cap) significant of his rank or office, but the entire apparel of the Efremetrum was more elaborate than that of the other.

On the right Kisare, in like manner, two individuals were represented as coming from the Deakeal, one a Deltsanz of State and the other a private Citizen, the two in close conversation. The Deltsanz carried a book in his left hand, which latter rested on his right breast. In stature, he represented an individual of about seven feet, and of stout build. His visage manifested an expression of meditation. The Citizen represented an individual who was about six feet six inches in height, but of a more slender build than the Deltsanz. He was posed in the attitude of earnest conversation and gesticulation. Their garments, as represented, were of the same style as those of the other group, but those worn by the Citizen were the plainest of them all.

The Cĕl-pŏr-tĭc'ĕs (Sculptural) work was of the highest Art, and was wrought by Adolphus, the greatest Celpor (Sculptor) of that period. The Uzie embossing on the letters of the Motto, was the work of Liusron, the greatest Calluth (Painter) of that period.

The Deakeal was not represented, in the sculptural assemblage of characters, on the Kisareze.

This entire Cemetteza was perfectly plain (though most of the Cemetteza' that gave entrance to other public and private grounds were elaborately ornamented with sculptures, representing the human, the animal, and vegetable life), excepting the above-described work of Adolphus and Liusron, which gave to it a noble and stately appearance, and being composed entirely of Wilse Signitie, symbolized "purity of action in the adjustment of all civil matters," and the whole assemblage of the Cemetteza, the "utility of the great Deakeal."

After the submergence of Atlantis, and therefore after the destruction of all the Gretictor, and memorials of it, except such as existed in the minds of the remnant people on the various borderlands, the Art of Architecture had to be re-established in the remnant world, by the descendants of the remnant peoples, aided by spirit influence.

The early generations who had passed to spirit life, and who alone had definite knowledge of the Atlantian Gretictor, had left to their descendants but a vague conception of the Art, such as tradition affords. This in turn was idealistically handed down through several subsequent generations, the narrations causing differences of opinion and ideas to be entertained by the peoples who migrated into different sections of the country.

Ultimately, individuals were born to the various tribes, who by nature possessed certain degrees of artistic genius. These were sought out by spirit-Gretictor, who inspired, influenced and guided them, according to their mental and local material conditions, to establish again the primitive work of Architecture.

Passing into the pre-historic region of Siloton (Egypt), we find manifest evidence of the first links which we must utilize in order to connect up and re-establish the continuity of the Great Cycle of Architecture. In the first place we must take the pre-historic Silotonian It'mä (Pillar or Column) or It'mäs (an Arch formed by combined pillars with a cap Itma. These were the inspired ideas of architectural structure in Siloton. (See Ex. No. 7, Plate I.)

There were three forms of the Itmas, viz., the first, consisting of two flat perpendicular Itmases, six feet wide and two feet thick, and twelve feet in height, and one horizontal Itma or top stone, the same width as those of the sides, but only about one and a half feet thick, thus to strengthen and hold the two perpendicular Itmases in place, which thus formed sort of a monolithic pylon. (See Ex. No. 7, Plate I.)

The second form or idea was similar to the Atlantian Cemetteza. (See Ex. No. 5, Plate I). The two, or side perpendicular Itmases, were five feet square, and twelve feet in height. Those that formed the pointed arch were three feet thick and five feet wide, and erected from the center of the perpendicular Itmases and meeting at an apex above, thus forming a triangle, with the base-angle omitted, which had its support at the apex and top of the two Itmases. (See Ex. No. 1, Plate I.)

The third was composed of two perpendicular cylindrical Itmases, that formed the sides of the structure, four feet in diameter, and one of a circular arched form that extended from one Itma to the other, thus forming a circular archway, twelve feet in height, computing from the top of the arch. (See Ex. No. 8, Plate I.)

The original use to which the Itmas was put, was to mark the entrance to cities, as gateways, minus extended walls, such as were constructed in other countries in subsequent times. The style first adopted was that of placing three Itmases in a line, which, if they had been surmounted with a cap Itma, would have formed a double portaled pylon. But they simply consisted of three erect Itmases, from six to eight feet in height, five feet wide and three feet thick. (See Ex. No. 2, Plate I.)

Another use to which the simple, erect Itmases were put, was to mark "cross roads," in the country, and served the same purpose as the modern guide-board at cross-roads. In this case there were four sets of Itmases, two in each, thus marking the square area formed by the junction of the two roads. These were from six to eight feet in height, five feet wide, and three feet thick. On the side of the Itmases, facing the approaching traveler, inscriptions were placed, that gave intelligence to the individual, in relation to directions and distances to adjacent sections of country, and the cities located therein. (See Ex. No. 9, Plate I.)

The development continued during several generations, until the above-named forms, or styles of Itmas, were the result, adopted and used for the same purposes, or utility, to a certain degree, in the construction of such buildings as tombs, temples, pylones, etc., all of which is evidenced by now known pre-historic remains.

The idea of the Egyptian Itmas, as represented by Ex. No. 8, Plate I, was re-embodied in the Kĭs-ăx'ēs (Arched Gateways, see Ex. No. 3, Plate I), of the pre-historic cities of Sū'räs (Nineveh), Quĭn-zī-ŏn'tō (Korasbad), Kē-nē-ō'shŏn (Nimroud), and Nē-ĕn-tō-cō'sy (Babylon), thus erected by the Sē-nō'dĕs, Mĕn-zō'acks, Cŏr-ĕn-tĕn-găn'tōes, and Sĭl'krŏns, respectively, who were descendants of the Esgenens, etc., thus establishing that style of Architecture in the region of Assyria, the only difference being that the Kisax had an additional plain, round base, and the capital. The general height of the Kisax was about fifteen feet.

The ideas of the Egyptian Itmases, such as we have represented by Examples Nos. 1 and 3, Plate I, were embodied in the Quinzeex (Gateways), as represented in Examples Nos. 4 and 6, of the pre-historic cities of Zanzureta (Greece), by the various descendants of the Icthieons; the principal difference being that the former column was characterized with a square base, and the latter rose, in the assemblage of two square blocks, from a square base, each extension less in thickness than the former, and the latter terminating in a plain, Doric capital. The pointed Arch was formed by a succession of four blocks of stone, jointed and cemented, one within the other, thus to support the pointed arched form that terminated in one slightly pointed stone, which formed the apex. The entire structure, from base to apex, was about twelve feet in height.

Thus, we see that the Atlantian Kisare (Column) led up to the Egyptian Itma, the Assyrian Kisax, and the Grecian Quinze; and we might add, was the influence from which the ideas of the Maenhirs, and their extension into Cē-clū'she-ēs (Alignments), etc., were re-conceived, through spirit influences, as will be shown later in this work. Also that the greatness of the remote Atlantian Gretictor, lost sight of by mortals, through the occurrence of the greatest cataclysm of conjunct cataclysms the world has ever known, is re-embodied in the Architecture of the 20th century of modern achievements, having been thus reborn by the erection of the pre-historic Itma and Itmas, as a new architectural embryo, developed and characterized through the Modern-Ancient, the Mediæval and the Modern periods of time, by the varied ideas, conceptions, and mental and physical energies, of the Architects, co-operative with the spirit influences, according to the spiritual development of the age in which they have lived and labored, and their individual ability to receive the same. Hence, by advanced spirit forces, and the mental development of architects, have arisen such wonderful architectural monuments as now exist, wherein the columns and arches are at once the chief characteristics, and the links that connect Atlantis to the Eastern and Western Continents, in the great Cycle of Architectural events.

In evidence of the columnar influence, in modern-ancient periods of time, such as links down from the pre-historic Itma, one has but to contemplate such structures as the Temple of Amenhotep, at Luxor, with its wonderful array of grey "lotus columns," or pillars, of 1500 years B. C., or that of Rameses III, with its huge but coarse and ugly columns, as in the Hypostyle Hall; or the Temple of Karnak, at Thebes, which Agatha informs us was a temple of "added National Temples," the additions being the works of, and used by, succeeding sovereigns. Of these the inferior sculpture and architecture are, alike, said to date from the period of Rameses II, along to the Ptolemies. The more beautiful carvings and workmanship characterizing the Twelfth Dynasty, and the more elegant work of Seti's time, 1300 years B C., and of Thothmes, or Queen Hatasu, 1600 years B. C., and the older work, which was of better architecture and more refined taste, all date back to the time of Menkara and his daughter, Agatha. Examples are, the wonderful Temple of Hathor, at Denderah, with its grand columnal facade and pronacs; the interior Hypostyle Court, originally of very great antiquity and restored by the Ptolemaic builders, situated on the site of a pre-historic temple by the name of Tel'zē-mäz, which was erected by a priest of the name, two hundred years before the reign of

Khufu, who, in his time built another temple on the site of Telzemas and this, in turn, gave place to the Temple of Hather; the ruined Temple of Thothmes III, 1500 years B. C., at Kom Ombo, with its facade of columns which brought out the idea of the Itmas; the great Temple of Edfou, with its platformed roof supported by massive columns, a work of the Ptolemies in reproduction of a more ancient edifice; the ancient Ptolemaic Temple of Esnah, with its vast Hypostyle Hall nearly buried below ground, the columns of which crowned with palm and papyrus-style Capitals, and covered with inscriptions and cartouches, are mostly those of the Ptolemies; the great Temple of Medinet Habu, south of the Colossi, erected by Rameses III, 1200 years B. C., with its Ptolemaic Gate, with two massive columns as guides to the entrance, which latter bear evidence of the advanced idea of the pre-historic Itmas of Siloton, as well as do the entrance to the pavilion and the massive columns that support the inner court of the Temple; the Temple of Queen Hathepsu at Dair-al-Bahari, with its fluted columns, origin of the first development of the Doric style, the colonnade of fluted pillars of which, pure in Doric style, are cut from the living rock, or built so as to veil the flat walls; the Temple of Isis, on the Island of Philæ, 380 years B. C., with its Hypostyle Hall of paneled columns, and double colonnade; Pharoah's Bed, which displays the advanced idea of the Itmas by its columns and portals, covered by a wall; the Temple of Hathor, the Egyptian Venus, and the colonnade of Nectanebo's Temple bearing out the same idea; the great Rock Tombs of Beni Hasan of the Dynasties XII and XIII, the columns of which support the facade and internal chambers, the earliest known form of architecture, the idea of which led up to the Greek Doric of 1000 years later.

Passing from the influence of the great achievements of the Atlantian Gretictor, to the subsequent pre-historic period, previous to and contemporaneous with, the now known primitive Aborigines, through which time, spirits of the Atlantian Greticze were influencing the minds of the people, we note them beginning their work of re-establishment of the Art of Architecture, the development of which, during that period, was only to the extent of their then greatest need.

It has been supposed that the Architectural influence first reached man through natural, objective, or visible creation, such as the nests of birds, the lairs of beasts, etc., when they were led to construct rude abodes, such as arbors, out of trees and their twigs; caves and huts of mud; tents, of poles covered with skins, especially by the migrating, hunting, fishing, and remnant local tribes, who led pastoral and nomadic lives. By modern thinkers and writers, this condition is generally placed at such times as immediately preceded and were contemporaneous with the Adomic Period; but as above shown, there was a rise, a development and a decadence of the art, the last condition, however, being by force of the submergence. Hence, it came into existence in remote, pre-historic ages, and not contemporaneously with what moderns term the "early period of Man's existence," as the term is generally accepted; for the Atlantians, nearly 17000 years ago, could refer to the antiquated origin of Gretictor and Greticze. There came a time, long after the submergence, when the re-establishment of the art became absolutely necessary; which seems to be the time that modern writers place as its origin; but it rightly belongs to, and even precedes, the Atlantian period of which we write. Therefore, when the remnant peoples of Atlantis were migrating to the various sections of Europe, Asia, Africa, North and South America, we note the spirit influence of those disembodied Greticze at work from the spirit side of life, endeavoring to inspire their mortal brethren with architectural ideas, such as they saw would achieve the greatness of the art as now extant over the Globe, if developed. Hence, the evolution from the crude state of architecture, as rendered by the original descendants of the remnant Atlantian peoples, to the greatness of the constructed art as displayed by subsequent peoples, wherein the Architects have harmoniously blended their imaginative and technical powers to the development of unity, power, grandeur, beauty, and harmony; all of which we recognize as individual and influential embodiments, manifesting through their structures, according to the age and locality in which they lived, through the inspirations given to them by their co-operative "spirit intelligences." So, while passings along on this review of architectural development, we pause at that period of pre-historic time, when the structures were raised, whose monumental evidences yet remain, though in ruins, or partly so, to connect the links that are to re-establish the great Architectural Cycle, or that part of its circumference that extends from the Atlantian period to that of the twentieth century.

Leaving Siloton, and the original influence of the Itma and Itmas ideas, we pass on to the Eastern Continent, to contemplate some of the monumental evidence of what is now termed, and understood, as the "works of primeval man," though far from being so.

First, let us consider the Monoliths, as single Maenhirs, Trilithons, and Alignments, or crude ideas of architecture, conceived and impressionally wrought out by descended tribes who migrated into various sections of country, now containing monumental evidences that are similar to the idea of Itmas, e. g.; take the best known of the Maenhirs and Trilithons, as at Carnac, Brittany, or about nine miles southwest from Auray, in the department of Morbiham, France, the former being a huge stone, sixty-three feet in height and fourteen feet in diameter, rudely shaped to a circular form, its weight estimated at two hundred and sixty tons. This marvelous stone, and the Trilithon standing near it, are the work of a descended tribe of the Conseanzes, who originally settled in the region along the now known Loire river, near its junction with the Vienne and the Indre rivers, and migrated westward from the original settlement, referred to above, to the mouth of the Loire, from which section they spread out into the district now submerged by the Bay of Biscay, lying west and northwest of the department of Vendee, Loire Inferieure, Morbihan and Finistere, and northwest into Morbiham, which submerged district and all the above-named departments, they termed E-shē-mē'lŭs, and called themselves the "E-shē-mē'lēs."

The great Maenhir, above referred to, originally stood nearly in the center of the then known district of Eshemelus. At that time, the El-jā'hä (god or supreme being) or Maenhir, representing the god, stood in the center of a great circle that was formed by erect, single Maenhirs, large enough to encompass several thousand people, for as many as that would assemble there on special occasions. Originally, the Eljaha was surmounted by a crude figure of a male human form, which represented the supreme principle, in adoration of which the people there met, and therefore was their idol, or "god representative," which they termed Eljaha. The image faced the rising sun, and the people entered facing the same way. The hour for worship was at sunrise, when the people would enter the Kē-rĕl'thē (circle) through the Rĭz'măth (gateway, or now known Trilithon), and as they entered, they would bow low to the rising sun, and then to the Eljaha, in which attitude they would remain in silence for some moments, then pass circularly around the image with their heads bowed in meditation, then pass out of the Rizmath, and away to their abodes. But when the people entered on special occasions, they paused for a moment at the inner side of the Rizmath, then gathered in a multitude about the Eljaha, and thus, in silence, awaited the impressions such as were intended by the "spirit guides" for their uplifting and unfoldment, generally. From this practice has descended the idea of all "silent worship," and it would be well if, in modern times, all religious orders and private individuals would go into secret silence when they wish to receive inspiration for all good. And invocations thus offered in silence would better open the door for such conditions, than in public sanctuaries, where much speaking and gaudy show divert the mind from the true source of inspiration. Therefore, it is better to "enter thy closet in secret." So with the Eshemeles, and as each individual felt the inspiration sought, he rose and passed silently out of the Kerelthe, and further by the Cē-clū'shē-ēs (alignment avenues), to his abode.

The Ceclushees in that and adjacent districts, of which fragmentary sections still exist, were roadways leading in from the surrounding country. These originally radiated from the Eljaha, or rather the Kerelthe, and led toward the four points of the compass, and intercepting avenues that led in from cross sections; thus they were traveling guides to the people who sought the place for worship.

Originally, the Ceclushees extended a long distance into the country, some of them being no less than 100 miles in length, though in case of extreme length, the stones forming them were placed farther and farther apart, as the distance lengthened. It was from the Ceclushe arrangement that the subsequent idea of "mile-stones" was conceived; and from the Kerelthe arrangement descended the idea of amphitheatres, circular stone inclosures, etc.

The fifty or more alignments still in France, all within a radius of a few miles, and centrally located in a district containing the most remarkable megalithic remains in the world, are but a small portion of the vast number of structures such as Kerelthees and Ceclushees, that had place throughout the western peninsula of France, and the northern portion of the submerged district of the Bay of Biscay.

Many of the single Maenhirs, or stones, that had place in the original construction of Kerelthees and Ceclushees throughout that region of country, have during subsequent time, been carried away by the peoples, for their subsequent construction. Hence the diminution, numerically and collectively, which has left the structures in smaller sections where they originally were compound, or in greater series, of Kerelthees and Ceclushees.

These megalithic remains are all constructions made by the descendants of the Eshemeles of Eshemelus, and varied in strueture according to the developed ideas of the various generations, hence the condition of 13, 11, 10, 4, or single rows or lines of alignments which mark the work of succeeding generations, in periods ranging from seventy-five to one hundred years apart, and their establishment in the various districts, under the leadership of a chief of the people, as there were, at that time, no governmental conditions to control the people, aside from that of a leader.

Therefore, in evidence of the "tribal constructions" of that region, and the varieties characterizing each, beginning with that at Menec, which was planned and constructed by O-mā-cĕl'lä, a non-historic leader of the people in that district, we find the Maenhirs that form those Ceclushees that are arranged in eleven rows, thus descending in length, grading along the line from ten to thirteen feet above the ground at first, and terminating at heights of about three to four feet, where they end with a Kerelthe whose longest diameter is three hundred feet. The structure at Kermario, planned and constructed by Wăn-zăl'zē, the non-historic leader of the people of that district, is one in which we find the group starting in about 350 yards from the former, and formed by ten lines or Ceclushees, the Maenhirs being of a more uniform length throughout the line, of about ten to twelve feet in height, now containing nine hundred and ninety-four stones, many of which are of great size, being eighteen feet in length, and extending four thousand feet. After a greater interval, at the village of Kerlescent, the structures were planned and constructed by E-cē-lĭc'sĭc, the non-historic leader of the poeple in that district, where we find the Ceclushees extending in thirteen rows, now composed of two hundred and sixty-six stones, which terminate with a Kerelthe, all together extending a distance of one thousand feet or more. At Erdevan there is a structure planned and constructed by Rä-chĕl'ōes, the non-historic leader of the people of that district, in which, originally, the Ceclushees were composed of about fifteen hundred Maenhirs, two hundred and ninety of which are still standing, seven hundred and forty having fallen, while the balance have disappeared by removal, or decay. At Peumarch, the structure was planned and constructed by Rē-zĭg'mä, a non-historic leader of the people in that district, in which we find the Ceclushees in four rows, now containing over two hundred Maenhirs, though originally there were more; others are formed by only one row of the Ceclushe, as at Loure, Camaret and Kerdowadec, the latter having a Ceclushe of about four hundred meters in length, which terminates with a kind of a *croix gammee,* and was planned and carried out by Rē-jĕd'ĭs, the non-historic leader of the people of that district. Between Camaret and the point of Toulinguet, the structure, situated on an elevated portion of land, was planned and constructed by Wĕl-tā-zō'ăm, the pre-historic leader of the people of that district, and here the line of Ceclushees, though originally much longer, is six hundred yards long now, and contains about forty stones, many others having been removed, probably for subsequent constructions. Close to this are a Dolmen and a prostrate Maenhir.

Subsequent to the establishment of the Cŭd'lĭngs-tŏns, in their section of Gŏn-sō-ē'sēs, or now known section of Haute Garonne, France, where the Ancestors settled in the vicinity of the now known city of Toulouse, some of their descendants migrated south-westward into the Pyrenees region, which section they termed Chä-hä'zēl A-ē-kĕl'lē̆y, meaning "the people of Chahazel." In this region there are Ceclushees of single file, mostly of straight setting, though some are of reptiliform. All these remnants are of the constructions established by the various tribes of the Chahazel people, under local leadership. The one at the ancient city of Peyrelade (Billiere) was planned and constructed by Zär-zăn'zē-bär, the leader of the Chahazel people who migrated to that section, and the Ceclushees that extended in a straight line from north to south, now apparently for three hundred yards, originally extended about double that distance; and while it now contains ninety-three stones, some of which are of great size, it originally contained about one hundred and fifty, placed at varying distances, farther apart in the section now extinct.

The one at St. Colomb, in Cornwall, England, called "Nine Maidens," now composed of eight quartz stones, or Ceclushees, that extend in a perfectly straight line for two hundred and sixty-two feet, originally extended about three hundred and fifty feet, and contained fifteen Ceclushees of the same material as those now standing. This structure was planned and established by Cē-lĕn'cē-ŭs, the leader of a tribe of Eshemeles who had migrated from their ancestral home of Eshemelus, or country of France.

Prior to the establishment of the English, Bristol and St. George's channels, the Eshemeles, who were very numerous, had spread throughout the districts now submerged by the above-named waters, and also that part of England now known as the Shires of Cornwall, Dover, Dorset and Somerset, and up into the now known section of Ireland, which they termed E-măn-mē'trū-zē, and called themselves the Kĕs-lä-ĕn'jŭs. Subsequent to their establishment in Emanmetruze (Cornwall), a tribe of their descendants migrated to the northeast and settled in the district now known as Wiltshire, and there established themselves as a nation. Their principal settlement was in the vicinity of what is now Avebury, which section they termed Dē-lĕn'zē-ŏn, and called themselves the Kū-lī'zē-ŏns. They were ruled by a leader whose name was Krū'ī-zōte, who planned and established the great Megalithic structures of Avebury, which are the most remarkable in England. These and the foregoing, named Ceclushees, or Alignments, are therefore fitting original links with which to aid us in the re-establishment of the great Architectural Cycle.

Another influence, leading up to the re-establishment of Architectural greatness, is that of the Cromlechs or Dolmens, such as the circular, the oval, the irregular, and the rectangular enclosures, formed by rude Monoliths; e. g., the Dolmen celebrated as "Kit's Cotty House," in England, formed of three large Monolithic supports, and a Megalith or top-stone, 11 x 18 feet, which was erected by Wĭl-zō-rō'măs, a non-historic ruler of a colony of Kulizeons who had migrated into the section of Mid-Kent, which section they termed E-kĭn-cū-bē'rē. This ruler built the Dū'zē (Dolmen) as a covering for his tomb, beneath which, ultimately, his body was placed in an underground tomb. This was the original form of tombs, and led up to all other ground forms, and all other Dolmens served the same purposes. He got his ideas from Dū'zē-ēs (Dolmens) that had been constructed by Sē'crē-dĕl, the first ruler of the Eshemeles, in the region of the now known Channel Islands, where Dolmens are found, and where every species of Megalthic monument occurs, all of which are the works of Secredel, his nation and their descended rulers and peoples. The adjacent districts, now submerged, were rich with Megalithic structures, but were lost to modern knowledge.

The Megalithic structures in France, numbering about three thousand four hundred and ten, located in Brittany, Aveyron, etc., are the works of the Eshemeles and the Falkaleits, the former having carried the influence into the Brittany section, after whom the latter people patterned, and ultimately carried the influence into Germany and Holland, by migratory conditions. Migrating Eshemeles from Cushemaza, or the Channel Island districts, carried the influence into the British Island districts. It found its way into Crimea and Circassia, by migrating Kintilucians, who got the idea from the pre-historic peoples in the section of Germany. (See migration of the Kintilucians.) Further influence, from the Megalithic structures, was carried into Central Asia and India, where Megalithic structures are widely diffused in the region east of the Jordan River.. However, the influence in the latter region was more particularly due to the Sĭn-ē'thōns (original ancestors of the Jews, the term "Jews" meaning "sect," and not "people"), who migrated into that region from their Tĭn-dĭn'zē-ōn (Germany). Therefore the influence was of a dualistic nature, viz: from the northeast, through the Kintilucians; and from the northwest through the Sinethons. The Megalithic structures found in Germany, the Danish-lands of Scandinavia, South Sweden, etc., were established by the influence of Falkaleits, who migrated into those regions. The structures seen, from the Pyrenees region, along the coast of Spain, through Portugal and Andalusia, where they are numerous, as also in Morocco, Algeria and Tunis, were established by migrating Chahazel Aekelley (people) who migrated into those sections from Chahazel, the now known Pyrenees region, and also some of the Eshemeles, of the subsequent submerged section of Eshemelus, northwest of France. Those in Arabia and Persia were established by the Sinethons, who migrated into those regions from the Jordan region. All the nude Dolmens were instituted as monuments that super-covered original underground tombs. Those covered with mounds, or so-called "burial mounds," were of later date or origin. Therefore, the Duzees, or Megalithic structures, now termed Dolmens, we have chosen as having constituted one of the principal links, with which to continue the re-establishment of the great Architectural Cycle, in the above-named geographical regions.

The original Kerelthees, or original circular enclosures, arranged by the placement of alignment stones into Cromlech and Dolmen forms, led up to an advanced idea of Kerelthe structures in pre-historic periods, e. g., such as the famous structure of Avebury, previously referred to, established by Kruizote and his nation for war purposes. It was fifty years under construction, and Kruizote ruled during the fifty years subsequent to its completion, and the completion of those adjacent to it, hence he was an aged ruler. The outer circle of one hundred set stones, varying from fifteen to seventeen feet in height, and forty feet in circumference, enclosing an area one thousand feet in diameter, answered the purposes of a fort, where Kruizote and his warriors gathered, before an engagement in battle. The great ditch and lofty rampart around the Kerelthe, were for protection against invaders from other nations, who sometimes sought to overpower them, during unguarded hours, and carry off the treasures and war implements there deposited. The Rĕz'lĕs (Stone Pillar or Maenhir), twenty feet in height, that stands centrally in one of the two inner Kerelthees, consisting of a double row of stones, was the outlook for approaching enemies, and a place from which the danger signal was given by the Skĭn'dër (trumpeter) on watch on top of the Rezles, by blowing a call with his Skin (trumpet), which would bring Kruizote and his warriors into the great Kerelthe. The long Ceclushe (avenue or alignment) of approach to the southwest, one thousand four hundred and thirty yards in length, now termed the "Kennet Avenue," consisting of a double row of Ceclushees, was constructed as a protection for the warriors, as they entered the great Kerelthe, when summoned by the Skinder for service. The Mĕz'lēs (Cromlech or Dolmen) in the other interior Kerelthe, was a receptacle for all war implements in time of peace, thus stored for quick access. The two other monuments on Hakpen Hill, or Haca's pen, and the artificial mound termed "Silbury Hill," originally belonged to the same group. The double oval of Hakpen Hill, 133 x 155 feet, was the original tomb of the chief warrior of the Kulizeons, and the artificial mound, or Silbury Hill, was the tomb of the private warriors of the nation, who had given their lives in its service. The great Ceclushees, or avenue, forty-five feet wide, now extending in the direction of Silbury Hill, originally connected the latter with Hakpen Hill, and marked the enclosed line of march taken by warriors at the burial of their dead. Therefore, these structures do not commemorate the last of the twelve Arthurian battles, 520 A. D., as supposed by Mr. Ferguson, nor are they the works of the Druids, as has been theorized, but date back to the conquests of the pre-historic Kulizeons of Delinzeon, about 1500 years B. C.

During the latter fifty years of Kruizote's rule, tribes of his nation migrated northwest into the section of Berkshire, England, though they remained under his leadership principally. At that time they were engaged in wars and contentions with the Zrineths of Cucula, or section now known as northern England. It was under the direction of Kruizote that the now known Alignments or Ceclushees, that have place in the "Vale of the White Horse," were established, wihch were intended to serve the same purposes as the great Kerelthe at Avebury, though the latter structure was never fully completed.

The famous Kerelthe, or Stone Circle of Stonehenge, situated in the Salisbury Plain, Wiltshire, England, was principally constructed by Cē-rĕt', ruler of the Kulizeons of Delinzeon, who succeeded Kruizote. It was a Temple then known as the Kē-tĕn-jĕt'ē-lūs. Ceret was more religiously inclined in his rulings than his predecessor (who constructed for war purposes and tombs), and therefore constructed after symbolic ideas, for religious purposes; hence, all parts of the structure symbolized some principle in creative nature, or conditions arising therefrom, each of which had its specific place, or utility, in forms of worship. The center circle, composed of upright stones, with others of smaller size placed horizontally on their tops, symbolized the gathering together and utility of unseen forces, such as pervaded the vast, encircling universe, especially so, those which passed from the east to the west, as the electric currents, movements of the planetary system, etc. The "inner circle" symbolized the assembly of the people into the influence of those forces, for the purpose of gathering knowledge from them. The "outer oval" symbolized the source of all provident utility, and was the place in which the speaker or teacher stood, when expounding the governing laws and principles. The "inner oval" symbolized the advancement, development and growth, in all creative operations and processes, and especially symbolized the spirit of all things, after disembodiment, or separation of soul and body; hence, was used as a fitting place to hold funeral services. The central stone, fifteen feet in length, was used for a double purpose; first, the east end of it was a rest or altar, upon which to place the body during the funeral services, and second, the west end was a place on which the priest stood, facing the morning sun, while he delivered the funeral oration, and conducted the services. The funerals were always held in the morning. The large central stone symbolized the "supreme force," which they recognized as coming from all points of the compass. The trilithons symbolized the "condition of opening the way to the minds and hearts of the people, that the light of knowledge arising from the supreme influences might enter their lives for that purpose, thus to benefit them mentally and spiritually." The Valum and Ditch that surrounded the entire Kerelthe, symbolized the necessity of individual effort, to ward off, or guard against besetting influences, such as might weaken or lessen their degree of morality. The avenue from the northeast, marked by a bank and ditch on each side, ultimately dividing into two branches, one going eastward up the hill between two group of barrows, and the other northward to the cursus, was the entrance and exit to the Retenjetelus, individually or processionally, according to the occasion. The eastward branch, up the hill, also led to the barrows on either side which were tombs. Those on the south side of the Ceclushe were tombs of the celebrities, and those on the north, of the common people, or people in general. The north branch led only to the Retenjetelus to and from the country. The now termed "cursus" did not exist at that time. It was constructed subsequently by the Druids, as a pleasure ground, where they held games and races of various kinds. The Cromlech, or "bowing stone," in the avenue, termed "Friar's Heel," originally was for two purposes, viz.: a place where sacrificial and circumcising instruments and paraphernalia were kept, and also a place for performing the operation. The large prostrate stone, within the area of the work and in line with the Cromlech, originally was used as the sacrificial stone.

One of the most sacred of the religious laws, laid down by Ceret, was that of circumcision of the males, and a similar operation on females, performed at the age of fifteen. To ignore this law was a crime, punishable with the individual's life; therefore, the above-named stone was the place upon which the victims were immolated, paying the penalty by being beheaded on the stone. When their blood flowed over the stone, it was not only considered the atonement for disregardment of the law, but as a warning to others to attend to the rite. The barrows that lie around, on all sides, are tombs, where the bodies of the immolated victims were placed, after the execution. Ceret was the first of the rulers in the region of Britain to establish the practice of circumcision. He had learned of it through Egyptians, who had migrated from Siloton into the region of his Ancestors, the Eshemeles of Eshemelus; and it was from the practice, instituted by Ceret and further handed down, that it became known to the more modern Jews, who, to this day, practice it as the initiatory rite of the Jewish Covenant. The same practice that anciently existed, and still exists, in Arabia and Persia, likewise came through the migratory influences from Egypt into those regions.

The Kerelthees at Stanton Drew, in Somersetshire, England, were constructed by Dĕl-hā'tī, leader of the Kulizeons who migrated there from Delenzeon, or the section of Wiltshire, England.

The one known as the "Stenis and Broger" circle, in the Orkney Islands, Scotland, was constructed by Pā-tä-mä'ū leader of the Eshemeles who had migrated to that section.

The five groups in the Shetland Islands, Scotland, three of which are in Unst, and two in the Fetler, were all established by Năn-zū'tŭs, leader of the Eshemeles who migrated to that section, but were completed by subsequent leaders of the same people.

The structure at Callernish, in the Lewis section of the Hebrides Islands, Scotland, commonly called "the stones of Callernish," were erected by A-kā-lī'jŭs, leader of the Eshemeles, who migrated to that section.

Nearly all the Ceclushees and Kerelthees, as all megalithic structures that existed pre-historically, were originally utilized for war purposes.

Submerged Atlantis Restored

All the foregoing structures we deem as suitable links, in their regions, with which to aid in the re-establishment of the great Architectural Cycle, and as having led up to the greater achievements of subsequent times.

PRE-HISTORIC CITIES, TEMPLES, AND THE ORIGIN OF THE PYRAMIDS.

TELTZIE XXVII.

Egypt was in the golden glow of its glory and greatness, between 10,000 and 12,000 B. C. Then came the dark clouds of degeneration, from which that country has never arisen; but the time is yet coming when evidences will reveal the fact of its past greatness, such as will again glorify all Egypt; for revealments, such as have resulted from excavations and researches, during recent historical events, are but the beginning of greater and more numerous facts, such as shall not only be obtained by excavations, upheavals, and natural material agencies, but by and through spirit revelation, as this book is now being compiled.

During the above-named period, the Cuzetens were the principal nation in Gasbia, or Lower Egypt. They had spread out along the Nile through the region now known as the Pyramidal Necropolis. Hence, they built many cities and towns throughout that section, and ultimately became very numerous there. It is the mortal remains of these people who are the disembodied populace of all the region now known as the Pyramidal Necropolis; theirs the intelligences that have survived the mortal knowledge of the cities in which they dwelt. Some of these we shall give further on, whose once surging population gave their mortal bodies, by millions, to the several entombments, or sepulchres, of Gasbia or Siloton, ultimately Lower Egypt.

Beginning with the period, 12,000 years B. C., and extendng up to that of 10,000 years B. C., while Egypt was in its greatness, the oldest, largest city of that region, then known as Mä-wilt'zä, had place north of the now known Abu-Roash Pyramid.

The principal city, then known as Shä-mĭs'rĕx, had place on the western shore of the Hăm'mō, or Nile river, opposite the now known city of Cairo. Their Necropolis extended southwestward toward the great Pyramid of Abu-Roash, which was the greatest Pyramidal work of the Cuzetens of Shamisrex, and was erected during the period between 9700 and 9000, B. C.

It was begun by an architect and ruler by the name of Kā-dĕl'sē-ĕc, and completed by another, by the name of Zoon'zăc, it having been under the direction of various architects and rulers during the period between the first and last-named rulers and architects above named, and became the entombment of all the rulers having in charge its construction.

During the period preceding 12000 and 9700 B. C., the entombment of bodies was mostly in the sepultures of the temples, which were of rectangular form and contained numbers of chambers, and in many cases, single tombs of the same shape as the temples were erected for individual entombments; and during the latter part of the above-named period, many small ones were built near Shamisrex, the Abu-Roash being the greatest.

About 9000 years B. C., the Cuzetens had become populous in the region now known as the "Sakkarah Necropic" section, whose principal city, then known as Jē-lū'cē-ăn, had place just south of the Sakkarah Că-zū'dăs (Pyramids).

During the next 3000 years a great many small Cazudas were erected by the succeeding rulers, and used principally as their tombs. These were modeled after the Abu-Roash.

Nearly all the pre-historic Sakkarah sepultures have been lost to mortal observation, being now beneath the earth's surface; as tombs thus entombed, themselves, by the changing of the soil, depressions, convulsions and natural decay.

The principal rulers, preceding those contemporaneous with the building of the large Cazudas of Sakkarah, were entombed in the small ones at first, but removed to the larger ones in subsequent time, by succeeding rulers, who wanted their ancestors' place in greater tombs, which fact was really the cause of the establishment of the "greater Pyramids" of Sakkarah.

About 6000 years B. C., the Great Step Cazuda was begun by A-ĕl-zē-ī'dŭs, an architect and ruler of the Cuzetens of that section, who had disembodied before the completion of the original portion of the structure.

Că-sī'thrĭck, ruler and architect who succeeded Aelzeidus, completed the original structure according to the plans made by Aelzeidus, and the Cazuda ultimately became the tomb of both Aelzeidus and Casithrick, the former having been placed in a small temporary tomb, where his body remained until the disembodiment of Casithrick, when their remains were placed in the Cazuda together. Super-coverings, to the extent of its present dimensions, were added to it by subsequent rulers.

The other Cazudas in that Necropolis, now in ruins, were erected from time to time, down to Dynasty VI, or about 3530 B. C., as history has it; and like the former, were burial tombs for the rulers.

About 4500 B. C., the Cuzetens had become numerous in the

section of the now known Abusir Pyramids, and their principal city, then known as A-bū'sĭr, had place east of the Abusir Cazudas, on the west shore of the Hammo, or Nile river, the name having descended, unchanged, to the present. These are the Cazudas, or Pyramids, that mark the Necropolis of that city.

It was from the Cuzetens of Abusir, that Menes or "Mena," the first King of Dynasty I, descended, and not from Thinis, upper Egypt, as claimed in history; and the city of Abusir was a part of the city subsequently termed Memphis, and occupied the same site in part, co-existing as a then ancient part of the portion added by Menes during his reign, and was lost, to mortal knowledge, by being covered with the sediment from the Nile's inundations and the shifting sands.

In the fourth generation of Memphis, after the rule of Menes, a small but beautiful Cazuda was erected, by the ruler of that period, in the center of the city. To this the remains of Menes were removed from his original tomb. It is therefore lost to mortal view, coverd beneath the earth's surface, with the remainder of the city.

The smaller of the two great Cazudas of Abusir was begun about 4500 B. C., by a ruler and architect by the name of Lī-ē-ū'sē-mŭs, whose long reign afforded him time to carry out the greater portion of the construction, which was ultimately completed by his nephew, a son of his youngest brother, who had studied the art of architecture under his uncle's instruction and guidance, from the time of his childhood. He was yet a youth when he began his office as ruler, and the completion of his uncle's Cazuda, the construction of which occupied nearly two hundred years from its beginning to its finish.

The "Great Cazuda of Abusir" was begun by Lieusemus II, in order to carry out the idea of greater work, which ability, vastness in concept, established the "choice of rulers" from the time of the construction of the Great Shemozan, or Sphinx at Gizeh, to that of the last Pyramid builders.

This Great Cazuda was four hundred years or more in process of construction, during which time there were several rulers who carried on the work after the plans laid down by Lieusemus I. It was ultimately completed by a ruler whose name was O'crē-dŏsh, and when completed was the tomb of all the rulers who had had charge of its construction, their remains being removed thither after the completion.

About 12000 years B. C., descendants of the Cuzetens who were a mixture of Kăz-ā-măn'zēs and Kăl-lū'thī-āns, began the erection of a great "Historic Temple," which was known to them as the Jĕlt'mŭs, or Sun God Temple, thus named for the architeet and builder, or first Shacha, of the Cuzetens. It had place about six miles to the east of the great Shemozan, or Sphinx, which latter was commenced about one thousand years later. The Jeltmus was constructed out of rocks taken from the strata that extend southward from the Shemozan or Sphinx, which fact established the original pre-historic excavations that separated the Sphinx from the now known strata that appear a short distance southward from it, and at nearly the same elevation. The first rock, taken from the strata, was used for the construction of the Great Jeltmus Temple; the remainder was taken out during subsequent periods, for the construction of the Tombs and Temples. At the time of the disembodiment of Jeltmus, his body was placed in a small tomb, built for him and his family.

The temple was about thirty feet in height, and terminated in a dome shape, formed by drawing in the four corners of the main structure. This was of pyramidal form at the base, which was about seventy-five feet wide on each side. The dome thus drawn in, curved outward again, and then extended to a still greater height in the form of an obelisk. The inward-drawn dome gave rise to the idea of, or origin of, the rounded domes that now have place on the tombs of the Caliphs, the Mosques of the Sultans, etc., with the change of form, from that of the indrawn pyramid sides, to the perfectly round diametrical form, with the apex extension above the dome . It likewise gave the original idea which later developed into the Obelisks; and the base of the Temple, that of the Pyramids.

The Jeltmus Temple contained three chambers above ground, and two in what might be considered the "basement." On the inside chambers above ground, and on the exterior of the structure, were historical records, such as pertained to general National matters, religious and political affairs, or general history, wrought in their language, with their alphabetic characters.

After the disembodiment of his family, the remains of Jeltmus, together with theirs, were removed to the Temple of Jeltmus, and placed in one of the lower chambers. It was from this procedure that the idea of entombment of the bodies of celebrities originated, and was more completely carried out, in the structure of the Great Shemozan, and later, in the Cazudas; the fact that forms the links to which we must connect the Atlantian practice of placing their mummified bodies in the Great Temple of the Illustrate Dead Bodies; though the original idea of entombing bodies is more properly to be traced back to the Hĕl'trō-plŏx-zē An-zē-rĕt'zē (Cave Tombs) of Atlantis.

About 4500 years B. C., the Cuzetens had become numerous in the district of the Dehshur Cazudas, and their principal city, then known as J-ē-hī'zĕr, had place southeast of these Cazudas. In that vicinty, originally, there were quite a number of small Cazudas and Tombs, erected long before the large ones that now remain. The smaller of the Stone Cazudas that yet have place in that Necropolis, was begun about 4500 B. C., and the larger one about fifty years later, and were therefore both under construction at the same time, the smaller one being completed first. The time consumed from the beginning of the smaller Cazuda, to the completon of the larger, was about twelve hundred years. Both structures were begun by the same architect and ruler, by name Heel'she-ŭs, whose mortal remains were placed in the smaller of the two Cazudas.

The occasion of the larger one was to satisfy the desire of the people who wanted a greater monument built in their Necropolis. Hence, to gratify them, and hold his position of greatness, the ruler planned and began, the larger Cazuda. Ultimately, it was completed by an architect and ruler by the name of E-lĭx'mŭs, whose mortal remains, with those of some of the intervening rulers, who had carried on the construction from the time of Heelsheus to that of Elixmus, were interred in this Cazuda. Some of these were removed from private and temporary tombs, some placed in during the construction; and the last, Elixmus, after the completion, and at the time of his disembodiment. However, the bodies of some of the earlier rulers, above referred to, were placed in small Cazudas, adjacent to the small Stone Cazuda; and these, excepting Heelsheus, were not removed to the large Cazuda.

The north Brick Cazuda was of much later date, it having been constructed by Usertesen III, and begun about 2650 years B. C.

The principal Cazuda of Lisht was begun by Usertesen, who, being an architect, drew the plans for the Cazuda and furnished the means with which to carry on its construction, but did not, as a ruler, superintend the work. He placed that in the hands of architectural servants, who wrought according to his plans. His remains were placed in the Cazuda before it was completed, for it was not finished until in the next generaton, and under the ruling of Usertesen II, of the Dynasty XII. There was no large town in the vicinity of the Lisht Cazuda, but the district had settlements at the time of its construction.

About 4500 B. C., the Cuzetens became numerous in the district of Aillahum, and their principal large city, then known as Nē-ī-cū'lŭs, had place on all sides of, or in other words, surrounded, the Necropolis of the city; hence the Cazuda of Aillahum was the central figure of the city.

The Cazuda was begun about 4500 years B. C., by an architect and ruler whose name was Rē-ū'zī-tĭng, a descended Cuzeten of that ctiy.

The Cazuda was about seventy-five years under construction. Reuziting I, however, did not live to complete the Cazuda, but his mortal remains were entombed there before its completion, which was carried out by his son, according to his father's plans. And the son, having succeeded his father as ruler, was also placed in the Cazuda at the time of his death.

This Cazuda was used for some of the succeeding celebrities, down to the time of Usertesen II of the Dynasty XII, 660 B. C., the last ruler therein entombed.

About 7000 B. C. the Cuzetens had become numerous in the district of Medum, and their principal city, first known as Rī-ā-crū'sĕr, named after their ruler, but afterwards changed to that of Kā-rĕn'tŭm, in honor of the subsequent ruler, of that name, had place east of the now known Great Pyramid of Medum.

The little village now existing to the right of the Cazuda, stands nearly central on the site of the pre-historic city of Karentum, but the latter was much larger, spreading out in all directions and limited only by the river's course, in that direction.

Some of the stones used in the construction of the now known village above referred to, were of excavations from some of the ruins of the city of Karentum, which latter is now an almost invisible ruin.

The great and marvelous Cazuda, as it stands enthroned upon its great rock platform, about two hundred and fifty feet above the river, surrounded by a great white mound, was begun by an architect and ruler of Cuzeten birth, by the name of Rī-ā-crū'sĕr, whose name as above stated had been given to the city under his reign. He lived to be over 200 years of age, and as the Cazuda was only about one hundred years under construction, he of course lived to complete it. Therefore the Cazuda was not, as is supposed by Dr. Petrie, built by Sneferu; but the latter-named king did build the Temple, in its vicinity, during his reign, 3990 B. C., hence, his name appeared on the internal passages of the Temple, as discovered by Dr. Petrie.

The Cazuda was used as a tomb for some of the celebrities, subsequent to the period of Riacruser.

The idea of "greatness," in architectural structure, such as gave to the rulers their positions, and supremacy of power, in the age of the Great Shemozan, or Sphinx, also became strongly impressive in the minds of the Kings of the Fouth Dynasty; hence the Great Cazudas of Gizeh. The idea relaxed at certain periods, and intensified at others, during the time that intervened between the construction of the Shemozan and the latter-named Cazudas, which was the principal cause of the variety, in size, of all the now known Cazudas.

As we have shown, by the foregoing data, the Great Cazudas, as supposed by historic writers, are of much more recent date than the others.

We have given the reason for their stupendous supremacy, in size, over that of the others, viz.: architectural ideas under guidance of spirit intelligences, according to the ability of the mortal brain, at the period of time, to conceive and carry out the same, and not as the original greater conception, or beginning of Pyramidal construction, which would have nothing leading up to the thought of such greatness, as some writers have supposed.

The first Great Cazuda of Gizeh, termed "The Splendid," was planned by Khufu, or Cheops, while he was yet only an architect. His original name was Sĕl'trĭx, and he had been entitled "Khufu" when he ascended the throne, as first King of Dynasty IV.

It was his great conception of the Cazuda, which he became possessed of through spirit aid, that elevated him in the minds of the people, who therefore made him their King.

He began the construction of the Cazuda immediately after he came in power, which was 4000 years B. C.

The construction of this great Cazuda, from beginning to finish, lasted through a period of one hundred years, though Khufu did not live in the mortal form to complete it, he having passed to spirit life about 3920 B. C., at which time his remains were entombed in the incomplete Cazuda.

During the next 20 years, the people under the direction of architectural supervisors, who were employed on the work at the time of the disembodiment of King Khufu, completed the great Cazuda, according to the original plan of Khufu.

Yermah informs us that Herodotus was vastly incorrect in his statement "that there were 100,000 men employed three months in the year for twenty years, on the construction of the Cazuda," for at no one time were there to exceed over seven hundred men employed on the entire detail of construction. But the suggestion made by Dr. Petrie, that "they were employed thus at the time of high Nile, when no labor could be done in the fields," is correct; only instead of its being a period of twenty years, such was the custom throughout the entire period of construction, both by order of the ruling King, and later by that of the supervisors who completed the construction. Thus, in its great dimensions of seven hundred and seventy-five feet on each side, and its original height of four hundred and eighty feet, stands this Pyrmid, evidence of one of the greatest conceptions of an Egyptian mind, through spirit guidance, leading up to that of Modern-Ancient, Mediæval, and Modern Architecture; all developments of which are but re-embodied ideas, under control of the same influence.

By the time of the completion of the first great Cazuda of Gizeh, another architect, whose name was Năn-dō'slŭm, originated the plan of the second great Cazuda of Gizeh, which fact caused him to be chosen as the next King; and he was therefore not a descendant, or relative, of the former King.

At the time of his enthronement, Năn-dō'slŭm's name was changed, and he received the title of "Khafra."

Khafra began the construction of the second great Cazuda, termed "The Great," as soon as he came in possession of the throne, which was immediately after the close of the year 3900 B. C.

This Cazuda was about seventy-five years under construction, and therefore complete about twenty-five years before the death of Khafra, who, at the time of his disembodiment, was one hundred and thirty years of age, he having become King at the age of thirty. His remains were placed in the Cazuda, in a tomb chamber prepared for that purpose, during its construction.

After the disembodiment of Khafra, A-glŏn'tō, who was the greatest priest of all the Nile region, then fifty years of age, was chosen King to succeed Khafra; this was on account of his great scientific learning; and he was raised to the degree of a King under the title of "Menkara," beginning with the period 3800 years B .C., and remained King for a period of one hundred and ten years.

As had been the custom of rulers and kings who preceded him, Menkara began his great Cazuda or ornamental tomb, soon after he ascended the throne, and was nearly one hundred years planning and constructing the Cazuda.

At his disembodiment the throne descended to Princess Agatha, his only child, and the first female who ever ruled over Egypt.

She began her reign at the age of seventy-five, having been born when her father was eighty-five years old.

Gē-ī'nā, her mother, was a second consort to Menkara, and was forty years of age at the birth of her daughter, Agatha.

Agatha passed to spirit life at the age of one hundred years, having reigned only twenty-five years as "Princess of the Nilus."

It was from this fact, of a female ruler, that other women,

in subsequent time, were allowed to ascend to royal power in Egypt, and later in other countries.

It has been supposed that Howard Vyse found the wooden mummy-case of Menkara, in the above-named Cazuda; also a few fragments, such as the ribs, vertebrae, the bones of the legs and feet, and some woolen wrappings of the King, which is not correct. They were the remains of Mĕl'tē-shä, Menkara's chief architect, and general superintendent of construction, under the royal direction of Menkara. He being a favorite of Menkara's, on account of his fine workmanship, and ability as a supervisor of construction, ordered that at the time of his disembodiment, his mortal remains should be placed in the Cazuda.

At the time of the writing of this section of the book, some sixteen years later than the writing of the message from Agatha (see page 214), she further informs us that the above supposition regarding the finding of Menkara's remains is incorrect, and further states that the entrance to her father's tomb is on the side facing the Second Great Cazuda, a little to the left of the center of that side, and that the labyrinthian passage leading to the tomb, in its wonderful intricate windings, descended by various flights of steps and landings, to a great depth, where there are several elaborate chambers of large dimensions. The first one of these is of triangular form, and is centrally located in the Cazuda. There are three doors, one at each angle of the triangle. One of the three makes the entrance to the chamber from the last landing. The other two open into another chamber. Upon entering the triangular chamber, the individual would be facing the south. The door on the left angle leads into the tomb chamber of Menkara, and is the tomb referred to, by Agatha, in her former message.

In the Menkara chamber, against the wall on the right side as one would enter, begins a series of stone receptacles; the first, and largest one, is square in form; the second one, long and narrow; the third one is of rectangular form.

The mummified body of Menkara lies in a stone case on the opposite side of the two receptacles first named, and the third-named receptacle is against the wall at the feet of the mummy case, which latter is also against the wall, receptacles and mummy case alike, having been sculptured from the solid rock which constitutes the walls.

In the three receptacles will be found the great wealth, referred to by Agatha, in her first message (see page 214), and the several chambers to which the door on the right, in the triangular chamber, leads, were never occupied.

Agatha further informs us that she was the only child of

Menkara, and that the three small Cazudas on the east side of the Menkara Cazuda are not, as has been supposed, those of the three daughters of Menkara, but of much later date; and furthermore, that her Cazuda was built upon the western side of the Menkara Cazuda, and is now completely covered with the shifting sands, similarly to the covering, from time to time, of portions of the great Sphinx.

At the time of the building of the three great Cazudas, the region about them was thickly populated by the Cuzetens. The principal large city, then known as Kleet'săm, had place southwest of the three Cazudas. Another large town by the name of Quĭn'dō, had place to the northwest of the first Cazuda, and one by the name of O-cū'tō, was located to the southwest of the third Cazuda.

PLACEMENT OF THE CAP-STONE ON MENKARA'S PYRAMID.

In the month of March, 1893, my venerable friend, Mr. Edward Shippen, placed the following question, with blank paper, in an envelope which he sealed, and addressed to the spirit of Menkara, for the purpose of obtaining an answer direct from said spirit, through the medial instrumentality of Mr. George Cole, now deceased, whose phase of mediumship was that of obtaining messages, and answers to questions from spirits thus questioned, under said conditions. The question and answer were:

Q.—"Will you gratify the world by giving us the method you employed when placing the cap-stone on your great Pyramid?"

A.—"I, Menkara, the Osirian, aforetime Pharaoh of the land of Kehm, will gratify my son of the Western Continent, and explain the method employed in raising the cap-stone upon the Pyramid named.

"For this purpose, I shall be obliged to employ your own language and phrases.

"The principle employed, my son, was that which you term the 'lever.' Masonry, to the height of one hundred feet, was constructed to be used as a fulcrum.

"A lever was prepared by splicing and joining trunks of trees, that their grains diverted; thus was a lever formed to the length of six hundred feet and to the thickness of fifteen feet, braced laterally with straps or bands, and elongated strips, to reduce bending. This lever was affixed to the top of the fulcrum, as on a pivot; made fast and secure. At the distance of fifty feet from where the cap-stone lay, was the fulcrum constructed. At the point of power, or six hundred feet distant from the cap-stone on the end of the lever, were galleries built, to the height of the fulcrum. To the top of these galleries were lifted large blocks of stone which were attached one by one to the point of power of the lever, and lifted one by one to the top of the galleries, to be used as weights to raise the cap-stone at the other end of the lever, thus accomplished by many men pulling down the end of the lever near the cap-stone, by means of ropes.

"After all this had been accomplished, metal straps were placed around the cap-stone, and made fast to the point near the fulcrum, which elevated the point of power of the lever high above the galleries, where lay the blocks to be used as weights; but many long metal straps were attached to that end of the lever, and each strap was placed around a block of stone, which was then swung from the galleries, one after another, until the tenth block of stone caused the cap-stone to rise to a balance. Each of those blocks of stone weighed five tons net, of your weight; therefore, fifty tons' weight lifted the cap-stone, and as the distance between the weight and the fulcrum was to the distance between power and fulcrum, so was the power to the weight.

"Therefore, 600 — 50 = 550 X 50 – 27500 ÷ 50 = 550 tons, the weight of the cap-stone; or twice 550,000 lbs., or 1,100,000 lbs.

"When the weight reached the ground, it was found that the cap-stone had not reached a sufficient elevation to crown the Pyramid. Men were then set to work to excavate under the weights to a depth that would allow the lever to raise the cap-stone to its proper elevation.

"After this had been done, elephants were strapped to ropes, which had been attached to the cap-stone and carried over the Pyramid so that they reached to the ground on the other side of the Pyramid, where the elephants were harnessed to them. These easily pulled the cap-stone over the place it was to rest, and upon one of the blocks of stone being detached in the excavation, the cap-stone, being guided, slowly settled in the place where it yet rests, a wonder to Moderns.

"I omitted to state that the mound was elongated, in form, and of a height equal to the Pyramid ,except superstructural fulcrum and galleries in the rear; and that the metal bands, to which the cap-stone was attached, were of sufficient length to slide upon the lever; hence, when the elephants on the other side of the Pyramid drew the suspended cap-stone over the top of the Pyramid, the metal bands permitted the cap-stone to rest above its bed; also, that the height of the fulcrum and galleries, located upon the mound, was equal to the height of the Pyramid.

"Now, my son, I trust I have used terms so plain and simple that they cannot be misunderstood; and if the revealing of ancient methods is a revelation to modern science, I am satisfied.

"MENKARA, OF THE LAND OF KHEM."

Passing from the Dolmens of underground tombs, we find their influence manifesting in various tumuli; e. g., the O-lĭn'dē-zăc-ĕs, or Burial Mounds, such as are found in Ireland, of which the New-Grange, near Droghead, is a good specimen, established by Zĕl'zĭc, a leader of the Eshemeles of that district.

Other instances are, the Y-ŏn'sy-ĕs, or Beehive Huts, that were established by Frū-dĭsh'ĕr, a leader of the Eshemeles of Cornwall, England; and subsequent leaders of the same people continued the construction, throughout Wales, Scotland, and the Lewis Islands, as they migrated to those districts. Originally they were built of mud, and utilized for dwellings; later, of stone, some being used as tumuli.

The Swĭsh-hĕl'dĭc-ĕs, or Pict's Houses of the Orkney Islands, Scotland, afford a further example. Some of these are chambered tumuli, and others underground dwelling that were established by Bĕl'tē-zŏc, a leader of the Eshemeles, descended from the main stock, and migrating to that section.

The Gē'mŏns, or Nurhags, found so numerously in the Sardinia Islands, which have been a puzzle to modern Archæologists, were tumuli; and were established by Jā-gĭl'dē-mŭs, one of the early leaders of the Kä-sĭn'käs, who settled in that distriet. (See migration of the Jeretheans.) Jagildemus was a spirit sensitive, and thus received his idea of the Gemons as a place in which to preserve the bodies of the departed spirits. Originally, and subsequently, the Gemons were erected on the sides of the mountains, when there would be a large Gemon, surmounted by the figure of a man, to represent the watchful care of the great ruling or protecting spirit, and other spirits who came to watch over the people. About the large Gemon were numerous small ones, tombs for the people generally, the large one being a tomb for the leaders or rulers of the people. The semi-circular stone structure on the side of the hill, that intercepted the Gemon in the center, from the two sides, was a flight of steps that led to the openings in the Gemon; and these further led to the tomb in which the bodies of the leaders were placed.

Links and Cycles

The Cĕ'lŏcks or Lake Dwellings, such as have been submerged in the lakes of Switzerland, Sweden, Italy and Ireland, were ideas of later descendants of the peoples whom we have shown elsewhere as having migrated to those regions, and were homes of the fishermen of that period.

Passing over to the Western Continent, into the Great Plains of North America, we find many specimens of pre-historic barrows of enormous magnitude, that in some respects resemble the "long barrows" of Great Britain. These were burial places for the bodies under conditions of both cremation and inhumation. Both customs were accompanied by the co-deposit of implements, weapons, food, ornaments, stone, bone, and pottery, the latter being, in many cases, elaborately ornamented—evidence of the high grade of development relative to taste and skill in workmanship, of the race that erected these hitherto mysterious constructions.

Some of these tumuli, and ramparts of earth that enclose areas of great extent, had much regularity of form, such as are found in the valleys of the Mississippi, and its mighty tributaries, the Ohio and the Missouri rivers. These were erected by the Shazas and their leaders, who migrated from their original section, of Anteshaza, in the now known district of Louisiana, and were descendants of the Congoes, from Shaltecongo, in the district now submerged by the waters of the Gulf of Mexico. (See migration of the Congoes.)

The first of the greatest of these mounds was established in the now State of Tennessee, southeast of Memphis, by O-sā-lĕn' gē-ō, a leader of a tribe of Shazas who migrated to that district. The second greatest (now in ruins) was established on the southeast side of the Ohio river, near its junction with the Mississippi, by Cĭl-zä-wä'shä, a leader of a tribe of Shazas who settled in that district.

The method employed by the Shazas, when constructing these mounds, and designing the utiilty of the same, was a peculiar one. After the establishment of a tribe, or settlement, in any of the districts where the mounds were built, and where mounds now exist, the body of the first member of the tribe, were he a private or a leader, who passed to spirit life, was placed, with his belongings, on the ground, and there covered over with a small mound of earth. This "burial" took place at sunset, and the exercises were closed with a circular dance about the mound.

On the occasion of the second disembodiment, the body and belongings of that individual were placed on the summit of the mound erected over the first body, and then covered as before, thus enlarging the mound in all its dimensions. After this the usual closing ceremony of dancing took place.

Then came a change in the order of burial. As the different individuals of the tribe passed to spirit life, their bodies were deposited at the base of the already made mound, in circular form, the heads of the latter to the feet of the former; then a circular base, in the form of a terrace, was thrown up so as to cover the bodies, one after the other, until the circle was complete. Then began another row of bodies on the top of the terrace, in the same form, until the circle was complete, and a second terrace had been formed, and so on, until the various subsequent terrace had formed a perfect circular mound again. Then the same order was begun again at the base of the mound, and so on, during the abode of the tribe in that district, or utility of the mound as a tomb, the same order of ceremonies being carried out at each burial, to the completion of the tomb.

Therefore, the now existing remains, known as the mysterious barrows, or "burial mounds" of North America, are the works of the Shazas, whose ancestors were the Congoes, from whom they had learned their art of ornamentation, such as was displayed on their pottery; as with the descended Congoes who settled in Central America, and established the marvelous sculptural, and other works of art, on the pre-historic structures throughout Central America, which have remained equally as mysterious to modern archæologists.

The Shäzäs, therefore, are the original "Mound Builders" of North America, and the ancestors of the aboriginal descendants, who by descended and migratory conditions, lost definite knowledge of the illustrious race from whom they had descended, but left the mounds as the only records, silent though as they are, of their past mortal achievements.

One of their mounds, in Mississippi, covers a base of nearly six acres. The ramparts, in that section, vary in thickness, and are from six to thirty feet in height, and usually enclose areas varying from one hundred to two hundred acres, while some contain four hundred.

One, on the Missouri river, has an area of six hundred acres. The enclosures are generally exact squares or circles, and sometimes a union of the two. Some are formed in parallelograms, or follow the sinuosities of a hill.

In Wisconsin, they assume the fanciful shape of men, quadrupeds, birds or serpents, delineated on undulating plains or wide savannahs.

In the State of Ohio, there are now no less than ten thousands of these barrows or mounds, and rampart remains, while those representing animals are far fewer than in Wisconsin.

There is one, in representation of a gigantic man, with two heads corresponding, in size, with that of the body which is fifty feet long and twenty-five feet across the breast.

This image was built by the descended Shazas to represent, or symbolize, the "great spirit," or "creative force of all things." The two heads were to represent the male and female forces, that are combined in all instances of material creation. They were in communion with spirits, and received much of their knowledge from that source; and therefore got the idea of a higher and more powerful spirit existence than the individual spirits, that ruled in all matters of creation.

On a slope near Brush Creek, there is a representation of a huge snake. It is well designed, with an oval ball in its mouth. The undulating folds of its body, and spiral of its tail, extend to the length of seven hundred feet. That image was established by the Shazas descendants, thus instituted from the fear they entertained of reptiles of that class, and as a danger signal, or reminder, to the people, of the reptile and its bite. The ball was placed in its mouth to represent the fact that everywhere, throughout the country, they were in danger of coming upon it, and to be inflicted with its bite; hence all should be on the watch as they traveled about, to avoid the danger. The great length of the image, and the coiling of its body, also represented the great extent of country wherein it might be found, in secret hiding. There was, however, a deeper meaning to the symbol, viz: to guard well all the undercurrents of evil of every kind, such as might beset them in their life existence, in unguarded hours; and this was taught to the youth of the people.

After the Shazas were well established, in these regions, and prior to the Adomic period, when they had become an illustrious people, they had established towns and hamlets throughout the great section.

Prior to the time of the great flood, or Biblical narrative, in which Noah figured, a great flood passed through the central portion of the now known United States of America, that had place through central British America and passed out into the southern waters of the globe, through the region now drained by the great rivers and their tributaries, of the central States. This great cataclysm carried with it so much earth and sand that it changed the surface greatly in many places.

As the sands whirled in about the buildings, through the streets and alleys, it lodged and filled in until it had completely covered many hamlets, on its course, leaving great piles, or mounds of earth, that covered acres of ground. This occurrence, therefore, was the origin of some of the great mounds that still exist, and many others that have passed from the knowledge of moderns, through subsequent natural causes.

Were complete excavations to be made, in some of the now known mound areas, evidences would be found to substantiate the facts, such as the yet remaining streets, leading to the structures or habitations, etc., etc.

Subsequently, the descendants of the Shă'zăs, who survived the flood conditions above referred to, erected all the now known barrows, or circular mounds; those also of square or rectangular form, or the combined forms of the two latter; and also the representations of birds, animals, reptiles, and human forms, which they did, as sacred symbols, in memory of their ancestors and their hamlets, that were lost in the great cataclysm.

The modern Indians have no traditions of having once belonged to the race who constructed the mounds of North America. This is due to the fact that the mounds were built by the original Shazas proper, who subsequently became extinct by the hand of invading tribes, that subsequently moved into other regions of country, and the Shaza descendants from these original mound builders, who had migrated into other regions and mixed with other races, through their thus descendent condition, lost all knowledge of the origin of their original part-blood ancestors, the Shazas, and of their works. That this could be a logical fact, the reader will only have to consider, for a moment, that even at the present time, were members of a family to move to other parts of the country and intermarry with other peoples, it would not be farther than the second or third generation until all knowledge of the preceding, original ancestors, would be unknown to the descendants, except by a carefully preserved genealogy—something that is seldom kept, even by the present generation, much less by the part-blood descendants of the "mound builders."

The variation in size, of these barrows or mounds, was usually occasioned by the size of the tribe, and the length of time they dwelt in a vicinity. Thus, constructed of earth and stone, the mounds varied from a few feet, in circumference and elevation, to structures with a base circumference of from one to two hundred feet, and an altitude of from sixty to ninety feet.

The pre-historic architecture and sculpture, examples of which still exist in Mexico and Central America, were the work of the Gurenzes, and their descendants, the Aztees, and their further descendants. (See migration of the Gurenzes to the districts of Hayti, Yucatan and Honduras.) It was this pure stock of Gurenzes (remnants from the Atlantians of Teltzie Zret), who retained the knowledge of the great cave structures, or temples of Atlantis, and who handed it down to their descendants and utilized it themselves, in connection with spirit revelations and inspirations, from which resulted the construction of most of the great pre-historic structures, the remains of which now exist, and will yet be discovered, throughout Central America and Mexico (and even many more that lie in ruins buried beneath the earth's surface or hidden in the fastness of the forests). Such, for instance, as the gorgeous buildings found on the table-lands of Anahuac, or Mexico; or in the humid valleys of Central America, and along the peninsula of Yucatan and the shores of Honduras; the great Mexican Pyramid; the wonderful remains, at Palenque and Papantla, or the many towns through Central America, Chiapas and Yucatan, discovered during the last century in the almost impenetrable forests of those regions, some of which were characterized with extensive and highly decorated structures, whose walls were of hewn stone, finely put together with mortar, and bearing hieroglyphical inscriptions, exactly resembing the Aztec Manuscripts (such as are now shown in the museums of Europe, and in the publications of Humboldt), or the well-executed roofs and obelisks there, covered with mythical figures, and pictorial or hieroglyphical inscriptions, all so densely concealed by the luxuriant vegetation of the region, that they remained totally unknown for ages, even by people living in close proximity to them.

The most conspicuous of the above-named ruins are the temples and the palaces, of "pyramidal form" in its various stages, widely intervening. The ascents to these are by grand flights of steps; the long chambers had no windows, but received light through the open doors, similar to buildings in Barbary, and other eastern countries, at the present time. But the latter have been influenced by the Atlantian remnant peoples, migrating eastward through Northern Sfury (see migration of that region), who retained ideas of the Atlantian cave temples.

The apartments of the Mexican pre-historic structure are in two parallel rows; a narrow corridor, or series of chambers runs along the front, thus bearing out the idea of cave chambers; the interior apartments are richly adorned with sculptures, ornamented with stuccos, and gaily-painted red, yellow, white and black, ideas that arose from a knowledge the Gurenzes had of the wonderful natural figures, and material colorings, that had place in the Atlantian cave temples.

Among the very magnificent ruins found at Uxmal and other places in Yucatan, similar to those above mentioned, are sculptured obelisks, the face of each being characterized with a human figure, on which is portrayed a benignant countenance, hands to the breast.

This figure was established by the Gurenzes, as a representation of their god, Er-ĭsh'fäl, the term implying "a great spirit," or "all-creative force," or "provident source of all good," and it was thus worshipped. The benignant countenance was given to the image as a symbol of good, benevolent, kind and gracious feeling for all humanity. The position of the hands represented the god as declaring that these good qualities were embodied within his being; and this was taught to the people.

The other sides of the obelisks are covered with hieroglyphical tablets, designed by the Gurenzes of that region, as the plains of Honduras and table-lands of Anahuac were both inhabited by descended Gurenzes.

The principal building at Uxmal, originally known as the Bä-bō'mē-ăz, so named after the original architect (who, by the way, did not live to complete the structure, but after his death it was continued by his son, under the original plan; and as the son did not long survive his father, the work was completed under the direction of the original architect's grandson), was first intended for a temple, and utilized as such by the Gurenzes. But later it was used as a fortress, against hostile invaders. It was in a magnificent pyramidal form, of three terraces, faced with hewn stone, and neatly rounded at the angles. The first terrace is five hundred and seventy-five feet long, fifteen feet broad, and three feet high, serving as a sort of plinth to the whole. The second terrace is five hundred and forty-five feet long, two hundred and fifty feet wide, and twenty feet high. The third terrace is three hundred and sixty feet long, by thirty feet wide, and nineteen feet in height. The upper part is gained by a vast flight of steps, one hundred and thirty feet wide, from the center of the second terrace. This structure leads to the temple, the facade of which is about three hundred and twenty-two feet long, with an elevation of about twenty-five feet. Its grandeur is enhanced by the rich sculpture that covers the upper part, above a fillet, or cornice, that surrounds the whole building at about half its elevation. The interior consists of two parallel ranges of chambers, eleven in each row. The front apartments are entered by doorways, enriched with sculpture, which gives sufficient light to the rooms. The roofs are stone and cement, supported on bearers of very hard wood, the latter being also covered with hieroglyphics, etc.

The ruins at Chichen, Yucatan, that extend over an area of two miles, were originally the homes of families, belonging to a large settlement of Gurenzes of that district.

One of the best preserved of these buildings was the work of an architect by the name of Jĕl-căz'dē-mŏs, and was the Palace or abode of Yĕz-dē'zē, the original priest and ruler, and also of those who superseded him in subsequent time.

The "Palace," with an ambit of six hundred and thirty-eight feet, was constructed in three terraces, the combined altitude being sixty-five feet. The buildings on the second terrace have highly sculptured facades, both above and below the horizontal fillet; and the doorways are highly adorned with mouldings, and truss-like ornaments, supporting a dip-stone. The staircase is fifty-six feet wide. The front apartments are forty-seven feet long and nine feet wide. The roofs are stone arches, and originally were painted in various colors.

The curious structure adjacent to the Palace, consisting of two parallel stone walls, two hundred and seventy-four feet long, thirty feet thick, and thirty feet apart, belonged to a more complete structure, then termed Wĭl'cŏm-sĭt, which means "playhouse," and answered the purposes of a modern theatre and a games enclosure.

The now termed *"casas caradas,"* meaning "shut-up house," i. e., supposed that the doorways had been walled up when the building was constructed, was originally termed In-drū-zett' signifying a "tomb." It was erected for the purpose of preserving the bodies of the priests and rulers, who dwelt in the Palace; and each doorway was closed after the chamber to which it led was filled with the "illustrate bodies," and not at the time of the construction, as has been supposed by modern writers. Were the tomb to be opened now, bodies and relics would be found, in evidence of our revelation.

The vast extent of the ruins at Copan, Honduras, join in evidence of the greatness of the Gurenzes, who were the builders in that district.

One of their Pyramidal structures, planned by an architect by the name of Shā-rā-zē'lăz, has an elevation of one hundred and fifty feet, measuring along its slope. This is occupied by small structures within an enclosure, similar to the temples of Egypt.

This structure, originally termed I-kĭn'dō-zĕt, was the temple of the Gurenzes of that district, and the abode of O-kĭn'try-mŏs, the original priest and ruler of that people.

The chief ornamental characteristics on the Ikindozet, are skulls of quadrumanous animals, in light relief, etc. Sculptured obelisks also occur, from eleven to thirteen feet in height, and from three to four feet wide. These are also highly ornamented with sculptures in bold relief.

The Gurenzes, of this district, were somewhat more crude in their religious ideas, than were those of some sections.

The worship might be called idolatrous. Kĕr-rĕl'tē-măs was the name of their god principle, which latter was the embodiment of the principles of animation, intelligence and strength, such as characterize nature, especially such as was manifested through animal forms. The animals were to them the most sacred of symbols, as they considered them the prime inhabitants and therefore owners of the land, it being their natural home. Trees were also symbols, representing the greater strength that characterized vegetable forms, and also expressing the intelligent characteristic, through their manifest growth. Hence trees and skulls of animals were among the principal ornamental designs on their structures.

The idea of obelisks and pyramidal forms of structure, and their ornamentation by sculpture and inscriptions, extended into both Egypt and Central America, through descendants of the Cuzetens in the former region, and that of the Gurenzes in the Atlantian influence, such as came through the knowledge the remnants of those two regions had, of the Atlantian monuments and temples that bore out similar forms, and were similarly ornamented and inscribed.

Furthermore, these remaining ideas under spirit guidance, revelation and inspiration, established the re-embodiment of the similar ideas in the minds of the architects of those two regions, in subsequent time. And thus having been wrought out by the people above named, in the structures of the two regions, the splendid ruins stand, a wonder to modern minds as to their origin and use.

In connection with the Palace there was originally a temple, then termed Rŭm'nĕt. At the rear of the inner chamber of the Rumnet was a large sculpture of a man, called "Kĭn'dĭs," meaning the "creating spirit of all things," and thus taught, by the priests, as representing a great spirit who created all things.

This established a sort of idolatrous worship. Therefore, had the Gurenzes survived as a nation, to continue their original beliefs and works, this Continent would have developed the same degree of supposed idolatry as existed in Egypt.

When the people entered the Rumnet, for worship, they

passed around in front of the Kindis, knelt before it, and offered a silent invocation in reverence to the "great creative spirit," and then arose and passed out and away from the Rumnet.

The Priests taught the people in the Rumnet, but this was the custom only on special, or stated days, during the months of the year.

So sacred was the Rumnet to the people, that when they passed it, they would turn to it, bow, or sometimes kneel to it, and silently repeat their invocation.

The influence of the Dū-zē'ĕs structures, especially upon the subsequent barrow, or mound tumuli, was very extensive, and was handed down by the descendants of the Dū'zē constructions; i. e., they appear in Great Britain, Scandinavia, Denmark, Sweden, Sythia, Siberia, and on both sides of the Mediterranean; in north Africa, Asia Minor, and across the plains of Mesopotamia; in the valley of Cabul and throughout India; a group of the largest barrows, or Cairins in Ireland, the burial place of the Kings of Tara, situated on the banks of the Boyne, above Droghead; the huge mound at New-Grange, of the same region, built of stone and earth, three hundred feet in diameter at the base, and two hundred and seventy feet in height with its base, are the remains of a Kē-rĕl'thē of large standing stones. Of this, the chamber twenty feet high in the center, is reached by a covered cē-clū'shē, seven feet in height.

The influence, as it has spread over the various countries, has through advanced ideas and spirit influence, established such structures as the vast tumuli of Alyattes, near Sardis of Lydia, in Asia Minor, together with those of Europe, and of Asia, as evidenced by the tombs in Mesopotamia, and the great mounds and ramparts at Babylon and Nineveh. While in Greece, it further led to the idea of the noted "Hippodrome" and "Amphitheatre" of the Greeks and Romans.

Submerged Atlantis Restored

ARCHITECTURAL DEVELOPMENT AND EXTENSION.

TELTZIE XXVIII.

The structures of Siloton (Egypt) are the oldest now known on the globe, and therefore are the proper ones to which we must link the Atlantian influence, since they had their origin in that section through the influence of remnant descendants of Atlantians who settled in the Siloton districts. Thus, Siloton was the place of the true origin of Egyptian architecture, and not India, as has been supposed by modern writers.

As the spirit influence, co-operative with that of the Tē-lī-ū'sä, became stronger and more comprehensive, to the latter, they accordingly conceived ideas of greater magnitude, which they developed according to the conditions and utilities of the various districts, and periods of time, during pre-historic and subsequent ages.

Before proceeding with the extension of the cycle, however, it might be well to state that during the time of Hĭl-lō'thē-ăn, and Căl-lū-ĕn'dĕn, and the period of our re-establishment of the cycle, the Teliusa had erected many structures throughout Siloton, that went to decay prior to the historic period, or were shattered, scattered, and entombed beneath the earth's surface, by the force of earthquakes in that region subsequent to their erection.

Passing from the influence of Hillothean and Calluenden, and that of the Teliusa who succeeded them in the generations contemporaneous with the various periods just preceding the historic, a period of about 2730 years, we find the links to which we must connect those of the more remote pre-historic and also those of the historic, in order to re-establish the extension of the Great Architectural Cycle. The development of this was one of the principal events in the pre-historic age of Egypt; a period the duration of which was from the time the Kăs-ā-măn'zēs entered Gasbia (Lower Egypt), or the Kăl-lū'thē-äns entered Kalluthea (Upper Egypt), to the time of the First Dynasty, under King Menes, a period of about 9000 years, and contrary to the proposed duration of 4000 years, as per M. Chabas.

Therefore we pass the crudities that existed, from the time the above-named people settled in those regions of Siloton, to the works of Hillothean, Calluenden, and subsequent pre-historic Teliusa, as given above, which we utilize as the proper links with which to make the connection of pre-historic events in the Cycle of Architecture, which must be done principally in the regions of Egypt where the pre-historic and historic Necropolis sections are marked with such remnant monumental evidences as are embodied in the great Mastabas, Pyramids, Temples, Obelisks, the great Sphinx at Gizeh, etc. For instance, leading up to the "Art of Construction," we note the great Embankments of the Nile, done under the influential reign of Menes, the first King of Dynasty I, who established the Temple of Ptah, at Memphis; also the great Mastabas of Sakkarah, the greater of which, a very archaic structure among pyramids, was established by Uenephus, fourth Trinite King, or of Dynasty I; the great Pyramids of Gizeh; those of Aboo-Seer; those of Dahshoor; the great Mastaba or Pyramid of Medum, or Meydoum, etc.

Passing on with the influence that the Siloton Teliusa had established by their Teliusatic, such as the Mastabas, Pyramids, and other tumuli, to the effect it had upon a further development of the Art, we find it manifested in various forms of Temples, with their accompanying Obelisks, in which the grandest ideas of the descended Tē-lī-ū'sa were embodied; marking an epoch that extended from the time of the establishment of Thebes, as a capitol city, about 2000 years B. C. down to the time of the Cæsars; an epoch embracing the so-called "Sanctuary Temples," those with single chambers; the "Peripteral Temples," those surrounded with columns in front; and those with a portico and many columns in front, as Esne, Dendera, etc., and many inner chambers; also those with large courts, and with Pyramidal towers, or propylons in front; the Great Temple at Karnak, that occupies an area of about four hundred and twenty thousand square feet, a propylon three hundred and seventy feet long, a hypostyle hall, a parallelogram of about three hundred and forty-two feet in length, and one hundred and seventy wide, acknowledged to be one of the most wonderful apartments in the world. It has fourteen rows of columns, nine in each row, forty-three feet high; two rows, six in each, of the enormous height of sixty-two feet, and eleven and a half feet in diameter, the capitals of which measure twenty-two feet across.

Another example is the Great Temple of Apollinopolis Magna, at Edfoo, upper Egypt on the banks of the Nile between Thebes and the First Cataract. Its doorway is fifty feet high; facade two hundred and fifty feet; propylon covered with many figures of colossal proportions, some of which are forty feet in height; court one hundred and sixty by one hundred and forty feet, and surrounded on three sides by columns thirty-two feet high; a covered portico one hundred and ten by forty-four feet, consists of three rows of six columns, each thirty-four feet high, etc. Other examples are, the ruined Temple of Amen-ra, at Thebes; the beautiful Temple of Athor, the Egyptian Venus, that stands on the mounds of Tentyra, one and a half miles from the Nile; the Temple of El-Uksur on the Nile, southwest of the Temple of El-Karnak, of which it is an appendage; the Setheum, a Temple of Setee I, and the Rameseum; the great Temple of Rameses II, of El-Kurneh; the group of Temples known as the Medemnet-Haboo, southwest of the former; between the two the ruins of Amenophium with its gigantic seated Colossi; the Great Temple of Isis, on the Island of Philæ; the Great Temple of Amen, near the town of Kharigeh, the ancient Hibe; the Temple of Esneh, of Dair-al-Bahari, and others.

Passing into Arabia, we find that the Arabs of modern times, though considered somewhat skillful as artificers, have no record as developed masons or architects, a fact evidenced by their clumsy, unstable constructions of coarse and ill-fashioned details.

In regard to utility and beauty, there are no structures in all Arabia, either public or private, of any architectural merit, that have place by Arabic construction proper; a proof conclusive of the decadence of the genius of the pre-historic Cicentues, and the degenerate condition into which their descendants have fallen, in regard to architectural inspirations, ideas, conceptions and developments.

About 5500 B. C., the various divisions of the people of El-tē'za (Arabia) became hostile to each other, when wars broke out among themselves, which caused destruction of their structures, and the people to scatter, migrate, and mix with other peoples, a condition that never was overcome by the remaining native peoples of Elteza, hence the present low condition of native architecture.

Passing into Persia, we note the influences that developed through architectural ideas, which manifest through such strue-tures as the Tomb of Cyrus, at Murgab, east of the Persian Gulf.

The tomb stands on seven bold steps of white marble, the lowest being forty-three by thirty-seven feet. The tomb proper is twenty-one by sixteen feet five inches outside, with bold mouldings to the door; it has a sloping roof of marble, with a pediment at either end, enriched with mouldings. The chamber itself is only seven feet by ten, the walls being built up with thick blocks of marble. Originally there was a colonnade of twenty-four columns, Grecian style, around the tomb.

This tomb was the work of a Persian architect by the name of Kä'zō, who being a spirit sensitive, got his idea of the structure from a Greek spirit, who was his general adviser; and therefore the tomb was not, as is supposed by modern writers, the work of a foreigner, or architect from a Greek colony in Asia Minor.

In the grand ruins of Persepolis and Susa, above the former, are chiseled the Tomb-chambers, in the steep rocks, of Persian kings. The platform on which the structures were built measured one thousand four hundred and twenty-five feet on the west side, and nine hundred and twenty-six feet on the north, and was raised to about forty feet above the adjoining country. The platform was approached by a flight of steps, the grandest known in the world, each being twenty-two feet long.

While modern writers place the development of Persian Art as contemporaneous with the Grecian, contemplating the fact that utterly different results exist in the development of the two, they cannot tell by what steps the Persian Architects arrived at the singular work at Persepolis and Susa.

But Yermah informs us that the Persian architects thoroughly understood the law of spirit communication, and therefore had their spirit counselors, who were the spirits of Grecian architects. These, after passing to spirit life, sought to bring out different, and if possible, even greater structures, in the Persian region, than they had been able to in Greece; hence, it was through that order of spirit counsel that the ideas and conceptions of the structures at Persepolis and Susa were obtained, and carried out by the Persian architects.

The great Tomb-chambers above referred to, originally were termed A-mē-dē'ŭm, meaning Tombs of the Illustrious Dead, and the entire structure was planned by Iz-rē-ĕl-nē'ăd, a spirit sensitive and architect; but ultimately completed by succeeding architects, who carried out the original plan of Izreelnead, a Persian by birth.

This great structure we have chosen, as one of the principal links with which to connect Ancient and Modern structures, thus to establish the extension of the great Cycle of Architecture into the latter period of time.

The famous walls of the ancient capital, Ecbatana, North Media, originally were about seventy-five feet broad, and one hundred and five feet high, the stones of which were nine feet by four feet and six inches, and its gateways one hundred feet high and sixty feet wide. The structure, originally, was termed Lă-pō'ōz, and consisted of six complete walls, with an inner row of fifteen monoliths, and a centrally located one. Each wall was built, successively, by subsequent rulers, at various periods of time, marking their reigns, which varied from seventy-five to one hundred years, and in some cases more. At the time of the completion of the Lapooz, the people of that district were a powerful nation, a fact which the great Lapooz symbolized in general. The several walls were built, one over the other, on the side of the conical hill, and were colored from the outer to the inner one, respectively, white, black, scarlet, blue, orange, and silver, and the inner row of monoliths were gilded. The colors on the various walls were national, belonging to the people and their rulers, at the period of time during which each wall was constructed. The fifteen gold-colored monoliths, then termed Căl'mā-zŭs (the "finale"), and the centrally located one, which latter served the purpose of an outlook, collectively, represented the "light and force of the sun," and also referred to gold as the most precious of metals, and thus symbolized the "greatness of the nation." The Lapooz, originally, was built for protection in time of war, and at that time there was an underground tunnel that led from the city to the inner walls of the Lapooz, through which the people could pass in safety in times of danger.

The great Ish'ĭn-făl, or Propylæum (the term at that period of time signified the "line between the earth and the spirit life"), was subsequently planned and erected by Xerxes, who intended it to be a tomb for himself and his family.

Originally, it was in the form of, or similar to, a terraced pyramid, excepting the facade, which was flat above the first terrace, the whole structure being drawn in at the top in an oval shape.

On the facade, above the first terrace, was sculptured a very large image of Xerxes, executed in bas-relief, beneath which was the entrance to the Ishinfal. On each side the entrance hall were two large rooms, one back of the other, making four in all, intended as tomb-chambers for the family.

At the rear of the hall was a large alcove chamber with an arched roof, in the center of which was a pedestal supporting a sarcophagus, which contained the body of Xerxes, preserved by a process that left the body more natural than is the case with the mummifying process. This was placed in an erect position on the pedestal, facing the entrance, the body at all times being visible to those who entered the tomb.

The Ishinfal structure was roofed with an arch of stone, as above mentioned, having been drawn in to an oval form.

A circular wall encompassed the Ishinfal, or Propylæum, of which there yet remain two grand tär-dĕs′try, or gateways (the singular of the term being tär′dĕs, meaning gate), twenty-four feet apart, with columns twenty-four feet high, and openings of thirteen feet, with fragmentary portions of the wall between.

Large images in the form of bulls, with human heads, crowned with coronets of leaves, adorned the piers.

The bodies of the bulls symbolized strength or force; the human heads, the nation in general; the leaf coronets, conquests won by the nation generally.

Beyond the Ishinfal was the grand O-gĕ-rĕn′zē, or Palace of Xerxes, and subsequent Kings of Persia, and is now termed the "Chehil Minar," "hall of forty columns" (an Eastern mode of expressing a great many). Originally there were seventy-seven, that being a mystic number with the early Persian people.

It was approached by a magnificent staircase, each step of which served as a pedestal to a figure, one foot nine inches high, in bas-relief, that symbolized united force of the people of the nation, and represented the various costumes of the period, generally speaking. The partitions on the interior of the structure were of stone, but the finishings were of wood of the Lebanon cedar.

The Ogerenze, as a whole, would be difficult to describe in our limited space and time, from the fact that it was a Palace of Palaces, so to speak. For each subsequent King added a part to the structure, which was marked by four series of columns, or divisions, the greater of which outlined the entrance to the Palace of Xerxes, and was the centrally arranged division, originally of thirty-seven columns. There were three more divisions, two of which had fourteen columns in two rows of seven each, and one of twelve columns in two rows of six each. These, as above stated, marked the entrances to the "additions" of the subsequent Kings, aggregating a total of seventy-seven columns.

Of all these, only ten are now standing, but the bases of most remain, and the whole ground is covered with the ruins of the columns that have fallen, the highest of which varied from sixty to sixty-seven feet four inches, including the capital and base.

Some of the gigantic columns bore capitals seven feet high, twelve feet two inches wide, while the shafts, fifty-four feet ten inches in height, are composed of only four marble blocks. The columnar divisions to the various additions to the Palace, answered the same purpose to that structure, that the pylons did to the ancient structures of Egypt.

The large enclosed building, now termed the "Hall of One Hundred Columns," of which gigantic fragments remain, was then known as the Shē-ō′mä. It was a large Government Hall, covering an area about two hundred and twenty-five feet square.

The great Palace of the ruins of Susa, built by Artaxerxes Mnemon, son of Xerxes, was originally known as the Mē-sē-ĕn′-dry. The columns of this, to a certain extent, exceeded in size those of the Ogerenze of Xerxes, for they varied from sixty-five to seventy feet in height, and were in four divisions, in lines of seven columns, as was the case with the Ogerenze. Therefore, the seemingly original Persian style of architecture arose through spirit guidance, which influenced the minds of the prehistoric Greticze, whose thus conceived ideas, co-operative with further Grecian, Egyptian, and Assyrian migratory influences, developed the peculiarities that characterized the pre-historic Gretictor, and the historic architecture. Hence, the columnar styles of the ancient ruins; the human heads seen on the bull statues; the plain architraves of the doors and windows of structures, with large roll, covetto, and fillet at the top, etc.

Passing from Persia into India, we note the Lats, or "Pillars of Aso-ka′, a grandson of Chandragupta, the earliest extant of architecture remaining in that region. These were erected in the locality where Asoka abjured Brahmanism, and caused Buddhism to become the religion of the state. The Lats bore the record of this edict.

The Buddhist Topes, such as at Sanchi, were originally established as burial chambers for the Buddhas, whose bodies were placed in the chambers. The remains are now found in those chambers, then called "dagobas."

The rock-cut Caves (Chaityas) or original temples, of which there are no less than one thousand in India, were for general use, such as that of Karli, near Bombay, with circular apse, divided into three aisles, by two rows of columns. Some, however, are square structures, with circular, or oval chamber at the end, and are entered by a small door.

The monasteries (Viharas) originally were the abode of the monks, and are more numerous than the Cave Temples. Originally these were square caves, supported by pillars of the natural rock, left in the original place, and surrounded by a number of small chambers, which were originally the sleeping apartments of the monks, and the students who sought to adopt the same life. There was also an apartment used as instruction room, and the whole edifice was a place of seclusion. There are found, at Ellora near Aurangabad, a series of hypogea or caves. sunk in the solid rock, extending a distance of three or four miles.

The now termed "Parasova Roma" and "Diajannata," halls supported by massive pillars, were not only entrance places, but apartments where the monks and students kept their paraphernalia, robed or disrobed when passing or repassing, in or out to the various adjacent rooms, on various occasions.

The caves termed "Indra," having a court open to the sky, containing small shrines, were where the monks taught the students, and held their religious ceremonies, which latter were numerous.

The Kylas or Kailasa, such as those of Ellora, that occupy a space sunk in the rock, two hundred and seventy feet deep and one hundred and fifty feet wide, with grand detailed appendages, have the appearance of forming a grand temple, which in fact they do.

The Jains temples, such as the famous temple at Somnauth, and that built by Vimala-Sah, on Mount Abu, and the temple at Sadre, the latter possessing twenty domes, varying from thirty-six feet to twenty-four feet in diameter, and supported by four hundred and twenty columns.

The "towers," a mark of victory, such as the Jaya Stamba, erected by Khumbo Rana, to commemorate the defeat of Mohammed of Malwa, in 1439, which is nine stories in height, and richly ornamented from bottom to top.

The great Hindu Temples, such as the one at Tiravalur, near Tanjore, the dimensions of which are nine hundred and forty-five by seven hundred feet, built by the Tamul races, considered to be the greatest temple builders in the world.

The great Pagodas or temples, such as at Tanjore, the greatest in India, resting on a base eighty-three feet square, that rises to a height of nearly two hundred feet, possessing a grand interior; also the Black Pagoda at Kannaruc, and the Shoemadoo Pagoda at Pegu.

The Ghâts, or landing places, that line the rivers of North India, such as the Ghoosla Ghat, at Benares, etc., etc.

The idea of grandeur, as displayed in the construction of these and other similar edifices, was a work sacredly wrought, in the cause of spiritual interest. An example of constructors, entering into that work and giving the artistic effects in favor of spiritual advancement, which they embodied in these spiritual edifices, a characteristic that has followed the races of India, through ages past, and even down to the most modern.

This spiritual idea was prompted by their teachings generally, especially that Heaven was very beautiful, a knowledge they gained from beholding spirits who manifested to the teachers, in conditions of light and beauty. These also taught them that they, as developed spirits, dwelt in corresponding conditions, in contradistinction with the state of undeveloped spirits, and the conditions in which they must necessarily dwell.

Passing from Siloton (Egypt) into Zăn-zū-rē'tä (Greece), we wish to note that as had been the case with the former, so it was with the latter—the architectural influence came through spirit inspirers and teachers, to the Zanzuretan Meltheon, until they had conceived the ideas of the Doric, Ionic, Corinthian and Caryatic orders of Meltheonses, and the peculiar mouldings connected with them, such as characterize the Greek temples, which latter were improved ideas, of similar structures that had been originated in the minds of the pre-historic Silotonian Teliusa, and partially carried out by them.

Therefore, the architectural ideas embodied in the Greek architecture, by spirit influence, were original with themselves, and not borrowed from Egypt, and though in subsequent time, knowledge of the various orders, by and through migratory aid, was known to both the Egyptians and the Greeks, as it was in both countries, yet each had originated ideas of the orders, to the extent of which they existed in the two countries, rerespectively.

In the first place, let us notice the oldest supposed existing structure in Greece; i. e., the one at Mycenae. This was constructed by Atrius, who was a descended ruler of the Kĕl'to-plăs, in which his remains, as those of his son, Agamemnon, were placed at the time of disembodiment. Thus, the structure was not, as has been supposed by modern writers, the treasury of Atrius.

In the same district we note the great "Cyclopean Walls," so termed by moderns for want of a better name.

These gigantic structures were erected by descendants of the Keltoplas and the A-zĕn-trū'sî-ăns, both of them descendants of the Ic-thī-ē'ŏns, who by diverse migration, had settled in that portion of Zanzureta now known as Argolis.

Originally these walls were termed Trū-cŏn-cy-lē'ŏn (protection against invaders), and primitively built about portions of the city such as were occupied by the rulers and the wealthy citizens, who thus protected themselves and their property from invasion; while the poorer classes were left unprotected in their homes without the walls.

Links and Cycles

About 4000 B. C., some descendants of the Keltoplas had settled on the fertile plains of Argive, where they built their principal town. They termed it Jĕl-cy-lā-ā'măs, and it had place on the site now occupied by the ancient city of Mycenae.

Contemporaneous with that settlement by the Keltoplas, in the above-named district, descendants of the Azentrusians had settled on portions of the marshy plain of Argolis, where they built a town which they termed Skĭt-chăn'zē. (It must be borne in mind that at that period of time that plain, or district of land, was not in its present marshy condition, which arose after the eruptions in that region, that shattered Greece.) This was on the site where subsequently the ancient city of Tiryns had place.

During periods of time subsequent to the above-named origin of the "Truconcylecon walls," the Keltoples and the Azentrusians, though of the same stock, had co-united and joined issues as a nation, under the name of Cē-rē'thăns (see migrating peoples of Greece), who continued the work of Truconcylecon structure and city building, on the two above-named sites, until the present known conditions of the two cities Mycenea and Tiryns, were fully established, and assumed even greater than the present known proportions, relative to structures, such as walls, palaces, other buildings, and constructions in general.

Subsequent to the arrival of the Azentrusians in their section of A-zĕn-trū'sĭ-ä (district of Achai of Morea), some of their descendants, prior to the formation of the now known Gulf of Corinth, migrated northeast into the territory of Phocis, where they settled in the vicinity of the now known ancient city of Delphi.

In due time they built a town which they termed Kē-lŭn'dry, on the site on which subsequently the ancient city of Delphi had place; and it was this branch of the Azentrusians that erected the Truconcylecon (or now known Cyclopean) walls in that vicinity, which are similar to those at Mycenae and Tiryns.

As the influence spread and developed during subsequent periods, we find it manifesting through the Grecian styles of Temples, e. g., Temples of the Doric order, the Theseum, the Parthenon and the Propylæum, at Athens; of Jupiter at Ægina; of Jupiter at Olympia; of Apollo at Bassas (ruins), all Greek proper. Other characteristic types are to be found, as of the Doric order in Sicily, such as Jupiter, at Selinus; Minerva, at Segesta; Minerva, at Syracuse; Juno, Concord, and Jupiter, at Agrigentum; of the Doric order in Asia Minor, as the Mausoleum at Halicarnassus; and of the Ionic order, as Diana, of Ephesus; while further instances in the Ionic order are, Apollo, at Branchidæ, Ionia; the Temple on the Ilissus, Athens; the Erectheum, and other examples of the Athenian Acropolis. Traces of the Corinthian are, the Temple of Apollo Didymæus, at Miletus, Ionia; the Monument of Lysicrates, at Athens, etc., and of the Caryatic order, or the third portion, or portico, of the Temple in the Athenian Acropolis, etc.

While these temples are said to date from 600 to 335 B. C., yet some of them were built upon sites, and in the vicinities, of pre-historic temples that date from one hundred years after the beginning of the Adomic period, to the oldest of the now known temples above referred to.

Prior to the convulsions that severed Greece from Asia Minor, on the east, and Italy and Sicily, on the west, the extensions of the Continent embraced southern Europe and Turkey, and subsequent to the establishment of the Ic-thī-ē'ŏns, in their section of Ic'kē-trūse (see later), tribes of their descendants migrated eastward into the district now submerged by the Ægean Sea. At the time of the submergence, portions of that race, of the same stock as the descended Greeks, were left in the district of what is now known as Asia Minor, whose descendants were the peoples modern writers suppose to have been the Greek colonists of Mysia. These populated the valley of Caicus or Cyzicus, on the shores of the Propontis; in fact, the whole of the sea coast thence round to the Gulf of Adramyttium, where so many supposed Greek towns were built; thus extending along the south shore of the Propontis, Hellespont, and Troad, where Parium, Lampsacus, and Abydos had their supposed origins, through descendants of the above-named remnant people in those regions, subsequent to the time of the convulsions and submergence above referred to; and likewise the original nucleus of the now known Greek colonies, that anciently occupied the sea coast from the Gulf of Adramyttium, to the mouth of the Caicus, and thence to the Elaitic Gulf.

The greater centers of the subsequent growth of architecture, resulted in the towns of Assos, Adramyttium, on the Gulf of Adramyttium, and Elæa, Myrina and Cyme, on the Elaitic Gulf.

Therefore, the supposed influence on the architecture in those regions, by Greek colonists, is not correct, but was that of inspiration, and guidance, by Grecian spirits who manifested to their brethren in their several localities, thus extending styles of the Grecian architecture, to a certain degree, in those regions of Asia Minor.

The appearance of the Greek influence, in the architectural

style of temples above referred to, in Sicily, like that in Asia Minor, was due to the influence of Greek spirits over the sensitive architects of Sicily, which latter had descended from the same original stock, as had the ultimate Greeks, i. e., from the Jē-rē-the'ăns.

For our Grecian links, by which to connect up the pre-historic and the historic Architectural Cycle, we have chosen, first, the great Parthenon of Athens, of the Doric Temples. This, the queen of the Doric Temples, was planned by Ictineus, under Pericles, and completed 438 B. C., and occupies the site of a ruined temple, that was pre-historically known as the Temple of Gē-mĕl'tē-zŏn, which was planned and established by an Icthieonian architect by the name of Cē-lĭr'ē-ŭs.

The Gemeltezon was the largest of the Temples in that section at the time it was constructed, which was about 3000 B. C., the term Gemelte meaning "great," and the term Gemeltezon, "greater," or "greatest;" hence the Temple received its name. In style, it was a combination of the Doric and the Ionic, the former being the greater. In form, it was rectangular, and a medium large structure. At that period of time, style was all more or less mixed up, in the orders, all four, viz: the Doric, the Ionic, the Corinthian and the Caryatic, being known, but under somewhat different utilities, etc.

In the second place, we have chosen the Erectheum of Athens, as one of the links with which to aid in the pre-historic and the historic connections of the Architectural Cycle.

This temple of the Ionic order was erected in the vicinity of a pre-historic temple then known as the Be-lō-ŏn'zō, planned and erected by an Icthieonian architect by the name of Frē-lē-ŏn'-tē-ĕt, about 3500 B. C.

The ruins of the Temple of Beloonzo were utilized in the construction of the ancient Erectheum, hence not now known to have existed. In style, it was square, with round corners, and embellished with a mixture of Ionic and Corinthian details, the former being in the majority. It was used as a funeral temple, on which occasions the services were always pantomimed, in complete silence. The term "Belo" signified "silence," which referred to the silent funeral services, and the compound term "Beloonzo," referred to the greater silence of the body after the spirit had departed; hence, the Temple received the name of Beloonzo.

In the third place, we have chosen the triple Temple in the Athenian Acropolis and the Choragic Monument of Lysicrates, as the links with which to make the pre-historic and historic connections in the Architectural Cycle in that region.

The last-named Temple was rebuilt, upon the site of a ruined temple that was pre-historically known as that of Jĕl'tē-cloise (Temple of the Gods), that was planned and constructed by an architect by the name of O-rä-zē-nē'tŭs, an Icthieonian by birth, 4000 B. C.

The Jĕl'tē-cloise was a square structure, of two stories, the whole presenting the outline of a truncated pyramid. The lower story was of Corinthian style excepting the two columns at the entrance, which were the Caryatic; and over the entrance were foliate designs, carved in low relief. The upper story, front and two sides, were of the Caryatic style. On the front there were three columns of the human form, the center one being that of a female, and the others male. The same arrangement had place on the sides of this story. These Caryatic columns were accompanied with various foliate designs over portions of the wall, etc. The rear of the story was characterized with three trees, that were sculptured in bas-relief, in place of the Caryatic columns, the largest one being in the center, and the wall was also ornamented with foliate designs.

In evidence of the greater antiquity of architecture in Zăn-zū-rē'tä (Greece) that is now known in history, we might give many other examples, but the three above named pre-historic Temples and their builders will suffice.

Celireus, Freleonteet, Orazenetus, and other Icthieonian architects, were all spirit sensitives, and therefore received their ideas through the inspiration and guidance of spirit influences who had long before entered the disembodied life; hence the early architectural influence in Zanzureta.

Passing from the architectural influence of Greece to that of Rome, we note that spirit influence caused the Roman architects to further develop the Grecian Arch, that had formerly been developed from the placement of the Quinzeex (columns) so as to form arches, etc.; a fact which led up to the construction of the famous Cloaca Maxima, or public sewers, by Tarquin the Great, and finished by Tarquin the Proud, 556 B. C.

From the idea of the Zanzuretan Quinzeex, such as marked the approach of rivers and streams, for the guidance of the traveler, the Roman architects developed the idea, until they had carried secure and permanent roads across the wide and rapid rivers.

Passing from the Zanzuretan or Grecian development of the Quinze (column) idea, to the Roman, we find the architects of that period conceiving ideas of inspiration, which caused them to deviate from the earlier works of the Doric, Corinthian and Ionic orders, and to develop the foliated Corinthian, which became their ultimate national style. (This influence came to the Romans through the inspiration of Icthieonian spirits, who had used it in the pre-historic Athenian Acropolis, etc.) In this way it was used with wonderfully varied distinctness from the Grecian, and even the Roman, as evidenced by the difference existing between the Choragic Monument of Lysicrates at Athens, the Temple of Vesta at Tivola, and the Temple of Jupitur in Rome, the three most beautiful examples of the Corinthian order in existence.

Therefore the foliate style, as first influenced at Athens, through the Icthieonian spirits, is to that extent natural in Greece; but the inspiration and guidance was more fully conceived and carried out by the Roman architects, who developed it as their National style or order. Then came the reflex influence of the Roman ideas, as developed by the architects of that period, who carried back the Corinthian styles into Iberia, Gaul, Istria, Greece, Syria, Egypt, etc.

It might be well to note here that the idea of the Caryatic order, originally, came from the use of human figures on the architectural structures of Atlantis, and thus influenced by Atlantian spirits, those who gave it forth to the sensitives of these periods. Even so that of the foliate Corinthian order, for the Atlantian structures were extensively characterized with that kind of ornamentation; likewise the Sphinxes, as the Atlantians used animal forms so much in connection with their monuments. All these ideas were given back to the world again by Atlantian spirits, to the pre-historic and historic builders.

The same might be said of the Columns and the Arches. For 1000 years before the Adomic period, the idea of the Arch was conceived and established, as before mentioned, by being placed in very crude form at points where travelers would cross streams of water, as a signal to them as they approached. Sometimes pillars were used for the same purpose, which also were in the original idea of Columns, used for other purposes in subsequent time, as at the entrances to grounds of private homes of the wealthy classes, and ultimately to temples, and further in a variety of ways.

One interesting link is that of the "flaming sword," as narrated in the biblical account of Adam, which though purely legendary, was based upon some facts.

At the beginning of the Adomic period, the idea of columnar

erection for marking entrances to private possessions, by means of pillars, in the form of gabled arches (see later). was conceived by Gŏn'thē-ōle (the biblical Adam), who placed at the entrance of the Valley of Cē-lī'tē (the biblical garden of Eden), two large pillars, supporting a gabled covering of stone monoliths, to which he caused to be suspended a golden sword, which flashed in the sunlight, thus giving it the appearance of fire, and all people passing in and out of the Valley, passed beneath the pillars and beneath the sword.

The sword was an emblem, intended by Gontheole to warn the people who entered the Valley that a sufficient force existed within to resist invaders; and to represent peace as reigning within the Valley; and furthermore, it was an ensign to that effect, and could be seen from a great distance by those who were approaching.

There was no shutting out of the Valley, excepting of invaders, and there was no "garden of Eden," excepting the fertile Valley of Celite in which Gontheole and his people dwelt (see later).

The above structure will serve the purpose of one of the links with which to connect the pre-historic Pillar, or Column strutures, with those of the Modern-Ancient.

As the Roman influence developed under both spirit and mortal guidance, we find it made manifest in such architectural structures as the Temple of Fortuna Virilis, at Rome; the Pantheon; the Temples of Peace and Venus; the Temple of Rome; the Temple of Minerva Medica, etc.; the Colosseum; the Mausoleum of Adrian; the Tunnel Sewer; the ancient Bridges on the Tiber; the Imperial or Triumphal Arches; the Cenotaph Columns of Trajan, and of Antonine; the Palace of the Cæsars; the Baths of Titus, of Caracalla, and of Diocletian; the Villa of Adrian and that of Mæcenas, at Tivoli; the Palaces of the Roman Emperors, and Patricians at Baiae, and in other parts of Italy; the structures of Herculaneum and Pompeii, etc., all of which stand as links to which we link the pre-historic and historic influences, in the Architectural Cycle, of those regions.

The Roman influence relative to the Corinthian order, extended in to Bena and in Gaul; in Islria and in Greece; and to the present time, Nismes, Pola, Athens, Palmyra, and to the banks of the Nile.

In further consideration of the Roman influence, we note its manifestation through such works as the Theatres, e. g., those of Pompeii, and Herculaneum, Rome, Verona, Pola, Taormina, Arles, Orange, and others in France, and in Sicily. We note it in the Amphitheatres, such as were erected by Julius Cæsar, Caligula and Nero; Vespasian, Titus, etc., as at Rome, Nismes, etc.; in the Forum, as at Pompeii, Rome, etc.; in the Aqueducts, such as stretch along the Campagna, span the Valley at Tarragona, the Pont du Gard, at Nismes, and others; in the Triumphal Arches, such as those of Titus, Severus, Janus and Constantine, at Rome, and that of Trajan, at Ancona; in the grand dwellings, such as the Villa of Hadrian, near Tivoli, and other Roman palaces and mansions of Italy, from that of Sallust on the Benacus or Lago di Garda, to those of the Roman nobles on the shores of the Bay of Baiae; in that of Diocletian, at Spalatro, and in the grand remains of Baalbec and Palmyra; again in the Basilicas, such as that of Trajan of Maxentius, and the remains as found at Pompeii, Herculaneum, Treves, etc.; in the further development by means of "Pointed Architecture," found in every part of Europe, such as at Paris, Cologne, the Fountains Abbey, England; structures in Spain; in the Cathedral of Trondjem, Norway, etc.

The Byzantine influence extended from Constantinople to Venice, the Pisan buildings, and those in the south of Italy, and of Spain; the early churches of Europe, as the San Clemente and San Lorenzo, at Rome; the San Miniato, at Florence; the Cathedrals of Torcello, San Zenone, Verona, and San Michele, Pavia; through which the old styles were being thrown off, and the new developed; ,old, pre-historic forms being re-embodied as new in a succession of circular buildings, e. g., re-embodied in the Pantheon and other circular temples at Rome; thence to the old Cathedral of Brescia and the magnificent church of San Vitale, Ravenna; the Cathedral at Achen, and further to that form of edifice throughout the world.

The influence of the grand Gothic style in architecture is as wonderful, and as far-reaching—from the Archway in the old Britford church, Wilts, to the framework on the steeple of Earl's Barton, Northauts, and in many other structures that existed in England before the Norman conquest; in the style developments that have been specified as Norman or Romanesque, along from 1066, the reign of William I, to the time of Henry VIII, 1546; transitional, from Norman to Pointed and Early English, the First Pointed or Lancet; transitional again from Early Pointed to Complete or Geometrical Pointed, Flowing or Curvilinear styles; transitional from Flowing lines of Decorated or Middle Pointed, to the stiff and hard lines of the succeeding styles—Third Pointed, Rectilinear (shape) or Perpendicular; from the rude work of the Norman styles, such as is displayed on the transept of Winchester Cathedral, to that of grandeur, as displayed on the Cathedrals of Peterborough, Durham, Norwich, Ely, etc., the best in England.

The Pointed style, best illustrated in the magnificent and beautiful edifice of Canterbury, began in 1175, by the architect, William of Sens.

The First Pointed style is manifest in the transepts of the York, Lincoln, and Salisbury cathedrals, and more especially Westminster Abbey, London; the most beautiful steeples of Gloucester cathedral and of St. Mary's, Taunton; the open roofs, such as at St. Peter, Mancroft; the beautiful transepts of Hexham Abbey Church, Pluscardine and Melrose Abbeys; the famous Chapel at Rosslyn; the Glasgow, St. Andrews, Kirkwall, Dunblane, and Elgin cathedrals, and the Abbeys of Pluscardine, Sweetheart, Kelso, Dryburg, Jedburgh, Holyrood, Dundrennan and Melrose of Scotland; Kilkenny Cathedral, Christ Church, and St. Patrick's of Dublin, Ireland, etc.

Passing into Asia Minor, the Architectural influence was manifest in such structures as the Rock Cut Tombs (the grandest being in Caria and Lycia), viz: those at Tantalais near Smyrna; those of Alyattes, King of Lydia, on the banks of the Hermus, near Sardis; the enormous Sarcophagi, such as those at Olinda, ranging on each side of the street leading to the city; those in Lycia, chiefly on the banks of the Xanthus; and those cut in the steep rocks which invariably overhang the city; the Obelisk Tombs, great high blocks of stone or marble on a square base, surmounted by a sarcophagus of great size, of later date than the rock-cut tombs; the Harpy Tomb, after 547 A. D., and near it the Chimaera Tomb, with a Gothic-headed sarcophagus and sculpture crest; and near this, another, called the "Winged Horse Tomb; those at Telmessus, Myra and Lycia; the Lyon Tomb at Cnidus, Caria; theTrophy Tomb at Xanthus; the Mausolus at Halicarnassus, Caria, one of the seven wonders of the world, and the grandest of all Greek tombs. All of these are architectural links by which we must connect the pre-historic to the historic works of those regions.

Passing into Assyria, we note the Architectural influence as having manifested through structures, now known as the "ruins" of the great Palace Temples of the ancient cities of Khorsabad, Nimroud, and Nineveh; the numerous tombs, such as those that have existence in Nimroud, Kouyurjik, Khorsabad, etc.; the enormous ruined Temples of Chaldea, such as the Birs Nimroud, near Babylon, and the one at Mugeyer.

Subsequent to the establishment of the Es'gē-nēns, in their

home of Es-gē-nĕn-ĕx (see later), south of the Taurus Mountains, a large tribe of their descendants migrated into the section of country now known as Mosul, Mesopotamia, east of the upper Tigris river, which section they termed Căc-wä-cō'tŭm, and called themselves the Sē-nō'dēs.

Subsequently, the Senodes erected their principal city on the site now occupied by the ruins of Nineveh, which they termed Sū'räs, which was the original Nineveh, or Kowyunjik.

Slăn'drō, a descendant of the Senodes, was the principal architect who originated plans of structures or the halls and temples of Sū'räs, the remains of which are now known to exist at Nineveh. He was himself co-operative in the work with Shū'lăx, a Senodes sculptor who assisted him in that part of the construction.

At that period of time, it was the custom with architects and builders to erect the cities and palace buildings on elevated portions of ground, or natural hills. Hence the appearance of the buildings as placed on artificial mounds, which modern writers suppose to have been parts, or sub-structures, of ruined edifices and buried cities.

The fortresses, of which remains yet exist, were originally intended as protective agencies to the cities and their inhabitants, against invading peoples. Some of the cities were originally entirely encompassed by the walls, while others were only partially so.

The general Architectural form of the structures, was rectangular, but strikingly narrow in proportion to length.

Most of the structures, of which their ruined forms are now termed "halls,"were simply homes of the people. The custom at that time, with these people, was for many families to occupy one building, similar to the modern plan of apartment houses; hence they built no private homes, excepting the Palaces occupied by celebrities, which in detail were similar to the apartment homes. Some of the structures were those erected for Temples, which, as to form, were similar to the home buildings. In these what now appears to be only a long, narrow hall, is the outline of the main structure, or first story, though the buildings varied from one to three.

The massive walls were thus constructed for two purposes, viz., great strength in support of the various stories and roofing of the structures; and as a protection against the then termed Kū'rō-winds, that came in through the valleys, twice a year, in the months of March and September.

What now appears to have been simply halls, generally speaking, were, originally, divided off into three or more apartments by cross-sectioned structure. A central wall extended lengthwise through the hall, which divided the basilica into rectangular apartments.

The two apartments in front of the building were entered by means of an arched or square portal, that led into a sort of vestibule, and thence into the apartments on either side by portals similar to that on the facade.

All the other apartments, in the rear of the front ones, were entered from the sides of the buildings, through an exterior portal; and further by interior portals on each side, right and left of the vestibule, as was the case with those in front.

The vestibule terminated in a flight of steps that led up to the second story, the landings of which had place on a platform that was built on top of the central wall. From the same platform, a second flight of steps, at opposite angles with the first flight, led on up to the third story, where entrances were made to the apartments of that story.

Every apartment had one large window, in front of a vaulted opening in the wall, through which the light was admitted into the apartment.

The two apartments, in the front of all the structures, were for the common use of all tenants, for general purposes, and therefore not private.

The roofs of the buildings were all flat, and were covered with wooden troughs, placed on in the manner of a modern tiling, and of the same use.

Over the front roof, in many cases, a sort of oval, and sometimes square, dome rose to a moderate height.

The structures were not, as has been supposed by some writers, columnarly supported, being of solid walls, excepting the vaulted openings through which light was admitted. What columnar characteristics the buildings possessed were simply those of ornamentation, of a sculptural order, and in bas-relief.

The Temples were similar to the tenement structures, so far as the division of rooms was concerned. They were of rectangular form, the larger of which was generally the entire front of the structure, and used as the general assembly room; but the rear third of the building was divided off into rectangular apartments, with hall in the center, rooms utilized by the priests for both living and sleeping rooms, with one apartment for the deposit of their paraphernalia.

It has been wondered at, by some writers, that no traces of "dwelling houses" now exist in the vicinity of the hall ruins.

This is easily accounted for by the fact that the inhabitants were collective dwellers, in tenement buildings, and therefore built no private dwellings, generally speaking. In case of the more wealthy individuals, some had structures to themselves; but these were, in detail, fashioned after those occupied by the collective dwellers; hence, remains of private dwellings would not now be recognized as such.

The ruined hall now known to exist at Kouyunjik, described as being two hundred and eighteen feet long, and twenty-five feet wide, was a Temple, originally known as Cä-sĕl-dō'ä, the term meaning "a place for spirit communion," or "manifestation." (The term was derived from the Atlantian term, Cä-cĕl'lä, which meant a spirit sensitive. The latter, however, referred to media, while the former referred to the place where the communication was held between the spirit and the mortal sensitive.)

About the time that the Senodes settled in their section of Căc-wä-cō'tŭm (Kouyunjik) a tribe of Esgenens, from their section of Esgenenex, settled near the Cacwacotum settlement, suburban as it was, termed that district Thū-rī-clē'ŏn (Korasbad), and called themselves the Mĕn-zō'ăcks. Subsequently they there built a village which they termed Quĭn-zī-ŏn'tō.

The now known ruins of Korasbad were originally structures erected by descendants of the Menzoacks, under the direction of an architect by the name of Sē-cŭn'zē, and a sculptor by the name of Crĕn-lū'ĕn, both being descendants from the Menzoacks.

About the same time that the above-named settlements were made, another tribe of Esgenens from Esgenenex, settled in the vicinity of the now known ruins of Nimroud, which district they termed O-zĕn'tō, and called themselves the Cŏr-ĕn-tĕn-găn'tōes, where subsequently, on the present site of the above named ruins, they built a large town which they termed Kē-nē-ō'shŏn. This was under the supervision of an architect by the name of Mĕn'thē-clŭs, and a sculptor by the name of Gĕl'sŭm, both of whom were Corentengantoes by birth.

About the time that the above-named tribes of Esgenens migrated to the several above-named portions of the now known eastern portions of Mesopotamia, another tribe of the same people, from the same region, migrated into the western portion of Mesopotamia. They settled near what is now known as the "Ruins of Babylon," which section they termed Pā-thä'dēs, and called themselves the Sĭl'krŏns; and there, in subsequent time, they built a large town which they termed Nē-ĕn-tī-cō'sy.

The now known ruined Temple of Birs Nimroud, of that district, was built by descendants of the Silkrons, planned and superintended by a wealthy leader and architect, by the name of Brō-děn'ziē, a Silkron, in co-operation with a sculptor by the name of Sū-rē-rŏn'sy, a descendant of the same people.

The rectangular form of the Assyrian buildings—the graceful curves, minarets, domes, octagons, circles, tower-like stories, raised from square bases, have been both re-embodied and developed from ideas, received and inspired by spirit aids, within the minds of the various tribe-descendants of the Es-ge-nen race, who had migrated into various parts of Assyria. But the influence came principally from Atlantian spirit architects and sculptors.

The Assyrian Architectural Art, generally speaking, has little analogy with the Egyptian. In contradistinction, there are no quantities of columns; no grand pylons; no enormous cloistered courts; nothing to equal the gigantic Pyramids, or Tombs of Egypt; the Sphinxes are superseded by winged bulls; and the slight-cut Intaglio, by magnificent sculptured slabs.

The idea of the winged bulls was to represent the principles of strength, power, and vehemence. The head of the human was con-junct with the body of the bull, in representation of various leaders of the peoples of that day, similar to those of the Egyptian sphinxes. The wings represented rapid activity, such as characterized their leaders in dispatch of service, as though by flight.

The slabs were for two purposes, viz., ornamentation, when a variety of subjects were chosen and outlined to fit the occasion, as vegetation, animal and human forms, and portrayals of historic events or conquests of a civic nature.

Therefore, the early Assyrian structures that give evidence of a high stage of artistic perfection, such as led up to the mythological display, as found in Greece, along the Tigris and Euphrates, etc., were re-embodied ideas, given to the architects and sculptors of the Senodes and the Menzoacks, the Corententgantoes, Silkrons, and other descendants of the Esgenens, by Atlantian spirits of that order. The architects and sculptors then planned and constructed their edifices, in accord with their conceptive forces and understanding of the same, as spirit sensitives.

Passing into China, we note that in pre-historic periods the structures were very crude indeed, being simply an assembly of poles or small trees, cut and formed into shape, and daubed over with mud or plaster; especially was this so with the structures of the Lăz'ĕr-ĕnds, of the northern portion, those of the southern being more open.

The development, therefore, was of a general order; individual ideas, rather than those of special architects being adopted, co-operated in whatever development had place.

The Kĕn'tĕr-sends and Lăz'ĕr-ĕnds (see later account of these peoples), up to within about two centuries of the time of Confucius, had no conscious knowledge of spirit communication or manifestation, in the sense of guidance; though they were unconsciously influenced through the force of impression, so far as the spirit forces were able to reach them mentally, under the then existing conditions, especially the Kentersends. The Lazerends were less progressive at that time than their southern brethren, in spiritual progress. But during the two centuries preceding the coming of Confucius, as the Christ of the Chinese nation, some knowledge had been gained, by sensitives, of spirit existence, and but for the interference of Confucius, through his teachings, this would have developed to a greater extent.

Passing from the pre-historic general influence, to the development, as now known, which, as was the case with the former, has reached its ultimatum through general ideas rather than through the influence of special architects, and has, with certain portions of impressional influence, resulted in such strue-tures as the Great Wall of China; the Temple of Confucius, at Shanghai; the Temples of Heaven, and the Temples of Agriculture, at Pekin; the Toov Tang, or Halls of the Ancestors, in all towns of China; the Pai Loo, or Pai Fung, Memorial Monuments; the Tombs, etc., all links that figure in the great Cycle of Architecture, the influence of which began with the crude works of the Lazerends in their section of Zĭn-tī-zăn'tŭm, or north of the Great Walls of China, and those of the Kentersends, in their section of Zăn-cŭs'tē-zŭm, south of the above-named walls. (See migration and descendants of these peoples later on.)

While the Esgenens, form Esgenenex, enroute to their distriet of Pā-thä'dēs (near Babylon), where they became the Silkrons, they halted for some time in the district now known as the town of Antioch, Syria. When the main colony proceeded on its migration, to the above-named section, a portion of the people remained in the district of Antioch and took to themselves the name of Tŭ'căns. Subsequently they built a small town on the site now occupied by Antioch, which they termed Nĭn-zä-tŭ'căn. Therefore the original inhabitants of the region, or districts, along the Orontes, were descendants from the Esgenens, through the migrating Tucans, their descendants; especially those who inhabited the original districts where subsequently the towns of Iopolis or Ione, Meroe, Bottia and Antioch had place, on which sites the Tucans had built their hamlets and towns, with others, along the banks of the Orontes, in pre-historic times. Most of these were destroyed by a series of great earthquakes that had occurred throughout that region about 450 B. C.; and many of the remains, after that calamity, were further destroyed by the series of nine great earthquakes that had place at various intervals from 148 B. C. to 588 A. D. Thus was the architecture of the Tucans rendered unknown modernly.

In subsequent time, a large tribe of Tucans migrated southeast, from Ninzatucan, into the district now known as Palmyra, which section they termed E-thē-lō'mä, and called themselves the Sĕn'thē-ŏns. There they built a hamlet on the site now occupied by the ruins of Palmyra, which they termed Sentheon, after their tribe name. In the early part of the Adomic period, the Sentheons were under the rule of a leader, by name Jĕn-zē-nō'sōs, who established the structures now known as the ruins of Palmyra; and a Sentheon architect, Zĕn'zē-lŏt, under appointment by Jenzenosos, planned some of these structures, especially the one now termed the "Temple of Sun." The pre-historic Sentheons, the Senodes, the Menzoacks, the Corentengantoes, the Silkons, the Tucans, and other descendants, became the prehistoric ancestors of the ancient Hebrews or Jews; and it was from the Sentheons that Zenobia, the Palmyrene Queen, descended, though Prince Odænathus, her husband, was of Roman descent.

In recognition of the Jewish influence, through the Art of Architecture, we note the great Temple of Solomon as described in the biblical narrative, I Kings, VI, VII; the Tombs of the Kings of Judea, hewn out from the solid rock; the Tomb of Absalom, and that of Zachariah, and the rock-cut building in the Valley of Jehoshaphat, near Jerusalem, etc.

These, especially in the concept and construction of the great Temple of Solomon, were established through spirit inspiration and direction. Thus guided, Solomon and his chief workers, who were spirit sensitives, carried out their spirit impressions and directions, to the ultimate erection of the temple, and establishment of its uses.

The St. Front at Periqueux (imitation of St. Mark's, at Venice), and the great Abbey Church of Cluny, and that of Vezelay, in Burgundy; the Old Domaine Royale (a perfection of the art); Notre Dame, Paris (a marvelous monument of art); the Cathedral of Chartres (the zenith of development), all of which

are representative monuments of the edifices of France, through which superb features of the Gothic style are made manifest, were thus established by the co-united influence and developing forces of spirit and material energy, in the region of France.

In the Architecture of Germany, the Romanesque influence appears, as embodied in such structures as those of Treves, as the Convent of Lorsch). The influence extending from the Lombard churches of North Italy, found embodiment in the churches of the Rhine region; e. g., St. Gereon and St. Cunibert, of Cologne; the cathedrals of Naumburg, Limburg, Gelnhausen, etc.

In the Architecture of Spain, the Roman influence is manifest in Santa Maria de Narance, near Oviedo; the French influence, as developed in the churches of St. Serrnin and Toulouse; and the Cathedral of Santiago; the remarkable edifices, San Isidero, Leon; San Vicente, Avila; those of Segovia, and the old Cathedral at Lerida; the local influence manifests in St. Millan, Segovia; the "central tower and lantern dome influence" is manifest in the old cathedrals at Salamanca; the Church at Toro; and the cathedral of Zamor; the transitional influence to Early Pointed works is manifested in the three great Spanish churches of that period, viz., the cathedrals of Toledo, Leon and Burgos. For great capacity, one may note the influence of Jayme Fabre, of Majorca, whose greatest works are in Catalonia; of these the cathedral of Gerona is the most remarkable, and thus there is a leading up to the real Spanish style of structure.

In the Architecture of Italy, passing from the influence of the Roman, the Romanesque, and the Byzantine influences when basilicas of the time of Constantine, such as those of Pompeii, that of Trajan, of St. Agnese and St. Lorenzo; San Clemente; St. Peter's and St. Paul's; Santa Maria; Opus; Alexandrenum, of Rome; the two remarkable basilicas of St. Apollenare in Classe, and St. Apollenare Nuovo, of Ravenna; those of Torcello; Toscanella; and Aquileia, etc., we note the influence manifesting through the round arched, be-domed, pointed arched and gothic Architectural transitions.

The transformation began its more marked influence in such edifices as St. Ambrogio, at Milan; St. Mark's, at Venice; the churches of San Zenone, Verona; San Michele, Pavia; and the cathedrals of Pisa.

The transformation from round arches to that of pointed work, though limited in Italy, is seen in such buildings as were first influenced by the architect, Nicola Pisano. As that influence spread, we see it manifested in such structures as the Ferrara cathedral and those at Genoa; the beautiful cloisters and porches of unsurpassed elegance, as at Verona; the Campaniles, such as mark the glory of Florence, of Giotto, and of art manifested in the tower of the cathedral at Florence; the cathedral of Milan; in Gothic interiors, such as the Pisan baptistery; the Frari, at Venice, and Santa Anastasia, at Verona; the palaces and mansions of Florence, Bologna, Vicenza, Udine, Genoa, and especially those of Venice; the Town Halls of Perugia, Piacenza and Siena, Corneto, Amalfi, Asti, Orvieto, and Lucca; the fountains of Peruga and Viterbo; the monuments of Bologna, Verona, Arezzo, etc.

In our assemblage of Architectural data, the events and influences of which, during the pre-historic and historic epochs of time, have been re-embodied in those of the Modern-Ancient and the Modern—and in making a connection between these epochs in the great Art zodiac, through which the Architectural Cycle has passed, we have chosen Callimanchus, Vitruvius, Palladio, and Street, as principal links with which to establish the re-embodiment, who, co-operative with a vast number of Architects who worked and influenced as epicycle links, on the deferent of the great Architectural Cycle that has extended into all quarters of the globe, have brought to the twentieth century its present condition of Architectural Art.

Callimanchus, of whom so little is known historically, was, as our spirit advisers inform us, a descendant of the Ic-thī-ē'ŏns who settled in the region now known as Argolis, Greece, and was born about 400 years, B. C., in the city now known as Corinth (see migration of the Icthieons); hence, would be considered Grecian by birth.

He was very talented both as architect and sculptor, and being a spirit sensitive, was taught and influenced, in his art work, by Atlantian spirit architects and sculptors, whereby he obtained his education in those arts, rather than by material influences. It was from spirit sources, exclusively, that he got his idea of the Corinthian Columns, and not, as has been supposed, "from having observed an Acanthus plant, surrounding a tile-covered basket which had been placed over a tomb."

As an architect and sculptor, he came into prominence between his twentieth and twenty-fifth years, and lived to work and influence for many years, for he arrived at the age of one hundred before he became mortally disembodied.

He was the first architect, of Greece, to plan ornamentation on the plain capitals that surmounted the fluted Doric order, as well as the originator of the Corinthian.

He being only four years the senior of the sculptor, Scopas, was therefore contemporaneous with him (though the latter did not come into prominence as early in life as did Callimanchus.

One of the principal results of the co-united work of these two celebrities was manifested in the temple of Athena Alea, at Tegea.

Strange as it may seem, Scopas, the sculptor, planned the architectural design of the building, but Callimanchus designed the columnar part.

These two celebrities further co-operated in the plans and construction of other edifices, in various parts of Greece, and as both were spirit sensitives, advised by Atlantian spirits, often consulted each other relative to plans, designs and styles, in the establishment of their proposed art works.

Marcus Vitruvious Pollio, architect, engineer, and author, was a Roman by birth, but moved to Athens, Greece, with his parents, when a child of eight years. There he remained permanently for forty-two years, during which time he traveled throughout various portions of Greece.

From these travels he gained much knowledge regarding Greek architecture.

During his youth, he had become acquainted with Caius Octavius (Augustus, the Roman Emperor), while the latter was a student in Athens. This resulted in a profound friendship between Vitruvius and Caius Octavius, that lasted to the close of the reign of Augustus.

Vitruvius returned to Rome, the place of his birth, at the age of fifty years, where he established his permanent home, about five years before the death of Augustus. He had been called there by the latter, to accept a position as superintendent of the balistæ and other military engines; and there he completed his great literary work, "*De Architectura,*" of ten books, which he dedicated to his friend Augustus, on account of their long, profound friendship.

This great work was his chief influence in an Architectural sense, long after he became disembodied mortally. The greatest of this might be said to date from the Renaissance period and to extend down to the present time; especially so throughout the period of the classical revival, when all architects recognized it in the sense of authority, and zealously accepted its precepts as final.

Bramante, Michael Angelo, Palladio, Vignola, etc., whose influence had great weight, architecturally, throughout nearly all the European countries, were close students of the principles laid down in "*De Architectura*" of Vitruvius. Hence, a re-embodiment of pre-historic ideas, known and practised in the Atlantian period, which were alive in the mind of Vitruvius, who represents an epicycle of his period, moved on the deferent of the great Architectural Cycle in the Augustan age, and in its influential orbit, rendered visible through so many centuries, embraced not only that period of time, but the present century as well.

Co-operative influences with these, through various periods of time, might be mentioned, such as that of the architects who designed the churches in the era of Christian Rome, beginning with the time of Constantine and extending to the twelfth century; or the works of the Cosmati family and their pupils, who influenced in the thirteenth century (not only as architects, but sculptors and mosaicists), the manifestations being through churches and palaces, and campaniles as well; the further influence of such individuals as Baccio Pintelli Giuliano da Majano, Francesco di Borgo, San Sepolcro, Bramante, one of the greatest architects the world has ever known; San Micheli, one of the best architects of the early part of the sixteenth century, as proved by his works at Verona, Venice, etc., which embraced churches, palaces, tombs, fortifications, and other military designs, besides which his great written work on classical architecture, *"Li Cinque Ordini dell' Architectura,"* added to his influence. Then Peruzzi, of Siena, architect and painter, influenced through such works as the villa of Farnesina, on the banks of the Tiber in Rome; work, as architect, on St. Peter's at Rome, Palaces at Rome, and in southern Italy, etc.

Palladio Andrea was a native of Vicenza, North Italy, and was one of the chief architects of that city who studied the buildings of ancient Rome for an early practical knowledge of architectural drawing. He influenced through such designs as the Barbarano, Porti and Chieregati Palaces of Vicenza, and others, for the nobles of that and adjacent districts. His finest work was the Palazzo della Rogione, at Vicenza, which was of the Tuscan and Ionic orders.

Being famous throughout Italy, Pope Paul III ordered him to come to Rome, to report on the state of St. Peter's.

In Venice, he influenced through such creations as churches and palaces, among which the manifestations can be recognized, to the best advantage, in S. Giorgio Maggiore, the Capuchin church, and some of the large palaces on the Grand Canal.

He further influenced through country Villas, for which he established plans throughout Northern Italy. Among these the finest is the villa of Capra.

His last great work (completed by his pupil Scamozzi) was the Teatro Olimpico, at Vicenza, which he designed after a classical model.

Like Vitruvius, Palladio also greatly influenced through his literary works, especially by that of his greatest, under the title of *"I quatro libri dell' Architettura."* This extended into almost numberless editions, having been translated into every European language, hence, wielded an enormous Architectural influence throughout Europe. All of this established the "Palladian style," a revival of classicalism, such as belonged to the epicycle that moved on the deferent of the great Architectural Cycle of the sixteenth-century orbit, co-operative with such contemporaries as Vignola, Scamozzi and Serlio.

As contemporaneous, in architectural influence, in Rome and other districts of Italy, might be mentioned Barocchio, of Vignola, who succeeded Michael Angelo as architect on St. Peter's, and the author of the *"Five Orders of Architecture;"* Maderna of Rome; Bernini, of Naples, who designed the great colonnade of St. Peter's, Rome and the Palace of Pope Urban; Boromini, of Bissone, whose principal influence was manifest through the churches of St. Agnes, in Piazza Navona, the Colegio di Propaganda, and the restoration of San Giovanni in Laterano; the works of Carlo Fontana, and further extensions into the latter part of the Modern period.

George Edmund Street, one of the ablest architects of the nineteenth century, we have chosen to represent the latter links in the great Gothic Epicycle, that moved on the deferent of the Great Architectural Cycle during the nineteenth century, and Gothic influence originated by Adolphus of Atlantis, who planned his own palace in Atara, Atlantis, the sole structure, of that style, on the Lontidri at the time of the submergence, that is, of any note, re-embodied in the Pointed Architecture in the minds of the Roman architects; modified by the Romanesque, the Lombard, and the Byzantine of Europe; having thus arisen in the fourth century, and been subverted, in the twelfth, by the Pointed Arch, through various nations. The prime idea of it, however, was first re-conceived in the minds of the Egyptians, who re-embodied it in the Itmas, thus inspired by the spirits of the Atlantian Cemetteza constructors.

The development of the Pointed Arch, local and national, has manifested to a great extent through, the structures of Italy, England, France, Germany and Spain; with variations according to political geography, or physical conditions. But it is too vast an undertaking to treat individually, in this treatise, the transitions and development the style has sustained, through the various countries and periods of time.

The sketches of George Edmund Street are acknowledged to be masterpieces of spirit and brilliant touch; and his great taste and technical skill manifest monumentally through such edifices as the convent of East Grinstead, the Theological College at Cuddesden, and many churches, such as the St. Philipi and St. James at Oxford; St. John's at Torguay; All Saints at Clifton; St. Saviour's at Eastbourn; St. Margaret's at Liverpool, and the St. Mary Magdalene at Paddington.

His largest works are in evidence in the nave of Bristol cathedral; the choir of the cathedral of Christ Church, in Dublin; and above all, the New Courts of Justice, in London, the latter second only in architectural importance (during the century) to the House of Parliament.

Finally, in consideration of the Architectural influences, viz., those of disembodied spirits, co-operative with the yet embodied, or mortal spirits, through the establishment of the original and developed styles of Architecture, that have arisen and developed from the Atlantian Cemetteza or Arch, and the Kisare or Column, which led up to their exquisite Gretictor or Architecture, which in that period of time embraced the Tilze or Ionic, the Nuzeleth or Doric, the Admus or Corinthian, the Itheze or Caryatic, the Iothees or Composite, re-embodied in the original Itma or Column, and Itmas or Arches of Egypt, the Duzees or Doimens, the Kerelthees or Circles, the Cazudas or Pyramids, the Heltees or Tumuli, etc., that in process of development led up to the magnificent structures of the twentieth century, through the above-named styles or orders of the Greeks and Romans, and the dwellings of all nations, especially the palaces or mansions of the emperors, kings, potentates and other nobility; the monastic edifices, churches and cathedrals, edifices of governments, states and municipalities; corporate structures, including colleges, academies, schools, libraries, art galleries, museums, societies, railway stations, etc., among which, as representative epicycles of the whole Architectural Cycle, or links with which to connect the modern extension to that of the remote Ancient or Atlantian, the pre-historic, and the Modern-Ancient, in evidence of the ultimatum of the great originating and developing forces, and influences of the seen and unseen, or Spirit and Mortal workers, we have chosen such structures as the Mosques of Tooloon and Kaid Bay at Cairo, Egypt; the Temples of Confucius, Shanghai, of Heaven and of Agriculture at Pekin, China; the Kylas of Ellora, and the Temples at Tiravalur, and Tanjore,

India; the Royal Palace (Pentelic Marble) at Athens, Greece; the Parliament building, St. Paul's and Westminster Abbey, London, England; the Cathedrals of Winchester, York, Lincoln, Salisbury, Gloucester, Taunton, etc., England; the Cathedrals of Glasgow, St. Andrews, Kirkwall, Dublane, and Elgin, and the Abbeys of Pluscardine, Sweetheart, Kelso, Dryburgh, Jedburgh, Holyrood, Dundrennan and Melrose, Scotland, and including the Parliament buildings of that district of Great Britain; the Cathedral of Kilkenny and those of Dublin, and the Parliament buildings of Ireland; the Royal Palace, Government buildings, the Old Domaine Royal, the Cathedrals of Chartres, of Notre Dame, Paris, Bruges, Lemans, Rouen, etc., of France; the Royal Palaces, Governmental buildings, and Cathedrals of Cologne, Hildesheim, Magdeburg, Lubeck, Bamberg, Naumburg, Nuremberg, Vienna, Munster, Munich, etc., of Germany; the Royal and Governmental buildings, the Cathedrals of Toledo, Leon, Burgos, Siguenza, Lerida, Tarragona. Seville, Segovia, Salamanca, etc., Spain; the Royal Palaces and Governmental buildings, St. Peter's, and other Cathedrals of Rome, Ravenna, Torcello, Toscanella, Aquileia, Milan, Genoa, Pisa, Venice, Verona, and Florence, Italy; the Capitol at Washington, and its style-related State capitols, municipal buildings, cathedrals, churches, academies, colleges, schools, libraries, palaces and mansions, of the Western Continent, etc.

EX-IN-TON'ZE NUD U-RE'TA, OR AUTHORS AND PROSE.

TELTZIE XXIX.

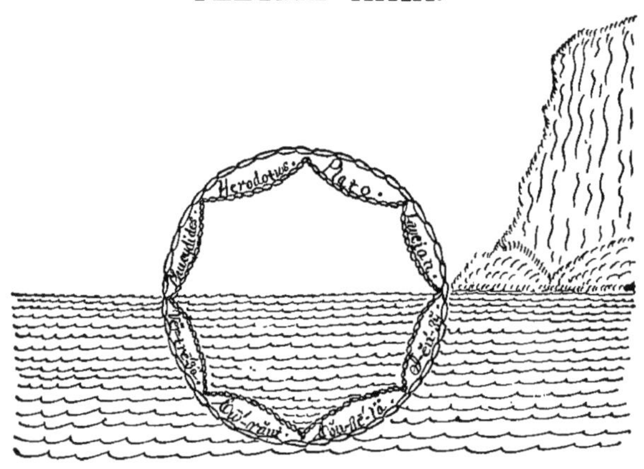

The following information relative to Art and Literature has been given to us by An'stä-ci-ä Prolex, our Atlantian Lē-ă'sä Dē-cĕlt' (spirit adviser), a daughter of Liŭ'srŏn Dĕl'zē-ō (her father) and E-mē'lŭ'cē-ŭs Hē'mē-lon (her mother), the wife of Alem Prolex, and the Sī-ĕs-tiē'lēte (sister-in-law) of Erothrodia.

During the latter part of the first Efremetrum, U-rē'tä (prose) was very crude and simple, and was written on the crude Dĕl'zĕc (paper) of that period. Compared with prose of the third Efremetrum, it would be as the crude writings of the Aborigines compared with those of authors of the twentieth century.

Clĭd'zē was the first noted of the Ureta Osk-ley'zē (authors or writers),* or Ex-ĭn-tŏn'ze (authors or writers),** of the Lontidri. His works began with the second Efremetrum, when he was at the age of twenty years. His first work was a sort of history of the first Efremetrum from as far back as he was able to gather data. Later in the same Efremetrum, his works be-

Note—*Term in the language of Teltzie Et. **Language of Teltzie We.

came more extensive, and at the age of one hundred he was a great historian. He lived in Neitz, the Kistrez aistie (Capitol city) of Teltzie We.

Sĭn'ĕx was a noted Exintonze, whose work began with the last twenty years of the second Efremetrum and extended about thirty years into the third. She wrote also some Chrĭs'tiē (Poetry),* yet not the strictly poetical, but in a similar style, which she interspersed throughout her Christie and Ureta, which established a style peculiarly her own. She was considered a very fine Exinton, who dwelt in the aistie of Desento, in the southwestern portions of Teltzie We.

Gē-is'trĭc (a fine fancy paper) was used principally for Metze coverings. It was made from the gluten of the Acetum and finely pulverized Teze. To give the covering body and durability, it was put over pieces of Zitley, or the coarse variety of Acetum. The Metze coverings were fastened by means of a silver wire, which was used to lace or stitch the leaves together, in the form of a Metz. The color of the Ceistric material was principally purple, but old gold or bronze, light blue, and some black were used, as varieties. The Metze were of various sizes, some being very large.

I-ĕn'zē was the originator of Sigris. He was born in Teltzie Zret, but during the middle portion of the second Efremetrum, at the age of about forty years, he moved to Atara. He brought all of his MSS. there with him. He was a Cacella (spirit sensitive), who wrote on themes portraying the simplicity of life, nature and spirituality, all of which he wove and blended together harmoniously.

Cŏn-zē'lä was the most noted Sigris Oskley of the fourth quarter of the second Efremetrum. He brought out a more perfect style of Sigris, and originated the use of Metze in a crude style. His themes assumed more of the philosophic, scientific, and historic character. As a Cacella, along these lines of thought, he was very gifted.

Çŭ'rănt came into great notoriety as an Oskley of Sigris, beginning in the first period of the third Efremetrum. He was a Cacella, whose themes were of a scientific nature, generally, but he dwelt especially on the spiritual. His thoughts were generated by his soul's deepest research, and sent forth by its force of reflection, thus to be recorded on the pages of his Metze.

Vĕr-trē'zä was a noted Sigris Oskley, and a contemporary of Curant's who wrote more on the sciences of Astrology and Astronomy. He was a talented and intellectual person, and con-

*Term in the language of Teltzie We, given to her peculiar style of writing.

sidered more of a spirit than a mortal. And he was a Cacella of the highest order. He co-labored with Curant in perfecting the enterprise of Metz-making, which condition lasted throughout the third Efremetrum. Through their influence the enterprise grew to great usage, and the styles and qualities were various. They established the then noted Cū'rē-tēen (the term meant "to build and scatter"), Acetum and Metz manufactural building, near the Opsite Kelete at Atara, that supplied the entire Lontidri with these products.

Vertreza and Curant continued the work of Os-kley'zē during the time they were superintendents of the Cureteen workmen. They were assisted by sub-officers who officiated as heads of the different departments.

The styles of Sigris were very different from those of modern times. The ideas or thoughts, on the subject, were briefly stated in individual paragraphs, and sometimes followed by a sort of descriptive paragraph, very brief and concise. The subjects usually were historic, descriptive, imaginary, scientific and philosophic.

Religion was never discussed in Metze, as that was placed on Maretuxze (Monuments), where everybody could read as they passed by. The Atlantians knew nothing of the term "religion," in its modern signification; but the term Cĭt-rē'zē (spirituality) was used instead.

There were no romances, or sensational Oskleyze. Many wrote from inspiration.

History was one of the greatest of subjects during the third Efremetrum. There were contemporaries, in all parts of the Lontidri, who wrote historic facts of their localities, which were sent to the Acetum for compilation.

Libraries, both private and public, were established throughout the Lontidri. They were thus dispersed from the great Cureteen of Atara.

Vĭn'tē-zĕn was a noted female Ureta Exinton, or Oskley, whose work began with the third Efremetrum. Her productions were narratives in Gē'hĕt (book) form. She wrote many Gē-hĕt'ze on various themes, embracing those of fact, fiction, imaginary, spiritual, the secular, etc. She was considered a fine Exinton. She continued her work through the third Efremetrum, to the time of the final submergence of the Lontidri.

Wër-ĕn'tāge was the most noted Ureta Exinton, or Oskley, of the third Efremetrum. His work began with the very last of the second Efremetrum, and continued through the third until the final submergence of the Lontidri. His works were of an extremely fine and artistic character. They were on sacred and spiritual subjects. He also wrote biographic sketches, especially of the various Că-cĕl-lă'zē (spiritual advisers) of the Lontidri, during its historic periods. He was also a Deltsanz (teacher) of the art of Ureta. One of his strong points, when writing, was the power of his descriptive genius, which he made manifest in a beautiful, diffusive way, no matter what the subject, or the theme. Thus gifted, he established a style in descriptive and narrative writing. He dwelt in Kē-rĕn'te-zē, an aistie on the northeastern border of Teltzie Et, but he held his school, where he taught the "Art of Ureta writing," in Atara, the Kistrez aistie of the Lontidri.

These Exintonze had many contemporaries in the period of their greatness, and owing to the progress of the art of Sĭ'grĭs (prose), all styles were made manifest during the latter part of the third Efremetrum.

As the style of prose writing advanced, the term for prose was changed from Ureta to that of Sigris, a distinction between the ancient and modern styles; and the authors of the Sigris style became the greatest influence in the art, in the latter epoch of Atlantian greatness; hence our division of Exintonze nud Ureta, and Oskleyze nud Sigris, preceding and following this paragraph, as into first and second periods.

In the "second period" we note that Sigris became permanently established during the latter part of the third Efremetrum. With the knowledge of Sigris writing, came also the establishment of Mĕt'zē (books), for they were never used to record Prĕt'lĕx (poetry) prior to that time. The establishment of Metze, therefore, had place during the latter part of the second Efremetrum, when Sigris was established and developed with it, during the third, in regard to style, etc. This differed greatly from books of modern times, both in material, construction, and the printed contents.

The material for printing on was known as A-cē'tŭm, and was of two qualities. One known as Kē'lĭst, very fine, was used for Metze only, and the other, a coarse, spongy one, called Zĭt'-ley, was used for drawings, paintings, and illustrations, and also as a part of the material for covering the Metze. The Kelist was made from the gluten of Acetum stalks, compounded with powdered E-trĕx (a mineral). The Zitley was made from the gluten of the Acetum and pulverized Tē'zē, a product of the Acetum. The Teze was a vegetable cotton, such as the modern Gossypium, or more commonly known "cotton plant," produces. The pods grew pear shape, instead of a perfect oblong, as is the case with the Gossypium, and the shells of these dropped off when ripe, leaving the Teze on the shrub, something like the modern cotton plant, only the latter simply bursts open, thus exposing the cotton. The blossoms were similar to those of the modern Jimson weed. Acetum was cultivated in fields similarly to the modern cotton plant, and was not fibrous, but succulent. The gluten was pressed from the young plants and spread on metal sheets, and prepared for the different kinds of paper by further sprinkling on the other ingredients, after which they were pressed together with powerful machinery. The gluten gave to the paper a beautiful, glossy appearance. Fine machinery was necessary for the preparation of the Teze for use.

The first records and historic writings, of Atlantis, were placed on tablets and monuments of stone. In the first Efremetrum, however, writing was done on pieces of bark, especially prepared for that purpose from the Sĕd'wĭck, a tree that grew abundantly in the Aelkedze of the Lontidri. These writings were made in sizes that could be easily transferred at pleasure, and to suit the occasion.

In the second Efremetrum, the people began to make crude paper from the Sedwick bark, which was pressed into sheets and dried. This somewhat resembled modern veneering, especially in the quality of stiffness and thickness. When used, it was cut into tablets varying in length form six to eight Unx-zē (inches), and from four to six in width. Being stiff and hard they could not be folded.

At the beginning of the third Efremetrum, the art of paper-making had advanced considerably. The quality was similar to the vellum leaves used by the ancient Grecians and Romans, and still used in the leaflet form. Later in the Efremetrum, a fine quality was being made, and converted into booklets similar to those of the later Greeks and Romans.

The art of printing was discovered a few years before the last of the great convulsions that caused the total submergence of Atlantis. The type was made of metals, and formed in the same style as the characters used in chirographic work. Therefore the written and printed pages were the same in appearance. The printing was done by machinery, the motive force of which was electricity.

At the time of the submergence of Atlantis, nearly all the knowledge, and achievements, of Literature and Art, were archived beneath the waters of the Atlantic Ocean, with the peoples. All that remained was in the memory of a few educated individuals who survived the submergence, and dwelt on the remnant islands or border-lands of the Continents. Many of the islands went down from time to time, in the immediate future, subsequent to the submergence of Atlantis, which caused a terminal loss of the products and records of the artists, in all branches.

During the long ages that intervened between the submergence of Atlantis and the Modern-Ancient historic period, literature and literary styles were re-established in Arabia, Egypt, Greece, etc., as will be seen by our data, given under the various sections.

As the pre-historic ancients, who dwelt on the yet remaining islands in the Atlantic Ocean, and the border-lands of Atlantis, now the Eastern and Western Continents, who had some knowledge of the great achievements of the Atlantian Zeuleze, passed from the material life, their descendants, through various changes during a period of four thousand years, became ignorant of the Zeuleus, so highly developed by their Atlantian ancestors. Hence, the total loss of all manuscripts, records and even knowledge of the Arts and Literature, and the remote Zeuleze, who had established the same in their remote and so-called "lost historic periods" (not lost, but being restored again by those illustrate spirits).

Just here we are informed by the spirit of Al'chē-lĕt an Abdula of El-tē'zē (a portion of which is now known as Arabia), that soon after the expiration of the four thousand years, above referred to, through the influence of Atlantian spirits, his then mortal people received inspiration and instruction relative to the hidden arts and literature, such as enabled them to re-establish and develop similar products, and producers, in accord with the conditions of the country and peoples of that period; hence, the re-establishment of Art and Literature such as had place in Elteze, or Arabia, 12,000 or 10,000 B. C. All of which makes Arabia the "mother country" of the descended arts and literature of modern times.

In subsequent pre-historic time, the people of Elteze became great and numerous; and among these were many Mĕl-sä'ī-ĕsts (Artists) of all kinds, who had arrived at the zenith of their greatness in relation to literature and art, but had not so far developed as their remote ancestors, the Atlantians.

Ultimately there began a decadence in the El-tē-zē'ăn Mĕl-sä'ēs and Cē'lē-măsh (Eltezean arts and literature). As the people became numerous, portions of them wandered into sections of adjacent country where they established settlements, grew into new nations and took to themselves new names, which severed them from the influence of their mother country.

At first there were but few people who formed the settlements that afterwards progressed into nations; and of necessity, from want of utilities to carry on their then knowledge of life's habits, in a measure, they lost their civilization, attained in the influence of the greatness of Elteze. Besides, the majority of emigration was among the less intellectual and cultured people who formed the colonies, and these, by virtue of their limited numbers, were compelled to turn their attention to the means of subsistence. Thus no time could be devoted to entertainment, or to mental development, for the time being, and ages again intervened between this decadence and the rise of new literatures and arts in the nations which came, in subsequent time, through the same sources, viz: spirit influence and manifestation; and furthermore, to the present period, on some islands and continents there are peoples who have never risen from the crude conditions into which they fell, by that separation from the mother country.

During the time of dispersement of the people from Elteze, who formed other nations, their "beginning" of progress, or state of uncivilization, as the case was, there came great changes also to Elteze, the mother country, by convulsions of the earth, The going down and coming up again of portions, which established deserts; destroyed the people, and their achievements; and made decadence inevitable. Therefore Elteze, or pre-historic Arabia, dates its fall, in national greatness, back to the time of the formation of the Great Sahara Desert, which took place twelve thousand years ago, during the reign of Al′chē-lĕt, the Abdula of that period.

From that time, for a period of six thousand years, there was a decline in everything, including all the arts. There was little or no progress during that period.

There were great changes in bodies of both land and water, portions went down and others came up.

At that time nearly all Europe was water. Later came convulsions and upheavals, which threw up land at different points. This, by immigration, was afterward re-inhabited, and in due time, through spirit influence, each section took up progression, which condition developed more rapidly than it had formerly done.

The origin of Cecacen, or prose writing, in Elteze, dates back to about 6500 B. C., when descendants of the Re-zĕn′dĕths (see migration of the people) erected their great As-kä′ĭ-lĕt. This was a monument, of vast dimensions, which they erected for three purposes:

First, as a place of protection to travelers who, when passing, could enter the rooms of its interior.

Second, as an observatory or outlook, from which to look over the surrounding country, for the purpose of prospecting, or discovering travelers in want, as well as for a guide to all travelers passing through that region.

Third, as a place on the walls of which to record the history of ancient Rezendeths, or rather their religious ideas, which were few in number. Their god, or up-builder, they termed E'tē-lŏy.

Thus was the idea of Cecacen or "prose writing" instituted, and it was continued, as a custom, by their subsequent pre-historic descendants, by further display on their monuments, wrought in their alphabetic characters. (See description of the mounnment later.)

Guī'tŏn was the most noted Cecacen Kelt (prose writer) who lived and wrote about the period of 6950 B. C. He remained in the mortal form to quite an advanced age. He further developed the Cecacen style of writing, and continued to place it on the monuments constructed for that purpose, in his time; thus taking as model the custom of his ancestors, the Rezendeths, who had placed the records of their god, Eteloy, on the inner walls of the great Askailet monument. Guiton was a resident of a pre-historic Chī'zŏn (city) then known as Tĕl-too'ney, located in the eastern-central portion of Elteze, on or near the site of the town of Wab. His principal themes were those of Nature, and narratives portraying the customs of the people, conditions of the country politically and religiously, and the general "life principles," as understood at that period.

I'zone was the most noted Cecacen Kelt who lived about 6000 B. C., and came into notoriety immediately after the aged Guiton had passed to spirit life. She wrote both Cecacen and Ee'tū (prose and poetry). Her subjects were principally of a historical nature, though she wrote on some religious themes. Her writings were classical, and had they been preserved, would have been a wonder to modern readers. She was a resident of the pre-historic Chizon, Dĕl-hē'drĭck, in northwestern Elteze, on or near the site where now is the town of Kaaf.

O-rē-ĕn'tē was a very distinguished Cecacen Kelt who lived about 5950 B. C. He wrote on historic, religious and secular themes, and subjects in general. He also wrote Eetu. He was the first of that period to use paper, and established the use of Mĕs'sē (an attachment of MSS. to take the place or books). The

Messe sheets were about two by one and a half feet in size and were fastened at the top by a metal frame. When reading, the individual held the frame, to which the sheets were attached, if he so desired; and as he read, he threw them one after another over the frame. The library case was simply the wall of the room, on which the frame sheets were hung, one on top of the other in the same series. This was done by means of brackets that extended out from the wall far enough to admit of the sheets being turned, as they were read, without taking them down from the wall. He lived at El-lī-trē′ty, the Chä-ta-pa za Chī-zŏn (Capitol city) of Elteze.

Cē′kĕth was a contemporary of Oreente's, who wrote on the same themes, and was, in every respect, equally famous. He lived in a small Chizon then known as Es′cūe, in the northern portion of Elteze, or the country now known as Asia Minor (at that time Elteze embraced the northwestern portion of the now known country of Turkey), on the Sihon river, near where the town of Hadjim now stands.

Sĭn′gē-rĕt was a distinguished Cecacen, and also Eetu Kelt, who lived 5900 B. C., and wrote on general themes. She lived in Ellitrety, the Chatapaza Chizon of Elteze.

Cĭn-cū′thē was also a noted Cecacen writer who lived from 5850 to 5800 B. C. She wrote wholly on imaginary themes, and in modern times would have been termed a novelist. She dwelt in a small Chizon then known as Cĕn-tū′sĕn, which was in the southern portion of Elteze, near the now known Damasir river, and between the towns of El-Landah and Hamden.

Passing from the attainments of the Cecacen Keltmes, and the influence of their works, in Elteze, into the region of Siloton (Egypt), to which section some of them had migrated, we find the Lē-ĕl′vä (art) of Tĕs-cŏn′ō-mĕs (prose) under spirit influence and co-operative with that of the incoming influence from Elteze, being established about 5000 B. C.

Ac-rō-jō′vĭs was the most noted Fē-lī-zō-măt′ī (author) of that period, who influenced the people by his writings. General subjects—religion, nature, social and political issues of the day—were his principal themes. He dwelt in a large Celzic (city) by the name of Nĕl-nū′shŏn, in central Siloton, in the vicinity where now stands the town of Kailub. He was born early in the century, and lived in the mortal until nearly its close. He modelled his literary methods after the Eltezean Keltmes, in the particular of recording his writings, which he placed on sheets of prepared barks and dried skins.

At that time "writings" were done in a style difficult to explain so the reader may get a full idea. Sometimes an entire thought, or idea, was expressed by means of symbols or signs, quite different from those of monumental preservation, that revealed a far deeper significance than the casual contemplation of a modern translator would discern. For at the present time, little beyond the seeming crudity of the signs and symbols, would be cognized because the "word and sentence symbols," by which ideas are expressed, do not require the reader to reach so far into the soul and spirit of things, in order to understand the ideas conveyed. Hence a quicker and less meditative process is that of modern transmission, of thoughts and ideas, through the medium of literary utilities.

The symbols and signs of the above-named period were, to some extent, interspersed with some of their alphabetic symbols; in an abbreviated way, though perfectly understood by the reader.

Throughout the century there arose contemporaries who influenced events of the different epochs, especially in the latter half of the century, each of whom wrote, in a progressive form, in accord with his or her individual style and chosen themes, a practice that continued during a period of about three hundred years.

O-lē-ăn'nä was the most noted Felizomati who appeared at the head of the Felizomatius about 4550 B. C. He lived, in the form, to about the middle of the following century, through which time, and long after, his works influenced the minds of the people. He resided at a small Celzic by name of Frĕt-zē-ū'lŭs, in the northern portion of Siloton, on the site of Girgeh, or near it. This author chose his subjects chiefly from Nature. His writings were considered decidedly classic. In fact, in modern times, he would have been termed a naturalist. He contrasted "human nature," quality and attributes of being, with "phenomenal nature," respecting form and its process of materialization, soul, body and spirit, thus bringing them under one common whole, as having arisen from the same source. All material form he brought into the subjects, as evidential proof, or representations of the principle of life, and its development and unfoldment. He continued the use of barks and skins for keeping the records, whereon he placed his thoughts and ideas, as his ancestors had done, with the additional development of fastening them into a lengthened form. These he folded in a lapped form, a development that led up to the establishment and utility of the papyrus-rolls of ancient and historic Egypt. He further developed the idea of representing his thoughts in the "word form." Therefore he discontinued the use of so many symbols and signs, with which to express his ideas, a change that was soon taken up and followed by his contemporaries, and the writers of subsequent time. However, when recording history and religious data, on the monuments, he held largely to the symbolic and sign forms of expression, from the fact that it was necessary to abbreviate more, in that, in order to come within the limit of the space, and furthermore, because it was much easier to execute writing in that form.

To the pre-historic peoples of Siloton, as of Egypt, the "sign," and the "symbolic" and hieroglyphic" writing characters, represented the soul, spirit and life of the subject—a more profound meaning than modern contemplators are wont to give to them. Hence, the translation, in all its profound meaning, is never fully reached, and therefore has been virtually lost.

During this century Tesconomes Felizomatius had increased in number, and dwelt in various parts of Siloton, each writing in his or her special style, and on chosen themes, accordingly, and it was in this period of time, and from among these Felizomatius, who migrated into Zanzureta (Greece), that the influence of prose writing first entered that country.

Passing from the pre-historic attainments of the Tesconomes Felizomatius, and the influence of their Siloton works, into Zanzureta, we find the I'ō-ŏn (art) of Hā'sŭms (prose) writing, under spirit influence, and co-operative with the influence of immigrant Cecacen Keltmes, from Siloton, an event in the epoch of literature, beginning about 4500 B. C.

Gĭb'dē-ŏn was the first noted Hasums Kumnel (Prose Author) of that period. He had migrated from Siloton to Zanzureta, and became a resident of a small Ducē'lē (city) in the then known eastern portion of Zanzureta, east of the present coast of Greece, in the region submerged by the Ægean sea, between what is now known as the Skopelos and the Skyros Islands, the submergence having taken place about the beginning of the Adomic period.

Gibdeon lived in that section, where he produced most of his works, and influenced the people until the latter part of the century.

By nature he was capricious, and wrote in that style. While he displayed, through his writings, changeable, freakish, fantastical, and even whimsical characteristics, yet his strongest were brought out in such subjects as demanded the fanciful in idea to carry out the details. Hence, at the present time, he would be termed a fanciful author.

He was thus led, in his imaginary or visionary conceptions, through various spirit influences, who manifested through his clairvoyant sight, in such a manner as to lead him to see symbols, from which he conceived the various ideas which he, from time to time, embodied in his writings; and it was from the fact that he was influenced by so many different spirit intelligences, who thought, and understood general principles so differently, one from the other, that he displayed so changeable a character in his writing; a condition, and a law, of spirit manifestation, that will last as long as time moves on, and spirits come back to the worlds they have passed through, to influence subsequent dwellers in the forms adapted to the world in which they dwell.

Through his writings, Gibdeon greatly influenced the people of that period, whose minds were not only open to spirit teachings directly, but were also in a condition to receive changeable ideas, such as arose from conflicting influences, according to the varied ideas of controlling intelligences. He chose his subjects or themes from general life principles and surrounding aspects in Nature. He had quite a number of contemporaries, some of whom were from his own country, and others natives of Zanzureta. Thus the "Ioon of Hasums" writing slowly developed, throughout the next three hundred years, under the influence of various Cumneloes, who wrote on various subjects, in styles harmonious with their own characteristics, or that of independent individuality.

Hĭm-mī'rŭs was the greatest Hasums Cumnel in the period beginning about 4200 B. C. He dwelt in northern Zanzureta, in the small Ducely of Rēn-cē-ĭ'lŭs, on or near the site where is now the town of Palamas. He lived and wrote throughout the century, and was therefore nearly one hundred years old when he passed to spirit life. In his time he was considered a great dramatic writer. His subjects were chosen from social life and political and governmental affairs, themes he would work out in a classic form. He was a blood relative, or ancestor to the historic Hermes, on the latter's paternal side, the name having sustained several changes through the generations that intervened from the time of Himmirus to that of Hermes, and it terminated in the latter.

Passing from the links in the great pre-historic Cycle of Authors and Prose, to those of the historic, we note four great influences whom we have chosen as principal links in our Cycle of Authors and Prose:

Thucydides, the greatest Greek historian of antiquity, as evidenced by his *History of the Peloponnesian War,* and his MSS.

on various themes, through which he influenced by complex and intricate thought, intellectual brilliancy and intense feeling, the political ideas, sense of government, generalship, devotion to truth, etc.

Herodotus, the noted Greek historian, as evidenced by his records of the struggles between Greece and Asia, or between the Greeks and the barbarians; also his history of the struggles between Greece and Persia; his description of the countries and peoples of Lydia, Media, Assyria, Babylon, Egypt, Scythia, Thrace, etc. His influence was largely through diligence, candor and impartiality, political dispassionateness, normal national pride, broad conception of romantic ideas, vivid and picturesque description, harmonious language, etc.

Plato, the great Greek philosopher and father of idealism; the embodier of ethical and political, metaphysical, scientific and mystical, philosophical ideas, made manifest in his various dialogues, in which he re-embodied idealistic characteristcs of both real and supposed celebrities, as in his *Laches, Chasmides, Lysis; Protagoras, Io, Meno; Euthyphro, Apologia, Crito, Phaedo; Symposium, Phaedrus Cratylus; Gorgias, Republic; Euthydemus, Parmenides, Theaetetus, Sophist, Statesman, Philebus; Timaeus, Critias; The Laws,* etc.

Lucian, the great essay writer, who in prose literature, stands without a rival; a satirist, noted as a fluent, easy and unaffected composer; elegant and correct as a linguist, a strong rhetorician, as evidenced by his *True History,* narratives, dialogues, etc.

We further note, in the great Cycle of Authors and Prose, such influential links as the historians, Antiphon, Xenophon, Livy, Sallust, Tacitus, Villehardouin, Froissart, Hallam, Macaulay, Josephus, Vellius, Hacataeus, etc., as in the philosophic portion, such influential links as Socrates, Aristotle, Epictetus, Anaxagoras, Pythagoras, Marcus Aurelius, Seneca, etc., and in the dramatic, Plautus, Statius, etc.; in the satirical, Persius, Petronius etc.; in rhetoric such as Longinus and Quintilian; in logic, such as Zeno (its inventor); pathos, such Euripides; men of letters, such as Varo; in the biographic, Plutarch; in the geographic, Strabo; as writers, Cicero; Pliny; and Suetonius.

Passing into France, we note such influential links as Guizot, the historian; Descartes and Cousin, the philosophers; Dumas and Sand, the novelists; Moliere, Racine and Corneille, the dramatists ;Rabelais, the humorist; Montaigne, the essayist, etc.

Passing into Germany, we note such influential links among prose writers as Grimmelshausen, Moscherosch, Balthasar

Schupp; Buchholtz, Anton Ulrich, Leibnitz, Wolf, Moses Mendelssohn, Geo. Sulzer, Abbt, philosophers; Justus Moser J. J. Winckelmann, Leopold Ranke, Gervinus, Giesebrecht, Hauser, historians; Gustave Treytag, Frederick Spielhagen, Fritz Reuter, etc., novelists.

Passing into Italy, we note such influential links as the historians, Giovanni Pontano, Bernardino Coro, Leonardo Bruni; Machiavelli, Guicciardini; such philosophers as Galileo Galilei, Giovan Battista Vico, etc.; scientists, Telesio, Giordano Bruno, Tommasi, Campanella, Venini, etc.; such writers as Boccaccio, and as writers of tales, Geovanni Fiorentio, etc.

In England, we note such influential links as the philosophers Lombard, Locke, Hume, Collins, etc.; the historians, Macauley, Freeman, etc.; the men of letters, Voltaere, and Carlyle; other writers, King Alfred and De Quincey; Darwin, the physicist; Butler, the theologian; Richardson, the novelist; Fielding, in fiction; Wickliff, in general philosophy and science, etc.; together with the vast number of similar links as mentioned under the head of Authors and Prose, in these and other countries, too vast a number to mention, who have influenced the extension of the great Cycle of Authors and Prose, down to the twentieth century.

PRET'ZE NUD PRET'LEX
OR
POETS AND POETRY.

TELTZIE XXX.

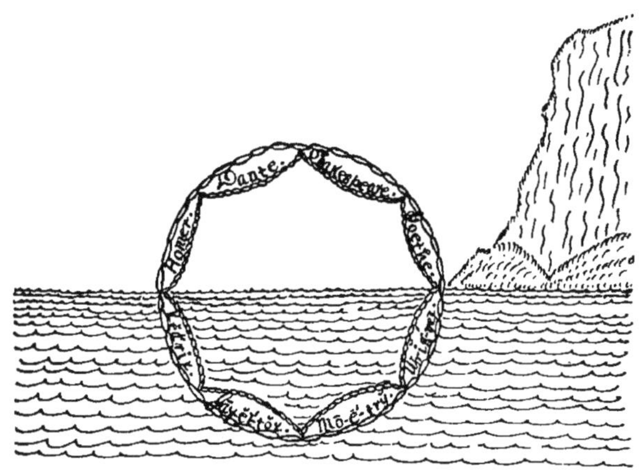

Beginning with the early part of the second Efremetrum of Atlantis, there were various Prĕt'zē (Poets) in the northern and northeastern portions of the Lontidri, and especially in the vicinity of Atara, as that was the center of Atlantian Art and Literature.

Wrĭg'vĕx, a female, was one of the most noted of the then ancient Pretze, a Lyric Oskley nud Pretz (Author and Poet) who chose her themes entirely from nature. Her thoughts were gathered from universal objective and expressive Nature, scenery and landscapes being her favorite themes, of which she wrought in masterly fashion. To her, the inspiration of melody flowed through the waters, where it expressed itself in the motion of the billows, waves and riplets, qualified with conditions of light and shadow. It was as one of Nature's modes of manifesting emotion, a quality further expressed in the breezes that wafted the airs of springtime among the verdant trees, or the fiercer winds that caused them to writhe and bend their unclothed forms in the winter season; in the falling rain drops and soaring snowflakes, as they found place on the bosom of the earth; in the natural forms that characterize, or the lights and shadows that envelope, the universe, by day and by night, and are as a counterpart of individual, objective nature. In fact, to her, all objective life expressed, from the heart and soul through the spirit and language of melody, that which she as a Cacella (spiritual teacher), under the guidance of spirits of the then past, caught up and reproduced in her lyrics.

Later, in the second Efremetrum, the epic style was added to the lyric, both of which developed into more artistic forms as the minds of the people developed, in literary thought, a condition due to the influence of the various talented pret-ze, who likewise were influenced by spirit intelligences.

Mō-ē'try was a most noted epic Pretze of this period, who wrote on themes of a religious character, or of spirit and soul ideas, in which he blended the styles of blank verse with rhythm, or metre, even in the same poetic production. In relation to form, he developed each thought or impression at the time it was received (for he was a Cacella, inspired by spirits of the then past ages), blending them in the above-named form, thus causing his Pretlex to possess beauty in style and character. His religious themes were principally on the "God principle," as governing creation, motive force, and the principle of purity in opposition to evil; also as in the universal sense, and the profound sublimity of creation in all of its aspects, which profundity and sublimity were religion to him; therefore, being so broadminded, he drew his themes from all existence.

Jā-ĕl'tŏx was one of the most noted female Pretze of the second Efremetrum, and wrote in didactic verse. Her themes or subjects were of a general or universal character, though most of them were chosen so as to bring out gayety and mirth, merriment and joyousness, as characteristics of life, in strong contrast to sadness or the sombre. Her style of writing was rhythmical, in character broad and far-reaching. As a Cacella, she was inspired by spirits from the realms of light, with the brightness that radiates from nature. This, to her, was the magnet and mainspring, the force of existence, which she utilized as a model for her Pretlex. And she influenced the people of Atlantis by her expressions of light, and thus drew them from the sombre confines of life into conditions more elevated and spiritual.

During the third Efremetrum, the Epic and Lyric styles passed through a mythical, legendary and astronomical version, such as related the gods and goddesses, in natural exploits, to romance and heroism, through themes relative to social and political life; and further, by themes relative to nature and its processes, a broader view of astronomical aspects, and didactics of a philosophical and scientific nature—the development of which continued to the close of the Efremetrum.

Xĕd'rĭx was one of the most noted among Pretze who made themselves famous through versification on various subjects. He was a didactic Pretz who wrote in blank verse on themes of nature and its visible aspects. He portrayed heroism—but more when of the sentimental order than the tragic—thus bringing out happiness and joy, and their contrasts, such as conditioned certain kinds of romance and noble life characters, mixing the individual and nature into beautiful and profound creations,. in a literary sense. He was also a Cacella endowed with the love of nature, of a heroic character, strong sentimentality and purity of purpose, and therefore was inspired by such spirits as brought influences from the realms of purity, light and love.

Passing from the greatness of the Ev'li-ăm Osk-ley-zē' (Literary Authors) of Atlantis, through the epi-cycle of Pretlex, under the ascendant influence of Jayeltox, Xedrix and their contemporaries, together with influences coming to them more ancient, as of Wrigvex, Moetry and their ,contemporaries, who during subsequent ages, from the spirit realm of the Cycle, held their severed links to the surface of the briny deep, as it were, for the purpose of re-welding and reconstructing, literature, and for the continuity of the literary influence; until, so to speak, the pre-historic celebrities, alert in that period of time, literally caught sight of the "gleaming links" through the white crests of the blue ocean waves, and felt at last the influence of the Pretz Oskleyze, of the long submerged Atlantians; heard the "spirit-echoes" from their submerged lyrics and epics, as they vibrated over the spirit epi-cycle, in continuation of the songs and recitation models of the long past.

Thus were the poets inspired with re-embodied ideas, which resulted in re-conception, re-connection, and re-establishment, of the spiritual-ideal links, of the past, to the establishment of those of the material epi-cycle of the present. Which, thus established, on the earth-plane, are still revolving on the deferent of the great Literary Cycle. Hence, by the spirit influences of the past, have the embodied spirits of the present been attracted, impressed, inspired and influenced, with ideas of the hidden Arts and the re-establishment of the Poetic epi-cycle on the material plane.

Entering the pre-historic period, some time between Atlantis and the time of Homer, we find the poetic spirit-influence began its work in the region of Arabia, where the idea was conceived by the Eltezean or pre-historic Arabian sensitives. Therefore E-ĕl'dŭ (Poetry) had its pre-historic re-embodiment and rise in Elteze, or Arabia, and E-ĕl-dū'ē-ăn (Poets) developed throughout the period, until in the latter part of it there were many, who wrote in the various styles and on various themes.

Krē-ĕs'ty was a most noted E-ĕl-dū'ä (Poet) of that period, who wrote in both lyric and epic styles. His themes were of a sacred nature. He was also a great humorist, hence many of his productions were thus characterized

Jăn'zy Krē-ĕs'ty, daughter of the above-named Eeldua, whom she followed, was considered the greatest Eeldua of the pre-historic epoch, in that country. Her works were mostly lyrical, but her themes embraced all grades of sentimentality and the humorous as well; and one of her strong characteristics was to arrange idiomatic expressions in the form of Eeldu

Kreesty and his daughter, Janzy, were each Mē-lŏs-dū'ăn (Seers*), and influenced the people by and through the Eeldu they wrote, inspired by their ability to see spirits and "spirit symbols," from which they got their impressions and inspirations. These they embodied in their Eeldu.

Passing from the influence of the great Kreesty and his daughter, and their contemporaries, through the migratory conditions into Siloton or Egypt, we find material influences developing under spirit-impression and inspiration, which led up to the establshment of the pre-historic Egyptian Bră (Poetry). Soon there appeared in that part of the country a goodly number of Bră-zō-ĕts' (Poets), who influenced the people through versification, lyric and epic, of various subjects.

Cē-ē-tī'zō was one of the most noted pre-historic Brazoets, who wrote both lyric and epic verse. He chose subjects from the characteristics of nature, and dealt with both terrestrial and celestial regions, embracing astronomically and astrologically conceived ideas. He was a noted Nĕt'rē-ŏs** (spirit conversant), able to influence the minds of the people by and through knowledge thus gained, which he embodied in his Bră. He also embraced heroism and religion, among his subjects, generally in relation to the Sun-god, and the various idols, celebrated then as representing spirits of departed celebrities.

Mĕl-tē'zä, a female Bră'zō (Poet), contemporary with Ceeti-

*As was the case with the Atlantians, the pre-historic people never used the term "Medium," as now. To the pre-historic Arabians the term "Melos" meant "one who saw spirits, from whom he received the ideas embodied in his Eeldu" (Poetry.)

**The term "Netreos" meant "an individual who repaired to quiet regions in the mountains, to talk with the spirits on various subjects, and then returned to teach the people accordingly."

zo, was the greatest, and most admired lyric Brazo among Egyptian Brazoets of that period. She was also a great Netreos, and frequently retired into the mountains where she gathered much knowledge from her spirit advisers.

Her Bra was of a very peculiar conception, difficult to describe. It was rythmical, gliding, and waving, in style. It might be likened unto movements of the air, and the waters, when she was dealing with material subjects, or with those of spiritual, or mortal and emotional characteristics, that qualify them. This fact was always made clearer during the rendition of the Bra, by gesticulations, or movements of the body, especially if recited with lyric accompaniment.

Subsequently, the prehistoric-poetic influence, by migrating peoples, extended along the developing cycle, in Zanzureta or Greece, where in due time Lā-lō'lä (Poets) and Lā-lō'-läs (Poetry) were well established.

Zē-wĭs'tē-nä was among the most noted of the pre-historic Lalola, who wrote in all the styles. His epics dealt with such heroism as was in harmony with the political and religious sentiments and events of the period. His lyrics embodied characteristics of nature, and particularly themes that portrayed the sentimental qualities belonging to all lifehood. His didactic verse embraced general principles of a moral and social nature. He being a Mō'dē-lĕn, or Mŭl'zē* (as they then termed Media), was able, by spirit vision, to catch ideas symbolically, from that influence; hence he, as a Modelen, influenced the people by and through his spiritual knowledge, which he made manifest through his Lalolas (Poetry).

Jā-ū'sā-lä, a contemporary of Zewistena, was another great Modelen, and female Lā'lō (Poet), who was the most celebrated of pre-historic Lalola of Zanzureta, in that period. She wrote principally in the lyric and epic styles. Her themes in the lyric were gathered from the popular folk-lore stories, in which she contrasted the superstitious tales and legends with facts of a historical nature, such as she received through her Modelen powers. This did much to influence the minds of the people against their superstitious beliefs, as well as the belief in tales and legends not founded on facts.

Her epics also, but more elaborately and logically, dealt with legendary subjects. Her narrations were based on issues of the day, in which she took real personages as her heroes and hero-

*The terms "Modelen" and "Mulze" meant "one who could see beyond the stars, and reveal that which was shown him by the spirits."
*The plural is formed only by changing the accent to the second syllable.

ines, in connection with their works, and contrasted them with the religious narratives, thus influencing the minds of the people along religious, social and political lines.

Her greatest and most celebrated works were based upon principles embraced in Astronomy; her themes, the Sun, the Moon, the Planets, the Constellations, etc. In these she blended the profound, scientific forces and laws of nature, governing the planetary realm, into the splendor of the sidereal aspect, as she, by and through her spiritual powers, was inspired to do, in such a way as not only to influence the minds of the people in that period of time, but in subsequent time; for she was the light that shone along the developing regions of the Cycle, to illumine the Astronomical intellect of pre-historic and ancient Greece, whereby they saw, conceived, and further developed, the science of Astronomy in its ascendency characterizing the Greeks, the continuance of which has even been the connecting links down to the modern realm of the Cycle.

Beginning with a period about 1000 B. C., we note Homer, the great "father" of Greek epic poetry, whom we choose as the principal connecting link in the Poetic Cycle between pre-historic Zanzureta (Greece) and subsequent periods. We select Homer because of the quality, made manifest through his writings on heroic and war themes; his description of the "conflict" between the Trojan army and the Greek heroes, Achilles and Agamemnon; the "interposition of the gods "as discoursed of in his "Iliad." Other representative writings of Homer, through which he influenced, are his heroic romances, as the "Odyssey," in which the long wanderings and final return to Ithica, of the aged warrior, Ulysses, are related; and further, his "Hymns" and "Epigrams," in which various subjects are discussed.

We note next Hesiod, the "father of Greek didactic poetry," whom we find at a period somewhere between Homer and the sixth century B. C., described as a "commissioned prophet" and "poet of the Muses," who influenced through proverbial philosophy; his writings of experiences of life afield; interweavings of episodes of fable, allegory, personal history, etc.; a Bœotian shepherd's calendar, embracing the adherency of ethical enforcement of honest labor dissuasive of strife and idleness; hints and rules as to husbandry; and a "religious" calendar, pointing out the lucky or unlucky days for rural or nautical undertakings; his famous "Works and Days;" and also his systematic arrangement of the legends of the gods, goddesses, and their offspring, in his "Theogony."

In the eighth century B. C., we note Arctinius, who continued the theme of "heroism" in the story of the Trojan war from the point at which the "Iliad" had laid it down; the School of Cyclic poets; the influence of the early Lays (or os-called "cantilenes," sung with the lyre, by Achilles and Patroclus, and those preceding; and interspersed through these centuries.

We note, during the seventh and sixth centuries B. C., the influence of the "Rhapsodists," who recited epic poetry, wand in hand, at festivals.

Passing from these more ancient Greek poets and their works, to those of the fifth century B. C., we find the ascendency assumed by five masters, viz., Aeschylus, the father of Greek tragic drama, who combined naval heroism with lyric poetry, as in his "Parsaius," moral and religious subjects, as in his "Agamemnon," "Prometheus," and "Eumenides;" Pindar, the great lyric poet of Greece, as manifest in his "Epinicæ;" Sophocles, the skilled tragic dramatist whose concentrated force is displayed through depiction of the personal emotions, and destinies, of his fabulous heroes, as in his "Oedipus Tyrannus," "Oedipus Colenus," "Philocteles," "Antigone," etc.; Euripides, the mediating poet, between the Hellenic and modern Romantic Drama, who established the transition by typical impersonation of heroic servitude, romantic character, pathetic nature, and subjects of fate, as in his "Alcestis," "Medea," "Hippolytus," "Ion," "Iphigenia in Aulis."

Passing from the epic, elegiac, iambic and lyric influences, of the fifth century B. C. (when literary prose as a re-embodiment began), and the tragic and comic of the Attic period (contemporaneous with historical, philosophical and oratorical prose) to the Alexandrian, or beginning of the decadence in the third century B. C., we note Lycophron who, through enigmatic verses, puzzled the people; Artus, in versified lore, on themes astronomical and medical; Callimachus, whose erudite influence was given forth in hymns, epigrams, and elegies; Nevius, the father of Roman political satire and censorious criticism; Plautus, the greatest comic and dramatic genius of Rome, and one of the greatest of the world, as proven by his comedies, "Amphitruo," "Asenoria," "Captivi," etc.; Ennius, the great elevator of tragic drama through "Saturnian Verse," and epic poems such as the "Annals;" the Bucolic poets, headed by Theocritus, the most famous of the pastoral writers who, through a sense of natural beauty, produced rural ideas, epics, or "cabinet pictures" of mythology, sketches of contemporary life, courtly compositions, expressions of personal kindness, and attachment; Bion, who touched and charmed the people by the music and pathos of his pastoral poetry; etc., etc.

Passing from the Alexandrian period to that of the Gracco-Roman in the latter part of the second century B. C., when the influence spread into Rome through Greek literature, we find the first part in harmony with the Free Republic, under the ascendency of Lucretius, the imaginative, emotional, scientific and philosophic poet, as evidenced by his books "De Rerum Natura;" Catullus, the last poet of the Free Republic, whose range of influence embraced themes of sensation, passion, warm affection, the amatory, personal and political animosities, as in his "Coma Berenices," "Ephuhalamium;" and "Attis," writing of passion love, and verses expressing savage indignation against Lesbia, his mistress, and Caelius Rufus his rival.

In the first century B. C., entering the Augustan age, we find the poetic art further matured under the influence of two principal masters, viz.: Virgil, the great epic genius, idealizer, blender of past, present and future greatness, dispeller of discord, establisher of order, harmony and peace, the portrayer of national glory, beauty in nature, and the intellectual herald of Grecian learning to the Roman and the modern mind, through his expressions in epos; and the display of conviction, seriousness, sympathy, natural sublimity and affection, as in his "Pastoral Hymns," the "Georgics," the "Æneid," etc.

Horace was the great lyric satirist, the idealist and realist, of his age; the revealer of public lives and the manners and ways of the Roman republic, as set forth in his "Satires and Epodes," through which works he also became the inspirer of fancy and imagination, and the reflector of the force of Greek influence.

Passing from the golden period of creative impulse to the last of the Augustan age, we find poetic styles changing to the imitative and popularism, under the influence of Ovid, the last of the Augustan poets, whose remarkable facility governed him in his choice of themes, viz.: fashionable romance, passionate love, immorality, fancy and fascination, social pleasure, popular aspects of science, immortality, etc., as portrayed in his "Heroids," "Amores," "Ars Amatoria," "Remedia Amores," "Festi," "Tristia," "Ex Ponto," "Ibis," "Metamorphoses," etc.

Later, in the silver age, we find the poetic influence to be in accord with the life of the age, the chief representatives being, first, Silius, whose imitative impulse led him into portrayals of personal heroism, as in his "Renica," a work of fourteen thousand lines, on scenes of the second Punic war; Statius, whose pathos and pictorial fancy are portrayed in his "Silvae;" Martial, whose themes of sensual frivolities, Roman life, individual motives, social caste and luxury, are recorded in his "Epigrams;" and lastly Juvenal, the reforming satirist, whose morose disgust is manifest through social satires, indignation, character portrayal, realism and grotesque humor, as set forth in his "Books of Satires," and who closed the poetic book of the Roman productive hour, and set its spirit free, to find in the creative and imitative geniuses of other climes, its reincarnation.

Finally, the decay of originality, the mechanical influence of critics, commentators, compilers and imitators, and the supremacy of prose works up to the fourth century, A. D., reduced poetic works to a lower grade, as the versification of Æsopic "Fables," by Babrius; the didactic poems on fishing and hunting, by Oppian; some elaborate essays in epic verse, by Nonnus and Quintus Smyrnaeus; poems and hymns of a mystic character, inspired by Orphic lore; the so-called "Sibylline Oracles," in hexameter verse, influenced by the expression of Jewish longings for the restoration of Israel, and by predictions of the triumph of Christianity and the short poems on Greek anthology.

The last stage in the decay of literary Hellenism, which was rapid and continuous, can be traced from 400 A. D. to 529 A. D., when the teaching of Pagan philosophy was brought to an end by the Edict of Justinian, which proclaimed the death warrant of Greek literature.

In the Byzantine period, beginning with the sixth century, we note the influence of Georgius, of Pisidia, who, in iambic verse, celebrated various wars; Cosmos, and Joannes Demascenus, of the eighth century, celebrated as hymn writers in theological motif; Leo VI., of the ninth century, who versified astronomical and eclesiastical subjects; Theodorius, of the tenth century, who narrated the "Capture of Crete" in iambic trimeter; Nicatas Eugenianus and Constantine Manasses, of the twelfth century, who versified in fiction and romance; Tzetzes, who wrote in verse of history, fact, fiction, custom and incident; Theodorius Prodromus, who wrote satirical and humorous didactic poems, and romances in iambic trimeter; Manuel Philes, of the thirteenth and fourteenth centuries, who wrote in didactic poetry of the great deeds of his patrons, or their moralities and virtues; Rhegas, of the eighteenth century, famed as a lyric, who wrote of liberty, and war songs; Christopoulos, of the eighteenth and nineteenth centuries, noted for his songs of love, of wine, etc.

Passing to the era of the independence of Greece, we note the influence of such great writers as Panagiotis Sontsos, a lyric writer, whose ideality, patriotism and love of liberty led him to sublime conceptions, such as his "The Traveller," "The Messiah," both based on the subject of dreams, and his plays, "Vlachavas," "Caraiscakis," "The Unknown," and his many lyrics; Alexander Sontsos, a satiric writer, who was idealistic, patriotic and possessed of a love for liberty, as evidenced by his conceptions, "The Wanderer," and comedies, "The Prodigal," "The Premier," "The Untamed Poet," "The Constitutional School," his numerous "Odes," "Lyrics," etc.; Alexander Rizos Rangabe, the great regenerating poet of Greece, whose great beauty and purity of thougth can be traced in his hymns, odes, songs, narratives, poems, ballads, tragedies, comedies, etc.

Passing into Gaul, we note that the Celts, through Phoenician commerce, were influenced by Greek poetry, rhetoric and the arts —and subsequently the furtherance of poetic influence, viz.: the Grecian, through the Gauls, and the Asiatic, through the Teutons; the German influence, with the Goths and other Teutons, which established didactic, epic and lyric poetry in alliterative verse, on subjects of commemoration, mourning, triumph, etc.

We note, in the twelfth and thirteenth centuries, the influence of the poets through themes of legendary romance, which they vivified with the spirit of chivalry, and adapted ancient heroes to the subject of their mediaeval hero stories.

Near the close of the twelfth century, we note Wolfram von Eschenbach, the sentimental and spiritual, mystic and passionate idealist, and his chief influential work "Parzival," in which he reveals strivings of a restless but noble spirit, to rise from idyllic simplicity to higher and purer aims. The spiritual significance of this poem is best understood by those readers who find discontent in their own lives, along natural lines, and who sense the loveliness embodied in that of the spiritual. To such it is an influence toward high and spotless aims. Gottfried, the contemporary and contrast of Wolfram von Eschenbach, who influenced by the results of human passion, as evidenced by his *"Tristan and Iseult,"* love of material things, secrets of the human heart, immoral tendencies, penetration of character, so widely different from the spiritual conceptions of the other, as revealed in "Parzival."

Passing from the influence of these, the two greatest poets of mediaeval romance, we note Conrad von Wurzburg, one of the most artistic of the writers of that period, as manifest in his works on the Trojan war, etc.

The Minnesingers were imitators of the Troubadours, as Heinrich von Morungen, Reinmar der Alte, Gottfried von Neifen, who wrote upon the favorite theme, *Minne,* or love, embracing sadness, evanescence of human pleasure, intense feeling, love, both elevating and sentimental, or extravagant and fantastic;

loyalty of vassal to lord, Christian to church, continuity of life, mental conditions through the aspects of nature and the seasons, etc. But the most illustrious of the *minnesanger* was Walter von der Vogelweide, whose didactic and lyrical poetry embraced general themes relative to his native land, embracing strife between spiritual and secular powers, rebuke against the extravagant ambitions of the papacy, humanity and freedom, art simplicity, grace, spontaneity, which latter conditions were displayed in his *"Unter den Linden an der Heide,"* and *"Tandaradei,"* its musical refrain; Thomasin Zerkler, who influenced moral enthusiasm, as in his *"Welsche Gast"*; Freidank, that of a high conception of duty, as in his *"Bescheidheit"*; Hugo von Trimberg, that of satire, as in his *"Renner."*

Heller, the famous didactic poet, who combined science, imagination and sympathy in the themes of his poems, as *"Die Alpen,"* etc.; Hegedorn, one of the most distinguished poets of the century, exerting an influence by didactic, satirical and moral verses, epigrams, odes, fables and songs, as manifested in the collections under the titles of *"Versuch einiger Gedichte, oder erlesene Proben poetischer Nebenstunden"*; *"Versuch in poetischen Fabeln und Erzählungen"*; and in his lyrics under the titles *"Sammlung neuer Oden und Lieder,"* and his *"Moralische Gedichte," etc.*

Passing the *Halla* school of poets, of which Glenn, Utz and Götz were original members, and the *Sturm und Drang* times, whose poets voiced hostility to all conventionalities, and clung to the truths of nature, we note Goethe, who in the influential Poetical Cycle stands in the modern German realm co-important with Shakespeare in the English, or Dante in the Italian mediaeval, and Homer with the great spirits of antiquity.

Goethe, whom we have chosen as one of the principal links in the great Poetic Cycle, was noted for being a poet of culture, possessing a great imaginative faculty; sympathy in creative impulse; activity, ideal vitality, and a universality, whereby he weighed the elements of human life; combined idealism and realism through his theme-pictures of the world generally, and portrayed languid sentimentalism, passionate despair, jealous agony, warm love of nature, the sweetness and unreasonableness of young passion, weariness of youthful life, etc., as in his *"Die Leiden des Jungen Werthers,"* satire, as in his *"Peter Bray," "Gods, Heroes, and Wieland,"* as in *"Satyros;" imagination, Christianity*, and the struggle between truth and falsehood, as in his *"Iphigenie;"* sorrows of a poetic nature, and the blending of realism and idealism in his *"Tasso;"* profound human experience, as in his *"Egmont;"* contrast between humble love and the desolation of the distant revolutionary wars—as in his *"Hermann und Dorothea;"* the spirit of chivalry, as in his *"Gotz von Berlichingen;"* and the mysteries of human life, its allurements and sorrows, innocence and its fall, antagonism of sensual and moral principles, characters, soul development through torment, affliction, repellant and disturbing elements, happiness in accord with the development of soul, contrasted with sorrows likewise conditioned, philosophy, religion, etc., as set forth in his *"Faust;"* the subtle charms of his lyrics delineate in themes of joy, longings and regret of the human heart, purification of passing emotions, reflected experience through his pictures of nature, indifference to hopes and fears, etc.

Here, at the zenith of the German Poetic Cycle, we note Schiller, Goethe's greatest friend, contemporary and contrast link—as was the case with Shakespeare and Marlowe on the English—famed for his chivalrous mind, revolutionary ardor, non-conventional character, strong will and passion, unselfish, possessing a soul filled with lofty aspiration for his race; contrasting ideality and reality, as may be seen in his lyric poems, such as *" An die Freude," "Die Gootter Griechenlands," "Die Kunstler,"* etc., produced in the middle period of his life; and *"Lied von der Glocke," "Das Ideal und des Leben," "Die Ideale," "Der Spazierzang," "Der Genius; Die Edwartung," "Das Eleusiche Fest," "Cassandra,"* etc., of his last and greatest period; his satirical epigrams against contemporary writers, as in the series *"Xenien;"* those embracing truths deduced from experiences in life, as in the series *"Votivtafeln;"* dramatic poems of revolutionary themes and destructive force, as in *"Die Rauber," "Tiesco," "Cabale und Liebe;"* intellectual and moral growth; imagination, social and political progress, etc., as in *"Don Carlos;"* misleading passion, lofty courage, and enthusiastic purpose, as in *"Die Jungfrau von Orleans;"* the combination of romantic and classical elements, as in *"Wilhelm Tell;"* hate, superstition, dark career, love, tragic pity, hopeless passion, spiritual freedom, integrity, etc., as set forth in his great trilogy, *"Wallenstein."*

After Goethe and Schiller, the two great poetical influences, had passed from the material realm, and the development of the Romantic, Schwabian, Fatalist and Patriotic schools, we find the poetic influence diverging, through themes of co-relation of mind and matter, probabilities of mysteries in human life; and the external world; spiritual emotions, mysticism, religious asprations, philosophical speculation, reconciliation of religion and science, etc. Searchlights were thrown backward, upon the works of preceding ages, thus revealing models for the present use, until the poetic influence was blended into the general literature of the day.

In the eighteenth century arose another lyric star, destined to follow, in greatness, Goethe and Schiller. It was that of Heinrich Heine. Imagination, love of freedom, enthusiasm for the beautiful, all these found expression through his lyrics,as in his *"Buch der Lieder."* Satire caused him to mock, through many themes, and to chisel from the works of his predecessors and contemporaries, and club Germany's despotic government. His influence illumined the minds of the school known as "Young Germany," at the head of which was Karl Gutskow.

Leaving Germany, through the works of the lyric poets of the nineteenth century, we ask the reader to consider the libraries and the archives containing the works and manuscripts of the members of the Poetic Epi-cycle of Germany, for a greater understanding of the profound influence and force, thus yielded in behalf of the great Literary Cycle.

Passing from the age of chivalry, at the fall of the Hohenstaufen dynasty, the period of poetic decline caused by wars and contentions which dethroned the influence in the castles of the princes, and the towers of the nobles—we note the effort at ascendency of the art, which of necessity had to come through the new conditions among the energetic inhabitants of the growing bergs and cities, who established the *"Tabulatur,"* or "rules of the guilds" for poetic song compositions.

Toward the end of the fifteenth century we note the *"Reineke Vos,"* a noted satirical epic of the age; *"Raynard the Fox,"* and *"Isengrim the Wolf,"* an epic modelled after the old Holland prose, with the theme changed from the social life of animals, to satire, and its enduring tendencies of human nature, the chastisement of vice, truth and justice, etc., a poem which has been vast in its influence, from the fact that it has been used as a model by the Franks, and for High and Low German works, the most noted of which were the hexametres of Goethe; *"Narrenscheff"* (ship of fools), by Sebastian Brandt, which was a noted allegorical poem in which the vices were satirized as fools; popular poetry, originating from conditions of strife and contention, was abundant, such as the verses of Veit Weber on the battles of Granson, Murten, and Nancy, and themes touching every aspect of the humble grades of daily life, in appropriate lyrics, were passed from section to section by the generations, and were as precursors to the grander conceptions of the subsequent German classics, that sprang up during the period of reform.

In the sixteenth century, we note Hans Sachs, the chief meistersinger of that age, whose thousands of poems comprised all the then known styles of verse, and touched on all the principal elements of the age. His verse in fables, parables, tales, dialogues, and his dramatic poems, such as the *"Shrove Tuesday Plays,"* were characterized with vivid imagination, sly humor, didactic power, satire, moral sentiment, ideas and controversion of the public, etc. His hymns displayed spiritual aspiration, as in *"'Warum betrübst du dich, mein Herz?"* and spiritual reverence for Lutheran reform, as in his poem beginning *"Die. Wittenbergisch Nachtigall, Die man jetz höret überall."* Johann Fischart, the greatest satirist of the century, who was ever vigilant in opposition to the evils of his day, and in favor of their reformation, as manifest in his many poetic and prose writings, we also note.

During the seventeenth century, many of the court poets influenced through the medium of satire, choosing for their model, Boileau, the French writer.

Passing from the seventeenth century, which was the termination of literary decay, along to the eighteenth century, the period of revival, we note Gunther, whose lyrics vibrated in harmony with the voices of nature, to awaken the life that had grown fruitless under the aforesaid dismal formalty of the court poets.

Under the influence of Frederick the Great, the German people were restored to vigor and confidence, intellectually, from the conditions following the Thirty Years' War. Thus, above the mediæval decay, they arched the future poetic structure in harmony with the cycle of antiquity, in which that branch of literature had been the chief prime factor in its framework. Schools arose in the service, whose aim it was to penetrate the meaning of ancient classics, regarding styles, imaginary effects and idealistic virtues; and to comprehend the lives of the Greeks and Romans in regard to the aspect of religion, art, and philosophy, as manifested through the ancient works; hence, through education, their intellectual germs responded to a growth of higher ideas. As the German mind turned back over the ancient cycle, it not only came in touch with Greek and Roman intelligence, but with that manifested through the great minds of Italy, Spain, France, and England, and new life was consequent by the counion of these mental emanations that arose from the laws of form, and the powers of imagination and reason. As poetry had been the prime factor in the creation and establishment of literature, in all nations, so it has been the chief aid in its revival.

Entering Britain, in the sixth century, we note the Anglo-Saxon influence on poetic development. Widseth, a poet of the Myrging race, narrated tales of the nations he had visited, as a Gleeman, and with them an account of their kings. *"Deor's Complaint"* is a poem that referred to Wieland, the Teutonic demi-god, and was the lament of a bard, displaced by a rival, in his lord's favor.

With the spread of the Christian spirit over the kingdom, came the Anglo-Saxon poetry in alliterative verse, on national and religious subjects, as collected and compiled in the famous Exeter Codex of the eighth century. Beda, the monastic poet of the same century, displays the hexametre, iambic, and trochaic styles, in writing on the subjects of *St. Cuthbert, Justin Martyn, Day of Judgment,* etc., thus lending an influence toward moral character.

In the tenth century Cardmon, the earliest English poet and precursor of the Milton style, produced the works known as *"Pharaphrase,"* which treat of the rebellion of the Angels, and the fall of Man.

In the eleventh century we come in touch with the Anglo-Norman influence, on poetic development. Turoldus produced his heroic *"Chanson de Roland."* Benoit wrote his vast *"History of the War of Troy."* Wace wrote his famous *"Brut d' Angleterre,"* historic of the Kings of Britain, from Brutus to Cadwalader. Through the Anglo-Norman poets, historical chronicles were blended into romances, a transformation that developed the romance of revenge, slaughter, race hatred, unlawful love, magic and witchcraft, into a series of mythical legends, symbolizing the dogmas and creeds of the Roman Catholic faith, such as the San Graal legend.

Later, in the bardic poetry of Wales, under the influence of Gwalchmai, Elidir, Gwion, etc., the patriotic triumphs of the Princes were portrayed.

Passing the detail of mixtures in the development of poetic styles arising from the amalgamation of races and linguistic differences, the alliterations, imitations, translations, and new versions of the twelfth and thirteenth centuries, to the fourteenth, we find Langland at the head of the Teutonic affinity, or alliterative poets, and Chaucer, Goueer and Lydgate, at the head of the Franco-Latin affinity or rhyme poets.

Chaucer, the intellectual giant of this period, caught the Franco-Latin spirit, evidenced by his *"Canterbury Tales," "As-*

sembly of Foules," "House of Fame," "Book of the Duchesse," "Court of Love," "Legends of Goode Women," etc.

In the fifteenth century, the period of renaissance and reform, when the revival of Greek learning spread into England and France, we find Surray and Wyat the principal reformers in metre and poetic style.

In the sixteenth century we find an opposition to the Roman-Christian influence in the Puritan, which sought to suppress English poetry; hence, a strife between the poets and the enemies of their art, Spenser and Shakespeare being leaders, which eventually led to moral reform in poetry.

Here, in the Elizabethan age, when great minds began to turn the literary machine, together with the influx of thought influence from adjacent regions, that came of ancient models and was pressing its way into the literary throng, where the brain soil was ready for new propagation, came development of new poetic conceptions, such as the romantic advancement of the brave knights and ladies of Spenser's *"Föerie Queene,"* and the allegorical and moral, virtues displayed, gains influence through Burns, as by his *"Cotter's Saturday Night,"* or by Byron in his *"Childe Harold,"* etc.

Two great headlights lead the dramatic and poetic styles of this age—the first, Marlowe, father of English tragedy, and establisher of blank verse, as displayed in his epic tragedies, as *"Tamburlane the Great," "Doctor Faustus," "Jews of Malta," "Edward the Second,,"* and *"The Massacre of Paris."* Second, the immortal Shakespeare, whom we have chosen as one of the principal links in the great Poetic Cycle. He was and is known to the world, through his great repertory of romantic comedy based on woodland haunts and styles in sylvan life, as *"A Midsummer Night's Dream," "As You Like It," "Love's Labours Lost," "Merry Wives of Windsor,"* etc.; his Roman plays, portraying the perplexities of human life, as *"Coriolanus," "Julius Caesar," "Anthony and Cleopatra,"* etc.; his historical dramas, based on British national life, loyalty, patriotism, struggles and fates of the rulers, etc., as *"King Richard II"* and *"King Richard III," "King Henry IV,"* and *"King Henry V,"* etc., and his great tragic pieces, in which he portrays the sublime agony, as in *"Hamlet;"* terrors, as in *"Macbeth;"*profound passion, as in *"Othello;"* grandeur and pathos, as in *"Lear."*

Passing the "phantasy and conceit" poets of the age, and entering the seventeenth century, we find Milton expressing, in blank verse, episodes embracing moral energy, great imagination and conception, where invention takes the place of tradition, legend and history, as evidenced in his masterpiece, *"Paradise Lost."* Dryden, the great poetic-controversialist, whose themes deal with the political and religious reactions of the day—rebellion, faction, disobedience, anarchy, etc., as set forth in his *"Absalom and Achitopel,"* an argument against democracy and the absolute right of majority; in *"Threnodia Augustalis,"* against senates; in *"Hend and Panther,"* against the clergy, who were dissatisfied at having to become obedient and submissive to the arbitrary acts of James II.; in *"Religio, Laici,"* relative to religious belief, its extent and authority in private judgment, etc.

In the eighteenth century, in the age of Queen Anne, we note Addison, the Whig poet, who wrote of the heroism and victory in the battle of Blenheim, as set forth in his *"Campaign;"* Parnell, in *"Didactics;"* Rowe, in *"Pastorals;"* Defoe, in satirical poems; Pope, whose classical taste led him to follow the model of Horace, as evidenced by his *"Essay on Criticism,"* of which *"Ars Poetica,"* by Horace, is said to be the model; Swift, the upholder of compromise and unbelief in revealed religion, as apparent in his *"Tale of a Tub;"* Cowper, of amiable piety and spiritual despair, as established by his *"Task," "The Castaway,"* etc.; Burns, the genius who spoke straight from the heart of Nature—as a child of nature, endowed with sagacity, logical faculty and judgment, exposing hypocrisy and fanaticism of the ministers, and giving expression to pathos, melody and beauty, as in his many songs, etc.

In the latter part of the eighteenth and first of the nineteenth centuries, we find Scott, the romantic poet, exercising an influence in favor of return from French revolution, to chivalry, feudalism, etc., as evidenced by *"Marmion," "Lay of the Last Minstrel," "Lady of the Lake,"* etc.

In the nineteenth century we find Shelley, the famous and imaginative poet in rhetoric metre, the consummate producer of lyrics on subjects of ideality, sublimity, beauty, goodness, and intellectual passion, as *"The Revolt of Islam"* (favoring bloodless revolution); *"Julian and Maddalo"* (reality of ordinary things); *"The Cenci"* (grand tragedy); *"Prometheus Unbound"* (sublimely dramatic imagination and ideality); *"The Witch of Atlas"* (roving imagination controlled by beauty"), etc.

Passing briefly into Italy, we note the Franco-Italian poems, which are the links to pure Italian works—the poems of Giacomino and Bonvecino, of religious influence in the north; love songs, such as *"Contrasto,"* attributed to Ciullo d' Aleamo, characteristic of the sensuality of the southern people; the rhymes of the Sicilian school; the political poetry of Guittone d'Arezzo;

the philosophic poetry of Guido Guinicelli, embracing chivalry, love, and mental nobility; the allegorical, visionary and moral styles of the thirteenth century, as *"Tesoretto,"* by Brunetto Latini; the *"Documento d'Amore,"* and *"Del Reggimento e die Costumi delle Donne,"* of Francesco da Barberino; the Tuscan lyric poetry, which began the true Italian art; the works of Guido Cavalcanti, such as his famous *"Sulla Natura d'Amore,"* of a philosophic character, a treatise on amorous metaphysics; the love poems of Cinoda Pistoia, etc.

Dante, the distinguished mediæval poet, whom we have chosen as one of the principal links in the great Poetic Cycle, was a lover of nature; a dweller in scientific, philosophic and astronomic atmospheres, of expressive and descriptive ability, and adherer to conceptive unity, of religious earnestness, rich symbolism and scholastic attainments; capable of passionate love, as manifest in his *"Vita Nuova,"* or Young Life; of philosophic comment, as evidenced by his *"Convito;"* a master of lyric style, as set forth in his *canzoni ballate* and *sonnetti;* in sympathy with Ghibellinism, as shown in the Latin treatise, *"De Monarchia;* a promoter of linguistic and poetic composition, as per the treatise *"De Vulgari Eloquio;"* a genius in the portrayal of allegory and romance and the contrast of sadness and cheerfulness; of lofty things and the lowly, fear and hope; strong in portrying incontinence, violence, fraudulency, purgatory, paradise, temporal and eternal happiness, civil and religious confusions in society, vice, envy, fickleness, pride, avarice, light and reason, artistic grandeur and delicacy, hatred and love, consciousness and fancy, etc., as embodied in his *"Divina Commedia,"* and other productions.

Petrarch was the first humanist and lyric poet, of the modern school, as manifest in his *"Africa,"* a long poem in hexametres, on the campaigns of Scipio; and his *"Canzoniere,"* in which love is the principal embodiment of the poem, with varied conceptions and natural impressions. Then come the comic poetry of the thirteenth and fourteenth centuries, by such authors as Bindo Bonichi, Orgagna, Antonio Pucci, etc., the political poetry of the fourteenth century, by such authors as Teziodegli Uberti; the *ballate* (poems sung to dancing); the Petrarchist love songs; the Romanistic poems of the fifteenth century; the *cantari* (romantic poems); elegiac poems, as *"Margante Maggiore,"* by Luigi Pulci; heroic poetry, as *"Italia liberata dai Goti,"* by Trisino; the lyric poetry of the sixteenth century, represented by many authors, both male and female; the didactic poems, as *"Costigiano,"* by Baldassare Castiglione, etc., embracing too many authors and subjects to further note, but these all go to make up the complete link, of the Italian portion of the great Poetic Cycle, and its influence on the people of that region.

Passing briefly into France, we note the influence of the Troubadours, from every stage and rank of feudal society, who sang songs to the accompaniment of musical instruments; the Jongleurs, who sung the songs of their disembodied brothers; the songs known as *chansons,* of a religious character; the *servente,* embracing subjects of love or war; the *tensons,* or discussions on love questions; the *aubade,* or provincial songs, portraying the passing of darkness and the dawning of light, and religious, and love themes; the *ensenhamen,* dealing with conduct and etiquette; the *epitre,* embracing petitions, thanks, advice, moral suasion and instruction; the *tresons,* embracing facts of art and science; the early epics of the *trouveres,* such as the *"Chansons de Geste,"* the *"Chanson de Roland,"* the *"Roman des Loherains,"* etc.; the rhyming chroniclers, the poems of the classical cycle, as *"Histoire des dues de Normandie,"* of thirty thousand lines, by Benoit de Sainte-Maure; satirical poems, such as *"Housse Partie," "Le Mantel Mautaillie," "Landri," "Roman de Renart,"* etc., etc.; the early lyrics of various styles; songs and poems of the fourteenth century, as the *rondeau.* the *triolet,* etc.; the didactic poetry of the sixteenth and seventeenth centuries, as influences that led up to the finals of more renown, as the poet Boileau, of the seventeenth century, who wrote elaborate *epitres* to his friends; Racine, of the seventeenth century, who wrote *"Thebaide,"* portraying rivalry; *"Alexandre,"* a tragedy; *"Andromaque,"* of the Shakespearian order and various other productions, Next we note the great Romantic school, as Victor Hugo, Alphonze de Lamertine, Alfred, Count de Vigny, Alfred de Musset, Auguste Barbier, etc., of the greatness of whom the reader can learn from history, as space forbids further comment on the poetic influence, so widely extended among the various peoples of the earth, which we accept as principle links in the great Poetic Cycle.

HET-ZEN'ZE NUD KREST-E-ON'ZE,
OR
TONE POETS AND MUSICIANS.

TELTZIE XXXI.

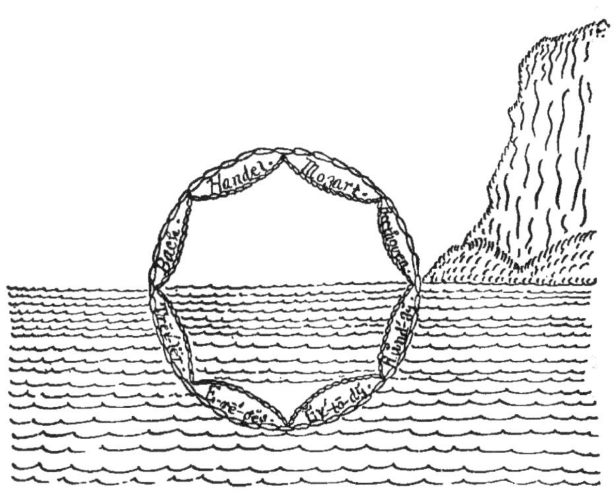

Krĕst (music), at the beginning of the first Efremetrum, was simple in style, and the instruments were crude; the most popular of these was the Cī-cō'nî-ä. It was constructed out of a shell of wood, cylindrical in form, the ends of which were closed with prepared skin, from an animal known as the Cē-ĕt'trē. A hole was made in the center of the cylinder, to give quality to the sound. The cylinder was graded in thickness from one end to the other, which gave the instrument power to differ in pitch at the points where it was struck on the surface, which was done with a wooden hammer, by the operator. This condition gave quality of tone, and also degrees of dynamic force to the tones. The Ciconia was principally used to accompany the voice when rendering chants.

During the latter part of the first Efremetrum this instrument was considerably improved, in various ways. With this development, Hĕt'zĕn (music composers) arose, in accord with the advancement of the art, a condition which lasted until about the middle of the second Efremetrum.

Rŭnd'zey was the name of the most noted Krĕst'ē-ŏn (musician) of that period, and he was the celebrity to whom is due the original progress made in the Art of Music and development of musical instruments. He came into the knowledge of instrumental tone production accidentally—though through spirit influence. Once while sitting on some fallen timber in the forest, meditating upon the beauties of nature that surrounded him, and listening to the songs of the birds and their graduation of sound, Rundzey was carelessly striking here and there upon the timber with a stick that he had in his hand, when his attention was drawn to the fact that he was producing different qualities and pitches of sound, and that he could produce different degrees of power, by the stroke. From this fact he began a series of experiments, which ultimately resulted in the construction of the Ciconia.

Ex'tō-dy was a Kresteon who flourished in the middle of the second Efremetrum. His special influence was in the improvement of the then known musical instruments, and the composition of music adapted to them. He was the originator of the Kăth'ā-rŏn-zä, from which the E'thē-rē-lē-ŭm was developed. At first the Katharonza was a crude and simple instrument. It was composed of five strings, played by picking them with the fingers, from the underneath end. The form of the instrument was that of a modern table. The crude or original construction of this instrument was from Gē'sē, a fibrous wood. For a long time, Extody experimented, in order to bring out this instrument, which was at last done by taking a piece of the tree, cutting away the woody part from beneath the fibres, so as to leave them in various lengths to produce pitch of sound. By careful cutting and trimming, the ends of the wood that held the fibres fast, he was able to produce differences in the quality of tone. Thus, he continued to improve the instrument until the time of the third Efremetrum, when it had become so perfect that it was lost in the origin and adoption of the Ethereleum, which latter was established under the supervision of his son Zeluth, who carried out his plans for its construction.

Extody possessed a nature that vibrated in unison with sounds, and therefore he was an instrument easily influenced by the spirit forces who sought to bring out in him the knowledge of the pitch of sound, and its utility, in the art of music, to a greater degree of perfection than had been; hence, the origin and perfection of the Katharonza.

Contemporaneous, with Zelūth' was a celebrated Kresteon by

the name of Cĕl'ĕt-ĭck. During the first part of the third Efremetrum, they worked together, voicing the Ethereleum. Zeluth would work at the instrument during the process of its tuning, or voicing, while Celetick, standing near the instrument, listened and directed the changes to be made in the pitch to perfect the scale. Zeluth used the tone of his own voice as a guide to tune by, and Celetick would indicate the changes necessary to bring the strings into unison or harmony, by raising or lowering his hand; and the point of unison, by its repose. This not only made the work less laborious, but the result more accurate and perfect.

E-rē'gĕs was a noted Gĕl-ĕs'try (singer) and Kresteon, whose influence was felt in the early part of the third Efremetrum. He modelled after Zeluth as a public performer of vocal and instrumental krest, but not as a builder of instruments. He was educated, by Extody, in the art of composition, as well as that of krest, and was an expert at correcting manuscripts of krest, and at harmonizing melodies.

Trĕx'lĕr was the most noted Kresteon of the latter part of the third Efremetrum. He represented completeness in both vocal and instrumental krest, in all their details. He was a deltsanz in the krest sĭl-dä'zĭc (music school), or Kē-nĭs'try (college) of Atara, to whom persons came from all parts of the Lontidri, in order to place themselves under his instruction.

Atlantian krest was represented to be read by the krĕst-ē-ŏn'zē (musicians) in a different manner from the methods employed by modern musicians and composers; therefore, we will, in part, represent and explain the Atlantian methods, so the reader may have a better idea of the principal characters they employed; i. e., the characters representing the krest, and their signification in relation thereto.

Their Cēet (staff) consisted of right oblique gŭt'zē (lines), from four to seven in number, according to the number of crē'sy (syllables) that were to be used in the quĭn'tō-zē (measure), which latter was represented by the space between two left oblique gutze, which they termed sĕl-sō'zē (single bars). The beginning of the ceet was indicated by two perpendicular parallel gutze, that were about one-quarter the length of those of the ceet, and were termed sū'mē (beginning bars). The relt (close) of the ceet, was indicated by three left oblique gutze, one-half the length of the ceet gutze, drawn parallel with each other, after the last sĕl'sō (bar).

In some compositions, as above stated, a uniformity of four ceet gutze was employed; six in some, seven in some, while others were irregularly formed or mixed, the different quintoze of the composition varying in the number of eect gutze, per quintoze, from four to seven, as the words in the composition required. This was fixed in accord with the metre of the poem, or syllables in the stanzas. More uniformity was adhered to in the representation of instrumental score than the vocal.

The ceet, in addition to the variances that arose, syllabic uniformity, such as established the mixed order of quintoze of four, five, six, or seven gutze, were also characterized with ĕl′fĕt gutze, or quarter-lengthed ledger lines, that represented the higher krū-ĕn′zē (tones) of the frū-gē′zē (scale) names, such as ŭt, bū, su (a, b, c), etc., were not used to designate the absolute pitches of the frugeze, but the cardinal numbers were used instead, similar to the modern order; e. g., the ceet began with the introductory short line or gutze, which was called ĕt (one), then followed four right oblique gutze, then the left oblique long gutze or selso, thus forming a quintoze. Then followed four short right oblique gutze, then another selso, which established another quintoze, and so on, forming quĭn-tō′zē* of short gutze, until enough had been made to contain the kruen or tones of the scale.

The introductory short gutze or line at the beginning of the wĭs′sī-lō ceet or treble staff, represented the first tone of the frū′-gē-zē sū, or scale of C, and was recognized as ĕt or one, of that fruge, or what modernly is termed "middle C." The same gutze on the mā-sī′lō ceet, or bass staff, represented the octave lower than middle C, etc.

When transposing to the various ō-rŭm′zē or frugeze (keys or scales) of Atlantian krest or music, the order was the same as that of the modern transposition, viz: by fourths and by fifths, the former thus establishing the first kruen in the frugeze of lutze (first tone in the scale of flats), and the latter in that of sharps; i. e., four tones higher than one, or C, inclusive, would be four of the original fruge of tū, or one of the scale of F. Likewise, zret kruenze, or five tones higher than one, or C., inelusive, would be zret of the original fruge or five of the scale of C, which would establish ĕt of the frugeze gū, or one, of the scale of G.

The sĕn′gĕr frugeze nud orumze, or minor scales and keys, were only known to a portion of the highly educated Atlantian Krĕs-tē-ŏn′zē (musicians), and at the time of the submergence were about to be established by them for practical and general use, when the principle would have been brought out in their compositions. But alas! it, with them, was cut off from further

*The plural is formed only by changing the accent to the second syllable.

development by that awful submergence, hence practically left not understood by the kresteonze of the Atlantian period of time.

The rĕt'zē (notes) were all formed with a triangular head, and a stem or left oblique gutze. The fĕt rĕt (whole note) had a filled head and full-length stem. The sĕl'fĕt rĕt (half note) had an open head and a stem three-fourths the length of that of the whole note. The ĕt'fĕt rĕt (quarter note) had an open head and stem one-half the length of the whole note. The ĕstz'fĕt rĕt (eighth note) had an open head and stem one-fourth the length of the whole note. The sŏt-zē'fĕt rĕt (sixteenth note) was the same as the eighth note, with the addition of one short gut (line) beneath the stem. The wĕz nŭd thrĭst-zē'fĕt rĕt (thirty-second note) was the same, with the addition of two gutze. The kätz nŭd cē-rēte-zē'fĕt (sixty-fourth note) was the same, with the addition of three gutze, as represented below·

Fĕt rĕt	 Half-note
Sel'fĕt rĕt	 whole-note
Et'-fĕt rĕt	 quarter-note
Estz'fĕt rĕt	 eighth-note
Sŏt-ze'fĕt rĕt	 sixteenth-note
Wĕz nŭd thrĭst-zē' fĕt rĕt	 thirty-second note
Kĕtz nŭd cē-rĕte-zē'fĕt rĕt	 sixty-fourth note

The Zĭlt'zē (rests) were formed by the use of long, right-oblique gutze, and short horizontal gutze, and horizontal elliptic gutze, the latter consisting of the under-curve, as follows:

Fĕt-zĭlt — whole rest

Sĕl′fĕt zĭlt — half rest

Et′fĕt zĭlt — quarter rest

Estz′fĕt zĭlt — eighth rest

Sŏt′zē fĕt zĭlt — sixteenth rest

Wĕz nud cē-rēte-zē′fĕt zĭlt — thirty-second rest

Kĕtz nŭd cē-rēte-zē′fĕt zĭlt — sixty-fourth rest

The Krĕst El-tē-mĕt′zē (music symbols) were as follows:

Sū′mē — beginning bar

Sĕl′sō — single bar

Sĕl-sō′lŏs — double bar

Rĕlt — close

Gĕst — sharp

Lūt — flat

Wrĕt — natural

Wĭs′sī-lō zŏn — treble clef

Mā′sī-lō zŏn — bass clef

Zĭg — tie

Yō — legato mark

Vĭst, or Cūm — pause or hold

Dō-rĕt — dotted note

Clĭnt — time signature

The mĕt'zä (scale signature), as is the case with modern music, consisted in gĕst'zē (sharps) lŭt'zē (flats) or wrĕt'ze (naturals), that were written in a line above the sūme, at the beginning of the composition, and were from one to seven in number, in accord with the key to be represented, as the Atlantian krest, like the music of modern time, was written in fifteen keys; i. e., the natural, and from one to seven gestze, and from one to seven lutze.

The clĭnt (time signature) was represented by dō'zē (dots) placed one above the other, and after the zŏn'ze (clef), i. e., two dots to indicate double time, three to indicate triple time, four to indicate quadruple time, and also to indicate the number of beats in the quintoze (measure); but instead of a lower figure to indicate the kind of a note that was to receive one beat, the ret (note) that represented the unit value was placed after the doze; i. e., if a quarter note was to receive one beat, the estz'fĕt rĕt was used. If the eighth note was to receive one beat, the estz'fet ret was then used.

AT'LAN-TI-AN MEL'ZIC (Example).

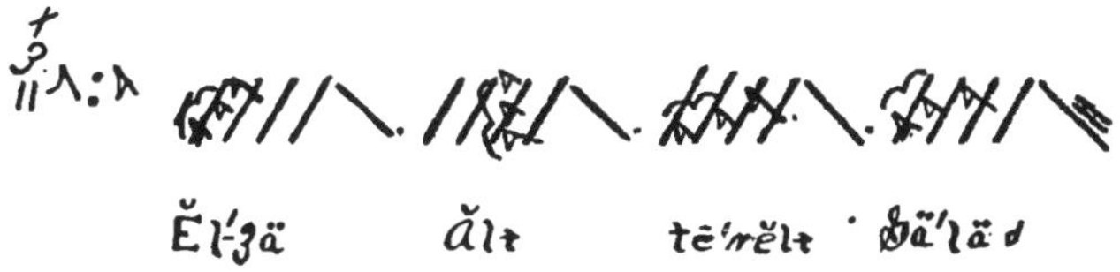

Ĕl'zä ălt tē'rĕlt bä'lä d

TRANSLATION.

My soul be thine God.

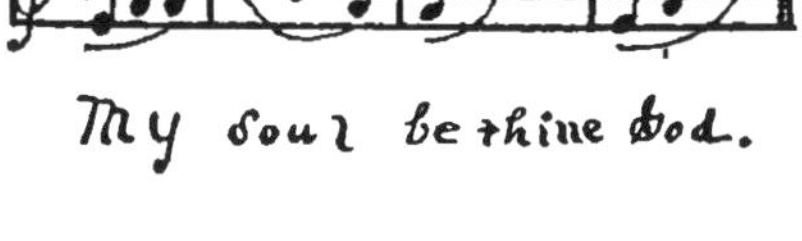

O'RUM PRE'ZE
OR
KEY NAMES.

Atlantian.	English
Gē gĕst'zē o'rum zē Sū.	No sharps, key of C.
Et gest o'rum ze Gū.	One sharp, key of G.
Wē gĕst'ze o'rum ze Dū.	Two sharps, key of D.
Sĕt gest'ze o'rum ze Ut.	Three sharps, key of A.
Kĕt gest'ze o'rum ze Iē.	Four sharps, key of E.
Zrĕt gest'ze o'rum ze Bū.	Five sharps, key of B.
Sŏt gest'ze o'rum ze Tū gĕst.	Six sharps, key of F sharp
Zŭm gest'ze o rum ze Sū gĕst.	Seven sharps, key of C sharp.
Et lūt, ŏ'rŭm zē Tū.	One flat, key of F.
Wē lut'ze o'rum ze Bū lŭt.	Two flats, key of B flat.
Sĕt lut'ze o'rum ze Iē lūt.	Three flats, key of E flat.
Kĕt lut'ze o'rum ze Ut lūt.	Four flats, key of A flat.
Zrĕt lut'ze o rum ze Dū lūt.	Five flats, key of D flat.
Sŏt lut'ze o'rum ze Gū lūt.	Six flats, key of G flat.
Zŭm lut'ze o'rum ze Sū lūt.	Seven flats, key of C flat.

yc es

MET'ZA NON'ZA NUD CLINT'ZA, OR SCALE SIGNATURES, CLEFS, TIME AND SIGNATURES.

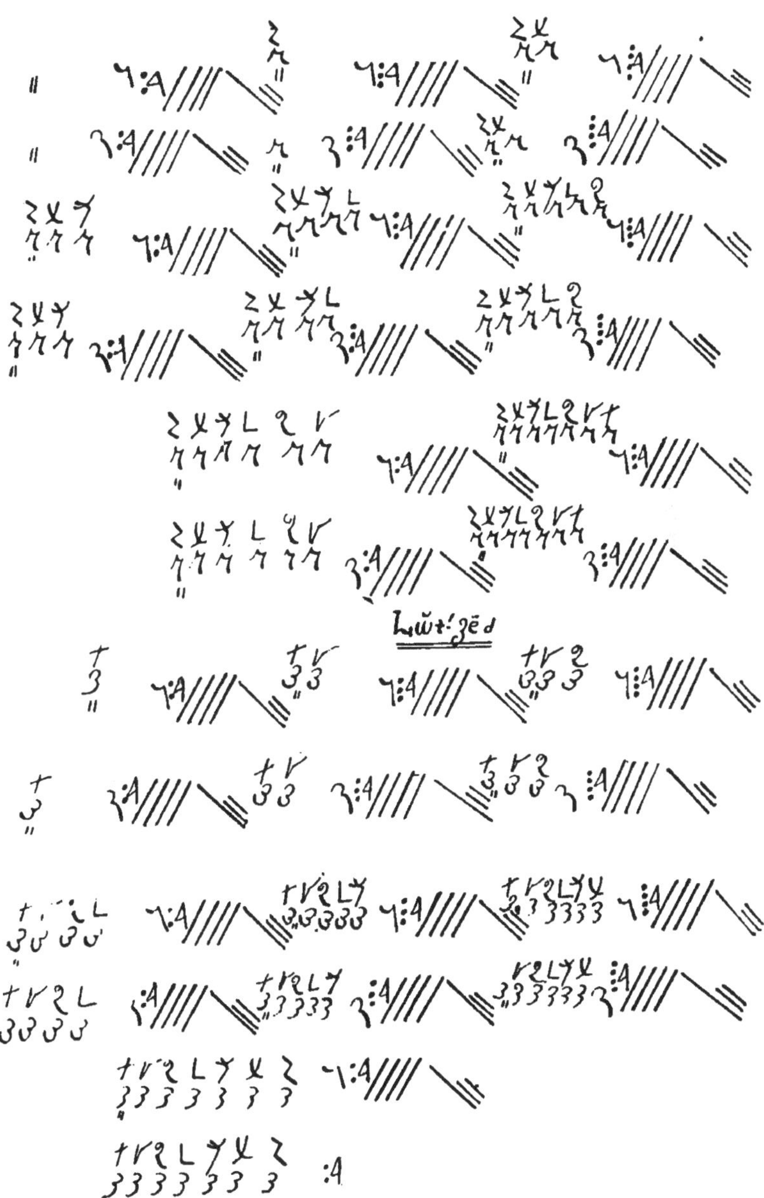

WRET FRU'GE ZE SU,

CES

CE-NO'ZE NUD MEL-THO-ON'ZE,

OR

NATURAL SCALE OF C.

BY

FIGURES AND LETTERS.

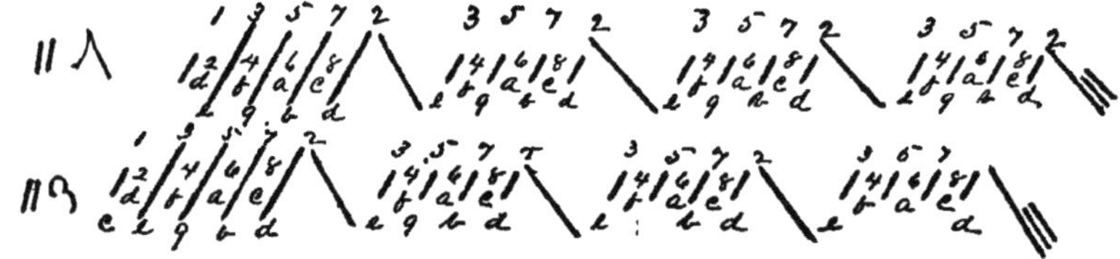

WRET FRU'GE ZE SU NU'GER,

CES

RET-ZE'

OR

NATURAL SCALE OF C MAJOR

BY

NOTES

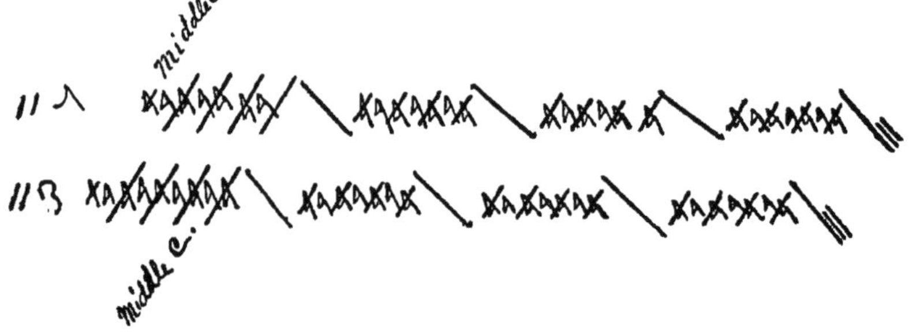

FRU'GE ZE TU,
OR
SCALE OF F.

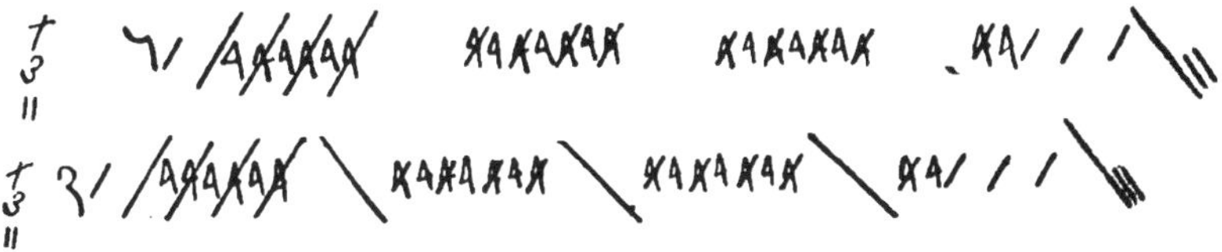

FRU'GE ZE GU,
OR
SCALE OF G.

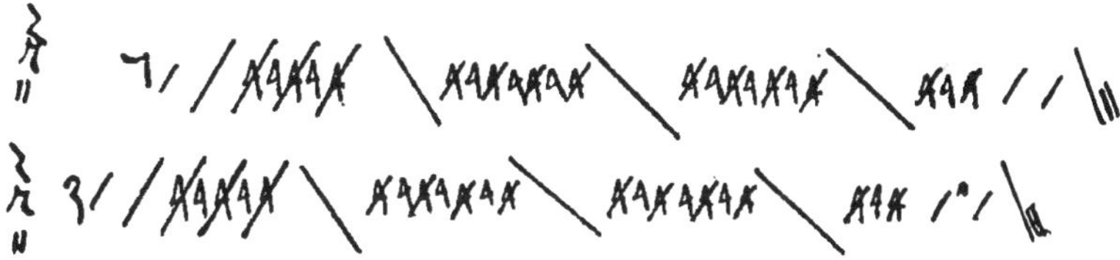

In the latter part of the third Efremetrum, the en'sä-zē krĕst (art of music) was in a high state of cultivation with the Atlantian people. They used both sē'thăck (vocal)) and trä'ō (instrumental) krest in their homes, temples and places of amusement. The sethack that they used in their Agalteze (temples) was much like the modern chants, though like most of the Atlantian krest, was rendered in a gliding or waving style, but in strict rythm. Much care was taken, by the authors, to make the melody attractive, leaving the spiritual sense of the words for consideration, by the individuals who gave them utterance during the song. A number of specially educated crytzē' (plural of cryt, a male singer and crytz, a female singer), led the assembly in that part of the worship.

USH I-E'TONE, U-RA-THE'A NUD E-THE'RE-LE-UM.

TELTZIE XXXII.

The I-ē'tōne, to a certain extent, resembled the class of instruments now known as the Lyre and the Harp, especially in the placement of the strings, and the method of manipulating them. When complete, it stood about three and a half coitex in height. It consisted of a quō'sĕx (frame) wrought out of golden-colored zeī'tē (a combination of ū'ziē, jĕt'ney and kī-zē'tä material). The quosex had four signitie (marble) foo'zē (legs) that stood on rolling balls of the same material, thus adding greatly to the resonant quality of the tones produced on the trä (instrument). Extending upward, from the signite fooze, were two perpendicular sections of the quosex, which, further extended into an irregular or wave-like form, that established the upper portion of the quosex. Across the lower half of the quosex, above the signitie fooze of the quosex, in right-oblique form, was a cross section or hollow body that formed a sound chest. To this trŭm-vē'zē (ten strings) were attached in the upper side by means of ū'ziē tī'yē (golden keys). At the top of the quosex, in left-oblique form, was a cross-bar, to which the upper ends of the veze were made fast by means of ū-ziē rū-īte'zē (golden hooks). The entire quosex, as was the case with the cross section or sound chest, was of hollow form, the hollow condition making a complete circuit through the quosex and the sound chest, by means of their inter-connection at the ends of the sound chest, a device that had much to do with the quality of the sound produced on the tra. At stated points, on the upper portion of the quosex, were zrēt ūziē tī-yē (five golden keys) that opened and closed inner valves, thus giving different qualities to the sound. The upper tiye of the five, however, operated an external valve to the quosex, for the purpose of indefinitely extending vibration of sound, a fact that also affected the quality of sound. The trum veze were made of clē'tiē (silver) principally, with a slight combination of zelet and jetney. They were placed or strung in a half-fan form with connections as above stated, and varied in size, from the finest wire that could be made from that combination of materials, up to the required weight of the lowest-toned veze. The veze were tuned by means of the uzie tiye that fastened them to the sound chest, and the pitch of tone was obtained by the tension brought to bear upon the veze, in connection with their length and weight. The highest-toned vē-zē' were strung nearest to the player, and graded down, so that the lowest or deepest-toned were farthest from him. Both hands were used when picking the veze, the right manipulated the highest-toned, and the left the lowest. They were also used as dampers, to shorten the duration of the tones, and to produce harmonic embellishments. The tra was made in its irregular waved-form for a certain vibratorial effect.

The Krest produced from the Ietone, was extremely soft and melodious, as if coming from fairy land. It was only a home tra, and was played mostly at eventide.

The idea of the Ietone was carried, by the Atlantian remnant migrators, into the Egyptian and Asiatic countries, where in long subsequent time, by spirit influence, the idea of the Lyre was conceived, and brought out in its crudest state. But after further development, in those regions, it was carried into Greece, where it figured extensively in association with the rendition of the Hellenic poetry.

In the music of the Æolian and Ionian colonies, it figured in accompaniments, and also found further improvement. It was used by the mythical Masters—Orpheus, Musæus, Thamyris, etc. It figured in the ceremonies of Greece, where it was changed into various styles, among which are the known Chelys and the lyre of Hermes, and also the cithara of Apollo from which the phormix was conceived. Into Egypt, and Semitic Asia, likewise descended the Egyptian lyre of fan-shape, that ultimately, in the eighteenth, nineteenth and twentieth dynasties, sustained various changes in form and utility.

The Harp, of great antiquity, had its origin in Egypt, through traditional influences, carried into that region by prehistoric migrators, who had descended from the remnant Atlantians on the Eastern Continent. Some of these had knowledge of the Ietone, and established the tradition of the instrument. This was in turn handed down to the pre-historic Egyptians, who ultimately, through spirit influence, brought to bear, co-operatively, with the traditional idea of the Atlantian Ietone, the concept of the primitive harp, and thus brought forth the instrumental child in the crude state known as the "bow form." This was far inferior to the Ietone, from which it had descended, through the then understanding of the mortal mind, or inventor, and unlike the Ietone, was played horizontally, while being borne upon the shoulder of the musician. Crude as it was, owing to the inability, at that period of time, of the mortal mind in its then stage, and the conditions that limited it, to catch the spirit impressions, that were intended to inspire invenion of a more perfect instrument, yet it must be accepted as one of the broken links, in the cycle of instrumental music, severed by the great Atlantian submergence, as fared also the ancient lyre.

As time passed, and the mortal mind became more clearly receptive to spirit influence and impression, inventors were inspired, as is the case in modern times, with ideas of improvement, until we find improved varieties that have had place throughout the ages, ranging from the most crude forms, of primitive representation, to the grand varieties of vertical harps used in the time of Rameses III, such as are portrayed in the frescoes of that period, in the tombs of Thebes. These had from ten to thirteen strings, with a sound-body below, thus approaching the idea of the Atlantian Ietone sound-chest, which was a spirit impression given the inventor in accord with his ability to receive the same. The harp of the ancient Assyrians, with the sound-body uppermost, and the earliest known use of the "sound holes" in the same, was another spirit impression, of the valves that existed on the upper portion of the quosex of the Ietone. The cross-bar to which the strings were fastened and tuned, though reversed from top to bottom, was a spirit impression; especially in the fact of fastening and tuning the strings below, as was the case with those on the Ietone. From further developments and extensions, through spirit aid, impressions and ideas were received, and conceived, which established the varieties known as the Irish "clairseach," the Highland Scotch "clarsach," the Welsh, Cornish and Breton "telyn," "teleiu," "telen," etc.—hence, the Celtic harps.

Furthermore, through the ninth century, by European influence in co-operation with spirit inspiration, improvements were made by sensitives, of that period. Likewise in the seventeenth, by a Tyrolese maker; in the eighteenth, by Hochbrucker, a Bavarian maker, and by two Frenchmen by the name of Cousineau. Ultimately, in the nineteenth century, by the same influences, through the intelligence of Sebastian Erard, the famous modern "Erard harp" was perfected, and stands in evidence of the developments that arise from spirit inspiration, and the influence thus brought to bear upon the mortal intelligence; the co-operation of which has been the means of bringing out all the mechanical devices attributed to the genius of mortal inventors.

Therefore, from descended traditions, of the Atlantian

Ietone, influenced by spirit inspiration and impression, have resulted the gathering up of Ideal Links, by descended mortals. These they have utilized in the development of kindred instruments, equal to the demands of the people throughout the ages with which they were contemporaneous, intervening bstween the Atlantian period and the Modern. Thus have evolved the instruments that rendered accompaniment to primitive songs, prior to the earliest known historical periods, from and through the latter, down to the perfected Harp, which so beautifully characterizes the instrumentation of such orchestral compositions as those of Meyerbeer, Gounod, Berlioz, Liszt, Wagner, etc.

Thus are we, by the Atlantian Ietone, and the Harp of modern times, able to connect up the Cycle of Lyre and Harp Instrumentation.

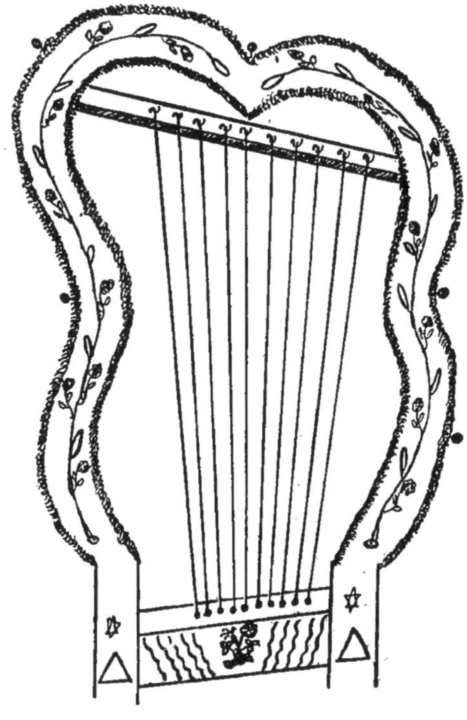

USH I-E'TONE.

The U-rä-thē'ä resembled that class of instruments modernly known as the guitar and mandolin, especially in the manner of its use. The body of the instrument was rectangular in form, and of a thin, light material, termed zeite, a compound of its three materials, uzie, jetney and kizeta. (This compound was sometimes reduced to the consistency of modern gold-leaf, and sometimes even to a liquid form, and then it was used as a wash or plating, and would never change color, or tarnish.) The top of the body was a flat surface, but the bottom was slightly convex. On two of the corners were floral, or other designs, inlaid with uzie, above which were openings similar to those on a modern violin, to give a certain quality to the tones. It possessed eight strings, that extended diagonally across its body. The neck of the instrument was at the opposite diagonal corner, parallel with the strings. To this the strings were fastened, by a set of uzie tiye (golden keys), and were made fast at the other extremity by means of uzie ruiteze (golden hooks). The tra was held on the lap of the kresteon (player) who played in a soft, sweet, melodious, and gliding style, when rendering trao krest (instrumental music), or when accompanying sethack (vocal) compositions. This style now characterizes Hawaiian musicians, in the use of the guitar and mandolin, a style re-embodiment inspired by the influence of Atlantian spirits, or kresteonze, of the long-agone submerged Atlantis, who have never lost or forgotten the beautiful, concordant, soft, gliding and attractive qualities, that characterized the krest of that period, in the great Art Cycle.

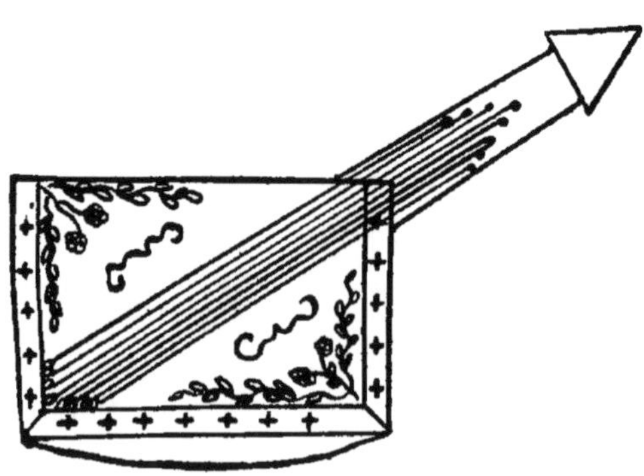

USH U-RA-THE'A.

The Ethereleum resembled the modern piano-forte, to a certain extent, and served the same purposes. It was the favorite tra in many of the Atlantian wēl-chĕ'zē, a-găl-tĕ'zē nud sĭl-tĕr'zē (homes, temples and entertainment or concert halls). When completely constructed, it was not portable, for it was built permanently against the wall. The quosex was composed of a compound in which uzie and jetney were the principal materials. The underneath portion of the quosex was without casing, so constructed as to admit of an easy adjustment of the inner mechanical parts of the action. The frūgē (scale) range was from five to seven sen-tū-rē'zē (octaves), as the occasion required. Those in welcheze varied, according to the financial condition of the purchaser; but those in the agalteze and silterze were usually of seven. The veze were fastened at the upper end to a stationary quosex. This in turn was permanently fastened to the wall, across the upper back center of the open quosex of the tra; and at the bottom to a projecting part of the tra quosex, where now the extended keyboard of the modern piano-forte is located. The veze were of three kinds of metal, and grouped accordingly in color alternations, and were each characterized with the color peculiar to itself, one set being of ē'trēz (copper), one of clē'tiē (silver), and one of ū'ziē (gold); then each possessed the qualities of sound peculiar to itself, facts that made a rich blending of tones, and gave to the tra a fine appearance. The veze were strung in groups, of three each, by alternation of colors; i. e., beginning at the left were three of copper color, then three of the silver, then three of the golden, thus alternating throughout the entire fruge or scale. The mechanism of the tra was such as to produce either very deep, or very high qualities of tone, as the occasion required. The tones, in all their qualities of sound, were very different from those now produced upon the modern piano-forte, and by the use of sympathetic vibration, under control, they were able to give to their music a waving quality not possible to the piano-forte, which passed from a low to a high pitch, and *vice versa,* at the will of the performer, he controlling this by mechanical attachments and devices. That is, by their use, they allowed the beautiful deep vibrations of the lower veze, sympathetically, to vibrate over the fruge; and further taken up by the rear veze, in like manner, caused the tra to sound as if played upon by many hands. From this characteristic quality, in the instrumental music, they conceived the idea of a wavy rendition of their vocal chants, as rendered in their agalteze services. Instead of a manipulation of keys, to set the strings into vibration, as when playing on the piano-forte, the vibration was established by picking the veze of the Ethereleum, direct, which was done by means of loops formed by a continuation of the veze, near the lower extremity. Back of and between the fundamental veze, was another set of veze, similarly arranged. These were smaller than the front ones, and were used for a triple purpose; viz., first, on which to produce intermediate tones; second, to serve as echoing and re-echoing agents, thus acted upon by sympathetic vibrations from the fundamental or front veze, which condition was controlled by mechanical attachments, thus preventing a mixture of sounds, or inharmony of tones. There were pedals located and operated similarly to those of a piano-forte, thus to govern the vibrations, and to produce a very soft tone from either the front or back veze. Loud tones were produced by picking the open vezé, and soft ones obtained by means of the adjustment tiye; and a still softer one by means of the pedals, as above stated. An additional adjusting pedal, connecting with a mechanical device, that was connected with the front veze of the upper half of the tra, was used to control the over-tones. On the front of the tra, at the corresponding location of the keyboard on the piano-forte, was arranged a set of ĕl-tē-mĕt'zē (symbols), which, in their symbolic sense, referred to the absolute pitches of the fruge (scale). These they termed sŏn lĭch'zē (tone pitches), and they would correspond to the arrangement of letter-names as on the keyboard of the piano-forte. (See diagram of the Ethereleum.) Furthermore, it will be observed, that there are eleven characters and that there are but eight sōn or tones, in the fruge; therefore eight of the eleven represent the sōn lĭch-zē', and were symbols for that specific purpose, as the Atlantians neither used letters, syllables, nor number names, to designate the pitches of sound in this sense. Hence, when singing, they never used the relative "pitch names," as "do, re, mi, fa, sol, la, si, do," as do modern singers, but simply gave utterance to one syllable, for the different sounds, or pitches, as moderns sometimes use the one syllable "ah" continuously. The remaining three of the eleven eltemetze were placed at the beginning and ending of each senturi, or in alternation with each senturi of the fruge, throughout the entire compass of the tra. Thus were located the mechanical adjustments, that admitted sympathetic vibrations to take place as above stated, from one octave to another, over the front veze, while the pedals governed the echo attachment that controlled that characteristic of the rear veze.

The entire complication of the mechanical part of the Ethereleum, as well as that of the other Atlantian träze, is far beyond our present ability to reproduce in diagram form, as we have not time to delineate, or narrate them in detail, so as to give a complete expression to them as they have been shown to us, clairvoyantly, to have been. In reality, they were so much more perfect and complete—so much more scientifically and artistically constructed and wrought out, that we, especially with our present limited capacity for drawing, such as would insure a perfect representation of the mechanical parts, can do so only in part. But enough has been given, herewith, to afford the reader some idea of the instruments then in use.

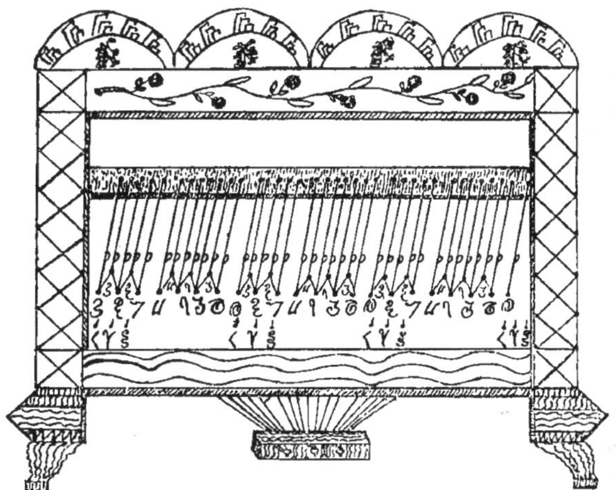

USH E-THE'RE-LE-UM.

The Atlantians had their traze smaller than those already described, that were principally adapted to the rendition of melodic krest, and time-beating purposes, especially such as were utilized in their fē-lĭn'zō (military) and qū-ī-ĭs'trăl (orchestral) organizations. For as before stated, everything pertaining to the art of krest was being wrought out and utilized, at the time of the overthrow of the Lontidri.

Among the felinzo and quiistral traze, we will name some of the most important ones, leaving many of the smaller ones out, for want of space.

The El-ē'zē was a sĕt tī-yē'o (three-keyed) wind tra, that would somewhat answer the description of the modern bugle-horn.

The Rūt'zē was another wind tra, that would compare favorably with the modern flute or piccolo, it being, in size, intermediate between the two, but in quality of tone more like the flute.

The I-zē'tŏn finds similar representation in the modern drum, though in shape and size it differed, being square-form, and only about one cŏi'tĕx in length.

The E-lū'tēs has its partial representation in modern violins, and like them, varied in size, as is the case with the viola, violoncello, and double bass. It also differed in having a broader body, which came down to a point that formed the extension, and served the purpose of the neck of the modern violin. It was held, by the player, in various ways, similar to the modern style, though more often laid upon a table or stand, for convenience in manipulating the strings, etc. There were two sound holes in the top, but characters were inlaid over the neck of the tra, that when fingered by the player, indicated the pitch points, as the frets, on the modern guitar.

The Kĕl'dä was a tra that was quite similar to the modern music boxes. It had three metal rollers, the central one of which was longer, and the outer two of the same length, which were the mechanical part of the tra, that operated the tone-producing parts. These were set into action by means of a crank, turned by the operator.

USH LE'ZO KREST K-EN'THRUP, OR THE GREAT MUSIC FACTORY.

TELTZIE XXXIII.

In regard to the manufacture of Krĕst'ō (musical) traze, and the composition of sē'thăck and tră'ō krĕst (vocal and instrumental music), Anstacia informs us that in the aistie of Almorthia, in Teltzie Zret, was the principal location of the enterprise.

The main K-ĕn'thrŭp was an enormous structure that extend-fronting along the main xŏn'tĭs (street) for three ĭx-rōl' tä (squares). It was divided into compartments by halls, that extended from the rear to the front of the structure, and these were subdivided into smaller Teltzie, or sections, by other halls that extended at right angles with the former. To each compartment was assigned the manufacture of some particular tra; and to the sections, from rear to front throughout the compartment, the various grades of its construction—from the rear section, where began the work on the rough material, to the front section where all the traze of that variety were completed. Centrally, in front of the great structure, was located the salesroom on either side of which was a large room to which all completed traze were brought for final expert inspection. Six or seven individuals, well versed in the science of mechanism, were employed in each of the two rooms, to render that service. These were not allowed to leave their offices, at night, until the day's consignmnt to them had been thoroughly tested, and their judgment passed upon the workmanship. Back of the salesroom were two large rooms, occupied by sē'thăck tră'ō and prĕt'lĕx sĕn-dē'zēr (vocal, instrumental and poetry composers), who composed all the vocal and instrumental music, and the words that accompanied the vocal score, used throughout the entire Lontidri. No one, except those proficiently qualified, could be employed in these capacities. The Pretze and sendezer of the sethack krest, occupied the same room, that they might the more readily confer, one artist with another, when adapting the words to the music. However, there were alcoves in each room, to which any of the sendezer could retire, for greater concentration of thought, and to receive spirit-inspiration, for they composed under spirit guidance, a fact they were fully conscious of. The surroundings, therefore, in those rooms, in every detail, were such as would bring the brightest and most perfect conditions possible, to aid the sendezer in their work, for they sought superiority in all matters pertaining to the Art of Music. Towers, as from a great Cathedral, rose above the central portion of the great Kenthrup. A great dome-shaped roof covered the entire structure, composed of an aggregate of lesser domes, that rose individually from the various sections and compartments of the entire structure, thus constructed to be self-protective from the force of the wind and storm. The entire kenthrup received its interior light through the dome of domes, that were composed of transparent materials, while windows, in the outer walls, gave the additional side lights.

In recognition of the morning sunlight, when the day's work was about to begin, fifteen minutes were devoted to the rendition of grand krest. This took place in the salesroom, when every kind of instrument manufactured in the kenthrup was used to accompany the voices in a service of praise and thanksgiving, unto the great Solar Light, a principle as sacred, to the Atlantian people, as is God to modern peoples.

Passing from the principal epochs, and periods of events, in the pre-historic Atlantian portion of the sī-ĭ'kĕl ze krĕst (cycle of music), with Trexler and Ereges as the last greatest kresteonze, to the subsequent pre-historic period, through which the remnant peoples descended, Anstacia informs us that the knowledge of the Art of Music was retained by Atlantian spirit intelligences, which enabled them, as such, by mental influence, to establish characteristics and ideas for development, within the minds of subsequent descended mortals, in accord with the ideas and conceptions of the spirit-influence, or mind. Therefore, the re-embodiment influence of the "art music" began its development in the minds of the remnant Atlantian descendants, in the region of Siloton (Egypt), in the early pre-historic period, when E-dăm-ĕt'kär'ă-mär* (instrumental music) and Zŭx kär'ă mär* (vocal music) were established in Egypt; which facts entitle that section to be considered the "mother country of pre-historic music, and the welding link in music" between Atlantis and ancient and modern countries, though the influence was soon after felt in the many regions to which the descended peoples were migrating.

*Pre-historic Egyptian term.

During the time, therefore, that intervened between the submergence of Atlantis and the historic time of Egypt, karamar, both vocal and instrumental, had developed to a considerable degree, under the influence of the then known mortal karlamar or instrumentalists, and zexes or vocalists. Among these, just prior to the historic period, the most celebrated of the former class were, a male by the name of Kĕl'zĭc, and a female by the name of A-zē-ī'dä; and of the latter at that period, a male by the name of Nĭn'zŏt, and a female by the name of Sĕl'zy.

The only true law of so-called re-incarnation, in the code of laws that govern the present existence of mortal or spirit, of itself profound, logical, and operative throughout the spheres of eternal existence, for the sole purpose of unfoldment and development of all intelligence, is a silent, and in the majority of cases, unrecognized "teacher," or "influence" of spirit minds upon mortals, whereby the latter conceive and bring forth new-born ideas, by manifest new characteristics, which can be recognized as having belonged to another individual or a predecessor. Nor is this law operative from the spirit side of life wholly, reverting backwards (for the mind of an incarnate spirit or intelligence can reach out to disembodied ones), thus causing the latter to awaken unto the same thought, which establishes within their minds new-born ideas, inducing their further unfoldment and development, which is a reconceived and re-embodied characteristic quality, and not an individuality.

In the same ratio, it is an operative law throughout the realms of spirit, and the regions of worlds; for mental influence is not limited to one of these. It operates as an agent beyond, to aid in the higher spheres; and reverts back, through the spheres of spirit, to the mortal plane, thus to influence higher development.

The same law is exercised by one incarnate intelligence upon another, likewise incarnate, whereby one mortal is assisted in development by another. It is also operative between disembodied intelligences, whereby one spirit is assisted in his or her development or unfoldment, by another. Therefore, a so-called "re-incarnation," "re-insoulment," or "re-embodied characteristic" quality, of this kind, does not reverse the natural law of birth, either in the mortal or spirit existence. Hence, it is naturally logical, for natural law never reverses operatively, to fit some specific case, or fancy of creedists or ismists.

Therefore, there is no reincarnation of the individual spirit and soul proper, but simply a reconceived, redeveloped characteristic quality, as a result of the influence of one mind over another, which qualifies the influenced individual, with similar mental conditions to those of the influencing intelligence. This in turn further influences the mortal soul and body, or the spirit-soul, in development, as well; hence mistaken as a reincarnation of the influencing individual.

The Chamboret′ was a pre-historic edam of Egypt, an impressional, or conceived idea, received by the inventor, though imperfectly, from a spirit influence who sought to impress the former with an idea of the Atlantian Ethereleum, but the inventor's idea being thus imperfectly received, diverged, by a conception of the idea which resulted in the production of the pre-historic Egyptian chamboret, which through the remainder of the pre-historic and historic periods of time, sustained several changes, until it became linked into the modern instrument known as the Mär-ĭm′bä of general use in South America, and also Central Amer, ica, an instrument such as is used at the present time by the famous Marimba Band, now touring the United States.

The Chamboret, of pre-historic time, was constructed in the form of a table, from wooden material, and was about two feet by three feet in size; the lower octave of bass strings were of gut or fibre. The remaining octaves were each of a different kind of material, set into vibration by means of percussion hammers in the hands of the player.

The influence of the chamboret passed westward, from Egypt and Africa, across the islands of that region, to the West Indies, thence into South America where it developed into the idea of the above named Marimba, and thence into Central America.

The influence of the chamboret, likewise, passed eastward from Egypt, into Persia and India, where it was lost in the changes that took place in those regions, and thus developed into various stringed and percussion instruments of that region.

From the chamboret, also, descended the idea of the dulcimer, and other instruments such as the zither, etc.

The Dē-nŏn′drĭck was a pre-historic Egyptian e-dam, which similarly to the chamboret, was an impression (though imperfectly received by the inventor) intended by the spirit influence to have given the idea of the Atlantian Ietone; but, instead, the idea of the Denondrick was conceived, and brought out; it was the chief influence from which, through the subsequent changes and developments, arose the lyre and the harp of the Egyptians.

The denondrick was constructed with a body similar to that of the frame of the modern tambourine, or an open, hoop-shaped frame, across which were stretched seven strings, made fast at both ends by means of upper and lower horizontal pieces of wood.

It was held on the lap of the karlamar, supported by his left arm, and manipulated by the fingers of the right hand.

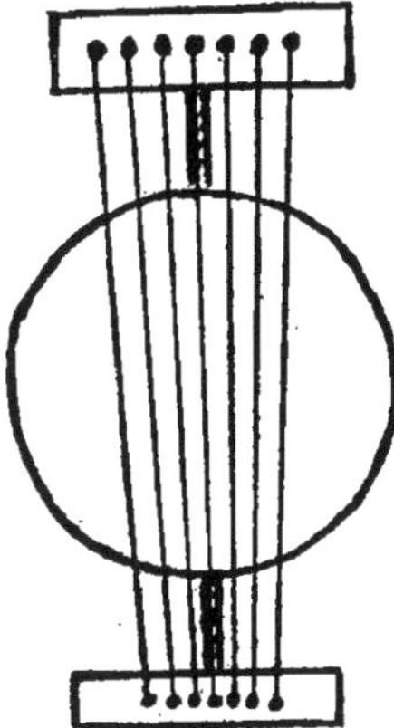

THE DE-NON'DRICK.

Passing along the great Cycle of Music, into the region of Arabia, we find the same re-embodied principles as in Egypt, manifesting through developing ideas conceived by the pre-historic Arabians, who, to a certain extent, invented forms of nē-ĕs'ī-tē (music), though they never became so far advanced in the art as their ancestors, the Atlantians, or even their less remote brethren, the Egyptians.

The jĕs-ō-lĕts (instruments) of the Arabians were crude in comparison with those of the Atlantians, hence less expensive.

The Dĕs'sē was their largest jesolet, and in some respects it resembled the Atlantian Etherelеum, but was much more crude. It was constructed as if combined with a table; the cē-ō-lets' (chords of strings) that produced the tones were made from the fibres of a tree, then known as the Cī-lē'tē, that grew in the northern portion of the country. The quality of tone produced on the ceolet was greatly influenced by the age of the tree from which the fibre was taken, a fact that was necessarily considered in its utility throughout the scale.

The ceolets were set into vibration by a sĕl-frē-ī'dē (musician), who picked them with his fingers, as was the case with the Atlantian Etherelеum, only from the under side of the instrument.

Arabian jesoletes neesite was never brought to perfection, from the fact that among that people there were so many sweet and talented krĕs-nĕt′ĕs (vocalists or singers), whose krīs′es (voices) have never been excelled, on the earth plane, so far as quality and compass are concerned, therefor vocal music became the favorite amusement among the masses, and the cultivation of the kris (voice) was more zealously practised than was the construction and improvement of musical instruments.

The two most noted krisnetes were a male by the name of Cĕn-ē-ī′tō, and a female by the name of E-kī′tō. They were located at El-lī-trē′ty, the capital city of pre-historic Arabia.

These celebrated krisnetes were also ăl-kē-trî′ĕs (teachers of vocal music), and each was also a noted sĕl-frē-ī′dō (musician), who played on the various Arabian jesolets, especially the desse. Their school of neesite was located at Ellitrety.

Subsequently, within the minds of the people who had descended from the Atlantian remnants in the Egyptian and Arabian regions, or migrated farther into the orient (see our lines of migrations), musical ideas were reborn under, the same re-embodied condition of spirit-influence. And in the regions of Greece it found its most profound establishment, or rooting and development.

Thus came, from the crude art of "time keeping" by stamping the feet, and clapping the hands, as practised among the eastern pre-historic descendants from Atlantis, something that opened the door, or the descended minds, for the conception of rythmic masurement, which they manifested by the adoption of instruments of percussion, as drums, cymbals, bells, and triangles, that have led up to the present modern perfection, by a development of that pre-historic re-incarnation of mental influence. This in time, further opened the idealistic chamber, to receive impressions of "wind instruments," when spirit influence, aided by nature's sighing breezes as they passed over beds of reeds, or the stronger winds as they whistled through the forest branches, conveyed to the mortal intelligence, the re-conceived idea or thought of producing tones by instruments of breath. An idea that has, in its development with the new co-operative mind, led up to the flute, the flageolet, the hautboy, oboe, bassoon, clarionet, horns, trumpet, and greatest of all, the Organ, that caused the walls of our finest temples and halls to vibrate in praise and honor of the spirit forces or intelligences, who have wafted back to the children of earth, ideas of musical knowledge, that the mind and spirit of mortal man might be benefited.

Through the qualities of tension and vibration, though in crude forms, under the inspiration of spirit-influence, the mortal mind was led to conceive the idea of tone production from tensioned fibres and sinews, which, in its further development, has led up to the lyre, the lute, the harp, the dulcimer, the clavichord, the harpsichord, and greatest of all, the grand Piano-forte. The marvelous qualities of this instrument sound forth, giving expressions of praise and thanksgiving, to the spirit-influences which, along this line, have labored by means of natural law, to impress, inspire, and influence, the minds of embodied spirits, or mortals, that we of the twentieth century might feast our incarnate spirits within the melodic and harmonic tones, that through the law of vibration, issue from the now grandest of all stringed instruments, the piano-forte, as did our far removed ancestors, the Atlantians, fill their musical selves through their Ethereleums.

As was the case in Egypt, regarding conceived ideas of music and the establishment of musical instruments, and of musicians and vocalists in the pre-historic periods, so it was in the regions of Greece. As the influence passed eastward from Egypt, by migrating peoples, ultimately, in subsequent pre-historic time, the art of flō-rē′ci (music) was further developed and continued among the Grecian people, among whom there developed many flō-rē′ci-ăns (musicians) and shŭlt′ē-zē (vocalists) and flō-rē′ci-ĕs kū-zē-ĕl′tics (musical instruments).

The most noted among the pre-historic Grecian shulteze were a male by the name of Nĕn′sĭc, and a female by the name of Nĕl′-sĭc. The most noted of the florecians were a male by the name of Trĕl′zē-vŏx, and a female by the name of Cē-trē′cy. The principal florecies kuzeeltics were the lĕz′rō and the cĕl-cē-rĕt′.

With the influence above mentioned, that passed eastward into Greece by migrating peoples from Egypt, a knowledge of the Egyptian Denondrick was carried into Greece, where in subsequent pre-historic time, from it, the idea was conceived which resulted in the invention and development of the lezro and the celceret, which by further spirit-influence, were changed and developed into the historical "chelys," "cithras," or "phorminx," or the class of instruments modernly known as the lyres.

The story or legend, giving credit to Hermes as being the inventor of the lyre, and as having gotten his idea from having stretched the sinews of a tortoise across its shell, is not wholly a fact, for his principal idea was taken from the denondrick; but the inventor changed the form of the frame, or circular body, to that of one in resemblance of the tortoise shell, which latter became the support of the strings, instead of being attached to a base, as was the case with the denondrick, and was a much inferior instrument to the lezro or the celceret, that had preceded it, and also, idealistically, descended from a knowledge of the Egyptian denondrick.

The Lezro was a pre-historic Grecian kuzeeltic (instrument) that preceded the celceret, and the ultimate historic chelys, cithras or phorminx, of Greece, and was the material influence that led up to all the Grecian lyres.

In form, the lezro was characterized by a triangular body that supported the strings at their upper end; and it stood erect, upon a box-like base or sound chest, to which latter the lower ends of the strings were made fast. There were eight strings, the lengths of which, relative to their difference in pitch, were governed by the lower sides of the triangular form of the frame over which they were strung, co-operative with the degree of tension and quality of the material, of the different strings.

This arrangement of the strings brought the longer, or lower-toned ones, in the center of the scale, and were therefore manipulated with the thumb of the left hand and the fourth finger of the right. The remainder of the fingers were utilized when manipulating the higher-toned strings.

The kuzeeltic, when played upon, stood in an upright position, similar to that of the harp, though not tipped, and the florecian (musician), likewise, stood at the side of the kuzeeltic.

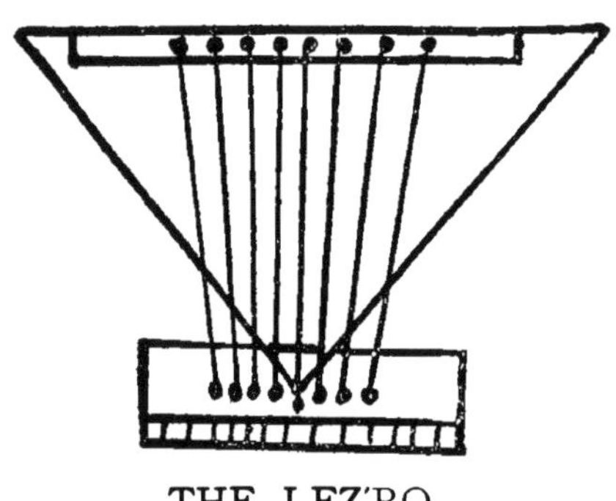

THE LEZ'RO.

The Cĕl-cē-rĕt was also a pre-historic Grecian kuzeeltic that had its origin through changed ideas of the lezro, under spirit-influence. This instrument, in its construction, or establishment, became the link by which we are able to connect the Atlantian ietone through the ideas of the Egyptian denondrick, and the Grecian lezro, to the historical variety of lyres.

In form, the celceret had a body or sound-chest very much the shape of a miniature gondola, the terminal of which was ornamented with various designs, as triangles, globes, scrolls or leaves, the latter being the most common (see diagram). There were nine strings, the length of which, relative to pitch, was governed by an arched frame that extended in that form from one terminal of the sound-chest to the other, and to this they were attached at their upper ends, the lower ends being made fast to the body or sound-chest; therefore, by length, tension, and the material quality of the open strings, they vibrated in different pitches of tone.

The kuzeeltic, when being played, was held diagonally across the lap of the florecian, its right end resting against his or her right side, and as the lower-toned strings were in the center of the kuzeeltic, they were manipulated by the florecian in the same manner as when playing upon the lezro.

THE CEL-CE-RET'.

Passing into the Christian era, through the influence of the Egyptian and Grecian musical celebrities, we find the influence re-embodied in subsequent minds, who conceived the ideas that developed into a chant, in its crude state, which had a great influence upon the minds of the church folowers, throughout the first three hundred years, A. D., though checked by the persecutions of Nero and Diocletian.

In the latter part of the fifth century, A. D., St. Ambrose re-embodied the idea of the Ambrosian chant, that influenced the church followers, through two hundred years.

During the next seven hundred years, we find St. Gregory the Great, and his works, as the principal influence, who had further re-embodied his ideas of church music, in co-operation with that of St. Ambrose. This gave rise to the epoch of the Gregorian or Roman chant, which aided the spirit-influences to open the minds of many mortals, who also received impressions that led up to a greater development and utility of the Art of Music, when we find the people of England influenced by such celebrities as St. Augustine and Pope Vitalian, Italian singers; King John of Fornset, who established the first English school, and King Alfred, who founded a professorship of music at Oxford. The Organ was constructed; musical theories were written, and five eminent musicians headed the developing influence.

France was also influenced by the Kings; coronation masses were composed; part-singing, notation, *minim* and *semiminim,* old French school, were introduced, and nine eminent musicians, and many troubadours headed the developing influence.

Germany and the Netherlands were influenced by the cultivation of sacred or passion Plays, and tournaments of Song, but no musicians of especial note were then in the musical ascendency.

Italy was influenced by the requiems of Celanos; the organ was improved by Pope Sylvester, and Guido stood as the principal musician, who through conceived, or re-embodied ideas, was led to invent the modern Scale.

Through the fifteenth and sixteenth centuries, entering the epoch of the Polyphonic schools, we find the influence greatly developed.

In England, the second, third, fourth, fifth and sixth English Schools of Music were founded, by John Dunstable, J. Hamboys, Robt. Fayrfax, J. Redford and Christopher Tye, respectively, and also their official boards. Further influence came through the Kings of these periods, and thirty or more noted musicians. O. Gibbons was the brightest light of the latter part of the sixteenth century.

France was under the influence of the Kings; the later French School of Music was established; the lute and guitar assumed their modern forms; books of masses were written, and the *Odes* of Horace were published; sixteen or more eminent musicians headed the developing influence that marked the condition of musical events.

Germany and the Netherlands influenced through their Gallio-Belgian; first, second, third and fourth Flemish schools, as founded by Dufay, Okenheim, Josquindes, Gombert, and Lassus; also the first, second and third Dutch schools, as founded by Arkadelt, Hollander, and Suelink, respectively; the German Polyphonic schools, schools of Munich and Nuremburg, founded by A. de Fulda, O. de Lassus and Hasler, respectively. These faculties, with thirty or more eminent musicians, wielded a great influence over the German and Dutch people.

Italy was influenced by her schools of music, as the Venetian, Lombardy, Early Florentine, Early Roman, Late Roman, Early Neopolitan and Late Neopolitan, founded by Willaert, Gafwrius, Costeccia, Festa, Palestrine, Tinctor, and Francesco, respectively. These, with twenty or more eminent musicians, represented the developing influenc in Italy in the musical events of that period.

Passing on into the seventeenth century of the Great Musical Cycle, we find the influence of the Monadic school of Florence, and the epoch of the Polyodic schools, especially effecting invention; the rise and development of the Opera, under the influence of Peri, Caccini, and Galieli, in the first period; Monteverde, who invented the *dominant seventh,* and *pizzicato* passages for stringed instruments, and influenced, through operatic renditions in the second period; establishment of the Opera House, at Venice, by Farrari and Manelli; rythmic melody, in the Opera, as improved by Cavelli in the third period. In the first period, Cavaliere influenced by his production, at Rome, of the first *Oratorio,* in representation of the Soul and of the Body. In the second period, the influence was strengthened by the *Allegorical Drama,* as established by Kayosterger. In the third period, Carissimi, the most conspicuous celebrity of the period, influenced through an elevation of Sacred *Dramas,* or *Cantatas,* and*Oratorios*. In the first period, the influence of the clavichord, upon the rise of instrumental utilities, was established, and the harpsichord aided in the accompaniment of the first operas. It served Handel and Bach, and their contemporaries, in support of the *recitative Secco*, and was the chief material influence to the conception of the impressional idea of the pianoforte.

In England, during this epoch, the influence was further felt by the establishment of songs for the lute; *motteats* and grave "chamber music" and the *madrigal,* during the reign of Queen Elizabeth; art publications, the establishments of Organists, books of Psalms, Church music, rounds, catches and canons, fantasias, compositions of music for the coronation of King Charles II, and his March; the Cathedral service, origin of the "Verse Anthem," and the Anglecian chant; the Divine service, origin of the English opera by Purcell, etc. These influences, with ten noted English musicians, with Purcell as the greatest light, that stood at the helm of progress, inspired by spirit-impression, wielded a great power in the restoration of the Musical Cycle during that period.

In France, during this epoch, the influence was felt through the requiem, masses and preludes, the writing of treatises on acoustic harmony, and a history of music; orchestral accompaniment of the Mass, Court ballets, the founding of the French school of Music of the seventeenth century, by Jean Lulli; origin of the Grand Opera and the French *Overture*. These, with nine or more eminent musicians, with Lulli as the leading celebrity, under spirit-influence, elevated the music of France.

In Germany, some eighteen eminent musicians, with H. Schutz at the head, struggled for the rise of music, but the ThirtyYears' War greatly retarded the progress. Yet, operas, of which the "Dafne" of Rinuccini, was the first, were set to music, by Schutz, and "Passion compositions" were published; Singspiels and "Evening music" wielded the best influence under the conditions of the country.

Italy, as stated above, was influenced by the Opera, as invented by Peri, who also invented thorough bass; by other operas by various composers; the invention of the *oratorio* by Cavaliere; *pizzicato* passages, invented by Monteverde; the improvement of the orchestra, by Legrenzi. The terrible plague in 1630, that devastated the principal cities of Italy, greatly retarded the progress of music in that region, but occasioned the composition of the Mass for six choirs, to be sung for the cessation of the plague, at Rome. In addition to the many operas composed, appeared sacred and secular *sonatas;* opera houses were opened to the public; dramatic music, and sacred dramas were written. These conditions, co-operative with about twenty-two eminent musicians, with A. Scarlatti at their head, inspired by spirit-influence, gave material aid to the rise of the Art of Music through the first three periods of this epoch.

Entering the latter part of the seventeenth century, or the fourth period, and beginning of the Classical epoch, we find Scarlatti influencing through his Simple recitative, Accompanied recitative and the regular *Aria,* and further development of the *Overture,* while many of his contemporaries influenced through the rise of meagre preluded, into well-formed overtures. Scarlatti reached the zenith of his genius in oratorio and recitative compositions.

In this period, Jean P· Rameau was added to the principal celebrities of France. Eleven celebrities were added to Italy, with Duranke and Marcello at the head.

In Germany, during this period, two great lights appeared in the Cycle of Music: G. F. Handel and J. S. Bach. These, the first greatest celebrities in the epoch, we have chosen as fitting subjects to join hands with Trexler and Ereges, the last two greatest of the Atlantian kresteonze of that classical, pre-historic epoch, as periodical links in the great Cycle of Music, by which we are able to continue the influence of the art of krest or music, that was established in Atlantis, and re-established by the remnant descendants, whose genius, under spirit-influence, and further development through the first seventeen centuries of the Christian era, has welded the links in the broken cycle and restored the greatness of the Atlantian Art, though under modified conditions and utilities.

John Sebastian Bach, the founder and father of German

music, we have chosen as one of the principal links in the great cycle of Tone Poets and Musicians. Bach, in his earlier life work, influenced chiefly through his wonderful pianoforte and organ playing. Later, as a composer of Sacred oratorios, cantatas, and choral works, in which he displayed such emotional, passionate, pious fervor of religious devotion. Further, he influenced in his co-operation with the ideas of Luther, who planted the earliest germs of the oratorio, in which Divine passion was recited, especially in North Germany, thus continuing to influence the German people through that style of Church music, as is evidenced by his having set portions of St. Matthew's gospel to music, in oratorio form. This, while in keeping with the incidental narration, he characterized with reflective passages, under especial "harmonic" treatment, and made the whole more effective by his grand display of airs, duets, and choruses, all written for the occasion. Furthermore, he was an influence by his setting Passion music to the words of St. John and St. Matthew. His cantatas for church use, peculiarly adapted to every Sunday's requirements, in the Lutheran service; his secular cantatas, masses, pieces for the Roman church, the organ part never having been equalled in intrinsic qualities, or as material for masterly display; concertos and suites for the orchestra, a vast number of pieces for the harpsichord or clavecin, preludes, fugues, etc., are among the influences, like those of Handel, that will never cease, by impression, to influence minds throughout coming generations; hence, re-incarnation of the musical ideas of these great men.

George Frederic Handel, one of the greatest of all musicians, we have chosen as one of the principal links in the great cycle of Tone Poets and Musicians. Handel influenced chiefly through the artistic development of England, thus affecting both private and political life; and the more in regard to natural issues, as he co-operated with the sentiment of English poetry, and natural and religious life. Through his genius as an organist, orchestral master, composer of operas, "water music," tedeums, anthems, etc., he was an influence; but his greatest influence was felt through his oratorios and secular works, such as dealt with national epics, as evidenced by his didactic oratorios, *"Judas Maccabaeus"* and *"Israel in Egypt," "L'Allegro il Penseroso," "Alexander's Feast,"* and those dealing with deep religious feeling as his *"Messiah,"* etc.

"The music of Handel, for its simple, massive, perspicuous grandeur, may be likened to a Grecian temple; and that of Bach to a Gothic edifice, for its infinite involution of lines and intricacy of detail. The great complexity of the one makes it more difficult of comprehension, and more slow in impression, while the sublime majesty of the other displays itself at a single glance and is printed at once on the mental vision. Handel wrote for effect, and he produces it with certitude upon thousands. Bach wrote as a pleasurable exercise for mastery, and gives kindred pleasure to those who study his work in the spirit that incited him to produce it."

In this "epoch of his genius," in the fifth period of Operatic events, Handel produced many of his operas in England, and greatly elevated Dramatic music. Logroscino invented the *Concerted finale,* and others improved Italian music, while Rameau elevated the Opera from the traditions of Lulli.

In the sixth period, Gluck completely reformed Music-drama in France and Germany, and George Benda invented Melodrama.

Wolfgang Mozart, one of the greatest musicians the world has ever produced, whom we have chosen as one of the principal links in the great Cycle of Tone Poets and Musicians, influenced all Europe from his childhood to matured age. His great talent and genius, under profound development, brought him into notoriety with kings and queens, emperors, popes, and celebrities of high rank. It established them as his patrons and admirers, while the whole music-loving world bowed at the shrine of his accomplishments, and sought his "inspirational" influence, which was greatly felt through his operas, concertos, masses, symphonies, sonatas, and in other important works, both vocal and instrumental. Through all of these he manifested a fertility of invention, quality of natural dramatic instinct, graceful melody, force of expression and shapely, beautiful and well-constructed composition; pure and refined taste, affectionate quality, constant development of noble ideas, technical perfection, true genius, the soul's expression, mental elaboration, etc., as evidenced by his various works.

In the seventh period Mozart reached his zenith, as a composer of operas; Gretry and Mehul excelled in French opera; Cherubini and Cimarosa in the Italian.

In the fifth period of oratorio production, Handel, Bach and Graun embodied the oratorio with its most perfect ideas.

In the sixth period, Haydn, Jomelli and Paosiello were the ones who kept alive the ideas of their predecessors.

During this epoch, the pianoforte and organ were greatly improved. J. S. Bach, Handel and D. Scarlatti together, but particularly Bach, perfected the style in instrumental polyphonic music. His *Fugues* were the most perfect models in existence;

monophonic music, in the form of dance tunes, reached highest significance in the *suite*, and was a precursor to the *sonata*. Emanuel Bach established the *sonata* form, and Haydn re-characterized it, by improvements; Mozart glorified Haydn's achievement by perfecting, to a logical limit, its symmetry and proportion, its elegance of detail and wealth of melodic beauty.

Ludwig von Beethoven, the Shakespeare of Tone-Poetry, who represents the climax of musical history, and whom we have chosen as one of the principal links in the great Cycle of Tone Poets and Musicians, influenced through embodied ideas, and character qualities made manifest, such as artistic ideality, inspiration of truth and reality, personal emotion, depth of feeling, force of genius, artistic expansion, depth of pathos, dramatic force, love and emotion, independent thought, poetic ideas, etc. as evidenced by his great works, as by trios, sonatas, concertos, symphonies, masses, overtures, quartets, quintets, etc.

In the Classical-Romantic period Beethoven gave to music the romantic element, with little change of the sonata form, as established by Haydn and Mozart, and made it a medium of emotional expression, placing that principal in the ascendency of form.

In this epoch, Violin music and Orchestral music, alike, under the influence of Corelli, Scarlatti, Bach, Handel, and their contemporaries, were greatly improved during the first half of the century; Gluck, Haydn, Mozart and Beethoven made the orchestra a powerful feature in the portrayal of dramatic character and situation; Haydn created the Symphony and String quartet, and, in co-operation with Mozart, founded the modern orchestra; Beethoven developed the classic forms of Haydn and Mozart to the logical limit, and stands pre-eminent as a composer of Orchestral symphonies.

In Germany, during the eighteenth century, under the influence of Emperors Joseph I, Charles VI, Charles VII, Joseph II, and Leopold II, and their contemporaneous celebrated musical subjects, great influence was felt. Over one hundred lights rose to correspondingly celebrated heights, on the Musical cycle, the two greatest being Mozart and Beethoven, whom we have chosen, in co-operation with Gluck, J. A. Hiller, Haydn, Vogler, Dussek, T. A. Hiller, Cramer, Hummel, Spohr, von Weber, Meyerbeer, Hauptman, Moscheles, and Schubert, to represent the greatness of the latter part of the cycle, and to join hands with Rundzey and Extody, the first greatest noted Kresteonze of Atlantis, thus to connect up the pre-historic and historic events of this Cycle.

In Italy, during the eighteenth century, under the influence of Popes Innocent XIII, Clement XII, Benedict XIV, Clement XIII, and Pius VI, and the eminent Italian musicians of that epoch of the Classical school, of which there were seventy or more, Martini, Piccini, Simarosa, Clementi, Cherubini, Spontini, Rossini, Donizetti, and Scarlatti being the most noted among them, great advancement was made in that region, especially through the influence of operas.

In England, during the eighteenth century, music, under the influence of Queen Anne and Kings George I, II, and III, and Handel and his great works, his oratorios, water music, and coronation anthems, his historic, cathedral music, glees, anthems, harpsichord and dramatic music, and other publications, in co-operation with some thirty other eminent musicians, headed by J. Field, in the latter part of the century, greatly elevated that portion of the Musical cycle.

In France, during the eighteenth century, musicians, under the influence of the Kings, Louis XV and XVI, the court players, the suite, operas comique, treaties on Harmony, and other publications, by Rameau; Mozart's appearance in the country; Gluck's greater compositions; and various others, co-operative with some fifty eminent musicians, among whom the most noted were Gretry, Mehul, Baillott, Rode, Boieldieu, Auber, Herold and Halevy; who likewise under spirit-influence, elevated that part of the Musical cycle, and left their characteristics reincarnate, as it were, in their works, to influence modern minds.

During the latter part of the eighteenth century, the greater lights, in theMusical cycle, began to pass from the material side of life, to the spiritual, and we find J. S. Bach, Handel, Gluck, and Mozart, and a vast number of their contemporaries, going from the earth, having left only the influence of great genius, embodied in their works, which is still a commanding influence, upon modern minds, and such as could be felt only through characteristics as marvelous as theirs, from both the mortal and spirit.

Passing into the nineteenth century, the epoch of the Romantic schools, composers embodied their moods, peculiarities and experiences; intense feeling was expressed in all departments of technique, in opposition to classic ideals of good proportion and universal validity of type, such as had been embodied in the works of the masters, in the preceding century.

With the eighth period, therefore, begins the influence of Grand Opera proper, expressive of heroism and glory, such as manifested through Spontini's *"Vestale,"* Auber's *"Masieniella,"*

Rossini's *"Tell,"* Meyerbeer's *"Huguenots,"* Weber's *"Der Freishutz,"* and *"Oberon,"* which prepared the way for Weber, in the ninth period. He took up the embodied ideas of his predecessors, as evidenced by his *"Rienzi,"* and embodied his own idealistics in such works as the *"Flying Dutchman," "Tannhauser;"* expressed his nature through German folk-lore, myths, etc., and still further, through his novelty of harmony, orchestration, and stage effects, thus portraying his wonderful conceptions, as attained through spirit-influence of preceding celebrities.

In the seventh period of development in the Oratorio production, we find Haydn's embodied ideas in *"The Creation,"* and *"The Seasons;"* Beethoven's in *"Mount of Olives"* and *"Messa Solemis."* Through this embodiment, they influenced the minds of that and succeeding periods, with degrees of profound feeling, unprecedented since the embodied ideas of Bach. Even the orchestral rendition confirms the profundity in tone language, such as can only be read, understandingly, by the emotional powers of the listener.

In the eighth period, we find Mendelssohn embodying his ideas of Dramatic orchestral characterization beyond that of Haydn and Beethoven, as evidenced by his *"St. Paul"* and *"Elija;"* the same was true of Berlioz, only more extensively, as evidenced by his *"Damnation of Faust"* and *"Infancy of Christ."*

During this epoch, wonderful improvements attended the development of both the organ and the pianoforte.

Through the stronger emotion, embodied in Beethoven's later works, and the improvements made in the pianoforte, the door opened for the modern Romantic school, when brilliant compositions, and piano playing, had alike a reproductive influence upon the musical minds of that period, and those of the present as well, as evidenced by the embodied ideas, in the composition and rendition of works by such celebrities as Mendelssohn, Schuman, Tausig, Rubenstein, etc.

During this epoch, influence was felt, and embodied, through the genius displayed in the violin and orchestral compositions, of such celebrities as Weber, Mendelssohn and Berlioz, which caused a rise from such novelties as the fairy, spectre or demon styles in music, that developed, and influenced through the descriptive power of the opera and symphonic poems, in England, during the first half of the century.

The general development of the musical cycle, of this century, was under the influence of the Kings, George IV and William IV, and Queen Victoria, together with some forty eminent musicians. Among the latter the most noted were Balfe and Novello, Bennett and Sullivan.

During this period eighteen or more eminent English musicians, the greatest among them Field, passed into the spirit realm of the Cycle.

During the second half of the century England, and cognate nations, were influenced by these masters and their works, co-operative with schools, colleges, etc.

Some twenty-five of the eminent musicians of England passed into the spirit realm of the Cycle, among whom the most noted were Balfe and Bennett, during the latter half of the nineteenth century.

In Germany, and among cognate nations, during the first half of the century, we find people under the influence of Emperor William IV; schools, operas, oratorios, symphonies, sonatas, masses, overtures, songs, concertos, treaties on Harmony, societies, conservatories, all co-operative with about one hundred eminent musicians. Among these the most noted were Mendelssohn, Schuman, Liszt, Hiller, Wagner, Henselt, Gade, Kullak, Rubinstein, von Bulow, Brahms, Tschaikowsky, Tausig, Millocker and Grieg.

In this period, some sixty of the eminent musicians passed to the spirit realm of the Cycle, among whom the most noted were Haydn, Dussek, Beethoven, Schubert, Weber, Hummel and Mendelssohn.

In the second half of the century, we find the works of these, and other celebrities and their works, wielding an influence in the minds of Germany and among the cognate nations.

Some fifty-five or more of the eminent musicians passed into the spirit realm of the Cycle, among whom the most noted were Schuman, Cramer, Meyerbeer, Hauptman, Moscheles, Kullak, Wagner, Hiller and Liszt.

In France, during the first half of the the nineteenth century, the development of the Cycle was under the influence of Emperor Nepoleon Kings Louis XVIII and Charles X, and thirty or more eminent musicians, the most noted among whom were Berlioz, Chopin, Thalberg, Gounod, Saint-Saens, and Godard.

During this period some twenty-five of the most noted musicians passed to the spirit realm of the Cycle, among whom the most noted were Mehul, Herold, Boieldieu, Leseveur, Boillit, Chopin, and Kelkbenner.

In the second half of the century, we find these celebrities influencing, through ideas embodied in their compositions, the histories, schools, conservatories, academies, etc.

During the latter part of the century, forty or more of the eminent musicians passed to the spirit realm of the Cycle.

In Italy, during the first half of the nineteenth century, the people were influenced by Rossini's cantatas and operas, and similar compositions by Belleni, Donizetti and Verdi, etc. These were co-operative with some thirty eminent musicians, the most noted among whom were Maria and Verdi.

During this period, some twenty-five of the eminent musicians passed to the spirit realm of the Cycle, among whom the most noted were Clementi, Ballini, Paganini and Cherubini.

During the same half of the century, we find these celebrated musicians, and their works, influencing the people of Italy and cognate nations.

About twenty of the eminent musicians passed on into the spirit realm of the Cycle, among whom the most noted was Rossini.

In the nineteenth century, America, with one hundred and fifty or more prominent musicians, co-operative with the current musical works of the preceding masters, their own compositions and literature, schools, societies, conventions, conservatories, academies, associations, public-school music, etc., influenced the development of the Musical Cycle, in this region, throughout the first half of the nineteenth century.

During this period, about sixteen of the prominent musicians passed to the spirit realm of the Cycle, in America.

In the second half of the century, twenty-five or more prominent musicians were added to the developing core, who co-operated with the works and influence of their ancient and immediate predecessors, and the vast number of music dealers, schools, academies, conservatories, societies, journals, and other exponents, and instrumental facilities of every kind, all of which have been an influence in the development of the Cycle, in this region, and links by which certain aids have been given, in connecting up the present with the pre-historic conditions of the Cycle. The influence of this period, co-operative with the development of the past, is manifest in the establishment of a greater amplitude of expression; a wider range of poetic ideas have been brought into brighter coloring through the musical rendition, modulations, dissonances, greater distribution of voices, sensational effects, etc. As proof, mark the change in the operas, oratorios, songs, orchestration, and concertos, and especially the treatment of music for solo instruments.

In this period Wagner stands master in the Operatic zone of the Cycle, as is evidenced by his conception of such ideas as are displayed in *"Lohengrin," "Tristan and Isolde," "Niebelungen Ring,"* and *"Parsifal"*—all poetic, lofty in sentiment, in word expression, musical phraseology, tone-coloring and scenic details, as previously unknown; Gounod, likewise, climbed the hill of development by his sensuous conceptions, as evidenced in his creation of *"Faust."* Contemporaneous with him, on the same heights of musical conception, is Goldmark, evidenced in his *"Queen of Sheba;"* but the taste of the general public called for lighter Romance, hence the departure of some eminent writers. such as Suppe, Strauss, Lecocquet, and others, who expressed through lighter operas.

The Oratorio of "real poetic greatness," was terminated by authors who departed from such conceptions of it, as Mendelssohn's *"Elija,"* and its like, etc., and the people of the period were influenced through sensational creations, as *"The Tower of Babel"* and *"Paradise Lost,"* by Rubinstein; *"The Deluge,"* by Saint-Saens, *"Te-Deum,"* by Berlioz," or the *"Requiem,"* by Verdi, etc.

Still further development, diverging from the works of the great masters in the Cycle into a light, lyrical zone, is evidenced in Max Bruch's *"Oddysens"* and *"Frith Jof;"* Mackenzie's *"Rose of Sharon,"* and others; Dudley Buck's *"Light of Asia;"* Hoffman's *"Fair Melusena,"* etc.

As Mendelssohn's *"Elija"* marked the zenith of the modern Oratorios, and Wagner's *"Lohengrin"* of the Opera, Schuman and Chopin hold the altitude banner of poetic pianoforte playing and works; and no modern writers have influenced by superior conceptions and creations.

The principal influence has been through popularizing works of previous masters, addition of arrangements, such as Liszt's arrangement of Schubert's songs, and the ascendency that arose through the development of expression, brilliancy, and general effects.

As to violin and orchestral music, the influence is felt most in the revolution wrought in the Art of Orchestration, such as is evidenced by the sensational character given to it by the works of Berloiz; the elegant, poetic and organ-like characteristics displayed by Wagner, as in the prelude to *"Lohengrin," "Ride of the Valkyries," "Waldweben,"* the prelude to *"Tristan and Isolde,"* the score of the *"Gotterdammerung,"* the *"Symphonic Poems"* of Liszt, Saint-Saens, etc.

During the second half of the century, about fifty of the prominent musicians passed into the spirit realm of the Cycle.

BE-DES'ZE NUD BE-DES-TRE'ZE, OR PAINTERS AND PAINTINGS.

TELTZIE XXXIV

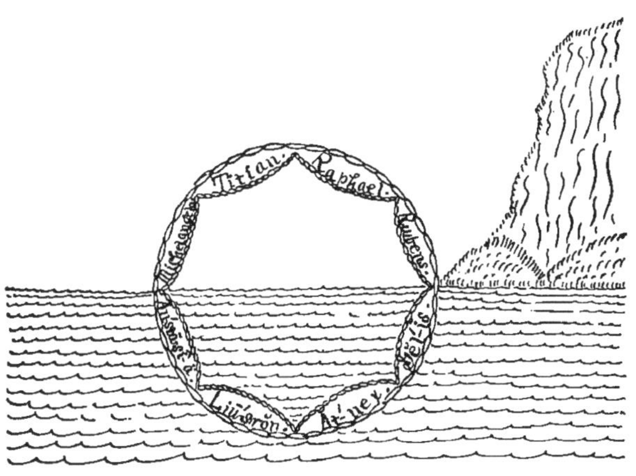

The Zē-ū'lē-ŭs zē Bē-dĕs'trē (art of painting) in the latter part of the first Efremetrum, was crude, both in design and material with which to execute the bē-dĕs-tre'zē.

The early work of the bedesze was modelled after natural landscapes, which began with certain specimens of vegetation, and was utilized for purposes of interior ornamentation, and wrought upon crude paper, the product of that period.

Gĕl'ĭs, a noted bē'dĕs (painter) of that epoch, was the originator of the zeuleus ze bedestre. As a child he was a Că-cĕl'lă, being influenced by spirit guides, to lay the foundation on which the great structure of bedestre, as an art, rested in subsequent time.

While at play, he collected some vegetable juices, which he daubed upon a chip of wood. As he continued this amusement, he caused the colors to blend, and naturally to assume various forms. As he grew older, he was led by the same influence, to see and conceive the idea of blending colors, and to utilize them in the process of imitating objective forms in representation of the scenes about him. Had he lived beyond the years of middle life, he would have greatly improved the art; but his passing out of the form made it otherwise.

There were many bedesze who, during that Efremetrum, modelled after his works; but as to the point of art, their productions remained thus crude during that epoch.

Gelis was located at El'thē-rē-zō, the original aistie in Teltzie Set, on the site of Enididstro of the third Efremetrum.

At'nĕx was a celebrity who rose at the beginning of the second Efremetrum, and who continued the zeuleus as originated by Gelis. He was further influenced, to improve it, which he accomplished by combining minerals and clay substances with vegetable juices. He originated, and adopted, the use of brushes, which were of three different sizes. They were made from parts of the body of the E'thē-lĕts, a low fibrous shrub of that region. Strips were cut the size of the brush, the ends were pounded until the woody part could be removed, which, when done, left the fibrous part to form the brush. The fibres were as fine as the finest of thread. His subjects were principally landscapes, and mountains and water scenes, his favorites. He painted direct from natural scenes, and when occasion afforded opportunity, his easel was an adjacent rock or fallen tree. He also discovered the art of making colorings to appear changeable in the light, which made them much more attractive. The effect was produced by a finish which he put on his bedestreze. The preparation was an oil he made, from a shrub then known as the Zĕth'tē-lĭn. It was similar to a modern varnish, and applied the same way.

Through the influence of Atnex, bedestre sildazic (painting schools) were established in various parts of the Lontidri, during which time the zeuleus greatly advanced toward perfection.

He dwelt at E-ū'tī-sē, the original aistie in Teltzie We, of the Lontidri, but this, in the latter part of the third Efremetrum, was changed to Neitz, the Kistrez aistie of the Teltzie.

Liū'srŏn was the most noted bedes of the third Efremetrum. He was a pupil of Kĕrt'zē-lĭn, who had been formerly a pupil of Atnex. He was a man of great genius, noted for his universality in bringing out the subjects and models he chose for his bedestreze. His designs and productions were for both interior and exterior ornamentation. His greatest achievements were in the aistie of Atara, adjacent to which his bedestre sildazic had place. He wrought elaborate bedestreze, modelled after various subjects and also after his own creation. His imagery, and perspective effects, were alike as perfect as life itself. His portraits were so fine, both in perspective and blend of colors, that the individual representation seemed ready to speak and move, as it were, so akin was it to the natural subject from which the portrait was modelled.

Crĕt'zē-lū was one of Liusron's most noted pupils, whose work was to retouch the carvings of Ax'trey, with whom he was contemporaneous, on the musical instruments. This art made the carvings realistic, in appearance, and much more beautiful than modern carvings appear.

Through the influence of Liusron and his renowned school, similar ones were established by his pupils, which strengthened the progress of the zeuleus throughout the Lontidri.

Anstacia, the daughter of Liusron, who became classically proficient under the influence of her father, continued his work, until the final submergence of the Lontidri.

Her most famous bedestre, which was a dramatic scene, portrayed in massive detail, was presented by her to the Kĕn'tî Klĭn'tĭc (a Dramatic society) of Atara, and was placed in the then famous Rĭz'tĭc (playhouse or theatre) of the Kenti Klintic, on the occasion of one of their grand National conventions of art. These were held annually in honor of the Masters of all arts, and their great works. The latter were displayed in the Riztic, during the convention, for the purpose of leading artists to higher aspirations in regard to the perfection of their works.

Therefore, there were many painters and paintings throughout the Lontidri, in the last period of Atlantian greatness. Could the adornments of habitations, both private and public, have been viewed by mortal Art lovers, of modern times, the fact of the greatness attained by the Atlantian artists would be recognized as far excelling the works of modern artists.

Passing from the Atlantian influence, through painters and paintings, into El-tē'zē (Arabia), to about 5500 B. C., we find a very crude idea of the art of painting, then existing in Elteze, having its re-embodiment by spirit inspiration and guidance.

After about five hundred years, through which time but little advancement had been made, the art took a start toward greater perfection, through the influence of Căl-lū'thēs (painters) co-operative with spirit guidance.

After the Mĕl'sä (art) of Căl-lū-thē'ăn (painting) had become well established in Elteze, it was utilized for both interior and exterior ornamentation, a fact which necessitated two classes of calluthes, viz: one for the interior, and one for exterior work.

El-ī-thē'nē was the first noted cal'lūth (painter) whose work and influence began about 5000 B. C. In his day, he was a master calluth of national repute, and was the originator and designer, in that melsa, in Elteze, especially for the ornamentation on buildings. He designed from all nature, as the occasion required, or admitted. He lived in the chizon of Jĕl-kĕs-trī'sō, then centrally located in the section of Elteze, between the now known Skemmar and Dehanah mountains, northeast of the town of Haill. He lived and worked until the middle of the fourth quarter of the century.

Crē'ēs was the most noted female calluth whose influence began about 4900 B. C. She first resided in the chizon of Jelkestriso, but later moved to a chizon, by the name of Quĭn-tē-zē'ŏx, then located in the southeastern portion of the now known country of Turkey, between the Euphrates and the Tigris rivers, and about half way between the now location of Bagdad and Samara. She had a school for pupils who came from all parts of the country. She chose her subjects, for calluthean, from various things in nature, embracing the vegetable, the animal, the bird, and human creations, astronomical and landscape scenes, etc., in which she far excelled the painters of the historic periods. She was a descendant from Elithene, lived to be aged, and still worked at her profession, when nearly one hundred years old.

At'nër was the most noted male calluth of Elteze, whose influence began about 4650 B. C. He resided in the southwestern portion of that country, in a small chizon by the name of Zăn-tō-zĕl'zĭc, on or near the site where the town of Hamdan has place. His chief work was in the production of human portraiture, though he did considerable in the representation of animal forms. He was the founder of progressive portrait calluthes, especially in the art of fine coloring and blendings. He had a school of melsa at Zantozelzic, and at that time was considered a fine melsaest. He passed to spirit life at an early age, for he did not enter the next century in the mortal.

Passing from the influence of the latter period of Atlantis, to the Sĕn-nër'zē (painters) kĕn Sĕn'trĭx (and paintings) sī Sī-lo'-tŏn (of Egypt), we are further informed, by Anstacia, that the art of painting as also of sculpture, had its more remote origin in that country, and subsequently was re-established, in various pre-historic sections of the country, through spirit influence upon the minds of sensitives in those regions, who were artistically inclined. Among these she mentioned the following pre-historic celebrities, and their developments as leading up to, or as connecting links, artistically speaking, with the Modern-ancient and Modern.

Brō-măn'zē, a pre-historic sĕn'nër (painter), and a descendant from the Kăl-lŭ'thē-äns of Kăl-lŭ'thē-ä, in the country of Siloton, came into the earth life about 1500 years before the Adomic period. He lived to the mortal age of one hundred, dwelt in the large pre-historic town of Bā-gĭl'lē-ä, that then had place on both sides of the now known White Nile river, west of the town of Senner, or about one hundred miles south of Khartoum, or the junction of the Blue and the White Nile rivers. He wrought his sentrix on both wood and stone. This was at first very crude, much as a child would delineate its ideas, in its first attempts at copying from a diagram. He attempted representation of animal and human forms, trees and various kinds of vegetation; in fact, any material object that appealed to his fancy.

His sentrix were all of a black, outlined style, as he never attempted the filled, or complete form representation, or used other colors. There was no special use made of his sentrix; in fact, he simply originated the black outlined style of sentry (painting).

Nē-ī-tăn'zä, a pre-historic senner, a grandson of Bromanze, came into the earth life about 1450 years before the Adomic period, and lived in the mortal form one hundred and fifty years, and therefore was a descendant from the Qū-zē'täs of Gŭstz. He dwelt in a large town by the name of Scăl-văn'tŭs, on the site of the now known town of Edfoo. He wrought his sentrix on barks, which he specially prepared for that purpose. At first he copied after the style of his grandfather's sentrix, and therefore only produced his subjects in black outline. Subsequently, he established the use of a red coloring matter, which he extracted from a plant stalk and its berries, then existent in that section of the country.

As was the custom of his grandfather, he utilized natural forms or objects, for his subjects, and also originated a crude form of landscape sentry, one of the best of which was a very large sentry, on which he represented a very high and steep mountain with a plateau near its base and a large spring of water gushing from the mountain side, which was falling to the plateau below. Above this were many trees, interspersed over the mountain side, among which were jutting rocks; a general disbursement of flowers, natural to that country; and a female, vessel in hand, was in the act of catching water from the spring on its course down the mountain side. On a portion of the plateau, to the right of the scene, he represented himself, as in the act of outlining and painting the scene. His sentrix were used for home ornamentation exclusively.

Mē-nā'rä, a pre-historic sĕn'nĕr, was a descendant from the

Kăl-lū′thē-ăns, of Kăl-lū′thē-ä, who came into the earth life about 1350 years before the Adomic period, lived to the mortal age of one hundred years, and dwelt in a pre-historic town by the name of Căl-ē-nō′thē-ŭs, that then had place on the eastern side of the Nile river, and on the site where the town of Berber now has place. His sentrix consisted simply in the representation of his subjects by sand tracings, which he did on natural beds, or those that he prepared for that purpose. He chose subjects from all natural life, or objects such as met his fancy, which in many instances he represented to the life.

There was no special use made of his sentrix, practically speaking, only as he would ornament the grounds about the homes of his friends, and his own, by means of prepared beds on which the traced sentrix of that period, took the place of flower-beds and shrub assemblies. These became pre-historic links, leading up to that class of ornamentation practised in ancient and modern times, and were the means of developing his own artistic nature, which had an influence on the advancement of ornamental art, of that kind, and therefore a link that conneets Atlantis with Ancient and Modern development of lawn decoration.

Mā-thē′ŭs, a pre-historic senner, was a son of Menera, who lived to the mortal age of a hundred and twenty-five years. He was a descendant from the Kallutheans of Kalluthea, in the country of Siloton, and at first dwelt in Calenotheus, but subsequently moved to the town of Mā-ā-thē′ŭs, on the site where the now known town of Meshra has place, where, on account of his notoriety as a senner, he was renamed Mā′thē-ŭs, after the town—with the slight change of dropping the second vowel of the word. He wrought his sentrix on wood, principally. At first he used only black coloring, but later he discovered a piece of soft stone which was of a bright color, and which he combined with the black. He then established a new feature in the art of coloring sentrix. He chose things in general for his subjects, especially animals, serpents and reptiles. The only use made of his sentrix was that of ornamental gifts from friend to friends, who would set them up in conspicuous places in their homes. It became an influence that led up to the more perfect representation of living creatures, and better ornamentation, as practised in subsequent ages, and evidenced by the beautiful home art adornments of past and present times.

Returning to Siloton (Egypt) about 4500 B. C., we find the Lē-ĕl′vä rĭl Lē-ŭth-mä′ĕt (art of painting), not only under further development, but sustaining changes relative to nomenclature, as well, which the reader will note by the terms now employed, etc.

E-quē'ä was the most noted Lē-ĕl-vä-zē'ĕt (artist) whose work and influence, began with that period of time contemporaneous with the latter days of Atner, the aged melsaest of Elteze.

Having migrated from Elteze to Siloton, he settled in the northern part of the country, in a small celzic (city) by the name of Căs-ī-dī-o'nä, then located on the west side of Nile river, on the site opposite to the now known town of Minieh Beni, and now extinct. He lived and worked during the first fifty years of the century, and being an Eltezean, had spent the first twenty-five years of his life in Elteze, where he was under the tutorship of Atner, which made him about seventy-five years of age, when he passed to spirit life. His principal subjects for leuthmaet were landscapes, and all natural scenery. Many of these were imaginary, though many times he modelled after real scenes. He continued and improved the style of color-blending, such as he had learned from Atner. His first and most famous leuthmaets were in representation of such scenes as by moonlight, sunrise, and sunset, with accompanying landscape conditions. His work was all interior, being portable pictures, and general stationary ornmentation.

Jĕn'tē-nōs, a contemporary of Equea, who was an Eltezean, while a youth, migrated northwestward out of the country of Siloton, into the secton now known as Barca, northeastern Tripoli, where he settled in a small celzic, by name Kĭn-try-ĭn'dŭs, now extinct. He lived to be about seventy-five years of age, and worked nearly to the close of his mortal life. His leuthmaets were of a general class, or of various subjects, embracing interior and exterior work, such as landscapes, human portraits, animal representations, etc. Some subjects he took from natural scenes, and others were purely imaginary. He had a school where he educated pupils in the leelva of leuthmaet (art of painting).

Soon after the influence of Equea and Jentenos had passed into antiquity, in Siloton, or from about 1000 years before the Adomic period, there began a great deterioration in the ability of the leuthmas, so that their leuthmaets were very inferior, in comparison with those of the above-named leelvazeets (artists). This condition continued, with the work of each succeeding leuthma, until about the time of the Adomic period, when the products of the leuthmas were simply a collection of very crude leuthmaets.

Passing into Mē-quē'thŭs (Assyria) we find the art of Cŭm-zō'lĕnd* under development through the influence of the Cŭm-zō'ĕst (painters), in co-operation with spirit guidance.

Fē-rē-nō'sō, a pre-historic cumzo, was a descendant from the Hĭm'mā-lēs of Jī'ĕn, in the country of Mē-quē'thŭs, and came into the earth life about 1200 years before the Adomic period, and lived to the mortal age of eighty-five years. He dwelt in a pre-historic town of Quĕl'zŏt, west of the Euphrates, on the site where now stands the town of Hillah. At first he wrought his cumzolend on the green bark of a standing tree, similar to the modern poplar; i. e., of a whitish-gray color. His first work was to delineate the alphabetic characters of the Himales language, by means of portraying his thoughts and ideas. Later in life, he began the representation of various material objects, both animate and inanimate, as his fancy prompted, which resulted in his having adorned all the trees for some distance around his home, and in adjacent sections. At first, he wrought with pencils formed of a black substance, but later, added a blue clay preparation. His great quantity of work gave him such thought and practice, that he ultimately produced some very fine cumzolend, which were made more attractive by having been wrought on living bark on the trees. These epidermal surfaces, as it were, became an arboreous "art gallery." He had to prepare some very fine pencils with which to bring out the perspective of his best landscapes, and all of his development, in the art of cumzolend, was due to the influence of spirit guides, who sought to bring about that condition through his organism. This became a pre-historic link between Atlantian art, and that of Ancient and Modern times, especially the principle of outlining and complete Crayon work, in portrait and landscape pencilling; and further, it led up to the art of representations in Oil, as produced by the countless artists of modern times.

Yunt, a pre-historic cumzo, was a son of Ferenoso, who lived to the age of fifty years. After migrating from the home of his father, he dwelt in a pre-historic town, by the name of Bŭl'bŭs, east of the Euphrates, on the site where the now known town of Zibda has place. Therefore, he became an inhabitant of the section of An-dē-lă-tō'lĕt, occupied by the descendants of the Mā-zā-tĭl'lē-ăns. At a later period he utilized papyrus leaves on which to represent his cumzolend. In addition to the black and blue materials, such as his father used, he established a pink color, which he obtained from a material substance, and also a green, which he extracted from vegetable matter; hence he fur-

*The term "lend," as affixed to Cum-zo, meant quantity.

ther developed the art of coloring, in that country. His cumzolend were utilized for interior ornamentation exclusively, and were pre-historic links that connected Atlantis with Ancient and Modern art, relative to coloring and home decorations.

Qū'zĕl, a pre-historic cumzo, was a descendant from the Hĭm' mā-lĕs of Lā-măn'tō, in the country of Mē-quē'thŭs, who came into the earth life about 1100 years before the Adomic period, and lived to the mortal age of one hundred years, and dwelt in a pre-historic town by the name of Tĭm'bē-zē, on the banks of the Tigris river, on the site where Bagdad has place.

Regarding his subjects for representation, he at first modelled after the style of Yunt, but later he originated the art of blending colors, in that region of the country. He represented the full form, by filling in the outlined space, in contradistinction with that of simple outlining, and therefore gave origin to the art of expression, in that country, relative to cumzolend produced. By this means, he brought out a more lifelike appearance to the eyes, and gave color to the lips, of the human visage, nostrils of animals, and hair of the head, etc. His landscapes were also an improvement over those of former cumzo, on account of this art of blending colors, etc. His cumzolend were utilized for house-decoration, and were in excess of those wrought by Yunt. His work was the pre-historic link, connecting Atlantis with the Ancient and Modern art of Full Form representation," "blending of colors," and "expression,' 'which they led up to.

Dĕl-cū'zŏt, a pre-historic cumzo, was a descendant from the Zē-ūes of Zū-yī-thē'us, in the country of Mē-quē'thŭs. He came into the earth life about 1050 years before the Adomic period. lived to the mortal age of ninety years, and dwelt in a large town by the name of Dĕl-cū'sa,* on the site where now the town of Abu Kuba has place. He wrought his cumzolend on the exteriors of doors to buildings, and did no interior work. He used a sort of staining process, the color being white and gray. It was, however, non-endurable where exposed to the exterior elements. At first he represented the human form as a subject for his cumzolend in both single and Grouped Posings, which latter style he originated, in that country.

In addition to the colors black, white, pink, and green, already utilized in that country, he originated or established the use of a cloudy orange. This he obtained from a mineral substance, by pulverizing it and mixing it with water.

He further developed the art of blending colors, which he did by use of a gluten, or solution which he extracted from trees of that kind. This, after hardening, not only gave body and lustre to his cumzolend, but added greatly to their durability.

He continued his development as a cumzo, until he became quite expert in the principle of life-expression; and his cumzolend, thus developed, made the pre-historic link that connects Atlantis with the Ancient and Modern art, of grouping human form-subjects in painted representations, life-expression, and the ultimate use of oil body work, and varnish finishings, such as are used in the development and completion of paintings.

His name was given him after the name of the town, the difference being in the last syllable which was a part of his mother's name, in exchange for the last syllable of the name of the town, a custom in those days, of honoring the mother's maiden name.

Passing into Zanzureta (Greece) we find the art of bū-dē'nū (painting) under development by the influence of bū'dĕns (painters), co-operative with spirit guidance.

Pī-ē'trŭs, a pre-historic buden (painter), was a descendant from the Ic-thī-ē'ŏns of Ic'ē-trūse, and came into the earth life about six hundred years before the Adomic period, and lived to the mortal age of seventy-eight years. He dwelt in the pre-historic city of An-clē-ō'ŭs, in the now known northeastern portion of Greece, on the site of Lamia. At first, he wrought his bū-dē'-nŭs (paintings) on the bark of standing trees, of grayish color, as was the custom of Ferenoso, the early cumzo of Mequethus. He first portrayed his ideas by alphabetic character-drawing. Subsequently, he conceived the idea of outlining human portraits, beyond which style he never developed. At this stage of his profession, he sought his subjects from all visible nature, which added greatly to his collection of "visage representations." He never ceased utilizing the living bark, on trees, on which to portray his budenus, which he did wherever, for the time being, he chanced to sojourn, and his permanent place or abode was a scene of prolific art of that order, which in modern times would seem odd indeed. Yet, it was more in keeping with reason than is the modern custom of defacing trees with nomenclature, and improper carvings, which has often brought about, as done, and made manifest upon public buildings as well, a condition not known in the time of Pietrus, for then all representation was purely artistic, that passers-by might study, enjoy and profit. He wrought all of his outlining in black, by means of a mineral substance, which he formed into pencils for that purpose. During his latter years as a buden, he became very proficient in his representation of homes, landscapes, animals, birds and the human form. His art work, like that of Ferenoso, was a link that led up to general art delineation, thus connecting Atlantis in that respect, with the art that belongs to Ancient and Modern times.

Ac-rē-mē'dēs, a pre-historic buden, and son of Pietrus, lived to the mortal age of ninety years.

After completing his studies, relative to budenus, under the tutorship of his father, he dwelt in a pre-historic city by the name of Běn-rī'dē, in the now known eastern-central section of Greece, on the site where the now known town of Chalkis has place. At first he wrought his budens on bark. This he removed from trees, and fastened together smoothly for that purpose. As his father had done, he chose various subjects from nature, and human and animal forms. In portrayal thereof, he used black mineral crayons, and a green-colored gluten that he extracted from a vegetable bark in that region. These he applied with a fibrous stick, which he made into the form of a brush. The chief utility of his budens was the ornamentation of his friends' homes.

E-zĭn'dä, a pre-historic buden, was a descendant from the Kěl'tō-pläs, of Kěl-tō-plä'sŭs, in the country of Zanzureta, who came into the earth life about five hundred and thirty years before the Adomic period, and lived to the mortal age of ninety-six years. He dwelt in a town by the name of Mĭn-nē-măt'ŭs, in the section of Greece now known as Argolus, on the site of Nemea. In the production of his budenus, he modelled after the works of Acremedes. He, also, used papyrus leaves on which to portray his thoughts, and the colors black and green. He originated and added to these the use of an old gold, or bronze color, which further developed the art of coloring. His productions were utilized for interior home ornamentation. But, during the last period of his profession, he wrought his subjects on the exterior of doors, to various buildings, and this was a pre-historic link, connecting the Atlantian art of exterior decoration on buildings, with that of Ancient and Modern usage.

Těl'gŭs, a pre-historic buden, was a descendant from the Ic-thī-ē'ŏns of Zē-căn'dē-zōte, in the country of Zanzureta, who came into the earth life about five hundred years before the Adomic period, and lived to the mortal age of seventy-nine. He dwelt in a large, pre-historic town by the name of E-ā-ŏn'thē, in that section of Greece now known as Thessaly, on the site of the now known town of Vourgareli, which at that time was the largest, most ancient, and most important town in Zanzureta, or Greece. He portrayed all his budens on layers or sheets of a mineral substance, then known as jer ser, found in smooth, thin layers, or elastic *laminae,* of various colors and degrees of transparency—the substance now known as mica. At that period of time jerser was used as is modern glass, the latter not being known to the pre-historic peoples.

On the above-named jerser window, Telgus wrought many patterns from various subjects, particularly of landscapes; also large aquatic scenes, as lakes and rivers, on which water fowls were represented in graceful floating, or in groupings upon the shores. Some of these were beautifully and artistically wrought, in process of which he utilized the black and old gold colors, mineral preparations, and vegetable green, white, blue and red; the latter two he himself originated and established the use of, thus further developing the art of coloring.

At first his work was all wrought on the interior of buildings, but subsequently he placed his budenus on the windows, as well, which styles were pre-historic links, connecting that class of Atlantian art with that of the Ancient, and leading up to the vast styles of interior and window ornamentation and glass painting, so popular throughout the continents in Modern times.

Returning to Zanzureta, about 4000 B. C., we find the frĭs-cŏn'sū tūse frĭs-cŏn- sū'nūce (painters and paintings) further developed, and under a change of nomenclature, as was the case in Siloton, or Egypt.

Aside from the early spirit influence, in Zanzureta, which established the art of budenu, in that section, there was some influence that aided in its further development, at a later period, which arose from international migratory conditions, brought into Zanzureta from Elteze and Siloton. For prior to the Adomic period, Elteze, Siloton and Zanzureta, were the three greatest nations on the earth.

At the time of the establishment of the Mediterranean and Ægean seas, peoples from the three nations were passing and repassing from Elteze and Siloton, into Zanzureta, and vice versa, by which means the influence of the ī-ō'ŏn (art) of frisconsunu was being established in Zanzureta, and it was at that time, and as occasioned by the submergence, the seas above mentioned were established, that separated Zanzureta from Siloton, and Elteze, that caused the Ioon of frisconsunu to begin its development, for the better.

Pō-lū-grū'tŭs was the most noted friscon (painter) who led in the Ioontis frisconsunu, about 4000 B. C. He dwelt in a small se-ma sa (town) by the name of E-non-dĕs-trē'ŭs, situated north of the now known Mt. Kathavothra, or between it and the river Hellada. He lived and produced frisconsunuce (paintings) until into the fourth quarter of the century. He first wrought portraits, and painted landscapes of a general character. He was a natural ioonso (artist) and therefore was easily inspired by spirit intelligences, who sought him out for that purpose, and who used him as their instrument through whom to establish the art of coloring, in that region of the country. He had many pupils from various parts of the country, who attended his school at Enondestreus.

Lū'si-ŭs was the most noted friscon about 3500 B. C. He dwelt in a semasa by the name of Zū-zē-rē-lē'ŭs, north of the now known Mt. Liakovra, on the site where now the town of Velitsa has place. He was a Zanzuretan, by birth, and lived through the century, and entered the first quarter of the next; therefore he was quite aged when he ceased his material work. His style of frisconsunu was that of interior and exterior decoration, embracing portable portraits, stationary landscapes, or wall scenic decorations, in which he displayed great brightness or brilliancy of colorings. It was his mission, under the guidance of spirit influence, to greatly advance the art of coloring, as established by Polugrutus, wherein he used deeper colors and heavier-bodied material, to which he gave the bright or glistening quality, above referred to; all far in excess of the same as found in modern paintings. His ability to blend the glistening quality almost as perfectly as the natural body-colorings, re-blending the whole with great perfection, made his creations very attractive, and himself celebrated among the ioon-loving people of that period. He was further celebrated for having developed the ioon to a greater perfection than Polugrutus, and it was an acknowledged fact that his inspiration came from spirit guides (as is the case with the writing of this book); hence, sacred to them, as one whose works should serve them as future models. He had a large school in his resident semasa, as pupils came to him from various parts of the country.

Passing into Et-zĕn-tū'an (Italy), we find the art of Păl-ză-co'ä (painting) under development by the influence of the Păl-ză-cō'äs (painters), co-operative with spirit guidance.

Păl-cē-'rō, a pre-historic pal-ză'-cō (painter) was a descendent from the Sĭn-ē'thŏns of Tĭn-dĭn'zē-on (Germany), who came into mortal life about six hundred years before the Adomic period, and who lived to the mortal age of one hundred years.

Early in life he migrated from Tindinzeon to Etzentuan, where he dwelt in a pre-historic town by the name of Fră-rea ro, in the now known southern portion of Italy, on the site where now the town of Beneento stands. His palzacosa was wrought on gray or light-colored rocks. He represented himself as seated upon the ground, by a rock, executing the outlines of a subject, which he was doing, by means of a small, hard stone, in the same manner as a stone cutter, of modern time, would use his hammer.

His palzacosa were in simple outlined alphabetic characters, thus giving expression to his thoughts and ideas. After the characters were thus outlined, with the concussion stone, he painted the black with a substance then known as bā-sī-ē', the same as what is now known as carbon, and with sēl'cē-lĭc, now known as graphite.* This style of cutting, and painting characters, as originated in Etzantuan, was one of the pre-historic links that connects Atlantis with the ancient and modern Art of Monumental marking, whereby religious and historical ideas, epitaphs, memorial records etc., have been, practically speaking, expressed in innumerable instances.

Băl-zā'rĭc, a pre-historic palzaco, was a descendant from the Jē-rē-thē'ăns of Etzentuan, who came into the earth life about five hundred and fifty years before the Adomic period, and lived to the mortal age of sixty-five. He dwelt in a pre-historic town, by the name of Qū-ër'rër, situated on the site of ancient Rome. He continued his production of palzacosa, in the same style as that of Palcero. He wrought on marble, instead of the gray stone. His early work, therefore, was to delineate alphabetic characters. But, in the latter period of his profession, he added the representation of leaves, vines and flowers, which he wrought upon the exterior casings of doorways. This was a pre-historic link, connecting Atlantis with Ancient and Modern periods, and led up to the ultimate ornamental work, of that style, both in Painting and Sculptural Carving, now known as one of the modern Arts.

Sĕn-sē-cō'zy, a pre-historic palzaco, was a descendant from the Jeretheans of Etzentuan, and came into the earth life about five hundred years before the Adomic period, and lived to the mortal age of one hundred years. He dwelt in a pre-historic town, by the name of Pŭn'zū-lăc, in the section now known as Campania, west of the known town of Agropoli, now submerged by the waters of the Mediterranean Sea, or rather the Gulf of Salerno.** He continued the art of pelzacoa by the use of basie and celcelic. His style of pelzacoa was to represent the human form, trees, flowers, birds, etc. He used the colors black

*The material used by nearly all the pre-historic painters when black coloring was desired.

**At that time the river now known as the Eboli Sele extended beyond its present mouth southward into the now known submerged section, above referred to, east of the city of Punzulac, now submerged.

and gold, or canary yellow, which latter he established, or originated the use of. It was not durable if placed on the exterior, or where it was exposed to the elements; hence was of interior utility, principally upon the jerser, or window-panes. A strange feature of his execution of the palzacosa thereon was that he painted from the inside of the jerser, so as to have the subjects visible from the outside, a process similar to the ancient and modern methods of weaving certain tapestries, which latter are woven from the rear of the fabric, a process at which he became very proficient, and which forms a pre-historic link connecting that Atlantian art to the Ancient and Modern idea of Exterior visible painting, on glass, and in tapestry weaving.

Plā-ī'zō, a pre-historic palzaco, was a descendant from the Cĭn-ē-tō'ī-ĕns of Cĭn-ē-tō'ī-ē, in the country of Etzantuan, who came into earth life about four hundred and fifty years before the Adomic period, and lived to the mortal age of one hundred and five years, and dwelt in a pre-historic town by the name of Răd'zō, in the section now known as Tuscany, on the site where now the town of Terontola has place, and who was, therefore, influentially contemporaneous, during the first half of his professional career, with the latter part of that of Sensecozy of Punzulac.

Subsequent to the time that Sensecozy passed to spirit life, Plaizo had developed the art of window ornamentation, and the material used for that purpose, so the subjects could be placed on the exterior of the jerser (panes) which he did by adding a gum substance, or white gluten, which he extracted from trees. This was transparent when dry, and not materially affected by change of weather.

His favorite style, for window decoration, was the zig-zag delineation over a yellow background, and thus to cover the entire surface; this he sometimes bespangled with flowers and leaves, which he represented as promiscuously strewn; perspectively, in front of this, he represented the human form in various posings, in accord with his fancy. This style, or class, of palzacosa, was extremely beautiful, and wonderfully wrought.

Anstacia says that no one in all the subsequent periods of time, has ever represented his subjects so beautifully and artistically, as did this pre-historic palzaco, despite his limited utilities. Therefore, Plaizo established the pre-historic link that connects Atlantis with the ancient and modern periods, in regard to the knowledge of mixing paints, an art that has led up to the marvelous art of staining and ornamenting glass, so universally wrought and utilized, in ancient and modern times.

Passing into Tĭn-dĭn'zē-ŏn (Germany), we find the art of prĕlt'zū (painting) developing under the influence of prĕlt'zē (painters), co-operative with that of spirit inspiration and guidance.

Rĕn'hĕr-bürg,* a pre-historic prĕlt (painter), was a descendant from the Făl'kā-leĭts of Făl-kā-leĭt (France), who came into the earth life about 1000 years before the Adomic period, and lived to the mortal age of one hundred years. He spent the first quarter of his work as a sănd'pē (painter), in Falkaleit, after which he migrated to northern Tindinzeon, where he began his work as a Tindinzeonan prelt. He dwelt in a pre-historic town by the name of Wī-cŭs'bĕrg, on the Warthe river, in Prussia, or Eastern Germany, on the site where the town of Posen now has place. He having learned the art of alphabetic "character painting" in Falkaleit, established that branch of the art in Tindinzeon, and began prĕlt'zŭs (paintings) on large leaves, which, after completion, he filed in packages, and fastened them together, in the form of a book, with leaf contents. He delineated his subjects in large and small alphabetic characters, the large ones as capitals, similar to the Atlantian style of writing and MSS.

Subsequently, he used sheets prepared of bark, on which he executed his preltzus, which he fastened together at one end with fibres of bark, in the form of a book; and with a fibrous cord, he suspended them against the wall, when not in use. His coloring was black only, and during the latter part of his career as a prelt, in addition to the other matter he had printed or crayoned, and placed in book form, he established a method of recording and filing deeds, events historical and otherwise. He conceived this idea from having kept a daily account of his migration, from Falkaleit to Tindinzeon, and also of facts that he had recorded, relative to his father's estate in Falkaleit.

His efforts as a prelt, and the manner in which he preserved his preltzus, were important pre-historic links connecting the art of literature, establishment of books, and character-writing, with those of ancient times, and the ultimate linguistic utilities, such as led up to the compilation of modern works of literature, so vast, throughout all countries, as to be almost beyond comprehension; hence an influential result, beyond special specific reference in this treatise.

*It may seem strange that an individual born in, and migrating from, the section we now know as France, should have a name so decidedly German. The terminals "berg, burg, burgh," etc., belonged to the Falkaleit nomenclature, and descended into the German region by the migration of "Ren-her-burg," where it has by further conditional descendancy established other forms than "burg."

E-chür'hăm, a pre-historic prelt, was a descendant from the Sĭn-ē'thōns of Tindinzeon, and came into the earth life about nine hundred and twenty-five years before the Adomic period, He lived to the mortal age of seventy-five years, and dwelt in a pre-historic town by the name of Wĕl'tĕr-bĕrg, in the section now known as Northeastern Germany, on the present site of the city of Hanover.

He wrought his preltzus on prepared barks; his subjects being chosen from among animals, which he represented in their natural abodes, and customs of life. This caused him to further conceive ideas in relation to landscape representation, such as of the seasons, etc., and many of his preltzus embraced a combination, of landscape scenery and animal life and abodes. This caused him to establish other colorings than black, to which he added the green and the red; therefore, his influence upon subsequent preltze was very advantageous, and a pre-historic link that connected Atlantis with the art of ancient and modern painting, such as has portrayed natural landscapes in all seasons of the year; wild and domestic animal life; and set the law for artistic principles laid down in perspectography, especially that of the art of representing, or delineating on plane surfaces, objects as they appear to the eye, from any given distance or situation.*

Anstacia informs us that had the mortal life of Echurham continued longer, his artistic productions, already very fine, would have been still superior, from the fact that he was highly developed at the time of his disembodiment.

Lĭn'tē-zōn, a pre-historic prelt, and a descendant from the Sinethons of Tindinzeon, came into the earth life about eight hundred and sixty years before the Adomic period, and lived to the mortal age of one hundred years. He dwelt in a pre-historic town by the name of Wĭn'tōn-bürg,** on the site where is now the town of Krailsheim.

He was a pupil of Echerham, during the last ten years of the latter's material life, having entered that study-period at the age of fifteen years. At the age of twenty-five, he left Welterberg,** and migrated to Wintonburg, where he began his professional labors as a prelt. At first he wrought his preltzus on prepared barks; and subsequently, on wood or portable board panels, prepared by hand. During his early work, he modelled kinds of birds, which he represented as the life subjects in landscape scenes; also single subjects, and those posed in groups. In after the style of Echurham, but later, he added to that all

*Anstacia informs us that this princ'ple was better known to the Atlantian painters than those of modern times.
** Soft g.

the former, he represented his subjects as variously occupying arborical places, aquatic regions, etc.

In the production of this class of preltzu, he used black, green, red, blue, and a bright golden color (the latter having been introduced into that country by himself), and some of his preltzus was very fine indeed.

During the latter part of his professional work, he wrought on jerser (mica). His subjects were various, but his specialties were landscape and fine bird representations. He further developed the art of preltzu (painting), the influence of which affected the subsequent preltze of that section of the country. He was also the establisher of the custom of temple ornamentation, in that region of country, both exterior and interior. His exterior work was on the facades of temples. One, it might be well to mention, was a scene in which two mortals, a male and a female, stood in a religious attitude, looking skyward as a white dove was descending to them. Its every detail expressed to the life, hence it was a fine production of art.

The descent of the white dove was symbolic of the great spirit force, whch at that time was recognized as coming from above. The Sinethons of Tindinzeon worshipped the sun, moon and stars, and believed that from them, and their realms, came a greater spirit force than that which they received from individual spirits, whom they knew attended them, in pursuance of life on the earth plane. The two mortals, as posed in the preltzu, represented the fact that human beings were the recipients of such aids, in life, as came from the celestial realm; and the endowment of that blessing was further symbolized by the coronet of leaves, worn by the female figure; and it still further represented the continuation of good, from the provident source, to the coming generations.

The preltzus of Lintezone were pre-historic links that connect Atlantis with Ancient and Modern life and landscape representation, by the art of painting; and especially the representation of temples, churches, and other public buildings, and the interior and exterior ornamentation, on their facades and windows, so vastly represented throughout the districts of the earth.

Sĕl'dĕr-ĭch, a pre-historic prelt, and descendant from the Sinethons of Tindinzeon, came into the earth life about seven hundred and forty-five years before the Adomic period, and lived to the mortal age of eighty-eight years. He dwelt in a large town by the name of Dē-cō'sĕn, on the site where the city of Berlin has place. He was contemporaneous with the last fifteen years of Lintezon's period, and modelled after him, in every respect.

His influence, therefore, was solely for a further development of the art of preltzus, already established, a fact that led up to the same linkings, thus connecting Atlantis with the ancient and modern art developments.

Passing into Fäl'kā-leĭt (France), we note the art of sănd'pē (painting), under development by the influence of sănd-pŭs'ēr (painters), co-operative with spirit guidance, in that section of country.

Zē-wän'dī, a pre-historic sandpus (painter), was a descendant from the Găn-hē-lē'măns of Fĕl-tē-nē-zē'tēs, in the country of Falkaleit, who began his earth life about 1100 years before the Adomic period, and lived in the mortal form ninety-five years. He dwelt in a pre-historic town by the name of Zĕl-mŏn'dā, in the section now known as Cantal, on the site where the town of Aubillac has place. He first wrought his sandpe on gray or light sandstone. It was exclusively alphabetic character outlining, and executed in black only, which he did with basie and celcelic, in connection with a dark brown juice which he extracted from the bark of a tree, glutinous in character, that became darker and thicker as it dried. The sandpe, thus originated by Zewandi, is a pre-historic link that connects Atlantis with the ancient character-writing, and the ultimate monumental inscriptions of both ancient and modern times.

Rē-ĭn'chy, a pre-historic sandpe, was a descendant from the Falkaleits of Falkaleit, who came into the earth life about nine hundred and fifty-five years before the Adomic period, and lived to the mortal age of one hundred years. He dwelt in a pre-historic town by the name of Rē-īn-chy-lĕnd.* This was on the Loir river in the now known section of Loir Etchir, on the site where the city of Blois has place. His sandpe were wrought on bark exclusvely. His subjects were those of the human form only. At first, he simply outlined them with black color. Later he originated the use of white and green. The latter he used when representing the earth, on which the forms stood. These were wrought in white, and the background of the sandpe (paintings) was the original color of the prepared bark.

During the latter part of his period as a sandpus, he advanced the style, by outlining the form, and then filling in the surface in representation of the full form. Though he made no attempt at life expression, he made considerable advance in the principles of pose and form perfection.

* Was then the largest and most important town in France. He was named after the town, with the additional syllable, which was a part of his mother's name added to the name of the town.

While he executed the forms all in white, he represented the hair and beard in black; and the forms were nearly all represented as nude, though in his later productons, he draped the loins with black garments.

His sandpe were pre-historic art links that connected Atlantian art with that of Ancient and Modern periods, respecting the representation of the human form, in all developments from the former to the latter, embracing both the nude and the draped paintings.

Cĭn′nē-căs, a pre-historic sandpus, the son of Reinchy, lived to the mortal age of seventy-five years. He migrated from his home city to a pre-historic town by the name of Vĭn-zĭ′ō, south of the now known D'yeu or Ile Dieu, in the district submerged by the waters of the Atlantic, west of the now known section of Vendee, at which time the city was lost to mortal knowledge, with that portion of land, about the beginning of the Adomic period. He first wrought his sandpe on prepared barks, but later, he used slabs of slate-stone. He chose the various homes as his subjects, which embraced the buildings, and grounds that surrounded them, with their accompaniment of trees. The domestic dog was often represented in front of the home, in various posings. In the production of these sandpe, he used the black, white, green, red or brick, and brown colors, which made quite an advance, in the art of coloring. His productions were used by his friends and patrons as home ornaments, and were pre-historic links connecting Atlantis with ancient and modern periods, in the art of coloring and architectural painting. We might say, the great style of photographic representations, of such subjects as are known to moderns in Modern times.

Clē-cē-ĭ′ĕt, a pre-historic sandpus, was a descendant from the Falkaleits of Falkaleit, who began his earthly career as a sandpus during the latter part of Cinnecas' time; hence, contemporaneous with him during that time. He dwelt in a town by the name of Zĕl-mŏn′dā, in the now known section of Cota D'or, on the site where the town of Dijon has place. He wrought his sandpe on laminae of jerser, and on the exterior of buildings, To the colors used by Cinnecas, he added a dingy blue, and a yellow. He first modelled after the human form, but later he represented landscapes, and in fact, any design in nature that met his fancy he painted, and therefore, ultimately, became very proficient as a sandpus.

One of his most famous sandpe was a very large landscape (twelve by twenty feet), in which he made a very perfect representation of the sky, the setting sun, mountain range, lake valley, etc. This was a very fine piece of art work, and was a prehistoric link, connecting the Atlantian art with that of the Ancient and Modern in landscape work, so extensively wrought in said periods.

Passing into Sĕd'ē-rōne (Spain) we find the art of celetiu (painting) under development by the cē-lē'tŭs (painters) co-operative with spirit influence, in that section of the country.

Zē'wŏnk, a pre-historic celeti (painter), was a descendant from the E-sĕl'trĭx, of Trū'sä, in the section of Sĕd'ē-rōne. He came into the earth life about 1000 years before the Adomic period, lived to the mortal age of fifty years, and dwelt in a prehistoric town by the name of Ur'lĕnd, in the now known section of Albacete, on the site where the town of Albacete has place. His first works were simply drawings, or animal form outlines, represented on the sands of the sea, or elsewhere, as beds of sand were to be found.

Subsequently, he used black slate-stone, reduced to the form of a pencil. All his works were simply outlined representation. At a still later period, he wrought on smooth leaves, and his process caused him to seek a coloring matter with which to represent forms of the animals. This resulted in his obtaining the juice from a red berry, which, in contrast with the green leaves on which he outlined, made attractive celetius.

During the latter part of his career, as a celeti, he conceived the idea of producing full form representations, in contrast with the simpler style of outlined celetius on slates and leaves.

His outline work was wonderful for that period of time, and had a great influence with subsequent celetus. Anstacia says that the people of modern times have no conception of the ideas conveyed through the style of outline representation such as was used in pre-historic periods, for it was vast and of great utility; and it is a great pre-historic factor link in the connection of Atlantian alphabetic characters, which in time, led up to modern writing and geometric outlining, as well as having figured in all kinds of drawing and drafting, by painters, architects, mechanics, etc.

Sā-răs'cō, a pre-historic celeti, was a descendant from the Sĕd'ē-rōnes of Sĕd'ē-rōne, and came into the earth life about nine hundred and thirty-five years before the Adomic period. He lived to the mortal age of ninety-six years, and dwelt in a prehistoric town by the name of Cē-lĕd'sē-ō,* in the now known section of Estremadura, Portugal, on the site of the city of Lisbon.

*Meaning "down by the sea coast." The city was so located and that name was therefore given to it.

He was contemporaneous with the last ten-years' period of Zewonk, and therefore copied somewhat from his methods, especially in the use of black slate-stone body and pencil outlining.

He prepared large pieces of slate stone, two feet or more square, on which he outlined the heads and busts of noted personages, and others who sought his service as a portrait outliner. Beneath each celebrity's portrait he recorded the name of the individual by use of the alphabetic characters of the Sederones. He worked from real subjects, and never attempted imaginary visages, or heads and busts.

He developed the art of simple outlining, as far as possible, and became very proficient in the art of prolific representation. He represented the hair, eyebrows, and eyes with white outlines, and the visage and other portions of flesh, such as the bust, etc., by the natural color of the slate, which he highly polished, so as to give it a glossy appearance. His influence upon subsequent celetus became a pre-historic link connecting Atlantian Zeuleus Ze Bedestre (art of painting) with that of ancient periods and ultimate modern times, having led up through the mural style, human form outlining, and ultimate modern portrait painting, so vastly extensive throughout various sections of the world.

Sē-rä-mĕn'sä, a pre-historic celeti, was a descendant from the Sederones of Sederone, and came into the earth life about nine hundred years before the Adomic period. He lived to the mortal age of seventy-five years, and dwelt in the town of Celedseo (home of Sarasco), where, for twelve years, he was under the tutorship of that celeti, after which he migrated to the then known section east of Sederone, now submerged, where he dwelt in the twin cities then known as Sā-măn'sä and An'tē-gĕn.**

He modelled after the style of Sarasco, and also utilized the slate and pencil materials; but his chief mission was to further develop the art, which he did by establishing the style of full form representation, in that country, in contradistinction to the outline representations of Sarasco. This he did in natural flesh colors, and further developed the natural appearance of the eyes.

Subsequently, in his career as a Celeti, he conceived the idea of representing the full, or round-form, body of the individual, after which he ceased to produce the head and bust representations (or style of his earlier works), in order to develop and per-

**Now submerged by the Mediterranean Sea. These two cities had place on the banks of the then known Ge-nan-gush river, which was an extension of the now known Guadalaviar river that in its then extension, flowed south east, west of the now known Ivica Island. The city of Samansa was located on the north east side of the river and of Antegen on the south west, about half way between the now known Ivica Island and the city of Valencia Del Cid, on the coast of the section of Valencia.

fect the new style, which, in an artistic sense, he reached in a high degree of perfection.

In order to obtain the above-named condition, he was led to conceive the idea of color-blending, and the principles embodied in perspective art, both of which he originated and developed in that section of the country, and therefore influenced the subsequent celetus, a fact which established the pre-historic link that connects Atlantian painting to the ancient and modern, thus leading up to the great art of representing life expressions, physical form representations, color blending and perspective art characterization.

Jŭt'sä, a pre-historic celeti, was a descendant from the Sederones of Sederone. He came into the earth life about eight hundred years before the Adomic period, and lived to the mortal age of one hundred years. He was a pupil of Seramensa during the last twenty-five years' period of the latter's mortal life, therefore dwelt, at that time, in the twin cities of Samansa and Antegen; but, after Seramansa's disembodiment, he migrated to the now known section of Cordova, where he settled in a pre-historic town by the name of Rā'gē, on the site where now the city of Cordova has place.

His celetius, like Seramensa's, were in the first place, bust and full form representations; but later he added to these styles other subjects, all of which he further improved.

He introduced the use of his celetius into the temples for ornamental purposes. Some, however, were symbolic representations, which usually were wrought in the niches, alcoves, etc.

Among his most celebrated celetius was one wrought in a large canopied niche, or alcove, on the rear wall of the temple. The canopy was beautifully wrought, in representation of the sky at early morning, as the stars were beginning to fade out of sight by the light of the sun, just coming up. The lower portion of the niche was in representation of the interior of the temple. Five persons, two females and three males, were represented as standing near the foreground, in the attitude of looking out at the fading stars and rising sun, each of whom was characterized with sublime countenance, and adorational attitude. The picture was sublime in every detail, and symbolized the sun and star worship of the Sederones, for they adored the sun and stars as being the source from whence all light and provident force came.

On each side wall of the temple were two very large panels, each possessed of a fine celetiu (painting). On one was represented spirit forms in the act of entering the temple. They were of various sizes, from childhood to maturity. On a blue vaulted canopy above the panel, the stars only, were represented, and there was a night scene of that order. All things considered, it was a beautiful and well-wrought production. On the companion panel, a fine representation of evening was wrought. The changing shadows and illumined tints, such as express from such a scene in nature, were represented, to the life, in this celetiu. Two male spirits were represented as standing in the foreground, looking upward at a large white bird, the latter having been represented as descending to them, which the celeti intended to represent or symbolize as spirit force returning from the departed sun, thus to brood over them, for their protection during the coming night.

On the other side wall of the temple, opposite to the above-described celetius, were two similar companion celetius. One was a landscape that disclosed a marine scene, valley and mountain range, and three spirit forms, two of which were kneeling, one on each side of the third, as the latter was standing with uplifted hands and upturned face. The two kneeling spirits were looking far away over the ocean, at the full moon, represented as having just arisen on the sky horizon, from beneath the waters. Back of the spirit forms was the valley; and in the distance, the mountain range, draped with the twilight shadows and tinted pall of evening. The moonbeams pierced through, lighting the ecene into loveliness akin to spirit beauty, and thus they fell over the spirit faces and their white robes, characterizing them with transparent splendor. The companion to this celetiu represented a landscape scene. Centrally, a high and massive mountain was represented in the distance, behind which the sun sank at eventide. From behind its peak was represented radiating golden light, piercing the sky regions, thus illuminating the cloudlets that were hovering near the peak of the mountain, while the crimson tints and purple sky blended in harmonious perspective. On the area of the valley, near the front of the celetiu, was represented a congregation, or vast multitude of people, solemnly watching the scene, as if having congregated to witness the going down of the sun. A spirit fŏrm was represented rising from behind the mountain peak, as if having come back from the departed sun. Further down the mountain side was represented the same spirit as floating or descending down the mountain side, through the tinted lights, thus approaching the multitude. This symbolized, to the people, the idea of a higher and greater light, which they termed Tĭsh'ă, meaning the light of the Great Spirit being brought to them in the form of a spirit, for they well understood the phenomena of spirit return and manifestation. This knowledge they had gained through clairvoyant and clairaudient powers, so generally used in those days, as a means of obtaining knowledge of natural principles. They were recognized by them as provident, helpful, pure and holy sources of providence, in all things brought to them in the material realm, and consequently manifold greater, in the spirit realm, from whence they came to administer·

Anstacia further informs us that these fine celetius, and some of the smaller ones that accompanied them, in that temple, were the finest productions in the art of painting, wrought by painters of any age the earth has ever known since the time of the works of the Atlantian bedesze (painters) were submerged.

Briefly following the influence of pre-historic ideas as em braced in the paintings of the past, their re-embodied extensions as influential links in the epi-cycles that move on the deferent of the great Cycle of Painters and Paintings, we make the connection in Etzentuan, through such links as the Byzantine influence of the twelfth and subsequent century, known to have prevailed in Pisa and Lucca, which manifested through mural paintings, representing the Crucifixion.

Entering the thirteenth century, Giotto wielded a great influence by inaugurating the Renaissance style of the Byzantine art, and the establishment of the true and the natural representation of a subjeet. This he, by co-operative spirit guidance, embodied in his paintings, the manifestation of which, by further re-embodiment, in productions by his pupils and imitators, governed Florence, artistically speaking, throught the thirteenth century.

In Siena, during the first half of the fourteenth century, great influence was felt by the ideas embodied in the paintings of such artists as Simone di Martino and Lippo Memmi, but more especially those of Ambrogio Lorenzetti, as evidenced by the ideas that manifest through their panel paintings and large fresco creations, which give evidence of both great imagination and technical skill, co-operative with spirit guidance.

The great works of Sano di Pietro and Matteo di Geovanni embodied great artistic ideas. The fifteenth century possessed many excellent artistic links, among which were the paintings of Peruzzi and Beccafumi. Masolino and Masaccio embodied naturalistic ideas that induced development of high artistic splendor. Orcagna conceived, embodied and developed, the idea of decorative style as wrought in bright colors, which in turn was re-embodied in the paintinge of subsequent artists over whom he yielded an artistic influence. Fra Angelico embodied sacred and decorative ideas, thus influenced by Orcagna, which in turn the latter influenced a re-embodiment of, in the works of his pupil, Benozzo Gozzoli. Masolino, Masaccio, Lippo Lippi, Botticelli, Filippino Lippi, etc., all embodied ideas that depict strong action, dramatic force and passionate expression, which first re-embodied in the works of pupils and imitators. Baldovinetti, Roselli and Ghirlandaio embodied ideas portraying the principles of realistic truth, and vigorous individuality, re-embodied, in turn, in the works of their pupils, through the former influence.

Signorelli embodied ideas, in his paintings at Orieto and Monte Oliveto, near Siena, in masterly representation of the nude human form, as evidenced by his most wonderfully and beautifully wrought easel picture, the so-called "School of Pan." Ideas not only of pre-historic painters were re-embodied by him, in his paintings, through spirit guidance; but, by further influence through the latter, he attracted the attention of Michelangelo, who re-embodied the idea in his primitve creations and developed the same, to the fullest capacity of his gigantic genius. This, in later life, co-operative with a powerful spirit influence, caused him to produce the most original and wonderful creations in the art of painting, known to the modern world, as evidenced by his fresco of "Isaiah," and other gigantic representations in fresco art, in the Sistine Chapel at Rome.

Piero della Francesca embodied ideas, such as manifest the art of delicate modelling, tender coloring, beautiful expression, etc. Perugino, one of the most advanced of Italian painters of his period, embodied ideas in his establishment of oil painting, such as superposed layers of color (as the Van Eycks), which greatly influenced, in the quality production of his and subsequent paintings, as smooth tinting, softness of form, graceful spaciousness to landscape distances, perspective, as viewed and governed by the rule of two centers of vision, etc. A still further influence was felt, through his frescoes, cartoons, etc., executed in stained glass. (See Encyclopædias for his grand works.)

Pinturecchio, a pupil of Perugino, yielded great influence by the re-embodied ideas in his vast number of paintings, through artistic traditions. He further developed the style of the older Perugian painters, such as Bonfigli, Fiorenzo di Lorenzo, Lo Spagna, and the early works of Raphael, due to the indelible impression of the individual ideas of Perugino upon his school of young artists—hence, the re-embodiment of his artistic nature, within the minds and lives of others. (See Encyclopædias for his great works.)

Timoteo Viti, an Umbrian painter, re-embodied in his excellent works the pre-historic idea of painting in red and black,, as was the custom of Sē-rä-mĕn'sä of Sederone (Spain), who blended his tints onto a black background, so as to produce a flesh color.

Mantegna embodied original ideas that greatly advanced Italian art, as evidenced by his manifestation of inventive force, gorgeous splendor of subject-matter, accuracy of detail, remote aspect, systematic consistency, etc.

The Bellini family, who influenced subsequent artists, re-embodied their ideas of science and spirit in the animation and dignity of the processional group, figure representation, perspectivity, precision and fine coloring; religious ideas; solemn splendor; energy without harshness; richness without luxury; intensity and vehemence of expression; firmness and strength of character; passionate energy in the solution and conception of the art principles, such as the perspective; the art of drapery; sculptural imitations, and re-embodiment of the antique; thus linking the pre-historic and the spirit influences, with those of the ancient and modern times, which we link back to the same ideas as manifested in the works of the Atlantian Bedesze.

Palma, of the fifteenth century, influenced by his re-embodied ideas; but he further influenced by a development of quality, which is made manifest through the richness and suffusion of his coloring, and his establishment of the flesh golden hue.

Giorgione, of the fifteenth century, crowned the art with greater effects, through faultless design; melting and harmonious coloring; life and glory, manifest through subjects, in contradistinction to solemn dreams and religious imagination; charming human grace and distinction; mutual joy of life and its rulings in the golden sunlight, extent throughout the regions of woodlands and meadows, a development that came to his sensitive organism, thus acted upon by spirit influence and inspiration; for his early pastoral life had tuned his physical and mental organism into touch with the vibrations of spirit forces, hence his supremacy as related to the art of that period of time.

Titian, of the fifteenth and sixteenth centuries, whom we have chosen as one of the principal links in the great Cycle of Painters and Paintings, and one of the greatest painters in the world, and a typical representative of the Venetian school, yielded a great influence through re-embodied and embodied ideas; at first, in his early works, as manifested by his representation of "Hercules," in the Morosini Palace; the "Virgin and Child," in the Vienna Belvidere, and the "Visitation of Mary and Elizabeth" (from the convent of E. Andrea), now in the Venetian Academy.

At a later period, he influenced through such frescoes as he executed on the re-erected Fondaco de' Tedechi; by his popular painting, "Christ Carrying the Cross," in the chapel of S. Rocco, Venice; "The Tribute Money" (Christ and the Pharisee), Dresden Gallery; "St. Mark Enthroned," along with S. S. Sebastian, Roch, Cosmo and Domiano, in the church of Salute; the "Three Ages," represented by a woman guiding the fingers of a shepherd, on a reed pipe, two sleeping children, a cupid and an old man with two skulls, with a second shepherd in the distance. This is one of his most poetically impressive works, and is now in the Bridgewater House. Further, are his "Worship of Venus," representing a statue of Venus, two nymphs, numerous cupids hunting a hare, and other figures (in the Madrid Museum); "The Holy Family," "St. Catherine" and the "Noli Me Tangere," in the London Gallery; the famous "Bacchus and Ariadne," in the National Gallery; the "Flora" of the Ufizzi; the "Venus" of Darmstadt; and the lovely "Venus Anadyomene" of the Bridgewater Gallery; the stupendous "Entombment of Christ," in the Louvre; the "St. Peter Martyr," for the Church of S. S. Giovanni e Paola (destroyed by fire, 1867); the "Madonna del Coniglio," in the Louvre; his series of frescoes in the Scuola di S. Antonio; the one in representation of St. Christopher carrying the infant Christ, havng place at the foot of the "Doge's steps," in the ducal palace at Venice; his paintings in likeness of five successive doges; the "Assumption of the Madonna," one of his world-renowned masterpieces, for the high altar of the church of the Friar (now in the Venetian Academy), which had a great influence in Italy relative to the art of executing colors, which marked the zenith of his fame, and is a re-embodied idea, conceived inspirationally, from the pre-historic works of Quzel and Delcuzot of Mesuethus; of Telgus, Polugrutus and Lusius, of Zanzureta; of Plaizo of Etzentuan; of Lintezon and Selderich of Tindinzeon; of Cinecas and Cleceiet of Falkaleit; of Seramensa and Junsa, of Sederone, between the Atlantian and the Ancient and Modern art of coloring. Furthermore, his painted figure of "St. Sebastian," for the papal legate in Brescia, having numerous replicas; his great painting in representative record, life size, of the battle of Cadore (burned in 1577), representing the moment at which the Venetian, Captain D'Alviano, fronted the enemy with horses and men crashing down into the stream, a work which elevated him, artistically, to the rank of Raphael and Michel Angelo, and of Rubens of a later period. Other famous achievements are his portraits of Charles V, and Philip II; his singular painting, called "Divine and Human Love," in the Borghese Gallery, Rome; the "Venus," of Florence; the "Portraits of Twelve Cæsars;" the representation of the "Virgin in the Temple," Venetian Academy; S. Spiritio, in the Church of the Salute; "Cain killing Abel," the "Sacrifice of Abraham," and "David and Goliath," and "Ecce Homo," Venice Gallery; the "Venus and Cupid," of Florence; the "Venus" of Madrid, and the "Supper of Emmaus," the Louvre; a trinity, representing Charles V, with his family and others, as in shrouds, praying to the God-head, Moses, and other persons, is also portrayed; the "Martyrdom of St. Laurence," "Christ" crowned with thorns, the Louvre; "Diana and Callisto," "Jupiter and Antiope," the "Magdaline," "Christ in the Garden," and the "St· Jerome," in the Brera gallery, Milan; the "Battle of Lepanto," of the Madrid.

His further influence, in relation to the perfection of portrait painting, by spirit aid and pre-historic inspired ideas, he manifested through his works in stately style, as embodied through simple perception and feeling, as evidenced by his representation of Alphonso, Duke of Ferrara, at Madrid; the same Duke and his wife, Laura Dianti, commonly caled "Titian and his Mistress," in the Louvre; of Frances I, in the Louvre; various likenesses of himself; the one of Paul III, also the same Pope with his grandsons, Cardinal Alessandro, and Duke Ottavio, Naples; Pietro Aretino, the Pitti Palace; Titian's daughter, Lavina, with a fan, in the Dresden Gallery; and the same with a jewelled casket, in the Lord Cowper's collection; the "Cornaro Family," Alnwick Castle; "L'Homme au Gant," in the Louvre; an historically unknown personage, youthful and handsome, the *ne plus ultra* of portraiture. Anstacia informs us that the personage above referred to, as being unknown by modern artists, was an adopted son of Titian, an orphan, whose original name was El-sin-is-ter, of Italian birth, but after adoption, was called Zĕnt' zër-lä, a term that referred to his spirit sensitiveness.

He became the adopted son of Titian at ten years of age, and passed to spirit life in his twenty-third year.

This youth had been attracted to Titian through his wonderful artistic ability, as made manifest at that early age, and also by his pure and innocent life, which characteristics he maintained to the last day of his earth life, for he was more a spirit than a mortal during that period of time, and was therefore adopted and educated by Titian, as an artist or painter. If he had remained in the mortal form, through his great talent and sensitive organism, attuned to spirit influence, as it was, he would have made one of the world's greatest painters.

After his disembodiment he was greatly missed and mourned by Titian, who painted the portrait of him, above mentioned, as a memorial of his beautiful life—a monument, that when thus understood, should yield its influence upon the lives of all who look upon and admire it.

His "Sansobino," "Eleonora, Duchess of Urbino;" "Francesco, duke of Urbino," "Catherine Cornaro, queen of Cyprus," all four of which are in the Uffizi Palace, etc., are further grand acquisitions.

In the art of coloring, handling and assemblage of subjects, creative invention, harmonious effects, Titian stands an unrivaled representation of the art of painting, which as an epi-cycle of influence, moving on the deferent of that of the greater Art Cycle of Painting, is an important link connecting the great Atlantian achievements, through the above-named pre-historic artists and their works, co-operative with the epi-cycles established by Bellini, Carpaccio, Giorgione, Tintoretto, etc., etc., to the more modern epi-cycles.

He caught the idea of Atlantian landscape, in its grandeur, in advance of the ideas re-embodied by the above-named prehistoric artists, or rather in supremacy to theirs, which he re-embodied in the representation of his home country, the region of the hill-summits of Cadore, to the Adriatic Sea. In these he portrayed the turreted Dolomite Alps, in lifelike grandeur, causing them and all their accompaniments of objective nature, to command the admiration of the observer, who, through the sense of sight, has been charmed with the artist's force therein embodied.

His paintings, being numerous, have been a great influence upon the artistic world, as evidenced by the great collection throughout the country. In the London National gallery there are nine; eighteen in the Uffizi; seven in the Naples Museum; eighteen in the Louvre; eight in the Venetian Academy; forty-one in the Madrid Museum, etc., etc., all of which manifest in favor of his great faculty in color and surface achievements. His first pictures were confined to the grade of red and green; his latter to that of deep yellow and blue, co-operative with common pigments. In his minglings of white, black and red, as a body, replicating various tints and mingling the colors to the ultimatum of carnation, or flesh colors, he re-embodied the Atlantian ideas of producing flesh colors, which they had perfected to a higher degree; an art which was, to a certain extent, re-embodied in the pre-historic works of the above-named pre-historic artists. Therefore, from the Atlantian development, through spirit guidance, co-operative with the influence of Giorgione's knowledge of the principles that "red comes forward to the eye," "yellow retains the rays of light," and that "blue assimilates to shadow" (which latter he gained knowledge of at the time of his co-partnership with Giorgione), Titian was led to further develop the principle into grander utility, wherein, by his genius in the management of colors and blendings, he was able to represent to the life, the glow of the late afternoon, the passionate ardor of early sundown, and general effects, such as lighting or illuminating his pictures.

Therefore all the foregoing works of Titian give evidence of his great influence over contemporary and subsequent artists, through his technical usage, both in fresco and oil painting, regarding color tone, luminosity, richness, texture, true representation of subjects, dignity and grace of pose, profound expression, sublime beauty, and the rendition of technical art, grand and beautiful in every detail; all of which afford him the honor of being one of the most important epi-cycle links, influentially, that connects the great artistic works of Atlantis, re-embodied in the works of the pre-historic artists, with the Ancient and the Modern epi-cycles that move on the deferent of the great Art Cycle of Painting.

Paul Veronese, of the sixteenth century, last of the great cycle of painters who composed the Venetian School, influenced through re-embodied ideas, which he further developed.

In evidence of his greatness, such qualities have been pointed out as manifested through his works, embracing the representation of palatial splendor, architectural grandeur and stately vista; personal dignity in sumptuous costumes; crowded assemblies; luxuriant environments; graceful poise of action and limb; rythmic movement; tints in sweet and lordly variation; pictorial inspiration born of the comprehensive eye and magical hand, rather than of the mind; comeliness and beauty of form and face, as drawn from life subjects; supreme representation; richness of drapery and transparency of shadows; exuberance, co-operative with soberness and serenity; brilliant coloring; high lights and mellow hues, etc., which make his works important links with which to connect the greatness of Atlantian art, through the pre-historic re-embodied ideal epi-cycles, their rise and development, and further re-embodiment, into the ancient, and ultimate condition of the Modern on its artistic course along the deferent of the great Art Cycle of Painting.

Tintoretto, of the sixteenth century, one of the greatest painters belonging to the Venetial School, self-taught, influenced at first through mural paintings and frescoes, and re-embodied ideas which he had embraced through the influence of Michelangelo's designs, and the colorings of Titian. By his numerous works he greatly influenced his contemporaries, and subsequent artists, because of manifest characteristics and genius which he embodied in them, e. g., audacious intrepidity, majestic greatness as a colorist; prodigious execution, wonderful imagination, as conceiver of ideas beautiful and suave, or those of a romantic and heroic nature, turbulent and reckless developments, powerful central thought and great inventive force, concretional imagination, picturesque ideality, perfect and natural treatment of action, gesture, and life-like principles, belonging to form or figure representation, to the exclusion of stiffness or immobility, etc.; all of which are important links in the establishment of the connection between the Atlantian epi-cycle of painting, and those of the pre-historic, Ancient and Modern, as they move along the deferent of the great Art Cycle of Painting.

Moretto and Moroni of the Brescian school, in the sixteenth century, influenced through their forceful embodied ideas, relative to the principles of portrait painting, and altar pieces. These were done by the former artists, and were remarkable for their silver-grey tones and refined modelling.

Romanio, of the same school and period, embodied great influential ideas in his fresco and easel paintings.

Domenico, of the latter part of the fifteenth century, influenced through ideas embodied in his frescoes and mosaic subjects.

Correggio, of the sixteenth century, one of the most celebrated painters of this period, greatly influenced his contemporaries and subsequent artists, through the embodiment of his ideas, especially such as, in their developed manifestations, revealed his genius relative to the force of vivid, impulsive invention, fine execution of pose, and general expression. He wrought both in oil and fresco, for churches and cathedrals.

A dual spirit influence brought to bear upon his sensitive organism, was the cause of his changeable representations, as have been termed "the faults of his excellences," wherein his works have been said to represnt "sweetness lapsing into mawkishness, and affection empty in elevated themes, and lasciviously voluptuous in those of a sensuous type; rapid and forceful action lapsing into posturing and self-display; fineness and sinuosity of contour lapsing into exaggeration and mannerism; daring design lapsing into incorrectness." This, therefore, makes him and his works fitting links with which to connect Atlantian art, through the pre-historc, the Modern-ancient and the Modern epi-cycles, that move on the deferent of the great Art Cycle ot Painting.

Ambrogio Borgognone, of the latter part of the fifteenth century and the early part of the next, an artist of great merit, foremost in the Milanese school, and contemporaneous with Leonardo da Vinci, lent a great influence through the re-embodiment of the ideas of Foppa, and of Zenale; and further developed the artistic quality of facial expression such as ultimated in the manifestation of calm beauty, and of delicate coloring.

Influentially, he becomes a systematic link in favor of faint and clear coloring in fresco, temperament, and oil productions. And as a re-embodier of Teutonic ideas in the qualities of sentimentality, slender and pallid types, fide lity of portraiture, placid and calm expression, storied and minutely diversified backgrounds, etc., he becomes a representative in the epi-cycle of art, moving on the deferent of the Greater Cycle, such as aids in the blending of Atlantian pre-historic art, with the modern-ancient and modern ultimatum.

Leonardo da Vinci, of the fifteenth and sixteenth centuries, primarily of the Florentine school, but creator of the later Milanese school, and the most accomplished painter of his period, extended a great influence to artists who came a century later. These re-embodied his creative ideas, and further developed them, especially those known as the "Lombard painters," of his own and succeeding generations; among these the closest re-embodiers were Salaino, Luini, Cesare da Sesto, Beltraffio, Marco d'Oggiono, etc.

Notwithstanding his many unfinished and lost works, through the force of mixed conditions both from the spirit and the mor tal sides of life, co-operative with his diverse ideas in favor of sculpture, architecture, music, letters and criticism, his influence as a painter was profound and lasting, through the knowledge of ideas which he embodied in his works. He was a student of nature, and wrought more to the life in that respect, and is therefore famed as having co-operated precision with freedom; subtle accuracy of definition with vital movement, and flow of line; adopter of light and shade, as essential elements in perspective art, in contradistinction with the simple elements of color and line. Especially so in modern times, which was in reality a re-embodied idea from the works of the pre-historic artists, Fē-rē-nō'sō of Mē-que'thŭs (Assyria); E-chĕr'hăm of Tindinzeon (Germany); Seramensa of Sederone (Spain), who originated or established and developed, the principles of perspectology, in their respective sections of country, principles thus brought to the ancient artists through spirit inspiration, and influential guidance.

He first influenced by his powerful talent for drawing, sketching, etc., thus further operated upon by siprit influences which caused him to reconceive, and re-embody ideas that had been embodied in the pre-historic works of sand-tracings of Menara, of Siloton (Egypt); the pencil drawings of Ferenoso of Mequethus; the portrait outlining of Pietrus of Zanzureta; the alphabetic delineations and leaf, vine and flower representations, of Balzaric of Etzentuan (Italy); the zig-zag delineations for window decoration by Plaizo of Etzentuan; the alphabetic delincations of Zewanda of Falkaleit; the outlined subjects of Reinchy of Falkaleit; the sand-tracings of Zewonk of Sederone; the slate-outlining of subjects, by Serasco of Sederone, and the same style of work by Seramensa, of the same country, etc.; all of which make him and his works important links, or epi-cycles of art, co-operative with the Great Art Cycle of Painting and Drawing, as they incidentally have moved on the deferent from the Atlantian period of time to the Modern.

Michel Angelo Buonarroti, of the fifteenth and sixteenth centuries, the last and most famous of the great artists of Florence, we have chosen, as one of the principal links in the representative epi-cycle, on the great cycle of painters and paintings. This artist, through the embodied and re-embodied ideas in his works, not only in painting, but in sculpture as well, has been one of the world's greatest influencers through artistic principles that have been, and shall forever be, extended through subsequent artistic minds and their re-embodiments of his ideas and influence, as he was by that of the remote Atlantian artists, extended through the pre-historic, and the ancient, by the embodiments and re-embodiments of the artists of those periods of time, co-operative with the inspiration and guidance of spirit artists contemporaneous with those times long since agone, who silently worked through his sensitive organism. This is evidenced by manifestations that speak forth, in silent declaration of his mighty genius, through such works as his panel painting of circular form in portrayal of the "Holy Family"; in which the Madonna is represented as kneeling on the ground, holding up the Child on her right shoulder, and accompanied by nude figures having place in the background (now in the Uffizi, Florence); his cartoon, or companion to that of Leonardo da Vinci, for the great hall of the Municipal Council, in representation of an incident of the Pisan war, when the soldiery, in the act of bathing, had been surprised by the enemy (incomplete), a work at the time greatly influenced through his re-embodied ideas of violent action, energetic movement, as adopted in Leonardo's battle cartoon, and developed into representation of the spirit of tempestuous fury, as a manifest expression thereof in his cartoon representing the incident in the Pisan war; his representation of the "Virgin and Child with Four Angels", though unfinished, embodies ideas of great grace, severity of feeling and design (National Gallery, London); his representation of the "Entombment of Christ," also unfinished, bears some influence through the more excellent and grander points, as made manifest through the principle of action, etc (National Gallery, London). His great plan, submitted to Pope Julius, for the decoraton of the Sistine Chapel, Rome, is a design of many hundred figures, embodying all the history of creation and of the first patriarchs; with accessory personages of prophets and sibyls dreaming on the new dispensation to come; and in addition, the forefathers of Christ, the whole to be executed, and divided by an elaborate frame work of painting architecture, with a multitude of nameless human figures supporting its several members, or reposing among them, etc. In the main field of the ceiling of the Sistine Chapel, which is divided into four larger, alternating with five smaller fields, he depicted a number of subjects in the following order: (1) the dividing of the light from the darkness; (2) the creation of sun, moon, and stars, and of the herbage; (3) the creation of the water; (4) the creation of man; (5) the creation of woman; (6) the temptation and expulsion; (7) an enigmatical scene, said to represent the sacrifice of Cain and Abel, but rather resembling the sacrifice of Noah; (8) the deluge; (9) the drunkenness of Noah.

In numbers 1, 3, 5, 7 and 9, the field of the picture is reduced, by the encroachment of the architectural framework and supporters. These subjects are flanked at each end by the figure of a seated prophet, or sibyl, alternately; two other prophets are introduced, at each extremity of the series, making seven prophets and five sibyls in all. In the angles to right and left of the prophets, at the two extremities, are the "Death of Goliath," the "Death of Judith," the "Brazen Serpent," and the "Punishment of Haman." In the twelve lunettes above the windows, and in the same number of triangular vaulted spaces over them, are mysterious groups, or pairs of groups, of figures, which from Michelangelo's own time have usually been known as "Ancestors of Christ." The army of nameless architectural and subordinate figures, is too numerous here to be spoken of. The work represents all the powers of Michelangelo as at their best. Disdaining all the accessory allurements of the painter's art, he has concentrated himself upon the exclusive delineation of the human form and face, at their highest power. His imagination has conceived, and his knowledge and certainty of hand have enabled him to realize, attitudes and combinations of unmatched variety and grandeur, and countenances of unmatched expressiveness and power. But he has not trusted, as he came later to trust, to science and acquired knowledge merely; neither do his personages, so much as afterwards, transcend human possibility, or so far leave the facts of actual life behind them. In a word, his sublimity, often in excess of the occasion, is here no more than equal to it; moreover it is combined with the noblest elements of grace, and even of tenderness. As for the intellectual meanings of his vast design, over and above those which reveal themselves at a first glance, or by a bare description—they are, from the nature of the case, inexhaustible, and can never be perfectly defined. Whatever the soul of this great Florentine, the spiritual heir of Dante, with the Christianity of the Middle Age not shaken in his mind, but expanded and transcendentalized, by the knowledge and love of Plato—whatever the soul of such a man, full of suppressed tenderness and righteous indignation and of anxious questionings of coming fate, could conceive, that has Michelangelo expressed, or shadowed forth, in this great and significant scheme of paintings. Their details, it must remain for every fresh student to interpret in his own manner."

Furthermore, his subsequent representation of the colossal and multitudinous "Last Judgment," the most famous of single pictures in the world, which has place on the great end wall above the altar of the Sistine Chapel, to supersede the frescoes there wrought by Perugino, is one through which his embodied ideas manifest influentially the characteristics and qualities of artistic science; fiery and daring conceptions; nudity in artistic human form; extremity of action and predicament, to the abandonment of moderation, beauty and tenderness, a condition as compared with that which guided his brush in the execution of the great ceiling ornamentaton, shows a conflicting spirit influence, that not only controlled the vibrations of his own mind, at the time, but further influenced, by the thoughts proceeding from the minds of the great populace. This, impregnated by the passionate and embittered theological temper of the times, is one of the greatest controlling mediums of result, directly, reversely, adversely, or diversely, in accord with circumstantial conditions, in all the pursuits and avenues of life; hence, one should look well to opposing, as to harmonious influences, in view of their aspirations for ascendency or supremacy, etc.

In further consideration of the fact, artistically speaking, we note the difference, influentially, between the grander and purer inspiration manifesting through the frescoes on the ceiling of the Sistine Chapel, and that of the representation of "The Last Judgment" on the end wall, or the frescoes in the Capela Paulina (another chapel in the Vatican), where the athletic, unclothed human forms, are represented in every variety and extremity of action and predicament. Void of moderation, beauty and tenderness, in contrast with the consolatory aspects of Christianity, the picture gives evidence of influence, in harmony with the passionate and embittered theological temper of the times, which through his indignant nature, found lodgment in the mental organism of the artist, to the extent of a conception, and creation of ideas, not harmonious in the oneness of purpose. Hence his apparent decline in art development, noticeable through the process work, in its extension from that of the frescoes on the ceiling of the Sistine Chapel, to "The Last Judgment," on the end wall, and further manifest in his frescoes in representation of "The Conversion of Paul," and the "Martyrdom of Peter," in the Capela Paulina, or Pauline Chapel in the Vatican. This great artist, through his varied styles of work, extended a dual influence, one, a condition arising from his embodiment of the grander and purer ideas, as manifest through his former works, and that of the frescoes on the Sistine Chapel ceiling, and the other, arising from the embodiment of such ideas as are incorporated in the representation of "The Last Judgment," on the end wall, manifesting an influence, to weaker individuals, whose idealistic natures vibrate in harmony with improper energy, violent action, terribleness; departure from nature and its pure laws, in the various manifestations of action, holding rigidly to scientific deductions from the abstract laws of structure and movement; degeneration of qualities, in coloring and general expression, hence a lowering in the scale of charm and grace.

Finally, as the mixed thought vibrations, emanating from both spirit and mortal minds, cease to vibrate through his sensitive brain, each having found repose in its own realm, the influential condition becomes less changeable.

The above-named masters, from the list of three hundred and

fifty-eight celebrated painters, representing the seventeen principal districts or divisions in the Italian school of Painting, from the thirteenth to the sixteenth century inclusive, viz: Lucca and Pisa, Siena, Florence, Umbria, Padua, Arezzo, Venice, Brescia, Verona Ferrara, Bologna, Modena and Parma, Cremona, Milan, Rome, and Naples, give evidence of the powerful influence thus extended, and make them proper links, with which to connect up the epi-cycle of Painting, in that region, while moving over the deferent of the Great Art Cycle, throughout all time.

Raphael Senzio of the fifteenth and sixteenth centuries, whom we have chosen as one of the principal representative links, in the Great Cycle of Painters and Paintings, is acknowledged to be the most universally popular artist of the world, since the time when written history began. His works, through both embodied and re-embodied ideas, have held a profound influence, both contemporaneously and subsequently, relative to the development of the art of painting, as well as that of fresco and cartoon productions.

In the days of his youth, Raphael re-embodied such ideas as influenced religious sentiment, and grace of motive; an adopted usage through the influence of his father's works and instruction, also delicacy and great care in general detail, from ideas embodied in the works of the Van Eycks, which in extension he re-embodied in his own, he having made a study of them in the ducal residence of Umbino. Later he was also influenced bv general ideas, embodied in the works of Perugino, his tutor.

In the sixteenth century, he entered upon his independent influental mission, as evidenced by his four pictures, for the churches at Citta di Castello. The first of these is a guild-banner, painted on one side with the "Trinity," and below, kneeling figures of St. Sebastian and St. Rocco. On the reverse side is a "Creation of Eve," through which beautiful grace and breadth of treatment are manifested; second, "The Coronation of S. Niccole Tolentino" (now destroyed); third, "The Crucifixion" (now in the Dudley collection), which is a fine panel, eight feet six inches in height, five feet five inches in width, in representation of "The Virgin," "St. John," "St. Jerome" and "St. Mary Magdalene;" fourth, his extremely beautiful and highly finished "Sposalizio" (now in the Brera Gallery, Milan), through which he manifests an influence in favor of the qualities of "sweetness of expression" and "grace of attitude;" the Connestabile "Madonna," his finest painting during his Perugenian period, is a round panel on which he represents the Virgin reading from a book of hours, which in fact is a re-embodied idea of his father's.

During his Florentine period, he influenced through such works as his two panels, in representation of "St. George" and "St. Michael," now in the Louvre, which give evidence of a transition from the mannerisms of Perugino, to quality ideas, as embodied in the works of other artists and sculptors, and which he re-embodied in favor of development. This fact broadened his influence in the art of drawing, beautifying color, adding gracefulness to composition, giving dramatic expression and precision of line, and a better representation of the human form; subtleties of modelling and soft beauty of expression; nobility of composition, and skillful treatment of drapery in dignified folds; and general perspective qualities, which ultimated in the creation of a new style of an eclectic order, manifest through such works as his large picture of the "Coronation of the Virgin," now in the Vatican, a beautiful production, renowned for its strong religious sentiment, and therefore it thus influenced. His "Dudley Graces," and his "Knight's Dream of Duty and Pleasure," in the National Gallery, London; "Apollo and Marsyas," a lovely panel, rich in color and graceful in arrangement, in the Louvre, are also sources of influence.

Furthermore, a great influence is manifest through such chief paintings, purely his own, as the "Madonna del Grand Duca" (Pitti); "Madonna del Giardino" (Vienna); the "Holy Family with the Lamb" (Madrid); the "Ansidei Madonna" (National Gallery); the Borghese "Entombment;" Cowper's "Madonna" at Panshanger; "La bella Giardiniera" (Louvre); the Eszterhazy "Madonna del Cardellino" (Uffizi); the "Tempi Madonna (Munich); the "Colonna Madonna" (Berlin); the Bridgewater "Madonna" (Bridgewater House); the Orleans "Madonna" (Duc d'Aumale's collection); the "Entombment of Christ" (Palazzo Borghese, Rome), etc.

During his Roman period, we find him supremely positioned, thus influencing contemporaneously with such artists as Michelangelo, Signorelli, Perugino, Pinturicchio, Lorenzo, Loretto, Peruzzi, Sodoma, etc., etc., through such embodied and re-embodied ideas as are made manifest or expressive through such works as his exquisitely wrought portraits of Bindo Altoviti, now at Munich; his famous paintings and frescoes in the Vatican, Rome, a series having place over the Apastamenti Borgia, to supersede the fresco decorations already there, which had been executed by the great artists, Bonfigli, Perugino, Piero della Francesca, Andræ del Casiagno, Signorelli, and Sodoma. Julius II. had caused these to be removed, and to be replaced by new designs by Raphael.

Regarding their general assembly, and the influence thereof, we note his works in the section known as the Stanzà, della Segnatura (Papal signature room), (1) his famous "Disputa", a magnificent decorative scheme, in representation of the hierarchy of the Church on earth, and its glory in Heaven. Angels are represented on the upper tier, while nude cherubs are represented as in the act of carrying the books of the Gospels, and are very beautifully wrought. The gilt ground on the Vault, like Perugino's in the "Stanza dell' Incendio," marked with mosaic-like squares, a style commonly practised by decorative painters, was an influential re-embodied idea, under further influence by spirit inspiration, co-operative with the re-embodied ideas of the mosaic art, that had developed from the embodied ideas of Theonzy and Emucu, the Atlantian Zī'tē Zē-ū-lē-ŭs'zē (mosaic artists), and still further extended through the influence of the pre-historic works of Elongo and Puuco, the Săc'cĕn Et-sī-ĕs'sä (mosaic artists) of Etzentuan, and their subsequent mosaic artists, of Italy. His Medallions on which he portrayed very graceful female figures, representing "Theology," "Science," "Justice" and "Poetry," with small accompanying subjects, respectively harmonious with each.; his noble fresco entitled the "School of Athens," in the Stanza della Segnatura, opposite his "Disputa," in which he has depicted celebrities contemporaneous with the events of Ancient Greece. This list embraces Philosophers, Poets, and men of Science, whom the Church admitted were "inspired from Heaven," who by their zealous works became precursors to the light of Christianity. But who were, in fact, guided and inspired by disembodied spirits, co-operative with their several mental qualities, by which they developed their respective embodied and re-embodied ideas. The truths of spirit return, various manifestation, inspiration, and guidance were even then known to some of the leaders of the Church, but for purposes known to themselves, they put these things in the light of divine revelation, etc.

The central figures of this work are Plato and Aristotle. Below these, on each side, are groups of literary celebrities, skillfully arranged, including the whole *"filosofica famiglia"* of Dante, with Bramante, as the aged Archimedes, represented as stooping over a geometrical diagram. On the left, is a representation of Francesco Maria della Rovera, Duke of Urbino, and on the right, figures of Raphael and Perugino. Over one window is represented a group of poets and musicians, on Mount Parnassus, round a central figure of Apollo, the aggregation being an assembly of finely wrought heads, among which are those of

Dante and Petrarch. Over the opposite windows are graceful figures of the three chief Virtues; Gregory IX is shown giving decretals to a jurist, and on the other side, Justiinan is represented as presenting his code to Trebonianus.

His fine painting, in representation of the "Flaying of Marsyas," is a re-embodied idea from the influence of antique sculpture; hence, an extended influential idea re-developed from the works of Uthre, Axtrey, Adolphus and Entize, of Atlantis, and through those of Conetry of Elteze (Arabia); Edelmaze and Ledelmoz, Denvoses and Tonoka of Siloton (Egypt); Debalbus and Tindegin of Mequethus (Assyria); Therenze, Chalsemenus, Melseos and Secolus, of Zanzureta (Greece); Prozelzo and Callenze, of Etzentuan (Italy); Pedizeustes of Falkaleit (France); Kitrecon and Multsy of Sederone (Spain); and further re-embodied, through the works of ancient sculptors, under spirit inspiration and guidance. Thus was reached the sensitive brain of Raphael—by way of the mental vibratory law in nature—who conceived the idea and re-developed it accordingly. His beautiful small picture in representation of the "Temptation of Eve," is a re-embodied idea co-existent with the same ideal subject, conceived by his contemporary, Dürer, through the same natural law of thought conception.

The same may be said of his fresco representation, of the expulsion of Heliororus from the Temple, having place in La Stanza d'Elidoro, or the one of the repulsion of Atila, from the walls of Rome, by Leo I, who is miraculously aided by the appartition of St. Peter and St. Paul; or the scene of the "Miracle at Bolsena," in which the "real presence" was proved to a doubting priest by the appearance of bloodstains on the Corporal. In this Julius II is represented as kneeling behind the altar, and on the lower space, on each side of the windows, are two groups, one of women and the other of officers of the guard. His fresco painting, in representation of the "Deliverance of St. Peter from Prison," is a wonderful combination and contrast of different qualities of light—as that from the moon, the glory around the angels, and that emanating from the torches of the sentinels.

His representation, in Stanza dell 'Incendio, is of the Incendio del Borgo, miraculously stopped by Leo IV, who is appearing and making the sign of the cross, at a window in the Vatican. The motive for one group on the left foreground was a re-embodied idea taken from the burning of Troy. This has a fine nude figure of Æneas, who is represented as issuing from the burning house, bearing on his back the old Anchises, and also leading the boy, Ascanius, by the hand.

Other finely wrought representations are, the "Madonna of Foligno" (Vatican); the Gervagh "Madonna" (National Gallery); the "Diademed Virgin" (Louvre); the "Madonna del Pesce" (Madrid); portraits of Julius II (Uffizi); the so-called Fornarina (Palazzo Barberini); the Baldassare Castiglione, of the Louvre, etc.; his fresco representing the "Triumph of Galatea" (in the palace of Agostino Chigi, by the Tiber banks); the "Villa Farnesina;" his designs from "Apuleius' Romance of Cupid and Psyche;" his celebrated fresco painting in representation of Sibyls, in Santa Maria della Pace; his "Madonna della Seggiola" (Pitti Palace); his "St. Cecilia" (Bologne); the miniature "Vision of Ezekiel" (Pitti Palace); the "Lo Spasimo," or "Christ Bearing His Cross;" the Madonna called "Della Perla," and the "Madonna della Rosa" (Madrid Gallery); the portrait of Leo X, with Cardinals de' Rossi and de' Medici (Pitti Palace); his large representation, "St. Michael and the Devil" (Louvre); his portrait of a Violin player (Sciarra-Colonna, Palace, Rome); his life-size portrait of the painter Timoteo della Vite, in black and red chalk (British Museum), etc.

Furthermore, there is his extended influence through subjects for cartoon designs, for tapestry copies, such as "Scenes from the Acts of the Apostles;" "Christ in the Delivery of the Keys to St. Peter;" the "Martyrdom of St. Stephen;" "The Conversion of St. Paul;" "Saint Paul in Prison at Philippi," etc. These sixteenth century works, though few, when compared with the marvelous number of works that he produced during his Perugian, Florentine, and Roman periods of greatness, yet represent his marvelous influence through embodiments and re-embodiments, both received and extended, in behalf of the great development of the Art of Painting, through which his wonderful genius and artistic qualities of being, made themselves manifest to the world in such characteristic principles as grand drafting, elegant designing, beautiful coloring, graceful composition, wide range of subjects, varieties of style, profound adherence to the higher spiritual effects and sacred sources of artistic inspiration in all the details of professional art, historically, religiously, politically, mythologically and scenically, and in the broadest sense of the latter; versatility of power, ranging through a scale from the minute to the colossal in representation of subjects.

Therefore, these manifestations of influential genius, added to the characteristics of personal beauty; charm of manner; deep kindliness of heart; sincere modesty; spiritual sensitiveness, subject to profound inspirational guidance; qualities of being that during his short life of thirty-seven years, made him known and loved among men and women, of his day, in all pursuits of life, make him a fitting choice for one of the principal epi-cycle representatives of Art, revolving on the deferent of the Great Cycle of Painting, and therefore an essential connecting link, in the establishment of the same, from the Atlantian period, to the present time.

His versatile nature, tuned in harmony with general art principles, made him susceptible to various spirit influences, who sought him out as a fitting instrument through whom to operate, in pursuance of embodiments and re-embodiments, which they sought to accomplish for the great good of the inhabitants of the material sphere. Hence arose his adaptation, mentally and physically, to the development of various branches of art (like Aristotle of old whom no man has ever surpassed in versatility of genius); hence, his transition of styles from the Perugian to the Florentine, and to the Roman; his adaptation to architectural, sculptural and even to the lesser art designs; and also his love for archæological pursuits in which he was particularly influenced by spirits, who when in the mortal, had been contemporaneous with remote and antequated periods of time.

Therefore, Raphael, being so universally popular, renowned for his merits as a great painter, draughtsman, colorist, and master of graceful compositions; of wide range of subjects and wonderful varieties in style; versatility of power displayed in various subjects, according to occasion; large range of scale, from minute figures, to those of colossal dimension, in co-operation with breadth and vigor; and being personally kind of heart, modest, physically beautiful, charming in manner, was possessed of qualities of being that endeared him to all classes of people, and made him known and loved among men and women of high rank or position in life, the Government and the State., among whom were classed the princes of the Church, distinguished artists and scholars of every kind, in fact, the world-famed men of every class, who influenced through the courts of Julius II. and Leo X.; ambassadors of princes, withal, a father to his pupils—etc., are facts, the aggregation of which, render him a principal link in the representative epi-cycle, not only of Painting, but of Sculpture, Architecture, and the Lesser Arts, as designer of silver service, tersia- work, wood-carving, supervisor of engraving, and also as an archæologist. He was one of the world's greatest influences through embodied and re-embodied ideas and a developer of artistic principles, co-operative with spirit inspiration, holding so great an influence over not only the artists and admirers of art, of the age in which he lived and wrought as a mortal artist, but through the generations intervening between that and the present period of time, as evidenced by his marvelous work, continuous upon the earth plane during its existence as a world, and extending into the great beyond, where from world to world, as a spirit, his qualities of being will continue to develop and extend. They will thus reach out, not only to the realms beyond, but will be reflected back upon the earth, with those of all the other great artists, to inspire the minds of subsequent children of the earth, not only in art, but general spiritual developments through re-embodiments; hence to further aid, in the great connection to be made in the establishment of the epi-cycle of Painting and its movement on the deferent of the Great Cycle of Art.

Peter Paul Rubens of the sixteenth and seventeenth centuries, whom we have chosen as one of the principal links in the great cycle of painters and paintings, was the most eminent representative of Flemish Art, and one of the greatest painters of all the schools. He was under a powerful mortal influence, extending from the works of Michelangelo, Raphael, Titian, Giulio Romano, Tintoretto, Baroccio, Parmigiano, Paul Veronese, etc., co-operative with spirit influence and guidance, and is therefore chosen by us as one of the principal links in the representative epi-cycle of Painting, as one who, through the embodied and re-embodied ideas in his works, established an influence that has reached out, for further extension, to subsequent artists, like that of Michelangelo and Raphael, which will live on forever in the realms of time, space and life. Living quality evidenced by his multitude of works, through which his great genius is made manifest, shows in his representation of "Magdalene Anointing Christ's Feet" (now at Hermetage in St. Petersburg); a re-embodied idea, influenced through the works of Otto Voenius; his religious paintings, the "Invention of the Cross," "The Crowning with Thorns," and "The Crucifixion" (Hospital at Grasse, in Provence); his "Mercury and Psyche," a re-embodied idea of Raphael (Museum at Pesth); his "Heraclitus and Democritus" (Madrid Gallery); the immense picture, the "Baptism of Our Lord" (Antwerp, Gallery); "The Transfiguration" (Museum, Nancy); the portrait of Vincenzo and his Consort, kneeling before the Trinity (Library at Mantua); the large altar-piece, "The Circumcision at St. Ambrogio," at Genoa; the Virgin in a glory of Angels, and two groups of Saints, painted on the wall, at both sides of the high-altar in the Santa Maria, in Valicella, Rome; his large, famous, original representtion of the "Adoration of the Magi," which in dimension is twelve by seventeen feet and contains twenty-eight life-sized figures, arranged in gorgeous attire—warriors in steel armor, horsemen, slaves, and also camels, etc. (Madrid Gallery); the "Raising of the Cross" and the "Descent from the Cross," and the accompanying representation of the "Visitation" and "Presentation in the Temple," on the interior wings (Antwerp Cathedral), embodied and re-embodied ideas, under extended influence, from the fresco work of Ricciarelli, at Trinita de' Monti, and the magnificent picture of Baroccio in the Cathedral of Perugia.

His great influence in Gothic church decorations on ceilings, with the use of fore-shortened figures, thus blending the religious art with the colossal pictures between the twisted columns of the high-altars, extended influences from the works of such masters as Titian, Veronese and Tintoretto, are ideas under embodied and re-embodied conditions, and through further influence of spirit inspiration upon the sensitive brain of Rubens. His twenty-four pictures illustrating the life of Mary de'Medici (queen mother) of France (Louvre); the "Triumph of Henry IV." (Pitti Palazzo), is an extended influence from Mantegna as embodied in his "Triumph of Cæsar" (now at Hampton Court), and further re-embodied by Rubens; his "Assumption of the Virgin," at the high-altar of the Antwerp Cathedral, a peculiar conception and idealistic embodiment, similar to that of Titian's "Assunta," in the cathedral of Verona, each of which is artistically qualified, according to the conditions material and spiritual, co-operative with the genius of the artists, in evidence of receptive inspiration, by two individuals at a considerable distance apart. In his wonderful representation of the "Massacre of the Innocents," he portrays the mothers, defending their children, with nails and teeth (Munich Gallery). His representation of St. Francis attempting to shield the Universe from the Savior's wrath, was a re-embodied idea, influenced through the writings of St. Germain (Brussels Gallery). The "Blessing of Peace" (National Gallery, England); forty or more portraits of his beautiful wife, Helena (in Munich, St. Petersburg, Blenheim, Lichtenstein, Louvre, etc.); the "Feast of Venus;" his portrait of Helena Fourment, ready to enter the bath, or the "St. Ildefonso" (Vienna Gallery); the "Martyrdom of St. Peter," at Cologne; the "Martyrdom of St. Thomas," at Prague; the "Last Judgment of Paris," at Madrid; the "Garden of Love" (Madrid and Dresden); the "Village Feast" (Louvre); and his numerous etchings, such as the head of Seneca, and the beautiful figure of St. Catharine, etc., are other masterpieces.

The foregoing works are but a few of his more than one thousand, the distribution of which has given them place as property of the Kings of Spain, to the number of thirty-two; the Madrid gallery possesses one hundred or more; smaller numbers are in all the principal galleries of Europe, as at Antwerp, Brussels, Paris, Lille, Dresden, Berlin, Munich, Venice, St. Petersburg, London, Florence, Milan, Turin, etc.

The great genius of Rubens is made manifest by the "silent language" of "expression," or characteristic qualities thus embraced, in his thousand and more works, written upon wood, canvas, and other materials, to adorn walls and easels, by the magic of his brush and pencil. These were invisibly guided by the hands of spirit artists, whose mental forces also were in equilibria with his own receptive brain. Hence we look and read therefrom the forceful characteristic quality—manifestations of vigorous design; decorative skill; force of brightness and glow of coloring; energy of character; boldness of composition; striking attitudes; effective grouping; breadth of touch; pictorial conception; perfect design; magnificent drapery; portrayal of life and nature; conceptive fancy of subjects; prodigious faculty in execution; co-blendment of religious and decorative art styles, to the ultimatum of united principles; mixture of the sacred with the mythological, etc., all of which are re-embodied qualities, that further inspired the minds and governed the works of the Flemish school of Artists, for more than a century subsequently.

Likewise was his influence brought to bear upon the epicycle of Engraving, as manifest through the plates of such artists as Soutman, Vorsterman, Pontius, Witdoeck, the two Bolswerts, Peter de Jode, N. Lauwers, etc., who further re-embodied his embodied and re-embodied ideas, upon their plates. Furthermore, the influence extended into the Antwerp school of Engraving, a further extension which linked him influentially into Modern schools, relative to styles, etc.

Finally, the great influence of Rubens, the great master-link in the epi-cycle of painting, not only brought him into favor with various courts, such as at Mantua, and under the patronage of Mary de' Medici, the Duchess of Gonzoga and Louis XIII. of France; Philip IV, of Spain; Charles I, of England; Isabella, of Spain; Ferdinand, of the Netherlands, etc., but established him as a model art influence, worthy to be followed by artists and art-loving patrons, for all time to come.

Yea, truly! The light of this great artistic star, in co-operation with the influence of other spirit artists, like that of all the other great representative stars, or epi-cycles of Art, will continue to illumine the progress of Painting, on the Earth plane, and each his own, as they eternally move on the deferent of the Great Art Cycle, thus to blend with that of the worlds and planets having place throughout immeasurable space, incalculable time, and endless life! A mission belonging to spirit artists, while they, during their onward progression and attraction as art epi-cycles, pass from sphere to sphere, world to world, planet to planet, and through the endless zones of eternity, thus making the linkings that must establish the infinite condition and endless existence of each, co-operative with the Great Spirit Art Cycle, on whose deferent they move, to regions beyond, or zones counterpart to the material; representing an assembly of epi-cycles, as it were, to form a Great Art Zodiac Cycle, beginning with the Atlantian period, passing into the pre-historic, the Ancient, the Mediæval, and the Modern, thence on into the epi-cycle divisions, or zones embracing the myriads of worlds, throughout the regions of space, which are the influential signs of the great Zodiacal, or Art Cycle.

Space will not permit of further comment on the influence, through the embodiments and re-embodiments of the ideas, belonging to the art, as having developed in the various other countries, so we leave the reader here, to search history for further links in the great cycle of painters and paintings that will make the extension into the twentieth century of the art zone.

NOTE:—The author of this work permits an explanation here that he too modestly withheld in earlier parts of this work. He has written of the Great Art of the world only after a long, careful and painstaking study of it, made in its own chief centers and high places, England Ireland, Scotland, Belgium, Holland, Switzerland, Germany, France and Italy. Mr. Leslie prepared for his foreign tour and made it for the central purpose of studying various forms of Art, but especially celebrated Paintings in the Galleries, Churches and Royal Palaces of the old world.—EDITOR.

USH ZI'TE ZE-U'LE-US ENT AT'LAN-TIS, OR THE MOSAIC ART IN ATLANTIS.

TELTZIE XXXV.

The Zī'tē Zē-ū'lē-ŭs or Tessellate style of Art work, had its origin, or remote ideal embodiment, in Atlantis, where before the close of the third Efrementrum, or the time of the great submergence, it had developed into quite a degree of perfection, in regard to condition and practical usage.

Theonzy, a zite zeule (mosaic artist) who was a native of Teltzie Et, and who dwelt and worked in the aistie of Atara, principally, beginning with the last half of the second Efremetrum, and extending beyond the first half of the third, was the original establisher and developer of that style of art in Atlantis. He wrought extensively and also instituted a large school, in the aistie of Atara, where he taught many pupils, both the local people and from adjacent Teltzie'. He first wrought from wood, when he harmoniously co-mingled and blended various colors into tessellated order. At a later period, however, he conceived the idea of co-mingling precious stones, with marble, but he never wrought with common stone, or prepared clay.

During his work in the third Efremetrum, he had advanced in the zite zeuleus, so that his productions were in representation of many subjects, as his fancy prompted. These were relative to, or harmonious with, the occasioned utility, the product being chiefly of ornamentation on floors, tables, and the surfaces of similar furniture, but never for mural or pictorial purposes, such as portraits.

E-mū'cū, a pupil of Theonzy, and also a native of Teltzie Et, came into great renown during the second quarter of the third Efrementum. At first he continued to develop the style of his tutor, Theonzy; but being of a progressive turn of mind, he developed the characteristics of the art as already attained, and embodied such ideas as made his product more beautiful, the designs more varied and the utility more extended. In fact, much of the style of the ancient, mediaeval and modern re-embodiments.

Passing into Siloton (Egypt), we find the zā'thŭs lē-ĕl'vä

(mosaic art) under development by zā'thŭs lē-ĕl-vä-zē'ĕts (mosaic artists), co-operative with spirit guidance and impressional influence.

Crē-nē-ăl'lŭs, a Silotonan, was the first noted pre-historic zathus leelvazeet (mosaic artist) of Siloton, who came into the earth life about five hundred and fifty years before the Adomic period. He lived to the mortal age of about one hundred and seven, and dwelt in the pre-historic town of Căs-ī-dī-ō'nä, the home of Equea, the painter.

At first, through the influence of the works of the lē-ŭth'mäs (painters) co-operative with spirit guidance and inspiration, he was led to conceive the idea of placing pieces of white, red, black and dark grey colored woods together, which ultimately gave him the idea of reducing the pieces to the form of squares, and finally to that of cubes. These he wrought into his zathus patterns, but designed no special subjects or representations, excepting an arrangement of alternate colors; but this resulted in a ground or body of squares, bordered with a line of triangles, having place as ornamental work on the surface of tables, shelves, and similar pieces of furniture.

Gē-lē'sŭs, a son of Creneallus, was born when his father was fifty years old, and lived to the mortal age of ninety-five. He spent the first twenty-five years of his life in pursuit of the study of the leelva of zathus, under the tutorship of his father, after which he continued the art independently, in the town of Casidiona. At first he held to the style of his father's works, which he further developed artistically.

Later in life, he conceived the idea of taking squares of various colored slate-stone, to which he added painted ones, of other colors, thus to form floor steps, and the walks leading up to them, and about the buildings (the latter three, or the exterior work, having no painted zā-thŭs'ĕts, but all of the natural colors of the slate-stone). These he ornamented in various ways, by zig-zag, diagonal or bias layers, of various colored zathusets (mosaics).

Further influence, from the pre-historic works of Gelesus of Siloton, whose ideas were re-embodied in the works of subsequent zathus leelvazeets, and later mosaic artists of Egypt, until the more complete establishment of the art, had extended throughout Northern Africa, Spain, Asia Minor, Syria, etc., as evidenced by the remnant, antequated, and later mosaic work, found in Algeria, Tunis, and Carthage, of North Africa, all equally elaborate in detail even as those of Rome, the chief difference being in the change of materials from which the *tesserae* were formed, in accord with the products of the country, viz: being marble of various colors and varieties of tints, natural to these regions, e. g., four different shades each of red, green, and yellow; deep black, various shades of brown, and of bluish greys, pure white, white slightly striated with grey, etc. Those of Carthage were especially beautiful, being wrought with large spaces between the tessellated designs, ornamented with exquisitely wrought, sweeping curves of acanthus and other leaves, in rich design, co-operative with a gradation of tints, in development of the principles of light and shade.

The remote style of mosaic ornamentation of jewelry, ivory thrones, and other furniture, in close resemblance to the cloissonnee enamel, such as royal cartouches; ornaments formed of papyrus, and other plants; figures of deities; ivory carvings in low relief, enriched by inlay of fragments of lapis-lazuli; colored glass, and other gem-like stones. These, when utilized in representation of the eyes, to large heads, made them expressively noticeable, co-existent with the figured panels, borders to the dresses; the thrones on which figures are seated; the ornaments above the cartouche; and symbols upon the latter, thus inlaid with colors; on carved staffs and sceptres; heads of animals, griffins, etc., as wrought in Nineveh and Egypt (specimens of which are now in the British Museum, London); the pre-historic column-caps, wall tiles, and other objects, executed at Tel al Yahudiya, in Lower Egypt, the designs of which are in some form of the Papyrus plant. These are wrought into form by means of brilliantly colored bits of glass, or enameled earthenware, sunk into tiles or columns. The idea being the same as that re-embodied in the pre-historic and ancient works of Greece; all of which are re-embodied ideas in further extension of those conceived by Creneallus and Gelesus, and their subsequent pre-historic and remote ancient zathus leelvazeets, and mosaic artists, of Siloton and Egypt.

The wood-mosaics, of the fourteenth to the seventeenth centuries, were considerably used in Egypt, in the process of decoration in Mohammedan buildings, as evidenced by the idea made manifest through the magnificent pulpits and the woodwork in the mosques, at Cairo and Damascus. The patterns are wrought by the process of inlay, and the materials utilized are small pieces of various colored woods, some being further characterized with an ornamentation of bits of mother-of-pearl, and minutely carved ivory. The ultimatum is a marvelous assemblage of magnificence, established by the co-union of beautiful materials and exquisite workmanship; grace and idealistic design; monuments in evidence of modern re-embodiment, of styles that had been formerly re-embodied by the ancient Copts of that region, who thus ornamented their grand *inconostases* and other screens, in their churches, etc.

Passing into Zanzureta (Greece), we find the zŏn'där ī-ō-ŏn (mosaic art) under development by zŏn'där ī-ō-ŏn-sō'ēs (mosaic artists), co-operative with spirit guidance and impressional influence.

Dăn-frē'sä, a Zanzuretan, was the first noted pre-historic zŏn'där ī-ō-ŏn'sō (mosaic artist) of Zanzureta, whose influence began about 3340 B. C., and who lived to the mortal age of one hundred and twelve years, dwelling in the pre-historic sē-mä'sä (town) of Zŭ-zē-rē-lē'ŭs, the home of the frĭs'cŏn (painter), Lusius, about fifty years after the latter had passed to spirit life.

During the time intervening between the close of the earth life of Polugrutus, the noted friscon, and the beginning of the earth life of Danfresa, there was a style of painting being produced, simliar to the pre-historic zondar ioon, which was the chief influence that gave rise to the zondar ioon proper, as established by Danfresa.

His first zondar works were all wrought of wood, and consisted in the placement of various sized cubes, of white, yellow, red, walnut, or shades of brown or dark gray, and black wood, in tessellated form, alternating the colors, not only to form a beautiful groundwork, but so as to represent geometrical figures in ornamental patterns, and the borders to them, which when made had place on table surfaces and similar furniture surfaces.

During the latter portion of his artistic career (for he worked until nearly the close of his earth life), Danfresa had perfected his work by a marvelous system of joining the Zondarnuc, and final polishment of the tessellated surface, so as to render it extremely beautiful. In fact, in those two respects, no finer work has been done in any subsequent age.

E-ză-ĕn'drĭc, a son of Danfresa, was born when his father was fifty years of age. He lived to the mortal age of eighty-five years, and continued to reside in the semasa of Zuzereleus. At first, he wrought entirely from wood and in the style that his father had.

Later, he conceived the idea of moulding clay into Zondar forms, or cubes, which he dried, hardened, and then painted in various colors. These he used principally for doorsteps, and walks leading up to them. Still later, he used marble material for the same purposes; and further, used them for forming floors to buildings, in which latter he changed the style by forming large squares of block representations, by the assemblage of the small zondarsu (mosaics) by alternating the colors, which in turn he represented by the interlaying of two different colored lines of zondarsu, which formed a very handsome surface.

Further influences, from the pre-historic works of Ezændric, of Zanzureta, and Elongo of Etzentuan, were re-embodied in those of subsequent zondar ioonsoes, and later mosaic artists of Greece and Italy; until the more complete establishment of the art had spread out into various countries, as England, Germany, France, etc. This is evidenced by the antique, and later mosaic works, of those regions, as at York, Woodchester, Cirencester, etc. These are as elaborately wrought as those at Rome, and those of other countries, equally as elaborate in detail, but with changes, such as were occasioned by the utility of materials, natural to the locality in which the mosaic work was wrought.

Other mosaics are, the Ancient and Mediæval pavements, formed by cubes of marble, glass, and clay, of sectile process and style; the walls and vaults designed by an assemblage of pieces of opaque glass in small cubes, so arranged as to form complicated patterns of the fictile or vermiculate process and style; the ancient specimens of tessellated work, such as in Sparta, Athens, Olympia, etc., all of which are but re-embodied ideas, having extended to the period of their establishment, thus influenced by the works of Ezaendric, subsequent zondar iconso, and later mosaic workers.

Furthermore, the mosaic work in the pavements of the early temples, as in the pronaos of the Temple of Olympia, re-embodied ideas extending down from the pre-historic influence of Danfresa, and his son, Ezaendric. The work of Sosus, of Pergamus, subsequent to the time of Alexander, who was celebrated in history as having introduced the style of "floor decoration" with imitations of characteristic objects, was a still further extended idea, having been re-embodied from the same source, when it spread out into the towns of Pergamus, Ephesus, Alexandria, etc., of the Macedonian period.

Again, the ornamentation on column-caps, wall tiles, and other objects (as was the custom in Egypt), by placing bits of brilliantly colored glass, or enameled earthenware wrought in representation of papyrus plants, sunk into tiles or columns, as in the Erectheum at Athens, fifth century B. C., whose white marble columns had bases ornamented with a plant-like design, in which pieces of colored glass were inserted to enhance the beauty of the main line of the pattern—all of which are re-embodied ideas, in further extension of those conceived and wrought out by Danfresa, Ezaendric, and subsequent pre-historic zondar ioonsoes, of Zanzureta.

The Roman mosaics, both of marble and opaque glass, so extensively used for ornamentation of floors and walls, are also re-embodied ideas, having extended from the influence of Ezændric, of Zanzureta, co-operative with that of Elongo, the prehistoric saccen etsies of Etzentuan.

Other influences and re-embodiments are made manifest in such extensions as that at the Isola Farnese, nine miles from Rome, which is formed of tile-like slabs of green glass; the sectile pavement on the Palatine Hill, formed of various shaped pieces of glass, in black, white, and deep yellow; at Pompeii, where nearly every house gives evidence of the extended influence of mosaic art, as manifested through the designs wrought on floors, walls, and even in vestibules; glass and marble mixtures, of *tesserae* mosaic work, beam forth in brilliantly colored expressions; graceful flowing patterns, geometrical designs, and picture-like subjects of great elaboration, have place in many places of note. In the "House of the Faun," is to be seen one of the most noted. It is a minutely-wrought scene of "The Battle of Isis," in representation of the moment of Alexander's victorious charge against the cavalry of Darius. The skillfully executed and famous mosaic pictorial piece, known as "Pliny's Doves," found in Hadrian's Villa, at Tivoli (in the Capitoline Museum), in which art manifests through such qualities as the light on the gold bowl, the plumage of the doves, and the reflection in the water of the drinking dove, which give evidence of wonderful proficiency in the Art of Mosaic Designs, etc., at that period of time.

Other splendid instances are the mosaic decorations on the vault of the Ambulatory of the circular church, of S. Cartanza, built by Constantine the Great, outside the walls of Rome, fourth century; those on the main compartment of the vault of S. Cortanza, the surface of which is covered with vine branches laden with grapes, gracefully twined in curves over the space, the center figure being that of a large medallion on which is represented a life-size male bust, beneath which the artist wrought vintage scenes, oxen carts transporting grapes, and boys treading them in the vat. Geometrical designs of circles, framing busts, and full-length figures, with gracefully wrought borders, are an accompaniment, on other parts of the vault; in the ruined Christian Chapel, discovered by M. Renan, there was a fine mosaic pavement that covered the nave and aisles, which was characterized by a design of circles enclosing figures emblematic of the seasons, the months, and the winds; the same being co-existent with similar styles, discovered on the site of Roman Italica near Seville, Spain; others at Ephesus and Hallicarnassus, in Asia Minor, and at Neby Yumas near Sidon, Syria. The whole constituting a condition that exists through the influence of the works of Danfresa and Ezaendric, of Zanzureta, and Elongo and Puucu of Etzentuan, co-operative with the various spirit influences and inspirations from the departed artists of Zanzureta, and also of Siloton. Hence, the idea's wide distribution into the above-named countries, in co-operation with the influence of mortal artists, who conceived, developed, and re-embodied the same, in their works, above referred to.

The gorgeous mosaics and inscriptions on the walls of the great mosque of S. Sophia, Constantinople, Turkey, and on the walls and dome of S. Saviour's in the same city, of Byzantine influence, are even richer than the mosaics at Ravenna and Pal ermo. Those in the monasteries of Mt. Athos, at Salonica, and at Daphne, near Athens, identical in style with those in Italy of the same date, are evidence conclusive of the mortal and spirit influence, re-embodied, from the pre-historic works of Danfesa and Ezændric of Zanzureta; and of the mosaic artists that re-embodied their ideas during the time intervening between the sixth and fourteenth centuries, in those regions. There are other examples, as the even more beautiful mosaic work in the "Dome of the Rock," at Jerusalem, from the seventh to the eleventh century; those in the sanctuary of the great mosque of Cordova, of the tenth century; in the Cathedral of S. Gereon at Cologne, Germany, and at Parenzo, Austria-Hungary; the grand display of mosaics over the nave columns in the Church of the Nativity, at Bethlehem, Palestine, similar to those in Monreale; the extremely minute diptych of the eleventh century, originally in the Imperial chapel, in Constantinople, now preserved in the "Opera del Duomo," Florence, a work in *tesserae* of glass and metal, said to be the only existing example of *tesserae* wrought of solid metal; it is in representation of saints, and the portrayal of inscriptions, each tessera thereof, being scarcely larger than a pin's head.

Passing into Etzenzuan (Italy), we find the săc'cĕn ĕt'sī (mosaic art) under development by săc'cĕn ĕt-sī-ĕs'sä (mosaic artists), co-operative with spirit inspiration and further guidance.

E-lŏn'gō was the first noted pre-historic saccen etsies (mosaic artist) in Etzentuan, whose influence began about five hundred years before the Adomic period, and therefore was contemporaneous with the palzaco (painter) Senzecozy, and lived to the mortal age of one hundred and five. He was a descendant from the Jē-rē-thē'ăns, of Etzentuan, and dwelt in the pre-historic town of Qū-ĕr'rĕr, the home of the palzaco Balzaric.

His first saccensa (mosaics) were wrought in wood, at which time he established the style of co-uniting natural colored woods, such as red, white, black, dark grey, and those of peculiar grain. These he at first matched, and laid together in squares, with which to form the top surface of tables, etc.

At a later period, he conceived the idea of utilizing small cubes of soft stone, and finally of marble, for the purpose of constructing floors to buildings. He never developed the ornamental style to any marked degree, yet he carried out the idea of tessellated form, for the ground or body, by the alternation of colors, which to a certain extent beautified the work, and he did some zig-zag formations, thus approaching the ornamental idea.

Pū-ū'cō, an Etzentuan saccen etsi, was a descendant from the Jeretheans, a pupil of Elongo, and a native of Querrer, who was born about four hundred and twenty-five years before the Adomic period, and lived in the mortal ninety-five years. His first work was in continuation of the styles of Elongo, with further development of the same. At a later period, he conceived the idea of placing jerser saccensa of square, circular and oval foms, so the assemblage formed window panes, and the alternation of colors, viz: the natural tints of the jerser, with saccensa of the same material, which he stained with various colors, formed patterns and designs, which served the purpose of window ornamentation, as well as that of light-giving mediums, similar to the stained glass windows of modern times.

As the ages went by, the influence of these and subsequent saccen etsiessa, spread out through Italy, Sicily, etc., causing embodiment after embodiment, re-embodiment after re-embodiment, of the mosaic art, in all its developed forms and diverse styles until the above-named regions, contemporaneous with various others, have been and are richly possessed with antequated, mediæval and modern products, in glorious testimony of the powerful influence of disembodied spirit intelligence, through their silent co-operation with that of the embodied spirit intelligence, operating through the power of genius, talent, and sensation. The latter law, alone, can roll up the curtain on the stage of pre-historic antiquity, thus to reveal the hidden links, as they formed that portion of the Art Cycle belonging to past or remote ages, and therefore to make possible the connections that are to re-establish a more complete Historical Cycle, which can only be done through data links, re-assembled from the events of time, replaced and verified by spirit knowledge and revelation, to form the Great Cycle of Art. The extension of this has given rise to ancient, mediæval, and modern products of mosaic art, such as adorned the villas and palaces, baths and forums, floors and pavements of Rome, e. g., the large mosaic, found on the Aventine Hill (now in the Laterano), in representation of all manner of remains, from a feast. It was wrought by Heraclitus, and is a re-embodied idea from the extended influence of a pre-historic saccen etsies and his pupil, Puucu, co-operative with spirit influence.

The representation, of a battle between Alexander and the Persians, found in the Czsa del Fauno, at Pompeii, is a still further extension of the re-embodied idea of saccensa.

The inlaying of wood, known as *tarsia-work,* or marquetry, in process of development and usage from remote time, is also an extended idea from the influence of the works of the above-named pre-historic saccen etsies.

Passing into the mediæval period of Italy, we find the influence of the pre-historic saccen etsiessa of Etzentuan, in a condition of prolific extension, and conditioned development, as evidenced by the glass cube decorations on the walls and vaults. The large pieces of marble and small *tesserae* have been assembled to form pavements; the small rectangular and triangular pieces of glass beautifully adorn the marble pulpits, columns and other architectural designs, and the mosaics of wood, etc., such as cronologically had adoption, development and usage, from the fifth to the fourteenth century, of the Christian era.

These are the wonderful adornments of vaults, apses, arches, and walls of sanctuaries, with mosaic representations, or "motives," such as the "Majority," or the colossal center figure of Christ, with Saints standing on each side; Christ represented as a Lamb, to whom the twelve Apostles, in the form of sheep, are paying adoration; Christ the Good Shepherd, portrayed as a beardless youth, seated among a circle of sheep, e. g., as represented in the tomb of Galla Placidia; the Virgin Mary, or the patron saint of a church, centrally located in the apse, with other saints on each side; the "Doom," or "Last Judgment," as adornment of domes, as in the Baptistery of Florence; the scene of Christ's baptism, the river Jordan being sometimes personified as an old man with flowing beard, holding an urn from which a stream of water flows forth; a representation of Justinian and his Empress Theodora, attended by a numerous suite of courtiers and ladies, as in the church of S. Vitale, Ravenna; scenes from both the Old and the New Testaments, or the lives of the saints, represented in a vast number of varieties, on the walls of the bodies of churches, or arranged in square-shaped pictures, of one or more tiers, over the nave columns or arcades, etc., etc., expressive of artistic ideas, embodied and re-embodied through delicate grades of colors and tints; brilliant encrustations, magnificent beyond description; decorative splendor displayed in the blending of gold, and colors that glisten, in mosaic form, over the surfaces of soffits, angles, and in vaulted ceilings; garments and draperies enriched with golden tints; rich jewels; gold and silver embroidery; sparkling reds, blues, and other colors, such as blend harmoniously, to the ultimatum of figure perspective and drapery adornment; thus marking the artistic development of the various motives, designed and developed in such works as the above-named having placement in Rome, as in the Triumphal arch of S. Paola fuori le Mura; over the nave column and the triumphal arch of S. Maria Maggiora; in the apse of S. S. Cosmas and Damian; in the apse of S. Agnese fuori le Mura; in the Baptistery of S. Giovanni, in the Laterano; in the apse of S. Cecilia, in Trastevere; St. Marco, St. Maria della Navicella, and the "Chapel of the Column;" in the triumphal arch of S. Pressede; in the apses of S. Clementi; St. Francesca Romana, St. Maria in Trasteen, St. Paolo fuori le Mura; in the triumphal arch of St. Clementi; in the apse of St. Giovanni in Laterano, by Jacopo da Turrita; in the apse of St. Maria Maggiore, by Jacopo da Turrita and Taddeo Gaddi, through whom the influence of the pre-historic saccen etsiessa, Elongo and Puuco, and their subsequent embodiers and re-embodiers, sought further extension and continuity.

In Milan, the influence was made manifest through such works as those in the "Tribune of St. Ambrogio," in representation of Christ, in the center piece, and the history of St. Ambrose at the sides; in the Chapel of St. Aquilinus, to the right of the church of St. Lorenzo, in representation of Christ and the Apostles and Annunciation to the Shepherds.

The influence spread, and made itself manifest in various cities and towns of Italy.

In Florence, in the apse of the Battistero, or church of S. Giovanni Battesta, are fine mosaics; those in the choir-niche wrought by Fra Jacopo; and those in the dome by Andrea Tafi, Apollonio Greco, and others; and on the pavement also are mosaic designs; in the apses of the cathedrals of Fundi, Naola, and Capua; in those of the Torcello and Murano islands, Venice, are fine specimens.

In Sicily, in the apses of the cathedrals at Salerno and

Cefalu; in the vault of the church of La Martorano, and on the whole walls of the Capella Palatin, in Palermo.

In Ravenna, on the roof of the baptistery adjacent to the Metropolitan church, in representation of the Apostles; in the vault of the tomb of Galla Placidia; in the vault of Archbishop Chapel; in the apse and nave of S. Apollenare Nuovo, acknowledged to be the triumph of mosaic art, in represenation of, two processions of Virgins and of Martyrs marching—the former from the city of Classis, and the latter from the palace of Theodoric, to the Savior. In the first group, Christ is represented as sitting upon his mother's lap, and the Magi are interposed between him and the procession of Virgins. In the second, Christ is represented as enthroned in glory, guarded by four ministrant Angels, etc.; in the apse and whole sanctuary of S. Vitale, are mosaic representations, of an interesting character; among them full-length contemporary portraits in representation of Justinian and Empress Theodora, surrounded by ecclesiastics, courtiers, and soldiers of the guard; in the apse and nave of S. Apollinare, in Classe, as if peering from behind the great marble columns, mosaic representations that silently proclaim to the on-looker, the greatness to which that Art, influentially speaking, had attained, in the sixth century. Among the most conspicuous of ideas, embodied and re-embodied, thus manifesting, is the "Great Jeweled Cross," symbolizing the Savior on the Mount of Transfiguration, with Moses and Elias represented as leaning forth, from the clouds on either side; while in the valley below, the Apostles wait, thus represented symbolically, as sheep.

Numerous mosaic portraits of Bishops of Ravenna, have place upon the walls of the church, and a mosaic picture in representation of Constantine Pogonatus and his brothers, in the act of bestowing a *privilegium* on Bishrop Reparatus, aecompanics them.

The great Cathedral of Monreale, Sicily, of the twelfth century (on the site of pre-historic and later edifices) is one of the most beautiful structures in the world, and is dedicated to the "Assumption of the Virgin Mary. It is a structure whereupon and within which the Norman Kings established a great influence through manifestations of their wealth and artistic taste, having caught the inspiration or ideas of gilding and mosaic grandeur, from the developments of those arts that had place through the pre-historic and Modern-ancient embodiments and re-embodiments, led on by further spirit influence and inspiration. The silent, but powerful evidence of this fact is made manifest through such qualifications as the pointed arches, covered with marble inlay; its two hundred and sixteen white marble columns decorated with bands of patterns in gold, silver and blending of colors established by glass *tesserae,* that extend in vertical or spiral form from end to end over each column; the exterior of its doorways; its pointed archways, so magnificently encrusted with inlay, embracing the Norman, French, Byzantine, and Arabic styles; its high dado composed of marble slabs, encrusted with bands of mosaic; its minute picture, wrought in brilliantly colored mosaics on a gold ground and arranged in tiers divided by horizontal and vertical bands of flowing mosaic ornamentation, thus assembled to cover the surfaces of the interior walls. The same covering is upon the soffits and jambs of the arches, so wonderfully encrusted with mosaics or *tesserae.* Through and amid these, one beholds the array of minute pictures thus assembled, like spirits, as it were, of the past, from many nations, arrayed as an Heavenly Host, speaking with a multitude of tongues, as it were, in evidence of the continuity of life, and its influence, in the past and the present, relative to Art Inspiration, and the conception and idealistic establishment, embodiment, and re-embodiment of facts, to the ultimatum of art connection through the Epicycle of periodical events, as they have moved on through time, over the deferent of the Great Art Cycle.

In fact conclusive, its 80,630 square feet of enclosed grandeur, like a jewel-encrusted cave, glittering with splendor by the power of its myriad glass mosaics whose brilliant colors dazzle the eyes as if gleaming forth from a throne of gold, each representing a thought or inspiration, sent forth from the spirit world to attract the mortal mind, and in it to awaken new ideas; embody or re-embody thoughts intended for further development into facts; and to possess the observer with greater knowledge. The same impression is made by the glass *tesserae* that adorn the edges of the arches and jambs, thus giving softness to the great mosaic garment—as to the high lights on painted art, that give perspective to fabric folds and draperies of textile placement; thus enhancing the great golden form of the wall to the ultimatum of artistic blending. The whole is symbolic of the force that lies back of united and co-operative mortal and spirit intelligences, relative to the Ideal conception of Art, its birth and development into an epicycle, thence to move on the deferent of the Great Cycle, and to influence the world symbolically, e. g., the magnificent assemblage of marble and porphyry mosaics that compose the pavement, of the triple choir, impresses one with the profundity, the solidity and the durability, of artistic principles, cemented together with the force of truth, polished with knowledge, and illumined with spirit light. It becomes a symbol aggregating in the base or foundation of a higher and more marvelous condition of life, disembodied and arisen to various realms above, and the grades of development thereunto, as laterally symbolized by the magnificent walls and domes above. The reflection of light and brilliancy that descends from the latter, meeting that of the former, symbolizes the co-operative blendings of spirit and mortal thoughts—the generative force of idealistic conception, and birth into embodied and re-embodied forms under the title of artistic principles, from the material and spiritual wombs of life, where the development of embryotic art matures. Thus through the ocular sense, aided by mental contemplation of the represented embodied or re-embodied subjects in full likeness of the developed idea, that condition is afforded which renders possible the continuity of mental generative principles, hence the Productive Epicycle, infinite as Life, lasting as Time, and profound as Space.

Among the conspicuous pictures in the half dome of the central apse, is one of a colossal half-length figure of Christ as a central figure, with the Virgin and Child seated below. Full length colossal figures of St. Peter and St. Paul adorn the other apses; subjects of the Old Testament, types of Christ and his scheme of redemption, accompanied by representations of those who prophesied his coming; subjects from the New Testament. in representation of Christ's miracles and suffering, with Apostles, Evangelists, and Saints, in accompaniment.

In Venice, the famous church of St. Marco, on the narthex, apse, walls of nave and aisles, are encrustations of mosaics covering an area of 45,790 feet, that in their brilliant glow blend in beauty with the profuse decoration of gilding, bronze, and the oriental marble. The placement of this marks the mosaic influence from the tenth to the sixteenth century. It is as a glorious school of encrusted architecture; grand emblem of durability and harmonious blending of beauty, virtue, knowledge, and spiritual attainments; an expression in the language of colors, in all their shades, tints and hues; an assembly of glass alabaster, marble, gold and general mosaic forms, symbolic of subtle, variable, inexpressible, transparent, polished, lustrous, qualities of pure life and its developments.

Thus it is, that one, when beholding the grandeur here assembled, is reinspired with the spirit of the past, and feels the force of de-carnate spirit upon the incarnate senses, and can better understand the Truth of spirit guidance and its inspiration.

The mosaic art here manifests, or expresses and influences, through such works as "The Last Judgment," having place over the main entrance; to the right, the "Embarkation of the Body of St. Mark at Alexandria," and its "Arrival at Venice;" to the right, the "Veneration of the Saints," and "Deposition of the Relics of the Saints in the Church of St. Mark;" above, on the right and left, the four mosaics in representation of the "Descent from the Cross," "Christ in Hades," the "Resurrection," and the "Ascension." Again, in the Entrance Hall, in the vaulting, the mosaic representation of Old Testament subjects, on the right, as, First Dome, "Creation of the World and the Fall of Man;" in the following arch, "The Deluge;" in the Second Dome, in the second arch, "Noah," and the "Tower of Babel;" in the Third Dome, the "History of Abraham;" in the Fourth Dome, "Joseph's Dream," "Joseph Sold by his Brethren," and "Jacob's Lament;" in the Fifth and Sixth Domes, "Joseph in Egypt;" and in the Seventh Dome, the "History of Moses."

The interior reached, one is charmed and inspired with the beauty of the main lines of art; the grandeur and nobility of the perspective; the magnificence of the decorative spirit manifested through the assemblage of embodiments and re-embodiments, embraced in the mosaics on the walls and other elevated positions. When standing upon the great tessellated pavement, one is reminded of the continuity of life, and its association, not only with the past, but the future, blendings of soul with soul, and spirit with spirit, to the ultimatum of lasting natural art, which needs no restoration from decay.

Above the door of the St. Marco are representations of "Christ," "The Virgin," and "St. Mark;" in the arch above, "The Apocalypse;" in the right aisle, a representation of "Christ in Gethsemane," with "Legends of the Apostles" above; in the First Dome, "The Descent of the Holy Ghost," in the left aisle, "Paradise," and "Martyrdom of the Apostles;" in the center dome of the Nave, a representation of the "Ascension," and on the south and west ribs "Scenes from the Passion;" in the dome behind the high-altar, a representation of "Christ surrounded by Old Testament Saints;" in the apse, "Christ Enthroned;" in the sacristy, on the vaulting, other fine mosaics. In the vaulting, to the left of the altar, are some fine mosaics of the thirteenth and fourteenth centuries, as in the central dome, Christ is represened as commanding his disciples to baptise the gentiles in his name; other representations are relative to the life of John the Baptist, etc., all of which give evidence of the force of embodiied and re-embodied idea, giving expression through the mosaic art, and having its first embodiment in Atlantis; pre-historically re-embodied through the saccensa of Elongo and Puuco, and their subsequent saccen etsiessa; therefore proper links with which to connect the Remote, Ancient, Mediæval and Modern periods of the Great Art Cycle influence.

ALLIED OR VARIED INFLUENCES.

From the influence of the Atlantian zite zeuleze, through the zathus leelvazeets of Siloton; the zondar ioonsoes of Zanzureta; and the saccen etsiessa of Etzentuan; co-operative with various spirit influences, contemporaneous with the various periods of time and events, conditions have given rise to the variations that characterize the mosaic art, and allied styles diverging from it, yet belonging to it, relative to the principle of embodied and re-embodied ideas, their conception into the mortal brain, or mental womb, by aid of influence and inspiration; their development and ultimate birth into art form; ultimate utility; and subsequent influence, e. g., the art of Inlaying, embracing ornamentation by the process of incrustation, or otherwise inserting one material substance or several substances into another, differing in color and nature; thus to establish fabrication of furniture and other objects, of an ornamental kind, the styles of which are numerous and effective in the extension of the Mosaic Art, relative to its allied conditions.

Further contemplation leads us to note the various styles of Inlay that have arisen from the above-named influences, as diverge from the main cycle of mosaic extension, e. g., the *Niello* style of decoration, a black compound consisting of silver, lead, copper, sulphur and borax; the design being hatched with a steel point upon a foundation of gold or silver; then engraved with a burin, into which hot *Niello* was poured; the superfluitant deposit, when cold, being cut down to the surface of the body with pumice stone; the leaving this, the engraved design on the plate or body, with the effect of a print, ultimating in an Ornamental Art, long since established, and practised to the present time, to a great extent, in Europe, Russia and India. The influence of this is evidenced by such works as the ornamentation on the dress and armor of a bronze statue representing a Roman General (first century), British Museum; a silver casket or lady's toilet box, fourth century (British Museum); the silver of the *Baldacchino,* over the high-altar of S. Sophia at Byzantum (Constantinople) in the Byzantian period; the Pala d' Oro, at S. Mark's, Venice (tenth century); the decorated paten in the church at Hanover Palace; ornamentations of the same kind in the cathedral of Hildesheim, Hanover, Prussia; some ecclesiastical plate, preserved records in church investuries, of the middle ages in France, such as existed in Notre Dame, Paris, and Cluny cathedrals (eleventh century), whose columns and sanctuaries were covered with *Niello.* This was in the form of decoration of personal ornaments, as worn by the Teutonic and Celtic races, eighth to the eleventh centuries, in Britain and other countries (European Museums); *fibulae* of silver and gold, ornamented with *Niello,* as worn by the Scandinavians and Britains; gold rings, as worn by the Saxons, e. g., that of Ethelwalf, King of Wessex (British Museum); and one of Alhastan, Bishop of Sherborne (South Kensington Museum); the croziers, shrines, *fibulae,* etc. (tenth to twelfth centuries), wrought by the Irish workmen, of Ireland.

Later, the vast amount of decorated church plate and silver altar frontals, of Italy, of mediæval influence, as at Pistoia cathedral, Florence. The piece is in representation of the "Coronation of the Virgin," and microscopic in minuteness, but four inches in length, and three in breadth, but embraces forty figures, accurately drawn and minutely finished; the silver beaker, said to be the finest example of German *Niello* of the sixteenth century (British Museum), a piece covered with graceful scroll-work, which forms medallions in which are figures of cupids employed in various occupations.

The influence arising from these and similar products, through respective ideal embodiments and re-embodiments, co-operative with spirit influence, further aided in the conception and development of the idea of engraving on metal plates. The extension of this art has been and is too vast to enumerate in this work; but suffice it to say that the influence, in reality, trends back to the Atlantian period, when similar work was practised in the Monumental and other Engravings, and through the works of Theonzy and Emucu, of Atlantis; re-embodied in the pre-historic tracings of Menara and Matheus, of Siloton; Ferenoso of Mequethus; Pietrus and Telgus of Zanzureta; Palceiro and Balzaric of Etzentuan, and painters of regions previously named.

Furthermore, the marvelous inlay of the Japanese, on mineral surfaces, viz: of fine bronzes with gold and silver; large articles and cast hollow ware; common metals and alloys; while their famous lacquer work is inlaid with mother-of-pearl and other substances, similar to the lacquered papier-mache of Western sections.

A variety, to this idea, which might be said to have arisen, and been thus embodied in, is that of inlaid mosaics, where the colored designs are inserted in spaces cut in solid ground, or the basis, e. g., the Florentine mosaic, consisting of the veneers of precious colored stones set in slabs of marble.

Again, the decoration known as *Pietra Dura* is of mosaics, composed of inlaid hard and expensive stones, pebbles, agates, lapis-lazuli, carnelian, amethysts, etc., laid in relief in marble, an influence arising from similar sources as those above mentioned, under local and conditional changes.

The *Bidri* decorative art of India is a reverse idea to the *Niello* art, relative to placement of colors; e. g., the silver is on a *Niello* ground, in a way that when completed leaves a beautiful contrast, between the bright inlaid silver and the dead black ground.

The *Damaskeening* decorative art, of Persia and India, embraces the adornment of iron and steel, by the mode of manufacture, etchings, or by inlaying with gold or silver, for the ornamentation of arms and armor, blades of swords, locks of pistols, etc. This is known in India as *Kuft-work,* or *Kuftgari,* and is wrought by the process of inlaying gold or silver wire in iron or steel, as above stated. In Kashmir the style of inlaying vessels of copper and brass with tin was prevalent in time agone.

The Buhl-work, or ornamentation of cabinet-work, of the sixteenth century, is a re-embodied idea, as manifested through the works of Andre Charles Boule, of France, the famed originator of the style, who by the assemblage of Indian and Brazilian woods, brass, ivory, gold, tortoise-shell, etc.' extended a great influence in this class of art mainly through his beautiful representations of various species of animals, flowers, fruits and historical scenes; as battles, hunts, landscapes, etc., which he wrought upon furniture, in arabesques and pictures.

This style of decorative art, as re-embodied in the works of Boule, was a compound of re-embodied ideas, through the influence of spirit inspiration, which embraced co-operative ideas, of both painting and mosaic origin, as having extended from such works, of the Atlantian arts, as had place in architecture, on furniture, and especially on the bodies of musical instruments. Ideas further re-embodied in the choice and execution of ideal subjects, as represented in the works of Crece, the pre-historic Arabian painter, which were precursors to the idea of Arabesque Ornamentation, which under further spirit influence, found way into the later Arabian and Moorish architectures, and was ultimately adopted as an ornamental style on cabinet work, by Boule of France.

Furthermore the pre-historic ideas of Danfresa, the mosaic artist of Zanzureta, as manifest through his tessellated ornamention on tables and similar pieces of furniture, and also the prehistoric ideas of Elongo, the mosaic artist of Etzentuan, as manuifest through his style of co-uniting colored woods to form the tops of tables and other similar furniture, etc., extend subsequently, through the works of ancient and modern mosaic or inlay artists, until when passing along the spirit epi-cycle, counterpart to the material, the sensitive brain of Boule caught the idea of his own famed style of ornamentation, from the influences that were moving along with the spirit epi-cycle, over the deferent of the Great Spirit Cycle of Art, thus causing him to conceive and develop the ideas, that have so beautifully manifested through what is now known as the Buhl-work, co-existent with similar ideas, conceived and developed by the Egyptians and some Asiatic races, and further re-embodied by the Greeks and the Romans, in their works of similar art.

The Certosian-work, or "ornamental inlay" of ivory into solid cypress and walnut woods, embraces the Italian work on choir-fittings, and the Persian and Indian styles, represented by geometrical figures.

The Renaissance-work embraces the styles of gilding and painting on wood, inlay of agate, carnelian, lapis-lazuli, marble of various tints, ivory, tortoise-shells, mother-of-pearl, and various woods.

Further influences might be said to extend into the embodiment of the ideas of veneer-work, such as marble in wall decorations, and woods in cabinet-work, etc.

The Bombay-boxes, of India, display geometrical patterns on wood, etc., all of which are re-embodied ideas, under extended development; thus influenced by remote, ancient, mediæval, and modern works, through spirit influences.

The Tarsia-work consisting of different pieces of inlaid woods of various colors, exclusively, a style dating from remote periods, and practised later by the Romans, Italians and Spaniards.

In the fifteenth century, Italian artists conceived the idea of representing architectural scenes, landscapes, fruit, and flowers, by *Tarsiatura* work, using ivory, ebony, box, palm, birdseye maple, beach, and other woods, which they wrought into panels of walnut wood.

This influence developed into the allied style known as Marquetry, consisting of different pieces of diverse colored woods of small thickness, glued onto a ground of oak or fir. It was thus used in pictorial and ornamental designs, figure subjects, architectural views, quaint interiors, etc., throughout Italy and

Spain, and in the domains of Charles V, and his successors. At first only two or three different woods were utilized, but in the last century the developed idea of Marquetry embraced the use of tulip-wood or mahogany, with that of lime and pear tree, holly, beech and other varieties of light woods; while in Italy, ebony and ivory were utilized, and ebony and mother-of-pearl in Holland.

The embodied idea of Marquetry representations, formerly manifested through its utility, conjointly with cabinet work; but it is now principally confined to floors, checkered-work, inlaid woodwork, etc., so extensively used in various countries.

This style, in time, influenced a diverse idea of the art, embodied in what is now known as Damaskeened ornamentation, which is wrought by placing precious stones and metallic amalgums onto bronze articles.

Therefore, Tarsia, Marquetry and Damaskene ornamentation, constitute an ultimatum, or developed idea, first embodied by Creneallus, of Siloton, Danfresa of Zanzureta, Elongo, of Etzentuan and mosaic artists of those sections, and the subsequent mosaic artists, throughout ancient, mediæval, and modern periods of time. Artists each and all, held by the influence, inspiration and guidance of spirit artists, who, in their love for mortal humanity, leave their realms of spirit art to bring to man such knowledge of the past, present and future, as shall broaden his mental capacity or capabilities, and enlighten his spiritual being. Thus opened the door of knowledge and wisdom, letting man out into the unbounded realms of time, space, and life, endowed with natural artistic glory in grades of development and unfoldment, that are boundless and divine, in their process of revolution, as epi-cycles moving on the deferent of the Great Art Cycle, whose circumference finds no end or limit, in its extent through time, space, and life.

The so-called "Opus Alexandrinum," a second mediæval class of mosaic pavements of the thirteenth century and later, are common throughout Italy and the East. They consist of small marble *tesserae* for the main line of the pattern, and large pieces for the ground or matrix, designed in large flowing bands which interlace and enclose circles, etc. The materials used are mostly white marble, with green and red porphyry and occasionally glass; as manifest by the beautiful pavements of the countless churches throughout Italy, as St. Mark's at Venice; S. Lorenzo, S. Marco, S. Maria Maggiore and S. Maria, in Trastevere, Rome; front of the high-altar in Westminster Abbey, London; front of the shrine of Becket, at Canterbury; in the cathedral of

S. Sophia at Tubizond, Turkey, a piece of work wrought of beautiful materials and elaborately designed.

This Opus Alexandrium style for pavements was not only a re-embodied idea from pre-historic and spirit influences proper, but was further influenced in its re-embodiment, by the delicate panellings in wood, or as wrought upon pulpits, doors, etc., of that period. A co-union of these influences established the style of glass mosaic ornamentation on ambones, pulpits, tombs, bishop's thrones, *baldacchino* columns, architraves, and other marble objects, as wrought and utilized by Italian artists. Of this there is evidence in the cloisters of S. Geovanni, in Laterano, S. Paolo fuori le Mura, and the church of S. Maria in Ara Coeli, Rome; and in the S. Clemente, St. Lorenzo, and the Salerno cathedrals.

The "Florentine style," of sectile mosaic, influenced not only in Italy, but extended into India, where it manifests through the decorations in Mohammedan buildings. The finest examples of these are at Agra, such as have place in the grand tomb, Taj Mehad.

The so-called "Roman Mosaic" style, consists in short, slender pieces of colored glass, set in cement. The ends of these form the pattern, which is finished by grinding down to a polish. It is a modern re-embodied idea, influenced by preceding styles, etc. The idea of this "wood mosaic" work, known as *"Intassiatura"* of the fifteenth and sixteenth centuries, was a re-embodiment by the artists of Tuscany and Lombardy. They utilized it in the decoration of stalls and lecterns in the church choirs. It was wrought by the use of minute pieces of various colored woods, in geometrical patterns and figure subjects. Views of buildings, with strong perspective effects, and some landscapes, were wrought, by the use of larger pieces of material, thus manifesting through such work as that on the panels of the stalls at the Certosa, or Carthusian monastery, near Pavia—work beautifully wrought by the artist, Borgognone; and on the stalls in Siena cathedral and in the S. Pietro de Casinensi, at Perugia. These latter are among the finest of the re-embodied ideas, so numerous in Italy, all of which are extended, developed, idealistic re-embodiments, whose original conceptions date back from Atlantis, borne along on the epicycles of mosaic art, as they have rotated on the deferent of the Great Mosaic Art Cycle throughout the Pre-historic, the Ancient, the Mediæval and the Modern periods of time.

CEL-POR'ZE NUD CEL-POR'TIC, OR SCULPTORS AND SCULPTURE.

TELTZIE XXXVI.

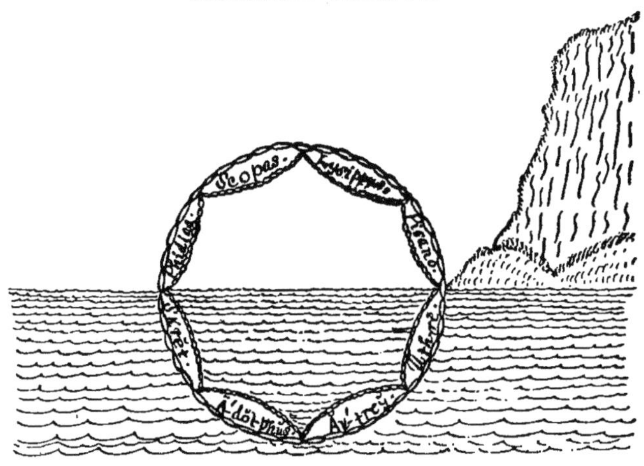

The Kĭd* of Zē-ū'lē-ŭs zē Cĕl-pör'tĭc (art of sculpture) was not extensively manifested until about the middle of the second Efremetrum.

During the early part of the first Efremetrum, kid was very crude, simply the putting together of sticks to form ornamentations, which were placed, in the desired form, on portable pieces of wood ready for ultimate placement on structures.

During the latter part of the first Efremetrum, the idea of cutting little images, usually of animals, from stone, was conceived; and finally, during the first half of the second Efremetrum, kid had developed, until the images were wrought in a much larger size, greater perfection of form, and general life-like expression.

Uth'rē was the first noted cĕl'pör (sculptor) of the Lontidri. He was located at Miezietori, the seat of commerce in Teltzie

*The term "kid" was the ancient Atlantian word for art; kid-stry for artist, and kid-stry-ze for artists; while ze-u-le-us, ze-u-le and ze-u-le-ze respectively, were their modern terms.

Ket. He reached the zenith of his greatness in the middle of the second Efremetrum. He passed from the mortal plane early in the third quarter of the second Efremetrum.

His work was manifested both on the interiors and exteriors of structures, the former being largely carvings of a picturesque design. Bas-reliefs were in marble, stone or other mineral substances, and were all of a symbolic character; those in the temples being religious and astronomical, from which sources he chose his models. In all, he sought to represent, through his kid productions, higher and nobler aspirations of man,—thus to lead and influence earth's children, to cultivate their taste for beautiful and artistic adornments, both material and spiritual.

One of his finest pieces of work was in the then known great A-găl'tē zē Yĕz'dūe (Temple of Yezdue) in the aistie of Miezietory. It was titled Cūt'zē Fē-lŏn'zē (spiritual progress). It represented a mountainous landscape, rising from a low plain. A winding pathway led from the plain to the apex of the highest mountain. Along the path, a profusion of flowers were represented, the graded variety and charming quality of which, attended the characteristics of the entire ascent. Many people were represented as on a pilgrimage up the pathway to the top of the moutain. The chief symbol in the detail, was to convey the idea of the soul and spiritual principles; and the process of individual effort necessary to gain entrance into the higher life, on the material plane; and the ultimate condition necessary to pass more fully into the higher realms of the spiritual, after disembodiment. Above the summit of the mountain, were represented "spirits of light," whose bended forms and outstretched hands symbolized the aid that comes from disembodied intelligences, to all earthly pilgrims, in their efforts to climb to the realms of spirituality, and the life beyond.

His interior work was principally in Governmental and other Public buildings, and in harmony with the utility of them. His general exterior work was on monuments, shafts, walls, etc., in accord with the object for which the structure had place. His first monumental work was on the great E-lŏn-kĕt'rō, in the aistie of Miezietory. Many of his helpers, or pupils, developed into fine workmen under his tutorship, who subsequently influenced a greater development of the kid, throughout the Lontidri.

Ax'trĕy was the most noted celportic of ĕ-ĕs-tĭn'zē (statuary) known to the Atlantian people. As a youth he lived at Miezietory, and was a pupil of Uth'rē, in the latter years of the second Efremetrum. His influence lasted through the third Efremetrum, which made him of an advanced age, modernly compared.

At the beginning of the third Efremetrum, he removed to the Aistie of Atara, where he remined until the submergence of that aistie. His most noted work was the ĕ-ĕs'tĭn ze Găl'thä-zä (statue of Galthaza), the first Efremetrum* of Atlantis. This the sculptor chiseled out from a block of ty-ăn'zä (granite). The tyanza used for the eestin, in quality, resembled the modern Scotch granite, only in place of the pink shade being mixed with gray, it was more of a golden hue. The eestin was placed in the great Dē-ăk'ē-äl at Atara.

All the public buildings possessed eestinze of political and national characters, the most of which were wrought by this master, or under his supervision. His most renowned exterior work was that of the numerous eestinze that had place on the ĭx-rōl-tä'zē (public squares) at the junctions of all the xŏn-tĭs'zē (streets) of the aistie; those in the cĕr-gū'zē (parks) and on the public edifices of the aistie. His natural talent for designing and finishing, won for him the most profound extolation from the critics of the Lontidri.

A-dŏl-phŭs was the most noted celpor of wood, known to the people of the third Efremetrum. He lived in the latter part of that period. His early work was on signitie (marble), but at odd times he would carve on wood for amusement, and soon conceived the idea of bringing out greater perfection in that branch of the zeuleus, which he did later on. Therefore, he was the originator of wood-carving, in Atlantis. His work was considered to be very fine, especially on subjects of flowers, vines, landscapes, and such ornamentation as would be placed on elaborate furniture, panellings, mantles, etc. His great talent won for him the superintendency of all the carving done at the great vĕx'ē-rŏn (music factory), in the aistie of Almorthea. He wrought the finest work to be done on the cases of the musical instruments, where the greatest artistic skill was required. Many of his carvings were so fine that they closely resembled paintings. Many of his helpers at the vexeron became his most ardent pupils, and as they became proficient under his guidance, they branched out into other parts of the Lontidri, thus to strengthen the growth of that branch of the zeuleus in other aistieze. He passed from the mortal sphere in the latter part of the third Efremetrum.

Skrĕt was a celpor, noted for his talent displayed in the celportic representing animals and birds. His works were mostly in signitie, as best fitted the requirements of fine buildings and monuments. He was an expert in the execution of celportic in

*It will be observed that the term "Efremetrum" was used for both the period of a dynasty, and the ruling teacher or president of the period.

representation of birds and animals, and he wrought also many fine specimens of flowers and fruits; the designs of these were generally original. He also did some work in wood-panelling, and bas-reliefs; some of the latter he wrought from clay, in plastic process. His most noted work had place in Neitz, the Kistrez aistie of Teltzie We, but he had sĭl-dä-zĭc'zē (schools) in the aistieze of Atara and Almorthea. These also rendered him famous as a deltzans (teacher) of celportic. He continued his work until the close of the third Efremetrum, or until the final submergence of the Lontidri.

En'tī-zē was one of Atara's most famous celporze, whose celportic consisted principally in human form representations, which he chiseled to the life. He also made some celportic in representation of animal forms. He wrought mostly from signitie, and many of his works had place throughout the aistie of Atara, especially in the public places. They were zeuleus rivals, in contrast with the great works of the aged Axtrey. He chose his subjects principally from the more modern Atlantian celebrities. His work as a deltsanz of celportic, was done at his studio, in his own mansion. He continued his labor and influence until the time of the great submergence, when he and all of his works, together with all the other great achievements of Atlantian zeuleze, with his beloved Atara and the Lontidri of Atlantis, sank beneath the waves of the now mighty Atlantic Ocean.

Passing into Elteze (Arabia), we are further informed by the spirit of Alchelet, that the Eltezean cistareeres ma cinstry (Arabian sculptors and sculpture) were not as plentiful in Elteze, or as fine, as in Atlantis, excepting in some of the monumental works of the cistareeres.

Their monuments were about equal to those of modern time and workmanship, but of different style and construction. They made no pretensions with Statuary, except in combination with monumental and edificial ornamentation. Their work, in style, was principally ornamental, raised design, or bas-reliefs, and figures on the public buildings and other edifices. They erected monuments in public places, especially in the deserts. The grandest of these were located at the Resting Places of the people, there erected according to the conditions surrounding them. These were intended for the guidance of the people when, on their journeys, they sought resting places.

Generally speaking, their monuments were of rectangular form and built of masonry; and therefore the work of the cistareeres was principally in the ornamentation of them, which was wrought from plastic material. This was in designs or models of flowers, animals, personages, trees, shrubs, birds, etc. After the main structure was complete, their cistareeres, by means of a plastic substance that was much finer than that of which the blocks were composed, moulded the ornamentation on the structures, as plaster of paris mouldings have placement in modern construction. This work was very finely wrought in all its details.

Passing the crude ideas conceived and wrought by early remnant descendants of Atlantis, or the cinstry established through the influence of primitive spirit impressions, we take up the cycle of cinstry about 6000 B. C., there to begin the re-establishment of the mĕl'sä (art), by connecting the links of the Atlantian celportic and the Eltezean cinstry.

Cŏn-ĕt'ry was the most noted cistareer of that period. He first dwelt east of what is now known as the Dehanah mountains, southwest of the "Ruins of Babylon," in a small chison by the name of Mŏn-ā-lăn'sŭm. Later, he moved to El-lē-trē'tē, the capitol city of Elteze, then located in what is now known as the Valley of Yabrin, north of the Menakib mountains. He was the founder of the melsa of cinstry, in Elteze, and had a large school in Ellitrete, composed of pupils who came from all parts of the country. His great force came to him through inspiration, or spirit influence, of which he was conscious. Hence, he was looked upon by the Eltezeans as a wonderful character. He lived and worked into the fourth quarter of the century. His style of cinstry was representation of life subjects, such as birds, animals, and the human form, which he wrought from wood, stone, and marble—the materials respectively marking the events of his progress.

The melsa of cinstry was subsequently of very slow development, under various mĕl-sä'ī-ĕsts (artists), in accord with the styles of the times with which they were contemporaneous.

Passing from the celporze nud ush zeuleus ze celportic of the last days of Atlantis, to the mā-răs'zē kĕn mā-rä'sĕs sī Sī-lō'tŏn, or sculptors and sculpture, of Egypt, Anstacia informs us that the Art of Sculpture had its rise in that country, and after the submergence of Atlantis; and that it was re-established in various pre-historic sections of the Eastern Continent, through spirit influence, co-operative with mortal spirit sensitives, whose minds were artistically inclined. Among these she gives the following, as some of the principal artists and their developments, as leading up to the Modern-ancient, and the Modern, but during the first five hundred years, very crude.

E-dēl-mä'zē, a pre-historic maras, a descendant from the Qū-zē'tās of Gŭstz, in the country of Siloton, came into the earth life about one thousand years before the Adomic period, and lived to the mortal age of one hundred and twenty-five years, dwelling in a pre-historic town by the name of Trū-ī-zăn'ŭm (now extinct); but then located west of the now known Fifth cataract of the Nile river.

His works, generally speaking, were in wood carving, and at first quite crude, in an artistic sense. All his subjects were those in representation of the human form; which, when completed, he placed on the tops of poles, erected for that purpose, and similar to those now known as "totem poles." They at that time were placed in front of individual homes, and in the center of areas, as where two streets crossed, and were thus utilized as "idols" by the inhabitants of Truizanum. This idea not only led up to the totem pole of later periods, but the placement of human forms as images, in public places, as temples, gateways to cities, etc.

Lē-dĕl'mŏz, a prehistoric maras, who descended from the Cuzetens of Cuzetenne, the next most noted maras, was born about five hundred years after Edelmaze, and lived to be a hundred and thirty years old. He resided in a town by the name of U-trō'mē-ŭs, on the north side of the Nile river, on the site of Damietta.

His work, principally, was of a plastic order, or the process of moulding clay into forms, afterward dried by the heat of the sun. His subjects, principally, were both animal and human forms, some of which were utilized as idols, and some for ornamental purposes. The distribution of these was either by erection, on street corners, or over the doors of private dwellings belonging to the more wealthy class. Some were even placed in the same position on public buildings,—ideas that continued the link of human idol erection, and the introduction of the animal—which ultimately led up to the idea of co-uniting, in representation, human and animal forms—such as ultimated in the erection of all kinds of Sphinxes, in later periods of time, as in Egypt and other countries.

Returning to Siloton (Egypt), about 5500 B. C., we find the cū-nū-lä-ĭs'ăns nūce cū-nŭ-lä-ĭs'tĭc (sculptors and sculpture) under further development, and changes of nomenclature, which the reader will observe.

Dĕn'vō-sēs was the most noted cū-nūlä'ĭs (sculptor), whose works and influence began about 5500 B. C., in Elteze. He was a native of that country and lived there the first fifty-five years of his mortal life, but the last fifty years of it in Siloton, to which country he had migrated. When in Siloton, he dwelt in a small celzic by the name of Sĭn'kō-pēs, then located south of the mountains, or between the Tropic of Cancer and the Oasis of Dachel, about the same latitude as that of the First Cataract of the Nile. His style of cunulaistic was principally that of images, or idol forms, which he wrought from moulded clays, or chiselled from sand stones or soap stones. The subjects were the human form and also that of animals. These represented the gods, and the religious teachings of that period of time. He was greatly inspired by his religious beliefs, and being a spirit sensitive, received inspired ideas from disembodied spirits, who were in sympathy with the same religious teachings.

Tō-nō'kä was the most celebrated cunulais whose work and influence began about 5400 B. C. He was a resident also of Sinkopes, the abode of Denvoses. He lived and worked through the century, hence was a venerable man. He was a Silotonan by birth, a pupil of Denvoses, and took the place of the latter, influentially and otherwise, at the time of his disembodiment. Being a very talented individual, and a spirit sensitive, he became an excellent instrument, in the hands of the spirit intelligences, who used his forces for the purpose of improving styles previously established, as by Denvoses. One of the principal improvements was the discarding of the soft materials used in his creations, and in their stead the use of hard material, such as marble, granite and other hard stones. He also improved the general form and expression of the images, bringing them nearer to real life representations.

Cunulaisans (sculptors) slowly increased. But under their influence the art developed gradually, until the historic period, when the remnant monuments, representatives of their work, were the evidence thereof.

Passing with the influence of the above-named marasze ken marases, of the early period in Siloton, through that of the cunulaisans nuce cunulaistic, of the second pre-historic period of Siloton, contemporaneous with, and under similar conditions with the re-embodiment and development of the art of painting, in order to establish the sectional epi-cycles that have moved and are still moving, on the deferent of the Great Art Cycle, of Sculpture, we take for our ancient links, the divine, calm, and mysterious immensity of Egyptian sculpture, with all its developments, and weld it into the pre-historic cunulaistic of the later period, and the marases of the earlier leelva of Siloton. We weld them into the remote celportic, wrought by the celporze of the latter days of Atlantis.

Therefore, the extension of the epi-cycle of Sculpture is cognizable by and through the existing remnants and preserved sculptures of ancient Egypt, as in other countries, the cognition being in the embodied and re-embodied ideas that manifest through them, and the archæoligic conditions under which they were developed, and still have their existence; e. g., we note such works as the establishment of the Quarries and Grottoes opposite El-Minyeh, of Fourth and Sixth Dynasties. The Sepulchral grottoes of Benei-Hasan, in the face of the eastern mountains, which are adorned with sculptures and paintings of the Twelfth Dynasty; tombs of monarchs and governors; pillars cut out of the rock; figures of celebrities, in their various occupations, as fishing, hunting, game, feasts, processions of agriculture, etc.; figures of birds and beasts, those of birds being more numerous; an assemblage of marases, arising from the work of Hër-măn'ly, the original and principal maras, who executed the sculptural work in those grottoes, aided and further extended by his pupils and helpers, whose influence extended still further subsequently. Other instances of his sculpture are to be found in the ancient grottoes that honey-comb the promontory known as Gabel-esh-Sheykh Sa'eed, on the western banks of the Nile, thus established and further extended by Cĕl-cē-lō'pē-ŭs, the original and principal maras, and subsequently further influenced and extended by his pupils and helpers and their descended influences; the Sepulchres and Grottoes, or tombs of the Kings and their courtiers in the mountains behind the very ancient ruins of the Capitol of Khunaten, of Eighteenth Dynasty, which was a seat of pure Sun workship. The sculpture of this was originated and further extended by Shan'fa, the original and principal maras of that dynasty; and his pupils and helpers, who also further influenced subsequently. The sculpture, also, in the Crocodile,—Mummy catacombs, in the eastern range opposite Manfaloot, the work of Mĕn'gē-lō, the original and principal maras of that period, and his pupils and helpers, who likewise influenced in the leelva, subsequently; the sculptural adornment in the Grottoes, in the mountains back of Asyoot, one subject being of enormous size, wrought by Bō-lū-dē-ĕn'dō, the chief maras of that period, and his pupils and helpers, and their further extended influence, to its completion. The stone portals in the temple of Athor, the Egyptian Venus, adorned with sculptures in representation of the emperors, Domitian and Trajan; the full-faced sculptures in representation of Athor, on each of the four sides of the capitals of the twenty-four enormous columns that support the portico; on the portico, as on the portals; the mystical subjects relative to Astronomy; the famous Zodiac; the whole interior, encrusted with sculptures and inscriptions, of a religious character; the sculptures in the roof-chapel representing the Legends of Osiris;

the exterior of the temple sculptures, equal to those interior, the figures being such as those of Cleopatra and Ptolemy Cæsar; all of these are among the great evidences found in Egypt, while the last-named seems truly a re-embodied idea, in part, of the great Atlantian Pĕl'zō ŭsh zē Mĕn-sē-cū-lŭs Shĕlts (Temple of the Illustrate Dead Bodies), work of Pū-cū-lĕn'dale, the original and principal maras of that section. His work was continued by his pupils and helpers, not only in this temple, but in subsequent structures. Other evidences are, the great sphinx at Ghizeh (see illustration); the long line of sphinxes that leads up from the temple of El-Uksur, the work of Sĕp-sē-ŭs, one of the principal marasze of the region, aided by his pupils and helpers. The portion of the sphinx row as it leads to El-Karnak (now wholly ruined), was the work of Pay-hăn'nē-ŭs, one of the original and principal marasze of the district, likewise aided by his pupils and helpers. Further, the great Obelisk of red granite, that originally guarded the portals or propylæum to the Temple; the Obelisk that formerly stood on the west side, now in the place de la Concord, Paris; and the two were the work of Lē-Cŏmp'tē, one of the principal marasze of that section and that period.

Other notable groups and evidences are: the three seated statues, of red granite, representing Rameses II, which are accompanied by representations of incidents in the "War of Rameses II. with the Kheta or Hittites," that covered the wings of the portal—those on the left wing depicting the Egyptians, led by their King, defeating the "confederate peoples," under the walls of the Hittite stronghold Ketesh, on the Orontes. This great work was wrought by, and under direction of, Sŭn-lē'gĕl, a principal maras of the period and that region, also assisted by his pupils, and their subsequent extended or descended, influence. Sunlegel is credited, also, with the work, gigantic in proportions, of the King, standing up in his chariot, which he has forced into the midst of the hostile army whose members have fallen to right and left under his well-aimed arrows. The same sculptor did the scene on the right wing, representing the Egyptian camp. All of these are beautifully-wrought sculpture, in sunk-relief, and are works that link back, as re-embodied ideas, to such as those of the avenues of enormous columns, with their capitals of bell-shaped flowers of the papyrus plant, and the multitudes of columns of various sizes and their sculptural accompaniments, period of Setee I., wrought and influenced by Gē-lū'cē-ĕn, and his pupils and helpers of that period; those of Rameses II, wrought and influenced by Purucu, and his pupils and helpers, of that period; those of Rameses III, who was the same person as Rameses II, under a new title, wrought and influenced by Purucu, who, like Rameses, was celebrated in two dynasties.

Other sculptures influenced, by the force of the great Pharaohs, such as are on walls, and representing these great monarchs making offerings to the gods; similar subjects having place on the columns; those that adorn the exterior of the walls, in evidence of their conquests; e. g., those of Setee I, on the north wall. He is represented as being of gigantic size, charging in his chariot, thus routing his enemies and capturing their strongholds. The Adversary Host embraces the Hittites, the Ruten of Syria; the Shasu of Arabia; Khalu of Syria; the Remenen of Armenia. The Monarch's return in triumph forms part of the grand whole. On the south wall is Remeses II, represented with his conquests, prisoners, etc.

The beautiful red granite Obelisk (and its companion, now in ruins), of Thothmes I; the enormous granite Obelisk of El-Karnak; monument of Queen Hatshepu, of Dynasty Seventeen, and its companion now in scattered fragments; the colossal rams, lions, and sphinxes, on the southern approach to the temple of El-Karnak, from that of El-Uksur; those forming the avenue in front of the temple; those that branch off to the east from the Avenue of Rams, leading to the temple of Khuns, thus intercepting another avenue of Ciro-sphinxes at right angles to it; the great Obelisk of the Temple of Amenra at Thebes; the columns of that temple, with sculptural accompaniments, now heaped up in ruins; the Columns of the Sotheum, or Temple of Setee I, at El-Kurneh, with accompanying sculpture in harmony with the worship of Rameses II—all form evidences of the strong stand taken by Sculpture in the genius of Ancient Egypt.

The spirited sculpture that had place in the great temple of Rameses II, or that popularly known as the Rameseum of El-Kurneh (second only to that of El-Karnak), is the work of Purucu and Geluceen, principal marasze of that period and section, co-operative with their pupils and helpers; and their subsequent descended influence, under spirit inspiration and guidance. Examples are to be found, as that on the back of the Propylon, representing a battle, and other scenes of the conquests of the King; the colossal and wonderful statues of Rameses, in the court of the temple (now broken in pieces); and the largest statue now known among the remains of Egypt, being of one block of red granite, of eight hundred and eighty-seven tons, five and a half hundredweight, and sixty feet in height. This mammoth stone represents the king seated on his throne, with accompanying court, characterized with colonnades, composed of columns, adorned with capitals in the form of the papyrus buds; and the Osiridean pillars formed of square blocks, having in front a figure of Rameses as Osiris. The Art instinct, traceable to the same artist-group, created, in addition, the remarkable sculpture, that had place on the walls of the court, representing the battles between the Egyptians, led by Rameses II, and the Kheta or Hittites, near the city of Ketesh, where the King of Egypt is portrayed as routing the chariots of the enemy who are fleeing in disorder toward Ketesh, across a double moat, protected by a force of infantry; the representation of priests, bearing small statues of Kings, the first of which is Menus, first sovereign known in written history; the second that of Munt-hotp, of the Eleventh Dynasty, and subsequent Kings of the Eighteenth and Nineteenth Dynasties, as far as Rameses II, who terminated the series; the marvelous assembly of columns with capitals in the shape of papyrus flowers, and buds of the same plant, placed in the Hypostile hall of the great Rameseum; the curious sculpture on the front wall of the hall, in representation of the putting to rout of a hostile force; the capture of a town by the Egyptians scaling its walls, using ladders, while Rameses and six of his sons led the army.

The religious subjects, and a series of the twenty-six sons and three daughters of Rameses II, etc., work planned and begun, especially the colossal statue of Rameses, was by Purucu and his pupils and helpers; but subsequently carried out and completed by Kĕn-thē-ū'sē, one of the principal marasze of the later period. The gigantic Obelisks and Statues, such as stood on either side the approach to the magnificent Temple of Amenophis III, southwest of the great Rameseum of El-Kurneh; e. g., the one in representation of King Amenophis III, seated on his throne; another, the famed "Vocal Memnon;" the colossal standing statues of Queen Mut-em-wa, the King's mother, and Queen Tai, his wife, in accompaniment, etc., are the work of Trē-lū'sy, one of the principal marasze of that period and section.

The sculptures representing the sovereign of Eighteenth Dynasty, including Queen Hatshepu, found in the sanctuary of one of the temples of Medeenet-Haboo, are the work of Lŭd'sō, the principal maras of that section and period, who, co-operative with pupils and helpers, wrought other sculptors in those temples; e. g., the representation of Rameses III, as in the act of slaying his enemies before Amenra; a series of captures of chiefs of the Hittites, Amorites, Teucrians, Sardones, Etruscans, and other peoples, as portrayed on the towers of a palace south of the great temple leading to it; the sculptures on the chamber walls representing the private life of Rameses; the Osiridean pillars and many Columns, having capitals in the form of papyrus flowers and buds, that adorned the great temple of Medeenet-Haboo; sculptures on the walls, relating to the wars of Rameses III; sculpture groups, on the exterior of similar subjects, Rameses going to war; the rout of the Tamhu, a Lybian people; prisoners of the Tamhu, Mashuasha, and Libyans, being brought before the King, while the scribes counted the hands which had been cut from the slain soldiers, numbering 12,535 individuals; a great battle with the Takkaru or Tencrians, whose army is defeated by the Egyptians; the Takkaru fight in chariots of two horses, and in wagons, drawn by oxen; the remarkable sculpture in relief, representing the King as passing through a marshy country in his chariot, his encounter with three lions, and when having slain two with his javelins, turns around to meet the third which is posed ready to spring upon him; the sea-fight, in which the Egyptian fleet defeated that of the Shardana and the Takkaru, while Rameses and his army fought them from the shore; then as leading the captives before the gods of Thebes. All of these are works of the foregoing marasses and their descended, and extended, influence through subsequent marasze, in that section.

The grottoes on the low spurs of the Libyan chain behind the Setheum; the pillars that support their roofs and the sculptures that adorn their chambers, are the works of Quinzeon, the principal maras of that section and period. The sculptures of the Twenty-sixth Dynasty, in the tract beyond the Asaseef, of hieroglyphic form, in the excavated tombs at the terminals of the western spurs, such as that of Petanum-apt, a priest, are the works of El'tē-mŭs, the principal maras of that section and period. The sculptures in the Tombs of the Queens and Princes of the Eighteenth, Nineteenth and Twentieth Dynasties, are the work of Mŭ'dī-sĕn, the principal maras, who originated the plan, and wrought, in these tombs, during his earth life, a work continued by his pupils and helpers, and ultimately by their pupils and co-operative influences. The Tombs of the Kings, adorned with painted sculpture (too extensive for individual mention at this time); the sculptures in slight intaglio (an art dating from the fourteenth century B. C.), as in the tombs of Beni Hassan, are works originated, planned and wrought upon by Hĕr-măn'ly, the maras above mentioned, and further carried into completion by his pupils and helpers, and descended marasze in subsequent time. The four gigantic statues, sixty-six feet in height, representing Rameses the Great, with children standing about his feet, figures that flank the entrance doorway to the rock-cut facade of the Temple of Aboosimbel; the most wonderful of all the temples of Rameses the Great, in Nubia, hewn from the solid rock, dating from the fourteenth century B. C.; the carvings, inscriptions, and sculptural adornment, that characterize both interior and exterior, in pictorial description of the life and conquest of Rameses II; the statues of various Kings, and the sculptured Throne of Rameses, etc., that have place within the structure are works of Mŭn-zū'rĭc, the principal maras of that sectoin and period, co-operative with his pupils and helpers, and subsequent marasze influences, of that section and period.

The statue of Chephren, found in the rock-cut temple at Ghizeh, and other sculptural work, originated, planned and wrought, by Lē-cŏmp'tē, a maras of that section and period; the great Sphinx at Ghizeh (See chapter dealing with Sphinx); the Sitting Memnon in the sepulchre of Osymandys (the Memnonium), a colossus sixty feet in height, with face seven feet in length, ears three feet six inches long, and shoulders twenty-six feet across, work of Cŏn'trē-zĕl, one of the principal marasze of that section and period; the two colossal statues of Rameses the Great that formerly stood before the great temple of Ptha, in the ancient city of Memphis, now lying on their backs amid the palms, the only remains of the once famous city of Memphis, are the work of Mĕn-zē-ū'lēs, the principal marasze of that section and period, who, in co-operation with his pupils, and their subsequent descended influences, gave rise to most of the sculptural works of that ancient city.

The wonderful sculptures found in the temple of Athor, at Denderah, such as those on the portal entering the outer wall, representing Domitian and Trajan, engaged in acts of worship before various deities; the twenty-four columns supporting the portico, fifty feet high and seven feet in diameter, with capitals, on the four sides of which are sculptured the full face of Athor, representing the Cæsars making offerings; the sculptures of a religious character that cover the whole interior, in harmony with the utility of the various chambers; bas-reliefs of Augustus, in the interior of Hypostyle Hall; Cleopatra and her son, Cæsarion, on the exterior of the temple, etc., are the works of I-chĭl'zō, a maras of the first period of the temple, and the descended influence from his pupils and subsequent marasze in that section.

The portrait-statues of Khafra, carved in Diorite, and other works in his temple, were wrought by Kā-lū'zä, a noted maras of that section and period; the statue of Rameses the Great, from

Abydos, was the work of Nĕn-dū'săc, a noted maras of that section and period, and is now in the British Museum; the Tablet Ancestors, in Sete's temple; list of Names; statues of Isis and Hor, and accompanying sculptural decorations in this Abydos temple, works also of Nendusac; the pictorial representations, beautifully sculptured in low-relief, and colored with exquisite taste, in the temple of Queen Hatasu, at Deir-el-Bahari, work portraying her commercial and scientific expeditions to the land of Punt, are the work of Wĭsh'ū-lŭs, a noted maras of that section and period. The representions of Ptolemy and the two Cleopatras; carvings on the columns; wall decorations; and the sculptures of food offerings, in the temple of Kom Ombe, are all the work of Gē-nō'thē-ŏn, a noted maras of that section and period.

From all the above and foregoing, the Wall Depictions and Decorations, such as characterize the temple of Karnak, Thebes, the temple of Denderah, the temple of Thothmes III, the temple of Khonsu, Karnak; the temple of Abydos; the tomb of Setee I; the tomb of Ti; the interior of the tombs of Naklet, Thebes; the capitals of the temple at Philæ; the temple of Edfu; the historical scenes and hieroglyphics on the temples of Medeenet-Haboo; on the pylons and in the sanctuary, of the temple of Kahonsu, Karnak; the colossal granite head of Thothmes III (British Museum); the Julius Cæsar and Augustus (British Museum); Mark Antony (Louvre); Cleopatra's Needle (London); Cleopotra's Needel (Central Park, N. Y.); the colossal Hawk, from Pithom (the park, Ismailia); the Triad, from Tanis (Ismailia); the Obelisk of Usertesen I, at Begig; the Obelisk at Heliopolis, erected by Usertesen I, etc., etc., are the links, among the vast number that existed during the decades of time intervening between remote pre-historic time and the remote ancient and modern-ancient periods, by which we establish the Epi-cycle of Sculpture, as extending from the Atlantian to the Historic period, as having been influenced and guided by spirit inspiration and guidance, as it moved along on the deferent of the Great Art Cycle.

Passing into Mequethus (Assyria), we find the clăn-nā'zō shū clăn'thŭs (sculptors and sculpture) under development, and the clannazo co-operative with spirit influence, and also the influence of migratory conditions.

Dē-băl'bŭs, a pre-historic clăn'nā (sculptor) was a descendant from the Cuzetens, in the country of Siloton, was born about seven hundred years before the Adomic period and lived to the mortal age of one hundred years. At the age of thirty-five he migrated to Mequethus, where he settled in a pre-historic city by the name of Bē-mŏn'tē, on the west side of the Upper Euphrates, or Flat river, on the site of Kalaat En Nejim.

He having lived in Siloton at a period three hundred years later than Edelmaze, he was influenced by artistic conditions that had developed among the marasze during the period of time subsequent to Edelmaze's transition, and his departure into Mequethus. The work of Debalbus was principally in wood carving.

His subjects were representations of animal and human forms, and were, when completed, utilized as idols, having place on the interior of buildings, and in exterior meeting or gathering places, such as were utilized for worship. In the latter case, a pole, about five feet in height was erected, on the top of which an image, as of a man, was placed in standing posture, with arms extended out and up to the right and the left. From the center pole, four branches, in the form of candelabra, bore one at each extremity, an image. These varied in form, e. g., on one was a large bird; on another, a dog; on another, a fish; and on another, a lion. These representations were at first crude, in an artistic sense, but gradually developed into better conditions in that respect.

These images were representations relating to the religion of the people of that section of Mequethus, at that period of time, which was that of the life principle that animated all material things.

Tĭn'dē-gin,* a pre-historic clanna, was a descendant of the Es'gē-nĕns of Es-gē-nĕn'ĕx, in the country of Clē-ăn-di'ci-ä (Asia Minor), who was born about twenty-five years before the transition of Debalbus, and lived to the mortal age of ninety-five.

About the time that Debalbus passed to spirit life, Tindegin came into notoriety as a clanna, and migrated to Mequethus, where he settled in Gŭn'gŭs, on the eastern bank of the Tigris river the present site of Bagdad. His youth was spent in the society of Debalbus, from whom he received many ideas relative to the art of clanthus.

His first work, in Gungus, which brought him notoriety, was of the plastic order (which he and Debalbus had planned just prior to the transition of the latter); being of clay, moulded into images of animals, bird and human forms, the same as the subjects adopted by Debalbus. These he completed by the process of sun-drying, and when finished, they were utilized for the same purposes as the clanthus wrought from wood by Debalbus, which

*Soft sound of g.

latter had developed simultaneously with Tindegin, during his last days as a clanna.

In the latter part of his work as a clanna, he was influenced, or inspired, to chisel his images out of stone, though his work in that respect was somewhat crude at first. These were utilized as idols, and were placed both on poles, and on private and public buildings; but had no placement on exterior public grounds, excepting in a few instances, when they were placed in the yards of private homes of the more wealthy inhabitants.

Thus was originated, in Mequethus, the influence of clanthus; such as led up to the idol and ornamental statutary that had place in ancient Assyria, and further linked to allied types of Modern times, in the style of both single and grouped subjects.

Passing with the pre-historic influence of the clannazo shu clanthus so Mequethus, we make connecting links through such works as the Sculpture in alabaster that adorned the buildings of that region: e. g., the golden image of Bel; the two other golden statues that accompanied it in its shrine; the two that had place in the shrine at the base of the temple, in ancient Babylon; all of these the work of Rē-sō-cŏn'dī, one of the principal clannazo of that section and period, who wrought in metals, by plastic processes. Another link would be the wall sculpture in the royal palaces of Nineveh, wrought by Et-rī-zē-ī'nō, one of the principal clannazo, and his pupils of the earlier periods, and later by descended influencing clannazo, who followed in the same styles; and those of Babylon, wrought by In-so-ū-tĕl'lŭs, one of the principal clannazo, and his pupils, of the same period as those in Nineveh. The latter group were the chief originators of that class of sculpture, in that region, whose influence, co-operative with subsequent clannazo and their works, under spirit inspiration and guidance, through the periods extending from the time of Sennacherib to that of Sardanapalus (705-625 B. C.). To them is due the class of work executed still later, carved in very low-relief, on enormous slabs of marble, of sacred subjects, as that of the King worshipping one of the many Assyrian gods, of colossal size; others, illustrations of the King's life, amusements, prowess in war or hunting; long processions of prisoners and tribute-bearers, as coming to do him homage, which latter, in scale, range from medium to the minute in the figure sizes, etc.

This art was made manifest in bird and animal subjects, to a greater degree of reality, than through the human form; the principal reliefs are in representation of horses, mules, hounds, goats, lions, and many other animals; e. g., the one in the British Museum, in representation of a lioness, wounded by an arrow in her spine, dragging helplessly her paralyzed hind legs, is most expressive, in artistic reality; likewise the horses, in the relief on a marble wall-slab from the palace of Sardanapalus at Nineveh. The bas-reliefs wrought in the time of Assur-nasir-pal's reign, are especially famous for animal figures, such as the representation of the lion-hunts depicted on that celebrity's slabs. The elaborate backgrounds to the groups, wrought from the time of the second empire to the reign of Essar-Haddon, which support rich and intricate groupings; the skillfully-wrought vegetable form representations and landscape outlinings, in the period of the reign of Assur-bani-pal; scenes from the harem, as the King reclining, with his wife at his side, banqueting under the shade of vines, etc.; the bas-relief sculpture characterized with colorings of red, blue, black and white, principally to represent eyes, hair, and garment fringes (the same idea conceived by the Greeks, though not borrowed from the Assyrians, but under direct spirit inspiration, etc., which fact is wholly responsible for the seeming transition of the one into the other); the female head in high relief, Nineveh collection (British Museum); the sphinx, in high-relief, and a plaque, Nineveh collection, wrought from ivory, etc., all form evidential links of inherent life of an Art.

Through the pre-historic influence, as extended by the foregoing clannazo of Mequethus, and that of their clanthus, Sculpture reached its culmination about the ninth century B. C. In heroic times, the Pheonicians carried Asyrian wares into Greece, which they sold to the Greeks, and *vice versa*.

The work in wood, ivory and metals, wrought by the Assyrians and Greeks, influenced by the commercial exchanges through the trading Pheonicians, brought an amalgamation of alphabetic character representations, viz: those of the Mequethuses (Assyrians); the Zanzuretans (Grecians); the pre-historic Phı-an-ı cı-ans of Phī-nēä (ancestors of the Pheonicians of Syria. This constituted an influence that, in the art of carving, led up to sculpture in low-relief and in parallel horizontal bands, as practised in the seventh century B. C.; then on up to the art statuary in marble and bronze, a result, as was the case in Egypt and other countries, made manifest in Assyria and Greece, relative to the development of sculptural styles, due not only to spirit influence inspirationally, etc., but by and through migratory conditions, of pre-historic and historic peoples of those regions, which likewise brought the spirit influence of those various peoples and their original sections, into co-operation from the spirit side of life; hence the greater extension, etc.

AR'ZETS LUS AR-ZE'TUS LE ZAN-ZU-RE'TA, OR SCULPTORS AND SCULPTURE OF GREECE.

TELTZIE XXXVII.

Passing into Zanzureta, we find the art of är-zĕ'tŭs under the development through the influence of är'zĕts, co-operative with spirit inspiration and guidance.

Thē-rĕn'zē, a pre-historic är'zĕt (sculptor) was a descendant from the Ic-thī-ē'ŏns of Ic'ē-trūse, in the country of Zanzureta. He was born about six hundred years before the Adomic period, lived to the mortal age of a hundred and fifteen years, dwelling in a town by the name of Quĭn'zē—now submerged by the waters of the Gulf of Corinth—which had place in that portion of the now known submerged district west of the town of Khostia.

His work, exclusively, was of the plastic order or process—the moulding of clay into arzetus (Sculpture; i. e., figures), which he dried by the heat of the sun. His subjects, generally speaking, were first of a geometric character, that resulted in the moulding of figures, on flat surfaces, as circles, angles, alphabetic characters, etc., accompanied by many forms of ornamental meanderings which led up to all that class of low-relief ornamentation, that was further extended by subsequent arzets of Zanzureta; and which, by migratory influence, spread out into other countries. The prime utility of his arzetus was for the interior ornamentation on buildings.

Chăl-sē-mē'nŭs, a pre-historic arzet, was a descendant from the Skrŏx-ā-jō'läs of Skrox-ā-jō'lä, in the country of Zanzureta, who was a pupil of and contemporaneous with, Therenze; and who lived to the mortal age of one hundred years. During his most noted period of time, he dwelt in a town by the name of Lĭn-cū'zē, now submerged by the Ionian Sea, then located in that portion of the submerged district, west of the mouth of the Aspru river.

His arzetus was all wrought from soft stone, thus in advance, materially speaking, of the work of Therenze. His prime noted arzetus was in representation of any subject in nature; i. e., it embraced the animal, the bird, and the human forms. He wrought these in full form, while landscapes and vegetable subjects he wrought in low-relief, thus leading up to the idea of full-form sculpture and the relief styles as they developed into greater perfection in later periods. At first his work was crude, but he developed it to quite a perfection during his latter material period. His last work embodied the idea of placing raised, or relief subjects, on earthenware, which led up to the great development of that exquisite branch of this art, in subsequent time.

Returning to Zanzureta, about 4400 B. C., we find the ăl-sy′sū tūse ăl-sy-sū′mŭs (sculptors and sculpture) under further development through the influence of not only Zanzuretan alsysu, co-operative with spirit influence, but that of Siloton cunulaisans, as well; and a change of nomenclature as had been the case in Egypt, and has been with all the languages, during subsequent periods of time; conditions that led up to the establishment of the local alsysu tuse alsysumus, in Greece, at that period.

Mĕl′sē-ŏs was the most noted ăl′sy (sculptor) of Zanzureta, whose work and influence began about 4350 B. C. He was a Silotoan by birth, and in his early youth a pupil under Tronoka; but in his later youth he migrated into Zanzureta. He resided in a large sē-mä′zä (town) by the name of At-lăn′tī-cŏn, located west of Mt. Delphi, about half way between it and the Talanta channel, south of the river, between the towns of Politika and Cholkis. Melseos lived and worked, into the early part of the first quarter of the next century; hence was over a hundred years old when he passed to the spirit realm.

His style of alsysumus differed from that of the Silotonan cunulaisans, especialy in form. At that period they constructed triangular monuments, ranging from twelve to fifteen feet in height, built with a triangular apex that terminated point upwards. Each corner, at the top of the triangular shaft, was sur mounted by an image of a human form, male or female, or of some animal, in representation of some celebrated personage, or a principle; and from the center of the three images, rose the point of the apex triangle, to an harmonious height, above the images.

Sē-cō′lŏs was the most noted alsy whose works and influence began about 4200 B. C. He was a Zanzuretan by birth, and a pupil of Melseos, and spent his youth in the semaza of Atlanticon, which was in the latter days of Melseos. Subsequently, he resided in a large semaza by the name of Tăl-lē-sī′cŏn, now submerged by the Gulf of Lepanto or Corinth, in the open waters of the Gulf, in the district that then lay centrally between the now known coast towns of Galazidi to the north, and Akrata to the south. He lived to about eighty-five years of age, and continued his work up to nearly the time of his dis-embodiment.

His mission, through spirit guidance, was to further develop the Zanzuretah ioon alsysumus (Grecian art of Sculpture) established by Melseos. But he also established new styles and designs, one of which was the placement of alsysumus tuse telsusics (sculpture and pillars) by the doorways or entrances of edifices, from which idea developed the more extensive pillars or columns of the Grecian order.

Passing with the pre-historic influence of the arzets lus arzettus, we make the connection with such links as the following:

In Greek legend we have the account of a Greek sculptor by the name of Daedalus, who wrought before the time of Homer, but supposed by historians to have been a legendary representative of the art of carving and sculpture in Greece, but who, on the contrary, was a real person. In passing through the legendary conditions, the real name of the person, which was Dăl-zăn'ŭs, became changed to Daedalus, as above. Some points in the legend relative to him and his work are only ideas carried out by the pre-historic narrators; but, we are informed by Anstacia, others are true. As, for instance, that he wrought wooden images of deities; originated tools with which to carve; was the first to open the eyes of statues so they seemed to look at the spectator; was the first to separate the legs of the statues so they might walk; that he operated in Crete and Attica in the time of Minos. These are facts; but such ideas as his statue of Hercules having to be tied to keep it from running away, when the hero, angry at its resemblance to himself, threw a stone at it; or that he fled from Athens after having killed his skillful nephew, Talus; had gone to Crete, etc., * * * and his ultimate arrival in Sicily, are purely legendary.

We are also informed by Anstacia, that Dalzanus (Daedalus) was a wonderfuly gifted sculptor; a spirit sensitive of great force, that he never studied his art under a mortal tutor, but wrought from clairvoyant representations given him by spirit guides; therefore he could change from one subject to another at will. His whole being was endowed with conceptive conditions, as it were, and was, therefore, a more wonderful mortal than the people of that period, or subsequent times, ever knew.

The greater freedom which early Greek artists introduced into their figures, was always contrasted with the stiffness of Egyptian statues; and that the legend represented Daedalus as having been some time in Egypt, arose from the fact that Dalzanus was at times controlled by an Egyption spirit sculptor; hence the contrast.

Anstacia also informs us that Dalanus, now as a spirit, is greatly advanced as such; and that, as a spirit, he is surrounded by various halos or colored lights, indicative of that advancement; and that his spirit home is one of splendor; yet at the present time, as has been the case during intervening ages, he returns to mortal sculptors, to aid them in their works, by inspiration; and also that his work on the mortal plane is now nearly ended, when he will pass on to influence in the higher zones.

The cutting and jointing of the great stones that had place in the marvelous "Cyclopean walls" of Tyrinthia, under the direction and workmanship of Nū-mē'lēs, a non-historical sculptor, and his helpers; those at Mycenea, under the direction and workmanship of Mē-sūl'lēs, also a non-historical sculptor, and his helpers; the reliefs of two Rampant Lions, from above the gateway to the citadel of Mycenea (Homeric poems); also the work of Mesulles; the wood and ivory carvings, rich ornamentation on furniture and armor, such as is on the "Shield of Ajax," by Tychus (Iliad vii, 222); "Penelope's Chair," by Icmalius (Odyssey, xix. 60); the "Couch of Odysseus" (Odyssey xxiii, 189); the beautiful "Sidonian crater" (Odyssey iv, 617), wrought by non-historical sculptor, Hĕl'sē-ŭs. When the workmanship of an object is of surpassing beauty, and the artist unknown, as in this case, it was ascribed to the artist god, Hephaestus.) The so-called "Treasury House," of Atreus (see page —— for our account of the structure), by the non-historical sculptor Jĕl'dē-sŭn, and his helpers, all stand as evidential links.

Others are, the antequated Acropolis remains, Athens, Attica, Ionia, Ægina, Selinus Etruria, Xanthos; the ruins of the Mausoleum at Halicarnassus; representations in drawings and specimens, removed to the British, Munich, and Pelermo Museums; specimens brought to knowledge by excavations in Greece, at Camerus and Jalyssus; in Rhodes, Sicily, the Cyrenaica, and in Cyprus—all of which is due, not only to the efforts of the Archæological Societies, but to explorations by private individuals, who have sought to link the arts of the present with that art of the past, which not only gave to the world specimens of early sculpture on metopes and friezes, of archaic style, but established a great influence through literary works narrative thereof, which together form important links in the Great Art Cycle of the Ages, and therefore are important to the Historic.

Of the first historic period, some interesting specimens are, the colossal statue of Jupiter, executed at Corinth, and dedicated at Olympia, the work of a non-historical sculptor by the name of Prăx-ī-tĭl'ēs and the Cedar Chest, in which the infant Cypselus was concealed. The latter was ornamented with gold and ivory figures, arranged in parallel horizontal bands, in representation of heroic legends and scenes from daily life, the names being inscribed *boustrophedon;* i. e., in the manner characteristic of early times, by descended pre-historic letters of the Zanzuretans, used in early times; the enormous Caldron (Herodotus iv, 152), with projecting gryphons' heads, and a support formed of kneeling figures seven ells in height, alluded to as "the oldest example in bronze which he had seen," which was the work of a non-historic sculptor by the name of Quĭn-tē-ni'ŭs; the statue of Jupiter, at Sparta, as described by Pausanius (iii, 17, 6), the work of Clearchus, of Rhegium, made of plate bronze beaten out to form the whole figure, and fastened together with nails. Another example of the influence is the bronze bust found at Polledara, near Vulci, now in the British Museum; the fictile Vases discovered, with figures of animals and flowers arranged in parallel horizontal bands; ideas received by the Greek sculptors and also by the Assyrian, resulting from spirit influences, operating through local and migratory conditions, somebeing decorated with human figures, as principal subjects, the representations of which were taken from the heroic legends of Greece, and further ornamented with accompanying floral designs, the names of the heroes being written in characters from the old Corinthian alphabet. This latter finds its link in the alphabet of the pre-historic Zanzuretans.

We pass from the sculptural influence, as affected by the style of ornamental wooden and bronze reliefs, of Egypt, Assyria and Greece, as a link from the Pre-historic, through the Homeric, to the second period of Classical Art, when a more perfect representation of the human form was established, and the re-born idea of Atlantian Celportic became apparent, in such re-embodiments as were manifested through marble sculpture, in advancement over the art in wood and bronze—as draped figures of goddesses and other subjects; a more natural form of roundness, etc., as evidenced in the works of such sculptors as Archemus, and his sons Bupalus and Athenis, of the Island of Chios (heads of the school of Chios).

The examples of the genius of Archemus and his sons are those that had place in Chios, Delus, Iasus and Smyrna, e. g., the "Graces," or goddesses (nude figures), draped by Bupalus, for the temple of Tyche (Fortune) in Smyrna, and many now non-existing examples, then in Asia-Minor and on the Greek

Islands, that, could they be restored, would give evidence of the great achievements of this art, at that period of time—as developed through conceptions of the sculptors, thus re-embodied through Atlantian spirit inspiration and manifest influence,—more than six centuries B. C.

The influence was not small, of Bathycles, the Greek sculptor of Magnesia on the Mæander, 600 B. C., who, at the head of that school, re-embodied such ideas as were manifest through his statue of Apollo; reliefs; and figures on the colossal "Throne of Apollo" at Amyclæ, near Sparta.

Likewise, the influence of Diphoenus and Scyllis, of Crete, who wrought sculpture groups and statues of deities, from wood, ivory and marble. Not only these two sculptors are to be credited with this class of work, but others not known to history; among whom, the two most noted of that period were, Gē-sē-lē'-ŭs and Tē-băl-bŭs'dĕn, whose works with those of Diphoenus and Scyllis, had place in the Greek towns of Sicyon, Cleonae, Argus, Tyrinthia, and Ambracia.

Although both Diphoenus and Scyllis are now known as traditional, yet they, as many others, our guides inform us, were real persons, and wrought even more than is accorded to them through tradition.

Doryclidas and Dontas influenced through re-embodied ideas, thus influenced through the works of the above-named sculptors. Traditional genius they made manifest through their figures and groups of deities, wrought in cedar and gold, as at Olympia, for the Heraeum, and for the Treasuries of the Epidaurians and Megaraeans.

Other influences, in the art, were the sculptors Clearchus of Rhegium, who wrought in bronze; Tectaeus and Angelion, who wrought the figure of Apollo at Delus, and whom Callon, the celebrated Aeginetan sculptor and his helpers, re-embodied and modelled after; Smilis of Aegina, and Gitiades of Sparta, the former having produced a group of "Horae," to be placed with the figure of Themis, executed by his contemporary, Doryclidas; Smilis, who wrought the figure at Samus; the sculptor of the figure of the Goddess, of the temple of Athene, Chalkioikos; likewise, the sculptor of the reliefs on the plates of bronze, representing scenes from the legends of Hercules and Perseus; and mythical incidents among them at the "Birth of Athene"—all these we accept as real personages, who influenced the high Art genius in those periods.

Canachus, re-embodied the ideas, as induenced by Dyhoenus and Scyllis—original heads of the Sicyon School—which he further extended by manifestations through statues of dieties, which he wrought, sometimes of gold and ivory, as per that of Aphrodite at Sicyon (Pausanias ii, 10, 4), and others of bronze, as per the celebrated statue of Apollo Philesius at Miletus. The latter was influenced, during his earth life, by an Egyptian spirit sculptor, by the name of Gō-lo-ō'dŭs, who dated back to a period remote from the time of the production of the above-named "Apollo." The same spirit had likewise influenced the production of the statue of Apollo at Thebes, Egypt; the two statues differing only in the material from which they were wrought, the latter being of wood and the former of bronze.

In the school of Argus and of Ægina, through which the influence of bronze sculpture was felt, we find Ageladas, the sculptor who was the instructor of the three great masters, Myron, Polycletus and Phidias, by which means he greatly extended the epi-cycle of sculpture, and also influenced through his own works, such as his two statutes of Zeus, etc.

Aristomedon, Glaucus and Dionysius, who influenced in Argus, through bronze works (Pliny, N. H., xxxiv. 2.5.10; 19, 75).

Callon, who headed the bronze sculptural influence in Ægina, as per his statue of "Athene," at Troezene, and his tripod with a figure of "Cora," at Amyclae.

Onatas, of Ægina, greatly influenced through bronze works of large compositions, and also through single statues of gods and heroes.

Anaxagoras, the Greek sculptor, influenced through such bronze works, as his statue of "Zeus," fifteen feet high, for Olympia, in commemoration of the battle of Plataeae.

The bronze statue of "Poseidon," ten and one-half feet high, for the temple of the deity on the Isthmus, was the work of a non-historical sculptor by the name of Clē-ŏm-ē-dēs, a native of Ægina.

The golden tripod that stood on a bronze support, formed of three serpants, for the entrance of the temple of Delphi, was the work of a non-historic sculptor of Ægina, by the name of U-săm'-ā-jes.

Antenor influenced through bronze groups and statuary, such as the group representing "Tyrannicides, Harmodius, and Aristogiton," erected in the Agora at the foot of the Acropolis at Athens.

Pythagoras, the Greek sculptor, influenced through bronze statues and groups, such as his "Philoctetes," at Syracuse, through which he portrayed a marvelous expression of pain, muscular action under strain, veins and sinews, of the human form.

Just here we are informed, by A'lĕm Prō'lĕx, that the existence of so many sculptural monuments, which cannot be traced to the real artists of the early periods who wrought them, at the present time, is on account of there being no written records, officially kept of them at the time of their production, only in such cases as when the sculptor chanced, from a fancy of his own, to record his name on the work which he had wrought, and these were comparatively few in number compared to the great production of that period of time. He further informs us that the masters then enjoyed the title of greatness, and were therefore gratly honored by the people contemporaneous with them; but from lack of literary records, their names passed into oblivion, and did not follow their works, as was the case also with many non-historical facts of antiquity, a condition that has rendered any right modern solution of them difficult and impossible, aside from the revelation through spirit manifestation; and he further states, that the above works as referred to, do not belong to sculptors of the more recent historic times, or known sculptors.

The sculptures from the Temple of Athene, at Ægina, (now in Munich), were the works of two non-historical sculptors, of whom E-drăm'ē-tēs was the original and older. These two, with helpers, wrought the scenes of the western pediment. Sár-dē'-rē-ŭs, a pupil of E-drăm'-ē-tēs, with his helpers, wrought those of the eastern pediment. Those of the western, were in portrayal of the combat over the dead body of Achilles; those of the eastern, a combat, characterized with similar features, in which, as was the case with the former, the central figure represented a fallen hero, with the goddess, Athene, appearing on the scene. This piece is, as has been supposed, a representation of the combat of "Hercules and Telamon," Greeks, against "Leomedon," of Troy.

The marble *stele* found in east Attica (now in the Theseum at Athens), representing, in low relief, "Ariston," an armed warrior, standing in profile, was wrought by Artistocles.

The marble *stele* in Orchomenus, representing in low, flat relief, and profile, an aged man wearing a mantle, standing, resting on his staff and holding a beetle towards the dog at his feet, was by Anxener, of Naxus.

The marble *Stele* in Orchome, representing in low flat relief, the work of a non-historic sculptor by the name of Sy-phō'-dēs.

The fragment of a metope, from the temple of Selinus, in Sicily, represents "Athene," and not as supposed, "Artemis." In this the goddess is trampling on an armed giant whom she had hurled to the ground. It is a wonderfully expressive piece of art, portraying anguish on the face of the giant, etc., and was the work of the non-historic sculptor, Am-brä'zä.

The marble relief, found on the Acropolis of Athens, and there preserved, representing a female figure stepping into a car, (Friderichs, *Bausteine,* i. p. 25.), not a goddess, as supposed, but an imaginary personage, was wrought by a non-historic sculptor by the name of Tē-nō'süs.

The reliefs of the so-called "Harpy Tomb," discovered at Xanthrus in Lysia, in the British Museum, (Friederichs, *Bausteine,* i. p. 37.), was the work of a non-historic sculptor by the name of Tē-nō'thüs.

The fine frieze, from Xanthus, representing a procession of chariots, in which the horses are splendidly wrought, British Museum, (Prachov, Antiquissima Monumenta Xanthiaca, 1872), was the work of a non-historic sculptor by the name of Jĕd'ē-sŏn. sculptor by the name of Jĕd'-ē-sŏn.

The marble relief, in Thasus, representing "Apollo, Hermes, and Nymphs," (Ovebeck, Gesh. d. Griech. Plastik, 2d ed,; i. fig. 28.), was the work of a non-historic sculptor by the name of Nu-de-zon.

These, and many others not here accounted for, were works that led up to the art of Gem-cutting, an ally to the art of sculpture, etc.

Phidias, the most famous of Greek sculptors, the "Michelangelo of Antiquity," whom we have chosen to represent the first great sectional link in the Epi-cycle of Sculpture, at the period of 500 B. C., influenced through such works as he wrought of bronze, wood, gold, ivory, etc., as per his two bronze productions, the first being a large group, dedicated at Delphi, and the second that of the colossal statue of Athene, the "Promachos," erected on the Acropolis, between the Propylaea and Erechtheum. In this the goddess is represented so that the top of her spear and the crest of her helmet are visible at sea, from Cape Sunium (Pausanias i, 28, 2); his Athenian monument at Delphi, commemorating the battle of Marathon; his colossal, chryselephantine figure, of "Athene Areia," of wood, gilt, and marble, at Plataea, the wood of which is covered with gold, and the face, hands and feet, of Pentelic marble; his statue of "Aphrodite," in gold and ivory at Elis; his statue of Athene, ("the Lemuian," "the beauty,") for the Acropolis of Athens; his colossal statue of "Athene," for the Parthenon at Athens, and his "Zues," for the temple at Olympia, wrought of gold and ivory, one of the grandest of all his works. His wonderful statue of "Zeus," the "supreme god of Greece," in the temple at Elis, when finished, was over forty feet high; it represented the god seated on his throne, his right hand holding forward a figure of "Victory," and his left resting on a sceptre, on which an eagle was perched; the head of the deity was crowned with an olive wreath, while his drapery was of gold, highly ornamented with enameled figures and designs of flowers. The throne in this was of ebony and ivory, inlaid with precious stones, richly sculptured with reliefs, and in part painted; and but for the description given by Pausanias, this great work of Phidias would be unknown, to the historic world, as nothing of it now remains. Such is the case with many grand works of the past, that, could they but be replaced, for the consideration of artists of the twentieth century, a more sublime and appreciative estimation would be entertained for the greatness of remote, pre-historic, and antequated peoples and their achievements, in comparison with those of our times, and in comparison with other historical periods.

So great was the influence of this work, as well as that of other sculptors, that imitations were placed on the coins, of their sections, thus acquainting the public, in general, with the ideas therein and thereon embodied, which is also a descended link, to the extended custom of our times, representing governmental celebrities, and other ensigns, on the currency; and, therefore, it is the greatness of the past, the re-embodiments of the ideas of those periods, re-born through spirit influence in the minds of the subsequent celebrities, that has given the twentieth century its greatness. And only a hidden link, in the cycle of all events, the obscurity of which having been in part removed, along the extension of time, affords its present manifestations.

The sculptural figures in the round, from the pediments, the metopes in high relief, and the friezes in low, flat relief, of the Parthenon, were not wrought by Phidias, but were re-embodied ideas from his influential works, carried into effect by subsequent non-historical sculptors, and their helpers, who modelled after his style, etc., e. g., the subjects of the eastern pediment, especially that of the "Birth of Athene," were principally wrought by a non-historic sculptor, by the name of Dī-ăm'ē-dēs, and by his helpers; those of the western, in representation of the "Contest of Athene with Poseidon," for the supremacy over Attica, was principally wrought by a non-historic sculptor by the name of Bē-rĭn'sky, and his helpers; the metopes, ninety-two in number, and the accompanying sculptue thereof, were the works of a non-historic sculptor, by the name of Thē-ō-nō'clēs, and his helpers, the subject being a combat between Centaurs and Lapithae; those on the east and west sides, yet on the building; those of the north, preserved in Athens; those of the south, removed to the Louvre and to Copenhagen, constitute other grand remains.

Theonocles superintended his helpers, and also himself wrought on the great frieze, five hundred and twenty-four feet in length, and forty feet in height, from the ground, which is in very low, flat relief, representing a long festal procession, and characterized with every variety of movement of horse and foot, of young and old, men and women, gods and goddesses, all bearing out national dignity and pride.

Anstacia informs us that this procession was, as it has been supposed by some individuals, to have been, "in representation of the victors at the Pan-Athenaic games, advancing to the Panthenon to receive their prizes, and to attend a sacrifice in honor of victory," and not that "in which it was usual to accompany, annually, the newly-made robe for Athene Polis."

Myron was one of the chief sculptors of the old Attica School, fifth century B. C., and pupil of Argos, who influenced principally through bronze works, excepting the wooden statue of "Hecate," at Ægina. His most famous works were those in representation of the Cow; the runner, Ladas, and "The Discobolus" (copy life size in the Massimi Palace, Rome), etc.

Polycletus, a contemporary of Phidias and Myron, influenced through his creation of ideal athletes and deities, his greatest work being the chryselephantine statue of "Hera," at Argos, etc.

Alcamenes, a pupil of Phidias, an Athenian sculptor, famed by Cicero, Pliny, Pausanias, Lucan, etc., between four and five centuries B. C., influenced through such works as his masterpiece, a statue of "Venus Urania," in the temple of that deity at Athens; figures of deities; his statue of "Aphrodite" for her temple; that of "Triple Hecate;" that of "Aesculapius," "Hephaestus," "Ares," etc.

Agoracritus, of Porus, also a pupil of Phidias, influenced through such works as his figure of "Nemesis," in Rhamnus; his statue of "Rhea," in the Metroon at Athens (Pausanias i, 3, 5); his bronze statues of "Athene Itonia" and "Zeus," in the temple of the goddess, between Alalcomenae and Coronea (Pausanias ix, 34, 1).

Further extension, of the influence of Phidias, was felt through the re-embodied ideas in the works of Colotes and Thrasymedes of Parus, and stil further by Theocosmus, of Megara.

Polycletus, of Sicyon, who co-operated, influentially, with

Phidias and Alcamenes, thus forming a great triumviate link among the Greek sculptors, influenced through such works as his great chryselephantine statue of Hera, at Argus, which was an embodied idea co-related with that of the statue of Zeus at Olympia, by Phidias. Of these the former is said to yield to the latter, in grandeur and imposing aspect, and vice-versa, but the latter outrivaled, in finish, the former.

Of the three colossal marble heads, copies of the head of the statue of "Hera," at Argus, the one at Naples was wrought by a non-historic sculptor by the name of Grăph'ī-māze; the one in the British Museum, by a non-historic sculptor by the name of Frē-nū'lŭs; the one in the Villa Ludovisi, by a non-historic sculptor by the name of Lū-crē'dŭs.

Polycletus further influenced through his works in representation of athletes, such as his "Doryphorus" and "Canon" (the latter, Alem Prolex informs us, was a distinct subject, and not meant by Pliny as "Doryphorus," as has been supposed).

The marble copy of "Diadumenus," found at Valson, France (now in the British Museum), was the work of a non-historic sculptor by the name of O-cle-mus.

His bronze group of boys playing with knuckle-bones, which afterwards stood in the palace of Titus, Rome, was one, the nature of which was re-embodied in the works of subsequent sculptors; e. g., the small group in terra-cotta representing two women playing at the game, etc., which was the work of a non-historic sculptor by the name of Quē'ley.

Other works of his are, the statue of "An Amazon," executed for Ephesus; his bronze statue of maidens, carrying sacred vessels on their heads, possessed by Heius the Mamertine, from whom they were taken by Verres (Cicero, *in Verr* iv, 3, 5); his statue of "The Samian," "Artemon," etc.

Polycletus, the younger, influenced through re-embodied ideas and styles as influenced by the elder Polycletus, above named, as evidenced by his statues of "Victors at Olympia," and a statue of "Zeus Philius" (Pausanias viii, 31, 4), in which the expression is said to resemble that of Dionysus.

The marble relief in Athens, found at Eleusis, representing Demeter, Cora, and boy (*Monumenti,* vi. pl. 45), was the work of a non-historic sculptor by the name of Hĕl'cē-ŭs.

The upper part of a female figure, supporting a basket on her head (Calathephorus), now in Cambridge (Wieseler, *Denkmaler* ii. pl. 8, No. 92), was the work of a non-historic sculptor by the name of I-cē-lō'nŭs.

The marble relief of "Orpheus and Eurydice," in Villa Albani, and its two replicas, in Naples and Paris, was the work of a non-historic sculptor by the name of Lē-dī-ōn'sēe.

The metopes from the Temple of Zeus, at Olympia (now in Paris), were the work of a non-historic sculptor by the name of Y-yŏn'sō-my, who was co-operative with the Phidias who wrought the great statue of Zeus for the temple; Alchemenes, who wrought the figures for the western pediment, and Paeonius of Hende, who wrought the figures for the eastern Pediment.

The metopes and inner frieze of the temple of Theseus at Athens, yet in their original place, were the work of a non-historic sculptor by the name of Sā'krātes.

Scopas, native of Parus, upon whom, co-extant with Praxiteles, the mantle of Phidias fell, influentially, further influenced through such works as his bronze statue of Aphrodite, sitting on a goat, in Elis (Pausanias vi, 25, 2); his statue of a Maenad, at Athens, in the attitude of rushing with her head thrown back and streaming hair, holding a slain kid in her hand. In this the artist manifested excited passion and bodily agitation; his statue of "Apollo Citharoedus," with long flowing robe, head thrown back as in a dreamy enjoyment of the strains from his lyre, is a work made to manifest a passion of peaceful inspiration; his work co-operative with Bryaxis, Ceochares, and Timotheus, in the production of the sculptural works on the monument which Queen Artemesia, of Caria, erected at Halicarnassus, in memory of her husband; his sculpture for the towns of Cnidus, Ephesus, and Chryse in Troad, Asia-Minor; and his representation of Poseidon, Thetis and Achilles, attended by Nereids, the latter riding on dolphins and hippocampuses; and by tritons and other mamaleous creatures of the sea, a work that had place in the Temple of Neptune, at Rome, etc.

Praxiteles influenced through sympathetic types of human or divine beings; and emotional pleasures, as evidenced by his marble statue representing Hermes as carrying the infant Dionysus, found at Olympia.

We are informed by Anstacia that Praxiteles was not a pupil of Scopas, as has been supposed, but contemporaneous, and a co-worker with him, during the last half of his career as a sculptor.

She also informs us that Scopas did not originate, in Greek Art, the ideal types of those marine beings that personified the element of the sea; but, the origin was of a date two or more generations previous, and by a non-historic sculptor, by the name of Căr'ad-a-nō'nŏn; and this latter was followed by another non-historic sculptor, by the name of Cĕn'dū-lĕx, of Athenian birth, and note, who improved the idea and further developed the art, and from whose works and influence Scopas further wrought, and influenced.

Furthermore, in relation to his large composition, representing the slaughter of the children of Niobia, which had place on the Temple of Apollo, Rome (the authorship being ascribed to Scopas by some writers, and to Praxiteles by others), we are informed by Alem Prolex that Scopas designed the composition. and was the principal developer of it; but at the same time he received ideas from Praxiteles, as well as from other contemporaries, relative to its general detail and these he carried into effect as suggested to him by them.

Just here we are informed, by the same spirit, that Praxiteles was not a son of Cephisodotus, as supposed, but of E-rē'tē-nŏs, a noted sculptor and painter of that period, who was particularly famous for the perfect wooden models he wrought, for his pupils and helpers to follow or copy in bronze or marble. Yet some of his best wooden sculptures he painted white, and worked down to a glossy finish, which were considered very fine, and also, it was from his father that Praxiteles learned the art of sculpture.

Furthermore, Anstacia informs us, the statue of "Leucothea," in the Glyptotheke of Munich, was not the work of Cephisodotus, but that of Praxiteles. It was, however, a re-embodied idea, further developed by him, having been influenced through the idea of Cephisodotus, who wrought a statue, for Athens, of Irene, with the boy Plutus in his arms, which subsequently had place as a copy on the coins of Athens; hence, the idealistic influences.

Again, he influenced through the expression of sensual beauty, natural to youthful feminine ideal life, in the highest type, true to nature; these subjects he wrought mostly in marble, and softened the aspect of them by a process of encaustic, adorned with colored draperies; and also tinted accompaniments of marble form. These were ideas that he had gathered from his father's works, under tints and colored developments, in evidence of which we note such works as his marble statue of "Aphrodite," at Cnidus, which Pliny declared to be the most beautiful statue in the world. The re-embodied ideas of this can be traced to such copies as the "Venus" of the Capitoline Museum, "Venus de Medicis," and other representations and copies of "Aphrodite," as in the Louvre, etc.; his statue of "Aphrodite," at Thespiae; his celebrated "Satyr," in Athens; his "Apollo Sauroctonus;" his statue of "Artemis Brauroria," at Athens, etc., were strong and influential ideas, that continued the extension of sculptural ideas, such as led up to a more perfect expression, in the art.

The works of Cephisodotus and Timarclu, sons of Praxiteles, heads of the Athenian school, who wrought statues of various deities; and their contemporaries, who produced portrait sculpture, influenced in the extension of the art.

Bryaxis, 345 B. C., was a contemporary of Scopas and Praxiteles, with whom he took part in establishing the sculptures in the mausoleum at Halicarnassus, and who influenced through such works as five colossal figures of gods: at Rhodes, "Bacchus" (*Liber Pater*); at Cnidus, a group of "Aesculapius and Hygeia"; at Megara, "Apollo in the Grove of Daphne"; at Antioch, a statue of "Pasiphae," and a portrait of "Seleucus."

Anstacia informs us that the group of Jupiter and Apollo with the lion, at Patara, and the statue of Serapis, were originated and begun by a non-historic sculptor by the name of Hē-lĭp'tĭs, and subsequently completed by Bryaxis; and that it was Heliptis also who wrought a statue of "Aesculapius, God of Healing;" and that it was he who introduced the type of these deities, viz., Aesculapius and Serapis, into that region, and not Bryaxis, as has been thought by some writers. The statue of Apollo, at Daphne, however, representing the god in his character of "Musagetes," with long-flowing drapery, girt at the waist, was originated and completed by Bryaxis; and it was through the style of draped and mature forms that Bryaxis influenced mostly, as Praxiteles had done, in contrast, by his display for nude and youthful figures.

Timotheus, a contemporary of Scopas, and Praxiteles, Bryaxis and Leochares, through ideas of large composition, such as his colossal, acrolithic statue of "Ares," at Halicarnassus, held a comparative influence in that period of time. (Anstacia informs us just here that this piece of sculpture was not the work of Leochares, as some modern writers have thought, but of Timothens, hence we so assign it.)

Leochares, contemporary and co-operative sculptor, with Scopas, Bryaxis, Timotheus and Pyihis, on the mausoleum above referred to, about 356 B. C., influenced through such works as the frieze on that edifice (fragments of which are now in the British Museum); his statue of "Irocrates," at Athens; his bronze representation of Alexander the Great, engaged in a lion hunt, co-operative with his contemporary Lysippus; his ivory and gold group, in the Philippeion at Olympia, representing the family of Philip and Alexander; his portraits; his ideal chryselephantine statues; his ideal of Zeus, one for the Acropolis, one at Piraeeus, and one removed to Rome; other ideal conceptions, including deities, portraits, mythological and allegorical subjects; and his masterpiece, the "Rape of Ganymede," etc.

Euphranor influenced, during the middle of the fourth century, B. C., through many pieces of sculptural work, ranging from colossal life figures to drinking cups; and also through his modification of canonical proportions, of his subjects, in contradistinction to those of Polycletus.

Lysippus, who influenced during the period between 372 and 316 B. C., re-embodied ideas made manifest through the works of Euphranor, which he developed and further extended, especially the favorite type of idealistic athletic statuary and portraiture, as evidenced by his more than fifteen hundred statues and groups of bronze, said to have gone forth from his workshop. Two of these are of colossal size, viz., the "Jupiter," at Tarentum, which is sixty feet high, and that of "Hercules," in the same place; re-embodied ideas influenced through the works of Polycletus, with developed physical form, as evidenced by works of his, and his subsequent followers, who wrought statues and heads in bronze and marble; his bronze statuette of "Hercules," famed in antiquity and called "Epitrapezius," a copy of which, in stone, formerly from Babylonia (now in the British Museum) was, as per his signature, wrought by a sculptor by the name of Diogenes. Further, his group of "The Muses," for the town of Megara, etc., all of which had an influence, relative to styles and types, with his contemporaries and the subsequent sculptors, e. g., the statue of Alexander the Great, in Munich, standing with one foot, raised on a helmet, which was the work of a non-historic sculptor by the name of Ar-tēm'mē-ŭs; the so-called "Jason," in Lansdowne House, the work of a non-historic sculptor by the name of Cē-lē-cō'sy, who re-embodied the idea from the same type on the Parthenon. The Parthenon work was accomplished under the supervision of Thē-ō-nō'clēs, and his helpers, who wrought the frieze on that temple, the same style having been, subsequently, re-embodied by Lysippus, in the creation of his new type as of the "god of Neptune," for his temple on the Isthmus of Corinth; and further re-embodied in the attitudes of draped female figures, such as in the existing statues of the Muse, "Melpomene," standing with one foot raised on a rock, which was the work of a non-historic sculptor by the name of Au-thō-grā-phē'rē; therefore the style became an extended influence, from Theonocles, through the works of Lysippus, and later by that of various non-historic sculptors.

We are here informed, by Anstacia, that Lysippus was influenced greatly by Athenian types, from which he re-embodied similar ideas in his works, especially that which had descended from the hand of Praxiteles.

Furthermore, the influence of Lysippus was extended, through such works as the bronze statuettes of Neptune and Jupiter, found at Paramythia, in Epirus (British Museum), which were the work of a non-historic sculptor by the name of E-ĕn'sē-lōpe; the large bronze of "Hercules," from Byblus (British Museum), re-embodied ideal work, by a non-historic sculptor by the name of Lĕt-sē'mŭs; the series of portrait sculpture of this period, originated by a non-historic sculptor by the name of O-cē-lĭn'dä, who was followed, in the work, by his son Jăn-shū'-lŭs, and still later by another non-historic sculptor by the name of Wĭck'ē-dē-sĕnd, who represented three generations of time; and the colossal bronze head found at Satala, in Armenia (now in the British Museum), which was the work of Wickedesend, who had gone from Athens to that section of the country. The head was wrought for a place of worship, and was in representation of the goddess, Creanthus, representing the evening star, according to that position of the various planets during the twelve months of the year, etc.

The marble head of Alexander the Great, from Alexandria, now in the British Museum, was the work of a non-historic sculptor by the name of Lăm-ī-lū-mē'les, who influenced subssquent to the sculptors, Mys, Mentor, Acrogas, and Boethus, who preceded the Alexandrian period, and it was from the works of Lamilumeles that the ideas of die-sinking and gem-engraving were established in that region, and carried out by such engravers as Cimon and Euaenetus, Euclides, Eimenus, Eumelus, Phrygillus, Sosion, etc. This art manifested especially on the Greek coinage of that period of the Macedonion Kings, Philip and Alexander, and extended to that of the Chalcideans of Thrace, and to Cydonia, in Crete, etc., where such engravers as Neuantus and Lesbus re-embodied the idea. It was also the works of Lamilumeles that influenced Pyrgoteles, gem-cutter and court engraver to Alexander the Great, to cut the portrait of Alexander the Great on an emerald, an act which further influenced the adoption of the portrait of Alexander on the coins of his successor, Lysimachus. The above-named marble head of Alexander, therefore, was preserved in Alexandria, in memorium of its sculptor, Lamilumeles. But the records of this artist, which were lost, with many others, had they been preserved, would have thrown much light upon historic facts, now so vague and uncertain.

The reliefs on the "Lantern of Demosthenes," a building in

Athens, representing Bacchus and his suite, transferring the Tyrrhenian priests into dolphins, were the work of a non-historic sculptor by the name of Săn-dī-ēna'cŭs, of greatness, artistically speaking, and a contemporary of the above-named sculptor, Janshulus.

The sculptures of the so-called "Nereide monument," discovered at Xanthus, Lycia (British Museum), which represent a series of female figures, in the round, of life size, wearing a thin drapery through which the forms are entirely visible, are the work of a great non-historical sculptor, by the name of Quĭn-cē-lŏs, who originated that style of work. When Quincelos was in Greece he was associated, in the art of sculpture, with Janshulus.

He, by chance, conceived the idea of the style. When engaged in certain drafting and cutting of lines and figures, he discovered that representations could be made of inner and outer designs, wherein both were rendered visible. From this fact, under further spirit inspiration, he finally conceived the idea of thus representing the human form, with other accompaniments, in group, which ultimately brought out works similar, and finally the above-named Nereid representation.

Following the influence into the fifth period of classical art, transformed as it was from ideal types of deities, to those of allegorical figures, with a re-embodiment of figures of deities and heroes from the preceding old types, and the further development of the portrait belonging to the Hellenistic and Roman periods, we find the influence extended, by such sculptors as the sons of Praxiteles, Cephisodotus and Timarchus, at the head of the Athenian school, who influenced through portrait sculpture; and Euthycrates, son of Lysippus, and Tisicratis, a pupil of Euthycrates, who headed the Sicyonion school, whose influence was re-embodied in such works as the bronze statue representing the river, Eurotas, by Eutychides, who expressed the mobility of water by the human form (Pliny, N. H. xxxiv, 8, 78), and the highly praised statue of Tyche (Pausanias vi, 2, 7), for the town of Antioch; the colossal bronze statue of "Helius," at Rhodes, by Chares of Lindus, a work which for its size, has been recorded as one of the wonders of the world; which when found stood seventy cubits high (destroyed by an earthquake about 224 B. C.); the influence of which led down to other colossal works of that region, as re-embodied by Apollonius and his brother Tauriscus, who wrought the famous colossal marble group known as the "Farnese Bull," which represents Amphion and Zethes, in the act of tying the revengeful Dirce to a wild bull, in the presence of his mother, Antiope (Naples Museum); the bronze group representing Athamas, seized with insanity after slaying his son, Learchus, by Aristonidas, of the Rhodian School; the large groups and compositions representing battle scenes, such as portrayed the victory of Attalus over the Gauls, 239 B. C., a work through which were manifested such characteristics as dogged submission under captivity, grim expression under pain, and abject misery of the wives of the warriors when a battle had been lost; the four groups, presented by Attalus to Athens, in representation of battles, between the gods and the giants; between Athenians and Amazons; between Greeks and Persians at Marathon; and between his own army and the Gauls in Mysia, etc.

We find the influence again in Pasiteles, who influenced through staturia, sculptura, and caelalura, including chryselephantine figures, re-embodiments of former period ideas; Stevanus, who influenced through statuary, from living models, and re-embodiments of previous ideas, that had manifested through the works of Pasiteles, as per his "Orestes," in the Villa Albani (*Annali dell' Inst.* 1865, pl. D; Freiderichs, *Bausteine* i, p. 112), which is a co-related idea, with the male figure, in the group of "Orestes and Electra," in Naples, by Menelaus.

These, celebrities of their day, along with others of influence, such as Arcesilaus, Posidonius of Ephesus, Zopyrus, Pytheas, Teucrus, etc., formed important links in the Sculptural Epi-cycle, through the influence of Revival; i. e., through copy extension, of ideas that had been made manifest through the works of preceding masters; and which, in turn, paved the way for gem-engraving, silver glass, and precious stone ornamentation, vases, statuettes and utensils of various kinds in bronze and silver, all re-embodiments, idealistically, from Greek models, as evidenced by the influence of gem-cutting. Some examples of this, which exist, in onyx, sardonyx, agate, etc., as worn by the Egyptians, Greeks, and Romans, show imitative designs engraved upon them in bas-relief, or figures raised above the surface, such as are known as Cameos; e. g., the large one now in Vienna, fashioned both from allegorical and literal ideas, in representation of the "Suppression of the Pannonian revolt by Tiberius and Germanicus" (Müller, *Denkmäler* i, pl. 67, No. 377); the cameo in the Cabinet of Medals, in Paris (Müller *ibid.* No. 378); the drinking cups of onyx, and other precious stones, such as the "tezza Farnes," in Naples (*Mus.* Borb. xii, pl. 47); the glass ornamentation, in place of precious stones, such as characterizes the celebrated "Portland Vase," in the British Museum, etc.

The bronze group of Athamas seized with insanity after having slain his son Learchus, work of Aristonidas of the Rhodian School; the group of Laocoon, work of the sculptors, Agesander, Athenodorus, and Polydorus; the works of Polycles, of Athens, his son, Timarchides, and his grandson, Dionysius, of the "New Attic school," etc., with further influence extending into Rome.

Passing into Clē-ăn-di'cï-ä (Asia Minor), we note the influence of the pre-historic ē-sĕn'sŏn shū ē-sĕn-sŏn'rĭx* (sculptors and sculpture), through engraved hieroglyphics, or Rock-Sculpture (*boustrophedon*), of pre-historic origin, through Lydia, Phrygia, Cappadocia, and Lyconia, never yet deciphered. They were chiefly the works of the pre-historic Dĕn-cī'ēs. (See migrations in Asia-Minor, later in this work.) Those of Lydia were influenced by Sĕl-ăn'shē-ī, a descendant from the Dencies, who was the most noted sculptor of that period, as aided by his pupils and helpers. Those of Phrygia were influenced by the pre-historic sculptor, Cŭm' bē-ăn, a descendant from the pre-historic sculptor Trĭs-tī-lō'sy, a descendant from the Dencies, and his pupils and helpers, and those from Lyconia, by the pre-historic sculptor Nū-drē-ĕn'sĭc, a descendant from the Nō-cō'trăns, and his pupils and helpers.

In evidence of the influence throughout that section of country, we note the sculpture, on the rock faces of a plateau fifty to two hundred feet in height, surrounding a great pre-historic city by the name of Dĭ-jō'nŏsh, on the road from Pteria to Sardis, inscribed, "Midras The King," thus sculptured by Cŭm'-bē-ăn, the principal sculptor of that city, at the time that Midras was made king, though he was contemporaneous with the latter period of the reign of the previous pre-historic King Kānō'jŏsh. and executed sculptural designs on the rocks in that period, having been influenced by sculptors of a still earlier period.

The city of Dī'jō-nosh was built by the descendants of the Eltaclucians, whom we have shown as having settled in that region of the country, and the sculptural designs, of this city, were principally, as before stated, planned and partly wrought, by Cumbean and his pupils and helpers, whose subsequent influence extended to the establishment of other sculpture, of the old Phrygian kingdom of the Senforeus Valley. Those sculptors, for a time, had been influenced by the old Cappadocian supremacy, under the extended influence of the pre-historic sculptor, Tristilosy, and his pupils, co-operating with the influence, which originally had been handed down from the above named sculp-

*Anstacia informs us that the Dencies language, at that period of time, had no preposition "of."

tural influences. (See migrations of peoples into Phrygia and Cappadocia.)

The existing monuments, in evidence of the above named facts, belonging to Phrygian greatness, in the sculptural arts, and otherwise, appear in two classes, that which bears the inscribed name, "MIDRAS THE KING," the most remarkable of the one class. The detailed sculpture exists in geometrical patterns, of squares, crosses, and meanders, surmounted by a pediment, supported in the centre by a pilaster in low relief, and is thus delineated on the surface of a huge perpendicular rock; other designs portray the subjects of vines, floral patterns, etc., that ornament the surface of the rock; some are characterized with sphinxes, of a remote and archaic type, that were sculptured on two sides of the pediments, some were characterized with carved doorways, leading to small chambers, on the back of which, in low relief, was sculptured a rude female image, then termed Cĕl-dē-cē'nä (supposed by modern writers to be a mythological representation of the "mother goddess," Cybele, or "mother of Zeus"), having on each side of her a lion, which rests his paws on her shoulders, and places his head against hers. This is, in reality, and originally was intended to represent, the goddess Celdecena, which term, in the language of the Eltaclucians, meant "purity;" while the lion represented the characteristic of "cruelty," or the cruel element in all its phases, and the posing of the group represented the characteristic of cruelty as brought under subjection by spiritual purity. As a people, the Eltaclucians were very spiritual; hence they worshiped the Celdecena, as presiding over the principle of Spiritual purity, and its force, in both the mortal and the spirit spheres; and for this it was represented on the doorways leading to these sepulchral chambers.

The second class is marked by the heraldic type, of two animals, usually lions rampant, facing one another, but divided by a pillar or some other device. These have place on the monuments of an earlier date than the former class, and were symbols relative to national conditions, i. e., the people, being of a spiritual turn of mind and understanding, abhorred wars and contentions generally which conditions they symbolized by the rampant lions; while the standards separating them represented barriers, or influential forces, especially those of spirit intervention, having descended between the contending forces, to aid in subduing the hostile conditions, thus to restore peace and harmony in both national and domestic affairs. Therefore, this type was a very sacred symbol to the people.

The influence of the heraldic type extended into the geometrical, and further, into the designs of the inscribed monuments, as the people advanced in their spiritual and more scientific knowledge. But this was not to the exclusion of symbolism, which gives evidence of the linking influences, that followed in the descending generations of those peoples and their works.

The Phrygians possessed a high artistic faculty, very similar to that of the Greeks; caused probably by the lines of ancestral lineage of both nations, from remote periods. (See our migrations and establishment of both races.)

The influence of such art ideas as those displayed on Midas' Tomb, was re-embodied in various ways, by the Cappadocians, even in the patterns employed in cloth and carpets. It was also re-embodied in the patterns in apparel, etc., that ornamented the priests of that period, as evidenced by the embroidered robe on the priest, in the rock-cut sculptural design at Ibriz. This was similar to the patterns on the Midas Tomb, and a style that originated with the Eltaclucians, whose descendants became the now known Phrygians.

The heraldic influence was further carried into Assyria, partly by migratory conditions (see our descendants and migrations of that people), but it was also under development, in that section, by spirit inspiration and guidance. Therefore the style, to a degree, was orginal with the Phrygians, and thus it spread throughout Asia Minor into Assyria, and ultimately linked with that type in the early Grecian sculptural art, as evidenced by the heraldic type of two lions, in the device over the principal gateway of Mycenae, and at Tiryns, or Tirynth, Greece, etc.

The rock monuments in the Phrygian style, and the votive reliefs of an Anatoline type found near Phocaea, Asia Minor, have their existence under the same conditions as the former named subjects, and all are important links with which to conneet up the extension of the Epi-cycle of Sculptural Art, as it was moving along in that region, on the deferent of the Great Art Cycle.

Passing into Etzentuan (Italy), we find the rē-ĕn'täs tŭs rē-ĕn-cū'sä (sculptors and sculpture) under development through the influence of reentas, co-operative with spirit advisers.

Prō-zĕl'zō, a pre-historic reenta (sculptor), son of Chăl-ĕs-mē'nŭs; the Zanzuretan arzet (sculptor), migrated from his home in Skrō-jā-ō'lä, into Etzentuan, when but a lad of fifteen years. There he began the development of his artistic gifts, and lived to the mortal age of eighty-nine years, in a pre-historic town by the name of Frē-nō'zē, in the section now known as Basilicata, Italy, on the site of the town of Pescopagano.

His first reencusa was wrought on soft stone, as was his father's custom; but his work was much finer, artistically speaking. He generally chose a variety of objects for his subjects, as his father had done, the utility of which was for interior ornamentation, or bric-a-brac use.

Later in life he began ornamental work on stone buildings or structures, in relief style, as well as that in the architectural idea of laying stone in projections, etc., so as to appear ornamental on the main structure, by jutting and other zig-zag forms. His efforts were crude at first, but afterwards he developed the idea to considerable perfection, until it not only led up to subsequent sculptural advancement, but to certain architectural growths and original ideas, especially those of the "greater pillar" and "column" ideas, of subsequent time.

Căl-lĕn'zē was a pre-historic reenta and a descendant from the Je-re-the'ans, of Etzentuan, who was a pupil of Prozelzo. He lived in the form one hundred and ten years, and ultimately dwelt in a pre-historic town named Gŏtch'lĕnd, then located in the now known district submerged by the waters of the Bay of Naples, a town which was at that time the greatest in Etzentuan, Italy.

His first work, as a reenta, was to advance ornamental, architectural construction in stone. Later in life he originated the execution of the relief style, on marble, when he chose such subjects as those of the human form. This work was utilized for exterior ornamentation on buildings. Later he originated the idea of representing the full form, or round Re-en-cu-sa, standing on a pedestal and wrought from one block of marble. His lines were crude at first, but he developed that branch of the art up to a better condition, artistically, before his transition to spirit life, and thus established the link that led up to the great production of an order of Statuary that so universally adorns every country's places for Art, in modern times.

We pass into Tindinzeon (Germany) and find the art of mĕn-zoi'tŭs (sculpture), under development by the menzoits (sculptors), co-operatively influenced by their spirit advisers.

Strĕn-bĕrg'ĕr*, a prehistoric menzoit (sculptor), was a

*Give g the soft sound.

As we are writing this biography of Strenberger, he presented himself to Mrs. Van-Duzee clairvoyantly, and said, "You have called me up from the long ago existence—the conditions of which life I have long since freed myself, and in exchange for which I have developed into this, of greater light and beauty." She described him as a wonderfully bright, beautiful, and advanced spirit—all light.

descendant from the Sĭn-ē'thŏns of Tindinzeon, who began his mortal life about nine hundred years before the Adomic period, and lived in the form one hundred and fifty years, and dwelt in a town by the name of Crū-shĕn'hĕn, on the site where now the town of Arenshausen, Prussia, or Eastern Germany, has place.

His menzoitus was wrought of wood, and, properly speaking, belonged to the carved order that was utilized in the bodies of the musical instruments that he originated. At first his work was quite crude, but by means of faithful study and untiring experimental effort, he ultimately reached quite a perfect development in that line of manufacture.

He not only originated the bodies of several musical instruments, but was led to discover the principle of melodics, and therefore to establish various pitches of sound. This he did while making two different instruments that were minipulated by a process of concussion, viz: the Lē-ĕl'sō, an instrument similar to the now known violins, guitars and mandolins, only the body of the Strenberger instrument was rectangular in form, no neck, and had three strings.

Ultimately this instrument linked with the violin class. He was the author, also, of the Frĭz, which was of a hollow wooden body, about two inches in diameter, about sixteen inches in length, and slightly elliptical but tubelike. A long opening, bearing out the same elliptical form, was cut on top of the central portion of the body, and parallel with it. From the inner edge of the opening, next to the player, rose a metal strip, so placed as to extend diagonally from the centre of the lower end of the opening to the upper front of the same. This arrangement was to assist in the melodic grade of the sounds of the instrument—higher or lower. Seven keys, or small hammers, in a line, at various distances, were attached to the back and outer-side of the body, by springs; the hammer part being adjusted so as to rest directly over the top of the metal strip, which the player, by finger manipulation, caused to strike on top of it, similar to the action in the stroke of piano hammers upon the wires. The body of the instrument was suspended, at each end, upon a frame, so as to allow free vibration, and was an instrumental link that led up to the class of instruments modernly known as the dulcimer, clavichord and the piano.

He further established a crude order of metal plastic ornamentation, which he hammered into form to be placed on the instruments, and ultimately he formed other single ornaments for various purposes, all of which led up to greater advancement in the plastic art of metal order, such as is known to people of modern times.

Hā'gūte, a pre-historic menzoit, and a descendant from the Sinethons, of Tindinzeon, was born about 800 years before the Adomic period, and lived in the body one hundred years. He dwelt in a large town by the name of Wĭn'gĕr-bürgh, in the now known section of Brandenburg, Prussia, Eastern Germany, on the site where now the town of Kustrin has place.

His first menzoitus was wrought by the process of moulding clay, which he hardened by the heat of the sun. Later, he used soft stone for the same purpose; and during the latter period of his career as a menzoit, he used both hard stone and marble for his menzoitus.

His subjects for representation were peculiar, in that he moulded and carved after models of drapery, such as hung in graceful folds and was of many patterns; but usually in representation of portal and window portieres, or screens, in which case a projected canopy or marble or stone crowned the hanging, or sculptured drapery. The canopies were beautifully carved with representations of leaves and vines, executed in relief style.

The finest of his menzoitus was wrought from white marble. The utility of all of it was for exterior and interior ornamentation, the former having place on the facades of buildings, and the latter, as the taste of the purchaser suggested. All of his latter period productions were magnificently perfect, and beautiful in every detail. His creations were links that led up to the idea of window and portal drapery, as well as all classes of ornamental drapery, such as has developed during subsequent ages and which is of such great utility in modern times.

Passing into Falkaleit (France), we find the pē-dī'zĕr-ŭs bĕnz pē-dī-zĕr-ŭs'tēs (sculptors and sculpture) under the influence of pedizerus, co-operative with spirit influence.

Plĭn'tōne, a pre-historic pē-dī'zĕr (sculptor), was a descendant from the Gŭd'lĭng-stŏns of Gŏn-sō-ē'sēs, in the country of Falkaleit, who came into the earth life about 1000 years before the Adomic period, and lived to the mortal age of seventy-five years, and dwelt in a pre-historic town by the name of Prĭn-ī'dĕt, on the site of the now known town of Damazan, on the Gironne river.

His pedizerustes was wrought of wood, and was very simple. His subjects, principally, were animals and fishes, and such landscapes as portrayed water scenes with ship accompaniments. In fact he chose such subjects as met his fancy, excepting that he did not attempt representation of the human form.

The only utility made of his pedizerustes, was for interior home decoration.. His creations were links that led up to the representation of naval scenes, and monumental animal subjects, as they now have place throughout subsequent time.

Rĕn'sŏc, a pre-historic pedizer, and a descendant from the Cō-sē-ăn'zēs of Kō-lä'ĭs, in the country of Falkaleit, who came into notoriety, was contemporaneous with the last half of Plintones period. He lived to the mortal age of one hundred and five years, and dwelt in a large town by the name of Sĕn'lŏss, in the now known section of Indre Et Loir, on the site where the town of Tours has place.

His pedizerustes was also wrought of wood, for in his first period as a pedizer, he was influenced by the works of Plintone; but during his latter period he made great advancement, improving the ideal works of the latter. During that time, he chose the human form largely for his subject. He wrought in relief at first, but later created the full forms of individuals, standing on pedestals.

As to the art of carving to the life, his proficiency has not been excelled during the ages that have passed, ancient or modern; and no sculptor, of those periods, has ever brought out such expressive eyes, or such visage representation of the beard and hair of the head, such perfect bodily form and graceful pose, as was manifested through the pedizerustes of this Rensoc. The first utility, made of his creations, was for exterior ornamentation on the facades of buildings.

Later, he conceived the idea of grouping his subject figures, in representation of various scenes and conditions of life. These were utilized for interior decorations, e. g., one of his most beautiful representations was of a happy family, the father, the mother and the children, posed in an evening gathering at the fireside.

No modern sculptor could have wrought a more perfect idea of such a scene as he portrayed in that group of 7000 years agone. Therefore it became an important link, spanning that period of time, in support of the marvelous product of individual and grouped statuary, a type such as now crowds public and private assemblage places of Sculptural Art, throughout the continents of the earth.

Passing into Sĕd'ē-rōne (Portugal and Spain), we find the sā-wā'nē sent sā-wā-nē-ŭs' (sculptors and sculpture), under the influence of the sawane, co-operative with spirit inspiration and guidance.

Săn-zū'lŭs, a pre-historic Sā'wāne (sculptor), was a descendant from the Mā-lĭn'gōes of Dĕl-cör'tō, in the country of Sederone, who came into the earth life about 1200 years before the Adomic period, and lived to the mortal age of one hundred and seven years.

As a sawane, he dwelt in a pre-historic town by the name of Sĕn-mā'lŏs, located near the junction of the now known Ebro and Segre rivers, on the site where now the town of Mequinenza has place. His sawaneus was all wrought of wood, and his subjects were those of the animal form, exclusively, especially of the larger species, which he posed both singly and in groups, according to his own fancy, and the further representation of their life traits and characteristics. He attained considerable proficiency in the production of this order of sawaneus, during the latter part of his career.

His creations were utilized for ornamenting yards, and public squares, and especially as central ornaments to the area where streets crossed, as various sculptural monuments now adorn such places. The art of Sanzulus was the re-embodied link connecting that style of adornment, through the ages, down to its Modern ultimatum and utility.

Kĭt'rē-cŏn, a son of Sanzulus, and therefore a descendant from the Malingoes, lived to the mortal age of eighty years. After completing his studies under his father, he migrated to the section of Sederone now known as the section of Jean, then occupied by Sederones who had migrated there from Sederone. Here he settled in a town by the name of Jĕn-tä-cē'nä, on the site where now the town of Villargorde has place.

His sawaneus was all wrought from wood, his favorite subject the human form. This he represented by carvings on panels, in relief style. The panels, he further ornamented with leaf and vine patterns, and their borders with scrolls and meanderings, thus giving his sawaneus the appearence of being framed. He utilized a wood of reddish tint, similar to modern rose wood, cedar, and cherry, which he beautified by a very high polish, giving his carvings life-like appearance.

Anstacia says, "No better sculpture, of that order, exists even today, than the sawaneus wrought by this Kitrecon, whom the world would call an undeveloped man."

Mŭlt'sy, a pre-historic sawane, was a descendant from the U-cē'dē-ăns of U-cē'dĕ-ä, in the country of Sederone, who came into the earth life about one hundred years after Kitrecon had passed to spirit life. He lived to the mortal age of only forty years, during which time, as a sawane, he dwelt in a town by the name of Căn-sā'dēs, in the section now known as Salamanca, on the site now occupied by the city of Salamanca.

This artist was, physically speaking, of medium stature, slender, frail, and of delicate form; but, being sustained by spirit forces that attended his labors, as well as being thus influenced and sustained mentally, he was able to accomplish his earth mission as a sawane. His best work was the establishmet of sawaneus, wrought from stone.

His subjects, generally speaking, represented the human form. He used figures posed in groups, typifying ideas which were conveyed to his intelligence by the transmission of thought, which he caught from his spirit advisers. That he was conscious of the fact, and being in continuous communication with them, caused him to conceive the idea of representing spirit forms as angelic subjects. Such ideas became his chief production, all of which were exceptionally fine, and well wrought in an artistic sense, and representatively considered.

One of his most beautiful and most artistically wrought groups, was in representation of twelve spirits, grouped about the couch of a mortal whose spirit was in the act of leaving the body, or at the hour of so-called death. It was a masterly piece of art. The spirit, as is the case when it leaves the body, was represented as having passed out from the mortal head, and could be seen as a white cloud, in the process of unfolding into the soul form, or spirit body.

The twelve spirits were represented with outstretched arms and open hands, waiting to receive the new born spirit, and as ready to bear it away to its spirit home.

A companion group to this was next created, representing the spirit form as in the arms of the twelve spirits, who were now looking with angelic countenances upon the new born soul as it lay in their arms.

The idea of the "groups" as above described, intended by the sawane, was to portray mortal dissolution, and spirit transition; or the separation of the soul-body from the mortal, or the birth of soul and spirit into spirit life. The latter group, Anstacia informs us, was one of the finest sculptural representations ever wrought by a leading sculptor of any nation, since those men of Atlantis, so long before, submerged from mortal sight. She also adds, "Could the mortal career of Multsy have been prolonged to the length of some of the pre-historic sculptors, already mentioned, he would have brought about even a more wonderful advancement in the art of his period, thus to influence subsequent ages." For, being under spirit guidance, his greatest thought was tuned in harmony with spiritual ideas. This, in turn, influenced his hand, in his manifest representations of art, all through his wonderful productions of sawaneus; and this not only led up to the idea of "grouping subjects," in the sawaneus of his period of time, but to that of the Adomic period, and even of later periods, to the Biblical representations of the Christian era, and ultimately to the variety of "groupings" known to Modern times.

SCULPTURE AND SCULPTORS OF THE MIDDLE AGES AND MODERN TIMES.

TELTZIE XXXVIII.

Passing from the Pre-historic, and the beginning of the Modern-Ancient, to the Middle Ages, and later into Modern periods, we note the low grade of Pagan plastic work of the fourth century A. D., and the rise instituted by Christian workers of the same century, and its influence, through embodied and re-embodied ideas that were still under the guidance of spirit inspiration, as well as through direct communication. Influenced or "inspired" treatment is manifest through such works as "the leaf from an ivory consulor diptych," portraying the noble figure of an Archangel holding an orb and sceptre (British Museum), the work of a non-historic sculptor by the name of Cē-ī-mā'lē-ä; the decorative reliefs on sarcophgi, similar to those on the Pagan tombs; reliefs portraying scenes from the Old Testament, in subjects such as the "Meeting of Abraham and Melchisedec;" the "Sacrifice of Isaac;" "Daniel among the Lions;" "Jonah and the Whale," etc.; of New Testament scenes, such as were typical of the early life of Christ, or as illustrating His power and beneficence, as a Cä-cĕl'lä (spirit sensitive, or medium); e. g., "The Sermon on the Mount;" "The Triumphal Entry into Jerusalem" (Spirit work through his organism as a Cacella); many fine examples to be seen in the Vatican and Old Lateran museums; similar sarcophagi sculptural decorations, such as were wrought in the provinces of Rome, especially in Gaul; some splendid specimens extant in the museums of Arles, Marseilles, and Aix, France.

Of the fifth century's influential extensions, we note the reliefs in ivory and wood, as decorations on Episcopal thrones in Italy, such as the so-called "chair of St. Peter," in his great basilica; the small panel reliefs on the doors of S. Sabina, on the Aventine Hill at Rome, representing scenes from Biblical history, carved in wood, and the work of a non-historic sculptor by the name of Lĕt'sŭs, who thus extended the old classic style; the ivory throne of Bishop Maximianus, in S. Vitale, Ravenna, portraying the Bishop and the Four Evangelists in front of this

Episcopal throne. This was the work of a non-historic sculptor by the name of Mŭl-cō-mō'ŭs; and the bands, that encompass the above-named representation of the Bishop and the Four Evangelists, representing carved vines and foliage throughout which are interspersed animals and birds, was the work of a non-historic sculptor, by the name of Dĭn-mō'thō, a contemporary and co-worker with Mulcomous. It was also Dinmotho who wrought the capitals in the same edifice, in representation of vines and foliage, with birds drinking from chalices.

In the sixth century the development was under the influence of the works of the foregoing sculptors and their contemporaries, and subsequent Byzantine conditions. The above-named style of ornamentation was continued, and also a new class of decorative sculpture introduced, such as the portrayal of subjects, in low relief, on slabs of marble for screens, altars, pulpits, etc., co-ornamentative with the style of the bands, in representation of flowers, foliage, animals, etc., as described, this being a development extending from the early influence, or treatment, of the acanthus or thistle, as seen on the capitals of S. Sophia, at Constantinople, the "Golden Gate," at Jerusalem, and many other Oriental buildings, and really an extended influence from Atlantian sculpture, the ideas of which were re-embodiments, through spirit inspiration and guidance, and made manifest again through the works of pre-historic and non-historic sculptors, in the various sections where it developed.

The development in Plastic Art, which became so famous under the Byzantine influence, was precursored by such work as the bronze statue of "St. Peter," in his Roman basilica, which early work influenced future impressions relative to the production of metal work. This, famous in the early Byzantine period, as wrought of bronze, marble, gold, and silver, even to the extent of surface ornamentation of bronze and marble products, was also a re-embodied idea, having arisen from Atlantian works, through spirit inspiration and guidance, as above stated.

From the sixth to the twelfth century, there was an opposition, owing to the rigid influence of the Church, and its hostility to sensual beauty, especially as toward the Christ subjects, which, by edict, must be "without form or comeliness." It was thus impiety to carve or paint Him with any of the beauty and nobility of the Pagan gods. Therefore, among the Byzantine artists, subject to such rigid rules relative to the manner in which they must pose or portray each sacred figure, progressive details were retarded for the time being. Every saint, according to religious decree, had to be portrayed in a stated attitude, with one fixed expression of visage, draped in a special style, and of prescribed colors. Hence, the conservative and non-progressive development of Art, during a period of time that reared a monotonous monument to the dogmatic unity of the Catholic Church, its great monastic system and consequent results. A condition, however, which counts as but one item in the great combination of religious events that have retarded the progress of truth, influenced wrong conceptions, and given birth to ideas relative to spiritual powers, such as have developed into religious monstrosities, that scare, force and rule, intelligent people into acceptance of theories and dogmas, rather than into a state of being led by the spirit influences, such as represent truth and knowledge relative to the God principle, in all things—its conditions naturally and historically, in the past, at the present, and for the future.

The extensive vandalism that went on in former times, due to the use of precious metals in the establishment of the plastic art of that period, robbed modern times of many specimens; hence, the few that remain. But among these, dating from the eighth century, might be mentioned as important, the series of colossal wall reliefs executed in hard stucco, in the Church of Cividale (Friuli) near Trieste, Austria-Hungary. This is a work representing rows of female saints, bearing jewelled crosses, crowns, and wreaths, etc., in which the costuming, attitudes and general arrangement of the scene closely resemble those of the gift-bearing mosaic figures of Theodora and Herladie's, in St. Vitale, Ravenna. The former was the work of a non-historic sculptor, by the name of Dinmotho, a son of the non-historic sculptor of the same name, previously mentioned.

Vandalism, relative to spiritual principles and possessions, by creeds, sects, and individuals, who have remodelled them to fit the ideas of the new possessors, utilizing them to the extent of displacing the original idea, intent, and utility, of the spirit intelligences and forces who first established them, has resulted in a decadence, for a time, in true spirit manifestation and the historic keeping thereof; a state of affairs, which, like the Arts, is rising again from its oblivion, so to speak, through the same spirit inspiration, guidance and manifestation; and again being brought to the inhabitants of the earth plane by said denizens of the spirit zones, for the good of humanity generally, and the downfall of erotic works, both as from the mortal and from non-developed spirit influences, who seek to aid in the extension of ignorance, falsehood, and degenerate conditions.

Passing into the Mediæval period, we find the influence extending throughout various portions of Europe, through works wrought from gold, silver, gilt, copper, etc.; e. g., in the Saxon period, that influence spread into England, which gave place to such developments as the tall Churchyard Crosses, of the Northern provinces, which were carved from stone material, as that in the churchyard of Goshforth, in Cumberland. On this, in a small scale, reliefs are rudely carved, a process in sculpture which shows a traditional state, from the worship of Odin to that of Christ. The old Norse symbols and myths, also sculptured upon it, assume a semi-Christian form, which shows the force of re-modelling ideas, as above mentioned. This was the work of a non-historic Scandinavian sculptor, by the name of Cē-clū-ăn'dŭs, who migrated into Cumberland from Scandinavia.

We are here informed, by Anstacia, that the art of "cross sculpture," as above named, practised by the Scandinavian, the Norse and the Celtic sculptors, was originally influenced by migrating sculptors, from Italy, who passed through Germany into Scandinavia and Norway; and that ultimately, through descended influences from those regions, the idea extended into England, Ireland and Scotland; and that Cecluandus, of the latter part of the tenth century, having then settled in a small town originally known as Al-tā-mōs-lănd, now known as Gosforth in Cumberland, was the principal one to establish this art in England.

The crosses of Cornwall, Ireland, and in Scotland, ornamented with intricate patterns of interlacing knot-work, are of Norse origin, and not of that Christian style or origin, as manifests through such works as the two large stone reliefs now in Chichester cathedral, England, the work of an Italian sculptor by the name of Rĕn-dī-sō'nō, who, in the eleventh century, migrated from Northern Italy into Germany, and subsequently into Chichester, England, the town then being known as Sā-lū'sā.

We are also here informed, by Anstacia, that the tradition now in existence, that the above-named reliefs came from the pre-Norman church at Selsy, is not truth; but that they were wrought by Rendisono, for the original church that had place on the site of the now existing Chichester cathedral; and at the time of the destruction of the old church and excavation for the new cathedral, the reliefs were preserved, and ultimately placed in the latter edifice. This fact gave rise to the tradition, and is an instance that proves how many changes and erroneous ideas come about, that mystify and becloud, and render history of antequated times so uncertain in many respects. She also informs us that Rendisono was not only a sculptor, but a priest of a roaming nature, who sought the vicinity of different peoples whom he might teach, and thus extend his religious ideas; hence his residence in Salusa, now Chichester; and it was the fact that he had come from the Northeast, where he became acquainted with Byzantine art, that caused him to re-embody ideas, from that style, into his reliefs above referred to, which represent Christ at the tomb of Lazarus, in portrayal of two scenes in the raising of Lazarus. The figures are stiff, attenuated, and ugly, the pose very awkward, and the drapery of exaggerated Byzantine character, with long, thin folds, and the eyes are represented by pieces of glass, or colored enamel, inserted, and the treatment of the hair is in long, rope-like twists, etc.

Further influence led to the Tympanum reliefs, over the doors of churches, representing "Christ in Majesty," "The Harrowing of Hell," "St. George and the Dragon," etc.; reliefs representing the Zodiacal signs, such as established the richly-sculptured arches of the twelfth century; the exquisitely-carved ornamentation in slight relief, on the churches of Norway and Denmark, of the eleventh and twelfth centuries, showing a stage where the sculptors displayed great skill in the representation of Dragons, and of interlacing foliage in grandly sweeping curves.

The principal non-historic sculptor in Norway, of the eleventh century, was a native Norwegian by the name of Jĕn'ăck, and the principal one of the twelfth century was also a Norwegian, by the name of Sĕl'mŭck, whose influence, contemporaneous with that of others, established the development of the art in that region; while in Denmark the eleventh century influence was headed by a non-historic sculptor who was a native of that section, by the name of Dū-vĕr'gī-nēs; while in the twelfth century the influence was headed by a non-historic sculptor, also of Denmark, by the name of Am-nō-mĕn'dăb.

The Monumental Sculpture of the twelfth century, such as the effigies in representation of various Knights Templar, clad in military costume and chain-mail armor, i. e., in the round Temple Church, London, where the figures are cut in hard Purbeck marble, the work of a non-historic sculptor by the name of Tē-līs'kē, and a native of Norway, who migrated to that section.

The effigy of Robert, Duke of Normandy, carved in oak and decorated with painting, which has place in the cathedral at Gloucester, was the work of a non-historic sculptor by the name of Jĕn'stŏck, a native of that section.

The two bronze effigies in Westminster Abbey, were modelled and cast by William Torell, a goldsmith of London, who influenced in the thirteenth century.

The two bronze effigies, those of King Henry III and Queen Eleanor, on their tombs, in Westminster Abbey, were modelled and cast by the same William Torell, who influenced in the fore part of the thirteenth century. An embellishment with Lucca gold, with noble, well modelled features and crisp, wavy curls, characterizes the head of Henry, while the remarkable characteristics on the effigy of Queen Eleanor, manifest classic beauty, which alike give evidence of the ideal types of that century.

The sculptural decorations in the church facades of that century, such as the one of the west end of Wells cathedral, which is carved with more than six hundred figures in the round, or in relief, arranged in tiers, and of varying sizes; the reliefs that embellish the tympana of the doorways, and those above them, wherein are portrayed kings and queens, bishops, knights, saints both male and female, as colossal statues standing in rows, are sculptural work done under the direction of a non-historic sculptor by the name of Gā-lĭn'dŭs, and a re-embodied idea of decoration brought out by him, through spirit inspiration and guidance. He was by nature a Cacella (medium), who was influenced by the spirit of Quĭn'tē-lōz, the principal Celpor (sculptor), who designed and carried out the Celportic (sculpture) on the Temple of the Illustrate Dead, in Atlantis.

Furthermore, there are the fine examples that have place in the cathedrals of Peterborough, Lichfield Salisbury, Lincoln, etc.; e. g., the spandrels of the wall-arcade in the Chapter house of the Salisbury cathedral, with some sixty reliefs, of subjects from Bible history, the work of a non-historic sculptor by the name of Tĕr-rĕl'lŭs, a thirteenth century influence of that district; the celebrated, large, massive reliefs of Angels, in the spandrels of the choir arches in the Lincoln cathedral, work of a non-historic sculptor by the name of Gĕl'sŭck, who influenced in that district during the latter part of the thirteenth century; the work in Lichfield cathedral, which was under development by a non-historic sculptor by the name of Sā-năl'lŭs; and that in the Peterborough cathedral, done by a non-historic sculptor by the name of Re-rock.

Similar subjects occur in the transepts of Westminster Abbey, London, the earliest of which was under the development of a non-historic sculptor by the name of Its-līne'dy. Here, mediæval sculpture, in an unbroken succession from the thirteenth to the sixteenth century, is represented by a complete collection, by various geniuses of sculptural ability.

The bronze effigies of royal persons, and rich nobles, with the whole surface heavily gilded; hammered plates of copper nailed on a wooden core, richly decorated with champlave enamels in various bright colors, used in the form of effigies having place in sepulchral purposes, at at Limoges, in France, were the result of the sculptural influences between the thirteenth and fourteenth centuries, which were exported to various sections of the country. Of this, an instance is the effigy of William of Valence, now in Westminster Abbey, London, which was the work of a non-historic sculptor, a native of France, by the name of El'dī-ŏn.

The royal effigy of Henry V, of the fourteenth century, formed of beaten silver fixed to an oak core, but with a cast head (the silver of which was originally decorated with enamel, having been removed in the time of Henry VIII), was the work of a non-historical sculptor of English descent, by the name of Borg-man (pron. soft g).

The decorating style of all sorts of sculpture in stone, with gold, silver and colors, applied over the whole surface, and the ornamentation of drapery with crystals, false jewels, and polished metallic foil, constitute a style extended in France and England by a non-historic sculptor by the name of Stĕl'ē-phŏn, a Grecian by birth, who in his youth had migrated to France. His first idea of the style of decorated sculpture was, therefore, conceived through Grecian influence; but later, he being a spirit sensitive, he was further influenced by Grecian spirits. This accounts for the similarity of this style, gilt painted and jeweled sculpture, to the colored sculptural decorations; and in other respects, to the works of the ancient Greek sculptors; and it was Stelephon who planned and wrought the sculptural ornamentation on the tomb of Aymer de Valence, of the fourteenth century, at Westminster Abbey. The tomb of Prince John of Eltham, his recumbent effigy and the small figures of mourners all around the arcading, wrought of alabaster (Westminster Abbey), was the work of a non-historic sculptor by the name of Sē-cō'lŭs.

The influence of wooden sculpture is seen in such examples as the life size effigy of the young knight, George de Cantelupe, in Abergavenny church, which is decorated with gilt and colored in the same style as the stone figures, with graceful tunic drapery, carefully carved armor, etc., which was the work of a non-historic sculptor by the name of Bā-săm'frä. The original high stone canopy of open work, on this tomb, further influenced the re-embodied idea of arches, canopies, and pinnacles, or architectural sculpture, such as the richly wrought tomb of Edward II, at Gloucester, the work of a non-historic sculptor by the name of Săc-rē-mŏn'dē. Other examples are the De Spencer tomb at Tewkesbury, the work of a non-historic sculptor by the name of Am-wĕz'kā, and the tomb of Lady Eleanor de Percy, at Beverly, of later influence, with magnificently sculptured foliage. This work, unrivaled by any continental example, was done by a non-historic sculptor by the name of Dē-ō'pē-lēs, who, being a spirit sensitive, was influenced by an Atlantian spirit sculptor, who had been, in Atlantis, an expert at foliage sculpture.

The colossal figure of an Angel, now in the South Kensington Museum, supposed to be Italian sculpture of the fourteenth century, was wrought by a non-historic sculptor by the name of Dĭs-cō'lī.

The large stone statue, in South Kensington Museum, of the fourteenth century, an example of the art finished with a stamped *gesso,* and an inlay of painted and glazed foil, was the work of a non-historic sculptor by the name of Nō'lā-mŭn, of French descent.

The colossal recumbent figure of Jesse, in Abergavenny church, which originally formed the lower part of what was known as the "Jesse tree," out of which a great tree was represented as growing, on the limbs of which were figures of the illustrious descendants of Jesse's line, was an early work of the non-historic sculptor, Bā-săn'fā. Of this, only the stump of the tree, springing from the side of Jesse, now remains. The piece, which is ten feet long, was cut from a solid block of oak; and the figure of an Angel, at the head, was worked out of the same piece of wood.

The influence of the wood sculpture of Mediæval Europe was re-embodied in the idea of wood carving generally, and lives in the ornamental decoration of church stalls, canopies, screens, and roofs. This work, in England, reached its zenith of perfection in the fifteenth century.

The influence of figure decorative sculpture having extended to the fourteenth century, and having attained a higher degree of perfection by the models of that period, we find it manifesting through such works as the gilt bronze portrait effigies of Edward III, which were the work of a non-historic sculptor by the name of Ar—ĕs-thē'nō.

The bronze effigy on the tomb of the "Black Prince," at Canterbury, was the work of a non-historic sculptor by the name of A-thŭs-ē-ăn'ŭs; that of Richard II, and his Queen, Anne of Bohemia (made in 1395), was the work of Nicolas Broker and Godfred Prest, goldsmiths of London.

The recumbent stone figure of Lady Arundel, with two angels at her head, in Chichester cathedral, manifesting a calm and peaceful pose and beauty of drapery, was the work of a non-historic sculptor by the name of Pĕr-ī-ŏd'ā.

The tomb figure of "William of Wykeham," in the cathedral

at Winchester, was the work of a non-historic sculptor by the name of Tŭl-ī-căn'tē.

Similar influences were extended throughout England, which were made manifest through sculptural effigies in such sections as Lichfield, York, Lincoln, Exeter, and in other ecclesiastic edifices, works wrought in the fourteenth century.

The bronze effigy of Richard Baucamp, in his family chapel at Warwick, of the fifteenth century influence, a noble portrait figure, richly decorated with engraved ornaments, was the work of William Austen of London; gilded and engraved by Bartholomew Lamespring, a Netherlands goldsmith and others.

Co-operative with the sixteenth century influence, we note the beginning of conditions of rapid decline, made manifest by such works as the series of life size statues high up on the walls, and on various minor altars, of Henry VII.'s chapel at Westminster Abbey. Of these there were, originally, over one hundred in the interior, and a large number on the exterior. There now remain ninty-five, in representation of Saints, and Doctors of the Church. These were chiefly the work of three non-historic sculptors, viz: Hĕl'drĭdge, a German; It-lō-ī'tĭs, an Italian, and Beē-rē'lĭs, a native of England. But the magnificent tomb of Henry VII; the recumbent effigies of himself and his queen, which still exist in the Lady Chapel of Westminster Abbey; the black marble altar upon which they lie, decorated with large medallion reliefs in gilt bronze, each with a pair of saints, the patrons of Henry VII. and Elizabeth of York, and other enrichments in bronze; the altar and its large marble *baldacchino* surmounted by terra-cotta angels, and records on which was a large relief in representation of the Resurrection of Christ in terra-cotta, etc., etc., these were the works of Torrigiano, the Florentine sculptor. This artist also influenced through such works as the bronze effigy of "Margaret of Richmond," in the south aisle of the same chapel; the terra-cotta effigy in Rolls chapel; his co-operation with Pinturicchio in modelling the elaborate stucco decorations in the Apartamenti Borgia, for Alexander VI.. etc.

The idea of the interior and exterior statuary ornamentation, on the Chapel of Henry VII, was an inspiration received by the above named non-historic sculptors, and further carried into effect by the influence of an Atlantian spirit sculptor; and therefore was an extended idea link from his knowledge of the statuary on the great Temple of the Illustrate Dead, of Atlantis.

In the seventeenth century, the influence was extended through such work as the effigy of Sir Francis Vere, in the north transept of Westminster, the work of Nicholas Stone.

The fine bronze statues of Charles Villiers, Duke of Buckingham, his wife and kneeling children, having place northeast of Henry VII.'s chapel, was chiefly the work of a non-historic sculptor by the name of Mōse'ley. This artist was of English descent, and co-operative with Nicholas Stone who directed part of the work; hence its appearance of having been the work of two different sculptors, who worked in very opposite styles.

Other examples and instances of the highest importance, may be briefly classed in the following:

The marble and alabaster tombs in various sections of England, with effigies and rich architectural ornamentation.

The equestrian statue of Charles I. at Charing Cross, by Hubert LeSoeur.

The standing statue of James II. behind the Whitehall banquet room, work of Grinling Gibbons, whose farther works including carvings in representation of realistic fruits and flowers, in pear and other white-woods, have place in Trinity College, Oxford. at Cambridge, Catsworth, Lincoln, and in other parts of England.

The influence of the eighteenth century, such as shows through the works of the Flemish, and other foreign sculptors, as Roubiliac, Scheemakers, Rysbrack, etc.

The Vases covered with delicate cameo-like reliefs, of great beauty, copied from antique gems and sculpture, produced by John Flaxman, under the employ of Josiah Wedgwood, the potter.

The relief illustrations, in outline, to the poems of Homer, Æschylus, and Dante, by Flaxman, based on drawings on Greek vases, etc.

The nude marble figure of "Eve," by Baily, a pupil of Flaxman.

The influence of the nineteenth century was extended through such works as those of Francis Chantrey, especially his Sepulchral Monuments; and through those of his contemporaries, Cunningham and Weeks, who were at times co-operative with him.

The works of John Gibson, who influenced through re- embodied ideas of polychromatic decoration of sculpture, in imitation of the *circumlitio* of classical times, as manifest through his tinted "Venus Victrix," etc.

The works of the elder Westmacott, who modelled the "Achilles," in Hyde Park; of R. Wyatt, who cast the equestrian statue of Wellington (lately removed from London); of Macdowell, Campbell, Marshall, Banks, Bell, etc.

The works of Alfred Stevens, a sculptor of the highest talent, who made the influence manifest through such works as his Duke of Wellington monument, which is composed of magnifi- bronze groups, having place principally in St. Paul's Cathedral, London (the complete models and the design of the monument are now in the Kensington Museum); in his original style and idealistic conceptions, evidenced by the sarcophagus supporting the recumbent bronze effigy of the duke; in the arched marble canopy on delicately enriched shafts; in the bronze groups at each end of the upper part of the canopy, one of which represents "Truth tearing the tongue out of the mouth of Falsehood," and the other, "Valour trampling Cowardice underfoot." In these the two virtues are represented by stately female figures, through which is the manifestation of beauty and vigour, and the vices are represented by two nude male figures of massive treatment. His mantle piece supported by nude female caryatides, in Dorchester House, Park Lane, is another concept in influence.

The works of Sir Frederick Leighton, whose influence is evidenced through such works as his bronze statue representing an Athlete struggling with a Python,—a work of very great merit, now in the South Kensington Museum.

The works of Sir Edwin Landseer, whose influence speaks forth from his colossal bronze Lions, in Trafalgar Square, etc.

Passing with the prehistoric influence of the Pē-dī'zĕr-ŭs Bĕnz Pē-dī-zĕr-ŭs'tĕs Dē Făl'kā-leīt (sculptors and sculpture of France) and making our connections with the twelfth century links in the extension of the Epi-cycle of Sculpture, we note the great influence of great sculptors as manifested through their works, the finest in the world and of great profusion, as on the facades of the large cathedrals covered with sculptural reliefs and thickly set rows of statues in niches; in fact the whole front a huge composition of statuary, which idea was re-embodied by the various sculptors, under the influence of Atlantian spirit celporze (sculptors), who had wrought on the great Temple of the Illustrate Dead, in Atlantis; e. g., one of the best and richest is that of the facade of the Poitiers cathedral, with foliated carved surface interspersed with rows of colossal statues, both seated and standing, that reach high up the front of the church, which was originally the plan and work of Frē-dē'lī, a non-historic sculptor, and his contemporary helpers. We note the following, as living links:

The sculpture on the three western doors of the Chartres cathedral, embracing fine tympanum reliefs, and colossal statues attached to the jamb-shafts of the openings, which were the works of Dĕl-sē'rŭs, a non-historic sculptor.

Links and Cycles

The sculptured doors of the north and south aisles of Bourges cathedral, the work of Jā-rū'shā-nĕr, a non-historic sculptor.

The west doors of the Notre Dame in Paris; the once stately Row of Kings on the west end of the same cathedral, deteriorated in effect by subsequent restorations; the magnificent series of statues and reliefs round its great western doorways, among which there are upwards of thirty life size figures, principally the work of Frā-rē'rŭs, a non-historical sculptor and his contemporary helpers.

The influence of the thirteenth century, termed the Golden Age of Sculpture in France, is made manifest through such works as the exquisitely beautiful Angel Statues around the Parisian Sainte Chapelle, the work of Lē-rä-ā'sŭs, a non-historic sculptor.

The sculpture on Amiens cathedral, rich in detail, e. g., the noble and majestic statues of Christ and the Apostles at the west end, and the sculpture on the south transept, manifesting dignity in combination with soft beauty, work of Al-tā-mū'sā, a non-historic sculptor.

The statues of the Child and Virgin, in various churches.

The facade of Laon cathedral on which the sculpture manifests the characteristics of grace and beauty, the work of E-rī'sŏn, a non-historic sculptor.

The grand sculpture in the cathedral at Rheims, especially the statue of Christ, of graceful and noble form, and the nude figure of Sebastian, work of Nē-rō'sō, a non-historic sculptor.

The very large collection of monumental effigies in the Abbey church, of St. Denis, and the portraits of the Early Kings in said church, works of Clē-mĕr'rī-ŭs, a non-historic sculptor, and his contemporary helpers.

The fourteenth century influence under decline, manifests through such works as the reliefs on the choir screens of the Notre Dame, at Paris, work of Sē-lā-cō'sä, a non-historic sculptor; the sculpture on the transepts of Rouen cathedral, work of Lā-mō'sä, a non-historical sculptor; and that on the west end of the Lyons cathedral, work of Quĭn'trĕl,, a non-historical sculptor.

Claux Sluter, a Netherlands sculptor, influenced through such works as his great "Moses' Fountain," in the cloister of the Carthusian Monastery, at Dijon, with its six life size statues of the Prophets, in stone, painted and gilded in mediaeval style; his magnificent altar tomb for Philip the Bold, composed of white marble, surrounded with arcading, which contains about forty small alabaster figures representing mourners of all classes, and the recumbent portrait-effigy of Philip in his ducal mantle, with folded hands,—an example which manifests great power and delicacy of treatment.

The influence in the latter part of the fifteenth century, is evidenced by such manifestations as through the rich reliefs and statues on the choir scenes of the Chartres cathedral, work of Për-mō'sī, a non-historic sculptor.

The sixteenth century influence, manifested through such works as the nude figure of "Diana" reclining by a stag, now in the Louvre, the work of Goujon; also his fine monument to Duke Louis, at Rouen, and his sculptural decorations on the Louvre.

The marble group of "Three Graces," bearing on their heads an urn containing the heart of Henry II, work of Germain Pilon for Catherine de' Medici, and his monument of Catharine and Henry II, at Denis.

The noble monument of Albert of Carpi, in the Louvre, work of the sculptor, Ponce.

The portrait-effigy, or recumbent figure, of the Duke of Montmorency, in the Louvre, wrought by Barthelemy Prieur.

The large statues and reliefs in ivory, of boys and cupids, wrought by Il Fiamingo.

The seventeenth century influence is manifest through such works as the representation of "Milo devoured by a Lion," wrought by Pierre Puget.

Extended influence manifests by such sculptors as Simon, Guillain, Francois, Michel Anguier, etc.

Charles Ant. Coyzevox influenced through portraiture and busts.

Clodion influenced through statuary groups, models, etc., such as his Bacchanal group, in terra-cotta.

The influence of the eighteenth century was made manifest through the works of such sculptors as Jean Antoine Houdon, who paved the way for a development in the Modern school of French sculpture, as evidenced by such works as his standing colossal statue of S. Bruno, in the S. Maria degli Angeli, at Rome, and his seated statue of Voltaire, in the foyer of the Theatre Francais.

In this century, through re-embodiments of Antique styles of Sculpture, an influence was established to the extent of a revolution in the art, which resulted in pseudo-classicism, thus hindering the progress of original talent and the further development of modern art, as evidenced through such works as the bronze spiral reliefs around the Column of the Place Vendome, and the statue of Napoleon on the top, and the classical Quadriga on the Triumphal Arch in the Place du Carrousel, wrought by Joseph Bosio.

The Chained Prometheus, of the Louvre, and the noble group, by Jacques Pradier, are other evidences.

The bronze "Mercury" in the Louvre; the statue of Marshal Ney, in the Luxembourg Garden, and that of General Cavaignac, in the cemetery of Montmartre, by Francoise Rude, are others.

The reliefs on the pediment of the Pantheon, by Pierre Jean David, are farther instances, as also the bronze statue of a Dancing Fisher-lad, modelled by Francois Joseph Duvet, now in the Luxembourg collection; the works of other French sculptors of note, such as Ottin Courtet, Simart, Etex, and Carpenaux, especially the last named, who was an artist of great ability and wrought many sculptures, some of which, however, were offensive, and a typical example of sad degeneration in the taste which prevailed under the rule of Napoleon III.

The nineteenth century influence, in France, was forcibly made manifest through such works as the lifelike representation of the human form. In these an excess of sensual realism is apparent through nude figures, such as adorn the various structures of France, and especially in Paris; though there are works, by some of the sculptors, that manifest more beauty, purity, technical skill, and original thought; facts that can be better understood by comparison of the Franch sensual treatment of the nude, with the purer treatment of the Greek, etc.

Passing with the pre-historic influence of the Mĕn'zoitz Unch Mĕn-zoi'tŭs Ot Tĭn-dĭn'zē-ŏn (sculptors and sculpture of Germany), we make the connections in extension of the Epi-cycle of Sculpture, with such links as were influenced through the Byzantium style, prior to the twelfth century, or by some re-embodiments of ideas, formerly embodied in the classical models of Italy, as evidenced by such works as the bronze Pillar reliefs, attributed to Bishop Bernward; the metal sculpture that was developed in the twelfth century, in Hildesheim and Cologne; in fact, in all the entire Rhine provinces; e. g., the beautiful bronze Front, at Liege, the design being that of various baptismal scenes from the New Testament, the figure-subjects of which were wrought, in relief, by Lambert Patras of Dinant; the fronts to the Osnabrück and Hildeshim cathedrals, works of and under the direction of Bī-steīn'ĕr, a non-historic sculptor, and his contemporary helpers of that period.

The exquisite bronze Candelabra, in the Abbey Church of Comburg, wrought by Rĭch en-le, a non-historic sculptor; and those at Aix-la-Chapelle, wrought by Sō'dĕn-nĭg, a non-historic sculptor.

The sepulchral figure of Rudolf of Swabia, in the cathedral at Merseburg, wrought by Mā-lī'gē, a non-historic sculptor.

The bronze effigy of Bishop Frederick, at Magdeburg, which has the body treatment as a relief; the head detached from the surface, etc., wrought by Dĭn'swă, a non-historic sculptor.

The choir scenes of the Hildesheim cathedral, in which is embodied the first plastic work of the century, being wrought in hard stucco, and originally ornamented with gold and colors, and further characterized with a series of large reliefs in representation of various saints, of which the forms and drapery are of much excellence and nobility. Hĭns'bĕrg, a non-historic sculptor, was the creating artist.

The progress of the thirteenth century was influenced by re-embodied ideas as manifest through such works as the "Golden Gate," of Freiburg cathedral, which has sculptured figures as ornaments on the jambs; the statues of the Apostles on the nave pillars; and particularly the representation of the Madonna, at the east end, which is of great beauty and sculpturesque merit. This was wrought by Ī'dĕn-wōld, a non-historic sculptor.

The statues on the interior and exterior of the Bamberg cathedral, of noble design, which were the work of Nā-hī'gĕn, a non-historic sculptor.

The Equestrian statue of Conrad III, in the market-place of Bamberg, which is supported by a foliated corbel, manifesting vigorous and original ideas therein re-embodied, also by the sculptor, Nahigen.

The statues of Henry the Lion, and Queen Matilda, at Brunswick, the forms of which express the re-embodiment of a high conception of beauty and dignity, as wrought by Bratch, a non-historic sculptor.

The tympanum relief of the "Death of the Virgin," surrounded by the sorrowing Apostles, beautifully wrought on the cathedral of Strasburg, which also possesses a large assemblage of other fine sculpture, various decorative carvings designed from nature, and varied realistic foliage models of great merit, originally planned and wrought by the son of Brătch, above referred to, and his contemporary helpers.

The re-embodied influence of the fourteenth century sculpture is made manifest through such works as the multitude of reliefs and statues that adorn the edifices of Nuremburg, e. g., at the church of St. Sebald the work of Shălt-zăc; those at the Frauenkirche, wrought by Mĕnt'rōe; and the west facade of the St. Lawrence, wrought by Lū'gĕck,—three pre-historic sculptors of that period.

The very beautiful statuary which adorns the "Beautiful Fountain," through which the sculptor, Heinrich der Balier, re-embodied his idea of grace and beauty, and further aided by the painter Rudolf, who decorated it with gold and color.

The wooden statues in the Museum at Augsburg, which have been endowed with re-embodied ideas of nobility and dignity by the sculptors—the chief of whom was a non-historic sculptor by the name of Augs'bürg, the name having descended from his ancestors to the above-named town, etc.

The colossal figure of the Virgin, on the exterior of the choir of the church of Marienburg Castle, wrought of hard stucco and adorned with glass mosaics, the work of Wĭn'tĕn-bĕrge, a non-historic sculptor.

The equestrian bronze group of St. George and the Dragon, in the market place at Prague, which expresses the re-embodied idea of vigor, wrought by Mĕn-trū'zē, a non-historic sculptor.

The effigy of Archbishop Conrad, in the cathedral at Cologne, and other military effigies, in Germany, in plate armor, wrought, by Shen-drac, a non-historic sculptor.

The sepulchral effigy of Gunther of Schwarzburg, in the Frankfort cathedral, work of Türn-lō'gă, a non-historic sculptor.

The re-embodied ideas in the fifteenth century, established a higher class of sculptural work, the influence being manifest in such works as the wooden altars, and *rerodoses,* gorgeously painted and gilded, carved with subject-reliefs and statues (re-embodiment of ideas that extended into Spain, Scandinavia, and Denmark); wooden screens, stalls, and other church-fittings, re-embodying the ideas of many sculptors, such as Jörg Syrlin, who wrought the gorgeous choir stalls in the Ulm cathedral, decorated with statues and canopied work; the elaborate sculptured stalls, and the great pulpit in Ulm cathedral, by his son and namesake.

The high altar, the tabernacle, and the stalls, of the Frauenkirche at Cracow, through which the re-embodied ideas of Veit Stoss are manifested, as in one of his masterpieces, viz: the large piece of wooden panelling on which he carved central reliefs of the "Doom" and the "Heavenly Host," framed by minute reliefs, scenes from Bible history (now in Nuremburg Town hall).

The exquisitely carved relief of Christ in Majority between the Virgin and St. John, in the chapel of the Monastery of Landau, and miniature reliefs of Christ, cut in box-wood and hone-stone, through which the re-embodied ideas of Dürer are made manifest (example in British Museum).

The great Schreyer Monument, for St. Sebald's at Nuremberg, and the great Tabernacle for the Host, eighty feet high, covered with statuettes, in the Ulm cathedral and the very spirited "Stations of the Cross," on the road to the Nuremburg, wrought by Adam Kraft.

The fifteenth and sixteenth century influence, bore evidence of the re-embodied ideas that manifest through the works of the Vischer family, who for three generations were considered among the ablest of sculptors in bronze, e. g., the bronze Front, at Wittenberg church; the four Episcopal Effigies, in relief, in Banberg cathedral (and fine bronze sculptural monuments of various dates by other masters), by Herman Vischer; the tomb of Archbishop Ernest, Magdeburg cathedral, by Peter Vischer, surrounded with fine statuettes of the Apostles under semi-Gothic canopies; the magnificent shrine of St. Sebald's at Nuremberg, which displays a tall canopied bronze structure, accompanied by many reliefs and statuettes, and portrait figure of the saint himself; dragons, grotesques, little figures of boys, mixed with graceful scroll foliage, that crowd every possible part of the canopy and its shafts, all of which manifest the elaborate ideas of Peter Vischer (the most renowned of the Vischers), as re-embodied in them.

The monument of Cardinal Albert, in the church at Aschaffenburg, and the tomb of Frederick the Wise, in the Castle Chapel at Wittenberg, manifest the re-embodied ideas of both Peter Vischer and his sons.

The bronze sculptural influence of the sixteenth century is manifest through such works as the fine series of bronze statues known as the Colossal Figures, round the tomb of Emperor Maximilian, at Innsbruck, in representation of a succession of heroes and ancestors of the emperor; the bronze statue of King Arthur of Britain, at Innsbruck, etc.

The bronze "Augustus fountain," by Hubert Gerhard, and the "Hercules fountain," by Adrian de Vries, at Augsburg.

The bronze influence of the seventh century is manifest through such works as the bronze reliefs, and accessories, of Andreas Schlüter, and his colossal statue of Frederick III, on the bridge at Berlin.

The influence in the latter part of the eighteenth century was manifest through such works as re-embodied the classical style, evidenced by the portrait-figures by Johann Gottfried and Friedrich Tieck; the recumbent Queen Louisa, at Charlottenburg; and statues of Generals Bülow and Scharnhorst, at Berlin, by Christian Rauch.

The colossal bronze equestrian statue of King William of Prussia at Cologne, by Friedrich Drake; the equestrian portrait of King Ernest Augustus at Hanover, and a Horseman attacked by a Lion (Berlin Museum), by Albert Wolff; the celebrated "Amazon and Panther" in bronze; the fine group of St. George and the Dragon" in a courtyard of the Royal Palace at Berlin, St. George and his horse being wrought in bronze, and the Dragon of gilt plates of hammered iron, work of Augustus Kiss.

The reliefs, by Hähnel, at Dresden; the reliefs and statues in the Glyptothek, at Munich and in Walhalla, and the colossal bronze statue of Bavaria, by Schwanthaler, etc., thus linking up to the present period.

Passing with the pre-historic influence of the Sā-wā'nē Sĕnt Sā-wā'nē-ūs Fō Sĕd'ē-rōne (sculptors and sculpture of Spain), we make the connections with such links as:—

The re-embodied sculptural ideas, as under French mediæval influence, made manifest through such works as the Cathedral of Santiago de Compostella, one of the grandest specimens in the world, the western portal and three doorways being so wonderfully adorned with statues and reliefs, all richly decorated with colors, among which are represented, round the central arch, figures of the twenty-four Elders; a noble relief of "Christ in Majesty" between Saints and Angels, has place in the tympanum, and the jamb-shafts are decorated with standing statues of Saints, with St. James the elder, the patron saint of the Church, posed against the central pillar. Mastei Mateo, of French descent, though a native of Spain, was the sculptor cooperative with a non-historic French sculptor by the name of Nĕn-sē-cō'lūs, which accounts for the thoroughly French style of the work. Anstacia, who informs us of this fact, also states that these two sculptors were influenced in their work by Atlantian spirits who had influenced similar art, in the far distant period of Aeginetan pediment sculpture, 500 years B. C., now come again to influence these sculptors of the mediæval period in France. Hence the fact that the works of the early Greeks and the mediæval Spaniards were produced at a somewhat similar stage, in these two far distant periods of artistic development, as noticeable in the heads with pointed beards and a fixed mechanical smile, together with the stiff drapery arranged in long narrow folds, etc.

The re-embodied influence of the fourteenth century is manifest in such works as the great silver Retable, at the Gerona cathedral, divided into three tiers of statuettes and reliefs, richly framed in canopied niches, the work of Peter Bernec, a Valencian silversmith.

The fifteenth century development, under German and French

influence, is manifest through such work as the very rich sculptural decorations that adorn the main door of Salamanca cathedral, the work of Mĕl'trĭs, a non-historic sculptor; the facade of S. Juan, at Valladolid, wrought by Nē-ä-mĭs'sū, a non-historic sculptor; and the Church and Cloisters of S. Juan de los Reyes, at Toledo, under the direction and sculptural work of Rē-lī-ĕn'dō, a non-historic sculptor, and his co-operative helpers. The most gorgeous example of architectural sculpture in the world is contained in the S. Juan de los Reyes.

We are informed by Anstacia that the carved foliage of this period, marked by such beauty and spirited execution, and the realistic forms of plant growth, as mingled with other more conventional foliage so masterfully wrought, are directly due to the influence of Atlantian spirits, through inspiration and revelation, brought to bear upon the sculptors of this period; for much of that class of sculptural style was wrought by the Atlantian Celporze (sculptors). Reliendo, who wrought on the S. Juan de los Reyes at Toledo, being one of the fifteenth century sculptors who was thus inspired and controlled.

The very noble bronze monument of Archdeacon Pelays, in the Burgos cathedral, supposed to be the work of Simon, of Cologne, and an architect of the Certosa, at Miraflores near Burgos, was, as we are informed by Anstacia, planned and partly wrought by the father of the above-named Simon, which latter completed it after the transition of his father; hence the monument was the work of two individuals by the name of Simon.

The Altar-tomb of King John II, and his Queen, one of the richest monuments in the world, in the Church of the Monastery of Cortosa, at Miraflores, was wrought by Gil de Siloe, who displayed great talent in under-cutting, and the shaping of the marvelously rich alabaster canopy work.

The re-embodied sculptural idea in the early part of the sixteenth century, under German and French influence, was made manifest through such works as the magnificent tomb of Ferdinand and Isabella, in the Granada cathedral, the work of Sē-mĕn'tē-ri, an Italian non-historic sculptor, who wrought in the Renaissance style. Therefore, this Temple was not the work of Torrgiano, as some have supposed.

The Choir reliefs, at Toledo cathedral, and those in the Colegio Mayor, at Salamanca, were by Alonso Berruguete, who wrought in those vicinities subsequent to the non-historic sculptors, Reliendo and Meltris.

The elaborate Retables, carved in wood with subjects in relief, and richly wrought in gold and colors, by Esteban Jordan,

Gregorio Hernandez, and other Spanish sculptors, and the great sumptuous masses of Polychromatic sculpture, re-embodied ideas of that style, have also been influentially extended, from the German style of retable of the fifteenth century.

The fine relief of the "Madonna and Saints" on the altar in the university Church of Seville, and in the chapel in the cathedral of St. Augustine, done by Montanes, one of the ablest Spanish sculptors of his time.

Passing with the pre-historic influence of the Rē-ĕn'täs Tŭs Rē-ĕn-cū'sä pā Et'zĕn-tū-ăn (sculptors and sculpture of Italy), and from old Byzantine extensions to the middle of the thirteenth century, we make the connections with the following links.

The very rude sculpture on the facade of the S. Andrea, at Pistoia, work of Gruamons and his brother Adeodatus; and other old Byzantine influential developments, such as are to be found at Pisa, Parma, Modena, and Verona, e. g., at Parma, the reliefs for the pulpit of that cathedral, wrought by Benedetto Antelami; other twelfth century developments in the abovenamed places, through which the great influence of sculptural ideas in plastic and graphic art, manifested and express themselves, resulting in such work as on the pulpit in the cathedral of Ravello, wrought by Nicolaus di Bartolomeo di Foggia. The principal figure among the rich sculpture here, is that of a large female head crowned with a richly foliated coronet, thus expressing lifelike vigor combined with largeness of style.

The bronze doors at Monreale Pisa, and elsewhere, are among the chief plastic work of Italy during the twelfth century, the original work of the former being by Pē-rū'sĭc; and of the latter, by Jĕn'drō-sŏn, non-historic sculptors of those sections; and we are here informed by Anstacia that though in history the former is supposed to be the work of Barisanos of Trani, who wrought the north door, and of Bonanus, who wrought the western, they simply completed the work originally planned and partially wrought by Perusic; and that the southern bronze door of the Pisa cathedral, was originally planned and partially wrought by Jendroson, and completed by Bonannos, and furthermore, that the bronze doors of the cathedrals of both Trani and Ravello, were wholly the work of Barisanos, there being no non-historic originator in these cases.

The influence, during the thirteenth century, was chiefly extended through the works of the Cosmati family, manifest from the twelfth to the fourteenth century, by their sculptural and mosaic adornments on the altars, *baldacchini,* choir-screens, paschal candlesticks, ambones, tombs, thrones, doors, etc., in Rome.

Pisano Andrea influenced in the twelfth and thirteenth centuries, through bronze works, as one of the three world-famed Bronze Doors of the Florentine baptistery, the finest in the world; with quatrefolio panels; containing single figures of the Virtues, and having scenes from the life of "The Baptist," wrought with the finish of a piece of gold jewelry; his beautiful Panel reliefs for the grea t Campanile, representing the Four Great Prophets, the Seven Virtues, the Seven Sacraments, the Seven Works, Mercy, and the Seven Planets, etc., a re-embodied influence extended from Giotto, and his brother Giovanni.

Pisano Giovanni, who influenced in the twelfth and thirteenth centuries, through such works as his sculpture in the Campo Santo at Pisa; the magnificent marble high altar and reredos, adorned with countless figures and reliefs illustrating the life of St. Gregory and St. Donato; his beautiful Tomb of Benedict I, with a sleeping figure of the Pope guarded by Angels, who draw aside the curtain, accompanied above with a sculptured plinth supporting canopied figures of the Madonna and Saints; a re-embodied influence thus extended by his father, Niccola.

Pisano Niccola, of the thirteenth century, one of the chief sculptors of Mediaeval Italy, influenced through re-embodied ideas, extended from the eleventh and twelfth centuries, conceptions of sculptors who had wrought bronze doors, marble pulpits, and other great works, in such cathedrals as the Salerno, Bari, Amalfi, Rabello, etc., as evidenced by his relief of "The Deposition from the Cross," at San Martino, at Lucca; his "Adoration of the Magi," on one of the panels in the pulpit of the Pisan Baptistery; his reliefs and statues on the pulpit at Siena, representing the Nativity; "The Adoration of Magi;" "The Presentation in the Temple;" "The Crucifixion," and "The Doom," etc; his last great work was the Fountain, in the piazza opposite the west end of the cathedral of Perugia, where two series of basins, rising one above the other, are adorned with sculptured bas-reliefs.

The fourteenth century influence effectively culminated in the establishment of artistic conditions, such as further manifested centrally in Florence, during the fifteenth century. Wealth and perfection now became the principal links with which to connectedly extend that portion of the Epi-cycle of Sculpture, with that of Athens, Greece, in relation to Plastic Arts of the fourth and fifth centuries B. C., of the latter named district; and the fourteenth and fifteenth centuries of the former; the analogy of which, though seemingly free from copyism, is due to spirit inspiration and influence brought to bear upon the minds of various sculptors, noticeable in various points embodied in the work of such artists as Donatello, Luca della Robbia, and Vittore Pisanello, which so strongly resembles the sculpture of Ancient Greece, and suggests the Phidean school; and rendered dissimilar, principally through the difference in the types of national faces and costumes having place in the two districts, at periods of time far apart. Therefore, the influence in Greece at that period of time, was under direction of Atlantian spirit cĕl-pör'zē, who re-established their influence in Italy during the fourteenth and fifteenth centuries, a fact which led up to the Perfection of Art in both Greece and Italy.

The chief mortal influence leading up to the Athenian greatness, of that period, through whose organism the Atlantian spirit celporze worked, was that of a non-historic sculptor by the name of Jĕl-sē-lō'ĭs, an Athenian by birth, who preceded Phidias, and after whom the latter copied, or modelled. And the chief non-historic mortal sculptor, through whose organism the Atlantian spirit celporze worked, which established the influence leading up to the Florentine greatness of that period, was that of a non-historic sculptor by the name of Ri-ĕm-bī'nō, of Florentine birth, preceding the Pisano family, after whom they copied or modelled.

In the fourteenth century, the influence was further extended by various schools in Northern Italy, as at Verona and Venice, that differed from the art of Tuscany, though Milan and Pavia, on the other hand, possessed sculptors who followed closely the style of the Pisani family. In evidence of this, we note the manifestation through such works as the magnificent shrine of St. Augustine, in the cathedral of Pavia, which presents the Saint life-size in pontificial robes, surrounded by a profusion of bas-reliefs, and minor figures representing Saints of his order, the Liberal Arts, and Cardinal Virtues, aggregating about four hundred and twenty heads, the work of a non-historical sculptor by the name of Sä-cē-lī'ō; the white marble Shrine of Peter the Martyr, in the church of St. Eustorgio, at Milan, grandly decorated with statues and subject reliefs, the work of Balduccio, of Pisa; the wellknown tombs of the Scaliger family at Verona, work of a non-historic sculptor by the name of Mē-jĕt'nē.

In the fifteenth century the influence manifested through such works as the Noble Figures in high relief, which decorate the lower story and angles of the Palace of the Doges, and the magnificent marble tympanum relief (recently added to the South Kensington Museum), having a noble colossal figure of the

Madonna, represented as sheltering under her mantle a number of kneeling worshippers. The back-ground of this is enriched with foliage and heads, forming a "Jesse tree." It is the work of Bartolomeo Bon.

The lofty monument of King Robert, behind the high altar of S. Chiara, Naples (fourteenth century work), and other tombs, in the same church, work of a non-historic sculptor by the name of Dō-ĕr'thē-ry, under whose supervision it was done.

The beautiful Sculptural Effigies, in low relief throughout Italy, especially at Florence, e. g., the tomb of Lorenzo Acciaioli, in the Cortosa near Florence, on which is wrought a marble effigy in low relief, and which is the work of a non-historic sculptor by the name of Nē-lī-tū'sî, and not of Donatello, to whom it has been erroneously attributed.

Orcagna, one of the chief sculptors of the fourteenth century, influenced through such works as his great White Marble Tabernacle, in the church of Or San Michele, in Florence, in which influence is made manifest through the assemblage of the combined splendour evidenced by the detailed sculptural work, as the reliefs and statuettes; minute glass mosaic enrichments laid in white marble; combines and altars; shrines and reredos, baldacchino and vaulted canopy; richly decorated gables and pinnacles; the figure of St. Michael surmounting the summit of the tabernacle; statues of the Apostles on the roof; relief of "Hope," between panels with the "Marriage of the Virgin," and the "Annunciation;" reliefs of the "Birth of the Virgin," and her "Presentation in the Temple;" "The Nativity," and "Adoration of the Magi;" the "Presentation of Christ in the Temple;" the "Angel warning the Virgin" to escape into Egypt; reliefs of the "Death of the Virgin," surrounded by the Apostles, and the "Assumption;" Heads of Prophets, Angels, and Virtues, wonderfully executed, all combined stand as one of the most magnificent sculptural works in Italy.

Ghiberti, of the fourteenth and fifteenth centuries, the great Florentine sculptor, who influenced through such works as his world renowned Baptistery Gates, of the San Giovanni, the first one of which was sculptured in representation of the "Sacrifice of Isaac," re-embodied ideas, artistically speaking, of Old Greek Art. On this the artist worked for twenty years. The second of the two Gates was in representation of Old Testament subjects (work lauded by Michelangelo a century later, as "worthy to be the gates of Paradise"). His three statues, of St. John the Baptist, St. Matthew, and St. Stephen, for the church of San Michele, etc.

Links and Cycles

Donatello, of the fourteenth and fifteenth centuries, a re-embodier of Grecian Art, influenced through such works as life-sized or colossal statues; large bas-reliefs crowded with figures, such as the statues of the Church of St. Michele; those on Giotto's belfry; the pulpit of St. Lorenzo; those in the Baptistery; his further influence through conceived ideas relative to styles, such as drapery, painted figures, treatment of proportion perspective, flatness of the figures to his bas-reliefs, and general Renaissance sculptural effects; his wide extent of individual works, as at Rome, Padua, Venice, Siena, Modena, Mantua, Ferrara, etc., e. g., his equestrian statue of Gottamelata, in Padua, one of two of the noblest the world has ever seen (the other being that of Colleoni, at Venice, by Verrocchio and Leopardi); his statue of St. Louis of France, for the St. Croce; his statue of St. George, outside the church of Or San Michele, at Florence, etc.

The head of the colossal statue of David, at Florence, by Michelangelo; the magnificent tomb of Giovanni Galeazzo Visconti, at Cortosa, near Pavia, work of a non-historic sculptor by the name of **Wĕn-dā̆-sō̆'sŏn.**

The works of Baccio Bandinelli, Giacomo della Porta, Montelupo, Ammanati, Vincenzo de'Rossi, etc., who re-embodied the Idealistic styles of Michelangelo, which latter raised the Art of Sculpture, as well as that of Painting to its highest pitch of magnificence, as a Modern link in the Epi-cycle, but diverse ideas already embodied in his works brought rapid decline, in the following extension, of the Epi-cycle of Sculpture.

The monuments to ancient Romans, as of the two Plinys, on the facade of the Como cathedral, work of a non-historic sculptor by the name of Bē-lĕs'kī; the *"heora"* to unsaintly mortals, such as that erected at Rimini, by Sigismondo Pandolfo, in honor of Isotta; and shrines dedicated to the saints.

The sixteenth century influence was manifest through such works as the bronze statue of "Mercury" flying upwards, by John of Douay (Giovanni de Bologna), in the Uffizi; his representation of the "Carrying off of a Sabine Woman," in the Loggia de' Lanzi; his great Fountain, at Bologna, on which he represented two tiers of boys and mermaids, the whole being surmounted by a colossal statue of Neptune; his fine bronze equestrian statue of Cosimo de' Medici, at Florence; and his very rich decoration on the west door of the Pisa cathedral.

The sculpture on the west facade of the church at Loreto and the elaborate bronze gates of the Santa Casa, works of great merit, resulting from re-embodied ideas extended by Girolamo Lombardo and his sons.

The bronze statue of "Perseus and Medusa," in the Loggia de' Lanzi, at Florence, wrought by Benvenuto Cellini; the colossal bronze seated statue, of Julus III, at Perugia, by Vincenzo Danti, one of the best portrait-figures of its period.

The seventh century influence was largely extended by the numerous works of Neapolitan Bernini, and in co-operation with a large school of helpers. Subjects and styles, therefore, varied greatly. His chief early work, the "Apollo and Daphne" of the Borghese Casino, manifests his skill for technical and delicate high finish, combined with soft beauty and grace; diverse to which, technically speaking, are his coarser works, the clumsy colossal figures, but partly clad in wildly fluttering garments, as have place in the churches of Rome, the Colonnade of St. Peter's, and on the bridge of S. Angelo, representing a decline in plastic work.

The figure of the dead St. Cecilia, under the high altar of her Basilica, re-embodied idea of the great repose that attends the body after its spirit transition, work of Stefano Maderna.

The eighteenth century influence is made manifest through such works as by Canova, e. g., the group of the " Three Graces;" "The Hebe;" and the very popular "Dancing Girls" in contrast, artistically, with his finest colossal marble group of "Theseus slaying a Centaur," at Venice; his Christian sculpture, such as the monument to Pope Clement XIII, in St. Peter's, Rome; that of Titian, at Venice; and his tomb of Alfieri, in the Florentine church of S. Croce.

The works of Bastianini, whose great talent was turned, in the tide of re-embodied fifteenth century ideas, and further influenced by his contemporary, Mino di Fiesole, whose methods he adopted.

Links and Cycles

USH MIZ-I-AM'BI-Ä ZE-U-LE'US ZE AT'LAN-TIS

OR

THE TERRA-COTTA ART OF ATLANTIS.

TELTZIE XXXIX.

The Mĭz-ī-ăm'bi-ä Zē-ū-lē'ŭs At'lăn-tĭs had its origin in the ā'ĭs-tiē of A'tä-rä, in Tĕlt'ziē Et, or Section One, during the latter part of the second E-frē-mē'trŭm.

Bā-rē'ăl, was the first noted Mĭz-ī-ăm'bi-ä Zē-ū'lē (Terra-Cotta Artist), whose works began in the latter part of the second E-frē-mē'trŭm, and who lived to the mortal age of about eighty years. He was the originator of the art, in Atlantis, and at first his works were simple as compared with those of his latter years. He utilized a red clay to form miniature pyramids, but subsequently, he conceived the idea of moulding clay in low relief style, when he chose various subjects for representation, such as vines and vegetation generally; and at a still later period, he wrought half columns, of those in high relief, which were then utilized for general architectural ornamentation.

In the latter half of his professional career, he established a school of Miziambia Zeuleus, in Atara, where he taught the Zeuleus to many pupils, through whom its influence spread out into various parts of the Lontidri.

Dē-rē'zē, a pupil of Bareal, began his public work in the first part of the third Efremetrum, and lived to the mortal age of eighty-eight years, and dwelt in the aistie of Almorthea, in Tĕlt-ziē Zrĕt, or Section Five, to which section he had moved after completing his course of study in the school at Atara.

He began work for himself by imitating the styles and utilizing the subjects as employed by Bareal, though under considerable further development and improvement.

Subsequently, he conceived the idea of moulding human and animal figures, in high-relief; but never produced his subjects in the round.

He also had a large school in Almorthea, for many years. The pupils from this disbursed themselves throughout various parts of the Lontidri, which further strengthened the development and advancement of this zeuleus, until it was generally practised and utilized as one of the Fine Art ornamentations in the aistieze of the Lontidri. Especially was it valued in its use on homes, temples, and public buildings, both interior and exterior, as the half column, brick and tiling, are used in modern times for ornamentation on facades, cornices, etc. The style was used for interior adornment, where colored materials are modernly interspersed.

The Spī'dē Lē-ĕl'vä Rĭl Sī-lō'tōn (the Terra Cotta Art of Egypt) had its origin in that country about 800 years before the Adomic period.

Quĭl'bĕx, was the first noted Spī'dē Lē-ĕl-vä'zē-ĕt (Terra-Cotta artist) in that country who came into note about 800 B. C., lived to the mortal age of seventy years, and dwelt in the pre-historic town of Sū-bī'tō, on the Bar-el-Jebel, on the site where the town of Ghaba Shambeh now has place.

His first conception relative to the origin of the Lē-ĕl'vä, was influenced through the placement of twigs, from shrubs and trees, in a picturesque form on pieces of prepared wood. From this, later, he conceived the idea of moulding Dĕltz (the name then used for a dark blue clay) into similar styles, as he had done with the twig arrangements. Thus he wrought in low relief, upon a base of slate-stone, zig-zag, pyramidal, and other outline figures. He modelled some other subjects, as the snake species, in its various coilings and crawlings, but he never attempted animal or human forms.

Sĕg'ā-wä, was the next Spide Leelvazeet ril Siloton, who came into note about 775 B. C., lived to the mortal age of about eighty-five years, and dwelt in the pre-historic town of Bä-vä-bä'yä, then located on the eastern shore of the now known small lake of Mbaringo, in British East Africa (town now extinct).

His first work was very simple, though he had some knowledge of the work of Quilbex, as he had migrated from the town of Sū-bi'to, to that of Bavabaya; and through curiosity, he began the practise of clay moulding experimentally. The material used by him was a clay of grayish or ashen color, which he prepared by a combination of lava and natural clay. He finally settled upon the idea of low-relief style, in representation of letter characters, which he utilized for all inscription work that was practised at that time. But he never developed general subject representations, such as human or animal figures, etc.

Therefore, Quilbex and Segawa, under the co-operative influence of spirit inspiration and guidance, originated and established the pre-historic Spide Leelva in Siloton (Egypt), thus embodied and re-embodied by them and their subsequent Leelvazeets from the extended Atlantian influence from the spirit side of life; is a fact which makes them fitting links with which to connect up the Epi-cycle of Terra-Cotta Art, from Atlantis, through pre-historic and ultimate extensions, into the Ancient and Modern establishments of the Art whereby and through which, manifestations have been made, and left as archaeologic evidence of aforetime history influence, during the events of past time in extension of this Art. Hence, passing from the pre-historic works of Quilbex and Segawa, we find the influence as having existed principally in the offspring idea of Wall Lining, with glazed brick or tile, as was the case in Assyria and extended into Persia. It was made manifest through the Sasanian works; and later, in the twelfth century, the Moslem. The same style manifest through the so called Rhodian and Damascus wares, whereon the rose, the hyacinth, the carnation, and the natural growth of trees and flowers of vast variety, speak in silent but beautiful language, in evidence of past greatness, as on the "Meea Wall," in the Mosque of Ibrahim Agha, Cairo; other Mosques in Persia, as at Tabriz; the ruined tomb of Sultan Khodabend, at Sultanieh; in the palace of Shah Abbas I. and on the tomb of Abbas II. at Ispahan, representing influences of the twelfth to the seventeenth centuries. Further extension of it are found in Spain, as in the *"azulejos,"* or wall tiles, manufactured by the Moors of the fourteenth century, in imitation of mosaics, manifest in such placements as seen in the Alhambra, and in the Generalife palace, at Granada; the Alcazar, at Seville, etc.

The Cē-lē'gŭs Mĕl'sä E'ū El'tē-zē (terra cotta art of Arabia), had its origin in that country about 600 years before the Adomic period.

Mī-ĕn'gō, was the first noted Celegus Melsaest, who came into note about 600 years B. A.,* lived to the mortal age of about fifty years, and dwelt in the pre-historic town of Bō-yē-wä'yä, in the northeastern portion of Elteze (Arabia), where now the town of Leina has place.

When but a child he began to play with mud, as is the case with many children of modern times, and on one of those occasions he chanced to make a figure, in partial representation of a man's body, i. e., he had made the body with a head and what he called legs, but no arms. Of course this was very crudely moulded, but seeing that it resembled a human form, he was delighted at what he had made, and at seeing that it would hold together, he ran to his mother, shouting at the top of his voice, "Cē'lē-gŭs! Cē'lē-gŭs!" (See! See!). And it was from this

*B. A., or before Adam.

event that the term "celegus" was adopted as the name for terra-cotta art, Miengo being the original worker in the art of moulding clay, or the establisher of the terra-cotta art, in that country.

He continued to develop the art, as time went by, until he had made much proficiency in representing human and animal forms, all of which he wrought in the round style, and never attempted any representations in relief.

While he developed to a considerable degree of proficiency, in form representation, there was yet no practical utility made of his works, and they served only as novelties to those who saw or possessed them. But in time they became the stepping-stones to the greater achievements and utilities of the subsequent celegus melsaiests of that country.

Hā-ū-cū'thī-ō, a son of Miengo, was the second Celegus Melsaest of Elteze, who lived to the mortal age of eighty-three years, and continued the work in the city of Boyewaya.

At first he wrought in the style of his father, by the use of natural clays, but he further conceived the idea of painting his pieces in various colors, some brown and some red, which he did, with vegetable juices, and other blacks, by mixing graphite with his clays.

Subsequently he continued to further perfect human and animal form representation, in the round. But those of the animal were far superior to the human; the latter being somewhat grotesque, and more on the comical order, especially the visages, which he characterized with gross mouths and ungainly teeth; and the limbs he rendered shapeless, according to the occasion of representation, etc.

His best animal subject, for representation, seemed to be of the Lion species, and these he made to appear quite natural.

The Wē-mŭl'cy Kā-rī'ĕl Sō Mē-quē'thŭs (terra cotta art of Assyria), had its origin in that country about 100 years before the Adomic period.

Săn-ăn'sē-lŭs, was the first noted wē-mŭl'cy kā-rī-ĕl'ĕst whose works began about 100 years B. A., and who lived to the mortal age of 110 years, and dwelt in the pre-historic town of Nä-vī-ō'bī, on the site where the now known ruins of Circesium have place, south of the junction of the Khabur (Chaboras), affluent of the Euphrates.

He was then known as a Sen-thic (wanderer), having migrated from El'tē-zē (Arabia). He therefore had some knowledge of plastic work from the Karielests (artists) of that country.

His first representations were those of the human form which he wrought in the round. His first subject, was the image of a man which stood up against a tree, during the process of moulding the form. The material he used was a blue clay.

Subsequently he made a plastic pavement or walk for his own premises. On this he wrought landscapes or natural geographical views in the low relief style, and the whole, when complete, was a fine piece of work. From this he conceived the idea of Stucco work, on architectural structures, and he carried it to a good degree of perfection, using such natural subjects as vines, trees, etc.

Gĭn-cē-cŏf′fy was the second noted wemulcy kariel of Mē-quē′thŭs, who came into noteriety about fifty years before the Adomic period, and lived to the mortal age of ninety-five years. He also dwelt in the city of Nā-vī-ō′bî, being an immigrant from the then known city of Crē′zä, on the site of the now known city of Van, on the eastern central side of the pre-historic lake Bŏs′trä. now known as lake Van. Therefore, he was a descendant from the Bostras, who then dwelt in that section, and which they termed Bä-sē-ā-răn′ĕr.

He was a pupil of Sananselus, and after completing his studies with said artist, began work in the same city for himself. He conceived the idea of further representing various subjects, and in addition to his landscapes, vegetation, and the human form, he added animals and birds, which he not only wrought in low and high relief, but in the round as well. He utilized his works for architectural and individual home ornamentation and decoration, and artistically, his products were very fine.

Therefore, the influence that extended from the embodied and re-embodied ideas of Săn-ăn′sē-lŭs and Gĭn-sē-cŏf′fy, co-operative with spirit influence and inspiration, and further extended through the works of subsequent wemulcy karielests, and later made manifest through ancient models, some of which were of great beauty, and the offspring ideas of which were embodied in the arts of brick enameling, plat moulding, gem cutting, etc. Evidences are manifest through the statues, brick edifices, bas-reliefs, low and high-reliefs, of various subjects and utility; e. g., the Terraced Temples of Ur Erech, etc., of the Chaldeans, which are adorned with enameled brick that had been colored, glazed, and hardened by fire; the Terra-Cotta cones of various hues, embedded in plates for external ornamentation on structures; the Colossal Half Columns at Warka (Erech), for exterior purposes; in Sargon's palace at Khorsabad, which influenced the establishment of the great and wonderful varieties of Pillars, in Assyria, etc., etc., all of which mark events which link the terra-cotta work, of antequated time, to that of the third Efremetrum of Atlantis; and its influence as having extended into the modern, thus to establish the Terra-Cotta Art, and all its offspring ideas, as they have been and are now moving, with their respective epi-cycle influences, on the deferent of the Great Art Cycle.

The Crĕn'chē I-ō'ŏn Lē Zăn-zū-rē'tä (terra-cotta art of Greece) had its origin in that country about three hundred years before the Adomic period.

Dĕl'dē-mŭnd was the first Crĭn'chē Ioonso (Terra-Cotta artist) of Zanzureta, who came into note about 300 B. A., and who lived to the mortal age of about one hundred years, and dwelt in the pre-historic town of E-deēr'dŏm, now submerged by the waters of the Ta Lanta channel, northeast of the now known mouth of the Hellada river.

He was a descendant from a people who dwelt in the northeastern portion of Zanzureta.

He was a spirit sensitive, and therefore was easily inspired with artistic ideas; and he thus received that of the Crenche Ioon, which was occasioned and further influenced by a natural scene he once witnessed; viz:—as he stood at twilight looking up over a hill at the clear but tinted sky, and at a beautiful tree crowning the summit of the hill, that in appearance stood out in relief from the sky, he conceived the idea of representing natural scenes, by natural means; i. e., by the use of clays, with which he could make the scene appear in perspective, as had been the case with the landscape he witnessed. Therefore, he set to work with yellow and blue clays, moulding in exact represntation of the above-named scene, which he chose for his first model, persevering until he had completed it, by what later ages came to look upon as the Low Relief Process.

From this experience, he developed representations of other landscape scenes, always taking his subjects from Nature, with their accompaniments of flowers, vines, trees and shrubs. Therefore, his was an art taken from nature, wrought with natural material, by a natural artist, inspired by spirit intelligence cooperative with natural law, etc., which ultimated in a proficiency that created some very fine and beautiful work.

Pē-ō'trä was the second noted Crenche Ioonso of Zanzureta, who came into note about 275 B. A., and who lived to the mortal age of about ninety years, and dwelt in the city of Edeerdom.

He was also a descendant from the people of the race of Deldemund, and studied under his tutorship, and therefore was contemporaneous with him.
temporaneous with him. But after completing his course of

study, he worked independently of Deldemund, and thus established a profession to himself.

At first he continued in the style of his master's works, but soon conceived the idea of representing the human form in the round style, a departure from the landscapes in relief, as his earlier works had been. He now utilized red and blue clays, and he painted the lips and cheeks of the clay representations red, like nature; and the eyes of both he painted to have a more lifelike appearance.

Subsequently he used a Sē-tī'le (soapstone) material of yellowish, reddish, and grayish-green colors, which he moulded into forms of various Idols, a process at which he became quite expert.

The Terra-Cotta Art, or baked clay figures, as the idea is re-embodied in the latter part of the nineteenth century, is of remote origin, having been practiced by the pre-historic artists of the various sections, and continued anciently by subsequent artists respectively, as in this case,—in Zanzureta (Greece), in the style of statues, busts and reliefs, by the Greeks and Romans, who also created colossal statues and groups. In evidence of the pre-historic and ancient usage, we have the products from the excavations, in 1873, of the tombs of Tanagra, a Boetian town on the highway from Athens to the north, and later, from excavations at Corinth, Smyrna, Cyme, Tarentum, the Cyrenaica, etc., etc. The specimens from Tanagra are statues varying from the minute, to dimensions that vary from eight to nine inches; those from the latter excavations are figures, of various styles and dates; the majority being of the last half of the fourth century B. C., while still earlier ones embraced the round, and the half styles, for wall and frieze ornamentation. Those belonging to the pre-historic period, small, idol-like figures of the crudest form, had almost shapeless trunks, with stick-like extensions for limbs. The breasts and eyes were roughly indicated by round dots, and the figure decorated with coarse stripes or cheques, in ochre color. Other specimens of these have been found at Hissarlik (Troad), Cyprus, and in other Islands, and in the Citadel of Tiryns. Very archaic figures varying from two to three inches in height, have been exhumed in various parts of the Ægean Islands, some of which are represented as stiff, seated deities (thought to be links between the Oriental and Hellenic arts), like the statues of the Sacred Way at Branchidae (south of Miletus), but which are, in reality, influences arising from the embodied ideas of Peotra, and re-embodied by subsequent artists.

The advancement in the Grecian terra-cotta art, is evidenced by such works as the relief, 18 x 12 inches, dating from the first half of the fifth century, in representation of two female mourners at a sepulchral *stale,* one standing and the other seated. On the other side of the *stale* two youths are represented as standing by the side of a horse, etc. (Louvre); the statuette of a girl, playing with the infant "Eros," who flies to her for shelter and is received with welcome half tinged with dread, from the Tanagra antiquities (St. Petersburg); "Aphrodite" and "Cupids," from the Castellani sale, in representation of a half nude figure of Aphrodite resting on a couch, with two cupids behind, holding up a veil, thus to disclose her form (South Kensington Museum); the many fine specimens of terra-cottas, ranging in date over a long period of time, that have been excavated at Corinth, all of which are influential links which we must utilize in connecting up the Epi-cycle of Terra-Cotta Art.

The statuettes and reliefs, both of pre-historic Zanzureta and of subsequent Greece, influenced the idea of Ornamental Jewelry, conceived by the artists of the latter-named section. This is but an offspring from the terra-cotta art, such as the necklaces and ear pendants, made of clay and covered with gold leaf (examples in the Louvre)

Another influence, or offspring idea from the foregoing, is embodied in terra-cotta ornamentation for architectural utility, such as has been found at Olympia and in the ruined temples of Selinus.

Further influence resulted in the embodied idea of Hard Stucco for wall covering, such as had place on the early Greek temples, manifest on the Doric temples at Ægina, Phigaleia, Paestum, and Agrigentum; the moulded reliefs on the interior walls of the Greek and Roman buildings; some tombs in Magna Graecia of the fourth century B. C.,—figure representations of nymphs, cupids, animals and insects; in the Baths of Titus, and various tombs near Rome; on the Moslem structures of the Middle Ages, such as geometrical patterns wrought in low and high-relief, wonderfully rich and beautiful, accompanied by flowing ornamental bands, or long Arabic inscriptions. These are seen in the Mosque of Tulum, Cairo, of the ninth century; the Moorish towers at Segovia in Spain; the Alhambra at Granada, and in the Alcazar at Seville; in the beautiful reliefs that encrust the Pillars and other parts of the Court, in the Florentine Palazzo Vecchio, representing vines and other plants winding spirally round columns, sixteenth century; in the English examples, as on the exterior of the old half-timbered house in the marketplace at Newark-upon-Trent, fifteenth century; others through the counties of Essex and Suffolk; Hardwick Hall (Derbyshire), with life sized stucco figures in high-relief, thus forming a deep frieze all around, etc. Thus specimens are found on down to the Modern stucco work, of all sorts, designs, and utilities, establishing the fact of extended influences direct and also diverse, through the ages, such as give aid in connecting up the Epi-cycle of Terra-Cotta Art, as it has moved along on the deferent of the Great Cycle of Art.

Passing with the terra-cotta influence of Zanzureta, or Greece, into Clē-ăn-dē′cï-ä, or Asia Minor, it having been thus extended originally in pre-historic time, we note that large quantities of terra-cotta figures have been found in western Asia Minor. This gives evidence, in that region, of the fact of their being similar in size to those of Tanagra, but of different style, they being thoroughly sculpturesque, rather than pictorial in style; and from six to ten inches in height, especially those of Smyrna, Cyme, Myrtina, etc., as evidenced by such specimens as the copy of a statue of Aphrodite from Megara, which stands on a moulded pedestal, instead of on a thin slab of clay, as was the style with the figures found at Tanagara (British Museum). This was a re-embodied idea from the works of various sculptors, in Asia Minor and adjacent sections; and as conceived by Qū-cē-lăn′ze, the originator of the art of terra-cotta in Asia Minor, a very intelligent individual, who traveled extensively in Asia Minor, and therefore came into touch with the incoming sculptural influences, from which, as before stated, he conceived the idea of terra-cotta work.

Very elaborate groups are among the yield,—subjects Dionysiac and Bacchanal; scenes from mythology, as the labors of Hercules, are chosen, the productions dating from the fourth century B. C., supposed to be copies from sculpture of the school of Praxiteles, or of Scopas, were really influenced by Hib-ē-lŭn′ēs, a pre-historic terra-cotta artist, who had learned the art from, or was influenced by, the works of Qucelanze. But he further developed the style, and to a greater perfection than the former artist had done; e. g., a fine nude figure of "Eros as a Youth," shows the little god leaning against a cippus, holding a bronze arrow in his hand (collection of M. Brantegem, Rome); the beautiful figure of a "winged Victory," a re-embodied motive idea of the colonial "Victory," of Samothrace island (Louvre); the very remarkable group, in representation of a Soul, led by Hermes Prychoprompus to the bark of Charon, which she is about to enter, Hermes being represented as a graceful nude figure, gently urging the shrinking soul,—the latter a draped female figure, to the boat at the brink of the rush-grown Styx; while Charon is represented as an aged man, in stooping attitude, awaiting the entrance of the Soul upon his bark (Prince Liechtenstem's collection, Vienna).

In evidence of the fact that fads arose in those days, as in modern time, are the deviations and degenerations from the true art principles, in like manner serving different purposes, we note the "caricature figures," exhumed at Smyrna and Ephesus, modeled in response to humorous ideas. These strange figures are characterized with attenuated limbs, large heads, flapping ears, and goggle eyes. Some are represented as playing musical instruments, others as actors, an idea handed down even to the twentieth century, as evidenced by such fads as the "Teddy bears," the "Billy O-Possums," the "Billikens," and other caricature images and figures, which are diminutive and degenerate art, under the guise of comique entertainment, or the society fad, over which less deep-thinking people go to excess.

These fad figures, which we term "satellites," or satellitish sub-epicycles of sculpture, or diminutive offsprings from the parent epi-cycle, serving two purposes, i. e., that of bric-a-brac and ornamentation, and for comique entertainment; and closely allied to the sub-epicycle of Fads found in all branches of Art, as referred to under the several subject articles on decadence from True Art.

The Bĕl-zē-ī′lĕt Pâ Et-zĕn-tū′ăn (Terra-Cotta Art of Italy) had its origin in that country about two hundred years before the Adomic period.

Cē-lī′zē-ō was the first Belzeilit Etsies (Terra-Cotta artist) of Etzentuan, who came into note about 200 years B. A., and who lived to the mortal age of about eighty-seven years, and dwelt in the pre-historic city of Querrer, on the site of ancient Rome. He was a descendant from the Jeretheans of Etzentuan.

He having been principally influenced through the works of pre-historic sculptors, conceived the idea of the Belzeilit Etsi, or moulding forms from natural clays, when he attempted various subjects.

His work, however, was chiefly experimental, and therefore had no practical value or utility. But it was sufficient to establish, or originate, that class of sculpture in that section of the country.

Săn-dē-ī′ē was the second noted Belzeilit Etsies Pa Etzentuan, who was a pupil of Celizeo, who lived to the mortal age of about one hundred years, and dwelt in the city of Querrer. He was a descendant from the Jeretheans of Etzentuan, and contemporaneous with Celizeo.

After leaving his master, his first work was that of the representation of a complete form of a man, in the round style, the figure being, in size, that of a lad of fourteen or fifteen years. It was finely executed, and of a beautiful physical form.

He was a natural artist, and a spirit sensitive, therefore susceptible to inspirations from that source, which rendered him a great success in his profession; and therefore his images were utilized for home decoration by the people generally.

Subsequently, he conceived the idea of representing human figures, and groups, which he interspersed with natural lawn adornments, as trees, shrubs, flowers, etc., such as characterize the home life. These he wrought in low relief for interior decoration to buildings. They were wonderfuly wrought and extremely beautiful, artistically speaking.

The influence of these pre-historic Belzeilit Etsiessa of Etzentuan, having extended with that of the Crinche Ioonsoes of Zanzureta, and further, through the works of subsequent terra-cotta artists of this section, is manifest in such works as the many fine specimens of the terra-cotta statuettes, and busts of herioc style, taken from the tombs of Tarentum, Italy, some of which date back to 400 B. C., and others to even an earlier time. We hold them the re-embodied ideas from the Atlantian terra-cotta works, through the influence of those of the pre-historic artists who had likewise re-embodied them; and further, through the ancient artists, many of the latter being ideal representatives in commemoration of their ancestors.

Furthermore, the many thousand "votive" figures and reliefs in clay, as found in the *temeni* of the temples of Clethonian deities at Tarentum and other places.

The influence of Etruscan terra-cotta, as re-embodied under similar circumstances, is greatly manifest, when clay, or painted terra-cotta for special sculpture, took supremacy over marble and stone. This is evidenced by such works as the clay Quadriga on the pediment of Capitoline Jupiter, one of the seven precious relics on which the safety of Rome depended (destroyed 83 B. C.); the great statue of Jupiter in the central *cella* of the Triple Temple, and many other statues of the early temples of Rome; the large terra-cotta Sarcophagi with recumbent portrait-effigies of the deceased, decorated with painting; a re-embodied idea of the Egyptian mummy preservers (examples in the Louvre and British Museum), e. g., in the latter, the Sarcophagus from Caere, Etruria; the moulded heads of satyrs and scroll foliage relief on friezes (Museo Gregoriano, Vatican); the large asci, covered with terra cotta statues found in the tombs of Canosa (Canusium) Cales, etc., dating from the fourth century B. C. (British Museum), etc.

Greek influence caused the Romans to re-embody many ideas relative to statuettes, placques, reliefs and architectural ornamentation of this art, as evidenced by the collections in the Berlin and British Museums, and in the Louvre; e. g., the scene of "Orestes" taking refuge at the Sacred Omphalos, at Delphi (Louvre), a plaque of the second century A. D.; a Chariot race in the Circus, same period (Louvre); the Friezes and Corinthian Columns, with elaborate acanthus capitals, in Rome, such as those of the Ampitheatrum Castrense; many busts, on the Via Latina, and the barracks of the Seventh Cohort of the Guards, in Trastevere; the terra-cotta sculptures, such as seated female figures from tombs, small sized (Capitoline Museum); large statues in terra-cotta, as the Torso of a nude male figure, representing Hercules; some terminal figures of Bacchus, and the beautiful statue of Urania, first century (British Museum).

The grand influences of the fourteenth, fifteenth and sixteenth centuries, in North Italy, re-embodied ideas from the foregoing influences, under spirit inspiration and guidance, as evidenced by such works as on the West Facade of the cathedral of Monza, so wonderfully, richly, elaborately, and minutely wrought in clay, in the fourteenth century; the cathedral of Crema, the Communal buildings of Piacenza; the St. Maria delle Grazie, in Milan, arrayed in a splendor of terra-cotta work; the Cortosa, near Pavia, which makes manifest the influence through its gorgeous terra-cotta adornment, of the sixteenth century; the Ducal Palace, and the churches of S. Francesco and S. Maria del Carmine, of Pavia, that manifest through their rich terra-cotta ornamentation; the rich terra-cotta adornment on the Cornices of many buildings in Rome, from the fourteenth to the sixteenth century; e. g., on the south side of the S. Maria in Ara Coeli, and the front of S. Cosimato in Trastevere; the manifestation through such terra-cotta works as statuary, reliefs, busts, and groups of many life size figures, of the fifteenth and the sixteenth centuries, by such artists as Ambrogio Foppa, for S. Satiro, at Milan, Guido Mazzoni and Begarelli for the churches in Modena, etc., etc., which afford us sufficient links with which to establish the continued extension of the Epi-cycle of Terra-Cotta Art, as it has moved on the deferent of the Great Art Cycle from the time of Atlantis to the present century, under the influence of mortal and spirit artists, in co-operation with the laws governing Natural Art.

Finally, passing into England, in the sixteenth century, we note the influence manifested in such examples as in Essex, e. g., that of the richly moulded Windows and Battlements, of the Manor House of Lawyer Marney, in the reign of Henry VIII; the richly decorated terra-cotta tomb with recumbent effigy, in the church of Lawyer Marney; the Collegiate church of Wymondham, in Norfalk, where the art manifests through the large and elaborate Sedilia, with lofty canopied niches of clay, sixteenth century; the terra-cotta sculpture wrought by Torrigiano, fragments of which have place in Westminster Abbey; the Colored Heads of the Caesars, at Hampton Court, and the recumbent effigy in the Chapel of the Rolls, of Italian re-embodiment, wrought during the reigns of Henry VII. and Henry VIII.

Coming into the more modern part of the epi-cycle, we find this art manifesting through architectural designs, on buildings, as those that ornament the museum of South Kensington, Albert Hall, etc., and the great utility of terra-cotta in architectural ornamentation, in all its varied styles, which is an ultimatum arising as a diversity from the embodied and re-embodied ideas of Terra-Cotta Sculpture, having its origin in Atlantis, as evidenced by their architectural ornamentation, and thus extended down through the Pre-historic and Ancient conceptions, to the Modern, monumental evidences of which, architecturally and otherwise, are widely disbursed over Europe and other countries, on and within existing buildings of public utility; and collectively, as reminiscent evidences of past greatness, as in the Louvre; the British Museum; the Museums of Berlin and Athens; South Kensington Museum; the famous Sabarouff collection in the Hermitage Palace at St. Petersburg; at Florence, Perugia, Capua, Rome and in other public places in Italy and the great distribution of the Tanagra figures, individually and collectively, as the collection of Prince Liechtenstein, at Vienna, etc.

Passing into Germany in the fifteenth century, and extending to the sixteenth, we find the art influencing and manifesting, as was also the case in various parts of Europe through magnificent and elaborate architectural utility, as evidenced on the church of St. Catherine, and the Town Hall, so elaborately and delicately traced and characterized with string-coursed cornices, enriched with foliage moulded in clay; the churches of St. Stephen, Tengermünde, and other edifices, so wonderfully decorated in the terra-cotta style.

Passing into France, the terra-cotta influence was made manifest in the sixteenth century, through re-embodied ideas, by

Italian artists, or immigrant sculptors from the northern and central portions of that country, under the patronage of Francis I.

Passing into Spain, we find the terra-cotta art of the sixteenth century, also under Italian influence, by immigrant sculptors from that region.

Here we leave the reader to search the historic zones of the Great Art Cycles, for other influential links than we have pointed out, thus to strengthen the extension of each, and further aid in the revealment of facts that shall ultimately make the restoration of Atlantis and its greatness, to such an extent as to establish in the minds of mortals the fact of its influence upon the minds of pre-historic peoples, similarly extended unto the peoples of Ancient and Modern periods, thus brought them through the force of Spirit intelligence, manifesting through the mortal.

USH DEL-ZE-MAR'IC SI ATLANTIS,
OR
THE GOVERNMENT OF ATLANTIS.

TELTZIE XL.

The following general information in regard to Atlantis and the various links leading up to modern times, has been given to us by Alem Prolex, our Dĕl'zō (chief) Atlantian Spirit Director, son of Entitha and Atcelina Prolex, and third Efremetrum of the Lontidri of Atlantis, who bore a threefold title by which he was recognized among his people. First:—a Deltsanz from Gabala, or Gala, who expounded moral and religious principles; second:—a Guide, whose mission it was to advise the people in all the avenues of social life; third:—the Originator of Governing Laws that were to control them in all matters of State and Nation.

In regard to the Dĕl-zē-mär-ĭc-sēs (Governmental) affairs of Atlantis, in comparison with those of other Dĕl-zē-mär-ĭcs (Governments) of ancient and modern times, we are informed by Alem Prolex, that each Teltzie had its Kistrez aistie (Capital city) where the Deltsanz (Teacher or Governor) presided, as is the case with Capital cities and Governors of the United States of America.

The In-thă-ō-ză Kĭs-trĕz sī ŭsh Lŏn-tī-drī (national capital of the continent), was Atara, located in Teltzie Et, where the Efremetrum (Supreme Teacher or President) lived, and presided over the Government, as is the case with our national capital city, Washington, D. C., where the President of the United States of America presides.

The Kistrez aistieze, (Capital cities) and the presiding Deltsanze (Teachers or Governors) over the various Teltzie' (Sections) at the time of their submergence, were as follows:—

Tĕltzie Et, A'tä-ră, the In-thă-ŏ'ză Kĭs'trĕz, and A'lĕm Prŏlĕx as E'frē-mē-trum.

Tĕltziē Wē, Neĭtz the Kĭs'trĕz ā-ĭs-tiē, and Yĕr'măh the Dĕlt'sănz.

Tĕltziē Sĕt, Hŭ'lĭtz the Kĭs'trĕz ā-ĭs-tiē, and Fört'zē the Dĕlt'sănz.

Tĕltziē Kĕt, Hā'drĕy the Kĭs'trĕz ā-ĭs-tiē, and Utz'ly-ĕr the Dĕlt'sänz.

Tĕltziē Zrĕt, Wĕx'trä the Kĭs'trĕz ā-ĭs-tiē, and O-rŏn'dō the Dĕlt'sänz.

Tĕltziē Sŏt, Gē'trĕx the Kĭs'trĕz ā-ĭs-tiē, and Sā'gōts the Dĕlt'sänz.

Alem Prolex further informs us that the Atlantian Delzemaric was a Stĕl'zä (Republic), hence as above stated, the principal administrators of the Lontidri were the Supreme Efremetruzem, corresponding with the Presidents of the United States of America, Mexico, France, etc., etc., and the Sub-Efremetruzem to the Governors of the States, each ruling over his own respective Teltzie. There were no intervening officials, such as Congressmen and Senators,, who were elected for a term of years, but in their stead, advisers were chosen by the several Sub-Efremetruzem for their special assemblies, etc., held semi-annually at the Kistrez aistie, where they, with the Supreme Efremetrum, entered into Congressional consultation upon matters of common interest to the people, enacted the laws, and transacted such business as lawfuly came before the assembly.

It was the power intrusted to the Supreme Efremetrum to make final decision upon all questions the Sub-Efremetruzem failed to agree unanimously upon.

Should questions arise among the people, such as demanded immediate settlement, special sessions were called, at which to adjust them.

Both the Supreme Efremetrum and the Sub-Efremetruzem were chosen by the people, and in accordance to their standing morally and educationally. The term of office was one hundred years, or during their natural life if less than that; providing they maintained justice and honor in all their rulings and acts in life, and were not physically rendered incapable of filling the office.

Regarding the development of the three Efremetrumze* (dynasties), our Guide futher informs us, that prior to the three hundred years of their existence, the people were more or less uncivilized, according to the locality, and circumstances governing their livlihood, and were democratic, or self governing. At this period of time, they began to see their need of stated laws for civil and social government; and a better understanding or knowledge of religious principles. This feeling prompted the steps that were taken, that ultimated in the establishment of the first (dynasty), and the choice of Galthaza as supreme Deltsanz, or Efremetrum, who established the Delzemaric, over which he presided about one hundred years.

Goetlez, the second Efremetrum, was chosen by the people after the disembodiment of Galthaza, and remained in office one hundred years. He was more progressive, in every way, than his predecessor; hence, during his term of office and under his teachings, the people became much more enlightened, and began the erection of public buildings, and the establishment of various commercial enterprises. Being some what advanced in years before he began his term of office, and having served the Delzemaric for one hundred years, Goetlez was considered too aged to continue his services as Efremetrum, and therefore was retired by order of the people.

Alem Prolex was then chosen, as the third Efremetrum, and served nearly one hundred years, which lawful term he probably would have completed but for the great submergence of the Lontidri.

It might be beneficial to the reader to know that the term, "Efremetrum" was used to signify both a "Supreme Teacher" of the Lontidri, and the "Dynasty;" the only difference being in the pronunciation, as governed by the accent marks, viz: the first syllable is accented, when the term is used in the former sense; and the third, when for the latter. The term "Efremetrumze," is the plural for the term when used in the latter sense, and is accented on the fourth syllable; and "Efremetruzem," for the plural of the former, with the accent on the third syllable.

During the progress of the third Efremetrum, great light burst upon the Delzemaric; and with it came a steady advancement in both civil and religious government. The Sciences, Arts, and Education, were generally sought after.

During the first fifty years of this Efremetrum, the great Dē-āke′äl or Dĕl-zē-mär′ic building, the Agalte Si Neceletus Mĕl′-zē Cō-dī′zē, and the Trūne Agalte Si Quesa, were erected; and electricity became much utilized for various purposes, which during the following fifty years, developed into a far greater use, as the people became better versed in machinery. That this would naturally be the case, can be readily comprehended, by calling to mind the great advancement that has been made in electric and other machinery, and the control of electric forces, during our last fifty years of Modern civilization. Looking back over that period of time, in our country, as well as in others, we can realize the great changes in every avenue of civilization; and thus the better understand what the same condition brought to us in the space of three hundred years.

The Atlantians of this period had a monetary system that differed somewhat from systems of modern times. Especially as they did not use U'ziē (gold) and Clē'tiē (silver) for their Gē'trex (money), but for ornamental and other purposes.

The Getrex was made from Zĭn'dē-lēte (a black and white crystallized substance)).

The valuation of the Atlantian Getrex was determined by measurement, i. e. (by means of machinery), the Zindelete was cut into cylindrical sections, of five denominations, one-quarter inch, one-half, three-quarters inch, one and one-quarter inches, and one and one-half inches. The diameter of each was equal to its length, and given a name significant of value. These corresponded very nearly, to the amounts, as compared with United States money, according to the following table:—

San-lĭp'	$ .25
San-mĭt'	$ .50
San-sĭt'	$1.00
San-lĭt'	$1·25
San-dĭt'	$2.00

It will be observed that there is no piece whose denomination is less than twenty-five cents, which in modern times would be inconvenient, according to the small amounts of some purchases now practised. Alem Prolex informs us that the Atlantian people seldom made exchanges, commercially, for quantities less than the worth of a Sanlip; but when it became necessary to have a smaller amount, e. g., twelve and one-half cents worth, a purchase of some other article, of the same amount, was made at the same time, and the Sanlip given for the two articles. Were the amount less than twelve and one-half cents, articles enough were taken to bring the amount up to the value of a Sanlip, etc.

We are furthermore informed that the Atlantian people owned their lands and homes, upon which the Delzemaric levied a tax, with which to defray expenses of the Sĭl-dä-zĭc' Sī Ush Dĕl-zē-mär'ĭc, (Schools of the Government), and the Pĕl-zē-cō'zē and the A-găl-tē'zē (Temples), similarly to America, only here the religious orders are self-supporting.

During the first Efremetrum, they used hand woven cloth for garments, made from the fibrous part of a tree called Ye'tra. Near the close of tihs Efremetrum, the people began to cultivate O'-ēze, a plant, or kind of grass, the fibers of which were as fine as silk.

In the second Efremetrum, Oeze became very plentiful, and was then woven into textures. The people of this period had learned how to beautify these fibers with brilliant colorings, which gave rise to the style of adorning the body with attractive garments.

The Oeze plant was much like varieties of the Bromelia fiber, of tropical America, commonly known as "pita," or silk grass, or the Caraguata, of Brazil, Guiana, Paraguay, and Argentina, and the "pita" of the Philippine Islands; in fact these plants are but a continuation of the original Oeze, under descended conditional changes, and therefore a connecting link in that branch of the Botanic Cycle.

As both Yē'trä and O'ēze were very plentiful at this period of time, they together became the chief influence that caused the people to invent machinery with which to weave textures. At first the machines were crude, yet they greatly aided in the production of textures.

But with the passing of time, entering the third Efremetrum, weaving had become a fine art. The colorings, grades of material, variety of patterns, and such utilities as were necessary to bring more perfect development, and ultimate perfection, reached a high state before the time of the destruction of the Lontidri by submergence.

In the latter part of the third Efremetrum, the Atlantian people had begun a compilement of their history, but that with all else belonging to the greatness of the Lontidri, was destroyed at the time of the great cataclysm.

Alem Prolex further informs us, that they had found data of more than 1000 years preceding the period of the beginning of the first Efremetrum, upon some ancient mounds and in caves. These were recorded in hieroglyphics, or the ancient Atlantian method of writing. Various excavations disclosed articles that had been used by former peoples, and these were preserved among collections of Atlantian antiquities. He furthermore informs us, that after passing to spirit life, he and others who cared to seek for them, learned many facts concerning the antiquity of Atlantis, that had never been discovered by the people of the latter age of the Lontidri.

FLAGS OF ATLANTIS

There were in all, six Delzemaric Gē-el'ze (Government Flags) as represented on the following page. The Gē'el of the Lontidri as also of Teltzie Et, was composed of six stripes extending in right-oblique form across the Geel, in the following order; first, beginning with a deep purple one at the upper left hand corner; second, a bright shade of violet; third, a medium shade of pink; fourth, an azure or sky blue; fifth, a very bright orange; sixth, pure white; but this composed the body of the flag, and thus separated the colored stripes.

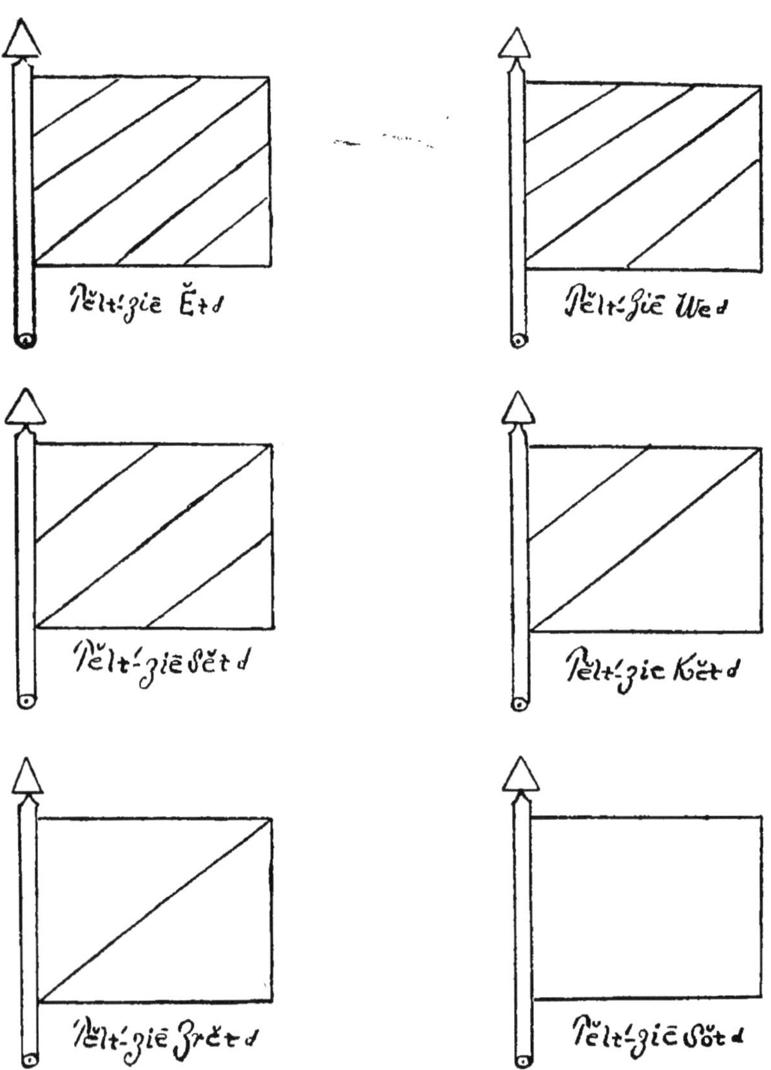

The geelze that belonged to the other Teltzie' individually, were characterized by the absence of the upper or first color that belonged to the Teltzie preceding it, in number; thus characterizing each subsequent geel with one less colored stripe, until the sixth geel was of white; i. e., the geel of Teltzie We had five colors—violet, pink, azure, orange, and white; Teltzie Set, four colors—pink, azure, orange, and white; Teltzie Ket, two colors —azure and orange, on the upper half and center, the lower portion being white; that of Teltzie Zret, simply the orange, that extended through the center, the upper and lower portions being white; and that of Teltzie Sot, plain white.

The upper color of the geel was the ensign of the Teltzie to which it was assigned; and the number of colors displayed on the Delzemaric geel represented the number of Teltzie in the Lontidri.

The Rē-ĭt-ēr′zē (standards) were painted and gilded in accord with the rank of the geelze and the colors belonging to them, e. g., the Delzemaric Reiter in combination of colors, was characterized, first, by that portion above the upper edge of the geel being solid uzie (gold); descending, that portion joining the purple stripe was painted purple, that joining the pink, and that joining the azure, were painted correspondingly; while the lower portion of the Reiter was composed of cletie (silver); therefore that color, and the various others on the reiter, were separated by bands of uzie.

The remainder of the reiterze were of celite, or painted in that color. That of Teltzie We had three colored bands, viz; violet, pink and azure; Teltzie Set, pink and azure; Teltzie Ket, azure and orange; Teltzie Zret, orange; and Teltzie Sot, entirely silver color. These various bands of color were separated by narrow bands of silver color, or un-painted sections of the uzie reiterze; in case of wooden reiterze', they were painted the silver color.

The metal reiterze were principally used on all Kistrez and Delzemaric affairs; but many of those used by private individuals, and for general decorative purposes, were composed of wood.

USH NE-RE'GES SI AT'LAN-TIS, OR THE RELIGION OF ATLANTIS

TELTZIE XLI.

In regard to the Atlantian Nereges (religion), Alem Prolex informs us that there were various sects among the people in certain portions of the Lontidri, during the first Efremetrumze, as has always been the case, in countries both ancient and modern.

There was a low and ignorant class of people in the northeastern portion of Teltzie Sot, who were looked upon by the more enlightened people of the Lontidri, as Idolaters.

These worshipped hideous characters, made of wood and stone, which they elevated in conspicuous places, where they passed and re-passed daily, to represent their adorational ideas. Some of the images were designed and wrought out in representation of the human form, which they termed Rĕn-hĕn-ĕl'gy, and after the form of the E-zō'tä, a very ferocious Atlantian animal that inhabited their Teltzie, that closely resembled the Orang-outang of modern times. This they termed "Ex-ăn'drä."

Their worship, however, was more in the sense of amusement or pleasure, than of a religious character; for of the latter, they in their crude state, had little or no idea. They adored a two-fold idea, viz; the condition of war or contention, and peace or pleasure. The former was represented by the image of Exandra, and the latter by that of Renhenelgy. They had stated days for their adorational gatherings, at the beginning of the new moon. The periods lasted for two days and one night, during which time there was no sleep indulged in. They congregated at these shrines, held their dances about the images, to which they made obeisance by means of crude, strange courtesies, grimaces, and movements of their bodies, giving utterance to sort of a chant, suitable to the occasion; i. e., if unto the image of Renhenelgy, they gesticulated and chanted in tones of voice in harmony with the idea embodied in the image,—peace and pleasure; if to the image of Exandra, they proceeded with gesticulation and a style of chant in accord with the sentiment of war and contention, the idea embodied in the image. The images were all erected in elevated positions, so that at times of adorational exercises the people would be compelled to look upward, which they did; and at the same time they extended their hands, palms together in front of their faces, when they chanted and courtesied as described.

It was from this form of adoration that the idea of the elevation of idols was handed down, through the ages of time, by descended races of people of that section of the globe; and further continued, under spirit inspiration, from those departed peoples, until it reached the extended practise of "Totemism," during Ancient and Modern times.

There was also a very peculiar race of people in the northeastern quarter of Teltzie We, who adored the moon, as a provident though mysterious source. They termed the orb E-ū'tiē, in that sense.

Their reverence for it was far greater than for the Sun, from the fact that they considered the changes in its disc, or its phases, more mysterious and wonderful than the unchanging Solar orb. They recognized the waxing of the Moon as symbolic of increase, in all matters pertaining to livlihood and welfare, and its waning, the opposite; and therefore they sought to shun it, and ignore it as evil, by non-recognition of it at such periods of its phases, and they termed it "O'nër, as the opposite of "Eutie."

When the new moon would first appear however, they began a series of nightly adorations, which consisted in singing, dancing, and body gesticulation. These lasted until the moon was full. At the first sight of its waning, they immediately dispersed to their respective abodes, to await its coming again.

There was another sect who dwelt in the northwestern portion of Teltzie Set, who recognized the marvelous forces made manifest through the Seas, Oceans, Lakes, and all moving waters. This principle they adored under the title of "Hĕl-tër-măn'zē," in representation of the mysterious force that moved the waters. They held their adorational exercises, originally, at the shores of the various water districts, at stated times in the year. Their exercises were usually marked with silent meditation upon the principle they adored, as they sat in assembly, by the water's edge.

At a later period this sect became more widely distributed over the Teltzie, when they changed the adorational exercises, and the name of the principle from Heltermanze, to Zē-rēt'. They built shrines to their deity in all parts of the Lontidri, which were in the form of A-găl-tē'zē (temples), and varied in accord with the wealth of the people of the vicinity. In the place of images, they erected maretuxze monuments), in representation of their Zeret. These consisted of square bases, with octagonal shafts, on which they sculptured spiral wreaths of leaves, extending from base to summit. Animals and birds were represented as in the act of ascension. The animals were on the lower parts of the shaft, and birds on the upper, usually with a large one on the apex. This would have spread pinions and upturned eyes, as if ready to soar away to the sky, which was to symbolize elevation, and ascension in all spiritual things.

The main Agalte and Maretux of the brotherhood were in the aistie of Enididstro, the Kistrez of Teltzie Set. The Agalte was very large, and therefore supported many towers, which in themselves, bore out the idea of elevation and ascension. The Maretux was about one hundred coitex in height, with proportionate base, about which were tanks or basins of water for use at the semi-annual feasts. The people were there twice a year for a general service, at the beginning of Summer, and of Winter.

These services would last two days and nights. The people came from great distances, bringing food. The nights were spent in singing, dancing and various social amusements. The day's service consisted of responsive services, at which the people all knelt, while one individual read the service, and they repeated the responses. Water was then sprinkled over the people while yet kneeling, as an emblem of cleansing and purity, a rite that has been handed down, to both ancient and modern worship. All little children were dipped into one of the pools of water adjacent to the monument, at which time an impressive and interesting service took place. After the sprinkling of the people, came the rite of washing feet, a practice also handed down to the Ancient peoples of the East. When meeting, and before the "clasping the hand of brotherhood," they dipped their hands into water, as a token of purification.

There were other sects who adored the principle of light and heat, as made manifest through the rays of the Sun, which principle they originally termed Dĕn-zē-mĕn′zē; and held adorational exercises in the open air, at stated times, providing there were no clouds to obstruct the view of the Sun at the time, and the sky entirely clear. The exercises began at sunrise and lasted until sunset, consisting in dancing and chanting at both sunrise and sunset, with feasting and pleasure during the middle of the day.

At a later period the term was changed to "Tĕl-tiē′," when they established the image of the Sun, as a representative symbol of the Teltie principle. They elevated this symbol on their public buildings, gateways, and arches leading to their Agalteze. At this period of time, they added to their symbol's representation by the sun's disc, the idea of the positive and negative principles or forces that characterize nature. They held a short devotional service twice a day at the temples, morning and evening. Those who were passing and had not time to enter the Pelzoze (temples), would halt, face the image of the sun over the gateway, as though looking upon the real solar orb, and give adoration for the spiritual light, and for the light of day which they received from Teltie. In the morning when the natural Sun was shining, they turned to it instead, and kneeling upon one knee, they offered the following prayer. "Tŭn rĕdz rē'chĕt nălt Tĕl-tiē'lĕth nĕz ĕt ŭn, ŭn*loo ĕt thŭn," which translated is as follows: "Thou, great light that God hath given to us, we bow to thee." In the evening, when the sun was setting, in the same manner, they repeated the following:—"Tĕs tŭn ĕt-lăn'dĕs quĕt rē'chĕt ĕt jĕn'trĕs nălt nĕlt gēl lĕn'gō mĭn-dē-săn' wĕltz nŭd tīz 'frĕl si Tĕl-tiē';" the translation, "As thou departest, give light to others, that they may become enlightened thereby, and know more of God." Then with low, bent bodies, they made obeisance, rose, turned and went their ways. They had various modes of service in the Pelzoze, one of which was by means of a circle, suspended horizontally on a standard, that represented the sun—so arranged as to continuously revolve. Its circular motion was silently watched by the worshippers, while they stood encircling it, thus contemplating the "Cycles of Creation," and the force of "Teltie" by which they were operated, or the All Power and All Force, symbolized by the moving circle. The order of disbursement was preceded by various gyrations, at the close of which they audibly repeated the morning or evening prayer, in accordance with the hour of service. Then reverently bowing, they would turn and depart.

Some sects embraced the Planets and Stars in connection with the Sun, as being possessed with mysterious forces of provident order, which principle, they termed Yăn-tĕr-măn'zē. But at this period, the people of the Lontidri, generally, reverenced the Sun as their Kā'lä, Gā-hä'lä, or Gä'lä, which to them represented the Universal Creative Force in all nature, especially in the time of the third Efremetrum. Some recognized this force in a more mysterious sense than others, in accord with their degree of enlightenment a condition that exists even among modern peoples; for there are many creeds and isms, theories and beliefs, relative to the God principle, its processes and developments; its reality and identity,

*The pronouns "us" and "we" were both written "un."

and its mysteriousness, or "degrees of being understood," according to the ignorance or eductation of mankind, in accord with suppositions and beliefs, or scientific and logical reasonings.

There was a sect in the northwestern portion of Teltzie Ket, who conceived the idea of a personal Gabala, or Individual Being of the Anthropomorphic order, which they originally termed Grăf′thē-ăm, an idea that was, in subsequent time re-conceived in the minds of ancient peoples, and widely spread among peoples of modern times, and is the connecting link between Graftheam—adoration, by those Atlantians, and the creedists of modern times, who are extending that Epi-cycle of the great Religious Cycle, having gone astray from the Universal Cycle of Natural Law.

In the latter part of the second Efremetrum, as the sect grew more numerous, the term was changed to Kitranda; but they still held to the idea that Kitranda was the ruler of the universe, and that he made manifest through the developments of natural form, or through nature. At this time they began the erection of Pelzoze (temples), which they dedicated to the adoration of Kitranda. Their principal Pelzo, which they termed Ex-ā-lĕn′-trē, a magnificent structure, was located at Hadrey, the Kistrez aistie of Teltzie Ket, where they assembled four times a year at the beginning of spring, summer, autumn, and winter, for worship and adorational exercises.

The Exalentre was a circular structure, or colosseum, built of golden-tinted stone, with many pointed turrets as ornamental qualifications, intended to carry out the idea of the rays of the sun, as emanating from the main body of the structure. The people, when assembled for worship, were always seated in a circle around the Exalentre. In the center of this Auditorium was a massive base and pedestal upon which four discs of the sun were elevated, one facing each of the four cardinal points. The service consisted principally in graceful movements in accompaniment to the rythm of the chant employed in the service. They stood facing the emblems of Kitranda, with right arm extended, parallel with the shoulder; then together they all turned once around to the left, facing the images again. The left arm was then extended, and a complete turn made back to the right, again facing the images. Both hands were then raised above the head, palms open, fingers extended, in radiant position, while they lowered the body perpendicularly. In this attitude they knelt upon both knees. They then clasped their hands behind them, and rose to their feet again. They then formed in a circle in single file about the image of Kitranda. One of the number led the march, and the rest followed, in circular movement, around the images, until they had passed three times around them. Then they halted in the position from which they had started, after which they dispersed at pleasure. On entering or departing from the Exalentre, they made obeisance to the statue of Kitranda, a god concept, in representation of the human form, which was placed on the front of the Pelzo, or Exalentre.

This condition lasted with the Graftheam or Kitranda sect, until the Atlantian In-thä'ō (nation) became more highly enlightened, when the idea was wholly abandoned, a condition that must come to modern peoples, before they can comprehend the full meaning of the God principle, and its existence as the life-giving, life-preserving, or the Great Creative Cycle, as the All of the Universe.

After the Graftheam and Kitranda ideas were abandoned, the Atlantians recognized a Universal Law, or Force, that governed all things, in a creative sense, materially, and the ever-existent and everlasting universality of Spirit and Nature, as the embodiment, through which the individualized portions of the universal spirit manifested, and revealed itself; which Universal Law, or Supreme Spirit, they termed Gala, and recognized it as existing as a whole in Universal Nature.

There was a sect, a division of which dispersed throughout portions of the Lontidri, who conceived the idea of a plurality of Gahala principles, viz: Kiantha, as Gahala Supreme, the source of never-failing light, and the Father Principle in Nature, as manifested through the Sun from morning until evening. With this was Mĕn'scŏt, as a female Gahala Supreme, the source of the lesser or borrowed light, and the Mother Principle in nature, as manifested through the Moon, from evening until morning. Quē-ziē-ĕn'zie, a goddess representing the source of education, science, and material birth, symbolized or manifested through the light of the morning star; Quē'ziē, a goddess, the source of knowledge, wisdom, and material disembodiment, symbolized or manifested through the evening star.

There were those to whom the Sun, the Moon, and planets gave the idea of parentage and offspring, and who considered them as emblematic of a family, the Sun and Moon being the father and mother, or heads of the family, and therefore representatives of the highest conception of creation, and of religious, moral, mental, and scientific principles. The planets, aside from being represented as the children of the Kiantha and Menscot, principles, were, in turn, representatives of the heads of descending families, which latter consisted of satellites, and certain portions of the constellations. These "families" represented principles, qualities of being, and the universal processes by which the creative forces manifested.

Alem Prolex further informs us that the Atlantians had no Sunday, in the sense of the term, as known from the Biblical standpoint of ancient and modern usage; but, instead, they had a stated In-thă-ō'ză Yēte (National Day) which might be said, to a certain degree, to correspond with it; and to be the connecting link between the customs of the Atlantian period and those of the Biblical, which latter are but re-embodied ideas of the former, under descended and conditional change.

The Atlantian day of pleasure was established by Goĕt'lĕz, when he became Efremetrum, of the second Efremetrum, or Dynasty, who, seeking the pleasure and good will of the people, instituted the Dăl-zō'tă Yete, which was then termed Sĕl'dē-rĕn, meaning "day of pleasure." This was observed once a month, on the day of the return of the new moon, when, in every town or city, public gatherings were held, for pleasure, amusement and feasting. The people of the country had gatherings for the same purpose, though some of them, who dwelt near the cities and towns, came in and joined the people there assembled. At the close of the day the people dispersed to their respective abodes, ready to resume their daily avocations on the following morn, which had been discontinued for the holiday, Selderen.

At the beginning of the third Efremetrum, when Alem Prolex became the Efremetrum, it was thought best for the country, by himself and his Efremetruzem, to make a change in the time of the Dalzota Yete, and exercises thereof, in such a way as to divert the minds of the people from feasting and general pleasure, to fasting and the receiving of ethical teaching of a more profound nature than had hitherto been the Delzemaricses (Governmental) enforcement. He therefore established an Inthaoza Yete, which they termed Mĕn-zē-rā'ŭs, meaning "day of education," and changed the time from the date of the new moon, as of the former Efremetrum, to that of the first day in the Ashnor (month), and the custom of feasting to that of fasting, and proclaimed it as an Inthaoza edict.

This condition of religious understanding, the spirit denizens whose mission it is to visit the mortal dwellers of the earth, are seeking to establish in the mind of every individual, thus to unveil the truths, now partially hidden from mortal sense, such as will extend the Great Religious Cycle, as one of Universal Spirit made manifest through All Nature; and it is from the great Book of Nature, they command us to read and learn, and not the books of idealistic creedism. Observe, and re-observe;

think, and continue to think, incessantly; open the windows of the Soul, and the doors to Intelligence; breathe into the being the atmosphere of truth; hear the voice of inspiration, and heed its teachings; then shall God be better recognized and understood.

From the beginning of Time has man been subject to Nature, and never the dominant influence; hence, it has been given us that "Nature is God, and God is Nature."

The Atlantians, as a people, were ultimately undivided in Religious matters, as they were in those of State. They were more a brotherhood than otherwise, especially in the portions of the Lontidri under government and education.

Marriage was not a civil, but a religious contract, instituted by the Deltsanza (teachers) of the most sacred order, originally speaking; but, later in the history of the Lontidri, laws governing the Atlantian marriage rite were enacted by the National Government, that were very strictly carried out, viz: no invalids of a chronic order, or cripples of a serious kind, were ever permitted to marry, on account of the influence that might thereby be extended, physically, into the organism of their offspring. No second marriages were ever permitted where there were children on either the paternal or maternal side, having been born to the first marriage, on account of conflicting interests of those and following offspring that might be born to the second marriage, to which the latter might lead; therefore, to such as above mentioned, only one husband or wife was allowed, and the penalty dealt out to those who disregarded the law, was imprisonment, or exile from the country, the duration of the penalty being governed by the ages of the offenders. In cases where they were beyond the middle period of life, the duration was made comparatively short, to that of the middle-aged or more youthful, whose term was extended accordingly.

It might be well to state here that all violation of National Laws of any kind whatever, was punished either by imprisonment, confinement to hard labor, or exile. No human life was ever taken, by order of the Atlantian National Government, for the violation of any law whatever. The only instance wherein disembodiment was officially assisted was at the birth of an infant, seriously deformed, the medical attendant being authorized to allow or assist its disembodiment, believing that to be the best condition for the unfortunate infant, all things considered; thus preventing inconvenience and discomfort individually, through the material life, and further offspring from a deformed parent, in case of marriage.

Virtue was held in such high esteem among the Atlantians that an adulterer was severely punished; i. e., the male offender was placed in Kĕn-dō'zi (prison) at hard labor for a term not less than two years, or more than ten, according to the conditions attending the offense. The female was placed in a Shăn'dē-lăs (Work House, Maternal Home, or place for moral training) for a term of not less than two years, or more than five, according to conditions, etc.. the greater limit being reduced, according to the good behavior and disposition of the individual to reform.

In case of an offspring resulting from the act of adultery, it was immediately, at birth, taken from the mother and placed in a Bĕn-zăn'tä (Orphan or Foundlings Home), where it was clothed, fed and educated, and never allowed to know of the conditions attending its birth, or its parentage, that its material life might be spared the mortification that otherwise would have attended the knowledge of the immorality of its parents, and the influence thus placed on its birth conditions, which would have had a tendency to destroy its high and noble aspirations of emulation, socially, mentally and religiously. Thus it was able to rise from and above the vortex of vice and dissipation, into a condition of social standing of purity.

Such unfortunates usually remained in the Benzanta until of age, when they went forth, fully equipped with moral and other educational qualifications, and a limited amount of means necessary to their start and success in life.

The women of Atlantis, under the Atlantian laws, were equals of men, morally, socially, religiously, and politically, and an Atlantian mother was regarded with the utmost reverence and affection. Her mortal brows, after disembodiment, were covered with laurel wreaths, entwined with the choicest flowers, regardless of the rank or station she had occupied during her earth career. The reader will thus understand that Atlantian greatness was founded on virtue, and purity of the social system.

The education of Atlantian children was a free system, but compulsory, the expenses being borne by the local Governments, with funds raised by taxation of various enterprises carried on by property owners. No one was barred from school on account of poverty, or insufficient means; in other words, the Atlantian was a Public School System exclusively, excepting the schools of Art, which were generally carried on by their patronage. Every Teltzie had its Agalte (temple) of learning, and instruction was commenced when the child exhibited signs of comprehension. Their passions and inclinations were carefully watched over, corrected and guided. Their instruction included precepts of morality and reason, and it was the aim of the Deltsanza to inspire youths with the principles which formed the true character of the Atlantian people, submission to parents and love of country. Literature, eloquence, science, mathematics, geography, botany, zoology, ornithology, etc., were among the chief studies taught in each public Sĭl-dä'zĭc (school), while the Fine Arts, such as painting, mosaics, sculpture, terra-cotta, architecture, etc., were among the principal subjects taught in the private Sĭl-dä-zĭc'zē (schools).

Furthermore, the Atlantian Nereges of the third Efremetrum was originally based upon certain phenomenal and social principles, the former, as revealed through physical or objective nature individually, and through spirit phenomenon, revelation and manifestation, when the people were rightly taught by aid of Cacellaze, who were developed for that purpose. These basic influences, co-operative with science, as taught by the Deltsanz' (teachers) who made calculations terrestrially, celestially, and naturally, and thereby influenced and controlled the minds of the people, thus established a Nereges void of creeds and illogical "isms," that came closer to the truth in relation to the God principle they reverenced, than many of the teachings in modern times.

The Atlantians recognized many trinity principles, the principal ones being those of Gala, Delzota nud In-drō-săn'trä (God, Nature and Creation); Nencie, Lemaz nud Wotz (Time, Space and Life); Leasa, Cletz nud Codize (Spirit, Soul and Body), a trinity of trinities, the symbol of which, as well as that of the sub-trinities, was the triangle. Separately considered, these principles were symbolized as follows; Gala, by the image of Ush Kĕn (the Sun), adored as the source of life and light as existent upon the Earth, and throughout the space in which it moves; Delzota, by landscape scenes, in which various material objects were portrayed, and understood as having their existence through natural processes; Indrosantra, by a landscape where the small streams in their fluvial conditions ultimated in the formation of the larger waters; males and females of the human race with their offspring; the same of the animal and the bird orders; flowers, shrubs and trees of various degrees of growth, co-existent with other developing objects in nature; Năn'ciē, by a monolith, on which was portrayed the image of Ken above a representation of Ush Et'zē Ash-nör'zē ĕnt ŭsh Zĕlt (the twelve months in the year) which were arranged on a Gēlist' (dial), in place of the Lŏut'zē sī ŭsh Yēte (hours of the day*), as follows:—Beginning with Quĭn (March), the first month of the Atlantian Zelt (year); Dĭn (April) the second; Lŭll (May) the third; Rē-sĕt' (June) the fourth; Lūte (July) the fifth; Gē-ĭst (August) the sixth; Sĭn-lēte' (September); the seventh; Ar'bŭt (October) the eighth; Kā-mūté (November); the ninth; Emblēze' (December); the tenth; Yĕr (January) the eleventh; and Altz (February) the twelfth; Lemaz (Space) by a representation of the image of Ken centrally, around which were numerous circles, one within the other as they extended outward, and recognized as limitless divisions of space extending beyond the earth; Wōtz (life) by a perfectly formed evergreen tree, in the front of a beautiful landscape scene, beneath which stood a human male and female, and a spirit, descending to them, hovering over them, just above the tree. This was understood by the Atlantians to represent both the material and the spiritual existence of life, as inhabiting two realms, viz: the terrestrial and the celestial. Lē-ā'sä (spirit), was symboled by a host of spirits represented as descending to the earth plane, where those having reached it had disbursed themselves into various material objects co-relative with the scene, which was to represent the principle of spirit as existing in co-relation and co-operation with all material forms in creation; Clētz (soul), by the representation of the soul and spirit in the process of passing, or having just left the material body, at the time of dis-embodiment; and Cōdīze (body), by the material body, after the soul and spirit had passed from it, lying in the repose of non-animation.

Alem Prolex further informs us that no nation on the face of the earth has ever come closer to the great "Over Spirit" and "Over Soul," or attained a greater knowledge of their manifestations through nature, than did the Atlantians, and that the deltsanza of Atlantis, were not only well versed in all spirit phenomena, or manifestations, but, in the Sciences, as Astronomy, Astrology, Physiology, Botany, etc.; from which, by observation and close analysis, they gained much useful knowledge regarding the precesses of Nature, and the general causes leading up to general effects, etc. They understood the science of Psychology, and the laws governing Psychomancy, to a greater

---

N. B.—After the first paragraph, page 180, should have been given the translation of the Atlantian terms for the days of the week, as follows: Rĕnz (Sunday); Nĕn'dī (Monday); En'dĭs (Tuesday); Fĕnz (Wednesday); Quĭntz (Thursday); Wĕltz (Friday); and Yŭn'zy (Saturday).

extent than modern peoples, which revealed much truth to them in all matters pertaining to Leasa, Cletz, nud Codize (spirit, soul and body), of the manifestations of Wotz (life), in In-drō-săn′-trä (creation), and so the people were taught.

Communion with Leasa′ (spirits) was a fact, that sense by which Leasa′ could manifest to mortals, was in the latter highly developed as an individual quality of being among Atlantians, a condition which, to a certain extent, was retained, or developed, by their southern remnant descendants, the Indians, who have never lost sight of the Great Spirit principle, or ceased to commune with departed spirits. Even in their crudest and most untutored conditions, they have recognized the workings of the Great Spirit, in Nature; which was in harmony with the teachings of their Atlantian predecessors.

The Egyptians and the Arabians—their northeastern remnant descendants—also maintained a zealous adherence to the practice of Psychomancy. Both these peoples, to this day, hold communion with departed spirits, and other racial examples might be mentioned.

This Epi-cycle, among the list of manifesting principles or connecting links between spirit and mortal life, though eclipsed for a time, on the mortal side, by the establishment of creeds, is fast coming to light again by its influence, through varied phenomenal manifestations, which fact will so re-establish links of Truth, in the place of those belonging to long accepted Creeds, as to remove the eclipse that has so long overshadowed the truth; and the Spirit Cycle, in all its glorified illumination will encircle humanity on the mortal side of life, as well as in the spiritual, as was the case in the glorious period of Atlantis.

Therefore, the Atlantian people were more spiritual, and came closer, as before stated, to the Gala si Dalzota (God of Nature), or, the Divine All in All, than any nation since. The spiritual laws governing manifestation were better understood by them, which enabled them to come closer, or more *en rapport* with the spirits and their existence as such, in a world of spirit life. The veil between them and the so-called "unseen," was more transparent than it is generally with modern mortals, and so it was, as before stated, with their descendants to a certain degree, who reached other continents in those ancient days; a condition that would have remained, and extended more generally into modern periods, but for the intercepting by creeds and isms—conditions that came in to destroy those that governed spirit manifestation.

To use the words of Alem Prolex in evidence of the nearness of the Atlantians to the spirit existence, might be well. They are "We spoke, and it was spoken unto us," (referring to clairaudient manifestations); "we looked, and it was made visible unto us" (clairvoyant manifestation); "we walked, and behold! a companion was made tangible" (materialization of forms).

The Atlantians, having no opposition from other sects, had a more complete system of communication with spirits than that of modern times. Spiritual principles were ideals with them; and all things pertaining to them were as principal conditions in the foundation of their religion. The latter rose to a high standard of attainment much greater than that of any religion of modern times. Their Pĕ-zō-zē′ and Agalteze were dedicated to spiritual uses exclusively; as were their civil edifices, to the principles of Justice and Truth. They not only received spirit communications in their Pelzoze and Agalteze, but at private homes throughout the community, where rooms were prepared for visitations from the spirit world. These apartments were furnished with spiritual decorations, such as Angelic subjects, represented in Art. Vines and blooming plants, such as would emit sweet fragrance and so perfume the pure atmosphere, were admitted. These rooms were principally in the homes of wealthy people who could afford to make such conditions; but no mortal, however lowly in life, was denied the privilege of coming to those sacred places at the stated hours for manifestation, if he so desired, for the purpose of learning, and so that he might be thereby elevated in the scale of humanity. Rich and poor alike went into them, with a sacredness of purpose which justified better conditions. They had music, which has ever been known to harmonize conditions for spirit communication or manifestation. They opened these exercises with sacred devotion to the "visiting spirits," then they quietly waited until manifestations were made in various phases; received their messages of love and greetings, and general instructions; walked and talked with the materialized forms of departed friends and guides, thus blending life existence material, with the spiritual, into one extended Epi-cycle, and thus they recognized Eternity—by the continuity of Life thus made manifest.

The Atlantians were taught by the Spirit Guides, that the great Book of Nature was the source from which to obtain true knowledge of the sciences and arts.

By the teachings through spirit revelations, co-operative with nature through all its manifestations visible, symbolic and scientific deductions and cognitions, made plain through these sources, the people were led to reverence all principles governing the material universe, and the spiritual principles that lay back of its movements, as the motive, developing force, or cause, leading up to individual material form and existence.

The people reverenced this great influential principle, worshipped, and built their Pelzoze nud Agalteze nud Maretuxze (temples and monuments) in acknowledgement and recognition of it, and not unto the material object or idol representing it, as has been the supposition of moderns in regard to the images set up by their ancient ancestors, which latter should be understood to have re-embodied the Atlantian idea, rather than that of material idolatry, as is now the case with moderns, who erect their temples in sacred reverence for the god they worship, and their monuments to the memory of their departed illustrious heroes.

The Atlantian idea of Ush Kĕn (the sun), as a Divine emblem, was conceived by them through its qualities of heat and light as dispersed throughout the universe, as understood by them at the time. As they saw its sheen upon the waters, and the minerals of the aelkedze, and felt its warmth in the atmosphere, they realized it as the provident source of their good, as well as the good of the beasts of the field and vegetation of the land; and most of all, a force uncontrollable as a whole, by mortal man, and unlimited in its service. Therefore, Ush Ken, as well as Ush Lĕt-tē'zŏn (the planets) having great influence on all Nature, was reverenced as symbol of the Divine Principle, known to them as Gala. Hence, every morning, as Ush Ken rose to view, they bent the knee in adoration of his force and benificence, and as a representative of Gala, the Divine Principle in all nature.

They then repaired to the Agalte, and when they entered the vestibule, they beheld the image of Ken, protrayed in radiant beauty, above the door. Then they uncovered their heads and offered the following invocation: "Tŭn nêh ŭsh rē'chĕt sī yēte eūel ŭn ēll ŭsh rē'chĕt sī Gälä lĕs lĕs'ĕt ŭsh kĕn Gälä (Thou art the light of day, fill us with the light of God, like unto the sun, God). They then entered the Agalte, while sweet strains of krĕst (music) came from the E'thē-rē-leŭm (musical instrument), as rendered by the Krĕs'tē-ŏn (musician). Then the Dĕlt'sänz spoke to the people, after which they went forth to their daily avocations, singing and chanting as they left the Agalte. Again, as Ush Ken sank from view, behind the Aelkedze, at eventide, a short devotional exercise was held in the Agalte, or privately, as the occasion afforded—when the following invocation was uttered. "Ul tŭn ĕt quĕt rē'chĕt ĕt nē'sŭt lū nē ĕnt dĕz'ry nŭd ĕl-ĕn'dē tŭn ĕsh'lĕnd ĕn'gĕl gĕl ŭn lē er-re er ŭlt sī rē'chĕt lĕs lĕs'ĕt trĭst jĕnā'qūes" (Go thou to give light to those who are in darkness; and when thou comest again, may we be more full of light like unto thyself, God, ours only).

The Atlantian Nereges (religion), contained so many symbols, that it really would be considered "symbolic" in itself. Religious thoughts, and recognition of life in all its manifestations, are but re-embodied or re-born ideas from one generation to another, through natural observation and inspirational influence, given by spirit intelligences who have lived in the mortal form during some past age. These teach as they had learned, or as they have progressed in the spirit realm; for some spirits are long ages in spirit life, before they relinquish old theories, in exchange for scientific truths, even as on the mortal plane—some advance, while others cling to creeds and dogmas. Therefore it is best to listen to logical truths, when receiving inspiration or information from the spirit side of life. Taking evidences from exalted, learned and wise spirits, in connection with an understanding of Nature's processes in creation, we then place oruselves in the hands of two powerful Că-cĕl-lä'zē (mediums), between God and Man; likewise, Mortal becomes the Că-cĕl'lä (spirit sensitive), between spirit and mortal, a source through which knowledge of the past, present, and future, may be given to humanity.

In the force of the sunlight, in the roar of the mighty ocean, in the silence of the majestic mountain range, by the glimmer of the starry sky-dome, we may read sermons mightier than were ever uttered by the lips of men.

A-E'RIC NUD A-E'MUS RIN'GA NUD SI-I'KEL, OR ETHNOGRAPHIC AND ETHNOLOGIC LINKS AND CYCLES.

TELTZIE XLII.

In considration of the A-ĕ'rĭc Nŭd A-ĕ'mŭs Rĭn'gä Nŭd Sī-īkĕl,' we must contemplate the characteristic differences that have existed and do exist, in the peoples of the earth, which condition has arisen from various natural causes, viz: from the two original colors black and white, through hybrid, sustentacle, and latitudinal influences, wherein we find the causes and effects, which give rise to conditional pre-historic characteristics of the race, by and through which we are enabled to reproduce facts and to re-establish them as history re-extended. For instance, as the zones have various geographic and geologic differences, in the various sections of the Eastern and Western continents, or in the four hemispheres of the Earth's Sphere, so we have specific or characteristic nations that occupy them; and most of these have some Ethnologic ideas, though some may be very crude indeed.

Likewise, in contemplation of the Islands of the Oceans and Seas, whose submerged bases rest upon areas of earth that were once peopled Continents, remnants of whom now have place, through descendancy, here and there upon these remnant earth monumental surfaces, as a part of the great distribution of modern humanity, as evidential links from past and present periods of time, in further extension of the Ethnographic and Ethnologic Epi-cycles that move on the deferent of Great Cycle of Life.

Therefore, as is the case with the geographic and the geologic links and cycles, so it is with those of the ethnographic and the ethnologic changes, which condition is responsible for their seeming mysteries and lost histories.

Go therefore, dear reader, unto all the peoples of the earth; note the present ethnographic and ethnologic conditions. Contemplate the remnant Aborigines whose present existence and condition give evidence of pre-existent nations, and the law of descending change, in contrast with Modern peoples at large. Yet the latter represent, conditionally, the once greater nations from whom the aborignal remnants have descended; and who once represented the greatness of illustrious races, destined to suffer degenerate results, as such, through their descendants, under natural causes and as such was the case once, so will the time come again, when present and future greatness, of certain nations must likewise suffer through similar causes, and their remnants must again establish a rise to greatness, through the ages to come.

Alem Prolex further informs us, that each of the six Teltzie' of the Atlantian Lontidri were divided into A-ē'rĭc (ethnographic), Aē'mŭs (ethnologic), and Sĭl'dē-măz (philologic), conditions, as follows:—

TELTZIE ET.

In Teltzie Et there was but one race of people, generally speaking, viz: the Atlantians proper, excepting in the eastern portion, or that portion east of the aistie of Atara, known as the Kĭn'tī-lū-ci-äns.

In height, the Atlantians varied from six to eight feet, were well proportioned, quite muscular, heavy built, and strong. They were characterized with both white and brunette skins; blond, black, brown, and in some cases red hair, some straight and some curly; of full beards generally; eyes, gray, blue, brown, and black. In fact, their physical conditions varied similarly as those of the Anglo Saxon race of modern times, excepting that the former exceeded the latter in height.

The Kintilucians were about the same as the Atlantians, physically, only in complexion; their hair was pure white, their eyes pink, and their complexion a clear pinkish white.

TELTZIE WE.

In Teltzie We, there were four divisions of people—divided not so much on account of their different, social, religious, and political ideas, as in these matters the entire Lontidri was governed by general laws; but, rather from a desire to change, migrate, and to further reach out for new conditions generally. The divisions were as follows:—

The Cĕl-ĕx-dĕn'trys occupied the northern and the northeastern portions of the Teltzie (in the earlier periods however, the latter named portion was divided into three uncivilzed tribes, viz: the Yō-săn′zēs, the Hū-bĕr-aŭs′tĕns and the Flū-zăn′zēs, who were similar to the now known Indian tribes, hostile to each other as tribes); the Cĕl-trē-zō′näs the eastern; the Nĭn-kä′zĭts the southern; and the Lĕl-tä′zăts, the southeastern.

In height, the Celexdentrys, generally, were about six feet. They were large boned and jointed, and very muscular. They were characterized with black skins; dark brown, or black eyes; black, but not long hair; straight, thin, crinkled beards; full oval faces, yet sharp, and projecting through the centre, from the forehead down; which, on account of the strong projection, caused their eyes to appear deep-set, and piercing; noses broad at the upper portion; nostrils very much drawn in, yet protruding and sharp; lips thick. They were a very energetic people.

The Celtrezonas generally, were somewhat taller than the Celexdentrys. In color, they were a shade lighter, which was caused by a slight mixture with peoples who came among them from the outskirts of Atara; and from the Ninkazits, in the southern portion of Teltzie We. Their hair was the same, in character, as that of the Celexdentrys, excepting longer and they possessed more of it over their bodies. Their eyes were about the same color, in fact their general features were about the same.

The Leltazats, who, by the way, were principally Celtrezonas migrators, from the eastern portion of Teltzie Set, and the northeastern border of Teltzie Et, were about the same as the Celtrezonas and border Atarians. In fact, they possessed about the same physical appearance as their neighbors, the Ninkazits, excepting their straighter hair, which condition came through the Atarian and the Celtrezonas influence.

The Ninkazits who migrated to the southern portion of Teltzie We from the northern portion of Teltzie Set, or the Săn-năn′zēs people, were about the same as the Sannanzes in general appearances; and were closely alied to the Atarians from the fact that the people of Teltzie Set were formerly inhabitants of the Atarian border, or Teltzie Et; therefore, not as civilized as the Atarians of the interior of Atara, a quality which ultimately stood as the chief distinction between the Atarians and the Sannanzes; and furthermore, between the Sannanzes and the Ninkazits.

The Celexdentrys and the Celtrezonas adopted about the same style of clothing, and utilized the same material, viz: skins from a mountain animal then known as the Gō′zō; a mild, handsome animal, about the size of a large dog, with dark gray or mouse-colored fur. The style adopted was that of an irregularly formed cape of furred skin, thrown loosely over the shoulders, that hung down to the waist. Another skirt-like garment was fastened or girted to the waist and that came down below the knees. This was also fastened about the legs with straps of skin, and formed a garment much like those worn by the ancient Turks. The feet were also wrapped with furred skins, up to the former named garment, which were fastened with straps of skin. The Celexdentrys always went with uncovered heads.

The Ninkazits and the Leltazats adopted the same style of clothing, the materials were hair, fibers, and soft barks; the fibres and the bark being used for the warp and the hair for the woof, and varied in colors, viz: black, brown, gray, and white. The style was a loose cape thrown about the shoulders. The lower garment was a very narrow or scant skirt, that hung down to the knees. They went barefoot, excepting in very cold weather, when they covered their feet with skin wrappings. They also went with uncovered heads, They generally wore the colored garments, and white material was never worn except by the Deltsanza.

The Ninkazits and the Leltazats, of Teltzie We, adopted the same form of worship, as follows:—They recognized a protective force as being above and beyond visible creation, which they termed "Yē-ĕl'tŭm," a term used in the same sense that Moderns do the term "God." They represented this Principle by means of pyramidal structures, which they used at their daily worship. These were about ten feet in height, some being rectangular, some hexagonal, and some octogonal, in form, which, as above stated, were used in representation of the principle they termed Yeeltum.

Some of the Yeeltumze were constructed out of moulded mud, and others sculptured from stone. They were placed on the thoroughfares, or public high-ways, where the people could have easy and constant access to them, as they passed to and fro on their daily missions.. Small Yeeltumze of the same style as those placed on exterior sections, about three feet in height, sculptured from gray stone, were placed in homes and private sacred shrines to Yeeltum. These the families approached, in the early morning and evening for the purpose of rehearsing the inscribed invocation unto Yeeltum.

The following characters constituted the inscription sculptured upon all the Yeeltumze, and at all times recited or read audibly, by those who approached the shrines, either private or public, for worship. The characters and the terms they represented, together with a translation of the same, were as follows:—

Kĕl'tă Sĭn'dä En'dry
Look we ask

El-tē'nä Crē-ĕn-dä Guĭl'dä
thy protection God.

The first word of the sentence, viz: "Kelta," was used as an exclamation, always uttered when they first caught sight of the Yeeltum.

The last word, viz: "Guilda," was an expression which referred to the protective principle, and was used in the same sense that Moderns use the term "Amen."

The Celexdentrys of the northern and northwestern portions and the Celtrezonas of the eastern portion of Teltzie We, held to the same form of worship, used the same terms in reference to the protective principle, and used the same Yeeltum representations, and inscriptions, as did their neighbors, the Ninkazits of the southern and Leltazats of the southeastern portions of Teltzie We; the only difference being that they added the triangle to the apex of the Yeeltumze, in the center of which was a representation of the sun and its rays, and this to them symbolized the Beneficent Principle of Light.

TELTZIE SET.

In the extreme northern portion of Teltzie Set, there was a tribe then known as the Bē-tĕn'ū-zĕns, who were ignorant and uncultivated, subsisted on fish and animal flesh, and clothed themselves with skins and furs. In physique and general appearance, they were much like the now known Kamchatkan people.

In Teltzie Set there were four general divisions of people, viz: the Lĕx-tē-lŏn'zäs, who occupied the southwestern third of the Teltzie; the Clē-trē-zŏn'zēs, the southeastern; and the Săn-năn'zēs, the northwestern.

This division of these peoples resulted from their desire to develop mining enterprises; hence, small parties of the Lextelonzas, which latter first settled, as above stated, in the southwestern portion of the Teltzie, migrated, to the southeastern and northwestern parts of the Teltzie

As time passed on, they were joined by other parties from the Lextelonza portion of the Teltzie, as well as from Teltzie Et, which soon resulted in the establishment of two new peoples, of the Teltzie, then known to the Atlantians proper, as the Celtrezonas of the southeastern, and the Sannanzes of the northwestern portion of the Teltzie.

In regard to physical characteristics, such as stature, color of skin, hair and eyes, general manners, etc., they were almost the fac-simile of the Atarians, from the fact that they primarily migrated to the southwestern portion of Teltzie Set, from Teltzie Et, or Atara. Therefore, they were practically one and the same race of people, the only difference being such as climate, locality, and general livelihood would influence.

The only difference in dress was such as comes to people who go to new and undeveloped sections of the country; hence, economy was practiced in this respect, by and through home manufacture; yet, to some extent, they imported from Atara such garments and other utilities as their means would afford; and kept the styles, to a certain extent, of their native Teltzie.

The Sannanzes, the Celtrezonas, and the Lextelonzes of Telt-Set, being considerably in advance of the peoples of Teltzie We, so far as civilization is concerned, were in advance of them in religious ideas, and therefore erected more elaborate shrines and symbols, representing the God principle, which they termed; Jăs-săn'nä, the term meaning "light."

The Jassanna principle was represented throughout the Teltzie by monumental symbols as follows:—There were four public monuments in the Teltzie, the largest of which was erected in the aistie of Cör-tĕl-dĕl'lō, located in the center of the Teltzie, in a large circular Sē-lŏn'dē-ŭs (square), containing several acres. The monument was constructed out of white signite (marble), and consisted of a great platform raised to the height of three steps, on top of which was placed a circular pedestal, from which rose a triangular shaft tapering to a point at the apex. The latter was surmounted with four horizontal bars of uzie (gold), that pointed to the four cardinal points, and one perpendicular bar that pointed heavenward. The whole structure was about forty feet in height. On the face of the third Signiti step, an inscription was sculptured, which read and translated as follows:—

Guĭl'dē Hä-rä'mä
Greater Knowledge.

The four horizontal bars were to represent the source from which each individual might gather knowledge, from the supreme force, or Jassanna, throughout the invisible or spiritual part of material creation, and that of the spiritual proper. The perpendicular bar represented the regions of the latter, whence each individual was to receive the benefits to be bestowed by that force, or Jassanna, who also dispensed light, not only in the common sense of the term, but the Light that gives understanding of all Truth made manifest through the knowledge of the stars and the planets, whereby not only the mentality of man was enlightened, but the soul and spirit illumined and beautified, both in mortal and the spirit existence.

The three small monuments symbolizing the Jassanna principle, were located, one at the aistie of Yezery, in the western portion of the Teltzie, one in the aistie of Soueldes, in the southeastern, and one in the aistie of Enididstro, in the southwestern.

Once a year, at the time of the vernal equinox, people from all over the Teltzie came to Corteldello for a three days feast, and to hold adorational exercises in honor of Jassanna.

The feast consisted of one meal only, per day, which was served at the mid-day hour, and consisted chiefly of fish, fruits and vegetables, but no cereals.

The adoration of Jassanna, as the Great Principle, was also connected with that of social, political, and educational attainments, and the order of the devotional exercises was as follows:— In the morning, the people, led by the Deltsanza, marched and countermarched in various figures, mostly in circles however, around the Jassanna monument, thus forming a great massive circle of human forms about it, when in concert, they repeated the following invocation: Jăs-săn'nä, gē-ĭ'lĕt cĕl-tĭnge rē'chĕt nŭd guĭl'dē hä-rä'mä which translation is, to wit: God, give greater light and more knowledge. They then dispersed for the day, to engage in such social intercourse as they most desired. At sunset, the same adorational exercises were repeated, as those of the morning.

About twenty-five years before the submergence of that portion of the Lontidri, this monument to Jassanna was re-modelled by adding to it the statues of two male and two female figures, in representation of the Deltsanza, who imparted education and knowledge, to the people, and further influenced them regarding wisdom in all life proceedings, as deduced from the laws of nature.

The figures were in stature, about nine feet, those of the two females were placed on opposite corners of the platform, and stood posed with folded hands in front, across their waists, and with up-turned faces, looking, as it were into the great vault of heaven. The two male figures likewise, were placed on the other two corners of the platform, opposite to each other, and stood posed with the right arm extended to the right, with the forearm forming a right angle with the upper arm, at the elbow, the palm of the hand being open front toward the people, and the head posed so as to appear as though the individual were looking far out to that cardinal point of the country, as it were, to gather from nature's terrestrial realm, inspiration, as they stood and taught the people.

The other three monuments were a fac-simile of the above described, except that they were smaller, and were used as daily local shrines for the people in the portions of the Teltzie in which they were located.

Miniature Jassanna monuments of the same style had place in the homes of the people generally, that were used for the morning and evening adorational exercises, etc.

TELTZIE KET.

The Nothosis of the southern portion of Teltzie Ket, at first, gave little attention to religious beliefs, rites or ceremonies, for they entertained no particular ideas of a God principle, but in time, they conceived or adopted more of the ideas of the Atarians, in regard to religious principles.

The Kasmancees of the northern portion of Teltzie Ket, lost nearly all knowledge of religion. They had some idea of a Supreme Force, but they had no form whatever of worship, and never did advance in religious ideas. They were much in the same condition of the Esquimaux of ancient and modern times, which latter are, as stated elsewhere in this work, descendants of the former, through a long line of ancestors.

In Teltzie Ket there were only two divisions of people proper, viz: the Nō-thō'sĭs, who occupied the southern portion of the Teltzie, who originally migrated there from Teltzie Et, or Atara, and the Kăs-măn'cē-ēs, who occupied the northern portion, and who were a mixed race of Nothosis from the southeastern portion of Teltzie Ket, and the Sannanzes, who migrated to the northern portion of Teltzie Ket, from the northwestern portion of Teltzie Set, and the Celexdentrys of the northern portion of Teltzie We.

The southeastern portion of the Nothosis people, mingled races with some of the Lextelonzas of the southwestern portion of Teltzie Set, and it was from this mixed race of Nothosis people who migrated to the northern portion of Teltzie Ket, who mixed races with the Sannanzes who migrated there from the northwestern portion of Teltzie Set, which ultimately established the Kasmancees people.

No special cause induced the migration of the various peoples to Teltzie Ket, other than their desire to spread out in pursuit of new possessions and accomplishments.

The Nothosis proper, in stature, size, complexion, etc., were about the same as the people of Teltzie Et, or Atara, from whom they originally descended, which condition continued in the southwestern portion of the Teltzie.

Those who occupied the southeastern portion, were about the same in stature and size, but in complexion, were of a swarthy or light brown color much in resemblance to the modern Italians, in that respect.

As to dress, the Nothosis carried out the Atlantian styles, as far as local conditions would permit.

The Kasmancees in stature, were about the same as the Nothosis, though much more slender in form. Their hair was darker and longer; eyes much larger and deeper set in the head; and fore-heads more protruding. They were also darker, from the fact that they were a race resulting from, as before stated, a mixed race of Nothosis and Celexdentrys, the former being dark and the latter black, and the Sannanzes who were white, the blendings of which mixture, resulted in various complexions, dark, medium, and light shades, e. g., as is the case with the peoples of North America, by the mixing of the Anglo-Saxon and African races in modern times.

The people of Teltzie Ket were more highly cultured in the arts, agriculture, sciences, etc., and had very fine architecture, especially so on the eastern side of the Miezietory terranzi (see that mountain range on the map). The peoples on the western side of the terranzi, though a great people, were not so highly cultured. They subsisted principally on fruits, were naturally indolent, and non-enterprising, when compared with those of the eastern section. Those in the northern portion, in the vicinity of the Reeta terranzi, were principally engaged in mining enterprises. They were not considered an educated people, though enough so that they were able to carry on a successful commercial exchange, so far as mineral products were concerned. They made no pretence in the arts and sciences.

TELTZIE ZRET.

In Teltzie Zret, there were three divisions of peoples, viz: the Mū'tī-zĕs, who occupied the northern and northeastern portions of the Teltzie; the Gū-rĕn'zĕs, the southern; and theMĕl'trē-zĕns, the southeastern.

The people in the northeastern portion of Teltzie Zret, though being cultured to a certain degree, were not so much so in general education, as in fine mechanics, or machinery, creating designs, constructing and erecting things of beauty, etc. Books they cared little for, but they were highly cultured in the arts, it being generally a natural gift to them. Their divisions, as was the case in the other Teltzie, was owing to a desire on the part of the migrators, to obtain new possessions, and to engage in new developments.

Regarding physical characteristics, the Mutizes were about the same as the Atarians, from the fact that they originally migrated from Teltzie Et to Teltzie Zret. In regard to dress, they carried out the styles of the Atarians, especially so after they had regained civilization, and were possessed with greater wealth.

The Meltrezens who migrated from the southeastern portion of Teltzie Et, to the southeastern portion of Teltzie Zret, and who were a mixed race of the southeastern Atarians and the Mellenthes of the northeastern portion of Teltzie Sot, in stature, were from six to seven feet, and were very broad shouldered and well proportioned, but not overly fleshy. Their hair was very dark brown, in some cases, and black in others, worn long, some being wavy, would have been nearly straight, had it been properly cared for. The males all wore long bushy beards. As to the colors of their skin, they resembled the now known Mulattoes of the southern United States of America, that characteristic having been caused by race mixture between the Mellenthes and Atarians. Their eyes were either dark gray, brown, or black. Their fore-heads were high, but narrow through the region of the temples; their features were long; their noses prominent, though well formed; their lips varied, some being thin, and others were somewhat pouched; their mouths were broad, and they showed their teeth considerably.

As to their manner of dress, they utilized the same textures, and retained the same styles as adopted by the Atarians, as near as their simplicity of life, means, and possession of utilities would permit.

The Mutizes, at first, became degenerated to a certain degree, from the religious ideas and customs of the Atlantians, yet they partially held to the knowledge they had of the God principle. In time, Deltsanza were sent among them from Atara, which resulted in a revival of the ideas and customs of their ancestors in Teltzie Et, at which time they began the erection of Agalteze (temples), and were rapidly developing their religious understanding, at the time of the final submergence of that portion of the Lontidri. Prior to this however, the Mutizes, as a people, recognized a God principle which they associated with the facts of life and creation, and which as a principle, they termed Kĕ'-dĭsh, which meant Creator, or that principle which creates all things. As a symbol or representation of Kedish, they erected a large Hū'lē-zŏn (pyramid), in a large Zelondeus (park), having place in the aistie of Listrio. It was about twenty feet in height, and was constructed out of blocks of gray signiti (marble) closely matched and highly polished, and stood in the centre of a great circle, the area of which was about two acres, centrally located in the Zelondeus, and out-skirted with beautiful trees. On the front of the Hulezon, in bas-relief, was carved the image of a powerfully built man, who represented the qualities of power and strength. The image was represented as being erect, in stature about ten feet. It was intended to represent Kedish, their God principle, therefore, beneath his feet, on the face of the Hulezon, the following inscription was carved.

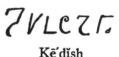

Kĕ'dĭsh
Creator.

This shrine was originally intended as a place for daily recognition and adoration of the great Kedish principle, by the people as they were passing to and fro through the Zelondeus, to which they expressed their adoration by a manner of bodily obeisance, but there was instituted the custom of general assemblies of the people of that portion of the Teltzie, that convened once a year at the Hulezon, which occurred at the time of the winter solstice, which was the beginning of their new year. The assembly was only for one day, and the principal Kedish exercises were held at sun-set, at the close of the day's feasting and social intercourse throughout the aistie. The order of the exercises at the Hulezon was that of a military movement. The people formed a great circle about the Hulezon two abreast, and marched seven times around it. Each couple as they passed the image of Kedish, made obeisance to it, by hand gesticulations, bowing, kneeling, and rising quickly in order not to break the movement of the remainder of the circle. As each couple arrived the seventh time before the Kedish image, having made their obeisence, turned and stepped out of the circle, and dispersed through the trees and shrubs, to their respective abodes. Thus circle after circle was formed, until all the people had gone through the exercises.

Similar Hulezonze, though smaller, were erected in the larger aistieze of that portion of the Teltzie, for local daily use, and annually for those who could not convene at the national exercises in the aistie of Listrio. Miniature Hulezonze were also placed in the homes, for family use as daily shrines.

The Meltrezens, as was the case with the new colonies, degenerated from the Atarian ideas of the God principle, and forms of worship, from the fact that, only a few people migrated at a time, hence gradually lost their interest in religious matters, giving their thoughts mostly to the maintenance of the body, and development of social and commercial enterprises.

At the time of the submergence, the Atarians were preparing to send Deltsanza to the Meltrezens and the Gurenzes, but this, like all the great plans of the Atarian people was thus prevented. The Gurenzes, like the Meltrezens, degenerated from all religious principles, or ideas, and never re-established any definite form of worship or instituted any representative of the God principle. They being a mixed race from the co-mingling of the Kä-cē'dricks of the southern portion of Teltzie Sot, and the mixed race of Meltrezens of the southeastern portion of Teltzie Zret, in stature, were shorter than the Meltrezens, the tallest of them not exceeding six feet. The majority, however, were medium sized, though not very fleshy. As to their color of skin, they would compare very favorably with modern Egyptians. They had small features; small, round heads; dark, straight hair, like the American Indians; black and also chestnut colored eyes, deep set and close together; small noses; high cheek bones; normal mouths; medium thin lips; and the males had exuberant beards that extended high upon the face.

In Teltzie Sot, there was a hostile tribe, then known as the

Drĕz-ā-lăn'cō-shăns, who inhabited the Gä-sib'bēe Aelkedze (mountains), remnants of whom occupied the now known Guadeloupe Islands, in the Leward Group of the Caribbe Islands. There is yet a remnant of the descendants of that people in the southern portion of that island, not known to moderns, though by explorations already made, fossil remains of skeletons and rude weapons have been found, which belonged to the descendants of that people, whose original link was the Drezalancoshans of the southern portion of Teltzie Sot of Atlantis. These people were partly civilized, and therefore not so crude as those on the southeastern portion, which latter were extremely quarrelsome.

There were four general divisions of people in Teltzie Sot, viz., the Schī'rănts, who occupied the northern portion of the Teltzie; the Mĕl-lĕn-thēs, who occupied the northwestern and the Schä-năn'dä-rīts and the Kä-cē'drīcks, who occupied the southwestern. These divisions were caused by two conditions, viz: the Schirants and the Mellenthes were very desirous to possess homes, and to have an opportunity to develop certain enterprises; and the Schanandarits and the Kacedricks, who were very contentious or quarrelsome among themselves, reached division through their hostilities, which made separations among them.

The Schirants and Mellenthes, originally from Teltzie Sot, migrated there from the southern portion of Teltzie Et; and some Meltrezens who returned to Teltzie Sot from Teltzie Zret, after their migration to the latter; ultimately, some of the Schanandarets of the southern portion of Teltzie Sot, and some of the Kacedricks from the southwestern portion, migrated to the north and northwestern portions of the Teltzie, and mixed races with the Schirants, the Mellenthes, and the Meltrezens, a fact that ultimately developed race conditions characteristic of the northern, and the northeastern portions of Teltzie Sot.

The migration of the Schanandarits and Kacedricks, of the southern portion of Teltzie Sot, to the northern, was occasioned by the going of the Schirants and the Mellenthes, of the northern portion to the South Sea coast, for the purpose of establishing fishing industries, which influenced some of the Schanandarits and Kacedricks to accompany them on their home return, for the purpose of transporting their supplies of fish to market.

Therefore, the Schirants and the Mellenthes, though occupying separate portions of the Teltzie, were by virtue of race characteristics, one and the same. In stature, they varied from six to seven feet; in physique and manner, they were very coarse;

the color of their skin very dark, but not a shiny black; their hair generally, was both black and curly, though sometimes brown; their features were thin, or slender; their foreheads low; their eyes were dark, quite large, obliquely placed, and strikingly long, even more so than those of the ancient Chinese; their noses were broad at the nostrils, but flat on the upper part; their cheek bones were broad and extended backward as if in harmony with the position of their eyes; their lips were thick, and naturally remained open, thus disclosing their teeth considerably; their chins were receding. The males had scant beards, that grew in tufts on their necks, principally. In regard to dress, so far as conditions would permit. They followed, in a crude way, the styles and utilities of the Atarians, or peoples of Teltzie Et, their original home. Before the submergence, however, they had made quite an advancement in this respect, as well as in conditional matters.

The Schanandarits of the southern portion of Teltzie Sot, and the Kacedricks of the southwestern, were remnants of an extremely low and ignorant, uncivilized but numerous, people, without tribe or national name, who before the submergence that established them as such in Teltzie Sot, dwelt in a section of country now known as the Tristan d' Acunha Islands in the South Atlantic Ocean, that then extended north of the Tropic of Capricorn, to the region of the now known St. Helena Island; which latter, after the first submergence that established the Tristan d' Acunba Islands, was a part of the southern portion of Teltzie Sot, which accounts for the fact that the remnant of that people were in the southern section of the Teltzie.

The Schanandarits and the Kacedricks, of the southern portion of the Teltzie, as was the case with the northern peoples, being remnants of one race, did not differ physically in their original condition. In height, like the northern people of the Teltzie, they varied from six to seven feet; but physically they were not built the same, being of more slender form, while the northern people were heavily built. Their skins were very black and shiny; their hair was black and curled tightly to their heads, like the hair of the modern negroes; their heads were quite round in form; their foreheads were low; their faces were broad; their eyes were black, and characterized with a sharp, piercing look; their noses were broad and flat; their ears small; their lips quite thick; and their mouths broad. The males had very little beard, and that curled tightly to the face. They were, in fact, a people of very ferocious appearance.

The majority of these people went without clothing. Some,

however, wore a short skirt-like garment, fastened at the waist, the rest of the body being nude. Their feet and heads were ungarmented.

The Schanandarits and the Kacedricks, of Teltzie Sot, never to any extent, manifested religious ideas, or established any forms of worship. Their chief thought was of obtaining food, which was principally flesh and fiish of various kinds.

Portions of the Schirants and the Mellenthes, of Teltzie Sot, held to the Atarian idea of Gala (the God principle) to a certain extent, which term they changed to Gabala, which to them meant "God, the Great Spirit."

The remainng portion of the people ceased, for a time, to entertain religious ideas; but, eventually, as the religious class became more advanced along this line of thought, its development began to spread out among the people again.

At this period of time, they instituted and erected, small monuments in their principal settlements, which they fashioned after the monumental styles in Atạra, though they were crudely constructed at first. The only inscription on these monuments was as follows:

Gä-hä'lạ̈
God the Great Spirit.

Just before the submergence that destroyed the Teltzie, they had begun the erection of Agalteze (temples), at the aistie of An-tē-swär'ăp, a place of about 1000 inhabitants, on the northern border of the Or'zër Kelete (lake), in the northewestern portion of the Teltzie. At the time of the above-named submergence, the foundation was complete, and portions of the structure nearly so.

Finally, in regard to the inhabitants of Atlantis, as is the case on all continents, there were degrees of development and civilization among them, according to local conditions, and the periods of time with which they were contemporaneous.

During the three Efremetrumze (dynasties), education, art, science, literature, architecture, in fact everything that goes to make up the National development and civilization of a people, existed in certain portions of the Lontidri; yet there were some districts where the people had not received the sufficient intellectual light to bring them to such a degree of civilization as would qualify them to join issues, to any extent, with those of higher civilizations.

Teltzie Et or One, was the seat of culture, art, science, architecture, mechanics, agriculture, and the embodiment of all kinds of commerce. The people were busy, harmonious and intelligent, and highly civilized in every way. The greater quality of which was that of soul growth, spiritual attainment, and a strong adherence to the teachings of Gala, in and through the divine principles of Nature, in creation. Knowledge of this was obtained through the processes leading up to the ultimate establishment of material form, and their endowment with life and energy.

Great as are the Nations of the twentieth century, yet they have not equalled those of this portion of Atlantis, in Art, Sculpture, Architecture, and the Sciences. No modern musician, painter, sculptor, engraver, or worker in mosaics has arrived at the sublime perfection, in their productions, reached by those of this Teltzie, so far as regards form, and general expression necessary to a more lifelike representation, and general grandeur of the subject. No architectural production of modern or ancient ages, gives evidence of greater ability to create plans, or to carry them out in structures, complete in all their grandeur, than existed in the time of Atlantian greatness. No monuments have been erected to the memory of modern celebrities, or religious and scientific principles of higher reach in any subsequent time, but they were more than equalled by the Atlantian people. No greater approach has ever been made to mechanical perfection than the Atlantians had made in the long ago.

To modern peoples, these statements may seem strange and perhaps overdrawn; but when they awaken to the fact that all these accomplishments have come to mortal man, of all ages, through spirit influence, inspiration and revelation, as mental re-conceptions and that the Atlantian people were in much closer communication with the spirit world, at large, than is the case with those of the twentieth century, it will not be hard to cognize or deduce the facts.

Links and Cycles

LIM'PIRE, A-THU'RO, A-E'RIC, NUD A-E'MUS FRE-DEN-CE-ZE

OR

GEOGRAPHIC, GEOLOGIC, ETHNOGRAPHIC AND ETHNOLOGIC EXTENSIONS.

TELTZIE XLIII.

In order to properly trace the Geographic, Geologic, Ethnographic and Ethnologic extensions from Atlantis, as they really had place during the time intervening between that period and the twentieth century of the Christian era, we shall be governed in that of the former two by the order in which the convulsions occurred, in the variouse regions at various periods of time and place, which resulted in the present contours of land and water on the earth's sphere; and the latter two, by the migratory conditions of the remnant peoples, resulting in the present distribution of the various races of peoples, thus linking the Atlantian, the pre-historic, the modern-ancient and modern racial events, in the establishment of the historic cycle belonging to these subjects.

At the time of the submergence of Teltzie Set, a portion of the Lextelonzas, of the southern portion, and the Cletrezonzes of the eastern, were left as remnants on the islands now known as the Azores. They termed the islands "Zē-lä-si-ōs," and called themselves the "Kē-sēl'zäs. Subsequently they became one people by mingling and mixing races.

After many ages of wandering to and fro through what are now known as the Madeira Islands, and the Canary Islands, which they termed Kër-i-wänsk (*ker-i* in their language meant "to move" or "to change," and *wansk* "to straggle" or "to wander"), a colony of the Keselzas by means of maritime migration, reached that portion of country now known as Morocco, Africa, termed Section Cō'jel; but they retained their former tribe name, Keselzas. By this time their ethnographic characteristics had undergone considerable change.

In the Islands of Zelasios, before their establishment in Cojel, they were of larger physique and taller in stature than were the Zanranzans. Their skins were of a lighter hue, in fact, they might have been termed quadroons. Their hair was straight and light, and many of the males characterized with considerable hair over their bodies. They wore long, heavy beards, as nature had abundantly bestowed it. Their eyes were blue or gray. They were an indolent people, from the fact that they had no means of cultivating the soil and therefore lived on animal, fish and oil foods.

At the time of the submergence of Teltzie Sot, a remnant number of the Schirants, who at that time occupied the northern portion of the Teltzie, were left on the section now known as the Cape Verde Islands. These they termed Zanranza, and called themselves the Zanranzans. In stature they were tall, heavy set, and well proportioned. They, however, were a very coarse people, characterized with black skins; frizzled, curled and disorderly black hair; beards of the same style; very little hair on their bodies; black or brown eyes; noses very flat at the upper portion, but broad and prominent nostrils; large mouths, with lips that were drawn tightly across their teeth, which latter were large, and always visible; Their ears were round and large.

At the time of the submergence of Teltzie Et, a few Atarians were left on the Zanranza Islands. They were large in physique, large boned and tall of stature. They had light colored skins; straight hair, some being light color, and some of different shades of brown; blue, gray or brown eyes; full beards in harmony with their hair; males had considerable hair on their bodies, as is the case even with peoples of modern times.

These people mixed races, through the many ages that followed, until the Zanranzans and the remnant Atarians were lost as distinct or separate peoples, by having mixed and blended into one race, who continued to exist under the original name of Zanranzans. In stature they were about the same as their ancestors, though a little more fleshy. In color they were a shade or two lighter than the black. Their eyes generally were black and light brown, the gray color that had characterized their ancestors being entirely lost. Their hair, however, was characteristic with that of both races of their ancestors, and so also were their features. They had very thick feet, but generally speaking not large. They wore skins about their loins, but the young people and the children went nude. In character, they were slightly hostile, but not among themselves, for on the contrary, they had much love and affection for each other, especially in regard to family relations.

SFŪ'RY
OR
AFRICA.

TELTZIE XLIV.

Sfū'ry,—the first pre-historic name of the great continent of Africa, was given by the Hŏr-zī-ē'thăs, or the people of the last tribe of the southern branch of the two nations who carried out the great Găs-bi-ăn migration, when they had reached their Cŏn-zăn-dē'ză, or that section of country now known as Abyssinia and Nubia.

Kă-năn'ziē,—its second pre-historic name, was given by the Kă-di-ōes, after their leader, the main tribe of the northern branch of the two nations enroute on the above-named migration, when they had reached their Kă-di-ō, or the section now known as Algeria, and Tunis.

In-thī-clē'ō-ny,—the third pre-historic name, was given by the Jĕ-rē-thē'ăns, who survived the submergence of the southwestern portion of their Cō'jĕl, or district, now submerged by the Mediterranean Sea, and who were left as remnants along the northern coast of Algeria and Tunis, after which they were known as the Kĭn-măn'zēs, and the section as Kĭn-măn-zĕs.

Subsequently, when pre-historic time merged into the ancient and historic, the Libeyhans, or Libyans, who were descendants of the Kinmanzes, changed the name of the continent to "Libeyah," after that of the people, the term then meaning, *the unknown.* The name then referred to the unexplored country south of them.

Later in the historic period, the Greeks termed the same country "Libya," from their word *"libs,"* meaning "south wind," and still later, they termed it *"a-pike,"* meaning, *"without cold;"* and their close allies, the Romans, termed it *"aprica,"* meaning, *"sunny."*

Later, it was changed by the Romans and Arabs, to "Afrygah," or "Afrikiyah," which was then only the section name of the district in Africa, now known as Tunis, and from which the term "Africa" ultimately became the name of the continent.

Submerged Atlantis Restored

The ethnographic, geographic, and historic, conditions relative to this great continent, are complicated, and in many respects, characterized with vagueness by both ancient and modern writers; a fact due to the absence of the pre-historic links necessary to the establishment of these cycles.

About 1000 years subsequent to the final submergence of Atlantis, there began a system of two sectional convulsions, to the south and southeast of the now known coast of Africa.

The first of the two convulsions had place in the section of country now known as the Mt. Amber, off the northeastern coast of the now known Island of Madagascar.

At the time of the convulsion, which was circular in form, and of marvelous force and great dimension, that portion of Africa, between 5″ N. Lat., and about 60″ S. Lat., extended east into what is now known as the Indian Ocean, and the South Indian Ocean, and as far east as to about 90″ E. Lon., from Greenwich. This territory was very mountainous, especially that portion lying between the equator, on the north, and the the southern extremity of Madagascar, and also southeast of the southern extremity of Africa. The principle Zē'lăg (mountain) ranges in this section were, first, the Wă-ĕn'tō-dē Zelag, which extended northeast from, and including Madagascar, the remnants of which are now known as the Mahe Archo., and all the islands and banks that then lay northeast of Madagascar.

The second was the En-tō-sō-zīn'gō Zelag, that extended eastward from Madagascar, whose remnants are that of the now known Mascarenhas group of Islands.

The third was the Căl-cŭ-lĕn'thē Zelag, that extended southeast from the southern extremity, of Africa, whose remnants are now known as the Marion, the Crozet's Islands, and the Kerguelens Land, or Islands of Desolation. The force of the marvelous convulsion, on its whirl of destruction, established the great Madagascar Island, by tearing it from the main land of Africa, and forming the Mozambique Channel; the eastern coast line of Africa, from the equator in the north, to about 30″ S. Lat., the inlet waters of the same, and all the islands east of the above named latitudes, etc.

The second sectional convulsion occurred about 500 years subsequent to the first, and had place in the section modernly known as Mossel Bay, on the southern extremity of Africa.

The force of the convulsion established the southern, southwestern, and southeastern coast lines of Africa, from the southern boundry line of the first convulsion, on the eastern coast, to north of the mouth of the now known Orange river, on the western, or Atlantic coast. The force further extended out, and along the Calculenthe range, thus completing the establishment of the Marion, the Crozets, and the Desolation Islands.

These two great convulsions, therefore, are responsible for the ultimate connection of the Indian, and South Indian Oceans, and their conjunction with the waters of the Southern Ocean, and the South Atlantic, and the island systems of that section.

All the rest of the western coast of Africa, was formed by the Atlantian convulsions, as described under that head.

First, let us consider the southern branch of the Gasbian migration. Subsequent to the establishment of the Zăn-răn'zăns in Zăn-răn'ză, or the Cape Verdi Islands, a tribe of that stock, or race of people, entered Sfury by maritimal migration, in the section now known as Senegambia, which section they termed E-lŏn'gē-tē-zē, and called themselves the Hör-zī-ē'thäs, who in subsequent time became the pre-historic ancestors of the aborigines of parts of southwestern Africa.

Ultimately, a colony of the Horziethas descendants instituted the beginning of the southern branch of the great Gasbian migration across Sfury, along the southern coast of the then known Kä-rŭn'tĭc Gä-zĕt'ē (Inland Sea), that in subsequent time gave place to the now known Great Sahara Desert, to the section of country now known as Nubia and Abyssinia, which section they termed Con-zăn-dē'zä, but retained their former tribe name of Horziethas.

At this period they had changed somewhat in physical appearance. In height, they were about six feet; large-boned; both muscular and fleshy. Their skins were dark, as well as their hair, both resembling those of the Negro. Their beards were also similar. They had low foreheads; large full, peculiar, but expressive black eyes, that were set closely together; large straight, but not broad noses; thick lips, and feet that were large, flat, and broad. In regard to dress, they wore only a loose draping of short furred skins about their loins; but the children as a rule went nude. They advanced no special religious ideas, and instituted no forms of worship, from the fact that their ancestors before them, the Horziethas of Sfury, had lost all knowledge of religious principles, by divergence in pursuance of migration.

The Horziethas, of Conzandeza, or Nubia and Abyssinia, became the pre-historic ancestors of the primitive stock of Abyssinians, and the Barabra, or Berberines, including the Nuba, the Kenons and the Dongolawi tribes in the region of the Nile, from the southern limits of Egypt, to Sennaar.

Submerged Atlantis Restored

About 7000 years before the Adomic period, a colony of the Horziethas migrated eastward from Conzandeza, into the section of country now known as the submerged district of the Red Sea, which they termed Săn'cŭt, and called themselves the Wē-zĭn'thēs.

After a few generations, the Wezinthes became considerably changed, in their physical appearance; in stature they would average about five feet, and five inches, some being slender, and some more fleshy. They had very dark skins; waving black hair that extended down to the shoulders; black eyes; slim faces; low foreheads; broad and prominent noses; thick lips, and separated so as to expose their teeth. They were a very ferocious people, even among themselves. They practised cannibalism, especially when disposing of the bodies of their enemies, or of such individuals as were passing through their section of country. In regard to dress, none whatever was needed, as they were naturally clothed with a heavy suit of hair that hung loosely down from their hips to their thighs, They also had a suit of hair that hung down from their shoulders, and from under their arms, but the remainder of their bodies was comparatively nude, hence they wore no clothing.

The Wezinthes of Sĕn'cŭt (*now district of the Red Sea, submerged*), recognized an unknown cause for the manifestations of nature, though their ideas were shadowed with crudeness and vagueness. They were attracted more from the mysteriousness, that to them shrouded everything in nature, rather than by the real creative cause, as a principle. They had no special place or time for recognization, or adoration of the mysterious presence, or its marvelous manifestations. They however, went through the act of crude dancing, and gesticulations, with both hands and feet; then sat singly, or in groups, upon the ground, as the case might be, uttered some sentences and gave vent to hideous sounds of the voice, whenever, and wherever, any thing strikingly strange arrested their attention, such as might be made manifest in, or through nature. After a period of about 500 years, the Wezinthes became partially lost, by the submergence of the country of Sancut, which event established the now known Red Sea. Only two portions of these were left, (remnant), one on the eastern, and one on the western border of the Sea. The eastern remnant established themselves into a small nation; termed the body of water Dĕg'ī-lĕt, meaning Red Sea; retained their former name of Wezinthes as a nation, and termed the borderland in which they dwelt, Türg'nĕy.

The separation of the Wezinthes, by the Degilet or Red Sea,

or the submergence of portions of Sfury, when tribes of them were forced into Turgney, was the severed link that otherwise would have welded Africa, in her motherhood, to the Eastern continent, or Asia, and its people.

Secondly, let us consider the northern branch of the Great Găs'bi-ăn migration. Many generations after the establishment of the Kē-sĕl'zäs in the Zē-lăs'si-ŏs, or the Azores Islands, a colony of the descended Keselzas, by maritimal migration, or passing from one island to another (which subsequently were submerged), entered Sfury or Africa, in the section now known as Morocco, which section they termed Cō'jĕl, but retained their former tribe name of Keselzas. After the ultimate mixture of races on the islands of Zelassios and Kĕr'ī-wănsk, and when the Keselzas in Cojel, they had sustained some ethnographic changes. Ultimately, they became larger physically, in fact they might have been termed then a gigantic people. In stature they averaged from six to seven feet, those of the latter height being in the majority. Their skins were dark and swarthy; their heads large; their hair bushy, a fact due more from non-dressing, and care, than from a specific race condition, some being black, some dark brown, and some red. Their eyes were small, dark brown, dark gray, and black; their fore-heads were medium in height, but they wore their hair low, thus concealing a part of their foreheads. Their faces were broad; their noses much like those of the Negro; their cheek bones were high, a condition that made their eyes seem deep set. Their feet were large, the ball and heel being flat and broad. They displayed great muscular development, especially from the knees down to the feet. They were very hostile to other pople, but not among themselves.

Regarding their manner of dress, while inhabiting the islands of Zelassios, their style was very crude and simple. The men wore a clout about the loins and upper part of the thighs, and the women a short skirt to cover the same parts of the body. These simple garments were made from skins (the fur worn next to the body), of an animal then known as the *Haldia.* This animal was about as large as a medium sized modern dog. Its fur was soft, short, and of a mouse color. Although the animal was wild, originally, yet the inhabitants domesticated it, for the purpose of breeding, thus the better able to secure its skin and fur for the utility of garmenting themselves.

After their establishment in *Cojel,* however, their style of dress sustained some change. Here, as they had done in Zelassios, and in Keriwansk, they utilized the skins and the hair of a wild, prolific, mountain animal, then known as the An-tē-zĭl'ĭng, for their raiment. The animal in size, was about as large as a Newfoundland, or St. Bernard dog, with thick, heavy, but not long hair, some of which was spotted with brown and white, and some was a silvery gray. The garments were made in a sort of combination suit, at first, very crude, by being joined together with thorn pins; but, later, by means of skin strips that answered the purpose of threads, or lacings. Very little difference was displayed between the garments worn by the men, and those of the women. The skin of the stern of the animal was utilized to form the seat of the lower garment, as worn about the loins and thighs; the skins of the legs of the animal to form the short legs of the lower garment, that was fastened down to the legs of the individual, as well as to form sleeves for their arms, while the skins from the main body of the animal were used as coverings for the upper parts of their bodies. This was done by cutting a hole in the middle of the skin, through which they put their heads, the skin, thus pendant, forming the covering for their backs and breasts, the ends of the skins being fastened to the lower garment, thus was formed the combination for the upper part of the body garment. Stockings were then made for the feet and lower legs; these were also fastened to the upper garment, which thus completed the combination.

The infant, or new born babe, was swaddled in skin, the hair being placed next to the child. In cases where the skins were not readily obtainable, the babies were swaddled in a mass of the cotton, or soft fiber, gathered from the pods of a plant, much resembling the modern milk weed, then known as Rī'kŏsh and which was, in subsequent time, largely used in the construction of cloth. After the children were large enough to have these swaddlings removed, they were replaced with new garments similar to those worn by the adults, but were made from the scraps of skins left from the manufacture of the adult garments.

In regard to religion, the Keselzas of pre-historic Cojel, as a people, generally recognized the light of the sun as their most sacred benefactor in life. They had no stated public gatherings in adoration of the principle of light, or no public form of worship. All was confined to individual recognition. At their first sight of the rising sun, wherever he, or she might be, the individual made obeisance to the sun at its first appearance in the morning. With the palms of their hands raised high above their heads opened toward the sun in front of them, thus posing, they bowed low three times to the rising sun, and each time they rose to the perpendicular, the hands were raised as above stated, at which time they would cry out, Cē-dē-sä!, meaning in their language, *great light*. *Cē*, alone, was their word for sun; *dē*, for the moon; and *sä*, for the stars.

After abiding many years in this section of country, they became a numerous people, and the desire to reach out still further for changes in life, caused a large colony of them to migrate beyond what modernly are known as the "Atlas Mountains," which they termed Kä-dī'ō, meaning cold, and also termed that section of country Kadio, and called themselves the Kä-dī'oes. Here eventually, they became a famous poeple, who had advanced greatly in every way.

Here, they were physically, about the same as were their ancestors, the Keselzas, of Cojel, or modern Morocco; however, they adopted more clothing, on account of the climate, which at first they made out of furred skins, etc. Subsequently, however, they learned to weave fabrics from fibres, and grasses, which they utilized in making their garments, and which they also formed into mats, etc. They learned to mould a blue clay substance into useful dishes. In fact they became more civilized in many ways, and were mentally in advance of their Ancestors. They were harmonious among themselves, but very hostile to intruders, or individuals that came among them, whom they were sure to kill. When migrating, they were ever ready to fight for possession.

The Kadioes of Kä-dī'ō, in the vicinity of the now known Atlas Mountains, recognized all Solar lights as a principle for adoration, or worship. These they termed Kū-zĭn'too, referring to the greater lights of heaven, *Kū*, meaning the sun, in the Kadioan language; *Zin*, the moon; and *Too*, the stars. The difference between their recognition of light as the principle for adoration, and that of their ancestors, the Keselzas, was that the latter only recognized one luminary, viz; the sun, and the Kadios combined the three, sun, moon, and stars, in which their adoration was centered.

They erected an emblem, or idol, in representation of the principle of Kuzintoo, which was formed by a perpendicular pole, or piece of wood, similar to that of the perpendicular piece. On the left point of the triangle, was represented the disc of the sun; on the right that of the moon; on the top point was placed a representation of a star· The radiations of light were represented, as emanating from them, by means of small sticks, so placed around the discs of the sun and moon, and on the outline of the star. The emblem, or idol, was not placed perpendicularly, however, but leaned against, and supported by, a triangular mound, or bank of earth, a little taller than the emblem. They held adorational assemblies and exercises twice a year, viz: at the times of the vernal and autumnal equinoxes, lasting for two days, from sunrise of the first morning, until sunset of the following day. The order of exercises, at such times was to assemble at sunrise and at sunset, by the emblem of Kuzintoo, when each individual would pass three times in a circular manner around the emblem, and each time as he came in front of it so as to face the south, he would triangle himself, e. g., would, with the right hand, starting at the throat, trace down obliquely to the waist, then horizontally across the waist to the right, then up obliquely, to the left, again to the throat, thus having traced, or pantomimed the outline of a triangle upon his breast. After this obeisance was made, in the form of a low bow, to the emblem; the third time, the individual would pass back to the assembly, thus giving place for another to go through the form. At the last sunset assembly, however, the whole company, formed into a circle around the emblem, passed once around; and as each individual came in front of the image or emblem, he would triangle himself, make obeisence, retire from the circle, and depart to his abode.

Each afternoon, as the sun passed down the western sky, they held a great feast. As they sat in groups, so arranged as to form a circle, they feasted on fruits, meats and fish.

During the year, whenever an individual passed the emblem, he would make obeisance to it in the same manner as above described.

While the Kadioes of Kadio, did not fully comprehend the meaning of the emblem, or mode of triangling themselves,—which was that the motion across the waist located the seat of life; and the obliques from the throat that formed the upper part of the triangle, as pointing up to the mental faculties,—as did the priesthood in subsequent generations; yet the principle was given them, through spirit influence for the purpose of further development; e. g., in the beginning, given them in crudity and ignorance, it was further developed by the priesthood, ultimately to find its more perfect analysis and understanding, through the philosophical and scientific researches and teachings of the present time and in the future.

The mode of triangle obeisance and emblematic representation, was not changed, in reality, until the time of the crucifixion, and then it was done by the priesthood of that period, and retained by priests of the Roman Catholic church, and their offspring of modern time.

After they had dwelt many generations in Kadio, or east of the Atlas Mountains of Morocco, a colony of their descendants migrated eastward along the range into the section of country now known as Algeria, but they did not change their colony, or section name. There they dwelt for many generations and grew to be a large nation; but not so numerous in population as their mother nation had been. Physically speaking, they remained about the same as their ancestors, the Kadioes of Morocco; but mentally they advanced considerably.

The Kadioes of Kadio, in the now known section of Algeria, conceived the idea of a great man, in their own likeness, as the creator of the planets, which creative principle they termed Gī-dī'ō. Among themselves, especially to their children, they taught the idea that the sun and the moon were the father and the mother of the stars. *Gi,* in the Kadio language, meant "father;" *Di,* "mother," and *O,* "child." Whenever they saw a falling star, they took it to be a new born star-child. Their representation therefore of Gidio, of the Creative Principle, was changed from planetary emblems, such as their ancestors, the Kadioes of Kadio, in the Atlas Mountain region, employed, to the full form of a man, in representation of Gidio, or Gi, the Father of Lights. They therefore established an image of Gidio for special use in their adorational exercises, which was very crudely wrought in the full form of a man, standing erect, with his right elbow against his side, the forearm raised to a perpendicular with the body, and the open hand turned to the front. The image was placed upon a perpendicular pole, erected much in resemblance of the "Totem" poles, which latter idea was handed down through the generations, to the ancient peoples of modern time, who erected them, not knowing the precursor to have been the image of Gidio.

The image of Gidio was made portable, so it could be moved at pleasure; and when erected was always set facing the north, thus to appear as if coming to the people from the south. The stated gatherings, for adorational exercises, or worship, were convened at three different periods during the month; viz: the first, at the first appearance of the new moon; the second, which was their greatest gathering and feast, at the time of the full moon; the third, the first night of the dark of the moon. General and individual adorations were always practised at the option of people, who felt so inclined, at the noon day hour, or when the sunlight was at its glory. At the stated gatherings, the people were assembled by means of vocal demonstration, accompanied by resonant wood, blowing through a sort of wooden horn, and shouting through a long stone tube with rising and falling tones of voice, aggregating a most hideous loud noise, that was continued until they reached the shrine of Gidio.

When assembled, the people formed circles within circles, about the image of Gidio, according to the number of people assembled, and their cast in society, viz; the leaders formed the centre circle; the higher class the next; and so on until all were formed into circles, the children at all times forming the outer circle. Thus formed, the great noise was resumed, and the adorational march begun. The latter was as follows:—the Chief of the leaders started to march first, from his position in the circle, diagonally across to the next outer circle, and back in advance diagonal form, to his own circle, thus forming two sides of a triangular movement, or the point of a star. Each leader followed suit in the tracks of the Chief, from his position in the circle, thus continuing the march, until the Chief, and each leader, had returned to the position from which they started. Thus the circles followed suit, one after another, until all had returned to their starting points. The noise accompanying the march was continuous from beginning to finish. When the last circle had finished its round, all the people knelt upon both knees, and bowed low, with the face to the earth, then rose and dispersed in a promiscuous manner. The feast, which consisted of meats, fish, fruits, and nuts, was always held late in the afternoon, before the time for the adorational march.

There were, in addition to the principal Gidio image, smaller ones, placed throughout the village, or settlement, and miniature ones were placed in the homes, for more convenient use, etc.

Gidio, of the Kadios, was the earliest conception of Anthropomorphism, the idea of which, like that of "triangling," in connection with the adoration of Kuzintoo, by their ancestors, that led down to the crucifix, was conceived through spirit influence, for the same purpose, beginning in crudity, such as would reach the undeveloped minds of the people, further developed by the priesthood. This concept of deity is being investigated, by master minds of the present, and will be more fully comprehended in the future through truthful teachings of philosophy, and scientific reasoning, such as shall cause the annihilation of such a belief, which is still taught by Anthropomorphists.

Ultimately, a colony of Algerian Kadioes migrated to the section of country now submerged by the waters of the southwestern half of the Mediterranean Sea, which section they termed Cō'jēl, after the pre-historic Cojel of their Keselza ancestors, in

Morocco, and they called themselves the Jē-rē-thē'äns. There they dwelt for ages, and became a great nation.

A short time after the Horziethas, of the southern branch, were established in their section of Conzandeza; and the Kasamanzes, of the northern branch in Găs'bî-ä, a descended tribe of the Horziethas migrated northward, along the now known Nile river. This latter they termed Gē-lĭ'ŏt, and they traveled to the section of what is now known as the First Cataract, which section they termed Kăl-lū'thi-ä, and called themselves the Kăl-lū'thi-äns. After several generations, a tribe of their descendants migrated still farther north, along the Geliot river, to the section adjacent to Gasbia, occupied by the Kasamanzes. Ultimately, the Kalluthians and the Kasamanzes mixed races, after which, their descendants re-named the section Cŭz-ē-tĕn'nē, and called themselves the Cŭz'ē-tĕns, but they continued to call the river Geliot.

The Cuzetens were unlike their ancestors in some respects, especially in their physical development and their life habits, a result of their having been a mixed race in general. In height they were from five to six feet; they had dull black skins; straight, scant, black hair that hung in thin shreds down to their shoulders; small, round, black eyes. Some had narrow noses with high bridges, and some had broad nostrils with flat bridges, large mouths, with medium, thick, and pouched lips; short, receding chins; short, scant beards toward the back of their cheeks and on the chin, but no moustache; low foreheads; quite large, broad hands and feet. In regard to dress, some wore skins about their loins, though the majority went nude; they had considerable hair on their bodies, especially across their abdomens and about the upper part of their legs; the heavier suit being about the loins, which grew shorter as it extended up the breast. They were a wild, roving people, and had no religious ideas.

Prior to the submergence that established the now known Arabian Sea, a remnant of the Gū-bĕv'ĕls, who were a mixed race of Hăn'grŏts and Wĭn'gŭs, migrated westward along the then known Lä-plä-lĭn'gō Krū'shĭc (mountain) range, to the region of the then un-named Krushic range, that extended eastward from the now known section of Cope Guardafui, Africa (an extension of the now known Singali Mountains), where they dwelt, for a time, by a beautiful Sāke (lake), which they termed Zē-tĭn'zä, in the then known extension of the great Tishhan of Azan, south of the Laplalingo Krushic, and east of the now known section of the Socotra Island.

Subsequently, they resumed their migration, when they followed the above named extension of the Somali range, until they entered the section of country south of the Singali range, where they settled in the section now known as Somali Land, Africa. They termed this section A-fĕc'to, and called themselves the A-fĕc'tōes. They were a quarrelsome people. In stature, some were about six feet tall, they were of athletic build; some were in height about six feet five inches, and of fleshy build. They generally had large heads, which they carried as if thrown back on the shoulders; dull black skins; black hair both curly and profuse; curly beards; dull eyes, and drooping lids; low, and very receding foreheads; noses with broad nostrils that lay flat on the face, and over flat bridges; generally small mouths, thin lips, pointed and protruding; flat, broad and thin hands and feet, with long fingers and toes. They all wore skins about their loins, and had considerable hair on their bodies. They were a contentious people, and were especially hostile to other tribes, upon whom they would make frequent raids. They had no religious ideas or ceremonies.

About the time that the Afectoes had settled in Afecto, there appeared in the same section a tribe of Cuzetens, who had migrated there from Cuzetenne, Siloton (Egypt), who ultimately mixed races with the Afectoes, which brought to them an ethnographic change, when they retained both their former section and tribe names of Afecto and Afectoes. They and their descendants became the pre-historic ancestors of the Somali race, whose origin heretofore has been a mystery to ethnographic students and historians, and whose difference physically, from the original people of Socotra, or the descendants of the pre-historic Ar-ē-tū'bēs, is due to their race mixture with the pre-historic Cuzetens.

The Somali are a fierce, lawless people. All go armed with spears and short swords; the latter exactly like those of the ancient Egyptians, whom the Somali resemble more than any other of the African people. This is on account of the infusion of Cuzeten blood into that of the Afectoes, their ancestors.

The legends, of the Gallas of Gojam, tell of their savage ancestors as "having come from the southeast," from a country on the other side of a "bahr" (lake or river). This had its origin from the fact of the migration of the Gū-hĕv'ĕls, or Afectoes, from their home on the eastern side of Sāke (lake) Zē-tĭ'zā, then known in the northern section of the great Tĭsh'hăn (valley) of A'zăn.

Likewise the Yedju, and the Raia Galla, point toward the

east, and commemorate the passage of a "bahr," a custom that had its origin from the same facts, relative to the Afectoes and their migration from Sake Zetinza.

The southern Gallas refer to the "expulsion of the race" from the country now occupied by the Somali, which legends had their origin in the facts arising from the great convulsion that had place off Cape Guardafui, when the islands of Abd el Kuri and Socotra were established, when portions of the people bed inland from Somali.

The Somali, the Afars, the Abyssinian, Agau and Bejas (Bishari), are closely allied to the Gallas, both in physical type and speech; and like them are a fine race, tall, active, robust, with fairly regular features, but not free from an infusion of negro blood, as shown by their dark, often almost black complexions, and still more by their kinky and even woolly hair. The latter sometimes is short, and sometimes long enough to be plaited in tresses that hang down to the shoulders. They have oval faces, high and round foreheads, full lips, strong and regular teeth, bright, restless eyes, etc.

Prior to the convulsions that established the now known Socotra Island, some of the Rezendeth race from southern Qureston had migrated southeast to the same section of the great Tishhan of Azan, where the Guhevels had halted, and where a portion remained after their brethren had passed on into their section of Afecto, and ultimately mixed races with the remnant Guhevels.

At the time of the great convulsion that sunk the eastern extremity of the now known Singali range of mountains, and formed Socotra and Abd-el-kuri islands, a portion of the Guhevels, who had remained in the northern section of the great Tishhan of Azan, at the time their brethren passed on into their section of Afecto, were left upon the Socotra Island, which section they termed Săl-sē'vī-ā, and called themselves the Ar-ē-tū'bēs.

The Aretubes, and their descendants, became the pre-historic ancestors of the original natives of Socotra, who in their nomad pursuits, inhabited the uplands of the island. They are a well-built race, with good features, and have long curly hair, but not woolly. They are a peculiar race, and differ from their brethren, the Somali, through their race condition mixed with the Rezendeths, which also made changes in their native speech.

Subsequent to the great convulsion that established the Socotra Islands, and Cape Guardafui, and that coast region of Africa, where as before stated, portions of the Afectoes were, from fear, driven inland to the northwest, they formed themselves into a new tribe in the region now known as Galla, which section they termed O-ā-nŏn'gä, after their leader, and called themselves the O-rē-ăn'ī-mēs.

Subsequently, a tribe of the Hör-zī-ē'thās, from southern Conzandeza, or Abyssinia, came into the section of Oanonga, where they ultimately became mixed with the Oreanimes, but retained the section and tribe names of Oanonga and Oreanimes. In stature, they were from five to six feet; they had light black skins; small heads, with narrow, projecting foreheads; some straight, and some curly black hair, of medium length; scarcely any beard, only a little under their chins and up the back side of their cheeks, which extended up to their hair; they had considerable on their bodies; deep set, medium-sized, black and very piercing, or sharp eyes; noses with small nostrils with more of a rounded bridge; large mouths, with drawn lips; pointed chins; long, narrow flat hands and feet, with long fingers and toes. In regard to dress, they all wore skins about their loins. They had no religious ideas, and were a quarrelsome people among themselves, and were of a nomadic nature. They and their descendants became the pre-historic ancestors of the Galla race, who like the Somali race, mystified the ethnographic and historic writers of modern times, in regard to their origin and migration.

Likewise, the ethnographic and philologic affinities that now exist between the Somali, the Galla, the Afars, or Donkoli and the Abyssinians, have come from the race mixture of the original stock of Horziethas in Africa, with that of the Jeretheans, after their long migration into Asia, thence south into Hindustan, west through the Tishhan of Azan, into Somali Land, through various tribes, and that of the Rezendeths (which was really from the Horziethas stock, they being descendants of the Wezinthese whose ancestors were Horziethas), through their migration south across western Arabia, to the great Tishhan of Azan, where they were lost as an infusion into the blood of the Guhevels, and further transferred through that of the Afectoes.

All the ethnographic and philologic affinities, therefore, existing in the original, and sub-stocks, are due to the mingling and overlapping of the above-named peoples in a race sense, during the ages that have passed by since Eastern Central Africa was peopled with the Horziethas, and Northeastern, or Egypt, by descendants of the same race, who sustained an infusion of blood from the great Jeretheans nation, through the Libyan and Phianician races.

The Gallas have nothing in common with the negro type. They are a powerful race; the musculation of their arms, thighs, and calves, is altogether different than that of the negro, and they have none of the fetor, developed by the negro skin. They have large, powerful frames; dark brown complexion; lofty, broad brows; lively, deep-set eyes; not infrequently, regular, and finely-shaped features, and are a nomadic pastoral people.

At the time of the submergence of the southern portion of Teltzie Sot of Atlantis, and prior to the arrival of the A-dăl'nī-ĕns, in their Nĭc-ā-phī-lĕ'tŭs, a remnant of the Schanandarits ĕns, in their Nĭc-ā-phī-lō'cŭs, a remnant of the Schanandarits from the southern portion of Teltzie Sot, were left upon the islands that then had place along the coast of the section of country now known as Angola, Africa, who soon passed from the islands into various parts of the latter-named section, and in subsequent time, congregated into a tribe, at which time they termed the now known section of Angola A-năn'dēs (meaning the barren land), and called themselves the Sĕn'dē-lănds (meaning "saved from the waters"). Their principal settlement, or hamlet, which they termed Mä-zĕn'tūp, was in the immediate vicinity of the now known town of Benguela.

In subsequent time, descendants of the Sendelands, migrated northeast, into the western half of the section now known as the Congo Free State, their eastern boundary line being that of the now known Sankuri river and lake, and further north into the crescent section that is formed by the course of the Congo river, or between it and the Kassai. Other tribes of the descended Sendelands migrated north from their Anandes, through the now known French Congo region, through sections of that region of the Soudan country, as far north as to the now known Sahara Desert district.

The original stock of Sendelands and their descendants, who like the Kintilucians of the northern branch of migrators across Sfury) did not mingle races with the southern migrators from the Horziethan nation, generally speaking, excepting a few straggling tribes, hence (like the Kintilucians, or Caucasians, and the Cuzetens, or Egyptians) retained, as far as possible, under the conditions of new locations and many ages of descendancy, the characteristics of their primitive ancestors, the Schanandarits of Teltzie Sot; and therefore, are the ancestors of the now known thirty-eight tribes, as classed in the "Western Group," of South African Negroes, and direct descendants from Teltzie Sot, of Atlantis.

The Horziethas, who migrated eastward through the now known country of Soudan (which time was subsequent to the establishment of the Sendelands through western central Africa, and their migrations southward into Southern Africa), are the primitive ancestors of the vast Negro race that now exists throughout Western Soudan and Guinea; Central Soudan and the Chad Basin; East Soudan and the Upper Nile; and slight mixture with some of the tribes of Sendelands, in that of South Africa, or Bantu Family. The Moors, the Kaffirs, the Hottentots and the Bushmen, have herein, been especially accounted for.

Subsequent to the establishment of the Horziethas, in E-lŏn'-gē-tē'zē, or the now known section of Senegambia, W. Africa, and their migration across Sfury, to the now known region of Nubia, and Abyssinia, a tribe of those Horziethas, in divergence to the course pursued by their easterly migrating brethren, began a migration southward through the region now known as Bagirmi, or Afawawa, from whence they followed the Zelag ranges to the district now known as French Congo, from whence they turned eastward, and settled in the section west of the now known Congo river, or rather between the now known Ubangi, or Mobangi, and the Sangha, affluents of the Congo, which section they termed Jăn'dō-zē, and called themselves the Jăn'dō-zēns, where they ultimately became a large nation.

When the Horziethas, who were on the eastern migration, had arrived in the section of country now known as the region of the upper waters of the Chadda, or Bende river, in the vicinity of the town of Yola, or N. E. of the now known Mt. Atlantika, where they halted for a time, factional contentions arose among them, which caused a large tribe to secede from the main body, who in divergence to the eastern course taken by the main body, established a migration southward, when they followed the Chadda river to its junction with the Niger; and thence they passed eastward into the section now known as Adamawa, thence into that of French Congo, until they arrived on the western side of the Sangha river, which they followed to its affluence into the Congo. They followed the latter on its western side until they arrived in the vicinity now occupied by the town of Brazzeville, where they settled, termed the section Dē-vō'măn, and called themselves the Kä-shē'äns. Here they multiplied, until they became a large nation, who occupied that portion of the now known section of French Congo, and along the western side of the Congo river, from about the latitude of the Equator, to the mouth of the Congo. Their principal hamlet which they termed Nī-cä-rō'nēls, was located on the site where now the town of Brazzeville has place.

Subsequent to the establishment of the Jendozens in Jendoze, between the Ubangi and the Sanga rivers, a tribe of their descendants migrated east and south, when they followed the course of the Congo river, and the zelag ranges, to the S. E. portion of the section now known as the Congo Free State, where they settled on the west side of the now known Iramba Kone mountains, near the north line of British Central Africa, which section they termed A-brăn'cěs, and called themselves **the Ăr-ā-băs'căns.** Their principal hamlet, which they termed **Săg-măl'li-ŏn,** was located on the site of their first settlement.

Ultimately, the Arabascans spread out through the northeastern and eastern portions of the Congo Free State to the regions of the lakes, especially the one now known as Bangweolo, which they termed O-prō-nŏ'sěs, where a large tribe of Arabascans settled, established a hamlet which they termed An'vō-nēse, which latter name they also gave to that section, but retained their former tribe name of Arabascans. They were fond of hunting and fishing, the latter being their chief enterprise, therefore sought the then termed zelags and sakes (mountains and lakes) as their centers of abode.

Subsequent to the establishment of the Arabascans in Abrances, a tribe of the Kasheans crossed the Congo river, passed eastward into the section now known as the Congo Free State, until they came to the now known Kuango river, the course of which they followed southeast, into the section now known as the eastern central portion of Angola, in the vicinity of the now known town of Cobungo, where they halted for a time, then resumed their migration eastward through what is now known as between British Central Africa and the Congo Free State, until they arrived in the vicinity of Abrances, then occupied by the Arabascans. In this section they also settled, and being descendants from the same race, viz., the Horziethas, only separate branches of the migration, soon joined issues and therefore became as one people. As the Arabascans had arrived in the section first, and were the larger tribe of the two, the united people adopted the same name of Arabascans as a tribe, and continued Abrances as the section name. Here they multiplied until they became a large nation, and had spread out through the northern and eastern portions of the section now known as British Central Africa, as far as to the now known Zambesi river.

Ultimately, a large tribe of the Arabascans from Abrances, migrated into the now known section of British South Africa, when they settled between the above-named section and that of the South African Republic, south of the Tropic of Capricorn, in the section between the now known towns of Shoshong and Molopolole, which section they termed Nĭc-ā-phī-lĕ'tŭs, and called themselves the A-dăl′nī-ēnes, where they multiplied until they became a large colony, and where they established their principal hamlet which they termed Săck′ī-lŭm.

The Adalnienes of Nicaphiletus, and their descendants, became the pre-historic ancestors of the Khoi Khoin (men of men) or Quae Quae, Kwekhena, t'Kuhkeub, as they term themselves, or now known Hottentots, and their original distinctness, as a primitive race, from all the other African races on the continent, is due to the fact that they are a direct descended race from the Horziethas, not having mingled races with the Sendelands, or ancestors of the Negro race proper; the mixed race of Atarians and Schirants, or ancestors of the Bushmen; or the U-rē-ăn′-lĕns, who were the ancestors of the Kaffres; hence, are close representatives of the Zanranzans of Zanranza, or Cape Verdi Islands, and more primitively speaking, the mixed race of the better class of Schirants of Teltzie Sot and Atarians of Teltzie Et, who at the time of the submergence of Teltzie Sot, were left as a remnant on the Islands, and therefore, as the Caucasians, through their having descended from the Kintilucians, and the Egyptians, through their having descended from the Cuzetens, were direct descendants from the Lontidri of Atlantis, so were the Hottentots by having descended from the Horziethas, especially so, the pure Namaqua and Oerlaama tribes.

The Hottentot possesses his mild, peaceable, affectionate and hospitable characteristics, and endowment with ingenious capability, through the continuation of the same, though in a modified degree, through descendancy, from his primitive ancestors, the Atarians. His indolent and non-energetic character is a modified continuation, from that of his primitive ancestors, the Schirants. His physical dimensions have been considerably degenerated from that of his primitive ancestors, through the influence of mixed race and local migratory conditions. His leather brown-colored skin; oval face; prominent, projecting cheek bones; black, dark chestnut, wide-apart eyes; broad, thick nose, flat at the roots; pointed chin; large mouth, with thick, turned-up lips, woolly hair that grows in short, thick, curly tufts on his head, and very scant beard, are conditioned characteristics, modified and varified, and thus developed through the mixture of the Schirant and the Atarian races, together with the influences that have arisen from the migration pursued from Atlantis to Southern Africa.

Prior to the convulsion that separated the now known Island of Madagascar from the main land of Africa, and established it as such, a tribe of the Afectoes from Afecto, or what is now known as the Somali Land, eastern Africa, migrated southward through the section of country now submerged by the western portion of the Indian Ocean, to about forty-four degrees longitude east from Greenwich, and eleven degrees south latitude, or northeast of the now known Comoro Islands, where they settled, termed the section Ab-ăm'hä-nēse, and called themselves the Jū'läs. Their principal hamlet, which they termed Jū-lī-ĭs'tĭc, was located on the site of their first settlement.

About the time that the Julas had become settled in Abamhanese, a tribe of the descendants of the Arabascans, from their Abrances, migrated southeast, into the district of country now submerged by the waters of the Mozambique Channel, then a great Kĕt'zĭl-ly (valley), where they settled, at a point in the Ketzilly about twenty degrees south latitude and forty degrees longitude east from Greenwich, which section of country and Ketzilly they termed Gŏn-thā-nē'sŭs, and called themselves the Gŏn'thā-nēs. Their principal city, which they termed Kŭl-ē' dŭsh, was located on the site of their first settlement.

At the time of the establishment of the Mozambique Channel, which caused the separation of Madagascar from Africa, and submerged the then known district of Gonthanesus, remnant Juras from their Abamhanes, were left in the section now known as Mozambique, where in time they mixed races, termed the section El-tĕr'rŭs, and called themselves the U-rē-ăn'lĕns, whose ultimate descendants became the pre-historic ancestors of the now known Kaffres or Kaffirs of Kaffraria, Africa.

At the time of the submergence of the district now known as the Mozambique Channel, and when the Island of Madagascar was established, remnants of the Julas from their section of Abamhanese, who had migrated as far east and southeast as to the now known borderlands of the northern portion of the Island of Madagascar, were left as a scattered people along the northwestern portion of the island; but, ultimately, they established a settlement at the point now known, as half way between the Narunda Bay, and the then known great range of zelags (mountains) that lay through the center of the island east of it, which zelag range they termed Ex'tĭs, named the section Fū'lä, and called themselves the Fū'läs. Their principal hamlet, which they termed Fula, was located on the site of their first settlement.

At the time of the establishment of the Mozambique Channel, as was the case with the Julas of Abamhanese, remnants of the Gonthanese, from Gonthanesus, who had migrated east and the Gonthanes from Gonthanesus, who had migrated east and lands of Madagascar, were left as a scattered people upon the western portion of the Island; but, ultimately they established a settlement in the section now known as the Sakalava country, at a point east of the Barlow Island, or between the now known Mailampaka, and the Morondana rivers, and half way between the western ranges of hills and the coast line in that section, which they termed Gĭt-ē-wä'bä, and called themselves the Gitewabas. Their principal hamlet, which they termed Gitewaba, was located on the site of their first settlement.

In subsequent time, the Fulas and the Gitewabas intermingled and mixed races, and spread out over various portions of the island south of the peak where now the town of Antongodrahoja has place, when they termed the Island Gō'lĕth, and called themselves the Shăn'trōs. Their principal hamlet, which they termed Dī-ā-mĕz'tēs, was located on the site where now the town of Antongodrahoja has place. The Gitewabas, the Fulas and their descended mixed race of Shantros, became the pre-historic ancestors of the Malagasy, collectively speaking, whose slight variances physically are due to mixed race conditions that have attended their descension during past ages.

That the Malagasy people of Madagascar seem not to have been peopled from Africa, and to belong to the Malayo Polynesian stock, a fact inferred from their similarity to the people of the Pacific Archipelago in regard to their physical appearance, mental habits, customs, and especially in their language, arises first from the fact that, since through the Gitewabas, who were descendants from the Horzietha nation (see the migrations through southern Africa); and secondly, since the Malayo Polynesian stock were descendants from the Horziethan nation (see their various migrations and descendant conditions across Asia), it will readily be seen how the influence was carried into Madagascar, and also into the great Eastern Archipelago.

What apparent African and Arabic elements that exist among the western and the northwestern and southeastern sections, respectively speaking, on the Island of Madagascar, is due to the fact that since the Gonthanes of Gonthanesus, in the now submerged district of the Mozambique Channel, were descendants from the Arabascans of Abrances, or the region of the now known Kongo Free State, and British-central Africa, and that at the time of the establishment of the Mozambique Channel, the Gitewabas, who were a remnant of the. Gonthanes, who were Gitewabas, who were a remnant of the Gonthanese, who were left on the island, carried the African element, such as belonged to the Horziethan descendants, into the island (and also the reflection back into Africa by the Gonthanes who, as a remnant, were left on the African side at the time of the establishment of the Mozambique Channel, and who became the ancestors of the Kaffirs). Further infusion by the mixture of races, between the Gitewabas and the Fulas on the Island, carried that element to various parts of the Island.

The Arabic elements, such as are visible in the northwest of the island, is due to the fact that since the Fulas of the northwest were descendants from the ancestors of the Arabians (see our migrations through Arabia into Hindustan, India, and westward through the great Tishhans of Nä-sĕn'dō and A'zŏff, to the Afectoes who settled in the Somali Land in Africa, and thence to the Julas of Julaistic, and ultimately the remnant tribe of Fulas in the northeastern portion of Madagascar), the influence was carried into the northwest of the Island. That of the southeastern coast was carried there by migrations of the Fula element, and by mixed race conditions during subsequent time.

Philologically speaking, the seeming virtual unity that exists in the inhabitants of Madagascar, arises from the mixture of the Fula and the Gitewaba languages, the latter being the stronger, into one general language, the dialects of which have arisen from the mixed conditions of the two languages as used in different localities, and under different conditions on the island. The same conditions were carried into the Pacific Archipelago region, by virtue of similar conditions attending the eastern migrations by peoples of the same stock.

Prior to the great convulsion that caused the submergence of Teltzie Sot, Atlantis, there was a very low tribe who dwelt in the northeastern portion of Teltzie Sot, who through contentious conditions, were caused to secede from the main colony of Schirants, of north Teltzie Sot, and therefore migrated to the extreme northeast portion of the Teltzie where they, as a very small tribe, led a nomadic life, under crude and degenerate conditions.

Subsequently, a small tribe of the very lowest class of Atlantians, from the southern portion of Teltzie Et, migrated into the northeastern portion of Teltzie Sot, where they met and mingled with the agove-named seceded tribe of Schirants, which condition ultimately established an inferior race of people who, to the Atatians, were known only as a peculiar race of low, ignorant people, who dwelt in that portion of the Lontidri, without tribe, or section names.

At the time of the submergence of Teltzie Sot, that portion of the western coast of Africa lying between the Tropic of Capricorn and about ten degrees south latitude, extended much farther westward, which formed a long point into what is now known as the North Atlantic Ocean, upon which a remnant of the above-named mixed race was left.

Soon after, a small convulsion occurred on the point of land above referred to, which frightened the remnant people, and caused them to migrate farther inland, when they halted at a point or section now known as the Angola region. In a short time after they had arrived in the above-named section, another convulsion occurred which cut the extended point of land off from the present continent of Africa, and practically submerged it (excepting a few small islands, that soon afterwards disappeared altogether). This again gave the tribe fear lest another convulsion would occur in that section, and destroy them, so they migrated still farther southward, to between the Tropic of Capricorn, and the twentieth degree south latitude, where they as a distinct race, in very low conditions, multiplied and soon spread out southeast into what is now known as the section of Cape Colony and other parts of South Africa as the ages passed by. They and their descendants became the pre-historic ancestors of the Saab, or Saan (so called by themselves), aboriginal race of South Africa, now known as the Bushmen, or Bosjesmans. They, as a dwarfish, low existing type of mankind, have become thus through the long ages of degenerate conditions through which they have passed, from the time of the submergence of Teltzie Sot, to the present time. Their dirty, yellow-colored skins have been thus characterized through the descended conditions arising from the co-infusions of the white Atarian and black Schirants blood, as established in their primitive home of Teltzie Sot, Atlantis, and their other physical characteristics are due to the same degenerate conditions.

SI-LO'TON
OR
EGYPT.

TELTZIE XLV.

Gasbia, was the first pre-historic name of Lower Egypt, so given by the Kasamanzese of that section.

Kalluthea was the first pre-historic name of Upper Egypt, so given by the Kallutheans of that section.

Gustz was the first pre-historic name of Middle Egypt, so given by the Quzetas of that section.

Siloton was the first pre-historic name of the entire country of Egypt, and was thus established about 1000 years before the Adomic period.

At that time there were five well-established nations in northeast Sfury, viz., the Cuzetens of Cuzetenne; the Ogerets of Siwin; the Creitons of Yunthrox; the Quzetas of Gustz; and the Horziethas of Conzandeza.

The people of those various sections were then in communication with each other, and held stated national conventions at Jīs-tē-lē'zōn, the then capital city of Conzandeza, or of the Horziethas nation.

At one of these conventions, the chief rulers of the five nations were summoned for the purpose of giving a name to the entire country, or to the northeastern section of Sfury, viz: Kū'jā, Sĕl-ī-ĕn'gō and E-lī-jĕ'tē, from Sĭn-tī-ăn'sō, the capital Witeze (city) of Cuzetenne in the section of the Cuzetens; Trĕs-tĕr-ĭs and Nŭn-dĕr-sŭn from Lā-thür-rū'gē, the capital Witeze of Siwin, in the section of the Ogerets; Häs-săl-lăn'gä and On-gē'lōw, from Sĕn'tī-soū, the capital Witeze of Yunthrox, in the section of the Creitons; Jĕr'tē-zē and Sĭs-tū'rē, from Yoū'thrŏl, the capital Witeze of Gustz, in the section of the Quzetas; and Al-lä-măn'zä, Lūt-zē'ra, Nun-ka-dris, Lū-cī'ciăn and Băsk'-hō-lĭt, from Mĭn-ē-tē'zăn, the capital Witeze of Conzandeza, in the section of the Horziethas. It was at that convention that the term "Siloton" (the term meaning many tribes) was chosen to be the name of northeastern Sfury (Egypt), thus covering a larger territory than Egypt does at the present time.

Submerged Atlantis Restored

In the latter part of the Adomic period, the Cuzetens, or original Egyptians, who had long before changed their section name, or that of Lower Egypt, from Gasbia to Cuzetinne, renamed that part of Siloton now known as Egypt, and termed it Kem as the name now appears in hierglyphic, or picture-writing records of Ancient Egypt. The term signified "dark," which not only referred to the dark land, or darkness of the cultivable soil, of Kem, or Egypt, but also referred to the people, who were of a very dark complexion. A striking coincidence—that of a dark section of country, inhabited by a dark race of people. The term "Kem," however, sustained a change of form in the demotic character-writing of Egypt, to that of Kemi, used in a dual sense, and referred to the color of both soil and people. In the hieroglyphic records of Ancient Egypt, the valley of Upper Egypt is termed "to-res," the term meaning "south land," and the plains of Lower Egypt are likewise termed "to-mehit," the term meaning "the north land." The Hebrews termed all Egypt Mizraim; the term being dual, referred to both Upper and Lower Egypt, collectively. Mazor was their name for Lower Egypt, and Pathros for that of Upper Egypt.

In making the ethnographic and philologic connections from Atlantis to Siloton, through Sfury, thus re-establishing and re-extending the facts relative to the above-named principles, or epi-cycles, as they evolved in pre-historic time, we must do so through the great Gasbian dual migration, and its mixed race conditions; e. g., let us begin with the remnant tribe of Schirants from Teltzie Sot, and that of the Atarians from Teltzie Et, of Atlantis, who crossed to Sfury; viz., the remnants of the Atlantian Lontidri, now known as the Cape Verde Islands of the Atlantic Ocean* and their descendants, the Zanranzans and Horziethas who crosses central Sfury, and their descendants, who ultimately became the Kallutheans of Kalluthia.

Likewise, the remnant tribes of Lextelonzes and Cletrezonzes from Teltzie Set, of Atlantis, who crossed to Sfury via: the remnants of Atlantian land, now known as the Azores, the Madeira and the Canary Islands of the Atlantic Ocean, and their descendants, the Keselzas and the Kadioes who crossed northern Sfury, and their descendants who ultimately became the Kasamanzes, of Gasbia, where the blood of the Kalluthians and the Kasamanzes was united by race mixture.

*As was the case with many of the submergences in past time, there were many more islands and necks of land existing as remnants at the time the remnant Atlantian tribes passed over them to Sfury, than at the present, they having been submerged one by one, from time to time, during the ages that have intervened; hence the migration was made possible.

Links and Cycles

Furthermore, in the evolution of the epicycle, their descendants the Cuzetens likewise became the prehistoric ancestors of the Ancient Egyptians, a fact therefore, that connects the Atlantian influences to a certain degree, through the pre-historic Cuzetens, to their ultimate descendants, the Egyptians, which latter are the strongest stock representatives on the continent of Sfury, of the pre-historic and long since submerged Atlantian nation, having thus been characterized by a few broken, remnant links from the ethnographic and philologic epi-cycles as they evolved from Atlantis through the great eastern dual migration, during many pre-historic ages, by which we are able to connect the Atlantian people of the northern and southern Teltzie of the Lontidri, with the Ancient Egyptians ethnographically and philologically.

The Egyptians have retained much of the physical and linguistic characteristics that were possessed by their near ancestors the Cuzetens, but being thus far removed from the cycle of Atlantian greatness, such as characterized certain Teltzie of the Lontidri, especially that of Atara could not therefore, exactly correspond ethnographically or philologically with Atlantis and its peoples generally speaking, but enough of the Atlantian influence has descended through the above named races and their migration, to not only effect the physical appearance of the original Egyptians, but their philologic characteristics as well. Hence it is that, their language and the characters by which it is represented are similar to, and originated from that of the Atlantians.

At the time of the establishment of the Red Sea, when the Wē-zĭn′-thē nation was principally submerged, the remnant portions left on the eastern and western shores of the submerged district, the remnant on the western shore eventually separated and formed themselves into two tribes, the separation being caused by social differences. The cruder, the real seceding tribe, occupied the southwestern border of the sea, which section they termed Sī-wĭn, and called themselves the O′gē-rĕts.

The more intelligent portion of the remnant occupied the northern border of the Sea, which section they termed Yunthrox, and called themselves the Creitons.

The Ogerets of Siwin, and their descendants, became the pre-historic ancestors of the now Bishari tribes of the Eastern Nubians, who at first were characterized with the less civilized conditions of their ancestors, the Ogerets.

The Creitons of Yunthrox, and their descendants, ultimately became the pre-historic ancestors of the now known Ababdeh tribes of the Eastern Nubians, who at first were characterized with the more civilized conditions of their ancestors, the Creitons.

After the establishment of the Kaluthians in Kalluthia, portions of them mixed races with the Ogerets, which fact gave rise to a new tribe who settled in the region of the Gē-lĭ'ŏt Ri'gër (Nile River) between Kaluthia and Gasbia, or Upper and Lower Egypt, which section they termed Gŭstz, and called themselves the Quzetas. They were a race of wild natured people, and treacherous in their dealings with other tribes. In stature, they were about six feet, and were full formed, or stocky in build, and were very muscular. They had quite dark skin; broad flat heads on top; low foreheads; black, and tightly curled hair; very scant beards; considerable short hair on their bodies; large black, full eyes; short, flat, but not broad noses; broad mouths and thick lips that turned up angularly, so as to show their teeth; receeding chins; large, broad and flat hands and feet, with long and flat toes and fingers. In regard to dress, generally speaking, they practised nudity. They had no religious ideas, hence no adorational gatherings or ceremonies. Their descendants became the prehistoric ancestors of the now known Copts, or more properly speaking, Ckoobt or Ckobt of Egypt. The modern Copts have, in a modified sense, retained considerable of the principal characteristics of their immediate ancestors, the Quzetas, and also some influences that date as far back as to the Horziethas, or more remote ancestors of the Quzetas, through the Kalluthians and the Ogerets, hence their dark skins; flattened fore-heads; soft woolly hair; short thick noses; wide mouths and thick lips; large, black, upward bent or angular eyes; high cheek bones; thin beards; bigoted dispositions; sullen temper and faithless characters.

Returning to the northern branch of the great Gasbian migration, we note the folowing ethnographic and philologic influences that arose from the local remnant tribes who did not complete the migration to Gasbia. In the first place, the above named influences were taken into Zē-läs-si-ŏs and Kër'i-wänsk, or the Azores, Maderia, and Canary Islands by the Lextelonzas and the Cletrezonzes of Teltzie Set, Atlantis, where the mixture of each characteristic had its beginning. This condition being established, was farther extended into Cojel number one, or Morocco, by the Keselzas, and their descendants, who ultimately became the prehistoric ancestors of the Mauri (black man), or Mauretanians of Ancient Mauretania, or Mauriessa, who likewise became the ancestors of the Berbers of the Atlas Mountain district of that region, with futher extension to the Shulu, or Shilhas in the southern tracts, and to some extent, to the Moors, who are descendants from the Ancient Mauretanian stock, with an infusion of Arabic and Spanish blood.

The influence was farther carried into Kadio, or Algeria, by the Kadioes of that section, whose descendants became the prehistoric ancestors of the Ancient Numidians (so named from the term *"nomades,"* meaning, in its Latinized form, a wandering tribe), who being of the same stock as the Mauretanians, likewise became the Kabyles of Tunis.

The influence was still extended eastward along the Mediterranean Sea region by the Jeretheans who were the same stock as the Keselzas and the Kadioes, whose descendants became the pre-historic ancestors of the Berbers of Tripoli, and by farther migration, brought the influence into Fezzan.

Again, the same Influence of the Keselzas and the Kadioes spread southward to the southern slopes of the Ze'lăgs (mountains), that then faced the wide expanse of the Great Kä-rŭn'tĭc, or inland sea now the Sahara Desert, whose descendants became the pre-historic ancestors of the Ancient Galtulians of that region, whose further extension is represented by the Twaricks, or Tamashek of the Sahara region.

Returning to the region of northern Algeria and Tunis, the same influence was spread north, and northeast out into Cogel number two, or that part of the submerged country now known as the western half of the Mediterranean Sea, and further into the country now known as Italy, Turkey in Europe, Greece, Asia Minor, etc.

At the time of the convulsions that established the southwestern section of the Mediterranean Sea, a portion of the Jeretheans who had not migrated into the Kĕt'zĭl-ly (plain), of Tĭm-ī-cū'lĕs, east of the Sardinia Islands, or the Ketzilly of Kō-rĕs'sä west of it, with their brethren were left as a remnant in the region of country now known as along the Mediterranean coast from the river Mulucha, or Muluya, east to what is now known as the Carthagenian territory, which section they termed Kĭn-măn'zĕs, and called themselves the Kinmanzes, whose descendants became the pre-historic ancestors of the Ancient Lĭbeyhans, or Libyans, whose further influence extended to the Massyli, on the eastern coast of Numidia, and the Massaesylia on the western, the limit between the two territories being the river Ampsaga which enters the sea to the west of the famous promontory called Tretum, now known as the "Seven Capes," which latter was formed at the time of the second of the ten great convulsions that formed the Mediterranean Sea.. The

Berbers therefore, are a nation of great antiquity, and from the time of pre-historic ages, and of the earliest history, have spread out over the same extant of country, as at the present time, viz: from the Atlantic, to the confines of Egypt, excepting that district now known as submerged by the waters of the Mediterranean Sea.

Through the local and terminal influences of the people who were variously distributed throughout the great Gasbian mirgation, has arisen that branch of philology now known as the Hamitic language which exists in the northeastern corner of Africa and the border-lands of that continent extending westward along the whole shore of the Mediterranean Sea, and southward to beyond the Equator, and falls in three districts, viz: The Ancient Egyptian and its descendant, the Modern Coptic; The Libyan, or Berber languages of Northern Africa; and the Ethiopic languages of eastern Africa. Gasbia, the terminal of the first great dual eastern migration therefore, not only represents the terminal location where the ethnographic influences met, as they had evolved through the first great dual migration, but is also the district where the philologic influences, through the same migration, met and were re-established by the Cuzetens, so far as was possible after the changes they had sustained through migratory and mixed race conditions, who further extended the influences to their descendants the Egyptians, in the region of the delta, and Ketzilly of the Nile, who have held fast to the original influences of their ancestors, the Cuzetens, as they had received them after having been handed down from age to age by the direct line of descendants and migrations from Atlantis to Gasbia. Therefore, the Egyptian language and the characters representing it, are the closest representatives of that of Atlantis in evidence of the philologic re-establishment, and re-extension of that principle must be made on the continent of Africa. In fact, the Egyptian are the only preserved ancient records of the Hamitic language, and bear evidence of the broken epi-cycle that had evolved from Atlantis to Egypt.

The Kalluthians who had retained the influence of the hieroglyphic sculpture or picture representations, such as had been handed down through the southern migration, from the Schirants of Teltzie Sot, and the Atarians from Teltzie Et, through the Zanranzans and Horziethas of central Sfury, further extended the practise to the Cuzetens, and they in turn to the Egyptians, hence, the use of the art in ancient Egyptian monumental records.

Likewise, the Kasamanzes who had retained the influence of

demotic character writing, as handed down through the northern migration, from the Lextelonzes and the Cletrezonzes of Teltzie Set, through the Keselzas and the Kadioes of northern Sfury, further extended the practise to the Cuzetens, and they to the Egyptians, hence the use of that art in common among the ancient Egyptians.

The hieratic character writing was of subsequent origin, having been instituted by the Egyptian priests for sacred use, and was a tachygraph or abridged form of the hieroglyphic signs.

EL'TE-ZE AND RE-IS'TA,
OR
ARABIA AND PERSIA.

TELTZIE XLVI.

Türg'nĕy, was the first pre-historic sectional name of Arabia, so given by the Wē-zĭn'thēse, prior to the formation of the now known Red Sea, which included the area of the latter, and further extended east to the border-lands of Arabia, on its present eastern shore.

Qū-rĕs'tŏn, was its second name, so given by the Rē-zĕn'-dĕths, who were a remnant of the Wezinthese, subsequent to the establishment of the Red Sea, and embraced that portion of Arabia now known as the Province of Hedja Yemen, or Elhejaz.

El'tē-zē was the third, or general name for the entire section of Arabia, so changed and given, about 2000 years before the Adomic period, by A- chē-lĕt', the first pre-historic rule of the Arabian country, which he did at the time he came into the office of ruler. The country, therefore, bore the name of El'tē-zē until about the modern ancient time when it was changed to Arabia.

Returning to the Wezinthes as a nation, we find that during a long period of time subsequent to the formation of the Red Sea, the eastern and western remnants both ultimately, became a numerous people, or great nation occupying two districts, from which other nations subsequently descended. Those of the Eastern division, who dwelt in the high-lands of Turgney, retained that section name as given.

About 6000 years before the Adomic period, the Rezendeths had also descended into a numerous people, at which time various conditions caused dissensions to arise among them, which resulted in a secession of three tribes from the nation, viz: the Ack'rē-deths; the Hĭs'ŏcks; and the I-ŏx'ĕns, who ultimately migrated farther eastward into the high-lands of the section of country now known as Arabia, which they termed Qureston.

A colony of the Rezendeths proper, who were not hostile to their seceding brethren, also migrated to the same section of Qureston, or Arabia, but retained their former name. At that time, the Hisocks recognized an invisible provident source upon which their success in all things depended, especially light, which they recognized as the principal guardian spirit of their general success, which they worshipped usually at sunset, by giving thanks for the day's good. As a symbol or image representing the principle they worshipped, they chose the large wild animal then known as the Wīl-kīe-trē'zē, which was a kind, docile or harmless animal, having short, fine brown hair, and was an inhabitant of the mountain regions. On account of its kind and docile quality of being, it was chosen as the representative of the benevolent spirit. They looked on other animals with fear. They made wooden images of the Wilkietreze, to use in their worship when traveling from place to place, and in localities where the animal did not range.

The Ioxens, like the Hisocks, reverenced light as a great benefactor, but held their devotional exercises at the noon-day hour. Their provident spirit was embodied in the term Quĕl-tĕr-dō'sĕr, meaning All Glorious. Their order of worship was by kneeling at the noon-day hour, whether in assembly, or individually, some even bowing to the earth, when they would repeat the term Quelterdoser over several times, and then arise and depart.

The Ackredeths, like the Hisocks and the Iozens, recognized an invisible provident benevolence, as coming from above, which to them was as a ministering spirit of good to the earth, and especially to them as a people.

The symbol, or image representing this principle, as used by them, was that of a bird, large as the American Eagle. It was very beautiful, its plumage being principally blue, tipped with a golden hue, especially on its back and wings, but its breast was a dove color or light gray. It was a speedy bird, that soared high in the heavens, but came to the earth, and among the people for its food. It was then known as the Its-tē-lō'ny, the term meaning high and low. They recognized it as a wonderful bird, in being able to ascend and descend also, from such great altitudes in flight, seeking the blue, golden, or gray heavens for light, possessing the same hues of plumage, and descending among the people for food, which latter fact was at all times a signal for them to kneel in reverence of the principle it represented.

In all their journeyings, or assembly processions, they carried a captive Itstelony with them, and when the natural bird was not attainable, wooden images were carved, stained, and carried like modern ensigns, in reverence of the religious principle they adored. This was one of the principal examples, from the many, whence Ancient and Modern Idolarty was instituted.

The Rezendeths had no special worship; though, they had a sublime adoration for the grandeur of the rising sun, which they termed Zē-grĭs-tĭl'lĭs, the term meaning Great Light, in recognition of which, it was their custom to either congregate, or to stand individually facing the East, when they saw the first rays of light on the orient sky, and before the disc of the sun was visible, to stand with clasped hands in adoration awaiting the appearance of the wonderful beautiful orb, until it had fully disclosed itself by having arisen above the horizon, when they made obeisance to it, repeated audibly the name Zegristillis, and departed.

In subsequent time, descendants of these colonies, migrated in tribes further eastward. When they left Qureston, they did so via: the central section of the country, for at that time, the northwestern section was an inland sea, then termed Kŭl'tē-zĕn, modernly known as the Syrian Desert area, and the southeastern section was also an inland sea, then termed Al-ăm-thā-iē modernly known as the Great Arabian Desert area. They passed over the section now occupied by the waters of what is now known as the Persian Gulf, which was a subsequent submergence, into the section of country now known as Laristan, southwestern Persia, which section they termed Rŭn-dē-rū'sănd. After a long period of time, they had spread out until they were halted by the waters of an inland sea, which they termed Bĕl-tĕr-thĕr'sē, which occupied the area now known as the Lut Desert.

The original remnants of the Rezendeths, Ackerdeths, Hisocks and Ioxens of the northern and central sections of Qureston, after their descended tribes had migrated eastward, became the ancestors of generations, from whom ultimately descended the now known Mustareb Arabs of the northern section of modern Arabia.

The original remnant of Rezendeths of the southeastern section of Qureston, after ages of intermingling races with their remnant ancestors, the Wezinthese, had descended into a new nation, whose further descendants ultimately became the ancestors of the Pure Arabs of the southern section of modern Arabia.

The Wezinthese, being the ancestors of the Rezendeths, and the ultimate absorption of the former, by the latter, in the sense of race conditions, embodied the characteristics of both in their descendants, which likewise, was re-embodied in the race of Pure Arabs of the south.

The fact that the blood of the Wezinthese and the Renzendeths, through the Ackredeths, the Hisocks and the Ioxens, descended to the northern Arabs, and that of the two first to the southern Arabs, caused the two branches of Arabs to possess physical, mental and linguistic characteristics, which mark their affinity with each other.

The seeming divergences of Asiatic impress between the two races, before they left Qureston, their home country, which was carried further into Asia by the descended, migrating tribes, instead of being re-flected from Asia upon the Arabs, as some modern writers are wont to fix it, e. g., the Rezendeths who migrated to the north, carried their characteristics with them. Their descendants, the Ackredeths, the Hisocks, and the Ioxens, who by means of diverse opinions and characteristics, became separated from their original ancestors, carried their characteristic influence to the peoples of other sections. Ultimately, by the comixture of their remnants with those of the original ancestors, the divergences of opinion possessed by the former descendants, became embodied with that of the characteristics of the latter, which accounts for the existence of the same in the Mustareb Arabs of the north.

The Ackredeths and the Rezendeths who migrated farther into Asia, the descendants of the Hiscocks into Hindustan, and the Ioxens into Persia, etc., carried the above named re-embodied characteristics into those sections; hence, the conditional impress is one of radiation, instead of that of re-flection, as generally accepted and understood by moderns.

Therefore, the Mustareb Arabs, in addition to the above named characteristics of their northern brethern, are diverse from them, in pastoral tendencies, and proneness to nomad life! idiomatic peculiarities, drawing near to the modern Hebrew; strong clannish inclinations, and disposition to oppose regal power, or settled comprehensive organization. Their history, institutions, past and present, are identical, so far as basic principles are concerned, with those of their southern brethren, and have appeared in the traits of the Hebrew, Syrian, Chaldean and other descendants of modern times.

Thus we find in the modern Arabs, the Ahl Bedoo, or as commonly known, the Bedouin, who dwell in the open land, under tents in a vast circle of country, between the coast and the central plateau joining the Syrian Desert on the north, and the Ahl Hadr, or dwellers in fixed localities.

Subsequently, the Ioxens migrated to the northwest, followed the mountains modernly known as the Pushtikoh range, which they termed A-lĕn'cō, the term meaning a long low range, into the section now known as Luristan, which section they termed Si-ä'zä, and called themselves the Cĭl'zys.

About 4000 years subsequent to the submergence of Atlantis,

there occurred two sectional convulsions between the countries now known as Egypt and Arabia, that were simultaneous with each other. At that time there was a Kĕd-yĕd'tŏn Dŏsh (Wezinthian term for Mountain Range), then known as the Skĕn'sĭc, that extended south and southeast from the section now known as the Sinaitic Peninsula, between the now known Gulfs of Suez and Aden, to which the now known mountains Horeb and Sinai belong, to the now known straits of Bab-el-mandeb, at the entrance of the Gulf of Aden.

A large Kĕt-sē-ä'nŏ (valley), then known as the Gĕn-dĕl-cä'-tō, lay extent on the eastern central side of the Skensic Dosh. Another large Ketseano, then known as the Gĕn'dē-grăf, lay extent on the western central side of the Skensic Dosh.

A large Rĕnz (Lake) also, then known as the Skensic (named after the Kĕd-yĕd-tŏn'zē) lay extent between two large Kedyedtonze, in the Skensic Dosh, about 26 deg's. N. Lat. whose waters were red. That color also characterized the rocks of the Kedyedtonze in that section. In fact, to a greater or less extent, throughout the entire Dosh. The soil also possessed the same quality, hence the Kedyedtonze were termed the same as the lake, a term which meant red in the Wezinthean language.

The principal one of the two sectional convulsions had place in the Skensic Dosh, at a point about 20 degrees N. Lat. The force of the convulsion sank the main portion of the Dosh, N. northwest, and S. southeast of the point of the convulsion, and submerged the Ketseanoze of Gendelcato and Gendegral, thus establishing that portion of the Dĕg'ī-lĕt Sē'ziē (later term for Red Sea). The present coast line of the Red Sea, however, was further established by many small convulsions and submergences that have occurred from time to time, during the ages that followed the sectional convulsions above mentioned.

The other one of the two sectional convulsions had place in the now known section of Syria, near the location of the present city of Gaza. The force of that convulsion, which was of a subterrene order, extended southward until it met the force of the principle convulsion, which latter was extending northward, at the northern extremity of the Skensic Renz, where the conjunction of forces and mingling of fire and water, caused a re-action of the forces, and the force of the principal convulsion spent itself in the further establishment of the Gulf of Aden, and the other forces, by reaction, established the Gulf of Suez.

For the first 5000 years after the estableshment of the Red Sea. no material life existed in its waters, from the fact that, they contained from twenty-five to thirty different strong mineral solutions that were washed in from the surrounding Kenyedtonze, and also from its sub-terranean sources, that impregnated the waters to such an extent as to establish a liquid compound in which no material life could exist; but, about the time above mentioned, material life began to make its appearance, a condition that was brought about by a subterrene convulsion that occurred partially beneath the area of the Sea, and the country to the west of it. This let in waters from the Atlantic sources on the west side, which came in through subterrene streams, thus weakening the mineral compound, and the poisonous effect which from that time to the present, rendered life possible in the Red Sea waters.

The Sea is characteristized with its coloring by subterranean influences, as is the Ocean by subterrene salt beds. It is an inland Sea, with no visible tributaries. The water comes up from the bottom through a peculiar mineral substance that gives it its specific coloring. There is nothing on the earth's surface just like the soil, or material through which the water passes on its way into the body of the sea. There is an immense quantity of that material embedded in the earth beneath this body of water, and it is a formation which has been established by volcanic eruptions far beneath the surface of the earth. The peculiar color has been given it through metamorphic conditions, or burning of the earth formations. The time will come when the Sea will be lost again as such, through the volcanic conditions that still are breeding and developing beneath its surface.

The unhealthful condition of the country surrounding this Sea, is caused by a miazma that comes from the water, that is produced by volcanic fires beneath the earth's surface. The fires, even now, are very near the surface, and the time is near at hand when an eruption will take place, that will be considered of a very peculiar nature. Lava will be thrown up, that in subsequent time will be much sought after, as was the case with similar eruptive material in Atlantis, by the Atlantians, it being very useful for both ornamental and substantial constructing purposes. It will vary in color, thus established through the influence of heat and motion, such as will make it very attractive in appearance. You may go from one eruptive condition to another of the past, so continuing to do, and you will find no two whose remnant deposits of lava, or erupted material are characterized with exactly the same coloring; hence, the specific influences that exist in the various localities, will each develop their own specific colorings.

An Egyptian spirit geologist, whom Alem Prolex brings

to us, by the name of Gĕlt'mŭs, speaks as follows:—"As a spirit, who has studied largely into metamorphic conditions, I say unto you that, by this process, all minerals are characterized with color, either primarily, or by subsequent influences arising from the primary condition; hence, you can better understand the formation and coloring processes that have established the Minerals and Gems of your own mountains, and qualified them as such. Coming through different stratas of earth, the lava partakes of the color of these stratas of earth. This, with its own heat combined, form the ultimate color. This principle applies to all minerals. Each has a certain condition through which it has to pass during the process of formation; hence, the varieties of mineral products. Perhaps you can understand better by an illustration, e. g., you can recognize the impregnated qualities of different springs of water, through the sense of taste. The springs receive their characteristics by coming in contact with the same conditions that qualify the minerals. Passing through crevices, and rocks, some of the fluids are retained in holes, or basins containing those mineral qualities, and by the retention they are thus impregnated and ultimately find their way into, and mingle with the water of the springs.

"As to crystals, they are formed by slow dripping, or the dropping of water containing certain mineral qualities; but, conditioned by having been filtered through clear sand, such as contains no sediments, or coloring material, which thus produces a pure crystal.

"Crystals having a symmetrical shape, and packed together as if so placed by means of human hands, were so arranged by means of circulating air that passed through and around them during the process of formation.

"Stalactites and stalagmites, such as have place in the great caverns or caves of earth, were formed and qualified with color by the same process, in accord with the perculation, pendant flow and dripping of the impregnated water, and those of the crystal form, by non-impregnated water that finds its way into their confines.

"Colors sometimes blend with clear srystals, which condition has been caused by the influence of rays of light, that thousands of years ago, during their formation, penetrated the liquid substance.

"The Moss Agate is formed by the finest of mosses being caught and imbedded in the crystalizing mass as the drippings fall to form them, or as they lie in the impregnated water. Since the varities in the mineral kingdom are, to a greater or less extent, due to the conditions of water and air that surround them during the period of their hardening, so it is with the Agate.

"Topaz is formed where the water has been impregnated with sulphuric conditions, produced by volcanic action. The erupted lava lying in the impregnated water, becomes colored through the process of crystalization, or hardening, thus forming the topaz.

"By these, and other evidences manifest in the formation of minerals, and precious stones, you may better understand the meaning of the term, 'Nature's God,' or Nature's process in formation, by its working laws.

"There is no art so beautiful as that of Nature. From this manifestation, man may catch glimpses of the inner, or infinite expression, which is in harmony with Nature's wonderful outward demonstrations. So much beauty and grandeur is imbedded within the extended forms of the mountain ranges; beneath the waves of the oceans and the seas; and far out into space, beyond the vision of the mortal eye, therefore, the human conception of realities, such as exist in the general sense of the term, is meagre indeed, and the knowledge of man thereby, greatly retarded."

THE GREAT TISH'HANS OF A'ZOFF AND NA-SEN'DO, AND THE EL-RE'ZOX SE-ZIE'.

A'zoff was the pre-historic name of the northern portion of the then known section, or Tishhans (valleys), the area of which is now submerged by the waters of the Arabian Sea, such as the sections or Gulf of Oman, Cambay and Cutch, and centrally between Arabia and India in that latitude.

Nä-sĕn'dō was the pre-historic name of the southern portion, or great Tishhan that had place centrally between Africa and South Arabia on the west, and India on the east, between the tenth and twentieth degrees N. Lat., or from Cape Guardafui, Northeast Africa, to Cape Comorin in Southeast India, thus embracing the western branch of the great Tishhan of Nasendo, now submerged by the waters of the Gulf of Aden.

Prior to the submergence, however, the term Azoff was discontinued for the northern portion of the section between India and Hindustan, or India, when the term Nasendo was adopted, and used as embracing the entire country now submerged by the waters of the Arabian Sea, and so remained until the time of the submergence.

About 2000 years, subsequent to the submergence of Atlantis, a system of five periodical convulsions began in the region of what is now known as the Arabian Sea section.

Prior to the convulsions, the country of the coast line of the Arabian Sea, was bordered by a low range of zig-zag mountains, with occasional high peaks, then known as Lă-plă-lĭn'gō, that extended in conformity with the modern coast line from the now known Gulf of Cambay, Hindustan in the east, to Cape Fartak, Arabia, in the west. Another range of the mountains, not named, extended from the now known Cape Guardafui, Africa, east and south in conformity with the extension of the then known Laplalingo range, thus embracing the islands now known as Abd-elkuri and the Socotra. Low short ranges and spurs extended southwest from the Laplalingo range, that terminated in the great Tishhan Nasendo, which latter extended south, thus blending into the area of country in its extent to the shores of what was then known as the Squä'shä (meaning big water), now known as the Indian Ocean.

The first of these four periodical convulsions had place southwest of the now known Cape Fartak, in one of the highest peaks belonging to the Laplalingo range, in a cross section that extended from Cape Fartak, to the now known Cape Guardafui, Africa, that formed a junction with the head of the then known Păl-tō-ē'sĕr, and the Un'rand range that extended from Cape Guardafui. The force of the convulsion extended west, thus forming the now known Strait of Bab-el-Mandeb, and the Arabian and African coast-lines of that section, and east from the coast-line, as far as to Cape Mandraki, southeast from this point, and east of the Paltoeser range, to the Tishhhan then known as Mä-sĕn'dō.

The second of the five periodical convulsions occurred about fifty years subsequent to the first, and had place at Cape Guardafui, Africa. The force of the convulsion extended along the Unrand range, south to the then coast line of the Squasha Sezie, thus leaving the islands now known as Abd-el-kuri and Socotra, as their remnants, thus letting the waters in from the Squasha Sezie, which established them as such, and submerged the section of the first convulsion, which completed the establishment of the Gulf of Aden, and inundated the southwestern portion of the then known Tishhan of Masendo. The force also established the eastern coast line from Guardafui, south to about two degrees north of the Equator.

The third of the five periodical convulsions occurred about one hundred years subsequent to the second, and had place in the western section of what is modernly known as the Gulf of

Oman. The force of the convulsion established the southern coast of what is modernly known as the province of Beloochistan, in Asia, from the mouth of the now known Indus river, in the east, to, and including the now known straits of Ormuz, which latter condition connected the then known fresh water lake of Sē-zē-quē'zăn, to the now known Gulf of Oman, when the lake became what is modernly known as the Persian Gulf, and further established the coast of Arabia, from the northwest point of the Persian Gulf, as far south, and southwest, as to the now known Cape Mandraki, and then southeast into the then known Tish-han of Mă-sĕn'dō, which further admitted the waters of the Squasha Sezie, from a line running southwest and south from the then known mouth of the Indus river, to the border line of the first periodical convulsion.

The fourth of the five periodical convulsions occurred about a hundred and seventy-five years subsequent to the third, and had place in the region now known as the Gulf of Cutch. The force of the convulsion extended northwest and west to the line of the third periodical convulsion, and southwest to the Tishhan of Masendo, and thus established the western coast line of Hindustan, from northwest of the now known Cutch peninsula to the vicinity of what is now known as Bejapore, on the Malabar, or western coast of India, and further established the Sea district, to and southeast of Bejapore.

The fifth of the periodical convulsions occurred about one hundred years subsequent to the fourth, and had place on the Malabar, or eastern coast of India, south of what is now known as the old town of Gad. At that time a range of mountains, then termed Lū-kĭ'dĭsh, extended from that section of India, southward, which now, by its remnant, forms the Laccadive and the Maldive Islands. The force of the convulsions followed the northern remnant of the Lukidish range, to the establishment of the Laccadive Islands, and submerged the land between them and the now known coast of India, from the point of the convulsion to that of the convulsion that formed the Maldive Islands, above mentioned.

The fifth periodical convulsion, therefore, with a few smaller ones that occurred subsequently, along the coast of the countries bordering the Arabian sea, completed the establishment of the above-named sea, and blended its waters in their conjunction with those of the great Squasha Sezie, ultimately known as that of the Indian Ocean, and the Arabian Sea.

Prior to the establishment of the El-rē'zŏx Sē-ziē' migrators (but not in tribes) from the eastern, western and northern sections of country, had inhabited or settled in families throughout the tish-hans of Azoff, and Masendo, and in portions of the mountainous sections, where they dwelt as rural peoples for many ages, but never established any particular nation, or built any hamlets of note, notwithstanding they became mixed as a race of people by various inter-marrying.

Si-ä'zä was the first pre-historic name of Persia, so given by the Ioxens, who first settled in that section.

Rē-ĭs'tä was the second pre-historic name of Persia, so changed and given by the Cĭl'zys (descendants of the mixed race of Rezendeths and Ioxens) and so remained until it was further changed to Persia, or Persis, by the ancient Parsas; ultimately to Persia, by the Achaemenian Monarchs who came forth from Persia.

When the Ioxens or Cilzys reached their destination, they found the country inhabited by a very crude race of people whom they termed Tō-lū'ciēs, who had inhabited the southern section of that part of the country for ages. They were descendants of the Zil-lē'zōs of Săb-măn'thä (pre-historic people of the Norwegian section), who migrated from that cold climate, southward, in search of greater warmth. When they began their migration from Sabmantha, they were quite a large tribe, but finally, when they reached the region where many ages later they were invaded by the Ioxens, there were but three males and two females left, who had survived the hardships of the migration; but at the time the Ioxens entered their land, they had multiplied to the number of a large tribe. During their migration and establishment in the section of Luristan, they had greatly degenerated both physically and mentally. They had bodies that much resembled that of a modern bear, but their heads were more in likeness of the human race. They had grown wild and ferocious. The greater portion of them became extinct by the hands of the Ioxens in battle, which latter was the first of the many conflicts entered into by the Ioxen nation.

The Cilzys and their descendants became the pre-historic ancestors of the Persian people, and being a mixed race from three distinct peoples, were therefore physically conditioned accordingly. In stature they were generally about six feet in height, broad-shouldered, bony and muscular; in color, they would compare favorably with the modern quadroons; their eyes were dark brown generally, though some were very dark gray; their hair was black, kinky and matted; their beards black and thick; their lips were thick, mouth broader than the modern Negro; their teeth large, wide and prominent; their noses differed.

Some were heavy and broad, while some were more on the aquiline order; they were very quick to learn, especially by their own observation, hence progressed rapidly. They might have been called an intellectual people, naturally; they might also be said to have had classical natures, a fact that caused them to develop along those lines in their latter time as a distinct people, or before they were lost in the mixed race that followed their blood union with the Esgenens, which latter condition was reached about 1000 years subsequent to the coming of the Cilzys into Esgenenex. As a people, generally speaking, they were quite peaceable.

In regard to dress, they manufactured fibres into a kind of cloth or texture which they used to manufacture into raiment. The women wore but one garment; this was sort of a narrow, loose gown that hung down from the neck and shoulders, to half way below the knees. The men had two styles of dress. First, some wore a loose narrow jacket, that came down below the thighs. Some, in addition to the jacket, which was not as long as the former named, wore a narrow skirt that hung from beneath the jacket. A few, however, wore the skirt without the over jacket. Both males and females dressed their feet with what they called brō-kī'ĕsh. This was formed by wrapping the feet and lower limbs, to the upper part of the calf, with the same material as that used in making their garments, which was held in place by cross wrapping and twining the same with a sort of cord, that terminated by being tied around the upper part of the brokiesh. The huntsmen wore brokiesh made from skins of animals, with the hair shaved off, and were laced and tied with leather or skin cords. In addition to the manufacture of cloth for their garments, they also made rugs and mats, by combining grasses and fibres in the process of plaiting, while only fibres were used in the manufacture of the cloth.

The Cilzys of Siaza were an idolatrous people. At first they worshipped Nature, such as landscapes—particularly the mountainous portions of the country—and the very large trees, one variety in particular, which they termed Chăn'sēse, and was characterized with drooping limbs, like the modern willow, was considered sacred by them, and they made obeisance whenever they passed it.

Their shrine was in the form of an arch, made of trees, vines and flowers, so planted as to possess a rock background, usually against the mountain side, on which was carved, or drawn, a coarse, crude, massive face, which was to represent their God Principle. This they termed Sĭn-glī-ō'tī, meaning the Great

Worker, which they thought was the builder of the hills, mountains, and all Nature's landscape scenes. They also had small shrines, varying in size, and in local places, but the above-named large shrine was for public assemblies. The specified time for the general assembly was at the evening hour, but more especially on the evening of the full moon. The order of their adorational exercises was to bow low before the shrine, rise again, turning the body facing the moon, when it was visible, gesticulating with their hands and body in a joyful manner, keeping time to a chant or sort of hymn, that was more like groanings and grunts than music. Individuals visited the shrine daily, especially if they had grief or sorrow of any kind. When the sorrow was of such a nature as to interest several individuals, then they went in groups or families. They were very devoted to their religious beliefs and ceremonies. At the side of the shrine a reservoir of water was always placed, or, when possible, a natural spring or stream of water was there located, from which they drew the water and sprinkled all around the shrine before entering into the form of services. This was to convey the idea of cleansing and purity. They likewise sprinkled themselves before entering the shrine for worship.

After the generations who worshipped the principle of Singlioti, the term representing the builder of landscape scenery was changed to that of Yăl'ly, meaning a Great Force, greater than that of Singlioti, that created all things visible in the universe. The term Yally was continued by their descendants in the Esgenen nation, into which, by blood mixture, the Cilzys were ultimately lost, as before mentioned, until about the immediate pre-historic period of time that preceded the modern ancient.

The physical condition of the four nations at the time their further migrations were established from Siaza, was as follows The Ioxens of Siaza averaged in stature about six feet. Some were fleshy, and others slender. Their skins were a dull black; their hair was black, curly and shaggy, and extended down to their shoulders; their eyes were black, large and full; their noses were flat and broad; their lips were thick and their ears large; their feet were narrow through the instep, their heels broad and projecting backwards, and the foot was broad across the toes; their hands were quite large, their fingers long and tapering, and considerably spread apart.

The Rezendeths of Siaza averaged from five to six feet in stature, the former height prevailing. They were small in body, but their heads were massive, so to speak, in comparison. They had black skins; coarse black, shaggy hair, though it would have been straighter if it had been properly cared for; their eyes were black; their features coarse; ears large and flabby, and they wore full beards; their feet were long and broad; hands short, but broad and large. They were a wandering people, and not generally hostile; but would protect themselves when wandering from the attack of other peoples. In warm climates or weather, most of them went nearly nude; but when it was cold they used the skins of such animals as they were able to obtain, which they wore with the fur next to their bodies. The skins were worn in two parts; viz., one about the loins and waist, and another about their shoulders.

The Hisocks of Siaza averaged in stature from about five and a half to six and a half feet. They were large-boned and quite muscular in build. Their skins were a dull black; their hair black, curly or bushy; their eyes black, small and deep set; their eyebrows and lashes were heavy; their foreheads narrow, low and retreating; their noses broad and flat; mouths large, and lips thick; ears normal in size; some wore beards and some did not; and their bodies were characterized, on certain parts, with considerable hair, which was soft, silky, and glossy. Their feet were quite large, flat, broad and bony; their hands large, and fingers long. In regard to dress, they generally went nude in warm weather, but in the cold, they wore skins wrapped about their loins and shoulders.

The Ackredeths of Siaza, averaged in stature about six feet, and in physique were broad, bony, muscular and very strong. Their complexions were a little lighter, and features somewhat better, generally speaking, than those of their neighbors, the Rezendeths, a fact having arisen from conditions in descendancy, which had their origin at the time of their withdrawal from the main tribe of Rezendeths in Qureston, influenced by the fact that the lighter complexioned, straighter-haired and finer-featured of the Rezendeths, became thereby clannish in disposition, and therefore at the time of the contentions that made the other divisions, seceded under the title of Ackredeths. Their hair was straight, and of both brown and black color. Their eyes were black or brown; the males wore full, regular beards; their noses were large and prominent; mouths broad and lips pouched; their ears were wide at the top, and extended back beyond a normal size; their hands were normal in size, feet broad and insteps high. They were a very peaceable people, unless wronged by others, when they would fight for justice, or their rights. They were great lovers of anything that bore the semblance of music. Everything was utilized from which they could produce tones, or sounds of any kind, the latter condition being in the majority, that more often terminated in hideous noises, rather than music. The non-musical sounds were employed mostly as a means by which they assembled the people on important occasions.

They plaited their hair into fabrics, that in the process of construction, they characterized with ornamental designs, or patterns. These fabrics they wore across their breasts, or over their shoulders, but wore furred skins about the waist and loins. Later on, they learned to make cloth from fibres, which they ornamented with a fringe by letting the warp extend beyond the woof, or woven edge of the cloth. The fringe was then stained so as to hang in stripes, in harmony with the ornamental patterns of the fabric.

Subsequent to the general migration of the Ioxens to Luristan, and the original stock of Rezendeths, Hisocks, and Ackredeths from the section modernly known as Fars, to their northern homes, small remnants of each nation remained in the Fars, and the section now known as Laristan, who in subsequent time blended by mixture, into one race, at which time a portion of them also came in touch with some of the tribes of Cilzys, with whom they also mixed races, which had a tendency to make some physical changes in the above-named peoples, before their migrations to other parts of the world.

Ultimately, the descendants of the last-named mixed race established a migration to the northwest, when they followed along the western foothills of the mountain system that now separates Turkey and Persia, until they had arrived about thirty-six degrees north latitude and about forty-three degrees longitude east from Greenwich, when they left the mountain range, and passed westward into the valleys, until they came to the junction of the now known Zab tributary with the Tigris river. Here they halted for a time in the section now known as the site of the old Nimrud Ruins, from whence they permanently settled in the vicinity of the now known city of Mosul, from which location they spread out northwest, through that portion of the Tigris valley, where ultimately they became a large nation.

In subsequent time, their principal city which they termed Căl'vŭs was located on the site where now the city of Mosul has place. Their descendants became the pre-historic ancestors of the great nation of Kurds, and their close allies, or offshoots, who occupy the great mountain tracts of Kurdistan, and certain sections of Turkey and Persia, etc.

From the fact that the general migratory line of all the tribes and colonies, from the time of the final submergence of Atlantis to the meeting and separation of the Rezendeths, the Hisocks, the Ackredeths and Ioxens in Siaza, that section is the link between the East and the West, which welds pre-historic and antequated migratory conditions, to those of the modern or present time.

Subsequent to the departure of the Hisocks on their migration from their Rŭn-dē-rū'sand (Laristan), a remnant of their tribe in Runderusand became slightly mixed with stragglers from the remnants of the Rezendeths and Ackredeths from the Fars section. Ultimately, the descendants from this mixed condition became the pre-historic ancestors of the tribes in the interior of Laristan, now known as the Mezaijan, the Bekoi, and the Tahuna, having place ethnographically, between the Tajiks, and the Kurds. This fact is easily accounted for by comprehending the various migratory and mixed race conditions, which we have given of the four nations or peoples, viz., the Rezendeths, the Ackredeths, the Hisocks and the Ioxens, from the section of Arabia and Laristan, Fars, etc. Though originally from one race, the Rezendeths, had changed in many ways physically and otherwise, from livelihood and local conditions, together with those of the descending generations, which had their effect upon the several individual nations, and their ultimate descendants, who likewise were under physical changes from the same causes, etc.

Subsequent to the establishment of the Ioxens in Luristan, descendants of the Rezendeths and the Ackredeths migrated from Runderusand or Laristan to the vicinity of Luristan, or the home of the Ioxens. The Ioxens, fearing that their section of the country might eventually be possessed by the invaders, instituted wars against them, which ultimately resulted in the expulsion of the Rezendeths and the Ackredeths from their Siaza home, or the Luristan section, when they established a migration northeastward, to the highlands of the now known country of Persia, or via the western border of the Gerest, or then known inland sea, now the area or country known as the Great Salt Desert. Here they first settled along the foothills of the mountain system that separates the now known province of Mazanderan, from those of Khorassan and Irak Ajami, at the point of the dividing line between the latter two provinces, which section they termed Hō'ĕt, and called themselves the Kā-lăc'ā-dives. The term meant secession; i. e., "Kalac" meant secession, and "Adive" meant a separation of the people into sections of both hamlet and country.

Subsequently, their principal city, which they termed Hăs'sēs, was located in a large valley northeast of the now known town of Semnoon. After a generation, when the main colonies of the Rezendeths and Ackredeths, or the two branches of the Kalaccadives migrated further eastward. The remnants of the two races blended into one, by mixture, when their descendants became the pre-historic ancestors of the Persian race proper.

Links and Cycles

GU'LEM, KEL-THE'DAT NUD KE-I-EL-WI'THE, OR TURKEY, AFGHANISTAN AND BALUCHISTAN.

TELTZIE XLVII.

Gū-'lĕm, was the first pre-historic name of the entire section of country east and south-east of the now known Taurus Mts., known as Turkey in Asia, so given by the mixed race of Cĭl-'zys and Es'gē-nĕns, and so remained until it was changed at the beginning of modern ancient time.

Subsequent to the formation of the now known Mediterranean Sea, from fear of further submergence, a large colony of the Rezendeth people migrated from the north highlands of their ancestral home, into the extreme south-western section of what is now known as Syria.

In subsequent time and at various intervals, their descend ants migrated along the waters of the Mediterranean Sea, northwestward through the section now known as Syria, leaving remnants at various points, until, ultimately, the last colony had reached the southern boundary of the Taurus mountains, which they termed Văc'kŏns, called themselves the Es'gē-nĕns in honor of their leader, and therefore termed the country Es-gē-nĕn'ĕx. The mountains were termed Vackons, after an animal of that name, that inhabited them, which they utilized for their principal food.

Subsequent to the time that the Esgenens became established in Esgenenex, a colony of Cilzys established a migratory system from their home in Siaza or Persia, northwestward, halting for a time at various points, where they left remnants and established new tribes of descendants, until the last tribe had arrived in the same vicinity already occupied by the Esgenens.

The original Esgenens of Esgenenex were not as fine a race of people as were the Cilzys. In regard to their physical condition, they were very similar to their ancestors, the Rezendeths. They were very quarrelsome among themselves, would even kill their own wives and children, or other females of the colony. For weapons, they used clubs with stone heads, or axes. Being the stronger of the two peoples physically, they outlived the Cilzys by race absorption; but ultimately the descended tribes from this mixture became in every way a finer race of people than were their ancestors, the Esgenens, and their general appearance was much more like that of the Cilzys. A strange fact was that when the Cilzys and Esgenens intermarried, if the female was of the former people, and the male of the latter, their offspring were of a much finer type than when the condition was reversed. This fact was caused by the males being the stronger physically.

The Esgenens, like most of the pre-historic peoples, lived to advanced ages, that ranged from one hundred years upward. They wore furred skins about their loins and thighs, and sometimes across their backs and breasts.

The original colony of Rezendeths who ultimately became the Esgenens of Esgenenex, were thus established about 5500 years before the Adomic period. Being of the pure original stock, they retained the characteristics of their ancestors, as nearly as was possible, by strict descendancy, during so many ages; a fact due to their isolation from other peoples or nations, so far as intermingling of races is concerned, up to the time of the invasion of the Cilzys into Esgenenex, which latter-named people ultimately became lost, as a race, in that section, by intermarriage with the Esgenens. The descendants of this amalgamated or blended condition of the two peoples, became the pre-historic ancestors of the ancient Cilicians, whose further descendants became the Modern Ancient Turks proper.

The Cilicians, the Cappadocians, the Syrians and the Turks proper, have their identity as descendants from the same original stocks, viz., the Cilicians and the Turks from the Esgenens of Esgenenex, which latter were descendants from the Rezendeths and the Cilzys, the latter being descendants from the Ioxens of Siaza or Persia. The Cappadocians proper, from the Esgenens and Rezendeths, and the Syrians proper, from the remnant Rezendeths who were migrating into Esgenenex, and the mixed race of Esgenens and Cilzys who migrated into the valleys south of Esgenenex, and east of the now known Cyprus Island, who were left as remnants in Syria, at the time of the establishment of the eastern portion of the now known Mediterranean Sea.

From the fact that the modern Turks and the Mongolian races are similar to each other in regard to ethnographic and linguistic conditions, and possess characteristics similar to each other, a link is thus established that proves their indubitable affinity, which exists in the fact that the Turks are descendants from the Rezendeths and Ioxens, and the Mongolians from the

Rezendeths and Ackredeths, the Rezendeth influence being the strongest.

Furthermore, minglings of the Hisocks, Ackredeths and Ioxens, with the Rezendeths throughout Qureston, or Arabia, and in the vicinity of Runderusand, or Laristan, also some of the characteristics of the Hisocks, whose descendants ultimately peopled India, and migrated to the eastern Islands from thence, as well as from the eastern coast of the Pacific, through the Lăz'-ĕr-ĕnds and the Kĕn'tĕr-sĕnds, are found in the Turks and the Mongolians.

The Cilzys of Esgenenex, while they had no adorational assemblies, erected no images or idols, and had no modes of worship, yet, like the Indians who worship "The Great Spirit," supposed that some great invisible being, like unto themselves, ruled over them and all things visible in nature, and was also the builder or creator, and therefore controller of the same. Being of the cruder portion of the Cilzys of Siaza, who migrated to Esgenenex, they did not hold to the full idea of their kindred of Siaza.

The Esgenens of Esgenenex, originally, had no religious aspirations, but after the Cilzys had become absorbed or blended into the former nation by mixture, the religious ideas of the latter had an influence upon the Esgenens and their descendants, a condition that lasted for many generations after the Cilzys were lost as a distinct nation.

MIGRATION OF THE ESGENENS.

In subsequent time, the descendants of the mixed race of Cilzys and Esgenens separated into various tribes, who instituted migrations into all parts of the country now known as Turkey in Asia, excepting that portion now known as Bagdad.

Subsequent to the formation of the Island now known as Cyprus, dissensions and wars broke out between the lower and higher classes of the Esgenens in the southern section of Gū'lĕm, or Turkey, when a small tribe of the lower class crossed to the Island of Cyprus, by passing over the smaller islands that then existed between the now known northern coast of Cyprus and the main land of Gulem, that were remnants of the southern portion of the now known Taurus mountains, subsequently submerged, therefore now unknown. After a time, they termed the Island Tĕr'sē-sĕnd, and called themselves the Tĕr'sĕx. They were a very peculiar people, of little civilization, but being quite prolific, soon became a large colony. They were, in height, from five to six feet; large-boned and muscular, and had dark skins. Their heads were large; foreheads low; their cheek bones high; eyes black or brown, and deeply set; their hair and beards were black or brown, straight and of medium length; their lips were thick; noses quite flat; ears large, and extending backward at the top, and were characterized by considerable hair on the outer rims of the lobes, and protruding from the inner part of the ear. Their bodies, also, were heavily suited with hair, especially under the arms and about the loins, it being long enough to take the place of garments with which to shield the private parts of the body; their necks were short, and when walking they stood very erect; they were quick and active in movement; very passionate; had no civilization, and spoke a very peculiar language. They went nude at all times, and lived on nature's supplies, such as fruits, nuts, fish and animal flesh.

The first mixture that occurred in their race was with a tribe of Rezendeths, who came among them from Rē-ī-ĕn'dē (Candia Island), which ultimately resulted in their further degeneration, a condition that lasted until migrators came in from the now known country of Syria, at which time, through mixed descendants, they began to rise again from their degenerate conditions. A fact that is known to exist with peoples, as is the case with the animal races, viz: through race mixture, the descendants will at times, either advance or retrograde, generally speaking, in accord with the ruling circumstances and conditions. They had very little religious conception, hence no manifestation of that principle was carried out by them.

Subsequent to the submergence and formation of the section modernly known as the eastern portion of the Mediterranean Sea, a large tribe of Esgenens from Gulem, or Turkey, had migrated to a large valley that then lay extent between the now known section of Rut, Syria, and the Cyprus Island, which they termed Sē-dē-zĕl'lä, the term meaning Valley of Silence, and retained their former name of Esgenens.

At the time of the submergence that established the eastern portion of the Mediterranean Sea, a large remnant of the Esgenens of Sedezella were left upon the western coast of Rut, Syria, who subsequently began a migration southward through the now known section of Palestine, to the section now occupied by the waters of the now known Dead Sea, which section they termed Phī-nē'ä, and called themselves the Phī-ăn-ē'ci-äns, in honor of their leader whose name was Phī-ăn-ē'cī-ä; a term, however, that sustained some change in its extension into Modern Ancient time, but only in an orthographic sense, viz: to Phoenicia, and Phoenicians.

Links and Cycles

At the time of the formation of the Red Sea, a large portion of the Phianecians were lost by the convulsion and submergence, though a small remnant was left in its eastern border, and a large one on the western; these ultimately became the pre-historic ancestors of the Phoenicians of modern ancient history. The Phianecians of Phianecia were about six feet in height. They had large frames, and were heavily built; their color was that of a greenish yellow; their heads were broad through the temples and heavy through the back brain; foreheads quite high; hair a dark brown, chestnut or black, and long and straight; their beards were soft and silky; eyes black, brown, dark blue, or hazel, and large and expressive; their noses were long thin and sharp, but turned up some at the point; their ears were normal; feet quite large and flat, and their toes long; their hands and fingers were the same. They wore long, loose garments that extended down from the neck, somewhat in the Grecian style, and were made from a soft texture, wrought from hair and fibres. They thought themselves to be the chosen people. They believed in a great ruling force, which they termed I'thē-kä, meaning Protecting Spirit, from which origin has been re-embodied the idea of a personal God of ancient and modern times. They erected an idol or image to represent the Itheka principle, which was formed by seven perpendicular, hexagonal shafts of wood, six of which stood circling the seventh, or central one, which latter was the taller, on the front of which was carved the image of a man in full form, who thus symbolized the spirit of Itheka. The stated times for their adorational exercise were not regular. They were held by appointment as the occasion demanded. When the exercises were held, they were opend by all the people bowing before the image of Itheka, each offering thanks for his or her protection and benefit, as the case demanded. This was then followed by a great feast, after which they departed for their homes. Small images of Itheka, in likeness of the public ones, were made and placed in the homes of the people for private use. As a people, generally speaking, the Phianecians were highly civilized. They cultivated the fields, built their homes and public structures out of stone and a sort of brick, where the former was not of easy access, which they had learned to manufacture.

Prior to the time that the Esgenens, from whom the Adomic races descended (see account of Gontheole), a colony of the Esgenens from Esgenenex migrated southeast, until they came to the Euphrates river, when they continued their migration down along its western shore until they reached the section about thirty-two and a half degrees north latitude, and forty-four and a half degrees longitude, east from Greenwich, where they settled, termed the section Jī'ĕn, or that vicinity in which the now known town of Hillah has place and called themselves the Him'mā-lēs.

Subsequently, a tribe of their descendants migrated further up the Euphrates, to about thirty-four and a quarter degrees north latitude, and forty-two and a quarter degrees longitude east from Greenwich, or in the vicinity of the now known town of Zibda, where they settled. They termed the section An-dē-lă-tō'lĕt, and called themselves the Mā-zā-tĭl'lē-ăns.

Another tribe of the Himmales, from Jien, migrated northeast to the Tigris river, to about thirty-three and a half degrees north latitude, and forty-four and a half degrees longitude, east from Greenwich, or into the vicinity of the now known town of Bagdad, which section they termed Lā-măn'tō, and retained their former name of Himmales.

Another tribe of Himmales migrated southeast from Jien, down the Euphrates river, to about thitry-one degrees north latitude and forty-six degrees longitude, east from Greenwich, or in the vicinity of the now known town of Abu Kuba, which section they termed Zū-yi-thē'ŭs and called themselves the Zē'ŭes.

In establishing the links, and making the connections and extending the great ethnographic and ethnologic cycles of human existence, from the pre-historic to the Adomic periods, and even later, we do so between the events belonging to the Esgenens of Esgenenex, in the region now known as south of the Taurus mountains, and those of Gōn'thē-ōle, one of their principal descendants, his migrations and descendants, and their migrations and descendants, as well as that of the same conditions of other tribes and colonies who subsequently descended from the original Esgenens, who migrated into other sections of the Continent.

In many of the Biblical narratives, or myths, the principal events were founded upon facts, as is the case with novel writing at the present time, but clothed in mythical and idealistic narration, and substituted nomenclature, especially in regard to the individuals who figure in the narrative, such as were used in the Biblical writings relative to the "Creation of the World," and the destruction of its peoples by the "Deluge," etc.

Gontheole, whose migrations, and descendants were taken by the Biblical narrator, as "Adam," the chief character of his subject, as figuring with "Eve," in the "Garden of Eden," was a real personage, and therefore was not a myth in that sense, though parts of the narration were. He, as before stated, was a descendant of the Esgenens of Esgenenex, south of the Taurus mountains (near Pood). He was one of the principal leaders of those people, and at the time of their contentions and wars, he fled alone from that section to save his life. He passed east until he came to the now known Euphrates river, which he followed southeast, to its junction with the Tigris river, where he tarried in a beautiful valley which he termed Cē-lī'tē, meaning a beautiful valley (and was really the Eden Land referred to by the Biblical narrator), and took unto himself the name of Gontheole, meaning the lone man.

At the age of one hundred years, he had met some of the inhabitants of central Siaza or Persia, who were remnant descendants from the Ackredeths and Rezendeths, who dwelt in the then known section of Zĕv-ër-ĕn'dēs, where now the city of Yezd is located, who extolled their country to him to such a degree that he decided to go on a prospecting journey through that section of country. He therefore passed eastward from the valley of Celite, to Zeverendes, where he met an Ackredeth woman by the name of Cly-ē'thē, whom he married, and returned with her to the valley of Celite, where they dwelt together for nearly six hundred years. Gontheole survived Clyethe about two hundred years, and at the age of nine hundred years, passed on to spirit life.

To Gontheole and Clyethe, were born five children, three sons, and two daughters, viz: Kā-nŏn'zi-ä, the first son, (or Cain, as termed in the Biblical narrative); Dī-zŏn'zū, the second son (or Able); Zĭn'ī-sēse, the third son (or Seth); Zē-ä-lĭn'thä, the first daughter, and Cīl-ī-ĕn'zä, the second, the two daughters being the youngest children.

Like most of the mythical parts of the Bible narrative of the Creation, the killing of Dizonzu by his brother Kanonzia, was among the rest. There was no murder committed. Gontheole, when his two sons Kanonzia and Dizonzu became of mature age, desired that they go hence and possess themselves with certain sections of land as their own, and therefore sent them away for that purpose, which they did. Kanonzia therefore, passed over to the east side of the now known Tigris river, thence followed its course for a time, northeast, until he came to a large valley which he termed Nō'dē-gĕnt, meaning, the lone land, (which the Biblical writer changed to Nod), that lay east about forty-five degrees Longitude, east of Greenwich, and about thirty-six and one-half degrees, North Latitude, where he located at the western foothills of the mountains.

After a sojourn for about ten years in that locality, he went on a prospecting journey to see what he could discover on the eastern side of the mountain range. While en route on the eastern side of the mountains, he came into a settlement of Rē-zĕn'-dĕths, who during the migration of the main stock, had branched off from them when they halted near the now known mountain Damavend, Persia, which halting place they termed Sī-ăm'nīng, where he remained for a time, and associated with the tribe during his prospecting expedition. During his stay, he became acquainted with a woman of the tribe of Rezendeths, whom he married, and with her returned to his home in the Nodegent valley, on the western side of the mountain range. On returning however, he moved further northwest from his Nodegent home, and called the new section Mā-mō'pä.

Subsequently, there were born to Kā-nŏn-zî-ä and Rē-ĕz'dĕth, two sons and one daughter. Thē-rē'zy was the first son (or Enoch of the Biblical narration); Al'tē-zōne the second, and Hē-ō-di-ä the daughter, which latter was the second child by birth.

When Therezy came to maturity, as his father before him had done, he migrated farther northeast, in order to possess himself with land, etc., until he came to a valley that lay extent west of what is now known as Mount Ararat, which latter he termed Hĭn'kĕl-ty and named the valley Es-gē-nĕn'ĕx, in memory of the Esgenenex of his ancestors, the home of the original Esgenens, and therefore of his grand-sire Gontheole. After a time, he returned to his own people, and from them took to himself a wife by the name of Kä-shē'lä, and returned to his valley of Esgenenex.

Therezy and Kashela were the paternal and maternal ancestors of one son by the name of Mär-rē'zä, who subsequently begat a son by the name of Gē-lĭn'gĕt, which latter was the pre-historic personage represented in the Biblic narrative as Noah, who figured in the great Deluge.

Dizonzu the second son of Gontheole, migrated into that section of country now known as below the confluence of the Euphrates and the Tigris rivers, east of the continuation of the Euphrates, where he settled in a large valley which he termed Mŭn-zō'mŭns, which name extended down to the time of the Mussulmans. He followed the occupation of a shepherd, and when he became well established in Munzomuns, he made a journey into Cĕn-rē'shä (Fars), in order to meet his mother's people, and while there, took a woman by the name of E-lĭth'ē-ŭs to be his wife, who was a descendant from the Ackredeths of Cenresha, as was also Clyethe, his mother, and returned with her to Munzomuns, his home valley. To them were born two sons and two daughters, viz: Zē-rī'thē, a daughter, who was the first born; Gē-rŏn'zō, a son ,the second born; Mē-hĕt'ley, a daughter, the third born; and Zū'rŭm, a son, the fourth born.

Subsequently, straggling people began to settled in Munzomuns, from east of the mountains of Cenreshaor Fars, and Dĕ-rĕ-shŭ′ shăn (Luristan), of whom Dionzu became a leader. The Ackredeths and Rezendeths in the vicinity of Cenresha, became jealous of the settlers in Munzomuns, on account of so many of their people having migrated there, who had placed themselves under the rule of leader-ship of Dionzu, which condition led to serious contentions and wars between the two peoples. The Ackredeths and Rezendeths fearing that the people under command of Dionzu, would eventually seek to rule Cenresha, as well as Munzomuns, decreed to destroy Dionzu's nation and power, by killing all the infant male descendants.

An infant son of Zerithe, the eldest daughter of Dionzu, by the name of Nī-ŭ′tĭs, was secreted in order to prevent his possible fatality at the hands of the hostile nation, whose life was therefore preserved, and when he came to the years of maturity, was not known outside of his immediate family, to be the son of Zerithe. At that time, there were a few people in the section of Munzomuns, of the Rezendeth and Ackredeth immigrants, who differed in their opinions, generally speaking, from their hostile brethren, of Dereshushan and Senresha, who colonized themselves together, Niutis being among them and recognized as being a very intellectual person, was chosen by them to be their leader. This fact and person were used by the Biblical writer, for his theme, when narrating the life of Moses.

The above named colony, under the leadership of Niutis, finally instituted a long migration westward. En route from Munzomuns, they crossed the Euphrates, and followed it toward its source, until after long journies, and various haltings they had reached the section of country about forty degrees longitude east from Greenwich, and thirty-five degrees north latitude in the country now known as Syria, where they remained for a considerable time. Later on, they passed southwest, to the now known Anti Lebanon range, thence west through the great pass, to the western side of what is now known as the Jebel Esh Sharki mountains, thence southwest between the Jebel Esh Sharki and the Jebel Libnan and the Lebanon mountains, thence down to, and along the eastern shores of the now known Sea of Galilee, thence along the river Jordan, to the section now known as the Ford of Abarah, near Beisan, where, in the fordable season they crossed the Jordan and went into what is now known as the Ghor, or the valley of Jordan, where they settled, termed the valley Al-lĕ-bär′dĭn, meaning, Land of Promise, and called themselves the Shăn-dĕ′ŏes, who in after time were known as the Israelites.

Submerged Atlantis Restored

When Mareza, the son of Therezy and Kashela came to maturity, as his ancestors had done, he sought to possess lands of his own, and therefore moved from his parental home in the valley of Esgenenex, and located in another valley northwest of Hinkelty, or Mount Ararat, which he termed Jĕn-tī-ū'sĕn, meaning a beautiful valley. He took to himself a wife by the name of Mĕl-ē'tĭsh, and to them was born a son whose name was Gē-lĭn'gĕt, the ultimate life conditions of whom, furnished the theme for the Biblical myth, or narrative of Noah and the Flood. When Gelinget arrived at maturity, he also followed the example of his ancestors, and sought home possessions of his own. He therefore migrated southeast of Mt. Ararat, into a valley which he termed O-kā-lĕn'tŭs (meaning a rich, fertile valley), and later, took to himself a wife by the name of Zō-rĭl'ī-thy.

While many of the pre-historic migrations were instituted by virtue of tribal conditions; seeking the source of the Sun; overcrowded sections and hamlets; or a desire to search for new conditions of livelihood, those instituted by Gontheole's descendants, down to the time of Gelinget, were purely in search for homes and land possessions. As was the case with parts of the ethnographich myths, being founded on facts, so it was with that of Noah and the Flood.

At the time that Kanonzia's descendants still occupied the valley of Nodegent; Dionzu's that of Munzomuns; Therezy's that of Esgenenex; Marreza's that of Jentiusen; and Gelinget's were fully established in Okalentus, all that section of country now known as extent from the Caucasian mountains, between the Caspian and the Black Seas, south through Turkey, Persia, and Syria, especially through the region of Palestine, was conditioned with a general rain storm, that had no cessation during its period of precipitation, which Alem Prolex informs us was about sixty days and nights, a period of time, some twenty days longer than given by the Biblical narrator.

As the valleys and lower lands gradually became inundated by the water that was flowing down from the higher sections, and mountains, and the valley courses overflowing their banks, the families of the above named peoples, took their principal possessions, especially their cattle, and moved to the uplands for safety. So also, was it the case with the wild beasts and domestic animals of the country. As the waters came higher and higher, the people and animals were forced to ascend the mountain peaks for further safety of life and possessions, a fact that accounts for their transportation to those localities, instead of being carried there in an "Ark," as stated by the Biblical narrator, hence, that part of the narrative is myth.

After the storm ceased, and the waters began to recede, the people followed their descent to the valleys, in order to look after their land and home possessions. As they descended, they found that the soil and sand that formerly had place on the mountain sides were washed away in certain sections, thus leaving the rocky condition that now characterize those sections of the mountains of that region.

When finally they arrived in the vicinity of their hamlets and homes in the valley, they found that the sand and soil had been transported to the valley below, by the great fluvial power and force of the flood, and had therefore buried their homes out of sight, and were it not for the process of decay, that destroys such materials when they are buried beneath the earth's surface, many of the possessions of those people could be found to-day by means of excavation.

The above named flood was almost as disastrous as was that wihch submerged Atlantis, the difference being only in the final removal of the waters from the earth's surface in that section at the time of the flood, and the non-occurrence of severe convulsions beneath the earth's surface at the time of the flood. The same condition of removal of sands from the mountain sides took place throughout Palestine, and their deposits established the now known deserts, south of Palestine, especially that of El Tiah, which was not an inland sea formation. It is claimed by the pre-historic spirits, who are assisting us in this revelation, that the two above named cataclysms were the greatest and most marvelous natural disasters of the world's unwritten history.

The now known Lake Van, bordering the section of Van, on the northwest, Bitlis on the east and Erzerum on the south, between Armenia and Kurdistan, Turkey, and Lake Erivan, or Cotcha, in Trans-Caucasia, Russia, are remnant water sections of the prehistoric flood above referred to; but, Lake Urumiah was subsequently established by a large convulsion that had place in the now known "Kashaga Dagh Mountains" soon after the establishment of the Caspian Sea.

Kĕl-thē'dăt was the first pre-historic name of the entire portion of country now known as Afghanistan , so given by the descendant Hisocks of Căn-lăn-jū'na, their home in Kelthedat. Subsequent to the establishment of the Hisocks in Runderusand, (Laristan), the main colony established a system of migrations, when they passed into the section of Cenresha (Fars). Meeting with opposition from the local tribes of Rezendeths and Ackredeths, they therefore continued their migration from that section, which diverged from that of the migration of the Rezendeths and the Ackredeths. They passed eastward over the high-lands that then separated the Gĕ'rĕst and the I-cē-lĕn'tē inland seas, the area of which is now known as the Lut and the Great Salt Deserts, into the section of country now known as Afghanistan, east of lake Seistan or Zurrah, when they settled between the Helmund and Khash rivers, termed the Helmund and also the Lake I-rĭn'dē-crūse and the section, Căn-lăn-jū'nä, where they dwelt for many generations under the name of Hisocks, and became a large nation, and in time had built a principal city which they termed Häs'sĕn, on the site where the town of Dooshack has place, on the eastern coast of Lake Zurrah.

In stature, they averaged from five and one-half, to six and one-half feet, they were large boned and muscularly built; had dull black skins; abundant long, black, wavy hair, and their bodies, like those of their ancestors, were characterized with considerable. They had low receding foreheads; heavy eyebrows and lashes; small, roundish and deep set eyes; broad feet but shorter than those of their ancestors, which was also the case with their hands. They were very indolent, went nude, sat about on the ground in listless groups, with their feet folded under them. They were very hostile among themselves, a condition caused by their extreme selfishness.

Subsequently, some of their descended tribes migrated further east along the Helmund river and its tributaries, until they came to the western slopes of the Solymaun mountains, which range they termed Hăz'dĕl, and settled in that section north of the now known Gomal river, in the district of Dera Ismae Khan, which section they termed Mĕl-thā-lē'ŏn, and called themselves the Hä-ē'zĕls, and in time had built their principal city, which they termed A-kī'dō, which was located on the site of their first settlement. They being descendants from the Hisocks of Canlanjuna, physically speaking, were similar to their ancestors, with such changes as would naturally come to them through the influence of climate and livelihood in that section, through their long sojourn there, which was for many generations. During their sojourn in Hazdel, some of the Tĭm'mē-nŏns from Shăf'fi-ŏn, their home on the western slopes of the Hindu Kush range, wandered southeastward to the vicinity of Hazdel, and mixed races with the Haezels, which fact established further physical changes in the Haezel tribes, who carried the new characteristics into Gē-rŭn'dī-ŭs (the Punjab section), and later into Swän'sō (Hindustan).

Subsequent to the establishment of the Kā-lăc-ca-dives in Hō'ĕt (see their migration to the section between Irack Ajami and Khorassan, Persia, descendant tribes of the Rezendeths and the Ackredeths migrated further eastward into the section now known as Afghanistan. En route, they passed along the southern slopes of the now known Paropamisus mountains, or north of the then known Ge-rest, or inland Sea, until they arrived in the section now known as ancient Aria (Herat), where they halted for a time in the vicinity of the now known town of Herat on the Heri river.

Subsequently, the main portion of the two tribes continued their migration eastward, but a portion of each remained in the above named section, where in time, they mixed races, termed the section Kū-rē-ăn'ŭm, the river Wĭt'zē, and called themselves the Kū-rē-ăn'ŭms, and ultimately, they had built their principal city, which they termed Gē'trĕth, and was located on the site where now the city of Herat has place.

As the main portion of the Rezendeths and Ackredeths, or the Kalaccadives, migrated farther eastward from the section of Kureanum, they continued along the Paropamisus mountains, to the vicinity of the now known Hindu Kush mountains, in northeastern Afghanistan.

The Ackredeths settled south of the range, termed that section Ry-kĕn-stŏn, and called themselves the A'glŏnsts. Physically speaking, they being immediate descendants of the Ackredeths, were similar to the latter, only in such changes as might occur through climate and livelihood, etc. Subsequently, they had built a principal city which they termed Kĭng'tō-nēse, which was located on the site where the city of Cabool has place.

The Rezendeths settled north of the range, about fifty-nine degrees longitude, east of Greenwich, which section they termed Cŏn'sĕg, and called themselves the Cŏn-sĕg'ĕns. Their physical conditions were very much like their ancestors, the Rezendeths of Siaza, being in stature, about five feet. However, they were more fleshy, and chubby in appearence. They had black skins; black, curly and shaggy hair; black eyes, set closely together; noses with scarcely any bridge, and quite flat at the nostrils; broad mouths, and pouched lips; and large heads. Many of them practised nudity, but some followed the custom of their ancestors who wore skins of animals.

Subsequent to the arrival of their ancestors, the Rezendeths, in the section of Hindu Kush mountains, and their change of name to that of Consegens, and the establishment of the section of Conseg, there was a division among the people, caused from race difficulties. When they arrived in the section which they afterwards named Conseg, they found a portion of it inhabited by a small, then aboriginal tribe, that bore no name and retained no knowledge of their past history, ancestors or original home. They had come from the north, and had occupied the district of Conseg for many generations, a fact known traditionally to them, where they had lived in a condition of degeneration, until they were more like animals, than human beings.

After a time, some of the lower class of the Consigens mixed races with the above named wild tribe, from which condition there descended off-spring that further developed into a small tribe or mixed race. The better class of the Consegens refused to recognize them as belonging to their race, hence, contentions arose which caused the mixed race to move into a section a little further east from Conseg, along the Hindu Kush range, where they were known by the people of that section as the Grē-ī-ĭl'tĭs, so named by the Consegens, where they eventually became extinct. They were a very peculiar people. In some respects, they bore resemblance to the Consegens. However, there were two striking differences, viz: in that their foreheads were very receding, and their heads or skulls projected upward at the beck. Second, a very strange feature was that a line of long hair extended up and down, along their spines, much as does the mane along a horse's neck. Some short hair extended from the line of long hair around their sides, and over their breasts; but, the remainder of their bodies was comparatively free from hair, conditions which came from the influence of race mixture between the Consegens and the wild hairy tribe. In subsequent time, they had built a principal hamlet, which they termed Tour-jac, located on the site of their first settlement.

After several centuries, three distinct nations had descended from the Aglonsts and the Consegens, viz: the Kentersends, the Lazerends, and the Timmenons, the latter being a mixed race that descended from the Aglonsts and the Consegens.

The Kentersends occupied the southern slopes of the Hindu Kush range, in the section modernly known as the Tibetan Plateau, which section they termed Thū-rī-ĭs'tĭc, near Ry-kĕn-stŏn, the home of the Aglonsts, their ancestors, and termed the mountains In-dē-grĭs'tē. The Kentersends being immediate descendants of the Aglonsts, physically speaking, were about the same as their ancestors, the Ackredeths and the Aglonsts, the only difference being such as came to them through livelihood conditions. They practised nudity in the warm seasons, but in the cold, they wore skins about their loins and over their shoulders. In regard to religion, they in their home in Thuriistic, and during their eastern migration, worshipped the stars as representatives of the principle of continuous light, which they termed Gō-lō'thrā, meaning, one, two, three, and was symbolic of the three wondrous lights of the heavens, viz: the Sun, the Moon and the Stars. The Stars were chosen as the principal symbol, because they shone at night, when no sunlight, or even moonlight was visible; hence, considered a continuous condition of light, that brightened the condition of night, which latter also symbolized the benefit derived from dispelling evil, or darkened conditions of life.

As the term Golothra meant one, two, three, they instituted an image, or symbol of the principle, for use in their shrines at times of worship. They took the idea of it from the form of their own bodies. It consisted of three pieces of wood, one of which they placed in a perpendicular position like unto their bodies when erect, and the other two pieces they placed on the top of the perpendicular piece, and at oblique angles with it like the arms would appear from the shoulders, when they were partially raised, from the body, and the apex of the oblique pieces posed like the head of the body. On each of the three pieces of wood, were three sets of stars, and three stars in each set. From the base, on both sides of the perpendicular piece of wood, rose three lesser pieces of wood each of which terminated with three radiating points that were tipped with a star.

At the time of their stated assemblies for adorational worship, which was four times a year (or at the first full moon of the incoming season), they convened, for a day and night, in the open air, at their public shrine of Golothra, which was located in a public part of their hamlet grounds. The assembly began at the rising of the sun the first day, and closed at its rising on the following day, thus making a session of one day and night. The form of worship was as follows: — The image was placed on the south side of the campus. The people formed in semi-circles on the north side, facing the image. The first gesture, was to point to the centre of their breasts, from the fact that their breath issued from that section of their bodies, and furthermore, that the sun stood in the south when its light was the grandest. The second, was to point to their left shoulders, because they considered the left side the seat of life, and as they stood facing the south, that was the eastern side, from whence the sun made its morning appearance. The third, was to point up to the heavens, which they considered the source of all light, both day and night. With each of their gestures, they pronounced one syllable of the term

Golothra at a time, thus: "Go," "lo," "thra" (one, two three), after which they disbanded for social details, and the preparation of their general feast, which latter was partaken of only once during the twenty-four hours' assembly, and that at the close of the day. Their feast consisted principally of meats, which they hung over fires until they were roasted very brown. They had some fruits, and a sort of bread, or flat baked loaves of mixed, pulverized fruits.

The Lazerends occupied the northern slopes of the same range, or the section modernly known as Pamir Plateau, which section they termed Sĕn'ē-cūtes, near Conseg, the home of their ancestors the Consegens. They being immediate descendants of the Consegens, were physically about the same. They generally went nude, excepting in the cold weather, when they wore skins about their loins and shoulders. In regard to religion, notwithstanding the original ideas of their ancestors the Aglonsts, Consegens and Swansoans, by virtue of migratory and descendant conditions, they lost that influence, and therefore manifested no religious ideas, and established no form of adorational worship, yet the Lazerends of this section, recognized the principles of strength, force or power, and protection, as their ideal for adoration, which principal, they termed Eū'trē-zē, like that of Golothra, as used by the Kentersends, also translates, *one, two, three,* and referred to the three above named principles. They erected images, or idols as symbols of Eutreze, for use in their shrines, the principal one having place in the central part of their settlement, where they held their general adorational assemblies. It consisted of three pillars, about six inches apart, and three feet in height. They were formed from limbs of trees, from which the bark had been removed, and were joined at the top and the bottom, by pieces of limbs of the same kind as those that formed the pillars. Back of the pillars, was represented the head and shoulders of an animal then known as the Jĕm'ī-ēse, that resembled the modern lion, that appeared to be gazing at the people from behind the pillars. The idea conveyed by that representation was that they as a people, had control over the animal, hence represented as being placed behind the pillars. Thus they worshipped it in that sense, and also as representing the condition of protection, such as came from some unknown source, or greater being than themselves.

The shrine of the principal Eutreze, located in the central part of the settlement, was constructed out of barks, which constituted the roof, there being no sides to the structure, excepting the posts that supported the roof, which latter was of gable form, very slight pitch, and as before stated, thatched with bark, on top of a rustic frame of limbs. The idol was made portable, so they might at any time, carry it with them from place to place, when changing their abode. It was always placed in the centre of the shrine. The stated time for the adorational exercises, or worship, was once every day, generally at eventide, but whenever an individual passed the shrine, he or she would make the usual obeisance to it. The order of the exercise was to pass three times around the idol, in a circle, each individual making obeisance to the imprisoned Jemiese, as they passed its gazing eyes. As each person passed around the third time, and made the third obeisance to the idol, he or she withdrew from the circle, and departed hence. Sometimes, however, parties would tarry for sports or games, and, at times, even linger to settle contentions, which often ultimated in a quarrel, being settled in favor of the hero of the fight. In addition to the principal Eutreze, several smaller ones were placed throughout the settlement, for general use by the people, who recognized the God principles, as represented by Jemiese, as they passed the sub-shrines on their daily missions.

The Timmenons occupied the western slope, which they termed Shăf'fi-ŏn, in distinction from their Ancestors, the Aglonsts, and the Consegens, as a mixed race. In stature, they averaged from five to five and one-half feet, were slender in build, yet their bodies were large; they were quick, active, and stealthy in motion, and were also very strong; their hair was black, long and straight; their skins dark; eyes quite large, some being black, and some brown; their noses were broad at the top, but were drawn in at the nostrils; their mouths were large, and their lips thick; foreheads were low and somewhat receding; ears were quite large, and their beards quite scant, but what they did have was soft, silky or fuzzy; their feet were quite large and broad; heads normal, but their fingers were long and tapering.

In regard to dress, they plaited barks and fibres into a sort of fabric which they wore in the form of a narrow skirt, that extended from the waist, half way down to the knees. Some of the women would throw a fabric over their shoulders in addition to their skirt. The children always went nude. They recognized the lunar light as their beneficial God Principle, and therefore worshipped the Moon in all its phases of light, objectively, in assemblies in the open air, and continued the same theoretically, during the time of its dark phases, individually, at any place where they chanced to be at the time. Their general assemblies for adorational worship always convened at the first appearance of the new Moon, which they termed Y-yō'kä-lĕt, which referred both to the God Principle and the phases of the Moon, i. e., Kä meant dark, Lĕt meant light, and the prefixes Y, and Yō referred to the greater light, or full moon, its return and departure. They made no images of the God Principle, as nature, by the moon and its phases, was adequate to the occasion. They considered the moon superior to the stars, and capable of moving to other regions for the purpose of giving light to other peoples, during which time they only had the light of the stars as a substitute for that of the moon. Their order of adorational exercises was to form themselves into crescent lines, according to the number of people assembled, in which position they spent considerable time, repeating audibly their adorational invocations; then they bowed low to the moon, and returned to their homes. As before stated, the greatest assembly was on the night of the first appearance of the full moon, yet the assemblies, ad libitum, occurred each night during the light phase of the moon, or individually at any place where the individual chanced to be.

The Hisocks of Canlanjuna, or ancient Drangiana (Seistan), and their descendants became the pre-historic ancestors of the now known Afghan clans proper, such as the Durranis, or original Abdalis, who occupy the whole of the south and southwest of the Afghan Plateau; the strong and brave Ghilzais who occupy the high Plateau north of Kandahar, and extend eastward to the Sulimani mountains and north to the Kabul river, and down the river to Jalalabad; the Yusufzais who occupy the hills and valleys north of Peshawar, including part of the Peshawar plain; the Kakars who occupy the elevated country in the southeast of Afghanistan, among the spurs of the Toba and Sulimani mountains, etc.

The Ackredeths, one of the two tribes of Kalaccadives, of Hō'ĕt, or ancient Aria (Herat), and their descendants, became the pre-historic ancestors of the Hazara tribes, who principally dwell in the wild mountainous country on the northwest of Afghanistan proper, including the western extension of the Hindu Kush, or Paropamisus mountains, and it is from their ancestors, the Ackredeths, that they are endowed with the Mongol type, dialects, and speech, as were the Mongols proper of China, in later migrations and descendancy of the Ackredeths.

The Rezendeths, the other one of the two tribes of Kalaccadives, of Hoet, and their descendants of that vicinity, became the pre-historic ancestors of the Eimak tribes, and also the Tajiks, or Parsiwans, who dwelt principally in the western portion of Afghanistan, and who also are intermingled with the Afghans over the country, who have retained most of the physical characteristics of their ancestors, the Rezendeths, except that in color they have grown lighter, caused by subsequent race mixture and climatic influences.

A mixed race of Haezels and Aglonsts and their descendants, are the pre-historic ancestors of the Turis and Jajis tribes of Kuran.

Kē-ĭ-ĕl-wī'thē was the first pre-historic name of Baluchistan, so given by the Pō'ly-ăns of **Pō-ly-nō-nī-dy** about the beginning of the the Adomic period, and so remained until it was changed by the descendants of the Polyans, about the close of the Adomic period, to that of Baluchistan, at which time the people changed their name to that of Bră-hō'ēs; at the same time, the U-stē'mē-ŏns changed their name to that of Bā-lū'chēs, a derivative term from the new section name.

Subsequent to the establishment of the Swăn-sō'ăns in Swăn-sō, or northwestern Hindustan, a large tribe of their descendants migrated westward into the section of country now known as eastern Baluchistan, where they settled in a valley in the Province of Gileh-Gundava, between the now known rivers of Bolan and Moola, and the spurs of mountains that extend northeast and southwest of the Bolan river, which sections they termed Polynonidy, and called themselves the Polyans. Subsequently, their principal hamlet, which they termed Poo'tē-lĭm was located on the site where the town of Gundava now has place.

After the establishment of the Polyans in Polynonidy, a small tribe of Hisocks from their Calanjuna, or western Afghanistan, migrated southward into the section of western Baluchistan, where they settled in the now known Province of Mekran, in the valley north of the eastern branch of the Dasti river, between it and its junction with the northwestern branch, and the now known Bushkerad mountains, which section they termed U-stē'-mē-ŏn, and called themselves the U-stē'mē-ŏns.

Still later the Ustemeons became mixed as a race with a portion of the Polyans, which changed the characteristics of the new race in some respects, but they still retained the name of Ustemeons as a tribe, and Ustemeon as their section name, until it was changed, as above stated. In time, they had built a principal hamlet, which they termed Tĕl'ĕn-săc, on the site of their first settlement.

The Polyans proper, of Polynonidy, and their descendants, became the pre-historic ancestors of the now known Baluches of Baluchistan.

SHIN'DER-SHAN NUD U-ISH'TE-COS
OR
HINDUSTAN, INDIA AND DESERTS.

TELTZIE XLVIII.

Subsequent to the time when the Timmenons, or their descendants, the Haezels, migrated to northwestern Hindustan, which section they had named Swanso, and called themselves the Swansoans (see below), there was a separation of the Swansoan colony into two sects or factions, one the Hĭn'dŭs, and the other the In'drä, thus named after the leader of each faction.

Hindus led his faction or tribe from Swanso proper, northeast along the now known upper southern basin of the Ganges river, which section they termed Hindustan, and called themselves the Hindus, in honor of their leader. They and their descendants became the pre-historic ancstors of the Hindus people who preserved the Hindo language as existing anciently and modernly, north of the Vindhya Mountains, and more strictly speaking, to the upper basin of the Ganges. Therefore, the term Hindustan, as established by the pre-historic Hindus of the above named section of country, has descended from that pre-historic period to the modern, practically unchanged.

Indra led his faction, or tribe, from Swanso to the southeast, into the section of country now known as eastern Ajmeer, Hindustan, where they settled, but at first retained their former name of Swansoans, and their section name of Swanso; but, about three hundred years later, the descended Swansoans termed the entire section of country now known as Hindustan, Shĭn'dĕr-shăn.

Prior to the race mixture between the Dĕl'kä Sä'dĕls and the Swansoans, which established the Hĭn'tŏx race (see below), the portion of Swansoans who became the Indra tribes, and who greatly adored their leader Indra, during his mortal career, still worshipped him after his disembodiment, as a spirit benefactor of their people. This fact further influenced the Hintox and their descendants to such an extent that they ultimately discarded the Shindershan term, for that of Indra, originally belonging to the Ajmeer district, which unlike that of Hindustan, sustained several changes during various periods of time, viz: to Indrus, later to Indus, and ultimately to India; hence, both the terms, Hindustan and India, have found way into modern utility and nomenclature, in regard to the Peninsula.

Subsequent to the establishment of the Hä-ĕ'zēls in Mĕl-thā-lē'ŏn, of Kĕl-thē'dăt (Afghanistan), a large tribe of their descendants migrated eastward, via what is modernly known as Jalalabad, and the Kayber Pass, into the section now known as the Punjab, where they settled at the junction of the now known Jhelum and the Chenaub rivers, termed the section and the rivers Gē-rūn'dī-ūs, but retained their former tribe name of Hä-ĕ'zēls, and there established a hamlet which they termed Dŭm-rū'shy, *dŭm* meaning, in their language, quiet, and *rū-shy* meaning rapid. In its broadest sense the term, as a whole, referred to the swift but quiet condition of the waters that characterized the three rivers of the Punjab.

In subsequent time, a large tribe of their descendants had migrated southeast into the section now known as southeast Rajputana, India, where they settled on the shores of the now known Chumbul river, at a point south of the now known city of Karauli, or Capitol of the State of Karauli, which section they termed Swanso, and called themselves the Swansoans. There they established a hamlet, which ultimately became their principal pre-historic town, which they termed A-zĕn-zū-ĕn'dă, meaning *a shelter among the mountains*; that is, in its practical sense, A'zĕn was their word for sheltered, and Zū-ĕn'dă, for mountains. The hamlet and ultimate city of Azenzuenda, was located in the section now known as the Native State of Karauli, or Kerowley, in Rajputana, India, on the site where now the city of Karauli, the Capitol of the above-named State, has place.

The Swansoans of Swanso, in stature, were five and a half to six and a half feet; some were slender, but generally they were of an athletic form, being muscular, large-boned and jointed. Their skins were a dull black; their heads were normal in size, when compared with their bodies, though they were flattish on top, and their foreheads were low, and projected over the eyes considerably. Their hair was black, some being straight and long, and some long and wavy; their beards were short, and grew principally under the chin and around the neck, and their bodies were also characterized with considerable hair. Their eyes were black, round in appearance, and far apart; their noses were short and broad, their mouths broad, and their lips thick; their feet were thin, flat, or flabby, and their toes were long; their hands were characterized the same as their feet. They were a selfish people, contentious with other tribes or peoples, but were quite harmonious among themselves. All the children, and some of the adults, went nude, and both the men and women who were clad at all, simply wore a short skin apron in front. In regard to religion, from the influence they had received from their ancestors, the Hisocks of Canlanjuna, which latter people had degenerated from the religious and adorational ideas of their ancestors, the Hisocks of Runderusand, had lost all adorational ideas and forms of worship by the time they had become settled in Swanso; hence they held to no religious ideas, and had no forms of worship.

From Shaffion, the Timmenon descendants established a migratory system. The first migrating tribe, as did the Haezels, entered the section of country now known as the Punjab region, and passed northeast until they came to the now known Himalaya mountains. In subsequent time, various tribes, at various periods of time, migrated along the southern boundary of the Himalaya range, until they came to the region where the now known Brahmaputra river flows through the range, whence they followed its course westward; and then southward to the now known Ganges river, from whence, in subsequent centuries, they spread out into the section of country now known as Bengal, which section they termed Cē-rē'gĕs, and called themselves the Dĕl'kä Sä'dĕls. In time, they had established their principal city, which they termed U-rī-ē'zĕl. It was located northwest of the now known city of Calcutta, on the Tropic of Cancer, near the now known town of Burdwan, west of the river Hugli.

The Delka Sadels of Cereges in stature, on an average were about six feet; they were slender, though quite muscular, and had large bones and joints. The women, however, were more fleshy than the men. They had dark skins, but not as dark as their neighbors, the Swansoans of Swanso. Their hair was short and frizzled, generally speaking, but some possessed that which was curly. Their heads were flattish on top, but projected at the back, and their foreheads were receding. Their noses were thin and sharp. Their eyes were black; the auricle of their ears was very peculiar, being long at the top with scarcely any lower lobe, and were smooth, or void of folds. Their mouths were broad; lips short, thus exposing a very long and large set of teeth. Their feet were thick and short; hands small, but their fingers were well proportioned.

About five hundred years before the Adomic period, or at the time the Delka Sadels had become settled in Cereges, they had sustained but little change in their livelihood, but there was no marked intellectual change in them.

By the time of the Adomic period, however, they had become quite intellectual, and were then seeking for greater knowledge, caring more for that than for their physical or national advancements. At first they adhered to the style adopted by their ancestors. Later, however, they learned the art of braiding and twisting the long hair of what was then known as the Qū-zĕn'-tŏx, for both the warp and woof of fabrics. The Quzentox was the pre-historic ancestor of the animal of Thibet now known as the Cashmere Goat. The downy wool or hair of the Quzentox thus made into fabrics, was utilized as material from which to form their garments, which latter consisted of two pieces, one worn like a cape, and the other formed into a narrow skirt, that came down just below the knees. They also wrapped their ankles and legs up to the knee with the same material, and fastened the wrappings at the top and the bottom with bark strings, thus forming a sort of legging, that they called Qū'ĭst. Subsequently, they invented a sort of loom with which to aid them in forming and weaving their fabrics. It was made by placing four posts perpendicularly, thus forming a square. A cord was extended from the top of one to that of the other of the rear post, to which the warp was fastened. In like manner was a cord stretched from the tops of the front posts, over which the other ends of the warp was drawn by several individuals, who thus constantly held the warp threads in that position, while several others, beginning at the rear ends of the warp, wove in the woof by passing the threads to each other, who in turn drew the threads through, and beat them back into the warp, thus forming the fabric. This was the first invention of the loom, and form of weaving in that country, an idea that was re-conceived through spirit influence, and brought out, re-embodied and developed, down to the present-time utilities and products belonging to the textorial art.

In regard to religion, the Delka Sadels seemed to be the people in whom lost ideas of a religious character could be revived; therefore, in their early existence in Cereges, they conceived the idea of a great being, an invisible man, who had built all things visible, and whom they termed U-kī'dĭsh, which term, in their language, meant Great Builder. Subsequently, other generations of their descendants changed the name to A-gŭs'tä, the term meaning *All Force,* or *All Power,* Again, about the time of the Adomic period, the people of that generation changed the name to A-gē'lī, meaning *The Unseen.* These changes were made by virtue of the advanced ideas of the new leaders, and the influences brought to them by immigration from other nations, or peoples, which ultimated in a progression of religious ideas.

The first form of adorational exercises was, to wit: they assembled each month, on the date of the first appearance of the full moon, in the evening, or at the hour of its rising. The place arranged for their assemblies was at their Quintezon; i. e., a very crude structure in the form of an oblong square, with open sides and a thatched roof. In the front center of the Quintezon a platform was erected, on which was placed an idol, or image of Ukidish, about three feet in stature, wrought of wood. It was a crude, coarse, massive image of a man, represented in a standing posture, the hair being represented by a black staining of the head, the cheeks by red, and the forehead by white. As the platform on which the Idol stood answered the purpose of a facade to the Quintezon, they usually held their adorational exercises on the exterior of the structure, or in the front of the Idol, especially in fair weather, but when it was inclement, they held their exercises in the interior. The order of the exercises was to form a circle in front of Ukidish, about which they danced for some time and mumbled a crude chant in honor of the Great Builder. This was accompanied by musicians who stood between the circle of dancers and the Idol, and who drummed on pieces of resonant wood, and played a crude instrument composed of a square frame of wood, over which two strings, one shorter than the other, were stretched perpendicularly, which they set into vibration by picking them with their fingers. The musicians joined with the dancers in mumbling the chant. This was one of the first links, or re-conceived ideas of stringed instruments, which they termed Cŏl'lŏsh, and while the frame was square, the one string was made shorter by an additional strip of wood being placed across the frame sufficiently far enough down to obtain the length of the string required to make the tone required. When the moon was fully arisen, the exercises ceased, and the worshippers departed hence. A small image of Ukidish was placed in every home, to which the occupants made their family obeisance, and requests for personal aid.

The second Quintezon was a much finer structure than the first, and A-gŭs'tạ, the Idol, though wrought from wood, was more artistic, in a sculptural sense, than that of Ukidish in the first Quintezon, and the third Quintezon was still finer than the second, being built out of stone; and the Idol Ageli, was sculptured, or beautifully wrought from marble. During the time of their worship of the god Ukidish, the Delka Sadels had migrated or spread out westward and southward, to the now known British District of Jabalpur, or Jubbulpore, of the Central Provinces, where they established a hamlet which in subsequent time became their principal pre-historic city, which they termed Al-tä-shū'zä (Alta, in their language, meaning climbing, and shuza, rocks, and referred to their climbing to the rocky basin in which Altashuza was built), which was located on the site where now the town of Jabalpur, the capitol of the above-named district now has place. They retained their former name of Delka Sadels, but termed the section Bĕl-zrän'dō.

Subsequently, the Swansoans of Swanso and the city of Azenzuenda, spread eastward until they had reached that section of Belzrando, and the hamlet of Altashuza, as above described, when they came among the Delka Sadels, where the two races mingled, which gave rise to a new nation, who termed themselves the Hintox, retained the name of Altashuza for the city, and Belzrando for the section.

The Hintox of Belzrando, on an average, were about six feet in stature, though some were shorter, and some even taller. They were heavily built, having broad shoulders and decidedly roundish bodies, and were very muscular. They were of a lighter complexion than their ancestors, the Delka Sadels, and the Haezels, though they might have been considered a dark-skinned people. Their heads were normal in size, when compared with the condition of their bodies. Their foreheads likewise, but were quite full through the upper portion. Their hair was black, long and bushy, the latter condition caused more from want of care than otherwise. Their eyes were black or dark brown, large and full, and displayed a piercing expression. Their eyebrows were heavy, and their lashes long. Their noses had a deep sunken bridge at the upper portion, but full and somewhat puggy at the lower. The mouths of some were large, and characterized with thick lips, while others had short lips, which caused them to reveal both sets of teeth. Their ears were peculiar from the fact that the upper portion of the auricles were large and lopped forward. Some of them had feet with extremely high insteps and large ankles that seemed to join very closely onto the instep, which gave to them a very peculiar appearance; and the portion of the foot forward of the instep was quite long, which fact made the foot look very peculiar, indeed. Their hands, however, were normal in size, if compared with the body. The men wore a sort of trousers made from a texture which they wrought out of fibres, mixed with the soft hair or wool from an animal then known as the Kē-lī-ŭx'try. It somewhat resembled both the small deer, and the sheep of modern times, the body being more like that of the sheep, but the legs small horns, etc., were more like those of the deer. The head, however, was some larger than either the deer or sheep. It has been long since extinct, which fact was occasioned through hybrid conditions. The women wore long narrow skirts that extended to below their knees, and a sort of cape that they formed by throwing a strip of the texture around their shoulders, with the ends crossed over their breasts.

In subsequent time, contentions arose among the Hintox, which caused them to separate, and to migrate in tribes from the vicinity of Altashuza, and other portions of the section of Belzrando. One division, however, remained in the section of Belzrando, and the city of Altashuza. The first migrating division passed southeast to the section now known as west of the Eastern Ghats mountains, at a point about eighty degrees longitude east from Greenwich, and about nineteen degrees north latitude, or on the site where now the town of Sironcha has place, near where the Penganga and the Indravati rivers flow into the Godavari, between the Penganga and the Indravati, where they settled, retained their former section and tribal names of Belzrando and Hintox respectively, and established a hamlet that subsequently became their principal pre-historic city of Sentoese. The second migrating division passed southwest, east of the now known Western Ghats mountains, about seventy-five degrees longitude east from Greenwich, and about eighteen and a half degrees north latitude, where they settled, retained their former section and tribe names, and established a hamlet, which later became their principal city, Tŭsh-ĕs-ī-ăn′go. Physically and idealistically speaking, they more particularly resembled their Swansoan ancestors, than they did the Delka Sadels, hence they followed more closely the modes of living and general ideas of the former; but the Hintox of Sentoese, on the contrary, resembled the Delka Sadels the most, and therefore followed more closely their modes of livelihood and general ideas.

In subsequent time, a large colony of Hintox from the city of Sentoese migrated southward along the foothills of the then known Reendicon range, or now known Eastern Ghats mountains, until they arrived at the now known sacred river Kistna, when they entered into a contention as to whether they should proceed farther southward, or follow the river eastward, the ultimatum of which was that the smaller portion of the colony followed the river course eastward, when they passed through the Eastern Ghats, to their eastern side, out into the great alluvial plane, or valley lying between the mountains and the Bay of Bengal, east of the now known town of Bezwara, where they settled, retained their former section and tribal names, of Belzrando and Hintox, respectively, and established a hamlet which they termed Sĕn′dū-zē. The main portion of the colony crossed the Kistna, followed the western side of the Reendicon mountains, until they arrived in the now known section of the southeastern Mysore, where they settled, and also retained their former section and tribe names of Belzrando and Hintox, and established a hamlet on the site where now the town of Bengalore has place, which ultimately became their principal pre-historic city of Săn-năn′zy.

After several generations, a tribe of the Hintox, of Tushesiango, migrated southward to the vicinity of the city of Sannanzy, where the two descended peoples of the Hintox nation met again, but without knowledge of their ancestors having previously descended from the same nation, or the same people of Altashuza, and by mingling races, or tribes, blended again into one and the same race again, that more strongly resembled the Hintox of Sannanzy, on acount of their having been the more numerous, hence the stronger tribe. There were but a few of the Tushesiangoes, who came into Sannanzy.

The Hintox of Sentoese and Sannanzy, in stature, were generally about six feet; were broad shouldered, large boned, and had dingy black skins; heads nordmal with the size of the body; black, long and curly hair; perpendicular foreheads, of normal height, but wore their hair low; eyes black, round and full; noses long and pointed; mouths large and lips full; ears roundish, not large; chins somewhat receding; feet and hands large, and large finger joints; large joints all over the body; and considerable hair on the body. The men clad themselves in a low-necked, loose garment, that extended down to their knees, and in some cases even lower. The women wore a narrow skirt that extended down to the knees, and in addition they threw a texture over their shoulders, which they brought to one side, where they fastened it. Their textures were made from a soft material. They used no fibres, but only hair and wool from an animal then known as the Celistin, that resembled the modern goat, but now extinct.

The leaders, as distinct from the people, wore two textures, one thrown over the right shoulder and fastened on the left side, and the other over the left shoulder and fastened to the right side. On each side of their breast, extending down from the shoulders to the front of the waist, was outlined the form of a spear head, by means of three shells, one on each side, and one at the point. Below the point was a circle in solid mass, wrought with small white shells. Each side of the circle was suspended two strings of a sort of beads, one of the loops being shorter than the other, thus causing it to hang within the longer. Around the neck and down in front, hung two longer and larger strings, or loops, one within the other, formed of teeth from an animal then known as the Nē-ĭ'clĭsh, which much resembled the modern dog, a sacred animal to the Hintox. It had fur however, instead of hair, which was gray, or sort of a maltese color. Some were striped, some nearly black, some white, with marks of the maltese mixed. Though now extinct in the now known dog race of animals, it was far superior to them in every way.

In regard to religion, the Hintox of Sannanzy, at first, retained the ideas of the original Delka Sadels, but later, they established an idol worship, or rather used an idol as the representative of a provident principle which they termed Al-trä'gish, the term meaning, *Helper,* or *Guide.* It was in the form of a man, posed as sitting with his feet folded under him. At his feet, crouched the form of an animal then known as the Neiclish.

Their I-cŏn'nä (temple), was formed by a frame work of sticks, placed together in the form of panels, alternating with open spaces the same size as the latticed panels, or in other words, one panel woven with sticks, and the other an open space, and the roof was thatched with bows and rushes.

Neiclish, the idol, was placed on the front of the Iconna, above which also was designed a crude half circle that was intended as a representation of the forces that came down upon Neiclish, and that he in turn was endowed with the forces that came from within the circle of the heavens, as outlined by the circular horison, for further dispensation unto the people. Within the semi-circle was the crude design of the stars, which was to represent that Neiclish also drew forces from them which he utilized and further dispensed unto the people as beneficiary endowments.

They held their adorational exercise twice a year, which was at the Spring and Autumn periods of the year. Sometimes they would hold special exercises, but never more than four times a year, which then were held, one at the beginning of each of the four seasons, viz: Spring, Summer, Autumn, and Winter. The exercises would last for one day, or from sunrise in the morning until midnight. A great feast was served at sundown, when they placed a barbecued animal on the center of a large table, about which were placed fruits and vegetables, and as the sun went down and the twilight came on, they ate and made merry. They assembled at the rising of the sun, took their positions before Neiclish, in the form of a semi-circle within semi-circles, until all the people were thus assembled. They then raised their open hands with outstretched arms, toward Neiclish, and then bowed their heads in obeisance to him. This was done by the people of one circle at a time, beginning with those of the one in front, extending back until all had made their obeisance to Neiclish. The order of obeisance was accompanied with crude music, rendered by musicians on instruments formed by hollow pieces of wood, with square holes through from the surface to the central hollow, similar to the modern flute or fife, and the hands and fingers were utilized to open or close the holes in order to produce the pitch of tone required. This re-conceived idea of wind instruments, was the first that came to the pre-historic people of this section through spirit influence, and in turn led up to the further development of such instruments in subsequent time. The musicians also rendered a chant in harmony with the playing of the instruments, during the adorational exercises, as they sat beneath Neiclish, or the idol, and the people. After the obeisance exercise was completed, they disbanded from the semicircles, and spent the day preparing the feast for the evening, and further social pleasures.

Subsequent to the establishment of the Kentersends in Thuriistic, a large tribe of the most civilized and intellectual portion of the Kentersends seceeded from the main colony and instituted a migration to the southeast, in divergence to that of their brethren. In pursuance of their migration, they passed southward from the now known Karakarum mountains, until they came to the upper Indus river, when they followed its upper course into the section now known as Little Tibet, where they settled in the valley between the Indus, and the Shyok rivers, which section they termed Rĕd'ē-zĕnt, but retained their former tribe name of Kentersends. They dwelt in Redezent for about two hundred years, when the entire descended colony continued the migration southeastward, along the upper course of the Indus, to about eighty degrees longitude east from Greenwich, when they turned southward, crossed the mountain range lying parallel with the main Karakarum mountains, into the valley between the latter named mountains, and the Himalayan range, thence west, around the western extension of the latter, into the section now known as the Punjab, viz: the rise and course of the now known Sutley river, which they followed southeast for about seventy-five or one hundred miles, where they settled in the valley lying extent between the river and the mountains, which section they termed Yĕs-tī'ä, and called themselves the Kä-lĭs'-tŏns.

When the Swansoans of Swanso had waxed strong as a nation, and began to spread out for new possessions, they invaded Yestia, waged war against the Kalistons for possession of their lands, and being the stronger nation, overpowered the Kalistons, killed most of the males, took the remainder, and part of the women as spoils of war, and left the remainder destitute of support, who therefore soon became extinct from exposure and starvation. The few captives by virtue of race mingling, and natural causes, became lost as a distinct race, in the blood of the Swansoans; therefore, the Kalistons were known in subsequent pre-historic time, as "THE LOST TRIBE."

Being descendants of the Kentersends, the Kalistons compared favorably with their ancestors, and their style of dress, and modes of living were similar, only being changed as their advancement in civilization, and the climate would occasion. They were a people who were superior in every way to their ancestors, and to their oppressors as well, and but for their untimely extinction, they would have developed into a great nation. They worshipped the Sun as the Great Light, which principle they termed Zăn-tō-zi'an, which term in their language meant, The *Great Light*. They erected an image or symbol in representation of the principle Zantozian, which was that of a triangular shaft of light brown stone, which they termed Zī-nī'ē, meaning *Monument*. The shaft was three feet wide on each triangular side, for about eight feet high, when it tapered to a point at the apex, the taper being about one quarter the length of the main shaft. On each corner of the shaft, where it began to taper, was extended a small triangular piece of the same material as the shaft, at an angle of about forty-five degrees, to the height of the apex. Each piece tapered at the point in harmony with the apex of the shaft. On the three sides of the shaft, between the point where it began to taper and the apex of the shaft, was represnted, by means of mineral colorings, the same tint as the sun, its full disc, and radiant light. They had no special stated assemblies for invocational, or adorational exercises. The principle of Light was looked upon as a source of general benefit and aid in all matters pertaining to life, and whenever the individual had matters of importance come up, he or she would go before the shrine, there kneel and ask protection and help from Zantozian, relative to the specific case. Also, whenever the people, individually or collectively, passed the shrine, on their various missions or meanderings, they would kneel before it in obeisance, thus showing their reverence for the principle of which it was symbolic.

In regard to the U-ĭsh'tē-cŏs (pre-historic Arabian term for Deserts), we find that every U-ĭsh'tē (Desert), exists as such, through a series of developing processes, such as the inundation of divisions of land from subterrene and fluvial sources, the origin of which was caused by convulsive, or natural drainage, in, or to the sections they now occupy, thus first establishing Rē-ĕn'dē-zone (pre-historic Arabian word for Inland Seas), or Dĕl-mĕr'shä (Marshes), as the pre-historic peoples of that section termed them.

The Reendezone and Delmarsha were, subsequent to their establishment as such, drained off by convulsive agencies, such as rendered outlets for their waters. Then by further absorption and evaporation, their districts were ultimately transformed into the various uishtecos.

The reader has only to scan the geographic area of the Eastern and Western Continents, especially Africa and Asia, contemplating the now known deserts, characterized with aridity of soil; absence of running water; dryness of atmosphere; comparative absence of vegetable and animal life; the general appearance of a boundless sea of sand, whose arid coast lines are marked with rocky fragments, and ranges of barren mountains, having their non-aqueous bays, and commanding promontories; nave-like mounds of sand; varied surfaces; irregular reliefs that range in altitudes from one hundred feet below, to from 5000 to 8000 feet above the sea level; sand dunes; oases, that contain rocky plateaus; vast tracts of loose stones and pebbles; ranges of hills of dissimilar types, and valleys through which abundance of water once flowed, when such as the Great Sahara area was land; great frontiers, such as those of Soudan and Barbary in Africa, and similar conditions in Asia, and the southwestern portion of the United States of America, to be able to find the missing links that will restore the aquatic epi-cycles of the past ages, thus proving their service in the establishment of the geographic changes in the past, as their cogs have turned in the great cycles of time on the deferent of the cycle of Life.

Furthermore, by considering all monumental evidences, such as above mentioned, the reader may be able to also link convulsive and aquatic changes of the past, into those of the present, and still contemplate the future, for all nature repeats itsself limitlessly, throughout the boundless ages of time. The great system of inland waters that had place over the earth's surface in the pre-historic, and more remote ages of the past, their transformation into desert wastes, in pre-historic, antiquated periods of time; the re-establishment of inland seas, by submerging new sections of land, with the same waters that have rolled on with the billows of time from the pre-historic ages to the present periods in which we recognize, not only the desert monuments, wrought and erected by aquatic changes; but a great system of marshes; lakes; seas and oceans, facts similar, that existed prior to the desert monuments, to be deduced from the present monumental aspects, such as exist modernly on the surface of the earth, that prove the force of convulsive and aquatic epi-cycles, and the changes they have wrought, by their evolutionary revolutions on the deferent of the great cycle of time, thus linking the past, present and future aqueous and convulsive forces of nature into the supreme cycle of causation. Therefore, as in the past, so it is in the present and will be in the future, that the same causes, viz: the subterrene earthquakes that never of themselves reach the earth's surface, but are convulsive seeds as it were passing to and fro throughout the body of the earth, opening up sources for greater eruptions, that cause the surface to rise and fall, and further develop into powerful convulsions, which ultimately establish depressions; upheavals; drainage; submergence; etc., such as have and will continue to misplace waters; re-establish lands, fertile and arid; mountains; lakes, and seas throughout the great cycle of time on which the records of remote ages are kept by the spirit scribes contemporaneous with that division of time, and those of the modern ancient, the present and the future, by mortal scribes contemporaneous with these periods of time, on the pages of history, and also reproduced by spirits on the eternal pages of the great book of facts and truth.

At the time of the formation of the Red Sea, the then known Rḛ-ĕn'dē (Inland Sea) of Tē'zē, now known as the Desert of Judah, was partially drained off at the time of each of the convulsions that established the Red Sea, and finally came to its present arid condition, through continual evaporation and absorption.

Just previous to the time of the great flood in which the Biblical narration pictures Noah as the principal character, that portion of the country lying south, and southwest of Judea and Idumea, was a great low marshy section, then known as Gē-rŏn'-dē-zē (the term meaning uninhabited country).

At the time of the great flood that had place throughout what is now known as the "Holy Land" (previously mentioned), great changes came to the entire country, which caused many of the fluvial sources to become extinct, and others to be established, as the waters of the flooded sections passed south, and southwest during the subsidence of the flood, and much of the soil and sand was washed down from between the ranges of mountains into the country of Gerondeze, southeast of Judea, which established the now known deserts of Beer Sheba, and El Tih, and at the same time the ultimate drainage of the country of Gerondeze, established the two rivers now known as Wady es Sunny, and Wady Khuberah, of the Desert El Tih district; the Wady el Khulil and its outlet into the Mediterranean Sea, though a part of it existed before the flood, and was the boundary between Judea and the country of Gerondeze. All the water courses between Syria and Egypt were changed to either larger or smaller dimensions by the effects of the flood. Even the Nile was rendered larger at that time.

Passing into the country of Arabia, we note the Syrian desert in the northwest, and the Sandy, in the southeast. The inland sea that gave place to the former, was pre-historically known as the Kŭl'tē-zĕn Sē'ziē, and the latter, as the Al-ăm-thā'ĭc Sē'ziē.

At the time the Wezinthes inhabited the now known Red Sea area, the Kultezen and the Alamthaic Seas, practically speaking, were one great body of saline water, for the section of high land between them, was very nearly inundated, therefore the body of water was known to the Wezinthes as one Sea, which they had originally termed Jä-rĕl'lă, but subsequently, the Wezinthe descendants descovered that the sea was divided by a section of land which they ultimately occupied in portions, when they gave the divisional names, as above.

We are further informed by Alem Prolex that the cause, source and process, by which the above named seas were established are unobtainable, not being known by the spirit intelligences contemporaneous with that time; but, in remote ages, the two seas were one, and so remained until convulsions occurred that rendered upheavals and uprisings of the land throughout the central portion of Arabia, thus causing the separation of the waters of the Jarella Sezie into two bodies of water. Prior to this separation, the higher portions of the Qū-sō-zū'stăc (mountains) of central Arabia, were Islands in the great Inland Sea of Jarella.

At the time of the convulsion that established the now known Persian Gulf, and the Straits of Oman, the Kultezen Sezie was drained off into that division of country, thus completing the establishment of the Persian Gulf, and their further aquatic blendings with the now known Arabian Sea, through the Straits and the Gulf of Oman.

At the time of the first of the five convulsions that established the now known Arabian Sea, the waters of the Almathaic Sezie, were partially drained off southward, and ultimately, were lost in the Arabian Sea, as the latter became fully established, and by further aquatic blendings with the now known Indian Ocean.

Passing into Persia, we note the two deserts, viz: The Great Salt, and the Lut, in the section of country now known as Kerman. These two deserts were established originally, as Reendezone, or great saline Delmarsha, by the force of three great convulsions.

The first of the three had place in the section now known as Fars, west of the now known Lake Bakhtegan, at the southeast section of the Zagros mountains, or about fifty-two and one half degrees longitude, east from Greenwich, and twenty-nine degrees north latitude, which caused a slight inundation of the section of country now known as the Lut, or Kermania Desert, in southeastern Persia. The second of the three convulisons occurred about fifty years after the first, and had place about thirty-six degrees north latitude, and fifty-three degrees longitude east from Greenwich, near the southern point of the Alburz mountains, which caused the inundation of the section now known as the Great Salt Desert, in northeastern Persia. The third of the three convulsions occurred almost simultaneously with the second, and had place east of the section of the Zagros chain of mountains, at about thirty-seven degrees north latitude, and forty-seven degrees longitude east from Greenwich, which inundated portions of the section now known as Irak Ajemi, and blended into the inundations of the second convulsion in the section of Khorasan. As the ages passed by, evaporation had reduced the inundations to two sections, viz: the Khorasan, then known as the Gē-rēst' Rē-ĕn'dē, or saline Dal-Mar, now known as the Great Salt Desert; and the Kerman, then known as the I-cē-lĕn'tĭc Rē-ĕn'dē, or saline Del Mar, and now, as the Lut, or Kerman Desert. The Great Salt Desert was entirely established by the disappearance of the saline water of that portion of the Gerest Reende but the Icelentic was partially established by draining off the saline waters of that portion of the Gerest Reende, into the Gulf of Oman, at the time of the formation of the latter, and ultimately completed to its present condition by evaporation and absorption as the ages went by.

Passing into Afghanistan, we note the Sandy Desert in the southwestern section. About eighty-five years subsequent to the first of the three convulsions that established the Lut of Persia, there occurred two convulsions that established the Reende, or fresh water Delmar, then known as the Thür-ī-ĕn'des Rē-ĕn'dē, now known as the Sandy Desert, southeastern Afghanistan. The first of the convulsions had place in the section now known as the Zarah Hollow, or Lake Zurrah, in the tract of Seistan, on its northeastern side, which in part, established the ancient "Hollow," and inundated the land south, and southeast of it. About five years later, the second convulsion occurred, and had place at the same point where the first one occurred, which inundated the section west, and northwest of it. Ages of natural evaporation and absorption has left the now known rivers and the great depression with its lake and several marshes, as connecting links in evidence of the transformation that takes place between submerged districts of the past, and the desert conditions of the present.

Passing into China, we note the Great Gobi Desert, in the northeastern section, which was established as such, by two convulsions, that caused the partial drainage of a great natural Delmar, then known as the Căs-cū-dē-rĕn'gē. The first occurred about twenty-five years after the first one that formed the Lut Desert of Persia, and had place in the section north of the now known Nan-Shan mountains, or about thirty-nine degrees north latitude, and ninety-one degrees longitude east from Greenwich. The force of the convulsion caused a partial drainage of the southearn portion of the Cascuderenge Delmar, the waters of which found dispersement over the low-lands of the country now known as Tibet. The second of the two convulsions occurred about sixty-three years after the first, and had place east of the Kin-Gan mountains, about forty-five degrees north latitude, and one hundred and nineteen longitude, east from Greenwich. The force of the convulsion extended throughout that section of the Kin-Gan mountains, especially to their southern boundary, which opened a partial drainage for the waters of the northeast section of the Cascuderenge Delmar, viz: the section of country lying between the extremity of the Kin-Gan mountains and the eastern extremity of the Inshan, and thence to the now known Gulfs of Lea-tong and Pe-chili, by the river courses of that region. Ages of evaporation and absorption have ultimately reduced the great Cascuderenge Delmar to the section now known as the Great Gobi Desert.

Ages prior to the submergence of Atlantis, that portion of country now known as the Great Sahara Desert district, Africa, was somewhat mountainous. At that period of time, a great convulsion occurred, that had place in the Zē'lăgs (mountains) then known as Sierra Antilla, about twenty-four degrees north latitude, and five longitude, east from Greenwich. The force of the convulsion extended through those ranges of the Zelags, thus sinking and submerging portions of them, and also leaving others, which latter ultimately became Islands. Beneath the surface, in the region of the convulsion, was a great subterrene lake. When the convulsion occurred and sank the land about it, its waters burst forth to the surface, and in time, submerged that portion now known as the Great Sä-hä'rä Desert, which body of saline water then became known to the Atlantians as the great Skä'dăsh (inland sea or lake), of Kä-rŭn'tĭc.

At the time of the various Atlantian convulsions that occurred on the eastern side of the Lontidri, the waters were partially drawn off, and at the time of the final submergence of Atlantis, the Great Sahara Desert district was practically drained, which after further absorption and evaporation, took on its present condition as a desert. At the time that the Horziethas were migrating across, and settling in the regions of central Sfury (Africa), they termed the desert Sahara, which has been handed down from that time, with but little change, i.e., only in the pronunciation of the vowels, the name having been suggested to the people by the sound of a water-fall of a stream in the mountainous section, near the subterrene lake, or Skadash above referred to. The great cave that contained the waters of the subterrene Skadash still exists. It can be found extending from about twenty-five to thirty degrees north latitude, and about three longitude, west from Greenwich, to about seventy longitude, east from Greenwich. The formation in the subterene district still exists, and if ever explored, will be found to be of most wonderful, and beautiful formation, which was due to a process caused by the infusion of steam through the fissures in the rocks and earth, at the time when the convulsion took place.

Prior to the establishment of the Great Skadash of Karuntic, a system of Zelags, then known as the Sierra Antilla, a section of which is now known as the Ahaggar or Hoggar, extended east and southeast through the central portion of Africa, from the now known section of Barbary and Soudan. Another Zelag range, then known as Prĭn'kĕl-ty, now as the Atlas, extended from Atlantis, through the country now known as Morocco. About seventy-five years after the establishment of the Karuntic Skadash, there began a system of three peridocal convulsions in the section of country now known as Egypt. The first had place in the now known region of the mouth of the Nile river. The second occurred about twenty years after the first, and had place about fifteen degrees north latitude, and thirty degrees longitude east from Greenwich, in the section now known as Egyptian Soudan. The third occurred about two years after the second, and had place about twenty degrees north latitude, and thirty-five longitude, east from Greenwich, in the now known country of Nubia.

Prior to this convulsion, there existed an immense subterrene thermal, saline Skadash, which in its extension, was like a great system of caves beneath the Zelag ranges that followed the course of the Gē-lī'ŏt Sĕl'tăsh (Nile River), extending from the region of the ancient lake of Mareotis, to that of the Birk-el Karn, or Lake Eel-Karn, at the extremity of the Feyoon, or Oasis west of the Geliot Seltash, to which an opening in the Zelags leads. At the time of the first convulsion, the waters were forced out from the subterrene Skadash, through a subterrene Seltash, that led from the Skadash to the opening in the Zelags now known as the lead to the Feyoon, which partly inundated that part of the country west of the Zelags. The force of the second convulsion, completed the submergence, thus forming the Yă-că-too' Skadish, or inland sea, now the Syrian Desert.

The depressions that now exist between the Zelag ranges, were caused by the Typhoon winds, which swept in through them from the southeast to the northwest. Were this region to be subterenely explored, the great caverns and caves that constituted the walls of the above named great saline Skadish, or Lake, would yet be found to exist, though they are filling up as the ages go by.

Regarding the source of the waters that formed the great Skadish, or inland sea, then known as the Căl-dē-gĭs'tic, that gave place to the now known Nubian Desert, Alem Prolex says that the information given him by the spirits contemporaneous with the time of its formation, is so conflicting, that a definite conclusion cannot be reached at this time, as to the source of its formation; but, the general conclusion is that, as the convulsion followed so close to the one that completed the formation of the Yacatoo Skadash, west of it, that the force of the convulsion opened subterrene connections with the Yacatoo Skadash, from which the Caldegistic Skadish was formed. At the time of the formation of the Red Sea, the waters of the Caldegistic Skadash were practically drained off, and by further evaporation and absorption, the Nubian Desert was formed.

The similarity existing between the sources of the waters that established both the Sahara and the Libyan Deserts, viz: by subterrene Skadashes, is due to the similarity of the existing Zelag ranges, and their extension southeastward. Both have left a small lake at their extremity, one southeast of the section now known as Morocco, and the ancient lake Mareotis of Egypt, from which subterrene streams flowed into their respective subterrene Skadashes, and both the latter had subterrene outlets that terminated in Oases at the southeastern extremity, viz: the section of Air, or Asben of the Sahara, and the Feyoon, or Lake Elkard, of the Libyan.

The Skadash that gave place to what is now known as the Desert of Kalahari, South Africa, was first known as Kä-sō'tä. At the time of the convulsion that established the island of Madagascar, and the Mozambique Channel, the force shot inland, so as to partially establish the Kasota Skadash, which ultimately became fully established by inland subterene convulsions, which let the water in from the Indian Ocean, through subterrene fissures in the earth. Later convulsive forces in the same region, cut down the earth so as to shut off the incoming waters from the Indian Ocean, which left the Kasota Skadash in an evaporating condition, that in time rendered its area, or district that of a desert, some parts of which, have never been explored.

The Kasota, as a Skadash, was impregnated with two principal substances, known to the Atlantians and the natives of Africa, as Bē'zĕr (salt) and I-ĭn'tä (a crystal), which latter does not now exist in any other part of the world, but abounds in that vicinity, and in a simple solution, is very poisonous, on account of which, it was much feared by the natives, and invariably shunned by the animals, and was very destructive to vegetation when in its crystallized state, or in a simple solution; but when in a compound solution, with the Bezer, it became less harmless, hence the deposits, after evaporation of the water of the Kasota, that section became uninhabited and non-vegetabled.

The Arabs have long been in the habit of tapping the subterranean waters, by sinking wells, a copious supply being usually obtainable at depths varying down to two hundred feet. The water in many cases rises so rapidly often times when the aqueous strata, or caverns are pierced in certain localities that the well sinkers are sometimes drowned ere they reach the surface.

In the Algerian Sahara, the French have sunk a large number of these wells, and the fact that plentiful waters can be had from subterrene sources, by way of the spring outlets and artificial wells, goes to prove that the subterranean Skadashes, or lakes still exist, whose outlets form the many Oases of the Deserts from the western coast of Africa to central Asia, and the great convulsive forces that opened large outlets to them, were the means by which the pre-historic Skadashes, or inland seas were established.

Prior to the eighth of the eleven great periodical convulsions that had place in the now known Golden Gate region, California, or in the beginning, the convulsive conditions that were making the changes along the coast of California during the 1000 years that intervened between the seventh and the eighth of the eleven great periodical convulsions above referred to; the convulsive forces, as they radiated east, and southeast into the sections of country now known as California, Nevada, Utah and Arizona, caused subterranean inlets from the Pacific Ocean, which ultimately established a great body of water throughout the regions of those now known states, which in its uprising from the subterranean inlets, established, as before stated, a great inland sea, which ultimately became known as the Shä-run-tre'zōn Cet (Sea) by the tribes of Shin'tō-lōns, who first migrated into the Sierra Nevada mountain regions. The principal convulsions that caused the draining off of the waters of the Sharuntrezon Cet, were two in number, which we will term the southern and the northern.

Prior to the establishment of the Sharuntrezon Cet, a great subterrene fluvial water course extended from the Rockies, westward to the Pacific Ocean. Its course was from its source in the Rockies of Colorado, thence southwestward, to the now known northeastern portion of the Colorado River, or where it enters the state of Arizona from Utah, thence followed the course of the Colorado River through the now known region of the Grand Canyon of the Colorado to the southwestern extremity of the latter, when it left what is now known as the southern course and outlet of the Colorado river and passed southwestward through the state of California to the region of the now known Bay of San Diego, where it had its outlet into the Pacific Ocean, the subterrene system of the great river and its outlt, having been established at the time of the establishment of the Bay of San Diego, the Channel of St. Barbary, and the Islands south of the latter.

The southern of the two convulsions that established the drainage of the great Sharuntrezon Cet, occurred about two hundred years prior to the eighth of the eleven of the great periodical convulsions, and had place beneath the waters of the Sharuntrezon Cet, in the region of the now known southwestern portion of the Grand Canyon of the Colorado, and extended along the subterrene fluvial source, to the northeastern extremity of the Great Canyon, when it burst forth in mighty convulsive force all along the source, thus establishing the greatest, grandest Canon on the face of the earth known to modern peoples, by throwing up the great walls of the Gorge that now exist for three hundred miles along the now known Colorado River, whose walls vary from 3000, to 6000 feet in height, which latter at that time held the waters of the northern portion of the great Sharuntrezon Cet, or those north of the now known Colorado River, from receeding southward. In subsequent time, the waters south of the now established Colorado River, were drained off by subterrene sinks and fluvial conditions into the now known Gulf of California.

The second, or northern convulsion occurred at the time of the eighth of the eleven great convulsions above referred to, and was caused by subterranean radiations from the latter, that burst forth principally, beneath the waters of the remnant, or northern portion of the Sharuntrezon Cet, in the region south of the now known Humboldt mountains, the latter being raised at the time, and further shattered the earth's surface throughout the now known states of Nevada and Utah, thus leaving subterrene outlets southwest to the Pacific Ocean, which were headed by depressions in the earth that are now known as the Walkers; Pyramid; Carson; Humboldt lakes or sinks, of Nevada; those in California; Southern Oregon; the Sevier; the Utah, and the Great Salt Lake of Utah, which served as a system of drainage, that reduced the remnant of the Sharuntrezon Cet, and parts of its waters also found their way to the Pacific coast by fluvial agencies southward into the now known Gulf of California, and further, by evaporation and absorption, was the great Sharuntrezon Cet reduced to the now known Great American Desert, and the Great Salt Lake of Utah, which latter is the principal remnant among the above named lakes of the Sharuntrezon Cet, that existed in remote pre-historic ages.

During the ages that passed, as the waters of the Sharuntrezon Cet were being drawn off and dispersed, there occurred many smaller convulsions and earth-quakes that rendered changes in the now known Great American Desert regions, which caused lands to sink, and others to rise, thus establishing valleys and whole individual mountain ranges, which fact not only assisted in holding some of the waters of the great Sharuntrezon Cet, thus establishing the lakes and sinks, but materially changed the aspect of the land portions throughout those northwestern states.

All the thermal springs of those regions are off-springs from the eruptive fires, or convulsive condition of that period, whose primal mineral, and thermal qualities have arisen from the lava deposits of those convulsions.

THE GREAT TISH'HANS OF A'ZAN AND GELV'THRIC, AND TRU'DOX, OR FURTHER INDIA.

TELTZIE XLIX.

A'zăn, was the pre-historic name of a great Tishhan (Hintox term for valley), that extended north and south between the now western coast of British India, and the eastern coast of the Laccadive and Maldive Islands, (so termed by the Gū-ĕv'ĕls). The southern portion of the Tishhan lay extent between the then known Sē-grĭs'tĭc, and the Dē-sănc'tō ranges; and the northern portion between the Desancto and the now known Western Ghats.

About the time that the Hintox began their migration from the city of Altashaza, and the northwestern section of Belzrando, to the central and southern sections, or location of the cities of Sentoese and Sannanzy, wars and contentions had also arisen among the Swansoans of Swanso, which caused a large tribe of them to migrate southwest from Swanso, when they passed over what was then known as the Sĕd'wĭck system of mountains modernly known as the Vindhya; thence westward, when they passed through the great gorge between the Sedwick and the then known Skä-gi'ĕn range, modernly known as the Western Ghats; thence southward into the northern portion of the great Tishhan, now submerged by the Indian Ocean, that then lay extent between the Skagien and the then known Dē-sănc'tō range, now submerged, the remnants of which form the now known Laccadive and the Maldive Islands, where they settled, retained their former section name of Belzrando, and called themselves the Hăn-grō'tēs. They established their hamlet about fourteen degrees north latitude and about seventy-two degrees longitude east from Greenwich, or in the area now submerged by the Indian Ocean, west of the modern towns of Honauwar and Coondapoor, southwest India, which hamlet subsequently became their principal pre-historic city, which they termed Wĭl-ā-mēde.

Subsequently, and long after the Hintox had migrated from Tushesiango and Sentoese, to that portion of Belzrando where they built their city of Sannanzy, a colony of their descendants migrated from that section of Belzrando, and the city of Sannanzy, over the Skagien and the then known Segristic ranges, which latter extended southwest and south, from the now known Malabar Coast, near Goa, India, parallel with the Desancto range, into the southern portion of the great Tishhan, where the Hangrotes dwelt, in the now known submerged area of the Indian Ocean, or Nine Degree Channel, west of the city of Purcah, India, where they settled, retained their former section name of Belzrando, and called themselves the Wĭn-gū'ĭs, and there established their principal city which they termed Hä-ä-ē'zĕl. Ultimately, the Hangrotes and the Winguis mixed races, which established a new race of people, who finally termed the great Tishhan, A'zăn, and called themselves the Gū-hĕv'ĕls.

At the time of the convulsion that caused the submergence of the great Tishhan of Azan, a large number of the Guhevels, who dwelt along the foothills of the Desancto range, and in the southern portion of the Tishhan, were left as remnants on the higher portions of the range, which now form what is known as the Maldive Islands, southwest of India. Subsequently, they became a large tribe, termed the islands Um'rĕz, and called themselves the Mag-ō-lū'tēs. In stature they were about five feet, generally fleshy. They had very dark skins; long, black, disheveled or undressed hair, that extended its growth, not only from the head, but all along the spine, and back, down as far as to the hips, thence forward over the loins and abdomen, though shorter on the latter-named parts of the body. That strange freak of nature made it unnecessary to provide themselves with raiment. Their heads were normal; eyes black; noses broad and flat; and the upper part of the ear auricle was pointed more like that of animals, and was characterized with considerable hair; their foreheads were very low; eyebrows and lashes quite long and heavy, there being no parting or space between the brows; their mouths were normal, but their lips were thick; their feet and hands were broad, and their toes and fingers spread apart; they were quarrelsome among themselves, and would fight unto death in defense of what they thought to be their rights. They practised cannibalism, but never victimized an individual over the age of twelve years. Their conditions in every way were degenerate when compared with their ancestors, the Hintox and the Swansoans.

At the time of the submergence of the Tishhan of Azan, the Guhevels dwelt along the northern portion of the section of the Desancto range, which latter now forms the Laccadive Islands, and which they subsequently termed Drĕx, and called themselves the Zŏn'zā-ăcs. They were short in stature, varying from four to five feet, and were quite fleshy, a fact that made them appear very odd; their skins were very dark; heads large, another odd feature; their hair was black, bushy, and the men possessed beards of the same nature; their eyes were black, penetrating, and might be said to be very handsome. Their foreheads were low; noses not as flat and broad as those of the Magolutes; their mouths were large, lips thick, and rolled outwards, so as to display both sets of teeth; they had small ears; short and thick feet and hands, their toes and fingers the same. They were a very low race of people, were scattered and few in number; they went entirely nude, which caused considerable hair to develop over their bodies, which was of a fuzzy character. They were peaceable among themselves, but hostile to intruders.

At the time of the second of the four convulsions of the second division, or at the time of the establishment of the now known island of Ceylon, southeast of India, a small remnant of the Hintox who had migrated to that section from Belzrando, or the region of the city of Sannanzy, were left on the island, who called themselves the A-gōs'tōns. Being few in number, existing under adverse circumstances as to climate, ill health, and non-sustenance, they soon became extinct.

Subsequently, by maritimal migration, another tribe of Hintox from the same section of Belzrando, entered and possessed themselves of the Island, which they termed Tē-zē'lōn, and called themselves the Hăs'drī-cōns, and established a hamlet for themselves, on the upper Măl-wät'tä oya (river), on the site where the now known town of Anuradhapura has place, which ultimately became their principal pre-historic town, which they termed Il-līn'drī-ŭs. In stature, they were from five feet six inches, to six feet; stood erect, and were well formed bodily, which latter was very plump; they had dark skins; long, straight, black hair; scant beards, except under the chin, and about the throat and neck; black or brown eyes, that were set back in the head, and somewhat projecting foreheads; sharp and well-formed noses, and they held their chins back against their necks, which gave them an important appearance. Their faces were broad, especially so across the cheek bones. The men were clad only with a sort of diaper, and painted their arms and breasts in characters of zig-zag lines and crossmarks. The women wore a sort of cloth, made from the tissue of trees, thrown over their shoulders, crossed in front, one end hanging down the back, and one down the front, belted or tied about the waist, and the sides down the limbs left open. They lived solely on the products of their hunting and fishing, and the fruits and nuts that the Island naturally afforded. They were careless, indolent, and quarrelsome among themselves, probably on account of there being but one race of people on the Island at that time, which caused jealousies to arise among themselves.

Gĕlv'thrĭc was the pre-historic name of a great Tishhan (so named by the Hintox) that extended southwest and northeast, between the then known Mŭsk-lŏn'gō range, and the now known eastern coast range of British India, and the Island of Ceylon, and the western coast of the Andaman and Nicobar Islands.

After the Delka Sadels of Cereges, the Hintox of Sentoese, and of Sannanzy, had become a numerous people, the Delka Sadels spread out into the northern portion of the great Tishhan of Gelvthric, that section being a part of their Cereges, where they had built a large city which they termed Kĭl'zërve, which was located about seventeen degrees north latitude and eighty degrees longitude east from Greenwich, now submerged by the waters of the Sĕt Bĕt'gäl, or now known Bay of Bengal.

The northwest portion of the Tishhan was inhabited by Hintox settlers, who had spread out from the city of Sentoese, and that section of Belzrando. The entire southern portion of the Tishhan was populated with Hintox from the city of Sannanzy, and that section of Belzrando, where they built a large city which they termed O-rī-zō'cŭm, now submerged by the waters of the Set Betgal, or Bay of Bengal.

Furthermore, the Hintox of the southern portion of the Tishhan of Gelvthric spread farther out beyond the then known Musklongo range, the remnants of which are now known as the Andaman, Nicobar and Sumatra Islands, into the then known Tishhan of Kä-ĭs'mä, which extended north and south between the Musklongo and the Sĕn-quĭs'trä ranges, the remnants of which are now known as the Mergui Archipelago, where they built a large town which they termed Cĭn'zä, which was located about ninety-five degrees longitude east from Greenwich, and directly east of the now known Great Andaman Island, now submerged by the waters of the Set Betgal, or Bay of Bengal.

About 11,000 years subsequent to the final submergence of Atlantis, there began a great compound system of convulsions that had place in different portions of the section now known as the Bay of Bengal, and was the next greatest system of convulsions to that of Atlantis, excepting that of the Great Eastern Archipelago, the world has ever known.

The above-named system of convulsions we will divide into two sections, viz., the southern or primitive, and the northern, or secondary, the southern being characterized by four sectional convulsions, and the northern by seven. At that time a range of mountains, then known as the Desancto, extended northwest, and then curved a little northeast from about a hundred and fifty-three degrees longitude east from Washington, to about eighteen degrees north latitude, where it was connected with the now known coast of India, and whose southern heights now form the Maldive and the Laccadive Islands. Another range, then known as the Segristic, extended a little south from the now known Malabar Coast, near Goa, India, then south parallel with the Desancto range, to near the region of the Equator, when it diverged a little southwest to the boundary line of the now Indian Ocean. Another range then called the Lukidish, which was then an extension of the now known Western Ghats range, extended a little southwest, to a close proximity with the Segristic range, thence southward parallel with the latter, to the point of its divergence southwest, where the former range diverged southeast from the latter, to the boundary line of the Indian Ocean.

The first of the southern section convulsions had place in the section now known as between Cape Comorin, India, and the Atollan Tilla, Kalay and Dou Matis Islands of the Maldive group, in the then known Segristic range. The force of the convulsion extended northwest along what is now known as a portion of the Malabar Coast, India, and out into the Desancto range, thus establishing the whole of the Maldive Islands, and brought the waters of the Indian Ocean from their then coast boundary, west of the Desancto range, to its present coast line of southwestern India.

The second of the southern section convulsions occurred about 1500 years subsequent to the first, and had place in the section now known as Palk Straits, between Ceylon and southeastern India. The force of the convulsion cut Ceylon off from the main land of India, established its southern coast line, that part of its Coromandel coast, as far north as to about fifteen degrees north latitude, established the Island of Ceylon, and brought the Indian Ocean coast boundary from the southern extremity of Ceylon, to that of India.

The third of the southern section convulsions occurred about five hundred years subsequent to the second, and had place off the northwestern coast of what is now known as the Island of Sumatra, in the then known Musklongo range of mountains, which extended from central Sumatra, with a southern branch that extended from northwestern Sumatra to the now known Cape of Negrais of Farther India, embracing among its heights the now known Nicobar and Andaman Islands.

Another range of mountains, then known as the Sĕn-quĭs'tră, extended north and south, west of what is now known as Lower Siam, and British Tenasserim, Farther India, that embraced what is now known as the Margui Archipelago. The force of the third convulsion extended east, established the northern portion of "Sumatra," as far as to "Diamond Point;" southeast along the southern branch of the Musklongo range, thus establishing the southern coast of "Sumatra," and the "Hog," "Pulo Nias," "Baniak," and other islands south of "Sumatra;" northwest along the main Musklongo range, as far as to establish the "Nicobar Islands;" and west to the central portion of the great valley of Gelvthric, or to the line of the second convulsion of the southern section, thus establishing the "Indian Ocean" coast line as far north as to about ten degrees north latitude.

The fourth of the southern sectional convulsions occurred almost simultaneously with the third, and had place off the southwestern coast of what is modernly known as "Lower Siam," in the southern section of the then known Senquistra range.

The force of the convulsion established the northeast coast line of "Sumatra," from "Diamond Point," and that of the southwestern of "Malay," by forming the straits of "Malacca," thus leaving "Sumatra" an Island. The force further extended northwest along the Senquistra range to the southern extremity of the now known section of "British Tenasserim," thus establishing the western coast of "Lower Siam" and that portion of the now known "Mergui Archipelago," as far as to the "Saint Matthew Island."

The first of the northern section convulsions occurred about one hunderd years after the first of the southern, and had place in the section modernly known as "The Mouths of the Ganges," southeastern "Hindustan." The force of the convulsion established the present condition of the inlet waters at the point of the convulsion, formed the coast line of "Hindustan" southwest as far as "Point Palmyras," and of "Farther India," southeast as far as to "Teknauf" of "Arakan," and southwest into the then known valley of Gelvthric.

The second of the northern section convulsions occurred about three hundred years after the first, and had place on the eastern coast of "India," northeast of the town modernly known as "Vizagapatam." The force of the convulsion established that portion of the eastern coast of "India," northeast and southwest from the point of the convulsion that lies between "Point Palmyras," and the mouth of the "Godavari" river, which latter it also established. The force further extended southeast into the great valley of Gelvthric.

The third of the northern section convulsions occurred almost simultaneously with the second, and had place on the southeast coast of "India," between the rivers modernly known as "Kistnah," and "Pennair." The force of the convulsion established the eastern coast of "India," from the line of the second convulsion of the Southern Section, and southeast into the great valley of Gelvthric, thus completing the establishment of the eastern coast of "India," and "Hindustan," and the submergence of the western half of the valley of Gelvthric.

The fourth of the northern section convulsions occurred about one thousand years subsequent to the third, and had place in the northeast remnant of the Musklongo range, between what is modernly known as the "Preparis Island," and "Cape Negrais." The force of the convulsion extended southwest in the range, as far as to beyond the now known "Great and Little Coco Islands," thus reducing that part of the range to its now island conditions. The force further extended southwest into the remnant of the valley of Gelvthric, to the submerged district, established the mouth of the river "Irrawaddy;" the coast of "Farther India," from "Cape Negrais" to the now known town of "Yeh;" the "Gulf of Martaban," and its inlet waters, thus submerging that section with inlet waters from the western submerged section of the valey of Gelvthric.

The fifth of the northern section convulsions occurred almost simultaneously with the fourth, and had place with the then known Senquistra range, between what is modernly known as "Tavoy Point," and "King's Island," of the Mergui Archipelago." The force of the convulsion established the western coast of modern "British Tenasserim," "Farther India," and all the inlet waters from the southern boundary line of the fourth convulsion to the southern extremity of "British Tenasserim," that portion of the "Mergui Archipelago," in that section, and also extended southwest to the central portion of the then known valley of Kaizma, thus extending the submergence into that district, by inlet waters from that of the fourth.

The sixth of the northern convulsions occurred about fifty years subsequent to the fifth, and had place in the remnant of the Musklongo range, between what are modernly known as the "Little Andaman island," of the "Andaman" group, and the "Car-Nicobar" of the "Nicobar" group. The force of the convulsion extended east to the boundary line of the third and fourth convulsions of the southern section, and north to the boundary line of the fourth of the northern section convulsion, thus establishing the group of "Andaman Islands, and further extending the submergence of the valley of Gelvthric, to about fifteen degrees north latitude by the inlet waters from the "Indian Ocean."

The seventh of the northern section convulsions occurred almost simultaneously with the sixth, and had place off the southwestern coast of what is modernly known as "Arakan," the "British" division of "Burmah," in "Asia," between the islands of "Cheduba," and "Ramee," and the now known town of "Akyab." The force of the convulsion extended northwest to the boundary line of the first northern section convulsion, and southeast to "Cape Negrais," or the northern boundary line of the fourth northern section convulsion, thus establishing the silands and inlet waters of that coast section, and thus completing the establishment of the great "Bay of Bengal," its coast lines, inlet waters, and its junction with the "Indian ocean."

At the time of the submergence of the northeastern portion of the Tishhan of Gelvthric, a remnant of the Delka-Sadels were left on the borderland of the section of country now known as Farther India.

At the time of the submergence of the southern and central portion of the Tishhan of Gelvthric, the Hintox of those sections, especially those who were near the foothills of the then known Musklongo range fled to their peaks and summits, when they saw the waters coming into the Tishhan. After a time they established themselves as a tribe, on the remnant land, to which they had fled, now known as the Andaman islands, which latter they termed Chatleza, and called themselves the Chalts. After several generations, physically speaking, they were about five feet eight to five feet ten inches in stature. They had round, plump bodies; dark skins; their heads were flattish on top, but full and round above their ears; they had black and slightly curly hair; thick lips; long ears, small at the top, but the lower lobes were large; their eyes were mostly black or brown, though some were gray; they stood very erect; their feet and hands were unusually large. As a people, they were more intelligent than were the Wezenets of Ruencicon; they tilled the ground some, and lived in huts which they constructed of sticks and covered with mud. The men wore a sort of apron made out of animal skins, and ornamented with a fringe of pendant hair, but the rest of their body was nude. The women generally wore a short, loose sort of trousers, made from animal skins, that extended to just below their knees, and some wore the same garment as the men, but it was made from a texture they manufactured from grass and fibres. Some of the men and women wore no clothing, but were at all times nude.

At the time of the submergence of the Tishhan of Kä-iz'mã, and the reduction of the Musklongo range, the Hintox who dwelt along the eastern foothills of the range, escaped to its remnant sections, which are now known as the Andaman and the Nicobar Islands, and those on the eastern border of the Tishhan, and along the western slopes of the Senquistra range, escaped to their summits, which are now known as the Mergui Archipelago, and thence into the section now known as British Tenasserim, of Farther India, while some who were on the western side of the Tishhan, escaped to the remnants of the Musklongo range, or Andaman and Nicobar Islands.

At the time of the convulsion that separated the now known Island of Sumatra from the southeastern portion of the Musklongo range, some of the Hintox who dwelt along that section of the range, and in that portion of the Tishhan of Gelvthric, fled to the summits now known as the Nicobar Islands, which section in time, they termed Rū-ĕn'cī-cŏn, and called themselves the Wē-zē-nĕts. In stature they were about six feet; they were tall, angular, and long-limbed, and were a coarse, crude people; they had long, heavy features; their hair and beards were black and long, but they had very little hair on their bodies; their eyes were black or dark brown, and deeply set; their heads were large, and their foreheads low; their feet were very large, broad and flat, and their hands were thick and broad; their fingers thick, but long. They were contentious among themselves, and were a people of very little intelligence, or civilization. The men wore diapers, but the women wore a narrow skirt that extended to their knees, their bodies above their waists being nude. Both the men and women painted their breasts and arms in waved lines running in a circular form. From this practice of the Wezenets, the idea and custom of tattooing was carried out in subsequent ages. The texture from which they made their garments was wrought out of grasses.

Trū'dŏx was the first pre-historic name of the entire country now known as Farther India, so given by the Fĕs'ĕnts.

After the Delka Sadels had escaped from the Tishhan of Gelvthric, into the section now known as Farther India, and the Hintox from the Tishhan of Kaisma, by way of Mergui Archipelago into the section now known as British Tenasserim, Farther India, the two tribes met, mingled races and ultimately established a new race of people, who in time termed the section Trudox, and called themselves the Fesents. In stature they were about six feet, on an average; they were athletic in form, being very muscular and having large joints. They were considered a very strong people, but were very lazy and inactive. Their skins were a dull black; heads quite large, their rear skulls projecting back considerably; their foreheads were low and narrow; their hair was black and medium long, some being straight and some curly, the latter condition mostly among the women; their eyes were black, small and deep set; their noses were flat and large, and their lips thick, and rolling outward; their ears were large, the upper lobe was flabby and hung forward, and characterized with considerable short hair; in fact there was considerable hair on parts of their bodies; their feet were flat with heels projecting back considerably, and their toes were long, with big joints; their hands were large and bony, fingers long and large jointed. They were a fierce and hostile people when aroused by intruders, or by contentions among themselves; but, being naturally lazy, they never tilled the soil, but lived on animal flesh, fish and fruits. They went nude, excepting for the covering furnished by the natural hair on their bodies, it being long under their arms and about their loins. They had no religious ideas, or aspirations, hence no modes of worship or adorational exercises.

In Burmah, of Farther India, the Delka Sadels, the Hintox and their mixed race of Fesents and their descendants, became the pre-historic ancestors of the Burmese, who have retained some of the physical characteristics of their ancestors, such as being stout and well-proportioned; their hair, however, though retaining its black color, has grown coarser and more lank; their beards more scanty, and their complexions lighter—facts due to the conditions attending their descent from mixed races. Their migrating tribes northward have established the same Mongoloid characteristics in their descendants, viz: the Tibetans, and the tribes of the eastern Himalayas; the Paloungs, Toungthoos, Karens, and other tribes toward the east; the Kakhyens, or Singphos on the northern frontier; and along the mountain ranges that traverse the upper regions, whose square faces, strong jaws and oblique eyes, through descendant conditions, display a retention of mixed race characteristics.

Subsequent to the establishment of the Văck-ā-rē-ŏns of Tong-King, China, to that of the "Tantalam Islands," east of "Lower Siam," remnant tribes from the stopping points during the migration along the "Mekong River," migrated westward into the mountainous districts of the now known Siamese Shan States." Subsequently, their descended tribes migrated still further north into what is now known as the "Independent Shan States," whose descendants became the pre-historic ancestors of the pure Shan stock, or Thainyai, "Great Thai," so called by the Siamese who term themselves Thai-noi, or "Little Thai."

Subsequently, a tribe of Fesents from Burma migrated into the section now known as the Siamese Shan States, where they mixed races with the Vackareons of that section, whose descendants became the pre-historic ancestors of the Siamese; hence the physical similarity that exists between the Shans, and the Siamese of modern times.

During the southern migration of the Vackareons, through the now known section of Indo China, remnant tribes along the section of the now known Cambodia river, diverged eastward from the main migrating tribe, into the section now known as Anam, or Cochin China, whose descendants became the pre-historic ancestors of the Anamites.

Descendant conditions characterized these natives with such ill-built forms as to class them as the ugliest of all the Indo Chinese who belong to the Mongolian race. They are scarcely of middle height, being shorter and less vigorous than their neighbors; their complexions are tawny, darker than the Chinese, but clearer than that of the Cambodians; their skins are thick; foreheads low; their skulls slightly depressed at the top, but well developed at the sides; their faces are flat, with highly protruding cheek bones, and are lozenge-shaped, or eurygnathrous to such a degree as is nowhere exceeded; their noses are flattish, and the smallest among the Indo Chinese; their mouths are large, and lips thick; their necks are short, and their shoulders slope extremely; their bodies are thick-set, large, all in one piece, as it were, and wanting in suppleness; the pelvis is large, with a considerable separation of the upper part of the femora, which causes them to possess a curious swagger to their gait, a characteristic that suffices to distinguish them as Anamese from all the other Indo Chinese people without exception.

Another peculiarity which especially distinguishes the Anamese from the Indo Chinese branches, is a greater separation of the big toe from the other four, than is found to be the case in any of the peoples who walk barefooted. It is said to be "so general, and well marked, as to serve as an ethnographic test, and indicates that the people of Anam are not descendants, as some authors have asserted, from a mingling of indigenous savages with the Chinese, but have existed as a distinct race for a long time." According to Father Legrand de la Liraye (*Notes historiques sur la nation Annamite Saigon*, 1865), this curious feature has served to distinguish the people of Anam since the year 2285 B. C.; that is to say, sixty-three years after the Biblical deluge." The Anamese are idle, fond of ease, and incapable of emotion. They possess great love of their native soil and native village, and cannot remain long away from home. They are mild, or rather apathetic, but have great aptitude for learning. They are slightly religious, some Buddhism among the common people, but the learned hold to the Confucian doctrine. They have great respect for the dead, and hold ceremonies in honor of their ancestors, and inhumation is their mode of disposing of the body.

The Chams who dwell in the forests on the frontiers of Cochin China, are descendants of a tribe of Fesents who migrated to that section from Burma. Their tall stature, war-like qualities, love of fighting, gay, open character, and absence from theft, are characteristics that have descended to them from their ancestors, the Fesents, and not from the Arabians, as some authors have thought, though the Arabians possess the same qualities, or traits of character, which is easily accounted for. The northern Arabs descended from a mixed race condition, through the pre-historic Rezendeths, Ackredeths, Hisocks and Ioxens. The Ackredeths and Rezendeths migrated into Asia, where the descended Timmenons were endowed with some of the same characteristics which they handed down to their descendants, the Delka Sadels. The Hintox, likewise, brought some of the same characteristics into Hindustan, which were farther extended through the Hintox descendants, and which found a meeting and renewal in the mixed race of Delka Sadels, or Fesents.

About the time the Vackareons halted in the section now known as Cambodia, Indo China, or near the mouth of the Mekong, or Cambodia river, a remnant tribe of the Fesents, who were migrating toward the now known section of Malay, diverged eastward, and also settled in the same section.

Ultimately, after the main portion of the migrating Vackareons had established themselves in the vicinity of the Tantalam I., the remnant Fesents and Vackareons mixed and blended into one race of people, the descendants of whom became the prehistoric ancestors of the Khmer, or Cambojans proper, whose further spreading out during subsequent time, established the numerous wild, or degenerated tribes who now occupy the borders of the Cambojan plain. The Khmer still possess physical characteristics of both the Fesents and the Vackareons, as they are tall and straight of build, have less of the Mongoloid features than the Indo Chinese races generally, characteristics that descended from the Delka Sadels and the Hintox to them, through the Fesents, their ancestors, while their good nature, though qualified with an apathetic character, comes through the influence of the Vackareon blood infusion. During the latter part of the pre-historic, and during the Adomic period, they developed in civilization to a goodly degree, as is evidenced by their Architectural Antiquities.

Subsequent to the establishment of the Fesents in Trudox, as a nation, a tribe of their race migrated into the section of country now known as Malay, which section they termed Mā-lăy'gŏn, and called themselves the Sō-kăth'răns.

Subsequently, a tribe of the Kenthricks from Tĭn-kī-dō'ci-ä, also migrated to Malaygon, and there became a numerous people, but they retained their former name of Kenthricks. They were a hostile or contentious people, and the more hostile portions of them remained exclusively to themselves, and in subsequent ages they became the pre-historic ancestors of the now known Negritos, or Sakei aborigines of Malay.

Likewise, in subsequent ages, descendants from the Sokathrans, became the pre-historic ancestors of the now known Semang aborigines of Malay, who, according to history, have been divided, socially, into three distinct groups, viz: "the Orang Benua," or "Men of the Soil," also called "Orang Gunung," or "Hilanders," and sometimes, "Orang Utah," or "Wild Men," who are uncivilized tribes, and constitute the aboriginal Malay element. Being unaffected by immigrant influences, they remain in small tribes, conditioned with a very low stage of culture, and are almost destitute of social organization, living exclusively upon products of the chase. "The Orang-Laut," or "Men of the Sea," who constitute the semi-civilized floating population, said anciently, to have been a vile people who dwelt principally upon the sea, and obtained their livelihood by fishing and robbing, who still occupy the same low social position as then, excepting their piratic pursuits, which at the present time are not tolerated in the Eastern waters. Their nomadic influence, however, during past generations, spread out into the Bajau and Milanau Islands of the Sulu Archipelago and neighboring sea coast lands, whose inhabitants are still sea nomads; and "the Orang Malayu," or "Malay Men," who constitute the civilized Malays, who are the dominant indigenous aboriginal population, who under immigrant influence have developed a national life characterized with culture and religion, and possessed of a literature, the influence of which has extended into the Archipelago.

Subsequent to the establishment of the Fesents in Trudox, Farther India, a tribe of Vackareons from their section of Vackareon, in Swä-dĭs'kăn, or China, and their city of Cuzerox, in the now known Province of Kang-si, China, arrived in the vicinity now known as the Island of Tantalam, off the southeastern coast of Lower Siam. In pursuance of their migration, they left Vackareon from their city of Cuzerox, from which they passed southwestward through the now known section of Kwang-si, into the central portion of the Province of Tung-king, in Anam, or China, to about twenty-one degrees north latitude, and about one hundred and six longitude east from Greenwich, where they settled between the now known Tueduc, and Songka rivers, where they dwelt for many generations, retained their original section and tribe names of Vackareon and Vackareons, and established a hamlet on the site of their settlement, which in subsequent time became their principal pre-historic town, which they termed Dĭs-ō-lṓre.

Subsequently, a tribe of their descendants took up the migration, when they passed southwest over the range of mountains that characterized that geographical section, thence south, and southeast through the eastern portion of the section now known as Loas, to about fifteen degrees north latitude, where they came to the now known river of Mekong, or Cambodia, which they followed south and southeast through Cambodia, to about ten degrees north latitude, or to the section east of the now known mouth of the Cambodia river, when they turned their course slightly southwest, to the section now known as the Tantalam Island, off the southeastern coast of Lower Siam (that section now known as the Gulf of Siam was not then submerged, hence, their migration was not obstructed by water), which section they termed Tĭn-kī-dṓci-ä, and called themselves the Kĕn′thrĭcks.

At the time of the convulsion that separated the now known Island of Sumatra from Malaygon, or Malay, and established the now known Straits of Malacca, and the then known southeastern section of the Tishhan of Gelvthric, and of Kaisma, there were no people inhabiting the Island section. In subsequent time however, there were two tribes, who by maritimal migration, entered and established themselves on the Island. The first tribe was from the Sokathrans of Malaygon, who settled in the section now known as Atjeh, or Acheen, northeast of the Bukit Barican mountain chain, between the Tawar Lake, and the Peslak river, which section they termed Mŭt′zŏn, and which term later on, became the name of the entire Island, termed "The Straits," over which they passed to Gĭl′lē-găth, the term meaning a water road, and called themselves the Gū′rōtes. Being of a nomadic nature, they moved about from section to section, on their hunting and fishing expeditions, hence they built no principal hamlet, or town.

The second tribe was from the Kenthricks of Malaygon, who, prior to that time had migrated into Malaygon from their section of Tinkidocia. They settled in the section now known as Acheen, or in the district of Labuan Batu, between the Pineh and the Bila rivers. Finding the Island already occupied by the Gurotes, and also named by them, the Kenthricks simply changed their tribe name to that of Hăr-ĕ'tŏns, and adopted the name of Mŭt'zŏn for their section name. They, like the Gurotes, were of a nomadic nature, hence they also built no principal hamlet or town.

In subsequent ages, the descendants of the Gurotes became the pre-historic ancestors of the now known Ballak race, who, pre-historically, occupied the western half of the Island, a remnant of which modernly occupied the section of the Island now known as southwest of Aclim, where by further race absorption, they will soon become extinct as a race. Likewise, descendants of the Haretons became the pre-historic ancestors of the now known Kubus race, a remnant of which still exists in the interior of the Island, as a savage race.

The Gurotes, in stature, were quite tall. They averaged about from five feet eight inches, to six feet. They had coarse features, large frames, and yet some were quite slender in appearance. They had quite dark skins; large heads; black, bushy hair and beard; black eyes; low fore-heads; and flat noses. The men wore a sort of cloth about the loins, and some went entirely nude. The women wore a garment that was twisted over the body, and that hung down to the knees. They were a contentious people among themselves, and were very much opposed to the intrusion of the Haretons upon their premises.

The Haretons were also a large people, being about five feet eight inches in stature, though they were of a medium weight. Their skins were a bright brunette; their hair and beard were both black and brown; their eyes were very large, and dark gray; their features were more like people of modern times. The men wore their hair short and in ringlets. The women wore theirs in long curls. Both men and women wore their garments loose, and carelessly thrown about them. They lived upon flesh and fish, fruits and nuts, and did not cultivate the land. They were a very indolent people, but generatively speaking, were very prolific. Naturally, they were quite intelligent, but were uncivilized.

GE-LIN'SIC,
OR
EUROPE.

TELTZIE L.

Gē-lĭn'sĭc was the first pre-historic name of the country now known as Europe, so given by the Sĭn'ē-thŏns of Tin-dĭn'zē-ŏn (Germany), and at that time only embraced that immediate portion of the Continent, but continued, until it was adopted by the peoples of the eastern half of what is now known as Europe.

Ē-trē-thē'ŏn was the second pre-historic name of Europe, so changed by common consent of the peoples of the western portion of the country, about the beginning of the Adomic period, and so remained until the time of Roman and Grecian fame, when a shorter term was desired, and therefore was changed again to that of Europe, the term meaning binding or bound together.

About two hundred years subsequent to the final submergence of Atlantis, there began a system of seven periodical convulsions that occurred in northwestern Europe. The first had place at the northern head of the then known Dīs-kī-lĕn'zō mountain range, which latter was at that time separated from the southern head of the then known El'phär range, by a deep, broad gorge-like Qū-tä'zä (valley), then known as the Kăl'lĭ-ăn Klī-dĭs'tō, to the section modernly known as the Irish Sea, the submerged area of which was then known as the Qū-tä'zä of Mĕn-cō-nŏn'dĭsh. The force extended southwest through a range of mountains then known as the Mä-zē'lŏn, that extended northeast and southwest between Ireland and Wales, which completely cut Ireland off from the other British Isles, by the formation of the now known North, and St. George's Channels, and the Irish Sea, and further establishing the zig-zag coast of Ireland, and its inlet waters, as well as those of the western coast of Scotland, England and Wales.

The second occurred about one hundred years, subsequent to the first, and had place centrally in the section of country now known as the "Bristol Channel," northwest of "Devon," "England." The force of the convulsion established the "Bristol," and the "English Channels," the latter, up to, but not including, the "Straits of Dover," and the "Scilly," the "Ushant," and the "Channel" Islands. The third, which was in two sections, occurred about four hundred years subsequent to the second. The first section had place in that portion of the now known "North Sea," at about fifty-four degrees north latitude, and one degree east longitude from Greenwich. The second section, occurred at the same time and had place at the point modernly known as the "Mouth of the Humber River," south of "Spurn Head." At that time, the then known Brodinzie mountains, modernly known as the "Dover Fjord" of "Norway," extended to the eastern coast of "England," in the region of the inlet waters of the "North Sea," now known as "The Wash," between the southeast section of "Lincoln County," and the northwest section of "Norfolk."

The force of the convulsion in the first section, extended northeast along the Brodinzie range, to the now known southwest coast of "Norway," northwest to the now known "Kinnards Head," "Scotland;" southeast to the now known mouth of the "Scheldt River," in Belgium;" northeast, thus forming the coast-line of "Holland," and its "Zuider Zee;" the coast line of "Denmark," and severing it from "Norway" on the north, and "Sweden," on the northeast, by the establishment of the waters modernly known as the "Cattegat," and the "Skager Rack," not including those south of "Central Funnen" and the "Cattegat," however, they being the work of a smaller convulsion that followed immediately after the above-named sectional convulsion, it having place between the point of "Denmark," now known as "The Skaw," and the section of "Sweden," northeast of it.

The force of the convulsion in the second section, extended northwest, southeast, and southwest, to the line of the first section of the convulsion, thus establishing the eastern coast of Scotland, as far north as to the now known "Kinnard's Head;" the entire eastern coast of "England," and the "Straits of Dover," thus severing "France," and "Belgium" from "England." Therefore, these convulsions established the "North Sea," as far north as to "Kinnard's Head, Scotland," and the southwestern point of "Norway," as well as that of the coast line conditions of all the countries having their boundary along its waters.

The fourth occurred about five hundred years subsequent to the third, and had place in a low mountain, between what is modernly known as the "Faroe," and the "Shetland" islands. At that time, a range of mountains then known as the Cŏr'ā-lĕtz, extended in a zig-zag form from the southeastern coast of Iceland, to the then known El'phas range, that embraced the peaks now known as the Faroe and the Shetland islands, forming a junction with the then known Gĕn-dē-zō'mŏn range, at the Faroe islands, and the Elphas range at the Shetland. The force of the convulsion extended northwest along the Coraletz range, to, and including the Faroe islands, which it established by the sinking, and inundation of that section of the Coraletz range. Further extending southeast, along the Coraletz range, it entered the Elphas range, from which point it radiated northeast, and southwest, thus establishing the Shetland and Hebrides islands, by sinking and submerging the lower portion of the Elphas range, and further established the northeast coast of Scotland, its islands and inlet waters. Furthermore, the extension of the force northeast along the Elphas range, sunk and submerged that section, thus establishing the coast line of Norway from the line of the first section of the third periodical convulsion in the south, to about sixty-two degrees north latitude, and the open waters between that section and the Faroe, the Shetland and the Orkney islands, and the northeast section of Scotland, and their connections with the waters of the North Sea.

The fifth occurred about 1000 years subsequent to the fourth, and had place northeast of the section modernly known as the Bornholm islands, in the now known Baltic Sea, centrally between the southern extremity of the Oeland island and the point of land now known as the Leba Section, west of the Gulf of Danzig, on the northern coast of Prussia.

At that time a range of mountains then known as the E-clē-len-zē'ō, extended from the now known Rugen island, on the northwest coast of the section of Pomerania, in Prussia, to the western portion of the section now known as Esthonia, Russia, that embraced the section now known as the Rügan, the Oeland, the Gothland, the Oesel and the Dago islands. Another range then known as the Vĭth-lē'ŭm, whose northeast extremity formed a junction with the then known Eclelenzeo range, west of the section of Esthonia, Russia, extended northwest and northeast, near what is now known as the southwest, and western coast of Finland, to the northeast extremity of the now known Gulf of Bothnia. A spur, or small range extended from the junction of the Vithleum and Eclelenzeo ranges, through the region of land now submerged by the waters of the Gulf of Finland. The force of the convulsion extended southwest and northeast throughout the Eclelenzeo range, and thus established the above named islands, the coast lines and inlet waters of northern Prussia; the southeast half of Denmark, from the boundary line of the third periodical convulsion; southeast Sweden; and western Russia, to the latitude of the northern extremity of the Gothland island, and the northern extremity of the section of Courland, Russia, and that portion of the Baltic Sea, to the above named latitude.

The sixth occurred about one thousand two hundred years subsequent to the fifth, and had place in the section of the Vithleum range, at the point now known as the Aland islands, which latter were high points in the range.

The force of the convulsion, which was of a radiating character, extended east along the spur, or small range of mountains that extended from the Eclelenzeo and the Vithleum ranges, thus establishing the Gulf of Finland, its coast line conditions; southeast, along the northeastern extremity of the Vithleum range; then southeast and southwest, along the northeastern remnant of the Eclelenzeo range, to the boundary line of the fifth periodical convulsion, thus establishing the Dago, and the Oesel islands; the Gulf of Riga, and by farther extension, the waters of the Baltic Sea, to about sixty degrees north latitude. The radiating force farther extended northeast, along the Vithleum range, thus establishing the Gulf of Bothnia, and the coast line conditions of eastern Sweden, and western Finland, in its section, and the Islands of Aland, that stand as monuments, reared by nature, in commemoration of the event that united the trinity waters of the Baltic Sea, the Gulf of Bothnia, and the Gulf of Finland.

A few months subsequent to the sixth periodical convulsion, two subterranean convulsions, that developed from the conditions of the sixth, occurred northeast of the city now known as St. Petersburg, which formed the lakes of Ladoga, and Onega, and the inland waters northwest of the Gulf of Finland, and the above named lakes.

The seventh occurred about fifty years subsequent to the sixth, and had place in the section modernly known as the southeast portion of the Bay of Biscay.

Prior to the second periodical convulsion, a range of mountains then known as the Här-ăn'zăc, extended circularly from what is now known as Lands End, England, thus embracing the Scilly Islands, west and southeast, through what is now known as the Bay of Biscay, whence it formed a junction with what is modernly known as the Pyrenees mountains, near the southwest boundary of France, and its northwest junction with Spain. Another range then termed Dĭs-kī-lĕn'zō, extended from off the northwest coast of the now known country of Ireland, along the coast of the latter, to the section now known as Cape Clear, off its southwest coast, and further circled southeast, to the vicinity of the now known Cape Ortegal, Spain, where it formed a junction with the As-tū'ri-ăn mountains. The force of the convulsion, being of the circular form, extended along the Haranzac range, to the border line of that of the second periodical convulsion, thus establishing the coast lines of France, to the now known Cape Finisterre, or the northwestern point of Spain, thus establishing their coast lines, the inlet waters of that section, and furthermore, formed the Bay of Biscay, by sinking that portion of the Haranzac range, and submerging that area of land. The Diskilenzo range, however, was submerged by the Atlantian convulsions that had place in that section.

THE TRIPLE MIGRATION OF THE ZRIN'ETHS.

Prior to the submergence of Teltzie We of Atlantis, there began a mingling of races that brought quite a change ethnographically, to the remnant descending races, viz: the Nĭn'kä-zĭts of the southern portion of the Teltzie, had mixed to a certain extent with the Lĕl'tä-zăts of the southeastern portion, when the submergence took place in that section. At the time of the submergence of that section, remnants of the mixed race of Ninkazits and Leltazats together with a portion of the Cĕl'ĕx-dĕn-trys of the northeastern part, and also of the Cĕl-trē-zō'näs of the eastern, were left as remnants on that section of the Eastern Continent, now known as the British Islands. Ultimately, the Celexdentrys and the Celtrezonas mixed races to a certain extent.

After several ages, there was a general mix up by the descendants of the four races above mentioned, a fact that resulted in their blending into one general race of people, when they termed the British island section Cū-cū'lä, and called themselves the Zrĭn'ĕths. By this time their physical characteristics had undergone a considerable change. They became a people of fine stature, with muscular bodies. The average height of both male and female was fully six feet. They were also characterized with long, straight, black hair, of which they took much care. Their skins were of a dark brunette color; their eyes were black, and brown, and were large and expressive; their fore-heads were high and full, but quite narrow through the temples; their noses were of the Roman style, and thin at the nostrils; in youth, their beards were soft or fuzzy, and not very heavy, but the more aged persons were possessed with longer and heavier ones; their mouths were quite broad, but their lips were comparatively thin. By nature they were a rather fierce people, very destructive, especially when migrating, or when engaged in warfare with other peoples. In regard to their dress, that of the women was a narrow garment that hung loosely down from the neck to below the knees. That of the men was an outer garment that hung loosely down from the neck to the thighs, and also an under garment of the pantalet order, that covered their legs down to the ankles. In winter, they covered their feet with animal skins. They manufactured a very pretty cloth, by weaving hair and fibres into a combination, that when trimmed, resembled the modern plushes, or Brussel fabrics, only of a cruder texture of course.

In regard to religion, about the time that the four remnant nations from Atlantis, above referred to, had become established as the Zrineth nation, they recognized a Great Spirit as the ruling force of creation, which they termed Tē-rū'shē, which meant Great Spirit. They established a sort of an idolatrous worship, however, or symbolic representation of that principle. Their images were in the likenesses of a man, but their principal one was further represented in an equestrian attitude, mounted on the then known Eū-kī'dĕt, an animal that was a cross between the Atlantian Hĭt'trä-î-nä (horse) and the Tĕx'rŏnz (camel). The image was carved out of wood and placed in the center of the tribal abode, where the people assembled twice a year for adorational worship, the stated times being at mid-summer and at mid-winter. The assembly for that purpose convened for thirty-six hours, during which time there was no intermission. The exercises consisted in dancing and all kinds of physical contortions, or strange movements of the body. Only one meal was partaken of during the thirty-six hours of worship, and that was during the eighteenth hour, or middle of the session, when they had a great feast, consisting of animal, vegetable, and fruit viands. At the close of the thirty-six hours session, an appeal was made unto Terushe, for their betterment in relation to mental powers by kneeling en masse before the statue, or idol, when they repeated an invocation to that effect. They then closed the exercises with loud vocal chanting, which they accompanied with crude musical instruments, and then departed to their various abodes.

Aside from the occasion of the above named meetings, the statue of Terushe was recognized by each individual when passing by, which he or she did by kneeling, and pronouncing audibly the inscription it bore, which was simply "Terushe." Small images of the Terushe, not mounted on the Eukidet however, were used in the homes at morning and evening devotions, as representing the gods of the people.

The Zrineths dwelt in Cucula for ages, during which time, modern Ireland was not separated from England and Scotland by the St. George's Channel, or those Islands from the Eastern Continent by the now known North Sea, or English Channel. Before the submergence that gave place to those waters, contentions and wars among the Zrineths had caused three tribes of them to migrate further into the continent, a condition which was and ever has been the cause of nearly all migrations eastward on the continents, or from continents to islands, and vice-versa.

The first colony of Zrineths to begin the triple migration from Cucula, or the British Island region, passed into the northeastern section of the country now known as France, where they retained their original tribe name of Zrineths, but termed that section of country Bă-sĕl'tō, where during subsequent time, they mixed races with the Făl'kā-leīts, or terminal remnant of the main branch of the great Cĭn-ē-tō'ī-ĕn migration to France, from which condition descended a fine, and more intellectual race of people, who ultimately became a large nation, colonies from which, advanced farther into the section of country now known as Germany, where they in turn mixed races with the Sinethons, the terminal remnant of the northeast branch of the great Cinetoien migration to Germany, who were a small colony, and who in subsequent time, were lost as a distinct race of people by amalgamation with the Sinethons, a condition that in their descendants, was the cause of the establishment of a new nation of still higher development, who ultimately re-termed the section In-thī-clē'ō-ny, and called themselves the Bē-trē'mĕns.

The second colony passed from the northeastern section of Cucula, now known as Scotland, into that of Norway, where they settled northwest of the mountains, now known as Dover Fjord, which latter they termed Brō-dĭn'ziē, termed the section Zō'tĕm, and called themselves the Zĭl-lē'zĕs, which was the name of their leader. They formed no new nations, but in their wanderings, spread out into the section now known as Norway, Sweden, and Lapland, the northern section of which, collectively, they termed Săb-măn'thă, which meant, *the land of snow.*

The third colony passed from the eastern section of Cucula, now known as England, into that section of country that was subsequently submerged by the North Sea, where they settled, termed the section (then land) Jĕn'dī-zĕn, and called themselves the Cŏn'cĭn-dīns. At the time of the submergence of Jendizen, the Concindins were nearly all lost. The few that remained on the border-lands, in time, ceased to be a distinct race, through mixture into others, and by other natural extinctions.

After the above named submergence that formed the now known North Sea, it was termed Ad-lĕs'trŭs, by the non-migrating Zrineths who remained on the Cucula Islands, which latter section they termed Cŭt-zē-lŏn'zē, meaning *severed lands.*

THE EASTERN MIGRATION OF THE KIN'TI-LU-CI-ANS.

At the time of the submergence of Teltzie Et, or Atara of Atlantis, remnants of the Kĭn'tī-lū-ci-ăns, a sect who dwelt in the eastern portion of that Teltzie, were left on the land which ultimately became the now known Madeira and Canary Islands.

Prior to the submergence that formed the present coast line of Spain, and that established the now known Straits of Gibralter, there were high lands that then connected the above named islands with Spain, of that portion of the Eastern Continent, over which the Kintilucians passed into Spain, which they did in search of a section of country where they could be exclusively to themselves.

In Atlantis, they were known as possessing the peculiar characteristic, of remaining absolutely secluded from all the other Atlantian peoples, a fact that arose from their extreme sensitiveness, which latter was caused by their being a highly magnetic people, or electric by nature, either being productive of sensitiveness, according to the degree possessed, which caused them to shrink from all peoples aside from their own kindred, which latter they expressed great affection for.

Among all the nations of the earth, generally speaking, who have descended from the Atlantian people through the ages past, none have ever been as seclusive, and retained their originality so purely, and perfectly, as have the Kintilucians, whose descendants became the pre-historic ancestors of the now known Caucasians, of Caucasus, known to moderns. They have retained nearly the same color of skin, hair and eyes, the same twitching, or jerking of the latter, and activity of body, characteristics due to their sensitiveness, acted upon by the electric currents which they are very receptive of, or that pass through their organism, from nature's sources.

Subsequent to their arrival in Spain, the greater portion of them migrated from that section, into that modernly known as

France. A few of the less sensitive ones remained in the Spain region, and ultimately mingled with the Keselzas, who likewise had entered the Spain region, from that of Portugal, or more properly speaking, the Sederones of Sederone, which ultimately established a mixed race, who became the pre-historic ancestors of the Spanish people proper now known to moderns.

In subsequent time, the original colony of Kintilucians migrated from the France section, to that of Germany. Again, as was the case when they migrated from the Spain region, a remnant was left in that of France, who ultimately mingled races with the mixed race of Sederones and Cinetoiens, which latter had migrated into the France region from Cinetoia, or region of Genoa, Italy, and mixed races with the Sederones prior to the coming of the Kintilucians into the same section, which therefore, established a new race of people, pre-historically known as the Fäl'kā-leīts, whose descendants became the pre-historic ancestors of the French people proper, as known to moderns.

Again, the original Kintilucians took up their migration for the purpose of further secluding themselves from the incoming peoples, when they passed circularly, east and then south to the section of country now known as Caucasus, Russia.

As on the former occasion, a remnant of the colony was left in the Germany region, where, in time, they mingled races with the Sinethons of the Germany section, which resulted in the establishment of a new race of people, whose descendants became the pre-historic ancestors of the German people proper, as known to moderns.

Furthermore, that portion of the Sinethons who remained as the pure stock of Ganhelemans, by non-mixture with the Kintilucians, or with the mixed race of Ganhelemans and Kintilucians, as they descended, became the pre-historic ancestors of the German Jews, whose further migrations established those of Poland.

A descended tribe of the mixed race of Ganhelemans and Kintilucians from the section of Tindinzeon, or Germany, migrated to the section now known as England. In subsequent time they mingled races with the Zrineths of that section, which ultimately established a new race of people, from which descended the pre-historic ancestors of the Anglo-Saxon race proper.

Subsequently, the Anglo-Saxon race again mixed races with the Zrineth descendants in the Scotland, the Ireland, and the Wales regions, which established a race of people, whose descendants became the pre-historic ancestors of the Celts, and ultimately the now known Scotch, the Erse, and later the Irish, and the Cymry, or Welsh peoples.

It was the mixed race of Ganhelemans and Kintilucians that migrated to England, and there again mixing races with the Zrineths, that has established the present physical conditions of the Anglo-Saxon race, such as complexion, and the color of hair and eyes now characteristic with the white race.

After leaving the section of Tindinzeon, the Kintilucians circled east and south, through the now known southern portion of Poland, northeast of Galicia, and the Carpathian mountains, northeast of Moldavia, to the section in Russia, now known as Kherson, near the waters of the Black Sea, where now is located the town of Odessa, where they settled and dwelt for several generations, when they became dissatisfied with the location, and again resumed the migration of their ancestors, and pessed northeast to a point beyond the now known Sea of Azof, or Azov, into the section of Russia now known as Cis-Caucasus, north of the now known Caucasian mountains, where they perminently settled, termed the section Kintilucia, and retained the tribe name of Kintilucians, and as before stated, are the only people on the globe, who have preserved their true Atlantian type, or physical characteristics, through non-mixture with other nations during their ages of descendancy.

The term Kintilucia in the Atlantian language meant *white,* hence, on account of their complexion, and the color of their hair, the Kintilucians so named themselves, and their country as well, the latter being prompted by the snow that characterized the mountain peaks in summer time, and the country generally in winter.

Prior to the establishment of the Kintilucians in their section of Kintilucia, there was a small tribe of extremely crude, or so to speak, animal like people who inhabited the western slopes of what are now known as the Ural mountains, who at that time were without section, or tribe names, and no knowledge of their origin. After several generations, they had migrated along the eastern side of the now known Ural river, to a point north of the now known Caspian Sea, or about forty-nine degrees north latitude where they re-established themselves, and were then called the Sĕn'dĭx tribe, by the Kintilucians, the term meaning *from the snow land,* so they still had no tribal name of their own.

The Sendix, were, as before stated, a very crude people. In stature, they were about five feet, stood a little stooping, and their bodies were shaped more like that of the Orang-Outang, and were heavily clad with hair. Their hands and feet, however, were more like those of the human race. Their heads were flattish on the sides, and their skulls projected in the back, and also drooped downward somewhat, over which hung a long black suit of hair. Their features were long and slender, and they were visaged like the human. They carried their chins back tightly against their throats. Their eyes generally were black, but some were gray, and were placed very oblique in their heads. Their noses were slightly flat, their lips thin, and their skins were very dark, or chestnut color.

After several generations, some of the less reserved Kintilucians wandered into their midst, and in time mixed races with them, which fact caused a change in their physical characteristics as a race.

MIGRATION OF THE SED'E-RONES.

Soon after the arrival of the Keselzas in Cojel, number one, or in the region of Morocco, Africa, from the islands of Ze-läs'-si-ŏs, or Azores, a second colony of the same people, and from the same Island, by maritimal, and partial land migration, had reached the Eastern Continent, in the section of country now known as Portugal, at a point near the now known town of Lisbon, which section they termed Sederone, and called themselves the Sederones. After many years in this section, they grew to be a numerous people.

These Keselzas, being of the same race as those who entered Cojel, as above mentioned, possessed about the same physical characteristics as the latter, the only difference being in some of their life customs, that were occasioned by their location, as the Keselzas who migrated to Cojel, were from that section of the Zelassios Islands, now known as the Madeira and the Canary, while those who entered Sederone, or Portugal, were from that section of the Zelassios Islands now known as the Azores. At that period of time, the above named group of islands were accompanied by many smaller ones as well as narrow necks of land that, during the ages that have intervened between the migration and the present time, have been submerged, which made it easier for the Keselzas to migrate from island to island, hence, their existence upon the three known groups of islands, and ultimate migration to the Eastern Continent.

The Sederones were a contentious people, forever at war with themselves, and were very much degenerated, in comparison with their far removed ancestors, the Atlantians. In regard to dress, they wore two garments that they made by braiding and interlacing strips of soft bark into fabrics, which latter they shaped into sort of a skirt that was fastened about the waist, and that extended down to the ankles, and over gown that hung down loosely, from the neck to the thighs. The only distinction between the garments of the men and women, was that the latter girted their overgown down to the waist. In regard to religion, the Keselzas of Sederone, or Portugal, recognized some great creative force as being beyond their comprehension; but, they had no fixed ideas regarding it, or established forms of recognition, in the sense of worship.

Subsequently, a large colony of the Sederones migrated into the section now known as southwestern France, who, en route, left a few straggling remnants throughout the section now known as Spain, who ultimately became extinct through adversities, and mixture of races with the Kintilucians.

After the Sederones had become settled and established in the region of southern France, they were met by the Gudlingstons, the advancing tribe of the main portion of the great Cinetoien migration, with whom they mingled races, and took issue, in their migration to the section modernly known as northeastern France.

Subsequent to the establishment of the Keselzas, or Sederones in the now known section of Portugal, there were several principal migrations into various sections of the country of Sederone(Spain), as follows: One colony migrated southeast from Sederone, into the now known section of Jaen, but retained their former colony and section names of Sederones and Sederone. One migrated to the northeastern portion of Sederone, and settled near the junction of the now known Ebro and Segre rivers, termed the section Dēl-cör'tō, and called themselves the Mā-lĭn'-gōes. One migrated northeast, into the section now known as Salamanca, which section they termed U-cē'dē-ā, and called themselves the U-cē'dē-ăns. One migrated into the section now known as Albacete, which they termed Trū-sä, and called themselves the E-sĕl'trĭx. From these sections there was a general spreading out, to the establishment of the Spanish people generally, who are a mixture of Kintilucians and Keselzas through the ultimate race of Sederones.

About five hundred years prior to the submergence of Atlantis, a great convulsion occurred in two sections, and had place in the region between the now known islands of Iceland and Spitzbergen. At that time a range of mountains then known as the Shī-ăl'tĭc, extended in a circular form, northeast from Iceland, to the now known Jan Mayens Islands, including Iceland, now a remnant of the range. Another range, then known as the

Kä-sĭ'ĕn, extended in a zig-zag form from the Shannon Island section, to, and embracing the island of Spitzbergen.

The first of the two sectional convulsions had place in a low mountain in the Shialtic range, situated about half way between Iceland and the Jan Mayens Island. The force of the convulsion extended throughout the Shialtic range, sunk and submerged it, except those portions now known as Iceland, the Jan Mayens, and the Shannon islands, thus establishing them as such, as well as the eastern coast line and inlet waters of Greenland, to the region of the Shannon Island.

The second of the two sectional convulsions occurred about one hundred years subsequent to the first, and had place in the Kasien range, southwest of the section now known as South Cape of the Spitzbergen Island. The force of the convulsion extended throughout the Kasien range, which it sunk and submerged, leaving Spitzbergen, its coast line and inlet waters as a monumental remnant, to guard the now open waters of the Arctic Ocean, thus blending them with those of the North Atlantic, all of which, hold imprisoned beneath their aquatic briny forms, lands and peoples of the past ages, now lost, and silent beneath the waves, but who shall speak again from the lighted etherial realms, giving utterance to truths, eternal as God Himself.

CO'JEL, OR THE MEDITERRANEAN DISTRICT.

About five hundred years subsequent to the final submergence of Atlantis, there began a system of ten periodical convulsions, that occurred throughout southern Europe, and the great country of Cojel. At that time, a mountain range then known as the Săn'zā-măn-zä, that was a continuation of the mountains modernly known as the Sierra de Lousas, Sierra de Gata, and the Sierra de Estrella from Spain, through Portugal, extending circularly, southwest, and southeast, from north of the mouth of the now known Tagus river, to about thirty-three degrees north latitude off the coast of Africa. Another range then known as the Săn-grŭt'zē, a continuation of the now known Sierra de Monchique, extended circularly southwest and southeast in conformity with the Sanzamanza range, from the steep cliffs of the now known Cape St. Vincent, to about thirty-five degrees north latitude, off the coast of Africa.

The first of the ten periodical convulsions had place on the western coast of what is now known as Portugal, immediately southwest of the now known city of Lisbon. The force of the convulsion extended throughout the Sanzamanza and the Sangrutze ranges, caused their submergence, established the inlet waters from the North Atlantic Ocean, such as circle the southern coast of Portugal, southwest Spain, and northwestern Africa, in that section, and further separated Africa from Spain, leaving a great channel, that later in the ages became the Straits of Gibraltar.

The second occurred about three hundred years subsequent to the first, and had place northwest of the section modernly known as Sicily, midway between it and the southeast coast of the now known Sardinia Island. At that time, the section now known as the Mediterranean Sea, or that submerged district of country, was possessed with several ranges of mountains and plains, as follows: One known as the Yŭs-kē-lĭn'gō, then extended southwest from the now known Mt. Vesuvius district, and the vicinity of the Bay of Naples, to the lake modernly known as Benzart, in the northeast section of Africa. That range, for some time prior to the convulsions that sunk and submerged it, contained many inactive volcanoes and craters, but at the time of the convulsion, they resumed activity. Another range then known as Tē'tä, extended westward from the now known western coast of Sicily, until it formed a junction with the Yuskelingo range. Another range then known as the Jĕs'tä, extended northeast from the section modernly known as Tunis, Africa, until it formed a junction with the Yuskelingo and the Teta ranges.

A large plain then known as Tĭm-ī-cū'lĕs, extended from the north central portion of the Yuskelingo range, northwest to the foothills of the then known Vĭn'zē-leīt range, which are now known as having place in the Sardinia and the Corsica Islands. Another range of mountains, then known as the Trĭt-ăn'zĕs, extended from the section now known as the western coast of the Sardinia Island, to the eastern central portion of the country now known as Spain, whose high peaks formed the now known Balearic group of Islands.

A large plain then known as the Kō-rĕs'sä, extended westward from the Sardinia and the Corsica Island regions, to that of the Balearic Islands, and southward along the Tritanzes range. Another plain then known as the Gē-lī-gē'lōs, extended south of the Tritanzes range, toward what is now known as Algeria.

Another range then known as the Nĭm'nē, extended across from the section of country now known as the Tuscan Archipelago, to the northeastern portion of the now known Island of Corsica.

The Nimne range was a northeastern extension of the great Basso (Jerethean word for mountains) range of the lofty and rugged central range of mountains that extend north through the now known northern peninsula of Corsica, whose further extension northeastward was by the then known Nimne Basso and their spurs, from the regions of Cape Corse in the north, to the northern portion of Lake Bigugli, to the northwest coast of the now known province of Tuscany. The present condition of the lofty peaks and the low valleys throughout the island of Corsica is due to the tremendous action of the waters, at the time of the convulsions that established the islands of that region, and that portion of the Mediterranean Sea, which in their swoopings and transporting force, misplaced the soil and carried it away into the surging sea, for further distribution in the submerged sections. A large river then known as the Hăm′mō, coursed through the southern boundary of the territory now submerged by the waters of the Mediterranean Sea, which had its outlet into the Atlantic Ocean, where now exists the Straits of Gibraltar, and its rise in Africa, which southeastern portion, after the formation of the Mediterranean Sea, became known as the Ge-li-ot, and later, the Nile.

The force of the second periodical convulsion, originated at the junction of the Yuskelingo, Teta, and Jesta ranges. It radiated along them, thus causing depressions, and submergences of portions of them, as well as the plains in their regions, thus establishing the Sardinia and Corsica islands, which are remnants of the Vinzeleit range. It also submerged the Teta range to the northwest of Sicily, and the Jesta range, to the section now known as Tunis, Africa, and that section of the coast line and inlet waters of the latter, from the now known Cape Serrat in the west, to about thirty-six degrees north latitude, leaving Capes Blanc and Bon, as the severed remnants of that secton of land. When the Yuskelingo, the Teta and the Jesta ranges went down into the sea, many portions of them were but slightly submerged, which is the cause of the shallow water in the now known Mediterranean Sea.

The third occurred about one hundred years subsequent to the second, and had place in the section modernly known as the Lipari Islands, north of northeastern Sicily. At that time the great Apennines system of mountains that now extends throughout southern Italy and Sicily, was known as the A-tă-rē-că′tō system. The force of the convulsion being central in the section now known as the Lipari Islands, that were then a high point in the branch of the Atarecato system, being of circular form, severed the now known Island of Sicily from Italy, by establishing the straits of Messina, and its entire coast line conditions; extended to the northeast boundary of the now known Gulf of Policastro, Italy, thus establishing that section of the southwestern coast of Italy, and its inlet waters, as well as establishing the Lipari Islands; extended west to the boundary line of the second periodical convulsion; left the Ustica Island, and extended as far south and west of Sicily as to establish the now known Maltese group of islands, as well as those of Lampedusa, Linosa, and Pondellaria, west of them.

The fourth and fifth convulsions were almost simultaneous with the third convulsion. The fourth had place on the southwest coast of Italy, in the section now known as the Bay of Naples, and the fifth, in the section now known as the Gulf of Genoa, Italy, south of the now known city of Genoa. The force of those two convulsions established the coast of Italy from the southeastern section of France, in the north, to the boundary line of the third periodical convulsion in the southeast, or to the Gulf of Policastro, all its inlet waters, the island west of Campania, and the Tuscan Archipelago, west of Tuscany, etc., and the open water conditions west, to the eastern boundary line of the second periodical convulsion.

The sixth occurred about seventy-five years subsequent to the third, fourth, and fifth, and had place in the section of the then known Tritanzes range, between the eastern coast of Spain, and the now known Balearic Islands. The force of the convulsion extended east to the boundary line of the second periodical convulsion, thus establishing the now known Balearic Islands which then were but two in number, viz: the then known Cē-lĭn'dē-sō (now submerged) and the now known Ivica, the Majorca and the Minorca islands (then in one) which latter three were thus separated at the time of the convulsion that submerged the Celindeso Island, and in its varied circlings and radiations, established the eastern coast lines of France, Spain, and northern Africa, from the straits of Gibraltar to the western boundary line of the second periodical convulsion, and by submergence of the former established depression, through the Straits of Gibraltar, formed the open waters of the Mediterranean Sea, of that section. As above stated, there was, at the time of the formation of the now known Belearic Islands, one more in the group, or the two that then existed, and was known as the Celindeso Island. It was located a little northeast of the now known Minorca Island, and was very beautiful and attractive. About one hundred years before the Adomic period, a great convulsion had place in the Celindeso Island, when it, with all its inhabitants, slowly sank into the sea, and was totally lost to modern knowledge, and at which time its sister island was severed into the three parts now known as the Ivinca, the Majorca and the Minorca Islands.

The seventh of the convulsions, which in reality was in three sections, and was the most terrific of the ten, occurred about four hundred years subsequent to the sixth, during a period of about a hundred and twenty-five years from beginning to finish. At that time, a great range of mountains then known as the Căl-cē'ŭs, extended from the section now known as the peninsula of Istria, southwest Austria, along the coast of Dalmatia, Albania, and western Greece, thus embracing all of the now known Islands along the western coast of those countries; thence southeast to and including the now known Candia and Cyprus Islands, to the coast of the now known country of Syria. Another great system of mountain ranges, then known as the Cŏr-dē-cōn'gō, extended south, and southeast through the section now known as Turkey in Europe and Greece, two distinct branches of which then extended farther southeast from Greece to the western coast of the now known section of Asia Minor. A branch of the Calceus range extended from what is now known as the eastern coast of the Candia Island, to the coast of Asia Minor, through the section now submerged by the waters of the Gulf of Makry, thus establishing the Karapathos and the Rhodes Islands. A branch of the same range extended from what is now known as the northern coast of the Cyprus Island, through the section now submerged by the waters of the Gulf of Adalia, to Asia Minor.

The principal one of the three sectional convulsions had place in the eastern section of the country now known as the southeastern portion of the peninsula that separated the Soronicus Sinus, from the Argolicus, or modernly speaking, the Ægean, and the Nauplia Gulfs. The powerful force of the radiating convulsion, extending as it did, in all directions, shattered the entire country now known as Greece, established its coast line conditions, and inlet waters; extended east to the partial establishment of the now known Cyclades, or Archipelago east of Peloponnesus (which was completed by several smaller convulsions in subsequent time), to the coast of Asia Minor, thus establishing its western coast line, and inlet waters from the anciently known Ceramicus Sinus, or the now known Gulf of Kos, to and including the anciently known Propontis, or modern Sea of Marmora. The northeastern extension of the force further depressed and submerged the section of country now known as the Ægean Sea, the coast line and inlet waters of southern Turkey in Europe, from the section of northeastern Thessalia, Greece, to, but not including, the now known Bosphorus, or Channel of Constantinople; severed Turkey in Europe from Turkey in Asia by the establishment of the depression of land, or channel that became the Bosphorus Straits, or Channel of Constantinople, at the time of the complete formation of the now known Black Sea, when through it, the waters of the latter-named sea blended into those of the Marmora, thus completing the establishment of the Bosphorus Straits.

The second of the sectional convulsions occurred about fifty years subsequent to the first, and had place between what is modernly known as the Candia and the Cyprus Islands. The force of the convulsion extended northeast along the Calceus range, to the now known coast of Asia Minor, thus establishing the coast line and inlet waters of that section from the southern extremity of the anciently-known Craega's mountains, northwest to the line of the first convulsion, and south to the northeastern section of what is modernly known as Tripoli, Africa, thus establishing the now known Rhodes, Karpathos, and Candia Islands, and further extending the Mediterranean Sea eastward.

The third of the sectional convulsions occurred about twenty-five years subsequent to the second, and had place in the section modernly known as the northeastern coast of the Cyprus Island. The force of the convulsion extended west along the Calceus range, thus establishing the Cyprus Island, which latter stands as evidence of its work. It further extended northwest along that branch range, to its junction with the now known Lycian Taurus mountains of Asia Minor, and northeast along the Calceus range to their junction, with the southern branch of the now known Cilician Taurus mountains of Turkey in Asia, thus establishing the coast line of the latter, from the western coast of the now known Gulf of Adalia, to and including the Gulf of Iskenderoon, east to and including the coast line of the now known country of Palestine, as far south as to the now known Cape Carmel, thus establishing the coast line and inlet waters of Palestine, to that section. The force further extended southwest to the now known section of northern Egypt, and west to the eastern boundary line of the second convulsion, thus establishing the now known coast line of northern Egypt from the now known mouth of the Nile river, west to Tripoli, Africa, thus completing the eastern extension of the Mediterranean Sea, excepting the southeastern corner, which was established by a subsequent convulsion, elsewhere herein described.

During the one hundred and twenty-five years, there were other smaller convulsions that occurred throughout what is now known as Modern Greece, and along its western coast, that completed the now known Ionian Islands, and the Straits of Otranto. Before the formation of the southern half of the Mediterranean Sea, a large river then known as the Hammo, flowed westward throughout the new southern section of the Mediterranean Sea district, having its outlet into the North Atlantic, after the formation of the latter, where now is the Straits of Gibraltar. The river pre-historically known as Gē-lī'ŏt, and historically as the Nile, is the remnant source of the Hammo. Its course through the Mediterranean district was from the now known mouths of the Nile (which were established by radiations of the third periodical convulsion, and by smaller ones that opened the land between the foothills of the mountains), northwest, in a circular, but zig-zag form to the Calceus range of mountains, or at a point near the southeastern coast of the Candia Island; thence zig-zag southwest to about twenty degrees longitude east of Greenwich, to near the northeast coast of Tripoli, Africa, when it turned sharply northwest in a zig-zag course, passed between what is now known as the Maltese Islands, and those of the Pantellaria, Linosa, and Lanpedosa, and centrally between the now section of Cape Bon, Africa, and the western cost of Sicily; thence it cut through the then known Yuskelingo and Jesta ranges of mountains, and from thence westward in a zig-zag form, to its outlet into the North Atlantic Ocean, as above stated, in the section between the now known countries of Morocco, Africa, and Spain, or through what is now known as the Straits of Gibraltar.

The eighth of the ten periodical convulsions occurred about four hundred and fifty years subsequent to the seventh, and had place in the then known Calceus range, in the section of country now known as off the southwestern coast of Dalmatia, and the Islands now existing on the eastern shores of the Adriatic Sea. The force of the convulsion extended northwest and northeast along the Calceus range, thus establishing all the islands along the eastern coast of the Adriatic Sea, from the Gulf of Trieste in the north, to the border line of the seventh periodical convulsion on the western central coast of Greece, the Gulf of Taranto, southeastern coast of Italy, the western coast line of the Adriatic Sea, and the open waters of the Mediterranean Sea, south of the Straits of Otranto.

The ninth occurred about 2200 years subsequent to the eighth, and had place in the section modernly known as between the peninsula of Kertch, on the eastern coast of the peninsula of Corea, and the western section of the Dĕn-kŏn'sō-lēte, or what is now known as the western section of the Caucasian mountains. At the time of the convulsion, the now known Sea of Azov was the southeastern arm of an inland Sea, then known as Mĕrä-cō-ŏn'dĭsh, that then extended from it northeast to the now known region of the Caspian Sea, that portion of it that was formerly the pre-historic lake of Kĭnt'nō-zē. The force of the convulsion severd the peninsula of Kertch, and established the Straits of Enikale, through which the waters of the Meracoondish Sea were let in, to inundate portions of land, now the Black Sea district, which after the complete establishment of the latter, became the southwest remnant of the Meracoondish Sea, or the Sea of Azov, the Lake of Kintnoze being the northeastern remnant of the northern basin of the Caspian Sea. The force of the convulsion extended northwest and southwest, thus establishing the now known coast of the Crimean Peninsula, and the eastern coast of the Black Sea, which ultimated in the completion of the latter, by blending its waters with those of the Mediterranean, through the source of the Bosphorus straits, and submerging the land now occupied by the southern half of the Black Sea.

The tenth occurred about 1000 years subsequent to the ninth, and had place in the section now known as the eastern terminal of the Caucasian mountains, southeast of Cape Apsheron. At that time, the Caucasian mountains were known as the Denkonsolete range, and further extended southeast to the section now known as the Balkhan Bay, on the eastern coast of the Caspian Sea, where it diverged into two branches, one northeast and the other southeast, which caused the establishment of the Balkhan and the Adji Bojur Bays, and the extension of land that separates them. Another branch of the Denkonsolete range extended north from Cape Apsheron to the inlet waters on the eastern coast of the Caspian Sea, now known as Kara Bochazx.

At the time of the convulsion, the now known Northern Ural of the Caspian Sea was a fresh-water lake, then known as Kintnoze, into which the Volga river flowed from the west, the Ural from the north, and the Emba from the northeast, and the Kintnoze had its outlet from the now known Mertvy Kultu Bay, by a river then known as the Kĭ'dĕl-mŭsh, that flowed in a zig-zag course, southward into the Kidelmush Lake. It was a small body of water that had place on the northern side of the extremity of the branch from the Denkonsolete range, of that section, now known as the northern section of the inlet waters, termed Kara Bochaz. It had its outlet from its southeastern section, by a river that was also termed Kidelmush (then considered as a continuation of the former) that flowed in a zig-zag form south, southeast, north, and again southeast, along what is now known as the section of Ust Urt, where it was met by the Kăl'sŭs river, the outlet of Lake Kalceus.

Lake Kalceus, the term meaning *inland waters,* was at that time a body of fresh water, but is modernly known as the Aral Sea, which became a body of salt water after the establishment of the Caspian Sea, through subterrene drainage and mixture of waters, and assumed its present dimension and condition, as formerly, it was much larger than now.

The Kalsus river flowed in a zig-zag course southward to its junction with the Kidelmush river, from whence their conjunct waters flowed eastward, and were lost in those of an inland sea then known as the Delcranzo, which section having been later drained off, is now known as the Kara Kun Desert. Thus was the northeast half of the old course of the Ancient Oxus formed, as far as to the section of the anciently known Gulf of Aboughir, a southern extension of the Kalceus, or Aral Sea, now dried up.

At the time of the formation of the Caspian Sea, the waters of the Delcranzo Sea were drained off into the former, when what is now supposed to be the southwest half of the old course of the ancient Oxus, and its mouths, in the section of the Bays of Balkhan and Adji Bojur, were formed, which therefore was the course of the last retreating waters of the Delcranzo Sea, into the Caspian Sea, instead of, as has been supposed, the outlet course of the ancient Oxus.

Furthermore, there was no connection between the Aral and the Caspian Seas, through the old course of the ancient Oxus, as modernly supposed, but there was a connection of the waters of the Kalceus, and the Kintnoze Lakes, at the central point of the old course of the ancient Oxus, where they formed a junction, and flowed off to the Sea of Delcranzo.

The force of the convulsion extended east, along the Denkonsolete range, and its terminal diverging branches, thus forming the northern boundary of the Southern Basin of the Caspian Sea, by sinking and submerging that portion of the range, and further establishing the Bays of Balkhan and Adji Bojur, and the Balkhan peninsula, that separate them. Its further extension south from the point of the convulsion, to the base of the great Elburz range, established the southern marshy boundary of the Southern Basin, and on the east, the Gulfs of Enzeli and Kizil Agatch, and Cape Apsheron, as the western monuments contemporaneous structure with that of the Balkan peninsula, on the east, that stand in memory of nature's force and power to change land districts into seas, and vice versa. Further extension northeast along the branch, in that section of the Delkonsolete range, which formerly it sunk, took on the circular form in the region of Lake Kidelmush, thus, by connecting its waters with those of the Caspian Sea, established what is modernly known as the Kara Bochaz inlet waters, north of the Balkhan peninsula. Again, the force was resumed and extended along the eastern coast of the Caspian Sea, to the extremity of the now known Mangishlak Lake peninsula, whose high hills extended across to the western section of the now Caspian district, through which the force further extended, thus forming the Bay of Kuma on the west shore, sinking the hills between it and the point now known as the Mangishlak peninsula, the third monument in evidence of nature's work in connecting waters for the purpose of submerging lands. Whirling to the north, the force established the northern coast of the Mangishlak peninsula and that of the western and northern coast of Busatchi, which let the waters of Lake Kintnoze into the marshy lands now known as the Central Basin of the Caspian Sea, which completed the connection of the three basins of the Caspian waters, thus fully establishing the Caspian Sea, its coast lines and subterrene conditions.

MIGRATION OF THE JE-RE-THE'ANS.

As before stated, the Jeretheans were a great nation, who in their first tribal radiations from Cojel number Two, had spread out through that part of the then known district of country, now submerged by the waters of the northwestern section of the Mediterranean Sea, and at the time of the submergence, remnant tribes of them were left in the various localities along the western coast of Italy, on the Islands in the sea, and on the northeastern coast of Africa. They, like the Kadios, were a large people, who in stature averaged about seven feet, and were quite fleshy. Their skins were black, their eyes small, some being black and some brown; their hair, in the majority of cases, was straight, some being curly, and was black. The males had no beard to speak of, and little hair on their bodies; their lips were thick and peculiar-looking, as one rolled upward and the other downward; a condition that caused them to expose both their upper and lower teeth, displaying very broad incisors and canines that were remarkably long for a human mouth; their foreheads were low and narrow through the temples; their cheeks broad; noses narrow through the nostrils, but broader at the upper portion; their feet, hands, arms and legs were remarkably large.

Their style or manner of dress varied somewhat. Some wore short, narrow skirts; some wore strips of material that hung down from their shoulders to their knees, and some wore only a band around the waist, to which a pendant garment, or apron extended from the waist down the thighs. They used various materials for their raiment. Some garments were made from furred skins, and some from fibrous texture, which they ornamented with fresh green leaves. They ornamented their ears with white rings. As they never pierced their ears they hung the rings over them. The leaders of the tribe wore a sort of cap which they termed Zick, from which three white, pendant rings hung down to the forehead, the larger of the three being in the center. The Zick was further ornamented with green leaves. The people lived in huts which they termed Zē'lăshes, which at first were constructed by sticks being driven perpendicularly into the ground, and branches woven between them to form the wall, which latter was plastered over with mud, thus completing the Zelash in which they lived as families. The promiscuous dwellers, however, occupied tents in the fields, which former they termed Qŭishes, made from skins, and were very small and flat on top. When they moved, they took the skins off the frames, and left the latter behind.

As a rule, the people were peaceable among themselves, but hostile to outside tribes, who sought to trespass on their possessions. In regard to religion, those who occupied Cojel, or the southwestern Mediterranean section, recognized a being as superior to themselves, one in whom was embodied strength and protective force, which principle they termed U-tĭs'ē, which meant Builder of Nature. That being, or force, was symbolized by the image of the then known Terilen, an animal much in resemblance to the modern Lion, the term meaning strength, as by nature, the animal was a powerful beast; hence used as the symbol. The images were made of wood, and decorated with skins of the animal; however, they only represented the head and forequarters of the animal, thus displaying the heavy mane that hung down over its shoulders. The eyes and teeth on the image were represented, or wrought, with staining materials, similar to modern crayon work, only in a crude manner, however.

The principal image was always placed near the leader's Zelash, and a smaller one on top of the latter, and the families had small ones in representation of the same animal, in their homes. They had no stated call to assemble for worship, or adorational exercises in recognition of Utise, for the setting sun was always the signal for the people to meet at the shrine of the image for that purpose, and therefore was a daily occurrence. When assembled, either at the public image or in the presence of the images in the home shrines, they repeated an invocation for protection, which was embodied in the following audible language: El dos sy, Kel ka na fisht, Cre fa si li fi ca, Kel fre en ta, Ka se on sta. In this invocation they asked that they might be protected, guided, and helped in all things. "Onsta" was a word used in the same sense that a modern, when closing his prayer, or invocation, would say "Amen."

As the remnant Jeretheans, left on the northeastern coast of Africa, viz., the Kĭn-măn'zēs of Kĭn-măn'zēs, who became the ancestors of the Libyans, are accounted for in another section of the work, we will pass on to note the migrations of the Jeretheans eastward into Europe.

Prior to the second of the ten great periodical convulsions that established the Mediterranean Sea, a tribe of Jeretheans from the plain of Timicules, east of the now known Sardinia Island, and the then known city of Sŭt-rē-nĭn'go (principal city in the plain), migrated southeast, along the then known great river Hammo, or Nile, to the section of country now known as the mouth of the Nile river, which section they termed Găs'bî-ä, and called themselves the Kasamanzes.

Prior to the third, fourth and fifth great periodical convulsions that formed that part of the Mediterranean Sea, west of Italy, the great plain of Timicules, east of the now known Sardinia Island, was occupied by a large settlement of Jeretheans, whose principal city in the plain was termed by them, Sutreningo. Likewise, the great Qū-tä-zä' (valley) of Kō-rĕs'sa, that lay ex tent west of the Sardinia Island, was also inhabited by a large settlement of Jeretheans, whose principal city in the Qutaza they termed Kŭ'nŏx. At the time of the submergence of the plain of Timicules and the Qutaza of Koressa, and that established the Island of Sardinia, a large remnant of Jeretheans from both plain and Qutaza, were left upon the Island, which after a time they termed Kä-sĭn'kä, and called themselves the Kasinkas.

After several generations they became characterized as a crude and peculiar race of people. They inhabited the then known Zĭn-zē-lē'ĭt mountains, and lived principally in caves and excavations in the mountain sides, where they huddled together in harmonious families. In stature they were about five and one-half feet, and of small physique; had dark-colored skins; dark, straight, but disheveled hair and beards; dark eyes; long, pointed noses; wide mouths, and thick lips; low foreheads; ears with long lower lobes; and their hands and feet were large, thick and bony.

Prior to the formation of the northwestern section of the Mediterranean Sea, or the submergence that established the now known Balearic group of Islands, a mixed tribe of Sederones and Kintilucians, who migrated from the now known eastern section of Spain, inhabited the western and central sections of the now known Ivica and the Majorca Islands, and a mixed tribe of Sederones and Cinetoiens from southeastern France, likewise inbabited the now submerged pre-historical Island of Celindeso.

At the time of the convulsion that separated the section into two portions, and submerged the adjacent country, the remnant left upon the central section, now known as the Balearic Islands, termed the entire section Sĕl-lē-ō-ōn′sē, and called themselves the In-tī-lĕx′tō-ēse. They eventually became partially mixed with the Jeretheans, especially with those on the eastern portion of the Island, which as before stated, was inhabited by immigrant remnant Jeretheans from the great valley of Koressa; and in their further migrations, reached southern France and eastern Spain. Their ultimate descendants became the pre-historic ancestors of the now known Iberians of that region. The Intilextoese, in stature, were from five to six feet; they had large frames, broad shoulders, and were stockily built; their color was a dark brown; their heads were round, but flattish on top; foreheads low; hair black, curly or bushy, and some of the men had very slight beards; their eyes were black generally, but some were a dark brown, and were quite large and expressive, being somewhat sad in expression; their noses were broad, large and flat; mouths not broad, but their lips were thick and parted so as to expose their teeth; their ears were very large and prominent, especially the upper lobe; their feet were thick and broad, toes large, and nails long, which latter turned inward, or under; their hands and nails were conditioned the same. The peculiar characteristic of the nails was a natural feature, intensified by lack of care. They went nude, as a rule, but some wore skins about their loins, with the fur turned next to the body. They were a very indolent people. They recognized no religious principle, and therefore had no adorational seasons, nor exercises.

The mixed tribe of Sederones and Cinetoiens, left as a remnant on the now submerged island, termed it Celindeso, and called themselves the Celindes. In stature they were, on an average from five, to six feet, the latter being in the majority. They were tall and athletic; their color a dusky black; their heads were high on top, narrow through the sides; their foreheads were low; their hair was black, straight, and medium long; some of them had a thin, scant beard; their eyes were black, large, piercing, or sharp, and deep set, and were peculiar, from the fact that, like the modern Caucasians, there was a continuous twitching of the eye balls from side to side; their noses were of aquiline shape, though very thin; their mouths were broad, lips thick and rolled outward; their ears were normal; their feet broad, thin and flat; their hands were broad and their fingers long. They were quite an energetic people, fond of fishing and hunting. They mostly practised nudity, though some wore skins about their loins. They had no religious aspirations, hence no adorational assemblies, or exercises.

Prior to the establishment of the northwestern portion of the Mediterranean Sea, and the now known Sardinia and Corsica Islands, a tribe of Jeretheans from both the Scăn'dē-sēs (valley or plain) of Timicules and Koressa, migrated northward, until they arrived in a large Scandeses which they termed Rē-ĕx'tī-cōn, (now the submerged district of the Gulf of Genoa, Italy), where later they built their principal city which they termed Wĭn-gē-lĕt'. The greater portion of the tribe from the Scandeses of Timicules, however, passed over a range of Bas'so (mountains), which they termed Nĭm'nē, and a part of the tribe dwelt along the northern foothills of the range, and a part descended into the Scandeses, where they joined the tribe from the Scandeses of Koressa.

At the time of the submergence of the Scandeses of Timicules, and that of Koressa, a few remnants from the two, migrating tribes en-route to the Scandeses of Reexticon, who had settled along the way, and a small remnant of those who dwelt along the Nimne range, were left upon the now known Island of Corsica. Subsequently, by maritimal migration, a tribe of the Kasinkas from Kasinka, also inhabited the island, and ultimately termed it Al-tū'zū, the term meaning a small land within the waters, and called themselves the Al-tū-zū'ans. Being of the same race as the remnant already on the island, they soon became as one people, who bore out the same modes of livelihood, or characteristics of life, during ages that followed, and were the prehistoric ancestors of the Corsicans and the Sardinians, akin to the Iberians, Basques, Ligurnians, Sikans, Sikels, etc., all having descended from the Jeretheans.

Prior to the fourth of the ten great periodical convulsions that had place in Southern Europe, which established that portion of the western coast of Italy (the modern term Italy was derived from Etzentuan, by changing the first syllable Et, to It, and shortening the latter part of the word), bordering on the Bay of Naples, a large tribe of Jeretheans inhabited that section of country now submerged by the Bay of Naples, and its present border lands, which section they termed Mē-jĭn-ăn'tĭs, and their principal hamlet, As-tä-pä'sä.

At the time of the formation of the Bay of Naples, remnants of that people were left on its border-lands in the vicinity of what is now known as the city of Naples, who in subsequent time became a large nation, when they termed that section of the country Et-zĕn-tŭ'ăn, the term meaning, *a bit of land extending into the sea,* termed the Sea Zĕl-zä'tĭc, meaning, *an unknown body of water,* but retained their original tribe name of Jeretheans, in fact, they bore the name of Jeretheans until it was changed in the time of Modern Ancient nomenclature.

Several generations after the first tribe of Cinetoiens started on their great northern and western migration from Cinetoie, or from Genoa, Italy, another tribe of the remnant Cinetoiens of Cinetoie migrated northeast, into the section of country modernly known as Austria, where in time they mixed races with the Cĭn-grēt', which latter were descendants of the Falkaleits, who also had migrated from Falkaleit, through the northwestern portion of the country now known as Prussia, to the vicinity of Austria, where the above named Cinetoien migrators had settled. At that time the section now known as Germany, Austria and Turkey, in Europe, were all one section, and never were divided as above until Modern Ancient time.

After many years, the descendants of the Jeretheans and the Cingrets, in the vicinity of Austria, had so mingled races as to become entirely a new nation, or race of people, who termed the section Yĕm-sĭn'tŏ, and called themselves the U-yō'sĕns. In stature, they varied considerably in height, as they graded from five to seven feet. The medium in height were quite fleshy, but the taller and the shorter were quite slender, the latter being characterised wihch very short necks. They were quite dark skinned, much resembling the Egyptian people. Their hair was black, and dark brown, some being short, and some long, and generally was straight. Their eyes were black, and dark brown, large and full; their heads were peculiar, being quite flat on top; their foreheads narrow through the temples; their noses resembled somewhat those of the Negro; their features were slim; their cheek bones normal; their mouths large, and lips thick, and separated so that they disclosed their teeth, which displayed large incisors, and long canines in both upper and lower sets; their ears were quite round; their hands were in proportion with their bodies. They were quite hostile to other nations, or peoples, and remarkably quarrelsome among themselves. They mostly practised nudity, but some wore skins, which they formed into garments that were thrown loosely about their loins. They had no special idea of a God principle, therefore had no established adorational worship or exercises.

Prior to the establishment of the eastern and southern portions of the Mediterranean Sea, and the now known Island of Sicily, a large tribe of Jeretheans occupied the section of country now known as the Bay of Palermo, the Gulf of Caslel a Mare, and the Island of Ustica.

At the time of the submergence of that section, and the establishment of the Island of Sicily, a large remnant of those people were left on the western section of the island, who subsequently became quite numerous, and spread out into the eastern and southern sections of the island, termed it Quĭn'tēx, and called themselves the Lū'cē-rĕts. They never attempted a migration from the island, to any extent, for they were a very indolent people, and of a very low physical order. They were characterized with faces resembling those of the monkey tribe, more than otherwise, which was caused by a degeneration in that southern section of the country. In stature, they were about five feet; were fleshy, but small boned; their skins were so covered with thick short hair, that the color of their skin was not easily perceived; as above stated, they really were but a grade higher than the monkey race. Their hands and feet were more like those of the human race; their nature was quiet, and they carried their bodies like the human; their eyes were dazzling with brightness, and were characterized with a grayish green hue; their ears were short and roundish; their noses flat; mouths broad, and lips thick. They wore no garments, lived on fruits, animal and fish food, and all these, as a rule, uncooked.

Subsequently to the establishment of the Lucerets in Quintex (Sicily), a large tribe of Jeretheans migrated down through the section of country now known as southern Italy, and entered the eastern portion of Quintex, drove out a portion of the Lucerets of that section, and they established themselves under the name of O-cĕn'tē-zăns. Ultimately, the few remaining Lucerets of that section became absorbed by mixture with the Ocentezans, hence were lost as a distinct people. After many generations, the descendants of this mixed condition, or of these Ocentezans, became the prehistoric ancestors of the now known Sikels of Sicily.

About the same time that the Ocentezans became established in Quintex, a tribe of Jeretheans had entered the western portion of the same country, from their section of Etzentuan (the district now submerged by the Bay of Naples) via: an elevated neck of land that extended southwest from the Bay of Naples, to a then existing large island that lay extant about fourteen degrees longitude east from Greenwich, and thirty-nine degrees north latitude; and thence over small islands that then existed between the large island and the now known main land of Sicily, at the point now known as Palermo (all subsequently submerged). After they had entered Quintex, in that section, they there established themselves under the name of Kĕl-soots, where in time they waxed strong as a people, when they overpowered the Lucerets in that portion of Quintex, who ultimately, through continued fatality by the hostilities of the Kelsoots, and later absorption with the lower classes of the latter, became lost as a distinct race, and the descendants that followed in this mixed condition, which ultimately impregnated the whole race of Kelsoots, became the pre-historic ancestors of the now known Sikans of Sicily. Therefore, the Sikans and the Sikels of Sicily, are of the same race as the Iberians, the Basques, the Ligurians, the Corsicans, and the Sardinians, etc. They all descended from the Jeretheans, who were left as remnants on, or migrating to the various districts of their abodes, from their great country of Cojel, number Two, now submerged by the waters of the Mediterranean sea.

Prior to the eighth of the ten great convulsions in southern Europe, a tribe of Jeretheans and Etzentuans had migrated eastward into the section of country now submerged by the waters of the Adriatic Sea, who ultimately became a large colony, termed the section Thē-ō-lē'ŏn, and called themselves the Theoleons.

At the time of the formation of the Adriatic Sea, two principal remnants were left on its eastern shores, one in the region of the now known section of Trieste, and one in the section of Dalmatia, which we will call the northern and the southern families.

The northern remnant, in the section of Trieste, termed that section Kē-lī-zō-ĭs'tăn, and called themselves, or were so called by other people, the Kē-lō'zĭsts. They and their descendants became the pre-historic ancestors of the Liburnian races north of the Danube river, and their allies, the Lithuanians, and other Slavonic tribes of the northern family.

The southern remnant in the southern section of Dalmatia, termed that section Ic-thī-ē'sŭs, and called themselves the Ic-thī-ē'ŏns. They and their descendants became the pre-historic ancestors of the modern Ancient Illyrian races, south of the Danube river.

Links and Cycles

At the time that the tribe of Icthieons started on their migration from Dalmatia, to northwestern Greece, a tribe of the same people migrated farther east from their home in Icthieon, into the section now known as Illyricum, where they settled, termed the section E-ū-rē-thē-ä, and called themselves the E-ū-rē'thë-ăns. They and their descendants became the pre-historic ancestors of the Ancient Illyrians of that section, who, as above stated, spread out south of the Danube river.

Prior to the establishment of the now known Adriatic Sea, a tribe of Theoleons of Theoleon migrated south and southeast along the western foothills of the then known great Calceus range of mountains, to the section of the country now known as the submerged section, or then valley that lay extent east and west, north of the now known Candia Island, or between it and the now known Agean Ārchipelago. About the same time that they started on their migration, a tribe of Icthieons from Icthieus, or the now known section of Dalmatia, migrated south and southeast along the foothills of the same range of mountains, to the same section north of the Candia Islands. The two tribes arrived in the above named section or valley on the same day, the Theoleons, however, having preceded the Icthieons but a few hours. When the Theoleons saw the Icthieons descending into the valley, they were filled with amazement, and their leader cried out with a loud voice to the descending tribe of Icthieons, saying, "Ră-ĕs-păt'sä," meaning, *we seek for the unknown warm country,* to which, in the same manner, the leader of the Icthieons replied, saying, "Sō-rē'tĭs," which meant, *on time,* and also implied *in search for the same,* which was the case, both tribes having set out for that purpose.

The two tribes being of the same stock of people, soon joined issues, intermarried, and therefore, subsequently became as one tribe, when they termed that section, or valley, Nē'glē, meaning *home of the wanderers,* and called themselves the Sō-lē'tĭans, meaning, *united forces.* In subsequent time they had established their principal city, which they termed Săl-cū'sy, in that part of the Negle valley east from what was anciently known as the Taygetus Mountains, north of the now known Cape Malia, but their orgiinal hamlet consisted of huts along the foothills of the Taygetus range.

At the time of the submergence of the valley of Negle, and the establishment of the Candia Island, a large remnant of Soletians were left on the island, which they eventualy termed Rē-ī-ĕn'dē, and called themselves the Rē-ī-ĕn'dĕns. In stature, they were about five, to five feet and eight inches. The women were smaller than the men, their average being not above five feet. Their color was a pinkish red; their eyes dark brown, and some were gray; their hair was very long, straight, and some was dark brown and some was black. The men had beautiful, straight, silky, full beards, but no superfluous hair on their bodies. They took much pride in the care of their hair and beards. Their heads were large; noses broad and nostrils large; mouths, large, and their under lips were drawn back in conformity with their receding chins. Their feet were large and extremely broad; their hands were broad, and their fingers and toes resembled claws more than those of the human race, especialy those of the male sex. The men wore long loose robes that extended down to their knees, but were brought to the form of the waist by tying them with a sash. Beneath the robe they wore sort of trousers, the legs of which were broad at the bottom. The women wore robes gathered full about the neck and shoulers, and sashed down to the waist, and that extended below their knees. Both men and women, generally, wore a sort of sandal, but some wore a kind of shoe, or a combination of sandals with lacings about their ankles, and above them, the laces or strips being of various colored material. The sandals were worn in the home, and the laced shoes, when going out. They had no religious ideas, or adorational exercises of any inportance. Their descendants became the pre-historic ancestors of the ancient Eteocrates, mentioned in the Odyssey of Homer, who ultimately became lost in the blood of the ancient Cretans, and more modern race of Crete, or Candia.

Prior to the establishment of the now known Candia, Scarpanto, and Rhodes Islands, a tribe of Soletians from Negle had migrated norwestward along the mountain range, into that section of country on the southeast coast of the section now known as Asia Minor, now submerged by the waters of the deep and sheltered bay of Marmarice, lying between the anciently known mountains and rugged promontory of Cynossema (now Cape Alupe), and the frontier of Lycia, where they settled, termed the now submerged section Plē-ăn'cī, and called themselves the Plē-ăn-cī-ōes.

Subsequently, and before the establishment of the now known southwest coast of Asia Minor, a tribe of Pleancioes had migrated as far northeast as into the now known section of southeastern Caria, where they settled on the northwest side of the Calbis river, between it and the range of Mountains which rise northwest of it, or at about twenty-nine degrees longitude east from Greenwich, and about thirty-seven degrees north latitude, when they termed that section Qū-lī-ĕn'dō, and called themselves the Qū'dĭx. In subsequent time, they built their principal city, which they termed Mī-ĭn'jūs, upon the site of their first settlement, as above described. They and their descendants became the prehistoric ancestors of the Carian race proper, while a mixture of some of the Qudix people with some of the Chī-ē'bōns from Gū-zăn-tī-ăn (who at the time of the formation of the AEgean Archipelago were left on the main land of Caria) became the pre-historic ancestors of the Zeybecks or Xebeks, who migrated to the interior mountain districts of Caria, where they in their partial degenerate condition became possessed with certain peculiarities differing somewhat from the Carians proper.

MIGRATION OF THE CIN-E-TO'I-ENS.

At the time of the formation of the northwestern section of the Mediterranean Sea, a portion of the Jeretheans were left as a remnant in the section now known as northwestern Italy, near the point where now is located the city of Genoa, who remained in that section for several hundred years before the establishment of the great Cinetoien migration, who termed the section Cinetoie, and called themselves the Cinetoiens. Subsequently, a tribe of their descendants began the above-named migration, or system of migrations, which after years of pursuance by tribes of their descendants, one of the latter reached the vicinity now known as France.

During the ages that intervened between the establishment of the above-named system of migrations, and the ultimate arrival of the tribe in the region of France, as the descending tribes went forth to each new location, remnants of the various departing tribes were left in the local vicinities, thus to a certain extent peopling the country. The migratory course taken was through the following named sections of country. First, the Cinetoiens from Cinetoie started over the Hī-ā-dĭs'kā, ranges modernly known as the Alps, which they termed Mā-dū'rā, meaning in their language, mountains of snow.

This migration, all things considered, was the most marvelous attempt of all made mention of in this treatise. We were informed by the spirit of Kĭl-dŏn'ziē, who was one of the tribe, that but comparatively few of the tribe survived the terrible hardships they had to encounter during the migration.

After a time, the survivors arrived in the southern section of the country now known as Switzerland, where they and their descendants dwelt for many years, under the name of Mā-dū'rās.

Subsequently, a tribe of their descendants continued the migration by way of a circular course through the southwestern section of Switzerland, to the vicinity of the now known city of Geneva, where they established themselves as a colony, termed the section Tchĕt-treī'sŏn, and called themselves the Găn-hē-lē' măns.

After many years, a tribe of descended Ganhelemans continned the migration into the section of country now known as France, when they followed what is now known as the upper Rhone river, which they termed A-zē'lĕnd, to its junction with the now known Savon, where they left the water course in search of a warmer climate, and began a circular course, crossed the now known Cevennen range, in the vicinity of the section now known as Rhone, which range they termed the Căs-cū'thŏns, from whence they passed to the southwestern section of the country now known as Lot et Garonne, which entire country they termed Fĕl'tē-nē-zē'tĕs, by way of a mountain pass in the section of the now known Cantals, which they termed Găt-lŏn'giē, meaning, *gateway,* followed the now known Lot river, which they termed Tū-sū'lī-ŏn, to its junction with the now known Garonne, where they established a colony, termed the section Gŏn-sŏ-ē'sĕs, and called themselves the Gŭd'lĭng-stŏns.

After many years, a tribe of the Gudlingstons resumed the migration, but turned their course backward, circling westward, and northward, they passed from the section of Charente, to that of Vienne, via: the upper Charente river, between the mountain ranges, to the upper Vienne river, which they followed to its junction with the Loire, where they settled and established a colony, which eventually spread out along the Loire, to, and beyond its junction with the Indrie. They termed the Loire river, Dä-sănc'tō, the section of country, Kō-lä'ĭs, and called themselves the Cō-sē-ăn'zēs.

Many years later, a tribe of the Coseanzes descendants resumed the migration, until they arrived at the now known Sein river, at a point between its junction with the now known Oise, and Marn, where they settled, termed the Sein river Săd'wrĕtch, the section Fäl'kā-leīt (the term meaning a home resting place), and called themselves the Fäl'kă-leīts. They there multiplied, became very numerous, and spread out to, and far beyond the junction of the Oise and the Marn.

Passing through various changes physically, mentally and materially, such as had place during the migration of the Cinetoiens, the Maduras, the Ganhelemans, the Gudlingstons, and the Coseanzes, we find the descended Falkaleits possessing the section now known as France, about one hundred years before the Adomic period. Alem Prolex informs us that the Falkaleits were the true pre-historic ancestors of the now known French nation, though the latter have changed considerably in regard to physical characteristics, owing to the various conditions that attended their descent, during the ages intervening between the time of the Falkaleits and the modern French people. At first they were quite uncivilized, though later in the ages, they became greatly advanced. In stature, they were on an average, from six, to seven feet, and were slender built. They possessed quite dark skins; long features; straight, black, but long hair; full short, dark beards; black, brown, dark gray, small and deep set eyes; medium high foreheads, prominent, but narrow through the temples; medium high cheek bones; narrow and sharp, but prominent noses; peculiar ears, they being pointed at the top, instead of rounding; long arms, but hands and feet in proportion with their bodies. In regard to dress, they carried out, as far as possible, the styles of their Jerethean ancestors of Cojel, even to the last migrating tribe.

While the various migrating tribes depended upon local materials with which to form the farbics from which they made their raiment, the Falkaleits, upon entering Falkaleit, found an animal, that corresponded very closely with the modern goat, only larger, which they called Tăp'sē-găl, the hair of which they wove into the fabrics, from which they made their raiment. They at first, gave no thought to religious principles, or even had any idea thereof. Later on however, as they developed in various ways, there arose different opinions among them, regarding an invisible force that had created the sun, the moon and the stars, and especially the principle of light. They thought that some hand greater than their own, had formed the luminaries of the heavens, but they did not then recognize the God idea in its fullest sense. The difference of opinion among them caused some of them to choose the sun, some the moon, and some the stars, as special objects for admiration.

After a few generations, they conceived the idea of a great being, who was formed like unto themselves, as having formed all visible creation. This idea was brought about by a band of prospectors, who when exploring in the mountains, found at the base of one of the principal peaks, an opening that led to a marvelous cave, which later on, when light could be obtained, they explored completely. They imagined that the great being had prepared the cave for a home for them, hence the mountain to them, at once became sacred, to which they made their obeisance. They then termed the supposed being Thū'rĭc, and termed the mountain, Thū-rī-ĭs-tăn. For many years, the people passed to and fro from the settlement to the cave, which they adopted as their public shrine, and before, and in which, they held their adorational assemblies, or went individually, for the same purpose.

Subsequent to the migration of the Cinetoiens from Cinetoie, a tribe from the remnant colony of Ganhelemans in Tcbettreison, as their ancestors had done, established a branch migratory system, which was to the northeast, in a circular route. After many years of spreading out by their subsequent generations, and about the time that the Falkaleits had established themselves by the Sadwretch river, in Falkaleit, the last tribe of these wandering Ganhelemans had arrived at the central portion of the country now known as Germany, which they termed Tĭn-dĭn′zē-ŏn, and called themselves the Sĭn-ē′thŏns. They averaged from five and one-half, to six and one-half feet in stature. Their color was a swarthy hue. The dark complexioned were slim, and the light were fleshy. Some possessed black, curly hair; black eyes; and noses that resembled the now known German Jews; they had seemingly low forehads, but that was more owing to the style of wearing the hair, and were rather narrow; their cheek bones were normal; their mouths somewhat drawn down at the corners, and their lips were abovt the normal in thickness; their ears, hands and feet were also normal. Some possessed straight, long, dark brown hair; full dark brown eyes; high and broad foreheads; normal cheek bones; broad and square cut mouths, and their lips were thin; their ears, hands and feet were normal. The dark complexioned Sinethons could be said to resemble the German Jews. In fact, the German Jews are direct descendants from the dark complexioned Sinethons. Likewise, the light complexioned Sinethons resembled the modern Germans, for the same reason, they having descended from the light complexioned Sinethons. As a nation, they were somewhat quarrelsome among themselves, which was caused by jealousy between the light and dark factions, and both were hostile to anyone who chanced to trespass upon their possessions.

After the establishment of the Sinethons in their Tindinzeon (Germany), a tribe of the Zrineths migrated from their home in Cucula (British Isles) into Tindinzeon, where they ultimately mixed races with a portion of the Sinethons, which established a race of people whose descendants, with passing time, became the ancestors of the ancient Gauls. The women wore a sort of over-gown, and a short skirt beneath. The men wore clouts, principally, but when cold weather came, both men and women used skins, worn in the style of a blanket, and shoes made of the skins of a short-furred animal. They manufactured the fabric from which they made their raiment, the principal material being that of the long black hair of an animal then known as the Schanwreit, and which became extinct from the great slaughter that took place for the purpose above mentioned. The Schanwreit was a mountain animal, as large as the modern Bison, the latter in its almost extinct condition, being a comparison in that regard, from the fact of its having been slaughtered for its skin for robes, etc., with long black hair.

The Sinethons of Tindinzeon, or the region of Germany, had great adoration for the sunlight, and for fire, both of which they thought to be most wonderful. They conceived the idea that a great being, who had created all things, dwelt in the sun, which latter they termed Bĕn-ăn'drō-zĕn. They were really more attracted, however, to the flame that was produced by the fire, which latter they termed Bĕn-ăn'drō, than they were by the light, or the heat that radiated from the flame. They expressed their adoration of those two principles by a form of worship, as follows: As the sun began to disappear, they built their adoration fire, to take the place of its suspended light, from its departure, to its coming again. They built the fire in an open field. In preparing it, each person, when assembling, brought one stick of wood for that purpose. Beginning with the shortest sticks, they built them into a cone-shaped pile, from the center out, thus causing the cone to grow higher and higher, until all the material was placed on. As the sun was going down, fire was placed in the center base of the cone. The assembly then formed into a semi-circle on the eastern side of the cone, so as to have it between them and the setting sun, sacredly observing the rule never to pass between the burning cone and the sun, for they had certain superstitious ideas regarding the effect that would be produced upon their individual welfare, if they passed between the two great principles of light from the sun and the fire. After the fire was started, manifestations were made by individual jumping, or crude dancing. This was kept up until the cone was entirely consumed by the fire, nothing remaining but the hot embers, when they would disperse to their homes.

ZAN-ZU-RE'TA AND CLE-AN-DE'CI-A, OR GREECE AND ASIA MINOR.

TELTZIE LI.

Zăn-zū-rē'tä was the first pre-historic name of the entire country of Greece, as given by the Cē-drē'ŏns of Lē-ŏn-sĕd'rĭc, or Hellas, and the Cē-rē'thăns of Jē-sē-ē'thăn, or Morea (who at that time were practically under one government), in honor of their Kĕt'rē-dăd (ruler), whose name was Zanzureta.

Hē'lŏck was its second pre-historic name, as changed by the same peoples in honor of Helock, the son of Zanzureta, who succeeded his father as Ketredad of the two nations.

Hĕl'läs was its third pre-historic name, as changed by the same peoples, in honor of Hellas, the son of Helock, who succeeded his father as Ketredad of the two nations. The term Hellas, however, was handed down, from time to time, by the descendants of these nations, to ancient history.

Subsequent to the establishment of the Ic-thī-ē'ŏns in Ic-thī-ē'sŭs, a tribe of their descendants migrated southeast, along the range of mountains that separates the sections of "Herzegovina" and northern "Dalmatia," thence southward along the "Pindus" range, which they termed Cī-lĕn-dū'sky, until the last tribe of migrators had reached the region of now known "Acarnania," and "Aetolia," western Greece, where they settled east of "Lake Ambrakia," which they termed Jăn-tē'zŭs, and termed the section Zē-căn'dē-zōte, but retained their former tribal name of Icthieons. El-trū'lī was their principal city, which had place east of the "Aspru" river, about ten miles north of "Lake Trichonis.

Subsequently, a tribe of Icthieons from Zecandezote, migrated northeast into the section of "Thessaly," southwest of the "Tehanarty river, which latter they termed Kä-zū'trŭs, where they settled about half way between the now known cities of "Palamas" and "Pharsala," which section they termed Săn'krūt, and called themseves the Săn'krūts.* Gŏn'zī-ăc was their principal

*The Sankruts of Sankrut were the originators of the Sepulchral Mounds, or Tumulus Mounds, such as are found in Thrace, and on the planes of Marathon, the influence having been handed down to Attica, by persons migrating southward, and into Thrace, by the Cinthons, who were descendants from the Sankruts.

city, which was located south of the now known Salambia river, and west of, or in the vicinity of the city of "Larissa."

About the time the first tribe of Icthieons started from Zecandezote, on their migration to Sankrut, another tribe of Icthieons from Zecandezote migrated eastward to the section of country between "Phthiotis" and "Phocis," and "Attica" and "Boeotia," northwest of Lake Topolias, which latter they termed Ick′-ē-trūse, and also the section of country, but retained the tribal name of Icthieons. Fĕl-cŏn′sĕs was their principal city, which was located about fifteen miles northwest of Lake Topolias. Still later, their descendants spread out southward until they had reached the sections now known as Attica and Boeotia, and even to that of "Athens," in eastern Greece, but at that time they had made no change in their tribe or section names.

Subsequently, a tribe of Icthieons migrated southwest from the Athens region, into that of "Argolis" and "Corinth," of "Morea," west of the now known city of Corinth, which section they termed Kĕl-tō-plă′sŭs, and called themselves the Kĕl′tō-plăs. O-kā-lĕn′zy was their principal city, which had place northeast of "Nauplia," about one-third of the way between the now known cities of "Argos" and "Epidaurus."

About the time that these Icthieons migrated from the Athens section, another tribe of Icthieons from Zecandezote migrated eastward. When enroute, they circled round the eastern coast of Lake Trichonis, and entered the northern part of the section now known as "Achaia," of Morea, where they settled near the now known city of "Patras," which section they termed Az-ĕn-trū′sî-ä, and called themselves the Az-ĕn-trū′sî-äns. Tĕl-mŭz′iē was their principal city, which was located in the section now known as Achaia and "Elis," north of Mt. Olonos, about half way between it and the mountains that have place southeast of the city of Patras.

After several generations, the two tribes of Icthieons, who had migrated to northwestern and northeastern Morea, had spread out, one from the district of Corinth, northwest, and one from the district of Patras, southeast, until they met, and being of the same race of people, soon blended into one nation, when they termed the northern portion of what is known as Achai and Elis, and "Argolis" and "Corinth," Jeseethan, and called themselves the Cē-rē′thăns, in honor of their leader, whose name was Cerethan. These migrations were prior to the convulsions that shattered Greece into so many parts, and created so many inland waters; hence, the last-named migrators were not hindered from reaching their destination, by the waters of either the Gulf of Patris, or Corinth.

About the beginning of the Adomic period, a large tribe of the more intellectual portion of the Cerethans from Jeseethan (Morea), migrated southward through the section of "Arcadia." En-route, they passed still further southward, over the mountains that now separate Arcadia from "Laconia," into the latter-named section, by way of the pass that was formed by the course of the now known "Eurotas" river, which pass they termed Prū-sĕl'sĭc (a mountain pass), into the great valley that extends between the two ranges of mountains, anciently known as the "Taygetus" (the eastern chain), and "Paron" (the western), which they termed Kä-ū'zĭc (twin ranges), that then, in their southern extension, reached far out into the present sea area, thus forming the two promontories of "Taenarus" and "Malea," or Capes Malea and Matapan, which valley they also termed Pruselsic, after the mountain pass, when they followed the Eurotas river course on its eastern side, to the region east of the now known city of "Sparta," where they settled, termed the river Zū-ē'tä, the section Eū-zĕl'zăc, and called themselves the **Eu-zĕl'zăcs**. Their principal city, which they termed Cē-ū'tī-lĕn, was located between the now known Iris river and the mountains anciently known as "Taygetus," at a point southeast of the now known city of "Sparta," and about five miles north of thirty-seven degrees north latitude.

Prior to the formation of the Ægean archipelago, a tribe of Icthieons from Icketruse, migrated southeast (along the western branch of the great Cordecongo range, that extended throughout northern Greece, the Ægean archipelago region into Asia Minor), into the section now known as between the "Antiparos" and "Siphenos Islands," in the "Cyclades" region of the Archipelago, which section they termed Gū-zĕn'ti-ăn, and called themselves the Chī-ē'bōns. Their principal city which they termed Cū-rī'zō, was located in a valley that had place between the now known city of "Hermopolis" and the island of "Zea," in the Ægean archipelago. They spread out over the country now known as the Ægean archipelago, to the present coast lines of southeastern Greece.

Subsequent to the establishment of the Chiebons in Guzentian, and the Euzelzacs in Euzelzac, a tribe of Chiebons from Guzentian, migrated westward over the then known eastern chain of the Kauzic range, into Euzelzac (Laconia). Finding the Euzelzacs a hostile people, they migrated still further west, over the western chain of the Kauzic mountains, that extended southward, through "Messenia" to the sea, thus forming the Acritas Promontory, which section they termed Or-phŏ'cŭs, and called themselves the Mē-zŭ'rĭcs. Their principal city which they also termed Mezuric, was located between the now known city of "Soolima," or the ancient town of "Ira," and the southern shore of the Neda river that flows westward, into the now known "Gulf of Arcadia."

After the establishment of the Icthieons in Zecandezote, a tribe of their descendants migrated southwest, into a great valley that extended north and south, east of the section of "Kephalonia," of the "Ionian Islands," which latter are remnants of a great range of mountains that extended from the now known western portion of "Acarnania," south and southeast, to the island of "Cerigo," southern Greece, which valley they termed Skrōx-ā-jō'lä, the mountains Sĕn-trī'ŏx, and called themselves the Skroxajolas.

At the time of the establishment of the Ionian Islands, and the open water between them and the main land of Greece, remnants of the Skroxajolas were left on the islands. Their principal city which they termed Rŭ'dī-lĕn, was located in the section now known as Cephalonia, in the vicinity of the city of "Samo," or "Dilinati." As the Skroxajolas of Skroxajola, the Chiebons of Guzentian, and the Mezurirics of Orphocus, were all descendants from the Icthieons (see above), and their descendants peopled the now known sections of the Ægean archipelago, and it mainland coasts, and also in Messenia, and on the Ionian Islands; therefore, their ultimate descendants became the pre-historic ancestors of the modern ancient "Leleges" race.

About the time of the Adomic period, the Icthieons of Icketruse, re-named that section Leonsedric, and called themselves the Cedreons. They were more intellectual and civilized, in every way, than their brethren, the Cerethans, the super-development being largely due to the planetary conditions and solar light of that latitude. The influence of the civilization of the descended Cedreons of Leonsedric, through modern ancient Athens, as it reached the Cerethans of Jeseethan, brought to them a higher civilization, and at the beginning, and throughout the modern ancient periods, both the descended peoples from the section of Leonsedric and Jeseethan, gradually became more intellectual and more highly civilized, in every way. In fact, nearly all the descendants of the pre-historic Jeretheans, through their great migration from Cojel (as they settled in certain degrees of north latitude), usually advanced in their general ideas, as is the case with such circumstances in modern times; while those south of the line, became more crude as they mixed races, and existed under those climatic influences, and are facts that have established the race characteristics, belonging to the modern Italians, Greeks and Romans, physically and intellectually.

At the time of the formation of the Ægean archipelago, and the cutting up of the sections of Leonsedric and Jeseethan, many of the people were lost by the submergence that established those sections. The greater portion of the survivors, however, being in Jeseethan (Morea), as far as possible, held to their former attainments, intellectually and physically, while those in the Archipelago became more degenerate.

The Cedreons and the Cerethans practised nudity generally. The only difference being that the latter were characterized with more hair on their bodies, than the former. They had no idea of a God principle, in its modern sense, hence, they had no adorational exercises; but, the Cerethans adored the Sun, as the source of their benefits.

The disorder of land, infusion of waters, destruction of cities and records in Jeseethan, made it impossible for the people to re-instate themselves, in the same degree of civilization that they possessed prior to the convulsions and changes that they brought. The same might be said of the section of Leonsedric, and the Cedreons.

The Cerethans of Jeseethan, or southern Greece, and their descendants, became the pre-historic ancestors of the Ionian race, or Pelasgic peoples of ancient Greece.

The Cedreons of Leonsedric, or northern Greece, and their descendants, became the pre-historic ancestors of the Dorian race, or Hellenic peoples.

Subsequent to the establishment of the Sankruts in Sankrut, a tribe of their descendants started on a migration northeastward, when they followed the foothills of a range of mountains that then extended from the section now known as southern "Thessaly," circling northeast to the southeastern coast of "Thrace," which they termed E-măc'kä, and ultimately entered the section now known as Thrace, which they termed Cē-cĭn'thŭs, and called themselves the Cĭn'thons. Their principal city which they termed Jĕl-tä-crŭz, was located on the site where now the city of "Adrianople" has place. They and their descendants became the prehistoric ancestors of the ancient "Thracians."

When the Icthieons of Icthiesus were migrating southward, through the now known section of "Albania," a tribe seceded from the colony, when they halted for a time just north of what is now known as "Lake Ochrida," from whence they passed over the Pindus mountains, into the section of country now known as "Macedonia," and settled about twenty-two degrees longitude, east from Greenwich, and forty-one degrees north latitude to west of the now known "Gulf of Salonika," which section they termed Cĭl-cū'sĭc, and called themselves the Tăl-cū'si-ăns. Their principal city which they termed Vĕl'tē-săc, was located at the place where they first settled.

Subsequent to the establishment of the Sankruts in Sankrut, a tribe of their descendants migrated north into the section now known as Macedonia, until they came to the settlement of the Talcusians, where they also settled, and the two tribes soon became mixed and blended into one people. Their descendants became the pre-historic ancestors of the ancient Macedonians, and not the settlers from Thrace, as is supposed to be the case, by modern writers. The fact that the Thracians were migrators from Sankrut, and a part of the Macedonian blood was from the same nation, and the other part from an earlier tribe of the same stock, through the Icthieons, the descendants would be near enough alike to cause the error; therefore, the mixed race of Talcucians and their descendants became the pre-historic ancestors of the Macedonians.

Clē-ăn-dē'cī-ā was the first prehistoric name of the entire section of country now known as Asia Minor, given by the Dĕn'cī-ēs of central and western, and the Sō-cō'trūms, of eastern Cappadocia, who met in convention at Dē'jū, the capital of prehistoric Cleandecia, for that purpose. Clē'ăn, in their language, was a term that meant *climbing,* and the term dĕ-ci-ä, referred to *height,* and the compound word referred to the country generally, as being hard to traverse on account of its numerous mountain elevations. The Cleandecia, therefore, was used until about the time of the beginning of the Christian era, as the region of Cleandecia, or the now known section of Asia Minor, was little known by the peoples of Europe or Asia prior to that time, and therefore the name sustained no change until the time of the disembodiment of Attalus III, when a portion of Cleandecia was annexed to the Roman Dominions, under the name of Asia, 130 B. C., which during the early part of the Christian era, became more in use, until after the fifth century, when Orosius introduced the term in his writings in this sense.

Prior to the migration of the Rezendeth tribe to the section now known as Cilicia, which they termed Esgenenex, and called themselves the Esgenens, another tribe of Rezendeths migrated from the northern highlands of their ancestral home, northeast of the now known Red Sea, into Southeastern Syria; thence along the western coast of the Inland Sea, now known as the district or section of the Syrian Desert; thence west to the Dead Sea. Later they passed northeast into the section now known as the Province of Mesopotamia, until they came to the western shores of the Euphrates river, at about thirty-five degrees north latitude, which they followed northwestward until they had entered the section now known as Cilicia, in the Province of "Cappadocia," where they settled between the "Anti-Taurus" mountains and "Mount Argæus," termed the section E-dĕn'cy-cō'lis, and called themselves the Dĕn'cies. Their principal city, which they termed Dē'jū, was located on the site where the ancient town of "Mazaca," or later known as "Caesarae," has place. They and their descendants became the prehistoric ancestors of the Cappadocians proper, or the "Leucosyri" (white Syrians, so called by Herodotus, to distinguish them from their darker neighbors, in south Cappadocia).

When the tribe of Rezendeths were enroute to Edencycolis, or central Cappadocia, where they became the Dencies, a remnant of the main tribe were left in the section now known as "Melitene," in the northeastern portion of the province of Cappadocia, north of the Melas river, who retained the name of Rezendeths, but did not name the section.

Subsequently to the establishment of the Esgenens in Esgenenex (western Cilicia, Asia Minor), and also subsequent to the arrival of the Gonthementhans in Gonthementhe (Tyanitis, a province in Cappadocia), a tribe of the Esgenens migrated northeast, over the Taurus range, to about thirty-eight degrees north latitude, and thirty-five degrees longitude, east from Greenwich, or west of the Anti-Taurus mountains, which section they termed Ri-ăn'tī-cūs, and called themselves the Kū-zē'lăns. Their principal city, which they termed Kuzelan, was located on the site of their first settlement. In subsequent time, the Kuzelans and the Gonthementhans mixed races, when the former were lost as a distinct tribe, by the mixture. They and their descendants became the prehistoric ancestors of the "Tyanitis," or southern people of Cappadocia.

Subsequent to the migration of the Kuzelans, a tribe of the Esgenens, who dwelt in the eastern Esgenenex (Celicia), in the vicinity of the now known "Pyramus" river, migrated into Cappadocia, where they settled on the southern side of the Melas river, in a large valley which they termed Sŏ-cŏ'lŏm, and called themselves the Sŏ-cŏ'trŭms. Their principal city, which they termed Sō-cē'lă, was located on the cite of their first settlement. In future time, the Socotrums mixed races with the tribe of Rezendeths, in the section of Melitene, and became as one people, and their descendants bcame the pre-historic ancestors of the Cataonians and peoples of northeastern Cappadocia.

Subsequent to the establishment of the Dencies* in Edencycolis, a tribe of their descendants migrated westward into the now known province of "Phrygia," to about thirty-one degrees longitude east from Greenwich, and about thirty-nine degrees north latitude, in a valley northwest of the "Adoreus" mountains, which section they termed El-tă-clū'ci-ä, and called themselves the El-tă-clū'ci-äns. Their principal city which they termed Cū-rē-căn'ŭm, was located in the valley, on the site of their first settlement.

Subsequent to the establishment of the Cinthons in Cecinthus (Thrace), a tribe of their descendants migrated southeast, into the central portion of "Bithynia", where they halted for a time, north of the "Olympus" mountains. Not being satisfied with the location, they crossed over the mountain, and the now known "Sangarius" river, where the Eltaclucians also dwelt, and where, in time, the two peoples mixed; but their descendants retained the tribe name of Eltaclucians, and Eltaclucia and Curecanum respectively, as their section and city names. The mixed race of Eltaclucians and Cinthons, and their descendants, became the pre-historic ancestors of the ancient Phrygians.

Subsequent to the establishment of the Cinthons in Cecinthus, a tribe of their descendants migrated southeast, along the mountain range of southeastern Thrace, through the section of country, now the neck of land that, but for the Bosphorus, would connect Thrace and Bithynia (which was the condition at that time), when they passed into the section now known as central Bithynia, where they settled in a valley between the mountains east of lake "Ascania," or east of where the Gallus flows into the Sangarius, which valley they termed Et-ci'nē-ŭs, and called themselves the Et-ci'nē-ŏns. Their principal city which they termed Glē-ĭs'tă, was located on the site of their first settlement. They and their descendants became the pre-historic ancestors of the ancient Bithyni, and ultimate Bithynians.

Still later, a tribe of the Etcineons from Etcineus, migrated

*It was through the influence of the Dencies that the monuments of great antiquity have place throughout Cappadocia, Lydia, Phrygia and Lyconia, by migratory influences.

northeast into ancient Paphlagonia, where they settled in a great Valley, in the central portion of that province, about thirty-four degrees longitude east from Greenwich, on the east side of the now known Amrias river, termed the section Jĕt-ā-rĕn'gä, and called themselves the Jĕt-ā-rĕn'gäs. Their principal city which they termed En-gŏs'tiē, was located on the site of their first settlement. They and their descendants became the pre-historic ancestors of the very ancient Paphlagonians, that appear in the Homeric catalogue of the allies of Priam, during the Trajan War.

About the time that the Cinthons started on their migration to the Bithynian section, another large tribe of the same people migrated southeast, into the section of country known as ancient Mysia, where they located on the western side of Macestus river, in the valley where the river bends east, north and then west, below where the three upper tributaries flow into it, which section they termed Hy-ū-rā'tŭs, and called themselves the Hy-ū-rā'tŏns.

About the time that the Hyuratons became settled in Hyuratus, a large tribe of Kĕn'dē-cūs from Stĭl-căn'di-ŭs (Lyconia) migrated westward into the vicinity of the Hyuratons, where in time the two tribes mixed, and their descendants retained the terms Hyuratons and Hyuratus, as their tribal and section names respectively. Their principal city, which they termed Crē-cē'nä, was on the site of their first settlement. The descendants of this mixed race, became the pre-historic ancestors of the ancient Mysians.

When the Hyuratons, enroute to the Mysian section, arrived in the central portion of Phrygia, contentions arose among them as to the course they should pursue, which resulted in a separation of the tribe, when a part diverged from the original course of the route, and passed southwest, into the section of Lydia, and thence, south of the Temnus mountains, when they followed the Hyltus river to its confluence with the Hermus, where they settled in a valley east of the latter, and north of that portion of the former, which section they termed Lä'ci-ŭs, in honor of their leader, whose name was Lacius, and called themselves the Lä'ci-ăns. Their principal city they also termed Lacius, which was located on the site of their first settlement. They and their descendants became the pre-historic ancestors of the ancient "Maeonicians" of whom Homer wrote, or the "Meiones," who are recorded in the writings of Herodotus, and "Maeones," by other writers. Their historical descendants were the "Maeones," who inhabited the district of the upper "Hermus," where their town, anciently called "Maeonia" (now Mennen) existed, according to both Pliny and Hercules.

After the establishment of the Plē-ăn'ci-ōes in the valley of Plē-ăn'ci (now submerged by the Bay of Marmarice), remnants were left on the frontier of Lycia, where they settled in the central portion, or section anciently known as "Milyas," in a large marshy valley, north of the "Chimaera" mountains, which section they termed O-lē-cē-ĕn'tō, and called themselves the O-lē-cē-ĕn'tōes. Subsequently, they became scattered as a colony, and therefore as such, were practically lost; but a few were left, whose descendants became the pre-historic ancestors of the peculiar ancient race, now known as the "Zeybecks," who occupy the southern corner of the peninsula of Asia Minor, and also the "Milyans" of whom Herodotus wrote, who occupied the rugged mountain districts, in the northeast of Lycia.

After the scatterment of the Oleceentoes, a tribe of Esgenens from western Esgenenex (Cilicia) migrated into the section of Lycia, when they settled along the northern foothills of that portion of the Haurus mountain that has place in southern Lycia, between the "Climax" and the "Massicytes" ranges, or a little east of the thirtieth degree longitude east from Greenwich, which section they termed Nō-cō-tĭ-ä, and called themselves the Nō-cō'-ti-ăns. Their principal city which they termed Nocotia, was located on the southwestern side of the Massicytes range, south of their junction with the "Chimaera" mountains, or on the latitude, about parallel with the now known towns of "Pinara" and "Limyria," in southern Lycia, they having moved southward from their first settlement, prior to the establishment of their city of Nocotia. They and their descendants became the pre-historic ancestors of the ancient "Termilae," of whom Herodotus wrote, or "Tremilae," as Hecataeus called them, and as the name also appears in the native inscriptions, and known to the Greeks as "Syrians."

When the migrating Pleancioes were about entering the section of "Caria," they differed as to the course they should pursue in their further migration, which caused a separation of the tribe, when a portion of them diverged from the original plan, and passed eastward into the section of "Pisidia," where they settled in the western central portion, near the "Mountain Fortress," on "Crema," or in the anciently known Valley of "Cestrus," which section they termed Ic-thē-o'sĭs, and called themselves the A-măn'cō-chēs. Their principal city which they termed Gĕs-tī'lĭnth, was located on the site of their first settlement. They and their descendants became the pre-historic ancestors of the ancient Pisidians.

After the establishment of the Amancoches in Ictheosis, a tribe of their descendants migrated still farther eastward, into the section of "Lycaonia," where they settled in the southwestern portion, in the vicinity of the ancient town of "Lystra," which section they termed Nō-cō'trä, and called themselves the Nō-cō'träns. Their principal city, which they also termed Nocotra, was located on the site where the ancient town of Lystra subsequently had place. They and their descendants became the pre-historic ancestors of the ancient Lyconians.

After the establishment of the Nocotrans in Nocotra, a tribe of their descendants migrated still farther eastward, and entered the section of "Cappadocia," anciently known as "Tyanitis," where they settled along the river, near the town anciently known as "Tyana," which section they termed Gŏn-thē-mĕn'thē, and called themselves the Gŏn-thē-mĕn'thĕns. Their principal city, which they termed Cē-ō'sĭs, was located on the site where the ancient city of Tyana had place. They and their descendants became the pre-historic ancestors of the southern Cappadocians.

The original Gonthementhans became very much degenerated, and in a low condition; but as subsequent generations passed by, they rose from the degenerate condition of their ancestors, and therefore made considerable progress in many ways. In stature, they were from five to five and a half feet; were fleshy in body, but had slender limbs. They were of a peculiar color, their foreheads being dark, but their cheeks of a yellowish hue, the latter growing more intense, or marked, all over their bodies, as the generation descended. They had medium-sized heads, very low, receding foreheads; black, short, tightly-curled hair on their heads, and bodies also, to a certain extent; small, but sharp and piercing eyes; broad, monkey-like noses; large mouths, with thin lips; small feet and hands, but their fingers and toes resembled more the claws of animals, than those of the human. They were entirely nude. Their only protection from cold was the superfluous suit of hair on their bodies. At that time they had no religious ideas, but later, they practised superstitious rites, and adhered to the principle of sanctity, such as is known to have existed with the ancient Cappadocians, and other peoples of Asia Minor.

About the time of the Adomic period, a tribe of the Cinthons from Cecinthus (Thrace), migrated southeastward into Asia

Minor, when they settled in "Galatia," in the vicinity of the ancient town of 'Pessmus," whish section they termed Eth-bĕr-gū'dĕn, and called themselves the Eth-bĕr-gū'dĕns. Their principal city which they termed Klĭn-tī-cĭn'ză, was located on the site where the ancient town of "Pessmus" now has place. They and their descendants became the pre-historic ancestors of the ancient tribe of "Tolistobogii," of western Galatia.

Subsequently, a tribe of the Ethberguden descendants migrated southeast, into the central section of Galatia, where they settled about thirty-four degrees longitude east from Greenwich and forty degrees north latitude, east of the main central tributary to the Halys river, which section they termed Or-tī-lē'mŭx, and called themselves the Or-tī-lē'mī-ăns. Their principal city which they termed Tĕt'ū-ĕs, was located on the site of their first settlement. They and their descendants became the pre-historic ancestors of the "Tectosages" tribes, who anciently dwelt in central Gallatia.

About the time that the Chotians arrived in Neichotus (see below), a tribe of Gonthementhans from Gonthementhe (Cappadocia), migrated northeast into the eastern portion of Gallatia, where they settled east of the mountains, in the section of 'Trocmi" (southeastern Gallatia), which sectionthey termed Jă-lū'cī-ă, and called themselves the Jă-lū'cī-ăns. Their principal city which they termed Jalucia, was located on the site of their first settlement. They and their descendants became the pre-historic ancestors of the Trocmi tribes, who were known to have dwelt in eastern Gallatia.

After the establishment of the Ortilemians in Ortilemux, a tribe of their descendants migrated northeast, into "Pontis," where they settled in the valley east of the "Iris" river, near the point of its junction with the Lycus, which section they termed Nē-ī-chō'tŭs, and called themselves the Chō'tī-ăns. Their principal city which they termed Lē-y'ŏx, was located on the site of their first settlement. They and their descendants became the pre-historic ancestors of the "Chaldeans," or "Chalybes;" the "Tibareni," the "Mosynoeci," and the "Marotones," of northeastern "Pontis."

Subsequently, a tribe of Chotians migrated south from Neichotus, into Cappadocia, where they settled on the north side of the Halys river, at about thirty-six degrees longitude east from Greenwich, which section they termed Lī-dū-ē'tăs. Their principal city which they termed Lidueta, was located on the site of their first settlement. The Greeks termed this branch of Cappadocians "Leucosyri," or "white Syrians." This was on account of the yellowish hue that characterized their ancestors, the Chotians, which characteristic developed into a general or specific complexion, that characterized the Cappadocians of that section.

After the establishment of the Dencies in Edencycolis (Cappadocia), a large tribe of their descendants migrated eastward, to the foothills of the Anti-Taurus mountains, thence northeast, through a mountain pass, and entered the section of "Armenia-Minor," where they settled in a large valley, about thirty-eight and one-half degrees longitude east from Greenwich, which section they termed Chŏc'ē-täl, and called themselves the Chŏc'ē-täls. Their principal city which they termed Hī-ē-mā'nî-ä, was located on the site of their first settlement.

Subsequently, a tribe of the descended Chocetals of Chocetal, migrated southeast, to lake "Van," or "Aghtamar," which section they termed Bä-sē-ā-răn'ēr, and called themselves the Bŏs'träs, and termed the lake Bŏs'trä.

After the establishment of the Bostras in Basearaner, a tribe of Sokotras (who had become mixed with the remnant Rezendeths of Cappadocia, who were left in the section of Melitine) migrated eastward, until they arrived in the section of Basearaner, already occupied by the Bostras, whose descendants retained the tribe name of Bostras, and the section name of Basearaner. Their principal city, which they termed Crē'zä, had place where the ancient city of "Van" is located. They and their descendants became the pre-historic ancestors of the "Armenians" proper.

Links and Cycles

SWA-DIS'KAN AND E-NEN-DOR-NE'NE, OR CHINA AND SIBERIA.

TELTZIE LII.

Suă-dĭs'kan (the promised land) was the first prehistoric name of China, as given by the Kĕn'tĕr-sĕnds of Zăn-cŭs'tē-zŭm. The leaders of the migrating people promised them a final home, which was to be the region of the "rising sun." When they reached the Pacific waters, and could go no farther, toward the rising Sun, they abandoned the idea, settled in that region, and termed the entire country Swadiskan, a name it bore until about five hundred years after the beginning of the Adomic period, when it was changed to Sī-nă'ē, and still later to Sē-rĕs, which latter remained in use until it was known as the Empire of "Carhany."

After the establishment of the Kentersends in In-dē-grĭs'tē, the Lăz'ĕr-ĕnds in Sĕn'ē-cūtes, and the Tĭm'mē-nōns in Shăf'fi-ōn, their descendants established a system of migrations, viz: the Kentersends and the Lazerends eastward into China, and the Timmenons southward into "Hindustan."

The Kentersends migrated first into "Little Tibet." Enroute, they passed along the southern slopes of the "Hindu Kush" mountains, over the great plateau of "Tibetan," by way of the "Indus" river basin, along the Gorge of the western range of the Himalay mountains, through which the river bursts, into the section of Little Tibet, thence northeast to the "Kuen Lun" mountains, or about thirty-five degrees north latitude and thirty-eight degrees longitude east from Greenwich, to between the mountains and the northern portion of the "Lingzi" plane, where they settled, termed the mountains Grē-tē-zōn, the section Mŭn-kū-dū'sĕn, and retained the tribal name of Kentersends. After many generations, they became a numerous people.

Subsequently, a large tribe of their descendants migrated southward, form Munkudusen, to the region of the Himalay mountains, which latter they termed En-gŭs-tē-nĕn'gō, along which subsequent descended tribes continued the migration, until they had arrived in the section now known as the source of the "Pechoa" river, at the southern cross section of the "Yingling" mountains. During this part of the migration, small remnants from the main tribes were left in various sections along the northern border of the Himalayas, from which, descended tribes migrated northward, into southern and central Tibet, where they settled in various localities.

When the main tribe of Kentersends had reached the Pechoa river, they contended as to which course of migration they should pursue, which resulted in a separation of the tribe into two divisions, which we will term the northern and the southern. The northern passed northward, along the western slopes of the Yun-ling mountains, until they arrived at the northern section of the range, and the southeastern section of the "Siueh Shan" range, between which they passed. They then continued northward, along the eastern foothills of the Siueh Shan mountains; thence between the ranges lying to their northeast, and the "Peling" mountains, which latter they followed northward, on their eastern side, to about a hundred and nine degrees longitude east from Greenwich, where they settled for a time, termed the section Ar-ĭsk'ā-bī-lăs, and retained the tribe name of Kentersends.

Subsequently, the main portion of the colony continued the migration, when they passed eastward along the bank of the "Wei" river, to its confluence with the "Yellow" river, which latter they followed eastward on its south side, to about a hundred and fifteen degrees longitude east from Greenwich, where the river turns its course northeastward; where they left its course and passed northeast, into "Shan-tung," China. There they settled in the western central portion, on the "Ta-wan" river, between the "Yih" mountains and the now known "Grand Canal," which section they termed I-ŭ'tā-ny, the river Gē-lĭs'tī-sēs, and called themselves the Oc-tō-shăns. Their principal city, which they termed Am-nē'thŭs, was located on the site where the town of "Tain-gan" has place.

After the main tribe of Kentersends left their section of Ariskabilas, the remnant people multiplied, until they became a large colony, from which various tribes spread out into different sections of the now known provinces of "Shen-si" and 'Kan-suh."

The southern division of the main tribe, followed the now known "Kin-sha-Keang," or "River of the Golden Sands," which they termed Cē-lĭs-ī-cūse', to where the latter turns north, into the province of "Sez-chuen," China, where they halted for a short time. Contentions then arose among them as to the course for their further migration, which resulted in a division of the tribe. The main portion, however, followed the southern banks of the "Yang Tse Kiang" river, which latter they termed U-ĕl' tī-nŏn, until they arrived at about a hundred and nine degrees longitude east from Greenwich, in the southeastern portion of the section of "Sez-chuen," where they settled, termed th section Ar-phō'dēse, but retained their former tribe name of Kentersends.

After several generations, the main portion of the colony continued the migration, when they passed along the southern shores of the Ueltizon rīver, and finally arrived in the southeastern portion of the now known city of "Nankin," which section they termed Kē'chŭck, but retained their former tribe name of Kentersends.

Subsequent to the departure of the main tribe of Kentersends from Arphodes, or northern Sze-chuen, the remnant portion retained both tribe and section names, and their descendants ultimately spread out into the now known province of Sze-chuen, south, and southeast, into the province of "Kwei-chow."

When the southern division of the Kentersends separated at the north bend of the Ueltizon river, the branch of the main tribe passed southeast to the north side of the "Nanling" mountains, where they settled for a time, along their northern slopes, termed the mountains Lĭn-tă-shă'ză (a long winding range), the section Cŏn-sū'ĕn, but retained the tribe name of Kentersends.

Subsequently, the main portion of the descendants resumed the migration, when they left the mountain range at the eastern section of the province of "Kwang-se," and passed northward, until they came to the upper eastern tributary of the "Yuen" river, which latter they followed northeast, around the now known lake "Tung-ting," to the Ueltizon river, which they followed at different periods of time, until they arrived at the sectino now known as "Kiang-sŭ," or in the 'Nankin" vicinity, where their descended brethren of the main southern division had settled, but a short time prior to their arrival.

Ultimately, the two tribes joined issues, forgot the old contentions of their ancestors, and waxed strong as a nation, when they retained the section name of Kechuck, and the tribe name of Kentersends. Their principal city they termed Tū-gō'ry (four tribes), which term referred to the blending of the four tribes, viz. the Kentersends of Kuchuck and the Octoshans of Iutany, who were descendants from the Kentersends, and their migrating remnants, Kentersends of Arphodese, into southeastern China, of which Tugory was the capital. The name Tugory remained in use until in the first part of the Adomic period, when it was changed to Sĭn-ī-cū'lēse, and so remained until later, when it was again changed to "King-ling," as originally known under the Han dynasty about 206 B. C. At the time that the city was named Tugory, the entire portion of China south of the now known "Great Wall of China," was termed Zĕn-cŭs'tē-zŭm, a term in the Kentersend language, that meant "East, West, North and South, as did the term Zĭn-tī-zăn'tŭm of the Lazerends, or more particularly the four cardinal points toward which the four above-named tribes had spread out, who ultimately blended into one nation.

In the early part of the Adomic period, a tribe of the Octoshans of Iuthaney, migrated north into the section now known as the Province of Chih-li, where they settled north of the "Pei-Ho" river, in the vicinity of the now known city of "Pekin," which section they termed Hä-shū'shăn, and called themselves the Hashushans. Their principal city, which they termed Căl-tī-shū'ăs was located on the site where now the city of Pekin has place. About the beginning of the Adomic period, the name was changed to Tī-ŭn'gī-Shăn, which latter was retained until it was changed to Peking, and later to Pekin.

The early Kentersends of the pre-historic city of Tugory, and country of Zencustezum, were somewhat changed, physically, in comparison with their ancestors, the Kentersends of the region of Thuriistic.

In stature, they averaged about six feet, were slender, or angularly built; though they possessed very large joints. Their arms were long, hands normal, but their fingers were also long; their feet were large and flat; their skins very dark; their hair long and black, and they also had considerable on different parts of the body, especially up and down their spines, a fact that showed a development from the more animal, or low condition physically that had characterized some of their ancestors, toward the more human condition in that respect, that characterized the peoples of subsequent time. They had large, deep set, slightly angular, black eyes; receding foreheads, though they projected above the eyes, and their ears were large. The males wore simply a clout, and the females wore loose trousers that covered the hips and thighs. The garments were made from the furred skins of a species of animal then known as the Kĕ'dēnt (now extinct). It was an animal that inhabited the mountains principally, and was about the size of a modern hound; had soft, dark gray hair, about such as characterizes the modern maltese cat.

The early Kentersends of Zencustezum recognized light as a great principle that came to guide them in all matters. Therefore, they adored the sun, moon and stars as containing the principle of light, which latter they termed In'shā, meaning *light,* in the Kentersend language, and to which they erected an Idol, or Image, under the same name. Their general belief was that the planets had power over the earth and its people. They thought the sun to be their guide, or leader, by day, and the moon and star by night. When the sun was invisible during the day, and the moon and stars at night, they thought their leaders were lost, but that they would, in due time, return again. Strange as it may seem, the first appearance of the crescent moon was to them a sight more to be adored than was the glory of the rising sun; from the fact that they thought the greater help came from the light that led them at night. Therefore, the first appearance of the crescent new moon was the stated time for their adorational assemblies, worship, and feasting.

The idol worshipped as representing Insha, was constructed as follows: A large block of wood about five feet in height was erected on one of the commons of their settlement, on which was stained a large circle. Within the circle, on its center, was represented the half arisen disc of the sun. Above it, on each side, and beneath it, was represented sets of three stars. Below the lower set of stars was represented the crescent moon as lying on its back, and lastly, beneath the crescent moon was another set of three stars. The assembly and feast were always held, whether the moon appeared or not, as might be occasioned by clear or cloudy weather; therefore, when cloudy, they simply assembled and held their feast, from the fact that it was always prepared beforehand, but they entered into no adorational exercise.

The adorational and worshipful exercises consisted in gathering about Insha, when they would, in concert, give utterance to a sort of vocal chant, which was followed by dancing, when each individual proceeded in the style of his own idea. This was done as the moon was rising, after which they held their feast. Their feast consisted of roasted fowls, fish, and a quantity of various natural fruits. These were served upon a great table, or block of stone, the top of which had been cut down to a flat surface. After the feast was completed, they returned to their several abodes.

By this time, the Kentersends of Munkudusen began to change in regard to domestic life. Vegetables were added as an accompaniment to their fruit and flesh food. Plaited fabric garments took the place of a skin raiment, the former being made from the leaf and stem skins of a plant then known as the Kē-ū' gĕt, a juicy plant, in resemblance to the modern Rhubarb. The juice was made into a drink. The leaf and stem skins were made into warp, and hair was twisted into strips for the woof. The fabric was woven while the strips of skin from the Keuget were fresh, so that in drying, the contraction of the skins would hold the filling more tightly.

About two hundred years before the Adomic period, at the close of the long line of migration (see above), the Kentersends were confronted by the waters of the great Northern Pacific, and could go no farther; hence, turned their attention to a location and settlement, and to establish a hamlet, which at first consisted of mere huts, constructed from limbs of trees and sod. From this condition, a general development had place through subsequent ages, and ultimately resulted in the city of "Tiungi-Shan," and still later, the city of "Pekin."

The first morning after their arrival in the North Pacific region, worn and fatigued by their long migration in search of their promised home, where the sun rose, on awakening, they saw the sun rising, and as it appeared to them as coming from out the water, they were filled with wonder and new life; a fact which they expressed by shouting, "Sō-lĭs'trē, cō-lĭn'sē, sū-ĕn'zä" (We are still nearer to thee). As they developed livelihood utilities, intellectuality and civilization advanced and physical changes were brought about. They advanced in the idea of weaving, by the use of the cotton from a plant then known as the Klū'kĕt (which resembled the modern "milk weed"), in place of hair, and the bark of a shrub, much like the modern "Moose Wood" (then known as the Cīl'tī-zē), in place of the skins of the Keuget. These fabrics were made into two garments. The upper one was a sort of narrow blouse, and the lower one was a narrow skirt that extended to below the knees. Both the men and the women wore the same style of garments.

Later, they developed the idea of better weaving, and finer wrought fabrics. In the place of the cotton of the Kluket plant, they used the hair from animals then known as the Dē-kī'shē, long since extinct. They were then very plentiful, both wild and domestic, but harmless, and were about the size of a new born calf; had long shaggy hair, of black, brown, and were also ash, or dark gray colors; long, slender legs, and beautiful, expressive eyes. Their hair was annually cut from their bodies, similar to that of the wool from the modern sheep.

The Lazerends, in pursuance of their migration, passed along the northern side of the "Hindu Kush" mountains, over the great

Plateau now known as "Pamir," to the section of country also known as Pamir, from which they followed the watercourses, down the eastern slopes to the valleys below; thence to the southern slopes of the now known "Thian Shan" mountains, where they settled in the vicinity of the now known town of "Kutche," between the mountains and the "Tarim" river, which former they termed Chĭs-sŏn'dō, and the section E-u-rĭz'ĕl, but retained the tribal name of Lazerends. Their principal city, which they termed Bŭs-kē-lĕt', was located on the site of their first settlement.

The Lazerends and their descendants from Muckechan, spread out into the entire section now known as "Mantchooria," and ultimately became a large nation. They built their capital city, which they termed Kū-lĕnt'zî-ō, northeast of their earlier city of Buskelet, between the now known "Sikota" mountains, their western parallel range, which mountains they termed Klē-dĭs'tä (twin mountains). The site of the city was on the banks of the now known "Usuri" river, or southern branch of the "Amoor," which latter they termed Clī-ĭs'tä, or on the site where now the town of "Kimgoola" has place.

At the time of the departure of the Lazerends from Eurizel, on their migration eastward, a remnant of the tribe was left, who retained the original tribe and section names. Their principal city which they termed Al'bĕr-shăng, was located on the site where now the town of "Kutche" has place.

After the establishment of the Lazerends in northeastern Chinese Tartary, they termed all that portion of the Cihnese Empire north of the now known Great Wall of China, Zĭn-tī-zăn'-tŭm, which term in the Lazerend language (as was the case with Zencustezum of the Kestersends), referred to the four cardinal points, viz., East, West, North and South, in which directions the people of the cities of Buskelet and Kulentzio, and the section of Muckechan had spread out, inhabitants of Zintizantum, the region of the Amoor river, and further northeastward, along its course, and into the region of the now known western portion of the "Saghalien Island."

The section between the two cities represented the most civilized portion of the inhabitants, who were the people who originally established the idea of a dividing line between themselves and the Kentersends of the southern portion of the country, or Zintizantum, which condition in subsequent time (or after the breaking out of the Modern Chinese Wars) gave rise to the building of the Great Chinese Wall, which is a re-conceived idea of separation between the northern and southern portions of the country, and people, thus inspired and further influenced by spirit intelligences, who were, in their earth life, contemporaneous with the pre-historic idea as entertained, and to a certain degree, carried out by the pre-historic Lazerends and Kentersends, who are the pre-historic ancestors of the Chinese. The Lazerends of Eurizel were about the same, physically, as those of Senecutes. They had improved somewhat, in their modes of livelihood, and preparation for the same. They clad themselves more completely, though still with furred skins.

In the city of Kulentzio, and its vicinity, they grew to be more fleshy than muscular; a little lighter in color in some cases, and in others remained about the same. Their heads were not so large as those of their ancestors, the Rezendeths, but nearer the normal size. Their hair had grown to be a little straighter and longer. Their eyes, in some cases, had changed from black to a dark brown color, though the majority were still black, all being peculiar, from the fact that they had a squinty appearance, and were small. Their mouths were broad; lips pouching; ears normal; chins quite receding, and characterized with very thin or scanty beards. They had discarded the use of skin and fur raiment, and made their garments by plaiting rushes into aprons, using barks for the warp. Later on, they wore a skirt of the same material. Still later, they used the same material for their fabrics, excepting that in place of using bark for warp, the women prepared hair by pulling it out into rolls, which they twisted for that purpose, thus making the garments a little softer to the skin than the bark was. The preparation of both kinds of material was the work of the women; while hunting and fishing were the duties of the men.

In this section they got their first idea of cereal food, and its cultivation and utility as a food, in connection with that of flesh and fruits. The discovery was made by four huntsmen, who were digging in the earth for burrowed game. About them grew a cereal plant then known as the Sū-ĕn'ēz, that bore cereals about the size of a small navy bean, that was oblong, or one side curved, and the other right or left oblique form, which during the ages of its descendance has appeared in modern time as the now known "Buckwheat." As the huntsmen sat on the ground to rest the while, an animal then known as the Crū'lĭx, was eating of the Suenez. It was about the size of a modern sheep, and characterized with long, curly white hair; slender body, and limbs; long, bushy tail; large head, but pointed nose, much like the modern wolf; and long since extinct. The animal arrested the attention of the huntsmen who, seeing it eat of the cereals, also tasted of them, and found them good for food. Henceforth the people began the cultivation of the plant for that purpose.

The early Lazerends of the pre-historic cities of Buskelet and Kulentzio, and the country of Zencustezum, like the early Kentersends of Consuen and Zencustezum, had changed somewhat, physically, from the conditions that characterize their ancestors, of the region of Senecutes. In stature they were about six feet; were generally fleshy, of the flabby order; their legs from the knees down were massive, and the joints exceptionally large; their feet were large, short, broad and flat; their arms and hands were in harmony with their bodies; their skins were very dark; their hair black, and of various styles, that of the males being straight, but that of the females was wavy, or slightly curly; some thin, scattering hair characterized their bodies; their eyes were black, quite angular, and large, but had a squinted appearance; their foreheads were somewhat low, or perhaps medium; their heads flattish on top; their ears quite round and of medium size, and were characterized with a considerable growth of short hair on them, in harmony with a heavy growth around the lower part of the head, that partially covered them. They were a very indolent people, lived on animal food principally, hence fleshy and flabby in appearance. The raiment worn by both males and females was alike. It was simply a strip of fabric which they wove or plaited from fibers and hair, and was thrown carelessly around the waist, the ends of which hung down to the knees. At times, some of them went entirely nude, being clad or not, as they chose.

The early Lazerends of Zintizantum, being very ignorant, had no definite idea in regard to a God principle, and therefore erected no idols, and held no stated adorational assemblies. However, they felt that in the Sun, Moon and Stars, that shone above them, there was something marvelous, and far beyond their understanding, and therefore, individually, whenever they caught the first glimpse of either the Sun, Moon, or Stars, they would bow low to the ground, then proceed on their way.

Subsequent to the establishment of the inhabitants in the country of Zencustezum, two large tribes of Kentersends migrated southward to the southern border of Zencustezum. One from their section of Arphodese who, enroute, passed through the western portion of the now known Province of "Hoo-pi," and also of "Hoo-nan," to the eastern side of the northern bend of the now known Nanling mountains; thence southward into the now known Province of "Kuang-se," to the valley between the "Zwei-kiang," or "Cinnamon" river, and the "Se-keang," near their junction, which section they termed Văck'ā-rē-ŏn, the river Bē-thăn'thŭs, and called themselves the Văck-ā-rē'ŏns. After many generations, they had spread out westward, and northward, along the various tributaries of the "Ki-keang" river, and eastward into the western portion of the now known Province of "Kwang-tung." Their principal large city, which they termed Cŭz'ē-rŏx, was located on the site of their first settlement, and ultimately became the capital city of Vackareon.

About the time that the above-named tribe started from their section of Arphodese, the other of the two tribes of Kentersends started on their migration southward, from their section of Kē'-chŭck, when they passed through the now southeastern portion of the Province of "Gan-hwuy," and the western portion of the Province of "Che-keang," and followd the eastern slopes of the now known "Bohea Hills," into the northeastern portion of the now known Province of "Kwang-tung," where they settled on the western side of the now known "Tung-keang," or "east river," east of the now known town of "Sienpring," which section they termed Cĕl-lĕn'thē-cŏn, and for a time retained their former tribe name of Kentersends. Their principal city, which they also termed Cellenthecon, was located upon the site of their first settlement. After several generations, they had spread out westward and southward, in the now known Province of "Kwang-tung," at which time the two peoples, viz: themselves and the Vackareons met, and being of the same race, soon become as one people, when the Kentersends of the Cellenthecon section, changed their name to that of Vackareons, and their section to Vackareon.

They, being descendants of the Kentersends of the city of Consuen, and the country of Zencustezum, in a physical sense, were about the same as their ancestors, and so remained until about the time when began Modern history. They were an extremely indolent people, who never labored when they could avoid it, and therefore would lie around on the ground in groups, like cattle of the fields in modern times. They subsisted upon fruits, fish and animal food. They plaited, or wove by hand, a fabric consisting of grasses and fibers which they utilized as raiment. The women had two styles of dress. Some wore the fabric drawn about them in the form of a blanket, while others wore two garments; the lower consisted of a narrow strip of the fabric being hung from the waist like a very short skirt, while the upper was another piece of the fabric thrown about the shoulders. The men had one general style. They wore a narrow, pendant strip of the fabric that hung down in front, from the waist, as far as to the knees. The leaders of the people, however, were distinguished from the latter by a garment that consisted of a long strip of the fabric, in which a hole was cut in the center, through which they put their heads, thus forming a pendant strip both in front and back of the body, extending as far down as to the knees, and fastened at the waist. The front strip was ornamented with stained stripes that extended from the neck down to the waist. They, as well as the people, ornamented the nude parts of their bodies with the same staining, which was in diagonal stripes. The stripes, however, on the leaders' garments were perpendicular.

Though descendants from the Kentersends of Zencustezum, they did not retain the full idea of the guiding principle of light, as entertained by their ancestors. They recognized heat, or wormth, as their principal benefactor, and yet they recognized the light that came with the conditions of heat as being for their good. They termed their two principles, viz: heat and light, Kī-ĭs'us, Kī'ä, in their language, meant *heat* or *warmth,* and was always used as such, when speaking of fire; and Is'ŭs meant *light;* but in the use of the compound term, the vowel "a" was dropped. They had no stated place or time for adoration or worship, and made no idols in representation of Kiisus. Individually, they made obeisance to the natural Sun, as it rose above the horizon, and when it was well up on the eastern sky, they would stand facing it; then with backs turned to it, as in the attitude of receiving its warmth, they remained for a time, and then passed on. It was from this belief and custom of the Vackareons that the idea of Sun worship through the Adomic, and later periods of time, was adopted and handed down from generation to generation.

Subsequent to the establishment of the mixed race of Kintilucians and the Sendix, in the home section of the latter, north of the "Caspian Sea," a tribe of their descendants migrated from the "Ural" river section, to that east of the "Volga" near its outlet into the Caspian Sea, where they dwelt for about one hundred and fifty years, during which time they became a large tribe. Desiring to find a locality endowed with greater warmth, they as an entire colony, established a migration, in pursuance of such, when they passed eastward through the region that in subsequent time became the northern shores of the Caspian sea, thence southward through the section now known as between the Caspian and the "Aral Sea," to the southern portion of the former, when they turned their course eastward, passed through the section now known as "Turkestan," crossed the now known Himalaya mountains north of the Hindu Kush range, and entered what is now known as western "Mongolia," where they settled north of the now known "Kuen Lun" mountains, at about forty degrees north latitude and eighty degrees longitude east from Greenwich. They gave the section no name, but called themselves the Jē-rē' bads.

In stature they were from five and a half to six and a half feet. They possessed medium-sized bodies; their color varied from a dark reddish brown to a yellow, which was the first appearance of the yellow tint in the eastern continent, which in later generations changed to a copper color, thus caused by the influence of the sun's rays in that latitude, together with further mixture of races. Some of the people were even white. Their hair generally was long, straight, and varied in color, from a dark to a light brown; their eyes retained the same angular condition that characterized their ancestors, the Sendix, and were of black or brown color. Their heads were rather flat on top, broad through the forehead, which latter was low. Their eyelashes were quite long; their noses slightly flat; their mouths wide; their lips thin; their ears normal; their feet broad and long, and their hands the same. Their bodies were characterized with considerable hair, and they mostly went nude, though some wrapped themselves in skins.

They dwelt for ages along the Kuen Lun mountains, until finally they became lost as a distinct nation, by their minglings with the Kentersends and Lazerends throughout the Chinese Empire, and Chinese Tartary, which absorption of race has caused the present characteristics in the Chinese races, such as color, angular eyes, general visage peculiarities, etc., that are now possessed by the Chinese and Japanese people of modern time, only that as the generations have passed by, the above-named characteristics have grown less intense, and will continue so to grow in subsequent time.

At that time, the Jerebad blood mixture with the Kentersends, especially as it passed southward, in subsequent migrations, brought more of a reddish hue to the skins of the people. Those that descended from the mixture of blood with the Lazerends of the North, were possessed of skin of a darker hue. Therefore, the Japanese who were descendants from the Lazerends, are of a different shade from the Chinese and the Filipinos, which latter two are descendants from the Kentersends and, therefore, possess the lighter hue. The changes that came to the Chinese through the following generations, gave to them the copper hue, and the angular eyes that characterize them in modern time. Then as those influences spread out into the Great Eastern Archipelago, through degeneration, the black, the red, and various shades of color presented themselves, as the conditions of climate and livelihood influenced and further established them.

E-nĕn-dör-nĕ′dē was the first pre-historic name of the section of country now known as "Siberia," as given by the Shăl-tē-măn′-zēs of Shăl-tē-măn′go, the word being a compound term. The syllables "e-nen," translate snow; "dor," country; and "ne," fur. Enendor, therefore, in its compound sense, means additional fur, and the entire compound term, conveyed to the Shaltemangoes, the idea that in the snowy, or cold country of north Siberia (in contrast with the southern portion), it was necessary to put on additional furs, in order to obtain greater warmth.

Kă-sŭn′dĭx was the second pre-historic name of Siberia, as given by the descendants of the Shaltemanzes and the Sucaniums, about the beginning of the Adomic period. The term Kasundix is also compound. The syllables "ka-sun," signified cold or frozen; and "dix," land. Therefore, the compound term Kasundix, was known by those peoples, to mean the frozen land.

About 4000 years subsequent to the submergence of Atlantis, a powerful convulsion occurred, that had place in the section of country now known as the central portion of the "Yenisei Bay," south of "Nova-Zembla." At the time of that great convulsion, all the section of country between northeast Cape, and Nova-Zembla, and west, and southwest of the latter, was a land of frozen ice and snow, which by the power of the convulsion, became submerged by the now known "Arctic Ocean." A range of snow-clad Shŭl′tē-zōnes (mountains), then known as Krŏn′xŏt, extended northeast from the southwestern section of the now known "White Sea," to the southern coast of "Nova-Zembla," which latter belonged to the range, and further extended eastward, in a circular form, to northeast Cape, Siberia. The force of the convulsion extended southwest along the Kronxot range, sinking and submerging portions of it, thus establishing the White Sea, the Yenisei Bay, and the northern coast line, of "Europe," in that section, and severed Nova-Zembla from Europe, by establishing a water course between the Yenisei Bay, and the "Kara Sea," leaving the "Weigatz Island" as a severed link that formerly bound Nova-Zembla to the European Continent. The force of the convulsion further extended along the Kronxot range of Shultezones, formed the coast line of Nova-Zembla sank and submerged the section of land between Nova-Zembla and Northeast Cape, Siberia, thus forming the sea of "Kara," the zig-zag coast line of northeast Siberia, from "Cape North East," to "North Cape" of Norway, including the islands, the Gulf of "Obi," and all the inlet waters that accompanied the extension of land in that section, connected with the open waters of the Arctic Ocean, to the coast of "Russia" and "Siberia," in that section.

About two hundred years subsequent to the above named convulsion, another great one occurred that had place on the northern coast of Siberia, between "Cape Sviatoi," and the "Liakov Islands," or in the immediate vicinity of the "Liakov Island." At the time of the convulsion, there was a system of three ranges of Shultezones, then known as the Klō-zī-lĕ'nō system. One extended northeast from the section now known as the mouths of the "Lena" R.; one northwest from the section of Cape Sviatoi; and one northwest, parallel with the former, from the vicinity of the "Kolinia Bay." The force of the convulsion extended throughout the above named system, thus establishing the islands north of Siberia, the coast line and the inlet-waters of the latter, from North Cape in the west, to "Cape Chelakhskai" in the east, thus letting the open waters of the Arctic Ocean, south to the Siberian coast.

For many years subsequent to the coming of the Lăz'ĕr-ĕnds and the Kĕn'tĕr-sĕnds into what is now known as central Asia, the country of Siberia was only inhabited by wild animals. Eventually, a colony of the Lazerends migrated northeast, into that section of country now known as along the northern slopes of the Altai mountains, but gradually degenerated into very low conditions, on account of their surroundings, and subsisting, as they did on animal food. The colony was termed Gē-set's, so named by their brethren, the Lazerends, a term that, in the Lazerend language, meant a frozen portion. They continued in their degeneration, until about six hundred years before modern ancient history, when they were lost entirely as a nation, through their general physical degeneration. A few, however, wandered into the southern section, or vicinity of Eū-rĭz'ĕl, but being in such a low condition, did not associate with the Lazerends of that section, and, therefore, also became extinct.

Subsequent to the establishment of the section of Zintizantum, and the cities of Bŭs-kē-lĕt′ and Kū-lĕnt′zi-ō, a large tribe of huntsmen, migrated north into the section of Siberia, in pursuit of game. En route, they passed over the great mountain range now known as "Stanovoi," which they termed Găd-nō′sĭs, where they found a large vā-ä′yā (valley), which they termed Shăl-ē-măn′gō, that lay extent east of the now known "Orulgan range," which latter they termed Grē-sī-ĭl′tĭs, at a point about sitxy degrees north latitude and one hundred degrees longitude east from Greenwich, where they settled, and established a small nation of their own, and called themselves the Shăl-ē-măn′zēs.

About two hundred years subsequent to the establishment of the Shalemanzes nation in Shalemango, a tribe of their descendants migrated east of what is now known as the "Tas Khayakhiak" range, and northwest of the now known "Koly Mskiyo" range, where they settled in a vaaya, which they termed Sū-căn′-ĭ-ŭm, that had place at a point about sixty-six degrees north latitude and one hundred and fifty degrees longitude east from Greenwich, or west of the then known Gadnosis Shultezones, and called themselves the Sū-căn′ĭ-ŭms.

Descendants, both from the Shalemanzes and the Sucaniums, from Shalemango and Sucanium, continued to occupy those regions down to the Modern Ancient period of time, but from various causes, became coarse and degenerated.

TUSH NO'LUS GAN-DE-CU'LO GIN-DI-TE-HISH'AN, OR THE GREAT EAST INDIAN ARCHIPELAGO.

TELTZIE LIII.

Găn-dē-cū'lō (waters coming from below), was the first prehistoric name of the Great East Indian Archipelago, so termed by the Gĭs'trăz tribes of A-gŏn'thrus (Australia), about the beginning of the Adomic period. It, the greatest Gĭn-dī-tē-hĭsh'ăn (Gistrad term for Archipelago, meaning many islands) in the world, embracing what is modernly known as "Polynesia," "Australasia," "Malaysia," thus exists through the force and result of six great periodical convulsions, each of which was preceded and followed by smaller developing convulsions, as the ages passed by.

The first of the six occurred about three hundred years prior to the final submergence of Atlantis, and had place in the southeastern section of Polynesia. The greatest force of this convulsion had place in the "Tahiti" archipelago, of Polynesia, or better known as between the three islands, "Bora Bora," "Ulitea," and "Huahine," of the "Society Islands," which caused the inundation of land between them as well as that of the entire section.

Prior to this convulsion, and the submergence of this southeastern section of Polynesia, a system of mountains, then termed Lalengo, extended northeast and southeast, from the "Cook's" or "Harvey's" islands, thus embracing the Society group, and the "Low Archipelago." A branch also extended northwest, embracing the "Marquesas" group, and another branch extended southwest, embracing the "Austral" group.

A vast section of country, then termed Kūrā, characterized with mountains, valleys, rivers, and lakes, extended from "South America," "Central America," and "Mexico," west, and northwest, to the eastern sections of the now Polynesian islands. The powerful force of this convulsion extended along the Lalengo system, northeast, and southeast to the border lines of the convulsions that established the coast lines of South America, Central America, and Mexico, thus establishing the open waters of the Pacific Ocean, east of the Marquesas, and the Austral islands, as well as all of the islands belonging to the Polyesian system, east of the Cook's or Harvey's, the Society, and the Marquesas.

At the time of the first great periodical convulsion, that shattered and submerged portions of the Lalengo range, and its branches, thus establishing the southeastern portion of Polynesia, as far northwest as to the Cook's, Society and Marquesas Islands, remnants of the Kallutes were left upon the above named islands, whose descendants became the pre-historic ancestors of the "Sawaiori," or Malayo-Polynesian aborigines that inhabited the Cook's islands; the "Tahitians" of the Society or Tahiti archipelago; and the "Malayo-Polynesian" races of the Marquesas.

Prior to the submergence of that portion of the great country then known as Kura, that lay extent east of the America and Marquesas islands, in the northeast portion of the great Kĕl'tē-zĕc (valley) of Ac-clĭn'thē, that then had place between the Society, the Marquesas and America islands, was inhabited by a tribe of people who on account of their having no tribal name, Alem Prolex, has termed Găs'ticks, meaning *animal like,* who had migrated there from the Chăn-hăn'gōes settlement in Chä-hä-ē'zĕl, now the section of the Gulf of California, about the same time that the tribe of Chanhangoes migrated to the now known "Sandwich" island district, where as generations passed by, they degenerated into almost a state of animal existence. In fact, they were more like the now known Chimpanzee Ape tribe, excepting their lower limbs, which more closely resembled those of the human race. Being covered with a suit of hair, they wore no garments, lived a promiscuous life, having no idea of the sacred rites of marriage. They in their low condition, had no religious ideas, or adorational exercises.

Prior to the submergence of the great Keltezec, or country that extended from New Zealant, east and northeast, to the "Harveys" and "Austral" islands of southeastern Polynesia, a tribe of the In'drās race, or people of the then known section of Yĕl-lă-kū'dĕt, or modern "Guiana," South America, who in divergence to the original tribe's migration, passed southwestward along the then known Kē-lō'dŏsh range, as far as to the "Galapagos" islands, thence through the great country of Kura, to the then known Lä-lĕn-gō range, which they crossed, and passed along their southern foot-hills, to the region of country now known as the Pacific Ocean area, south of the Austral islands, which they termed Hă-zĕn-rē'nō, and called themselves the Sĕk-ā-lē'tŭs.

Submerged Atlantis Restored

At the time of the submergence of Hazenreno, by the Pacific waters, remnants of the Sekaletus tribe were left on the islands of that section. Physically, they were more like the human race, than were the Gasticks who dwelt in the Keltezec of Acclinthe. They had no superfluous hair on their bodies. They went entirely nude. They were large, bony, and yet of an athletic build, and had large feet and hands. Their foreheads were low; noses broad; mouths wide, with thick or heavy lips. Their eyes were dark and deeply set in their heads. Their hair was shaggy, and some was curly. They did not live promiscuous lives, as did the Gasticks, but having no form of marriage, they simply mated like animals, but not for any given length of time, which fact caused many quarrels, and contentions, especially so among the men. They had no religious ideas, hence no adorational gatherings or exercises.

The second periodical convulsion occurred about two hundred and seventy-five years subsequent to the first, and had place between the Fiji and the Navigators islands. Prior to this convulsion, a great mountain range, then termed Gĕ-sĕ-rĕn'zō, extended from New Zealand, northeast to the above named islands; thence forming a semi-circle northeast, and west, thus embracing the "America," islands.

Another range, then termed Kĕn-zĕ'tĕn, extended from the "Navigators" islands, the locality of its junction with the Geserenzo range, northeast, and west, in conformity to the course of the Geserenzo range, thus embracing the "Danger," "Bowditch," "Sidney," and the "Enderby" islands. A great Keltezec (valley), then known as the Strū-clē-zē'ŏn, extended northeast from between New Zealand and "Australia," to the now known section of the Fiji, "Friendly," and Navigators islands, at which latter point the great convulsion had place. Another, then known as the Acclinthe, that branched off from the Struclezeon, extended from north of the "Kermadec" islands, northeast from between the "Cook's or "Harvey's" and the "Savage" islands, to beyond the America and the Marquesas islands, into the country of Kura. Still another, then known as the Sē-grē'lĭn, lay extent between the Kenzeten and the northern section of the Geserenzo ranges. And yet another, then known as the Tē-zē-lē'ŏn, extended north from the Navigators, and the Fiji districts, to that of the "St. Pedro" island, where it branched off to the northeast, into the country of Kura, and northwest to the section now known as the Smyth's islands.

The greatest force of this convulsion had place in a low

mountain, centrally located between the Friendly, the Fiji, and the Navigators islands, which caused the mountain, and the land that joined it to the above-named islands, to sink, which subsequently established the water channels between them, by connecting the Struclezeon and the Acclinthe Keltezecus (valleys) by the removal of the mountain, which formed their terminus at that point. The force further extended throughout the Geserenzo and the Kenzeten ranges, southwest to, and including the "Tonga" islands, northeast to about five degrees south of the Sandwich islands, and as far east as thirty-four degrees longitude west from Greenwich, into the country of Kura, west to the Keltezec of Tezeleon, and southeast to the Keltezec of Acclinthe, thus establishing that section of Polynesia, from the Tonga islands in the southwest, to and beyond the America islands in the northeast.

At the time of the above named convulsion, which shattered and submerged the northern half of the Geserenzo range and its western neighbor, the Kenzeten, remnants of the Kallutes were left on the Friendly and Navigators islands, whose descendants became the pre-historic ancestors of the now known Samoans of Samoa, or the Navigators islands, and the Raratongas and other Malayo-Polynesians of the Cook's islands. This condition left the southwestern portion of the Geserenzo range, as far north as to the Tropic of Capricorn undisturbed, and yet connected to the main land of Australia, upon which was also left a small remnant of the Kallutes, who during the 1000 years that intervened the second and third periodical convulsions, had multiplied and migrated to the southern portion of the range, or now known section of New Zealand.

Prior to the convulsion that established the central portion of Polynesia, from northeast to southwest, the Kannanzes, had spread out into the great Keltezec of Tezeleon, south of the Sandwich islands, and were a numerous people. Tribes of the inhabitants of the Keltezec, established migrations southwestward along the Geserenzo range, and the Keltezec of Acclinthe, to the region of the Navigators, Society, and Cook's islands, or in the southwestern portion of the Keltezec, which they termed Acclinthe, and called themselves the Kallutes.

Prior to the establishment of the Fiji islands or "Viti" archipelago, the Friendly and the Navigators islands, some of the Kallutes had migrated into the Viti archipelago section, where they, after the formation of the islands, represented a Malayo-Polynesian race in opposition to the "Papuan" race of the Dĕtrē'-

mĕns, who also migrated to the Viti archipelago section. Further migrations westward, prior to the time of the fifth great periodical convulsion, by descendants of the Kallutes from the Friendly, the Navigators and the Fiji sections, ultimated in the establishment of the now known "Malayo-Polynesian race, as contemporaneous in existence with the Negrito-Polynesians, in the archipelago, from New Guinea in the west, to the Fiji islands in the east.

The third periodical convulsion occurred about 1000 years subsequent to the second, and had place in that section of the southern extremity of the Geserenzo range, now known as New Zealand, the exact location of the convulsion being between the "New-Ulster" and the "New-Munster" islands, when the two islands were severed, the portion of land between Cape "Farewell" and Cape "Egmont" was sunk, and the Cook's straits were formed, leaving the circular waters that encroach upon the North island, and form the "Golden" and "Tasman" bays of the South island. The force of this convulsion further extended along the Geserenzo range, northeast to the line of the second periodical convulsion, east to that of the first, and west into the Keltezec of Struclezeon, which established the New Zealand group of islands, including the "Raoul," the "Kermadec," and the "Macauley" islands.

At the time of the above named convulsion, remnants of the Kallutes were left on the North, or New Ulster island, where they settled in the northern section of the province of "Aucklnad," on the northern shores of the "Watemata Harbor" (an inlet of the "Hauraki Gulf"), and retained both their former tribe and section names. Their first pre-historic hamlet which they termed Rāy'jăb, was located on the site where now Auckland, capital city of the New Ulster island has place, it being the location of their first settlement. In subsequent time, they blended into a new race of people, by mixing with the Kŏn'nörts and the Körs, who had preceded them on the New Ulster island (see migration under the head of Australia), whose descendants became the pre-historic ancestors of the Maori aborigines.

After the establishment of the Gĭstrăz people in the province of "Queens- Land," Australia, and prior to the separation of New Zealand, from Australia, a tribe of their descendants migrated southeast to the section of the New Ulster or North Island of New Zealand, who in time termed that section Sör'zĕt, and called themselves the Kŏn'nŏrts. Subsequently, a tribe of the Gistraz descendants from "New South Wales," Australia, also migrated to the southern section of the New Ulster islands, who adopted the section name of Sorzet, as given by the Konnorts, but called themselves the Kors.

In evidence of the above named line of descendants, it will be observed by the reader that, the language of the "Maoris" is a dialect closely approaching that of the natives of the Sandwich islands, as well as that of the Navigators group, and the "Raratonga" of the Cook's; so much so, that natives of these mutually understand each other, a fact that proves their relationship ethnographically, and as having migrated from the same locality, and having descended from the same people, or ancestry.

Furthermore, the "Tahitians" of the Society; the "Marquesans" of the Marquesas; the "Raratongans" of the Cook's; and the "Samoans" of the Navigators" islands, are typical Malayo Polynesian races, closely connected physically, with the Maoris of New Zealand in the south, and the Sandwich islanders in the north, another set of links that hold together the ethnographic cycle of the Kannanzes from Kannanze (Sandwich islands), to Sorzet New Zealand

It was not until about the Adomic period that the now known New Munster islands, or that section of New Zealand was inhabited, which was first by migrators from both the Konnorts and the Kors, or the mixed race of Konnorts, Kors and Kallutes.

The fourth periodical convulsion occurred about fifty years subsequent to the third, and was in two sections, at periods of about seventy-five years apart. The first section had place southeast of the Clark's island, at about one hundred and seventy-two degrees west longitude north of the Tropic of Cancer, in what was then known as the En-tē-jŏ'thē-lĭc range.

Prior to this convulsion, the Entejothelic range extended from west of the Sharundusac point (heretofore described), slightly northwest to the "Rica de Plata" island, embracing the Sandwich, the Clark's and the Whale islands. The country immediately north of the Entejothelic range, was characterized with mountain spurs, undulated lands, rivers, and lakes, and was termed Chĭs'tī-sē, by the then inhabitants, who were not a distinct race of people, but stragglers from the various adjacent countries.

A great Keltezec then known as the Dĕn-bĕr-lē'tŭs, extended east and west (now beneath the open waters of the North Pacific Ocean), and was the dividing section between Chistise and the Entejothelic range, on its southern boundary, and the Nŏx'ī-nēne range and the country of Kör-dŭ-zŭ-lăc on its northern. Its southwestern section was a desert, and therefore nontillable. The west central section was deeply depressed, and trough like. The eastern section, west of northern California, and southern Oregon, was characterized with Dunes of various heights, from five feet, to about one hundred and fifty. Originally it was an inland sea, that prior to the second periodical convulsion, was known as Mĕn-tă-lē'să. Almost simultaneous with the second periodical convulsion, a powerful subterene convulsion occurred in the west central section of the sea of Mentalesa, which caused a subterranean outlet of its waters, which were drawn off into the submerged sections of the first, and second periodical convulsed districts, or into that part of the south Pacific Ocean, and thus left the Keltezec of Denberletus. Another great Keltezec extended northwest, and southeast, between the Entejothelic, and the northeastern section of the Fringuze triangular mountain system.

The force of the first section of the fourth periodical convulsion, extended throughout the Entejothelic range, east to the line of the convulsion that formed the present coast line of California and Mexico, north to the Keltezec of Denbeletus, west to the line of the convulsion that formed the "Japanese" islands, south, and southwest, to the Keltezec of Zē-dă'zē, which further extended the South Pacific waters northward, established the open waters of the North Pacific Ocean, by the inundation of the Keltezec of Denberletus, the "Rica de Plata," the "Whale," the Clark's and the Sandwich islands, and the section of the North Pacific Ocean, in which they stand.

The second section of the fourth periodical convulsion, occurred as above stated, about seventy-five years subsequent to the first section, and had place in the section of land between the "Rica d'Oro," "Guadalupe," "Sebastian Labos," and "Grampus" islands, in a small Keltezec then known as the Yă'tă-cŭs, that extended northeast from the Grampus, and the Sebastian Lobos islands, to beyond the Rica d'Oro. Prior to this convulsion, there was a great system of Dū-zī-ĕnd'lŭng (mountains), then termed the Frĭn'gū-zē, of a triangular course, whose extension embraced the now known "Magellans" archipelago, the "Ladrone" and the "Caroline" islands in its western and southern ranges, and the "Mulgrave," the "Anson's" archipelago, and the Rica d'Oro, and Sebastian Lobos, in the eastern and southern ranges. A large Keltezec, then known as the Kă-lō-zū'rĭc, had place in the center of the Fringuze system, and a large section of country then known as Fē-cō-lŭn'tē, lay extent southwest of the Fringuze range of Duziendlung, to the region of the Philippine islands. Another large Keltezec then known as the Tĕ-lănd'cĕst, extended east and west, south of the southern range of the Fringuze system.

The force of the above named convulsion extended along the eastern and western ranges of the Fringuze system (now the Caroline and the Mulgrave islands), which established the remainder of the western section of the North Pacific Ocean, as far west as to about one hundred and thirty degrees longitude east from Greenwich, south to the Caroline and the Mulgrave islands, and northeast to the line of the first sectional convulsion, and also established that section of the North Pacific Ocean, from the Rica d'Oro in the north, to the southern coast of the Caroline islands, and the Mulgrave archipelago, and northwest to the line of the convulsion that formed the Japanese islands.

Prior to the formation of the northern and northeastern portions of Polynesia a tribe of Chanhangoes who dwelt in the then known section of Chä-hä-ē'zēl, or the section now submerged by the "Gulf of California," migrated northwest along the border, or foothills of the then known Entejothelic range until they reached the section now known as the Sandwich islands, where they settled, retained their former tribe name, but termed the section Shī-tē-cŏn'gō.

At the time of the submergence of the country then known as Kör-dū-zū'lăc, south of Alaska, and west of North America (now submerged by the North Pacific Ocean), and the establishment of the islands that formerly were high portions of the Entejothelic range, remnants of the Kiroda nation, who dwelt in Korduzulac, were left on them, especially so on those composing the Sandwich group, who eventually became lost as a distinct race of people, by mixing races with the Chanhangoes, who were the most numerous of the two remnants, and who, as a mixed race, continued to exist under the same section and tribe names, but ultimately, they changed the section name to Kăn-năn'zy, and the tribe name to Kăn-năn'zēs. In stature, they were about six feet, and some a little more. They had very heavy bodies, but were well proportioned. They had dark skins; normal heads; black hair, some being straight, but the majority was bushy, and they had cansiderable on their bodies; black, full, sharp, or piercing eyes; broad, yet prominent noses that were quite thick near the forehead; large mouths; coarse, thick or heavy lips, that in parting, displayed their two sets of large teeth; heavy beards that grew high on their cheeks; broad, flat feet and hands; normal ears, that were characterized with considerable hair that grew out from the inner part of the auricle. They were a very quarrelsome people, using crude weapons in battle. They were very lazy, lived upon animal flesh, fish, fruits and roots. They went entirely nude. They had no religious ideas, and therefore had no adorational exercises, or forms of worship. They and their descendants became the pre-historic ancestors of the aboriginal Malayo Polynesian, or pure Hawaiian race of the Sandwich islands, whose reddish brown skins, or tarnished copper tint, came through the West Indies, and Mexican influences, viz: through the blood of the Chanhangoes, whose ancestors descended from that region. Through the influence of the Kiordas, Chanhangoes, and Kannanzes, with such additional changes as come with descending conditions, they were characterized with raven black hair, some straight, and some wavy; broad faces; flat noses and thin lips being the most strongly retained characteristics; while their thin beards and tarnished copper colored skins are modified characteristics, having arisen through the conditions of mixed races, change of climate and livelihood. Likewise with their stature, the bulk of the race had diminished to moderate size, excepting the chiefs and the women of their families, who had retained the remarkable stature of their remote ancestors, on account of the straight line of descendancy, yet the Hawaiian race, generally speaking, is considered among the finest races, physically, in the Pacific regions, bearing a strong resemblance to the New Zealanders in stature, and their well-developed, muscular limbs.

About the time that the Sĭn′dī-ŏx had become established in the Keltezec of Kalozuric, a tribe of Heckluces, who were descendants from the Sokathrans, had migrated from southern Extorn (the Philippine island district), to the section of the "Ladrone" or "Mariana" islands, which section they termed Chē-wä′dēs. At the time of the establishment of the Ladrone islands, a small remnant of the Sindiox race, from the Keltezec of Kalozuric, were also left on the island, who ultimately mixed races with the Chewades, and as the latter were the greater in number, the former were lost in the latter, by race mixture, thus leaving but a small change in the general appearance of the descendants, in regard to physical, or linguistic conditions. The Chewades and their descendants became the pre-historic ancestors of the "Chamorros" of the Ladrone islands, which latter became nearly exterminated by the Spaniards, when in conflict with them in the seventeenth century. The Chamorros of the Ladrone Islands were closely allied to the Tagals of the Philippines, from the fact that they were both descendants from the Sokathrans; i. e., the Tagals of the Philippines descended from the Sokathrans through the Heckluces, and the Chamorros from the Sokathrans through the Heckluces, and the Chewades, with a slight infusion of Sindiox blood; which latter accounts for the differences in these characteristics,

About the time that the Vackareons were migrating southward from Vackareon, a tribe of Jerebads were also migrating southeast from their home north of the "Kuen Lun" mountains of China, who, about the time that the Igentoses had established themselves in the then known Keltezec of Kalveno, and the Jerebads had also arrived there from the northwest, had settled in the section of the "Hogoleu," or "Rug" group of islands, which section they termed Kū'lyb, and called themselves the Kulybs. They and their descendants became the pre-historic ancestors of the "Red Race," now known to occupy (in contradistinction to the "Black Race") portions of the Hogoleu group, where they were left as a remnant when the Island was established, as was also the case with the Igentoses, or black race portion.

From the co-mixture, and further infusion of the Kintilucian and Sendix blood, through the Kentersends, the Lazerends and their descended migrating tribes, south and east, has come to southern and eastern Asia, and still farther to the Indian, and the Great Eastern archipelagoes, the characteristics of reddish, yellowish, brown and copper colors, or hues of skin, and angular eyes, or those Malay and Mongol features, in all their varied degrees of intensity, that now exist in the above-named sections.

From the attractive presence of the varied colors that have characterized the skins of the descending races, the idea of farther development of the idea led to the practice of tattooing the body, both of which have not only served as an ornamentation of the body, but as religious symbols, and to distinguish the rank of the individuals, clans and tribes who practised the art. (See Teltzie on Origin and Stigmatization.) Likewise, in the same sense, all modern civilized nations have extended the idea by adorning their wearing apparel with emblematic colors, and wearing emblematic attachments co-relatively.

The fifth periodical convulsion began its work about one thousand years subsequent to the fourth, and was in six sections, three in the northern portion, and three in the southern. The first had place southeast of the "Louisade" archipelago, or southeast of New Guinea. At that time, all the section of country, from and including New Guinea, the Solomon, the New Hebrides and the New Caledonia islands, was known to the inhabitants as Dĕt'rē-mēs, and also all the section of country now northeast and southeast of New Guinea, including the Solomon and the New-Hebrides Islands, to the Keltezecus (valleys) beyond, was known as Detremes, so named by the Chief, or Leader of the nation that then dwelt in that section, which latter, as a nation, bore his name. A Keltezec lay extent, northeast and southeast of the section of "New-Guinea," between it and a range of mountains that then embraced the Solomon, New-Hebrides, and New-Caledonia islands. Both the valley and the mountain range were termed Detremes, after the Chief or Leader Detremes, above mentioned. The force of this convusion established the Louisade archipelago, sunk the section of land between it and the New-Hebrides islands, and the southeastern coast of New-Guinea, as far west as the longitude of Cape York, in Australia, but not the "Torres Straits," and extended as far southeast as to form the coast line of Australia, north of the "Northumber" islands.

The second section of the fifth convulsion occurred about five hundred years after the first, and had place southeast of the "Island of Pines," in a Keltezec that extended northeast, between the Hunters and the Isle of Pines to the New-Hebrides and Fiji Islands. At that time a Dū-zī'ĕnd (mountain) range, then known as the Grĭs-tē-mī'ē extended from the district of the "New Caledonia" island, to that of the "South Cape" of Tasmania. At the time of this, and the former convulsion, a great Keltezec then known as Dĕn-trō-nō'sĭs, lay extent northeast of Australia. The force of this convulsion extended north to the establishment of the New-Hebrides Islands, east to the line of the second periodical convulsion, and extended along the Gristemie range to South Cape, established the Norfolk island, and those west of it, and the coast line of Australia from and including the Northumber island, to "Cape Otway," on the southeastern portion of the section of Australia, known modernly as "Victoria." It cut the great Island of "Tasmania" off from the mainland of Austraby the establishment of the "Bass Straits," leaving the "King," and "Hunter" islands on its northwestern boundary, the "Flinders" and the "Barren" on its northeastern.

The third section occurred but a few months later than the second, and had place in the section of land now submerged by the Gulf of "St. Vincent," which established the coast line, inlet and inland waters of the above-named section, and the coast islands, and inlet waters from Cape Otway, to Cape Leeuwin, on the southwest portion of West Australia.

The fourth section occurred about one hundred years after the third, and had place between the Radack and the Ralick chains of the "Mulgrave" archipelago. The force of this convulsion established the above-named archipelago, by severing it from the southern range of the Fringuze system of Dusiendlung, and submerged the country northeast and southeast, to the lines of the second and fourth periodical convulsions, and south to the line of the first, and second sections of the fifth.

The fifth section occurred about eighty years after the fourth, and had place just east of the Caroline Islands, in the "Torr Hope" group, which then belonged to the southern range of the Fringuze system. The force of this convulsion broke off that section of the range, from the Mulgrave archipelago, or line of the fourth sectional convulsion, to about a hundred and fifty degrees longitude east from Greenwich, extended north to the Keltezec of Kalozuric, south and southeast, across the Telandcest Keltezec, and further completed the devastation of the first sectional convulsion by the complete establishment of the "Solo mon islands."

The sixth section occurred about two hundred years after the fifth, and had place in the western remnant of the southern range of the Fringuze system of Duziendlung, between the "Yap" and the "Egoy" islands. The force of this convulsion extended east as far as the line of the fifth sectional convulsion, and west to beyond the "Pelew" and the "Andrews" islands, and south of the Andrew islands, thus completing the establishment of the triangular system of islands that originally were peaks in the triangular Duziend of Fringuze, and further established the North Pacific Ocean, north of the Equator, northeast of New-Guinea, and northeast of the Philippine Islands.

About two years after the sixth and last section of the fifth periodical convulsion, there occurred a powerful subterrene convulsive condition that extended from the region of the submerged section of the southern range of the Fringuze system, or better known as the group of "Caroline islands," beneath the submerged Keltezec, of Telandcest, and further sunk that section of land that lay north of New-Guinea, further completing the coast line of New-Guinea, its inlet waters, and established the islands between the "Solomon" and the "New-Hebrides," the Louisade archipelago, and completed the establishment of the Solomon islands.

Submerged Atlantis Restored

Prior to the complete establishment of the Philippine Islands, and the southwestern section of Polynesia, a portion of the Vackareons and Kenthricks, who were remnants on the Philippine Islands, migrated eastward along the northern side of the range of Duziendlung, which the Sintox termed Fringuze, to about a hundred and fifty-eight degrees longitude east from Greenwich, and twelve degrees north latitude, where they made their principal halting place and termed the section Kăl-vē′nō, and called themselves the I-gĕn′tō-sēs. From this point they wandered back and forth, east and west, for many generations, along the range whose remnants are now the Carolina islands, and the Mulgrave archipelago, until they became a mixed race of people. They became quite ferocious. The men would fight with each other for the possession of their wives, after making their choice, which was their custom, in the place of a marriage ceremony. After possession was gained, however, they were kind and loving to their wives. They were a people of medium size; had dark skins, large dark eyes, large mouths and teeth, and their lips were thick; they had dark hair, that of the women being very long, heavy and straight, but that of the men was shorter, and they had considerable on their bodies. As a rule, they went nude, though some wore pendant or apron-shaped skins about their loins.

After many years' dwelling in the section of Kalveno, a tribe of the Igentoses migrated north from Kalveno, into the great Keltezec that lay extent between the triangular ranges of Duziendlung, of the Fringuze system (whose remnants now form the Megellan's, the Anson's, and the Mulgrave archipelagoes, and the Caroline Islands), which Keltezec they termed Kalozuric, the triangular Duziend system, Fringuze, and called themseves the Sindiox, the latter term being derived from their word Sindi (fire or heat), which particularly referred to the sun, and its heat.

The Sindiox, in stature, were from five and a half to six feet. They were very broad-shouldered and of an athletic build; their heads were broad; cheek bones high; their color a dull black; hair black, short and straight; eyes black and round; noses thin through the bridge, but nostrils broad; mouths medium-sized and lips thick and pouching; beards short, frizzled, and full face; ears normal; feet flat and broad across the ball, but narrow through the instep, the heel also being broad and flat; their hands were normal. They were mostly nude; some wore a garment about their loins. They simply adored the sun, which they termed Sindi. They thought the warmth or heat was sent to them through it, for their comfort, and therefore adored it as a beneficent force.

The Igentoses and their descendants became the pre-historic ancestors of the "Tarapon" race that inhabits the now known Caroline, the Marshal, and the Gilbert islands. The Sindiox race, who were also descendants from the Igentoses, who migrated from their home in Kalveno, into the Keltezec of Kalozuric, and their descendants, became the pre-historic ancestors of the Tarapon race that inhabits the "Ladrone Islands."

The present Tarapon race of the above-named sections have retained many of the physical characteristics of their Asiatic ancestors, with such modifications as would naturally occur on account of their migration and conditions of livelihood. Those in the Caroline section have grown lighter in color, but have retained about the same stature as their ancestors, the Igentoses. Those of the Gilbert Islands have degenerated in stature and size, and have retained more of the dark color of their ancestors, the Igentoses, due to the fact that they were farther south, and therefore conditioned differently.

The Tarapons of western Polyesia, bear more resemblance to some of the Papua peoples of the Indian archipelago, because the Vackareons and the Kenthrick blood has reached both peoples through the migrations of the Vackareons, as hereinbefore stated, which is the root and branch that has established both races. The traditions of the Gilbert Islanders tell us that their islands were peopled from the west and also from the east; that those from the west were more numerous than those from the east, and that those from the east were from "Samoa." There are also traditions of the arrival of other strangers at some of the islands. The facts in the case are that those from the west were the migrating Igentoses who became the ancestors of the pre-historic peoples of the Gilbert islands. Those from the east were migrating Chăn-băn′gōes from their home in Shitecogo, or the Sandwich islands section, and the strangers, above referred to, were a few Detremens from Detremes, or the Solomon islands region.

At the time the now known "Pelew," or "Palu" islands were separated from the central portion of the Caroline islands, a remnant of the Igentoses of that section of Kalveno, and a remnant of the migrating tribe of Degilets from the Wetlog or Borneo section, were left on the Pelew islands, where ultimately they mixed races, and thus established a new people, who termed the island Gĕr-zē-ĕn'zē, and called themselves the Gĕr-zē-ĕn'zēs, whose descendants became the pre-historic ancestors of the "Pelewese," whose dark, copper color, said to give evidence of Malay and Papuan blood, arises from the mixture of the dark-skinned Igentoses, and the red-skinned Degilets, with a further modified condition arising from natural causes, through the ages of descendance. Prior to the establishment of the Caroline islands, a tribe of Degilets had migrated into Kalveno, from Wetlog, or the "Borneo" region, as far as to the central section of the Caroline Islands, or the "Hugoleu," or "Rug" group, where ultimately they called themselves the Dē-vō'măns. At the time of the formation of the Hugoleu, or Rug group, remnants of both the Igĕntōsēs and the Dēvōmăns were left upon the Islands where they became hostile to each other, having so remained through all subsequent time, with very little mixture of races, which fact has established two races of people, viz: the "Red," whose pre-historic ancestors were the Devomans, and the "Black," whose pre-historic ancestors were the Igentoses.

The sixth periodical convulsion occurred about one thousand years after the fifth, and was in four sections. The first section had place west of "Cape York," in the northeast section of the Gulf of Carpentaria.' The force of this convulsion extended south and northwest, through the southeastern spurs of the then known great Duziendlung ranges of the Mē-lië'cōn system. By bursting through the eastern side of the now Gulf of Carpentaria, the "Torres Straits" were established. As the force extended south and southwest, it formed the south section of the above-named Gulf, and left Cape York on the eastern, and Cape "Arnhem" on the west, the islands, inlet waters, and coast line of those sections of the Gulf. As the force extended northwest, it completed the separation of New-Guinea from Australia, and submerged the southeastern section of the then known Meliecon system of mountains, and established the zig-zag coast line of Australia, as far west as to "Cape Londonderry," those of the southwestern coast of New-Guinea, as well as all the coast islands, inlet waters, etc., of that section of Australia, and New-Guinea.

The second section occurred but a few months later than the first, and had place in the section now known as the "Sunda" Straits." The force of this convulsion extended north, along the coast of Australia, to the line of the first sectional convulsion, which established the present coast line inlet, and inland waters, as far southwest as to the "Exmouth Gulf."

The third section occurred but a few months after the second, and had place in the section now known as "Shark Bay," on the western coast of Australia. The force of this convulsion extended northeast to the line of the third section, and south to Cape Leeuwin, or the line of the third section of the fifth periodical convulsion, which completed the coast line of Australia, and all its inlet waters and coast islands.

The fourth section occurred about three hundred and fifty years after the first, and had place in the center of the section of country now submerged by the waters of the "Celebean Sea." At that time, there was a great system of mountain ranges, then known as the Meliecon, east and southeast of the island of "Borneo," that extended southeast and south of New-Guinea, into that section of Australia now submerged by the Gulf of "Carpentaria." Another great Duziend range was then known as the Fĕl-cō-nĕt, that extended in a circular form from the island of "Timor," northwest, thus embracing those of "Java," and "Sumatra," a branch of which extended northeast, through that section of Borneo. The convulsion being one of the radiating and circular forms combined, the forces shot out into all directions, and circled here and there throughout the Meliecon system, and thus formed the "Straits of Macassar," severed the Celebean islands from Borneo, and established those east, as far as New-Guinea, and also the "Java Sea," whose waters submerged the section of country then known as Frŏnt'lē-gī, rendered the highest portions of the Fĕl-cō-nĕt range, into the island of "Java," which was then cut off from Sumatra, by the formation of the "Straits of Sunda," and those eastward to, and including that of "Timor," and westward, including Sumatra.

THE GREAT VALLEYS OF GON-TA-CU'LO AND FRONT'LE-GI AND THE SEAS OF SE'LA-SAC AND CAN-I-EN'CES.

TELTZIE LIV.

Gŏn-tă-cū'lō was the pre-historic name of a large Keltezec that lay extent northeast of the section now known as the island of Borneo, and north of the Celebes.

After the submergence of the Keltezec of Gontaculo, the body of water that submerged its area was pre-historically known as the Sē'lă-săc Sē-zĭe, and so remained until just about the beginning of Modern Ancient time, when it was changed to the "Celebean Sea."

Prior to the submergence of the Keltezec of Gontaculo, a tribe of Sokathrans from the Keltezec of Jellatse and a tribe of Vackareons from Vackareon, or the "Indo China" section, had migrated to the Keltezec of Gontaculo, where they ultimately mixed races, termed the valley Gontaculo, and called themselves the Gontaculoes.

Prior to the time that the Celebes island was severed from Wetlog (Borneo) some of the Degilets, who were a mixed race of Sokathrans and Kenthricks, had migrated into the section of the Celebes island, where they settled, and were left as a remnant, at the time of the establishment of the island, when they retained their former tribe and section names.

At the time of the submergence of the Keltezec of Gontaculo, remnants of the Gontaculoes were also left on the island of Celebes, where in subsequent time they mixed races with the Degilets, termed the island Kăth'ā-gĕm, and called themselves the Kathagemens, whose descendants became the pre-historic ancestors of the "Macassars" of Celebes, whose natural environments, reunion of ancestral blood, etc., has modified them physically, to some extent. While they have remained well built, and muscular, their complexion has changed to that of a dark brown hue; their eyes are black, sparkling and expressive; their foreheads high; their noses flattish, with large nostrils; their mouths large; their hair black and soft, which they allow to fall down over their shoulders.

Subsequently, a tribe of the more intellectual portion of the descended Gontaculoes desiring, if possible, to find the source of the rising sun, migrated southeast along the range of Duziendlung, whose remnants are now known as the Solomon islands, until they arrived in the Keltezec now submerged, that lay northeast of the section of New-Guinea at about forty-eight degrees longitude, east from Greenwich, and about four degrees south latitude, where they settled, termed the Keltezec Detremes, and called themselves the Detremens. They dwelt in the valley of Detremes for ages, until they had spread out southeast to the mountains beyond, and along the foothills of the above-named mountains, and some had even penetrated the section now known as the southeast border of New-Guinea. They were a peculiar people, and lived entirely to themselves. They were very peaceable among themselves, more intelligent than most of the migrators to the various island districts. In stature they were about five and one-half to six feet. They were large-bodied, being both fleshy and large-boned; they were of a dark mulatto color; had normal heads; bushy, black and brown hair; low foreheads; shaggy, heavy beards; a good deal of hair on their bodies; black, dark brown and gray eyes; straight, sharp noses; normal mouths; quite thick lips; normal ears; large, short, or stubby feet, and short toes; small hands and short fingers. They tilled the soil to some extent; were very cunning, shrewd or sharp by nature. They lived in huts, principally, that were constructed of mud and sticks, though some of them excavated the earth from the sides of the mountains, thus forming holes in which they dwelt. They wore long-haired skins about their loins, so as to hang skirt-like. They adored all space as the mysterious something from whence came all their benefits, or aids in life. They therefore worshipped the entire heavens. The sun was the principal object of adoration during the day, and the moon and stars by night. Every planet to them, represented a wonderful force, intended for their good. Their mode of the recognition of that force, was to kneel upon both knees, raise their hands toward the heavens, and then utter a prayer, such as fitted their individual, or specific needs; then bowing, they rose and departed hence.

The Detremens of this section were controlled by means of a revelation which they claimed to have had from nature. As the peaks of the range of mountains that bordered the valley, were nearly always hidden by clouds and mists, phenomena, such as attend the sunshine back of, and through the mists and clouds in such regions, were not uncommon in that section. It was claimed by the Detremens, that on a certain occasion, there appeared amidst the mists and clouds, the following characters:

These were formed by openings in the mists and among the clouds, so as to reveal portions of the mountain's side, that were illumined with a golden light that came from behind the mists, so as to produce a gorgeous phenomenon in the form of the written word of Detremes, plainly portrayed in characters of their language, and was a parallel case, of Nature's writing upon the mountain's peak, with that of the spirit handwriting on the wall at Belshazzar's feast.

The word Detremes, therefore, became sacred to the people, who adopted it as their national name, and was also borne by the chief ruler individually. Therefore, he in turn termed the country, the valley, and the mountain range, Detremes, whose remnants are now known as the Solomon islands, and further ordered that the people be called Detremens, as the name had been handed down to them from Kä'drā, their god principle of space, whom they adored as their benefactor.

The migrating Detremens, who dwelt in the section of the New-Hebrides islands (before the fifth great periodical convulsion), further migrated into Polynesia, as far as to the section that now forms the Fiji Islands, or more correctly, the Viti archipelago, where they became degenerated, and whose descendants ultimately became the pre-historic ancestors of the now known Fijians.

At the time that the island of Papua or New-Guinea was severed from the section of Frontlegi, and from the then known section of Detremes (Solomon Island region), remnants of the Detremes were left on the eastern and northeastern sections of the island, and scattered migrating tribes of the Gontaculoes were left on the northern and northwestern, who became the ancestors of the pre-historic tribes, from whom have descended the various Papuan, or Melanesian, and Negrito races of New-Guinea, and from similar sources, those of the whole of Melanesia, in modified forms, as the term implies.

After a time, the original remnant descended Detremens termed the island Lĕz-grä'tē (Great Land), and called themselves A'gŏnths; but as the ages went by, the tribe names were changed to suit the natural conditions surrounding them, and new terms were adopted on the section, meaning Great Land, which was a custom that continued to be handed down among the various tribes to the present time; hence, preventing any real single native name from being adopted for the island.

The various ethnographic differences arising in the dark Melanesians, or Papuans, or the characteristics that distinguished them from the Polynesians, arise from mixture of blood that descended to them through the Detremens and the Gontaculoes, whose ancestors, both remote and near, were the Fesents, Delka Sadels, and the Hintox on one side, and the Vackareons on the other, or an amalgamation of both Malay and Mongol blood, through the long line of descendancy. Therefore, the Papuan element that exists in the "Aura" islands, and in western New-Guinea, is influenced more from the Gontaculoes, or their descendants direct; while those of the Solomon Islands, the New-Hebrides, and the Fiji, have been more influenced from the Detremens and their descendants, and the various conditional Papuan grades of the tribes and peoples of New-Guinea proper, are due to mixture in pre-historic time through the Detremens and the Gontaculoes, still further modified by modern mixtures, in connection with natural, and conditional influences.

In the region of the Fiji Islands the Sawaiori, or brown Polynesian element from the east, met that of the dark Papuan, or Melanesian, when the former influence radiated into the latter, thus causing a race modification by virtue of the infusion of Polynesian blood into that of the Melanesian.

As the Malayo Polynesian element spread westward through the descendants of the Kallutes, it brought mixed conditions into Detremes, or the Solomon island section, and at the time of the formation of the Solomon islands, remnants of both the Detremens and the Kallutes were left on them, the latter having established settlements in the section of the "Bellona" and the "Rennell" islands of the south, and the "Ongting Java" in the north, a descended migration from the former, whose further descendants became the pre-historic ancestors of the Malay, or pure Polynesian element in the Solomon Islands.

The Detremens who occupied the central portion (by degeneration, and race mixture with the tribes of Kallutes, who entered their section), developed a new race of people in that section, whose descendants became the pre-historic ancestors of the now known Melanesians, or Papuan races of the Solomon islands. Owing to the influence brought to bear upon them by the infusion of the Kallutes blood, or that part of the mixed race influence, their skins vary from black, or brown, to a copperish hue, the darker predominating. Their hair is dark, though often dyed red or fawn color, and is crisp, and inclined to the woolly condition; it hangs naturally in ringlets three to eight inches in length, but when trained, it usually forms one smooth bush form, the fashion for both sexes. Depilation is practised; little hair, as a rule, grows on their faces, but hairy men are not rare.

In the New-Hebrides, the western migration of the Kallutes, and the presence of the Detremens, and their race mixture, established two race conditions in the islands, which present both Papuan and Malay Polynesian characteristics. Where the infusion of the Malayo Polynesian blood has been made into that of the Negrito Polynesian, the descendants are the taller, fairer, and less savage as a people.

In the Caledonia islands as in the Solomon, and the New-Hebrides, there are two types of aboriginal people, viz: a Sub-Papuan, and a Sub-Sawaiori race. The former are descendants from their pre-historic ancestors, the Detremens, though in a degenerate condition. The latter, or Sub-Swaiori type, are descendants from a mixed race of Kallutes, who migrated to that section from the Tonga and the Friendly Island sections, before the establishment of the Caledonia islands and the Detremens, and therefore possess all the features of the Sub-Papuans, though modified by the infusion of Kallutes blood, which brought to their descendants a physique superior to that of the Sub-Papuans, and a lighter color, which gives them a close resemblance to the Polynesians. The Sub-Sawaiori people inhabit the eastern and southern portion of the island, principally, and represent the upper class of aborigines; but the two types mingle to some extent all over the island.

At the time that Australia was severed from New-Guinea by the establishment of the Torres Straits, a remnant of the Agonths was left on the northeastern portion of the Australian section. Subsequently, they termed the section A-gŏn'thrŭs, after their ancestors, the Agonths, with a slight change in the name, as above, and called themselves the Gĭs'traz.

Subsequent to the establishment of the Gistraz tribe in Agonthrus, a portion of the Hĕn'si-ŏcks passed from island to island, east of the now known section of Java until they reached the northern section of Agonthrus, where they settled and called themselves the Rĕg'ăl-tys.

In subsequent time, a tribe of the Gistraz people had migrated to the southeastern coast of the island, when they settled in the section between the northern portion of the Clark mountains and the sea coast, or between the now known Upstart Bay and Port Denison, where they retained their former tribe and section names. Their first pre-historic hamlet, which they termed Mŭn'-jăb, was located on the site where now the town of "Bowen" has place, in the province of Queens-Land.

Prior to the separation of New Zealand from Australia, the Gistraz people had spread out along the eastern coast of Australia, or the section of Queens-Land, west of the Northumberland Islands, or from "Cape Upstart" in the north, to the southern extremity of Broad Sound. Still later on, a tribe of the Gistraz people from the above-named section migrated southward into the now known province of New South Wales, when they settled northwest of the city of Sidney, near the foothills of the Blue mountains of that section, and still retained their tribe and section names. Their first pre-historic hamlet, which they termed E-nĭn'gē-sĭng, was located on the site where now the town of "Richmond" has place.

The Gistraz, the Regaltys, and their descendants became the pre-historic ancestors of the now known Melanesians, or Australian aborigines, from whom they inherited some of the Negrito similarities. The Regaltys having descended from the Sokathrans and the Kenthricks of Malaygon, through the blood of the Gurotes and Haretons of Mutzon (Sumatra); the Krehats and the Hensiocks of Katza (Java); and ultimate mixed race of Krehats and Hensiocks; therefore, being descendants through the same blood of pre-historic ancestors as that of the Gistraz, which latter pepole had descended from the Sokathrans, Kenthricks, and Vackareons of Trudox (Farther India), and the Indian archipelago regions; the Detremens of Detremes (Solomon island region), who were migrators from the same people, and finally through the Agonths of Papua or New Guinea, readily re-united the ancestral race blood, when they met again in Agonthrus or Australia. Physically speaking, by means of conditional descendancy, they are somewhat changed.

Front'le-gi was the pre-historic name of the large Keltezec that lay extent east and west between the sections of country now known as the Islands of Java and Borneo. After its submergence the body of water that covered its area, was pre-historically known as the Căn-ī-ĕn'cēs Sĕ'ziē, and so remained until the Adomic period, when it was changed and has been since known as the Java Sea.

Submerged Atlantis Restored

Prior to the establishment of the Caniences Sezie, a large tribe of Sokathrans, and a small one of the Kenthricks, migrated to that section of country then known as Frontlegi, which embraced the now known Indian archipelago, or the great Keltezec now submerged by the waters of the Java Sea, which Keltezec they termed Sĭn-tō-ĭ'lĭc (the term meaning *Warm Sun*), and called themselves the Mōn'gē-lēts. In time the two peoples mixed races, which condition established a new race of people in that section. At the time of the submergence, they were nearly all lost, but those who did escape, were left as a remnant on the islands now known as Java and Madura. They were a higher grade of people than those who migrated to the now known Polynesian, and Australasian sections, from the fact that they were of the more intelligent portion of the Sokathrans, and Kenthricks, who inhabited the then known section of Malaygon (Malay). They wore short furred skins about their loins during the cold seasons, and at other times went nude. They had some idea of worship, directed toward the Sun, at the time of its rising and setting. When it was just appearing above the horizon, they congregated, or stood individually, where they could see it, and as it rose to full view, they waved their hands above their heads as if to salute its coming, and at the same time would shout the word Es-lē'tĭsh (*He comes back*). When the sun was going down, they would again congregate, wave their hands as before, and shout E-lē'tĭsh (*He goes down*).

At the time of the formation of the Kanhanze Sezie (Japan Sea), when Java was severed from Sumatra, two remnant peoples were left on the island, who had migrated there from Mutzon (Sumatra), viz: the Gurotes and the Haretons. The Gurotes occupied the northern portion of the island, called themselves the Krehats, but did not give the section a name. The Haretons, occupied the southern section, which they termed Găth-ō-sē-lōn'zē, and called themselves the Hē-ĕn'sī-ŏcks. After a time, the Heensiocks and Krehats mixed races, to a certain extent, from which condition came a new race, who retained the name of Heensiocks but re-named the entire island Kăt'zä, which so remained until about the Adomic period, when it was changed to Jahava, and later to Java.

The Heensiocks and their descendants, became the pre-historic ancestors of the "Sundanese" of Java proper. The Javanese proper, are an amalgamate race, so established by the infusion of "Madurese" blood into that of the Sundanese, which has been further influenced by that of the "Hindus." From natural environments, mixture of races, etc., the complexion of all three races of Java, has developed into various shades of yellowish brown, with a touch of olive green, the darker shades in the Javanese being due to the mixture of races. The hair disappeared from their breasts and limbs, and their beard became almost extinct. The hair of the head sustained but little change, except that it became coarser, and more lank. In stature, there has been some degeneration, as well as in their general physique, the former being best retained by the Madurese and Javanese, and the latter by the Sundanese and Madurese. There has been but little change in the eyes, except that in some of the Sundanese, the oblique condition of the more remote Schirants of Atlantis, through the Zanranzans of the Cape Verdi remnants, the Horziethas of Africa, the Rezendeths and Ackredeths, and ultimate Kentersends of China, has re-appeared. The noses of the Madurese and Sundanese, show a return condition belonging to their more remote ancestors, in being flat and small, with wide nostrils, and in some of the Javanese the aquiline condition reappears. Their eyes and mouths have sustained but little change from those of their immediate ancestors, excepting the disappearance, of the thin lips that characterized some of the Heensiocks and Mongelets. In the Madurese the cheek bones are more strongly developed than in the Javanese and Sundanese, which shows the change their features have sustained through the generations from their remote ancestors.

THE GREAT VALLEYS OF JEL-LAT'SE AND TE-LE-KA-TOO', AND THE SEAS OF TAG'A-LU AND YU-LI-O'TEM.

TELTZIE LV.

Jĕl-lăt'sē was the pre-historic name of the great Keltezec that lay extent southwest and northeast between the now known section of Borneo and the Philippine islands, on the east, and "Malay" and "Anam," or "Cochin China" on the west, or northeast from the Malay and Borneo sections to the latitude of "Hong Kong" China.

Prior to the final establishment of Gandeculo, or the Great Eastern archipelago, and the seas that now have place along the eastern coast of Asia, a great range of mountains then known as the Hĕck'läs, extended southwest from the section of "Kamchatka," in the north, to the island of "Sumatra" in the south, where it blended into the then known Felconit range, and also the then known Meliecon system of Euzeendlung.

About four hundred years prior to the first periodical convulsion, that established southeastern Polynesia, a large convulsion occurred that had place in the section of country now known as the Natumas island, northeast of Malay. The force of this convulsion separated Java, and Sumatra, formed the "Gulf of Siam," and that portion of the "China Sea" northeast, to the southern section of the "Palawan" island of the Philippines, and "Cape Cambodia," of "Farther India."

About two hundred and fifty years subsequent to this convulsion, a second one occurred, and had place west of the western central section of the Island of "Luzon,' of the Philippines. The force of this convulsion established the northeast section of the "China Sea," and extended further northeast, to the establishment of the "Formosa Straits," and the "Formosa Island." A few months later, a branch from the former convulsion, occurred, and had place in a high range of mountains northeast of the "Hainan islands," at a point just southwest of the "Straits of Luichau." The force of this latter convulsion formed the Straits of Luichau, severed the Hainan island from the peninsula on the southwest section of "Kwangtung," "China," established the "Gulf of Tonquin," its coastline, inlet waters, and islands. The force of the two above named convulsions, further completed the establishment of the "Philippine Islands," and all those within, and along the coast of the "China Sea," the coast lines, and inlet waters of that section.

water that covered its area, was pre-historicially known as the
After the submergence of the Keltezec of Jellatse, the body of Tagula Sezie, and so remained until during the Adomic period, when it was changed, and since known as the China Sea.

Prior to the establishment of the Tagalu Sezie, that portion of the great Keltezec of Jellatse, north from "Cape Varela," on the eastern coast of "Indo China," north to the coast of "China," and east, including the northern half of the Philippine islands (then a part of the great Hecklas range), was inhabited by Vackareons, who had migrated thence from both Vackareon in the now known Province of "Kwang-se," China, and their Vackareon in the province of "Tung-King," Anam, and also by the Kenthricks of Malaygon (Malay), who were of the same blood, from the section of their Tinkidocia (Lower-Siam), who ultimately mingled as one nation, and were all known under the national name of Kenthricks.

All the southern section of Keltezec of Jellatse, from about the location of "Cape Varela," of Indo China, east, including the southern half of the Philippine islands, and south, including the island of Borneo was inhabited by Sokathrans, who as a large nation, had spread out into the above named section.

At the time that the now known island of Borneo was severed from the main land of Indo China, a remnant of the Sokathrans from Malaygon, who had spread out into the same section, were left on the Island of Borneo, and in subsequent time, mingled races to such an extent as to establish a new race, who termed the island Wetlog, and called themselves the Degilets. In disposition, they varied. They were quite peaceable at times, and then again they were quite contentious. They went mostly nude, but at times, some of them wore skins about their loins. They had no religious ideas, or conception of a God principle, hence no adorational exercises, symbols, or idols. The Degilets, who were a mixed race of Sokathrans from Malaygon, and the Kenthricks from Tinkidocia, and their descendants, became the pre-historic ancestors of the five branches of Dyaks, Dayaks, or Dayakkers, as classified by Kessel, and also of the brown, long haired Malay race now known to occupy the Island of Borneo.

Contentions that arose among them in their early pre-historic period, caused them to separate into two factions, the division being made according to the diversity of ethnographic conditions that arose through the descendancy from a mixed race, viz, the Sokathrans and the Kenthricks; hence the now known two races, viz: the Dyaka and the Malayan, who really belong to the same stock, though the latter consider the former as aliens, and themselves as original people. In stature and physical form, they have degenerated somewhat, from that of their ancestors, the Degilets, but their reddish brown color, has grown somewhat purer, and the women have taken on more of the Chinese color, which is a link down from the Vackareon ancestors, which latter descended from the Kentersends, who were also the ancestors of the Chinese. Their high cheek bones and *retrousse* noses bear out characteristics having descended from the Degilets, and the non-presence of a beard, a characteristic of most of the males, though some have a slight growth, is but still further degeneration of that characteristic, subsequent to the time of their ancestors, the Degilets, who possessed beards only under their chins and on their necks. Their foreheads have changed from the retreating form, to the high order. Their hair and eyes have remained nearly the same.

At the time of the establishment of the "Gulf of Ton-quin remnants of the Vackareons of their Vackareon in the section of "Tung-King, Anam, who had spread out into the Tonquin section, were left on the now known island of "Hainan," when they settled o nthe northwest side of the "Li-mou Shan," or "Wu Tchì Shan" mountains, when they termed the island Wŏg-nō'thre, and called themselves the Wŏg'nōse. The men generally wore loose robes. Some of them only wore a garment about the loins, and some even went nude. The women who clothed themselves, wore a loose robe, a part of which was thrown back over each shoulder, after being crossed on the breast. They were a great people to gesticulate when holding conversation with each other, and they were very harmonious as a people. They were at all times in adoration of the Sun, which they supposed to be the cause of all existence in creation. In reality, they worshipped the whole heavens, or the planets, the constellations, and fixed stars thereof. When they held their adorational services, they would kneel, raise their right hand toward the heavens, then bow to the earth, place their hands, palms downward, and then lay their faces on top of them, after which, they would utter a prayer, such as suited the occasion which usually was relative to their needs individually. During this exercise, their leader (who was always the tallest among them), stood in front of them, and when they had done with the prayer, he raised his hand, which was the signal for them to rise, which they did, and when standing erect, they uttered exclamations in adoration of the Sun, which was done in the form of a chant; then the leader and people together bowed three times, after which they dispersed. They and their descendants, became the pre-historic ancestors of the now known civilized aborigines of the island of Hainan. They being descendants from the Kentersends (from whom also descended the Chinese), through the Vackareons, therefore brought the Mongolian element into the island in its original state, the Chinese element of the present time having come through subsequent immigrations; hence, the Shu-li, while being about the same stature, as the Chinese, their skin is a more decided copper color; their cheek bones higher; and their features more angular. Their hair is long, straight, and black, a characteristic retained from as far back as to their remote ancestors, the Ackredeths and the Aglonsts. Their beards, however, are very scant, if any, due to a degeneration of that characteristic, that began to appear as far back in the ancestary, as the time when the Kentersends began their migration from Thuriistic, and continued down the line of descendants to the time of the establishment of the Chinese and Hainan aborigines.

At the time that the Philippine islands were severed from Wetlog, and the main land, remnants from the Kenthrick people of Tinkidocia, and of the Vackareons from Vackareon in the Tonquin section, were left on the northern portion of the islands, or principally upon the island of Luzon, which they termed Ex'tŏrn, and called themselves Trä'fĕns. There was also a remnant of the Sokathrans from the Keltezec of Jellatse, who were left on the southern portion of the islands, who finally adopted the name of Extorn as the section, originally given by the Trafens, as above stated, but called themselves the Hĕck'lu-sēs. Subsequently, they mixed races with the Trafens, which condition ultimately established a race of people whose descendants became the pre-historic ancestors of the "Aeta" or "Negrito" race, now known to exist sporadically throughout the Philippine archipelago, and by virtue of their mixed blood, having descended through seven races of people, viz: the Delka Sadels; the Hintox; the Fesents; the Sokathrans, and the Kenthricks, which latter had descended from the mixture of Kenthricks and Vackareons, and being under the influence of degeneration, brought them down to their present physical condition, viz: dwarfish in stature, a full-grown man being but about four feet eight inches.

Direct descendants from the Heckluces, and their descending tribes, who brought the Malay element into the archipelago, became the pre-historic ancestors of the "Tagals," now known to inhabit the "low-lands," in pile dwellings near the water, whose well developed bodies, round heads, high cheek bones, flattish noses, low brows, thick lips, large dark eyes, and strongly marked lines from the nose to the mouth, compare favorably with the same conditions of their ancestors, though degenerated.

Direct descendants from the Trafens, and their descended tribes, who brought the Mongol element into the archipelago, like-wise, became the pre-historic ancestors of the "Visayas," who are now known to inhabit all the lands south of Luzon, and were termed Pintodos (i.e., painted people), by the Spaniards in the fifteenth and sixteenth centuries.

The savage "Visaya" tribes who inhabit the mountains in the interior of some of the "Visaya" islands, are also descendants from the Trafens, whose lives, under migratory conditions, have degenerated to their present state of existence.

At a later pre-historic period, when the more decided Mongol characteristics had become established in the descendants of the Kentersends of the section of Zencustezum, some of their tribes, by maritimal migration, arrived on the island of Luzon, whose descendants became the pre-historic ancestors of the now known "Igorrotes," or "Igolotes."

The absence of the oblique eyes in the Shu-li race, is due to the fact that they are descendants from a tribe of Lazerends who had migrated into that section about the time that the Vackareons arrived there. The oblique eye condition of the Chinese comes through the Kentersend influence proper, and the slighter oblique of the Japanese eyes, comes through the mixed influence of Kentersend and Lazerend blood descendants.

At the time of the final establishment of the Hainan island, a remnant of the Fesents, who had migrated from Trudox (Farther India), into the Keltezec of Jellatse, were left as a remnant on the southern portion of the island, who termed that section of the island, Shrĭn'nĕr-zrĕt, and called themselves the Hä-zī-ĕ'-zăns, whose descendants became the pre-historic ancestors of the "Sheng-li," or the now known wild aborigines of the Hainan island.

The Fesents who were a wild and hostile people, endowed their descendants, the Shangli aborigines with the same characteristics, for among themselves they still carry on deadly feuds, and revenge is said to be an inherited duty, which they do not fail to perform. One of the physical characteristics of the Sheng-li race, is their drooping ears, which descended to them from their ancestors, the Fesents, or mixed race of Delka Sadels and Hintox, whose ears were characterized with flabby, or drooping auricles, a feature that had likewise descended to the Fesents from their ancestors the Delka Sadels, who had ears with drooping upper portions of the auricles, and the Hintox who had long auricles that also lopped forward at the top, so marked was the feature with the Shang-li race that, 111, B.C., when "Lu-Pe-teh," general to Emperor Wu-ti, first made the island of Hainan, subject to Chinese, he divided it into the two prefectures, "Tan-uhr," or "Drooping Ear," in the south, which was the original section of the Haziezans (so called from the long ears of their native King), and "Chu-yai," or "Pearl Shore," in the north. The "Laos" of lower Siam, and the "Lolos" of China, being also descendants from the Fesents, are therefore of the same stock.

Te-le-ka-too' was the pre-historic name of the great Keltezec that lay extent southwest and northeast, from the now known island of "Formosa" in the southwest, and the Japanese islands in the northeast, and branched north, and northwest between the now known sections of "Corea" and eastern "China" and between the now known provinces of "Shan-tung" and "Shing-King," China.

About one hundred and seventy-five years subsequent to the previously mentioned second convulsion that had place west of Luzon, another one occurred in the section of country now known as that of the northwest coast of the "Kyushu" islands, Japan. At the time of that convulsion, a large Keltezec then known as Telekatoo extended northeast from the Formosa island, and northwest from the "Loo Choo," and the "Madiicosima" islands, and northwest, thus established the now known "Yellow Sea," by the submergence of that section of the Telekatoo Keltezec, and the coast line conditions of that section of China, as far as to the eastern point of "Cape Macartney," and all the islands, and inlet waters along that section of "Corea," China. About thirty years after this convulsion, a sectional one occurred southwest of "Charlottes Point," of the southern portion of the province of Shing-king, and north of the town of "Tang-chau," China. The force of this convulsion extended west into the southeastern portion of the province of Chih-li, south into the province of Shan-tung, and northeast into the province of Shing-king, when it severed the provinces of Shing-King and Shan-tung, sunk that portion of the great Keltezec of Telekatoo, and submerged it with the waters of the now known "Yellow Sea," thus establishing the "Gulfs of Pechili" and of "Liautung," and further connected them with the Yellow Sea, at which time the principal portion of the waters of the then known inland sea of Căs-cū-dē-rĕn'gē, were drained off into the Yellow Sea, and after many years of evaporation and absorption of the remaining waters, the Cascuderenge area became the now known great "Desert of Cobi," in central Asia.

After the submergence of the Keltezec of Telekatoo, the body of water that covered its area, was pre-historically known as the Yū-ly-ō'tĕm Sē-ziē, and so remained until near the latter part of the Adomic period, when it was changed, and the main portion since known as the Yellow Sea, and that portion between the provinces of Shan-tung, Chih-li, and Shing-king, as the Gulfs of Pechili and Liautung.

At the time that the island of Formosa was severed from the main land, by the establishment of the straits of Formosa, a remnant of the Kentersends, who had spread out from their hamlet and section of Cellenthecon, in the northeastern portion of the province of "Kwang-tung," China, into the region of the Formosa island, were left upon it, who settled on the southwestern coast, in the vicinity where now the town of "Changhua," has place, when they termed the island Crŏs'tine, and called themselves the Trē-lū'tēs.

After several generations, another tribe of Kentersends from the section of "Fuh-kien" (by maritimal migration), entered the island and settled among their brethren, the Trelutes. After they had thus dwelt together for several generations, contentions arose among them, which ultimated in the establishment of two conditional factions. This caused them to spread out, when one faction went to the southern portion of the island, which they termed Rē-ĭd'ĭsh, and called themselves the E-cĕs'sĕts. The other faction occupied the northern portion of the island, and retained the name of Crostine for the section, and that of Trelutes for their tribal name. Physically, they were about the same as their ancestors, the Kentersends, there being at that time no further mixture of races. They were Sun worshippers, and believed (as did their remote ancestors), that by migrating, they ultimately, would arrive at the place of its rising, or find from whence it came; hence, their various changes of location. Whenever they beheld the Sun ascending from the horizon, they (in adorational obeisance to its marvelous coming forth to view), would throw up their hands and arms above their heads and give utterance to loud exclamations of joy and gladness.

The Trelutes, and their descendants, became the pre-historic ancestors of the "Pe-pa-hwan," semi-civilized, or subjugated aborigines of the island of Formosa.

The Ecessets, and their descendants, became the pre-historic ancestors of the "Chehwan," or wild aborigines; or as they are sometimes called, the "green savages," who dwell in many tribes or clans in the island of Formosa.

There was also a mixture of Sokathran blood with that of the Ecessets, who at the time of the submergence of the Keltezec of Jellatse, escaped to the southern portion of the island of Formosa, which has left the Malay characteristic influence with their descendants, the "Che-hwan" aborigines.

Prior to the establishment of the Yulyotem Sezie, that portion of the Keltezec of Telekatoo south of the northeastern section of the province of Shan-tung, China, including the southern portion of the great Keltezec of Nintsrushan, and that portion of the foothills of the Hecklas range, now known as the southern section, or half of the island of "Niphon," Japan, was inhabited by Kentersend migrators from Zencustezum, who termed all that section of the country Jä-sä'dē, and called themselves the Jä-sä'dēs.

The northern portion of the Keltezec of Teleketoo, now submerged by the waters of the Gulfs of Pechili and Liautung, and the northern half of the great Keltezec of Nintsrushan, as far north as to the southern section of the "Saghalien" island, including the foot-hills of the Hecklas range of the section now known as the northern half of the Niphon island, and the entire portion of the "Yezo," was inhabited by the Lazerend migrators from Zintizantum, who termed all that section Shadise, and called themselves the Shăd-ī-sēs.

At the time of the establishment of the Yulyotem Sezie, a remnant of the Jasades from Jasade, and one of the Shadises from Shadise, were left upon the peninsula of "Corea," or "Chosen," so called by the natives. Subsequently, the two remnants mixed races whose descendants ultimately termed the section or peninsula, In'gŭs (*In the great waters*), and also called themselves the In'gŭs, for the same reason. The influence of the Jasades was the stronger of the two remnants, hence, by their being direct descendants from the Kentersends, the modern Coreans, more closely resemble the modern Chinese people who were also descendants from the Kentersends.

THE GREAT VALLEYS OF NINT-SRU'SHAN AND JEL'DE-CO. AND THE SEAS OF KAN-HAN'ZE AND OK-HOT'SK.

TELTZIE LVI.

Nint-sru'shan was the pre-historic name of the great Keltezec that lay extent southwest and northeast between the Japanese slands in the east, and Corea and Mantchooria on the west.

About the time of the first periodical convulsion, that established the southeastern section of Polynesia, there occurred two principal convulsions, and several smaller ones, within the space of two years time, that had place in the section of the "Japan" islands. At that time, there was a large keltezec known as the Nintsrushan, that extended northeast from southern Corea, and the Niphon island, to west of the Yezo.

The first of the principal convulsions had place between the Noto Cape (western central portion of the Niphon island, of Japan), and the southwestern coast of the Sado island. The force of this convulsion cut the Sado island from Cape Noto, formed the Fuseno Bay; and extended west into the Keltezec of Nintsrushan, sunk that portion of the northern section of the Straits of Corea, thus forming the southwestern section of the Sea of Japan, by submergence of the sunken land, with the adjacent sea waters, and further established the eastern coast of Corea.

The second periodical convulsion had place south of the Yezo island, between it and the northern boundary of the Niphon island. The force of this convulsion, separated the two above named islands, extended north, separated the Yezo island from the Saghalien, by the establishment of "La Perouse Straits," and extended west across the Keltezec of Nintsrushan, to the now coast of Manchuria, and in co-operation with smaller sectional convulsions, established the sea of Japan, as far north as to the southern extremity of the Saghalien island, the coast line, inlet waters, etc., of that section of eastern Asia.

After the submergence of the Keltezec of Nintsrushan, the

body of water that covered its area, was pre-historically known as the Kanhanze Sezie, and so remained until the latter part of the Adomic period, when it was changed, and since is known as the Japan Sea.

Prior to the establishment of the Kanhanze Sezie, as before stated, the northern half of the great Keltezec of Nintsrushan, the southern section of the Saghalien island, including the foothills of the great Hecklas range, the northern half of the Niphon island, and the entire portion of the Yezo, were inhabited by the Shadises. At the time of the formation of the Kanhanze Sezie, a large remnant of the Shadises were left on the southern section of the island of Niphon.

The Shadises left on the Yezo (who practically speaking, remained the same race of people), retained the same sectional and tribal names, and their descendants became the pre-historic ancestors of the "Aino" tribes of the island of Yezo.

The Jasades, who were the most numerous, and the Shadises who were left on the island of Niphon, in time, mixed races, after which, their descendants, re-termed the islands Jăp'ā-kăn, and called themselves the Jăp'ā-kăns, whose further descendants became the pre-historic ancestors of the Japanese proper. It was during the latter part of the Adomic period that the descended Jasades changed the section and tribe names, from Japakan to Japan, and Japakans to Japanese. The Japakans made no further migrations eastward than the present known islands of Japan, prior to their establishment as such.

Jĕl'dē-cō was the pre-historic name of the great Keltezec that lay extent north and south between the Saghalien and the Kurile islands (the southern half), and between the now known section of Siberia and the Kamchatka peninsula (the northern half).

About six hundred years prior to the first periodical convulsion that formed southeastern Polynesia, there occurred three principal convulsions in the section of country now known as the Sea of Okhotsk.

The first had place in the section extremity of Cape Patience, on the eastern coast of the Saghalien island. At that time the large Keltezec, of Jeldeco, also extended northwest from the now known Kurile islands, to the foothills of the spurs of the then known En-tä-sä-zĕn'zō range, but modernly known as the Yabloni, and the Stanovoi mountains. The force of this convulsion established the southern half of the Sea of Okhotsk, severed the Saghalien island from the main land of Asia, completed the Gulf or "Channel of Tartary," and left "Cape Patience" as the silent witness of the convulsion and its results.

The second periodical convulsion occurred about fifty years after the first, and had place in the foothills of the spurs of the Entasazenzo range, south of the town of Okhotsk, in eastern Siberia. The force of this convulsion established the northern section of the "Sea of Okhotsk" (not including the Gijinsk Gulf, which latter was the work of a subsequent smaller convulsion), by submerging that section of the Keltezec of Entasazenzo, and also established the northwestern coast of the Peninsula of Kamchatka, and the coast lines of the "Sea of Okhotsk," on the Russian and Kamchatka sides.

The third periodical convulsion occurred about sixty-five years after the second, and had place between "Cape Lopatka" or the southern extremity of the Peninsula of Kamchatka and Paramushir of the "Kurile islands." At the time of this convulsion, a range of Duziendlung, then termed En-sĕ-mē'nī-ăl, extended southwest from the now backbone of Kamchatka and its southeastern branch, to the region of the now known Yezo island, where it became conjunct with the great Hecklas range, before described, the highest peaks of which are now known as the Kurile islands. The force of this convulsion extended along the Ensemenial range, to the establishment of the Kurile islands, and completed the work of the former convulsions by the final establishment of the Peninsula of Kamchatka, and the present open waters of the Sea of Okhotsk, and the southwestern section of the "Behring Sea."

After the submergence of the Keltezec of Jeldeco, the body of water that covered its area was pre-historically known as the Ok-hŏt'sk Sē'ziē, and has so remained until modern times, the name never having sustained a change, and therefore now known as the Okhotsk Sea. Prior to its formation, that portion of the great Keltezec of Nintsrushan, submerged by the waters of the now known northern portion of the Gulf of Tartary; the southeastern half of the island of Saghalien, or more properly, the island of Karaftu, or Karafuto; the southeastern portion of the then known Keltezec of Jeldeco, to about as far north as the fiftieth degree north latitude, and east to the foothills of the Hecklas range, on the Kurile islands, were inhabited by the Yū-ĭn'zăms of Gĭl-tī'zĕr.

The northwestern half of the Saghalien island, the central and the northwestern portion of the Keltezec of Jelteco, as far north as to about sixty degrees north latitude, and east to the section of the foothills of the Hecklas range, or the Peninsula of Kamchatka, were inhabited by Salemanzes migrators from Salemango. At the time of the formation of the Saghalien island, a remnant of the Salemanzes was left on the northern portion of the island, who ultimately termed it Jū-kū'lĭx, and called themselves the Tĕt'lybs, whose descendants became the pre-historic ancestors of that branch of the "Tungus" race, now known as the "Gilyaks," who occupy the northern portion of the island.

The Gilyaks, who still occuy the region of the "Amur river" of Manchuria, and "Saghalian Oula" of southeastern Siberia, are members of the same stock, having descended, as did the Salemanzes, directly from the Lazerends of Zintizantum; those from the Amur River region direct from Zintizantum, by migration to their Salemango home, northeast Siberia; thence to the Saghalien island, where now, as then, they subsist by fishing and hunting. About the same time that the "Ainoes" were settled in Yezo, and the Kurile island section, a tribe of the Ingus race from Ingus (Corea), from whence they wandered, while on a hunting expedition, finally became settled in the Amur basin; from whence they farther migrated into the section of the Saghalien island, and at the time of the establishment of the island, a very small tribe of them were left on it.

The descendants of the Ingus people, who possessed both Kentersend and Lazerend blood in their veins, and who slightly differed from the Gilyaks, who were of the pure Lezerend stock, became the pre-historic ancestors of the Oroks of the Saghalien island, and the Orotchons of the Amur river section, who also still live by fishing and hunting.

At the time of the formation of the Gulf of Tartary, and the establishment of the southern portion of the Saghalien island, a remnant of the Kuinzams of Giltizer (Kurile islands) was left on that portion of the island, and another portion was left on the southeastern coast of Siberia, whose descendants became the descendants of the Ainoes of southern Saghalien, and the region of the Amur river.

At the time of the establishment of the Kurile islands, a remnant of the Yuinzams were also left on them, whose descendants became the pre-historic ancestors of the Ainoes that now inhabit those islands, and who are a kindred race to the Ainoes of the Yezo and the Saghalien islands, and also those of the Amur river basin, descended from the Yuinzams of Giltizer, who were descendants from the Salemanzes who had migrated from Salemango (their home in eastern Russia), to the region of the Kurile islands, where they took the name of Yuinzams, and called the section Giltizer, and from whence they spread out westward, across the southern portion of the Keltezec of Jeldeco, the southern portion of the Saghalien island, and the northern extension of the Nintsrushan Keltezec, now the Gulf of Tartary, to the southern coast again.

The Ainoes of the Kurile islands, the Saghalien, and the Amur river sections, differ from all other Mongolian races by their luxuriance of hair and beard, a fact due to their having descended from the Lazerends, through the blood of the Salemanzes of the cold climate of Siberia, thus bringing the condition southward again to the Kurile and the Saghalien island sections, through their descendants, the Yuinzams.

Migrating tribes of the Salemanzes and their descendants became the pre-historic ancestors of the "Lamuts" (Sea People), or the Tungus tribes on the western coast of Okhotsk Sea. Also migrating tribes of Lazerends and their descendants became the pre-historic ancestors of the "Yupitatze," or Tungus tribes between the delta of the Amur river, and the Peninsula of Corea.

It is the infusion of the Kentersend and the Lazerend bloods, combined in the main stock of the "Tungusese" races, by various tribe mixtures, that has given rise to all the branches of the Tunga stock.

Descendants of the Lazerends also became the pre-historic ancestors of the "Manchus," or "Manchu" people (the term meaning *pure*), who inhabit Manchuria. They were of the better class of the aborigines, and were a shifting population, with no fixed location, but went in clans, named after their leaders, as, under the "Chow" dynasty (1122-1225 B. C.), they were known as the "Sew-Shin," in subsequent periods, as the "Yihlow," "Wuh-keih," "Moh-hoh," "Pohai," "Nuchin," "K'etan," etc., and in the thirteenth century, "Manchu," after a ruler who came to power at that time.

Subsequent to the establishment of the Sucaniums in Sucanium, northeast Siberia, a tribe of their descendants migrated eastward into the section now known as the western coast of Kamchatka. At the time of the formation of the Okhotsk Sezie, a remnant of the tribe was left in the "Penzhinsk" district of the "Kamchatka Peninsula," which latter they ultimately termed Zĕm'ā-trŭs (dark, or short days), and called themselves the Răm-ā-sĕns. They and their descendants became the pre-historic ancestors of the "Kamchadales," or the "Itelm," as they termed themselves. Though they have spread out into different localities of the Peninsula and yet in the Penzhinsk district (their native home), they to the present time have retained, to a great extent, the purity of their original language, the sound of which has been compared by Mr. Kennan to that of "water running out of a narrow-mouthed jug." They have also retained the characteristics of their ancestors, being a strong, hardy people, inured to the severities of the climate, and are capable of any amount of toil in the way of walking. They, as was the case with their ancestors, are affectionate, and even submissive to their women.

Submerged Atlantis Restored

QUIL-SE'RA, MER'SUR, MIC-NU'LU, KISH RE-COD'NY,
OR
STIGMATIZATION, TATTOOING, FACE PAINTING, AND FEATHER-WEARING.

TELTZIE LVII.

The origin of stigmatization, such as is so widely practised in Australia, in the place of tattooing, dates back to the time that the Gistraz tribe became settled in their section of Agonthrus, now known as the southeastern portion of Australia, and is more remote, pre-historically, than the practice of plain tattooing.

The facts leading up to the practice is as follows: On a certain occasion, as the evening star and the full moon made their appearance above the horizon, Kăl-săd'ē-ŭs, the leader of the tribe, was reclining in rest on the side of a mountain thus contemplating the scene until the stars of the entire heavens had become visible. Thus meditating upon the wonderful phenomena, he conceived the idea that the Sun was the father planet, the Moon the mother, and the stars their children.

Further thought upon the subject caused him to raise cicatrices on his face in the form of circles, to represent the sun; semi-circles, to represent the moon's phases; dots, to represent the stars, and lines by which he separated the various designs; all symbolic of the power of principle which he thought had given them existence, and which he thought to be greater than that possessed by himself, or his people. Later, his tribe and their descendants adopted the same practice, for the same symbolic purpose; but later, with the generations that followed, they also used the practice for the purpose of tribal distinctions, when they adopted the same forms of cicatrices as tribal badges. The custom was handed down from the Gistraz tribes, to the Modern Ancient aboriginal peoples of Australia, in connection with their great reverence for the planets and the stars, the latter especially, from the innumerable number of them, such as were visible upon a clear night. Thus they conceived the idea that the people on the earth plane, like the stars in the heavens, should be numerous, which fact led them to seek a greater increase of children.

The origin of the tattooing on the Eastern Continent and Great Archipelago, dates back to before the time of the convulsion that established northwestern Polynesia, and had place among the O-nō-ā-to'äs, who pre-historically inhabited the islands of O-nō-ä-tō'ä, group of the Gilbert islands, the name of the islands never having been changed through pre-historic, or Modern Ancient times, and so remains at the present time. They were a tribe of Igentoses, who had wandered southeast from their section of Kalveno, to the region of the now known Onoatoa group of islands, south of the Gilberts At the time of the convulsion that established the islands, a remnant of those people was left on them, when they termed them Onoatoa, and called themselves the Onoatoas.

The circumstances leading up to the origin of tattooing in this section was as follows: A member of the tribe, by chance got a portion of the purple juice of a plant, then known as the Qū'dūke (now extinct), on his forearm, which, apparently, was formed in the image of a snake. He finally discovered that the stain was indelible, and therefore could not be washed off. The people of the tribe, being superstitious, were possessed with fear, for they thought it an evil omen. Finally, to see how it would look on another individual, they took a member of the tribe, and with a sharp instrument they scratched the skin in diagonal lines across the arm, and then applied the juice of the Quduke, along the scratches. When the wounds had healed, they found that it had been a successful operation, and that by breaking the skin before making the application of the juice, it became the more indelible, for thus applied it never came out. Subsequently. they began to make images of trees and animals on their bodies by the same means.

Before the establishment of the Gilbert, the Marshall and the Onoatoa islands, some of the tribe of the Igentoses, or ultimate Onoatoas, (after they had established the practice of tattooing), wandered back into that portion of Kalveno, known as the Marshall islands, and therefore brought the idea of tattooing to the people of that region, who in turn, adopted the practice and further developed it by adding to the coloring property of the Quduke, that of mineral colorings; and also that of the juice from a native plant of theirs, by the name of Kŭn'dĭt (now extinct); and also that of a fruit by the name of Ute (also extinct) which was non-edible and was qualified by black skin and juice.

The compound thus made was of a very dark reddish color, thus making the tattooing much more attractive. Thus, the descending tribes who remained as remnants on the now known Marshall islands, improved the art of tattooing, both in designs and colorings, until in 1529, they were discovered by Saavedra who when observing the fine tattooing of the inhabitants called them "Los Pintados," meaning the painted people.

Before the fifth and sixth great convulsions that established western Polynesia, and Malaysia, some of the tattooed people of the Marshall island section, when migrating westward through the then known section of Kalveno, continued still further, until they arrived in Wetlog (Borneo), from whom the Degilets of Wetlog learned the art, and adopted it as a practice; the custom descended down to the period of time when Borneo was visited by sailors, who also adopted and practised the art, by tattooing their various ensigns and symbols on parts of their bodies, and by their changing from one region to another through the great watercourses, carried the knowledge of the art to other peoples.

The origin of the practice of tattooing in North America dates back to the time when a remnant of the tribe of Izoletes, who were migrating from their section of Izolete (Oregon), to their Quintezelon home (Admiralty island section), settled in the region of British Columia. The incidents leading up to the origin of the practice were as follows: Săg-ā-wä'ĭ-ăn, a member of the remnant tribe of Izoletes, when killing and dressing an animal then known as the In'kī-gĕn (now extinct) received a crescent-shaped wound on the back of his hand. Knowing that the leaves from a tree then called the O-kä'doo (now extinct) were medicinal, he plucked one with which to remove the blood from the wound. He then plucked some small leaves from a shrub then known as the Jä-dī'kä (now extinct), which he bound on to the wound with one of the large leaves of the Okadoo tree, causing the wound to turn a greenish color; and after it had healed, the green color could not be removed. Seeing that such a mark could be produced, the tribe, generally speaking, adopted the practice of green tattooing, which at that time was done purely for the purpose of ornamentation of the body. This condition lasted for nearly three hundred years, when it was discontinued in the British Columbian section proper.

Soon after the adoption of the green tattooing in the British Columbian region, however, Sagawaian, with a small tribe of his tattooed people, who looked upon him as a superior one among them, and chose him as their Chief, migrated farther northwest, into the region now known as Queen Charlotte's archipelago; there they settled and called themselves the Sagawaiens. In that locality they could not obtain the Okadoo, or the Jadika leaves, but they discovered a pool on the side of one of the mountains, the water of which was highly impregnated with a mineral substance which they found to be almost indelible whenever they got it on their skins. They, therefore, experimented as to its use for the purpose of tattooing, in place of the green leaves such as they had formerly used. Being successful, they ultimately found other mineral waters of different colors, that answered the same purpose.

Therefore, the practice of tattooing on the North American Continent originated with the Sagawaiens, by imitating Sagwaian's accident, and it was continued by their descending tribes, who became the pre-historic ancestors of the "Haida" Indians, known to exist modernly upon the Queen Charlotte's islands, off the coast of British Columbia, who had received the art from their ancestors long ages ago, or since before the establishment of the islands. The idea of ornamentation, as embodied in the original Sagawaien practice, however, has sustained some changes with the modern Haida Indians, who attach to the former the Totem markings.

The origin of the practice of tattooing in South America, is far more ancient than that of North America, and the facts leading up to its establishment in that region of the Eastern Continent, are as follows: After the Onoatoas had brought the art of tattooing into the section of Wetlog (Borneo), and it had also become a practice among the Degilets of that section, a tribe of tattooed people migrated from that section westward to the region of southern Hindustan; thence along the then known Lū-kī'-dĭsh, and Wä-ĕn'tō-dē ranges, to the region of southern Madagascar, where they permanently settled and called themselves the Wĭl-ā-wăs'tō-zēs. Subsequently, a tribe of their descendants migrated to the now known region of the "Cape of Good Hope," South America, but retained their former tribe name. Still later, a tribe of their descendants migrated to the region of the Tristan d' Acuha islands, the southern extremity of the then known Otessen range, who still retained their former tribal name. Subsequently, a tribe of their descendants migrated to the region of the St. Helena island, who also retained their former name of Wilawastozes. Ultimately, a tribe of their descendants migrated westward into the section of "Brazil," South America, who after many years, or at the end of the migration (through the descendants of the Onoatoas and the Wilawastozes), brought the influence or practice of tattooing into South America; hence, no modern ancient person, or tribe, can lay claim to the origination of the art, either on the Eastern or the Western Continents.

The origin of body, or face painting, such as is now practised in Java, the Nicobar islands, etc., or on the Eastern Continent, dates back to that period of time when the Vackareons were established in the region now known as the mouth of the Cambodia river, Farther India. The facts leading up to the origin of the practice are as follows: Shū'dŏck, a member of the tribe of Vackareons of that section, while sitting at night on the bank of the then known Vĭn-zĭck'ē-ăsh, or Cambodia river, contemplated the image of the Moon and the Stars, which he saw reflected in the water. Being therefore impressed with the strange phenomenon, which he thought came from an unknown force greater than that which he possessed, sought to show reverence to it by imitating, or reproducing the scene, which he did by painting, or staining it on little blocks of wood, and later, by placing it in the same manner on his face. This attracted the attention of Keī-rē'dŭz the then leader of the tribe, who when learning the cause of Vinzickeash's strange appearance, adopted the practice on his own person, for the same purpose, which was soon followed by other members of the tribe, and ultimately adopted as a tribe distinction.

Body painting or staining was first done by means of black and white clays, which the natives termed Zē-rē'tŏr, and which they first reduced to a solution. With it they represented scenes of the Moon and Stars. Later they added images in representation of birds; then serpents; and finally those of various animals. The birds were adopted first after the representation of the Moon and the Stars, on account of their ability to soar away toward the region of the Moon and the Stars; and therefore became symbolic of the unseen and unknown force that they recognized as being higher than themselves. In fact, everything they painted on their bodies was for some symbolic purpose; but in subsequent time, was endowed with a religious meaning. Next, they adopted the serpent, which, by the people, was the most reverenced, for to them it was an object to be feared. Hiding, and crawling upon the ground, as is its nature, they would come suddenly upon it, which at all times gave them a sudden shock. These facts they attributed to the cunning, or wisdom of the snake, which principle they reverenced with great sacredness, as being one far above their possession, and belonged to the mysteries of the unknown and the unseen. Hence it is that the image of the serpent and serpentine painting are favorites among all the superstitious peoples of the world, the idea having been handed down from generation to generation, and from peoples to peoples from remote pre-historic, to modern times.

The practice of body painting was among the Vackareons, the most ancient of all pre-historic peoples. It became quite artistic (being well wrought) before the time of the formation of the "Gulf of Siam," but at the time of that submergence, most of the people were lost, and therefore the better knowledge of the art. That which was preserved was in a cruder state, as practised among the islanders who survived the submergence.

In subsequent time, small tribes of the remnant Vackareons of that section migrated southwest, and also southeast, some into the section of the Nicobar islands who brought the influence of body painting among the Wezenets of that section. Some of the tribes passed into the section of Java, and likewise brought the influence to the Hē-ĕn'si-ŏcks of that region, who also adopted it; but improved the art by using the juice of the berries from a small shrub then known as the Cē'lid, which was of a rich crushed strawberry color, in addition to the white and black Zeretor, as originally used by the Vackareons. Therefore, the Vackareons, by their influence upon the pre-historic Wezenets of Ruencicon or the Nicobar islands, and the Heensiocks of Gathoselonze (Java), established the art of face or body painting known in modern times, as existing on the Eastern Continent, and its adjacent islands.

The practice of body or face painting among the North-American Indians had its origin in two ways and in two different sections on the Western Continent. First, in the Western States, and in Mexico. The incidents leading up to the origin in that region, are as follows: A tall, slender Chief by the name of Big Spăn-ză'lū (*big palm tree*) and his tribe of Lĭn'zōes, had settled in a beautiful valley near the western coast of Mexico. Soon after they had possessed themselves of that home, another tribe of the same race, under the leadership of a Chief by the name of Chē-ī-că'zō, came into and sought to possess the valley for their home, by driving Big Spanzalu and his tribe out of it. A great battle ensued, when Big Spanzalu and his tribe were victorious in holding the valley as their possession, but Big Spanzalu was badly wounded about the head during the battle. As the blood issued from his wounds, it flowed down his face, which caused it to be stained in red streaks and spots. Thus marked with his own life blood, he wore the stains for a time, in honor of his victory over Cheicazo and his tribe. As the stains were disappearing from Big Spanzalu's face, he replaced them by means of the juices from berries, and weeds, and it was from this fact that he received the idea of staining his face to further commemorate events having place among his people, who from that time on, stained their faces in representation of his blood-stained face, which representation he had continued in memory of their ancestors' victory over Cheicazo. The practice was further handed down among the descending tribes of Mexico, from generation to generation, and also those of the northwestern states and Alaska, such as is now known to exist in those regions.

Secondly, the practice of body and face painting had a similar origin in the eastern States and Canada. The incidents leading up to the Eastern origin are as follows: A large, heavy-set Chief, of commanding appearance, by the name of Och-ā-chē'tä, and his tribe of Kĭn'chŏcks (who had settled in the region now known as the Chesapeake Bay area) in order to make himself look braver and fiercer (thus to command greater respect from his tribe, and to be the more feared by other Chiefs and their tribes), painted his face (see description of the Kinchocks for the style). This was really an idea reconceived from Ochacheta, which he had received from the influence of departed spirits of more ancient time, who in their earth life had practised the art. And the same might be said of Big Spanzalu, for though he was possessed with physical wounds that aided in the conception of the idea of face painting, that was the means used by the spirit impressors who sought to establish the art among the western tribes, as they in their earth life had done on the Eastern Continent. After a time, the children of the descending tribes, when at play, would paint their faces to look like that of Chief Ochacheta from which fact it became a custom of the tribes to paint their faces, as did Ochacheta, for the purpose of making themselves look braver and fiercer. Therefore, from the influence of face painting, as practised by the Kinchocks, the Owaschetoes, and the Succeleons, of pre-historic time, who intensified their natural reddish-brown skins by further coloring, or staining their faces, the art was handed down to all the modern clans who dwelt in the eastern States and Canada.

Feather adornment is more ancient than that of body or face painting, such as was and is practised by the North-American Indians. It dates back to the time when the Meltrezens were in possession of the eastern and northern portions of the area now known as the Gulf of Mexico, and Cuban regions; and the establishment of the Shazas in their section of Anteshaza, or the now known section of the mouth of the Mississippi river. The circumstances leading up to the origin of the practice are as follows: As a chief by the name of Kĕl-lū-ăn'nē, and his tribe of Shazas were migrating through the area now submerged by the Gulf of Mexico, to their section of Anteshaza, they were opposed by Wĭn-kē-lū'shŏn, a leader of one of the tribes of Meltrezens of that section, when a battle ensued. Through the brave leadership of Kelluanne, the Shazas were victorious. After they had become settled in Anteshaza, the tribe coronated Kelluanne with feathers, in honor of his bravery and the victory won, and furthermore, in order that other tribes seeing him thus decorated, would recognize him as their leader, and fear him the more.

Subsequently, the descending tribes adopted the plan of wearing feathers in their hair when going to battle, thus to distinguish them from the opposing tribes, as Kelluanne and his tribes had done before them; but in addition the leaders were known and recognized both by having feather coronets and wearing a string of feathers down their spines, and one on the outside of each leg that extended from the hip down to the foot. Therefore the custom of feather wearing was handed down to modern ancient, and modern time as well, but worn more from the fact of recording and commemorating some achievement, than otherwise.

The ornaments worn by the Shazas in their ears and noses, originally had no specific signification aside from that of ornamentation, but after the tribes began to wear feathers, they added to the number of quills, or stones on the strings, one at a time, as they would accomplish something out of the ordinary, such as killing a bear, in contrast with the act of killing some little, or inferior animal, etc. Subsequently, or just prior to the modern ancient period, leaders of the Islanders conceived the idea of nose and neck ornamentation, in order to distinguish themselves from the under members of the tribes, which like that of feather-wearing, was also worn to some extent by members of the tribes in commemoration of some achievement.

Submerged Atlantis Restored

GU-I-O-I'TA AND SEN'LINS, OR NORTH AMERICA.

TELTZIE LVII.

The continent of "North America," as a whole, was not named until about the beginning of the Christian Era, when it was divided into two sections, viz: the Southern and the Northern.

Gū-ī-ō-ī'tä (sun land) was the first pre-historic name of the southern division, as given by the Lĭn'zōes, whose descendants peopled that portion of North America.

Sĕn'līns (little warmth) was the first pre-historic name of the northern division, as given by the descendants of the Shä'zäs, who peopled the northwestern portion of North America.

Thousands of years prior to the submergence of Atlantis, the continent of North America, was entirely submerged. This was caused by a series of convulsions and eruptions that began in the region of Labrador, Newfoundland and eastern Canada, and worked northwest through the region of British America, thence south through the same region and through the section of the Western United States, and further southwest from the Newfoundland region into the eastern United States, which caused a complete inundation of the Western Continent, or North America. The convulsive condition that spread over so wide a territory, was caused by under ground streams of moulten lava that then radiated throughout those regions, having their convulsive forces collected at various points along their radiating sources, thus making the great continental convulsive occurrence, that caused the great submergence.

Prior to the submergence of Atlantis, great subterrene convulsions throughout the submerged continent of North America, caused the land to rise and fall to a marvelous degree, in all parts of the continent, which in turn, caused the waters to divide, change position, and ultimately to run off into the Southern Pacific Ocean region which left the Continent of North America still connected to the Eastern Continent, the connecting land being that of Atlantis, on the East; and to that of Asia, by the land that now forms the Great Eastern Archipelago, and otherwise submerged by the great convulsions, upheavals and depressions. For proof of this revealed fact of inundation, the reader has only to contemplate the fact that, in all regions of the North American continent, even to the top of the highest mountains, great deposits of shells, sand, pebbles, sedimentary layers of rock, fossiliferous deposits etc. etc., exist, many of which are of far greater age than is supposed by modern geologists.

The fifth of the eleven great periodical convulsions (previously referred to), occurred about fifty years subsequent to the fourth, and had place in the section known as the state of Guerrero, Mexico, or where the inlet waters of Acapulco now have place. The force of the convulsion extended as far southeast as to the inlet waters near the town of Tutatepec, on the coast of the state of Oaxaca, into which the river Verde flows, and as far northwest, as to the inlet waters on the coast of the state of Colima, into which the river America flows.

Prior to the time of these convulsions, a Cŏn'zē (mountain) range, then known as the Dĕt-tlē'lŏn, extended from the then known Glē-tū'dē-zĕl Conze range, northeast from the Guadalupe island, to the vicinity of "Point Conception," with adjacent spurs accompanying it.

The sixth convulsion occurred about one hundred years after the fifth, in the region of the "Revillagigedo" islands. These islands were the terminal of the Conze range (then known as the Shä-rŭn'dū-săc) that extended northwestward from them, to the most northern portion of Mexico. The point of land, that terminated at the islands, was also termed Sharundusac. It extended northeast from the islands, to "Cape Corrientes," Mexico, and northwest from the islands, to "Cape St. Lucas," Lower California, thus connecting Lower California to the main land of Mexico. Prior to the time of the sixth convulsion (see later), there was no "Gulf of California."

The force of the convulsion extended from the Sharundusac point, along a branch of the range that extended from it to the inlet waters of "San Blas," into which the waters of the then known rē-ū'tĕr (river) of Jĕl'tī-zĕs (now the Santiago) flowed, and embraced the "Los Tres Marias" islands; also another conze range, that extended from the Sharundusac Point, to Cape St. Lucas, or south of the eastern section of the peninsula of California. The force of the convulsion continued its extension northwest, until it had formed that portion of the Gulf of California, as far northeast as to the island of "Carmin," on the western coast of Lower California, and the inlet waters, into which those of the river "Estrella" flow, on the southeastern coast of the state of "Sonora," Mexico.

Subsequent to this convulsion, at periods sometimes but a few months apart, there occurred three smaller convulsions throughout the section of country now occupied by the waters of the Gulf of California, that completed the formation of the latter. The first of the three, had place on the southeastern coast of the state of Sonora, Mexico, where the inlet waters now are, into which the river "Mayo" flows. The force of the convulsion extended southeast to the ultimate line of the sixth periodical convulsion, and southwest to the inlet waters into which the river "Yagui" flows, thus further establishing the Gulf of California, to that section of country.

The second of the smaller convulsions had place near the southwestern point of the island of "Tiburon." off the eastern coast of the state of Sonora, Mexico. The force of the convulsion extended southeast to the terminal of the first, formed the island of Tiburon and those in its vicinity, and further extended northwest to the north of the "Angeles" island, which latter, as well as the Gulf of California, it also established.

The third of the smaller convulsions had place in the section of country now occupied by the "St. Lais Bay," in the northeastern portion of the state of Oreoa in Lower California. The force of the convulsion extended southeast to the northwestern ultimatum of the second; and northeast to the establishment of the "George" islands, and further northwest to the present extremity of the Gulf of California, into which the famous "Colorado" river flows,

The seventh periodical convulsion occurred about five hundred years subsequent to the sixth, and had place about six degrees west of the "Guadalupe" island, on a conze range then known as the Glē-tū'de-zel that extended from it, to the Cedros island, and further connected to the main land of Lower California, where the Bay of St. Sebastian Vizcaino, and Point Eugenia have place. The force of the convulsion extended into the main land, along the Gletudezel Conze, established the Guadalupe and Cedros islands, and the southwest coast line, to and including the point northwest of the "Magdalena" Bay, having been formed by the force of the sixth periodical convulsion, which latter extended northwest to the establishment of that portion of the southwestern coast line of Lower California, to the point of land northwest of the Bay of Magdalena, which latter it formed at the time that the southern section of the Gulf of California was formed. The force of the seventh periodical convulsion also established the coast line, islands, and the inlet waters of the northwest coast of Lower California, and California proper, as far northwest as to "Point Conception. The terminal force of the convulsion took on a circular form, south of the County of Santa Barbara*, California, which established the "Santa Barbara Channel," and the islands of "San Miguel," "Santa Rosa," and "Santa Cruz." As the force was extending along the Dettlelon range, it also took on a circular force south of "Point Fermin," which forme dthe island of "Santa Catalina."

Prior to the occurrence of the seventh periodical convulsion, the entire coast of Lower California, California, Oregon, and Washington, extended much farther out into the Pacific Ocean, in conformity with the present general coast line, and was a mountainous section. During about 1000 years subsequent to the seventh periodical convulsion, smaller ones occurred in the section west of the present coast line of the above-named states, which caused various changes in the aspect of the then coast line, as well as that of the interior land, now submerged.

The eighth periodical convulsion occurred about 1,000 years subsequent to the seventh, or at the ultimatum of the small convulsions above referred to, which had place in the section known modernly as *"Golden Gate,"* in the vicinty of "San Francisco," California, or more definitely speaking, beneath the head of "Richardson's Bay," within the body of a high mountain belonging to a Conze range, then called Kä-kĭs-kĭd'ro in which also, the Angel island was then a prominent point. The convulsion was caused by a combination of radiating, and circular forces, which completed the work begun by the smaller convulsions, above mentioned, shot down and out from the southeastern section of Marin County, thus forming Richardson's Bay, as it sunk and submerged the portion of the Kakiskidro range there located. It further established the Raccoon Straits, and the Angel island, radiated southwestward and burst asunder the rocks and earth, thus forming the famous Golden Gate, that now gives a passage from the San Francisco Bay, to the Pacific Ocean. Radiations extended northwest, that severed Contra Costa and Marin Counties, and left the Brooks, the Molate, and the Marin islands. Also northeast, leaving Points San Pedro and San Pablo. The force took on a circular form that established the San Pablo Bay, and inlet waters connected to it, which latter were formed by radiations of the circular force that reached their locality, through subterrene fissures, in the rocks, of older con-

*Alem Prolex informs us that the time is not far distant, when another extensive convulsion will take place near "Point Salmas," on the southern coast of the County of "Santa Barbara," California.

vulsive origin, that led to their region. Likewise the force radiated southeast from Angel island, severed the Counties of Alameda, and San Mateo, leaving the Yerba island, tnen took on the circular form which established the southeastern center of the Bay of San Francisco, and further radiations from which lost their force in the establishment of the inlet waters that submerged the extremity of their devastations. The force further extended northeast, to the southwestern point of the County of Mendocino, California. By its extension out into the Pacific Ocean, and north to the terminal of the small convulsions that had formed the now coast line northwest from the line of the seventh convulsion, and northwest to the above named point, it formed the present coast line, inlet waters, and islands, to the region of the County of Mendocino.

The ninth periodical convulsion occurred about 1200 years subsequent to the eighth, and had place southeast of the "Vancouver island," centrally, where now the waters submerge the land between the "Whidbey" and the "Sland" islands. The force of this wonderful radiating convulsion, extended southward, thus establishing all the zig-zag system of inland waters to the northern section of the County of "Thurston," in the state of Washington. The force also extended to the northern section of "Birch Bay," which established the latter, and all the zig-zag system of waters in the region north of the Whidbey and the Sland islands, at the same time forming the latter named islands, as well as those of "San Juan."

The tenth periodical convulsion occurred about five hundred years subsequent to the ninth, and had place on the southeast point of "Cape St. James," or the lower extremity of the "Queen Charlotte" islands, the latter being high points in the Conze range then known as Et-těl'ē, that extended from "Prince William Sound," southeastern Alaska, along the now coast of Alaska, and British America, including the Vancouver island. The force of this convulsion extended southwest then southeast on a curve, along a Conze range then known as the Se-tē'lŏnz, which sunk and submerged the land southwest of the southern one of the Queen Charlotte islands, and severed the latter from the main land, which left the point that subsequently became the northern Queen Charlotte; and formed the body of waters between the two islands and the main land east and south of them, to the northwest section of the "Vancouver" island. It also established the inlet waters of British America, in that section; and further extended northeast, until it had completed the establishment of the Vancouver island, Queen Charlotte straits, and Archipelago, the Gulf of Georgia, and all the inland waters and islands north and west of the San Juan, and the straits of Juan de Fuca, which latter completed the separation of the Vancouver island, from the state of Washington.

The eleventh periodical convulsion occurred about one hundred years subsequent to the tenth, and had place between the islands of "Tchitchagoff," and "Baranoff," of the King George Archipelago, west of British America. The force of this convulsion extended circularly, northwest and south, along a Conze range then known as Kăl-zo-ē'lo, which sank and submerged the land west, and south of it, far out into what is now that section of the Northern Pacific Ocean, and established the Tchitchagoff, and Baranoff islands, and the inland waters northeast of them.

The eleventh periodical convulsion was followed by three successive convulsions, within a few months of each other, that completed the present coast line conditions. The first of the three successive convulsions, had place between the northwestern point of the northern Queen Charlotte island, and the coast of British America. The force of this convulsion severed the north Queen Charlotte island from Alaska and British America, and formed the waters northwest, and east of it.

The second successive convulsion had place between the "Prince of Wales," the "Baranoff," and the "Kaptianoff" islands. The force of this convulsion established the Prince of Wales and the Kaptianoff islands, and the inlet waters, and islands, east and southeast of them, to the line of the successive convulsion.

The third successive convulsion had place in the "Cross Sound" area, northwest of the Tchitchagoff island. The force of this, the greatest of the three successive convulsions extended northwest and southward, in a circular form along a Conze range, then known as Sĕn-sō-bī'tō; and also northwest along the Et-tĕl'ē range, to the southwestern boundary of "Prince William Sound," Alaska, when it submerged that section of land far out into the now North Pacific Ocean; established the "Middleton" island and all the inland waters from and including the Prince William Sound, to and including the Cross Sound, along the coast line of that section of Alaska.

About 1,100 years after the eleventh periodical convulsion, there began another system of five, that occurred during the subsequent six hundred years. The first had place in a Conze range, then known as Kî-ör'dä, that was a spur of the then known great Săng-măn'gŭs, the remnants of which are now known as the chain of Aleutian islands. The Kiorda range extended from the central section of the Kenay Peninsula, southwest to the Kukamak Trinity group of islands; thence curved southeast into the section then known as Kör-dū-zū'lăc, now submerged by the waters of the North Pacific Ocean. The exact location of the convulsion was in the now known North Strait, between the southwestern section of the Alnonak, and the northeastern section of the Kadiak island. The force of the convulsion extended out along the Kiorda range, and established the islands of Alnonak, Kadiak, and those to their southwest; submerged the great country of Kordusulac south and east of them, to the border line of the eleventh periodical convulsion, before named; the Kenay Peninsula; the southern coast of Alaska Peninsula; the open and inlet waters southeast of the Alaska Peninsula, and their islands, as far southwest as to Point Kupreanof; and the western coast of the Shumagin islands.

The second occurred about two hundred years subsequent to the first, and had place about half way between "Prybilov" islands, and the Bay of "Bristol," in the "Behring" Sea. At the time of the convulsion there was a Conze range then known as Ak-rĕn'tiē, that extended from the "Akoutan Pass," circled to the northeast, to about one hundred and sixty-five degrees longitude west from Greenwich, and the same latitude, as that of the St. Paul island, of the Prybilov group, which was the point of the convulsion; thence it curved northwest, to the island of Nounivak, off the southwestern coast of Alaska. The force of the convulsion extended south, along the Akrentie range, to that section of the Aleutian islands now known as the Fox group, and south into the country of Korduzulac, to the then known coast of the North Pacific Ocean, and north to Cape Vancouver; and northeast of the Nounivak island; sunk and submerged the greater portion of the range, excepting a few Conze peaks, that thus existed for a time pre-historically; but finally, by the force of smaller convulsions, were also submerged, one by one, until none excepting the Nounivak are left as remnants of the range. The force of the convulsion spread further eastward, to the ultimate establishment of the southeastern section of the Behring Sea, or submergence of the district of land from the then known Akrentie range, to Aliaska Peninsula on the southeast, and Alaska, on the east, as far north as Cape Vancouver, thus establishing the Bays of "Kuskokwim," "Kulwkak," and "Bristol," Capes "Newenham," and "Constantine," and all the islands and inlet waters along that section of western Alaska.

The third occurred about one hundred years subsequent to the second, and had place in the section of country that then lay between the now known "St. Paul," and the "St. George" islands of the Prybilov group. Aat the time of the convulsion, a Conze range, then known as the Gū-hū'lĕm, extended from Mt. Kovovin, on the eastern section of the island of "Aticha" (in the "Andreanowsky" group, of the Aleutian islands), which curved eastward to the Prybilov islands; thence continued its course northwestward, to the "Hall," St. "Matthew," and Pinnacle islands west of the "Nounivak" island. The force of the convulsion extended southwest along the Guhulem range to the vicinity of Mt. Kovovin, submerged the then known district of Pär-cĕl'tē-ūs, east to the border line of the second periodical convulsion, and established that section of the Andreanowsky group east of Mt. Kovovin, to the border line of the second convulsion; and further south into the country of Korduzulac, to the then known coast line of the North Pacific Ocean. On its northeastern course, along the Guhulem range, it established the Pribylov group of islands, and submerged the district of Parcelteus northward as far as west of the island of Nounivak, and eastward to the border line of the second periodical convulsion.

The fourth occurred about one hundred years subsequent to the third, and had place west of the Prybilov group, at a point about one hundred and seventy-eight degrees longitude west from Greenwich, and about fifty-eight degrees north latitude. This powerful convulsion occurred in the middle of a Conze range then known as the Săn-măn'drä-hăn, that extended in a zig-zag course from the island of Agattau, in the "Blijnie," or "Rat" group of the Aleutian island system, in a northeastern direction, to the St. Matthew island, west of Cape "Romanzof," Alaska, where it formed a junction with the Guhulem range. The force of this convulsion extended southeast, along the Sanmandrahan range, to the western extremity of the Blijnie, or Rat group which latter named group it established, and submerged that section of the country of Korduzulac that lay extent south of them, to the then known coast line of the Northern Pacific Ocean. On its northeastern extension, it established the Hall, and the St. Matthew islands; and further extended the Behring Sea as far northwest, and northeast, as to the Bay of "St. Gabriel," of Russia, and Cape "Romanzof" or southwestern Alaska.

The fifth occurred about twe hundred years subsequent to the fourth, and had place near the southeastern coast of what is now known as the Lawrence island. At the time of this great convulsion, there was a Conze range, then known as the Kĕn-gĕr-lūs'tĕn, that extended northeast from the now known Lawrence island, in a line with the Behring straits, to, and beyond Cape

Lisburne, of northwestern Alaska. Another Conze range then known as the Kĕl-ē-lē'zŏn, (thus named after its central highest peak, which bore that name, but now known as the St. Lawrence island), extended northwest, and southeast, to the northwestern section of the "Gulf of Anadir," of Russia, and to the eastern central section of "North Sound" in western Alaska. The force of this powerful convulsion extended in the form of a cross, along the Kelelezon, and the Kengerlusten ranges, which established the open sea, south, southeast and southwest of the Lawrence island; the North, and Kotzebue Sounds, on the western coast of Alaska; the Gulf of Anadir; the Behring Straits; and all the islands, and inlet waters of their coasts, by tearing asunder the land, leaving the Cape "Prince of Wales," of Alaska, and the "Tchuktches" peninsula of Russia, as the severed link that formerly connected that section of the Eastern and Western continents.

About 5,000 years subsequent to the submergence of Atlantis, a great system of four periodical convulsions occurred, and had place in the northern and eastern sections of British America. The first had place at the eastern point of "McClure straits," at its junction with "Perry Sound,' which formed all the islands and the inlet waters west of the point of the convulsion, to the Arctic Ocean; south to the Arctic Circle; and east to about ninety-five degrees longitude west from Greenwich, or the western coast line of "Boothia;" "North Somerset;" "North Devon," etc.

The second occurred about five hundred years subsequent to the first, and had place in the section of "Lancaster Sound,", between the southeast section of "Devon," and the islands to the southeast, which established the islands, and inlet waters, west to the eastern and northern extremity of the first convulsion; south to the extremity of "Boothia Gulf;" thence northeast, forming the channels north of the "Melville Peninsula," the "Murray Maxwell;" and "Scott inlets," and the portion of "Baffin's Bay," northeast of the latter inlets.

The third occurred about four hundred years after the second, and had place beteen "Cape Kater," and the northern extremity of "Cumberland," in the section of country now submerged by the waters of "Home Bay," this convulsion was the most extensive of the four, and completed the formation of "Baffin's Bay;" "Davis Straits;" and the entire inundation to the western coast of "Greenland;" the "Cumberland islands;" "Hudson straits;" "South Ampton island;" "Fox Channel;" "Hudson Bay," and all the islands and inlet waters of that section. The fourth occurred about fifty years after the third, and had place in the section now known as the "Gulf of St. Lawrence" off the southwest coast of "Newfoundland," which latter it established, with all its inlet waters; extended southwest and established the "Bay of Fundy;" thus leaving "Nova Scotia" and the "Cape Breton island" practically in the sea; and further established the "Prince Edward, the "Magdalen," and the "Anticosta" islands; as well as the broad delta of the famous "St. Lawrence," with its "Thousand islands."

About 1,000 years before the Adomic period, a system of nine great periodical convulsions began their operation in the eastern central portion of the North American Continent. The first had place in the section of country now known as "Prince Edward," in the province of "Ontario," northeast of "Picton," which established the now zig-zag coast conditions and the inlet waters of that section of country, and also those in the extension eastward along the present southwestern half of the St. Lawrence river; the present outlet of Lake "Ontario;" and that portion of the St. Lawrence to, and including the region of the Thousand islands. *Gī-ăl-li′tē, who gave the above inforamtion, also stated that at that period of time there were high Conzes (mountains) in that region, that were known to the Gī-ăl-li′tēs (his nation), as the Săn-tē-grăn′gē range, which extended from the point of the convulsion, northeast, through the trail of country now occupied by the waters of the St. Lawrence river. The convulsive force sunk the range and gave place to the inlet waters from the Gulf of St. Lawrence. Previous convulsions had established the eastern half of the St. Lawrence river.

Furthermore, he also informed us that, a system of rocky hills, known to him and his people, as the Kū-ā-lŭx′tŏn range, extended in a zig-zag course southwest from the region of the convulsion, to that of the present outlet of the Niagara waters into Lake Ontario. The force of the above named convulsion having extended along the Santegrange, and the Kualuxton ranges, completed the establishment of the St. Lawrence river, which the Giallites termed Cĕl-lăn-ti′sō (many islands in the big

*Giallite represented himself as the Chief of a great tribe of North American Indians, who went by the name of the Gialites (after having seceded from the Owaschetoes, who dwelt then in the St. Lawrence region) long since extinct through natural causes, and therefore never known, as a real nation, to the Indians of the present period of time.

Being fond of wandering in search of Nature's wonders, Giallite left his tribe, as a Chief, and traveled over the whole section of country now known as the Upper Lake regions.

In his course of conversation regarding the great Upper Lakes of North America, he said, "much gill, (gold) much giest, (silver) in the western Big Lake region, if pale face hunt much, he can find."

waters), and Lake Ontario, which they termed Kē-dĭ'tō** (big water trail), thus referring to the Cellantiso whose waters now have their outlet into the St. Lawrence river.

The second convulsion occurred about two hundred years subsequent to the first, and had place in the section of country now submerged by the waters of the western portion of Quinte Bay, between the Hubb island and the main land south of the town of Bellville. The force of this convulsion extended east to the Unger's and Forester's islands, which made connection with the already submerged section between Picton and Deseronto, which latter section had been submerged by the force of the first periodical convulsion; hence, the northern and southern course of that portion of the Quinte Bay.

Prior to the establishment of the Quinte Bay, all that portion of Ontario was inhabited by a large nation, separated into various tribes, who dwelt at various points throughout that area; but were under the rule of one great Chief by the name of A-pō-cō-gä'wä, the section and nation being of the same name, given by the Chief in honor of himself as such.

After the submergence, remnants of various tribes of the Apocogawaens were left along the borders of the bay. After many generations, they became a strong nation, and dwelt in various districts under the rule of a great descended Chief by the name of Quĭn-tē-gä'wä. The last two syllables of the term were added by the Chief himself, his original name having been Quĭn'tē. This he did from the traditional knowledge he had of the great chief Apocogawa. He also termed the nation, and the body of water (which had submerged the section formerly occupied by the Apocogawaens) Quintegawa. The present term, by which the bay is known, had its origin by traditional descent, from the term Quintegawa, with the last two syllables dropped.

Originally, the islands and ancient towns were all named with Apocogawaen and Quintegawaen terms, they having descended with these nations, as was also the case with the term "Quinte." All have been changed anciently and modernly, except one, viz that of the island of "Waupoose," southwest of "Point Pleasant," or the " Upper Gap."

The third convulsion occurred about three hundred years after the second, and had place in the region of "Rondeau Harbor," Ontario, off "Point aux Pins." Its force extended north-

**Giallite further informed us that, the Kedito, when first formed, was an inlet of salt water from the Gulf of St. Lawrence, and was a much lower body of water then, than since the waters of the upper lakes have forced their way out into the Atlantic Ocean, through the St. Lawrence River.

east to the region of Buffalo, New York; southwest to Toledo, Ohio; and established the coast line and inlet waters of Lake Erie (which body of water was first termed Shăl-tī'zä), not including the Detroit river, or the Niagara outlet of Lake Erie. This latter was formed about fifty years later by a smaller convulsion that had place in the vicinity of Grand island, which latter was first termed Dē'lash.

About five years later, a more severe convulsion occurred in the section now known as the Whirl-pool Rapids, in the Niagara river, which rapids subsequently were termed Năk'ā-thrĕn, (whirling waters), the river Kä-dē'tă, the falls, Măg'lĕt (*let the waters out*), i. e., for the Canadian side, but the American side was called Sē-dē'gē.

The powerful force of this convulsion extended down to the region of the mysterious Whirlpool, first termed Săk-wē-mä'shä (another whirling waters), where it spent its force in a circular form. The force and action of the convulsion, met by that of incoming waters, in co-operation with a great suction of air, established this marvelous condition, that still has place in the Niagara river. Likewise, the force extended in the opposite direction through the southern portion of the Niagara region, to the point of the former convulsion, or in the region of the rapids above the present location of the Falls, which established subterraneous and subaqueous conditions yet unknown to moderns who visit this famous section of country.

But a few months later than the last named convulsion, a smaller one occurred on the northeast border of the Whirlpool, mid-river, between the two points where now the angle of the river turns from the Whirlpool, on its course to Lake Ontario, which are guarded from the Canadian side, by the famous natural rock statue known as "The Demon of the Gorge." The force of this convulsion extended down what is now the river course, to a point below "The Giant Rock," which then received its present placement, and opened the new channel that now extends from the Whirlpool, to the Giant Rock, and further established what is known as "Devil's Hole Rapids."

The remnant of the river, to its outlet into Lake Ontario, has its existence through natural erosive and fluvial conditions operating in that section of the river during the ages past.

The fourth convulsion occurred about one hundred and fifty years subsequent to the third, and had place in the section of country now centrally located in "Lake Huron," east of "Thunder Bay." At the point of the convulsion, there was a high section of land, extensions of which reached southwest from it toward

"Saginaw Bay," and northeast to the present islands between "Huron peninsula," and the "Great Manitoulin island." The force of this convulsion formed the coast lines and inlet waters of Lake Huron, which was subsequently called Kä-soŭ'lĭt, (Big Spirit bring big waters), south of Huron peninsula and the eastern coast of the County of Presque Isle, Michigan, not including the "St. Clair," or "Detroit" rivers or the "St. Clair Lake."

The fifth convulsion occurred about seventy-five years subsequent to the fourth, and had place in the section of land that then connected Huron peninsula to the Great Manitoulin island. At that time, a high ridge of land extended from "Cape Hurd" to the northeast point of Michigan, that then included the "Owen," and the "Manitou islands," along which the force of the convulsion extended, which completed the northern, and western coast lines of Lake Huron to the eastern center of the "Straits of Mackinac," and the northwestern secton of "Hammond's Bay," and formed the coast line and inlet waters of the "Georgian," and the "Manitoulin Bays," and also the course of the "St. Mary's" river, as far northwest as to the "Falls of St. Mary."

About twenty-five "big moons*" later a small convulsion occurred, between the points known as "Mt. Clemens," and the "Waupole island," or locality of the northern inlet waters from Lake St. Clair, which established the lake, and its inlet, and outlet waters, viz: the Detroit and St. Clair rivers, the latter as far as to the St. Mary's Falls.

The sixth periodical convulsion occurred about four hundred and fifty years subsequent to the fifth, and had place west of "Little Traverse Bay," between it and the "North," and "South" "Fox islands." At that time a range of mountains, called Sē-tē'-lŏnz, extended from the Manitou islands, northwest of the County of Leelanau, Michigan; circularly northeast, to those of the Great Manitoulin, along which the force of the convulsion extended, which established "Green Bay," and the coast lines and inlet waters of "Lake Michigan," (called Sinzelanzic, meaning, big lake), as far south as the central section of the County of "Muskegon," and northeast to the complete establishment of the Straits of Mackinac, and the ultimate junction of Lakes Michigan, and Huron.

The seventh convulsion occurred about fifty years subsequent to the sixth, and had place in the section of land east of the state lines of Wisconsin, and Illinois, at a point now centrally located in the southern section of Lake Michigan. At the time

*Giallite, in giving the above information, used the term "big moons" to denote years, hence 25 big moons, meant 25 years.

of the convulsion, there was a high rocky section at the point of its occurrence. The force of the convulsion caused the land and rocks to sink, and thus further established the coast line and inlet waters of Lake Michigan to its southern boundaries.

The eighth convulsion occurred about seven hundred and fifty years subsequent to the seventh, and had place west of Canada, between the islands of "Michipicoten" and Caribou." At that time, high lands extended from "Keweenaw," northeast to the now coast of Canada, that embraced the Michipicoten, and Caribou islands. Another section of high lands extended from the same point, circularly to the now coast of "British America," or to the islands in the "Nepigon Bay." The force of the convulsion followed the course of these high lands, and established the coast lines and inlet waters of "Lake Superior," (called Măl-tā-rī'est, cold icy lake, no good), east of "Eagle river," or the northwestern section of "Keweenaw," Michigan, and the western coast of "Nepigon Bay," British America; and centrally, east of the "Isle Royale," off northeast point of Minnesota, and the St. Mary's river, or outlet of Lake Superior, as far southeast as to the Falls of St. Mary, where it met the extremity of the fourth convulsion's power, which had formed the southeast section of the St. Mary's river; established the Falls of St. Mary; and ultimate outline of the Lake Superior waters, into Lake Huron.

The ninth periodical convulsion occurred about eight hundred and seventy-five years after the eighth, and had place south of the Isle Royale. At the time of the convulsion, a high portion of land extended northeast from the "Apostles" islands, to the section of land west of the Nepigon Bay, to British America, and embraced the Isle Royale in the northern section, and the Apostles islands in the southwest section. The force of this convulsion established the southwest section of Lake Superior, its islands, coast lines and inlet waters, and were the last convulsive, and submerging links that connected up the waters of the Great Lakes of North America, and gave them fluvial power, to reach the Great Atlantic Ocean, through the St. Lawrence river, and the Gulf of St. Lawrence.

Prior to the submergence of Teltzie Zret, of Atlantis, a tribe of Kintilucians had migrated from the eastern portion of Teltzie Et, to the southern portion of Teltzie Zret, where in time, a portion of them had mixed races with the Gurenzes of that portion of the Teltzie. At the time of the convulsion that formed the now known Bermuda islands, the only remnant of Teltzie Zret, a portion of the Kintilucians and Gurenzes, and also a mixed race of the two peoples were left upon them, where in subsequent time, for want of proper means of subsistence, they degenerated into the state of wild tribes, who ultimately became extinct from want and disease.

About the time that the Kintilucians had arrived in Teltzie Zret, tribes of Meltrezens and Gurenzes had migrated farther southwest into the region now known as the West Indies islands.

At the time of the formation of the West Indies islands, remnants of the Meltrezens were left in the section of those islands now known as the Bahamas, and a remnant of the Gurenzes were left in the section now known as the northern portion of Hayti.

Subsequently, a tribe of the mixed race of Gurenzes and Kintilucians, also migrated to the section of Hayti, then occupied by the Gurenzes proper, where they accepted the section name of Guselsic, as given by the Gurenzes, but called themselves the Y-năn′dōes. At that time there was a chain of Islands, remnants of the range, that extended southward through Teltzie Zret, or from the now known section of the Bermudas, to the Hayti, over which they passed. In subsequent time, however, those remnant islands all went down by convulsive power, which also cut off considerable of the northeast portion of Hayti and Cuba, in evidence of which, let the reader note the fact that the range that existed and extended from the then known section, in Teltzie Zret, of the now known Bermuda, to the Hayti islands, it can be readily seen that the above named range of mountains extended in conformity with the ranges of North America, all the latter either extending south, southeast or southwest; hence, a geographical proof of the islands over which the mixed tribe of Gurenzes and Kintilucians passed to Hayti. The open water between Cuba and Florida was not fully established until about the period of between six, to eight thousand years B. C. In subsequent time, the Ynandoes and the Gurenzes of Guselsic, blended into one nation, or race of people, and retained the name of Gurenzes.

Prior to the convulsion and submergence that established the West Indies islands, and after many generations in that section, the Meltrezens had spread out into the region of the now known section of Cuba, principally in the section of San Juan, which section they termed Tū-yăn-ăng′ (*the unknown country*), which term became the name of the entire section of Cuba, as the Meltrezens spread out over its area. Subsequently, a large colony of the Meltrezens from the western section of Tuyanang migrated southwest, into Yucatan and the country surrounding it, which section they termed Shăl-tē-cŏn′gō, and called themselves the Cŏn-gōes, while other tribes of the same people had spread out into what is now known as the submerged northwestern portion of the Caribbean Sea.

About the same time that the Meltrezens migrated from western Tuyanang, another tribe of Meltrezens migrated from central Tuyanang (San Juan, Cuba), to the southern portion of the State of Florida, U. S. A., which section they termed Chē-rē-ĕs′tēs, and called themselves the En-grē-nē′mĕns, where they dwelt for many generations, until they had spread out northward through the states of Florida, Georgia, and the Carolinas; and further east of the Allegheny mountains to and including Virginia, leaving small remnant tribes in various sections, who held to their former tribal and sectional names as adopted by their ancestors during their course of migration.

At the time of the establishment of the island of Hayti, as before stated, a tribe of the Gurenzes were left on the northern half of the island, where they dwelt for many generations, from whence in subsequent time they spread out into the central section of the country now submerged by the waters of the Caribbean Sea. Finally, a tribe of Gurenzes, who were migrating still further south than Guselsic, arrived at the northern coast of the United States of Columbia, South America, which section they termed Shū′shăck, and called themselves the Shū′shăcks.

About the time that the Shushacks had settled in Shushack, a tribe of Gurenzes from the Carribbean Sea district, in divergence to the course taken by the Shushacks, migrated westward, into Yucatan, where in time they mixed races with the Congoes, which latter condition gave origin to the red, or light tawny hues that characterized the skins of their descendants, the Linzoes of Quintelinzo, from which latter people that reddish hue has descended to all the North American Indians, and also through their seceded tribe, the Chanhangoes of Chahaezel, to the eastern portion of the Great Eastern Archipelago, through their ultimate descendants, the Sandwich Islanders.

At the time of the complete establishment of the now known Caribbean Sea, peoples of that section were left as remnants, in various parts of the section now known as Central America.

Subsequent to the establishment of the Congoes in Shaltecongo, their descendants had spread out along the Conze ranges, and into the Cē-ī′lĕs-ĕs (valleys), of the central and southern half of the district now known as the Gulf of Mexico.

Ultimately, a tribe of pure Congoes from Shaltecongo, migrated north from that section, along the then known Genzerest Aelkede range (the Gulf of Mexico not then being in existence. See article on Mexico), to the section of country now known as southern Louisiana, west of the now known mouth of the Mississippi river, which section they termed An-tē-shä'zä, and called themselves the Shä'zäs.

Subsequently, the Shazas from Anteshaza, followed the great river of Năn-zē-lī-ē'tŭs (Mississippi), and its eastern source, the Tĕl-sē-oo'dŭc (Ohio), in various tribes, to various sections throughout the middle states as far north as Ohio, Indiana, Illinois, and Iowa, west to Nebraska, Kansas, and Indian Territory.

The descended tribes of the Shazas, and the Engrenemens passed westward from the Năn-zē-lī-ē'tŭs source and the Great Dē'lā-cäs (lake) regions; and those of the Shĭn'tō-lōns, and the I-zō-lē'tēs westward by way of the Cē-cĕl-lū'shē-ōn (Colorado), and the Kĭn'trā-sha (Columbia) rivers and their sources; and the Conze ranges. Their meeting and mingling races established the pre-historic Indian inhabitants from Arizona and New Mexico in the south, to Washington, Montana, Dakota, and Minnesota in the north, and from the Nanzelietus on the east, to the Pacific coast on the west; east to Alabama, Tennessee and Kentucky; south to Texas, Louisiana and Alabama.

About the same time that the Shazas migrated to Anteshaza, another tribe of the Congoes migrated southwestward from Shaltecongo, across the country now submerged by the Bay of Campeachy, to the now known section of Vera Cruz, and near that portion now occupied by the city of Vera Cruz, which section they termed Quĭn-tē-lĭn'zō, and called themselves the Lĭn'zōes.

The Engrenemens of Chereestes, and the Shazas of Anteshaza, both being descendants from the Meltrezens, were of a dark mulatto color; but, the blended reddish hue that characterized the eastern tribes of the North American Indians had arisen from their pre-historic blendings with the western, or from the migrating and race mixing influences of the Linzoes, as they passed north and west, with those of the Shazas and the Engrenemens, as they passed north and east, the intensities of the hue being established by further influence of the sun's rays in the different degrees of latitude.

During subsequent ages, all the southern and western sections of Mexico, were peopled by tribes of the Linzoes, who spread out from their section of Quintelinzo, who went by the same tribal and sectional names, excepting the Chăn-hăn'gōes of Chă-hä-ē'zĕl, who by nature, being contentious and hostile, sought to distinguish themselves from their brethren, the Linzoes, by taking new tribal and sectional names; therefore, called themselves the Chanhangoes, and termed the section Chahaezel, the latter being the now known district submerged by the waters of the Gulf of California, and also that of Lower California.

In subsequent time, a large tribe of Linzoes migrated from the section of Northwest Mexico, to the section now submerged by the waters of the San Diego Bay, which section they termed Shĭn'tō-lŏn, and called themselves the Shĭn'tō-lŏns. They dwelt in that section for many ages, from whence their descendants spread out into the Sierra Nevada mountain regions.

Subsequently, a large tribe of the Shintolons from Shintolon, migrated along the Pacific coast region, to the section of Mendocino, which they termed I-zō-lē'tĕs, and called themselves the I-zō-lē'tĕs. They dwelt in that section for many generations, and their descendants spread out eastward into the section of Oregon, and Utah.

Subsequently, a tribe of the Izoletes migrated northwest into the section of British America, now known as east of the Admiralty island, which section they termed Quĭn-tē-zē'lŏn (snow land), and called themselves the Tē-zē'lŏns.

In subsequent time, a descended tribe of Tezelons, who had mixed races with the remnant Kiordas of that section migrated northeast, from Quintezelon, to the section of Yukon, between the Rocky Mountains and Mt. St. Elias of Alaska, which section they termed Găn-gō-mĭn'gō, and called themselves the Găn-go-mĭn'gōes.

About the time that the Gangomingoes had settled in Gangomingo, a tribe of descended Shahaiens from the Cucokin migrations, settled in the section about one hundred and thirty-three degrees longitude west from Greenwich, and about sixty-four degrees north latitude, or south of the Mackenzie river.

In subsequent time, a tribe from the Gangomingoes of Gango mingo, migrated southwest, when they settled in the section about half way between the Mt. St. Elias, and the mouth of the Atna, or Copper river, where subsequent to the submergence of the then known country of Kör-dū-zū'lăc, remnants of the Ki-ör'dăs mixed races with them, but the mixed race still held to the section and tribe names of Gangomingo and Gangomingoes.

Subsequent to the establishment of the Engrenemens in Chereestis, or Florida, a tribe of their descendants migrated eastward, until they arrived in the section of the Chesapeake Bay, which they termed Kĭn'chŏc, and called themselves the Kĭn'chŏcs. After several generations, they had spread out northwest into the section of Pennsylvania; western New York, and the Lake Erie regions.

Subsequently, a tribe of the Kinchocs migrated into the section of Massachusetts, in that portion just west of the city of Boston, which they termed Sŭe-cī-lē'ŏn, and called themselves the Sŭc-cī-lē'ŏns, who in time, had spread out into New Hampshire; Vermont, eastern New York, and the Lake Ontario region.

In time, the Shazas from Anteshaza, who migrated north through the Central States, arrived in the great Wē-ute' (lake) regions; and the Kinchocs, the Succileons, and the Shazas mingled races through New York, northern Ohio, Michigan, Indiana, Illinois, and eastern Wisconsin and their descendants ultimately became the peoples of the great lake regions.

Subsequently, a tribe of the Succileons migrated into that section now known as the Gulf of St. Lawrence, which they termed O-wăs-chēe-tō, and called themselves the O-wăs-chēe-tōes.

At the time of the convulsion that separated Greenland from British America, remnants of the Kasmancees of the northern portion of Teltzie Ket, of Atlantis, who had migrated and settled in that district of country now submerged by the waters of the North Atlantic Ocean, south of Greenland, and east of Labrador, were left on both southern Greenland, and eastern Labrador. The remnant left on the British American side, occupied the eastern coast of Labrador, which section they termed U-ō'mĭng, and called themselves the U-ō'mĭngs.

Subsequently, they had spread out westward, and the Owascheetoes northwestward, until the two tribes met in that section of the Dominion of Canada, now submerged by the waters of the Hudson Bay, where they mingled races, which resulted in the establishment of a new race of people, who termed the section Cū-cō'kĭn, and called themselves the Shä-hä-ī'ĕns. In subsequent time, they had spread out further westward, into the Dominion of Canada, and the Tezelons from Quintezelon; the Gangomingoes from Gangomingo; and their descended tribes had migrated eastward over the Rocky mountains, where they met and minglied races, whose subsequent descendants further migrated into the section of the Dominion of Canada.

Prior to the convulsion that established the North Pacific Ocean (or that portion that now borders the southern, and the southeastern coast of Alaska), as far south as to about fifty degrees north latitude, and from north of the Vancouver island on the east, to the Aleutian islands on the west, was a great country occupied by a large nation of people, who termed the section Kör-dū-zū'lăc, and called themselves the Kī-ör-däs.

As before stated the Kiordas were a great nation, or numerous people who had spread out south from the now known southern coast of Alaska as far south as to the Vancouver island, west of British America, to, and including the Aliaska peninsula, and southern portion of the Alaska. At the time of the submergence of their country, as a nation, they were principally lost. However, remnants escaped to the borders of the sections of Alaska, British America, and the then known Shī-tē-cŏn'gō section, some of whom were further lost by cold and starvation, and mixture with incoming races.

Pre-historically, all that section now occupied by the waters of the central, or northeastern portion of the Behring Sea, or the inland sea, pre-historically known as the Krĕn'däh Sē'ziē, was known as Pär-cĕl'tē-ŭs, so termed by the Pär-cĕl'tĭcs, who first settled in that district.

Subsequent to the establishment of the Gangomingoes, in Gangomingo, and the Shahaiens in Tinicules, a tribe of the Gangomingoes migrated northeast over the O-lŭm'bē-quăsh Conze (Rocky mountains), and settled in Tinicules near the Shahaiens, where in time they mixed races.

Subsequently, a tribe of the mixed race of Gangomingoes and Shahaiens, migrated westward into the section of Alaska, at a point about one hundred and forty-eight degrees longitude east from Greenwich, on the line of the Arctic Circle, north of the Yukon river, which section they termed El-tī-shä'zä, and called themselves the El-tĭ-shä'zäs. Subsequently, they followed the Yukon river southwestward, to about sixty-five degrees north latitude west of the southwest extremity of the Yukon Hills, at the point where the Kouiak river flows into the Yukon, where they dwelt for a period of about one hundred and fifty years, where they retained their original tribe and section names.

Subsequently, a tribe of the Eltishazas migrated westward, north of the Yukon river, into a large Cē-ī'lĕs (valley), now submerged by the waters of North Sound, which valley they termed Pär-cĕl'tē-ŭs and called themselves the Pär-cĕl'tĭcs.

Later, a tribe of Parceltics migrated northwest, to the district of the Behring Straits, between Cape Kre-gugin and Nigchigan Point, where at the time of the establishment of the Behring Straits, they were principally lost. Another large tribe of Parceltics migrated southwest to the valley that then lay extent between the then known Guhulem and Akrentie Conze ranges, at a point about one hundred and sixty-eight degrees longitude west from Greenwich, and about fifty-eight degrees north latitude, or centrally in an imaginary triangle that would embrace the Prybilov, St. Matthew, and Nounivak islands, where they dwelt for many generations, under the same tribal and sectional names. During that time, a tribe of Kiordas had also occupied the valleys that then lay extent between the Akrentie range; the southwestern coast of Alaska; the Alaska peninsula, in the south, at a point east of the Prybilov islands, and the Bristol Bay.

Subsequently, a tribe of the Kiordas had migrated southwest, over the Akrentie range, into the valley that lay extent between tht, and the Guhulem range, at a point between the Prybilov islands, and Mt. Shishaldin, of the Aleutian islands, to which section a tribe of the last named Parceltics also migrated. Still later there was a mixture of races between those Parceltics, and Kiordas, but the Kiordas being in the majority, both in number and physical strength, the descended race held to the section and tribe names of their ancestors, the Kiordas.

From the Kiordas of the former named section, and the mixed race of Kiordas and Parceltics, remnants were left upon the peninsula, and its extension into the Aleutian islands, at the time of the convulsion that established that portion of the Behring Sea, and remnants of the Parceltics were left on the St. Matthew, the Nounivak, and the Lawrence islands.

THE MEL'TRE-ZENS AND THEIR EASTERN MIGRATION.

Returning to Tuyanang (San Juan, Cuba), and the Meltrezens of that section, we pass with a tribe of their descendants from their Tuyanang, on their migration northwestward to the southern portion of the state of Florida, here established, under the name of Engrenemens, in their section of Chereestes.

The Engrenemens and their descendants, became the prehistoric ancestors of the now classified *Appalachian Races,* who occupied the southeastern districts of the United States of America, westward to Arkansas and Louisiana; northward to Tennessee and South Carolina, all inclusive.

The linguistic condition of the ancient Timucuas of South Carolina and Georgia, arose from the fact that, prior to the submergence of the land that then connected Teltzie Ket and Zret of Atlantis, to the now known eastern portion of the United States of America, a large tribe of Gurenzes had migrated from the southern portion of Teltzie Zret, into the Tyngerze (valleys) that then had place in the district of country east of the states of Georgia and Florida, and a small tribe of Nothosis from the southern portion of Teltzie Ket, likewise had migrated into the Tyngerze east of the Carolina states.

Links and Cycles

At the time of the submergence, some of the Nothosis, and a large number of the Gurenzes were left as remnants on the remnant islands along the coast (now submerged), and on the mainland now the states of Florida, Georgia and South Carolina. In subsequent time, these remnant Gurenzes and Nothosis became mixed as a race, when they called themselves the Zĕn'dă-con-dā-cĕnds, and termed the region along the coast from Florida to South Carolina, Zĕn-dă'cŏn, and the language spoken was Atlantian, such as was in use by the Gurenzes of Teltzie Zret, with a dialect that grew out of the amalgamation of it and the language spoken by the Nothosis of Teltzie Ket. The Gurenze remnant being larger than that of the Nothosis therefore caused the amalgamate descendants to continue the language of the former, modified by the dialect condition that had arisen from the mixed race linguistic influence. Therefore the extinct Timucua language, formerly current along the eastern coast of Georgia, Florida, and as far south as to Cape Canaveral, is a linguistic link, hving its origin in Atlantis, and therefore is a stock language.

The principal dwelling center of the Zendacondacends was in Georgia (along the Altamaha river), which they termed the On-gē-gō-lăs'sē.

As the descendants of the Engrenemens migrated eastward, and the Shazas branched out westward along the then known Telseooduc (Ohio), river region, they blended races, and their descendants spread out into the regions of the states of Ohio, Indiana, Illinois and Kentucky, and were a blend between the Appalachian and the Dakota, or Sioux family.

Passing with the descended migrating tribe of Engrenemens, northeastward from the section of Chereestes (Florida), we find them established in the district now known as the Chesapeake Bay, Virginia and Maryland, under the name of Kinchocs, in their section of Kinchoc.

The Kinchocs and their descendants, became the pre-historic ancestors of the now classified southern branch of the *Algonquin Family.*

Passing with the descended migrating tribe of Kinchocs further northeast from Kinchoc (Virginia and Maryland), we find them established in the section of the state of Massachussetts, or in the vicinity of the City of Boston, under the name of Succileons, in their section of Succileon.

The Succileons and their descendants became the pre-historic ancestors of the now known Classified Eastern Branch of the *Algonquin Family.*

Passing with the descendants of the Shazas who migrated north from their Anteshaza, those of the Kinchocs from Kinchoc, who migrated northwestward; and the Succileons who migrated southwestward; we find the three branches as having mingled races from which condition we find the tribes established in the Great Lake Regions, whose descendants became the prehistoric ancestors of the now known classified Western Branch of the *Algonquin Family.*

Passing with the descended tribe of Succileons further northeast from Succileon (Boston vicinity), we find them established in the then known district of country, now submerged by the Gulf of St. Lawrence, under the name of Owascheetoes, in their section of Owascheeto.

The Owascheetoes and their descendants became the prehistoric ancestors of the now known classified Northern Branch *Algonquin Family.*

Passing with the descended migrating tribe of Owascheetoes from Owascheeto (Gulf of St. Lawrence district), northwestward, we find them in the district now submerged by the Hudson Bay.

Passing with a descended migrating tribe of the remnant Kasmancees from Teltzie Ket of Atlantis, or U-ō'mĭngs, from their section of U-ō'mĭng (eastern Labrador) westward, we find them also in the district now submerged by the Hudson Bay.

Subsequently, we find the Owascheetoes and the Uomings of the Hudson Bay district amalgamated into one race, under the name of Shä-hä-ĭ'ĕns, in their section of Cŭ-cō'kĭn.

The Shahaiens and their descendants became the pre-historic ancestors of the now known classified *Athabascan,* or *Tinney Family,* known to be the most widespread ethnical and linguistic group in North America, comprising most of Alaska and the Canadian Dominion, from the Eskimo domain to the Churchill river north and south, and from the Rocky mountains to the Hudson Bay west and east, besides isolated enclaves in Oregon, Arizona, New Mexico, Colorado, and North Mexico.

Passing with the migrating tribes of Uomings, who did not mingle with the Owascheetoes, throughout what is now known as northeastern and northern British America, we find them established throughout the now known Eskimo Domain, under the name of Hyc'tē-sēz, in their section of Sŭl'-lē-trōme, the latter being the section of country now known as about seventy degrees north latitude and a hundred and eight degrees longitude west from Greenwich, between what is now known as Wollaston Land and Victoria Land, that portion of country south, east, and west of the two above-named sections not then being shattered, and submerged, as is now the case.

The Hyctesez and their descendants, or one of the third developing branches of Kasmancees of Atlantis, through the Uomings, became the pre-historic ancestors of the now known Eskimo, or Innuits, of the Labrador region, and that of British America southwest of Greenland, whose close alliance with the *Hyperborean Races* of Alaska and British America, can be traced or easily accounted for through the migrations of their allies, the Shahaiens from their section of Cucokin, to northwestern British America, where they mixed races with the Gangomingoes, and passed into Alaska as the Eltishazas, from whom descended the Eskimo of northeast British America and north, and northeastern Alaska, and still further into Siberia and northeastern Asia.

THE CON'GOES AND THEIR NORTHERN MIGRATION.

Returning to the district now known as the submerged central and southern half of the Gulf of Mexico, and the pure Congoes from their section of Shaltecongo, we pass with a tribe of their descendants on their migration along the then known Gĕn-zē-rĕst mountains, to the district of southern Louisiana, west of the Mississippi river, where we find them established under the name of Shazas, in their section of Anteshaza.

The Shazas and their descendants became the pre-historic ancestors of the now known classified *Dakota* or *Sioux Family*, whose proper domain is the western Prairies between the Mississippi river and the Rocky mountains, east and west, and stretching from the Saskatchawan, British America, southward to the Red River of Texas.

Prior to the establishment of the Bahama Islands, a small tribe of Gurenzes and a larger tribe of Meltrezens had migrated from the southern portion of Teltzie Zret, of Atlantis, into the region of the Great Bahama Island, where the two tribes amalgamated into one race, who on account of the Meltrezen influence being the stronger, favored that type physically, and continued the Meltrezen language with some dialect influence from that of the Gurenzes.

Prior to the submergence of the district of land between the Bahamas and the now known states of Georgia and Florida, the mixed race had again migrated northwest into that portion of the state of Georgia where now the town of Brunswick has place.

When that portion of the country was inhabited by the Engrenemens, who were the stronger tribe of the two, they forced the mixed tribe, above referred to, to leave that portion of the country, and to migrate further westward. When they arrived on the banks of the Mississippi, they halted there for a time. Soon the Shazas, likewise, forced them to move still further westward. Taking up the line of migration again, they passed into the southeastern section of the state of Texas, where they settled along the Brazos river, in the district of Washington, termed the section El-grē-nä'dä, and called themselves the O-jä'zēnes.

The Ojazenes of Elgrenada and their descendants became the pre-historic ancestors of the *.Pawnee Family,* as classified with the Shoshones ethnically, but linguistically different from all other tribes, which latter fact is due to their having continued the Meltrezen language with its Gurenzes dialect influence, while the Shintolons, from whom the Shoshones descended, retained the ethnical type, but not the same linguistic conditions.

The Ojazenes ultimately spread out into the now known states of Texas, and Kansas, and now have a reserve in Indian Territory.

Passing (prior to the establishment of the now known Lake Superior) with a migrating tribe of Shazas from the region now known as south of the Minni Wakam or Devil's Lake, or along the upper course of the Tchan Sansan river, eastward, we find them established under the name of O-kā-lū'cî-ăns, in their section of Bĕd-ā-rä'zēs.

The Okalucians and their descendants became the pre-historic ancestors of the now known classified *Wyandot-Iroquois Family.* That the Wyandot-Iroquois are ethnically allied to the Algonquin Family, is due to the fact that they are both descendants from the original Meltrezens of the Caribbean region. That they are linguistically allied to the Dakotas or Sioux Famiy, is due to the fact that they descended through the migratory conditions of the Congoes and Shazas, as they passed north-westward through the United States, thence eastward; while the Algonquin Family descended through the migratory conditions of the Engrenemens, Kinchocs, Succileons and Owascheetoes, as they passed north-eastward through the United States, along the Atlantic regions.

Passing with the migrating tribe of Congoes, north-westward from the northwestern central portion of the district of country now submerged by the Gulf of Mexico, through the State of Texas; with the Shazas from the region of Arkansas, westward through the southern portion of Indian Territory and northwestern Texas; one of Ojazenes from Texas, northwest through that state; one of Izoletes south-eastward through Nevada and Utah, with other straggling tribes from North Mexico and South Colorado, into various valley districts of the state of New Mexico, who during subsequent ages, amalgamated into one ethnical race, we find the origin of the race of people whose descendants became the pre-historic ancestors of the now classified *New Mexico Pueblos.*

Passing with a tribe of descended migrating Shintolons from their section of Shintolon (San Diego Bay section) to the western side of the lower Colorado river, or near its junction with the Rio Gila; and a tribe of Congoes, who likewise migrated (from the district now known as the western central portion of the Gulf of Mexico), northwest through Texas, New Mexico, and Arizona, to the eastern side of the lower Colorado river, and its junction with the Gila, where in subsequent time they mixed races, and blended into one family, whose descendants became the pre-historic ancestors of the family now classified as the *Yuma Stock.*

Submerged Atlantis Restored

O-CE-A-LAN'GUS,
OR
CENTRAL AMERICA AND MEXICO.

TELTZIE LVIII.

O-eē-ā-län'gŭs was the first pre-historic name of the sections of country now known as Central America, and Mexico, as given by the Congoes of that region, about the time of the beginning of the Adomic period. About 1000 years subsequent to the submergence of Atlantis, a great system of nine periodical convulsions occurred, and had place in the region of the West Indies islands, Gulf of Mexico, and the Caribbean Sea, that occurred throughout a period of about 4500 years.

Prior to these convulsions, a mountain range known to the people of that period as the Meztrie range, extended from the section of "Trinidad," north of the coast of South America, embracing the Caribbee Islands, Porto Rico, Dominican Republic, Republic of Hayti, and Cuba, to the Bay of Honduras including the islands, reefs and bays on the eastern coast of Yucatan and Balize, and the Bay islands, on the coast of Honduras.

Another system of mountains, pre-historically known as the Mutize, embraced two principal ranges, viz: the eastern and the western. The eastern extended from the western and southern coasts of Hayti, circling westward and southward, which embrace the Quinto Seno Sand Banks, the Serrana Reef, Old Providence, and Andrew's islands. The western branch extended west and south, in circular form, from the southern central section of Puerto Principe, Cuba, to the northeastern coast; thus embracing the now known Gayman and Swan Islands and the protruding remnants now known as the Moaquito Banks, east of Honduras and Nicaragua, of Central America.

Another range then known as the Zē'dē-ā, extended to the Tobago Island, northeast of Trinidad; thus embracing the Tortuga and the Margarita Islands. Still another range then known as the Cŏr-dī-zū'lăc, extended eastward from the section now known as Gallinas Point, west of the Gulf of Maracaibo, to the region of the Tobago Island, where it terminated in a junction with the Zedea range, thus embracing the Oruba, the Curacao, the Buen Ayre, and the Los Roguez Islands.

A large valley then known as the Fū'gĕr, lay extent between the Meztrie range, and the western branch of the Mutize, in the northeast area of the Caribbean Sea. Another then known as the Wăn-zē-rĭck, lay extent between the eastern and western branches of the Mutize system, in the same section of the Caribbean Sea district. Still another, then known as the Mē'di-ă Plē'-ă-cĕlt (great valley), extended north and east from the Isthmus of Panama, to the region of the Leeward, and Windward, of the Caribbean islands, now submerged by the waters of the central, and the eastern sections of the Caribbean Sea.

A range then known as the Gĕn-zē-rĕst' extended a little northeast from the northeastern coast of the Tabasco, and the western coast of Campeche, Central America; to the southeastern coast of Louisiana, and the southwestern coast of Mississippi, U. S. A., the central extension being from Laralaria Bay, on the southeastern coast of Louisiana. A large valley then known as the Lĕx-ō'phĭs lay extent east of the Genzerest range, centrally in the section now known as the eastern half of the Gulf of Mexico.

The then known river of Năn-zē'lī-ē'tŭs (long and immense), flowed in a zig-zag course southeast through the Meztrie range, near the center of the Channel of Yucatan, between the latter and Cuba; thence circling eastward, it cut through the Mutize range, centrally between Southern Jamaica, and the Serrana Reef, east of Nicaragua; thence circling southeast, to about thirteen degrees north latitude, north of the Magdalena River, South America; thence coursing northeast about one degree north of the Gulf of Maracaibo or Venezuela; thence circling southeast and northeast to about twelve degrees north latitude and twelve degrees longitude east from Washington; when it turned on a course southeast and passed out into the North Atlantic Ocean, near the northeast coast of the Trinidad island, or between it and the Tobago Island.

The first of the nine periodical convulsions had place in the northwestern branch of the Meztrie range, in the section of the "Exuma Island," now one of the "Bahama" group. The force of the convulsion extended northwest to the southeast coast of "Florida," which severed the range from that section, established the "Straits of Florida," south, and southeast to the coast of "Cuba," and "Hayti;" sunk and submerged portions of the range, which thus established the "Bahamas."

The second in two sections, occurred about five hundred years after the first and had place, in the section of the "St. Vincent island," one of the "Windwards" in the "Lesser Antilles" group.

The force of the convulsion extended circularly, northwest to the eastern coast of "Porto Rico;" circularly southwest to, and along the coast of "Venezuela," thus establishing the entire group of "Caribbee islands," those off the coast of "Venezuela;" the "Gulf of Maracaibo;" and the coast line and other inlet waters of "South America," from "Gallinas Point" in the west, to that forming the northwest coast of the "Gulf of Paria" in the east.

The second section of the convulsion occurred almost simultaneously with the first, and had place on the eastern coast of the "Trinidad island." The force of the convulsion severed "Trinidad" from the main land; established the "Gulf of Paria;" the "Mouth of the Orinoco;" the "Serpents Mouth," the principal outlet of the "Orinoco;" and its accompanying islands; and established the northeast coast line of "South America," as far southeast, as to "Cape North."

The third periodical convulsion occurred about six hundred and fifty years subsequent to the second, and had place in the section now known as the northeast coast of the "Mona island," between "Porto Rico and "Hayti." The force of the convulsion severed the latter two named portions of land and established the "Mona island;" the "Mona Passage;" and the further extension of the force eastward, established the northern and southern coasts of "Porto Rico," and its separation from the "Virgin islands;" which latter were established partially by the second periodical convulsion, and partly by the third. The westward course of the force established the northern and southern coast lines of "Hayti," its inlet waters, accompanying islands, and severed it from "Cuba," and "Jamaica," to the line of the ninth periodical convulsion; and established the "Windward Passage" between "Cuba," and "Hayti."

The fourth convulsion occurred about five hundred years after the third, and had place in the northwest portion of "Vera Cruz," "Mexico;" between the main land and "Cape Roxo." The force of the convulsion established the entire western half of the "Gulf of Mexico," as far east as the then known Genzeret range, or to the "St. Vincent island," off the coast of "Louisiana;" and "Lake Terminos," and its islands, in the south; and in north, eastern "Tabasco," in "Mexico." At the time of the convulsion, a low mountain then known as Monzikolos, stood near the central portion of the then known valley of Quaindrel, which at the time of the convulsion, sank below the now level of the waters. It had been very slowly sinking during the ages that passed after the convulsion, a fact that rightly accounts for the great depth of the water in that section at the present time; as well as that of the gradual receding of the waters, which latter is a well known fact to moderns, and were it not for the constant inflow of water from tributary streams, along the coast, the submerged banks that exist in different sections of the Gulf, would now be above the water. The time will come when the moving downward of the submerged Mt. Monzikolos, will bring to view the banks above mentioned.

The fifth periodical convulsion occurred about nine hundred years subsequent to the fourth, and had place in the southern section of the Genzerest range, near the northwestern coast of "Campeachy," "Central America." The force of the convulsion extended northeast along the Genzerest range, to the southeast coast of "Louisiana," which sunk and submerged the range, leaving as its remnants, the islands in the lake of "Terminos," between "Tabasco," and "Campeachy," "Las Arcas," west of "Yucatan;" also the "Sunday island," northwest, and the "Great Campeachy Bank," north of "Yucatan." Further extension of the force eastward, established the coast line and inlet waters of western "Campeachy;" northern and eastern "Yucatan," as far south as to "Espiritu Santo Bay;" severed "Cuba" from "Yucatan," by sinking and submerging the land of that region; leaving the islands and banks on the cosat of "Yucatan;" and establishing the "Channel of Yucatan."

Simultaneous with this convulsion, at the southern section of the Genzerest range, there were three sectional convulsions in the northern region, viz: One in the section known as "Laralaria Bay;" one in the "Timbalier Bay;" and one in the "South West Pass" of the Delta of the Mississippi." The force of the three convulsions established the coast line, inlet waters and islands, from "Gaillou Bay," southern coast of "Louisiana," to "Apalachee Bay," "Florida;" and south to the line of the fifth periodical convulsion thus extending the open waters of the "Gulf of Mexico," to the line northeast from the western point of "Cuba," and to the western border of the "Apalachee Bay;" and therefore, established the present terminal of the Great Manzelietus, or Mississippi river, the mysterious Delta of which, with the five Passes, and five Bays remain as monumental evidence of the convulsive forces that shot in through the ravines, leaving the higher land, thus establishing the present radiating outlet of the Mississippi waters.

The sixth convulsion occurred about seven hundred years after the fifth, and had place in the section of the "Bay island," off the northern coast of "Honduras." The force of the convulsion formed the Bay islands; the Bay of Honduras; and the inlet waters, the banks, reefs, and islands on the eastern coast of Balize; as far north as to the southern boundary line of the fifth periodical convulsion; and northeast to the center of the Channel of Yucatan; and east to Cape Cameron, Honduras.

The seventh convulsion occurred about six hundred years after the sixth, and had place in the southern portion of the eastern branch of the Mutize range, in "Old Providence island," east of the coast of Nicaragua, Central America. The force of the convulsion extended throughout the branch northward to near the southwest coast of Jamaica; and southward to Costa Rica, and Panama; thus establishing the protrudings, islands, and reefs from Serrana Reef, to the Albuquerque Keys; the northeast coast line of Costa Rica, its inlet waters and islands, and the northern coast line, inlet waters and islands of Yucatan; the Gulf of Darien; and the South American coast, northeast to the Magdalena river. It further extended westward, following the western branch of the Mutize range, to the point between the Great Gayman, and the Swan islands; thus establishing all the islands and sand banks from the Swan island, in the north, to the eastern extremity of Costa Rica, which are remnants of the western branch of the Mutize range, and thus establishing the southern and southeastern portion of the Caribbean Sea as far north as to about sixty degrees north latitude, the southwestern portion having been formed by the sixth periodical convulsion, which linked its waters, into those of the Gulf of Mexico.

The eighth periodical convulsion occurred about three hundred years after the seventh, and had place in the section now known as amid the islands off the north central coast of Cardenas, Cuba. The force of the convulsion extended west, to the extremity of Cuba, east to the boundary line of the western department of Cuba, or the Yama Bay, to the boundary line of the first periodical convulsion, thus completing the establishment of the northern coast of Cuba, the inlet waters and islands. Further extension of the force north and northeast, to the Great peninsula of Florida, established all the islands and reefs from the Tortugas, to the main land of Florida, all the inlet waters, and islands on the western coast of Florida, to the Apalachee Bay, or eastern line of the fifth periodical convulsion; thus completing the Gulf of Mexico, and linking its waters with those of the North Atlantic Ocean.

The ninth periodical convulsion occurred about one hundred years subsequent to the eighth, and had place in the northern section of the western branch of the Mutize range, or in the section now known as off the southern coast of Santa Cruz, Cuba. The force of the convulsion formed the entire southern coast line of Cuba, its inlet waters, the Isle of Pines, and other coast islands, extended east to the boundary line of the third periodical convulsion; west to the boundary line of the fifth, and sixth; south and southeast to the seventh, which completed the sinking and submergence of the northern section of the two branches of the Mutize range; thus establishing the Jamaica island, its coast line, and inlet water canditions; the two Gayman islands; and completing the establishment of the Carribbean Sea, by linking the northwestern section to the portions already formed by the force of the sixth and seventh periodical convulsions.

THE PRE-HISTORIC OR ABORIGINAL AMERICANS.

Returning to the region of the great West Indies Archipelago; the district of the Caribbean Sea; the Gulf of Mexico; and the Meltrezen; the Yunandoes, or mixed race of Gurenzes and Kintilucians; and the ultimate Gurenzes who were a total blend by mixture with the Yunandoes, as the peoples who inhabited those sections pre-historically, and their further migrations into South America, Central America, Mexico, and North America, we have the root from which has sprung up and spread out the great tree of Aboriginal American or American Indian races whose first disbursement is represented by the numerous families, and tribes now existing throughout North America, Mexico, Central America and South America, and their adjacent islands.

Passing with the tribe of Meltrezens from the western portion of their Tuyanang (Cuba), into Yucatan, we find them established under the name of Congoes, in their section of Shaltecongo, whose migratory remnants of very small tribes inhabited the district through which they passed, now submerged by the northwestern portion of the Carribbean Sea; and further development of the main branch in the Shaltecongo section, extended out into the district now submerged by the Gulf of Mexico, hence, those now aquatic districts were pre-historically non-submerged and inhabited.

Passing with a tribe of seceded Gurenzes who dwelt in the Caribbean district, into Yucatan, we find them in an amalgamate condition with the Congoes of Shaltecongo, which condition brought a race change to the descendants.

Passing with other tribes, or remnants of the Meltrezen and Gurenzes of the Caribbean Sea district, at the time of the submergence that established it, we find remnants of the above named inhabitants who were near the main land of Central America, in various parts of the latter named country, whose evolved race conditions were also under the influence of amalgamation.

Passing with a descended migrating tribe of pure Gurenzes from Guselsic, southwestward through the district now submerged by the Caribbean Sea, to the now known section of Costa Rica, we find them established in the vicinity of Point Blanco, under the name of Teabaskans, in their section of Tubdeana. They as a mixed race of Gurenzes and Kintilucians, or Ynandoes, and ultimate amalgamation into the Gurenzes stock, spread out into the section now known as Nicaragua and the Peninsula of Panama, where they became the pre-historic ancestors of the now known classified *Central American Races.*

Passing with another tribe of Congoes from their Shaltecongo, (Yucatan), we find them established in the section now known as Vera Cruz, Mexico, as one of the first developed branches of the race, under the name of Linzoes, in their section of Quintelinzo. They and their descendants, became the pre-historic ancestors of the *Mexican Race* of the Modern Ancient period of time.

The mixed race of Gurenzes from the Caribbean district, with the Congoes of Shaltecongo (Yucatan), became the prehistoric ancestors of the *Maya Quiche,* of Yucatan and Guatemala, and their outlying branch in Vera Cruz and Tamaulipas.

Passing with a tribe of descended Linzoes from Quintelinzo, after the main tribe had branched out and inhabited various portions of the now known section of Mexico, and had established migrations from the northwestern portion of the latter named country, we find them established in the district now submerged by the San Diego Bay, as one of the second developed branches of the race, under the name of Shintolons, in their section of Shintolon. They and their descendants, became the pre-historic ancestors of the now classified *California Races of American Indians.*

Subsequent to the establishment of the drainage of the Great Sharuntrezon Cet (Inland Sea), and the establishment of that district into the now known Great American Desert, descendants from the Linzoes from their section of Quintelinzo (southwestern California) and the Shintolons from their section of Shintolon (southern and northwestern California), instituted small descended tribe migrations, eastward into the states of Oregon, Utah, Idaho, Nevada, Arizona, south, and southwest California, north Texas, New Mexico and north Mexico, whose descendants ultimately became the pre-historic ancestors of the now classified *Shoshone or Snake Family.*

Passing with the descended tribe of Shintolons from their Shintolon, on their migration northward, we find them established in the section now known as the County of Mendocino, California, under the name of Izoletes, in their section of Izoletes. They and their descendants, became the pre-historic ancestors of the now classified *Columbian Races.*

Passing with the descended migrating tribe of Izoletes, from their Izoletes, into British America, or the region of the Admiralty islands, we find them established under the name of Tezelons, in their section of Tezelon. They and their descendants, became the pre-historic ancestors of the now classified *Tlinket,* or *Tlinketantukwan Race.*

Passing with the descended tribe of Tezelons from their Quintezelon, on their migration into the Yukon section, between the Rocky mountains and Mt. St. Elias of Alaska, we find them slightly amalgamated with the Kiordas of that section, under the name of Gangomingoes, in their section of Gangomingo. They and their descendants, became the pre-historic ancestors of the now classified Eskimo peoples of that section of country.

Passing with the descended migrating tribe of the mixed race of Gangomingoes and Shahaiens from their Tinicules into Alaska, north of the Yukon river, we find them under the name of Eltishazas, in their section of Eltishaza. They and their descendants, became the pre-historic ancestors of the now classified *Hyperborean Races.*

Passing with two descended migrating tribes of Gangomingoes from their Gangomingo, we find one established in the vicinity of the Shahaiens, south of the Mackenzie river, who became lost in the blood of the Shahaiens; and one on their migration southwestward,into southeastern Alaska, between Mt. St. Elias and the mouth of the Atna, or Copper river, we find them as an amalgamated race, who had mixed blood with the remnant Kiordas of that section of Korduzulac, under their former name of Gangomingoes. This branch of the Gangomingoes, as they descended and migrated into the Aleutian island districts, became the pre-historic ancestors of the now classified, or two families of Aleuts, collectively known as the *Ungungun,* comprising the *Unalashkans,* who call themselves the *Kagataya Kung'n* ("Men of the East").

That the Ungungun family differ so greatly in linguistic and ethnic conditions, and to some extent physically, from the Eskimo of those regions, is due to the fact that, the former are amalgamate descendants from the Gangomingoes and Kiordas branches, and the Eskimo proper, are amalgamate descendants from the mixed races of Gangomingoes and Shahaiens.

Note. Owing to the great extent of this work, we have been obliged to leave out the general portion of the Teltzie on South America. In future editions however, we propose to amplify some sections already given, insert the Teltzie on South America, and publish the work in two volumes.

That the Ethnographic links may be not entirely severed at this point of the earth, we will give the pre-historic peoples, their locations and historic descendants, which are as follows.

A migrating tribe of Kacedricks in Dimtimzeon (Venezuela), became the Zimeons;o ne of Schanandarits into Geuselsic (Maracaibo Gulf section), became the Selsics; one of Zimeons into Indris (Guiana), became the Indris; one of Gurenzes into their Shushock (United States of Columbia), became the Shushocks; one of Indris into Quetese (southern Venezuela), became the Queteses; one of the Selsics into their Sanchon (United States of Columbia), became the Sanchons; tribes of Sanchons into Equador, and into Exkuien (Peru), became the Exkuiens; one of the Exkuiens into Getresan (southern Bolivia), became the Getresans; one of the Getresans into Zelgoliot (southern Chili), became the Zelgoliots; one of the Zelgoliots into Concoseshan (Tierra del Fuego), became the Concoseshans; a mixed race of Atlantians and Schirants into Tierra del Fuego, became a branch of the Chazahaens; a mixed race of the Sanchons and the Mellenthaes of Romarareya (north of Amazon), became the Triostes; a mixed race of the Sanchons and Mellenthaes of Wapeana (in the Minas Geraes region), became the Wapeanas; a tribe of Zanranzans into Lenitemo (section between the Sierra de Mar and the Sierra Monlequeira ranges), became the Haendeces.

The Concoseshans and their descendants became the pre-historic ancestors of the tribes that exist south of, and in Patagonia. The Selsics, of the Waraus, that of the Coast region. The Zimeons, that of the Arawacks of the Coast region. A mixed race of Schanandarits and Kacedricks, that of the Barre Family. The Shushocks and the Sancons, that of the now classified New Granada and Guiana Races of the United States of Columbia. The Sancons, that of the New Granada and Guiana Races in Brazilian Guiana, embracing the Carib Family. The Indris, that of the New Granada and Guiana Races, embracing the unclassified aborigines of the interior of the British, Dutch and German Guianas. A tribe of Queteses, that of the classified New Granada and Guiana Races, embracing the Wapeanas in the Savannah region. A tribe of Sancons of Equador, that of the classified Peruvian and Bolivian Races, embracing the primitive Cura tribes (now extinct.) A tribe of Shushacks of Equador, that of the classified Peruvian and Bolivian Races, embracing the primitive Puruha, of Equador; the Jivaros of Pastassa; and the Zaparos of the Upper Napo. The Exkuioes, that of the classified and Peruvian and Bolivian Races, embracing the Peruvians of the aboriginal Quichua Races, and the five nations, who collectively, are termed Antisians. The descended Getresans, that of the Classified Peruvian and Bolivian Races, embracing the civilized Quinchua and the Ayamara, or Inac Indians of the western highlands; the half civilized Indians of Molos and Chiquitos; the Samucus, Curaves, Tapiis and Corabaccas, originally in the south; the Saravccas, Otukes, Curmuminacas, etc., in the southeast; the Paiconecas in the northwest, etc. The Zelgoliots, that of the classified Austral Races, embracing the Auca of Chili and Patagonia; the Mouche or highlanders; the Lavquenche or coast people; the Huilliche or southerners. The Heltezas, that of the now classified Austral Races, embracing the Patagonians, Tchuelche, etc. The Concoseshans, that of the classified Austral Races, embracing the Alacaluf group of Fuegians. The Chazahaens, that of the classified Austral Races, embracing the Yahgans and Fuegians of Tierra del Feugo. A tribe of Wapeanas, that of the now classified Brazilian Races embracing the southern division of the Guariana Family. The Triostes, that of the classified Brazilian Races, embracing the Tupi Family. The Haendeces, that of the classified Brazilian Races, embracing the Non-Guarani element in Brazil, collectively known to the Tupis as Tapuyas The mixed race of Atlantians and Schirants, or branch of Chazahaens, that of the primitive Bushamen, or historic Bushmen.

Links and Cycles

E-UN'DU.

I, E-ŭn'dū, like Rē-mē'nä, always was, am now and forever
shall be;
For the cycles of evolution cease not to turn throughout Eternity.
What seemeth to be the end is only the process of Spirit and
Matter, returning
To the condition of development which made visible their state
of individual being—
Or generative periods, where cycles give forth their excess, by
offspring,
As a part of themselves, and never the image of some other created thing.
Though conditions may touch and mingle in the aura of cycles
as they meet,
And the influence of each cause the diverse development to be
replete;
Yet the hybrid cycle will re-embody the co-united parent
individualities,
As an offspring of combined forces, a part of each, and lasting
as Eternity.
The material cycle is ever turning, in the great zone of atomic
matter,
Throwing off particles which assume individual form, as offspring epi-cycles later;
Gathering them in again, when by natural process they ultimately disintegrate,
A wonderful law that supplies nature with conditions from which
it re-creates.
The spiritual cycle, in the great zone of universal spirit, ever
turns the same way,
But finally carries the individualized spirit and soul farther and
farther away,
Where the senses of the soul gather knowledge, that develops the
spirit intelligence,
And lights the path of progress, through which they move and
have existence;
It further extends its excess forces, new epi-cycles of life to
create,
Into zones where the material cycles furnish them with an individual, material, form-mate.

Submerged Atlantis Restored

A divine law of nature is this, that all existence may move in
cycles perpetually;
The material cycle over its disintegrated form, and other stores
of excess,
Into new ones, through which newly-created individual souls and
spirits express.
The spirit cycle, thus co-united with the material, in the process
of extension,
Makes all individual life endless, and therefore lasting, in regard
to duration.
While bodies and other form creations only last individually as
epi-cycles material and mortal,
The spirit and soul creations move on and out, as individualized
epi-cycles of God Eternal.
So material epi-cycles are created, disintegrated, re-blended, and
re-constructed,
And those of the spiritual, individualized and continued, as they
are naturally conducted—
On the deferent of the great Over Soul and Over Spirit cycles
of creation,
Each moved and governed by the principles of Animation, Extension and Duration.
Hence it is, that Rē-mē'nä and E-ŭn'dū, the conditions of beginning and ending,
Weld together the cycles of all created existence, while they are
meeting and blending.
Therefore, we conclude with the fact that E-ŭn'du is also Rē-
mē'nä, or a beginning,
And Rē-mē'nä, likewise, is E-ŭn'dū, which also establishes it as
an ending.
And as the two conditions in all life cycles, infinitely meet and
blend,
The process is logical proof, that the end is beginning, and the
beginning is end.

J. BEN. LESLIE.

Printed in Poland
by Amazon Fulfillment
Poland Sp. z o.o., Wrocław

58573936R00461